Infants and Children
Prenatal Through Middle Childhood

EIGHTH EDITION

Laura E. Berk

Illinois State University

Adena B. Meyers

Illinois State University

PEARSON

Boston • Columbus • Indianapolis • New York • San Francisco • Hoboken
Amsterdam • Cape Town • Dubai • London • Madrid • Milan • Munich • Paris • Montréal • Toronto
Delhi • Mexico City • São Paulo • Sydney • Hong Kong • Seoul • Singapore • Taipei • Tokyo

In loving memory of my parents, Sofie and Philip Eisenberg   L. E. B.
For my grandmothers, Rose Honig and Edith Polin, with love and gratitude   A. B. M.

Senior Publisher: Roth Wilkofsky
Managing Editor: Tom Pauken
Development Editor: Judy Ashkenaz
Editorial Assistants: Rachel Trapp, Devon Bacso
Supplements Editors: Rachel Trapp, Judy Ashkenaz, Kim Michaud, Jeanie McHale
Team Lead—Project Management, Communication/Psychology: Linda Behrens
Senior Project Manager, Psychology: Donna Simons
Senior Digital Product Manager: Thomas Scalzo
Associate Digital Product Manager: Christopher Fegan
Senior Product Marketing Manager: Lindsey Prudhomme Gill
Senior Operations Specialist: Diane Peirano

Photo Researcher: Sarah Evertson—ImageQuest
Interior Designer: Carol Somberg
Cover Designer: Joel Gendron, Lumina Datamatics
Project Coordination and Editorial Services: MPS North America LLC
Art Rendering and Electronic Page Makeup: Jouve
Composition Specialist: Jeff Miller
Copyeditor and References Editor: Margaret Pinette
Proofreader: Julie Hotchkiss
Indexer: Linda Herr Hallinger
Manufactured in the United States by RR Donnelley
Cover Art: "In My Grandmother's Village," Lia Anglina, 13 years, Indonesia. Reprinted with permission from the International Museum of Children's Art, Oslo, Norway.

Copyright © 2016 Laura E. Berk. Copyrights © 2012, 2008, 2005, 2002, 1999, 1996, 1993 Pearson Education. All Rights Reserved. Printed in the United States of America. This publication is protected by copyright, and permission should be obtained from the publisher prior to any prohibited reproduction, storage in a retrieval system, or transmission in any form or by any means, electronic, mechanical, photocopying, recording, or otherwise. For information regarding permissions, request forms, and the appropriate contacts within the Pearson Education Global Rights & Permissions department, please visit *www.pearsoned.com/permissions.*

Unless otherwise indicated herein, any third-party trademarks that may appear in this work are the property of their respective owners and any references to third-party trademarks, logos, or other trade dress are for demonstrative or descriptive purposes only. Such references are not intended to imply any sponsorship, endorsement, authorization, or promotion of Pearson's products by the owners of such marks, or any relationship between the owner and Pearson Education, Inc. or its affiliates, authors, licensees, or distributors.

Page 510: Photo © 2015 by Child Lures, Ltd. All Rights Reserved. Excerpted from Child Lures® Prevention's *Think First & Stay Safe*™ *School Program/Student Workbook/Parent Guide* by Kenneth Wooden, Rosemary Webb, and Jennifer Mitchell. Excerpted with permission of Child Lures, Ltd., Child Lures Prevention, 5166 Shelburne Road, Shelburne, Vermont 05482 (802) 985-8458, *www.childluresprevention.com.*

Library of Congress Cataloging-in-Publication Data
Berk, Laura E.
    Infants and children : prenatal through middle childhood /
Laura E. Berk and Adena B. Meyers — Eighth edition.
        pages cm
    Includes bibliographical references and indexes.
    ISBN 978-0-13-393672-8 — ISBN 0-13-393672-4
    1. Child development.   I. Meyers, Adena Beth   II. Title.
RJ131.B3863 2016
618.92—dc23
                                        2015002432

10 9 8 7 6 5 4 3 2
V011

Student Edition
ISBN 10: 0-13-393672-4
ISBN 13: 978-0-13-393672-8

Instructor's Review Edition
ISBN 10: 0-13-403568-2
ISBN 13: 978-0-13-403568-0

À la Carte Edition
ISBN 10: 0-13-403564-X
ISBN 13: 978-0-13-403564-2

www.pearsonhighered.com

About the Authors

© BARBARA ADELMAN, ÉLAN STUDIOS

Laura E. Berk is a distinguished professor of psychology at Illinois State University, where she has taught child, adolescent, and lifespan development for more than three decades. She received her bachelor's degree in psychology from the University of California, Berkeley, and her master's and doctoral degrees in child development and educational psychology from the University of Chicago.

Berk has been a visiting scholar at Cornell University, UCLA, Stanford University, and the University of South Australia. She has published widely on effects of school environments on children's development, the development of children's private speech, and the role of make-believe play in development. She has been featured on National Public Radio's *Morning Edition* and in *Parents Magazine, Wondertime,* and *Readers' Digest,* and has contributed to *Psychology Today* and *Scientific American.*

In addition to *Infants, Children, and Adolescents,* Berk's best-selling texts include *Child Development, Development Through the Lifespan,* and *Exploring Lifespan Development,* published by Pearson. Her other books include *Private Speech: From Social Interaction to Self-Regulation; Scaffolding Children's Learning: Vygotsky and Early Childhood Education; Awakening Children's Minds: How Parents and Teachers Can Make a Difference;* and *A Mandate for Playful Learning in Preschool: Presenting the Evidence.*

Berk is active in work for children's causes. She recently completed nine years of service on the national board of Jumpstart for Young Children and currently serves on the governing board of the Illinois Network of Child Care Resource and Referral Agencies. She is a fellow of the American Psychological Association, Division 7: Developmental Psychology.

Adena B. Meyers is a professor of psychology and member of the school psychology faculty at Illinois State University. She received her bachelor's degree in women's studies from Brown University and her doctoral degree in clinical-community psychology from the University of Illinois at Urbana-Champaign, and is a licensed clinical psychologist.

Meyers's areas of specialization include contextual influences on child and adolescent development, with an emphasis on family-, school-, and community-based interventions that promote children's social and emotional functioning. She has served as a consultant to the Collaborative for Academic, Social, and Emotional Learning (CASEL), and as a supervisor of mental health consultants working in Head Start preschool settings. She also supervises clinicians providing mental health services to elementary and secondary school students.

Meyers's publications have focused on school-based consultation; adolescent pregnancy, parenthood, and sexual development; school-based preventive interventions; and the role of pretend play in child development. Her clinical interests include therapeutic interventions related to stress and trauma, and mindfulness-based stress reduction. She has taught a wide variety of courses, including introductory psychology, child and adolescent development, human sexuality, introduction to women's studies, and statistics for the social sciences.

Berk and Meyers are faculty colleagues in the Department of Psychology at Illinois State University. They have collaborated on numerous projects, most recently coauthoring the chapter on make-believe play and self-regulation for the *Sage Handbook of Play and Learning in Early Childhood.*

Features at a Glance

Contents

chapter 4
Birth and the Newborn Baby   122

PART THREE
INFANCY AND TODDLERHOOD: THE FIRST TWO YEARS

chapter 5
Physical Development in Infancy and Toddlerhood   158

A Personal Note to Students

Our many years of teaching child development have brought us in contact with thousands of students like you—students with diverse college majors, future goals, interests, and needs. Some are affiliated with our own field of psychology, but many come from other related fields—education, sociology, anthropology, biology, family studies, social service, and health sciences, to name just a few. Each semester, our students' aspirations have proved to be as varied as their fields of study. Many look toward careers in applied work—teaching, caregiving, nursing, counseling, social work, school psychology, and program administration. Some want to teach, and a few want to do research. Most hope someday to become parents, whereas others are already parents who come with a desire to better understand and rear their children. And almost all arrive with a deep curiosity about how they themselves developed from tiny infants into the complex human beings they are today.

Our goal in preparing this eighth edition of *Infants and Children* is to provide a textbook that meets the instructional goals of your course as well as your personal interests and needs. To achieve these objectives, we have grounded this book in a carefully selected body of classic and current theory and research brought to life with stories and vignettes about children and families, most of whom we have known personally. In addition, the text highlights the joint contributions of biology and environment to the developing child, explains how the research process helps solve real-world problems, illustrates commonalities and differences among ethnic groups and cultures, and pays special attention to policy issues that are crucial for safeguarding children's well-being in today's world. Woven throughout the text is a unique pedagogical program that will assist you in mastering information, integrating the various aspects of development, critically examining controversial issues, applying what you have learned, and relating the information to real life.

We hope that learning about child development will be as rewarding for you as we have found it over the years. We would like to know what you think about both the field of child development and this book. We welcome your comments; please contact us through our textbook website: *www.infantschildrenandadolescents.com.*

Laura E. Berk and Adena B. Meyers

Preface for Instructors

A Message from Laura Berk

It is my pleasure to introduce **Adena B. Meyers,** new coauthor of *Infants and, Children,* Eighth Edition. How excited I was when she readily responded "yes!" to my invitation to join in preparing this edition. Adena and I live and work in the same community: We have been departmental colleagues for many years and have written together on numerous occasions. Our coauthorship of the eighth edition is a natural extension of our previous joint endeavors.

Adena brings to the text outstanding scholarship, areas of specialization that complement my own, a similar writing style, a shared commitment to research-based applications, and wide-ranging direct experiences with children and families. In addition to her talents as a teacher, researcher, and clinician, she is an exemplary parent of two remarkable teenagers.

Adena's gracious partnership throughout the journey of preparing this revision realizes my fondest hopes when I first set my pen to page to craft *Infants and Children:* that future editions will be numerous, and that instructor and student enthusiasm for the text will continue to be a deep source of author pride and satisfaction for many years to come.

Laura E. Berk

The Eighth Edition

In preparing this eighth edition of *Infants and Children,* we drew inspiration from the hundreds of students of child development with whom we have worked in our combined half-century of college teaching. As in previous editions, we aimed for a text that is intellectually stimulating, provides depth as well as breadth of coverage, portrays the complexities of child development with clarity and excitement, and is relevant and useful in building a bridge from theory and research to children's everyday lives.

The more than two decades since *Infants and Children* first appeared have been a period of unprecedented expansion and change in theory and research. This eighth edition represents these rapidly transforming aspects of the field, with a wealth of new content and enhanced teaching tools:

■ *Diverse pathways of change are highlighted.* Investigators have reached broad consensus that variations in biological makeup, everyday tasks, and the people who support children in mastery of those tasks lead to wide individual differences in children's paths of change and resulting competencies. This edition pays more attention to variability in development and to recent theories—including ecological, sociocultural, dynamic systems, and epigenesis—that attempt to explain it. Multicultural and cross-cultural findings, including international comparisons, are enhanced throughout the text and in revised and expanded Cultural Influences boxes.

■ *The complex, bidirectional relationship between biology and environment is given greater attention.* Accumulating evidence on development of the brain, motor skills, cognitive and language competencies, temperament and personality, emotional and social understanding, and developmental problems underscores the way biological factors emerge in, are modified by, and share power with experience. The interconnection between biology and environment is revisited throughout the text narrative and in Biology and Environment boxes with new and updated topics.

■ *Inclusion of interdisciplinary research is expanded.* The move toward viewing thoughts, feelings, and behavior as an integrated whole, affected by a wide array of influences in biology, social context, and culture, has motivated developmental researchers to strengthen their ties with other areas of psychology and with other disciplines. Topics and findings included in this edition increasingly reflect the contributions of educational psychology, social psychology, health psychology, clinical psychology, neurobiology, pediatrics, sociology, anthropology, social service, and other fields.

■ *The links among theory, research, and applications—a theme of this book since its inception—are strengthened.* As researchers intensify their efforts to generate findings that can be applied to real-life situations, we have placed even greater weight on social policy issues and sound theory- and evidence-based interventions and practices. Further applications are provided in the Applying What We Know tables, which give students concrete ways of building bridges between their learning and the real world.

■ *The educational context of development becomes a stronger focus.* The home, school, and community are featured as vital educational contexts in which the child develops. Research on effective teaching practices appears in all chapters and in new and revised Social Issues: Education boxes.

■ *The role of active student learning is made more explicit.* The *Take a Moment…* feature, built into the chapter narrative, asks students to think deeply and critically as they read. Ask Yourself questions at the end of each major section have been revised to promote four approaches to engaging actively with the subject matter: *Review, Connect, Apply,* and *Reflect.* This feature assists students in thinking about what they have read from multiple vantage points. The *Look and Listen* feature presents students with opportunities to observe what real children say and do and attend to influences on children in their everyday environments.

Text Philosophy

The basic approach of this book has been shaped by our professional and personal histories as teachers, researchers, and parents. It consists of seven philosophical ingredients that we regard as essential for students to emerge from a course with a thorough understanding of child development:

1. An understanding of major theories and the strengths and shortcomings of each. The first chapter begins by emphasizing that only knowledge of multiple theories can do justice to the richness of child development. As we take up each age period and domain of development, we present a variety of theoretical perspectives, indicate how each highlights previously overlooked facets of development, and discuss research that evaluates it. Consideration of contrasting theories also serves as the context for an evenhanded analysis of many controversial issues.

2. An appreciation of research strategies for investigating child development. To evaluate theories, students must have a firm grounding in research methods and designs. In addition to a special section in Chapter 1 covering research strategies, numerous studies are discussed in sufficient detail throughout the book for students to use what they have learned to critically assess the findings, conclusions, and implications of research.

3. Knowledge of both the sequence of child development and the processes that underlie it. Students are provided with a description of the organized sequence of development along with processes of change. An understanding of *process*—how complex interactions of biological and environmental events produce development—has been the focus of most recent research. Accordingly, the text reflects this emphasis. But new information about the timetable of change is constantly emerging. In many ways, children are considerably more competent than they were believed to be in the past. Current evidence on the sequence and timing of development, along with its implications for process, is presented throughout the book.

4. An appreciation of the impact of context and culture on child development. A wealth of research indicates that children live in rich physical and social contexts that affect all domains of development. In each chapter, students travel to distant parts of the world as we review a growing body of cross-cultural evidence. The text narrative also discusses many findings on socioeconomically and ethnically diverse children within the United States and on children with varying abilities and challenges. Besides highlighting the role of immediate settings, such as family, neighborhood, and school, we make a concerted effort to underscore the impact of larger social structures—societal values, laws, and government programs—on children's well-being.

5. An understanding of the joint contributions of biology and environment to development. The field recognizes more powerfully than ever before the joint roles of hereditary/constitutional and environmental factors—that these contributions to development combine in complex ways and cannot be separated in a simple manner. Numerous examples of how biological dispositions can be maintained as well as transformed by social contexts are presented throughout the book.

6. A sense of the interdependency of all domains of development— physical, cognitive, emotional, and social. Every chapter takes an integrated approach to understanding children. We show how physical, cognitive, emotional, and social development are interwoven. Within the text narrative and in a special series of Ask Yourself *Connect* questions at the end of major sections, students are referred to other sections of the book to deepen their grasp of relationships among various aspects of change.

7. An appreciation of the interrelatedness of theory, research, and applications. Throughout this book, we emphasize that theories of child development and the research stimulated by them provide the foundation for sound, effective practices with children. The links among theory, research, and applications are reinforced by an organizational format in which theory and research are presented first, followed by practical implications. In addition, a current focus in the field—harnessing child development knowledge to shape social policies that support children's needs—is reflected in every chapter. The text addresses the current condition of children in the United States and around the world and shows how theory and research have combined with public interest to spark successful interventions.

Text Organization

The chronological organization of this text assists students in thoroughly understanding each age period. It also eases the task of integrating the various domains of development because each is discussed in close proximity. At the same time, a chronologically organized book requires that theories covering several age periods be presented piecemeal. This creates a challenge for students, who must link the various parts together. To assist with this task, we frequently remind students of important earlier achievements before discussing new developments, referring back to related sections with page references. Also, chapters devoted to the same topic (for example, cognitive development) are similarly organized, making it easier for students to draw connections across age periods and construct an overall view of developmental change.

New Coverage in the Eighth Edition

Child development is a fascinating and ever-changing field, with constantly emerging new discoveries and refinements in existing knowledge. The eighth edition represents this burgeoning contemporary literature with more than 1,500 new citations. Cutting-edge topics throughout the text underscore the book's major themes. Here is a sampling:

CHAPTER 1 New chapter introduction, inviting readers to become acquainted with the coauthors • Revised and updated section on developmental neuroscience, with special attention to developmental social neuroscience • New Social Issues: Health box on how family chaos undermines children's well-being • Revised and updated Cultural Influences box on immigrant youths • Updated examples of research designs, including the benefits of massive longitudinal projects yielding multipurpose data banks • Inclusion of children's assent as part of informed consent guidelines for protection of human subjects

CHAPTER 2 Updated discussion of gene–gene interactions, including the distinction between protein-coding genes and regulator genes • Consideration of social and cultural influences on the male-to-female birth sex ratio • New evidence on older paternal age and increased risk of DNA mutations contributing to serious disorders, including autism and schizophrenia • Enhanced attention to the impact of poverty on development, with special attention to interventions that help children surmount developmental risks • Revised and updated Social Issues: Education box on the impact of worldwide education of girls • Updated research on neighborhood influences on children's physical and mental health • Expanded attention to the role of ethnic minority extended families in promoting resilience in the face of prejudice and economic deprivation • Current statistics on the condition of children and families in the United States compared with other Western nations • Enhanced discussion of gene–environment interaction • Expanded section on epigenesis, including the role of methylation

CHAPTER 3 Revised and updated section on motivations for parenthood • Enhanced attention to fetal brain development, sensory capacities, and behavior • Updated Biology and Environment box on the prenatal environment and health in later life • Expanded and updated consideration of a wide range of teratogens • New evidence on the long-term consequences of emotional stress during pregnancy • Updated Social Issues: Health box on the Nurse–Family Partnership—reducing maternal stress and enhancing child development through social support

CHAPTER 4 New statistics and research on benefits and risks of medical interventions during childbirth • Consideration of the role of chronic maternal stress in preterm and low birth weight • New findings on the risks of late preterm birth—as little as 1 or 2 weeks early • New research on parenting and development of preterm and low-birth-weight infants • Expanded and updated Social Issues: Health box on health care and other policies for parents and newborn babies • Updated findings on hormonal changes in both mothers and fathers around the time of birth, and in foster and adoptive mothers, that facilitate caregiving • New evidence on factors contributing to sudden infant death syndrome (SIDS), along with the importance of public education efforts • New research on the role of sleep in infant learning • Updated discussion of "proximal care"—extensive holding of young babies—in reducing infant crying • Enhanced discussion of techniques for reducing infant stress to painful medical procedures • New findings on prenatal influences on newborn taste perception

CHAPTER 5 Updated introduction to major measures of brain functioning, including the EEG geodesic sensor net (GSN) and near-infrared spectroscopy (NIRS) • Enhanced discussion of brain development, with special attention to the prefrontal cortex • Updated Biology and Environment box on early brain plasticity • New research on children adopted from Romanian orphanages, bearing on whether infancy is a sensitive period of development • Enhanced attention to cultural influences on infant sleep • New findings on long-term consequences of malnutrition in infancy and toddlerhood • New Social Issues: Health box on U.S. public policy changes that improve infant feeding practices in low-income families • Updated discussion of the controversy surrounding

newborns' capacity to imitate • New dynamic systems research on development of walking, reaching, and grasping • Updated findings on implications of infants' capacity to analyze the speech stream for later language progress • Enhanced discussion of the impact of crawling and walking experience on perception of depth-at-an-edge • New evidence on the perceptual narrowing effect in speech, music, and species-related face perception, and in gender- and race-related face perception

CHAPTER 6 Updated evidence on toddlers' grasp of pictures and videos as symbols, including experiences that enhance symbolic understanding • New research on infants' ability to discriminate and perform simple arithmetic operations on large sets of items • Revised section introducing information-processing concepts, including working memory, automatic processes, processing speed, and executive function • Updated Biology and Environment box on infantile amnesia, addressing contributions of neurological change, language, and adult–child conversations about past events to stable long-term memories • New research on cultural variations in scaffolding infant and toddler learning • New evidence on the importance of sustained, high-quality child care from infancy through the preschool years for cognitive, language, literacy, and math performance at kindergarten entry • Updated evaluation findings on Early Head Start • New Biology and Environment box on the capacity of deaf children to invent language when exposed to limited or grammatically inconsistent input • Updated findings on babies' participation in imitative exchanges and joint attention, revealing their developing capacity for effective communication • New research on toddlers' preverbal gestures, with implications for spoken language development • Enhanced attention to SES differences in early vocabulary development as a predictor of vocabulary size at kindergarten entry • New evidence highlighting the vital role of a responsive adult in early language development

CHAPTER 7 Enhanced discussion of cultural variations in infant emotional expressiveness, with special emphasis on the social smile • New research on consequences of effortful control for cognitive, emotional, and social development • Revised section on genetic and environmental influences on temperament, with updated section on ethnic and gender differences • New section on temperamental differences in toddlers' susceptibility to rearing experiences, highlighting research on the short 5-HTTLPR gene • Revised and updated section on consequences of early availability of a consistent caregiver for attachment security, with special attention to children adopted from Eastern European orphanages • New findings on the joint contributions of infant genotype, temperament, and parenting to disorganized/disoriented attachment, with evidence on the short 5-HTTLPR and DRD4-7 repeat genes • Revised and updated Social Issues: Health box on child care, attachment, and later development • Updated research on cultural variations in early self-development

CHAPTER 8 Updated consideration of early childhood brain development, with emphasis on the prefrontal cortex and executive function • New statistics and research on the health status of young children, including tooth decay and childhood immunizations • Updated Biology and Environment box on low-level lead exposure and children's development • Enhanced discussion of the contribution of sleep to early childhood physical growth and cognitive development • Expanded attention to the impact of adult mealtime practices on children's eating behavior and weight status • New evidence on parenting practices and young children's unintentional injuries • Expanded attention to cultural variations in development of drawing, including a new Cultural Influences box on why children from Asian cultures are advanced in drawing progress and creativity

CHAPTER 9 New research on young children's natural and supernatural beliefs, including cultural variations • Updated evidence on early childhood categorization, highlighting cultural differences • New findings on cultural variations in effective scaffolding • New Social Issues: Education box on children's questions as a catalyst for cognitive development • Expanded discussion of gains in executive function in early childhood, including attention, inhibition, and planning • New evidence on neurobiological changes in the cerebral cortex accompanying young children's more effective problem solving • New findings on cognitive attainments and social experiences that contribute to mastery of false belief, with attention to cultural differences • Updated Biology and Environment box on autism and theory of mind • Enhanced discussion of SES differences in emergent literacy and math knowledge • New evidence on benefits of universal prekindergarten programs • Revised section on strengthening preschool intervention, including findings on Head Start REDI • Updated discussion of effects of educational television and computer activities on academic learning • New research on preschoolers' strategies for word learning, including cultural variations

CHAPTER 10 New research on the influence of parents' elaborative reminiscing on preschoolers' self-concept and emotional understanding • Updated Cultural Influences box on cultural variations in personal storytelling and its implications for early self-concept • New evidence addressing contributions of sociodramatic and rough-and-tumble play to young children's emotional and social development • Enhanced discussion of cultural variations in sociodramatic play • Expanded and updated section on contributions of early childhood peer relations to school readiness and academic performance • New research on corporal punishment and children's adjustment, with special attention to children at high genetic risk for behavior problems • Updated Cultural Influences box on ethnic differences in the consequences of physical punishment • Expanded discussion of parent training programs in intervening with aggressive children, with special attention to Incredible Years • Updated evidence on hormonal influences on gender typing • New Social Issues: Education box on mother–child conversations as a source of children's gender stereotypes • Updated section on styles of child rearing, including Baumrind's distinction between confrontive and coercive control

CHAPTER 11 Updated findings on brain development in middle childhood • New evidence on factors contributing to obesity, including parents' demanding work schedules, frequent eating out, and children's capacity for self-regulation • New Social Issues: Health box on family stressors and childhood obesity • Enhanced consideration of the effectiveness of school-based obesity prevention programs • New findings on unintentional injury in middle childhood, with special attention to parental supervision and to school and community safety education programs as preventive strategies • Expanded attention to informal, child-organized games in middle childhood, including SES and cultural variations • Updated statistics on U.S. schoolchildren's physical activity levels and access to physical education and recess

CHAPTER 12 Updated research on school-age children's spatial reasoning, focusing on cognitive maps of large-scale spaces • New sections on executive function and working memory in middle childhood, with implications for academic learning • Updated Biology and Environment box on children with attention-deficit hyperactivity disorder • New findings on the contribution of societal modernization to children's performance on diverse cognitive tasks • Updated evidence on the school-age child's theory of mind, with special attention to recursive thought • New Cultural Influences box on the Flynn effect, dramatic gains in IQ from one generation to the next • New research on contributions of language skills to test bias, with special attention to African-American English • Updated findings on reducing cultural bias in testing through countering the negative impact of stereotype threat • Implications of recursive thought for language development, including understanding irony and sarcasm • Expanded discussion of the diverse cognitive benefits of bilingualism • Enhanced consideration of the benefits of cooperative learning in classrooms • Revised and updated section on educational media, with special attention to the influence of video game play on diverse aspects of cognitive development • Updated section on U.S. academic achievement in international perspective

CHAPTER 13 New evidence addressing effects of person praise and process praise on children's mastery orientation • Expanded coverage of cognitive and cultural influences on achievement-related attributions • Updated section on peer acceptance and rejection • Revised and updated Biology and Environment box on bullies and their victims, with special attention to cyberbullying • Recent changes in children's stereotyped beliefs about achievement • Updated evidence on children's development in gay and lesbian families • Expanded coverage of effects of fathers' employment on child development • Updated discussion of children's fears, including school refusal • Revised and updated Cultural Influences box on the impact of ethnic and political violence on children • Updated evidence on child sexual abuse, including global prevalence estimates and long-term developmental consequences • Enhanced discussion of resilience, introducing the concept of developmental cascade • New research on social and emotional learning interventions, with special emphasis on the 4Rs program

Pedagogical Features

Maintaining a highly accessible writing style—one that is lucid and engaging without being simplistic—continues to be one of our major goals. We frequently converse with students, encouraging them to relate what they read to their own lives. In doing so, we aim to make the study of child development involving and pleasurable.

Chapter Introductions and Vignettes About Children

To provide a helpful preview of chapter content, we include an outline and overview in each chapter introduction. To help students construct a clear image of development and to enliven the text narrative, each chronological age division is unified by case examples woven throughout that set of chapters. For example, within the infancy and toddlerhood section, we look in on three children, observe dramatic changes and striking individual differences, and address the impact of family background, child-rearing practices, parents' and children's life experiences, and child-care quality on development. Besides a set of main characters, many additional vignettes offer vivid examples of development among children.

End-of-Chapter Summaries

Comprehensive end-of-chapter summaries, organized according to the major divisions of each chapter and highlighting important terms, remind students of key points in the text discussion. Learning objectives are included in the summary to encourage focused review.

Ask Yourself Questions

Active engagement with the subject matter is supported by revised and expanded study questions at the end of each major section. Four types of questions prompt students to think about child development in diverse ways: **Review** questions help students recall and comprehend information they have just read. **Connect** questions help students build an image of the whole child by integrating what they have learned across age periods and domains of development. **Apply** questions encourage application of knowledge to controversial issues and problems faced by children, parents, and professionals who work with them. **Reflect** questions make the study of child development personally meaningful by asking students to reflect on their own development and life experiences. Each question is answered on the text's MyDevelopmentLab website.

Learning Objectives

New to this edition, learning objectives appear in the text margins next to each main head, guiding students' reading and study.

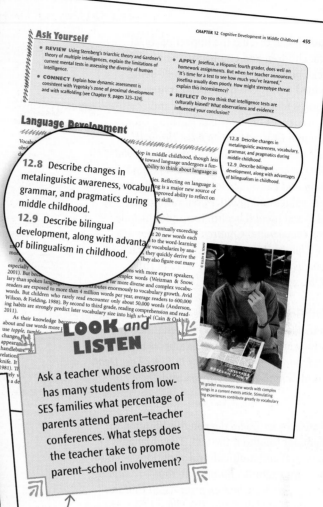

Take a Moment...

Built into the text narrative, this feature asks students to "take a moment" to think about an important point, integrate information on children's development, or engage in an exercise or an application to clarify a challenging concept. **TAKE A MOMENT...** highlights and reinforces the text's strength in conversing with and actively engaging students in learning and in inspiring critical thinking.

Look and Listen

This active-learning feature presents students with opportunities to observe what real children say and do and attend to influences on children in their everyday environments. "Look and Listen" experiences are tied to relevant text sections, with the goal of making the study of development more authentic and meaningful.

Three Types of Thematic Boxes

Thematic boxes accentuate the philosophical themes of this book:

Social Issues boxes discuss the impact of social conditions on children and emphasize the need for sensitive social policies to ensure their well-being. They are divided into two types: **Social Issues: Education** boxes focus on home, school, and community influences on children's learning—for example, *Children Learn About Gender Through Mother–Child Conversations; School Recess—A Time to Play, a Time to Learn;* and *Media Multitasking Disrupts Attention and Learning.* **Social Issues: Health** boxes address values and practices relevant to children's physical and mental health. Examples include *Family Chaos Undermines Children's Well-Being, U.S. Public Policy Changes Improve Infant Feeding Practices in Low-Income Families,* and *Family Stressors and Childhood Obesity.*

Biology and Environment boxes highlight growing attention to the complex, bidirectional relationship between biology and environment. Examples include *The Prenatal Environment and Health in Later Life, Deaf Children Invent Language,* and *Autism and Theory of Mind.*

Cultural Influences boxes deepen the attention to culture threaded throughout the text. They highlight both cross-cultural and multicultural variations in child development—for example, *Immigrant Youths: Adapting to a New Land; Why Are Children from Asian Cultures Advanced in Drawing Skills?;* and *The Flynn Effect: Massive Generational Gains in IQ.*

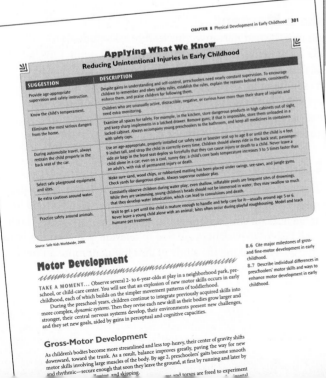

Applying What We Know Tables

In this feature, we summarize research-based applications on many issues, speaking directly to students as parents or future parents and to those pursuing different careers or areas of study, such as teaching, health care, counseling, or social work. The tables include *Supporting Early Language Learning, Helping Children Manage Common Fears of Early Childhood,* and *Regulating Screen Media Use.*

Milestones Tables

A Milestones table appears at the end of each age division of the text. The tables summarize major physical, cognitive, language, emotional, and social attainments, providing a convenient aid for reviewing the chronology of child development.

Enhanced Art and Photo Program

The art and page-layout style present concepts and research findings with clarity and attractiveness, thereby aiding student understanding and retention. Each photo has been carefully selected to complement the text discussion and to represent the diversity of children around the world.

In-Text Key Terms with Definitions, End-of-Chapter Term List, and End-of-Book Glossary

Mastery of terms that make up the central vocabulary of the field is promoted through in-text highlighting of key terms and definitions, which encourages students to review the terminology of the field in greater depth by rereading related information. Key terms also appear in an end-of-chapter page-referenced term list and an end-of-book glossary.

Acknowledgments

The dedicated contributions of a great many individuals helped make this book a reality and contributed to refinements and improvements in this eighth edition.

Reviewers

An impressive cast of reviewers provided many helpful suggestions and constructive criticisms, as well as encouragement and enthusiasm, for the organization and content of the text. We are grateful to each one of them.

For the First Through Seventh Editions

Scott Adler, York University
Mark B. Alcorn, University of Northern Colorado
Joseph Allen, University of Virginia
William Aquilino, University of Wisconsin
Armin W. Arndt, Eastern Washington University
Martha Arterberry, Colby College
Lamia Barakat, Drexel University
Cecelia Benelli, Western Illinois University
Kathleen Bey, Palm Beach Community College
Heather Bouchey, University of Vermont
Donald Bowers, Community College of Philadelphia
Michele Y. Breault, Truman State University
Jerry Bruce, Sam Houston State College
Kristy Burkholder, University of Wisconsin, Madison
Melissa Burnham, University of Nevada, Reno
Lanthan D. Camblin, University of Cincinnati
Joseph J. Campos, University of California, Berkeley
Linda A. Camras, DePaul University
Gustavo Carlo, University of Nebraska—Lincoln
Lynn Caruso, Seneca College
Nancy Taylor Coghill, University of Southwest Louisiana
Raymond Collings, SUNY Cortland
Diane Brothers Cook, Gainesville College
Nicole Campione-Barr, University of Missouri, Columbia
Jennifer Cook, Kent State University
Roswell Cox, Berea College
Ronald Craig, Edinboro University of Pennsylvania
Zoe Ann Davidson, Alabama A&M University
Sheridan DeWolf, Grossmont College
Matthew DiCintio, Delaware County Community College
Constance DiMaria-Kross, Union County College
Jacquelynne Eccles, University of Michigan
Jeff Farrar, University of Florida
Bronwyn Fees, Kansas State University
F. Richard Ferraro, University of North Dakota
Kathleen Fite, Southwest Texas State University
Peter Flynn, Northern Essex Community College
Trisha Folds-Bennett, College of Charleston
Nancy Freeman, University of South Carolina
William Friedman, Oberlin College
Jayne Gackenbach, MacEwan University

Eugene Geist, Ohio University
Sabine Gerhardt, University of Akron
Abi Gewirtz, University of Minnesota
Kristine Hansen, University of Winnipeg
Vivian Harper, San Joaquin Delta College
Algea Harrison, Oakland University
Janice Hartgrove-Freile, North Harris Community College
Vernon Haynes, Youngstown State University
Bert Hayslip, Jr., University of North Texas
Sandra Hellyer, Butler University
Joan Herwig, Iowa State University
Paula Hillmann, University of Wisconsin, Waukesha
Robert Hiltonsmith, Radford University
Shayla Holub, University of Texas, Dallas
Christie Honeycutt, Stanly Community College
Malia Huchendorf, Normandale Community College
Lisa Huffman, Ball State University
Clementine Hansley Hurt, Radford University
Jennifer Jipson, California Polytechnic State University
Scott Johnson, New York University
Joline Jones, Worcester State University
Kate Kenney, Howard Community College
Shirin Khosropour, Austin Community College
Elisa Klein, University of Maryland
John S. Klein, Castleton State College
Claire Kopp, Claremont Graduate School
Eugene Krebs, California State University, Fresno
Carole Kremer, Hudson Valley Community College
Gary W. Ladd, University of Illinois, Urbana–Champaign
Deborah Laible, Lehigh University
Linda Lavine, State University of New York at Cortland
Sara Lawrence, California State University, Northridge
Gail Lee, Jersey City State College
Judith R. Levine, State University of New York at Farmingdale
Miriam Linver, Montclair State University
David Lockwood, Humber College
Frank Manis, University of Southern California
Martin Marino, Atlantic Cape Community College
Mary Ann McLaughlin, Clarion University of Pennsylvania
Megan McLelland, Oregon State University
Annie McManus, Parkland College
Trent Maurer, Georgia Southern University
Cloe Merrill, Weber State University
Daniel Messinger, University of Miami
Rich Metzger, University of Tennessee at Chattanooga
Karla Miley, Black Hawk College
Joyce Munsch, California State University, Northridge
Jennifer Trapp Myers, University of Michigan
Virginia Navarro, University of Missouri, St. Louis
Larry Nelson, Brigham Young University
Peggy Norwood, Red Rocks Community College
Peter V. Oliver, University of Hartford
Behnaz Pakizegi, William Patterson University
Virginia Parsons, Carroll College
Karen Peterson, University of Washington, Vancouver
Julie Poehlmann, University of Wisconsin—Madison

Tom Power, Washington State University
Kavita Prakash, Heritage College
Joe M. Price, San Diego State University
Cathy Proctor-Castillo, Long Beach Community College
Verna Raab, Mount Royal College
Raghu Rao, University of Minnesota
Mary Kay Reed, York College of Pennsylvania
Michael Rodman, Middlesex Community College
Alan Russell, Flinders University
Pamela Schulze, University of Akron
Tizrah Schutzengel, Bergen Community College
Johnna Shapiro, Illinois Wesleyan University
Elizabeth Short, Case Western Reserve University
Delores Smith, University of Tennessee
Gregory Smith, Dickinson College
Laura Sosinsky, Fordham University
Thomas Spencer, San Francisco State University
Carolyn Spies, Bloomfield College
Kathy Stansbury, University of New Mexico
Connie Steele, University of Tennessee, Knoxville
Janet Strayer, Simon Fraser University
Marcia Summers, Ball State University
Daniel Swingley, University of Pennsylvania
Christy Teranishi, Texas A&M International University
Dennis Thompson, Georgia State University
Tracy Thorndike-Christ, Western Washington University
Connie K. Varnhagen, University of Alberta
Athena Vouloumanos, McGill University
Judith Ward, Central Connecticut State University
Shawn Ward, Le Moyne College
Alida Westman, Eastern Michigan University
Jayne White, Drury University
Colin William, Columbus State Community College
Belinda Wholeben, Rockford College
Sue Williams, Southwest Texas State University
Deborah Winters, New Mexico State University
Ilona Yim, University of California, Irvine
Nicole Zarrett, University of South Carolina, Columbia

For the Eighth Edition

Shannon Audley-Piotrowski, Smith College
Janet J. Boseovski, University of North Carolina Greensboro
Kate Fogarty, University of Florida
Dominic Gullo, Drexel University
Shanta Hattikudur, Temple University
Hiu-Chin Hsu, University of Georgia
Zsuzsa Kaldy, University of Massachusetts Boston
Sarah Kollat, Pennsylvania State University
Murray Krantz, Florida State University
Stuart Marcovitch, University of North Carolina Greensboro
Amy H. Mezulis, Seattle Pacific University
Amanda Morris, Oklahoma State University—Tulsa
Winnie Mucherah, Ball State University
Dara Musher-Eisenman, Bowling Green State University
Angela Nievar, University of North Texas

Maggie Renken, Georgia State University
Dorothy Sluss, James Madison University
Joan E. Test, Missouri State University
Virginia Tompkins, Ohio State University

Editorial and Production Team

We have been fortunate to collaborate with a highly capable editorial team at Pearson Education. It has been a great pleasure to work once again with Tom Pauken, Managing Editor, who oversaw the preparation of the fourth and seventh editions of *Infants and Children* and who returned to edit this eighth edition as well as its supplements package. We cannot capture in words Tom's amazing contributions: His careful review of manuscript, keen organizational skills, responsive day-to-day communication, insightful suggestions, astute problem solving, interest in the subject matter, patience, thoughtfulness, and sense of humor (at just the right moments) greatly enhanced the quality of the text and made it possible for us to keep pace with Pearson's tight revision time frame. Tom is truly our editor extraordinaire: We greatly look forward to working with him on future projects.

Donna Simons, Senior Production Project Manager, coordinated the complex production tasks for the seventh edition as well as for this eighth edition, transforming our manuscript into an exquisitely beautiful text. We are grateful for Donna's keen aesthetic sense, attention to detail, flexibility, efficiency, thoughtfulness, and incredible commitment. We cannot count the number of times Donna has been there for us, not just during typical working hours but virtually at all hours—finding a way to create a more convenient page layout, suggesting a more effective turn of phrase in our prose, improving on an artwork sketch to make the resulting figure more effective, and much, much more.

Rachel Trapp, Editorial Assistant, has been nothing short of amazing. In addition to spending countless hours expertly gathering and organizing scholarly literature, she assisted with so many editorial and production tasks that they are, literally, too numerous to list. Judy Ashkenaz, Development Editor, commented on each chapter prior to our revision, helping to ensure that we listened attentively to each of the reviewers' recommendations and suggestions. She also prepared the new Lecture Enhancements for the Instructor's Resource Manual and revised its chapter summaries and outlines. Our appreciation to Judy for her work on more editions of *Infants and Children* than any other member of the publishing team.

We thank Sarah Evertson for helping to identify the exceptional photographs that so aptly illustrate the text narrative. Margaret Pinette provided outstanding copyediting and Julie Hotchkiss, impeccable proofreading.

The instructor resources package benefited from the talents and diligence of several other individuals. Kimberly Michaud, Jeanie McHale, and Rachel Trapp prepared a superb Test Bank along with excellent MyDevelopmentLab and REVEL assessments. Rachel Trapp is also responsible for the beautifully illustrated PowerPoint presentation. Maria Henneberry and Phil Vandiver of Contemporary Visuals in Bloomington, IL, collaborated with us in producing an artistic and inspiring set of new video segments covering diverse topics in child development.

Rachael Payne prepared the ad copy and informative e-mails to the sales representatives and the field about *Infants and Children*, Eighth Edition. She also designed our text website, *www.infantschildrenandadolescents.com*. Rachael's insightful and creative work also appears within Pearson's product website, *www.pearsonhighered.com/berk-ica-8e-info*. We thank, as well, Lindsey Gill, Marketing Manager, for day-to-day marketing efforts aimed at ensuring that up-to-date information about the text and its instructor resources reaches Pearson Education's sales force.

Last but not least, our sincere thanks to Roth Wilkofsky, Senior Publisher of Arts and Sciences, for crafting a caring climate at Pearson in which to prepare this revision. We are indebted to Roth for valuing our work, bringing us to New York for the eighth edition planning meeting, visiting our community to get to know us in the everyday settings in which we work, and periodic problem solving and encouragement. We have benefited greatly from his wide-ranging knowledge and experience, and his cordiality.

Family, Colleagues, and Friends

Immeasurable gratitude goes to our families, colleagues, and friends for their patience, understanding, and support.

From Laura: I thank my family for being *there* for me during over a quarter-century of work on my suite of Pearson titles. My sons, David and Peter, grew up with my texts, passing from childhood to adolescence and then to adulthood as successive editions were written. David has a special connection with the books' subject matter as an inner-city elementary school teacher. Peter is now an experienced attorney, and his vivacious and talented wife Melissa joins a new generation of university faculty engaged in innovative teaching and research. All three continue to enrich my understanding through reflections on events and progress in their own lives. My husband, Ken, willingly put on hold much in our life together to accommodate the challenges and pace of this revision. His astute reflections and support made all the difference during the project's final months.

My appreciation, as well, to Richard Payne, colleague, friend, and fellow Pearson author, for many profitable discussions about the writing process, the condition of children and families, and other topics that have significantly influenced my work. Greg Simpson, Dean of the College of Arts and Sciences, has taught from my texts, repeatedly underscoring their importance to Illinois State University. In addition to warm friendship and advice on the cover image and design, Harold and Marlene Gregor have provided me with an unmatched model of lifelong creativity. Throughout the preparation of this project, my long-time friend Jana Edge ensured that a five- to six-mile early morning walk preceded my sitting down to write. For extraordinary counsel, I am immensely grateful to Paul LiCalsi and Devereux Chatillon.

From Adena: I am especially grateful to Cooper Cutting for encouraging me to pursue this project despite his own significant work commitments. I appreciate the many family dinners he prepared, rides to and from school he provided, and hours of homework he supervised while I was busy writing. My teenage children, Charlie and Isabel Cutting, are my best cheerleaders. As usual, they were good-natured about their mother's hectic schedule and periodic high stress levels. I also thank my parents, Barbara and Joel Meyers, for nurturing my writing skills, believing in me more than I believed in myself, and demonstrating all of the features of high-quality parenting that we describe throughout this text.

I am grateful to my friends and colleagues, Rocío Rivadeneyra, Maura Toro-Morn, Sue Sprecher, Rachel Bowden, Amy Wood, Corinne Zimmerman, and Renée Tobin, for camaraderie that kept me sane and balanced, and for understanding when I was too busy. In addition to being an especially supportive department chair and a good friend, Scott Jordan imparted some of the most important professional advice I have ever received. Karina Diaz and Amanda Rohan proved to be exceptionally reliable and conscientious graduate assistants, whose help was indispensable throughout my work on this project.

Finally, I thank Laura Berk for the opportunity to collaborate with her on this remarkable textbook. Her mentorship and example inspire my best work.

Laura E. Berk and Adena B. Meyers

mydevelopmentlab

MyDevelopment Lab is a collection of online homework, tutorial, and assessment products, integrated with the eText, that is designed to improve students' learning. Authored by Laura Berk and Adena Meyers, MyDevelopmentLab for *Infants and Children*, Eighth Edition, engages students through active learning and promotes in-depth mastery of the subject matter, thereby fostering more thorough preparation for class, quizzes, and exams.

- **A Personalized Study Plan** analyzes students' study needs into three levels: Remember, Understand, and Apply.

- **A Variety of Assessments** enable continuous evaluation of students' learning.

- **The Gradebook** helps students track progress and get immediate feedback. Automatically graded assessments flow into the Gradebook, which can be viewed in MyDevelopmentLab or exported.

- **The eText** allows students to highlight relevant passages and add notes. It can be accessed through a laptop, iPad®, or tablet. An app is available to facilitate download.

- **Extensive video footage** includes NEW segments produced by author Laura Berk.

- **Multimedia simulations** include NEW topics, with simulations designed by author Laura Berk to seamlessly complement the text.

- **Careers in Human Development** explains how studying human development is essential for a wide range of career paths. This tool features more than 25 career overviews, which contain interviews with actual practitioners, educational requirements, typical day-to-day activities, and links to websites for additional information.
- **Biographies** of major figures in the field. Examples include Erik Erikson, Jean Piaget, Lev Vygotsky, Eleanor Gibson, Lawrence Kohlberg, and Carol Gilligan.
- **MyVirtualChild** is an interactive web-based simulation that allows students to rear a child from birth to age 18 and monitor the effects of their parenting decisions over time.

For a sampling of MyDevelopmentLab's rich content, visit *www.mydevelopmentlab.com.*

REVEL™

Revel™ is an immersive learning experience designed for the way today's students read, think, and learn. Built in collaboration with educators and students nationwide, REVEL is Pearson's newest, fully digital method of delivering course content.

REVEL further enlivens the text by integrating into the authors' narrative interactive media and assessments, thereby offering students additional opportunities to engage deeply with course content while reading. Greater student engagement leads to more thorough understanding and improved performance throughout the course.

To learn more about REVEL, visit *www.pearsonhighered.com/ REVEL.*

Instructor Resources

In addition to MyDevelopmentLab and REVEL, several other author-produced student and instructor materials accompany *Infants and Children,* Eighth Edition.

Instructor's Resource Manual (IRM) This thoroughly revised IRM can be used by first-time or experienced instructors to enrich classroom experiences. Two new lecture enhancements accompany each chapter, presenting cutting-edge topics, with article citations and suggestions for expanding on chapter content in class.

Test Bank The Test Bank contains over 2,000 multiple-choice and essay questions, all of which are page-referenced to chapter content and also classified by type.

Pearson MyTest This secure online environment allows instructors to easily create exams, study guide questions, and quizzes from any computer with an Internet connection.

PowerPoint Presentation The PowerPoint presentation provides outlines and illustrations of key topics for each chapter of the text.

"Explorations in Child Development" DVD and Guide This REVISED DVD WITH 10 NEW SEGMENTS is over five hours in length and contains more than 50 four- to ten-minute narrated segments, designed for classroom use, that illustrate the many theories, concepts, and milestones of child development. The DVD and Guide are available only to instructors who are confirmed adopters of the text.

About the Chapter Opening Art

We would like to extend grateful acknowledgments to the International Museum of Children's Art, Oslo, Norway; to the International Child Art Foundation, Washington, DC; and to the World Awareness Children's Museum, Glens Falls, New York, for the exceptional cover image and chapter opening art, which depict the talents, concerns, and viewpoints of young artists from around the world. The awe-inspiring collection of children's art gracing this text expresses family, school, and community themes; good times and personal triumphs; profound appreciation for beauty; and great depth of emotion. We are pleased to share with readers this window into children's creativity, insightfulness, sensitivity, and compassion.

"A Child's Dream of Parents with More Time"
Mia Koch
16 years, Norway

REPRINTED WITH PERMISSION FROM THE INTERNATIONAL MUSEUM OF CHILDREN'S ART, OSLO, NORWAY

Infants and Children

History, Theory, and Research Strategies

REPRINTED WITH PERMISSION FROM THE INTERNATIONAL CHILD ART FOUNDATION, WASHINGTON, DC

"Me and My World"
Lizaveta Lenkevich
9 years, Belarus

With bold brush strokes and vibrant color, this artist conveys the energy and beauty of her town and the various pathways through it. Chapter 1 will introduce you to a multiplicity of ways to think about and study child development.

In a café not far from our university offices, we held our first meeting to discuss the exciting collaborative journey before us—preparing this eighth edition of *Infants and Children*. As we delved into the task, our conversation turned to child development as we had personally experienced it. We exchanged stories about our own children—the amusing things they had said as preschoolers, their varied personalities and interests, and the differences in their childhood experiences, given that our two families are a generation apart in age.

Three decades ago, Laura noted, a free day usually meant that her sons David and Peter hurried out the door after breakfast to join neighborhood playmates in climbing trees, organizing a game of pickup baseball, or building a backyard fort. The out-of-school hours of today's children, in contrast, are more often devoted to a flurry of prearranged learning opportunities—dance, music, and karate lessons; academic tutoring; and parent-organized play dates—leaving little time for unstructured play. Similarly, school life for present-day children seems speeded up: Charlie and Isabel, Adena's son and daughter, mastered in kindergarten much of what David and Peter had been expected to learn in first and second grade. And Charlie and Isabel's world is replete with high-tech media—fast-action video games, cell phones, iPads, iPods, and countless other modern gadgets that didn't exist when David and Peter were young.

As we talked, we touched on our own childhood experiences and how they contributed to who we are today. Laura remembered weekends helping her father in his downtown clothing shop, the year her mother studied to become a high school teacher, and Sunday outings to museums and the seashore. Adena described frequent moves to new cities as her father, a professor, changed jobs every few years, along with the excitement and challenges of adapting to new neighborhoods, schools, and peer groups.

We also spoke about our childhood friends and what we know about their present lives. Laura's high school classmate Phil—shy, anxious, and cruelly teased because of his cleft lip—now owner of a thriving chain of hardware stores and member of his city council. Adena's inventive, extroverted friend Ally, who grew up in a low-income family, served as Adena's campaign manager when she ran for student council, and saved for college by crushing and selling pop cans—today a successful CEO of a nonprofit organization. Julio, immigrant from Mexico who joined Laura's class in third grade—currently director of an elementary school bilingual education program and single parent of an adopted Mexican boy. And finally, Laura's next-door neighbor Rick, who picked fights at recess, struggled with reading, dropped out of high school, and moved from one job to another over the following 10 years.

As you begin this course in child development, perhaps you, too, are wondering about some of the same questions that crossed our minds during our café conversation:

- In what ways are children's home, school, and neighborhood experiences the same today as they were in generations past, and in what ways are they different?
- How are young children's perceptions of the world similar to adults', and how are they different?

- What determines the features that humans have in common and those that make each of us unique—physically, mentally, and behaviorally?
- How did Julio, transplanted at age 8 to a new culture, master its language and customs and succeed in its society, yet remain strongly identified with his ethnic community?
- Why do some of us, like Kathryn and Rick, retain the same styles of responding that characterized us as children, whereas others, like Phil, change in essential ways?
- How do cultural changes—employed mothers, child care, divorce, smaller families, and new technologies—affect children's characteristics?

These are central questions addressed by **child development,** an area of study devoted to understanding constancy and change from conception through adolescence. Child development is part of a larger, interdisciplinary field known as **developmental science,** which includes all changes we experience throughout the lifespan (Lerner et al., 2011). Great diversity characterizes the interests and concerns of the thousands of investigators who study child development. But all have a common goal: to describe and identify those factors that influence the consistencies and changes in young people during the first two decades of life. ■

1.1 What is the field of child development, and what factors stimulated its expansion?

1.2 How is child development typically divided into domains and periods?

The Field of Child Development

The questions just listed are not just of scientific interest. Each has *applied,* or practical, importance as well. In fact, scientific curiosity is just one factor that led child development to become the exciting field of study it is today. Research about development has also been stimulated by social pressures to improve the lives of children. For example, the beginning of public education in the early twentieth century led to a demand for knowledge about what and how to teach children of different ages. Pediatricians' interest in improving children's health required an understanding of physical growth and nutrition. The social service profession's desire to treat children's emotional and behavior problems and to help them cope with challenging life circumstances, such as the birth of a sibling, parental divorce, poverty, bullying in school, or the death of a loved one, required information about personality and social development. And parents have continually sought advice about child-rearing practices and experiences that would promote their children's development and well-being.

Our large storehouse of information about child development is *interdisciplinary*. It has grown through the combined efforts of people from many fields. Because of the need to solve everyday problems concerning children, researchers from psychology, sociology, anthropology, biology, and neuroscience have joined forces with professionals from education, family studies, medicine, public health, and social service, to name just a few. Together, they have created the field

© ELLEN B. SENISI

Child development research has great practical value. Findings on how children learn best in school have contributed to new approaches to education that emphasize exploration, discovery, and collaboration.

of child development as it exists today—a body of knowledge that is not just scientifically important but also relevant and useful.

Domains of Development

To make the vast, interdisciplinary study of human constancy and change more orderly and convenient, development is often divided into three broad domains: *physical, cognitive,* and *emotional and social.* Refer to Figure 1.1 for a description and illustration of each. Within each period from infancy through adolescence, we will consider the three domains in the order just mentioned. Yet the domains are not really distinct. Rather, they combine in an integrated, holistic fashion to yield the living, growing child. Furthermore, each domain influences and is influenced by the others. For example, in Chapter 5 you will see that new motor capacities, such as reaching, sitting, crawling, and walking (physical), contribute greatly to infants' understanding of their surroundings (cognitive). When babies think and act more competently, adults stimulate them more with games, language, and expressions of delight at their new achievements (emotional and social). These enriched experiences, in turn, promote all aspects of development.

You will encounter instances of the interwoven nature of all domains on nearly every page of this book. In the margins of the text, you will find occasional *Look and Listen* activities— opportunities for you to see everyday illustrations of development by observing what real children say and do or by attending to everyday influences on children. Through these experiences, we hope to make your study of development more authentic and meaningful.

Also, look for the *Ask Yourself* feature at the end of major sections, designed to deepen your understanding. Within it, we have included *Review* questions, which help you recall and think about information you have just read; *Connect* questions, which help you form a coherent, unified picture of child development; *Apply* questions, which encourage you to apply your knowledge to controversial issues and problems faced by parents, teachers, and children; and *Reflect* questions, which invite you to reflect on your own development and that of people you know well.

Physical Development

Changes in body size, proportions, appearance, functioning of body systems, perceptual and motor capacities, and physical health

Cognitive Development

Changes in intellectual abilities, including attention, memory, academic and everyday knowledge, problem solving, imagination, creativity, and language

Emotional and Social Development

Changes in emotional communication, self-understanding, knowledge about other people, interpersonal skills, friendships, intimate relationships, and moral reasoning and behavior

FIGURE 1.1 **Major domains of development.** The three domains are not really distinct. Rather, they overlap and interact.

Periods of Development

Besides distinguishing and integrating the three domains, another dilemma arises in discussing development: how to divide the flow of time into sensible, manageable parts. Researchers usually use the following age periods, according to which we have organized this book. Each brings new capacities and social expectations that serve as important transitions in major theories:

- *The prenatal period: from conception to birth.* In this nine-month period, the most rapid time of change, a one-celled organism is transformed into a human baby with remarkable capacities for adjusting to life in the surrounding world.
- *Infancy and toddlerhood: from birth to 2 years.* This period brings dramatic changes in the body and brain that support the emergence of a wide array of motor, perceptual, and intellectual capacities; the beginnings of language; and first intimate ties to others. Infancy spans the first year; toddlerhood spans the second, during which children take their first independent steps, marking a shift to greater autonomy.
- *Early childhood: from 2 to 6 years.* The body becomes longer and leaner, motor skills are refined, and children become more self-controlled and self-sufficient. Make-believe play blossoms, reflecting and supporting many aspects of psychological development. Thought and language expand at an astounding pace, a sense of morality becomes evident, and children establish ties with peers.
- *Middle childhood: from 6 to 11 years.* Children learn about the wider world and master new responsibilities that increasingly resemble those they will perform as adults. Hallmarks of this period are improved athletic abilities; participation in organized games with rules; more logical thought processes; mastery of fundamental reading, writing, math, and other academic knowledge and skills; and advances in understanding the self, morality, and friendship.
- *Adolescence: from 11 to 18 years.* This period initiates the transition to adulthood. Puberty leads to an adult-sized body and sexual maturity. Thought becomes increasingly complex, abstract, and idealistic, and schooling is directed toward preparation for higher education and the world of work. Young people begin to establish autonomy from the family and to define personal values and goals.

For many contemporary youths in industrialized nations, the transition to adult roles has become increasingly prolonged—so much so that some researchers have posited a new period of development called *emerging adulthood,* extending from age 18 to the mid- to late-twenties. Although emerging adults have moved beyond adolescence, they have not yet fully assumed adult roles. Rather, during higher education and sometimes beyond, these young people intensify their exploration of options in love, career, and personal values before making enduring commitments. Because emerging adulthood first became apparent during the past few decades, researchers have just begun to study it (Arnett, 2007, 2011). Perhaps it is *your* period of development.

With this introduction in mind, let's turn to some basic issues that have captivated, puzzled, and sparked debate among child development theorists. Then our discussion will trace the emergence of the field and survey major theories. We will return to each contemporary theory in greater detail in later chapters.

© UWE OMMER, *1,000 FAMILIES*, TASCHEN

Child development is so dramatic that researchers divide it into periods. This large South African family includes children in infancy (child in arms), early childhood (seated boys), middle childhood (girl standing in front row), and adolescence (boy standing at far left).

Basic Issues

1.3 Identify three basic issues on which theories of child development take a stand.

Research on child development did not begin until the late nineteenth and early twentieth centuries. But ideas about how children grow and change have a much longer history. As these speculations combined with research, they inspired the construction of *theories* of development. A **theory** is an orderly, integrated set of statements that describes, explains, and predicts behavior. For example, a good theory of infant–caregiver attachment would (1) *describe* the behaviors of babies around 6 to 8 months of age as they seek the affection and comfort of a familiar adult, (2) *explain* how and why infants develop this strong desire to bond with a caregiver, and (3) *predict* the consequences of this emotional bond for future relationships.

Theories are vital tools for two reasons. First, they provide organizing frameworks for our observations of children. In other words, they *guide and give meaning* to what we see. Second, theories that are verified by research often serve as a sound basis for practical action. Once a theory helps us *understand* development, we are in a much better position *to know how to improve* the welfare and treatment of children.

As we will see later, theories are influenced by the cultural values and belief systems of their times. But theories differ in one important way from mere opinion or belief: A theory's continued existence depends on *scientific verification*. Every theory must be tested using a fair set of research procedures agreed on by the scientific community, and its findings must endure, or be replicated over time.

Within the field of child development, many theories offer very different ideas about what children are like and how they change. The study of child development provides no ultimate truth because investigators do not always agree on the meaning of what they see. Also, children are complex beings; they change physically, cognitively, emotionally, and socially. No single theory has explained all these aspects. But the existence of many theories helps advance knowledge because researchers are continually trying to support, contradict, and integrate these different points of view.

Although there are many theories, we can easily organize them by looking at the stand they take on three basic issues: (1) Is the course of development continuous or discontinuous? (2) Does one course of development characterize all children, or are there many possible courses? (3) What are the roles of genetic and environmental factors—nature and nurture—in development? Let's look closely at each of these issues.

Continuous or Discontinuous Development?

A mother reported with amazement that her 20-month-old son Angelo had pushed a toy car across the living room floor while making a motorlike sound, "Brmmmm, brmmmm," for the first time. When he hit a nearby wall with a bang, Angelo let go of the car, exclaimed, "C'ash!" and laughed heartily.

"How come Angelo can pretend, but he couldn't a few months ago?" his mother asked. "And I wonder what 'Brmmmm, brmmmm' and 'Crash!' mean to Angelo. Does he understand motorlike sounds and collision the same way I do?"

Angelo's mother has raised a puzzling issue about development: How can we best describe the differences in capacities and behavior among small infants, young children, adolescents, and adults? As Figure 1.2 on page 8 illustrates, most major theories recognize two possibilities.

One view holds that infants and preschoolers respond to the world in much the same way as adults do. The difference between the immature and the mature being is simply one of *amount or complexity*. For example, little Angelo's thinking may be just as logical and well-organized as our own. Perhaps (as his mother reports) he can sort objects into simple categories, recognize whether he has more of one kind than of another, and remember where he left his favorite toy at child care the week before. Angelo's only limitation may be that he cannot perform these skills with as much information and precision as we can. If this is so, then

FIGURE 1.2 **Is development continuous or discontinuous?** (a) Some theorists believe that development is a smooth, continuous process. Children gradually add more of the same types of skills. (b) Other theorists think that development takes place in discontinuous stages. Children change rapidly as they step up to a new level and then change very little for a while. With each step, the child interprets and responds to the world in a qualitatively different way.

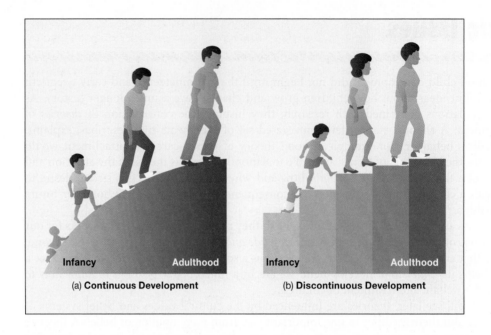

Infancy **Adulthood** **Infancy** **Adulthood**

(a) **Continuous Development** (b) **Discontinuous Development**

Angelo's development is **continuous**—a process of gradually adding more of the same types of skills that were there to begin with.

According to a second view, Angelo's thoughts, emotions, and behavior differ considerably from those of adults. His development is **discontinuous**—a process in which new ways of understanding and responding to the world emerge at specific times. From this perspective, Angelo is not yet able to organize objects or remember and interpret experiences as we do. Instead, he will move through a series of developmental steps, each with unique features, until he reaches the highest level of functioning.

Theories that accept the discontinuous perspective regard development as taking place in **stages**—*qualitative* changes in thinking, feeling, and behaving that characterize specific periods of development. In stage theories, development is much like climbing a staircase, with each step corresponding to a more mature, reorganized way of functioning. The stage concept also assumes that children undergo periods of rapid transformation as they step up from one stage to the next, alternating with plateaus during which they stand solidly within a stage. In other words, change is fairly sudden rather than gradual and ongoing.

Does development actually occur in a neat, orderly sequence of stages? This ambitious assumption has faced significant challenges (Collins & Hartup, 2013). Later in this chapter, we will review some influential stage theories.

One Course of Development or Many?

Stage theorists assume that people everywhere follow the same sequence of development. For example, in the domain of cognition, a stage theorist might try to identify the common influences that lead children to represent their world through language and make-believe play in early childhood, to think more logically and systematically in middle childhood, and to reason more systematically and abstractly in adolescence.

At the same time, the field of child development is becoming increasingly aware that children grow up in distinct **contexts**—unique combinations of personal and environmental circumstances that can result in different paths of change. For example, a shy child who fears social encounters develops in very different contexts from those of an outgoing agemate who readily seeks out other people. Children in non-Western village societies have experiences in their families and communities that differ sharply from those of children in large Western cities (Kagan, 2013a; Shweder et al., 2006). These different circumstances foster different cognitive capacities, social skills, and feelings about the self and others.

As you will see, contemporary theorists regard the contexts that shape development as many-layered and complex. On the personal side, these include heredity and biological makeup. On the environmental side, they include both immediate settings—home, child-care center, school, and neighborhood—and circumstances that are more remote from children's everyday lives: community resources, societal values and priorities, and historical time period. Finally, researchers today are more conscious than ever before of cultural diversity in development.

Relative Influence of Nature and Nurture?

In addition to describing the course of child development, each theory takes a stand on a major question about its underlying causes: Are genetic or environmental factors more important in influencing development? This is the age-old **nature–nurture controversy.** By *nature,* we mean the hereditary information we receive from our parents at the moment of conception. By *nurture,* we mean the complex forces of the physical and social world that influence our biological makeup and psychological experiences before and after birth.

Although all theories grant roles to both nature and nurture, they vary in emphasis. Consider the following questions: Is the older child's ability to think in more complex ways largely the result of a built-in timetable of growth, or is it primarily influenced by stimulation from parents and teachers? Do children acquire language because they are genetically predisposed to do so or because parents intensively teach them from an early age? And what accounts for the vast individual differences among children—in height, weight, physical coordination, intelligence, personality, and social skills? Is nature or nurture more responsible?

A theory's position on the roles of nature and nurture affects how it explains individual differences. Theorists who emphasize *stability*—that children who are high or low in a characteristic (such as verbal ability, anxiety, or sociability) will remain so at later ages—typically stress the importance of *heredity*. If they regard environment as important, they usually point to *early experiences* as establishing a lifelong pattern of behavior. Powerful negative events in the first few years, they argue, cannot be fully overcome by later, more positive ones (Bowlby, 1980; Sroufe, Coffino, & Carlson, 2010). Other theorists, taking a more optimistic view, see development as having substantial **plasticity** throughout life—as open to change in response to influential experiences (Baltes, Lindenberger, & Staudinger, 2006; Overton, 2010).

Throughout this book, you will see that investigators disagree, often sharply, on the question of *stability versus plasticity*. Their answers have great applied significance. If you believe that development is largely due to nature, then providing experiences aimed at promoting change would seem to be of little value. If, on the other hand, you are convinced of the supreme importance of early experience, then you would intervene as soon as possible, offering high-quality stimulation and support to ensure that children develop at their best. Finally, if you think that environment is profoundly influential throughout development, you would provide assistance any time children or adolescents face difficulties, in the belief that, with the help of favorable life circumstances, they can recover from early negative events.

A Balanced Point of View

So far, we have discussed basic issues of child development in terms of extremes—solutions favoring one side or the other. But as we trace the unfolding of the field in the rest of this chapter, you will see that the positions of many theorists have softened. Today, some theorists believe that both continuous and discontinuous changes occur. Many acknowledge that development has both universal features and features unique to the individual and his or her contexts. And a growing number regard heredity and environment as inseparably interwoven, each affecting the potential of the other to modify the child's traits and capacities (Goldhaber, 2012; Kagan, 2013b; Overton, 2010). We will discuss these new ideas about nature and nurture in Chapter 2.

Biology and Environment

Resilient Children

John and his best friend, Gary, grew up in a rundown, crime-ridden inner-city neighborhood. By age 10, each had experienced years of family conflict followed by parental divorce. Reared from then on in mother-headed households, John and Gary rarely saw their fathers. Both dropped out of high school and were in and out of trouble with the police.

Then their paths diverged. By age 30, John had fathered two children with women he never married, had spent time in prison, was unemployed, and drank alcohol heavily. In contrast, Gary had returned to finish high school, had studied auto mechanics at a community college, and became manager of a gas station and repair shop. Married with two children, he had saved his earnings and bought a home. He was happy, healthy, and well-adapted to life.

A wealth of evidence shows that environmental risks—poverty, negative family interactions and parental divorce, job loss, mental illness, and drug abuse—predispose children to future problems (Masten, 2007, 2011; Sameroff, 2006). Why did Gary "beat the odds" and come through unscathed?

Research on **resilience**—the ability to adapt effectively in the face of threats to development—is receiving increased attention as investigators look for ways to protect young people from the damaging effects of stressful life conditions. This interest has been inspired by several long-term studies on the relationship of life stressors in childhood to competence and adjustment in adolescence and adulthood (Werner, 2013). In each study, some individuals were shielded from negative outcomes, whereas others had lasting problems. Four broad factors seemed to offer protection from the damaging effects of stressful life events.

This teenager's close, affectionate relationship with his grandfather helps foster resilience. Strong bonds with family members can shield children from the damaging effects of stressful life conditions.

Personal Characteristics

A child's genetically influenced characteristics can reduce exposure to risk or lead to experiences that compensate for early stressful events. High intelligence and socially valued talents (in music or athletics, for example) increase the chances that a child will have rewarding

---

Finally, as you will see later in this book, the relative impact of early and later experiences varies greatly from one domain of development to another and even—as the Biology and Environment box above indicates—across individuals! Because of the complex network of factors contributing to human change and the challenges of isolating the effects of each, many theoretical points of view have gathered research support. Although debate continues, this circumstance has also sparked more balanced visions of child development.

Ask Yourself

- **REVIEW** What is meant by a *stage* of development? Provide your own example of stagewise change. What stand do stage theorists take on the issue of continuous versus discontinuous development?

- **CONNECT** Provide an example of how one domain of development (physical, cognitive, or emotional/social) can affect development in another domain.

- **APPLY** Anna, a high school counselor, has devised a program that integrates classroom learning with vocational training to help adolescents at risk for school dropout stay in school and transition smoothly to work life. What is Anna's position on *stability versus plasticity* in development? Explain.

- **REFLECT** Describe an aspect of your development that differs from a parent's or a grandparent's when he or she was your age. How might *contexts* explain this difference?

experiences at school and in the community that offset the impact of a stressful home life. Temperament is particularly powerful. Children who have easygoing, sociable dispositions and who can readily inhibit negative emotions and impulses tend to have an optimistic outlook on life and a special capacity to adapt to change—qualities that elicit positive responses from others. In contrast, emotionally reactive and irritable children often tax the patience of people around them (Vanderbilt-Adriance & Shaw, 2008; Wang & Deater-Deckard, 2013). For example, both John and Gary moved several times during their childhoods. Each time, John became anxious and angry. Gary looked forward to making new friends and exploring a new neighborhood.

A Warm Parental Relationship

A close relationship with at least one parent who provides warmth, appropriately high expectations, monitoring of the child's activities, and an organized home environment fosters resilience (Masten & Shaffer, 2006; Taylor, 2010). But this factor (as well as the next one) is not independent of children's personal characteristics. Children who are relaxed, socially responsive, and able to deal with change are easier to rear and more likely to enjoy positive relationships with parents and other people. At the same time, children may develop more attractive dispositions as a result of parental warmth and attention (Gulotta, 2008).

Social Support Outside the Immediate Family

The most consistent asset of resilient children is a strong bond with a competent, caring adult. For children who do not have a close bond with either parent, a grandparent, aunt, uncle, or teacher who forms a special relationship with the child can promote resilience (Masten & Reed, 2002). Gary received support in adolescence from his grandfather, who listened to Gary's concerns and helped him solve problems. In addition, Gary's grandfather had a stable marriage and work life and handled stressors skillfully. Consequently, he served as a model of effective coping.

Associations with rule-abiding peers who value school achievement are also linked to resilience (Tiet, Huizinga, & Byrnes, 2010). But children who have positive relationships with adults are far more likely to establish these supportive peer ties.

Community Resources and Opportunities

Community supports—good schools, convenient and affordable health care and social services, libraries, and recreation centers—foster both parents' and children's well-being. In addition, opportunities to participate in community life help older children and adolescents overcome adversity. Extracurricular

activities at school, religious youth groups, scouting, and other organizations teach important social skills, such as cooperation, leadership, and contributing to others' welfare. As participants acquire these competencies, they gain in self-reliance, self-esteem, and community commitment (Benson et al., 2006). As a college student, Gary volunteered for Habitat for Humanity, joining a team building affordable housing in low-income neighborhoods. Community involvement offered Gary opportunities to form meaningful relationships, which further strengthened his resilience.

Research on resilience highlights the complex connections between heredity and environment. Armed with positive characteristics, which stem from native endowment, favorable rearing experiences, or both, children and adolescents can act to reduce stressful situations.

But when many risks pile up, they are increasingly difficult to overcome (Obradović et al., 2009). To inoculate children against the negative effects of risk, interventions must not only reduce risks but also enhance children's protective relationships at home, in school, and in the community. This means attending to both the person and the environment—strengthening children's capacities while also reducing hazardous experiences.

Historical Foundations

1.4 Describe major historical influences on theories of child development.

Contemporary theories of child development are the result of centuries of change in Western cultural values, philosophical thinking about children, and scientific progress. To understand the field as it exists today, we must return to its early beginnings—to ideas about children that long preceded scientific child study but that linger as important forces in current theory and research.

Medieval Times

Childhood was regarded as a separate period of life as early as medieval Europe—the sixth through the fifteenth centuries. Medieval painters often depicted children wearing loose, comfortable gowns, playing games, and looking up to adults. Written texts contained terms that distinguished children under age 7 or 8 from other people and that recognized even young teenagers as not fully mature. By the fourteenth century, manuals offering advice on many aspects of child care, including health, feeding, clothing, and games, were common (Heywood, 2013; Lett, 1997). Laws recognized that children needed protection from people

KUNSTHISTORISCHES MUSEUM, VIENNA, AUSTRIA/ALI MEYER/BRIDGEMAN ART LIBRARY

As early as medieval times, adults viewed childhood as a distinct developmental period. In this sixteenth-century painting, *Children's Games*, by Pieter Bruegel the Elder, boys and girls wearing loose, comfortable clothing play lively outdoor games. [*Children's Games (Kinderspiele)*: Detail of top right-hand corner, 1560 (oil on panel) (detail of 68945), Bruegel, Pieter the Elder (c.1525–69).]

who might mistreat them, and courts exercised leniency with lawbreaking youths because of their tender years (Hanawalt, 1993).

In sum, in medieval times, if not before, clear awareness existed of children as vulnerable beings. Religious writings, however, contained contradictory depictions of children's basic nature, sometimes portraying them as possessed by the devil and in need of purification, at other times as innocent and close to angels (Hanawalt, 2003). Both ideas foreshadowed later views of childhood.

The Reformation

In the sixteenth century, the Puritan belief in original sin gave rise to the view that children were born evil and stubborn and had to be civilized (Heywood, 2013). Harsh, restrictive child-rearing practices were recommended to tame the depraved child. Children were dressed in stiff, uncomfortable clothing that held them in adultlike postures, and disobedient students were routinely beaten by their schoolmasters. Nevertheless, love and affection for their children prevented most Puritan parents from using extremely repressive measures (Moran & Vinovskis, 1986).

As the Puritans emigrated from England to the New World, they brought the belief that child rearing was one of their most important obligations. Although they continued to regard the child's soul as tainted by original sin, they tried to teach their sons and daughters to use reason to tell right from wrong (Clarke-Stewart, 1998). As they trained their children in self-reliance and self-control, Puritan parents gradually adopted a moderate balance between severity and permissiveness.

Philosophies of the Enlightenment

The seventeenth-century Enlightenment brought new philosophies that emphasized ideals of human dignity and respect. Conceptions of childhood were more humane than those of the past.

JOHN LOCKE The writings of British philosopher John Locke (1632–1704) served as the forerunner of a twentieth-century perspective that we will discuss shortly: behaviorism. Locke viewed the child as a *tabula rasa*—Latin for "blank slate." According to this idea, children begin as nothing at all; their characters are shaped entirely by experience. Locke (1690/1892) saw parents as rational tutors who can mold the child in any way they wish through careful instruction, effective example, and rewards for good behavior. He was ahead of his time in recommending child-rearing practices that present-day research supports—for example, the use of praise and approval as rewards, rather than money or sweets. He also opposed physical punishment: "The child repeatedly beaten in school cannot look upon books and teachers without experiencing fear and anger." Locke's philosophy led to a change from harshness toward children to kindness and compassion.

Look carefully at Locke's ideas, and you will see that he regarded development as *continuous*: Adultlike behaviors are gradually built up through the warm, consistent teachings of parents. His view of the child as a tabula rasa led him to champion *nurture*—the power of the environment to shape the child. And his faith in nurture suggests the possibility of *many courses of development* and of *high plasticity at later ages* due to new experiences. Finally,

Locke's philosophy characterizes children as doing little to influence their own destiny, which is written on "blank slates" by others. This vision of a passive child has been discarded. All contemporary theories view children as active, purposeful beings who contribute substantially to their own development.

JEAN-JACQUES ROUSSEAU   In the eighteenth century, French philosopher Jean-Jacques Rousseau (1712–1778) introduced a new view of childhood. Children, Rousseau claimed, are not blank slates to be filled by adult instruction. Instead, they are *noble savages,* naturally endowed with a sense of right and wrong and an innate plan for orderly, healthy growth. Unlike Locke, Rousseau believed that children's built-in moral sense and unique ways of thinking and feeling would only be harmed by adult training. His was a child-centered philosophy in which the adult should be receptive to the child's needs at each of four stages: infancy, childhood, late childhood, and adolescence.

Rousseau's philosophy includes two influential concepts. The first is the concept of *stage,* which we discussed earlier. The second is the concept of **maturation,** which refers to a genetically determined, naturally unfolding course of growth. In contrast to Locke, Rousseau saw children as determining their own destinies. And he viewed development as a *discontinuous, stagewise* process that follows a *single, unified course* mapped out by *nature.*

Scientific Beginnings

The study of child development evolved quickly in the late nineteenth and early twentieth centuries. Early observations of children were soon followed by improved methods and theories. Each advance contributed to the firm foundation on which the field rests today.

DARWIN: FOREFATHER OF SCIENTIFIC CHILD STUDY   British naturalist Charles Darwin (1809–1882) joined an expedition to distant parts of the world, where he observed infinite variation among plant and animal species. He also saw that within a species, no two individuals are exactly alike. From these observations, he constructed his famous *theory of evolution.*

The theory emphasized two related principles: *natural selection* and *survival of the fittest.* Darwin (1859/2003) explained that certain species survive in particular parts of the world because they have characteristics that fit with, or are adapted to, their surroundings. Other species die off because they are less well-suited to their environments. Individuals within a species who best meet the environment's survival requirements live long enough to reproduce and pass their more beneficial characteristics to future generations. Darwin's emphasis on the adaptive value of physical characteristics and behavior eventually found its way into important developmental theories.

During his explorations, Darwin discovered that early prenatal growth is strikingly similar in many species. Other scientists concluded from Darwin's observation that the development of the human child followed the same general plan as the evolution of the human species. Although this belief eventually proved inaccurate, efforts to chart parallels between child growth and human evolution prompted researchers to make careful observations of all aspects of children's behavior. Out of these first attempts to document an idea about development, scientific child study was born.

THE NORMATIVE PERIOD   G. Stanley Hall (1844–1924), one of the most influential American psychologists of the early twentieth century, is generally regarded as the founder of the child-study movement (Cairns & Cairns, 2006). Inspired by Darwin's work, Hall and his well-known student Arnold Gesell (1880–1961) devised theories based on evolutionary ideas. They regarded development as a *maturational process*—a genetically determined series of events that unfold automatically, much like a flower (Gesell, 1933; Hall, 1904).

Hall and Gesell are remembered less for their one-sided theories than for their intensive efforts to describe all aspects of child development. They launched the **normative approach,** in which measures of behavior are taken on large numbers of individuals and age-related

Theories of child development have sparked an extensive parenting-advice literature. These parents turn to an infant-care manual for guidance on how best to care for their new baby.

averages are computed to represent typical development. Using this procedure, Hall constructed elaborate questionnaires asking children of different ages almost everything they could tell about themselves—interests, fears, imaginary playmates, dreams, friendships, everyday knowledge, and more. Similarly, through observations and parent interviews, Gesell collected detailed normative information on the motor achievements, social behaviors, and personality characteristics of infants and children.

Gesell was also among the first to make knowledge about child development meaningful to parents by telling them what to expect at each age. If, as he believed, the timetable of development is the product of millions of years of evolution, then children are naturally knowledgeable about their needs. His child-rearing advice, in the tradition of Rousseau, recommended sensitivity to children's cues (Thelen & Adolph, 1992). Along with Benjamin Spock's *Baby and Child Care,* Gesell's books became a central part of a rapidly expanding popular literature for parents.

THE MENTAL TESTING MOVEMENT While Hall and Gesell were developing their theories and methods in the United States, French psychologist Alfred Binet (1857–1911) was also taking a normative approach to child development, but for a different reason. In the early 1900s, Binet and his colleague Theodore Simon were asked by Paris school officials to find a way to identify children with learning problems who needed to be placed in special classes. To address these practical educational concerns, Binet and Simon constructed the first successful intelligence test.

Binet began with a well-developed theory of intelligence. Capturing the complexity of children's thinking, he defined intelligence as good judgment, planning, and critical reflection (Sternberg & Jarvin, 2003). Then he created age-graded test items that directly measured these abilities.

In 1916, at Stanford University, Binet's test was adapted for use with English-speaking children. Since then, the English version has been known as the *Stanford-Binet Intelligence Scale.* Besides providing a score that could successfully predict school achievement, the Binet test sparked tremendous interest in individual differences in development. Comparisons of the scores of children who vary in gender, ethnicity, birth order, family background, and other characteristics became a major focus of research. And intelligence tests rose quickly to the forefront of the nature–nurture controversy.

LOOK and LISTEN

Examine several recent parenting-advice books in your local bookstore or library, and identify the stance each book takes on the three basic issues about child development.

Ask Yourself

- **REVIEW** Imagine a debate between John Locke and Jean-Jacques Rousseau on the nature–nurture controversy. Summarize the argument that each historical figure is likely to present.

- **CONNECT** What do the ideas of Rousseau, Darwin, and Hall have in common?

- **REFLECT** Find out whether your parents read any child-rearing advice books when you were growing up. What questions most concerned them? Do you think the concerns of today's parents differ from those of your parents' generation? Explain.

1.5 What theories influenced child development research in the mid-twentieth century?

Mid-Twentieth-Century Theories

In the mid-twentieth century, the field of child development expanded. A variety of theories emerged, each of which continues to have followers today. In these theories, the European concern with the child's inner thoughts and feelings contrasts sharply with the North American academic focus on scientific precision and concrete, observable behavior.

The Psychoanalytic Perspective

By the 1930s and 1940s, parents increasingly sought professional help in dealing with children's emotional difficulties. The earlier normative movement had answered the question, What are children like? Now another question had to be addressed: How and why do children become the way they are? To treat psychological problems, psychiatrists and social workers turned to an emerging approach to personality development that emphasized each child's unique history.

According to the **psychoanalytic perspective,** children move through a series of stages in which they confront conflicts between biological drives and social expectations. How these conflicts are resolved determines the person's ability to learn, to get along with others, and to cope with anxiety. Among the many individuals who contributed to the psychoanalytic perspective, two were especially influential: Sigmund Freud, founder of the psychoanalytic movement, and Erik Erikson.

FREUD'S THEORY   Freud (1856–1939), a Viennese physician, sought a cure for emotionally troubled adults by having them talk freely about painful events of their childhoods. Working with these recollections, he examined his patients' unconscious motivations and constructed his **psychosexual theory,** which emphasizes that how parents manage their child's sexual and aggressive drives in the first few years is crucial for healthy personality development.

In Freud's theory, three parts of the personality—id, ego, and superego—become integrated during five stages, summarized in Table 1.1 on page 16. The *id,* the largest portion of the mind, is the source of basic biological needs and desires. The *ego,* the conscious, rational part of personality, emerges in early infancy to redirect the id's impulses so they are discharged in acceptable ways. Between 3 and 6 years of age, the *superego,* or conscience, develops as parents insist that children conform to the values of society. Now the ego faces the increasingly complex task of reconciling the demands of the id, the external world, and conscience—for example, the id impulse to grab an attractive toy from a playmate versus the superego's awareness that such behavior is wrong. According to Freud, the relations established between id, ego, and superego during the preschool years determine the individual's basic personality.

Freud (1938/1973) believed that during childhood, sexual impulses shift their focus from the oral to the anal to the genital regions of the body. In each stage, parents walk a fine line between permitting too much or too little gratification of their child's basic needs. If parents strike an appropriate balance, children grow into well-adjusted adults with the capacity for mature sexual behavior and investment in family life.

Freud's theory was the first to stress the influence of the early parent–child relationship on development—an emphasis that continues in many contemporary theories. But his perspective was eventually criticized. First, it overemphasized the influence of sexual feelings in development. Second, because it was based on the problems of sexually repressed, well-to-do adults in nineteenth-century Victorian society, it did not apply in other cultures. Finally, Freud had not studied children directly.

ERIKSON'S THEORY   Several of Freud's followers took what was useful from his theory and improved on his vision. The most important is Erik Erikson (1902–1994), who expanded the picture of development at each stage. In his **psychosocial theory,** Erikson emphasized that in addition to mediating between id impulses and superego demands, the ego makes a positive contribution to development, acquiring attitudes and skills that make the individual an active, contributing member of society. A basic psychological conflict, which is resolved along a continuum from positive to negative, determines healthy or maladaptive outcomes at each stage. As Table 1.1 on page 16 shows, Erikson's first five stages parallel Freud's stages, but Erikson added three adult stages. He was one of the first to recognize the lifespan nature of development.

Unlike Freud, Erikson pointed out that normal development must be understood in relation to each culture's life situation. For example, in the 1940s, he observed that the Yurok Indians of the U.S. northwest coast deprived newborns of breastfeeding for the first 10 days,

TABLE 1.1	Freud's Psychosexual Stages and Erikson's Psychosocial Stages Compared	
APPROXIMATE AGE	**FREUD'S PSYCHOSEXUAL STAGE**	**ERIKSON'S PSYCHOSOCIAL STAGE**
Birth–1 year	*Oral:* If oral needs are not met through sucking from breast or bottle, the individual may develop such habits as thumb sucking, fingernail biting, overeating, or smoking.	*Basic trust versus mistrust:* From warm, responsive care, infants gain a sense of trust that the world is good. Mistrust occurs if infants are neglected or handled harshly.
1–3 years	*Anal:* Toddlers and preschoolers enjoy holding and releasing urine and feces. If parents toilet train before children are ready or make too few demands, conflicts about anal control may appear in the form of extreme orderliness or disorder.	*Autonomy versus shame and doubt:* Using new mental and motor skills, children want to decide for themselves. Parents can foster autonomy by permitting reasonable free choice and not forcing or shaming the child.
3–6 years	*Phallic:* As preschoolers take pleasure in genital stimulation, Freud's Oedipus conflict for boys and Electra conflict for girls arise: Children feel a sexual desire for the other-sex parent. To avoid punishment, they give up this desire and adopt the same-sex parent's characteristics and values. As a result, the superego is formed, and children feel guilty when they violate its standards.	*Initiative versus guilt:* Through make-believe play, children gain insight into the person they can become. Initiative— a sense of ambition and responsibility—develops when parents support their child's sense of purpose. If parents demand too much self-control, children experience excessive guilt.
6–11 years	*Latency:* Sexual instincts die down, and the superego strengthens as the child acquires new social values from adults and same-sex peers.	*Industry versus inferiority:* At school, children learn to work and cooperate with others. Inferiority develops when negative experiences at home, at school, or with peers lead to feelings of incompetence.
Adolescence	*Genital:* With puberty, sexual impulses reappear. Successful development during earlier stages leads to marriage, mature sexuality, and child rearing.	*Identity versus role confusion:* By exploring values and vocational goals, the young person forms a personal identity. The negative outcome is confusion about future adult roles.
Early adulthood		*Intimacy versus isolation:* Young adults establish intimate relationships. Because of earlier disappointments, some individuals cannot form close bonds and remain isolated.
Middle adulthood		*Generativity versus stagnation:* Generativity means giving to the next generation through child rearing, caring for others, or productive work. The person who fails in these ways feels an absence of meaningful accomplishment.
Old age		*Integrity versus despair:* Integrity results from feeling that life was worth living as it happened. Older people who are dissatisfied with their lives fear death.

© OLIVE PIERCE/BLACK STAR

Erik Erikson

ANTONIA TOZER/GETTY IMAGES

A child of the Kasakh people of Mongolia learns from her grandfather how to train an eagle to hunt small animals, essential for the meat-based Kasakh diet. As Erikson recognized, this parenting practice is best understood in relation to the competencies valued and needed in Kasakh culture.

instead feeding them a thin soup. At age 6 months, infants were abruptly weaned—if necessary, by having the mother leave for a few days. From our cultural vantage point, these practices may seem cruel. But Erikson explained that because the Yurok depended on salmon, which fill the river just once a year, the development of self-restraint was essential for survival. In this way, he showed that child rearing is responsive to the competencies valued and needed by the child's society.

CONTRIBUTIONS AND LIMITATIONS OF PSYCHOANALYTIC THEORY A special strength of the psychoanalytic perspective is its emphasis on the individual's unique life history as worthy of study and understanding. Consistent with this view, psychoanalytic theorists accept the *clinical,* or *case study, method,* which synthesizes information from a variety of sources into a detailed picture of the personality of a single child. (We will discuss this method further at the end of this chapter.) Psychoanalytic theory has also inspired a wealth of research on many aspects of emotional and social development, including infant–caregiver attachment, aggression, sibling relationships, child-rearing practices, morality, gender roles, and adolescent identity.

Despite its extensive contributions, the psychoanalytic perspective is no longer in the mainstream of child development research. Psychoanalytic theorists may have become isolated from the rest of the field because they were so strongly committed to the clinical approach that they failed to consider other methods. In addition, many psychoanalytic ideas, such as psychosexual stages and ego functioning, are too vague to be tested empirically (Crain, 2010). Nevertheless, Erikson's broad outline of psychosocial change captures the essence of personality development during childhood and adolescence. Consequently, we will return to it in later chapters.

Behaviorism and Social Learning Theory

As the psychoanalytic perspective gained prominence, child study was also influenced by a very different perspective. According to **behaviorism,** directly observable events—stimuli and responses—are the appropriate focus of study. North American behaviorism began in the early twentieth century with the work of psychologist John Watson (1878–1958), who wanted to create an objective science of psychology.

TRADITIONAL BEHAVIORISM   Watson was inspired by Russian physiologist Ivan Pavlov's studies of animal learning. Pavlov knew that dogs release saliva as an innate reflex when they are given food. But he noticed that his dogs started salivating before they tasted any food—when they saw the trainer who usually fed them. The dogs, Pavlov reasoned, must have learned to associate a neutral stimulus (the trainer) with another stimulus (food) that produces a reflexive response (salivation). Because of this association, the neutral stimulus alone could bring about a response resembling the reflex. Eager to test this idea, Pavlov successfully taught dogs to salivate at the sound of a bell by pairing it with the presentation of food. He had discovered *classical conditioning.*

Watson wanted to find out if classical conditioning could be applied to children's behavior. In a historic experiment, he taught Albert, an 11-month-old infant, to fear a neutral stimulus— a soft white rat—by presenting it several times with a sharp, loud sound, which naturally scared the baby. Little Albert, who at first had reached out eagerly to touch the furry rat, began to cry and turn his head away at the sight of it (Watson & Raynor, 1920). In fact, Albert's fear was so intense that researchers eventually challenged the ethics of studies like this one. Consistent with Locke's tabula rasa, Watson concluded that environment is the supreme force in development and that adults can mold children's behavior by carefully controlling stimulus– response associations. He viewed development as continuous—a gradual increase with age in the number and strength of these associations.

Another form of behaviorism was B. F. Skinner's (1904–1990) *operant conditioning theory.* According to Skinner, the frequency of a behavior can be increased by following it with a wide variety of *reinforcers*—food, praise, a friendly smile, or a new toy—or decreased through *punishment,* such as disapproval or withdrawal of privileges. As a result of Skinner's work, operant conditioning became a broadly applied learning principle. We will consider these basic learning capacities further in Chapter 5.

SOCIAL LEARNING THEORY   Psychologists wondered whether behaviorism might offer a more direct and effective explanation of the development of children's social behavior than the less precise concepts of psychoanalytic theory. This sparked approaches that built on the principles of conditioning, offering expanded views of how children and adults acquire new responses.

Several kinds of **social learning theory** emerged. The most influential, devised by Albert Bandura (1977, 2011), emphasizes *modeling,* also known as *imitation* or *observational learning,* as a powerful source of development. The baby who claps her hands after her mother does so, the child who angrily hits a playmate in the same way that he has been punished at home, and the teenager who wears the same clothes and hairstyle as her friends are all displaying observational learning. In his early research, Bandura found that diverse factors influence children's

© LAURA DWIGHT PHOTOGRAPHY

Social learning theory recognizes that children acquire many skills through modeling. By observing and imitating his father's behavior, this child learns an important skill.

LOOK and LISTEN

Describe an event you observed in which feedback from a parent or teacher likely strengthened a child's self-efficacy. How might the adult's message have influenced the child's self-perceptions and choice of models?

motivation to imitate—their own history of reinforcement or punishment for the behavior, the promise of future reinforcement or punishment, and even observations of the model being reinforced or punished.

Bandura's work continues to influence much research on children's social development. But today, like the field of child development as a whole, his theory stresses the importance of *cognition,* or thinking. Bandura has shown that children's ability to listen, remember, and abstract general rules from complex sets of observed behaviors affects their imitation and learning. In fact, the most recent revision of Bandura's (1992, 2001) theory places such strong emphasis on how children think about themselves and other people that he calls it a *social-cognitive* rather than a social learning approach.

In Bandura's revised view, children gradually become more selective in what they imitate. From watching others engage in self-praise and self-blame and through feedback about the worth of their own actions, children develop *personal standards* for behavior and a *sense of self-efficacy*—the belief that their own abilities and characteristics will help them succeed. These cognitions guide responses in particular situations (Bandura, 2001, 2011).

For example, imagine a parent who often remarks, "I'm glad I kept working on that task, even though it was hard," and who encourages persistence by saying, "I know you can do a good job on that homework!" Soon the child starts to view herself as hardworking and high-achieving and selects people with these characteristics as models. In this way, as children acquire attitudes, values, and convictions about themselves, they control their own learning and behavior.

CONTRIBUTIONS AND LIMITATIONS OF BEHAVIORISM AND SOCIAL LEARNING THEORY Behaviorism and social learning theory have had a major impact on practices with children. **Applied behavior analysis** consists of observations of relationships between behavior and environmental events, followed by systematic changes in those events based on procedures of conditioning and modeling. The goal is to eliminate undesirable behaviors and increase desirable responses. It has been used to relieve a wide range of difficulties in children and adults, ranging from poor time management and unwanted habits to serious problems such as language delays, persistent aggression, and extreme fears (Heron, Hewar, & Cooper, 2013).

In one study, researchers reduced toddlers' aggressive behavior in a child-care classroom by reinforcing them with adult attention and joint play when they behaved appropriately and punishing them for attacking other children or throwing objects by withdrawing adult attention and playing with nearby peers (Greer et al., 2013). In another investigation, children with acute burn injuries played a virtual reality game while nurses engaged in the painful process of changing their bandages. Visual images and sound effects delivered though a headset made the children feel as if they were in a fantasy world. As the game reinforced children's concentration and pleasure, it distracted them from the medical procedure, causing their pain and anxiety to drop sharply compared with dressing changes in which the game was unavailable (Das et al., 2005).

Nevertheless, many theorists believe that behaviorism and social learning theory offer too narrow a view of important environmental influences, which extend beyond immediate reinforcement, punishment, and modeled behaviors to children's rich physical and social worlds. Behaviorism and social learning theory have also been criticized for underestimating children's contributions to their own development. Bandura, with his emphasis on cognition, is unique among theorists whose work grew out of the behaviorist tradition in granting children an active role in their own learning.

TABLE 1.2	Piaget's Stages of Cognitive Development	

STAGE	PERIOD OF DEVELOPMENT	DESCRIPTION
Sensorimotor	Birth–2 years	Infants "think" by acting on the world with their eyes, ears, hands, and mouth. As a result, they invent ways of solving sensorimotor problems, such as pulling a lever to hear the sound of a music box, finding hidden toys, and putting objects into and taking them out of containers.
Preoperational	2–7 years	Preschool children use symbols to represent their earlier sensorimotor discoveries. Development of language and make-believe play takes place. However, thinking lacks the logic of the two remaining stages.
Concrete operational	7–11 years	Children's reasoning becomes logical and better organized. School-age children understand that a certain amount of lemonade or play dough remains the same even after its appearance changes. They also organize objects into hierarchies of classes and subclasses. However, children think in a logical, organized fashion only when dealing with concrete information they can perceive directly.
Formal operational	11 years on	The capacity for abstract, systematic thinking enables adolescents, when faced with a problem, to start with a hypothesis, deduce testable inferences, and isolate and combine variables to see which inferences are confirmed. Adolescents can also evaluate the logic of verbal statements without referring to real-world circumstances.

Jean Piaget

Piaget's Cognitive-Developmental Theory

If one individual has influenced the contemporary field of child development more than any other, it is Swiss cognitive theorist Jean Piaget (1896–1980). North American investigators had been aware of Piaget's work since 1930. But they did not grant it much attention until the 1960s, mainly because Piaget's ideas were at odds with behaviorism, which dominated North American psychology in the mid-twentieth century (Watrin & Darwich, 2012). Piaget did not believe that children's learning depends on reinforcers, such as rewards from adults. According to his **cognitive-developmental theory,** children actively construct knowledge as they manipulate and explore their world.

PIAGET'S STAGES   Piaget's view of development was greatly influenced by his early training in biology. Central to his theory is the biological concept of *adaptation* (Piaget, 1971). Just as structures of the body are adapted to fit with the environment, so structures of the mind develop to better fit with, or represent, the external world. In infancy and early childhood, Piaget claimed, children's understanding is different from adults'. For example, he believed that young babies do not realize that an object hidden from view— a favorite toy or even the mother—continues to exist. He also concluded that preschoolers' thinking is full of faulty logic. For example, children younger than age 7 commonly say that the amount of a liquid changes when it is poured into a different-shaped container. According to Piaget, children eventually revise these incorrect ideas in their ongoing efforts to achieve an *equilibrium,* or balance, between internal structures and information they encounter in their everyday worlds.

In Piaget's theory, as the brain develops and children's experiences expand, they move through four broad stages, each characterized by qualitatively distinct ways of thinking. Table 1.2 provides a brief description of Piaget's stages. Cognitive development begins in the *sensorimotor stage* with the baby's use of the senses and movements to explore the world. These action patterns evolve into the symbolic but illogical thinking of the preschooler

In Piaget's sensorimotor stage, babies learn by acting on the world. As this 1-year-old bangs a wooden spoon on a coffee can, he discovers that his movements have predictable effects on objects, and that objects influence one another in regular ways.

In Piaget's preoperational stage, preschoolers represent their earlier sensorimotor discoveries with symbols, and language and make-believe play develop rapidly. These 4-year-olds use a variety of props to create an imaginary birthday party.

in the *preoperational stage*. Then cognition is transformed into the more organized reasoning of the school-age child in the *concrete operational stage*. Finally, in the *formal operational stage*, thought becomes the abstract, systematic reasoning system of the adolescent and adult.

Piaget devised special methods for investigating how children think. Early in his career, he carefully observed his three infant children and also presented them with everyday problems, such as an attractive object that could be grasped, mouthed, kicked, or searched for. From their responses, Piaget derived his ideas about cognitive changes during the first two years. To study childhood and adolescent thought, Piaget adapted the clinical method of psychoanalysis, conducting open-ended *clinical interviews* in which a child's initial response to a task served as the basis for Piaget's next question. We will look more closely at this technique when we discuss research methods later in this chapter.

CONTRIBUTIONS AND LIMITATIONS OF PIAGET'S THEORY   Piaget convinced the field that children are active learners whose minds consist of rich structures of knowledge. Besides investigating children's understanding of the physical world, Piaget explored their reasoning about the social world. His stages have sparked a wealth of research on children's conceptions of themselves, other people, and human relationships. In practical terms, Piaget's theory encouraged the development of educational philosophies and programs that emphasize children's discovery learning and direct contact with the environment.

Despite Piaget's overwhelming contributions, his theory has been challenged. Research indicates that Piaget underestimated the competencies of infants and preschoolers. When

In Piaget's concrete operational stage, school-age children think in an organized, logical fashion about concrete objects. This 7-year-old understands that the amount of pie dough remains the same after he changes its shape from a ball to a flattened circle.

In Piaget's formal operational stage, adolescents think systematically and abstractly. These high school students participating in a robotics competition solve problems by generating hypotheses about procedures that might work and conducting systematic tests to observe their real-world consequences.

young children are given tasks scaled down in difficulty and relevant to their everyday experiences, their understanding appears closer to that of the older child and adult than Piaget assumed. Also, adolescents generally reach their full intellectual potential only in areas of endeavor in which they have had extensive education and experience. These findings have led many researchers to conclude that cognitive maturity depends heavily on the complexity of knowledge sampled and the individual's familiarity with the task (Miller, 2011). Furthermore, many studies show that children's performance on Piagetian problems can be improved with training—findings that call into question Piaget's assumption that discovery learning rather than adult teaching is the best way to foster development (Klahr, Matlin, & Jirout, 2013; Siegler & Svetina, 2006). Critics also point out that Piaget's stagewise account pays insufficient attention to social and cultural influences—and the resulting wide variation in thinking among children and adolescents of the same age.

Today, the field of child development is divided over its loyalty to Piaget's ideas. Those who continue to find merit in Piaget's stages often accept a modified view—one in which changes in children's thinking take place more gradually than Piaget believed (Case, 1998; Fischer & Bidell, 2006; Halford & Andrews, 2011; Morra et al., 2008). Among those who disagree with Piaget's stage sequence, some have embraced an approach that emphasizes continuous gains in children's cognition: information processing. And still others have been drawn to theories that highlight the role of children's social and cultural contexts. We take up these approaches in the next section.

Ask Yourself

- **REVIEW** What aspect of behaviorism made it attractive to critics of psychoanalytic theory? How did Piaget's theory respond to a major limitation of behaviorism?

- **CONNECT** Although social learning theory focuses on social development and Piaget's theory on cognitive development, each has enhanced our understanding of other domains. Mention an additional domain addressed by each theory.

- **APPLY** A 4-year-old becomes frightened of the dark and refuses to go to sleep at night. How would a psychoanalyst and a behaviorist differ in their views of how this problem developed?

- **REFLECT** Illustrate Bandura's ideas by describing a personal experience in which you observed and received feedback from another person that strengthened your self-efficacy—belief that your abilities and characteristics will help you succeed.

Recent Theoretical Perspectives

1.6 Describe recent theoretical perspectives on child development.

New ways of understanding the child are constantly emerging—questioning, building on, and enhancing the discoveries of earlier theories. Today, a burst of fresh approaches and research emphases is broadening our understanding of children's development.

Information Processing

In the 1970s and 1980s, researchers turned to the field of cognitive psychology for ways to understand the development of children's thinking. The design of digital computers that use mathematically specified steps to solve problems suggested to psychologists that the human mind might also be viewed as a symbol-manipulating system through which information flows—a perspective called **information processing** (Munakata, 2006). From the time information is presented to the senses at *input* until it emerges as a behavioral response at *output,* information is actively coded, transformed, and organized.

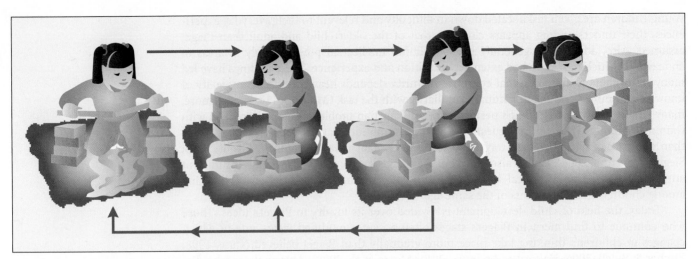

FIGURE 1.3 **Information-processing flowchart showing the steps that a 5-year-old used to solve a bridge-building problem.** Her task was to use blocks varying in size, shape, and weight, some of which were planklike, to construct a bridge across a "river" (painted on a floor mat) too wide for any single block to span. The child discovered how to counterweight and balance the bridge. The arrows reveal that even after building a successful counterweight, she returned to earlier, unsuccessful strategies, which seemed to help her understand why the counterweight approach worked. (Based on Thornton, 1999.)

Information-processing researchers often design flowcharts to map the precise steps individuals use to solve problems and complete tasks, much like the plans devised by programmers to get computers to perform a series of "mental operations." They seek to clarify how both task characteristics and cognitive limitations—for example, memory capacity or available knowledge—influence performance (Birney & Sternberg, 2011). To see the usefulness of this approach, let's look at an example.

In a study of problem solving, a researcher provided a pile of blocks varying in size, shape, and weight and asked school-age children to build a bridge across a "river" (painted on a floor mat) that was too wide for any single block to span (Thornton, 1999). Figure 1.3 shows one solution: Two planklike blocks span the water, each held in place by the counterweight of heavy blocks on the bridge's towers. Whereas older children easily built successful bridges, only one 5-year-old did. Careful tracking of her efforts revealed that she repeatedly tried unsuccessful strategies, such as pushing two planks together and pressing down on their ends to hold them in place. But eventually, her experimentation triggered the idea of using the blocks as counterweights. Her mistaken procedures helped her understand why the counterweight approach worked.

Many information-processing models exist. Some, like the one just considered, track children's mastery of one or a few tasks. Others describe the human cognitive system as a whole (Gopnik & Tenenbaum, 2007; Johnson & Mareschal, 2001; Westermann et al., 2006). These general models are used as guides for asking questions about broad age changes in children's thinking: Does a child's ability to solve problems become more organized and "planful" with age? What strategies do younger and older children use to remember new information, and how do those strategies affect children's recall?

The information-processing approach has also been used to clarify the processing of social information. For example, flowcharts exist that track the steps children use to solve social problems (such as how to enter an ongoing play group) and acquire gender-linked preferences and behaviors (Liben & Bigler, 2002; Rubin, Begle, & McDonald, 2012). If we can identify how social problem solving and gender stereotyping arise in childhood, then we can design interventions that promote more favorable social development.

Like Piaget's theory, the information-processing approach regards children as active, sense-making beings who modify their own thinking in response to environmental demands (Halford & Andrews, 2011; Munakata, 2006). But unlike Piaget's theory, it does not divide development into stages. Rather, most information-processing researchers regard the thought processes studied—perception, attention, memory, categorization of information, planning, problem solving, and comprehension of written and spoken prose—as similar at all ages but present to a lesser or greater extent. Their view of development is one of continuous change.

A great strength of the information-processing approach is its commitment to rigorous research methods. Because it has provided precise accounts of how children of different ages engage in many aspects of thinking, its findings have important implications for education (Blumenfeld, Marx, & Harris, 2006; Siegler, 2009). But information processing has fallen short in some respects. It has been better at analyzing thinking into its components than at putting them back together into a comprehensive theory. And it has had little to say about aspects of children's cognition that are not linear and logical, such as imagination and creativity (Birney & Sternberg, 2011).

Developmental Neuroscience

Over the past three decades, as information-processing research expanded, an area of investigation arose called **developmental cognitive neuroscience.** It brings together researchers from psychology, biology, neuroscience, and medicine to study the relationship between changes in the brain and the developing child's cognitive processing and behavior patterns.

Improved methods for analyzing brain activity while children perform various tasks have greatly enhanced knowledge of relationships between brain functioning and behavior (Blakemore et al., 2011). Armed with these brain electrical-recording and imaging techniques (which we will consider in Chapter 5), neuroscientists are tackling questions like these: How does genetic makeup combine with specific experiences at various ages to influence the growth and organization of the child's brain? How do changes in brain structures support rapid memory development in infancy and toddlerhood? What transformations in brain systems make it harder for adolescents and adults than for children to acquire a second language?

Recently, researchers spawned a complementary new area—**developmental social neuroscience**—devoted to studying the relationship between changes in the brain and emotional and social development. Developmental social neuroscience emerged later than its cognitive counterpart because techniques for measuring brain activity, which restrict movements in children, are hard to implement in most social situations, where children must move freely to interact with others (Zelazo & Paus, 2010). When researchers started to tap more convenient neurobiological measures that are sensitive to psychological state, such as heart rate, blood pressure, and hormone levels detected in saliva, an explosion of social-neuroscience investigations followed.

Active areas of investigation in developmental social neuroscience range widely. These include identification of the neural systems underlying infant gains in perception of facial expressions, risk-taking behaviors in adolescence, and individual differences in sociability, anxiety, aggression, and depression. A particularly energetic focus is the negative impact of extreme circumstances—such as early rearing in deprived orphanages or child abuse and neglect—on brain development and cognitive, emotional, and social skills (Anderson & Beauchamp, 2013; de Haan & Gunnar, 2009). Another burgeoning interest is uncovering the neurological bases of *autism*—the disrupted brain structures and networks that lead to the impaired social skills, language delays, and repetitive motor behavior of this disorder (Stoner et al., 2014). As these efforts illustrate, researchers are forging links between cognitive and social neuroscience, identifying brain systems that affect both domains of development.

Rapid progress in clarifying the types of experiences that support or undermine brain development at diverse ages is contributing to effective interventions for children with learning and behavior problems. Today, researchers are examining the impact of various treatment techniques on both brain functioning and behavior (Johnson, 2011; Schlaggar & Barnes, 2011). Although much remains to be discovered, developmental

© LAURA DWIGHT PHOTOGRAPHY

A therapist encourages a 6-year-old with autism to master the alphabet and interact socially, giving her a high five for progress. Developmental social neuroscientists are intensely interested in identifying the neurological bases of autism and using those findings to devise effective interventions.

neuroscience is broadening our understanding of development and yielding major practical applications.

Nevertheless, neuroscience research has so captivated the field that it poses the risk that brain properties underlying children's behavior will be granted undue importance over powerful environmental influences, such as parenting, educational, and economic inequalities in families and communities. Although most neuroscientists are mindful of the complex interplay between heredity, children's experiences, and brain development, their findings have too often resulted in excessive emphasis being placed on biological processes (Kagan, 2013b). Consequently, instances exist in which psychological outcomes in children have been wrongly attributed mostly or entirely to genetic and brain-based causes.

Fortunately, an advantage of having many theories is that they encourage researchers to attend to previously neglected dimensions of children's lives. The final four perspectives we will discuss focus on *contexts* for development. The first of these views emphasizes that the development of many capacities is influenced by the environments to which humans were exposed over a long evolutionary history.

Ethology and Evolutionary Developmental Psychology

Ethology is concerned with the adaptive, or survival, value of behavior and its evolutionary history. Its roots can be traced to the work of Darwin. Two European zoologists, Konrad Lorenz and Niko Tinbergen, laid its modern foundations. Watching diverse animal species in their natural habitats, Lorenz and Tinbergen observed behavior patterns that promote survival. The best known of these is *imprinting,* the early following behavior of certain baby birds, such as geese, which ensures that the young will stay close to the mother and be fed and protected from danger (Lorenz, 1952). Imprinting takes place during an early, restricted period of development. If the mother goose is absent during this time but an object resembling her in important features is present, young goslings may imprint on it instead.

Observations of imprinting led to a major concept in child development: the *critical period.* It is a limited time span during which the child is biologically prepared to acquire certain adaptive behaviors but needs the support of an appropriately stimulating environment. Many researchers have investigated whether complex cognitive and social behaviors must be learned during certain periods. For example, if children are deprived of adequate food or physical and social stimulation during their early years, will their intelligence be impaired? If language is not mastered in early childhood, is the child's capacity to acquire it reduced?

In later chapters, we will discover that the term *sensitive period* applies better to human development than the strict notion of a critical period (Bornstein, 1989; Knudsen, 2004). A **sensitive period** is a time that is biologically optimal for certain capacities to emerge because the individual is especially responsive to environmental influences. However, its boundaries are less well-defined than are those of a critical period. Development can occur later, but it is harder to induce.

Inspired by observations of imprinting, British psychoanalyst John Bowlby (1969) applied ethological theory to understanding the human infant–caregiver relationship. He argued that infant smiling, babbling, grasping, and crying are built-in social signals that encourage the caregiver to approach, care for, and interact with the baby. By keeping the parent near, these behaviors help ensure that the baby will be fed, protected from danger, and provided with the stimulation and affection necessary for healthy growth. The development of attachment in human infants is a lengthy process involving changes in psychological structures that lead the baby to form a deep affectionate tie with the caregiver (Thompson, 2006). In Chapter 7, we will consider how infant, caregiver, and family context contribute to attachment and how attachment influences later development.

© MARTIN HARVEY/GALLO IMAGES/CORBIS

Ethology focuses on the adaptive, or survival, value of behavior and on similarities between human behavior and that of other species, especially our primate relatives. Observing this mother cuddling her 8-day-old infant helps us understand the human infant–caregiver relationship.

Observations by ethologists have shown that many aspects of children's social behavior, including emotional expressions, aggression, cooperation, and social play, resemble those of our primate relatives. Recently, researchers have extended this effort in a new area of research called **evolutionary developmental psychology.** It seeks to understand the adaptive value of species-wide cognitive, emotional, and social competencies as those competencies change with age (King & Bjorklund, 2010; Lickliter & Honeycutt, 2013). Evolutionary developmental psychologists ask questions like these: What role does the newborn's visual preference for face-like stimuli play in survival? Does it support older infants' capacity to distinguish familiar caregivers from unfamiliar people? Why do children play in gender-segregated groups? What do they learn from such play that might lead to adult gender-typed behaviors, such as male dominance and female investment in caregiving?

As these examples suggest, evolutionary psychologists are not just concerned with the genetic and biological roots of development. They recognize that humans' large brain and extended childhood resulted from the need to master an increasingly complex environment, so they are also interested in learning (Bjorklund, Causey, & Periss, 2009). And they realize that today's lifestyles differ so radically from those of our evolutionary ancestors that certain evolved behaviors—such as life-threatening risk taking by adolescents and male-to-male violence—are no longer adaptive (Blasi & Bjorklund, 2003). By clarifying the origins and development of such behaviors, evolutionary developmental psychology may help spark more effective interventions.

In sum, evolutionary developmental psychology aims to understand the entire *person–environment system.* The next contextual perspective we will discuss, Vygotsky's sociocultural theory, serves as an excellent complement to the evolutionary viewpoint because it highlights the social and cultural dimensions of children's experiences.

Vygotsky's Sociocultural Theory

The field of child development has recently seen a dramatic increase in studies addressing the cultural context of children's lives. Investigations that make comparisons across cultures, and between ethnic groups within cultures, provide insight into whether developmental pathways apply to all children or are limited to particular environmental conditions.

Today, much research is examining the relationship of *culturally specific beliefs and practices* to development (Goodnow, 2010). The contributions of Russian psychologist Lev Vygotsky (1896–1934) have played a major role in this trend. Vygotsky's perspective, known as **sociocultural theory,** focuses on how culture—the values, beliefs, customs, and skills of a social group—is transmitted to the next generation. According to Vygotsky, social interaction—in particular, cooperative dialogues with more knowledgeable members of society—is necessary for children to acquire the ways of thinking and behaving that make up a community's culture. Vygotsky (1934/1987) believed that as adults and more expert peers help children master culturally meaningful activities, the communication between them becomes part of children's thinking. As children internalize features of these dialogues, they can use the language within them to guide their own thought and actions and to acquire new skills (Lourenço, 2012; Winsler, Fernyhough, & Montero, 2009). The young child instructing herself while working a puzzle or preparing a table for dinner has begun to produce the same kinds of guiding comments that an adult previously used to help her master important tasks.

Vygotsky's theory has been especially influential in the study of children's cognition. Vygotsky agreed with Piaget that children are active, constructive beings. But whereas Piaget emphasized children's independent efforts to make sense of their world, Vygotsky viewed cognitive development as a *socially mediated process,* in which children depend on assistance from adults and more-expert peers as they tackle new challenges.

In Vygotsky's theory, children undergo certain stagewise changes. For example, when they acquire language, they gain in ability to participate in dialogues with

COURTESY OF JAMES V. WERTSCH/WASHINGTON UNIVERSITY IN ST. LOUIS

According to Lev Vygotsky, shown here with his daughter, many cognitive processes and skills are socially transferred from more knowledgeable members of society to children. Vygotsky's sociocultural theory helps explain the wide cultural variation in cognitive competencies.

With her teacher's guidance, this Chinese child practices calligraphy. She acquires a culturally valued skill through interaction with an older, more experienced calligrapher.

others, and mastery of culturally valued competencies surges forward. When children enter school, they spend much time discussing language, literacy, and other academic concepts—experiences that encourage them to reflect on their own thinking (Bodrova & Leong, 2007; Kozulin, 2003). As a result, they gain dramatically in reasoning and problem solving.

At the same time, Vygotsky stressed that dialogues with experts lead to continuous changes in thinking that vary greatly from culture to culture. Consistent with this view, a major finding of cross-cultural research is that cultures select different tasks for children's learning, and social interaction surrounding those tasks leads to competencies essential for success in a particular culture. For example, in industrialized nations, teachers help people learn to read, drive a car, or use a computer. Among the Zinacanteco Indians of southern Mexico, adult experts guide young girls as they master complicated weaving techniques (Greenfield, 2004). In Brazil and other developing nations, child candy sellers with little or no schooling develop sophisticated mathematical abilities as the result of buying candy from wholesalers, pricing it in collaboration with adults and experienced peers, and bargaining with customers on city streets (Saxe, 1988).

Research stimulated by Vygotsky's theory reveals that children in every culture develop unique strengths. But Vygotsky's emphasis on culture and social experience led him to neglect the biological side of development. Although he recognized the importance of heredity and brain growth, he said little about their role in cognitive change. Furthermore, Vygotsky's focus on social transmission of knowledge meant that, compared with other theorists, he placed less emphasis on children's capacity to shape their own development. Followers of Vygotsky stress that children strive for social connection, actively participating in the conversations and social activities from which their development springs. From these joint experiences, they not only acquire culturally valued practices but also modify and transform those practices (Daniels, 2011; Rogoff, 2003). Contemporary sociocultural theorists grant the individual and society balanced, mutually influential roles.

Ecological Systems Theory

Urie Bronfenbrenner (1917–2005) is responsible for an approach to child development that has moved to the forefront of the field over the past two decades because it offers the most differentiated and complete account of contextual influences on children's development. **Ecological systems theory** views the child as developing within a complex *system* of relationships affected by multiple levels of the surrounding environment. Since the child's biologically influenced dispositions join with environmental forces to mold development, Bronfenbrenner characterized his perspective as a *bioecological model* (Bronfenbrenner, 2005; Bronfenbrenner & Morris, 2006).

Bronfenbrenner envisioned the environment as a series of interrelated, nested structures that form a complex functioning whole, or *system*. These include but also extend beyond the home, school, and neighborhood settings in which children spend their everyday lives (see Figure 1.4). Each layer joins with the others to powerfully affect development.

THE MICROSYSTEM The innermost level of the environment, the **microsystem,** consists of activities and interaction patterns in the child's immediate surroundings. Bronfenbrenner emphasizes that to understand child development at this level, we must keep in mind that all relationships are *bidirectional:* Adults affect children's behavior, but children's biologically and socially influenced characteristics—their physical attributes, personalities, and capacities— also affect adults' behavior. A friendly, attentive child is likely to evoke positive, patient reactions from parents, whereas an irritable or distractible child is more likely to receive impatience, restriction, and punishment. When these reciprocal interactions occur often over time, they have an enduring impact on development (Crockenberg & Leerkes, 2003).

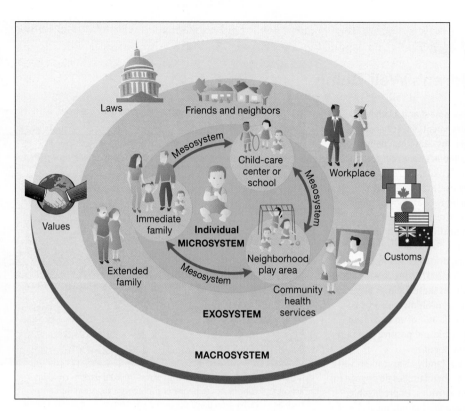

FIGURE 1.4 **Structure of the environment in ecological systems theory.** The *microsystem* concerns relations between the child and the immediate environment; the *mesosystem,* connections among immediate settings; the *exosystem,* social settings that affect but do not contain the child; and the *macrosystem,* the values, laws, customs, and resources of the culture that affect activities and interactions at all inner layers. The *chronosystem* (not pictured) is not a specific context. Instead, it refers to the dynamic, ever-changing nature of the child's environment.

Third parties—other individuals in the microsystem—also affect the quality of any two-person relationship. If they are supportive, interaction is enhanced. For example, when parents encourage each other in their child-rearing roles, each engages in more effective parenting. In contrast, marital conflict is associated with inconsistent discipline and hostile reactions toward children. In response, children often react with fear and anxiety or with anger and aggression, and the well-being of both parent and child suffers (Caldera & Lindsey, 2006; Low & Stocker, 2012).

THE MESOSYSTEM   The second level of Bronfenbrenner's model, the **mesosystem,** encompasses connections between microsystems, such as home, school, neighborhood, and child-care center. For example, a child's academic progress depends not just on activities that take place in classrooms but also on parent involvement in school life and on the extent to which academic learning is carried over into the home (Jeynes, 2012). Similarly, parent–child interaction at home is likely to affect caregiver–child interaction in the child-care setting, and vice versa. Each relationship is more likely to support development when there are links between home and child care, in the form of visits and cooperative exchanges of information.

THE EXOSYSTEM   The **exosystem** consists of social settings that do not contain children but that nevertheless affect children's experiences in immediate settings. These can be formal organizations, such as parents' workplaces, their religious institutions, and community health and welfare services. Flexible work schedules, paid maternity and paternity leave, and sick leave for parents whose children are ill are examples of ways that work settings can support child rearing and, indirectly, enhance children's development. Exosystem supports also can be informal, such as parents' social networks—friends and

This father says good-bye to his daughter at the start of the school day. Her experiences at school (microsystem) and the father's experiences at work (exosystem) affect the father–daughter relationship.

Social Issues: Health

Family Chaos Undermines Children's Well-Being

All of us can recall days during our childhoods when family routines—regular mealtime, bedtime, homework time, and parent–child reading and playtimes—were disrupted, perhaps because of a change in a parent's job, a family illness, or a busy season of after-school sports. In some families, however, absence of daily structure is nearly constant, yielding a chaotic home life that interferes with healthy development (Fiese & Winter, 2010). An organized family life provides a supportive context for warm, involved parent–child interaction, which is essential to children's well-being.

Family chaos is linked to economic disadvantage—especially, single mothers with limited incomes struggling to juggle the challenges of transportation, shift jobs, unstable child-care arrangements, and other daily hassles. But chaos is not limited to such families.

Surveys reveal that among U.S. families as a whole, mothers' time with children has remained fairly stable over the past three decades, and fathers' time has increased (Galinsky, Aumann, & Bond, 2009). But the way many parents spend that time has changed. Across income levels and ethnic groups, both mothers and fathers report more multitasking while caring for children—for example, using mealtimes not just to eat but also to check homework, read to children, and plan family outings and celebrations (Bianchi & Raley, 2005). Consequently, disruption in one family routine can disrupt others.

Possibly because of this compression of family routines, today's parents and children consistently say they have too little time together. For example, only slightly more than half of U.S. families report eating together three to five times per week (CASA, 2006; Opinion Research Corporation, 2009). Frequency of family meals is associated with wide-ranging positive outcomes—in childhood, enhanced language development and academic achievement, fewer behavior problems, and time spent sleeping; and in adolescence, reduced sexual risk taking, alcohol and drug use, and mental health problems. Shared mealtimes also increase the likelihood of a healthy diet and protect against obesity and adolescent eating disorders (Adam, Snell, & Pendry, 2007; Fiese & Schwartz, 2008). As these findings suggest, regular mealtimes are a general indicator of an organized family life and positive parent involvement.

But family chaos can prevail even when families do engage in joint activities. Unpredictable, disorganized family meals involving harsh or lax parental discipline and hostile, disrespectful communication are associated with children's adjustment difficulties (Fiese, Foley, & Spagnola, 2006). As family time becomes pressured and overwhelming, its orderly structure diminishes, and warm parent–child engagement disintegrates.

Diverse circumstances can trigger a pileup of limited parental emotional resources, breeding family chaos. In addition to *microsystem* and *mesosytem* influences (parents with mental health problems, parental separation and divorce, single parents with few or no supportive relationships), the *exosystem* is powerful: When family time is at the mercy of external forces—parents commuting several hours a day to and from work, child-care arrangements often failing, parents experiencing excessive workplace pressures or job loss—family routines are threatened.

A chaotic home life interferes with warm, relaxed parent–child interaction and contributes to behavior problems. Exosystem influences, such as excessive workplace pressures, can trigger disorganized family routines.

Family chaos contributes to children's behavior problems, above and beyond its negative impact on parenting effectiveness (Coldwell, Pike, & Dunn, 2008; Fiese & Winter, 2010). Chaotic surroundings induce in children a sense of being hassled and feelings of powerlessness, which engender anxiety and low self-esteem.

Exosystem and macrosystem supports—including work settings with favorable family policies and high-quality child care that is affordable and reliable—can help prevent escalating demands on families that give way to chaos (Repetti & Wang, 2010). In one community, a child-care center initiated a take-home dinner program. Busy parents could special-order a healthy, reasonably priced family meal, ready to go at day's end to aid in making the family dinner a routine that enhances children's development.

extended-family members who provide advice, companionship, and even financial assistance. Research confirms the negative impact of a breakdown in exosystem activities. Families who are affected by unemployment or who are socially isolated, with few personal or community-based ties, show increased rates of conflict and child abuse (Coulton et al., 2007). Refer to the Social Issues: Health box above for an additional illustration of the power of the exosystem to affect family functioning and children's development.

THE MACROSYSTEM   The outermost level of Bronfenbrenner's model, the **macrosystem,** consists of cultural values, laws, customs, and resources. The priority that the macrosystem gives to children's needs affects the support they receive at inner levels of the environment. For example, in countries that require generous workplace benefits for employed parents and high-quality standards for child care, children are more likely to have favorable experiences in their immediate settings. As you will see in later chapters, such programs are far less available in the United States than in other industrialized nations (Pew Research Center, 2013).

AN EVER-CHANGING SYSTEM   According to Bronfenbrenner, the environment is not a static force that affects children in a uniform way. Instead, it is ever-changing. Important life events, such as the birth of a sibling, the beginning of school, a move to a new neighborhood, or parents' divorce, modify existing relationships between children and their environments, producing new conditions that affect development. In addition, the timing of environmental change affects its impact. The arrival of a new sibling has very different consequences for a homebound toddler than for a school-age child with many relationships and activities beyond the family.

Bronfenbrenner called the temporal dimension of his model the **chronosystem** (the prefix *chrono-* means "time"). Life changes can be imposed on the child, as in the examples just given. Alternatively, they can arise from within the child, since as children get older they select, modify, and create many of their own settings and experiences. How they do so depends on their physical, intellectual, and personality characteristics and their environmental opportunities. Therefore, in ecological systems theory, development is neither entirely controlled by environmental circumstances nor driven solely by inner dispositions. Rather, children and their environments form a network of interdependent effects. Notice how our discussion of resilient children on pages 10–11 illustrates this idea. You will see many more examples in this book.

LOOK and LISTEN

Ask a parent to explain his or her most worrisome child-rearing challenge. Describe one source of support at each level of Bronfenbrenner's model that could ease parental stress and promote child development.

Development as a Dynamic System

Today, researchers recognize both consistency and variability in children's development and want to do a better job of explaining variation. Consequently, a new wave of systems theorists focuses on how children, in interacting with their complex contexts, alter their behavior to attain more advanced functioning. According to this **dynamic systems perspective,** the child's mind, body, and physical and social worlds form an *integrated system* that guides mastery of new skills. The system is *dynamic,* or constantly in motion. A change in any part of it—from brain growth to physical or social surroundings—disrupts the current organism–environment relationship. When this happens, the child actively reorganizes his or her behavior so the various components of the system work together again but in a more complex, effective way (Fischer & Bidell, 2006; Spencer, Perone, & Buss, 2011; Thelen & Smith, 2006).

Researchers adopting a dynamic systems perspective try to find out just how children attain new levels of organization by studying their behavior while they are in transition (Thelen & Corbetta, 2002). For example, when presented with an attractive toy, how does a 3-month-old baby who engages in many, varied movements discover how to reach for it? On hearing a new word, how does a 2-year-old figure out the category of objects or events to which it refers?

Dynamic systems theorists acknowledge that a common human genetic heritage and basic regularities in children's physical and social worlds yield certain universal, broad outlines of development. But children's biological makeup, interests and goals, everyday tasks, and the people who support children in mastery of those tasks vary greatly, leading to wide individual differences in specific skills. Even when children master the same skills, such as walking, talking, or adding and subtracting, they often do so in unique ways. And because children build competencies by engaging in real activities in real contexts, different skills vary in maturity within the same child. From this perspective, development cannot be characterized as a single line of change. As Figure 1.5 on page 30 shows, it is more like a web of fibers branching out in many directions, each representing a different skill area that may undergo both continuous and stagewise transformations (Fischer & Bidell, 2006).

© KABLONK!/GOLDEN PIXELS LLC/ALAMY

The dynamic systems perspective views the child's mind, body, and physical and social worlds as a continuously reorganizing, integrated system. In response to the physical and psychological changes of adolescence, this father and daughter must develop a new, more mature relationship.

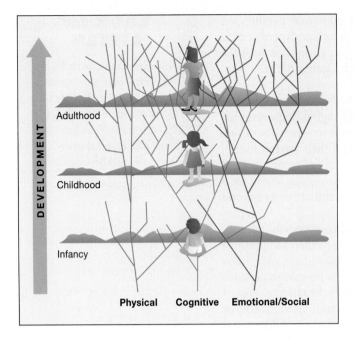

Adulthood

Childhood

Infancy

DEVELOPMENT

Physical   Cognitive   Emotional/Social

FIGURE 1.5 **The dynamic systems view of development.** Rather than envisioning a single line of stagewise or continuous change (refer to Figure 1.2 on page 8), dynamic systems theorists conceive of development as a web of fibers branching out in many directions. Each strand in the web represents a skill within the major domains of development—physical, cognitive, and emotional/social. The differing directions of the strands signify possible variations in paths and outcomes as the child masters skills necessary to participate in diverse contexts. The interconnections of the strands at each row of "hills" portray stagelike changes—periods of major transformation in which various skills work together as a functioning whole. As the web expands, skills become more numerous, complex, and effective. (Based on Fischer & Bidell, 2006.)

The dynamic systems view has been inspired by other scientific disciplines, especially biology and physics. It also draws on information-processing and contextual theories—evolutionary developmental psychology, sociocultural theory, and ecological systems theory. Dynamic systems research is still in its early stages. The perspective has been applied largely to children's motor and cognitive skills, but some investigators have drawn on it to explain emotional and social development as well (Fogel & Garvey, 2007; Kunnen, 2012). Consider the young teenager, whose body and reasoning powers are changing massively and who also is confronting a multiplicity of new academic and social challenges. Researchers following parent–child interaction over time found that the transition to adolescence disrupted family communication. It became unstable and variable for several years—a mix of positive, neutral, and negative exchanges (Granic et al., 2003). Gradually, as parent and adolescent devised new, more mature ways of relating to one another, the system reorganized and stabilized. Once again, interaction became predictable and mostly positive.

As dynamic systems research illustrates, today investigators are tracking and analyzing development in all its complexity. In doing so, they hope to move closer to an all-encompassing approach to understanding change.

Ask Yourself

- **REVIEW** Explain how each recent theoretical perspective regards children as active contributors to their own development.

- **CONNECT** Return to the Biology and Environment box on pages 10–11. How does the story of John and Gary illustrate bidirectional influences within the microsystem, as described in ecological systems theory?

- **APPLY** Mario wants to find out precisely how children of different ages recall stories. Anna is interested in how

adult–child communication in different cultures influences children's storytelling. Which theoretical perspective has Mario probably chosen? How about Anna? Explain.

- **REFLECT** To illustrate the chronosystem in ecological systems theory, select an important event from your childhood, such as a move to a new neighborhood or a class with an inspiring teacher. How did the event affect you? How might its impact have differed had you been five years younger? How about five years older?

1.7 Identify the stand taken by each major theory on the basic issues of child development.

Comparing Child Development Theories

In the preceding sections, we reviewed theoretical perspectives in child development research. They differ in many respects. First, they focus on different domains of development. Some, such as the psychoanalytic perspective and ethology, emphasize emotional and social development. Others, such as Piaget's cognitive-developmental theory, information processing, and Vygotsky's sociocultural theory, stress changes in thinking. The remaining approaches—behaviorism,

TABLE 1.3	Stances of Major Theories on Basic Issues in Child Development		
THEORY	**CONTINUOUS OR DISCONTINUOUS DEVELOPMENT?**	**ONE COURSE OF DEVELOPMENT OR MANY?**	**RELATIVE INFLUENCE OF NATURE AND NURTURE?**
Psychoanalytic perspective	*Discontinuous:* Psychosexual and psychosocial development takes place in stages.	*One course:* Stages are assumed to be universal.	*Both nature and nurture:* Innate impulses are channeled and controlled through child-rearing experiences. *Early experiences* set the course of later development.
Behaviorism and social learning theory	*Continuous:* Development involves an increase in learned behaviors.	*Many possible courses:* Behaviors reinforced and modeled may vary from child to child.	*Emphasis on nurture:* Development results from conditioning and modeling. *Both early and later experiences* are important.
Piaget's cognitive-developmental theory	*Discontinuous:* Cognitive development takes place in stages.	*One course:* Stages are assumed to be universal.	*Both nature and nurture:* Development occurs as the brain grows and children exercise their innate drive to discover reality in a generally stimulating environment. *Both early and later experiences* are important.
Information processing	*Continuous:* Children gradually improve in perception, attention, memory, and problem-solving skills.	*One course:* Changes studied characterize most or all children.	*Both nature and nurture:* Children are active, sense-making beings who modify their thinking as the brain grows and they confront new environmental demands. *Both early and later experiences* are important.
Ethology and evolutionary developmental psychology	*Both continuous and discontinuous:* Children gradually develop a wider range of adaptive behaviors. Sensitive periods occur, in which qualitatively distinct capacities emerge fairly suddenly.	*One course:* Adaptive behaviors and sensitive periods apply to all members of a species.	*Both nature and nurture:* Evolution and heredity influence behavior, and learning lends greater flexibility and adaptiveness to it. In sensitive periods, *early experiences* set the course of later development.
Vygotsky's sociocultural theory	*Both continuous and discontinuous:* Language acquisition and schooling lead to stagewise changes. Dialogues with more expert members of society also lead to continuous changes that vary from culture to culture.	*Many possible courses:* Socially mediated changes in thought and behavior vary from culture to culture.	*Both nature and nurture:* Heredity, brain growth, and dialogues with more expert members of society jointly contribute to development. *Both early and later experiences* are important.
Ecological systems theory	*Not specified.*	*Many possible courses:* Children's characteristics join with environmental forces at multiple levels to mold development in unique ways.	*Both nature and nurture:* Children's characteristics and the reactions of others affect each other in a bidirectional fashion. Layers of the environment influence child-rearing experiences. *Both early and later experiences* are important.
Dynamic systems perspective	*Both continuous and discontinuous:* Change in the system is always ongoing. Stagelike transformations occur as children reorganize their behavior so components of the system work as a functioning whole.	*Many possible courses:* Biological makeup, everyday tasks, and social experiences vary, yielding wide individual differences in specific skills.	*Both nature and nurture:* The child's mind, body, and physical and social surroundings form an integrated system that guides mastery of new skills. *Both early and later experiences* are important.

social learning theory, evolutionary developmental psychology, ecological systems theory, and the dynamic systems perspective—encompass many aspects of children's functioning. Second, every theory contains a point of view about child development. **TAKE A MOMENT...** As we conclude our review of theoretical perspectives, identify the stand that each theory takes on the controversial issues presented at the beginning of this chapter. Then check your analysis of the theories against Table 1.3.

Finally, we have seen that every theory has strengths and limitations. Perhaps you found that you are attracted to some theories, but you have doubts about others. As you read more about child development in later chapters, you may find it useful to keep a notebook in which you test your own theoretical likes and dislikes against the evidence. Don't be surprised if you revise your ideas many times, just as theorists have done throughout the past century. By the end of the course, you will have built your own personal perspective on child development. Very likely, it will be an *eclectic position,* or blend of several theories, since every viewpoint we have considered has contributed to what we know about children.

1.8 Describe research methods commonly used to study children.

1.9 Distinguish between correlational and experimental research designs, noting strengths and limitations of each.

1.10 Describe designs for studying development, noting strengths and limitations of each.

1.11 What special ethical concerns arise in doing research on children?

LOOK *and* LISTEN

Ask a teacher, counselor, social worker, or nurse to describe a question about development he or she would like researchers to address, as a means of facilitating applied work with children. After reading the rest of this chapter, recommend research strategies best suited to answering that question, citing their strengths and limitations.

Studying the Child

In every science, research usually begins with a *hypothesis*—a prediction drawn directly from a theory. Theories and hypotheses, however, merely initiate the many activities that result in sound evidence on child development. Conducting research according to scientifically accepted procedures involves many steps and choices. Investigators must decide which participants, and how many, to include. Then they must figure out what the participants will be asked to do and when, where, and how many times each will be seen. Finally, they must examine and draw conclusions from their data.

In the following sections, we look at research strategies commonly used to study children. We begin with common *research methods*—the specific activities of participants, such as taking tests, answering questionnaires, responding to interviews, or being observed. Then we turn to *research designs*—overall plans for research studies that permit the best possible test of the investigator's hypothesis. Finally, we discuss special ethical issues involved in doing research on children.

Why learn about research strategies? Why not leave these matters to research specialists and concentrate on what is already known about the child and how this knowledge can be applied? There are two reasons. First, each of us must be a wise and critical consumer of knowledge. Knowing the strengths and limitations of various research strategies is important in separating dependable information from misleading results. Second, individuals who work directly with children may be in a unique position to build bridges between research and practice by conducting studies, either on their own or in partnership with experienced investigators. Community agencies such as schools, mental health facilities, and parks and recreation programs sometimes collaborate with researchers in designing, implementing, and evaluating interventions aimed at enhancing children's development (Guerra, Graham, & Tolan, 2011). To broaden these efforts, a basic understanding of the research process is essential.

Common Research Methods

How does a researcher choose a basic approach to gathering information about children? Common methods include systematic observation, self-reports (such as questionnaires and interviews), clinical or case studies of a single child, and ethnographies of the life circumstances of a specific group of children. Table 1.4 summarizes the strengths and limitations of each of these methods.

SYSTEMATIC OBSERVATION Observations of the behavior of children, and of adults who are important in their lives, can be made in different ways. One approach is to go into the field, or natural environment, and observe the behavior of interest—a method called **naturalistic observation.**

A study of preschoolers' responses to their peers' distress provides a good example of this technique (Farver & Branstetter, 1994). Observing 3- and 4-year-olds in child-care centers, the researchers recorded each instance of a child crying and the reactions of nearby children—whether they ignored, watched curiously, commented on the child's unhappiness, scolded or teased, or shared, helped, or expressed sympathy. Caregiver behaviors—explaining why a child was crying, mediating conflict, or offering comfort—were noted to see if adult sensitivity was related to children's caring responses. A strong relationship emerged. The great strength of naturalistic observation is that investigators can see directly the everyday behaviors they hope to explain.

TABLE 1.4	Strengths and Limitations of Common Information-Gathering Methods		
METHOD	**DESCRIPTION**	**STRENGTHS**	**LIMITATIONS**
Systematic Observation			
Naturalistic observation	Observation of behavior in natural contexts.	Reflects participants' everyday behaviors.	Cannot control conditions under which participants are observed.
Structured observation	Observation of behavior in a laboratory, where conditions are the same for all participants.	Grants each participant an equal opportunity to display the behavior of interest. Permits study of behaviors rarely seen in everyday life.	May not yield observations typical of participants' behavior in everyday life.
Self-Reports			
Clinical interview	Flexible interviewing procedure in which the investigator obtains a complete account of the participant's thoughts.	Comes as close as possible to the way participants think in everyday life. Great breadth and depth of information can be obtained in a short time.	May not result in accurate reporting of information. Flexible procedure makes comparing individuals' responses difficult.
Structured interview, questionnaires, and tests	Self-report instruments in which each participant is asked the same questions in the same way.	Permits comparisons of participants' responses and efficient data collection. Researchers can specify answer alternatives that participants might not think of in an open-ended interview.	Does not yield the same depth of information as a clinical interview. Responses are still subject to inaccurate reporting.
Clinical, or Case Study, Method			
	A full picture of one individual's psychological functioning, obtained by combining interviews, observations, and sometimes test scores.	Provides rich, descriptive insights into processes of development.	May be biased by researchers' theoretical preferences. Findings cannot be applied to individuals other than the participant.
Ethnography			
	Participant observation of a culture or distinct social group. By making extensive field notes, the researcher tries to capture the culture's unique values and social processes.	Provides a more complete and accurate description than can be derived from a single observational visit, interview, or questionnaire.	May be biased by researchers' values and theoretical preferences. Findings cannot be applied to individuals and settings other than the ones studied.

Naturalistic observation also has a major limitation: Not all individuals have the same opportunity to display a particular behavior in everyday life. In the study just described, some children might have witnessed a child crying more often than others or been exposed to more cues for positive social responses from caregivers. For this reason, they might have displayed more compassion.

Researchers commonly deal with this difficulty by making **structured observations,** in which the investigator sets up a laboratory situation that evokes the behavior of interest so that every participant has an equal opportunity to display the response. In one study, 2-year-olds' emotional reactions to harm that they thought they had caused were observed by asking them to take care of a rag doll that had been modified so its leg would fall off when the child picked it up. To make the child feel at fault, once the leg detached, an adult "talked for" the doll by saying, "Ow!" Researchers recorded children's facial expressions of sadness and concern for the injured doll, efforts to help the doll, and body tension—responses that indicated remorse and a desire to make amends. In addition, mothers were asked to engage in brief conversations about emotions with their children (Garner, 2003). Toddlers whose mothers more often explained the causes and consequences of emotion were more likely to express concern for the injured doll.

In naturalistic observation, the researcher goes into the field and records the behavior of interest. This researcher observes children at a preschool. She may be focusing on their playmate choices, cooperation, helpfulness, or conflicts.

Structured observation permits greater control over the research situation than does naturalistic observation. In addition, the method is especially useful for studying behaviors—such as parent–child or friendship interactions—that investigators rarely have an opportunity to see in everyday life. When aggressive and nonaggressive 10-year-old boys were observed playing games with their best friend in a laboratory, the aggressive boys and their friends more often violated game rules, cheated, and encouraged each other to engage in these dishonest acts. In addition, observers rated these boys' interactions as angrier and less cooperative than the interactions of nonaggressive boys and their friends (Bagwell & Coie, 2004). The researchers concluded that aggressive boys' close peer ties provide a context in which they practice hostility and other negative behaviors, which may contribute to their antisocial behavior.

The procedures used to collect systematic observations vary, depending on the purpose of the research. Some investigators choose to describe the entire stream of behavior—everything said and done over a certain time period. In one study, researchers wanted to find out whether maternal sensitivity in infancy and early childhood contributes to readiness for formal schooling at age 6 (Hirsh-Pasek & Burchinal, 2006). Between age 6 months and 4½ years, the investigators periodically videotaped 15-minute mother–child play sessions. Then they rated each session for maternal positive emotion, support, stimulating play, and respect for the child's autonomy—ingredients of sensitivity that did predict better language and academic progress when the children reached kindergarten.

Researchers have devised ingenious ways of observing difficult-to-capture behaviors. For example, to record instances of bullying, a group of investigators set up video cameras overlooking a classroom and a playground and had fourth to sixth graders wear small, remote microphones and pocket-sized transmitters (Craig, Pepler, & Atlas, 2000). Results revealed that bullying occurred often—at rates of 2.4 episodes per hour in the classroom and 4.5 episodes per hour on the playground. Yet only 15 to 18 percent of the time did teachers take steps to stop the harassment.

Systematic observation provides invaluable information on how children and adults behave, but it tells us little about the reasoning behind their responses. For this kind of information, researchers must turn to self-report techniques.

SELF-REPORTS Self-reports ask research participants to provide information on their perceptions, thoughts, abilities, feelings, attitudes, beliefs, and past experiences. They range from relatively unstructured interviews to highly structured interviews, questionnaires, and tests.

In a **clinical interview,** a flexible, conversational style is used to probe for the participant's point of view. In the following example, Piaget questioned a 5-year-old child about his understanding of dreams:

> *Where does the dream come from?*—I think you sleep so well that you dream.—*Does it come from us or from outside?*—From outside.—*When you are in bed and you dream, where is the dream?*—In my bed, under the blanket. I don't really know. If it was in my stomach, the bones would be in the way and I shouldn't see it.—*Is the dream there when you sleep?*—Yes, it is in the bed beside me. (Piaget, 1926/1930, pp. 97–98)

Although a researcher conducting clinical interviews with more than one child would typically ask the same first question to establish a common task, individualized prompts are used to provide a fuller picture of each child's reasoning.

The clinical interview has two major strengths. First, it permits people to display their thoughts in terms that are as close as possible to the way they think in everyday life. Second, the clinical interview can provide a large amount of information in a fairly brief period. For example, in an hour-long session, we can obtain a wide range of child-rearing information from a parent—much more than we could capture by observing for the same amount of time.

A major limitation of the clinical interview has to do with the accuracy with which people report their thoughts, feelings, and experiences. Some participants, wishing to please the interviewer, may make up answers. When asked about past events, some may have trouble recalling exactly what happened. And because the clinical interview depends on verbal ability and expressiveness, it may underestimate the capacities of individuals who have difficulty putting their thoughts into words.

The clinical interview has also been criticized because of its flexibility. When questions are phrased differently for each participant, variations in responses may reflect the manner of interviewing rather than real differences in the way people think about a topic. **Structured interviews** (including tests and questionnaires), in which each participant is asked the same questions in the same way, eliminate this problem. These instruments are also much more efficient. Answers are briefer, and researchers can obtain written responses from an entire group at the same time. Furthermore, by listing answer alternatives, researchers can indicate the specific activities and behaviors of interest—ones that participants might not think of in an open-ended clinical interview. For example, when parents were asked what they considered "the most important thing for children to prepare them for life," 62 percent checked "to think for themselves" when this alternative appeared on a list. Yet only 5 percent thought of it during a clinical interview (Schwarz, 1999).

Nevertheless, structured interviews do not yield the same depth of information as a clinical interview. And they can still be affected by inaccurate reporting.

THE CLINICAL, OR CASE STUDY, METHOD An outgrowth of psychoanalytic theory, the **clinical,** or **case study, method** brings together a wide range of information on one child, including interviews, observations, and sometimes test scores. The aim is to obtain as complete a picture as possible of that child's psychological functioning and the experiences that led up to it.

The clinical method is well-suited to studying the development of certain types of individuals who are few in number but vary widely in characteristics. For example, the method has been used to find out what contributes to the accomplishments of *prodigies*—extremely gifted children who attain adult competence in a field before age 10 (Moran & Gardner, 2006).

In one investigation, researchers conducted case studies of eight child prodigies nationally recognized for talents in such areas as art, music, and mathematics (Ruthsatz & Urbach, 2012). One child began playing the violin at 28 months, had won regional competitions as a 5-year-old, and by age 7 had performed as a soloist at New York's Carnegie Hall and Lincoln Center. Another child started reading as an infant, took college-level classes beginning at age 8, and published a paper in a mathematics journal at 13. Across the eight cases, the researchers noticed interesting

Using the clinical, or case study, method, this researcher interacts with a 3-year-old during a home visit. Interviews and observations will contribute to an in-depth picture of this child's psychological functioning.

patterns, including above-average intelligence and exceptionally high scores on tests of memory and attention to detail. Notably, several prodigies in the study had relatives with autism, a condition that also involves intense attention to detail. The researchers concluded that although child prodigies generally do not display the social and cognitive deficits of individuals with autism, the two groups may share an underlying genetic trait that affects the functioning of certain brain regions, heightening perception and attention.

The clinical method yields richly detailed case narratives that offer valuable insights into the multiplicity of factors affecting development. Nevertheless, like all other methods, it has drawbacks. Because information often is collected unsystematically and subjectively, researchers' theoretical preferences may bias their observations and interpretations. In addition, investigators cannot assume that their conclusions apply, or generalize, to anyone other than the child or children studied (Stanovich, 2013). Even when patterns emerge across several cases, as occurred in the study of child prodigies, it is wise to confirm these with other research strategies.

METHODS FOR STUDYING CULTURE To study the impact of culture on child development, researchers adjust the methods just considered or tap procedures specially devised for cross-cultural and multicultural research (Triandis, 2007). Which approach investigators choose depends on their research goals.

Sometimes researchers are interested in characteristics that are believed to be universal but that vary in degree from one culture to the next: Are parents warmer or more directive in

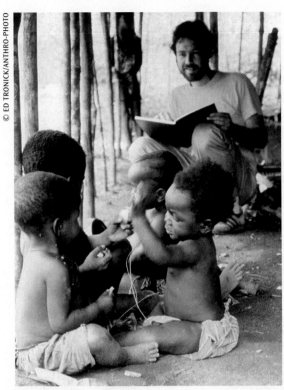

This Western ethnographer spent months living among the Efe people of the Republic of Congo. Here he observes young children sharing food. The Efe value and encourage cooperation and generosity at an early age.

some cultures than in others? How strong are gender stereotypes in different nations? In each instance, several cultural groups will be compared, and all participants must be questioned or observed in the same way. Therefore, researchers draw on the observational and self-report procedures we have already considered, adapting them through translation so they can be understood in each cultural context. For example, to study cultural variation in parent–adolescent relationships, the same questionnaire, asking for ratings on such items as "I often start a conversation with my parents about what happens in school" or "My parents can tell when I'm upset about something" is given to all participants (Qin & Pomerantz, 2013). Still, investigators must be mindful of cultural differences in familiarity with responding to self-report instruments that may bias their findings (van de Vijver, 2011).

At other times, researchers want to uncover the *cultural meanings* of children's and adults' behaviors by becoming as familiar as possible with their way of life. To achieve this goal, researchers rely on a method borrowed from the field of anthropology—**ethnography.** Like the clinical method, ethnographic research is a descriptive, qualitative technique. But instead of aiming to understand a single individual, it is directed toward understanding a culture or a distinct social group through *participant observation.* Typically, the researcher spends months and sometimes years in the cultural community, participating in its daily life. Extensive field notes are gathered, consisting of a mix of observations, self-reports from members of the culture, and careful interpretations by the investigator (Miller, Hengst, & Wang, 2003; Shweder et al., 2006). Later, these notes are put together into a description of the community that tries to capture its unique values and social processes.

The ethnographic method assumes that by entering into close contact with a social group, researchers can understand the beliefs and behaviors of its members in a way not possible with an observational visit, interview, or questionnaire. Some ethnographies take in many aspects of children's experience, as one researcher did in describing what it is like to grow up in a small American town. Others focus on one or a few settings, such as home, school, or neighborhood life (Calaff, 2008; MacLeod, 2009; Valdés, 1998). And still others are limited to a particular practice, such as uncovering cultural and religious influences on children's make-believe play. For example, ethnographic findings reveal that East Indian Hindu parents encourage preschoolers to communicate with "invisible" characters. They regard this activity as linked to *karma* (the cycle of birth and death) and believe that the child may be remembering a past life. In contrast, Christian fundamentalist parents often discourage children from pretending to be unreal characters, believing that such play promotes dangerous spiritual ideas and deceitful behavior (Taylor & Carlson, 2000). Researchers may supplement traditional self-report and observational methods with ethnography if they suspect that unique meanings underlie cultural differences, as the Cultural Influences box on the following page reveals.

Ethnographers strive to minimize their influence on the culture they are studying by becoming part of it. Nevertheless, as with clinical research, investigators' cultural values and theoretical commitments sometimes lead them to observe selectively or misinterpret what they see. Finally, the findings of ethnographic studies cannot be assumed to generalize beyond the people and settings in which the research was conducted.

Ask Yourself

- **REVIEW** Why might a researcher choose structured observation over naturalistic observation? How about the reverse? What might lead the researcher to opt for clinical interviewing over systematic observation?

- **CONNECT** What strengths and limitations do the clinical, or case study, method and ethnography have in common?

- **APPLY** A researcher wants to study the thoughts and feelings of children who have a parent on active duty in the military. Which method should she use? Why?

Cultural Influences

Immigrant Youths: Adapting to a New Land

Over the past several decades, increasing numbers of immigrants have come to North America, fleeing war and persecution in their homelands or seeking better life chances. Today, nearly one-fourth of U.S. children and adolescents have foreign-born parents, mostly originating from Latin America, the Caribbean, Asia, and Africa. Although some move with their parents, more than 80 percent of young people from immigrant families are U.S.-born citizens (Hernandez, Denton, & Blanchard, 2011; Hernandez et al., 2012).

How well are these youths—now the fastest growing sector of the U.S. youth population—adapting to their new country? To find out, researchers use multiple research methods: academic testing, questionnaires assessing psychological adjustment, and in-depth ethnographies.

Academic Achievement and Adjustment

Although educators and laypeople often assume that the transition to a new country has a negative impact on psychological well-being, evidence reveals that many children of immigrant parents adapt amazingly well. Students who are first generation (foreign-born) or second generation (American-born, with immigrant parents) often achieve in school as well as or better than students of native-born parents (Fuligni, 2004; Hao & Woo, 2012; Hernandez, Denton, & Blanchard, 2011). Findings on psychological adjustment are similar. Compared with their agemates, adolescents from immigrant families are less likely to commit delinquent and violent acts, to use drugs and alcohol, or to have early sex. They are also less likely to be obese or to have missed school because of illness. And they tend to report just as favorable, and at times higher, self-esteem as do young people with native-born parents (Fuligni, 1998; Saucier et al., 2002; Supple & Small, 2006).

These outcomes are strongest for Chinese, Filipino, Japanese, Korean, and East Indian youths, less dramatic for other ethnicities (Fuligni, 2004; Louie, 2001; Portes & Rumbaut, 2005). Variation in adjustment is greater among Mexican, Central American, and Southeast Asian (Hmong, Cambodian, Laotian, Thai, and Vietnamese) young people, who show elevated rates of school failure and dropout, delinquency, teenage parenthood, and drug use. Disparities in parental economic resources, education, English-language proficiency, and support of children contribute to these trends (García Coll & Marks, 2009; Pong & Landale, 2012).

Still, many first- and second-generation youths whose parents face considerable financial hardship and who speak little English are successful (Hao & Woo, 2012; Hernandez et al., 2011). Factors other than income are responsible—notably, family values and strong ethnic-community ties.

Family and Ethnic-Community Influences

Ethnographies reveal that immigrant parents view education as the surest way to improve life chances (Garcia Coll & Marks, 2009; Goldenberg et al., 2001). Aware of the challenges their children face, they typically emphasize trying hard. They remind their children that, because educational opportunities were not available in their native countries, they themselves are often limited to menial jobs. And while preserving their culture's values, these parents also make certain adaptations—for example, supporting education for daughters even though their culture of origin endorses it only for sons.

Adolescents from immigrant families internalize their parents' valuing of academic achievement, endorsing it more strongly than agemates with native-born parents (Fuligni, 2004; Su & Costigan, 2008). Because minority ethnicities usually stress allegiance to family and community over individual goals, first- and second-generation young people often feel a strong sense of obligation to their parents. They view school success as an important way of repaying their parents for the hardships they have endured (Bacallao & Smokowski, 2007; van Geel & Vedder, 2011). Both family relationships and school achievement protect these youths from risky behaviors (see the Biology and Environment box on pages 10–11).

Immigrant parents of successful youths typically develop close ties to an ethnic community, which exerts additional control through a high consensus on values and constant monitoring of young people's activities. The following comments capture the power of these family and community forces:

- *A 16-year-old girl from Central America describes the supportive adults in her neighborhood:* They ask me if I need anything for school. If we go to a store and I see a notebook, they ask me if I want it. They give me advice, tell me that I should be careful of the friends I choose. They also tell me to stay in school to get prepared. They tell me I am smart. They give me encourage-

These Tibetan-American children march in an international immigrants parade in New York City. Cultural values that engender allegiance to family and community promote high achievement and protect many immigrant youths from involvement in risky behaviors.

ment. (Suárez-Orozco, Pimental, & Martin, 2009, p. 733)

- *A ninth-grade boy from Haiti explains how his mother encourages and monitors his homework efforts:* When she's at work she's always calling me, asking if I am doing my homework or if I don't understanding something, . . . I just go to the library to look up some books and finish it because I know she's gonna ask about it. (Bang, 2011, p. 14)

- *A teenage boy from Mexico discusses the importance of family in his culture:* A really big part of the Hispanic population [is] being close to family, and the family being a priority all the time. I hate people who say, "Why do you want to go to a party where your family's at? Don't you want to get away from them?" You know, I don't really get tired of them. I've always been really close to them. That connection to my parents, that trust that you can talk to them, that makes me Mexican. (Bacallao & Smokowski, 2007, p. 62)

The experiences of well-adjusted immigrant youths are not problem-free. Chinese adolescents who had arrived in the United States within the previous year described their adjustment as very difficult because they were not proficient in English and, as a result, found many everyday tasks challenging and felt socially isolated (Yeh et al., 2008). Young immigrants also encounter racial and ethnic prejudices and experience tensions between family values and the new culture. In the long term, however, family and community cohesion, supervision, and high expectations promote favorable outcomes.

General Research Designs

In deciding on a research design, investigators choose a way of setting up a study that permits them to test their hypotheses with the greatest degree of certainty possible. Two main designs are used in all research on human behavior: *correlational* and *experimental*.

CORRELATIONAL DESIGN In a **correlational design,** researchers gather information on individuals, generally in natural life circumstances, and make no effort to alter their experiences. Then they look at relationships between participants' characteristics and their behavior or development. Suppose we want to answer such questions as, Do parents' styles of interacting with their children have any bearing on children's intelligence? Does attending a child-care center promote children's friendliness with peers? How do child abuse and neglect affect children's feelings about themselves and their relationships with peers? In these and many other instances, the conditions of interest are difficult or impossible to arrange and control and must be studied as they currently exist.

Correlational studies have one major limitation: We cannot infer cause and effect. For example, if we find that parental interaction is related to children's intelligence, we would not know whether parents' behavior actually *causes* intellectual differences among children. In fact, the opposite is possible. The behaviors of highly intelligent children may be so attractive that they cause parents to interact more favorably. Or a third variable that we did not even consider, such as the amount of noise and distraction in the home, may cause changes in both parental interaction and children's intelligence.

In correlational studies, and in other types of research designs, investigators often examine relationships by using a **correlation coefficient**—a number that describes how two measures, or variables, are associated with one another. We will encounter the correlation coefficient in discussing research findings throughout this book, so let's look at what it is and how it is interpreted. A correlation coefficient can range in value from +1.00 to −1.00. The *magnitude,* or *size, of the number* shows the *strength of the relationship.* A zero correlation indicates no relationship, but the closer the value is to either +1.00 or −1.00, the stronger the relationship (see Figure 1.6). For instance, a correlation of −.78 is high, −.52 is moderate, and −.18 is low. Note, however that correlations of +.52 and −.52 are equally strong. The *sign of the number* refers to the *direction of the relationship.* A positive sign (+) means that as one variable *increases,* the other also *increases.* A negative sign (−) indicates that as one variable *increases,* the other *decreases.*

Let's look at some examples of how a correlation coefficient works. One researcher reported a +.55 correlation between a measure of maternal language stimulation and the size of children's vocabularies at age 2 years (Hoff, 2003). This is a moderate correlation, which indicates that mothers who spoke more to their infants had children who were more advanced in language development. In two other studies, child-rearing practices were related to toddlers' compliance in consistent ways. First, maternal warmth and sensitivity during play correlated positively with 2-year-olds' willingness to comply with their mother's directive to clean up toys, at +.34 (Feldman & Klein, 2003). Second, the extent to which mothers spoke harshly, interrupted, and controlled their 4-year-olds' play correlated negatively with children's compliance, at −.31 for boys and −.42 for girls (Smith et al., 2004).

All these investigations found a relationship between parenting and young children's behavior. **TAKE A MOMENT...** Are you tempted to conclude that parenting influenced children's responses? Although the researchers in these studies suspected this was so, they could not be sure of cause and effect. Can you think of other possible explanations? Finding a relationship in a correlational study suggests that tracking down its cause—using a more powerful experimental strategy, if possible—would be worthwhile.

EXPERIMENTAL DESIGN An **experimental design** permits inferences about cause and effect because researchers use an evenhanded procedure to assign people to two or more treatment conditions. In an experiment, the events and behaviors of interest are divided into two types: independent and dependent variables. The **independent variable** is the one the investigator expects to cause changes in another variable. The **dependent variable** is the one the

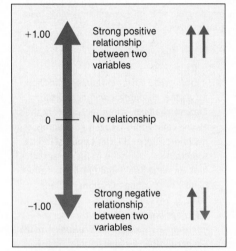

FIGURE 1.6 The meaning of correlation coefficients. The magnitude of the number indicates the *strength* of the relationship. The sign of the number (+ or −) indicates the *direction* of the relationship.

investigator expects to be influenced by the independent variable. Cause-and-effect relationships can be detected because the researcher directly *controls* or *manipulates* changes in the independent variable by exposing participants to the treatment conditions. Then the researcher compares their performance on measures of the dependent variable.

In one *laboratory experiment,* researchers explored the impact of adults' angry interactions on children's adjustment (El-Sheikh, Cummings, & Reiter, 1996). They hypothesized that the way angry encounters end (independent variable) affects children's emotional reactions (dependent variable). Four- and 5-year-olds were brought one at a time to a laboratory, accompanied by their mothers. One group was exposed to an *unresolved-anger treatment,* in which two adult actors entered the room and argued but did not work out their disagreements. The other group witnessed a *resolved-anger treatment,* in which the adults ended their disputes by apologizing and compromising. As Figure 1.7 shows, when they witnessed a follow-up adult conflict, more children in the resolved-anger treatment showed a decline in distress, as measured by fewer anxious facial expressions, less freezing in place, and less seeking of closeness to their mothers. The experiment revealed that anger resolution can reduce the stressful impact of adult conflict on children.

In experimental studies, investigators must take special precautions to control for participants' characteristics that could reduce the accuracy of their findings. For example, in the study just described, if more children from homes high in parental conflict ended up in the unresolved-anger treatment, we could not tell what produced the results—the independent variable or the children's backgrounds. To protect against this problem, researchers engage in **random assignment** of participants to treatment conditions. By using an unbiased procedure, such as drawing numbers out of a hat or flipping a coin, investigators increase the chances that participants' characteristics will be equally distributed across treatment groups.

Sometimes researchers combine random assignment with another technique called *matching.* In this procedure, participants are measured before the experiment on the factor in question—in our example, exposure to parental conflict. Then children high and low on that factor are assigned in equal numbers to each treatment condition. In this way, the experimental groups are deliberately matched, or made equivalent, on characteristics that are likely to distort the results.

MODIFIED EXPERIMENTAL DESIGNS: FIELD AND NATURAL EXPERIMENTS Most experiments are conducted in laboratories, where researchers can achieve the maximum possible control over treatment conditions. But as we have already indicated, findings obtained in laboratories may not apply to everyday situations. In *field experiments,* investigators capitalize on rare opportunities to assign participants randomly to treatment conditions in natural settings. In the experiment just described, we can conclude that the emotional climate established by adults affects children's behavior in the laboratory. But does it also do so in daily life?

Another study helps answer this question. Ethnically diverse, poverty-stricken families with a 2-year-old child were scheduled for a home visit, during which researchers assessed family functioning and child problem behaviors by asking parents to respond to questionnaires and videotaping parent–child interaction. Then the families were randomly assigned to either an intervention condition, called the Family Check-Up, or a no-intervention control group. The intervention consisted of three home-based sessions in which a consultant gave parents feedback about their child-rearing practices and their child's adjustment, explored parents' willingness to improve, identified community services appropriate to each family's needs, and offered follow-up sessions on parenting practices and other concerns (Brennan et al., 2013; Dishion et al., 2008). Findings showed that families assigned to the Family Check-Up (but not controls) gained in positive parenting, which predicted a reduction in child problem behaviors and improved academic achievement.

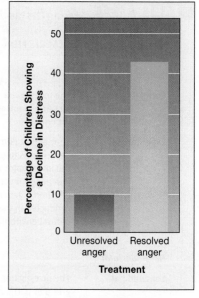

FIGURE 1.7 **Does the way adults end their angry encounters affect children's emotional reactions?** A laboratory experiment showed that children who had previously witnessed adults resolving their disputes by apologizing and compromising were more likely to decline in distress when witnessing subsequent adult conflicts than were children who witnessed adults leaving their arguments unresolved. Notice in this graph that only 10 percent of children in the unresolved-anger treatment declined in distress (see bar on left), whereas 42 percent of children in the resolved-anger treatment did so (see bar on right). (Based on El-Sheikh, Cummings, & Reiter, 1996.)

When researchers cannot randomly assign children to conditions in the real world, they sometimes conduct natural experiments using treatments that already exist. For example, the learning environments of different child-care centers might be compared to explore the impact of storybook reading on preschoolers' language and literacy development.

TABLE 1.5	Strengths and Limitations of Research Designs		
DESIGN	**DESCRIPTION**	**STRENGTHS**	**LIMITATIONS**
General			
Correlational	The investigator obtains information on participants without altering their experiences.	Permits study of relationships between variables.	Does not permit inferences about cause-and-effect relationships.
Experimental	Through random assignment of participants to treatment conditions, the investigator manipulates an independent variable and examines its effect on a dependent variable. Can be conducted in the laboratory or in the natural environment.	Permits inferences about cause-and-effect relationships.	When conducted in the laboratory, findings may not generalize to the real world. In *field experiments*, control over the treatment is usually weaker than in the laboratory. In *natural*, or *quasi-*, *experiments*, lack of random assignment substantially reduces the precision of research.
Developmental			
Longitudinal	The investigator studies the same group of participants repeatedly at different ages.	Permits study of common patterns and individual differences in development and relationships between early and later events and behaviors.	Age-related changes may be distorted because of biased sampling, selective attrition, practice effects, and cohort effects.
Cross-sectional	The investigator studies groups of participants differing in age at the same point in time.	More efficient than the longitudinal design.	Does not permit study of individual developmental trends. Age differences may be distorted because of cohort effects.
Sequential	The investigator conducts several similar cross-sectional or longitudinal studies (called sequences). These might study participants over the same ages but in different years, or they might study participants over different ages but during the same years.	Permits both longitudinal and cross-sectional comparisons. Reveals cohort effects. Permits tracking of age-related changes more efficiently than the longitudinal design.	May have the same problems as longitudinal and cross-sectional strategies, but the design itself helps identify difficulties.
Microgenetic	The investigator presents children with a novel task and follows their mastery over a series of closely spaced sessions.	Offers insights into how change occurs.	Requires intensive study of participants' moment-by-moment behaviors. The time required for participants to change is difficult to anticipate. Practice effects may distort developmental trends.

Often researchers cannot randomly assign participants and manipulate conditions in the real world, as these investigators were able to do. Sometimes they can compromise by conducting *natural*, or *quasi-*, *experiments*. Treatments that already exist, such as different family environments, child-care centers, or schools, are compared. These studies differ from correlational research only in that groups of participants are carefully chosen to ensure that their characteristics are as much alike as possible. In this way, investigators do their best to rule out alternative explanations for their treatment effects. But despite these efforts, natural experiments cannot achieve the precision and rigor of true experimental research.

To help you compare correlational and experimental designs, Table 1.5 summarizes their strengths and limitations. It also includes an overview of designs for studying development, to which we turn next.

Designs for Studying Development

Scientists interested in child development require information about the way research participants change over time. To answer questions about development, they must extend correlational and experimental approaches to include measurements at different ages. Longitudinal and cross-sectional designs are special *developmental research strategies*. In each, age comparisons form the basis of the research plan.

THE LONGITUDINAL DESIGN In a **longitudinal design,** participants are studied repeatedly, and changes are noted as they get older. The time spanned may be relatively short (a few months to several years) or very long (a decade or even a lifetime).

The longitudinal approach has two major strengths. First, because it tracks the performance of each person over time, researchers can identify common patterns as well as individual differences in development. Second, longitudinal studies permit investigators to examine relationships between early and later events and behaviors. Let's illustrate these ideas.

A group of researchers wondered whether children who display extreme personality styles—either angry and explosive or shy and withdrawn—retain the same dispositions when they become adults. In addition, the researchers wanted to know what kinds of experiences promote stability or plasticity in personality and what consequences explosiveness and shyness have for long-term adjustment. To answer these questions, the researchers delved into the archives of the Guidance Study, a well-known longitudinal investigation initiated in 1928 at the University of California, Berkeley, that continued for several decades (Caspi, Elder, & Bem, 1987, 1988).

Results revealed that the two personality styles were moderately stable. Between ages 8 and 30, a good number of individuals remained the same, whereas others changed substantially. When stability did occur, it appeared to be due to a "snowballing effect," in which children evoked responses from adults and peers that acted to maintain their dispositions. Explosive youngsters were likely to be treated with anger, whereas shy children were apt to be ignored. As a result, the two types of children came to view their social worlds differently. Explosive children tended to view others as hostile; shy children regarded them as unfriendly (Caspi & Roberts, 2001). Together, these factors led explosive children to sustain or increase their unruliness and shy children to continue to withdraw.

Persistence of extreme personality styles affected many areas of adult adjustment. For men, the results of early explosiveness were most apparent in their work lives, in the form of conflicts with supervisors, frequent job changes, and unemployment. Since few women in this sample of an earlier generation worked after marriage, their family lives were most affected. Explosive girls grew up to be hotheaded wives and mothers who were especially prone to divorce. Sex differences in the long-term consequences of shyness were even greater. Men who had been withdrawn in childhood were delayed in marrying, becoming fathers, and developing stable careers. However, because a withdrawn, unassertive style was socially acceptable for females in the mid-twentieth century, women with shy personalities showed no special adjustment problems.

PROBLEMS IN CONDUCTING LONGITUDINAL RESEARCH Despite their strengths, longitudinal investigations pose a number of problems. For example, *biased sampling*—the failure to enlist participants who adequately represent the population of interest—is a common problem. People who willingly participate in research that requires them to be observed and tested over many years are likely to have distinctive characteristics—perhaps a special appreciation for the scientific value of research, or a unique need or desire for medical, mental health, or educational services provided by the investigators. Furthermore, longitudinal samples generally become more biased as the investigation proceeds because of *selective attrition.* Participants may move away or drop out of the study for other reasons, and the ones who remain are likely to differ in important ways from the ones who do not continue. Also, from repeated study, people may become "test-wise." Their performance may improve as a result of *practice effects*—better test-taking skills and increased familiarity with the test—not because of factors commonly associated with development.

The most widely discussed threat to the accuracy of longitudinal findings is cultural–historical change, commonly called **cohort effects.** Longitudinal studies examine the development of *cohorts*—children born at the same time, who are influenced by particular cultural and historical conditions. Results based on one cohort may not apply to children developing at other times. For example, look back at the findings on female shyness described in the preceding section, which were gathered in the 1950s. Today's shy adolescent girls and young women tend to be poorly adjusted—a difference that may be due to changes in gender roles in Western societies. Shy adults, whether male or female, feel more anxious, depressed, have fewer

An 11-year-old helps his mother fix the grave of his father, who died in the typhoon that battered the Philippines in 2013. This powerfully destructive event is a cohort effect, with profound consequences for this child's development.

social supports, and may do less well in educational and career attainment than their agemates (Caspi et al., 2003; Karevold et al., 2012; Mounts et al., 2006). Similarly, a longitudinal study of social development would probably result in quite different findings if it were carried out in the second decade of the twenty-first century, around the time of World War II, or during the Great Depression of the 1930s.

Cohort effects don't just operate broadly on an entire generation. They also occur when specific experiences influence some children but not others in the same generation. For example, children who witnessed the terrorist attacks of September 11, 2001 (either because they were near Ground Zero or because they saw injury and death on TV), or who lost a parent in the disaster, were far more likely than other children to display persistent emotional problems, including intense fear, anxiety, and depression (Mullett-Hume et al., 2008; Pfeffer et al., 2007; Rosen & Cohen, 2010). A study of one New York City sample suggested that as many as one-fourth of the city's children were affected (Hoven et al., 2005).

Finally, longitudinal research, especially when conducted over multiple years, requires large investments of time, effort and resources. To maximize the benefits of these costly endeavors, investigators are increasingly carrying out massive longitudinal projects that gather information from large, representative samples on many aspects of development. Then they create multipurpose longitudinal data banks, which any researcher can access.

For example, the Early Childhood Longitudinal Study (ECLS), sponsored by the U.S. Department of Education in collaboration with other federal agencies, includes several nationally representative samples with thousands of participants, some followed from birth to kindergarten and others from kindergarten through eighth grade. The ECLS data bank has been used to study a wide variety of topics, including predictors of childhood obesity, effects of maternal stress during pregnancy on early development, the impact of family and preschool experiences on kindergarten readiness, and the influence of elementary school teaching practices on later academic performance. Investigations like the ECLS are enabling much more research to capitalize the unique strengths of the longitudinal design.

THE CROSS-SECTIONAL DESIGN The length of time it takes for many behaviors to change, even in limited longitudinal studies, has led researchers to turn to a more efficient strategy for studying development. In the **cross-sectional design,** groups of people differing in age are studied at the same point in time. Because participants are measured only once, researchers need not be concerned about such difficulties as participant dropout or practice effects.

An investigation in which students in grades 3, 6, 9, and 12 filled out a questionnaire about their sibling relationships provides a good illustration (Buhrmester & Furman, 1990). Findings revealed that sibling interaction was characterized by greater equality and less power assertion with age. Also, feelings of sibling companionship declined during adolescence. The researchers thought that several factors contributed to these age differences. As later-born children become more competent and independent, they no longer need, and are probably less willing to accept, direction from older siblings. And as adolescents move from psychological dependence on the family to greater involvement with peers, they may have less time and emotional need to invest in siblings. Subsequent research has confirmed these intriguing ideas about the development of sibling relationships.

PROBLEMS IN CONDUCTING CROSS-SECTIONAL RESEARCH Despite its convenience, cross-sectional research does not provide evidence about change at the level at which it actually occurs: the individual. For example, in the cross-sectional study of sibling relationships just discussed, comparisons are limited to age-group averages. We cannot tell if important individual differences exist. Indeed, longitudinal findings reveal that adolescents vary considerably in the changing quality of their sibling relationships. Although many become more distant, others become more supportive and intimate, still others more rivalrous and antagonistic (Branje et al., 2004; Kim et al., 2006; Whiteman & Loken, 2006).

Cross-sectional studies—especially those that cover a wide age span—have another problem. Like longitudinal research, they can be threatened by cohort effects. For example, comparisons of 5-year-old cohorts and 15-year-old cohorts—groups born and reared in different years—may not really represent age-related changes. Instead, they may reflect unique experiences associated with the time period in which the age groups were growing up.

Improving Developmental Designs

Researchers have devised ways of building on the strengths and minimizing the weaknesses of longitudinal and cross-sectional approaches. Several modified developmental designs have resulted.

SEQUENTIAL DESIGNS To overcome some of the limitations of traditional developmental designs, investigators sometimes use **sequential designs,** in which they conduct several similar cross-sectional or longitudinal studies (called *sequences*) at varying times. As the illustration in Figure 1.8 reveals, some sequential designs combine longitudinal and cross-sectional strategies, an approach that has three advantages:

- We can find out whether cohort effects are operating by comparing participants of the same age who were born in different years. In Figure 1.8, for example, we can compare the longitudinal samples at seventh, eighth, and ninth grades. If they do not differ, we can rule out cohort effects.
- We can make both longitudinal and cross-sectional comparisons. If outcomes are similar, we can be especially confident about the findings.
- The design is efficient. In our example, we can find out about change over a five-year period by following each cohort for three years.

In a study that used the design in Figure 1.8, researchers wanted to find out if family harmony changed as young people experienced the dramatic physical and psychological changes of adolescence (Baer, 2002). A questionnaire assessing emotional bonding among family members was given to three adolescent cohorts, each born a year apart. In longitudinal follow-ups, each cohort again responded to the questionnaire during the following two years.

Findings for the three cohorts converged: All reported (1) a slight decline in family harmony with grade and (2) similar levels of family harmony as they reached the same grade, confirming that there were no cohort effects. Therefore, the researchers concluded that family closeness diminishes steadily from sixth to tenth grade, noting, however, that the change is mild—not enough to threaten supportive family ties. **TAKE A MOMENT...** Turn back to our discussion of parent–adolescent communication as a dynamic system on page 30 and our

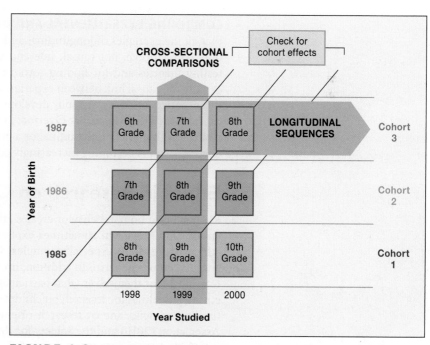

FIGURE 1.8 **Example of a sequential design.** Three cohorts, born in 1985 (blue), 1986 (orange), and 1987 (pink), respectively, are followed longitudinally for three years. Testing the cohorts in overlapping grades enables researchers to check for cohort effects by comparing participants born in different years when they reach the same grade (see diagonals). In a study using this design, same-grade adolescents who were members of different cohorts scored similarly on a questionnaire assessing family harmony, indicating no cohort effects. By following each cohort for just three years, the investigator could infer a developmental trend across five years, from sixth to tenth grade.

© ELLEN B. SENISI

How do these first graders make use of manipulatives to master place value in arithmetic? A microgenetic design, which permits researchers to follow children's mastery of a challenging task, is uniquely suited to answering this question.

consideration of adolescent sibling relationships on page 42. How are those results helpful in interpreting the outcomes of the sequential study just described?

EXAMINING MICROCOSMS OF DEVELOPMENT In the examples of developmental research we have discussed, observations of children are fairly widely spaced. When we observe once a year or every few years, we can describe development, but we cannot easily capture the processes that produce it. The **microgenetic design,** an adaptation of the longitudinal approach, presents children with a novel task and follows their mastery over a series of closely spaced sessions. Within this "microcosm" of development, researchers observe how change occurs (Flynn & Siegler, 2007; Kuhn, 1995; Siegler & Crowley, 1991). The microgenetic design is especially useful for studying cognitive development—for example, the strategies children use to acquire new knowledge in reading, mathematics, and science (Siegler, 2002, 2006). As we will see in Chapter 5, the microgenetic design has also been used to trace infants' mastery of motor skills.

Nevertheless, microgenetic studies are difficult to carry out. Researchers must pore over hours of recorded information, analyzing each participant's behavior many times. In addition, the time required for children to change is hard to anticipate. It depends on a careful match between the child's capabilities and the demands of the task. Finally, as in other longitudinal research, practice effects can distort microgenetic findings. But when researchers overcome these challenges, they reap the benefits of seeing development as it takes place.

COMBINING EXPERIMENTAL AND DEVELOPMENTAL DESIGNS Perhaps you noticed that all the examples of longitudinal and cross-sectional research we have considered permit only correlational, not causal, inferences. Yet causal information is also desirable, both for testing theories and for finding ways to enhance development. Sometimes researchers can explore the causal link between experiences and development by experimentally manipulating the experiences. If, as a result, development improves, then we have strong evidence for a causal association (Lerner & Overton, 2008). Today, research that combines an experimental strategy with either a longitudinal or a cross-sectional approach, with the aim of augmenting development, is becoming increasingly common.

Ethics in Research on Children

Research into human behavior creates ethical issues because, unfortunately, the quest for scientific knowledge can sometimes exploit people. When children take part in research, the ethical concerns are especially complex. Children are more vulnerable than adults to physical and psychological harm. In addition, immaturity makes it difficult or impossible for children to evaluate for themselves what participation in research will mean. For these reasons, special ethical guidelines for research on children have been developed by the federal government, by funding agencies, and by research-oriented associations such as the American Psychological Association (2010) and the Society for Research in Child Development (2007).

Table 1.6 presents a summary of children's basic research rights. TAKE A MOMENT... After examining them, read about the following research situations, each of which poses a serious ethical dilemma. What precautions do you think should be taken in each instance? Is either so threatening to children's well-being that it should not be carried out?

- In a study of moral development, a researcher wants to assess children's ability to resist temptation by videotaping their behavior without their knowledge. She promises 7-year-

TABLE 1.6	Children's Research Rights
RESEARCH RIGHT	**DESCRIPTION**
Protection from harm	Children have the right to be protected from physical or psychological harm in research. If in doubt about the harmful effects of research, investigators should seek the opinion of others. When harm seems possible, investigators should find other means for obtaining the desired information or abandon the research.
Informed consent/ assent	All research participants, including children, have the right to have explained to them, in language appropriate to their level of understanding, all aspects of the research that may affect their willingness to participate. When children are participants, informed consent of parents as well as others who act on the child's behalf (such as school officials) should be obtained, preferably in writing. Although minors cannot legally give consent, investigators are usually required to obtain children's written or verbal assent (agreement) for participation. Children, and the adults responsible for them, have the right to discontinue participation in the research at any time.
Privacy	Children have the right to concealment of their identity on all information collected in the course of research. They also have this right with respect to written reports and any informal discussions about the research.
Knowledge of results	Children have the right to be informed of the results of research in language that is appropriate to their level of understanding.
Beneficial treatments	If experimental treatments believed to be beneficial are under investigation, children in control groups have the right to alternative beneficial treatments (if available) or to the same treatment (if found to be effective) once the research is complete.

Sources: American Psychological Association, 2010; Society for Research in Child Development, 2007.

olds an attractive prize for solving difficult puzzles but tells them not to look at a classmate's correct solutions, which are deliberately placed at the back of the room. Telling children ahead of time that cheating is being studied or that their behavior is being monitored will defeat the purpose of the study.

- A researcher is interviewing fifth graders about their experiences with bullying. A girl describes frequent name-calling and derogatory comments by her older sister. Although the girl is unhappy, she wants to handle the problem on her own. If the researcher alerts the girl's parents to provide protection and help, he will violate his promise to keep participants' responses private.

Did you find it difficult to evaluate these examples? Virtually every organization that has devised ethical principles for research has concluded that conflicts arising in research situations do not have simple right or wrong answers. The ultimate responsibility for the ethical integrity of research lies with the investigator. But researchers are advised—and often required—to seek advice from others. Committees for this purpose exist in colleges, universities, and other institutions. These *institutional review boards (IRBs)* follow federal guidelines for the protection of human subjects, which balance the costs of the research to participants in terms of time, stress, and inconvenience against the study's value for advancing knowledge and improving conditions of life. If any risks to the safety and welfare of participants outweigh the worth of the research, then preference is always given to the interests of the participants.

The ethical principle of *informed consent* requires special interpretation when participants cannot fully appreciate the research goals and activities. Parental consent is meant to protect the safety of children whose ability to decide is not yet mature. In addition, researchers should obtain the agreement of other individuals who act on children's behalf, such as institutional officials when research is conducted in schools, child-care centers, or hospitals. This is especially important when research includes special groups, such as abused children, whose parents may not always represent their best interests (Fisher, 1993; Thompson, 1990).

Extra steps must be taken to protect children's research rights. Although this 8-year-old responds to the interviewer's questions, she may not know why she is being interviewed, or realize that she has the right to withdraw from the study without negative consequences.

As soon as children are old enough to appreciate the purpose of the research, and certainly by 7 years of age, their own informed *assent*, or agreement, should be obtained in addition to parental consent. Around age 7, changes in children's thinking permit them to better understand basic scientific principles and the needs of others. Researchers should respect and enhance these capacities by giving school-age children a full explanation of research activities in language they can understand (Fisher, 1993). Extra care must be taken when telling children that the information they provide will be kept confidential and that they can end their participation at any time. Even adolescents may not understand, and sometimes do not believe, these promises (Bruzzese & Fisher, 2003; Ondrusek et al., 1998). And in certain ethnic minority communities, where deference to authority, maintaining pleasant relationships, and meeting the needs of a guest (the researcher) are highly valued, children and parents may be particularly likely to consent or assent when they would rather not do so (Fisher et al., 2002).

Careful attention to informed consent and assent helps resolve dilemmas about revealing children's responses to parents, teachers, or other authorities when those responses suggest that the child's welfare is in danger. Children can be told in advance that if they report that someone is harming them, the researcher will tell an appropriate adult to take action to ensure the child's safety (Jennifer & Cowie, 2009).

Finally, because young children rely on a basic faith in adults to feel secure in unfamiliar situations, they may find some types of research particularly disturbing. All ethical guidelines advise that special precautions be taken in the use of deception and concealment, as occurs when researchers observe children from behind one-way mirrors, give them false feedback about their performance, or misrepresent the real purpose of the research. When these procedures are used with adults, *debriefing,* in which the researcher provides a full account and justification of the activities, occurs after the research session is over. Debriefing should also be done with children, and it sometimes works well. But young children often lack the cognitive skills to understand the reasons for deceptive procedures, and, despite explanations, they may leave the research situation questioning the honesty of adults. Ethical standards permit deception in research with children if investigators satisfy IRBs that such practices are necessary. Nevertheless, because deception may have serious emotional consequences for some youngsters, many child development specialists believe that researchers should use it only if the risk of harm is minimal.

Ask Yourself

- **REVIEW** Explain how cohort effects can distort the findings of both longitudinal and cross-sectional studies. How does the sequential design reveal cohort effects?

- **CONNECT** Review the field experiment on the impact of the Family Check-Up on page 39. Why is it ethically important for researchers to offer the intervention to the no-intervention control group after completion of the study? (Hint: Refer to Table 1.6. on page 45)

- **APPLY** A researcher compares children who went to summer leadership camps with children who attended athletic camps. She finds that those who attended leadership camps are friendlier. Should the investigator tell parents that sending children to leadership camps will cause them to be more sociable? Why or why not?

- **REFLECT** Suppose a researcher asks you to enroll your baby in a 10-year longitudinal study. What factors would lead you to agree and to stay involved? Do your answers shed light on why longitudinal studies often have biased samples? Explain.

Summary

The Field of Child Development (p. 4)

1.1 What is the field of child development, and what factors stimulated its expansion?

- **Child development** is an area of study devoted to understanding constancy and change from conception through adolescence. It is part of a larger interdisciplinary field known as **developmental science,** which includes all changes we experience throughout the lifespan. Research on child development has been stimulated both by scientific curiosity and by social pressures to better children's lives.

1.2 How is child development typically divided into domains and periods?

- Development is often divided into physical, cognitive, and emotional and social domains. These domains are not really distinct; rather, they combine in an integrated, holistic fashion.

© UWE OMMER, 1,000 FAMILIES, TASCHEN

- Researchers generally divide the flow of time into the following age periods: (1) prenatal (conception to birth), (2) infancy and toddlerhood (birth to 2 years), (3) early childhood (2 to 6 years), (4) middle childhood (6 to 11 years), and (5) adolescence (11 to 18 years). To describe the prolonged transition to adulthood typical of contemporary young people in industrialized nations, researchers have posited a new period of development, emerging adulthood, spanning ages 18 to 25.

Basic Issues (p. 7)

1.3 Identify three basic issues on which theories of child development take a stand.

- Each **theory** of child development takes a stand on three fundamental issues: (1) Is development a **continuous** process, or is it **discontinuous,** following a series of distinct **stages?** (2) Does one general course of development characterize all children, or are there many possible courses, influenced by the distinct **contexts** in which children grow up? (3) Are genetic or environmental factors more important in influencing development (the **nature–nurture controversy**), and are individual differences stable or characterized by substantial **plasticity?**

- Recent theories take a balanced stand on these issues. And contemporary researchers realize that answers may vary across domains of development and even, as research on **resilience** illustrates, across individuals.

Historical Foundations (p. 11)

1.4 Describe major historical influences on theories of child development.

- As early as medieval times, the sixth through the fifteenth centuries, childhood was regarded as a separate phase of life.

- In the sixteenth and seventeenth centuries, the Puritan conception of original sin led to a harsh philosophy of child rearing. The seventeenth-century Enlightenment brought a new emphasis on human dignity and respect that led to more humane views of childhood. Locke's notion of the child as a tabula rasa ("blank slate") provided the basis for twentieth-century behaviorism, while Rousseau's idea that children were noble savages foreshadowed the concepts of stage and **maturation.**

- Inspired by Darwin's theory of evolution, efforts to observe the child directly began in the late nineteenth and early twentieth centuries. Hall and Gesell introduced the **normative approach,** in which many measures were gathered on large numbers of individuals, yielding descriptions of typical development. Binet and Simon constructed the first successful intelligence test, which sparked interest in individual differences and made intelligence central to the nature–nurture controversy.

Mid-Twentieth-Century Theories (p. 14)

1.5 What theories influenced child development research in the mid-twentieth century?

- In the 1930s and 1940s, psychiatrists and social workers turned to the **psychoanalytic perspective** for help in treating children's emotional problems. In Freud's **psychosexual theory,** children move through five stages, during which three portions of the personality—id, ego, and superego—become integrated.

- Erikson's **psychosocial theory** builds on Freud's theory, emphasizing the development of culturally relevant attitudes and skills and—with the addition of three adult stages—the lifespan nature of development. Despite its extensive contributions, the psychoanalytic perspective is no longer in the mainstream of child development research.

ANTONIA TOZER/GETTY IMAGES

- **Behaviorism** focused on directly observable events (stimuli and responses) in an effort to create an objective science of psychology. B. F. Skinner's operant conditioning theory emphasizes the role of reinforcement and punishment in increasing or decreasing the frequency of behaviors.

- A related approach, Albert Bandura's **social learning theory,** focuses on modeling as the major means through which children and adults acquire new responses. Its most recent revision stresses the role of cognition, or thinking, in children's imitation and learning and is known as a social-cognitive approach.

- Behaviorism and social learning theory gave rise to techniques of **applied behavior analysis,** in which procedures of conditioning and modeling are designed to eliminate undesirable behaviors and increase desirable responses.

- Piaget's **cognitive-developmental theory** emphasizes that children actively construct knowledge as they move through four stages, beginning with the baby's sensorimotor action patterns and ending with the abstract, systematic reasoning system of the adolescent and adult. Piaget's work has stimulated a wealth of research on children's thinking and has encouraged educational programs that emphasize children's discovery learning.

Recent Theoretical Perspectives
(p. 21)

1.6 Describe recent theoretical perspectives on child development.

- **Information processing** views the mind as a complex symbol-manipulating system, much like a computer. This approach helps investigators achieve a detailed understanding of how children of different ages respond to tasks and problems and has important implications for education.

- Over the past three decades, researchers in **developmental cognitive neuroscience** have studied the relationship between changes in the brain and the developing child's cognitive processing and behavior patterns. More recently, investigators in **developmental social neuroscience** have examined relationships between changes in the brain and social development. Findings on the types of experiences that support or undermine brain development is leading to effective interventions for children with learning and behavior problems.

- Four contemporary perspectives emphasize contexts for development. **Ethology** stresses the adaptive value and evolutionary history of behavior and inspired the **sensitive period** concept. Researchers in **evolutionary developmental psychology** have extended this emphasis, seeking to understand the adaptiveness of species-wide competencies as they change over time.

- Vygotsky's **sociocultural theory,** which focuses on how culture is transmitted from one generation to the next through social interaction, views cognitive development as a socially mediated process. Through cooperative dialogues with more expert members of society, children come to use language to guide their own thought and actions and acquire culturally relevant knowledge and skills.

- **Ecological systems theory** views the child as developing within a complex system of relationships affected by multiple, nested layers of the surrounding environment—**microsystem, mesosystem, exosystem,** and **macrosystem.** Each of these levels is seen as a major influence on children's well-being. The **chronosystem** represents the dynamic, ever-changing nature of children and their experiences.

- Theorists who adopt a **dynamic systems perspective** seek to understand how children alter their behavior to attain more advanced functioning. According to this view, the mind, body, and physical and social worlds form an integrated system that guides mastery of new skills. A change in any part of the system prompts the child to reorganize her behavior so the various components work together in a more complex, effective way.

Comparing Child Development Theories (p. 30)

1.7 Identify the stand taken by each major theory on the basic issues of child development.

- Major theories vary in their focus on different domains of development, in their view of how development occurs, and in their strengths and weaknesses. (For a full summary, see Table 1.3 on page 31.)

Studying the Child (p. 32)

1.8 Describe research methods commonly used to study children.

- **Naturalistic observations** are gathered in everyday environments and permit researchers to see directly the everyday behaviors they hope to explain. **Structured observations** take place in laboratories, where every participant has an equal opportunity to display the behaviors of interest.

- Self-report methods can be flexible and open-ended like the **clinical interview,** which permits participants to express their thoughts in ways similar to their thinking in everyday life. **Structured interviews,** tests, and questionnaires are more efficient and permit researchers to specify activities and behaviors that participants might not think of in an open-ended interview.

- Investigators use the **clinical,** or **case study, method** to obtain an in-depth understanding of a single child. It involves synthesizing a wide range of information, including interviews, observations, and sometimes test scores.

- Researchers have adapted observational and self-report methods to permit direct comparisons of cultures. To uncover the cultural meanings of behavior, they rely on **ethnography,** engaging in participant observation.

1.9 Distinguish between correlational and experimental research designs, noting strengths and limitations of each.

- The **correlational design** examines relationships between variables, generally as they occur in natural life circumstances, without altering participants' experiences. The **correlation coefficient** describes how two measures, or variables, are associated with one another. Correlational studies do not permit inferences about cause and effect, but they can be helpful in identifying relationships that are worth exploring with a more powerful experimental strategy.

- An **experimental design** permits inferences about cause and effect. Researchers manipulate an **independent variable** by exposing participants to two or more treatment conditions. Then they determine what effect this variable has on a **dependent variable. Random assignment** reduces the chances that characteristics of participants will affect the accuracy of experimental findings.

- Field and natural, or quasi-, experiments compare treatments in natural environments. However, these approaches are less rigorous than laboratory experiments.

1.10 Describe designs for studying development, noting strengths and limitations of each.

- In a **longitudinal design,** participants are studied repeatedly at different ages, revealing common patterns as well as individual differences in development and the relationship between early and later events and behaviors. Longitudinal research poses several problems, including biased sampling, selective attrition, **cohort effects** (difficulty generalizing to children developing under other cultural and historical conditions), and the need for large investments of time and resources.

- The **cross-sectional design,** in which groups of children differing in age are studied at the same point in time, offers an efficient approach to investigating development. However, it is limited to comparisons of age-group averages and can be vulnerable to cohort effects.
- **Sequential designs** compare groups of children born in different years to find out if cohort effects are operating. When sequential designs combine longitudinal and cross-sectional strategies, researchers can see if outcomes are similar, for added confidence in their findings.

- In the **microgenetic design,** researchers present children with a novel task and track their mastery over a series of closely spaced sessions, seeking to capture processes of development. However, the time required for children to change is hard to anticipate, and practice effects can bias findings.
- When researchers combine experimental and developmental designs, they can examine causal influences on development. This combined strategy is increasingly common today.

1.11 *What special ethical concerns arise in doing research on children?*

- Because of their immaturity, children are especially vulnerable to harm and often cannot evaluate the risks and benefits of research. Ethical guidelines and institutional review boards that weigh the risks and benefits of research help ensure that children's research rights are protected.
- Besides obtaining consent from parents and others who act on children's behalf, researchers should seek the informed assent of children 7 years and older. The use of deception in research with children is especially risky because it may undermine their basic faith in the honesty of adults.

Important Terms and Concepts

applied behavior analysis (p. 18)
behaviorism (p. 17)
child development (p. 4)
chronosystem (p. 29)
clinical interview (p. 34)
clinical, or case study, method (p. 35)
cognitive-developmental theory (p. 19)
cohort effects (p. 41)
contexts (p. 8)
continuous development (p. 8)
correlational design (p. 38)
correlation coefficient (p. 38)
cross-sectional design (p. 42)
dependent variable (p. 38)
developmental cognitive neuroscience (p. 23)
developmental social neuroscience (p. 23)
developmental science (p. 4)

discontinuous development (p. 8)
dynamic systems perspective (p. 29)
ecological systems theory (p. 26)
ethnography (p. 36)
ethology (p. 24)
evolutionary developmental psychology (p. 25)
exosystem (p. 27)
experimental design (p. 38)
independent variable (p. 38)
information processing (p. 21)
longitudinal design (p. 41)
macrosystem (p. 28)
maturation (p. 13)
mesosystem (p. 27)
microgenetic design (p. 44)
microsystem (p. 26)

naturalistic observation (p. 32)
nature–nurture controversy (p. 9)
normative approach (p. 13)
plasticity (p. 9)
psychoanalytic perspective (p. 15)
psychosexual theory (p. 15)
psychosocial theory (p. 15)
random assignment (p. 39)
resilience (p. 10)
sensitive period (p. 24)
sequential design (p. 43)
social learning theory (p. 17)
sociocultural theory (p. 25)
stage (p. 8)
structured interview (p. 35)
structured observation (p. 33)
theory (p. 7)

Genetic and Environmental Foundations

REPRINTED WITH PERMISSION FROM THE WORLD AWARENESS CHILDREN'S MUSEUM, GLENS FALLS, NEW YORK

"Childhood"
Leticia Aparecida Da Silva
11 years, Brazil

As these children enjoy a summer day, their kite flying is influenced not only by their physical abilities but also by the direction and strength of the wind. Likewise, Chapter 2 addresses both genetic and environmental influences on child development.

"It's a girl!" announces the doctor, holding up the squalling newborn baby as her parents gaze with amazement at their miraculous creation.

"A girl! We've named her Sarah!" exclaims the proud father to eager relatives waiting for news of their new family member.

As we join these parents in thinking about how this wondrous being came into existence and imagining her future, we are struck by many questions. How could this baby, equipped with everything necessary for life outside the womb, have developed from the union of two tiny cells? What ensures that Sarah will, in due time, roll over, reach for objects, walk, talk, make friends, learn, imagine, and create—just like other typical children born before her? Why is she a girl and not a boy, dark-haired rather than blond, calm and cuddly instead of wiry and energetic? What difference will it make that Sarah is given a name and place in one family, community, nation, and culture rather than another?

To answer these questions, this chapter takes a close look at the foundations of development: heredity and environment. Because nature has prepared us for survival, all humans have features in common. Yet each of us is also unique. TAKE A MOMENT... Think about several children you know well, and jot down the most obvious physical and behavioral similarities between them and their parents. Did you find that one child shows combined features of both parents, another resembles just one parent, whereas a third is not like either parent? These directly observable characteristics are called **phenotypes.** They depend in part on the individual's **genotype**—the complex blend of genetic information that determines our species and influences all our unique characteristics. Yet phenotypes are also affected by each person's lifelong history of experiences.

We begin our discussion at the moment of conception, an event that establishes the hereditary makeup of the new individual. First we review basic genetic principles that help explain similarities and differences among children in appearance and behavior. Then we turn to aspects of the environment that play powerful roles in children's lives. As our discussion proceeds, some findings about the influence of nature and nurture may surprise you. For example, many people believe that when children inherit unfavorable characteristics, not much can be done to help them. Others are convinced that the damage done to a child by a harmful environment can easily be corrected. As we will see, neither of these assumptions is true. Rather, heredity and environment continuously collaborate, each modifying—for better or for worse—the power of the other to shape the course of development. In the final section of this chapter, we consider how nature and nurture work together. ■

Genetic Foundations

Within each of the trillions of cells in the human body (except red blood cells) is a control center, or *nucleus,* that contains rodlike structures called **chromosomes,** which store and transmit genetic information. Human chromosomes come in 23 matching pairs (an exception is the XY pair in males, which we will discuss shortly). Each member of a pair corresponds to the other in size, shape, and genetic functions. One is inherited from the mother and one from the father (see Figure 2.1 on page 52).

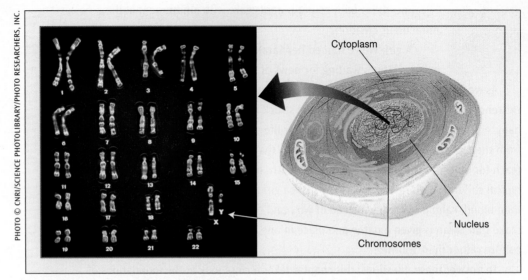

PHOTO © CNRI/SCIENCE PHOTOLIBRARY/PHOTO RESEARCHERS, INC.

Cytoplasm

Nucleus

Chromosomes

FIGURE 2.1 **A karyotype, or photograph, of human chromosomes.** The 46 chromosomes shown on the left were isolated from a human cell, stained, greatly magnified, and arranged in pairs according to decreasing size of the upper "arm" of each chromosome. The twenty-third pair, XY, reveals that the cell donor is a male. In a female, this pair would be XX.

2.1 What are genes, and how are they transmitted from one generation to the next?

2.2 Describe various patterns of genetic inheritance.

2.3 Describe major chromosomal abnormalities, and explain how they occur.

The Genetic Code

Chromosomes are made up of a chemical substance called **deoxyribonucleic acid** or **DNA.** As Figure 2.2 shows, DNA is a long, double-stranded molecule that looks like a twisted ladder. Each rung of the ladder consists of a pair of chemical substances called *bases.* Although the bases always pair up in the same way across the ladder rungs—A with T and C with G—they can occur in any order along its sides. It is this sequence of base pairs that provides genetic instructions. A **gene i**s a segment of DNA along the length of the chromosome. Genes can be of different lengths—perhaps 100 to several thousand ladder rungs long. An estimated 21,000 **protein-coding genes,** which directly affect our body's characteristics, lie along the human chromosomes. They send instructions for making a rich assortment of proteins to the *cytoplasm,* the area surrounding the cell nucleus. Proteins, which trigger chemical reactions throughout the body, are the biological foundation on which our characteristics are built. An additional 18,000 **regulator genes** modify the instructions given by protein-coding genes, greatly complicating their genetic impact (Pennisi, 2012).

We share some of our genetic makeup with even the simplest organisms, such as bacteria and molds, and most of it with other mammals, especially primates. About 95 percent of chimpanzee and human DNA is identical. And the genetic variation from one human to the next is even less: Individuals around the world are about 99.6 percent genetically identical (Tishkoff & Kidd, 2004). But these straightforward comparisons are misleading. Many human DNA segments that appear like those of chimpanzees have undergone duplications and rearrangements with other segments. So in actuality, the species-specific genetic material responsible for the attributes that make us human, from our upright gait to our extraordinary language and cognitive capacities, is extensive (Preuss, 2012). Furthermore, it takes a change in only a single DNA base pair to influence human traits. And such tiny changes generally combine in unique ways across multiple genes, thereby amplifying variability within the human species.

How do humans, with far fewer genes than scientists once thought (only twice as many as the worm or fly), manage to develop into such complex beings? The answer lies in the proteins our genes make, which break up and reassemble in staggering variety—about 10 to 20 million altogether. Simpler species have far fewer proteins. Furthermore, the communication system between the cell nucleus and cytoplasm, which fine-tunes gene activity, is more intricate in humans than in simpler organisms. Finally, within the cell, a wide range of environmental factors modify gene expression. Recent evidence reveals that many such effects are unique to humans and influence brain development (Hernando-Herraez et al., 2013). So even at this microscopic level, biological events of profound developmental significance are the result of *both* genetic and nongenetic forces.

The Sex Cells

New individuals are created when two special cells called **gametes,** or sex cells—the sperm and ovum—combine. A gamete contains only 23 chromosomes, half as many as a regular body cell. Gametes are formed through a cell division process called **meiosis,** which halves the number of chromosomes normally present in body cells. When sperm and ovum unite at conception, the resulting cell, called a **zygote,** will again have 46 chromosomes. Meiosis ensures that a constant quantity of genetic material is transmitted from one generation to the next.

In meiosis, the chromosomes pair up and exchange segments, so that genes from one are replaced by genes from another. This shuffling of genes creates new hereditary combinations. Then chance determines which member of each pair will gather with other chromosomes and end up in the same gamete. These events make the likelihood extremely low—about 1 in 700 trillion—that nontwin siblings will be genetically identical (Gould & Keeton, 1996). The genetic variability produced by meiosis is adaptive: It increases the chances that at least some members of a species will cope with ever-changing environments and will survive.

In the male, four sperm are produced when meiosis is complete. Also, the cells from which sperm arise are produced continuously throughout life. For this reason, a healthy man can father a child at any age after sexual maturity. In the female, meiosis results in just one ovum; the remaining genetic material degenerates. In addition, the female is born with a bank of ova already present in her ovaries, though recent findings suggest that new ova may arise from ovarian stem cells later on (White et al., 2012). Still, there are plenty of female sex cells. About 1 to 2 million are present at birth, 40,000 remain at adolescence, and approximately 350 to 450 will mature during a woman's childbearing years (Moore, Persaud, & Torchia, 2013).

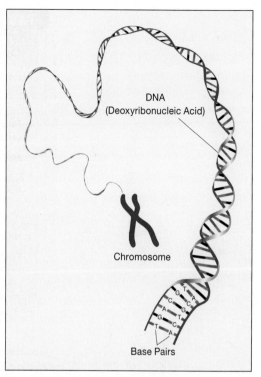

FIGURE 2.2 **DNA's ladderlike structure.** A gene is a segment of DNA along the length of the chromosome, varying from perhaps 100 to several thousand ladder rungs long. The pairings of bases across the rungs of the ladder are very specific: Adenine (A) always appears with thymine (T), and cytosine (C) always appears with guanine (G).

Boy or Girl?

Return to Figure 2.1 and note that 22 of the 23 pairs of chromosomes are matching pairs, called **autosomes** (meaning *not* sex chromosomes). The twenty-third pair consists of **sex chromosomes.** In females, this pair is called XX; in males, it is called XY. The X is a relatively large chromosome, whereas the Y is short and carries little genetic material. When gametes form in males, the X and Y chromosomes separate into different sperm cells. The gametes that form in females all carry an X chromosome. Therefore, the sex of the new organism is determined by whether an X-bearing or a Y-bearing sperm fertilizes the ovum. In fact, scientists have isolated a gene on the Y chromosome that initiates the formation of male sex organs during the prenatal period (Sekido & Lovell-Badge, 2009). But they also know that other genes, some yet to be identified, are involved in the development of sexual characteristics.

Multiple Offspring

Ruth and Peter, a couple your first author knows well, tried for several years to have a child, without success. When Ruth reached age 33, her doctor prescribed a fertility drug, and twins—Jeannie and Jason—were born. Jeannie and Jason are **fraternal,** or **dizygotic, twins,** the most common type of multiple offspring, resulting from the release and fertilization of two ova.

TABLE 2.1	Maternal Factors Linked to Fraternal Twinning
FACTOR	**DESCRIPTION**
Ethnicity	Occurs in 6 to 9 per 1,000 births among Asians and Hispanics, 9 to 12 per 1,000 births among white Europeans, and 11 to 18 or more per 1,000 births among black Africans[a]
Family history of twinning	Occurs more often among women whose mothers and sisters gave birth to fraternal twins, suggesting a hereditary influence through the female line
Age	Rises with maternal age, peaking between 35 and 39 years, and then rapidly falls
Nutrition	Occurs less often among women with poor diets; occurs more often among women who are tall and overweight or of normal weight as opposed to slight body build
Number of births	Is more likely with each additional birth
Fertility drugs and in vitro fertilization	Is more likely with fertility hormones and in vitro fertilization (see page 62), which also increase the chances of bearing triplets, quadruplets, or quintuplets

[a]Worldwide rates, not including multiple births resulting from use of fertility drugs.
Sources: Kulkarni et al., 2013; Lashley, 2007; Smits & Monden, 2011.

Genetically, they are no more alike than ordinary siblings. Table 2.1 summarizes genetic and environmental factors that increase the chances of giving birth to fraternal twins. Older maternal age, fertility drugs, and in vitro fertilization (to be discussed shortly) are major causes of the dramatic rise in fraternal twinning and other multiple births in industrialized nations over the past several decades—a trend that has recently leveled off with improved in vitro procedures (Kulkarni et al., 2013). Currently, fraternal twins account for 1 in about every 33 births in the United States (Martin et al., 2013).

Twins can be created in another way. Sometimes a zygote that has started to duplicate separates into two clusters of cells that develop into two individuals. These are called **identical,** or **monozygotic, twins** because they have the same genetic makeup. The frequency of identical twins is the same around the world—about 1 in every 350 to 400 births (Kulkarni et al., 2013). Animal research has uncovered a variety of environmental influences that prompt this type of twinning, including temperature changes, variation in oxygen levels, and late fertilization of the ovum (Lashley, 2007). In a minority of cases, identical twinning runs in families, but this occurs so rarely that it is likely due to chance rather than heredity.

During their early years, children of single births often are healthier and develop more rapidly than twins. Jeannie and Jason, like most twins, were born early—three weeks before Ruth's due date. And, like other premature infants—as you will see in Chapter 4—they required special care after birth. When the twins came home from the hospital, Ruth and Peter had to divide time between them. Perhaps because neither baby got quite as much attention as the average single infant, Jeannie and Jason walked and talked several months later than most other children their age. Most twins, however, catch up in development by early or middle childhood, as Jeannie and Jason eventually did (Lytton & Gallagher, 2002: Thorpe, 2006). Parental energies are further strained after the birth of triplets, whose early development is slower than that of twins (Feldman, Eidelman, & Rotenberg, 2004).

© F4FOTO/ALAMY

These identical, or monozygotic, twins were created when a duplicating zygote separated into two clusters of cells and developed into two individuals with the same genetic makeup. Identical twins look alike and tend to resemble each other in a variety of psychological characteristics.

Patterns of Gene–Gene Interactions

Jeannie has her parents' dark, straight hair; Jason is curly-haired and blond. The way genes from each parent interact helps explain these outcomes. Recall that except for the XY pair in males, all chromosomes come in matching pairs. Two forms of each gene occur at the same place on the chromosomes, one inherited from the mother and one from the father. Each form of a gene is called an **allele.** If the alleles from both parents are alike, the child is **homozygous** and will display the inherited trait. If the alleles are different, the child is **heterozygous,** and relationships between the alleles determine the phenotype.

DOMINANT–RECESSIVE PATTERN   In many heterozygous pairings, **dominant–recessive inheritance** occurs: Only one allele affects the child's characteristics. It is called *dominant;* the second allele, which has no effect, is called *recessive.* Hair color is an example. The allele for dark hair is dominant (we can represent it with a capital *D*), whereas the one for blond hair is recessive (symbolized by a lowercase *b*). A child who inherits a homozygous pair of dominant alleles *(DD)* and a child who inherits a heterozygous pair *(Db)* will both be dark-haired, even though their genotypes differ. Blond hair (like Jason's) can result only from having two recessive alleles *(bb).* Still, heterozygous individuals with just one recessive allele *(Db)* can pass that trait to their children. Therefore, they are called **carriers** of the trait.

Most recessive alleles—like those for blond hair, pattern baldness, or nearsightedness—are of little developmental importance. But as Table 2.2 on page 56 illustrates, some cause serious disabilities and diseases. One of the most frequently occurring recessive disorders is *phenylketonuria,* or *PKU,* which affects the way the body breaks down proteins contained in many foods. Infants born with two recessive alleles lack an enzyme that converts one of the basic amino acids that make up proteins (phenylalanine) into a byproduct essential for body functioning (tyrosine). Without this enzyme, phenylalanine quickly builds to toxic levels that damage the central nervous system. By 1 year, infants with PKU suffer from permanent intellectual disability.

Despite its potentially damaging effects, PKU illustrates that inheriting unfavorable genes does not always lead to an untreatable condition. All U.S. states require that each newborn be given a blood test for PKU. If the disease is found, doctors place the baby on a diet low in phenylalanine. Children who receive this treatment nevertheless show mild deficits in certain cognitive skills, such as memory, planning, decision making, and problem solving, because even small amounts of phenylalanine interfere with brain functioning (DeRoche & Welsh, 2008; Fonnesbeck et al., 2013). But as long as dietary treatment begins early and continues, children with PKU usually attain an average level of intelligence and have a normal lifespan.

In dominant–recessive inheritance, if we know the genetic makeup of the parents, we can predict the percentage of children in a family who are likely to display or carry a trait. Figure 2.3 illustrates this for PKU. For a child to inherit the condition, each parent must have a recessive allele. But because of the action of regulator genes, children vary in the degree to which phenylalanine accumulates in their tissues and in the extent to which they respond to treatment.

Only rarely are serious diseases due to dominant alleles. Think about why this is so. Children who inherit the dominant allele always develop the disorder. They seldom live long enough to reproduce, so the harmful dominant allele is eliminated from the family's heredity in a single generation. Some dominant disorders, however, do persist. One is *Huntington disease,* a condition in which the central nervous system degenerates. Why has this disorder endured? Its symptoms usually do not appear until age 35 or later, after the person has passed the dominant allele to his or her children.

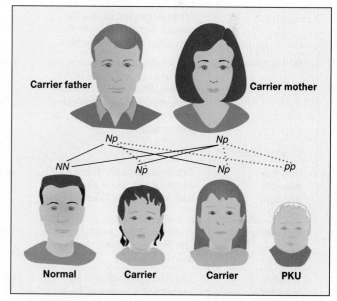

FIGURE 2.3   Dominant–recessive mode of inheritance, as illustrated by PKU. When both parents are heterozygous carriers of the recessive gene *(p),* we can predict that 25 percent of their offspring are likely to be normal *(NN),* 50 percent are likely to be carriers *(Np),* and 25 percent are likely to inherit the disorder *(pp).* Notice that the PKU-affected child, in contrast to his siblings, has light hair. The recessive gene for PKU affects more than one trait. It also leads to fair coloring.

TABLE 2.2 Examples of Dominant and Recessive Diseases

DISEASE	DESCRIPTION	MODE OF INHERITANCE	INCIDENCE	TREATMENT
Autosomal Diseases				
Cooley's anemia	Pale appearance, delayed physical growth, and lethargic behavior begin in infancy.	Recessive	1 in 500 births to parents of Mediterranean descent	Frequent blood transfusions; death from complications usually occurs by adolescence.
Cystic fibrosis	Lungs, liver, and pancreas secrete large amounts of thick mucus, leading to breathing and digestive difficulties.	Recessive	1 in 2,000 to 2,500 Caucasian births; 1 in 16,000 births to North Americans of African descent	Bronchial drainage, prompt treatment of respiratory infection, dietary management. Advances in medical care allow survival with good life quality into adulthood.
Phenylketonuria (PKU)	Inability to metabolize the amino acid phenylalanine, contained in many proteins, causes severe central nervous system damage in the first year of life.	Recessive	1 in 8,000 births	Placing the child on a special diet results in average intelligence and normal lifespan. Subtle difficulties in memory, planning, decision making, and problem solving are often present.
Sickle cell anemia	Abnormal sickling of red blood cells causes oxygen deprivation, pain, swelling, and tissue damage. Anemia and susceptibility to infections, especially pneumonia, occur.	Recessive	1 in 500 births to North Americans of African descent	Blood transfusions, painkillers, prompt treatment of infection. No known cure; 50 percent die by age 55.
Tay-Sachs disease	Central nervous system degeneration, with onset at about 6 months, leads to poor muscle tone, blindness, deafness, and convulsions.	Recessive	1 in 3,600 births to Jews of European descent and to French Canadians	None. Death occurs by 3 to 4 years of age.
Huntington disease	Central nervous system degeneration leads to muscular coordination difficulties, mental deterioration, and personality changes. Symptoms usually do not appear until age 35 or later.	Dominant	1 in 18,000 to 25,000 births to North Americans	None. Death occurs 10 to 20 years after symptom onset.
Marfan syndrome	Tall, slender build; thin, elongated arms and legs; and heart defects and eye abnormalities, especially of the lens. Excessive lengthening of the body results in a variety of skeletal defects.	Dominant	1 in 5,000 to 10,000 births	Correction of heart and eye defects sometimes possible. Death from heart failure in early adulthood is common.
X-Linked Diseases				
Duchenne muscular dystrophy	Degenerative muscle disease. Abnormal gait, loss of ability to walk between ages 7 and 13 years.	Recessive	1 in 3,000 to 5,000 male births	None. Death from respiratory infection or weakening of the heart muscle usually occurs in adolescence.
Hemophilia	Blood fails to clot normally; can lead to severe internal bleeding and tissue damage.	Recessive	1 in 4,000 to 7,000 male births	Blood transfusions. Safety precautions to prevent injury.
Diabetes insipidus	Insufficient production of the hormone vasopressin results in excessive thirst and urination. Dehydration can cause central nervous system damage.	Recessive	1 in 2,500 male births	Hormone replacement.

Note: For recessive disorders, carrier status can be detected in prospective parents through a blood test or genetic analyses. For all disorders listed, prenatal diagnosis is available (see page 64).
Sources: Kliegman et al., 2008; Lashley, 2007; National Center for Biotechnology Information, 2014.

INCOMPLETE DOMINANCE PATTERN In some heterozygous circumstances, the dominant–recessive relationship does not hold completely. Instead, we see **incomplete dominance,** a pattern of inheritance in which both alleles are expressed in the phenotype, resulting in a combined trait, or one that is intermediate between the two.

The *sickle cell trait,* a heterozygous condition present in many black Africans, provides an example. *Sickle cell anemia* (see Table 2.2) occurs in full form when a child inherits two recessive alleles. They cause the usually round red blood cells to become sickle (crescent-moon) shaped, especially under low-oxygen conditions. The sickled cells clog the blood vessels and block the flow of blood, causing intense pain, swelling, and tissue damage. Despite medical advances that today allow 85 percent of affected children to survive to adulthood, North Americans with sickle cell anemia have a life expectancy of only 55 years (Driscoll, 2007). Heterozygous individuals are protected from the disease under most circumstances. However, when they experience oxygen deprivation—for example, at high altitudes or after intense physical exercise—the single recessive allele asserts itself, and a temporary, mild form of the illness occurs.

The sickle cell allele is common among black Africans for a special reason. Carriers of it are more resistant to malaria than are individuals with two alleles for normal red blood cells. In Africa, where malaria is common, these carriers have survived and reproduced more frequently than others, leading the gene to be maintained in the black population. But in regions of the world where the risk of malaria is low, the frequency of the gene is declining. For example, only 8 percent of African Americans are carriers, compared with 20 percent of black Africans (U.S. Department of Health and Human Services, 2012).

X-LINKED PATTERN Males and females have an equal chance of inheriting recessive disorders carried on the autosomes, such as PKU and sickle cell anemia. But when a harmful allele is carried on the X chromosome, **X-linked inheritance** applies. Males are more likely to be affected because their sex chromosomes do not match. In females, any recessive allele on one X chromosome has a good chance of being suppressed by a dominant allele on the other X. But the Y chromosome is only about one-third as long and therefore lacks many corresponding alleles to override those on the X. A well-known example is *hemophilia,* a disorder in which the blood fails to clot normally. Figure 2.4 shows its greater likelihood of inheritance by male children whose mothers carry the abnormal allele.

Besides X-linked disorders, many sex differences reveal the male to be at a disadvantage. Rates of miscarriage, infant and childhood deaths, birth defects, learning disabilities, behavior disorders, and intellectual disability all are higher for boys (Butler & Meaney, 2005). It is possible that these sex differences can be traced to the genetic code. The female, with two X chromosomes, benefits from a greater variety of genes. Nature, however, has adjusted for the male's disadvantage. Worldwide, about 106 boys are born for every 100 girls, and judging from miscarriage and abortion statistics, an even greater number of males are conceived (United Nations, 2012).

In cultures with strong gender-biased attitudes that induce expectant parents to prefer a male child, the male-to-female birth sex ratio is often much larger. In China, for example, the spread of ultrasound technology (which enables prenatal sex determination) and enforcement of a one-child family policy to control population growth—both of which began in the 1980s—led to a dramatic increase in sex-selective abortion (Chen, Li, & Meng, 2013). Today, China's birth sex ratio is 118 boys for every 100 girls—a gender imbalance with adverse social consequences, such as rising crime rates and male competition for marriage partners.

In contrast, in many Western countries, including the United States, Canada, and European nations, the proportion of male births has declined in recent decades. Some researchers attribute the trend

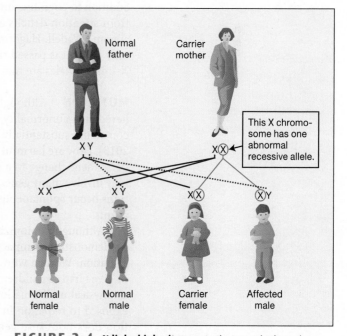

FIGURE 2.4 **X-linked inheritance.** In the example shown here, the allele on the father's X chromosome is normal. The mother has one normal and one abnormal recessive allele on her X chromosomes. By looking at the possible combinations of the parents' alleles, we can predict that 50 percent of these parents' male children are likely to have the disorder, and 50 percent of their female children are likely to be carriers of it.

to a rise in stressful living conditions, which heighten spontaneous abortions, especially of male fetuses (Catalano et al., 2010). In support of this hypothesis, a California study spanning the decade of the 1990s revealed that the percentage of male fetal deaths increased in months in which unemployment (a major stressor) also rose above its typical level (Catalano et al., 2009).

In sum, social and cultural factors can substantially modify the male-to-female birth sex ratio, in either direction. And they can readily undermine the ratio's assumed evolutionary role: compensating for males' greater genetic vulnerability.

GENOMIC IMPRINTING   More than 1,000 human characteristics follow the rules of dominant–recessive and incomplete-dominance inheritance (National Center for Biotechnology Information, 2014). In these cases, whichever parent contributes a gene to the new individual, the gene responds in the same way. Geneticists, however, have identified some exceptions. In **genomic imprinting,** alleles are imprinted, or chemically marked through regulatory processes within the genome, in such a way that one pair member (either the mother's or the father's) is activated, regardless of its makeup (Hirasawa & Feil, 2010). The imprint is often temporary; it may be erased in the next generation, and it may not occur in all individuals. The number of genes subjected to genomic imprinting is believed to be small—less than 1 percent (Isles & Wilkinson, 2011). Nevertheless, these genes have a significant impact on brain development and physical health.

Imprinting helps us understand certain puzzling genetic patterns. For example, children are more likely to develop diabetes if their father, rather than their mother, suffers from it. And people with asthma or hay fever tend to have mothers, not fathers, with the illness. Imprinting is involved in several childhood cancers and in *Prader-Willi syndrome,* a disorder with symptoms of mental disability and severe obesity (Butler, 2009). It may also explain why Huntington disease, when inherited from the father, tends to emerge at an earlier age and to progress more rapidly (Gropman & Adams, 2007).

Genomic imprinting can also operate on the sex chromosomes, as *fragile X syndrome*—the most common inherited cause of intellectual disability—reveals. In this disorder, which affects about 1 in 4,000 males and 1 in 6,000 females, an abnormal repetition of a sequence of DNA bases occurs in a special spot on the X chromosome, damaging a particular gene. In addition to cognitive impairments, the majority of individuals with fragile X syndrome suffer from attention deficits and high anxiety, and about 30 to 35 percent also have symptoms of autism (Wadell, Hagerman, & Hessl, 2013). The defective gene at the fragile site is expressed only when it is passed from mother to child (Hagerman et al., 2009). Because the disorder is X-linked, males are more severely affected.

MUTATION   Although less than 3 percent of pregnancies result in the birth of a baby with a hereditary abnormality, these children account for about 20 percent of infant deaths and contribute substantially to lifelong impaired physical and mental functioning (Martin et al., 2013). How are harmful genes created in the first place? The answer is **mutation,** a sudden but permanent change in a segment of DNA. A mutation may affect only one or two genes, or it may involve many genes, as in the chromosomal disorders we will discuss shortly. Some mutations occur spontaneously, simply by chance. Others are caused by hazardous environmental agents.

Although nonionizing forms of radiation—electromagnetic waves and microwaves—have no demonstrated impact on DNA, ionizing (high-energy) radiation is an established cause of mutation. Women who receive repeated doses before conception are more likely to miscarry or give birth to children with hereditary defects. The incidence of genetic abnormalities, such as physical malformations and childhood cancer, is also higher in children whose fathers are exposed to radiation in their occupations. However, infrequent and mild exposure to radiation does not cause genetic damage (Jacquet, 2004). Rather, high doses over a long period impair DNA.

The examples just given illustrate *germline mutation,* which takes place in the cells that give rise to gametes. When the affected individual mates, the defective DNA is passed on to the next generation. In a second type, called *somatic mutation,* normal body cells mutate, an event that can occur at any time of life. The DNA defect appears in every cell derived from the affected body cell, eventually becoming widespread enough to cause disease (such as cancer) or disability.

It is easy to see how disorders that run in families can result from germline mutation. But somatic mutation may be involved in these disorders as well. Some people harbor a genetic susceptibility that causes certain body cells to mutate easily in the presence of triggering events (Weiss, 2005). This helps explain why some individuals develop serious illnesses (such as cancer) as a result of smoking, exposure to pollutants, or psychological stress, while others do not.

Although virtually all mutations that have been studied are harmful, some spontaneous ones (such as the sickle cell allele in malaria-ridden regions of the world) are necessary and desirable. By increasing genetic variation, they help individuals adapt to unexpected environmental challenges. Scientists, however, seldom go looking for mutations that underlie favorable traits, such as an exceptional talent or an especially sturdy immune system. They are far more concerned with identifying and eliminating unfavorable genes that threaten health and survival.

POLYGENIC INHERITANCE   So far, we have discussed patterns of gene–gene interaction in which people either display a particular trait or do not. These cut-and-dried individual differences are much easier to trace to their genetic origins than are characteristics that vary on a continuum among people, such as height, weight, intelligence, and personality. These traits are due to **polygenic inheritance,** in which many genes affect the characteristic in question. Polygenic inheritance is complex, and much about it is still unknown. In the final section of this chapter, we discuss how researchers infer the influence of heredity on human attributes when they do not know the precise patterns of inheritance.

Chromosomal Abnormalities

Besides harmful recessive alleles, abnormalities of the chromosomes are a major cause of serious developmental problems. Most chromosomal defects result from mistakes during meiosis, when the ovum and sperm are formed. A chromosome pair does not separate properly, or part of a chromosome breaks off. Because these errors involve far more DNA than problems due to single genes, they usually produce many physical and mental symptoms.

DOWN SYNDROME   The most common chromosomal disorder, occurring in 1 out of every 700 live births, is *Down syndrome.* In 95 percent of cases, it results from a failure of the twenty-first pair of chromosomes to separate during meiosis, so the new individual receives three of these chromosomes rather than the normal two. For this reason, Down syndrome is sometimes called *trisomy 21.* In other, less frequent forms, an extra broken piece of a twenty-first chromosome is attached to another chromosome (called *translocation* pattern). Or an error occurs during the early stages of cell duplication, causing some but not all body cells to have the defective chromosomal makeup (called *mosaic* pattern) (U.S. Department of Health and Human Services, 2014). Because the mosaic type involves less genetic material, symptoms may be less extreme.

The consequences of Down syndrome include intellectual disability, memory and speech problems, limited vocabulary, and slow motor development. Measures of electrical brain activity reveal substantial disruption in connectivity among brain regions. This indicates that the brains of children with Down syndrome function in a far less coordinated fashion than do the brains of typical children (Ahmadlou et al., 2013). Affected individuals also have distinct physical features—a short, stocky build; a flattened face; a protruding tongue; almond-shaped eyes; and (in 50 percent of cases) an unusual crease running across the palm of the hand. In addition, infants with Down syndrome

An 8-year-old with Down syndrome, at right, plays with a typically developing classmate. Despite impaired intellectual development, this child benefits from exposure to stimulating environments and from opportunities to interact with peers.

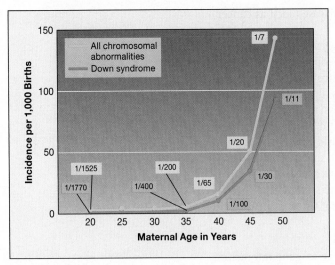

FIGURE 2.5 **Risk of Down syndrome and all chromosomal abnormalities by maternal age.** Risk rises sharply after age 35. (From R. L. Schonberg & C. J. Tifft, 2012, "Birth Defects and Prenatal Diagnosis," from *Children with Disabilities,* 7/e, M. L. Matshaw, N. J. Roizen, & G. R. Lotrecchiano, editors, p. 50. Baltimore: Paul H. Brookes Publishing Co, Inc. Adapted by permission.)

are often born with eye cataracts, hearing loss, and heart and intestinal defects (U.S. Department of Health and Human Services, 2014). Because of medical advances, life expectancy of individuals with Down syndrome has increased greatly: Today, it is about 60 years of age. However, more than half of affected individuals who live past age 40 show symptoms of *Alzheimer's disease,* the most common form of dementia (Davis & Escobar, 2013). Genes on chromosome 21 are linked to this disorder.

Infants with Down syndrome smile less readily, show poor eye-to-eye contact, have weak muscle tone, and explore objects less persistently (Slonims & McConachie, 2006). But when parents encourage them to engage with their surroundings, children with Down syndrome develop more favorably. They also benefit from infant and preschool intervention programs, although emotional, social, and motor skills improve more than intellectual performance (Carr, 2002). Clearly, environmental factors affect how well children with Down syndrome fare.

As Figure 2.5 shows, the risk of bearing a baby with Down syndrome, as well as other chromosomal abnormalities, rises dramatically with maternal age. But exactly why older mothers are more likely to release ova with meiotic errors is not yet known (Chiang, Schultz, & Lampson, 2012). In about 5 to 10 percent of cases, the extra genetic material originates with the father. Some studies suggest a role for advanced paternal age, while others show no age effects (De Souza, Alberman, & Morris, 2009; Dzurova & Pikhart, 2005; Sherman et al., 2005).

ABNORMALITIES OF THE SEX CHROMOSOMES Disorders of the autosomes other than Down syndrome usually disrupt development so severely that miscarriage occurs. When such babies are born, they rarely survive beyond early childhood. In contrast, abnormalities of the sex chromosomes usually lead to fewer problems. In fact, sex chromosome disorders often are not recognized until adolescence when, in some deviations, puberty is delayed. The most common problems involve the presence of an extra chromosome (either X or Y) or the absence of one X in females.

Research has discredited a variety of myths about individuals with sex chromosome disorders. For example, as Table 2.3 reveals, males with *XYY syndrome* are not necessarily more aggressive and antisocial than XY males (Stochholm et al., 2012). And most children with sex

TABLE 2.3	**Sex Chromosomal Disorders**		
DISORDER	**DESCRIPTION**	**INCIDENCE**	**TREATMENT**
XYY syndrome	Extra Y chromosome. Above-average height, large teeth, and sometimes severe acne. Intelligence, male sexual development, and fertility are normal.	1 in 1,000 male births	No special treatment necessary.
Triple X syndrome (XXX)	Extra X chromosome. Tallness and impaired verbal intelligence. Female sexual development and fertility are normal.	1 in 500 to 1,250 female births	Special education to treat verbal ability problems.
Klinefelter syndrome (XXY)	Extra X chromosome. Tallness, body fat distribution resembling females, incomplete development of sex characteristics at puberty, sterility, and impaired verbal intelligence.	1 in 900 male births	Hormone therapy at puberty to stimulate development of sex characteristics; special education to treat verbal ability problems.
Turner syndrome (XO)	Missing X chromosome. Short stature, webbed neck, incomplete development of sex characteristics at puberty, sterility, and impaired spatial intelligence.	1 in 2,500 to 8,000 female births	Hormone therapy in childhood to stimulate physical growth and at puberty to promote development of sex characteristics; special education to treat spatial ability problems.

Sources: Powell & Schulte, 2011; Ross et al., 2012; Saitta & Zackai, 2005.

chromosome disorders do not suffer from intellectual disabilities. Rather, their cognitive challenges are usually very specific. Verbal difficulties—for example, with reading and vocabulary—are common among girls with *triple X syndrome* and boys with *Klinefelter syndrome,* both of whom inherit an extra X chromosome. In contrast, girls with *Turner syndrome,* who are missing an X, have trouble with spatial relationships—for example, drawing pictures, telling right from left, following travel directions, and noticing changes in facial expressions (Otter et al., 2013; Ross et al., 2012; Temple & Shephard, 2012). Brain-imaging evidence confirms that adding to or subtracting from the usual number of X chromosomes alters the development of certain brain structures, yielding particular intellectual deficits (Bray et al., 2011; Bryant et al., 2012).

Ask Yourself

- **REVIEW** Cite evidence indicating that both heredity and environment contribute to the development of children with PKU and Down syndrome.

- **REVIEW** Using your knowledge of X-linked inheritance, explain why males are more vulnerable than females to miscarriage, infant death, genetic disorders, and other problems.

- **CONNECT** Referring to ecological systems theory (Chapter 1, pages 26–29), explain why parents of children with genetic disorders often experience increased stress. What factors, within and beyond the family, can help these parents support their children's development?

- **APPLY** Gilbert's genetic makeup is homozygous for dark hair. Jan's is homozygous for blond hair. What color is Gilbert's hair? How about Jan's? What proportion of their children are likely to be dark-haired? Explain.

Reproductive Choices

2.4 What procedures can assist prospective parents in having healthy children?

Two years after they married, Ted and Marianne gave birth to their first child. Kendra appeared to be a healthy infant, but by 4 months her growth had slowed, and she was diagnosed as having Tay-Sachs disease (see Table 2.2). When Kendra died at 2 years of age, Ted and Marianne were devastated. Although they did not want to bring another infant into the world who would endure such suffering, they badly wanted to have a child.

In the past, many couples with genetic disorders in their families chose not to bear a child at all rather than risk the birth of a baby with abnormalities. Today, genetic counseling and prenatal diagnosis help people make informed decisions about conceiving, carrying a pregnancy to term, or adopting a child.

Genetic Counseling

Genetic counseling is a communication process designed to help couples assess their chances of giving birth to a baby with a hereditary disorder and choose the best course of action in view of risks and family goals (Resta et al., 2006). Individuals likely to seek counseling are those who have had difficulties bearing children—for example, repeated miscarriages—or who know that genetic problems exist in their families. In addition, adults who delay childbearing are often candidates for genetic counseling. As maternal age rises beyond age 35, the rates of Down syndrome and other chromosomal abnormalities increase sharply (refer again to Figure 2.5). Older paternal age presents heightened risk of DNA mutations as well. After age 40, it is associated with increased risk of several serious psychological disorders (Zitzmann, 2013). These include *autism* (see page 23 in Chapter 1); *schizophrenia,* characterized by hallucinations, delusions, and irrational behavior; and *bipolar disorder,* marked by alternating periods of elation and depression. But because younger parents have children in far higher numbers than older parents, they still bear the majority of babies with genetic defects. Therefore, some experts argue that parental needs, not age, should determine referral for genetic counseling (Berkowitz, Roberts, & Minkoff, 2006).

Social Issues: Health

The Pros and Cons of Reproductive Technologies

Some couples decide not to risk pregnancy because of a history of genetic disease. Many others—in fact, one-sixth of all couples who try to conceive—discover that they are infertile. And some never-married adults and gay and lesbian partners want to bear children. Today, increasing numbers of individuals are turning to alternative methods of conception—technologies that, although they fulfill the wish for parenthood, have become the subject of heated debate.

Donor Insemination and In Vitro Fertilization

For several decades, *donor insemination*—injection of sperm from an anonymous man into a woman—has been used to overcome male reproductive difficulties. In recent years, it has also permitted women without a male partner to become pregnant. Donor insemination is 70 percent successful, resulting in about 40,000 deliveries and 52,000 newborn babies in the United States each year (Rossi, 2014).

In vitro fertilization is another reproductive technology that has become increasingly common. Since the first "test tube" baby was born in England in 1978, 1 percent of all children in developed countries—about 60,000 babies in the United States—have been conceived through this technique annually (Centers for Disease Control and Prevention, 2014a). With in vitro fertilization, a woman is given hormones that stimulate the ripening of several ova. These are removed surgically and placed in a dish of nutrients, to which sperm are added. Once an ovum is fertilized and begins to duplicate into several cells, it is injected into the mother's uterus.

By mixing and matching gametes, pregnancies can be brought about when either or both partners have a reproductive problem. Usually, in vitro fertilization is used to treat women whose fallopian tubes are permanently damaged. But a single sperm can now be injected directly into an ovum, thereby overcoming most male fertility problems. And a "sex sorter" method helps ensure that couples who carry X-linked diseases (which usually affect males) have a daughter. Fertilized ova and sperm can even be frozen and stored in embryo banks for use at some future time, thereby guaranteeing healthy zygotes should age or illness lead to fertility problems.

The overall success rate of assisted reproductive techniques, as measured by live births, is about 50 percent. However, success declines steadily with age, from 55 percent in women age 31 to 35 to 8 percent in women age 43 (Cetinkaya et al., 2013; Gnoth et al., 2011). Furthermore, assisted reproduction is associated with an elevated risk of pregnancy complications, miscarriage, and birth defects, due to the biological effects of in vitro techniques

AP IMAGES/HERALD & REVIEW, JIM BOWLING

Fertility drugs and in vitro fertilization often lead to multiple fetuses. These quadruplets are healthy, but babies born with the aid of reproductive technologies are at high risk for low birth weight and major birth defects.

and the older age of many people seeking treatment.

Children conceived through these methods may be genetically unrelated to one or both of their parents. In addition, most parents who have used the procedures do not tell their children how they were conceived. Does lack of genetic ties or secrecy surrounding these techniques interfere with parent–child relationships? Perhaps because of a strong desire for parenthood, caregiving is actually somewhat warmer for young children conceived through donor insemination or in vitro

---

If a family history of intellectual disability, psychological disorders, physical defects, or inherited diseases exists, the genetic counselor interviews the couple and prepares a *pedigree,* a picture of the family tree in which affected relatives are identified. The pedigree is used to estimate the likelihood that parents will have an abnormal child. For many disorders traceable to a single gene, blood tests or genetic analyses can reveal whether the parent is a carrier of the harmful allele. Carrier detection is possible for all the recessive diseases listed in Table 2.2, as well as others, and for fragile X syndrome.

Autism, schizophrenia, and bipolar disorder have each been linked to an array of DNA-sequence deviations (called *genetic markers*) distributed across multiple chromosomes. New *genomewide testing methods,* which look for these genetic markers, have enabled genetic counselors to estimate risk for these conditions. But the estimates are generally low because the

fertilization. Also, in vitro infants are as securely attached to their parents, and in vitro children and adolescents as well-adjusted, as their counterparts who were naturally conceived (Punamaki, 2006; Wagenaar et al., 2011). However, in one study, school-age children who had not been informed of their gamete-donor origins experienced less positive maternal interaction (Golombok et al., 2011). This suggests that families can benefit from open discussion with their children.

Although reproductive technologies have many benefits, serious questions have arisen about their use. In many countries, including the United States, doctors are not required to keep records of donor characteristics, though information about the child's genetic background might be critical in the case of serious disease (Murphy, 2013). Another concern is that the in vitro "sex sorter" method enables parental sex selection, eroding the moral value that boys and girls are equally precious.

Furthermore, about 45 percent of in vitro procedures result in multiple births. Most are twins, but 6 percent are triplets and higher-order multiples. Consequently, among in vitro babies, the rate of low birth weight is nearly four times as high as in the general population. In response, doctors have begun to reduce the number of fertilized ova injected into a woman's uterus, typically to no more than two (Kulkarni et al., 2013; Sunderam et al., 2013). Risk of pregnancy complications, miscarriage, and major birth defects also rises, due to the biological effects of in vitro techniques and the older age of many people seeking treatment. In sum, in vitro fertilization poses greater risks than natural conception to infant survival and healthy development.

Surrogate Motherhood

An even more controversial form of medically assisted conception is *surrogate motherhood*.

In this procedure, in vitro fertilization may be used to impregnate a woman (called a surrogate) with a couple's fertilized ovum. Alternatively, sperm from a man whose partner is infertile may be used to inseminate the surrogate, who agrees to turn the baby over to the natural father. The child is then adopted by his partner. In both cases, the surrogate is paid a fee for her childbearing services.

Most surrogate arrangements proceed smoothly, and the limited evidence available suggests that families usually function well, tell their children about the surrogacy, and stay in touch with and have positive relationships with the surrogate, especially if she is genetically related to the child (Golomobok et al., 2011; Jadva, Casey, & Golombok, 2012). The small number of children who have been studied appear to be as well-adjusted as agemates who were naturally conceived.

Nevertheless, because surrogacy usually involves the wealthy as contractors for infants and the less economically advantaged as surrogates, it may promote exploitation of financially needy women. In addition, most surrogates already have children of their own. Knowledge that their mother would give away a baby may cause these children to worry about the security of their own family circumstances.

New Reproductive Frontiers

Reproductive technologies are evolving faster than societies can weigh the ethics of these procedures. Doctors have used donor ova from younger women in combination with in vitro fertilization to help postmenopausal women become pregnant. Most recipients are in their forties, but several women in their fifties and sixties, and a few at age 70, have given birth. These cases raise questions about bringing

children into the world whose parents may not live to see them reach adulthood.

Currently, experts are debating other reproductive options. At donor banks, customers can select ova or sperm on the basis of physical characteristics and even IQ. And scientists are devising ways to alter the DNA of human ova, sperm, and embryos to protect against hereditary disorders—techniques that could be used to engineer other desired characteristics. Many worry that these practices are dangerous steps toward selective breeding through "designer babies"—controlling offspring traits by manipulating genetic makeup.

Although new reproductive technologies permit many barren couples to rear healthy newborn babies, laws are needed to regulate such practices. In Australia, New Zealand, and Europe, in vitro gamete donors and applicants for the procedure must undergo highly regulated screening (Murphy, 2013). Denmark, France, and Italy have prohibited in vitro fertilization for women past menopause. Pressure from those working in the field of assisted reproduction may eventually lead to similar policies in the United States.

The ethical problems of surrogate motherhood are so complex that 13 U.S. states and the District of Columbia have sharply restricted the practice (Swain, 2014). Australia, Canada, and many European nations have banned commercial surrogacy, arguing that the status of a baby should not involve profit making. At present, not enough is known about the consequences of being a product of these procedures. More research on how such children grow up, including later-appearing medical conditions and feelings about their origins, is important for weighing the pros and cons of these techniques.

---

genetic markers are found in only a minority of affected people. Also, the genetic markers are not associated with mental illness every time they appear. Their expression—as we will illustrate at the end of this chapter—seems to depend on environmental conditions. Recently, geneticists have begun to identify rare repeats and deletions of DNA bases that are more consistently related to mental illness (Gershon & Alliey-Rodriguez, 2013). In a small number of cases, these discoveries may lead to more accurate prediction of the likelihood of passing a psychological disorder from parent to child.

When all the relevant hereditary information is in, genetic counselors help people consider appropriate options. These include taking a chance and conceiving, choosing from among a variety of reproductive technologies (see the Social Issues: Health box above), or adopting a child.

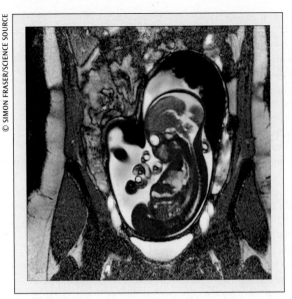

© SIMON FRASER/SCIENCE SOURCE

FIGURE 2.6 **Ultrafast MRI of a fetus, showing body structures.** Ultrafast MRI is increasingly being used as a supplement to ultrasound because it records detailed pictures of body structures, permitting greater diagnostic accuracy. In this colorized MRI of a 26-week-old fetus, the yellow area highlights a brain abnormality.

Prenatal Diagnosis and Fetal Medicine

If couples at risk for bearing a child with abnormalities decide to conceive, several **prenatal diagnostic methods**—medical procedures that permit detection of developmental problems before birth—are available (see Table 2.4). Women of advanced maternal age are prime candidates for *amniocentesis* or *chorionic villus sampling. Ultrasound,* commonly used during pregnancy to track fetal growth, permits detection of gross structural abnormalities. When ultrasound suggests problems but diagnosis is uncertain, *ultrafast fetal magnetic resonance imaging,* in which a scanner magnetically records detailed pictures of fetal structures, can be used for greater accuracy (see Figure 2.6). As Table 2.4 reveals, certain prenatal diagnostic techniques should not be used routinely because of risk of injury to the developing organism.

Prenatal diagnosis has led to advances in fetal medicine. For example, by inserting a needle into the uterus, doctors can administer drugs to the fetus. Surgery has been performed to repair such problems as heart, lung, and diaphragm malformations, urinary tract obstructions, and neural defects (Adzick, 2013; Bianchi, 2012). Fetuses with blood disorders have been given blood transfusions. And those with immune deficiencies have received bone marrow transplants that succeeded in creating a normally functioning immune system (Deprest et al., 2010).

These techniques frequently result in complications, the most common being premature labor and miscarriage (Danzer & Johnson, 2014). Yet parents

TABLE 2.4	**Prenatal Diagnostic Methods**
METHOD	**DESCRIPTION**
Amniocentesis	The most widely used technique. A hollow needle is inserted through the abdominal wall to obtain a sample of fluid in the uterus. Cells are examined for genetic defects. Can be performed by the 14th week after conception; 1 to 2 more weeks are required for test results. Small risk of miscarriage.
Chorionic villus sampling	A procedure that can be used if results are desired or needed very early in pregnancy. A thin tube is inserted into the uterus through the vagina, or a hollow needle is inserted through the abdominal wall. A small plug of tissue is removed from the end of one or more chorionic villi, the hairlike projections on the membrane surrounding the developing organism. Cells are examined for genetic defects. Can be performed at 9 weeks after conception; results are available within 24 hours. Entails a slightly greater risk of miscarriage than does amniocentesis. Also associated with a small risk of limb deformities, which increases the earlier the procedure is performed.
Fetoscopy	A small tube with a light source at one end is inserted into the uterus to inspect the fetus for defects of the limbs and face. Also allows a sample of fetal blood to be obtained, permitting diagnosis of such disorders as hemophilia and sickle cell anemia as well as neural defects (see below). Usually performed between 15 and 18 weeks after conception but can be done as early as 5 weeks. Entails some risk of miscarriage.
Ultrasound	High-frequency sound waves are beamed at the uterus; their reflection is translated into a picture on a video screen that reveals the size, shape, and placement of the fetus. By itself, permits assessment of fetal age, detection of multiple pregnancies, and identification of gross physical defects. Also used to guide amniocentesis, chorionic villus sampling, and fetoscopy. Sometimes combined with magnetic resonance imaging (see below) to detect physical abnormalities with greater accuracy. When used five or more times, may increase the chances of low birth weight.
Maternal blood analysis	By the second month of pregnancy, some of the developing organism's cells enter the maternal bloodstream. An elevated level of alpha-fetoprotein may indicate kidney disease, abnormal closure of the esophagus, or neural tube defects, such as anencephaly (absence of most of the brain) and spina bifida (bulging of the spinal cord from the spinal column). Isolated cells can be examined for genetic defects.
Ultrafast fetal magnetic resonance imaging (MRI)	Sometimes used as a supplement to ultrasound, where brain or other abnormalities are detected and MRI can provide greater diagnostic accuracy. Uses a scanner to magnetically record detailed pictures of fetal structures. The ultrafast technique overcomes image blurring due to fetal movements. No evidence of adverse effects.
Preimplantation genetic diagnosis	After in vitro fertilization and duplication of the zygote into a cluster of about 8 to 10 cells, 1 or 2 cells are removed and examined for hereditary defects. Only if that sample is free of detectable genetic disorders is the fertilized ovum implanted in the woman's uterus.

Sources: Hahn & Chitty, 2008; Jokhi & Whitby, 2011; Kollmann et al., 2013; Moore, Persaud, & Torchia, 2013; Sermon, Van Steirteghem, & Liebaers, 2004.

Applying What We Know

Steps Prospective Parents Can Take Before Conception to Increase the Chances of a Healthy Baby

RECOMMENDATION	EXPLANATION
Arrange for a physical exam.	A physical exam before conception permits detection of diseases and other medical problems that might reduce fertility, be difficult to treat during pregnancy, or affect the developing organism.
Consider your genetic makeup.	Find out if anyone in your family has had a child with a genetic disorder. If so, seek genetic counseling before conception.
Reduce or eliminate toxins under your control.	Because the developing organism is highly sensitive to damaging environmental agents during the early weeks of pregnancy (see Chapter 3), couples trying to conceive should avoid drugs, alcohol, cigarette smoke, radiation, pollution, chemical substances in the home and workplace, and infectious diseases. Furthermore, they should stay away from ionizing radiation and some industrial chemicals that are known to cause mutations.
Ensure proper nutrition.	A doctor-recommended vitamin–mineral supplement, begun before conception, helps prevent many prenatal problems. It should include folic acid, which reduces the chances of neural tube defects, prematurity, and low birth weight (see Chapter 3, page 112).
Consult your doctor after 12 months of unsuccessful efforts at conception.	Long periods of infertility may be due to undiagnosed spontaneous abortions, which can be caused by genetic defects in either partner. If a physical exam reveals a healthy reproductive system, seek genetic counseling.

may be willing to try almost any option, even one with only a slim chance of success. Currently, the medical profession is struggling with how to help parents make informed decisions about fetal surgery.

Advances in *genetic engineering* also offer new hope for correcting hereditary defects. As part of the Human Genome Project—an ambitious international research program extending from 1990 to 2003, aimed at deciphering the chemical makeup of human genetic material (genome)—researchers succeeded in mapping the sequence of all human DNA base pairs. Using this information, they are "annotating" the genome—identifying all its genes and their functions, including their protein products and what these products do. A major goal is to understand the estimated 4,000 human disorders, those due to single genes and those resulting from an interplay of multiple genes and environmental factors.

Already, thousands of genes have been identified, including those involved in hundreds of disorders of the heart, digestive, blood, eye, and nervous system; and many forms of cancer (National Institutes of Health, 2014). As a result, new treatments are being explored, such as *gene therapy*—correcting genetic abnormalities by delivering DNA carrying a functional gene to the cells. Recent testing of gene therapies for relieving symptoms of hemophilia and treating severe immune system dysfunction, leukemia, and several forms of cancer has been encouraging (Kaufmann et al., 2013). In another approach, called *proteomics,* scientists modify gene-specified proteins involved in disease (Ray et al., 2011).

Genetic treatments, however, seem some distance in the future for most single-gene defects and even farther off for diseases involving multiple genes that combine in complex ways with each other and the environment. Applying What We Know above summarizes steps that prospective parents can take before conception to protect the genetic health of their child.

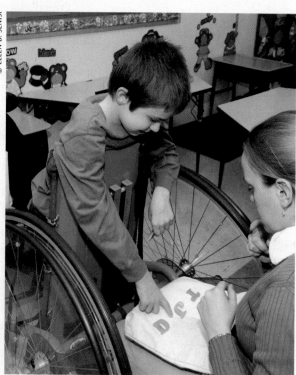

© ELLEN B. SENISI

This 10-year-old has Duchenne muscular dystrophy, a hereditary degenerative muscle disease that is likely to lead to early death. In the future, such children may benefit from gene-based treatments for hereditary disorders.

Adoption

Adults who are infertile, who are likely to pass along a genetic disorder, or who are older and single but want a family are turning to adoption in increasing numbers. Those who have children by birth, too, sometimes choose to expand their families through adoption. Adoption agencies try to ensure a good fit by seeking parents of the same ethnic and religious background as the child and, where possible, trying to choose parents who are the same age as typical biological parents. Because the availability of healthy babies has declined (fewer young unwed mothers give up their babies than in the past), more people in North America and Western Europe are adopting from other countries or accepting children who are past infancy or who have known developmental problems (Palacios & Brodzinsky, 2010).

Adopted children and adolescents—whether or not they are born in their adoptive parents' country—tend to have more learning and emotional difficulties than other children, a difference that increases with the child's age at time of adoption (van den Dries et al., 2009; van IJzendoorn, Juffer, & Poelhuis, 2005; Verhulst, 2008). Various explanations exist for adoptees' more problematic childhoods. The biological mother may have been unable to care for the child because of problems believed to be partly genetic, such as alcoholism or severe depression, and may have passed this tendency to her offspring. Or perhaps she experienced stress, poor diet, or inadequate medical care during pregnancy—factors that can affect the child (as we will see in Chapter 3). Furthermore, children adopted after infancy often have a pre-adoptive history of conflict-ridden family relationships, lack of parental affection, neglect and abuse, or deprived institutional rearing. Finally, adoptive parents and children, who are genetically unrelated, are less alike in intelligence and personality than are biological relatives—differences that may threaten family harmony.

Despite these risks, most adopted children fare well, and those with preexisting problems usually make rapid progress (Arcus & Chambers, 2008; Juffer & van IJzendoorn, 2012). In a study of internationally adopted children in the Netherlands, sensitive maternal care and secure attachment in infancy predicted cognitive and social competence at age 7 (Stams, Juffer, & van IJzendoorn, 2002).

Overall, international adoptees fare much better in development than birth siblings or institutionalized agemates who stay behind (Christoffersen, 2012). By middle childhood, those who were adopted in infancy have mental test scores resembling those of their non-biological siblings and school classmates, although they tend to achieve less well in school, to have more learning problems that require special treatment, and to be slightly delayed in language skills (van IJzendoorn, Juffer, & Poelhuis, 2005). Children adopted at older ages generally improve in feelings of trust and affection for their adoptive parents as they come to feel loved and supported in their new families (Verissimo & Salvaterra, 2006). As we will see in Chapter 5, however, later-adopted children—especially those with multiple early-life adversities—are more likely than their agemates to have persistent cognitive, emotional, and social problems.

By adolescence, adoptees' lives are often complicated by unresolved curiosity about their roots. Some have difficulty accepting the possibility that they may never know their birth parents. Others worry about what they would do if their birth parents suddenly reappeared. Adopted teenagers also face a more challenging process of defining themselves as they try to integrate aspects of their birth family and their adoptive family into their emerging identity. Nevertheless, the decision to search for birth parents is usually postponed until early adulthood, when marriage and childbirth may trigger it.

Adoption is one option for adults who are infertile or have a family history of genetic disorders. This couple, who adopted their daughters from China, can promote their children's adjustment by helping them learn about their birth heritage.

Despite concerns about their origins, most adoptees appear well-adjusted as adults. When parents have been warm, open, and supportive in their communication about adoption, their children typically forge a positive sense of self (Brodzinsky, 2011). And as long as their parents took steps to help them learn about their heritage in childhood, young people adopted into a different ethnic group or culture generally develop identities that are healthy blends of their birth and rearing backgrounds (Nickman et al., 2005; Thomas & Tessler, 2007).

As we conclude our discussion of reproductive choices, perhaps you are wondering how things turned out for Ted and Marianne. Through genetic counseling, Marianne discovered a history of Tay-Sachs disease on her mother's side of the family. Ted had a distant cousin who died of the disorder. The genetic counselor explained that the chances of giving birth to another affected baby were 1 in 4. Ted and Marianne took the risk. Their son Douglas is now 12 years old. Although Douglas is a carrier of the recessive allele, he is a normal, healthy boy. In a few years, Ted and Marianne will tell Douglas about his genetic history and explain the importance of genetic counseling and testing before he has children of his own.

Ask Yourself

- **REVIEW** Why is genetic counseling called a *communication process?* Who should seek it?

- **CONNECT** How does research on adoption reveal resilience? Which factor related to resilience (see Chapter 1, pages 10–11) is central in positive outcomes for adoptees?

- **APPLY** Imagine that you must counsel a couple considering in vitro fertilization using donor ova to overcome infertility. What medical and ethical risks would you raise?

- **REFLECT** Suppose you are a carrier of fragile X syndrome and want to have children. Would you choose pregnancy, adoption, or surrogacy? If you became pregnant, would you opt for prenatal diagnosis? Explain your decisions.

Environmental Contexts for Development

2.5 Describe family functioning from the perspective of ecological systems theory, along with aspects of the environment that support family well-being and children's development.

Just as complex as the genetic inheritance is the surrounding environment—a many-layered set of influences that combine to help or hinder physical and psychological well-being. **TAKE A MOMENT...** Think back to your own childhood, and jot down a brief description of events and people that significantly influenced your development. Do the items on your list resemble those of our students, who mostly mention experiences that involve their families? This emphasis is not surprising, since the family is the first and longest-lasting context for development. Other influences that make most students' top ten are friends, neighbors, school, and community and religious organizations.

Return to Bronfenbrenner's ecological systems theory, discussed in Chapter 1. It emphasizes that environments extending beyond the *microsystem*—the immediate settings just mentioned—powerfully affect development. Indeed, our students rarely mention one important context. Its impact is so pervasive that we seldom stop to think about it in our daily lives. This is the *macrosystem,* or broad social climate of society—its values and programs that support and protect children's development. All families need help in rearing children—through affordable housing and health care, safe neighborhoods, good schools, well-equipped recreational facilities, and high-quality child care and other services that permit parents to meet both work and family responsibilities. And some families, because of poverty or special tragedies, need considerably more help than others.

In the following sections, we take up these contexts for development. Because they affect every age and aspect of change, we will return to them in later chapters. For now, our discussion emphasizes that environments, as well as heredity, can enhance or create risks for development.

© LAURA DWIGHT PHOTOGRAPHY

The family is a network of interdependent relationships, in which each person's behavior influences that of others. As this family plays a game, warm, considerate parental communication encourages children's cooperation, which promotes further parental warmth and caring.

The Family

In power and breadth of influence, no other microsystem context equals the family. The family introduces children to the physical world by providing opportunities for play and exploration of objects. It also creates unique bonds among people. Attachments to parents and siblings are usually lifelong and serve as models for relationships in the wider world. Within the family, children learn the language, skills, and social and moral values of their culture. And people of all ages turn to family members for information, assistance, and pleasurable interaction. In cultures around the world, warm, gratifying family ties predict physical and psychological health throughout development (Khaleque & Rohner, 2012; Parke & Buriel, 2006). In contrast, a sense of isolation or alienation from the family, especially from parents, is generally associated with developmental problems.

Contemporary researchers view the family as a network of interdependent relationships (Bornstein & Sawyer, 2006; Bronfenbrenner & Morris, 2006). Recall from ecological systems theory that *bidirectional influences* exist in which the behaviors of each family member affect those of others. Indeed, the very term *system* implies that the responses of all family members are related. These system influences operate both directly and indirectly.

DIRECT INFLUENCES Recently, while passing through the checkout counter at the supermarket, one of us witnessed two episodes, each an example of how parents and children directly influence each other:

- Four-year-old Danny looked longingly at the tempting rows of candy as his mother lifted groceries from her cart onto the counter. "Pleeeeease, can I have it, Mom?" Danny begged, holding up a large package of bubble gum. "Do you have a dollar? Just one?"

  "No, not today," his mother answered. "Remember, we picked out your special cereal. That's what I need the dollar for." Gently taking the bubble gum from his hand, Danny's mother handed him the box of cereal. "Here, let's pay," she said, lifting Danny so he could see the cash register.
- Three-year-old Meg was sitting in the shopping cart while her mother transferred groceries to the counter. Suddenly Meg turned around, grabbed a bunch of bananas, and started pulling them apart.

  "Stop it, Meg!" shouted her mother, snatching the bananas from Meg's hand. But as she turned her attention to swiping her debit card, Meg reached for a chocolate bar from a nearby shelf. "Meg, how many times have I told you, don't touch!" Loosening the candy from Meg's tight little fist, Meg's mother slapped her hand. Meg's face turned red with anger as she began to wail.

These observations fit with a wealth of research on the family system. Studies of families of diverse ethnicities show that when parents are firm but warm, children tend to comply with their requests. And when children cooperate, their parents are likely to be warm and gentle in the future. In contrast, children whose parents discipline harshly and impatiently are likely to refuse and rebel. And because children's misbehavior is stressful, parents may increase their use of punishment, leading to more unruliness by the child (Stormshak et al., 2000; Whiteside-Mansell et al., 2003). In each case, the behavior of one family member helps sustain a form of interaction in the other that either promotes or undermines children's well-being.

LOOK and LISTEN

Observe several parent–young child pairs in a supermarket or department store, where parents are likely to place limits on children's behavior. How does quality of parent communication seem to influence the child's response? How does the child's response affect the parent's subsequent interaction?

INDIRECT INFLUENCES   The impact of family relationships on child development becomes even more complicated when we consider that interaction between any two members is affected by others present in the setting. Bronfenbrenner calls these indirect influences the effect of *third parties* (see Chapter 1, page 27).

Third parties can serve as supports for or barriers to development. For example, when a marital relationship is warm and considerate, mothers and fathers are more likely to engage in effective **coparenting,** mutually supporting each other's parenting behaviors. Such parents are warmer, praise and stimulate their children more, and nag and scold them less. Effective coparenting, in turn, fosters a positive marital relationship (Morrill et al., 2010). In contrast, parents whose relationship is tense and hostile often interfere with one another's child-rearing efforts, are less responsive to children's needs, and are more likely to criticize, express anger, and punish (Caldera & Lindsey, 2006; Pruett & Donsky, 2011).

Children who are chronically exposed to angry, unresolved parental conflict have serious emotional problems resulting from disrupted emotional security (Cummings & Davies, 2010). These include both *internalizing difficulties* (especially among girls), such as feeling worried and fearful and trying to repair their parents' relationship, and *externalizing difficulties* (especially among boys), including anger and aggression (Cummings, Goeke-Morey, & Papp, 2004; Goeke-Morey, Papp, & Cummings, 2013). These child problems can further disrupt parents' relationship.

Yet even when parental conflict strains children's adjustment, other family members may help restore effective interaction. Grandparents, for example, can promote children's development both directly, by responding warmly to the child, and indirectly, by providing parents with child-rearing advice, models of child-rearing skill, and even financial assistance. Of course, as with any indirect influence, grandparents can sometimes be harmful. When relations between parents and grandparents are quarrelsome, parent–child communication may suffer.

ADAPTING TO CHANGE   Think back to the *chronosystem* in Bronfenbrenner's theory (see page 29 in Chapter 1). The interplay of forces within the family is dynamic and ever-changing, as each member adapts to the development of other members.

For example, as children acquire new skills, parents adjust the way they treat their more competent youngsters. **TAKE A MOMENT...** The next time you have a chance, notice the way a parent relates to a tiny baby as compared with a walking, talking toddler. During the first few months, parents spend much time feeding, changing, bathing, and cuddling the infant. Within a year, things change dramatically. The 1-year-old points, shows, names objects, and makes his way through the household cupboards. In response, parents devote less time to physical care and more to talking, playing games, and disciplining. These new ways of interacting, in turn, encourage the child's expanding motor, cognitive, and social skills.

Parents' development affects children as well. The rise in parent–child conflict that often occurs in early adolescence is not solely due to teenagers' striving for independence. This is a time when most parents of adolescents have reached middle age and—conscious that their children will soon leave home and establish their own lives—are reconsidering their own commitments (Steinberg & Silk, 2002). Consequently, while the adolescent presses for greater autonomy, the parent presses for more togetherness. This imbalance promotes friction, which parent and teenager gradually resolve by accommodating to changes in each other. Indeed, no social unit other than the family is required to adjust to such vast changes in its members.

Historical time period also contributes to a dynamic family system. In recent decades, a declining birth rate, a high divorce rate, expansion of women's roles, increased acceptance of homosexuality, and postponement of parenthood have led to a smaller family size and a greater number of single parents, remarried parents, gay and lesbian parents, employed mothers, and dual-earner families. Clearly, families in industrialized nations have become more diverse than ever before. In later chapters we will take up these family forms, examining how each affects family relationships and, ultimately, children's development.

Social Issues: Education

Worldwide Education of Girls: Transforming Current and Future Generations

Malalah Yousafzai, a Pakistani schoolgirl, rose to international prominence for her persuasive activism favoring the rights of girls to education. Encouraged by her father, a schoolteacher and an educational activist himself, in 2009 at age 11 she wrote a blog for the BBC, using a pseudonym to protect her safety. In the blog, she described her experiences under rule of the Taliban, who had at times banned girls in her province from attending school. Later that year, the *New York Times* made a documentary about Malalah's life, and she started giving interviews that were broadcast around the world.

One afternoon in October 2012, a Taliban gunman boarded Malalah's school bus, asked for her by name, and fired three shots, critically wounding her. In the days following the assassination attempt, she hung between life and death, but gradually she recovered enough to travel to England for intensive treatment. The incident sparked worldwide support for Malalah and her cause. Among the outcomes of her persistent outspokenness was a United Nations petition called "I am Malalah," which demanded that all children be enrolled in school by the end of 2015. The petition led to Pakistan's first Compulsory Education Bill, passed by the National Assembly in 2012, which guarantees free education to all children between ages 5 and 16.

Over the past century, the percentage of children in the developing world who go to school has increased from a small minority of boys to a majority of all children in most regions. Still, some 57 million children of elementary school age, most of them poverty-stricken girls, are not in school, and 71 million of middle school age, again mostly girls, are out of school. Almost two-thirds of the world's 775 million illiterate adults are women (UNICEF, 2013b).

In research carried out in four countries—Mexico, Nepal, Venezuela, and Zambia—investigators examined the impact of variations in maternal language and literacy skills on family

Pakistani girls attend class on the first anniversary of the near-fatal shooting of Malalah Yousafzai, a teenage activist who advocates forcefully for education for girls. Malalah survived to see Pakistan's first compulsory education legislation and in 2014 was awarded the Nobel Peace Prize.

health, mother–child interaction, and young children's literacy skills (Levine et al., 2012). Participating mothers' average levels of schooling ranged from 5 years in Nepal to 8 years in Zambia, with some attending for as little as 1 year and most leaving school by age 13.

Nevertheless, some general patterns in family functioning do exist. In the United States and other industrialized nations, one important source of these consistencies is socioeconomic status.

Socioeconomic Status and Family Functioning

People in industrialized nations are stratified on the basis of what they do at work and how much they earn for doing it—factors that determine their social position and economic well-being. Researchers assess a family's standing on this continuum through an index called **socioeconomic status (SES),** which combines three related, but not completely overlapping, variables: (1) years of education and (2) the prestige of one's job and the skill it requires, both of which measure social status, and (3) income, which measures economic status. As SES rises and falls, parents and children face changing circumstances that profoundly affect family functioning.

SES is linked to timing of parenthood and to family size. People who work in skilled and semiskilled manual occupations (for example, construction workers, truck drivers, and custodians) tend to marry and have children earlier as well as give birth to more children than people in professional and technical occupations. The two groups also differ in child-rearing values and expectations. For example, when asked about personal qualities they desire for

Findings in each country, and across rural and urban areas, were the same: Educating girls had an especially powerful impact on the welfare of children and families. The diverse benefits of girls' schooling largely accrued in two ways: (1) through enhanced verbal skills—reading, writing, and oral communication; and (2) through the cognitive abilities that literacy promotes. Together, these capacities enable girls, as they become adults and mothers, to navigate health and educational settings more effectively and to teach their children in ways that foster school success in the next generation.

Family Health

Maternal education in developing countries has played a powerful role in the dramatic worldwide gains in child survival and health over past half century (Gakidou et al., 2010). In the four-countries study, the greater mothers' school attainment, the better their comprehension of radio and TV health messages and the more clearly they could to explain an instance of their own or their child's illness to a clinic health professional. And mothers' literacy competence explained this link between maternal schooling and health-related cognitive processing.

Clearly, education gives women the communicative skills and knowledge to benefit from public health information. As a result, it strongly predicts preventive health behaviors: prenatal visits, child immunizations, healthy diet, and sanitary practices (LeVine et al., 2004). In addition, because women with more schooling have more life opportunities, they are more likely to take advantage of family planning services, delay marriage and childbearing, and have more widely spaced and fewer children (Stromquist, 2007). All these practices are linked to increased maternal and child survival and health.

Mother–Child Interaction and Children's Literacy Skills

Making home visits to observe mothers interacting with their babies, researchers in the four-countries study found that schooling was positively associated with mothers' verbal responsiveness to their infants' and toddlers' vocalizations. And once again, maternal literacy skills accounted for this relationship. Follow-ups as the children grew older revealed that mothers who talked more had children with larger vocabularies. The more literate mothers had adopted a style of interaction that promoted language development.

In Nepal, the investigators looked closely at literacy-related parenting behaviors in the preschool and early school years. Regardless of family income or husband's schooling, mothers with more education—especially those with better literacy skills—reported that they more often taught their children academic skills, enriched the home with literacy materials, modeled literacy behaviors, and had higher expectations for their children's education. These home supports for education, in turn, predicted children's language and literacy progress.

Implications

The opportunity to advance in language and literacy skills—even in the limited doses available to women in the four-country study, many of whom attended low-quality schools for just a few years—alters maternal behavior, with substantial health and educational gains in the next generation. A recent United Nations report concluded that educating girls is the most effective means of combating the most profound, global threats to human development: poverty, maternal and child mortality, disease, gender inequality, and economic and social instability in the world's poorest countries (UNICEF, 2013b). But because of cultural beliefs about gender roles or reluctance to give up a daughter's work at home, parents sometimes resist sending their daughters to school.

An even larger barrier is that many countries continue to charge parents a fee for each child enrolled in school, often amounting to nearly one-third of the income of poverty-stricken families. Under these conditions, parents—if they send any children—tend to send only sons. But when governments abolish enrollment fees, provide information about the benefits of education for girls, and create employment possibilities for women, the overwhelming majority of parents—including the very poor—choose to send their daughters to school and are willing to make sacrifices to do so.

---

their children, lower-SES parents tend to emphasize external characteristics, such as obedience, politeness, neatness, and cleanliness. In contrast, higher-SES parents emphasize psychological traits, such as curiosity, happiness, self-direction, and cognitive and social maturity (Duncan & Magnuson, 2003; Hoff, Laursen, & Tardif, 2002; Tudge et al., 2000).

These differences are reflected in family interaction. Parents higher in SES talk to, read to, and otherwise stimulate their infants and preschoolers more and grant them greater freedom to explore. With older children and adolescents, higher-SES parents use more warmth, explanations, and verbal praise; set higher academic and other developmental goals; and allow their children to make more decisions. Commands ("You do that because I told you to"), criticism, and physical punishment all occur more often in low-SES households (Bush & Peterson, 2008; Mandara et al., 2009).

Education contributes substantially to these variations in child rearing. Higher-SES parents' interest in providing verbal stimulation, nurturing inner traits, and promoting academic achievement is supported by years of schooling, during which they learned to think about abstract, subjective ideas and, thus, to invest in their children's cognitive and social development (Mistry et al., 2008; Vernon-Feagans et al., 2008). In diverse cultures around the world, as the Social Issues: Education box above makes clear, education of women in particular fosters patterns of thinking and behaving that greatly improve quality of life, for both parents and children.

Because of limited education and low social status, many lower-SES parents feel a sense of powerlessness and lack of influence in their relationships beyond the home. At work, for example, they must obey rules made by others in positions of authority. When they get home, their parent–child interaction seems to duplicate these experiences—but now they are in authority. High levels of stress contribute to low-SES parents' greater use of coercive discipline (Belsky, Schlomer, & Ellis, 2012; Conger & Donnellan, 2007). Higher-SES parents, in contrast, typically have more control over their own lives. At work, they are used to making independent decisions and convincing others of their point of view. At home, they are more likely to teach these skills to their children (Greenberger, O'Neil, & Nagel, 1994).

As early as the second year of life, higher SES is associated with enhanced cognitive and language development and with reduced incidence of behavior problems. And throughout childhood and adolescence, children from higher-SES families do better in school (Bradley & Corwyn, 2003; Hoff, 2013; Melby et al., 2008). As a result, they attain higher levels of education, which greatly enhances their opportunities for a prosperous adult life. Researchers believe that differences in family functioning have much to do with these outcomes.

Affluence

Despite their advanced education and great material wealth, affluent parents—those in prestigious and high-paying occupations—too often fail to engage in family interaction and parenting that promote favorable development. In several studies, researchers tracked the adjustment of youths growing up in wealthy suburbs (Luthar & Latendresse, 2005a). By seventh grade, a substantial number (as many as 10 percent) showed multiple, serious problems that worsened in high school. Their school grades were poor, and they were more likely than low-SES youths to engage in alcohol and drug use, to have been involved with the legal system, and to report high levels of anxiety and depression (Luthar & Goldstein, 2008; Racz, McMahon, & Luthar, 2011). Furthermore, among affluent (but not low-SES) teenagers, substance use was correlated with anxiety and depression, suggesting that wealthy youths took drugs to self-medicate—a practice that predicts persistent abuse (Luthar & Sexton, 2004).

Why are so many affluent youths troubled? Compared to their better-adjusted counterparts, poorly adjusted affluent young people report less emotional closeness, less supervision, and fewer serious consequences for misbehaviors from their parents, who lead professionally and socially demanding lives. As a group, wealthy parents are nearly as physically and emotionally unavailable to their youngsters as parents coping with serious financial strain. At the same time, affluent parents of troubled youths often make excessive demands for achievement and are critical when their youngsters perform less than perfectly (Luthar & Barkin, 2012). Adolescents whose parents value their accomplishments more than their character are more likely to have academic and emotional problems.

For both affluent and low-SES youths, a simple routine—eating dinner with parents—is associated with a reduction in adjustment difficulties, even after many other aspects of parenting are controlled (see Figure 2.7) (Luthar & Latendresse, 2005b). Interventions that make wealthy parents aware of the high costs of a competitive lifestyle and minimal family time are badly needed.

Advanced education and material wealth do not guarantee a healthy family life. When children in affluent families lack parental supervision and emotional closeness, they are at risk for academic and emotional difficulties.

© INTI ST. CLAIR/GETTY IMAGES/PHOTODISC

Parental affection, acceptance, and monitoring of the adolescent's whereabouts and activities predict favorable adjustment in affluent young people, just as they do for youths in general.

Poverty

When families slip into poverty, development is seriously threatened. In a TV documentary on childhood poverty, a PBS filmmaker explored the daily lives of several American children, along with the struggles of their families (Frontline, 2012). Asked what being poor is like, 10-year-old Kaylie replied, "We don't get three meals a day.... Sometimes we have cereal but no milk and have to eat it dry." Kaylie said she felt hungry much of the time, adding, "I'm afraid if we can't pay our bills, me and my brother will starve."

Kaylie lives with her 12-year-old brother Tyler and their mother, who suffers from depression and panic attacks and cannot work. The children sometimes gather discarded tin cans from around their rural neighborhood and sell them for a small amount of cash. When money to pay rent ran out, the family moved from its small house to an extended-stay motel room. Before the move, Kaylie and Tyler had to give up their dog Noah. During the ride to the animal shelter, Kaylie whispered, "I love you, Noah," bursting into tears.

In the cramped motel room with family belongings piled haphazardly around her, Kaylie complained, "I have no friends, no places to play. I pass the time by." Her mother had postponed the children's school enrollment, expecting soon to move to a trailer court in a new school district. Kaylie and Tyler had few books and indoor games; no outdoor play equipment such as bicycles, bats and balls, and roller skates; and no scheduled leisure pursuits like swimming or music lessons or youth organization activities. Asked to imagine her future, Kaylie wasn't hopeful. "I see my future poor, on the streets, in a box, asking for money from everyone, stealing stuff. . . . I'd like to explore the world, but I'm never going to be able to do that."

Although poverty rates in the United States declined slightly in the 1990s, in recent years they have risen. Today, about 15 percent—46 million Americans—are affected. Those hit hardest are parents under age 25 with young children and older adults who live alone. Poverty is also magnified among ethnic minorities and women. For example, 22 percent of U.S. children—about 14.5 million—live in families with incomes below the federal poverty level, the income judged necessary for a minimum living standard (about $23,500 for a family of four). Poverty rates climb to 32 percent for Hispanic children, 34 percent for Native-American children, and 38 percent for African-American children. For single mothers with preschool children, the poverty rate is close to 50 percent (DeNavas-Walt, Proctor, & Smith, 2011; U.S. Census Bureau, 2014b).

Joblessness, a high divorce rate, a high rate of adolescent parenthood, and (as we will see later) inadequate government programs to meet family needs are responsible for these disheartening statistics. The poverty rate is higher among children than any other age group. And of all Western nations, the United States has the highest percentage of extremely poor children. Nearly 10 percent of U.S. children

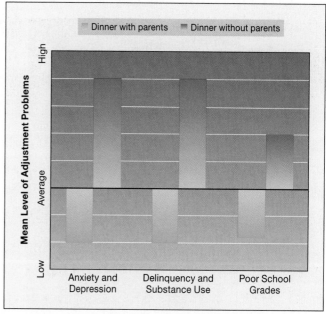

FIGURE 2.7 **Relationship of regularly eating dinner with parents to affluent youths' adjustment problems.** Compared with sixth graders who often ate dinner with their parents, those who rarely did so were far more likely to display anxiety and depression, delinquency and substance use, and poor school grades, even after many other aspects of parenting were controlled. In this study, frequent family mealtimes also protected low-SES youths from delinquency and substance use and from classroom learning problems. (Based on Luthar & Latendresse, 2005b.)

Homelessness poses enormous challenges for maintaining positive family relationships and physical and mental health. This mother and her three children prepare to move out of the motel room they share with her boyfriend and father.

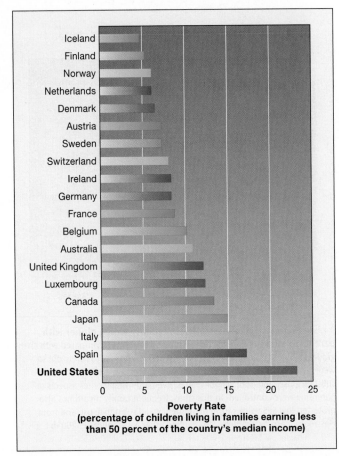

FIGURE 2.8 **Child poverty in 20 of the world's economically advanced nations.** Among the countries listed, the United States ranks last in having the highest percentage of children and youths under age 18 living in families with incomes below 50 percent of the national median income. (From UNICEF (2012). "Measuring Child Poverty: New League Tables of Child Poverty in the World's Rich Countries," *Innocenti Report Card No. 10*, UNICEF Innocenti Research Centre, Florence. Adapted by permission of UNICEF Innocenti Research Centre.)

live in deep poverty (at less than half the federal poverty threshold). In contrast, in most northern and central European countries, child poverty rates have remained below 10 percent for several decades (see Figure 2.8), and extreme child poverty is rare (UNICEF, 2013b). The earlier poverty begins, the deeper it is, and the longer it lasts, the more devastating are its effects. Children of poverty are more likely than other children to suffer from lifelong poor physical health, persistent deficits in cognitive development and academic achievement, high school dropout, mental illness, and impulsivity, aggression, and antisocial behavior (Morgan et al., 2009; Ryan, Fauth, & Brooks-Gunn, 2006; Yoshikawa, Aber, & Beardslee, 2012).

The constant stressors that accompany poverty gradually weaken the family system. Poor families have many daily hassles—the car breaking down, loss of welfare and unemployment payments, basic services—phone, TV, electricity, hot water—being shut off because of inability to pay bills, and limited or uncertain access to food—to name just a few. When daily crises arise, family members become depressed, irritable, and distracted; hostile interactions increase; and children's development suffers (Conger & Donnellan, 2007; Kohen et al., 2008). Negative outcomes are especially severe in single-parent families and families who must live in poor housing and dangerous neighborhoods—conditions that make everyday existence even more difficult while reducing social supports that help people cope with economic hardship (Hart, Atkins, & Matsuba, 2008; Leventhal & Brooks-Gunn, 2003).

A related problem—one that has become more common in the past 30 years—has reduced the life chances of many children. From 2.5 to 3.5 million people in the United States experience homelessness in a given year. The majority are adults on their own, many of whom suffer from serious mental illness. But about 40 percent of the homeless are children and youths (National Coalition for the Homeless, 2009). The rise in homelessness is mostly due to two factors: a decline in the availability of government-supported low-cost housing and an increase in poverty.

Most homeless families consist of women with children under age 5. Besides health problems (which affect the majority of homeless people), many homeless children suffer from developmental delays and chronic emotional stress due to their harsh, insecure daily lives (Kilmer et al., 2012). An estimated 25 to 30 percent of those who are old enough do not go to school. Those who do enroll achieve less well than other poverty-stricken children because of poor attendance, frequent moves from school to school due to time-limited shelters, and health and emotional difficulties (Cutuli et al., 2010; Obradović et al., 2009).

Although gaps in overall health, achievement, and emotional adjustment between poverty-stricken children and their economically better-off peers are substantial, a considerable number of children from financially stressed families fare well. In Chapter 1, we discussed a variety of factors that promote resilience in the face of environmental risks to development (see pages 10–11).

A host of interventions aimed at helping children surmount the developmental risks of poverty exist. In one, poverty-stricken families with preschool through adolescent children were randomly assigned to a family strengthening intervention or a no-intervention control group. The intervention involved 14 hours of intensive parent training devoted to learning about and practicing effective strategies for coping with stress, solving everyday problems, and engaging in positive family communication and parenting. Compared with controls, participating parents reported an improved capacity to manage stressful situations, lessening of economic strain, warmer parent–child interaction, and fewer depressive symptoms—benefits that translated into a reduction in child internalizing and externalizing difficulties (Wadsworth et al., 2013). Gains in family functioning, parent mental health, and children's adjustment were still evident 18 months after the intervention ended.

Some interventions, like the example just described, address family functioning and parenting skills, while others directly target children's academic, emotional, and social skills in preschools, elementary schools, and secondary schools. And an increasing number of programs recognize that because poverty-stricken children often experience multiple adversities, they benefit most from efforts that are multifaceted—that focus on family, parenting, and children's needs at once (Kagan, 2013a). We will discuss many such interventions, along with their impact on children's cognitive, emotional, and social development, later in this book.

Beyond the Family: Neighborhoods and Schools

As the concepts of *mesosystem* and *exosystem* in ecological systems theory make clear, connections between family and community are vital for children's well-being. From our discussion of poverty, perhaps you can see why: In poverty-stricken areas, community life is usually disrupted. Families move often, parks and playgrounds are in disarray, and community centers providing leisure-time activities do not exist. In poor urban neighborhoods, family violence, child abuse and neglect, children's problem behavior, youth antisocial activity, and adult criminal behavior are widespread (Chen, Howard, & Brooks-Gunn, 2011; Ingoldsby et al., 2012). And in poor rural communities—like the small town where Kaylie, Tyler, and their mother live—family isolation and scarcity of supportive services are especially high (Vernon-Feagans & Cox, 2013). In contrast, strong family ties to the community—as indicated by frequent contact with friends and relatives, organized youth activities, and regular church, synagogue, or mosque attendance—reduce family stress and enhance adjustment.

NEIGHBORHOODS   Let's look closely at the functions of communities in the lives of children by beginning with the neighborhood. **TAKE A MOMENT...** What were your childhood experiences like in the yards, streets, parks, and community centers surrounding your home? How did you spend your time, whom did you get to know, and how important were these moments to you?

Neighborhoods offer resources and social ties that play an important part in children's development. In several studies, low-SES families were randomly assigned vouchers to move out of public housing into neighborhoods varying widely in affluence. Compared with their peers who remained in poverty-stricken areas, children and youths who moved into low-poverty neighborhoods showed substantially better physical and mental health and school achievement (Goering, 2003; Leventhal & Brooks-Gunn, 2003; Leventhal & Dupéré, 2011).

Neighborhood resources have a greater impact on economically disadvantaged than on well-to-do young people. Higher-SES families depend less on their immediate surroundings for social support, education, and leisure pursuits. They can afford to transport their children to lessons and entertainment and, if necessary, to better-quality schools in distant parts of the community. In low-income neighborhoods, in-school and after-school programs that substitute for lack of other resources by providing art, music, sports, scouting, and other enrichment activities staffed by caring adults are associated with improved school performance and a reduction in emotional and behavior problems in middle childhood (Kataoka & Vandell, 2013; Peters, Petrunka, & Arnold, 2003; Vandell, Reisner, & Pierce, 2007). Neighborhood organizations, such as religious youth groups and special-interest clubs, contribute to favorable development in adolescence, including increased

Elementary school students learn chess in an after-school program. Neighborhood and school resources are especially important for economically disadvantaged children and families.

LOOK and LISTEN

Ask several parents to list their school-age children's regular lessons and other enrichment activities. Then inquire about home and neighborhood factors that either encourage or impede their children's participation.

self-confidence, school achievement, and educational aspirations (Barnes et al., 2007; Gonzales et al., 1996).

Yet in dangerous, disorganized neighborhoods, high-quality activities for children and adolescents are usually scarce. Even when they are available, crime and social disorder limit young people's access, and attendance is low (Dynarski et al., 2004). Furthermore, home and neighborhood obstacles often combine to reduce involvement. Parents overwhelmed by financial and other stressors are less likely to provide the stimulation and encouragement that motivate their children to participate (Kohen et al., 2008). In an investigation of a large sample of elementary school students diverse in SES and neighborhood residence, those living in the least stimulating homes and the most chaotic neighborhoods were least likely to participate in after-school and community-center enrichment activities (Dearing et al., 2009). Thus, the neediest children were especially likely to miss out on these development-enhancing experiences.

Just how do family–neighborhood ties reduce parenting stress and promote child development? One answer lies in their provision of *social support*, which leads to the following benefits:

- *Parental self-worth.* A neighbor or relative who listens and tries to relieve a parent's concern enhances her self-esteem. The parent, in turn, is likely to interact in a more sensitive and involved manner with her children.
- *Parental access to valuable information and services.* A friend who suggests where a parent might find a job, housing, and affordable child care and youth activities helps make the multiple roles of spouse, parent, and provider easier to fulfill.
- *Child-rearing controls and role models.* Friends, relatives, and other community members may encourage and demonstrate effective parenting practices and discourage ineffective practices.
- *Direct assistance with child rearing.* As children and adolescents participate in their parents' social networks and in neighborhood settings, other adults can influence children through warmth, stimulation, and exposure to a wider array of competent models. In this way, family–neighborhood ties can reduce the impact of ineffective parenting (Silk et al., 2004). Nearby adults can also intervene when they see young people skipping school or behaving antisocially.

The Better Beginnings, Better Futures Project of Ontario, Canada, is a government-sponsored set of community enrichment programs aimed at preventing the dire consequences of home and neighborhood poverty, including child and adolescent school failure and anti-social activity. The most successful of these efforts, using a local elementary school as its base, provided children with in-class and summer enrichment activities (Gershoff & Aber, 2006; Peters, 2005; Peters, Petrunka, & Arnold, 2003). Workers also visited each child's parents regularly, informed them about community resources, and encouraged their involvement in the child's school and neighborhood life.

Evaluations as children reached grades 3, 6, and 9 revealed wide-ranging benefits compared with children and families living in other impoverished neighborhoods without this set of programs (Peters et al., 2010). Among these were parents' sense of improved family functioning and child rearing, and gains in children's academic achievement and social adjustment, including positive relationships with peers and adults and a reduction in emotional and behavior problems.

SCHOOLS Unlike the informal worlds of family and neighborhood, the school is a formal institution designed to transmit knowledge and skills that children need to become productive members of their society. Children in the developed world spend many hours in school—6 hours a day, 5 days a week, 36 weeks a year—a total of about 14,000 hours, on average, by high school graduation. And today, because many children younger than age 5 attend "school-like" child-care centers or preschools, the impact of schooling begins even earlier and is more powerful than these figures suggest.

Schools are complex social systems that affect many aspects of development. Schools differ in their physical environments—student body size, number of children per class, and space available for work and play. They also vary in their educational philosophies—whether teachers regard children as passive learners to be molded by adult instruction; as active, curious beings who determine their own learning; or as collaborative partners assisted by adult experts, who guide their mastery of new skills. Finally, the social life of schools varies—for example, in the degree to which students cooperate or compete; in the extent to which students of different abilities, SES, and ethnic backgrounds learn together; and in whether classrooms, hallways, and play yards are safe, humane settings or are riddled with violence (Evans, 2006). We will discuss each of these aspects of schooling in later chapters.

Regular parent–school contact supports development at all ages. Students whose parents are involved in school activities and attend parent–teacher conferences show better academic achievement. Higher-SES parents, whose backgrounds and values are similar to those of teachers, are more likely to make phone calls and visits to school. In contrast, low-SES and ethnic minority parents often feel uncomfortable about coming to school, and daily stressors reduce the energy they have for school involvement (Grant & Ray, 2010; Reschly & Christenson, 2009). Teachers and administrators must take extra steps with low-SES and ethnic minority families and in urban areas to build supportive family–school ties.

When these efforts lead to cultures of good parenting and teaching, they deliver an extra boost to children's well-being. For example, students attending schools with many highly involved parents achieve especially well (Darling & Steinberg, 1997). And when excellent education becomes a team effort of teachers, administrators, and community members, its effects on learning are stronger and reach many more students (Hauser-Cram et al., 2006).

Schools are complex social systems that powerfully affect development. By encouraging students' active participation, this second-grade teacher promotes mastery of new knowledge and skills along with enthusiastic attitudes toward learning.

LOOK and **LISTEN**

Ask a teacher whose classroom has many students from low-SES families what percentage of parents attend parent–teacher conferences. What steps does the teacher take to promote parent–school involvement?

The Cultural Context

Our discussion in Chapter 1 emphasized that child development can be fully understood only when viewed in its larger cultural context. In the following sections, we expand on this important theme by taking up the role of the *macrosystem* in development. First, we discuss ways that cultural values and practices affect environmental contexts for development. Then we consider how healthy development depends on laws and government programs that shield children from harm and foster their well-being.

CULTURAL VALUES AND PRACTICES   Cultures shape family interaction, school experiences, and community settings beyond the home—in short, all aspects of daily life. Many of us remain blind to aspects of our own cultural heritage until we see them in relation to the practices of others.

TAKE A MOMENT... Consider the question, Who should be responsible for rearing young children? How would you answer it? Here are some typical responses from our students: "If parents decide to have a baby, then they should be ready to care for it." "Most people are not happy about others intruding into family life." These statements reflect a widely held opinion in the United States—that the care and rearing of young children, and paying for that care, are the duty of parents, and only parents. This view has a long history—one in which independence, self-reliance, and the privacy of family life emerged as central American values (Halfon & McLearn, 2002). It is one reason, among others, that the public has been slow to endorse government-supported benefits for all families, such as high-quality child care and paid employment leave for meeting family needs. And it has also contributed to the large number of U.S. children who remain poor, even though their parents are gainfully employed (Gruendel & Aber, 2007; UNICEF, 2012).

Cultural Influences

The African-American Extended Family

The African-American extended family can be traced to the African heritage of most black Americans. In many African societies, newly married couples do not start their own households. Instead, they live with a large extended family, which assists its members with all aspects of daily life. This tradition of maintaining a broad network of kinship ties traveled to North America during the period of slavery. Since then, it has served as a protective shield against the destructive impact of poverty and racial prejudice on African-American family life. Today, more black than white adults have relatives other than their own children living in the same household. African-American parents also live closer to kin, often establish family-like relationships with friends and neighbors, see more relatives during the week, and perceive them as more important in their lives (Boyd-Franklin, 2006; McAdoo & Younge, 2009).

By providing emotional support and sharing essential resources, the African-American extended family helps reduce the stress of poverty and single parenthood. Extended-family members often help with child rearing. As long as relationships with extended kin are warm, adolescent mothers of infants are more likely to complete high school and get a job than mothers living on their own—factors that benefit children's well-being (Gordon, Chase-Lansdale, & Brooks-Gunn, 2004).

For single mothers rearing children and adolescents, extended-family living continues to be associated with more positive mother–child interaction. Even after establishing their own home, single mothers often invite family members or close friends to live with them. This kinship support increases the likelihood of effective parenting, which is related to gains in children's academic performance, social skills, and emotional well-being and to reduced antisocial behavior (Simons et al., 2006; Taylor, 2010; Washington, Gleeson, & Rulison, 2013).

Finally, the extended family plays an important role in transmitting African-American culture. Compared with nuclear-family households (which include only parents and their children), extended-family arrangements place more emphasis on cooperation and on moral and religious values. And older black adults, such as grandparents and great-grandparents, regard educating children about their African heritage as especially important (Mosely-Howard & Evans, 2000; Taylor, 2000). Family reunions—sometimes

© JEFF GREENBERG/THE IMAGE WORKS

Three generations celebrate together at a neighborhood festival. Strong bonds with extended family members have helped protect many African-American children against the destructive impact of poverty and racial prejudice.

held in grandparents' and great-grandparents' hometowns—are especially common among African Americans, giving young people a strong sense of their roots (Boyd-Franklin, 2006). These influences strengthen family bonds, enhance children's development, and increase the chances that the extended-family lifestyle will carry over to the next generation.

Although the culture as a whole may value independence and privacy, not all citizens share the same values. Some belong to **subcultures**—groups of people with beliefs and customs that differ from those of the larger culture. Many ethnic minority groups in the United States have cooperative family structures, which help protect their members from the harmful effects of poverty. As the Cultural Influences box above indicates, the African-American tradition of **extended-family households,** in which parent and child live with one or more adult relatives, is a vital feature of black family life that has promoted resilience in its members, despite a long history of prejudice and economic deprivation.

Active, involved extended families also characterize other minorities, such as Asian, Native-American, and Hispanic subcultures. Within these families, grandparents play meaningful roles in guiding younger generations; adults who face employment, marital, or child-rearing difficulties receive assistance and emotional support; and caregiving is enhanced for children and the elderly (Jones & Lindahl, 2011; Mutchler, Baker, & Lee, 2007). In Hispanic extended families, for example, grandparents are even more likely to share in rearing young children than are African-American grandparents—a collaborative parenting arrangement that has physical and emotional health benefits for grandparents, parents, and children alike (Goodman & Silverstein, 2006). A likely reason for such far-reaching effects is that intergenerational shared parenting is consistent with the Hispanic cultural ideal of *familism*, which places an especially high priority on close, harmonious family bonds, frequent contact, and meeting family needs.

Our discussion so far reflects two broad sets of values on which cultures and subcultures are commonly compared: *collectivism* versus *individualism* (Triandis, 2005; Triandis & Gelfand, 2012). In cultures that emphasize collectivism, people stress group goals over individual goals and value *interdependent* qualities, such as social harmony, obligations and responsibility to others, and collaborative endeavors. In cultures that emphasize individualism, people are largely concerned with their own personal needs and value *independence*—personal exploration, discovery, achievement, and choice in relationships. Though the most common basis for comparing cultures, the collectivism–individualism distinction is controversial because both sets of values exist, in varying mixtures, in most cultures. In addition, cultural values are complex, differing in myriad additional ways (Chen & Eisenberg, 2012; Taras et al., 2014). Nevertheless, consistent cross-national differences in collectivism–individualism remain, with important consequences: The United States is more individualistic than most Western European countries, which place greater weight on collectivism. These values powerfully affect a nation's approach to protecting the well-being of its children and families.

PUBLIC POLICIES AND CHILD DEVELOPMENT When widespread social problems arise, such as poverty, homelessness, hunger, and disease, nations attempt to solve them by developing **public policies**—laws and government programs designed to improve current conditions. For example, when poverty increases and families become homeless, a country might decide to build more low-cost housing, provide economic aid to homeowners having difficulty making mortgage payments, raise the minimum wage, and increase welfare benefits. When reports indicate that many children are not achieving well in school, federal and state governments might grant more tax money to school districts, strengthen teacher preparation, and make sure that help reaches children who need it most.

Nevertheless, U.S. public policies safeguarding children and youths have lagged behind policies in other developed nations. As Table 2.5 reveals, the United States does not rank well on any key measure of children's health and well-being.

The problems of children and youths extend beyond the indicators in Table 2.5. The Affordable Care Act, signed into law in 2010, extended government-supported health insurance to all children in low-income families. But expanded coverage for low-income adults,

TABLE 2.5	How Does the United States Compare to Other Nations on Indicators of Children's Health and Well-Being?		
INDICATOR		**U.S. RANK[a]**	**SOME COUNTRIES THE UNITED STATES TRAILS**
Childhood poverty (among 20 economically advanced nations with similar standards of living)		20th	Canada, Iceland, Germany, United Kingdom, Norway, Sweden, Spain[b]
Infant deaths in the first year of life (worldwide)		37th	Canada, Greece, Hungary, Ireland, Singapore, Spain
Teenage birth rate (among 28 industrialized nations)		28th	Australia, Canada, Czech Republic, Denmark, Hungary, Iceland, Poland, Slovakia
Public expenditure on education as a percentage of gross domestic product[c] (among 30 industrialized nations considered)		13th	Belgium, France, Iceland, New Zealand, Portugal, Spain, Sweden
Public expenditure on early childhood education and child care as a percentage of gross domestic product (among 36 industrialized nations considered)		32th	Austria, Germany, Italy, Netherlands, France, Sweden
Public expenditure on health as a percentage of total health expenditure, public plus private (among 34 industrialized nations considered)		34th	Austria, Australia, Canada, France, Hungary, Iceland, Switzerland, New Zealand

[a]1 = highest, or best, rank.

[b]U.S. childhood poverty rates greatly exceed poverty in these nations, which have standards of living similar to the United States (see Figure 2.8 on page 74).

[c]Gross domestic product is the value of all goods and services produced by a nation during a specified time period. It provides an overall measure of a nation's wealth.

Sources: OECD, 2013b, 2014; UNICEF, 2012; U.S. Census Bureau, 2014b; U.S. Department of Education, 2014.

Upward Bound, a U.S. federally-funded enrichment program for high school students, serves as a pathway to college for many low-income students. Favorable public policies are vital for solving social problems and safeguarding development.

including parents, is optional for the states. Currently, 19 states have chosen not to participate, leaving millions of low-income parents without an affordable coverage option. Largely because uninsured parents lack knowledge of how to enroll their children, 11 percent of children eligible for the federally supported Children's Health Insurance Program (CHIP)—more than 5 million—do not receive coverage (Kaiser Family Foundation, 2014). Furthermore, the United States has been slow to move toward national standards and funding for child care. Affordable care is in short supply, and much of it is substandard in quality (Phillips & Lowenstein, 2011). In families affected by divorce, weak enforcement of child support payments heightens poverty in mother-headed households. When non-college-bound young people finish high school, many lack the vocational preparation they need to contribute fully to society. And 8 percent of 16- to 24-year olds who dropped out of high school have not returned to earn a diploma (U.S. Department of Education, 2014).

Why have attempts to help children and youths been difficult to realize in the United States? A complex set of political and economic forces is involved. Cultural values of self-reliance and privacy have made government hesitant to become involved in family matters. Furthermore, good social programs are expensive, and they must compete for a fair share of a country's economic resources. Children can easily remain unrecognized in this process because they cannot vote or speak out to protect their own interests (Ripple & Zigler, 2003). Instead, they must rely on the goodwill of others to make them an important government priority.

Without vigilance from child advocates, policies directed at solving a particular social problem can work at cross-purposes with children's well-being, leaving them in dire straits or even worsening their condition. For example, U.S. welfare policy aimed at returning welfare recipients to the workforce—by reducing or terminating their welfare benefits after 24 continuous months—can either help or harm children, depending on whether it lifts a family out of poverty. When welfare-to-work reduces financial strain, it relieves maternal stress, improves quality of parenting, and is associated with cognitive gains and a reduction in child behavior problems (Dunifon, Kalil, & Danziger, 2003; Gennetian & Morris, 2003; Jackson, Bentler, & Franke, 2006). In contrast, former welfare recipients who must take very low-paying jobs that perpetuate poverty often engage in harsh, coercive parenting and have poorly adjusted children (Smith et al., 2001).

LOOKING TOWARD THE FUTURE   Public policies aimed at fostering children's development can be justified on two grounds. The first is that children are the future—the parents, workers, and citizens of tomorrow. Investing in children yields valuable returns to a nation's quality of life. Second, child-oriented policies can be defended on humanitarian grounds—children's basic rights as human beings.

In 1989, the U.N. General Assembly, with the assistance of experts from many child-related fields, drew up the *Convention on the Rights of the Child*, a legal agreement among nations that commits each cooperating country to work toward guaranteeing environments that foster children's development, protect them from harm, and enhance their community participation and self-determination. Examples of rights include the highest attainable standard of health; an adequate standard of living; free and compulsory education; a happy, understanding, and loving family life; protection from all forms of abuse and neglect; and freedom of thought, conscience, and religion, subject to appropriate parental guidance and national law.

Although the United States played a key role in drawing up the Convention, it is one of only two countries in the world whose legislature has not yet ratified it (the other is Somalia).

American individualism has stood in the way (Scherrer, 2012). Opponents maintain that the Convention's provisions would shift the burden of child rearing from the family to the state.

Although the worrisome state of many children and families persists, efforts are being made to improve their condition. Throughout this book, we will discuss many successful programs that could be expanded. Also, growing awareness of the gap between what we know and what we do to better children's lives has led experts in child development to join with concerned citizens as advocates for more effective policies. As a result, several influential interest groups devoted to the well-being of children have emerged.

In the United States, one of the most vigorous is the Children's Defense Fund—a private, nonprofit organization founded by Marian Wright Edelman in 1973—that engages in research, public education, legal action, drafting of legislation, congressional testimony, and community organizing. It also publishes many reports on U.S. children's condition, government-sponsored programs that serve children and families, and proposals for improving those programs. To learn more about the Children's Defense Fund, visit its website at *www.childrensdefense.org*. Another energetic advocacy organization is the National Center for Children in Poverty, dedicated to advancing the economic security, health, and welfare of U.S. children in low-income families by informing policy makers of relevant research. To explore its activities, visit *www.nccp.org*.

Besides strong advocacy, public policies that enhance child development depend on policy-relevant research that documents needs and evaluates programs to spark improvements. Today, more researchers are collaborating with community and government agencies to enhance the social relevance of their investigations. They are also doing a better job of disseminating their findings to the public in easily understandable, compelling ways, through reports to government officials, websites aimed at increasing public understanding, and collaborations with the media to ensure accurate and effective reporting in news stories and radio and television documentaries (Shonkoff & Bales, 2011). In these ways, researchers are helping to create the sense of immediacy about the condition of children and families that is necessary to spur a society into action.

Ask Yourself

- **REVIEW** Links between family and community are essential for children's well-being. Provide examples and research findings from our discussion that support this idea.

- **CONNECT** How does poverty affect the functioning of the family system, placing all aspects of development at risk?

- **APPLY** Check your local newspaper or one or two national news websites to see how often articles appear on the condition of children and families. Why is it important for researchers to communicate with the general public about children's needs?

- **REFLECT** Do you agree with the widespread American sentiment that government should not become involved in family life? Explain.

Understanding the Relationship Between Heredity and Environment

2.6 Explain the various ways heredity and environment may combine to influence complex traits.

Throughout this chapter, we have discussed a wide variety of genetic and environmental influences, each of which has the power to alter the course of development. Yet children who are born into the same family (and who therefore share both genes and environments) are often quite different in characteristics. We also know that some children are affected more than others by their homes, neighborhoods, and communities. In some cases, a child who is given many advantages nevertheless does poorly, while another, though exposed to unfavorable rearing conditions, does well. How do scientists explain the impact of heredity and environment when they seem to work in so many different ways?

Children vary widely in intellectual abilities and personality traits. Contemporary researchers seek to clarify how heredity and environment jointly contribute to individual differences in these complex characteristics.

Behavioral genetics is a field devoted to uncovering the contributions of nature and nurture to this diversity in human traits and abilities. All contemporary researchers agree that both heredity and environment are involved in every aspect of development. But for polygenic traits (those due to many genes) such as intelligence and personality, scientists are a long way from knowing the precise hereditary influences involved. Although—as indicated earlier in this chapter—they are making progress in identifying variations in DNA sequences associated with complex traits, so far these genetic markers explain only a small amount of variation in human behavior, and a minority of cases of most psychological disorders (Plomin, 2013; Psychiatric Genomics Consortium, 2013). For the most part, scientists are still limited to investigating the impact of genes on complex characteristics indirectly.

Some believe that it is useful and possible to answer the question of *how much each factor contributes* to differences among children. A growing consensus, however, regards that question as unanswerable. These investigators believe that heredity and environment are inseparable (Gottlieb, Wahlsten, & Lickliter, 2006; Lerner & Overton, 2008). The important question, they maintain, is *how nature and nurture work together*. Let's consider each position in turn.

The Question, "How Much?"

To infer the role of heredity in complex human characteristics, researchers use special methods, the most common being the *heritability estimate*. Let's look closely at the information this procedure yields, along with its limitations.

HERITABILITY **Heritability estimates** measure the extent to which individual differences in complex traits in a specific population are due to genetic factors. We will take a brief look at heritability findings on intelligence and personality here and will return to them in later chapters, when we consider these topics in greater detail. Heritability estimates are obtained from **kinship studies,** which compare the characteristics of family members. The most common type of kinship study compares identical twins, who share all their genes, with fraternal twins, who share only some. If people who are genetically more alike are also more similar in intelligence and personality, then the researcher assumes that heredity plays an important role.

Kinship studies of intelligence provide some of the most controversial findings in the field of child development. Some experts claim a strong genetic influence, whereas others believe that heredity is barely involved. Currently, most kinship findings support a moderate role for heredity. When many twin studies are examined, correlations between the scores of identical twins are consistently higher than those of fraternal twins. In a summary of more than 10,000 twin pairs, the average correlation was .86 for identical twins and .60 for fraternal twins (Plomin & Spinath, 2004).

Researchers use a complex statistical procedure to compare these correlations, arriving at a heritability estimate ranging from 0 to 1.00. The value for intelligence is about .50 for child and adolescent twin samples in Western industrialized nations. This suggests that differences in genetic makeup explain half the variation in intelligence. Adopted children's mental test scores are more strongly related to their biological parents' scores than to those of their adoptive parents, offering further support for the role of heredity (Petrill & Deater-Deckard, 2004).

Heritability research also reveals that genetic factors are important in personality. For frequently studied traits, such as sociability, anxiety, agreeableness, and activity level, heritability estimates obtained on child, adolescent, and young adult twins are moderate, in the .40s and .50s (Caspi & Shiner, 2006; Rothbart & Bates, 2006; Wright et al., 2008).

Twin studies of schizophrenia, bipolar disorder, and autism generally yield high heritabilities, above .70. The role of heredity in antisocial behavior and major depression, though apparent, is less strong, with heritabilities in the .30s and .40s (Ronald & Hoekstra, 2014; Sullivan, Daley, & Donovan, 2012). Again, adoption studies support these results. Biological relatives of adoptees with schizophrenia, bipolar disorder, or autism are more likely than adoptive relatives to share the same disorder (Plomin, DeFries, & Knopik, 2013).

LIMITATIONS OF HERITABILITY The accuracy of heritability estimates depends on the extent to which the twin pairs studied reflect genetic and environmental variation in the population. Within a population in which all people have very similar home, school, and community experiences, individual differences in intelligence and personality would be largely genetic, and heritability estimates would be close to 1.00. Conversely, the more environments vary, the more likely they are to account for individual differences, yielding lower heritability estimates. In twin studies, most twin pairs are reared together under highly similar conditions. Even when separated twins are available for study, social service agencies have often placed them in advantaged homes that are alike in many ways (Rutter et al., 2001). Because the environments of most twin pairs are less diverse than those of the general population, heritability estimates are likely to exaggerate the role of heredity.

Heritability estimates are controversial measures because they can easily be misapplied. For example, high heritabilities have been used to suggest that ethnic differences in intelligence, such as the poorer performance of black children compared to white children, have a genetic basis (Jensen, 1969, 2001; Rushton, 2012; Rushton & Jensen, 2006). Yet this line of reasoning is widely regarded as incorrect. Heritabilities computed on mostly white twin samples do not tell us what causes test score differences between ethnic groups. We have already seen that large economic and cultural differences are involved. In Chapter 12, we will discuss research indicating that when black children are adopted into economically advantaged homes at an early age, their scores are well above average and substantially higher than those of children growing up in impoverished families.

Perhaps the most serious criticism of heritability estimates has to do with their limited usefulness. Though confirming heredity, these estimates offer no precise information on how intelligence and personality develop or how children might respond to environments designed to help them develop as far as possible (Baltes, Lindenberger, & Staudinger, 2006). Indeed, the heritability of children's intelligence increases as parental education and income increase—that is, as children grow up in conditions that allow them to make the most of their genetic endowment. In impoverished environments, children are prevented from realizing their potential. Consequently, enhancing these children's experiences through interventions—such as parent education and high-quality preschool or child care—has a greater impact on development (Bronfenbrenner & Morris, 2006; Phillips & Lowenstein, 2011).

Kasia Ofmanski, of Warsaw, Poland, holds photos of Nina (right), the identical twin from whom she was mistakenly separated at birth, and Edyta (left), who was assumed to be her twin and who grew up with her. When the twins first met at age 17, Kasia exclaimed, "She's just like me." They found many similarities: Both were physically active, extroverted, and earned similar grades in school. Clearly heredity contributes to personality traits, but generalizing from twin evidence to the population is controversial.

The Question, "How?"

Today, most researchers view development as the result of a dynamic interplay between heredity and environment. How do nature and nurture work together? Several concepts shed light on this question.

GENE–ENVIRONMENT INTERACTION The first of these ideas is **gene–environment interaction,** which means that because of their genetic makeup, individuals differ in their responsiveness to qualities of the environment (Rutter, 2011). Let's explore this idea in Figure 2.9 on page 84. Gene–environment interaction can apply to any characteristic; here it is illustrated for intelligence. Notice that when environments vary from extremely unstimulating to highly enriched, Ben's intelligence increases steadily, Linda's rises sharply and then falls

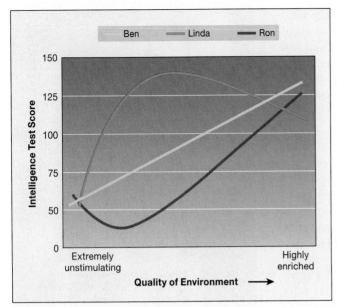

FIGURE 2.9 **Gene–environment interaction, illustrated for intelligence by three children who differ in responsiveness to quality of the environment.** As environments vary from extremely unstimulating to highly enriched, Ben's intelligence test score increases steadily, Linda's rises sharply and then falls off, and Ron's begins to increase only after the environment becomes modestly stimulating.

off, and Ron's begins to increase only after the environment becomes modestly stimulating.

Gene–environment interaction highlights two important points. First, it shows that because each of us has a unique genetic makeup, we respond differently to the same environment. Notice in Figure 2.9 how a poor environment results in similarly low scores for all three individuals. But when the environment provides an intermediate level of stimulation, Linda is by far the best-performing child. And in a highly enriched environment, Ben does best, followed by Ron, both of whom now outperform Linda. Second, sometimes different gene–environment combinations can make two people look the same! For example, if Linda is reared in a minimally stimulating environment, her score will be about 100—average for children in general. Ben and Ron can also obtain this score, but to do so, they must grow up in a fairly enriched home (Gottlieb, Wahlsten, & Lickliter, 2006).

Recently, researchers have made strides in identifying gene–environment interactions in personality development. In Chapter 7 we will see that young children with a gene that increases their risk of an emotionally reactive temperament respond especially strongly to variations in parenting quality (Pluess & Belsky, 2011). When parenting is favorable, they gain control over their emotions and adjust as well as or better than other children. But when parenting is unfavorable, they become increasingly irritable, angry, and poorly adjusted, more so than children not at genetic risk.

GENE–ENVIRONMENT CORRELATION A major problem in trying to separate heredity and environment is that they are often correlated (Rutter, 2011; Scarr & McCartney, 1983). According to the concept of **gene–environment correlation,** our genes influence the environments to which we are exposed. The way this happens changes with age.

Passive and Evocative Correlation At younger ages, two types of gene–environment correlation are common. The first is called *passive* correlation because the child has no control over it. Early on, parents provide environments influenced by their own heredity. For example, parents who are good athletes emphasize outdoor activities and enroll their children in swimming and gymnastics. Besides being exposed to an "athletic environment," the children may have inherited their parents' athletic ability. As a result, they are likely to become good athletes for both genetic and environmental reasons.

The second type of gene–environment correlation is *evocative.* Children evoke responses that are influenced by the child's heredity, and these responses strengthen the child's original style. For example, an active, friendly baby is likely to receive more social stimulation than a passive, quiet infant. And a cooperative, attentive child probably receives more patient and sensitive interactions from parents than an inattentive, distractible child. In support of this idea, the less genetically alike siblings are, the more their parents treat them differently, in both warmth and negativity. Thus, parents' treatment of identical twins is highly similar, whereas their treatment of fraternal twins and nontwin biological siblings is only moderately so. And little resemblance exists in parents' warm and negative interactions with unrelated stepsiblings (see Figure 2.10) (Reiss, 2003).

Active Correlation At older ages, *active* gene–environment correlation becomes common. As children extend their experiences beyond the immediate family and are given the freedom to make more choices, they actively seek

This mother shares her love of the piano with her daughter, who also may have inherited her mother's musical talent. When heredity and environment are correlated, the influence of one cannot be separated from the influence of the other.

© LOU CYPHER/CORBIS

environments that fit with their genetic tendencies. The well-coordinated, muscular child spends more time at after-school sports, the musically talented youngster joins the school orchestra and practices his violin, and the intellectually curious child is a familiar patron at her local library.

This tendency to actively choose environments that complement our heredity is called **niche-picking** (Scarr & McCartney, 1983). Infants and young children cannot do much niche-picking because adults select environments for them. In contrast, older children and adolescents are much more in charge of their environments.

Niche-picking explains why pairs of identical twins reared apart during childhood and later reunited may find, to their surprise, that they have similar hobbies, food preferences, and vocations—a trend that is especially marked when twins' environmental opportunities are similar (Plomin, 1994). Niche-picking also helps us understand why identical twins become somewhat more alike, and fraternal twins and adopted siblings less alike, in intelligence with age (Bouchard, 2004; Loehlin, Horn, & Willerman, 1997). And niche-picking sheds light on why adolescent identical twin pairs—far more often than same-sex fraternal pairs, ordinary siblings, and adopted siblings—report similar stressful life events influenced by personal decisions and actions, such as failing a course, quitting a job, or getting in trouble for drug-taking (Bemmels et al., 2008).

The influence of heredity and environment is not constant but changes over time. With age, genetic factors may become more important in influencing the environments we experience and choose for ourselves.

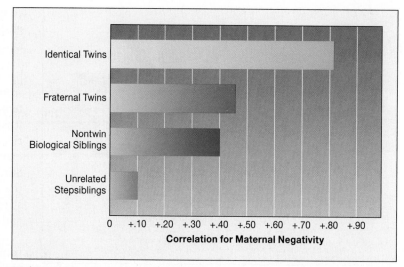

FIGURE 2.10 **Similarity in mothers' interactions for pairs of siblings differing in genetic relatedness.** The correlations shown are for maternal negativity. The pattern illustrates evocative genetic–environmental correlation. Identical twins evoke similar maternal treatment because of their identical heredity. As genetic resemblance between siblings declines, the strength of the correlation drops. Mothers vary their interactions as they respond to each child's unique genetic makeup. (Based on Reiss, 2003.)

ENVIRONMENTAL INFLUENCES ON GENE EXPRESSION Notice how, in the concepts just considered, heredity is granted priority. In gene–environment interaction, it affects responsiveness to particular environments. Similarly, gene–environment correlation is viewed as driven by genetics, in that children's genetic makeup causes them to receive, evoke, or seek experiences that actualize their inborn tendencies (Plomin, 2009; Rutter, 2011).

A growing number of researchers take issue with the supremacy of heredity, arguing that it does not dictate children's experiences or development in a rigid way. In one study, boys with a genetic tendency toward antisocial behavior (based on the presence of a gene on the X chromosome known to predispose both animals and humans to aggression) were no more aggressive than boys without this gene, *unless* they also had a history of severe child abuse (Caspi et al., 2002). Boys with and without the gene did not differ in their experience of abuse, indicating that the "aggressive genotype" did not increase exposure to abuse. And in a large Finnish adoption study, children whose biological mothers had schizophrenia but who were being reared by healthy adoptive parents showed little mental illness—no more than a control group with healthy biological and adoptive parents. In contrast, schizophrenia and other psychological impairments piled up in adoptees whose biological and adoptive parents were both disturbed (Tienari et al., 2003; Tienari, Wahlberg, & Wynne, 2006).

Furthermore, parents and other caring adults can *uncouple* unfavorable gene–environment correlations by providing children with positive experiences that modify the expression of heredity, yielding favorable outcomes. For example, in a study that tracked the development of 5-year-old identical twins, pair members tended to resemble each other in level of aggression. And the more aggression they displayed, the more maternal anger and criticism they received (a gene–environment correlation). Nevertheless, some mothers treated their twins differently. When followed up at age 7, twins who had been targets of more maternal negativity engaged in even more antisocial behavior. In contrast, their better-treated, genetically identical

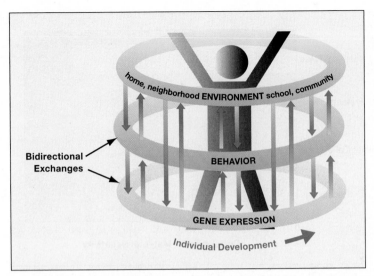

FIGURE 2.11 **Epigenesis.** Development takes place through ongoing, bidirectional exchanges between heredity and all levels of the environment. Genes affect behavior and experiences. Experiences and behavior also affect gene expression. (Based on Gottlieb, 2007.)

counterparts showed a reduction in disruptive acts (Caspi et al., 2004). Good parenting protected them from a spiraling, antisocial course of development.

Accumulating evidence reveals that the relationship between heredity and environment is not a one-way street, from genes to environment to behavior. Rather, like other system influences considered in this and the previous chapter, it is *bidirectional:* Genes affect children's behavior and experiences, but their experiences and behavior also affect gene expression (Diamond, 2009; Gottlieb, 2003; Rutter, 2007). Stimulation—whether *internal* to the child (activity within the cytoplasm of the cell, hormones released into the bloodstream) or *external* to the child (home, neighborhood, school, and society)—modifies gene activity.

This view of the relationship between heredity and environment, depicted in Figure 2.11, is called **epigenesis**, which means development resulting from ongoing, bidirectional exchanges between heredity and all levels of the environment (Gottlieb, 1998, 2007). Researchers are just beginning to clarify the precise mechanisms through which environment alters gene expression. One such mechanism is **methylation**—a biochemical process triggered by certain experiences, in which a set of chemical compounds (called a methyl group) lands on top of a gene and changes its impact, reducing or silencing its expression. Methylation levels can be measured, and they help explain why identical twins, though precisely the same in DNA sequencing, sometimes display strikingly different phenotypes with age.

A case study of a pair of identical-twin adults offers an illustration. Researchers reported that they had been highly similar in intelligence and personality throughout childhood. But after high school, one twin remained close to home, studied law, married, and had children, whereas the other left home, became a journalist, and traveled to war zones around the world, where she repeatedly encountered life-threatening situations and saw many people killed or wounded. Assessed again in their forties, the twins remained similar in intelligence. But compared with the "law twin," the "war twin" engaged in more risky behaviors, including drinking and gambling (Kaminsky et al., 2007). DNA analyses revealed greater methylation of a gene known to play a role in impulse control in the "war twin" than the "law twin"—a difference much larger than is typical for identical twin pairs.

Environmental modification of gene expression can occur at any age, even prenatally, with lasting consequences, as the Biology and Environment box on the following page reveals. And strong evidence exists, from both animal and human studies, that poor-quality parental care reshapes methylation levels of numerous genes, altering the expression of genes involved in children's neurological capacity to manage stress and, thus, elevating their risk for maladjustment (Devlin et al., 2010). The harsh conditions associated with chronic poverty, as well, are believed to exert their impact epigenetically, leaving behind a "biological residue" that compromises the child's potential for a physically and mentally healthy life (Miller et al., 2009). And at times, the impact can be so profound that later experiences can do little to modify the affected the characteristics. Furthermore, animal evidence indicates that some methylated genes are passed to offspring, affecting development in the next generation (Zhang & Meaney, 2010).

We must keep in mind, however, that epigenesis also operates positively: Favorable rearing experiences alter gene expression in ways that enhance development! And some negative epigenetic modifications in gene expression may be reversible through carefully designed interventions (van IJzendoorn, Bakermans-Kranenburg, & Ebstein, 2011). The concept of epigenesis reminds us that the genome is not static but is constantly in flux, both reflecting and affecting its ever-changing environment.

Epigenetics is still an emerging field, and clarifying its mechanisms may prove to be even more complex than efforts to understand DNA sequence variations (Duncan, Pollastri, &

Biology and Environment

Smoking During Pregnancy Alters Gene Expression

Maternal smoking during pregnancy is among the risk factors for *attention-deficit hyperactivity disorder (ADHD)*—one of the most common disorders of childhood, which we will take up in greater detail in Chapter 12. ADHD symptoms—inattention, impulsivity, and overactivity—typically result in serious academic and social problems. Some studies report that individuals who are homozygous for a chromosome-5 gene (DD) containing a special repeat of base pairs are at increased risk for ADHD, though other research has not confirmed any role for this gene (Fisher et al., 2002; Gill et al., 1997; Waldman et al., 1998).

One reason for this inconsistency may be that environmental influences associated with ADHD—such as prenatal exposure to toxins—modify the gene's activity. To test this possibility, researchers recruited several hundred mothers and their 6-month-old babies, obtaining infant blood samples for genetic analysis and asking mothers whether they smoked regularly during pregnancy (Kahn et al., 2003). At a 5-year follow-up, parents responded to a widely used behavior rating scale that assesses children for ADHD symptoms.

Findings revealed that by itself, the DD genotype was unrelated to impulsivity, overactivity, or oppositional behavior. But children whose mothers had smoked during pregnancy scored higher in these behaviors than children of non-smoking mothers. Furthermore, as Figure 2.12 illustrates, 5-year-olds with both prenatal nicotine exposure and DD genetic makeup obtained substantially higher impulsivity, overactivity, and oppositional scores than all other groups—outcomes that persisted even after a variety of other factors (quality of the home environment and maternal ethnicity, marital status, and postbirth smoking) had been controlled.

Another investigation following participants into adolescence obtained similar findings, suggesting that the genotype–prenatal environment effect persists (Becker et al., 2008). What processes might account for it? In animal research, tobacco smoke stimulates the DD genotype to release chemicals in the brain that promote impulsivity and overactivity (Ernst, Moolchan, & Robinson,

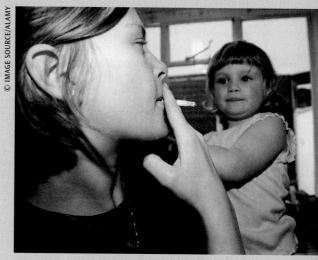

© IMAGE SOURCE/ALAMY

Because her mother smoked during pregnancy, this child may be at increased risk for attention-deficit hyperactivity disorder (ADHD). Prenatal exposure to nicotine seems to alter expression of a chromosome-12 gene in ways that greatly heighten impulsivity, overactivity, and oppositional behavior.

2001). These behaviors, in turn, often evoke harsh, punitive parenting, which triggers defiance in children.

The DD genotype is widespread, present in more than 50 percent of people. Thus, the majority of children prenatally exposed to nicotine are at high risk for learning and behavior problems (refer to page 106 in Chapter 3). Mounting evidence indicates that other genes, in epigenetic interplay with as yet unknown environmental factors, contribute to ADHD symptoms (Hudziak & Rettew, 2009).

FIGURE 2.12   Combined influence of maternal prenatal smoking and genotype on impulsivity and overactivity at age 5. In the absence of prenatal smoking, 5-year-olds who were homozygous for a chromosome-5 gene (DD) showed no elevation in impulsivity and overactivity (orange bar) compared with children of other genotypes (Dd or dd) (red bar). Among children of all genotypes, prenatal smoking was associated with an increase in these behaviors (green and purple bars). And the combination of prenatal smoking and the DD genotype greatly magnified impulsivity and overactivity (purple bar). Children's oppositional behavior followed a similar epigenetic pattern. (Based on Kahn et al., 2003.)

Smoller, 2014). But from what we already know, one lesson is clear: Development is best understood as a series of complex exchanges between nature and nurture. Although children cannot be changed in any way we might desire, environments are continuously transforming their genetic potential. The success of any attempt to improve development depends on the characteristics we want to change, the genetic makeup of the child, and the type and timing of our intervention.

Ask Yourself

- **REVIEW** What is epigenesis, and how does it differ from gene–environment interaction and gene–environment correlation?

- **CONNECT** Explain how each of the following concepts supports the conclusion that genetic influences on children's traits are not constant but change over time: somatic mutation (page 58), niche-picking (page 85), and epigenesis (page 86).

- **APPLY** Bianca's parents are accomplished musicians. At age 4, Bianca began taking piano lessons. By age 10, she was accompanying the school choir. At age 14, she asked if she could attend a special music high school. Explain how gene–environment correlation promoted Bianca's talent.

- **REFLECT** What aspects of your own development—for example, interests, hobbies, college major, or vocational choice—are probably due to niche-picking? Explain.

Summary

Genetic Foundations (p. 51)

2.1 What are genes, and how are they transmitted from one generation to the next?

- Each individual's **phenotype,** or directly observable characteristics, is a product of both **genotype** and environment. **Chromosomes,** rodlike structures within the cell nucleus, contain our hereditary endowment. Along their length are **genes,** segments of **deoxyribonucleic acid (DNA).** Protein-coding genes send instructions for making a rich assortment of proteins to the cytoplasm of the cell; **regulator genes** modify those instructions. A wide range of environmental factors also alter gene expression.

- **Gametes,** or sex cells, are produced through a cell division process called **meiosis,** which halves the number of chromosomes. In meiosis, genes shuffle to create new combinations, ensuring the uniqueness of individuals. Once sperm and ovum unite, the resulting **zygote** will again have the full complement of chromosomes.

- If the fertilizing sperm carries an X chromosome, the child will be a girl; if it contains a Y chromosome, a boy. **Fraternal,** or **dizygotic, twins** result when two ova are released from the mother's ovaries and each is fertilized. **Identical,** or **monozygotic, twins** develop when a zygote divides in two during the early stages of cell duplication.

© F4FOTO/ALAMY

2.2 Describe various patterns of genetic inheritance.

- Traits controlled by single genes follow **dominant–recessive** and **incomplete dominance** patterns of inheritance. **Homozygous** individuals have two identical **alleles,** or forms of a gene. **Heterozygous** individuals, with one dominant and one recessive allele, are **carriers** of the recessive trait. Most recessive genes have little developmental impact, but some bring serious consequences, such as PKU. In incomplete dominance, both alleles are expressed in the phenotype, resulting in a trait that combines aspects of both.

- **X-linked inheritance** applies when recessive disorders are carried on the X chromosome and, therefore, are more likely to affect males. In **genomic imprinting,** one parent's allele is activated, regardless of its makeup, at times profoundly affecting brain development and physical health.

- Harmful genes arise from **mutation,** which can occur spontaneously or be caused by hazardous environmental agents. Germline mutation occurs in the cells that give rise to gametes; somatic mutation can occur in body cells at any time of life.

- Human traits that vary continuously among people, such as intelligence and personality, result from **polygenic inheritance**—the effects of many genes. For such characteristics, scientists must study the influence of heredity indirectly.

2.3 Describe major chromosomal abnormalities, and explain how they occur.

- Most chromosomal abnormalities are due to errors in meiosis. The most common, Down syndrome, results in physical defects and intellectual disability. Disorders of the **sex chromosomes** are milder than defects of the **autosomes.**

Reproductive Choices (p. 61)

2.4 What procedures can assist prospective parents in having healthy children?

- **Genetic counseling** helps couples at risk for giving birth to children with genetic abnormalities consider appropriate reproductive options. **Prenatal diagnostic methods** allow early detection of genetic problems. Advances in genetic engineering and gene therapy offer hope for treating hereditary disorders.

- Reproductive technologies such as donor insemination, in vitro fertilization, surrogate motherhood, and postmenopausal-assisted childbirth permit many individuals to become parents who otherwise would not, but they raise serious legal and ethical concerns.

AP IMAGES/HERALD & REVIEW, JIM BOWLING

- Many parents who cannot conceive or who have a high likelihood of transmitting a genetic disorder decide to adopt. Although adopted children tend to have more learning and emotional problems than children in general, most fare well in the long run. Warm, sensitive parenting predicts favorable development.

Environmental Contexts for Development (p. 67)

2.5 Describe family functioning from the perspective of ecological systems theory, along with aspects of the environment that support family well-being and children's development.

- The first and foremost context for child development is the family, a dynamic system characterized by bidirectional influences, in which each family member's behaviors affect those of others. Both direct and indirect influences operate within the family system, which must continually adjust to new events and changes in its members. Warm, gratifying family ties, which foster effective **coparenting,** predict psychological health.

- **Socioeconomic status (SES)** profoundly affects family functioning. Higher-SES families tend to be smaller, to emphasize psychological traits, and to engage in warm, verbally stimulating interaction with children. Lower-SES families more often use commands, criticism, and physical punishment.

- Children's development in affluent families may be impaired by parents' physical and emotional unavailability. Poverty and homelessness undermine effective parenting and pose serious threats to children's development.

- Children benefit from supportive ties between the family and the surrounding environment, including stable, socially cohesive neighborhoods that provide constructive leisure and enrichment activities and that offer parents access to social support. High-quality schools with frequent parent–teacher contact are also vital.

- The values and practices of cultures and **subcultures** affect all aspects of children's daily lives. **Extended-family households,** which are common among many ethnic minority groups, help protect children from negative effects of poverty and other stressful conditions.

© JEFF GREENBERG/THE IMAGE WORKS

- Consistent cross-national differences in collectivism–individualism powerfully affect approaches to devising **public policies** to address social problems, including those affecting children. Largely because of its strongly individualistic values, the United States lags behind other developed nations in policies safeguarding children and youths.

Understanding the Relationship Between Heredity and Environment (p. 81)

2.6 Explain the various ways heredity and environment may combine to influence complex traits.

- **Behavioral genetics** examines the contributions of nature and nurture to complex traits. Some researchers use **kinship studies** to compute **heritability estimates,** which attempt to quantify the influence of genetic factors on such traits as intelligence and personality. However, the accuracy and usefulness of this approach have been challenged.

- In **gene–environment interaction,** individuals respond differently to varying environments because of their genetic makeup. **Gene–environment correlation** and **niche-picking** describe how children's genes affect the environments to which they are exposed. **Epigenesis** reminds us that development is best understood as a series of complex exchanges between nature and nurture.

Important Terms and Concepts

allele (p. 55)
autosomes (p. 53)
behavioral genetics (p. 82)
carrier (p. 55)
chromosomes (p. 51)
coparenting (p. 69)
deoxyribonucleic acid (DNA) (p. 52)
dominant–recessive inheritance (p. 55)
epigenesis (p. 86)
extended-family household (p. 78)
fraternal, or dizygotic, twins (p. 53)
gametes (p. 53)
gene (p. 52)

genetic counseling (p. 61)
gene–environment interaction (p. 83)
gene–environment correlation (p. 84)
genomic imprinting (p. 58)
genotype (p. 51)
heritability estimate (p. 82)
heterozygous (p. 55)
homozygous (p. 55)
identical, or monozygotic, twins (p. 54)
incomplete dominance (p. 57)
kinship studies (p. 82)
meiosis (p. 53)
methylation (p. 86)

mutation (p. 58)
niche-picking (p. 85)
phenotype (p. 51)
polygenic inheritance (p. 59)
prenatal diagnostic methods (p. 64)
protein-coding genes (p. 52)
public policies (p. 79)
regulator genes (p. 52)
sex chromosomes (p. 53)
socioeconomic status (SES) (p. 70)
subculture (p. 78)
X-linked inheritance (p. 57)
zygote (p. 53)

Prenatal Development

REPRINTED WITH PERMISSION FROM THE INTERNATIONAL MUSEUM OF CHILDREN'S ART, OSLO, NORWAY

"Pregnant Mommy"
Eliska Kocová
5 years, Czech Republic

In this painting, the rapidly growing fetus claims a central place in the parent's world. How is the one-celled organism transformed into a baby with the capacity to participate in family life? What factors support or undermine this earliest period of development? Chapter 3 provides answers to these questions.

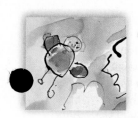

One fall, Yolanda and Jay enrolled in an evening section of our department's child development course, when Yolanda was two months pregnant. In their early thirties, married for several years, and with their careers well under way, they had decided to have a baby. Each week, they arrived for class full of questions: "How does the baby grow before birth?" "When is each organ formed?" "Has its heart begun to beat?" "Can it hear, feel, or sense our presence?"

Most of all, Yolanda and Jay wanted to do everything possible to make sure their baby would be born healthy. Yolanda started to wonder about her diet and whether she should keep up her daily aerobic workout. And she asked whether an aspirin for a headache, a glass of wine at dinner, or a few cups of coffee during the workday might be harmful.

In this chapter, we answer Yolanda and Jay's questions, along with a great many more that scientists have asked about the events before birth. We begin our discussion with these puzzling questions: Why is it that generation after generation, most couples who fall in love want to become parents? And what factors influence their decision to have just one child or more than one?

Then we trace prenatal development, paying special attention to supports for healthy growth as well as damaging influences that threaten the child's health and survival. Because the changes taking place during these nine months are so astonishing, the prenatal environment can exert a powerful, lasting impact—for better or for worse—on physical and mental health. Finally, we look at how expectant parents prepare psychologically for the arrival of the baby and start to forge a new sense of self as mother or father. ■

Motivations for Parenthood

TAKE A MOMENT... What, in your view, are the benefits and drawbacks of having children? How large would your ideal family be, and why? As part of her semester project, Yolanda interviewed her grandmother, asking why she had wanted children and how she had settled on a particular family size. Yolanda's grandmother, whose children were born in the 1960s, replied:

> We didn't think much about whether or not to have children in those days. We just had them—everybody did. It would have seemed odd not to! I was 22 years old when I had the first of my four children, and I had four because—well, I wouldn't have had just one because we all thought children needed brothers and sisters, and only children could end up spoiled and selfish. Life is more interesting and enjoyable with children, you know.

Why Have Children?

In the past, the issue of whether to have children was, for many adults, a biological given or a compelling social expectation. Today, in Western industrialized nations, it is a matter of true individual choice. Effective birth control techniques enable adults to avoid having children in most instances. And changing cultural values allow

3.1 How has decision making about childbearing changed over the past half century, and what are the consequences for child rearing and child development?

⇟ LOOK and **⇟**
⇟ LISTEN ⇟

Interview several parents of infants or preschoolers about the benefits and challenges of parenthood. Ask which issues they considered before starting a family. How deliberate about family planning were they?

people to remain childless with far less fear of social criticism than a generation or two ago (Scott, 2009). Nevertheless, the 6 percent of American 18- to 40-year-olds who currently say they do not want children is just slightly higher than the 5 percent who said so a quarter century ago. Despite media messages suggesting that Americans are increasingly preferring a childless lifestyle, the desire for children remains the norm: A survey of over 5,000 U.S. adults of childbearing age revealed that more than 90 percent already have children or are planning to have them (Gallup, 2013). Whether people actually become parents is affected by a complex array of contextual factors, including economic conditions, partnership changes, career goals, religious values, health conditions, and availability of supportive government and workplace family policies (Mills et al., 2011; Theil, 2006).

Besides these influences, a vital personal factor called *childbearing motivations*—each person's disposition to respond positively or negatively to the idea of parenthood—affects people's decision to have children as well as their psychological adjustment to pregnancy and the new baby's arrival. In Western nations, these motivations have changed over time, increasingly emphasizing individual fulfillment and deemphasizing obligation to society (Frejka et al., 2008).

When Americans and Europeans are asked about their motivations for parenthood, they mention a variety of advantages and disadvantages, which are listed in Table 3.1. Although some ethnic and regional differences exist, in all groups highly rated reasons for having children include personal rewards—for example, the warm, affectionate relationship and opportunities for care and teaching that children provide. Also frequently mentioned are social and economic returns, such as affirmation of one's adult status and children as a source of caregiving and financial support in later life (Guedes et al., 2013). Less important, but still mentioned, is a sense of future continuity—having someone to carry on after one's own death. And occasionally, couples look to parenthood as a gratifying opportunity to share in a challenging but important life task and to deepen their relationship.

Most adults also realize that having children means years of extra burdens and responsibilities. Among disadvantages of parenthood, they most often cite concerns about role overload (not enough time for both family and work responsibilities), doubts about their own readiness for parenthood, and worries about bringing up children in a troubled world. The financial strains of child rearing follow close behind. According to a conservative estimate, new parents in the United States today will spend about $300,000 to rear a child from birth to age 18, and many will incur substantial additional expense for higher education and financial dependency during emerging adulthood—a reality that has contributed to the declining birthrate in industrialized nations (U.S. Department of Agriculture, 2013a).

Greater freedom to choose whether, when, and how to have children (see the discussion of reproductive choices in Chapter 2) makes contemporary family planning more challenging as well as intentional than it was in Yolanda's grandmother's day. Still, about 30 percent of U.S. newborn babies are the result of unintended pregnancies, with most born to low-income, less educated mothers—circumstances associated with delayed prenatal care, premature birth, and child health problems (Guttmacher Institute, 2013). Yet opportunities to explore childbearing motivations in high school, college, and community-based health education classes and through family-planning counseling might encourage more adults to make informed and personally meaningful decisions—a trend that would increase the chances that they would have children when ready, find parenting an enriching experience, and rear physically and mentally healthy children.

© ALAN CAREY/THE IMAGE WORKS

One reason often given for having children is the opportunity for care and teaching that a young child provides.

TABLE 3.1	Advantages and Disadvantages of Parenthood Mentioned by American and European Adults of Childbearing Age (in general order of importance)
ADVANTAGES	**DISADVANTAGES**
Giving and receiving warmth and affection, providing care and teaching	Constant worries over and responsibility for children's health, safety, and well-being
Personal fulfillment, enhancing life's meaning	Role overload—not enough time to meet both child-rearing and job responsibilities
Creating one's own family	
Nurturing a new person and personality	Risks of bringing up children in a world plagued by crime, war, and pollution
Being accepted as a responsible and mature member of the community	Fear that children will turn out badly, through no fault of one's own
Having a source of caregiving and economic support in times of need	
Carrying on one's family name, lineage, heritage, or values	Financial strain
Strengthening the couple relationship through a shared project	Reduced time to spend with partner
Fulfilling a partner's desire for parenthood	Loss of privacy

Sources: Guedes et al., 2013; Miller, 2009.

How Large a Family?

In contrast to her grandmother, Yolanda—like most U.S. adults—plans to have no more than two children. And she and Jay are talking about whether to limit their family to a single child. In 1960, the average number of children per American woman of childbearing age was 3.1. Currently, it is 2.1 in the United States, 1.9 in the United Kingdom, 1.8 in Australia, 1.7 in Sweden, 1.6 in Canada, 1.4 in Germany, and 1.3 in Italy and Japan (U.S. Census Bureau, 2014a, 2014b). In addition to more effective birth control, a major reason for this decline is that a family size of one or two children is more compatible with a woman's decision to divide her energies between family and career. The tendency of many couples, like Yolanda and Jay, to delay having children until they are well-established professionally and secure economically also contributes to smaller family size. Furthermore, marital instability plays a role: More couples today get divorced before their childbearing plans are complete.

Popular advice to prospective parents often recommends limiting family size in the interests of "child-rearing quality"—more parental affection, involvement, and material resources per child, which enhance children's intellectual development. Do large families really make less intelligent children, as prevailing attitudes suggest?

For years, researchers thought that earlier birth order and wider spacing might grant children more parental attention and stimulation and, therefore, result in more favorable cognitive development. But recent evidence indicates that birth order and spacing are unrelated to children's intelligence (Kanazawa, 2012; Rodgers et al., 2000; Wichman, Rodgers, & MacCallum, 2007). Why is this so? Parents' differential treatment of siblings is far more responsive to children's personalities, interests, and behaviors than to these aspects of family structure.

Other evidence confirms that rather than parenting quality declining as new children are born, parents reallocate their energies. In a longitudinal study of Canadian two-parent families, new births led to a decrease in maternal affection toward older siblings, though most mothers probably remained generally warm. At the same time, the consistency of parenting—the extent to which mothers insisted older children meet their expectations for mature behavior, such as completing chores, doing homework, and treating others respectfully—rose over time (Strohschein et al., 2008). After a new baby joined the family, mothers seemed to reorganize their parenting practices to best meet all their children's needs.

Furthermore, the well-documented association between large family size and lower intelligence test scores of all siblings can be entirely explained by a

PHOTODISC/GETTY IMAGES

Average family size has declined in recent decades in most industrialized nations. But, contrary to popular belief, having more children does not reduce the intelligence or life chances of later-born children.

strong trend for low-SES mothers to give birth to more children. Among children of well-educated, economically advantaged mothers, the family size–intelligence relationship disappears (Guo & VanWey, 1999; Wichman, Rodgers, & MacCallum, 2007). In sum, although many good reasons exist for limiting family size, the concern that additional births will reduce parenting quality and, thus, impair children's skills and life chances is not warranted.

Is Yolanda's grandmother right when she says that parents who have just one child are likely to end up with a spoiled, selfish youngster? As we will see in Chapter 13, research also challenges this widely held belief. Overall, only children are just as well-adjusted as children with siblings.

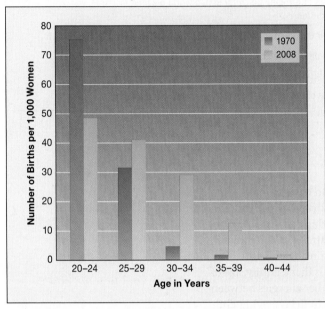

FIGURE 3.1 **First births to American women of different ages in 1970 and 2012.** The birthrate decreased during this period for women 20 to 24 years of age, whereas it increased for women 25 years of age and older. For women in their thirties, the birthrate rose nearly fivefold. Similar trends have occurred in other industrialized nations. (Based on U.S. Census Bureau, 2014b.)

Is There a Best Time During Adulthood to Have a Child?

Yolanda's grandmother gave birth to her first child in her early twenties. Yolanda, at age 32, is pregnant for the first time. Many people believe that couples should, ideally, have children in their twenties because the risk of having a baby with a chromosomal disorder increases with maternal age. Advanced paternal age is also associated with elevated risk of certain genetically influenced disorders, including autism and schizophrenia (see Chapter 2). Furthermore, younger parents have more energy to keep up with active children.

Nevertheless, as Figure 3.1 reveals, first births to women in their thirties have increased greatly over the past several decades. Many people are delaying childbearing until their education is complete, their careers are established, and they know they can support a child. Older parents may be somewhat less energetic than they once were, but they are financially better off and emotionally more mature. For these reasons, they may be better able to invest in parenting.

Nevertheless, reproductive capacity does decline with age. Fertility problems among women increase from age 15 to 50, with a sharp rise in the mid-thirties. Between ages 25 and 34, 12 percent of women are affected, a figure that climbs to 39 percent for 35- to 39-year-olds and to 47 percent for 40- to 44-year-olds. Age also affects male reproductive capacity. Amount of semen, concentration of sperm in each ejaculation, and quality of sperm decline gradually after age 35. Consequently, compared to a 25-year-old man, a 40-year-old is 12 times as likely to take more than two years to achieve a conception (Chandra, Copen, & Stephen, 2013; Lambert, Masson, & Fisch, 2006).

Women with demanding careers are especially likely to delay parenthood (Tough, Vekved, & Newburn-Cook, 2012). Many believe, incorrectly, that if they have difficulty conceiving, they can rely on reproductive technologies. But recall from Chapter 2 that the success of these procedures drops steadily with age. Although no one time during adulthood is best to begin parenthood, individuals who decide to put off pregnancy until well into their thirties or early forties risk having fewer children than they desire or none at all.

Ask Yourself

- **REVIEW** Explain why the common assumption that larger families reduce child-rearing quality, resulting in less intelligent children, is mistaken.

- **CONNECT** Why is it incorrect for couples who postpone childbearing until age 35 or later to conclude that medical advances can overcome fertility problems? (See Chapter 2, page 62.)

- **APPLY** Rhonda and Mark, a career-oriented couple in their early thirties, are thinking about having a baby. What factors should they keep in mind as they decide whether to add to their family at this time in their lives?

- **REFLECT** Ask one of your parents or grandparents to list his or her childbearing motivations. How do those motivations compare with your own? What factors—for example, education or cultural changes—might account for any differences?

Prenatal Development

3.2 List the three phases of prenatal development, and describe the major milestones of each.

The sperm and ovum that unite to form the new individual are uniquely suited for the task of reproduction. The ovum is a tiny sphere, measuring ¹⁄₁₇₅ inch in diameter, that is barely visible to the naked eye as a dot the size of the period at the end of this sentence. But in its microscopic world, it is a giant—the largest cell in the human body. The ovum's size makes it a perfect target for the much smaller sperm, which measure only ¹⁄₅₀₀ inch.

Conception

About once every 28 days, in the middle of a woman's menstrual cycle, an ovum bursts from one of her *ovaries,* two walnut-sized organs located deep inside her abdomen, and is drawn into one of two *fallopian tubes*—long, thin structures that lead to the hollow, soft-lined uterus (see Figure 3.2). While the ovum is traveling, the spot on the ovary from which it was released, now called the *corpus luteum,* secretes hormones that prepare the lining of the uterus to receive a fertilized ovum. If pregnancy does not occur, the corpus luteum shrinks, and the lining of the uterus is discarded two weeks later with menstruation.

The male produces sperm in vast numbers—an average of 300 million a day—in the *testes,* two glands located in the *scrotum,* sacs that lie just behind the penis. In the final process of maturation, each sperm develops a tail that permits it to swim

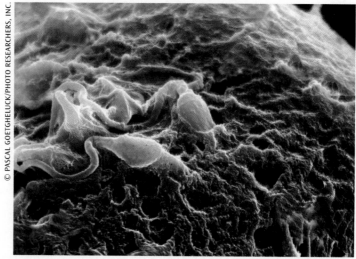

© PASCAL GOETGHELUCK/PHOTO RESEARCHERS, INC.

In this photo taken with the aid of a powerful microscope, sperm penetrate the surface of the enormous-looking ovum, the largest cell in the human body. When one sperm successfully fertilizes the ovum, the resulting zygote begins to duplicate.

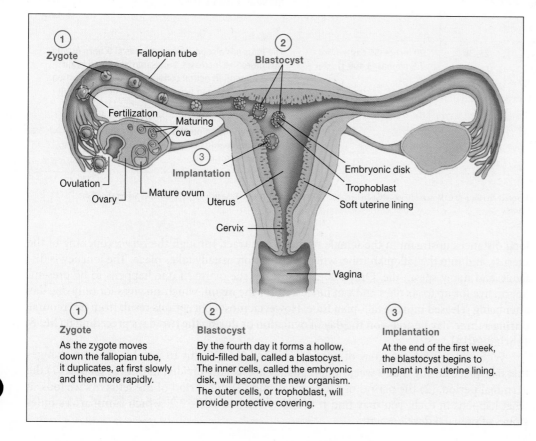

FIGURE 3.2 Female reproductive organs, showing fertilization, early cell duplication, and implantation. (From *Before We Are Born,* 6th ed., by K. L. Moore and T. V. N. Persaud, p. 87. Copyright © 2003, reprinted with permission from Elsevier, Inc.)

① **Zygote**
Fallopian tube

② **Blastocyst**

Fertilization
Maturing ova

③ **Implantation**

Ovulation
Mature ovum
Ovary
Uterus

Embryonic disk
Trophoblast
Soft uterine lining

Cervix

Vagina

① **Zygote**
As the zygote moves down the fallopian tube, it duplicates, at first slowly and then more rapidly.

② **Blastocyst**
By the fourth day it forms a hollow, fluid-filled ball, called a blastocyst. The inner cells, called the embryonic disk, will become the new organism. The outer cells, or trophoblast, will provide protective covering.

③ **Implantation**
At the end of the first week, the blastocyst begins to implant in the uterine lining.

TABLE 3.2	Milestones of Prenatal Development			
TRIMESTER	**PRENATAL PHASE**	**WEEKS**	**LENGTH AND WEIGHT**	**MAJOR EVENTS**
First	Germinal	1		The one-celled zygote multiplies and forms a blastocyst.
		2		The blastocyst burrows into the uterine lining. Structures that feed and protect the developing organism begin to form—*amnion, chorion, yolk sac, placenta,* and *umbilical cord.*
	Embryo	3–4	¼ inch (6 mm)	A primitive brain and spinal cord appear. Heart, muscles, ribs, backbone, and digestive tract begin to develop.
		5–8	1 inch (2.5 cm); ½ ounce (4 g)	Many external body structures (face, arms, legs, toes, fingers) and internal organs form. The sense of touch begins to develop, and the embryo can move.
	Fetus	9–12	3 inches (7.6 cm); less than 1 ounce (28 g)	Rapid increase in size begins. Nervous system, organs, and muscles become organized and connected, and new behavioral capacities (kicking, thumb sucking, mouth opening, and rehearsal of breathing) appear. External genitals are well-formed, and the fetus's sex is evident.
Second		13–24	12 inches (30 cm); 1.8 pounds (820 g)	The fetus continues to enlarge rapidly. In the middle of this period, the mother can feel fetal movements. Vernix and lanugo keep the fetus's skin from chapping in the amniotic fluid. Most of the brain's neurons are in place by 24 weeks. Eyes are sensitive to light, and the fetus reacts to sound.
Third		25–38	20 inches (50 cm); 7.5 pounds (3,400 g)	The fetus has a good chance of survival if born during this time. Size increases. Lungs mature. Rapid brain development, in neural connectivity and organization, enables sensory and behavioral capacities to expand. In the middle of this period, a layer of fat is added under the skin. Antibodies are transmitted from mother to fetus to protect against disease. Most fetuses rotate into an upside-down position in preparation for birth.

Source: Moore, Persaud, & Torchia, 2013.
Photos (from top to bottom): © Claude Cortier/Photo Researchers, Inc.; © G. Moscoso/Photo Researchers, Inc.; © John Watney/Photo Researchers, Inc.; © James Stevenson/Photo Researchers, Inc.; © Lennart Nilsson, *A Child Is Born*/Scanpix.

long distances upstream in the female reproductive tract, through the *cervix* (opening of the uterus), and into the fallopian tube, where fertilization usually takes place. The journey is difficult, and many sperm die. Only 300 to 500 reach the ovum, if one happens to be present. Sperm live for up to six days and can lie in wait for the ovum, which survives for only one day after being released into the fallopian tube. However, most conceptions result from intercourse during a three-day period—on the day of ovulation or during the two days preceding it (Mu & Fehring, 2014).

With conception, the story of prenatal development begins to unfold. The vast changes that take place during the 38 weeks of pregnancy are usually divided into three phases: (1) the germinal period, (2) the period of the embryo, and (3) the period of the fetus. As we look at what happens in each, you may find it useful to refer to Table 3.2, which summarizes milestones of prenatal development.

Germinal Period

The germinal period lasts about two weeks, from fertilization and formation of the zygote until the tiny mass of cells drifts down and out of the fallopian tube and attaches itself to the wall of the uterus. The zygote's first cell duplication is long and drawn out; it is not complete until about 30 hours after conception. Gradually, new cells are added at a faster rate. By the fourth day, 60 to 70 cells exist that form a hollow, fluid-filled ball called a **blastocyst** (refer again to Figure 3.2). The cells on the inside of the blastocyst, called the **embryonic disk,** will become the new organism; the thin outer ring of cells, termed the **trophoblast,** will become the structures that provide protective covering and nourishment.

IMPLANTATION   Between the seventh and ninth days, **implantation** occurs: The blastocyst burrows deep into the uterine lining. Surrounded by the woman's nourishing blood, it starts to grow in earnest. At first, the trophoblast (protective outer layer) multiplies fastest. It forms a membrane, called the **amnion,** that encloses the developing organism in **amniotic fluid,** which helps keep the temperature of the prenatal world constant and provides a cushion against any jolts caused by the woman's movement. A *yolk sac* emerges that produces blood cells until the developing liver, spleen, and bone marrow are mature enough to take over this function (Moore, Persaud, & Torchia, 2013).

The events of these first two weeks are delicate and uncertain. As many as 30 percent of zygotes do not survive this period. In some, the sperm and ovum did not join properly. In others, for some unknown reason, cell duplication never begins. By preventing implantation in these cases, nature eliminates most prenatal abnormalities (Sadler, 2010).

THE PLACENTA AND UMBILICAL CORD   By the end of the second week, cells of the trophoblast form another protective membrane—the **chorion,** which surrounds the amnion. From the chorion, tiny fingerlike *villi*, or blood vessels, emerge.[1] As these villi burrow into the uterine wall, the placenta starts to develop. By bringing the mother's and the embryo's blood close together, the **placenta** permits food and oxygen to reach the developing organism and waste products to be carried away. A membrane forms that allows these substances to be exchanged but prevents the mother's and the embryo's blood from mixing directly (see Figure 3.3).

FIGURE 3.3   **Cross-section of the uterus, showing detail of the placenta.** The embryo's blood flows from the umbilical cord arteries into the chorionic villi and returns via the umbilical cord vein. The mother's blood circulates in spaces surrounding the chorionic villi. A membrane between the two blood supplies permits food and oxygen to be delivered and waste products to be carried away. The two blood supplies do not mix directly. The umbilical arteries carry oxygen-poor blood (shown in blue) to the placenta, and the umbilical vein carries oxygen-rich blood (shown in red) to the fetus. (From *Before We Are Born,* 6th ed., by K. L. Moore and T. V. N. Persaud, p. 95. Copyright © 2003, reprinted with permission from Elsevier, Inc.)

© LENNART NILSSON, *A CHILD IS BORN*/SCANPIX

Period of the zygote: seventh to ninth day. The fertilized ovum duplicates at an increasingly rapid rate, forming a hollow ball of cells, or blastocyst, by the fourth day after fertilization. Here the blastocyst, magnified thousands of times, burrows into the uterine lining between the seventh and ninth day.

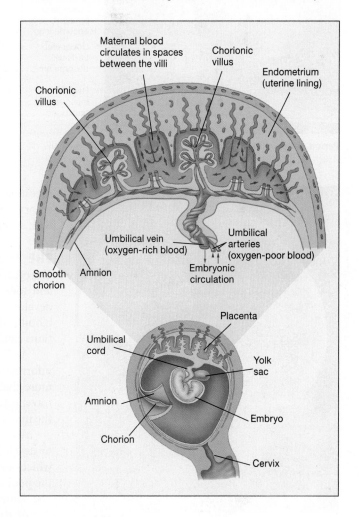

---

[1]Recall from Chapter 2 that *chorionic villus sampling* is the prenatal diagnostic method that can be performed earliest, at nine weeks after conception. In this procedure, tissues from the ends of the villi are removed and examined for genetic abnormalities.

The placenta is connected to the developing organism by the **umbilical cord,** which first appears as a primitive body stalk and, during the course of pregnancy, grows to a length of 1 to 3 feet. The umbilical cord contains one large vein that delivers blood loaded with nutrients and two arteries that remove waste products. The force of blood flowing through the cord keeps it firm, much like a garden hose, so it seldom tangles while the embryo, like a space-walking astronaut, floats freely in its fluid-filled chamber (Moore, Persaud, & Torchia, 2013).

By the end of the germinal period, the developing organism has found food and shelter. Already, it is a complex being. These dramatic beginnings take place before most mothers know they are pregnant.

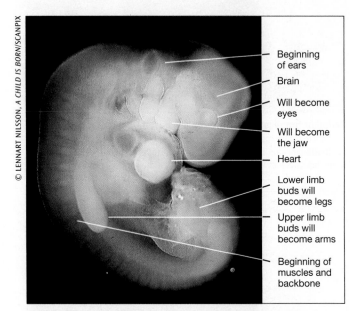

Beginning of ears

Brain

Will become eyes

Will become the jaw

Heart

Lower limb buds will become legs

Upper limb buds will become arms

Beginning of muscles and backbone

Period of the embryo: fourth week. This 4-week-old embryo is only ¼ inch long, but many body structures have begun to form.

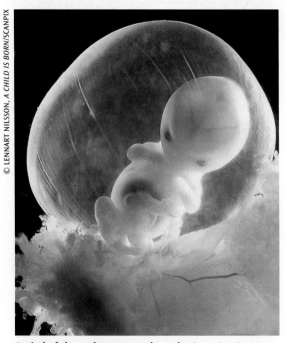

Period of the embryo: seventh week. The embryo's posture is more upright. Body structures—eyes, nose, arms, legs, and internal organs—are more distinct. The embryo now responds to touch. It also can move, although at less than one inch long and an ounce in weight, it is still too tiny to be felt by the mother.

Period of the Embryo

The period of the **embryo** lasts from implantation through the eighth week of pregnancy. During these brief six weeks, the most rapid prenatal changes take place, as the groundwork is laid for all body structures and internal organs. Because all parts of the body are forming, the embryo is especially vulnerable to interference with healthy development. But the short time span of embryonic growth helps limit opportunities for serious harm.

LAST HALF OF THE FIRST MONTH In the first week of this period, the embryonic disk forms three layers of cells: (1) the *ectoderm,* which will become the nervous system and skin; (2) the *mesoderm,* from which will develop the muscles, skeleton, circulatory system, and other internal organs; and (3) the *endoderm,* which will become the digestive system, lungs, urinary tract, and glands. These three layers give rise to all parts of the body.

At first, the nervous system develops fastest. The ectoderm folds over to form the **neural tube,** or spinal cord. At 3½ weeks, the top swells to form the brain. While the nervous system is developing, the heart begins to pump blood, and muscles, backbone, ribs, and digestive tract start to appear. At the end of the first month, the curled embryo—only ¼ inch long—consists of millions of organized groups of cells with specific functions.

THE SECOND MONTH In the second month, growth continues rapidly. The eyes, ears, nose, jaw, and neck form. Tiny buds become arms, legs, fingers, and toes. Internal organs are more distinct: The intestines grow, the heart develops separate chambers, and the liver and spleen take over production of blood cells so that the yolk sac is no longer needed. Changing body proportions cause the embryo's posture to become more upright.

At 7 weeks, production of neurons (nerve cells that store and transmit information) begins deep inside the neural tube at the astounding pace of more than 250,000 per minute (Nelson, 2011). Once formed, neurons begin traveling along tiny threads to their permanent locations, where they will form the major parts of the brain.

Around this time, ovaries in the female and testes in the male have begun to develop. By 8 weeks, the testes start to secrete the hormone testosterone, which will stimulate differentiation of male internal reproductive organs and the penis and scrotum during the coming month. In the absence of testosterone, female reproductive organs form.

At the end of this period, the embryo—about 1 inch long and ½ ounce in weight—can already sense its world. It responds to touch, particularly in the mouth area and on the soles of the feet. And it can move, although its tiny flutters are still too light to be felt by the mother (Moore, Persaud, & Torchia, 2013).

Period of the Fetus

The period of the **fetus,** from the ninth week to the end of pregnancy, is the longest prenatal period. During this "growth and finishing" phase, the developing organism increases rapidly in size, especially from the ninth to the twentieth week.

THE THIRD MONTH   In the third month, the organs, muscles, and nervous system start to become organized and connected. When the brain signals, the fetus kicks, bends its arms, forms a fist, curls its toes, turns its head, opens its mouth, and even sucks its thumb, stretches, and yawns. Body position changes are frequent, occurring as often as 25 times per hour (Einspieler, Marschik, & Prechtl, 2008). The tiny lungs begin to expand and contract in an early rehearsal of breathing movements.

By the twelfth week, the external genitals are well-formed, and the sex of the fetus can be detected with ultrasound (Sadler, 2010). Other finishing touches appear, such as fingernails, toenails, tooth buds, eyebrows, eyelids, and eyelashes. The heartbeat can now be heard through a stethoscope.

Prenatal development is sometimes divided into **trimesters,** or three equal time periods. At the end of the third month, the *first trimester* is complete.

THE SECOND TRIMESTER   By the middle of the second trimester, between 17 and 20 weeks, the new being has grown large enough that the mother can feel its movements. A white, cheeselike substance called **vernix** protects its skin from chapping during the long months spent bathing in the amniotic fluid. White, downy hair called **lanugo** also appears over the entire body, helping the vernix stick to the skin.

At the end of the second trimester, many organs are well-developed. And most of the brain's billions of neurons are in place; few will be produced after this time. However, *glial cells,* which support and feed the neurons, continue to increase at a rapid rate throughout the remaining months of pregnancy, as well as after birth. Consequently, brain weight increases tenfold from the twentieth week until birth (Roelfsema et al., 2004). At the same time, neurons begin forming *synapses,* or connections, at a rapid pace.

Brain growth means new sensory and behavioral capacities. The 20-week-old fetus can be stimulated as well as irritated by sounds. Slow eye movements appear, with rapid eye movements following at 22 weeks. And if a doctor looks inside the uterus using fetoscopy (see Chapter 2, page 64), fetuses try to shield their eyes from the light with their hands, indicating that sight has begun to emerge (Moore, Persaud, & Torchia, 2013). Still, a fetus born at this time cannot survive. Its lungs are immature, and the brain cannot yet control breathing movements or body temperature.

THE THIRD TRIMESTER   During the final trimester, a fetus born early has a chance for survival. The point at which the baby can first survive, called the **age of viability,** occurs sometime between 22 and 26 weeks (Moore, Persaud, & Torchia, 2013). A baby born between the seventh and eighth month, however, usually needs oxygen assistance to breathe. Although the brain's respiratory center is now mature, tiny air sacs in the lungs are not yet ready to inflate and exchange carbon dioxide for oxygen.

The brain continues to make great strides. The *cerebral cortex,* the seat of human intelligence, enlarges. Convolutions and grooves in its surface appear, permitting a dramatic increase in surface area that allows

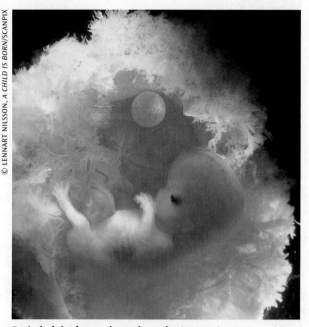

Period of the fetus: eleventh week. The organism grows rapidly, and body structures are completed. At 11 weeks, the brain and muscles are better connected. The fetus can kick, bend its arms, open and close its hands and mouth, and suck its thumb. Notice the yolk sac, which shrinks as pregnancy advances. The internal organs have taken over its function of producing blood cells.

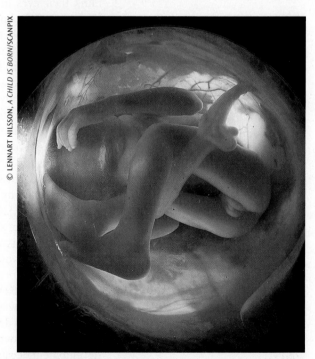

Period of the fetus: twenty-second week. This fetus is almost a foot long and weighs slightly more than one pound. Its movements can be felt easily by the mother and by other family members who place a hand on her abdomen. The fetus has reached the age of viability; if born, it has a slim chance of surviving.

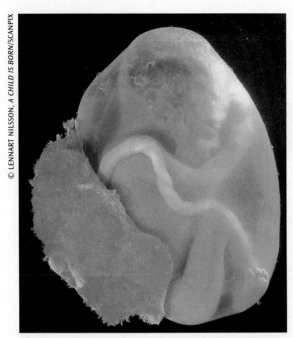

Period of the fetus: thirty-sixth week. This fetus fills the uterus. To support its need for nourishment, the umbilical cord and placenta have grown large. The vernix (cheeselike substance) on the skin protects it from chapping. The fetus has accumulated a layer of fat to assist with temperature regulation after birth. In two more weeks, it will be full-term.

for maximum prenatal brain growth without the full-term baby's head becoming too large to pass through the birth canal. As rapid gains in neural connectivity and organization continue, the fetus spends more time awake. At 20 weeks, fetal heart rate reveals no periods of alertness. But by 28 weeks, fetuses are awake about 11 percent of the time, a figure that rises to 16 percent just before birth (DiPietro et al., 1996). Between 30 and 34 weeks, fetuses show rhythmic alternations between sleep and wakefulness that gradually increase in organization (Rivkees, 2003). Around this time, synchrony between fetal heart rate and motor activity peaks: A rise in heart rate is usually followed within five seconds by a burst of motor activity (DiPietro et al., 2006). These are clear signs that coordinated neural networks are beginning to form in the brain.

By the end of pregnancy, the fetus also takes on the beginnings of a personality. Higher fetal activity in the final weeks predicts a more active infant in the first month of life—a relationship that, for boys, persists into early childhood (Groome et al., 1999). Fetal activity is linked in other ways to infant temperament. In one study, more active fetuses during the third trimester became 1-year-olds who could better handle frustration and 2-year-olds who were less fearful, in that they more readily interacted with toys and with an unfamiliar adult in a laboratory (DiPietro et al., 2002). Perhaps fetal activity level is an indicator of healthy neurological development, which fosters adaptability in childhood. The relationships just described, however, are only modest. As we will see in Chapter 7, sensitive caregiving can modify the temperaments of children who have difficulty adapting to new experiences.

The third trimester also brings greater responsiveness to external stimulation. As we will see later when we discuss newborn capacities, fetuses acquire taste and odor preferences from bathing in and swallowing amniotic fluid (its makeup is influenced by the mother's diet). Between 23 and 30 weeks, connections form between the cerebral cortex and brain regions involved in pain sensitivity. By this time, painkillers should be used in any surgical procedures performed on a fetus (Lee et al., 2005). Around 28 weeks, fetuses blink their eyes in reaction to nearby sounds (Kisilevsky & Low, 1998; Saffran, Werker, & Werner, 2006). And around 30 weeks, fetuses presented with a repeated auditory stimulus against the mother's abdomen initially react with a rise in heart rate, electrical brain-wave recordings, and body movements. Then responsiveness gradually declines, indicating *habituation* (adaptation) to the sound. If a new auditory stimulus is introduced, heart rate and brain waves recover to a high level, revealing that the fetus recognizes the new sound as distinct from the originally presented stimulus (Hepper, Dornan, & Lynch, 2012; Muenssinger et al., 2013). This indicates that fetuses can remember for at least a brief period.

Within the next six weeks, fetuses distinguish the tone and rhythm of different voices and sounds. They show systematic heart-rate and brain-wave changes in response to the mother's voice versus the father's or a stranger's, to their native language (English) versus a foreign language (Mandarin Chinese), and to a simple familiar melody (descending tones) versus an unfamiliar melody (ascending tones) (Granier-Deferre et al., 2003; Kisilevsky & Hains, 2011; Kisilevsky et al., 2009; Lecanuet et al., 1993; Lee & Kisilevsky, 2013; Voegtline et al., 2013). And in one clever study, mothers read aloud Dr. Seuss's lively book *The Cat in the Hat* each day during the last six weeks of pregnancy. After birth, their infants learned to turn on recordings of the mother's voice by sucking on nipples (DeCasper & Spence, 1986). They sucked hardest to hear *The Cat in the Hat*—the sound they had come to know while still in the womb.

TAKE A MOMENT... On the basis of these findings, would you recommend that expectant mothers provide fetuses with stimulation designed to enhance later development? Notice how risky it is to draw such conclusions. First, specific forms of fetal stimulation, such as reading aloud or playing classical music, are unlikely to have a long-lasting impact on cognitive development because of the developing child's constantly changing capacities and experiences, which can override the impact of fetal stimulation (Lecanuet, Granier-Deferre, & DeCasper, 2005). Second, although ordinary stimulation contributes to the functioning of sensory systems, excessive input can be dangerous. For example, animal studies indicate that a sensitive period (see page 24 in Chapter 1) exists in which the fetal ear is highly susceptible to injury. During that time, prolonged exposure to sounds that are harmless to the mature ear can permanently damage fetal inner-ear structures (Pierson, 1996).

In the final three months, the fetus gains more than 5 pounds and grows 7 inches. As it fills the uterus, it gradually moves less often. In addition, brain development, which enables the organism to inhibit behavior, contributes to a decline in physical activity (DiPietro et al., 1996). In the eighth month, a layer of fat is added to assist with temperature regulation. The fetus also receives antibodies from the mother's blood to protect against illnesses, since the newborn's immune system will not work well until several months after birth. In the last weeks, most fetuses assume an upside-down position, partly because of the shape of the uterus and partly because the head is heavier than the feet. Growth slows, and birth is about to take place.

Ask Yourself

- **REVIEW** Why is the period of the embryo regarded as the most dramatic prenatal period? Why is the period of the fetus called the "growth and finishing" phase?

- **CONNECT** How is brain development related to fetal capacities and behavior? What implications do individual differences in fetal behavior have for infant temperament after birth?

- **APPLY** Amy, two months pregnant, wonders how the embryo is being fed and what parts of the body have formed. "I don't look pregnant yet, so does that mean not much development has taken place?" she asks. How would you respond to Amy?

Prenatal Environmental Influences

Although the prenatal environment is far more constant than the world outside the womb, a great many factors can affect the embryo and fetus. Yolanda and Jay learned that parents—and society as a whole—can do a great deal to create a safe environment for development before birth.

Teratogens

The term **teratogen** refers to any environmental agent that causes damage during the prenatal period. Scientists chose this label (from the Greek word *teras,* meaning "malformation" or "monstrosity") because they first learned about harmful prenatal influences from cases in which babies had been profoundly damaged. But the harm done by teratogens is not always simple and straightforward. It depends on the following factors:

- *Dose.* As we discuss particular teratogens, you will see that larger doses over longer time periods usually have more negative effects.
- *Heredity.* The genetic makeup of the mother and the developing organism plays an important role. Some individuals are better able than others to withstand harmful environments.
- *Other negative influences.* The presence of several negative factors at once, such as additional teratogens, poor nutrition, and lack of medical care, can worsen the impact of a harmful agent.
- *Age.* The effects of teratogens vary with the age of the organism at time of exposure. To understand this last idea, think of the *sensitive period* concept. Recall that a sensitive period is a limited time span in which a part of the body or a behavior is biologically prepared to develop rapidly. During that time, it is especially sensitive to its surroundings. If the environment is harmful, then damage occurs, and recovery is difficult and sometimes impossible.

3.3 What are teratogens, and what factors influence their impact?

3.4 List agents known to be or suspected of being teratogens, and discuss evidence supporting their harmful impact.

3.5 Describe the impact of other maternal factors on prenatal development.

3.6 Why is early and regular health care vital during the prenatal period?

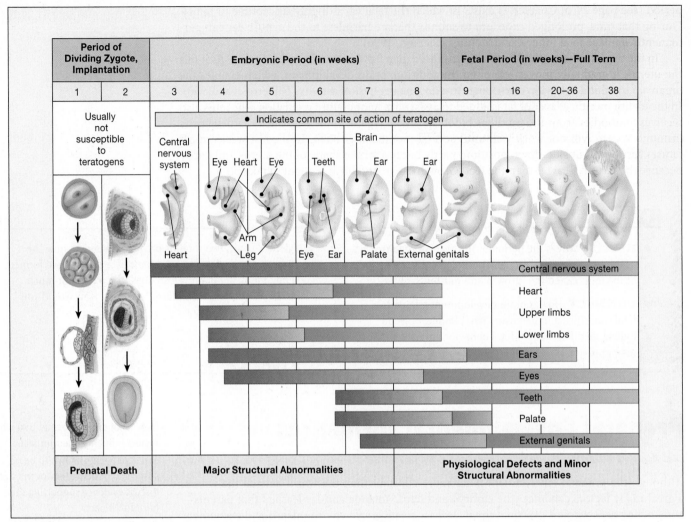

FIGURE 3.4 **Sensitive periods in prenatal development.** Each organ or structure has a sensitive period, during which its development may be disturbed. Blue horizontal bars indicate highly sensitive periods. Green horizontal bars indicate periods that are somewhat less sensitive to teratogens, although damage can occur. (Adapted from *Before We Are Born, 7th ed.,* by K. L. Moore and T. V. N. Persaud, p. 313. Copyright © 2008, reprinted with permission from Elsevier, Inc.)

Figure 3.4 summarizes prenatal sensitive periods. Look at it carefully, and you will see that some parts of the body, such as the brain and eye, have long sensitive periods that extend throughout prenatal development. Other sensitive periods, such as those for the limbs and palate, are much shorter. Figure 3.4 also indicates that we can make some general statements about the timing of harmful influences. In the *germinal period,* before implantation, teratogens rarely have any impact. If they do, the tiny mass of cells is usually so damaged that it dies. The *embryonic period* is the time when serious defects are most likely to occur because the foundations for all body parts are being laid down. During the *fetal period,* teratogenic damage is usually minor. However, organs such as the brain, ears, eyes, teeth, and genitals can still be strongly affected.

The effects of teratogens go beyond immediate physical damage. Some health effects are subtle and delayed. As the Biology and Environment box on the following page illustrates, they may not show up for decades. Furthermore, psychological consequences may occur indirectly, as a result of physical damage. For example, a defect resulting from drugs the mother took during pregnancy can affect others' reactions to the child as well as the child's ability to explore the environment. Over time, parent–child interaction, peer relations, and opportunities to learn may suffer. Furthermore, prenatally exposed children may be less resilient in the face of environmental risks, such as single parenthood, parental emotional disturbance, or maladaptive parenting (Yumoto, Jacobson, & Jacobson, 2008). As a result, their long-term adjustment may be compromised.

Biology and Environment

The Prenatal Environment and Health in Later Life

When Michael entered the world 55 years ago, 6 weeks premature and weighing only 4 pounds, the doctor delivering him wasn't sure he would make it. Michael not only survived but enjoyed good health until his mid-forties, when, during a routine medical checkup, he was diagnosed with high blood pressure and type 2 diabetes. Michael had no apparent risk factors for these conditions.

Could the roots of Michael's health problems date back to his prenatal development? Increasing evidence suggests that prenatal environmental factors—ones that are not toxic (as are tobacco or alcohol) but rather fairly subtle, such as the flow of nutrients and hormones across the placenta—can affect an individual's health decades later.

Low Birth Weight and Heart Disease, Stroke, and Diabetes

Carefully controlled animal experiments reveal that a poorly nourished, underweight fetus experiences changes in body structure and function that greatly increase the risk of cardiovascular disease in adulthood (Franco et al., 2002). To explore this relationship in humans, researchers tapped public records, gathering information on the birth weights of thousands of British men and women and the occurrence of disease in middle adulthood. Those weighing less than

5 pounds at birth had a 50 percent greater chance of dying of heart disease and stroke, even after SES and a variety of other health risks were controlled (Barker, 2009; Godfrey & Barker, 2000). The connection between birth weight and cardiovascular disease was strongest for people whose weight-to-length ratio at birth was very low—a sign of prenatal growth stunting.

In other large-scale studies, a consistent link between low birth weight and high blood pressure, heart disease, stroke, and diabetes in middle adulthood emerged—for both sexes and in diverse countries (see Figure 3.5) (Barker, 2009; Johnson & Schoeni, 2011). Researchers believe that complex factors associated with underweight are involved.

Some speculate that a poorly nourished fetus diverts large amounts of blood to the brain, causing organs in the abdomen, such as the liver and kidneys (involved in controlling cholesterol and blood pressure), to be undersized (Hales & Ozanne, 2003). The result is heightened later risk of heart disease and stroke. In the case of diabetes, inadequate prenatal nutrition may permanently impair the pancreas, leading glucose intolerance to rise as the person ages (Wu et al., 2004). Yet another hypothesis is that the malfunctioning placentas of some expectant mothers permit high levels of stress hormones to reach the fetus, which slows fetal growth, increases fetal blood pressure, and promotes excess blood glucose, predisposing the developing person to later disease (Barker & Thornberg, 2013).

Finally, prenatally growth-stunted babies often gain excessive weight in childhood, once they have access to plentiful food (Ojha et al., 2013). This excess weight usually persists, greatly increasing the risk of diabetes and heart disease.

High Birth Weight and Cancer

The other prenatal growth extreme—high birth weight—is linked to breast cancer, the most common malignancy in adult women (Barker et al., 2008). In a study of more than 2,000 British women, high birth weight—especially weight

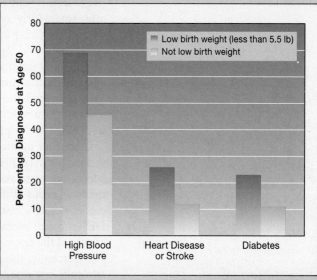

FIGURE 3.5 Relationship of low birth weight to disease risk in adulthood. In a follow-up of more than 2000 U.S. births at age 50, low birth weight was associated with a greatly increased incidence of high blood pressure, heart disease, stroke, and diabetes after many other prenatal and postnatal health risks were controlled. (Based on Johnson & Schoeni, 2011.)

above 8.8 pounds—was associated with a greatly increased incidence of breast cancer, even after other cancer risks were controlled (dos Santos Silva et al., 2004). The likely culprit is excessive maternal estrogen in the overweight expectant mother, which promotes large fetal size and alters the makeup of beginning breast tissue so that it responds to estrogen in adulthood by becoming malignant.

High birth weight is also associated with increases in prostate cancer in men and digestive, blood, and lymphatic cancers in both genders (Caughey & Michels, 2009; Cnattingius et al., 2009; McCormack et al., 2005). As yet, the reasons are unclear.

Prevention

The relationships between prenatal development and later-life illnesses do not mean that the illnesses are inevitable. Rather, the steps we take to protect our health can prevent prenatal risks from becoming reality. Researchers advise individuals who were low-weight or high-weight at birth to get regular medical checkups and screening tests that increase the odds of early disease detection. They also recommend consistent attention to diet, weight, fitness, and stress—controllable factors that contribute to cardiovascular disease, adult-onset diabetes, and cancer.

© BLEND IMAGES/ALAMY

Prenatal environmental factors can affect health in later life. This baby's high birth weight places her at increased risk for breast cancer in adulthood.

Notice how an important idea about development that we discussed in earlier chapters is at work here: *bidirectional influences* between child and environment. Now let's look at what scientists have discovered about a variety of teratogens.

PRESCRIPTION AND NONPRESCRIPTION DRUGS   In the early 1960s, the world learned a tragic lesson about drugs and prenatal development. At that time, a sedative called *thalidomide* was widely available in Canada, Europe, and South America. When taken by mothers 4 to 6 weeks after conception, thalidomide produced gross deformities of the embryo's developing arms and legs and, less frequently, damage to the ears, heart, kidneys, and genitals. About 7,000 infants worldwide were affected (Moore, Persaud, & Torchia, 2013). As children exposed to thalidomide grew older, many scored below average in intelligence. Perhaps the drug damaged the central nervous system directly, by modifying the expression of genes involved its development. Or the child-rearing conditions of these severely deformed youngsters may have impaired their intellectual development.

Another medication, a synthetic hormone called *diethylstilbestrol (DES),* was widely prescribed between 1945 and 1970 to prevent miscarriages. As daughters of these mothers reached adolescence and young adulthood, they showed unusually high rates of cancer of the vagina, malformations of the uterus, and infertility. When they tried to have children, their pregnancies more often resulted in prematurity, low birth weight, and miscarriage than those of non-DES-exposed women. Young men showed an increased risk of genital abnormalities and cancer of the testes (Goodman, Schorge, & Greene, 2011; Reed & Fenton, 2013).

Currently, the most widely used potent teratogen is a vitamin A derivative called *isotretinoin,* prescribed to treat severe acne and taken by hundreds of thousands of women of childbearing age in industrialized nations. Exposure during the first trimester results in eye, ear, skull, brain, heart, and immune system abnormalities (Yook et al., 2012). Isotretinoin's packaging warns users to avoid pregnancy by using two methods of birth control, but many women do not heed this advice (Garcia-Bournissen et al., 2008).

Indeed, any drug with a molecule small enough to penetrate the placental barrier can enter the embryonic or fetal bloodstream. Yet many pregnant women continue to take over-the-counter medications without consulting their doctors. Aspirin is one of the most common. Several studies suggest that regular aspirin use is linked to low birth weight, infant death around the time of birth, poorer motor development, and lower intelligence test scores in early childhood, although other research fails to confirm these findings (Barr et al., 1990; Kozer et al., 2003; Streissguth et al., 1987). Coffee, tea, cola, and cocoa contain another frequently consumed drug, caffeine. High doses increase the risk of low birth weight (Sengpiel et al., 2013). And persistent intake of antidepressant medication is linked to an elevated incidence of premature delivery and birth complications, including respiratory distress, and to high blood pressure in infancy (Lund, Pedersen, & Henriksen, 2009; Roca et al., 2011; Udechuku et al., 2010).

Because children's lives are involved, we must take findings like these seriously. At the same time, we cannot be sure that these frequently used drugs actually cause the problems just mentioned. Often mothers take more than one drug. If the embryo or fetus is injured, it is hard to tell which drug might be responsible or whether other factors correlated with drug taking are at fault. Until we have more information, the safest course of action is the one Yolanda took: Avoid these drugs entirely. Unfortunately, many women do not know that they are pregnant during the early weeks of the embryonic period, when exposure to medications (and other teratogens) can be of greatest threat.

ILLEGAL DRUGS   The use of highly addictive mood-altering drugs, such as cocaine and heroin, has become more widespread, especially in poverty-stricken inner-city areas, where these drugs provide a temporary escape from a daily life of hopelessness. Nearly 6 percent of U.S. pregnant women take these substances (Substance Abuse and Mental Health Services Administration, 2013).

Babies born to users of cocaine, heroin, or methadone (a less addictive drug used to wean people away from heroin) are at risk for a wide variety of problems, including prematurity, low birth weight, physical defects, breathing difficulties, and death around the time of birth

---

LOOK and LISTEN

On a trip to your grocery or drugstore, examine the fine print on nonprescription medication labels, such as pain relievers, and on energy drinks containing high levels of caffeine. Are the prenatal risks of these products clearly conveyed?

(Bandstra et al., 2010; Howell, Coles, & Kable, 2008; Schuetze & Eiden, 2006). In addition, these infants are born drug-addicted. They are often feverish and irritable and have trouble sleeping, and their cries are abnormally shrill and piercing—a common symptom among stressed newborns (Barthell & Mrozek, 2013). When mothers with many problems of their own must care for these babies, who are difficult to calm down, cuddle, and feed, behavior problems are likely to persist.

Throughout the first year, heroin- and methadone-exposed infants are less attentive to the environment than nonexposed babies, and their motor development is slow. After infancy, some children get better, while others remain jittery and inattentive. The kind of parenting they receive may explain why problems persist for some but not for others (Hans & Jeremy, 2001).

Evidence on cocaine suggests that some prenatally exposed babies develop lasting difficulties. Cocaine constricts the blood vessels, causing oxygen delivered to the developing organism to fall for 15 minutes following a high dose. It also can alter the production of neurons, formation of synaptic connections, and chemical balance in the fetus's brain. These effects may

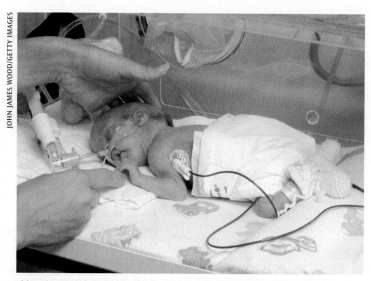

This 3-day-old infant, born many weeks before his due date, breathes with the aid of a respirator. Prematurity and low birth weight can result from a variety of environmental influences during pregnancy, including maternal drug and tobacco use.

contribute to an array of cocaine-associated physical malformations, especially of the central nervous system and heart; brain hemorrhages and seizures; and growth retardation (Cain, Bornick, & Whiteman, 2013; Li et al., 2013; Salisbury et al., 2009). Several studies report perceptual, motor, attention, memory, language, and impulse-control problems that persist into adolescence (Bandstra et al., 2010; Buckingham-Howes et al., 2013; Lester & Lagasse, 2010).

Other investigations, however, reveal no major negative effects of prenatal cocaine exposure (Ackerman, Riggins, & Black, 2010; Behnke & Smith, 2013; Hurt et al., 2009). These contradictory findings indicate how difficult it is to isolate the precise damage caused by illegal drugs. Cocaine users vary greatly in the amount, potency, and purity of the cocaine they ingest. Also, they often take several drugs, display other high-risk behaviors, suffer from poverty and other stresses, and engage in insensitive caregiving—factors that worsen outcomes for children (Jones, 2006; Molnar et al., 2014). But researchers have yet to determine exactly what accounts for findings of cocaine-related damage in some studies but not in others.

Another illegal drug, marijuana, is used more widely than heroin and cocaine. Researchers have linked prenatal marijuana exposure to attention, memory, and academic achievement difficulties; impulsivity and overactivity; and depression as well as anger and aggression in childhood and adolescence (Behnke & Smith, 2013; Goldschmidt et al., 2004; Gray et al., 2005; Jutras-Aswad et al., 2009). As with cocaine, however, lasting consequences are not well-established. Overall, the effects of illegal drugs are far less consistent than the impact of two legal substances to which we now turn: tobacco and alcohol.

TOBACCO   Although smoking has declined in Western nations, about 11 percent of U.S. women smoke during their pregnancies (Centers for Disease Control and Prevention, 2014f). The best-known effect of smoking during the prenatal period is low birth weight. But the likelihood of other serious consequences, such as miscarriage, prematurity, cleft lip and palate, blood vessel abnormalities, impaired heart rate and breathing during sleep, infant death, and asthma and cancer later in childhood, also increases (Geerts et al., 2012; Havstad et al., 2012; Howell, Coles, & Kable, 2008; Mossey et al., 2009). The more cigarettes a mother smokes, the greater the chances that her baby will be affected. If a pregnant woman stops smoking at any time, even during the third trimester, she reduces the likelihood that her infant will be born underweight and suffer from future problems (Polakowski, Akinbami, & Mendola, 2009). And the earlier she stops, the more beneficial the effects.

Even when a baby of a smoking mother appears to be born in good physical condition, slight behavioral abnormalities may threaten the child's development. Newborns of smoking mothers are less attentive to sounds, display more muscle tension, are more excitable when touched and visually stimulated, and more often have colic (persistent crying). These findings suggest subtle negative effects on brain development (Espy et al., 2011; Law et al., 2003). Consistent with this view, prenatally exposed children and adolescents tend to have shorter attention spans, difficulties with impulsivity and overactivity, poorer memories, lower intelligence test scores, and higher levels of disruptive, aggressive behavior (Lindblad & Hjern, 2010; Thakur et al., 2013).

Exactly how can smoking harm the fetus? Nicotine, the addictive substance in tobacco, constricts blood vessels, lessens blood flow to the uterus, and causes the placenta to grow abnormally. This reduces the transfer of nutrients, so the fetus gains weight poorly. Also, nicotine raises the concentration of carbon monoxide in the bloodstreams of both mother and fetus. Carbon monoxide displaces oxygen from red blood cells, damaging the central nervous system and slowing body growth in the fetuses of laboratory animals. Similar effects may occur in humans. Also, recall from Chapter 2 that nicotine-exposed fetuses with a certain genotype are at high risk for becoming impulsive, overactive, and oppositional children and adolescents (see page 87).

From one-third to one-half of nonsmoking pregnant women are "passive smokers" because their husbands, relatives, or co-workers use cigarettes. Passive smoking is also related to low birth weight, infant death, childhood respiratory illnesses, and possible long-term attention, learning, and behavior problems (Best, 2009; Pattenden et al., 2006). Clearly, expectant mothers should avoid smoke-filled environments.

ALCOHOL In his moving book *The Broken Cord,* Michael Dorris (1989) described what it was like to rear his adopted son Adam, whose biological mother drank heavily throughout pregnancy and died of alcohol poisoning shortly after his birth. A Sioux Indian, Adam was born with **fetal alcohol spectrum disorder (FASD),** a term that encompasses a range of physical, mental, and behavioral outcomes caused by prenatal alcohol exposure. As Table 3.3 shows, children with FASD are given one of three diagnoses, which vary in severity:

1. **Fetal alcohol syndrome (FAS),** distinguished by (a) slow physical growth, (b) a pattern of three facial abnormalities (short eyelid openings; a thin upper lip; a smooth or flattened philtrum, or indentation running from the bottom of the nose to the center of the upper lip), and (c) brain injury, evident in a small head and impairment in at least three areas of functioning—for example, memory, language and communication, attention span and activity level (overactivity), planning and reasoning, motor coordination, or social skills. Other defects—of the eyes, ears, nose, throat, heart, genitals, urinary tract, or immune system—may also be present. Adam was diagnosed as having FAS. As is typical for this disorder, his mother drank heavily throughout pregnancy.
2. **Partial fetal alcohol syndrome (p-FAS),** characterized by (a) two of the three facial abnormalities just mentioned and (b) brain injury, again evident in at least three areas of

TABLE 3.3 **Fetal Alcohol Spectrum Disorder: Criteria for Diagnosis**

	DIAGNOSTIC CATEGORY		
Criteria	*FAS*	*p-FAS*	*ARND*
Slow physical growth	Yes	No	No
Facial abnormalities: • Short eyelid openings • Thin upper lip • Smooth or flattened philtrum	All three are present	Two of the three are present	None are present
Brain injury	Impairment in a minimum of three areas of functioning	Impairment in a minimum of three areas of functioning	Impairment in a minimum of three areas of functioning

Source: Mattson, Crocker, & Nguyen, 2012.

impaired functioning. Mothers of children with p-FAS generally drank alcohol in smaller quantities, and children's defects vary with the timing and length of alcohol exposure. Furthermore, recent evidence suggests that paternal alcohol use around the time of conception can alter gene expression, thereby contributing to symptoms (Alati et al., 2013; Ouko et al., 2009).

3. **Alcohol-related neurodevelopmental disorder (ARND),** in which at least three areas of mental functioning are impaired, despite typical physical growth and absence of facial abnormalities. Again, prenatal alcohol exposure, though confirmed, is less pervasive than in FAS (Mattson, Crocker, & Nguyen, 2012).

Even when provided with enriched diets, FAS babies fail to catch up in physical size during infancy or childhood. Mental impairment associated with all three FASD diagnoses is also permanent: In his teens and twenties, Adam had trouble concentrating and keeping a routine job, and he suffered from poor judgment. For example, he would buy something and not wait for change or would wander off in the middle of a task. He died at age 23, after being hit by a car.

The more alcohol a woman consumes during pregnancy, the poorer the child's motor coordination, speed of information processing, reasoning, and intelligence and achievement test scores during the preschool and school years (Burden, Jacobson, & Jacobson, 2005; Mattson, Calarco, & Lang, 2006). In adolescence and early adulthood, FASD is associated with persisting attention and motor-coordination deficits, poor school performance, trouble with the law, inappropriate social and sexual behaviors, alcohol and drug abuse, and lasting mental health problems, including depression and high emotional reactivity to stress (Bertrand & Dang, 2012; Fryer, Crocker, & Mattson, 2008; Hellemans et al., 2010).

How does alcohol produce its devastating effects? First, it inter-

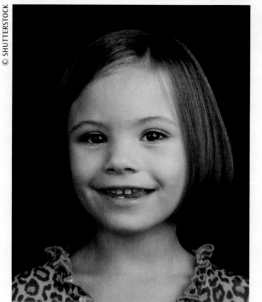

This 5-year-old's mother drank heavily during pregnancy. Her widely spaced eyes, thin upper lip, and flattened philtrum are typical of fetal alcohol syndrome (FAS).

This 12-year-old has the small head and facial abnormalities of FAS. She also shows the cognitive impairments and slow growth that accompany the disorder.

feres with production and migration of neurons in the primitive neural tube. Brain-imaging research reveals reduced brain size, damage to many brain structures, and abnormalities in brain functioning, including the electrical and chemical activity involved in transferring messages from one part of the brain to another (Coles et al., 2011; Memo et al., 2013). Second, the body uses large quantities of oxygen to metabolize alcohol. A pregnant woman's heavy drinking draws away oxygen that the developing organism needs for cell growth.

About 25 percent of U.S. mothers reported drinking at some time during their pregnancies. As with heroin and cocaine, alcohol abuse is higher in poverty-stricken groups. It is especially high among Native Americans, for whom the risk of a baby born with FAS is 20 to 25 times greater than for the rest of the U.S. population (Rentner, Dixon, & Lengel, 2012). Unfortunately, when affected girls later become pregnant, the poor judgment caused by the syndrome often prevents them from understanding why they themselves should avoid alcohol. Thus, the tragic cycle is likely to be repeated in the next generation.

How much alcohol is safe during pregnancy? Even mild drinking, less than one drink per day, is associated with reduced head size (a measure of brain development), slow body growth, and behavior problems (Flak et al., 2014; Martinez-Frias et al., 2004). Recall that other factors—both genetic and environmental—can make some fetuses more vulnerable to teratogens.

This child's deformities are linked to radiation exposure during the Chernobyl nuclear power plant disaster of 1986, when her mother was just a few weeks pregnant. Prenatal radiation exposure also increases the risk of low intelligence and language and emotional disorders.

Therefore, no amount of alcohol is safe. Couples planning a pregnancy and expectant mothers should avoid alcohol entirely.

RADIATION   In Chapter 2, we saw that ionizing radiation can cause mutation, damaging DNA in ova and sperm. When mothers are exposed to radiation during pregnancy, the embryo or fetus can suffer additional harm. Defects due to ionizing radiation were tragically apparent in children born to pregnant women who survived the bombing of Hiroshima and Nagasaki during World War II. Similar abnormalities surfaced in the nine months following the 1986 Chernobyl, Ukraine, nuclear power plant accident. After each disaster, the incidence of miscarriage and babies born with brain damage, physical deformities, and slow physical growth rose dramatically (Double et al., 2011; Schull, 2003). Evacuation of residents in areas near the Japanese nuclear facility damaged by the March 2011 earthquake and tsunami was intended to prevent these devastating outcomes.

Even when a radiation-exposed baby seems normal, problems may appear later. For example, even low-level radiation, resulting from industrial leakage or medical X-rays, can increase the risk of childhood cancer (Fushiki, 2013). In middle childhood, prenatally exposed Chernobyl children had abnormal brain-wave activity, lower intelligence test scores, and rates of language and emotional disorders two to three times greater than those of nonexposed children in the surrounding area. Furthermore, the more tension parents reported, due to forced evacuation from their homes and worries about living in irradiated areas, the poorer their children's emotional functioning (Loganovskaja & Loganovsky, 1999; Loganovsky et al., 2008). Stressful rearing conditions seemed to combine with the damaging effects of prenatal radiation to impair children's development.

Women should do their best to avoid medical X-rays during pregnancy. If dental, thyroid, chest, or other X-rays are necessary, insisting on the use of an abdominal X-ray shield is a key protective measure.

ENVIRONMENTAL POLLUTION   In industrialized nations, an astounding number of potentially dangerous chemicals are released into the environment. More than 75,000 are in common use in the United States, and many new pollutants are introduced each year. When 10 newborns were randomly selected from U.S. hospitals for analysis of umbilical cord blood, researchers uncovered a startling array of industrial contaminants—287 in all (Houlihan et al., 2005). They concluded that many babies are "born polluted" by chemicals that not only impair prenatal development but also increase the chances of life-threatening diseases and health problems later on.

Certain pollutants cause severe prenatal damage. In the 1950s, an industrial plant released waste containing high levels of *mercury* into a bay providing seafood and water for the town of Minamata, Japan. Many children born at the time displayed physical deformities, intellectual disability, abnormal speech, difficulty in chewing and swallowing, and uncoordinated movements. High levels of prenatal mercury exposure disrupt production and migration of neurons, causing widespread brain damage (Caserta et al., 2013; Hubbs-Tait et al., 2005). Prenatal mercury exposure from maternal seafood diets predicts deficits in speed of cognitive processing and motor, attention, and verbal test performance during the school years (Boucher et al., 2010; Debes et al., 2006). Pregnant women are wise to avoid eating long-lived predatory fish, such as swordfish, albacore tuna, and shark, which are heavily contaminated with mercury.

For many years, *polychlorinated biphenyls (PCBs)* were used to insulate electrical equipment, until research showed that, like mercury, they entered waterways and the food supply. In Taiwan, prenatal exposure to high levels of PCBs in rice oil resulted in low birth weight, discolored skin, deformities of the gums and nails, brain-wave abnormalities, and delayed cognitive development (Chen & Hsu, 1994; Chen et al., 1994). Steady, low-level PCB exposure is also harmful. Women who frequently ate PCB-contaminated fish, compared with those who ate little or no fish, had infants with lower birth weights, smaller heads, persisting attention and memory difficulties, and lower intelligence test scores in childhood (Boucher, Muckle, & Bastien, 2009; Jacobson & Jacobson, 2003; Stewart et al., 2008).

Another teratogen, *lead*, is present in paint flaking off the walls of old buildings and in certain materials used in industrial occupations. High levels of prenatal lead exposure are consistently related to prematurity, low birth weight, brain damage, and a wide variety of physical defects. Even at low levels, affected infants and children show slightly poorer mental and motor development (Caserta et al., 2013; Jedrychowski et al., 2009).

Prenatal exposure to *dioxins*—toxic compounds resulting from commercial waste incineration and burning of fuels, such as coal or oil—has particularly injurious effects. In addition to the problems just mentioned, it is linked to thyroid abnormalities in infancy and to an increased incidence of breast and uterine cancers in women, perhaps through altering hormone levels (ten Tusscher & Koppe, 2004). Even tiny amounts of dioxin in the paternal bloodstream cause a dramatic change in sex ratio of offspring: Affected men father nearly twice as many girls as boys (Ishihara et al., 2007). Dioxin seems to impair the fertility of Y-bearing sperm prior to conception.

Finally, persistent air pollution inflicts substantial prenatal harm. Exposure to traffic-related fumes and smog is associated with reduced infant head size, low birth weight, elevated infant death rates, impaired lung and immune-system development, and later respiratory illnesses (Proietti et al., 2013; Ritz et al., 2014).

INFECTIOUS DISEASE During her first prenatal visit, Yolanda's doctor asked her if she and Jay had already had measles, mumps, chickenpox, and several other illnesses. In addition, Yolanda was checked for the presence of several infections—and for good reason. As Table 3.4 indicates, certain diseases are major causes of miscarriage and birth defects.

This pregnant woman wears a face mask as protection against Singapore's smog, which occasionally hits life-threatening levels. Prolonged exposure to polluted air poses serious risks to prenatal development.

TABLE 3.4 Effects of Some Infectious Diseases During Pregnancy

DISEASE	MISCARRIAGE	PHYSICAL MALFORMATIONS	INTELLECTUAL DISABILITY	LOW BIRTH WEIGHT AND PREMATURITY
Viral				
Acquired immune deficiency syndrome (AIDS)	✔	?	✔	✔
Chickenpox	✔	✔	✔	✔
Cytomegalovirus	✔	✔	✔	✔
Herpes simplex 2 (genital herpes)	✔	✔	✔	✔
Mumps	✔	✗	✗	✗
Rubella (German measles)	✔	✔	✔	✔
Bacterial				
Chlamydia	✔	?	✗	✔
Syphilis	✔	✔	✔	?
Tuberculosis	✔	?	✔	✔
Parasitic				
Malaria	✔	✗	✗	✔
Toxoplasmosis	✔	✔	✔	✔

✔ = established finding; ✗ = no present evidence; ? = possible effect that is not clearly established.

Sources: Kliegman et al., 2008; Waldorf & McAdams, 2013.

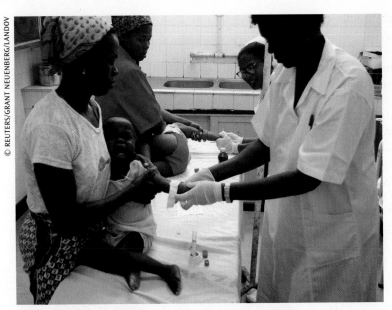

Babies are tested for the HIV virus in a clinic in Mozambique, Africa. Prenatal treatment with antiretroviral drugs reduces transmission of AIDS from mother to child by as much as 95 percent.

Viruses. In the mid-1960s, a worldwide epidemic of *rubella* (three-day, or German, measles) led to the birth of more than 20,000 American babies with serious defects and to 13,000 fetal and newborn deaths. Consistent with the sensitive-period concept, the greatest damage occurs when rubella strikes during the embryonic period. More than 50 percent of infants whose mothers become ill during that time show deafness; eye deformities, including cataracts; heart, genital, urinary, intestinal, bone, and dental defects; and intellectual disability. Infection during the fetal period is less harmful, but low birth weight, hearing loss, and bone defects may still occur. The organ damage inflicted by prenatal rubella often leads to lifelong health problems, including severe mental illness, diabetes, cardiovascular disease, and thyroid and immune-system dysfunction in adulthood (Duszak, 2009; Waldorf & McAdams, 2013). Routine vaccination in infancy and childhood has made new rubella outbreaks unlikely in industrialized nations. But an estimated 110,000 cases of prenatal infection continue to occur each year, primarily in developing countries in Africa and Asia with weak or absent immunization programs (World Health Organization, 2014b).

The *human immunodeficiency virus (HIV),* which can lead to *acquired immune deficiency syndrome (AIDS),* a disease that destroys the immune system, has infected increasing numbers of women over the past three decades. Currently, women account for one-fourth of cases in North America, Western Europe, and East Asia. Although the incidence of AIDS has declined in industrialized nations, the disease is rampant in developing countries, where 95 percent of new infections occur, more than half of which affect women. In South Africa, for example, nearly 30 percent of all pregnant women are HIV-positive (South African Department of Health, 2009). Untreated HIV-infected expectant mothers pass the deadly virus to the developing organism 10 to 20 percent of the time.

AIDS progresses rapidly in infants. By 6 months, weight loss, diarrhea, and repeated respiratory illnesses are common. The virus also causes brain damage, as indicated by seizures, gradual loss in brain weight, and delayed cognitive and motor development. Nearly half of prenatal AIDS babies die by 1 year of age and 90 percent by age 3 (Devi et al., 2009). Antiretroviral drug therapy reduces prenatal transmission by as much as 95 percent, with no harmful consequences of drug treatment for children. These medications have led to a dramatic decline in prenatally acquired AIDS in Western nations. And recently, several babies born with HIV who were given aggressive retroviral treatment within 2 days after birth appeared free of the disease (McNeil, 2014). Although distribution is increasing, antiretroviral drugs remain unavailable to about half of people needing treatment in impoverished regions of the world (UNAIDS, 2012).

As Table 3.4 reveals, the developing organism is especially sensitive to the family of herpes viruses, for which no vaccine or treatment exists. Among these, *cytomegalovirus* (the most frequent prenatal infection, transmitted through respiratory or sexual contact) and *herpes simplex 2* (which is sexually transmitted) are especially dangerous. In both, the virus invades the mother's genital tract, infecting babies either during pregnancy or at birth. Both diseases often have no symptoms, very mild symptoms, or symptoms with which people are unfamiliar, thereby increasing the likelihood of contagion. Pregnant women who are not in a mutually monogamous relationship are at greatest risk.

Bacterial and Parasitic Diseases. Table 3.4 also includes several bacterial and parasitic diseases. Among the most common is *toxoplasmosis,* an infection caused by a parasite found in many animals. Pregnant women may become infected from handling contaminated soil while gardening, contact with the feces of infected cats, or eating raw or undercooked meat or unwashed fruits and vegetables. About 40 percent of women who have the disease transmit it to the developing organism. If it strikes during the first trimester, it is likely to cause eye and brain damage. Later infection is linked to mild visual and cognitive impairments. And about 80 percent of affected newborns with no obvious signs of damage develop learning or visual disabilities in later life (Diav-Citrin, 2011; Jones, Lopez, & Wilson, 2003). Expectant mothers can avoid toxoplasmosis by making sure that the meat they eat is well-cooked, having pet cats checked for the disease, and turning over the care of litter boxes and the garden to other family members.

Other Maternal Factors

Besides avoiding teratogens, expectant parents can support the development of the embryo and fetus in other ways. Regular exercise, good nutrition, and emotional well-being of the mother are essential. Problems that may result from maternal and fetal blood type differences can be prevented. Finally, many prospective parents wonder how a mother's age affects the course of pregnancy. We examine each of these factors in the following sections.

EXERCISE   Yolanda continued her half-hour aerobic workout three times a week into the third trimester, although her doctor cautioned against bouncing, jolting, and jogging movements that might subject the fetus to too many shocks and startles. In healthy, physically fit women, regular moderate exercise, such as walking, swimming, biking, or an aerobic workout, is related to improved fetal cardiovascular functioning, higher birth weight, and a reduction in risk for certain complications, such as pregnancy-induced maternal diabetes and high blood pressure (May et al., 2010; Olson et al., 2009). However, frequent, vigorous exercise, especially late in pregnancy, results in lower birth weight than in healthy, nonexercising controls (Clapp et al., 2002; Leet & Flick, 2003). Hospital-sponsored childbirth education programs frequently offer exercise classes and suggest appropriate routines that help prepare for labor and delivery.

During the last trimester, when the abdomen grows very large, mothers have difficulty moving freely and often must cut back on exercise. Most women, however, do not engage in sufficient moderate exercise during pregnancy to promote their own and their baby's health (Poudevigne & O'Connor, 2006). An expectant mother who remains fit experiences fewer physical discomforts, such as back pain, upward pressure on the chest, or difficulty breathing in the final weeks.

Pregnant women with health problems, such as circulatory difficulties or a history of miscarriages, should consult their doctor about a physical fitness routine. For these mothers, exercise (especially the wrong kind) can endanger the pregnancy.

NUTRITION   During the prenatal period, when children are growing more rapidly than at any other time, they depend totally on the mother for nutrients. A healthy diet, consisting of a gradual increase in calories—an extra 100 calories a day in the first trimester, 265 in the second, and 430 in the third—resulting in a weight gain of 25 to 30 pounds (10 to 13.5 kilograms), helps ensure the health of mother and baby.

Consequences of Prenatal Malnutrition. During World War II, a severe famine occurred in the Netherlands, giving scientists a rare opportunity to study the impact of nutrition on prenatal development. Findings revealed that the sensitive-period concept operates with nutrition, just as it does with teratogens. Women affected by the famine during the first trimester were more likely to have miscarriages or give birth to babies with physical defects. When women were past the first trimester, fetuses usually survived, but many were born underweight and had small heads (Stein et al., 1975).

Prenatal malnutrition can cause serious damage to the central nervous system. The poorer the mother's diet, the greater the loss in brain weight, especially if malnutrition occurred during the third trimester. During that time, the brain is increasing rapidly in size, and for it to reach its full potential, a maternal diet high in all the basic nutrients is necessary (Hovdenak & Haram, 2012). An inadequate diet during pregnancy can also distort the structure of other

Prenatal malnutrition can damage the central nervous system and other organs. A government-supported farmers' market nutrition program enables this low-income expectant mother to purchase fruits and vegetables.

organs, including the liver, kidney, and pancreas, resulting in lifelong health problems (refer again to the Biology and Environment box on page 103).

Because poor nutrition suppresses development of the immune system, prenatally malnourished babies frequently catch respiratory illnesses (Chandra, 1991). In addition, they often are irritable and unresponsive to stimulation. Like drug-addicted newborns, they have a high-pitched cry that is particularly distressing to their caregivers. In poverty-stricken families, these effects quickly combine with a stressful home life. With age, delays in motor, attention, and memory development, low intelligence test scores, and serious learning problems become more apparent (Monk, Georgieff, & Osterholm, 2013).

Prevention and Treatment. Many studies show that providing pregnant women with adequate food has a substantial impact on the health of their newborn babies. Yet the growth demands of the prenatal period require more than just increased quantity of food. Vitamin–mineral enrichment is also crucial. For example, taking a folic acid supplement around the time of conception reduces by more than 70 percent abnormalities of the neural tube, such as *anencephaly* and *spina bifida* (see Table 2.4 on page 64). Folic acid supplementation early in pregnancy also reduces the risk of other physical defects, including cleft lip and palate, circulatory system and urinary tract abnormalities, and limb deformities. Furthermore, adequate folic acid intake during the last 10 weeks of pregnancy cuts in half the risk of premature delivery and low birth weight (Goh & Koren, 2008; Hovdenak & Hram, 2012).

Because of these findings, U.S. government guidelines recommend that all women of childbearing age consume 0.4 milligrams of folic acid per day. For women who have previously had a pregnancy affected by neural tube defect, the recommended amount is 5 milligrams (dosage must be carefully monitored, as excessive intake can be harmful) (Talaulikar & Arulkumaran, 2011). Since many U.S. pregnancies are unplanned (see page 92), government regulations mandate that bread, flour, rice, pasta, and other grain products be fortified with folic acid.

Other vitamins and minerals also have established benefits. Enriching women's diets with calcium helps prevent maternal high blood pressure and low birth weight. Adequate magnesium and zinc reduce the risk of many prenatal and birth complications (Hovdenak & Haram, 2012). Fortifying table salt with iodine virtually eradicates *infantile hypothyroidism*—a condition of stunted growth and cognitive impairment caused by prenatal iodine deficiency, that is a common cause of intellectual disability in many parts of the world (Williams, 2008). And sufficient vitamins C and E and iron beginning early in pregnancy promote growth of the placenta and healthy birth weight (Gambling, Kennedy, & McArdle, 2011; Klemmensen et al., 2009). Nevertheless, a supplement program should complement, not replace, efforts to improve maternal diets during pregnancy. For women who do not get enough food or an adequate variety of foods, multivitamin tablets are a necessary, but not sufficient, intervention.

When poor nutrition continues throughout pregnancy, infants usually require more than dietary improvement. In response to their tired, restless behavior, parents tend to be less sensitive and stimulating. Babies, in turn, become even more passive and withdrawn. Successful interventions must break this cycle of apathetic caregiver–baby interaction. Some do so by teaching parents how to interact effectively with their infants; others focus on stimulating infants to promote active engagement with their physical and social surroundings (Grantham-McGregor, Schofield, & Powell, 1987; Grantham-McGregor et al., 1994).

Although prenatal malnutrition is highest in poverty-stricken regions of the world, it is not limited to developing countries. The U.S. Special Supplemental Nutrition Program for Women, Infants, and Children (WIC), which provides food packages and nutrition education to low-income pregnant women, reaches about 90 percent of those who qualify because of their extremely low incomes (U.S. Department of Agriculture, 2012). But many U.S. women who need nutrition intervention are not eligible for WIC.

EMOTIONAL STRESS   When women experience severe emotional stress during pregnancy, their babies are at risk for a wide variety of difficulties. Intense anxiety—especially during the first two trimesters—is associated with higher rates of miscarriage, prematurity, low birth weight, infant respiratory and digestive illnesses, colic (persistent infant crying), sleep disturbances, and irritability during the child's first three years (Dunkel-Shetter & Lobel, 2012; Field, 2011; Lazinski, Shea, & Steiner, 2008). Prenatal stressors consistently found to impair infant physical and psychological well-being include chronic strain due to poverty, neighborhood crime, or homelessness; major negative life events such as divorce or death of a family member; community-wide disasters such as earthquakes or terrorist attacks; and fears specific to pregnancy and childbirth, including anxiety about the health and survival of the baby and oneself.

How can maternal stress affect the developing organism? TAKE A MOMENT... To understand this process, list the changes you sensed in your own body the last time you were under stress. When we experience fear and anxiety, stimulant hormones released into our bloodstream—such as *epinephrine* (adrenaline) and *cortisol,* known as the "flight or fight" hormones—cause us to be "poised for action." Large amounts of blood are sent to parts of the body involved in the defensive response—the brain, the heart, and the muscles in the arms, legs, and trunk. Blood flow to other organs, including the uterus, is reduced. As a result, the fetus is deprived of a full supply of oxygen and nutrients.

Maternal stress hormones also cross the placenta, causing a dramatic rise in fetal stress hormones (evident in the amniotic fluid) and, therefore, in fetal heart rate, blood pressure, blood glucose, and activity level (Kinsella & Monk, 2009; Weinstock, 2008). Excessive fetal stress may permanently alter fetal neurological functioning, thereby heightening stress reactivity in later life. In several studies, infants and children of mothers who experienced severe prenatal anxiety displayed cortisol levels that were either abnormally high or abnormally low, both of which signal impaired physiological capacity to manage stress. Consistent with these findings, such children are more upset than their agemates when faced with novel or challenging experiences—effects that persist into adolescence and early adulthood (Entringer et al., 2009; Van den Bergh et al., 2008).

Furthermore, maternal emotional stress during pregnancy predicts weakened immune system functioning and increased susceptibility to infectious disease in childhood (Nielsen et al., 2011). It is also associated with diverse negative behavioral outcomes, including anxiety, short attention span, anger, aggression, overactivity, and lower intelligence test scores, above and beyond the impact of other risks, such as maternal smoking during pregnancy, low birth weight, postnatal maternal anxiety, and low SES (Loomans et al., 2011; Monk, Georgieff, & Osterholm, 2013).

But stress-related prenatal complications are greatly reduced when mothers have partners, other family members, and friends who offer social support (Bloom et al., 2013; Luecken et al., 2013). The relationship of social support to positive pregnancy outcomes and subsequent child development is particularly strong for economically disadvantaged women, who often lead highly stressful lives (see the Social Issues: Health box on page 114).

LOOK and LISTEN

List prenatal environmental factors that can compromise later academic performance and social adjustment. Ask several adults who hope someday to be parents to explain what they know about each factor. How great is their need for prenatal education?

RH FACTOR INCOMPATIBILITY   When inherited blood types of mother and fetus differ, serious problems sometimes result. The most common cause of these difficulties is **Rh factor incompatibility.** When the mother is Rh-negative (lacks the Rh blood protein) and the father is Rh-positive (has the protein), the baby may inherit the father's Rh-positive blood type. (Because Rh-positive blood is dominant and Rh-negative blood is recessive, the chances are good that the baby will be Rh-positive.) If even a little of a fetus's Rh-positive blood crosses the placenta into the Rh-negative mother's bloodstream, she begins to form antibodies to the foreign Rh protein. If these enter the fetus's system, they destroy red blood cells, reducing the oxygen supply to organs and tissues. Intellectual disability, miscarriage, heart damage, and infant death can occur.

It takes time for the mother to produce Rh antibodies, so firstborn children are rarely affected. The danger increases with each additional pregnancy. Fortunately, Rh incompatibility can be prevented in most cases. After the birth of each Rh-positive baby, Rh-negative mothers are routinely given a vaccine to prevent the buildup of antibodies. In emergency cases, blood transfusions can be performed immediately after delivery or, if necessary, even before birth.

Social Issues: Health

The Nurse–Family Partnership: Reducing Maternal Stress and Enhancing Child Development Through Social Support

At age 17, Denise—an unemployed high-school dropout living with her disapproving parents—gave birth to Tara. Having no one to turn to for help during pregnancy and beyond, Denise felt overwhelmed and anxious much of the time. Tara was premature and cried uncontrollably, slept erratically, and suffered from frequent minor illnesses throughout her first year. When she reached school age, she had trouble keeping up academically, and her teachers described her as distractible, unable to sit still, angry, and uncooperative.

The Nurse–Family Partnership—currently implemented in hundreds of counties across 43 U.S. states, in six tribal communities, in the U.S. Virgin Islands, and internationally in Australia, Canada, the Netherlands, and the United Kingdom—is a voluntary home visiting program for first-time, low-income expectant mothers like Denise. Its goals are to reduce pregnancy and birth complications, promote competent early caregiving, and improve family conditions, thereby protecting children from lasting adjustment difficulties.

A registered nurse visits the home weekly during the first month after enrollment, twice a month during the remainder of pregnancy and through the middle of the child's second year, and then monthly until age 2. In these sessions, the nurse provides the mother with intensive social support—a sympathetic ear; assistance in accessing health and other community services and the help of family members (especially fathers and grandmothers); and encouragement to finish high school, find work, and engage in future family planning.

To evaluate the program's effectiveness, researchers randomly assigned large samples of mothers at risk for high prenatal stress (due to teenage pregnancy, poverty, and other negative life conditions) to nurse-visiting or comparison conditions (just prenatal care, or prenatal care plus infant referral for developmental problems). Families were followed through their child's school-age years and, in one experiment, into adolescence (Kitzman et al., 2010; Olds et al., 2004, 2007; Rubin et al., 2011).

As kindergartners, Nurse–Family Partnership children obtained higher language and intelligence test scores. And at both ages 6 and 9, children of home-visited mothers in the poorest mental health during pregnancy exceeded comparison children in academic achievement and displayed fewer behavior problems. Furthermore, from their baby's birth on, home-visited mothers were on a more favorable life course: They had fewer subsequent births, longer intervals between their first and second births, more frequent contact with the child's father, more stable intimate partnerships, less welfare dependence, and a greater sense of control over their lives—key factors in reducing subsequent prenatal stress and in protecting children's development. Perhaps for these reasons, adolescent children of home-visited mothers continued to be advantaged in academic achievement and reported less alcohol and drug use than comparison-group agemates.

Other findings revealed that professional nurses, compared with trained paraprofessionals,

The Nurse–Family Partnership provides a first-time, low-income mother with regular home visits from a registered nurse, who offers social support and help in accessing community services. As a result, this child has a considerably better chance of developing favorably.

were far more effective in preventing outcomes associated with prenatal stress, including high infant fearfulness to novel stimuli and delayed mental development (Olds et al., 2002). Nurses were probably more proficient in individualizing program guidelines to fit the strengths and challenges faced by each family. They also might have had unique legitimacy as experts in the eyes of stressed mothers, more easily convincing them to take steps to reduce pregnancy complications that can trigger persisting developmental problems—such as those Tara displayed.

The Nurse–Family Partnership is highly cost-effective (Dawley, Loch, & Bindrich, 2007). For each $1 spent, it saves more than $5 in public spending on pregnancy complications, preterm births, and child and youth learning and behavior problems.

MATERNAL AGE AND PREVIOUS BIRTHS In Chapter 2, we noted that women who delay childbearing until their thirties or forties face increased risk of infertility, miscarriage, and babies with chromosomal defects. Are other pregnancy complications also more common for older mothers? Research consistently indicates that healthy women in their thirties have about the same rates as those in their twenties (Bianco et al., 1996; Dildy et al., 1996). Thereafter, as Figure 3.6 reveals, complication rates increase, with a sharp rise among women age 50 to 55—an age at which, because of menopause (end of menstruation) and aging reproductive organs, few women can conceive naturally (Salihu et al., 2003; Usta & Nassar, 2008).

In the case of teenage mothers, does physical immaturity cause prenatal problems? The adolescent girl's rapid gain in body size precedes sexual maturity, indicating that nature tries to ensure that once a girl can conceive, she is physically ready to carry and give birth to a baby.

Infants born to teenagers have a higher rate of problems, but not directly because of maternal age. Most pregnant teenagers come from low-income backgrounds, where stress, poor nutrition, and health problems are common. Also, many are afraid to seek medical care. And in the United States, although the Affordable Care Act has greatly increased health insurance for pregnant adolescents, not all have full coverage.

The Importance of Prenatal Health Care

Yolanda had her first prenatal appointment three weeks after missing her menstrual period. After that, she visited the doctor's office once a month until she was seven months pregnant, then twice during the eighth month. As birth grew near, Yolanda's appointments increased to once a week. The doctor kept track of her general health, her weight gain, the capacity of her uterus and cervix to support the fetus, and the fetus's growth.

Yolanda's pregnancy, like most others, was free of complications. But unexpected difficulties can arise, especially if mothers have health problems. For example, the 5 percent of pregnant women who have diabetes need careful monitoring. Extra glucose in the diabetic mother's bloodstream increases the risk of pregnancy and birth problems, as well as brain damage and later learning difficulties (see the Biology and Environment box on page 116). Another complication, experienced by 5 to 10 percent of pregnant women, is *preeclampsia* (sometimes called *toxemia*), in which blood pressure increases sharply and the face, hands, and feet swell in the second half of pregnancy. If untreated, preeclampsia can cause convulsions in the mother and fetal death. Usually, hospitalization, bed rest, and drugs can lower blood pressure to a safe level (Vest & Cho, 2012). If not, the baby must be delivered at once.

Unfortunately, 6 percent of pregnant women in the United States wait until after the first trimester to seek prenatal care or receive none at all. As Figure 3.7 on page 117 shows, inadequate care is far more common among adolescent and low-income, ethnic minority mothers. Their infants are three times as likely to be born underweight and five times as likely to die as are babies of mothers who receive early medical attention (Child Trends, 2014b). Although government-sponsored health services for low-income pregnant women have been expanded, some do not qualify and must pay for at least part of their care. As we will see when we take up birth complications in Chapter 4, in nations where affordable medical care is universally available, such as Australia, Canada, Japan, and European countries, late-care pregnancies and maternal and infant health problems are greatly reduced.

Besides financial hardship, some mothers have other reasons for not seeking early prenatal care. These include *situational barriers* (difficulty finding a doctor, getting an appointment, and arranging transportation, and insensitive or unsatisfying experiences with clinic staff) and *personal barriers* (psychological stress, the demands of taking care of other young children, family crises, lack of knowledge about signs of pregnancy and benefits of prenatal care, and ambivalence about the pregnancy). Many also engage in high-risk behaviors, such as smoking and drug abuse, which they do not want to reveal to health professionals (Kitsantas, Gaffney, & Cheema, 2012). These women, who receive little or no prenatal care, are among those who need it most!

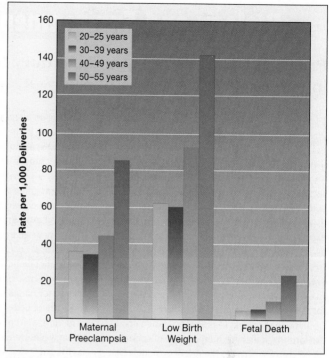

FIGURE 3.6 **Relationship of maternal age to prenatal and birth complications.** Complications increase after age 40, with a sharp rise between 50 and 55 years. (Based on Salihu et al., 2003.)

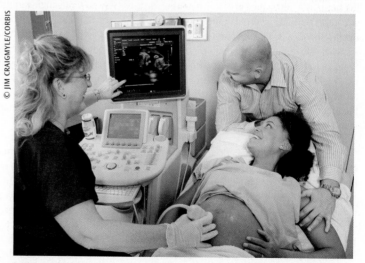

During a routine prenatal visit, a couple views an ultrasound image of twins. All pregnant women need regular prenatal care to protect their health and that of their babies.

Biology and Environment

Prenatal Iron Deficiency and Memory Impairments in Infants of Diabetic Mothers

Diabetes affects nearly 11 percent of Americans age 20 and older—a rate that has risen sharply over the past quarter century due to widespread overweight and obesity. Although its incidence is increasing among all sectors of the population, diabetes is at least twice as likely to affect low-income ethnic minority as white adults. Today, about 5 percent of expectant mothers are diabetic—twice as many as a decade ago. Most had the disease before becoming pregnant; others developed it during pregnancy (American Diabetes Association, 2014). In either case, their newborn babies are at risk for long-term developmental problems.

In the early weeks of pregnancy, when organs are forming, a diabetic mother's out-of-control blood glucose increases the risk of birth defects. Later in pregnancy, excess blood glucose causes the fetus to be "overfed" and to grow unusually large, often causing birth complications. Furthermore, to metabolize this flood of maternal glucose, the fetus secretes abnormally high levels of insulin—a circumstance that greatly increases demand for oxygen. To extract extra oxygen from the mother's system, the fetus increases production of oxygen-carrying red blood cells. This expanding red blood-cell mass requires extra iron, which the fetus can obtain only by taxing its own iron stores in the liver, muscles, heart, and brain.

In animal research on maternal diabetes, by late pregnancy iron stores decline sharply in the brain's temporal lobes (located on each side of the brain, just above the ears), which house structures centrally involved in memory development—specifically, the *hippocampus,* which plays a crucial role in the formation of new memories. Prenatal iron depletion interferes with growth of brain cells and their connections, permanently reducing the size and altering the structure of the hippocampus and impairing memory in laboratory rats (Jorgenson et al., 2005; Schmidt et al., 2007).

In human research, diabetic mothers bear children who, at later follow-ups, score lower than their agemates on intelligence tests (Nielson, Andersen, & Lundbye-Christensen, 2010). Is prenatal iron deficiency and resulting early damage to the brain's memory areas responsible? In a series of studies, Charles Nelson (2007a) and his collaborators recorded electrical brain waves to assess young infants' memory performance,

focusing on a particular slow brain wave in the temporal lobes believed to reflect memory processing.

Typically developing newborns come to recognize their mother's voice through repeated exposure during pregnancy (see page 100). In a comparison of newborns of diabetic mothers likely to have a brain iron deficiency (based on a measure of body iron stores) with normal-iron controls, brain waves were recorded as the babies listened to sound clips of their mother's or a stranger's voice (Sidappa et al., 2004). The controls showed a distinctive slow wave to each stimulus, indicating recognition of the mother's voice. The brain iron–deficient babies showed no difference in brain waves to the two stimuli, suggesting memory impairment of prenatal origin.

Maternal diabetes increases the fetus's risk of iron depletion and resulting damage to the brain's memory areas. This newborn of a diabetic mother is likely to have difficulty distinguishing his mother's voice from that of a stranger.

Do these memory deficits persist beyond the newborn period—evidence that diabetes-linked prenatal brain damage has lasting consequences? At 6 months, the researchers recorded brain waves while 6-month-old infants alternately viewed a videotaped image of their mother's face and that of an unfamiliar woman. Consistent with the newborn findings, control infants responded with distinct slow waves in the temporal lobes to the two faces, while infants of diabetic mothers displayed no difference (Nelson et al., 2000). Even after months of experience, they could not recognize their mother's facial image.

At an 8-month follow-up, babies were given a more challenging memory task. After feeling a novel object (an unusually shaped wooden block) held beneath an apron so they could not see it, the infants were tested visually: They viewed photos of the novel object interspersed with photos of familiar objects (Nelson et al., 2003). Again, infants of diabetic mothers showed no evidence of distinguishing the novel object from other stimuli. The control babies, in contrast,

responded to the novel object with a stronger temporal-lobe slow wave, suggesting an ability to recognize the novel stimulus, even when presented in a different sensory modality.

Nelson and his colleagues have followed their research participants through the preschool years, amassing additional evidence for poorer memory (especially more rapid forgetting) in children born to diabetic mothers than in controls (Riggins et al., 2009). The findings highlight a previously hidden pregnancy complication: As a result of iron depletion in critical brain areas, a diabetic pregnancy places the fetus at risk for lasting memory deficits and thus for long-term learning and academic problems. The researchers believe that damage to the hippocampus, located deep inside the temporal lobes, is responsible.

Nelson's research underscores the need for more effective ways of intervening with iron supplementation in diabetic pregnancies, as well as the importance of sufficient dietary iron for every expectant mother and her fetus. Diabetes prevention is also vital, through weight control, increased exercise, and improved diet beginning in childhood.

© ARIEL SKELLEY/BLEND IMAGES/CORBIS

Applying What We Know

Do's and Don'ts for a Healthy Pregnancy

DO	DON'T
Do make sure that you have been vaccinated against infectious diseases that are dangerous to the embryo and fetus, such as rubella, before you get pregnant. Most vaccinations are not safe during pregnancy.	Don't take any drugs without consulting your doctor.
Do see a doctor as soon as you suspect that you are pregnant, and continue to get regular medical checkups throughout pregnancy.	Don't smoke. If you have already smoked during part of your pregnancy, cut down or, better yet, quit. If other members of your family smoke, ask them to quit or to smoke outside.
Do eat a well-balanced diet and take vitamin–mineral supplements, as prescribed by your doctor, both prior to and during pregnancy. Gain 25 to 30 pounds gradually.	Don't drink alcohol from the time you decide to get pregnant.
Do obtain information about prenatal development from your doctor, local library, bookstore, and health organization websites. Ask your doctor about anything that concerns you.	Don't engage in activities that might expose your embryo or fetus to environmental hazards, such as radiation or chemical pollutants. If you work in an occupation that involves these agents, ask for a safer assignment or a leave of absence.
Do keep physically fit through moderate exercise. If possible, join a special exercise class for expectant mothers.	Don't engage in activities that might expose your embryo or fetus to harmful infectious diseases, such as toxoplasmosis.
Do avoid emotional stress. If you are a single expectant mother, find a relative or friend on whom you can rely for emotional support.	Don't choose pregnancy as a time to go on a diet.
Do get plenty of rest. An overtired mother is at risk for pregnancy complications.	Don't gain too much weight during pregnancy. A very large weight gain is associated with complications.
Do enroll in a prenatal and childbirth education class with your partner or other companion. When you know what to expect, the nine months before birth can be one of the most joyful times of life.	

Clearly, public education about the importance of early and sustained prenatal care for all pregnant women is badly needed. For women who are young, less-educated, low-income, or under stress and therefore at risk for inadequate prenatal care, assistance in making appointments, drop-in child-care centers, and convenient, free, or low-cost transportation are vital.

Culturally sensitive health-care practices are also helpful. Low-SES minority women often report depersonalizing experiences during prenatal appointments, including condescending interactions with medical staff and hurried checkups with no opportunity to ask questions. These behaviors are especially disturbing to women whose cultures emphasize warm, personalized interaction styles and a relaxed sense of time—causing many to avoid returning (Downe et al., 2009). In a strategy called *group prenatal care,* after each medical checkup, trained leaders provide minority expectant mothers with a group discussion session, which is conducted in their native language and encourages them to talk about important health issues (Massey, Rising, & Ickovics, 2006; Tandon et al., 2012). Compared to mothers receiving traditional brief appointments, participants engaged in more health-promoting behaviors and also gave birth to babies with a reduced incidence of prematurity and low birth weight—major predictors of newborn survival and healthy development. Applying What We Know above lists "do's and don'ts" for a healthy pregnancy, based on our discussion of the prenatal environment.

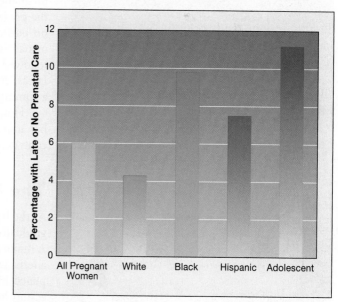

FIGURE 3.7 **Expectant mothers in the United States with late (after the first trimester) or no prenatal care.** More than 9 percent of low-income minority mothers, and about 10 percent of adolescent mothers, receive inadequate prenatal care. (Based on Child Trends, 2014b.)

Ask Yourself

- **REVIEW** Why is it difficult to determine the prenatal effects of many environmental agents, such as drugs and pollution?

- **CONNECT** How do teratogens illustrate the notion of epigenesis, presented in Chapter 2, that environments can affect gene expression? (See page 86 to review.)

- **APPLY** Nora, pregnant for the first time, believes that a few cigarettes and a glass of wine a day won't be harmful. Provide Nora with research-based reasons for not smoking or drinking.

- **REFLECT** If you had to choose five environmental influences to publicize in a campaign aimed at promoting healthy prenatal development, which ones would you choose, and why?

3.7 What factors contribute to preparation for parenthood during the prenatal period?

Preparing for Parenthood

Although we have discussed many ways that development can be thrown off course during the prenatal period, more than 90 percent of pregnancies in industrialized nations result in healthy newborn babies. For expectant parents fortunate enough to have stable relationships, sufficient income, and networks of social support, the prenatal period is not a time of medical hazard. Rather, it is a period of major life change accompanied by excitement, anticipation, and looking inward. The nine months before birth not only permit the fetus to grow but also give men and women time to develop a new sense of themselves as mothers and fathers.

This period of psychological preparation is vital. In one study, more than 100 U.S. first-time expectant married couples, varying in age and SES, were interviewed about their pregnancy experiences. Participants reported a wide range of reactions to learning they were expecting. Nearly two-thirds were positive, about one-third mixed or neutral, and only a handful negative (Feeney et al., 2001). An unplanned pregnancy was especially likely to spark negative or ambivalent feelings. But as the pregnancy moved along, these reactions subsided. By the third trimester, no participants felt negatively, and only about 10 percent remained mixed or neutral. Similarly, when a large sample of German expectant parents was followed over time, life satisfaction increased as birth approached (Dyrdal & Lucas, 2013). Couples' upbeat attitudes reflected acceptance of parenthood—a coming to terms with this imminent, radical change in their lives.

How effectively individuals construct a parental identity during pregnancy has important consequences for the parent–child relationship. Many factors contribute to the personal adjustments that take place.

For many expectant parents, feeling the fetus's movements initiates an emotional attachment to the new being.

The Baby Becomes a Reality

At the beginning of pregnancy, the baby's arrival seems far in the future. But gradually, as the woman's abdomen enlarges, the baby starts to become a reality. A major turning point occurs when expectant parents have concrete proof that a fetus is, indeed, developing inside the uterus. For Yolanda and Jay, this happened 13 weeks into the pregnancy, when their doctor showed them an ultrasound image. As Jay described the experience, "We saw it, these little hands and feet waving and kicking. It's really a baby in there!" Sensing the fetus's movements for the first time can be just as thrilling. Of course, the mother feels these "kicks" first, but soon after, the partner (and siblings) can participate by touching her abdomen.

Parents get to know the fetus as an individual through these signs of life. And both are likely to form an emotional attachment to the new being, especially when their relationship is positive, extended family members are supportive, and the mother reports favorable psychological well-being (Alhusen, 2008; Bouchard, 2011). In a Swedish study, the stronger mothers' and fathers' attachment to their fetus, the more positively they related to each other and to their baby after birth, and the more upbeat the baby's mood at age 8 months (White et al., 1999).

Models of Effective Parenthood

As pregnancy proceeds, expectant parents think about important models of parenthood in their own lives. When men and women have had good relationships with their own parents, they are more likely to develop positive images of themselves as parents during pregnancy (Deutsch et al., 1988). These images, in turn, predict harmonious marital communication and effective parenting during infancy and early childhood (Curran et al., 2005; McHale et al., 2004).

If their own parental relationships are mixed or negative, expectant mothers and fathers may have trouble building a healthy picture of themselves as parents. Some adults handle this challenge by seeking other examples of effective parenthood. One expectant father named Roger shared these thoughts with his wife and several couples, who met regularly with a counselor to talk about their concerns during pregnancy:

> I rethink past experiences with my father and my family and am aware of how I was raised. I just think I don't want to do that again. . . . I wish there had been more connection and closeness and a lot more respect for who I was. For me, my father-in-law . . . is a mix of empathy and warmth plus stepping back and being objective that I want to be as a father. (Colman & Colman, 1991, p. 148)

Like Roger, many people come to terms with negative experiences in their own childhood, recognize that other options are available to them, and build healthier and happier relationships with their children (Thompson, 2006). Roger achieved this understanding after participating in a special intervention program for expectant parents. Couples who take part in such programs feel better about themselves and their relationships, communicate more effectively, feel more competent as parents after the baby arrives, and adapt more easily when family problems arise (Glade, Bean, & Vira, 2005; Petch & Halford, 2008).

The Parental Relationship

The most important preparation for parenthood takes place in the context of the parents' relationship. Expectant couples who are unhappy in their marriages and who have difficulty working out their differences continue to be distant, dissatisfied, and poor problem solvers after childbirth (Houts et al., 2008; Kluwer & Johnson, 2007). Deciding to have a baby in hopes of improving a troubled relationship is a serious mistake. In a distressed marriage, pregnancy adds to rather than lessens family conflict (Perren et al., 2005). Furthermore, expectant couples experiencing prolonged anxiety and depressive symptoms influence prenatal development negatively (see page 113). They are in crucial need of intervention, starting as early as possible during pregnancy, directed at alleviating difficulties that contribute to poor family functioning.

When a couple's relationship is faring well and both partners want and plan for the baby, the excitement of a first pregnancy may bring husband and wife closer (Dyrdal & Lucas, 2013; Feeney et al., 2001). Parents who have forged a solid foundation of love and respect are well-equipped for the challenges of pregnancy. They are also prepared to handle the much more demanding changes that will take place once their baby is born. We will discuss the transition to parenthood in greater depth in the next chapter.

© BLEND IMAGES/ALAMY

Couples who have a warm, respectful relationship and who look forward to parenthood often find that pregnancy brings them closer. As a result, they are well-equipped to handle the changes that will come after the baby arrives.

Ask Yourself

- **REVIEW** List psychological factors during pregnancy that predict parenting effectiveness after childbirth.

- **APPLY** Megan, who is expecting her first child, recalls her own mother as cold and distant. Suggest steps she can take to form a confident, positive picture of herself as a new parent.

- **REFLECT** Ask your parents and/or your grandparents to describe attitudes and experiences that fostered or interfered with their capacity to build a positive parental identity when they were expecting their first child. Do you think building a healthy picture of oneself as a parent is more challenging today than it was in your parents' or grandparents' generation?

Summary

Motivations for Parenthood (p. 91)

3.1 How has decision making about child-bearing changed over the past half century, and what are the consequences for child rearing and child development?

- Adults in Western industrialized nations are freer today to choose whether, when, and how to have children. Motivations for parenthood have increasingly emphasized personal fulfillment and deemphasized societal obligations.

- In industrialized nations, family size has declined over the past half century, reflecting in part the need to balance career and family. Birth order and spacing are unrelated to children's intelligence. The greater number of births to low-SES mothers accounts for the link between large family size and children's lower intelligence test scores.

PHOTODISC/GETTY IMAGES

- Although older parents may be better equipped financially and emotionally to rear children, reproductive capacity declines with age, particularly as women reach their late thirties. Advanced maternal and paternal age is associated with increased risk of chromosomal and genetically influenced disorders.

Prenatal Development (p. 95)

3.2 List the three phases of prenatal development, and describe the major milestones of each.

- The first prenatal phase, the germinal period, lasts about two weeks, from fertilization and formation of the zygote through **implantation** of the **blastocyst** in the uterine lining. During this time, structures that will support prenatal growth begin to form, including the **placenta** and the **umbilical cord.**

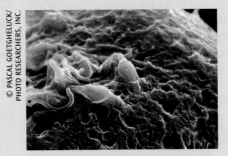
© PASCAL GOETGHELUCK/ PHOTO RESEARCHERS, INC.

- During the period of the **embryo,** from weeks 2 to 8, the foundations for all body structures are laid down. Initially, the nervous system develops fastest, forming the **neural tube,** the top of which swells to form the brain. Other organs, including the reproductive system, follow. At the end of this period, the embryo responds to touch and can move.

- The period of the **fetus,** lasting until the end of pregnancy, involves a dramatic increase in body size and completion of physical structures. At the end of the second **trimester,** most of the brain's neurons are in place. In the third trimester, between 22 and 26 weeks, the fetus reaches the **age of viability.** The brain continues to develop rapidly, and new sensory and behavioral capacities emerge: The fetus distinguishes different voices and language and musical sounds. Gradually the lungs mature, and the fetus fills the uterus.

Prenatal Environmental Influences (p. 101)

3.3 What are teratogens, and what factors influence their impact?

- **Teratogens** are environmental agents that cause damage during the prenatal period. Their impact varies with the amount and length of exposure, the genetic makeup of mother and fetus, the presence or absence of other harmful agents, and the age of the organism at time of exposure. The developing organism is especially vulnerable during the embryonic period. In addition to immediate physical damage, some health outcomes may appear later in development, and physical defects may have indirect psychological consequences.

3.4 List agents known to be or suspected of being teratogens, and discuss evidence supporting their harmful impact.

- Drugs, cigarettes, alcohol, radiation, environmental pollution, and infectious diseases are teratogens that can endanger the developing organism. Currently, the most widely used potent teratogen is isotretinoin, a drug used to treat severe acne. The prenatal impact of many other commonly used medications, such as aspirin and caffeine, is hard to separate from other factors correlated with drug taking.

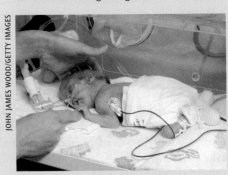
JOHN JAMES WOOD/GETTY IMAGES

- Babies born to users of heroin, methadone, or cocaine are at risk for a wide variety of problems, including prematurity, low birth weight, physical defects, and breathing difficulties around the time of birth. However, long-term consequences of maternal cocaine use are not well-established.

- Infants whose parents use tobacco are often born underweight and have attention, learning, and behavior problems in early childhood. Maternal alcohol consumption can lead to **fetal alcohol spectrum disorder (FASD)**. **Fetal alcohol syndrome (FAS)** involves slow physical growth, facial abnormalities, permanent intellectual impairment, and lasting mental health problems. Milder forms—**partial fetal alcohol syndrome (p-FAS)** or **alcohol-related neurodevelopmental disorder (ARND)**—affect children whose mothers consumed smaller quantities of alcohol.

- Prenatal exposure to high levels of radiation, mercury, PCBs, lead, and dioxins leads to physical malformations and severe brain damage; low-level exposure to these teratogens has also been linked to diverse impairments. Persistent exposure to air pollution also inflicts substantial prenatal harm.

- Among infectious diseases, rubella causes a wide variety of abnormalities. Babies with prenatally transmitted HIV rapidly develop AIDS, which leads to brain damage and early death; antiretroviral drug therapy dramatically reduces prenatal transmission. Cytomegalovirus, herpes simplex 2, and toxoplasmosis can also be devastating to the embryo and fetus.

3.5 *Describe the impact of other maternal factors on prenatal development.*

- Regular moderate exercise during pregnancy contributes to maternal health, fetal cardio-vascular functioning, and higher birth weight. However, very vigorous exercise results in lower birth weight.

- When the mother's diet is inadequate, low birth weight and damage to the brain and other organs are major concerns. Vitamin–mineral supplementation, including folic acid, before conception and continuing during pregnancy can prevent prenatal and birth complications.

- Severe emotional stress is linked to pregnancy complications and permanent alteration of fetal neurological functioning, resulting in impaired capacity to manage stress. Long-term outcomes include a weakened immune system, anxiety, short attention span, behavior problems, and lower intelligence test scores. The negative impact of prenatal stress can be reduced by providing the mother with emotional support.

- **Rh factor incompatibility**—an Rh-positive fetus developing within an Rh-negative mother—can lead to oxygen deprivation, brain and heart damage, and infant death.

- Older mothers face increased risk of miscarriage and babies with chromosomal defects, and, after age 40, a rise in other pregnancy complications. Poor health and environmental risks associated with poverty are the strongest predictors of pregnancy complications in teenage mothers.

3.6 *Why is early and regular health care vital during the prenatal period?*

- Unexpected difficulties, such as preeclampsia, can arise, especially when pregnant women have health problems to begin with. Prenatal care is especially crucial for those women least likely to seek it—in particular, those who are young or poverty-stricken. Among low-SES ethnic minority mothers, culturally sensitive health-care practices—such as group prenatal care—can lead to more health-promoting behaviors.

Preparing for Parenthood (p. 118)

3.7 *What factors contribute to preparation for parenthood during the prenatal period?*

- The nine months of pregnancy provide an adjustment period for expectant parents, who typically become increasingly positive about their new roles as childbirth approaches. Ultrasound images and fetal movements make the baby a reality, and parents may form an emotional attachment to the new being. They also rely on effective models of parenthood to build positive images of themselves as mothers and fathers.

- The most important preparation for parenthood takes place in the context of the couple's relationship. A troubled relationship usually worsens with expectant parenthood, while preparing to welcome a baby may strengthen a good relationship.

Important Terms and Concepts

age of viability (p. 99)
alcohol-related neurodevelopmental disorder (ARND) (p. 107)
amnion (p. 97)
amniotic fluid (p. 97)
blastocyst (p. 97)
chorion (p. 97)
embryo (p. 98)

embryonic disk (p. 97)
fetal alcohol spectrum disorder (FASD) (p. 106)
fetal alcohol syndrome (FAS) (p. 106)
fetus (p. 99)
implantation (p. 97)
lanugo (p. 99)
neural tube (p. 98)
partial fetal alcohol syndrome (p-FAS) (p. 106)

placenta (p. 97)
Rh factor incompatibility (p. 113)
teratogen (p. 101)
trimesters (p. 99)
trophoblast (p. 97)
umbilical cord (p. 98)
vernix (p. 99)

Birth and the Newborn Baby

"A Happy Day"
Natthanan Inhusub
9 years, Thailand

Safely held and nurtured by her parents, this baby thrives both physically and emotionally. In Chapter 4, we explore the birth process, the marvelous competencies of the newborn, and the challenges of new parenthood.

REPRINTED WITH PERMISSION FROM THE INTERNATIONAL MUSEUM OF CHILDREN'S ART, OSLO, NORWAY

Although Yolanda and Jay completed their child development course three months before their baby was born, both agreed to return to share with next term's class their reactions to birth and new parenthood. Two-week-old Joshua came along as well. Yolanda and Jay's story revealed that the birth of a baby is one of the most dramatic and emotional events in human experience. Jay was present throughout Yolanda's labor and delivery. Yolanda explained:

> By morning, we knew I was in labor. It was Thursday, so we went in for my usual weekly appointment. The doctor said, yes, the baby was on the way, but it would be a while. He told us to go home and relax and come to the hospital in three or four hours. We checked in at 3 in the afternoon; Joshua arrived at 2 o'clock the next morning. When, finally, I was ready to deliver, it went quickly; a half hour or so and some good hard pushes, and there he was! His face was red and puffy, his head was misshapen, but I thought, "Our son! I can't believe he's really here."

Jay was also elated by Joshua's birth. "I wanted to support Yolanda and to experience as much as I could. It was awesome, indescribable," he said, holding little Joshua over his shoulder and patting and kissing him gently.

In this chapter, we explore the experience of childbirth, from both the parents' and the baby's point of view. Today, women in industrialized nations have many choices about where and how they give birth, and hospitals go to great lengths to make the arrival of a new baby a rewarding, family-centered event.

Joshua reaped the benefits of Yolanda and Jay's careful attention to his needs during pregnancy. He was strong, alert, and healthy at birth. Nevertheless, the birth process does not always go smoothly. We will consider the pros and cons of medical interventions, such as pain-relieving drugs and surgical deliveries, designed to ease a difficult birth and protect the health of mother and baby. Our discussion also addresses the problems of infants born underweight or too early.

Finally, Yolanda and Jay spoke candidly about how their lives had changed since Joshua's arrival. "It's exciting and wonderful," reflected Yolanda, "but the adjustments are enormous. I wasn't quite prepared for the intensity of Joshua's 24-hour-a-day demands." In the concluding sections of this chapter, we look closely at the remarkable capacities of newborns to adapt to the external world and to communicate their needs. We also consider how parents adjust to the realities of everyday life with a new baby. ∎

The Stages of Childbirth

It is not surprising that childbirth is often referred to as labor. It is the hardest physical work a woman may ever do. A complex series of hormonal changes initiates the process. As pregnancy advances, the placenta releases increasing amounts of *corticotropin-releasing hormone (CRH)*, a hormone involved in the stress response. High levels of CRH trigger additional placental hormone adjustments that induce uterine contractions. And as CRH rises in the fetal bloodstream in the final prenatal weeks, it

4.1 Describe the three stages of childbirth, the baby's adaptation to labor and delivery, and the newborn baby's appearance.

stimulates fetal production of the stress hormone cortisol, which promotes development of the lungs in preparation for breathing (Li et al., 2014; Norwitz, 2009). An abnormal increase in maternal CRH in the third trimester of pregnancy is currently being evaluated as an early predictor of premature birth (Latendresse & Ruiz, 2011; Smith et al., 2009).

Several signs indicate that labor is near:

- Yolanda occasionally felt the upper part of her uterus contract. These contractions are often called *false labor* or *prelabor* because they remain brief and unpredictable for several weeks.
- About two weeks before birth, an event called *lightening* occurred; Joshua's head dropped low into the uterus. Placental hormone changes had caused Yolanda's cervix to soften, and it no longer supported Joshua's weight so easily.
- A sure sign that labor is only hours or days away is the *bloody show.* As the cervix begins to open, the plug of mucus that sealed it during pregnancy is released, producing a reddish discharge. Soon after, uterine contractions become more frequent, and mother and baby have entered the first of three stages of labor (see Figure 4.1).

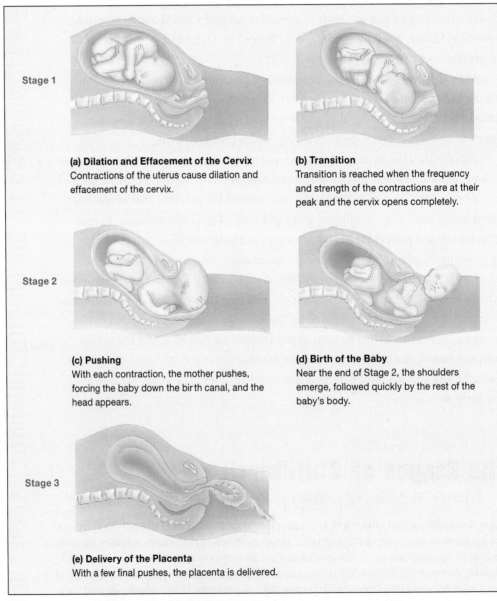

(a) Dilation and Effacement of the Cervix
Contractions of the uterus cause dilation and effacement of the cervix.

(b) Transition
Transition is reached when the frequency and strength of the contractions are at their peak and the cervix opens completely.

(c) Pushing
With each contraction, the mother pushes, forcing the baby down the birth canal, and the head appears.

(d) Birth of the Baby
Near the end of Stage 2, the shoulders emerge, followed quickly by the rest of the baby's body.

(e) Delivery of the Placenta
With a few final pushes, the placenta is delivered.

FIGURE 4.1 The three stages of childbirth.

Stage 1: Dilation and Effacement of the Cervix

Stage 1 is the longest, lasting an average of 12 to 14 hours with a first birth and 4 to 6 hours with later births. **Dilation and effacement of the cervix** take place—that is, as uterine contractions gradually become more frequent and powerful, they cause the cervix to open (dilate) and thin (efface), forming a clear channel from the uterus into the birth canal, or vagina. The uterine contractions that open the cervix are forceful and regular, starting out 10 to 20 minutes apart and lasting about 15 to 20 seconds. Gradually, they get closer together, occurring every 2 to 3 minutes, and become stronger, persisting for as long as 60 seconds.

During this stage, Yolanda could do nothing to speed up the process. Jay held her hand, provided sips of juice and water, and helped her get comfortable. Throughout the first few hours, Yolanda walked, stood, or sat upright. As the contractions became more intense, she leaned against pillows or lay on her side.

The climax of Stage 1 is a brief phase called **transition,** in which the frequency and strength of contractions are at their peak and the cervix opens completely. Although transition is the most uncomfortable part of childbirth, it is especially important that the mother relax. If she tenses or bears down with her muscles before the cervix is completely dilated and effaced, she may bruise the cervix and slow the progress of labor.

Stage 2: Delivery of the Baby

In Stage 2, which lasts about 50 minutes for a first baby and 20 minutes in later births, the infant is born. Strong contractions of the uterus continue, but the mother also feels a natural urge to squeeze and push with her abdominal muscles. As she does so with each contraction, she forces the baby down and out.

Between contractions, Yolanda dozed lightly. When the doctor announced that the baby's head was *crowning*—the vaginal opening had stretched around the entire head—Yolanda felt renewed energy; she knew that soon the baby would arrive. Quickly, with several more pushes, Joshua's forehead, nose, and chin emerged, then his upper body and trunk. The doctor held him up, wet with amniotic fluid and still attached to the umbilical cord. As air rushed into his lungs, Joshua cried. When the umbilical cord stopped pulsing, it was clamped and cut. A nurse placed Joshua on Yolanda's chest, where she and Jay could see, touch, and gently talk to him. Then the nurse wrapped Joshua snugly, to help with temperature regulation.

Stage 3: Birth of the Placenta

Stage 3 brings labor to an end. A few final contractions and pushes cause the placenta to separate from the wall of the uterus and be delivered in about 5 to 10 minutes. Yolanda and Jay were surprised at the large size of the thick 1½-pound red-gray organ, which had taken care of Joshua's basic needs for the previous nine months.

The Baby's Adaptation to Labor and Delivery

At first glance, labor and delivery seem like a dangerous ordeal for the baby. The strong contractions of Yolanda's uterus exposed Joshua's head to a great deal of pressure, and they squeezed the placenta and the umbilical cord repeatedly. Each time, Joshua's supply of oxygen was temporarily reduced.

Fortunately, healthy babies are equipped to withstand these traumas. The force of the contractions intensifies the baby's production of stress hormones. Unlike during pregnancy, when excessive stress endangers the fetus (see Chapter 3), during childbirth high levels of infant cortisol and other stress hormones are adaptive. They help the baby withstand oxygen deprivation by sending a rich supply of blood to the brain and heart (Gluckman, Sizonenko, & Bassett, 1999). And as noted earlier, they prepare the newborn's lungs to breathe. Finally, stress hormones arouse the infant into alertness. Joshua was born wide-awake, ready to interact with the surrounding world.

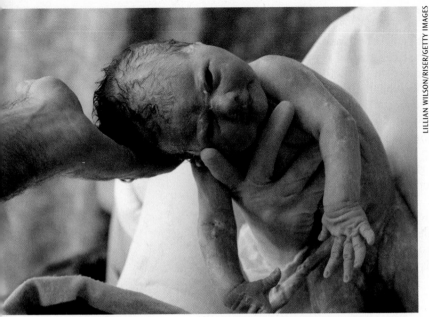

LILLIAN WILSON/RISER/GETTY IMAGES

To accommodate the well-developed brain, a newborn's head is large in relation to the trunk and legs. This newborn's body readily turns pink as she takes her first few breaths.

The Newborn Baby's Appearance

Parents are often surprised at the odd-looking newborn—a far cry from the storybook image they may have had in their minds. The average newborn is 20 inches long and 7½ pounds in weight; boys tend to be slightly longer and heavier than girls. The head is large in comparison to the trunk and legs, which are short and bowed. Proportionally, if your head were as large as that of a newborn infant, you would be balancing something about the size of a watermelon between your shoulders! This combination of a large head (with its well-developed brain) and a small body means that human infants learn quickly in the first few months of life. But unlike most other mammals, they cannot get around on their own until much later.

Even though newborn babies may not match parents' idealized image, some features do make them attractive (Luo, Li, & Lee, 2011). Their round faces, chubby cheeks, large foreheads, and big eyes make adults feel like picking them up and cuddling them.

Assessing the Newborn's Physical Condition: The Apgar Scale

Infants who have difficulty making the transition to life outside the uterus must be given special help at once. To assess the newborn's physical condition quickly, doctors and nurses use the **Apgar Scale.** As Table 4.1 shows, a rating of 0, 1, or 2 on each of five characteristics is made at 1 minute and again at 5 minutes after birth. A combined Apgar score of 7 or better indicates that the infant is in good physical condition. If the score is between 4 and 6, the baby requires assistance in establishing breathing and other vital signs. If the score is 3 or below, the infant is in serious danger and requires emergency medical attention. Two Apgar ratings are given because some babies have trouble adjusting at first but do quite well after a few minutes (Apgar, 1953).

TABLE 4.1	The Apgar Scale		
	SCORE		
Sign[a]	*0*	*1*	*2*
Heart rate	No heartbeat	Under 100 beats per minute	100 to 140 beats per minute
Respiratory effort	No breathing for 60 seconds	Irregular, shallow breathing	Strong breathing and crying
Reflex irritability (sneezing, coughing, and grimacing)	No response	Weak reflexive response	Strong reflexive response
Muscle tone	Completely limp	Weak movements of arms and legs	Strong movements of arms and legs
Color[b]	Blue body, arms, and legs	Body pink with blue arms and legs	Body, arms, and legs completely pink

[a]To remember these signs, you may find it helpful to use a technique in which the original labels are reordered and renamed as follows: color = **A**ppearance; heart rate = **P**ulse; reflex irritability = **G**rimace; muscle tone = **A**ctivity; and respiratory effort = **R**espiration. Together, the first letters of the new labels spell **Apgar**.

[b]The skin tone of nonwhite babies makes it difficult to apply the "pink" color criterion. However, newborns of all races can be rated for pinkish glow resulting from the flow of oxygen through body tissues.

Source: Apgar, 1953.

Ask Yourself

- **REVIEW** Name and briefly describe the three stages of labor.

- **CONNECT** Contrast the positive impact of the baby's production of high levels of stress hormones during childbirth with the negative impact of severe maternal stress on the fetus, discussed on page 113 in Chapter 3.

- **APPLY** On seeing her newborn baby for the first time, Caroline exclaimed, "Why is she so out of proportion?" What observations prompted Caroline to ask this question? Explain why her baby's appearance is adaptive.

Approaches to Childbirth

4.2 Describe natural childbirth and home delivery, noting benefits and concerns associated with each.

Childbirth practices, like other aspects of family life, are molded by the society of which mother and baby are a part. In many village and tribal cultures, expectant mothers are well-acquainted with the childbirth process. For example, the Jarara of South America and the Pukapukans of the Pacific Islands treat birth as a vital part of daily life. The Jarara mother gives birth in full view of the entire community, including small children. The Pukapukan girl is so familiar with the events of labor and delivery that she can frequently be seen playing at it. Using a coconut to represent the baby, she stuffs it inside her dress, imitates the mother's pushing, and lets the nut fall at the proper moment.

In most nonindustrialized cultures, women are assisted—though often not by medical personnel—during labor and delivery. Among the Mende of Sierra Leone, birth attendants are appointed by the village chief and are highly respected members of their communities. They visit expectant mothers before and after a birth to provide advice, can be called to help deliver a baby at any time, and practice traditional strategies to promote delivery, including massaging the abdomen and supporting the woman in a squatting position (Dorwie & Pacquiao, 2014). In Bolivia, a Siriono mother delivers her own baby in a hammock with a crowd of women close by, who keep her company. The father cuts the umbilical cord and joins the mother in tending to the newborn for the first few days (Jordan, 1993; Reed, 2005).

In Western nations, childbirth has changed dramatically over the centuries. Before the late 1800s, birth usually took place at home and was a family-centered event. The industrial revolution brought greater crowding to cities, along with new health problems. As a result, childbirth moved from home to hospital, where the health of mothers and babies could be protected. Once doctors assumed responsibility for childbirth, women's knowledge of it declined, and relatives and friends no longer participated (Borst, 1995).

By the 1950s and 1960s, women had begun to question the medical procedures that had come to be used during labor and delivery. Many felt that routine use of strong drugs and delivery instruments had robbed them of a precious experience and was often neither necessary nor safe for the baby. Gradually, a natural childbirth movement arose in Europe and spread to North America. Its purpose was to make hospital birth as comfortable and rewarding for mothers as possible. Today, most hospitals offer birth centers that are family-centered and homelike. *Free-standing birth centers,* which permit greater maternal control over labor and delivery, including choice of delivery

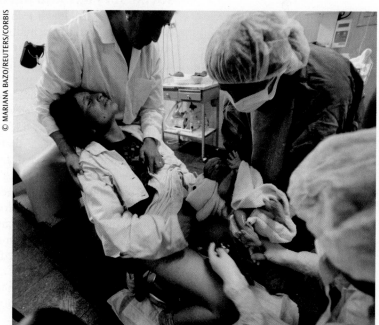

In this Peruvian health clinic, families are encouraged to incorporate practices of their village culture into the birth experience. Here, a familiar attendant supports and soothes a new mother as her baby is delivered.

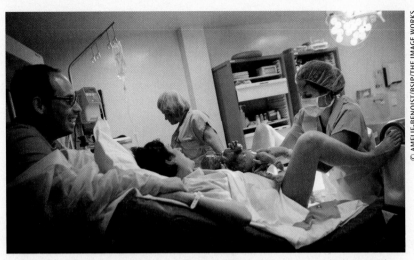

In a hospital birth center, a mother gives birth, assisted by the father. A companion's support is a vital part of natural childbirth, which is associated with shorter labors, fewer complications, and a more rewarding birth experience.

positions, presence of family members and friends, and early contact between parents and baby, also exist. And a small number of North American women reject institutional birth entirely and choose to have their babies at home.

Natural, or Prepared, Childbirth

Yolanda and Jay chose **natural,** or **prepared, childbirth**—a group of techniques aimed at reducing pain and medical intervention and making childbirth a rewarding experience. Most natural childbirth programs draw on methods developed by Grantly Dick-Read (1959) in England and Fernand Lamaze (1958) in France. These physicians recognized that cultural attitudes had taught women to fear the birth experience. An anxious, frightened woman in labor tenses her muscles, heightening the pain that usually accompanies strong contractions.

In a typical natural childbirth program, the expectant mother and a companion (a partner, relative, or friend) participate in three activities:

- *Classes.* Yolanda and Jay attended a series of classes in which they learned about the anatomy and physiology of labor and delivery. Knowledge about the birth process reduces a mother's fear.
- *Relaxation and breathing techniques.* During each class, Yolanda was taught relaxation and breathing exercises aimed at counteracting the pain of uterine contractions.
- *Labor coach.* Jay learned how to help Yolanda during childbirth by reminding her to relax and breathe, massaging her back, supporting her body, and offering encouragement and affection.

SOCIAL SUPPORT AND NATURAL CHILDBIRTH   Social support is important to the success of natural childbirth techniques. In Guatemalan and American hospitals that routinely isolated patients during childbirth, some mothers were randomly assigned a *doula*—a Greek word referring to a trained lay attendant—who stayed with them throughout labor and delivery, talking to them, holding their hands, and rubbing their backs to promote relaxation. These mothers had fewer birth complications, and their labors were several hours shorter than those of women who did not have supportive companionship. Guatemalan mothers who received doula support also interacted more positively with their babies after delivery, talking, smiling, and gently stroking (Kennell et al., 1991; Sosa et al., 1980).

Other studies indicate that mothers who are supported during labor—either by a lay birth attendant or a relative or friend with doula training—less often have instrument-assisted or cesarean (surgical) deliveries or need medication to control pain. Also, their babies' Apgar scores are higher, and they are more likely to be breastfeeding at a two-month follow-up (Campbell et al., 2006, 2007; Hodnett et al., 2012; McGrath & Kennell, 2008).

The continuous rather than intermittent support of a doula during labor and delivery strengthens these benefits for mothers and babies—outcomes evident in studies conducted in both developing and developed nations and among women of diverse ethnicities (Hodnett et al., 2012). Furthermore, this aspect of natural childbirth makes Western hospital-birth customs more acceptable to women from parts of the world where assistance from family and community members is the norm (Dundek, 2006).

POSITIONS FOR DELIVERY   When natural childbirth is combined with delivery in a birth center or at home, mothers often give birth in an upright, sitting position rather than lying flat on their backs with their feet in stirrups (the traditional hospital delivery room practice). Use of special seats to enable an upright birth has become more common.

© AMELIE-BENOIST/BSIP/THE IMAGE WORKS

LOOK and LISTEN

Talk to several mothers about social supports available to them during labor and delivery. From the mothers' perspectives, how did those supports (or lack of support) affect the birth experience?

When mothers are upright, labor is slightly shorter because contractions are stronger and pushing is more effective. The baby benefits from a richer supply of oxygen because blood flow to the placenta is increased, and fewer instances of infant heartbeat irregularities occur. Because the mother can see the delivery, she can work with the doctor or midwife, adjusting her pushing to ensure that the baby's head and shoulders emerge slowly, which reduces the chances of tearing the mother's tissues and, thus, the need for an *episiotomy* (incision that increases the size of the vaginal opening). Compared with those who give birth lying on their backs, women who choose an upright position are less likely to use pain-relieving medication or to have instrument-assisted deliveries (Gupta, Hofmeyr, & Shehmar, 2012; Romano & Lothian, 2008).

In another increasingly popular method, water birth, the mother sits in a warm tub of water, which supports her weight, relaxes her, and provides her with the freedom to move into any position she finds most comfortable. Among mothers at low risk for birth complications, water birth is associated with reduced maternal stress, shorter labor, lower episiotomy rate, and greater likelihood of medication-free delivery than both back-lying and seated positions (American Association of Birth Centers, 2014; Cluett & Burns, 2013). As long as water birth is carefully managed by skilled health professionals, it poses no additional risk of infection or safety to mothers or babies.

Home Delivery

Home birth has always been popular in certain industrialized nations, such as England, the Netherlands, and Sweden. The number of American women choosing to have their babies at home rose during the 1970s and 1980s but remains small, at less than 1 percent (Martin et al., 2013). Although some home births are attended by doctors, many more are handled by *certified nurse-midwives,* who have degrees in nursing and additional training in childbirth management.

The joys and perils of home delivery are well illustrated by the story that Don, a father of four, told us. "Our first child was delivered in the hospital," he said. "Even though I was present, Kathy and I found the atmosphere to be rigid and insensitive. We wanted a warmer, more personal birth environment." With a nurse-midwife's coaching, Don delivered their second child, Cindy, at their farmhouse, 3 miles out of town. Three years later, when Kathy went into labor with Marnie, a heavy snowstorm prevented the midwife from reaching the house on time, so Don delivered the baby alone. The birth was difficult, and Marnie failed to breathe for several minutes. With great effort, Don managed to revive her. The frightening memory of Marnie's limp, blue body convinced Don and Kathy to return to the hospital to have their last child. By then, the hospital's birth practices had changed, and the event was a rewarding one for both parents.

Don and Kathy's experience raises the question: Is it just as safe to give birth at home as in a hospital? For healthy women who are assisted by a well-trained doctor or midwife, it seems so because complications rarely occur (Fullerton, Navarro, & Young, 2007; Wax, Pinette, & Cartin, 2010). However, if attendants are not carefully trained and prepared to handle emergencies, the likelihood of infant disability and death is high. When mothers are at risk for any kind of complication, the appropriate place for labor and delivery is the hospital, where lifesaving treatment is available.

After a home birth, the midwife and a lay attendant provide support to the new mother. For healthy women attended by a well-trained doctor or midwife, home birth is as safe as hospital birth.

Medical Interventions

4.3 List common medical interventions during childbirth, circumstances that justify their use, and any dangers associated with each.

Medical interventions during childbirth occur in both industrialized and nonindustrialized cultures. For example, some tribal and village societies have discovered labor-inducing drugs and devised surgical techniques to deliver babies (Jordan, 1993). Yet childbirth in North America, more so than elsewhere in the world, is a medically monitored and controlled event.

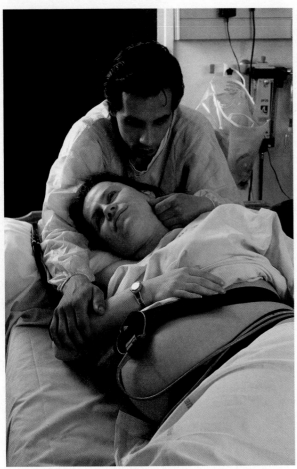

The fetal monitor strapped across this mother's abdomen uses ultrasound to record fetal heart rate throughout labor. In high-risk situations, fetal monitoring saves many lives. But it also may encourage unnecessary instrument and cesarean deliveries.

Use of some medical procedures has reached epic proportions—in part because of rising rates of multiple births and other high-risk deliveries, which are associated with increased maternal age and use of fertility treatments. But births unaffected by these factors are also medicalized.

What medical techniques are doctors likely to use during labor and delivery? When are they justified, and what dangers do they pose to mothers and babies?

Fetal Monitoring

Fetal monitors are electronic instruments that track the baby's heart rate during labor. An abnormal heartbeat pattern may indicate that the baby is in distress due to lack of oxygen and needs to be delivered immediately. Continuous fetal monitoring, which is required in most U.S. hospitals, is used in over 85 percent of U.S. births (Ananth et al., 2013). The most popular type of monitor is strapped across the mother's abdomen throughout labor. A second, more accurate method involves threading a recording device through the cervix and placing it directly under the baby's scalp.

Fetal monitoring is a safe medical procedure that has saved the lives of many babies in high-risk situations. But in healthy pregnancies, it does not reduce the already low rates of infant brain damage and death (Haws et al., 2009). Furthermore, most infants have some heartbeat irregularities during labor, so critics worry that fetal monitors identify many babies as in danger who, in fact, are not. Monitoring is linked to an increase in the number of instrument and cesarean (surgical) deliveries, practices we will discuss shortly (Wolfberg, 2012). In addition, some women complain that the devices are uncomfortable and interfere with the normal course of labor.

Still, fetal monitors will probably continue to be used routinely in the United States, even though they are not necessary in most cases. Doctors fear that they will be sued for malpractice if an infant dies or is born with problems and they cannot show that they did everything possible to protect the baby.

Labor and Delivery Medication

Some form of medication is used in over 60 percent of U.S. births (Osterman & Martin, 2011). *Analgesics,* drugs used to relieve pain, may be given in mild doses during labor to help a mother relax. *Anesthetics* are a stronger type of painkiller that blocks sensation. Currently, the most common approach to controlling pain during labor is *epidural analgesia,* in which a regional pain-relieving drug is delivered continuously through a catheter into a small space in the lower spine. Unlike older spinal block procedures, which numb the entire lower half of the body, epidural analgesia limits pain reduction to the pelvic region. Because the mother retains the capacity to feel the pressure of the contractions and to move her trunk and legs, she is able to push during the second stage of labor.

Although pain-relieving drugs help women cope with childbirth and enable doctors to perform essential medical interventions, they also can cause problems. Epidural analgesia, for example, weakens uterine contractions. As a result, labor is prolonged, and the chances of instrument delivery or cesarean (surgical) birth increase. And because drugs rapidly cross the placenta, exposed newborns are at risk for respiratory distress (Kumar et al., 2014). They also tend to have lower Apgar scores, to be sleepy and withdrawn, to suck poorly during feedings, and to be irritable when awake (Caton et al., 2002; Eltzschig, Lieberman, & Camann, 2003; Platt, 2014). Although no confirmed long-term consequences for development exist, the negative impact of these drugs on the newborn's adjustment supports the current trend to limit their use.

Instrument Delivery

Forceps, metal clamps placed around the baby's head to pull the infant from the birth canal, have been used since the sixteenth century to speed up delivery (see Figure 4.2). A more recent instrument, the *vacuum extractor,* consists of a plastic cup (placed on the baby's head) attached to a suction tube. Instrument delivery is appropriate if the mother's pushing during the second stage of labor does not move the baby through the birth canal in a reasonable period of time.

Instrument use has declined considerably over the past three decades, partly because doctors more often deliver babies surgically when labor problems arise. Today, forceps and (more often) vacuum extractors continue to be used in about 3 percent of U.S. births (Martin et al., 2013).

Using forceps to pull the baby through most or all of the birth canal greatly increases the risk of brain damage. As a result, forceps are seldom used this way today. Low-forceps delivery (carried out when the baby is most of the way through the vagina) is associated with injury to the baby's head and the mother's tissues. Vacuum extractors, which have rapidly replaced forceps as the dominant instrument, are less likely to tear the mother's tissues. Nevertheless, cup suction doubles the risk of bleeding beneath the baby's skin and on the outside of the skull compared with nonassisted deliveries. And the risk of more serious complications, including bleeding beneath the skull and seizures (which can damage the brain), increases tenfold (Ekéus, Högberg, & Norman, 2014). Consequently, neither instrument should be used when mothers can be encouraged to deliver normally and there is no special reason to hurry the birth.

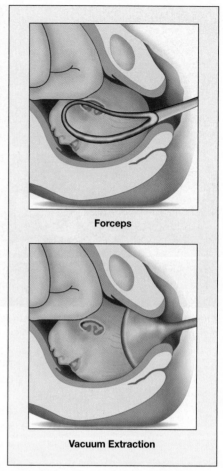

Forceps

Vacuum Extraction

FIGURE 4.2 **Instrument delivery.** The pressure that must be applied to pull the infant from the birth canal with forceps can injure the baby's head. An alternative method, the vacuum extractor, is less likely than forceps to injure the mother's tissues. Nevertheless, risk of infant scalp injuries and internal bleeding in the eyes and skull remains.

Induced Labor

An **induced labor** is one that is started artificially, usually by breaking the amnion, or bag of waters (an event that typically occurs naturally in the first stage of labor), and giving the mother synthetic oxytocin, a hormone that stimulates contractions. About 23 percent of American labors are induced—a figure that has more than doubled over the past two decades (U.S. Census Bureau, 2014b).

Induced labors are justified when continuing the pregnancy threatens the well-being of mother or baby. Often, though, they are performed for the doctor's or the patient's convenience—a major reason they have increased. An induced labor often proceeds differently from a naturally occurring one. Contractions are longer, harder, and closer together, increasing the possibility of inadequate oxygen supply to the baby. In addition, mothers often find it more difficult to stay in control of an induced labor, even when they have been coached in natural childbirth techniques. As a result, labor and delivery medication is likely to be used in larger amounts, and the chances of instrument delivery are slightly greater (Hoffman et al., 2006; Ramirez, 2011).

Occasionally, induction is performed before the mother is physically ready to give birth, and the procedure fails. When this happens, a cesarean delivery is necessary. The rate of cesareans is substantially higher in induced than spontaneous labors. Ripening of the cervix—initial dilation and effacement—is the best predictor of the success of labor induction (Simpson, 2011).

Cesarean Delivery

A **cesarean delivery** is a surgical birth; the doctor makes an incision in the mother's abdomen and lifts the baby out of the uterus. Forty years ago, cesarean delivery was rare. Since then, cesarean rates have climbed internationally, reaching 16 percent in Finland, 24 percent in New Zealand, 26 percent in Canada, 32 percent in Australia and Switzerland, and 37 percent in the United States (Martin et al., 2013; OECD, 2013a).

Cesareans have always been warranted by medical emergencies, such as Rh incompatibility, premature separation of the placenta from the uterus, or serious maternal illness or

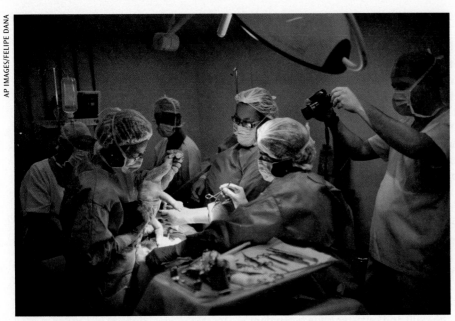

A new father records his baby's arrival by cesarean delivery. Cesareans have become increasingly common over the past forty years, largely because of medical control over childbirth.

infection (for example, the herpes simplex 2 virus, which can infect the baby during a vaginal delivery). Cesareans are also justified when babies are in **breech position,** turned so that the buttocks or feet would be delivered first (about 1 in every 25 births). The breech position increases the chances of squeezing of the umbilical cord as the large head moves through the birth canal, thereby depriving the infant of oxygen. Head injuries are also more likely. But the infant's exact position makes a difference. Certain breech babies fare just as well with a normal delivery as with a cesarean (Vistad et al., 2013). Sometimes the doctor can gently turn the baby into a head-down position during the early part of labor.

Until recently, many women who have had a cesarean have been offered the option of a vaginal birth in subsequent pregnancies. But growing evidence indicates that compared with repeated cesareans, a natural labor after a cesarean is associated with slightly increased rates of rupture of the uterus and infant death (Hunter, 2014). As a result, the rule "Once a cesarean, always a cesarean" has made a comeback.

Repeated cesareans, however, do not explain the worldwide rise in cesarean deliveries. Instead, medical control over childbirth is largely responsible. Because many needless cesareans are performed, pregnant women should ask questions about the procedure when choosing a doctor. Although the operation itself is safe, mother and baby require more time for recovery. Anesthetic may have crossed the placenta, making cesarean newborns sleepy and unresponsive and putting them at increased risk for breathing difficulties (Ramachandrappa & Jain, 2008).

Ask Yourself

- **REVIEW** Describe the features and benefits of natural childbirth. What aspect contributes greatly to favorable outcomes, and why?

- **CONNECT** How might use of epidural analgesia negatively affect the parent–newborn relationship? Explain how your answer illustrates bidirectional influences between parent and child, emphasized in ecological systems theory.

- **APPLY** Sharon, a heavy smoker, has just arrived at the hospital in labor. Which one of the medical interventions discussed in the preceding sections is her doctor justified in using? (For help in answering this question, review the prenatal effects of tobacco on pages 105–106 in Chapter 3.)

- **REFLECT** If you were an expectant parent, would you choose home birth? Why or why not?

4.4 What are the risks of oxygen deprivation, preterm birth, and low birth weight, and what factors can help infants who survive a traumatic birth?

Birth Complications

We have seen that some babies—in particular, those whose mothers are in poor health, do not receive good medical care, or have a history of pregnancy problems—are especially likely to experience birth complications. Inadequate oxygen, a pregnancy that ends too early, and a baby who is born underweight are serious risks to development that we have touched on many times. A baby remaining in the uterus too long is yet another risk. Let's look at the impact of each complication on later development.

Oxygen Deprivation

Some years ago, we got to know 4-year-old Melinda and her mother, Judy, both of whom participated in a special program for children with disabilities at our laboratory school. Melinda has *cerebral palsy,* a general term for a variety of impairments in muscle coordination caused by brain damage before, during, or just after birth. The disorder can range from mild tremors to severe physical and mental disability. One out of every 500 American children has cerebral palsy. About 10 percent experienced **anoxia,** or inadequate oxygen supply, along with a buildup of harmful acids and deficiency of vital blood substrates, as a result of decreased maternal blood supply during labor and delivery (Clark, Ghulmiyyah, & Hankins, 2008; McIntyre et al., 2013).

Melinda walks with a halting, lumbering gait and has difficulty keeping her balance. "Some mothers don't know how the palsy happened," confided Judy, "but I do. I got pregnant accidentally, and my boyfriend didn't want to have anything to do with it. I was frightened and alone most of the time. I arrived at the hospital at the last minute. Melinda was breech, and the cord was wrapped around her neck."

Squeezing of the umbilical cord, as in Melinda's case, is one cause of anoxia. Another cause is *placenta abruptio,* or premature separation of the placenta, a life-threatening event with a high rate of infant death. Factors related to it include multiple fetuses and teratogens that cause constriction of blood vessels and abnormal development of the placenta, such as tobacco and cocaine (Yamada et al., 2012). Just as serious is *placenta previa,* a condition caused by implantation of the blastocyst so low in the uterus that the placenta covers the cervical opening. As the cervix dilates and effaces in the third trimester, part of the placenta may detach. Women who have had previous cesareans or who are carrying multiple fetuses are at increased risk (Trønnes et al., 2014). Although placenta abruptio and placenta previa occur in only 1 to 2 percent of births, they can cause severe hemorrhaging, which requires that an emergency cesarean be performed.

In still other instances, the birth seems to go along all right, but the baby fails to start breathing within a few minutes. Healthy newborns can survive periods of little or no oxygen longer than adults can; they reduce their metabolic rate, thereby conserving the limited oxygen available. Nevertheless, brain damage is likely if regular breathing is delayed more than 10 minutes. **TAKE A MOMENT...** Can you think of other possible causes of oxygen deprivation that you learned about as you studied prenatal development and birth?

After initial brain injury from anoxia, another phase of cell death can occur several hours later. Placing anoxic newborns in a head-cooling device shortly after birth for 72 hours substantially reduces this secondary brain damage (detected through brain scans) and increases scores on a newborn behavioral assessment (Hoehn et al., 2008). Another alternative—whole-body cooling by having anoxic newborns lie on a precooled water blanket—leads to an impressive reduction in death and disability rates during the first two years (Allen, 2014).

How do children who experience anoxia during labor and delivery fare as they get older? Research suggests that the greater the oxygen deprivation, the poorer children's cognitive and language skills in early and middle childhood (Hopkins-Golightly, Raz, & Sander, 2003; Vohr et al., 2013). Although effects of even mild to moderate anoxia often persist, many children improve over time (Bass et al., 2004). In Melinda's case, her physical disability was permanent, but with warm, stimulating intervention services, she was just slightly behind in mental development as a preschooler.

When development is severely impaired, the anoxia was probably extreme. Perhaps it was caused by prenatal insult to the baby's respiratory system, or it may have happened because the infant's lungs were not yet mature enough to

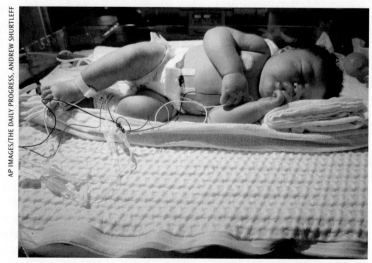

Treatment for this newborn, who experienced oxygen deprivation, includes a cooling water blanket to lower the baby's body temperature, which helps prevent brain damage.

breathe. For example, infants born more than six weeks early commonly have *respiratory distress syndrome* (otherwise known as *hyaline membrane disease*). Their tiny lungs are so poorly developed that the air sacs collapse, causing serious breathing difficulties. Today, mechanical respirators keep many such infants alive. In spite of these measures, some babies suffer permanent brain damage from lack of oxygen, and in other cases their delicate lungs are harmed by the treatment itself. Respiratory distress syndrome is only one of many risks for babies born too soon, as we will see in the following section.

Preterm and Low-Birth-Weight Infants

Janet, almost six months pregnant, and her husband, Rick, boarded a flight in Hartford, Connecticut, on their way to a vacation in Hawaii. During a stopover in San Francisco, Janet told Rick she was bleeding. Rushed to a hospital, she gave birth to Keith, who weighed less than 1½ pounds. Delivered 23 weeks after conception, he had barely reached the age of viability (see Chapter 3, page 99).

During Keith's first month, he experienced one crisis after another. Three days after birth, an ultrasound scan suggested that fragile blood vessels feeding Keith's brain had hemorrhaged, a complication that can cause brain damage. Within three weeks, Keith had surgery to close a heart valve that seals automatically in full-term babies. Keith's immature immune system made infections difficult to contain. Repeated illnesses and the drugs used to treat them caused permanent hearing loss. Keith also had respiratory distress syndrome and breathed with the help of a respirator. Soon there was evidence of lung damage. More than three months of hospitalization passed before Keith's rough course of complications and treatment eased.

Babies born three weeks or more before the end of a full 38-week pregnancy or who weigh less than 5½ pounds (2,500 grams) have for many years been referred to as "premature." A wealth of research indicates that premature babies are at risk for many problems. Birth weight is the best available predictor of infant survival and healthy development. Many newborns who weigh less than 3½ pounds (1,500 grams) experience persisting difficulties, an effect that becomes stronger as length of pregnancy and birth weight decrease (see Figure 4.3) (Baron & Rey-Casserly, 2010; Bolisetty et al., 2006; Wilson-Ching et al., 2013). Brain abnormalities, frequent illness, inattention, overactivity, sensory impairments, poor motor coordination, language delays, low intelligence test scores, deficits in school learning, and emotional and behavior problems are some of the problems that persist through childhood and adolescence and into adulthood (Aarnoudse-Moens, Weisglas-Kuperus, & van Goudoever, 2009; Hutchinson et al., 2013; Nosarti et al., 2011; Tanskanen et al., 2011).

About 12 percent of American infants are born early, and 8 percent are born underweight. The two risk factors often co-occur, and they can strike unexpectedly, as Keith's case illustrates. But the problem is highest among poverty-stricken women (Martin et al., 2013). These mothers, as indicated in Chapter 3, are more likely to be under stress, undernourished, and exposed to other harmful environmental influences—factors strongly linked to low birth weight. In addition, they often do not receive adequate prenatal care.

African-American babies are especially vulnerable to early and underweight birth: They have about twice the rates of white and Hispanic infants, even after accounting for SES and other potentially contributing factors, such as single parenthood and young maternal age (Martin et al., 2013). Although the disparity is not yet fully understood, researchers suspect that African-American pregnant mothers' greater exposure to multiple chronic stressors, such as job strain (long hours at tiring work), crime-ridden inner-city neighborhoods, crowded living conditions, and prejudice and discrimination, is involved (Dunkel-Shetter, 2011; Dunkel-Shetter & Lobel, 2012). Many studies confirm, for example, that race-related stressors—

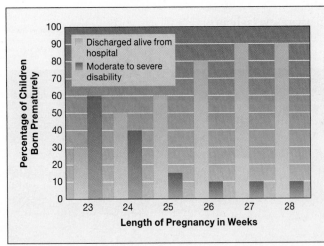

FIGURE 4.3 Rates of infant survival and child disabilities by length of pregnancy. In a follow-up of more than 2,300 babies born between 23 and 28 weeks gestation, the percentage of infants who survived decreased and the percentage who displayed moderate to severe disabilities (assessed during the preschool years) increased with reduced length of pregnancy. Severe disabilities included cerebral palsy (unlikely to ever walk), severely delayed mental development, deafness, and blindness. Moderate disabilities included cerebral palsy (able to walk with assistance), moderately delayed mental development, and hearing impairments partially correctable with a hearing aid. (Adapted from Bolisetty et al., 2006.)

biased treatment at school, at work, or in access to housing—predict lower birth weight, especially in African-American women (Giscombé & Lobel, 2005).

Furthermore, low birth weight is often transmitted across generations: Women who were underweight at birth themselves are twice as likely as other women to bear an underweight baby (Collins, Rankin, & David, 2011). The possible causes are diverse: They may be genetic, environmental, or epigenetic—for example, excessive prenatal stress may impair offspring's lifelong capacity to manage stress (see page 113 in Chapter 3). When a daughter becomes pregnant, she exposes her fetus to severe emotional stress and its negative consequences.

Finally, recall from Chapter 2 that prematurity is common in multiple births. About 60 percent of twins and more than 90 percent of triplets are born early and low birth weight (Martin et al., 2013). Because space inside the uterus is restricted, multiples gain less weight than singletons in the second half of pregnancy.

PRETERM VERSUS SMALL-FOR-DATE INFANTS Although preterm and low-birth-weight infants face many obstacles to healthy development, most go on to lead normal lives; about half of those born at 23 to 24 weeks gestation and weighing only a couple of pounds at birth have no disability (refer again to Figure 4.3). To better understand why some babies do better than others, researchers divide them into two groups. **Preterm infants** are born several weeks or more before their due date. Although they are small, their weight may still be appropriate, based on time spent in the uterus. **Small-for-date infants** are below their expected weight considering length of the pregnancy. Some small-for-date infants are actually full-term. Others are preterm babies who are especially underweight.

Small-for-date infants—especially those who are also preterm—usually have more serious problems. During the first year, they are more likely to die, catch infections, and show evidence of brain damage. By middle childhood, they are smaller in stature, have lower intelligence test scores, are less attentive, achieve more poorly in school, and are socially immature (Katz et al., 2013; Sullivan et al., 2008; Wilson-Ching et al., 2013).

Small-for-date infants probably experienced inadequate nutrition before birth. Perhaps their mothers did not eat properly, the placenta did not function normally, or the babies themselves had defects that prevented them from growing as they should. In some of these babies, an abnormally functioning placenta permitted ready transfer of stress hormones from mother to fetus. Consequently, small-for-date infants are especially likely to suffer from neurological impairments that permanently weaken their capacity to manage stress (Osterholm, Hostinar, & Gunnar, 2012). Severe stress, in turn, heightens their susceptibility to later physical and psychological health problems.

Even among preterm newborns whose weight is appropriate for length of pregnancy, just 7 to 14 more days—from 34 to 35 or 36 weeks—greatly reduces rates of illness, costly medical procedures, and lengthy hospital stays (although they need greater medical intervention than full-term babies) (Ananth, Friedman, & Gyamfi-Bannerman, 2013). And despite being relatively low-risk for disabilities, a substantial number of 34-week preterms are below average in physical growth and mildly to moderately delayed in cognitive development in early and middle childhood (Morse et al., 2009; Stephens & Vohr, 2009). In an investigation of over 120,000 New York City births, babies born even 1 or 2 weeks early showed slightly lower reading and math scores at a third-grade follow-up than children who experienced a full-length prenatal period (Noble et al., 2012). These outcomes persisted even after controlling for other factors linked to achievement, such as birth weight and SES. Yet doctors often induce births several weeks preterm, under the misconception that these babies are developmentally "mature."

CONSEQUENCES FOR CAREGIVING Imagine a scrawny, thin-skinned infant whose body is only a little larger than the size of your hand. You try to play with the baby by stroking and talking softly, but he is sleepy and unresponsive. When you feed him, he sucks poorly. During the short, unpredictable periods in which he is awake, he is usually irritable.

The appearance and behavior of preterm babies can lead parents to be less sensitive and responsive in caring for them. Compared to full-term infants, preterm babies—especially those who are very ill at birth—are less often held close, touched, and talked to gently. At times, mothers of these infants behave in an overly controlling fashion, resorting to interfering pokes and verbal commands in an effort to obtain a higher level of response from the baby (Feldman, 2007b; Forcada-Guex et al., 2006). This may explain why preterm babies as a group are at risk for child abuse.

Research reveals that distressed, emotionally reactive preterm infants are particularly susceptible to the effects of parenting quality: Among a sample of preterm 9-month-olds, the combination of infant negativity and angry or intrusive parenting yielded the highest rates of behavior problems at 2 years of age. But with warm, sensitive parenting, distressed preterm babies' rates of behavior problems were the lowest (Poehlmann et al., 2011). When they are born to isolated, poverty-stricken mothers who cannot provide good nutrition, health care, and parenting, the likelihood of unfavorable outcomes increases. In contrast, parents with stable life circumstances and social supports usually can overcome the stresses of caring for a preterm infant (Ment et al., 2003). In these cases, even sick preterm babies have a good chance of catching up in development by middle childhood.

These findings suggest that how well preterm babies develop has a great deal to do with the parent–child relationship. Consequently, interventions directed at supporting both sides of this tie are more likely to help these infants recover.

INTERVENTIONS FOR PRETERM INFANTS   A preterm baby is cared for in a special Plexiglas-enclosed bed called an *isolette*. Temperature is carefully controlled because these infants cannot yet regulate their own body temperature effectively. To help protect the baby from infection, air is filtered before it enters the isolette. When a preterm infant is fed through a stomach tube, breathes with the aid of a respirator, and receives medication through an intravenous needle, the isolette can be very isolating indeed! Physical needs that otherwise would lead to close contact and other human stimulation are met mechanically.

Special Infant Stimulation.   In proper doses, certain kinds of stimulation can help preterm infants develop. In some intensive care nurseries, preterm babies can be seen rocking in suspended hammocks or lying on waterbeds designed to replace the gentle motion they would have received while still in the mother's uterus. Other forms of stimulation have also been used—an attractive mobile or a tape recording of a heartbeat, soft music, or the mother's voice. These experiences promote faster weight gain, more predictable sleep patterns, and greater alertness (Arnon et al., 2006; Marshall-Baker, Lickliter, & Cooper, 1998).

Touch is an especially important form of stimulation. In baby animals, touching the skin releases certain brain chemicals that support physical growth—effects believed to occur in humans as well. When preterm infants were gently massaged several times each day in the hospital, they gained weight faster and, at the end of the first year, were more advanced in mental and motor development than preterm babies not given this stimulation (Field, 2001; Field, Hernandez-Reif, & Freedman, 2004).

In developing countries where hospitalization is not always possible, skin-to-skin "kangaroo care" is the most readily available intervention for promoting the survival and recovery of preterm babies. It involves placing the infant in a vertical position between the mother's breasts or next to the father's chest (under the parent's clothing) so the parent's body functions as a human incubator. Kangaroo care offers fathers a unique opportunity to increase their involvement in caring for the preterm newborn. Because of its many physical and psychological benefits, the technique is used often in Western nations as a supplement to hospital intensive care.

Kangaroo skin-to-skin contact fosters improved oxygenation of the baby's body, temperature regulation, sleep, breastfeeding, alertness, and infant survival (Conde-Agudelo, Belizan, & Diaz-Rossello, 2011; Kaffashi et al., 2013; Lawn et al., 2010). In addition, the kangaroo position provides the baby with gentle stimulation of all sensory modalities: hearing (through the parent's voice), smell (through proximity to the parent's body), touch (through skin-to-skin contact), and visual (through the upright position). Mothers and fathers practicing kanga-

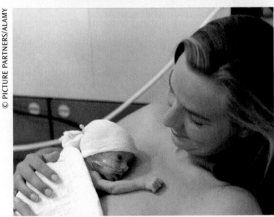

Top photo: A father in El Salvador uses skin-to-skin "kangaroo care" with his infant as part of a hospital program that teaches parents techniques for promoting survival and development in preterm and underweight babies. *Bottom photo:* In Western nations, kangaroo care may be used to supplement hospital intensive care. Here, a U.S. mother engages in the technique with her fragile newborn.

© ERNESTO BONILLA/XINHUA PRESS/CORBIS

© PICTURE PARTNERS/ALAMY

roo care feel more confident about caring for their fragile babies, interact more sensitively and affectionately, and feel more attached to them (Dodd, 2005; Feldman, 2007a).

Together, these factors may explain why preterm babies given many hours of kangaroo care in their early weeks, compared to those given little or no such care, are more likely to explore novel toys and score higher on measures of mental and motor development during the first year (Bera et al., 2014; Feldman, 2007a). Because of its diverse benefits, most U.S. hospital nurseries now offer kangaroo care to parents and preterm newborns.

Training Parents in Infant Caregiving Skills. Interventions that support parents of preterm infants generally teach them about the infant's characteristics and promote caregiving skills. For parents with the economic and personal resources to care for a preterm infant, just a few sessions of coaching in recognizing and responding to the baby's needs are linked to enhanced parent–infant interaction, reduced infant crying and improved sleep, more rapid language development in the second year, and steady gains in mental test performance that equal those of full-term children by middle childhood (Achenbach, Howell, & Aoki, 1993; Newnham, Milgrom, & Skouteris, 2009).

When preterm infants live in stressed, economically disadvantaged households, long-term intensive intervention is necessary (Guralnick, 2012). In the Infant Health and Development Program, preterm babies born into poverty received a comprehensive intervention. It combined medical follow-up, weekly home visits beginning soon after hospital discharge in which mothers received training in infant care and everyday problem solving, and cognitively stimulating child care from 1 to 3 years of age. More than four times as many intervention children as no-intervention controls (39 versus 9 percent) were within normal range at age 3 in intelligence, psychological adjustment, and physical growth (Bradley et al., 1994). In addition, mothers in the intervention group were more affectionate and more often encouraged play and cognitive mastery in their children—one reason their 3-year-olds may have been developing so favorably (McCarton, 1998).

At ages 5 and 8, children who had attended the child-care program regularly—for more than 350 days over the three-year period—continued to show better intellectual functioning. The more they attended, the higher they scored, with greater gains among those whose birth weights were higher—between 4½ and 5½ pounds (2,001 to 2,500 grams) (see Figure 4.4). In contrast, children who attended only sporadically gained little or even lost ground (Hill, Brooks-Gunn, & Waldfogel, 2003). A follow-up at age 18 revealed persisting benefits for the higher-birth-weight participants: They remained advantaged over controls in academic achievement, and they also engaged in fewer risky behaviors such as unprotected sexual activity and alcohol and drug use (McCormick et al., 2006).

These findings confirm that babies who are both preterm and economically disadvantaged require *intensive* intervention. And special strategies, such as extra adult–child interaction both at home and in infant–toddler and early childhood programs, may be necessary to achieve lasting changes in children with the lowest birth weights.

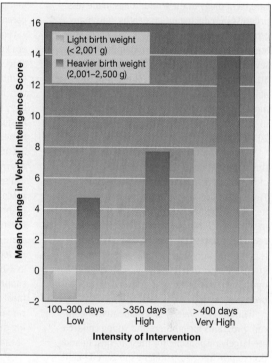

FIGURE 4.4 Influence of intensity of early intervention for low-income, preterm babies on intellectual functioning at age 8. Infants born preterm received cognitively stimulating child care from 1 through 3 years of age. Those who attended the program sporadically gained little in intellectual functioning (heavier-weight babies) or lost ground (lighter-weight babies). The more often children attended, the greater their intellectual gains. Heavier babies consistently gained more than light babies. But boosting the intensity of intervention above 400 days led to a dramatic increase in the performance of the light-weight group. (Adapted from Hill, Brooks-Gunn, & Waldfogel, 2003.)

VERY LOW BIRTH WEIGHT, ENVIRONMENTAL ADVANTAGES, AND LONG-TERM OUTCOMES Although very low-birth-weight individuals often have lasting problems, in a Canadian study, young adults who weighed between 1 and 2.2 pounds (500 to 1,000 grams) at birth were doing well in overall quality of life (Saigal et al., 2006). At 22 to 25 years of age, they resembled normal-birth-weight individuals in educational attainment, rates of marriage and parenthood, and (for those who had no neurological or sensory impairments) employment status. What explains these excellent outcomes? Researchers believe that home, school, and societal advantages are largely responsible (Hack & Klein, 2006). Most participants in this study were reared in two-parent middle-SES homes, attended good schools where they received special services, and benefited from Canada's universal health care system.

Social Issues: Health

A Cross-National Perspective on Health Care and Other Policies for Parents and Newborn Babies

Infant mortality—the number of deaths in the first year of life per 1,000 live births—is an index used around the world to assess the overall health of a nation's children. Although the United States has the most up-to-date health-care technology in the world, it has made less progress in reducing infant deaths than many other countries. Over the past three decades, it has slipped in the international rankings, from seventh in the 1950s to thirty-seventh in 2014. Members of America's poor ethnic minorities are at greatest risk, with African-American infants more than twice as likely as white infants to die in the first year of life (U.S. Census Bureau, 2014a, 2014b).

Neonatal mortality, the rate of death within the first month of life, accounts for 67 percent of the infant death rate in the United States. Two factors are largely responsible for neonatal mortality. The first is serious physical defects, most of which cannot be prevented. The percentage of babies born with physical defects is about the same in all ethnic and income groups. The second leading cause of neonatal mortality is low birth weight, which is largely preventable.

Widespread poverty and inadequate health-care programs for mothers and young children are largely responsible for these trends. In addition to providing government-sponsored health-care benefits to all citizens, each country in Figure 4.5 takes extra steps to make sure that pregnant mothers and babies have access to good nutrition, high-quality medical care, and social and economic supports that promote effective parenting.

For example, all Western European nations guarantee women a certain number of prenatal visits at very low or no cost. After a baby is born, a health professional routinely visits the home to provide counseling about infant care and to arrange continuing medical services. Home assistance is especially extensive in the Netherlands. For a token fee, each mother is granted a specially trained maternity helper, who assists with infant care, shopping, housekeeping, meal preparation, and the care of other children during the days after delivery (Zwart, 2007).

Paid, job-protected employment leave is another vital societal

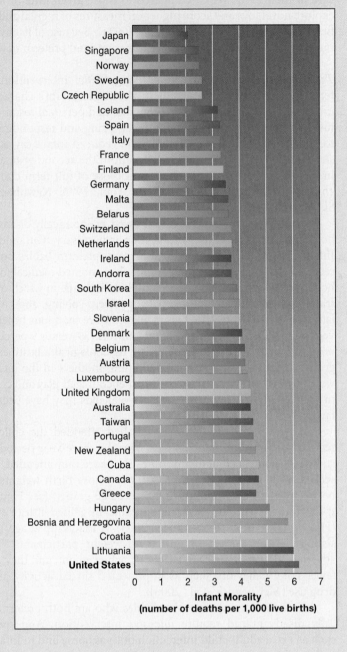

FIGURE 4.5 **Infant mortality in 37 nations.** Despite its advanced health-care technology, the United States ranks poorly. It is thirty-seventh in the world, with a death rate of 6.2 infants per 1,000 births. (Adapted from U.S. Census Bureau, 2014a.)

Nevertheless, even the best environments cannot always overcome the enormous biological risks associated with very low birth weight. Think back to Keith, the very sick baby you met at the beginning of this section. Despite advanced medical technology and new ways of helping parents, most infants born as early and with as low a birth weight as Keith either die or end up with serious disabilities (Larroque et al., 2008). Six months after he was born, Keith died without ever having left the hospital.

Keith's premature birth was unavoidable, but the high rate of underweight babies in the United States—one of the worst in the industrialized world—could be greatly reduced by improving the health and social conditions described in the Social Issues: Health box above.

intervention for new parents. Canadian mothers are eligible for 15 weeks' maternity leave at 55 percent of prior earnings (up to a maximum of $413 per week), and Canadian mothers or fathers can take an additional 35 weeks of parental leave at the same rate. Paid maternal and paternal leave is widely available in other industrialized nations as well. Sweden has the most generous parental leave program in the world. Mothers can begin maternity leave 60 days prior to expected delivery, extending it to six weeks after birth; fathers are granted two weeks of birth leave. In addition, either parent can take full leave for 15 months at 80 percent of prior earnings, followed by an additional three months at a modest flat rate. Each parent is also entitled to another 18 months of unpaid leave. Even economically less well-off nations provide parental leave benefits. In Bulgaria, new mothers are granted 20 months paid leave, and fathers receive three weeks (Robila, 2012). Furthermore, many countries supplement basic paid leave. In Germany, for example, after a fully paid three-month leave, a parent may take one more year at a flat rate and additional leave at no pay until the child reaches age 3 years (Ray, Gornick, & Schmitt, 2008).

Yet in the United States, the federal government mandates *only 12 weeks of unpaid leave* for employees in companies with at least 50 workers. Most women, however, work in smaller businesses, and many of those who work in large enough companies cannot afford to take unpaid leave. And because of financial pressures, many new mothers who are eligible for unpaid work leave take far less than 12 weeks. Similarly, though paternal leave predicts fathers' increased involvement in infant care at the end of first year, many fathers take little or none at all (Nepomnyaschy & Waldfogel, 2007). In 2002, California became the first state to guarantee a mother or father paid leave—up to six weeks at half salary, regardless of the size of the company. Since then, the District of Columbia, Hawaii, New

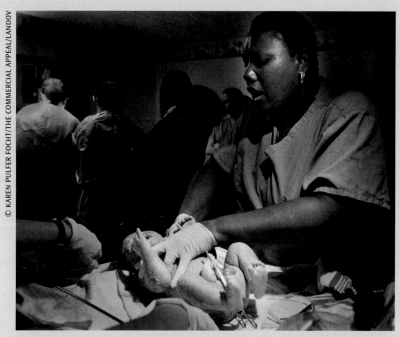

This doctor works with high-risk pregnancies, delivering infants whose poverty-stricken mothers have had little or no prenatal care. Nations with low poverty rates and government-supported, high-quality health care for pregnant mothers and babies outrank the United States in infant survival.

Jersey, New York, Rhode Island, Washington, and the territory of Puerto Rico have passed similar legislation.

Nevertheless, six weeks of childbirth leave (the norm in the United States) is not enough. When a family is stressed by a baby's arrival, leaves of six weeks or less are linked to increased maternal anxiety, depression, marital dissatisfaction, sense of role overload, and negative interactions with the baby. A longer leave (12 weeks or more) predicts favorable maternal mental health, supportive marital interaction, and sensitive, responsive caregiving (Feldman, Sussman, & Zigler, 2004; Hyde et al., 2001). Single women and their babies are most hurt by the absence of a generous national paid-leave policy. These

mothers, who are usually the sole source of support for their families, can least afford to take time from their jobs.

In countries with low infant mortality rates, expectant parents need not wonder how they will access essential resources for supporting their baby's development. The powerful impact of universal, high-quality health care; generous parental leave; and other social services on maternal and infant well-being provides strong justification for these policies. Responding to these findings, the Affordable Care Act provides generous grants to U.S. states to cover the cost of evidence-based home-visiting programs that provide comprehensive services to mothers, infants, and young children in high-risk families.

Fortunately, today we can save many preterm babies, but an even better course of action would be to prevent this serious threat to infant survival and development before it happens.

Birth Complications, Parenting, and Resilience

In the preceding sections, we considered a variety of birth complications. Now let's try to put the evidence together. Can any general principles help us understand how infants who survive a traumatic birth are likely to develop? A landmark study carried out in Hawaii provides answers to this question.

In 1955, Emmy Werner and Ruth Smith began to follow the development of nearly 700 infants on the island of Kauai who experienced either mild, moderate, or severe birth complications. Each was matched, on the basis of SES and ethnicity, with a healthy newborn (Werner & Smith, 1982). Findings showed that the likelihood of long-term difficulties increased if birth trauma was severe. But among mildly to moderately stressed children, those growing up in stable families with sensitive, involved parenting did almost as well on measures of intelligence and psychological adjustment as those with no birth problems. Children exposed to poverty, family disorganization, and mentally ill parents often developed serious learning difficulties, behavior problems, and emotional disturbance.

The Kauai study tells us that as long as birth injuries are not overwhelming, a supportive home can restore children's growth. But the most intriguing cases in this study were the handful of exceptions. A few children with both fairly serious birth complications and troubled family environments grew into competent adults who fared as well as controls in career attainment and psychological adjustment. Werner and Smith found that these children relied on factors outside the family and within themselves to overcome stress. Some had attractive personalities that drew positive responses from relatives, neighbors, and peers. In other instances, a grandparent, aunt, uncle, or babysitter provided the needed emotional support (Werner, 1989, 2001; Werner & Smith, 1992).

Do these outcomes remind you of the characteristics of resilient children, discussed in Chapter 1? The Kauai study and other similar investigations reveal that the impact of early biological risks often wanes as children's personal characteristics and social experiences contribute increasingly to their functioning (Werner, 2013). In sum, when the overall balance of life events tips toward the favorable side, children with serious birth problems can develop successfully. And when negative factors outweigh positive ones, even a sturdy newborn can become a lifelong casualty.

Ask Yourself

- **REVIEW** Sensitive care can help preterm infants recover, but they are less likely than full-term newborns to receive such care. Explain why.

- **CONNECT** List factors discussed in this chapter and in Chapter 3 that increase the chances that an infant will be born underweight. How many of these factors could be prevented by better health care for expectant mothers?

- **APPLY** Cecilia and Anna each gave birth to a 3-pound baby seven weeks preterm. Cecilia is single and on welfare. Anna and her husband are happily married and earn a good income. Plan an intervention appropriate for helping each baby develop.

- **REFLECT** Many people object to the use of extraordinary medical measures to save extremely low-birth-weight babies because of their high risk for serious developmental problems. Do you agree or disagree? Explain.

4.5 Is close parent–infant contact shortly after birth necessary for bonding?

Precious Moments After Birth

Yolanda and Jay's account of Joshua's birth revealed that the time spent holding and touching him right after delivery was filled with intense emotion. A mother given her infant at this time will usually stroke the baby gently, look into the infant's eyes, and talk softly (Klaus & Kennell, 1982). Fathers respond similarly. Most are overjoyed at their baby's birth; characterize the experience as "awesome," "indescribable," or "unforgettable"; and display intense interest in their newborn child (Rose, 2000). Regardless of SES or participation in childbirth classes, fathers touch, look at, talk to, and kiss their newborn infants just as much as mothers do.

Because effective caregiving is crucial for infant survival and optimal development, nature helps prepare mothers and fathers for their new role. Toward the end of pregnancy, mothers begin producing higher levels of the hormone *oxytocin,* which causes the breasts to "let down" milk; induces a calm, relaxed mood; and heightens responsiveness to the baby (Gordon et al., 2010).

Fathers show hormonal changes around the time of birth that are compatible with those of mothers—specifically, slight increases in *prolactin* (a hormone that stimulates milk production in females) and *estrogens* (sex hormones produced in larger quantities in females) and a drop in *androgens* (sex hormones produced in larger quantities in males) (Delahunty et al., 2007; Wynne-Edwards, 2001). These changes, which are induced by fathers' contact with the mother and baby, predict paternal positive emotional reactions and sensitivity to infants (Feldman et al., 2010; Leuner, Glasper, & Gould, 2010).

But do human parents require close physical contact in the hours after birth for **bonding,** or feelings of affection and concern for the infant, to develop—as many animal species do? Current evidence shows that the human parent–infant relationship does not depend on a precise, early period of togetherness. Some parents report sudden, deep feelings of affection on first holding their babies. For others, these emotions emerge gradually. And as successful adoption reveals (see pages 66–67 in Chapter 2), humans can parent effectively without experiencing birth-related hormonal changes. In fact, when foster and adoptive mothers hold and interact with their nonbiological infants, they typically release oxytocin (Bick et al., 2013; Galbally et al., 2011). And the greater their oxytocin production, the more they express affection and pleasure toward the infant.

Human bonding is a complex process that depends on many factors, not just on what happens during a short period after birth. Nevertheless, early contact with the baby may be one of several factors that help build a good parent–infant relationship. Realizing this, today hospitals offer **rooming in,** in which the infant stays in the mother's hospital room all or most of the time. If parents do not choose this option or cannot do so for medical reasons, there is no evidence that their competence as caregivers will be compromised or that the baby will suffer emotionally.

This father displays great affection for and involvement with his newborn baby. Like mothers, fathers typically express their elation by touching, looking at, talking to, and kissing the infant.

The Newborn Baby's Capacities

Newborn infants have a remarkable set of capacities that are crucial for survival and for evoking adult attention and care. In relating to the physical and social world, babies are active from the very start.

Reflexes

A **reflex** is an inborn, automatic response to a particular form of stimulation. Reflexes are the newborn baby's most obvious organized patterns of behavior. As Jay placed Joshua on a table in the classroom, we saw several. When Jay bumped the side of the table, Joshua reacted by flinging his arms wide and bringing them back toward his body. As Yolanda stroked Joshua's cheek, he turned his head in her direction. When she put her finger in Joshua's palm, he grabbed on tightly. **TAKE A MOMENT...** Look at Table 4.2 on page 142 and see if you can name the newborn reflexes that Joshua displayed. Then let's consider the meaning and purpose of these curious behaviors.

ADAPTIVE VALUE OF REFLEXES   Some reflexes have survival value. The rooting reflex helps a breastfed baby find the mother's nipple. Babies display it only when hungry and touched by another person, not when they touch themselves (Rochat & Hespos, 1997). And if sucking were not automatic, our species would be unlikely to survive for a single generation! At birth, babies adjust their sucking pressure to how easily milk flows from the nipple (Craig & Lee, 1999). The swimming reflex helps a baby who is accidentally dropped into water stay afloat, increasing the chances of retrieval by the caregiver.

4.6 Describe the newborn baby's reflexes and states of arousal, including sleep characteristics and ways to soothe a crying baby.
4.7 Describe the newborn baby's sensory capacities.
4.8 Why is neonatal behavioral assessment useful?

TABLE 4.2	Some Newborn Reflexes			
REFLEX	**STIMULATION**	**RESPONSE**	**AGE OF DISAPPEARANCE**	**FUNCTION**
Eye blink	Shine bright light at eyes or clap hand near head.	Infant quickly closes eyelids.	Permanent	Protects infant from strong stimulation
Rooting	Stroke cheek near corner of mouth	Head turns toward source of stimulation.	3 weeks (becomes voluntary head turning at this time)	Helps infant find the nipple
Sucking	Place finger in infant's mouth.	Infant sucks finger rhythmically.	Replaced by voluntary sucking after 4 months	Permits feeding
Swimming[a]	Occurs when infant is face down in pool of water.	Baby paddles and kicks in swimming motion.	4–6 months	Helps infant survive if dropped into water
Moro	Hold infant horizontally on back and let head drop slightly, or produce a sudden loud sound against surface supporting infant.	Infant makes an "embracing" motion by arching back, extending legs, throwing arms outward, and then bringing arms in toward the body	6 months	In human evolutionary past, may have helped infant cling to mother
Palmar grasp	Place finger in infant's hand and press against palm	Spontaneous grasp of finger	3–4 months	Prepares infant for voluntary grasping
Tonic neck	Turn baby's head to one side while infant is lying awake on back	Infant lies in a "fencing position." One arm is extended in front of eyes on side to which head is turned, other arm is flexed	4 months	May prepare infant for voluntary reaching
Stepping	Hold infant under arms and permit bare feet to touch a flat surface	Infant lifts one foot after another in stepping response	2 months in infants who gain weight quickly; sustained in lighter infants	Prepares infant for voluntary walking
Babinski	Stroke sole of foot from toe toward heel	Toes fan out and curl as foot twists in	8–12 months	Unknown

[a]Placing infants in a pool of water is dangerous. See discussion on the following page.

Sources: Knobloch & Pasamanick, 1974; Prechtl & Beintema, 1965; Thelen, Fisher, & Ridley-Johnson, 1984.

The palmar grasp reflex is so strong during the first week after birth that many infants can use it to support their entire weight.

Other reflexes probably helped babies survive during our evolutionary past. For example, the Moro, or "embracing," reflex is believed to have helped infants cling to their mothers when they were carried about all day (Kessen, 1967). If the baby happened to lose support, the reflex caused the infant to embrace and, along with the palmar grasp reflex (so strong during the first week that it can support the baby's entire weight), regain its hold on the mother's body.

Several reflexes help parents and infants establish gratifying interaction. A baby who searches for and successfully finds the nipple, sucks easily during feedings, and grasps when her hand is touched encourages parents to respond lovingly and feel competent as caregivers. Reflexes can also help parents comfort the baby because they permit infants to control distress and amount of stimulation. For example, on short trips with Joshua to the grocery store, Yolanda brought along a pacifier. If he became fussy, sucking helped quiet him until she could feed, change, or hold him.

REFLEXES AND THE DEVELOPMENT OF MOTOR SKILLS A few reflexes form the basis for complex motor skills that will develop later. For example, the tonic neck reflex may prepare the baby for voluntary reaching. When infants lie on their backs in this "fencing position," they naturally gaze at the hand in front of their eyes. The reflex may encourage them to combine vision with arm movements and, eventually, reach for objects (Knobloch & Pasamanick, 1974).

Certain reflexes—such as the palmar grasp, swimming, and stepping—drop out early, but the motor functions involved are renewed later. The stepping reflex, for example, looks like a primitive walking response. Unlike other reflexes, it appears in a wide range of situations—

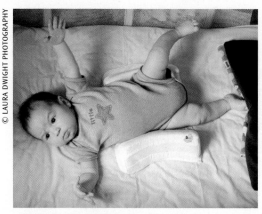

In the Moro reflex, loss of support or a sudden loud sound causes the baby to arch her back, extend her arms outward, and then bring them in toward her body.

In the tonic neck reflex, infants lie on their backs in a "fencing position," which may help prepare them for voluntary reaching.

When held upright under the arms, newborn babies show reflexive stepping movements.

with the newborn's body in a sideways or upside-down position, with feet touching walls or ceilings, and even with legs dangling in the air (Adolph & Berger, 2006). One reason that babies frequently engage in the alternating leg movements of stepping is their ease compared with other movement patterns; repetitive movement of one leg or of both legs at once requires more effort.

In infants who gain weight quickly in the weeks after birth, the stepping reflex drops out because thigh and calf muscles are not strong enough to lift the baby's chubby legs. But if the lower part of the infant's body is dipped in water, the reflex reappears because the buoyancy of the water lightens the load on the baby's muscles (Thelen, Fisher, & Ridley-Johnson, 1984). When stepping is exercised regularly, babies make more spontaneous stepping movements and are likely to walk several weeks earlier than if stepping is not practiced (Zelazo et al., 1993). However, there is no special need for infants to practice the stepping reflex because all normal babies walk in due time.

In the case of the swimming reflex, trying to build on it is risky. Although young babies placed in a swimming pool will paddle and kick, they swallow large amounts of water. This lowers the concentration of salt in the baby's blood, which can cause brain swelling and seizures. Despite this remarkable reflex, swimming lessons are best postponed until at least 3 years of age.

THE IMPORTANCE OF ASSESSING NEWBORN REFLEXES Look at Table 4.2 again, and you will see that most newborn reflexes disappear during the first six months. Researchers believe that this is due to a gradual increase in voluntary control over behavior as the cerebral cortex develops.

Pediatricians test reflexes carefully, especially if a newborn has experienced birth trauma, because reflexes can reveal the health of the baby's nervous system. Weak or absent reflexes, overly rigid or exaggerated reflexes, and reflexes that persist beyond the point in development when they should normally disappear can signal brain damage (Schott & Rossor, 2003; Zafeiriou, 2000). However, individual differences in reflexive responses exist that are not cause for concern. An observer must assess newborn reflexes along with other characteristics to accurately distinguish normal from abnormal central nervous system functioning.

States

Throughout the day and night, newborn infants move in and out of the five **states of arousal,** or degrees of sleep and wakefulness, described in Table 4.3 on page 144. During the first month, these states alternate frequently. The most fleeting is quiet alertness, which usually moves quickly toward fussing and crying. Much to the relief of their fatigued parents, newborns spend the greatest amount of time asleep—about 16 to 18 hours a day. Because the fetus tends to synchronize periods of rest and activity with those of the mother, newborns—even those who are 4 to 6 weeks preterm—sleep more at night than during the day (Heraghty et al.,

TABLE 4.3	Infant States of Arousal	
STATE	**DESCRIPTION**	**DAILY DURATION IN NEWBORN**
Regular, or NREM, sleep	The infant is at full rest and shows little or no body activity. The eyelids are closed, no eye movements occur, the face is relaxed, and breathing is slow and regular.	8–9 hours
Irregular, or REM, sleep	Gentle limb movements, occasional stirring, and facial grimacing occur. Although the eyelids are closed, occasional rapid eye movements can be seen beneath them. Breathing is irregular.	8–9 hours
Drowsiness	The infant is either falling asleep or waking up. Body is less active than in irregular sleep but more active than in regular sleep. The eyes open and close; when open, they have a glazed look. Breathing is even but somewhat faster than in regular sleep.	Varies
Quiet alertness	The infant's body is relatively inactive, with eyes open and attentive. Breathing is even.	2–3 hours
Waking activity and crying	The infant shows frequent bursts of uncoordinated body activity. Breathing is very irregular. Face may be relaxed or tense and wrinkled. Crying may occur.	1–4 hours

Source: Wolff, 1966.

2008). Nevertheless, young babies' sleep–wake cycles are affected more by fullness–hunger than by darkness–light (Davis, Parker, & Montgomery, 2004).

However, striking individual differences in daily rhythms exist that affect parents' attitudes toward and interactions with the baby. A few newborns sleep for long periods, increasing the energy their well-rested parents have for sensitive, responsive care. Other babies wake frequently and cry often, and their parents must exert great effort to soothe them. If these parents do not succeed, they may feel less competent and less positive toward their infant (Sadeh et al., 2007; Smart & Hiscock, 2007).

Furthermore, from birth on, arousal patterns have implications for cognitive development. Babies who spend more time alert probably receive more social stimulation and opportunities to explore and, therefore, may have a slight advantage in mental development. And as with adults, sleep enhances babies' learning and memory. In one study, eye-blink responses and brain-wave recordings revealed that sleeping newborns readily learned that a tone would be followed by a puff of air to the eye (Fifer et al., 2010). Because young infants spend so much time sleeping, the capacity to learn about external stimuli during sleep may be essential for babies' adaptation to their surroundings.

Of the states listed in Table 4.3 the two extremes—sleep and crying—have been of greatest interest to researchers. Each tells us something about normal and abnormal early development.

SLEEP   Observing Joshua as he slept, Yolanda and Jay wondered why his eyelids and body twitched and his rate of breathing varied. Sleep is made up of at least two states. During irregular, or **rapid-eye-movement (REM), sleep,** brain-wave activity is remarkably similar to that of the waking state. The eyes dart beneath the lids; heart rate, blood pressure, and breathing are uneven; and slight body movements occur. The expression "sleeping like a baby" was probably not meant to describe this state! In contrast, during regular, or **non-rapid-eye-movement (NREM), sleep,** the body is almost motionless, and heart rate, breathing, and brain-wave activity are slow and even.

Like children and adults, newborns alternate between REM and NREM sleep. However, they spend far more time in the REM state than they ever will again. REM sleep accounts for 50 percent of the newborn baby's sleep time. By 3 to 5 years, it has declined to an adultlike level of 20 percent (Louis et al., 1997).

Why do young infants spend so much time in REM sleep? In older children and adults, the REM state is associated with dreaming. Babies probably do not dream, at least not in the same way we do. But researchers believe that the stimulation of REM sleep is vital for growth of the central nervous system (Tarullo, Balsam, & Fifer, 2011). Young infants seem to have a special need for this stimulation because they spend so little time in an alert state, when they can get input from the environment. In support of this idea, the percentage of REM sleep is especially great in the fetus and in preterm babies, who are even less able than full-term newborns to take advantage of external stimulation (de Weerd & van den Bossche, 2003; Peirano, Algarin, & Uauy, 2003).

Social Issues: Health

The Mysterious Tragedy of Sudden Infant Death Syndrome

Millie awoke with a start one morning and looked at the clock. It was 7:30, and Sasha had missed both her night waking and her early morning feeding. Wondering if she was all right, Millie and her husband, Stuart, tiptoed into the room. Sasha lay still, curled up under her blanket. She had died silently during her sleep.

Sasha was a victim of **sudden infant death syndrome (SIDS),** the unexpected death, usually during the night, of an infant younger than 1 year of age that remains unexplained after thorough investigation. In industrialized nations, SIDS is the leading cause of infant mortality between 1 week and 12 months, accounting for about 11 percent of these deaths in the United States (Child Health USA, 2013).

SIDS victims usually show physical problems from the beginning. Early medical records of SIDS babies reveal higher rates of prematurity and low birth weight, poor Apgar scores, and limp muscle tone. Abnormal heart rate and respiration and disturbances in sleep–wake activity and in REM–NREM cycles while asleep are also involved (Cornwell & Feigenbaum, 2006; Garcia, Koschnitzky, & Ramirez, 2013). At the time of death, many SIDS babies have a mild respiratory infection (Blood-Siegfried, 2009). This seems to increase the chances of respiratory failure in an already vulnerable baby.

Mounting evidence suggests that impaired brain functioning is a major contributor to SIDS. Between 2 and 4 months, when SIDS is most likely to occur, reflexes decline and are replaced by voluntary, learned responses. Neurological weaknesses may prevent SIDS babies from acquiring behaviors that replace defensive reflexes (Lipsitt, 2003). As a result, when breathing difficulties occur during sleep, these infants do not wake up, shift their position, or cry out for help. Instead, they simply give in to oxygen deprivation and death. In support of this interpretation, autopsies reveal that the brains of SIDS babies

contain unusually low levels of serotonin (a brain chemical that assists with arousal when survival is threatened) as well as other abnormalities in centers that control breathing and arousal (Duncan et al., 2010).

Several environmental factors are linked to SIDS. Maternal cigarette smoking, both during and after pregnancy, as well as smoking by other caregivers, doubles risk of the disorder. Babies exposed to cigarette smoke arouse less easily from sleep and have more respiratory infections (Richardson, Walker, & Horne, 2008; Shah, Sullivan, & Carter, 2006). Prenatal abuse of drugs that depress central nervous system functioning (alcohol, opiates, and barbiturates) increases the risk of SIDS as much as fifteen-fold (Hunt & Hauck, 2006). Babies of drug-abusing mothers are especially likely to display SIDS-related brain abnormalities (Kinney, 2009).

SIDS babies are also more likely to sleep on their stomachs than on their backs and often are wrapped very warmly in clothing and blankets. Infants who sleep on their stomachs less often wake when their breathing is disturbed (Richardson, Walker, & Horne, 2008). In other cases, healthy babies sleeping face down in soft bedding may die from continually breathing their own exhaled breath.

SIDS rates are especially high among poverty-stricken minorities (Colson et al., 2009). In these families, parental stress, substance abuse, reduced access to health care, and lack of knowledge about safe sleep practices are widespread.

Public education efforts are vital for reducing the prevalence of SIDS. The U.S. government's Safe to Sleep campaign encourages parents to create safe sleep environments and engage in other protective practices. Among its recommendations are quitting smoking and drug taking, changing an infant's sleeping position, providing a firm sleep surface, and eliminating soft

BANANASTOCK/360/GETTY IMAGES

Public education campaigns encouraging parents to put their infants down on their backs to sleep have helped to reduce the incidence of SIDS, which has dropped by more than half in many Western nations.

bedding. An estimated 20 percent of SIDS cases would be prevented if all infants had smoke-free homes. Dissemination of information to parents about putting infants down on their backs has cut the incidence of SIDS by more than half in many Western nations (Behm et al., 2012; Moon, Horne, & Hauck, 2007). Another protective measure is pacifier use: Sleeping babies who suck arouse more easily in response to breathing and heart-rate irregularities (Li et al., 2006).

When SIDS does occur, surviving family members require a great deal of help to overcome a sudden and unexpected death. As Millie commented six months after Sasha's death, "It's the worst crisis we've ever been through. What's helped us most are the comforting words of others who've experienced the same tragedy."

Because newborn babies' normal sleep behavior is organized and patterned, observations of sleep states can help identify central nervous system abnormalities. In infants who are brain-damaged or who have experienced birth trauma, disturbed REM–NREM sleep cycles are often present. Both full-term and preterm babies with poor sleep organization are likely to be behaviorally disorganized and, therefore, to have difficulty learning and eliciting caregiver interactions that enhance their development. In follow-ups during the preschool years, they show delayed motor, cognitive, and language development (Feldman, 2006; Holditch-Davis, Belyea, & Edwards, 2005; Weisman et al., 2011). And the brain-functioning problems that underlie newborn sleep irregularities may culminate in sudden infant death syndrome, a major cause of infant mortality (see the Social Issues: Health box above).

Applying What We Know

Soothing a Crying Baby

TECHNIQUE	EXPLANATION
Talk softly or play rhythmic sounds.	Continuous, monotonous, rhythmic sounds (such as a clock ticking, a fan whirring, or peaceful music) are more effective than intermittent sounds.
Offer a pacifier.	Sucking helps babies control their own level of arousal.
Massage the baby's body.	Stroking the baby's torso and limbs with continuous, gentle motions relaxes the baby's muscles.
Swaddle the baby.	Restricting movement and increasing warmth often soothe a young infant.
Lift the baby to the shoulder and rock or walk.	This combination of physical contact, upright posture, and motion is an effective soothing technique, causing young infants to become quietly alert.
Take the baby for a short car ride or a walk in a baby carriage; swing the baby in a cradle.	Gentle, rhythmic motion of any kind helps lull the baby to sleep.
Combine several of the methods just listed.	Stimulating several of the baby's senses at once is often more effective than stimulating only one.
If these methods do not work, let the baby cry for a short period.	Occasionally, a baby responds well to just being put down and will, after a few minutes, fall asleep.

Sources: Campos, 1989; Evanoo, 2007; St James-Roberts, 2012.

To soothe his crying infant, this father holds the baby against his gently moving body and speaks softly. The combination of physical contact, motion, and gentle sounds causes infants to stop crying and become quietly alert.

© LAURA DWIGHT PHOTOGRAPHY

CRYING Crying is the first way that babies communicate, letting parents know that they need food, comfort, and stimulation. During the weeks after birth, all babies seem to have some fussy periods when they are difficult to console. But most of the time, the nature of the cry, combined with the experiences that led up to it, helps guide parents toward its cause. The baby's cry is a complex stimulus that varies in intensity, from a whimper to a message of all-out distress (Gustafson, Wood, & Green, 2000; Wood, 2009). As early as the first few weeks, infants can be identified by the unique vocal "signature" of their cries, which helps parents locate their baby from a distance (Gustafson, Green, & Cleland, 1994).

Young infants usually cry because of physical needs. Hunger is the most common cause, but babies may also cry in response to temperature change when undressed, a sudden noise, or a painful stimulus. Newborns (as well as older babies) often cry at the sound of another crying baby (Dondi, Simion, & Caltran, 1999; Geangu et al., 2010). Some researchers believe that this response reflects an inborn capacity to react to the suffering of others. Furthermore, crying typically increases during the early weeks, peaks at about 6 weeks, and then declines (Barr, 2001). Because this trend appears in many cultures with vastly different infant care practices, researchers believe that normal readjustments of the central nervous system underlie it.

TAKE A MOMENT... The next time you hear a baby cry, notice your own reaction. The sound stimulates strong feelings of arousal and discomfort in men and women, parents and nonparents alike (Murray, 1985). This powerful response is probably innately programmed to help ensure that babies receive the care and protection they need to survive.

Soothing a Crying Infant. Although parents do not always interpret their baby's cry correctly, their accuracy improves with experience. At the same time, they vary widely in responsiveness. Parents who are high in empathy (ability to take the perspective of others in distress) and who hold "child-centered" attitudes toward infant care—for example, believe that babies cannot be spoiled by being picked up—are more likely to respond quickly and sensitively to a crying baby (Leerkes, 2010; Zeifman, 2003).

Fortunately, there are many ways to soothe a crying baby when feeding and diaper changing do not work (see Applying What We Know above). The technique that Western parents usually try first, lifting the baby to the shoulder and rocking or walking, is highly effective. Another common soothing method is swaddling—wrapping the baby snugly in a blanket. The Quechua, who live in the cold, high-altitude desert regions of Peru, dress young infants in several layers of clothing and blankets that cover the head and body, a technique that reduces crying and promotes sleep (Tronick, Thomas, & Daltabuit, 1994). It also enables the baby to conserve energy for early growth in the harsh Peruvian highlands.

In many tribal and village societies and in non-Western developed nations, infants spend most of the day and night in close physical contact with their caregivers. Among the !Kung of Botswana, Africa, mothers carry their young babies in grass-lined, animal-skin slings hung on their hips, so the infants can see their surroundings and can nurse at will. Japanese mothers also spend much time holding their babies (Small, 1998). Infants in these cultures show shorter bouts of crying than their American counterparts (Barr, 2001). When Western parents choose to practice "proximal care" by holding their babies extensively, amount of crying in the early months is reduced by about one-third (St James-Roberts, 2012).

The Mongol people of Central Asia heavily swaddle their babies, a practice that reduces crying and promotes sleep while also protecting infants from the region's harsh winters.

Abnormal Crying. Like reflexes and sleep patterns, the infant's cry offers a clue to central nervous system distress. The cries of brain-damaged babies and those who have experienced prenatal and birth complications are often shrill, piercing, and shorter in duration than the cries of healthy infants (Green, Irwin, & Gustafson, 2000). Even newborns with a fairly common problem—*colic,* or persistent crying—tend to have high-pitched, harsh-sounding cries (Zeskind & Barr, 1997). Although the cause of colic is unknown, certain newborns, who react especially strongly to unpleasant stimuli, are susceptible. Because their crying is intense, they find it harder to calm down than other babies (Barr et al., 2005; St James-Roberts, 2007). Colic generally subsides between 3 and 6 months.

In an intervention aimed at reducing colic, nurses made periodic home visits, providing parents with help in identifying their baby's early warning signs of becoming overly aroused, in using effective soothing techniques, and in modifying light, noise, and activity in the home to promote predictable sleep–wake cycles (Keefe et al., 2005). Colicky infants who received the intervention spent far less time crying than no-intervention controls—1.3 versus 3 hours per day.

Most parents try to respond to a crying baby's call for help with extra care and attention, but sometimes the cry is so unpleasant and the infant so difficult to soothe that parents become frustrated, resentful, and angry. Preterm and ill babies are more likely to be abused by highly stressed parents, who sometimes mention a high-pitched, grating cry as one factor that caused them to lose control and harm the baby (Rautava et al., 2007; St James-Roberts, 2012). We will discuss a host of additional influences on child abuse in Chapter 10.

LOOK and LISTEN

In a public setting, watch several parents soothe their crying babies. What techniques did the parents use, and how successful were they?

Sensory Capacities

On his visit to class, Joshua looked wide-eyed at Yolanda's bright pink blouse and readily turned to the sound of her voice. During feedings, he lets Yolanda know by the way he sucks that he prefers the taste of breast milk to a bottle of plain water. Clearly, Joshua has some well-developed sensory capacities. In the following sections, we explore the newborn baby's responsiveness to touch, taste, smell, sound, and visual stimulation.

TOUCH In our discussion of preterm infants, we saw that touch helps stimulate early physical growth. And as we will see in Chapter 7, it is vital for emotional development as well. Therefore, it is not surprising that sensitivity to touch is well-developed at birth.

The reflexes listed in Table 4.2 on page 142 reveal that the newborn baby responds to touch, especially around the mouth, on the palms, and on the soles of the feet. During the prenatal period, these areas, along with the genitals, are the first to become sensitive to touch

(Humphrey, 1978; Streri, 2005). Newborns, even those born several weeks preterm, use touch to investigate their world. When small objects are placed in their palms, they can distinguish shape (prism versus cylinder) and texture (smooth versus rough), as indicated by their tendency to hold on longer to an object with an unfamiliar shape or texture than to a familiar object (Lejeune et al., 2012; Sann & Streri, 2007, 2008).

At birth, infants are highly sensitive to pain. If male newborns are circumcised, anesthetic is sometimes not used because of the risk of giving drugs to a very young infant. Babies often respond with a high-pitched, stressful cry and a dramatic rise in heart rate, blood pressure, palm sweating, pupil dilation, and muscle tension (Lehr et al., 2007; Warnock & Sandrin, 2004). Brain-imaging research suggests that because of central nervous system immaturity, preterm and male babies feel the pain of a medical injection especially intensely (Bartocci et al., 2006).

Certain local analgesics for newborns ease the pain of these procedures. As a supplement to pain-relieving medication, offering a nipple that delivers a sugar solution is helpful; it quickly reduces crying and discomfort in young babies, preterm and full-term alike (Roman-Rodriguez et al., 2014). Breast milk may be especially effective: Even the smell of the milk of the baby's mother reduces infant stress to a routine blood-test heelstick more effectively than the odor of another mother's milk or of formula (Badiee, Asghari, & Mohammadizadeh, 2013; Nishitani et al., 2009). And combining sweet liquid with gentle holding by the parent lessens pain even more. Research on infant mammals indicates that physical touch releases *endorphins*—painkilling chemicals in the brain (Axelin, Salantera, & Lehtonen, 2006; Gormally et al., 2001).

Allowing a baby to endure severe pain overwhelms the nervous system with stress hormones, which can disrupt the child's developing capacity to handle common, everyday stressors (Walker, 2013). The result is heightened pain sensitivity, sleep disturbances, feeding problems, and difficulty calming down when upset.

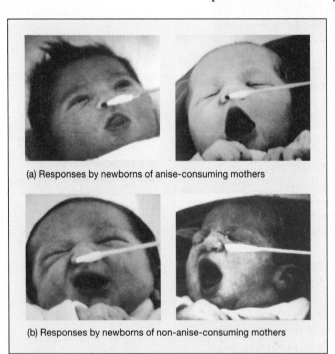

(a) Responses by newborns of anise-consuming mothers

(b) Responses by newborns of non-anise-consuming mothers

FIGURE 4.6 **Examples of facial expressions of newborns exposed to the odor of anise whose mothers' diets differed in anise-flavored foods during late pregnancy.** (a) Babies of anise-consuming mothers spent more time turning toward the odor and sucking, licking, and chewing. (b) Babies of non-anise-consuming mothers more often turned away with a negative facial expression. (From B. Schaal, L. Marlier, & R. Soussignan, 2000, "Human Foetuses Learn Odours from Their Pregnant Mother's Diet," *Chemical Senses, 25*, p. 731. Reprinted by permission of Oxford University Press, Inc., and Benoist Schaal.)

TASTE AND SMELL Facial expressions reveal that newborns can distinguish several basic tastes. Like adults, they relax their facial muscles in response to sweetness, purse their lips when the taste is sour, and show a distinct archlike mouth opening when it is bitter. Similarly, certain odor preferences are present at birth. For example, the smell of bananas or chocolate causes a pleasant facial expression, whereas the odor of rotten eggs makes the infant frown (Steiner, 1979; Steiner et al., 2001). These reactions are important for survival: The food that best supports the infant's early growth is the sweet-tasting milk of the mother's breast. Not until 4 months do babies prefer a salty taste to plain water, a change that may prepare them to accept solid foods (Mennella & Beauchamp, 1998).

During pregnancy, the amniotic fluid is rich in tastes and smells that vary with the mother's diet—early experiences that influence newborns' preferences. In a study carried out in the Alsatian region of France, where anise is frequently used to flavor foods, researchers tested newborns for their reaction to the anise odor (Schaal, Marlier, & Soussignan, 2000). The mothers of some babies had regularly consumed anise during the last two weeks of pregnancy; the other mothers had never consumed it. When presented with the anise odor on the day of birth, the babies of non-anise-consuming mothers were far more likely to turn away with a negative facial expression (see Figure 4.6). These different reactions were still apparent four days later, even though all mothers had refrained from consuming anise during this time.

Other evidence indicates that exposure to a flavor, either prenatally in the amniotic fluid or during the weeks after birth in breast milk, continues to influence taste preferences well into the first year and possibly beyond. Fetuses and newborns exposed to the flavor of carrots (because their mothers drank carrot juice) reacted more positively than did unexposed counterparts to carrot-flavored cereal at age 6 months (Mennella, Jagnow, & Beauchamp, 2001).

Furthermore, young infants will readily learn to prefer a taste that at first evoked either a negative or neutral response. Bottle-fed newborns allergic to cow's milk formula who are given a soy or other vegetable-based substitute (typically very sour and bitter-tasting) soon prefer it to regular formula. When first given solid foods several months later, these infants display an unusual liking for bitter-tasting cereals (Beauchamp & Mennella, 2011). This taste preference is still evident at ages 4 to 5 years, in more positive responses to foods with sour and bitter tastes compared to agemates without early vegetable-based formula exposure.

In mammals, including humans, the sense of smell—in addition to playing an important role in feeding—helps mothers and babies identify each other. At 4 days of age, breastfed babies prefer the smell of their own mother's breast to that of an unfamiliar lactating woman (Cernoch & Porter, 1985). And both breast- and bottle-fed 3- to 4-day-olds orient more and display more mouthing to the smell of unfamiliar human milk than to formula milk, indicating that (even without postnatal exposure) the odor of human milk is more attractive to newborns (Marlier & Schaal, 2005). Newborns' dual attraction to the odors of their mother and of breast milk helps them locate an appropriate food source and, in the process, begin to distinguish their caregiver from other people.

HEARING Although conduction of sound through the structures of the ear and transmission of auditory information to the brain are inefficient at birth, newborn infants can hear a wide variety of sounds—sensitivity that improves greatly over the first few months (Saffran, Werker, & Werner, 2006). At birth, infants prefer complex sounds, such as noises and voices, to pure tones. And babies only a few days old can tell the difference between a variety of sound patterns: a series of tones arranged in ascending versus descending order; tone sequences with a rhythmic downbeat (as in music) versus those without; utterances with two versus three syllables; the stress patterns of words, such as "*ma*-ma" versus "ma-*ma*"; happy-sounding speech as opposed to speech with negative or neutral emotional qualities; and even two languages spoken by the same bilingual speaker, as long as those languages differ in their rhythmic features—for example, French versus Russian (Mastropieri & Turkewitz, 1999; Ramus, 2002; Sansavini, Bertoncini, & Giovanelli, 1997; Trehub, 2001; Winkler et al., 2009).

Young infants listen longer to human speech than to structurally similar nonspeech sounds (Vouloumanos, 2010). And they can detect the sounds of any human language. Newborns make fine-grained distinctions among many speech sounds. For example, when given a nipple that turns on a recording of the "*ba*" sound, babies suck vigorously for a while and then slow down as the novelty wears off. When the sound switches to "*ga*," sucking picks up, indicating that infants detect this subtle difference. Using this method, researchers have found only a few speech sounds that newborns cannot discriminate. Their ability to perceive sounds not found in their own language is more precise than an adult's (Aldridge, Stillman, & Bower, 2001; Jusczyk & Luce, 2002). These capacities reveal that the baby is marvelously prepared for the awesome task of acquiring language.

Responsiveness to sound also supports the newborn baby's exploration of the environment. Infants as young as 3 days turn their eyes and head in the general direction of a sound. The ability to identify the precise location of a sound improves greatly over the first six months and shows further gains through the preschool years (Litovsky & Ashmead, 1997).

TAKE A MOMENT... Listen carefully to yourself the next time you talk to a young baby. You will probably speak in ways that highlight important parts of the speech stream—use a slow, high-pitched, expressive voice with a rising tone at the ends of phrases and sentences and a pause before continuing. Adults probably communicate this way with infants because they notice that babies are more attentive when they do so. Indeed, newborns prefer speech with these characteristics (Saffran, Werker, & Werner, 2006). They will also suck more on a nipple to hear a recording of their own mother's voice than that of an unfamiliar woman and to hear their native language as opposed to a foreign language (Moon, Cooper, & Fifer, 1993; Spence & DeCasper, 1987). These preferences may have developed from hearing the muffled sounds of the mother's voice before birth.

(a) Newborn View   (b) Adult View

FIGURE 4.7 **View of the human face by the newborn and the adult.** The newborn baby's limited focusing ability and poor visual acuity lead the mother's face, even when viewed from close up, to look much like the fuzzy image in (a) rather than the clear image in (b). Also, newborn infants have some color vision, although they have difficulty discriminating colors. Researchers speculate that colors probably appear similar, but less intense, to newborns than to older infants and adults (From Kellman & Arterberry 2006; Slater et al., 2010.).

VISION Vision is the least-developed of the newborn baby's senses. Visual structures in both the eye and the brain are not yet fully formed at birth. For example, cells in the *retina,* the membrane lining the inside of the eye that captures light and transforms it into messages that are sent to the brain, are not as mature or densely packed as they will be in several months. The optic nerve that relays these messages, and visual centers in the brain that receive them, will not be adultlike for several years. And muscles of the *lens,* which permit us to adjust our visual focus to varying distances, are weak (Kellman & Arterberry, 2006).

As a result, newborns cannot focus their eyes well, and their **visual acuity,** or fineness of discrimination, is limited. At birth, infants perceive objects at a distance of 20 feet about as clearly as adults do at 600 feet (Slater et al., 2010). In addition, unlike adults (who see nearby objects most clearly), newborn babies see unclearly across a wide range of distances (Banks, 1980; Hainline, 1998). As a result, images such as the parent's face, even from close up, look like the blurry image in Figure 4.7. Nevertheless, as we will see in Chapter 5, newborns can detect human faces. And as with their preference for their mother's smell and voice, from repeated exposures they quickly learn to prefer her face to that of an unfamiliar woman, although they are more sensitive to its broad outlines than its fine-grained, internal features (Bartrip, Morton, & de Schonen, 2001; Walton, Armstrong, & Bower, 1998).

Although they cannot yet see well, newborns actively explore their environment by scanning it for interesting sights and tracking moving objects. However, their eye movements are slow and inaccurate (von Hofsten & Rosander, 1998). Joshua's captivation with Yolanda's pink blouse reveals that he is attracted to bright objects. Nevertheless, once newborns focus on an object, they tend to look only at a single feature—for example, the corner of a triangle instead of the entire shape. And despite their preference for colored over gray stimuli, newborn babies are not yet good at discriminating colors. It will take about four months for color vision to become adultlike (Kellman & Arterberry, 2006).

Neonatal Behavioral Assessment

A variety of instruments permit doctors, nurses, and researchers to assess the behavior of newborn babies. The most widely used of these tests, T. Berry Brazelton's **Neonatal Behavioral Assessment Scale (NBAS),** evaluates the baby's reflexes, muscle tone, state changes, responsiveness to physical and social stimuli, and other reactions (Brazelton & Nugent, 1911). An instrument consisting of similar items, called the *Neonatal Intensive Care Unit Network Neurobehavioral Scale (NNNS),* is specially designed for use with newborns at risk for developmental problems because of low birth weight, preterm delivery, prenatal substance exposure, or other conditions (Tronick & Lester, 2013). Scores are used to recommend appropriate interventions and to guide parents in meeting their baby's unique needs.

The NBAS has been given to many infants around the world. As a result, researchers have learned about individual and cultural differences in newborn behavior and how child-rearing practices can maintain or change a baby's reactions. For example, NBAS scores of Asian and Native-American babies reveal that they are less irritable than Caucasian infants. Mothers in these cultures often encourage their babies' calm dispositions through holding and nursing at the first signs of discomfort (Muret-Wagstaff & Moore, 1989; Small, 1998). The Kipsigis of Kenya, who highly value infant motor maturity, massage babies regularly and begin exercising the stepping reflex shortly after birth. These customs contribute to Kipsigis babies' strong

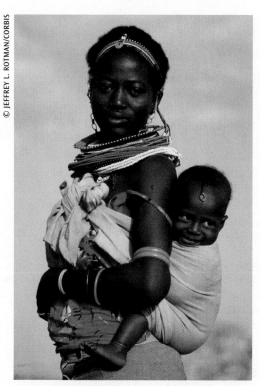

A mother of the El Molo people of northern Kenya carries her baby in a sling all day, providing close physical contact and a rich variety of stimulation. This practice, also adopted by many Western parents, promotes a calm, alert state in infants.

but flexible muscle tone at 5 days of age (Super & Harkness, 2009). In Zambia, Africa, close mother–infant contact throughout the day quickly changes the poor NBAS scores of undernourished newborns. When reassessed at 1 week of age, a once unresponsive baby appears alert and contented (Brazelton, Koslowski, & Tronick, 1976).

TAKE A MOMENT... Using these examples, can you explain why a single neonatal assessment score is not a good predictor of later development? Because newborn behavior and parenting styles combine to shape development, *changes in scores* over the first week or two of life (rather than a single score) provide the best estimate of the baby's ability to recover from the stress of birth. NBAS "recovery curves" predict intelligence and absence of emotional and behavior problems with moderate success well into the preschool years (Brazelton, Nugent, & Lester, 1987; Ohgi et al., 2003a, 2003b).

In some hospitals, health professionals use the NBAS or the NNNS to help parents get to know their newborns through discussion or demonstration of the capacities these instruments assess. Parents of both preterm and full-term newborns who participate in these programs, compared with no-intervention controls, interact more confidently and effectively with their babies (Browne & Talmi, 2005; Bruschweiler-Stern, 2004). Although lasting effects on development have not been demonstrated, NBAS-based interventions are useful in helping the parent–infant relationship get off to a good start.

Ask Yourself

- **REVIEW** What can newborn sleep patterns and crying tell us about the health of the central nervous system?

- **CONNECT** How do the diverse capacities of newborn babies contribute to their first social relationships? Provide as many examples as you can.

- **APPLY** After a difficult delivery, Jackie observes her 2-day-old daughter, Kelly, being given the NBAS. Kelly scores poorly on many items. Seeing this, Jackie wonders if Kelly will develop normally. How would you respond to Jackie's concern?

- **REFLECT** Are newborns more competent than you thought they were before you read this chapter? Which of their capacities most surprised you?

4.9 Describe typical changes in the family after the birth of a new baby, along with interventions that foster the transition to parenthood.

The Transition to Parenthood

The early weeks after a new baby enters the family are full of profound changes. The mother needs to recover from childbirth and adjust to massive hormone shifts in her body. If she is breastfeeding, energies must be devoted to working out this intimate relationship. The father must become a part of this new threesome while supporting the mother in her recovery. At times, he may feel ambivalent about the baby, who constantly demands and gets the mother's attention.

While all this is going on, the tiny infant is assertive about his urgent physical needs, demanding to be fed, changed, and comforted at odd times of the day and night. The family schedule becomes irregular and uncertain, and parental sleep deprivation and consequent daytime fatigue is often a major challenge (Insana & Montgomery-Downs, 2012). Yolanda spoke candidly about the changes she and Jay experienced:

> When we brought Joshua home, he seemed so small and helpless, and we worried about whether we would be able to take proper care of him. It took us 20 minutes to change the first diaper. I rarely feel rested because I'm up two to four times every night, and I spend a good part of my waking hours trying to anticipate Joshua's rhythms and needs. If Jay weren't so willing to help by holding and walking Joshua, I think I'd find it much harder.

Changes in the Family System

The demands of new parenthood—constant caregiving, added financial responsibilities, and less time for couples to devote to one another—usually cause the gender roles of husband and wife to become more traditional (Katz-Wise, Priess, & Hyde, 2010; Lawrence et al., 2010). This is true even for couples like Yolanda and Jay, who are strongly committed to gender equality and are used to sharing household tasks. Yolanda took a leave of absence from work, whereas Jay's career continued as it had before. As a result, Yolanda spent more time at home with the baby, while Jay focused more on his provider role.

For most new parents, however, the arrival of a baby—though often associated with mild declines in relationship satisfaction and communication quality—does not cause significant marital strain. Marriages that are gratifying and supportive tend to remain so (Doss et al., 2009; Feeney et al., 2001). But troubled marriages usually become more distressed after a baby is born (Houts et al., 2008; Kluwer & Johnson, 2007). And when expectant mothers anticipate lack of partner support in parenting, their prediction generally becomes reality, yielding an especially difficult post-birth adjustment (Driver et al., 2012; McHale & Rotman, 2007). For some new parents, problems are severe (see the Biology and Environment box on the following page).

Violated expectations about division of labor in the home powerfully affect family well-being. In dual-earner marriages, the larger the difference between men's and women's caregiving responsibilities, the greater the decline in marital satisfaction after childbirth, especially for women—with negative consequences for parent–infant interaction. In contrast, sharing caregiving predicts greater parental happiness and sensitivity to the baby (McHale et al., 2004; Moller, Hwang, & Wickberg, 2008). An exception exists, however, for employed lower-SES women who endorse traditional gender roles. When their husbands help extensively with child care, these mothers tend to report more distress, perhaps because they feel disappointed at being unable to fulfill their desire to do most of the caregiving (Goldberg & Perry-Jenkins, 2003).

Postponing parenthood until the late twenties or thirties, as more couples do today, eases the transition to parenthood. Waiting permits couples to pursue occupational goals and gain life experience. Under these circumstances, men are more enthusiastic about becoming fathers and therefore more willing to participate. And women whose careers are well under way and whose marriages are happy are more likely to encourage their husbands to share housework and child care, which fosters fathers' involvement (Lee & Doherty, 2007; Schoppe-Sullivan et al., 2008).

Biology and Environment

Parental Depression and Child Development

About 8 to 10 percent of women experience chronic depression—mild to severe feelings of sadness and withdrawal that continue for months or years. Often, the beginnings of this emotional state cannot be pinpointed. In other instances, depression emerges or strengthens after childbirth but fails to subside as the new mother adjusts to hormonal changes in her body and gains confidence in caring for her baby. This is called *postpartum depression*.

Although it is less recognized and studied, fathers, too, experience chronic depression. About 3 to 5 percent of fathers report symptoms after the birth of a child (Madsen & Juhl, 2007; Thombs, Roseman, & Arthurs, 2010). Parental depression can interfere with effective parenting and seriously impair children's development. As noted in Chapter 2, genetic makeup increases the risk of depressive illness, but social and cultural factors are also involved.

Maternal Depression

During Julia's pregnancy, her husband, Kyle, showed so little interest in the baby that Julia worried that having a child might be a mistake. Then, shortly after Lucy was born, Julia's mood plunged. She felt anxious and weepy, overwhelmed by Lucy's needs, and angry at loss of control over her own schedule. When Julia approached Kyle about her own fatigue and his unwillingness to help with the baby, he snapped that she was overreacting. Julia's childless friends stopped by just once to see Lucy but did not call again.

Julia's depressed mood quickly affected her baby. In the weeks after birth, infants of depressed mothers sleep poorly, are less attentive to their surroundings, and have elevated levels of the stress hormone cortisol (Field, 1998). The more extreme the depression and the greater the number of stressors in a mother's life (such as marital discord, little or no social support, and poverty), the more the parent–child relationship suffers (Simpson et al., 2003). Julia rarely smiled at, comforted, or talked to Lucy, who responded to her mother's sad, vacant gaze by turning away, crying, and often looking sad or angry herself (Feldman et al., 2009; Field, 2011). Julia, in turn, felt guilty and inadequate, and her depression deepened. By age 6 months, Lucy showed symptoms common in babies of depressed mothers—delays in motor and mental development, an irritable mood, and attachment difficulties (Hanington et al., 2012; McMahon et al., 2006).

When maternal depression persists, the parent–child relationship worsens. Depressed parents view their infants more negatively than independent observers do (Forman et al., 2007). And they use inconsistent discipline—sometimes lax, at other times too forceful. As we will see in later chapters, children who experience these maladaptive parenting practices often have serious adjustment problems. Some withdraw into a depressive mood themselves; others become impulsive and aggressive. In one study, children born to mothers who were depressed during pregnancy were four times as likely as children of nondepressed mothers to have engaged in violent antisocial behavior by age 16, after other stressors in the mother's life that could contribute to youth antisocial conduct had been controlled (Hay et al., 2010).

Paternal Depression

Paternal depression is also linked to dissatisfaction with marriage and family life after childbirth and to other life stressors, including job loss and divorce (Bielawska-Batorowicz & Kossakowska-Petrycka, 2006). In a study of a large representative sample of British parents and babies, researchers assessed depressive symptoms of fathers shortly after birth and again the following year. Then they tracked the children's development into the preschool years. Persistent paternal depression was, like maternal depression, a strong predictor of child behavior problems—especially overactivity, defiance, and aggression in boys (Ramchandani et al., 2008).

Paternal depression is linked to frequent father–child conflict as children grow older (Kane & Garber, 2004). Over time, children subjected to parental negativity develop a pessimistic worldview—one in which they lack self-confidence and perceive their parents and other people as threatening. Children who constantly feel in danger are especially likely to become overly aroused in stressful situations, easily losing control in the face of cognitive and social challenges (Sturge-Apple et al., 2008). Although children of depressed parents may inherit a tendency toward emotional and behavior problems, quality of parenting is a major factor in their adjustment.

This father appears completely disengaged from his wife and toddler. If this continues, disruptions in the parent–child relationship will likely lead to serious child behavior problems.

Interventions

Early treatment is vital to prevent parental depression from interfering with the parent–child relationship. Julia's doctor referred her to a therapist, who helped Julia and Kyle with their marital problems. At times, antidepressant medication is prescribed.

In addition to alleviating parental depression, therapy that encourages depressed mothers to revise their negative views of their babies and to engage in emotionally positive, responsive caregiving is essential for reducing young children's attachment and other developmental problems (Forman et al., 2007). When a depressed parent does not respond easily to treatment, a warm relationship with the other parent or another caregiver can safeguard children's development (Mezulis, Hyde, & Clark, 2004).

Applying What We Know

How Couples Can Ease the Transition to Parenthood

STRATEGY	DESCRIPTION
Devise a plan for sharing household tasks.	As soon as possible, discuss division of household responsibilities. Decide who does a particular chore based on who has the needed skill and time, not gender. Schedule regular times to reevaluate your plan to fit changing family circumstances.
Begin sharing child care right after the baby's arrival.	For fathers, strive to spend equal time with the baby early. For mothers, refrain from imposing your standards on your partner. Instead, share the role of "child-rearing expert" by discussing parenting values and concerns often. Attend a new-parenthood course together.
Talk over conflicts about decision making and responsibilities.	Face conflict through communication. Clarify your feelings and needs, and express them to your partner. Listen and try to understand your partner's point of view. Then be willing to negotiate and compromise.
Establish a balance between work and parenting.	Critically evaluate the time you devote to work in view of new parenthood. If it is too much, try to cut back.
Press for workplace and public policies that assist parents in rearing children.	Difficulties faced by new parents may be partly due to lack of workplace and societal supports. Encourage your employer to provide benefits that help combine work and family roles, such as paid employment leave, flexible work hours, and on-site high-quality, affordable child care. Communicate with lawmakers and other citizens about improving policies for children and families, including paid, job-protected leave to support the transition to parenthood.

A second birth typically requires that fathers take an even more active role in parenting—by caring for the firstborn while the mother is recuperating and by sharing in the high demands of tending to both a baby and a young child. Consequently, well-functioning families with a newborn second child typically pull back from the traditional division of responsibilities that occurred after the first birth. In a study that tracked parents from the end of pregnancy through the first year after their second child's birth, fathers' willingness to place greater emphasis on the parenting role was strongly linked to mothers' adjustment after the arrival of a second baby (Stewart, 1990). And both parents must help their firstborn child adjust. Preschool-age siblings understandably may feel displaced and react with jealousy and anger—a topic we will take up in Chapter 7. For strategies couples can use to ease the transition to parenthood, refer to Applying What We Know above.

Single-Mother Families

About 40 percent of U.S. births are to single mothers, one-third of whom are teenagers (Martin et al., 2013). Because most adolescent parents suffer from personal, family, and financial problems, their newborns are at high risk for developmental problems.

At the other extreme, planned births and adoptions by single 30- to 45-year-old women are increasing. These mothers are generally financially secure, have readily available social support from family members and friends, and adapt to parenthood with relative ease. In fact, older single mothers in well-paid occupations who plan carefully for a new baby may encounter fewer parenting difficulties than married couples, largely because their family structure is simpler: They do not have to coordinate parenting roles with a partner, and they have no unfulfilled expectations for shared caregiving (Tyano et al., 2010). And because of their psychological maturity, these mothers are likely to cope effectively with parenting challenges.

The majority of nonmarital births are unplanned and to women in their twenties. Most of these mothers have incomes below the poverty level and experience a stressful transition to parenthood. Although many live with the baby's father or another partner, cohabiting relationships in the United States are less socially acceptable than those in Western Europe,

LOOK and LISTEN

Ask a couple or a single mother to describe the challenges of new parenthood, along with factors that aided or impeded this transition.

involve less commitment and cooperation, and are far more likely to break up—especially after an unplanned baby arrives (Jose, O'Leary, & Moyer, 2010). Single mothers often lack emotional and parenting support—strong predictors of psychological distress and infant caregiving difficulties (Keating-Lefler et al., 2004).

Parent Interventions

Special interventions are available to help parents adjust to life with a new baby. For those who are not at high risk for problems, counselor-led parenting groups are highly effective (Gottman, Gottman, & Shapiro, 2010). In one program, first-time expectant couples gathered once a week for six months to discuss their dreams for the family and the changes in relationships sparked by the baby's arrival. Eighteen months after the program ended, participating fathers described themselves as more involved with their child than did fathers in a no-intervention condition. Perhaps because of fathers' caregiving assistance, participating mothers maintained their prebirth satisfaction with family and work roles. Three years after the birth, the marriages of all participating couples were still intact and just as happy as they had been before parenthood (Cowan & Cowan, 1997; Schulz, Cowan, & Cowan, 2006). In contrast, 15 percent of couples receiving no intervention had divorced.

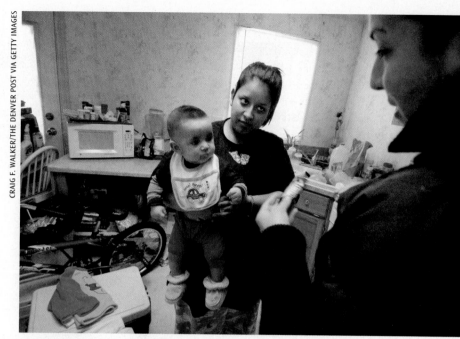

A counselor discusses options with this single mother for continuing her education. Parents struggling with poverty benefit from intensive intervention focusing on social support and effective parenting.

High-risk parents struggling with poverty or the birth of a child with disabilities need more intensive interventions. Programs in which a professional intervener visits the home and focuses on enhancing social support and parenting have resulted in improved parent–infant interaction and benefits for children's cognitive and social development into middle childhood (to review one example, return to page 114 in Chapter 3). Many low-income single mothers benefit from interventions that focus on sustaining the father's involvement and that provide training in effective coparenting (Jones, Charles, & Benson, 2013). These parents also require tangible support—money, food, transportation, and affordable child care—to ease stress so they have the psychological resources to engage in sensitive, responsive infant care.

When parents' relationships are positive and cooperative, social support is available, and families have sufficient income, the stress caused by the birth of a baby remains manageable. These family conditions, as we have already seen, consistently contribute to favorable development—in infancy and beyond.

Ask Yourself

- **REVIEW** Explain how persisting postpartum depression seriously impairs children's development.

- **CONNECT** Explain how generous employment leave for childbirth—at least 12 weeks of paid time off available to either the mother or father—can ease the transition to parenthood and promote positive parent–infant interaction. (*Hint:* Consult the Social Issues: Health box on pages 138–139.)

- **APPLY** Derek, father of a 3-year-old and a newborn, reported that he had a harder time adjusting to the birth of his second child than to that of his first. Explain why this might be so.

- **REFLECT** If you are a parent, what was the transition to parenthood like for you? What factors helped you adjust? What factors made it more difficult? If you are not a parent, pose these questions to someone you know who recently became a parent.

CRAIG F. WALKER/THE DENVER POST VIA GETTY IMAGES

Summary

The Stages of Childbirth (p. 123)

4.1 Describe the three stages of childbirth, the baby's adaptation to labor and delivery, and the newborn baby's appearance.

- In the first stage of childbirth, **dilation and effacement of the cervix** occur as uterine contractions increase in strength and frequency. This stage culminates in **transition,** a brief period in which contractions are at their peak and the cervix opens completely. In the second stage, the mother feels an urge to bear down with her abdominal muscles, and the baby is born. In the final stage, the placenta is delivered.

- During labor, the force of the contractions causes infants to produce high levels of stress hormones, which help them withstand oxygen deprivation, clear the lungs for breathing, and arouse them into alertness at birth.

- Newborn infants have large heads and small bodies. The **Apgar Scale** is used to assess the baby's physical condition at birth.

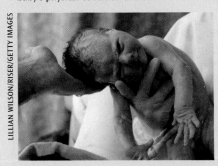

Approaches to Childbirth (p. 127)

4.2 Describe natural childbirth and home delivery, noting benefits and concerns associated with each.

- In **natural,** or **prepared, childbirth,** the expectant mother and a companion typically attend classes where they learn about labor and delivery, master relaxation and breathing techniques to counteract pain, and prepare for coaching during childbirth. Social support from a doula reduces the length of labor, the need for instrument-assisted births and pain medication, and the incidence of birth complications.

- Home birth is relatively rare in the United States but is common in some other industrialized nations. It is safe for healthy mothers who are assisted by a well-trained doctor or midwife, but mothers at risk for any kind of complication are better off giving birth in a hospital.

Medical Interventions (p. 129)

4.3 List common medical interventions during childbirth, circumstances that justify their use, and any dangers associated with each.

- **Fetal monitors** help save the lives of many babies whose mothers have a history of pregnancy and birth complications. But they also may identify infants as in danger who, in fact, are not, and are linked to an increase in cesarean deliveries.

- Use of analgesics and anesthetics to control pain during childbirth can prolong labor and cause newborns to be withdrawn and irritable. Instrument delivery using *forceps* or, more often, a *vacuum extractor* may be appropriate if the mother's pushing does not move the infant through the birth canal in a reasonable period of time. However, because they can cause serious complications, they should be avoided if possible.

- **Induced labor** is more difficult than naturally occurring labor and is more likely to be associated with the use of labor and delivery medication and instrument delivery. Inductions should be scheduled only when continuing the pregnancy threatens the well-being of mother or baby.

- **Cesarean deliveries** are justified in cases of medical emergency or serious maternal illness and when the baby is in **breech position.** A dramatic worldwide rise has occurred in cesarean deliveries, many of which are unnecessary.

Birth Complications (p. 132)

4.4 What are the risks of oxygen deprivation, preterm birth, and low birth weight, and what factors can help infants who survive a traumatic birth?

- Squeezing of the umbilical cord during childbirth, placenta abruptio, and placenta previa can cause **anoxia** (oxygen deprivation), with risk of brain damage and infant death. Effects of even mild to moderate anoxia on cognitive and language development are still evident in middle childhood, though many children improve over time. Infants born more than six weeks early commonly have respiratory distress syndrome, which can cause brain damage due to immaturity of the lungs and associated anoxia.

- Low birth weight is a major cause of **neonatal** and **infant mortality** and wide-ranging developmental problems. It is most common in infants born to poverty-stricken women. Chronic maternal stress likely contributes to the high rate of low birth weight among African-American babies. Compared with **preterm** babies, whose weight is appropriate for time spent in the uterus, **small-for-date** infants usually have longer-lasting difficulties. However, even minimally preterm babies experience mild to moderate developmental delays.

- Some interventions provide special infant stimulation in the intensive care nursery. Others teach parents how to care for and interact with their babies. Preterm infants in stressed, low-income households need long-term, intensive intervention.

- When babies experience birth trauma, a supportive family environment or relationships with other caring adults can help restore their growth. Even infants with fairly serious birth complications can recover with the help of positive life events.

Precious Moments After Birth
(p. 140)

4.5 Is close parent–infant contact shortly after birth necessary for bonding?

- Human parents do not require close physical contact with the baby immediately after birth for **bonding** and effective parenting to occur. Nevertheless, early contact supports parents' feelings of caring and affection. Hospital practices that promote parent–infant closeness, such as **rooming in,** may help parents build a good relationship with their newborn.

The Newborn Baby's Capacities
(p. 141)

4.6 Describe the newborn baby's reflexes and states of arousal, including sleep characteristics and ways to soothe a crying baby.

- **Reflexes** are the newborn baby's most obvious organized patterns of behavior. Some have survival value, others help parents and infants establish gratifying interaction, and still others provide the foundation for voluntary motor skills.

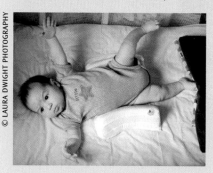

© LAURA DWIGHT PHOTOGRAPHY

- Although newborns move in and out of five **states of arousal,** they spend most of their time asleep. Sleep includes at least two states: **rapid-eye-movement (REM) sleep** and **non-rapid-eye-movement (NREM) sleep.** Newborns spend about 50 percent of their sleep time in REM sleep, far more than they ever will again. REM sleep provides young infants with stimulation essential for central nervous system development. Disturbed REM–NREM cycles are a sign of central nervous system abnormalities, which may lead to **sudden infant death syndrome (SIDS).**

- A crying baby stimulates strong feelings of discomfort in nearby adults. Once feeding and diaper changing have been tried, lifting the baby to the shoulder and rocking or walking is a highly effective soothing technique. Extensive parent–infant physical contact substantially reduces crying in the early months.

4.7 Describe the newborn baby's sensory capacities.

- The senses of touch, taste, smell, and sound are well-developed at birth. Newborns are sensitive to pain, prefer sweet tastes and smells, and orient toward the odor of their own mother's lactating breast and toward human milk rather than formula milk. Taste preferences developed through prenatal exposure to a mother's diet or through breast milk continue through the first year and possibly beyond.

- Newborns can distinguish a variety of sound patterns, as well as nearly all speech sounds. They are especially responsive to human speech, high-pitched expressive voices, their own mother's voice, and speech in their native language.

- Vision is the least developed of the newborn's senses. At birth, focusing ability and **visual acuity** are limited. Nevertheless, newborns can detect human faces and prefer their mother's familiar face to the face of a stranger. In exploring the visual field, they are attracted to bright objects but limit their looking to single features. Newborn babies have difficulty discriminating colors.

4.8 Why is neonatal behavioral assessment useful?

- The most widely used instrument for assessing the behavior of the newborn infant, Brazelton's **Neonatal Behavioral Assessment Scale (NBAS),** has helped researchers understand individual and cultural differences in newborn behavior. Sometimes it is used to teach parents about their baby's capacities.

The Transition to Parenthood
(p. 152)

4.9 Describe typical changes in the family after the birth of a new baby, along with interventions that foster the transition to parenthood.

- In response to the demands of new parenthood, the gender roles of husband and wife usually become more traditional. Parents in gratifying marriages who continue to support each other's needs generally adapt well. But a large difference between a husband's and wife's caregiving responsibilities can strain the marriage and negatively affect parent–infant interaction. Favorable adjustment to a second birth typically requires that fathers take an even more active role in parenting.

- Most nonmarital births are unplanned and to young mothers who have incomes below the poverty level and experience a stressful transition to parenthood. Planned births and adoptions by financially secure single women in their thirties and forties are increasing. These mothers typically adapt easily to new parenthood.

CRAIG F. WALKER/THE DENVER POST VIA GETTY IMAGES

- When parents are at low risk for problems, counselor-led parenting groups involving discussion of changing family relationships can ease the transition to parenthood. High-risk parents struggling with poverty or the birth of a baby with disabilities are more likely to benefit from intensive home interventions focusing on enhancing social support and parenting.

Important Terms and Concepts

anoxia (p. 133)
Apgar Scale (p. 126)
bonding (p. 141)
breech position (p. 132)
cesarean delivery (p. 131)
dilation and effacement of the cervix (p. 125)
fetal monitors (p. 130)
induced labor (p. 131)

infant mortality (p. 138)
natural, or prepared, childbirth (p. 128)
Neonatal Behavioral Assessment Scale (NBAS) (p. 150)
neonatal mortality (p. 138)
non-rapid-eye-movement (NREM) sleep (p. 144)
preterm infants (p. 135)
rapid-eye-movement (REM) sleep (p. 144)

reflex (p. 141)
rooming in (p. 141)
small-for-date infants (p. 135)
states of arousal (p. 143)
sudden infant death syndrome (SIDS) (p. 145)
transition (p. 125)
visual acuity (p. 150)

chapter 5

Physical Development in Infancy and Toddlerhood

"First Steps"
Irailde Alves Da Silva
14 years, Brazil

Encouraged and supported
by his mother, a baby takes
his first steps and experiences
the physical potential of
his growing body. During
the first year, infants grow
rapidly, move on their own,
increasingly investigate their
surroundings, and make sense
of complex sights and sounds.

REPRINTED WITH PERMISSION FROM THE WORLD AWARENESS CHILDREN'S MUSEUM, GLENS FALLS, NEW YORK

On a brilliant June morning, 16-month-old Caitlin emerged from her front door, ready for the short drive to the child-care home where she spent her weekdays while her mother, Carolyn, and her father, David, worked. Clutching a teddy bear in one hand and her mother's arm with the other, Caitlin descended the steps. "One! Two! Threeeee!" Carolyn counted as she helped Caitlin down. "How much she's changed!" Carolyn thought to herself, looking at the child who, not long ago, had been a newborn. With her first steps, Caitlin had passed from *infancy* to *toddlerhood*—a period spanning the second year of life. At first, Caitlin did, indeed, "toddle" with an awkward gait, tipping over frequently. But her face reflected the thrill of conquering a new skill.

As they walked toward the car, Carolyn and Caitlin spotted 3-year-old Eli and his father, Kevin, in the neighboring yard. Eli dashed toward them, waving a bright yellow envelope. Carolyn bent down to open the envelope and took out a card. It read, "Announcing the arrival of Grace Ann. Born: Cambodia. Age: 16 months." Carolyn turned toward Kevin and Eli. "That's wonderful news! When can we see her?"

"Let's wait a few days," Kevin suggested. "Monica's taken Grace to the doctor this morning. She's underweight and malnourished." Kevin described Monica's first night with Grace in a hotel room in Phnom Penh. Grace lay on the bed, withdrawn and fearful. Eventually she fell asleep, gripping crackers in both hands.

Carolyn felt Caitlin's impatient tug at her sleeve. Off they drove to child care, where Vanessa had just dropped off her 18-month-old son, Timmy. Within moments, Caitlin and Timmy were in the sandbox, shoveling sand into plastic cups and buckets with the help of their caregiver, Ginette.

A few weeks later, Grace joined Caitlin and Timmy at Ginette's child-care home. Although still unable to crawl or walk, she had grown taller and heavier, and her sad, vacant gaze had given way to an alert expression, a ready smile, and an enthusiastic desire to imitate and explore. When Caitlin headed for the sandbox, Grace stretched out her arms, asking Ginette to carry her there, too. Soon Grace was pulling herself up at every opportunity. Finally, at age 18 months, she walked!

This chapter traces physical growth during the first two years—one of the most remarkable and busiest times of development. We will see how rapid changes in the infant's body and brain support learning, motor skills, and perceptual capacities. Caitlin, Grace, and Timmy will join us along the way to illustrate individual differences and environmental influences on physical development. ■

Body Growth

TAKE A MOMENT... The next time you're walking in your neighborhood park or at the mall, note the contrast between infants' and toddlers' physical capabilities. One reason for the vast changes in what children can do over the first two years is that their bodies change enormously—faster than at any other time after birth.

Changes in Body Size and Muscle–Fat Makeup

By the end of the first year a typical infant's height is about 32 inches—more than 50 percent greater than at birth. By 2 years, it is 75 percent greater (36 inches).

5.1 Discuss major changes in body size, muscle–fat makeup, body proportions, and variations in rate of physical growth over the first two years.

Similarly, by 5 months of age, birth weight has doubled, to about 15 pounds. At 1 year it has tripled, to 22 pounds, and at 2 years it has quadrupled, to about 30 pounds.

Figure 5.1 illustrates this dramatic increase in body size. But rather than making steady gains, infants and toddlers grow in little spurts. In one study, children who were followed over the first 21 months of life went for periods of 7 to 63 days with no growth, then added as much as half an inch in a 24-hour period! Almost always, parents described their babies as irritable, very hungry, and sleeping more on the days before a spurt (Lampl, 1993; Lampl & Johnson, 2011).

One of the most obvious changes in infants' appearance is their transformation into round, plump babies by the middle of the first year. This early rise in "baby fat," which peaks at about 9 months, helps the infant maintain a constant body temperature. In the second year, most toddlers slim down, a trend that continues into middle childhood (Fomon & Nelson, 2002). In contrast, muscle tissue increases very slowly during infancy and will not reach a peak until adolescence. Babies are not very muscular; their strength and physical coordination are limited.

Shanwel at 7 weeks

Shanwel at 13 months

Shanwel at 17 months

Shanwel at 2 years

Mai at birth

Mai at 8 months

Mai at 11 months

Mai at 22 months

FIGURE 5.1 **Body growth during the first two years.** These photos depict the dramatic changes in body size and proportions during infancy and toddlerhood in two children—a boy, Shanwel, and a girl, Mai. In the first year, the head is quite large in proportion to the rest of the body, and height and weight gain are especially rapid. During the second year, the lower portion of the body catches up. Notice, also, how both children added "baby fat" in the early months of life and then slimmed down, a trend that continues into middle childhood.

Changes in Body Proportions

As the child's overall size increases, parts of the body grow at different rates. Two growth patterns describe these changes. The first is the **cephalocaudal trend**—from the Latin for "head to tail." During the prenatal period, the head develops more rapidly than the lower part of the body. At birth, the head takes up one-fourth of total body length, the legs only one-third. Notice how, in Figure 5.1, the lower portion of the body catches up. By age 2, the head accounts for only one-fifth and the legs for nearly one-half of total body length.

In the second pattern, the **proximodistal trend,** growth proceeds, literally, from "near to far"—from the center of the body outward. In the prenatal period, the head, chest, and trunk grow first; then the arms and legs; and finally the hands and feet. During infancy and childhood, the arms and legs continue to grow somewhat ahead of the hands and feet.

Individual and Group Differences

In infancy, girls are slightly shorter and lighter than boys, with a higher ratio of fat to muscle. These small sex differences persist throughout early and middle childhood and are greatly magnified at adolescence. Ethnic differences in body size are apparent as well. Grace was below the *growth norms* (height and weight averages for children her age). Early malnutrition played a part, but even after substantial catch-up, Grace—as is typical for Asian children— remained below North American norms. In contrast, Timmy is slightly above average in size, as African-American children tend to be (Bogin, 2001).

Children of the same age differ in *rate* of physical growth; some make faster progress toward mature body size than others. But current body size is not enough to tell us how quickly a child's physical growth is moving along. Although Timmy is larger and heavier than Caitlin and Grace, he is not physically more mature. In a moment, you will see why.

The best estimate of a child's physical maturity is *skeletal age,* a measure of bone development. It is determined by X-raying the long bones of the body to see the extent to which soft, pliable cartilage has hardened into bone, a gradual process that is completed in adolescence. When skeletal ages are examined, African-American children tend to be slightly ahead of Caucasian-American children in skeletal age. And girls are considerably ahead of boys—the reason Timmy's skeletal age lags behind that of Caitlin and Grace. At birth, the sexes differ by about 4 to 6 weeks, a gap that widens over infancy and childhood (Tanner, Healy, & Cameron, 2001). Girls are advanced in development of other organs as well. This greater physical maturity may contribute to girls' greater resistance to harmful environmental influences. As noted in Chapter 2, girls experience fewer developmental problems than boys and have lower infant and childhood mortality rates.

Brain Development

At birth, the brain is nearer to its adult size than any other physical structure, and it continues to develop at an astounding pace throughout infancy and toddlerhood. We can best understand brain growth by looking at it from two vantage points: (1) the microscopic level of individual brain cells and (2) the larger level of the cerebral cortex, the most complex brain structure and the one responsible for the highly developed intelligence of our species.

Development of Neurons

The human brain has 100 to 200 billion **neurons,** or nerve cells, that store and transmit information, many of which have thousands of direct connections with other neurons. Unlike other body cells, neurons are not tightly packed together. Between them are tiny gaps, or **synapses,** where fibers from different neurons come close together but do not touch (see Figure 5.2 on page 162). Neurons send messages to one another by releasing chemicals called **neurotransmitters,** which cross the synapse.

5.2 Describe brain development during infancy and toddlerhood, current methods of measuring brain functioning, and appropriate stimulation to support the brain's potential.

5.3 How does organization of sleep and wakefulness change over the first two years?

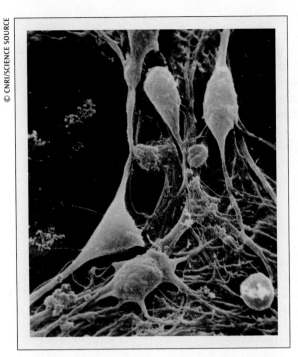

© CNRI/SCIENCE SOURCE

FIGURE 5.2 **Neurons and their connective fibers.** This photograph of several neurons, taken with the aid of a powerful microscope, shows the elaborate synaptic connections that form with neighboring cells.

The basic story of brain growth concerns how neurons develop and form this elaborate communication system. Figure 5.3 summarizes major milestones of brain development. In the prenatal period, neurons are produced in the embryo's primitive neural tube. From there, they migrate to form the major parts of the brain (see Chapter 3, page 98). Once neurons are in place, they differentiate, establishing their unique functions by extending their fibers to form synaptic connections with neighboring cells. During infancy and toddlerhood, neural fibers and synapses increase at an astounding pace (Gilmore et al., 2012; Moore, Persaud, & Torchia, 2013). Because developing neurons require space for these connective structures, a surprising aspect of brain growth is that as synapses form, many surrounding neurons die—20 to 80 percent, depending on the brain region (Stiles, 2008). Fortunately, during the prenatal period, the neural tube produces far more neurons than the brain will ever need.

As neurons form connections, *stimulation* becomes vital to their survival. Neurons that are stimulated by input from the surrounding environment continue to establish new synapses, forming increasingly elaborate systems of communication that support more complex abilities. At first, stimulation results in a massive overabundance of synapses, many of which serve identical functions, thereby ensuring that the child will acquire the motor, cognitive, and social skills that our species needs to survive. Neurons that are seldom stimulated soon lose their synapses, in a process called **synaptic pruning** that returns neurons not needed at the moment to an uncommitted state so they can support future development. In all, about 40 percent of synapses are pruned during childhood and adolescence (Webb, Monk, & Nelson, 2001). For this process to advance, appropriate stimulation of the child's brain is vital during periods in which the formation of synapses is at its peak (Bryk & Fisher, 2012).

If few neurons are produced after the prenatal period, what causes the extraordinary increase in brain size during the first two years? About half the brain's volume is made up of **glial cells,** which are responsible for **myelination,** the coating of neural fibers with an insulating fatty sheath (called *myelin*) that improves the efficiency of message transfer. Certain types of glial cells also participate directly in neural communication, by picking up and passing on neuronal signals and releasing neurotransmitters. Glial cells multiply rapidly from the end of

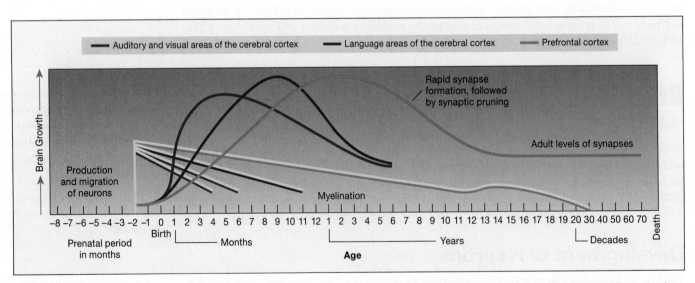

FIGURE 5.3 **Major milestones of brain development.** Formation of synapses is rapid during the first two years, especially in the auditory, visual, and language areas of the cerebral cortex. The prefrontal cortex undergoes more extended synaptic growth. In each area, overproduction of synapses is followed by synaptic pruning. The prefrontal cortex, responsible for thought (see page 165), is among the last regions to attain an adult level of synaptic connections—in mid- to late adolescence. Myelination occurs at a dramatic pace during the first two years and then at a slower pace through childhood, followed by an acceleration at adolescence. The multiple yellow lines indicate that the timing of myelination varies among different brain areas. For example, neural fibers myelinate over a longer period in the language areas, and especially in the prefrontal cortex, than in the visual and auditory areas. (Based on Thompson & Nelson, 2001.)

pregnancy through the second year of life—a process that continues at a slower pace through middle childhood and accelerates again in adolescence. Gains in neural fibers and myelination account for the overall increase in size of the brain, from nearly 30 percent of its adult weight at birth to 70 percent by age 2 (Johnson, 2011; Knickmeyer et al., 2008). Growth is especially rapid during the first year, when the brain more than doubles in size.

Brain development can be compared to molding a "living sculpture." First, neurons and synapses are overproduced. Then, cell death and synaptic pruning sculpt away excess building material to form the mature brain—a process jointly influenced by genetically programmed events and the child's experiences. The resulting "sculpture" is a set of interconnected regions, each with specific functions—much like countries on a globe that communicate with one another (Johnston et al., 2001). This "geography" of the brain permits researchers to study its organization and the activity of its regions using neurobiological techniques.

Measures of Brain Functioning

Table 5.1 describes major measures of brain functioning. Among these methods, the two most frequently used detect changes in *electrical activity* in the cerebral cortex. In an *electroencephalogram (EEG)*, researchers examine *brain-wave patterns* for stability and organization—signs of mature functioning of the cortex (see Figure 5.4). And as a child processes a particular stimulus, *event-related potentials (ERPs)* detect the general location of brain-wave activity—a technique often used to study preverbal infants' responsiveness to various stimuli, the impact of experience on specialization of specific regions of the cortex, and atypical brain functioning in children at risk for learning and emotional problems (DeBoer, Scott, & Nelson, 2007; Gunnar & de Haan, 2009).

Neuroimaging techniques, which yield detailed, three-dimensional computerized pictures of the entire brain and its active areas, provide the most precise information about which brain regions are specialized for certain capacities. The most promising of these methods is *functional magnetic resonance imaging (fMRI)*. Unlike *positron emission tomography (PET)*, fMRI does not depend on X-ray photography, which requires injection of a radioactive substance. Rather, when a child is exposed to a stimulus, fMRI detects changes in blood flow and oxygen metabolism throughout the

OLI SCHARFF/GETTY IMAGES

FIGURE 5.4 **Electroencephalogram (EEG) using the geodesic sensor net (GSN).** Interconnected electrodes embedded in the head cap record electrical brain-wave activity in the cerebral cortex.

TABLE 5.1 Measuring Brain Functioning	
METHOD	**DESCRIPTION**
Electroencephalogram (EEG)	Electrodes embedded in a head cap record electrical brain-wave activity in the brain's outer layers—the cerebral cortex. Researchers use an advanced tool called a geodesic sensor net (GSN) to hold interconnected electrodes (up to 128 for infants and 256 for children and adults) in place through a cap that adjusts to each person's head shape, yielding improved brain-wave detection.
Event-related potentials (ERPs)	Using the EEG, the frequency and amplitude of brain waves in response to particular stimuli (such as a picture, music, or speech) are recorded in the cerebral cortex. Enables identification of general regions of stimulus-induced activity.
Functional magnetic resonance imaging (fMRI)	While the person lies inside a tunnel-shaped apparatus that creates a magnetic field, a scanner magnetically detects increased blood flow and oxygen metabolism in areas of the brain as the individual processes particular stimuli. The scanner typically records images every 1 to 4 seconds; these are combined into a computerized moving picture of activity anywhere in the brain (not just its outer layers). Not appropriate for children younger than age 5 to 6, who cannot remain still during testing.
Positron emission tomography (PET)	After injection or inhalation of a radioactive substance, the person lies on an apparatus with a scanner that emits fine streams of X-rays, which detect increased blood flow and oxygen metabolism in areas of the brain as the person processes particular stimuli. As with fMRI, the result is a computerized image of activity anywhere in the brain. Not appropriate for children younger than age 5 to 6.
Near-infrared spectroscopy (NIRS)	Using thin, flexible optical fibers attached to the scalp through a head cap, infrared (invisible) light is beamed at the brain; its absorption by areas of the cerebral cortex varies with changes in blood flow and oxygen metabolism as the individual processes particular stimuli. The result is a computerized moving picture of active areas in the cerebral cortex. Unlike fMRI and PET, NIRS is appropriate for infants and young children, who can move within limited range during testing.

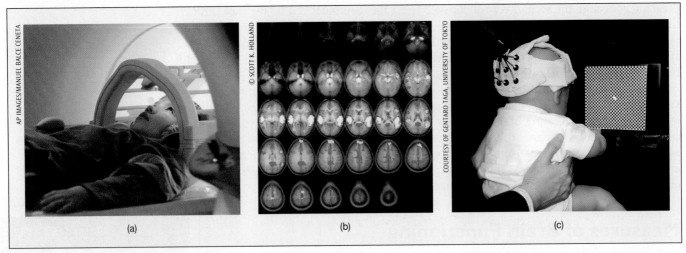

FIGURE 5.5 Functional magnetic resonance imaging (fMRI) and near infrared spectroscopy (NIRS). (a) This 6-year-old is part of a study that uses fMRI to find out how his brain processes light and motion. (b) The fMRI image shows which areas of the boy's brain are active while he views changing visual stimuli. (c) Here, NIRS is used to investigate a 2-month-old's response to a visual stimulus. During testing, the baby can move freely within a limited range. (Photo (c) From G. Taga, K. Asakawa, A. Maki, Y. Konishi, & H. Koisumi, 2003, "Brain Imaging in Awake Infants by Near-Infrared Optical Topography," *Proceedings of the National Academy of Sciences, 100,* p. 10723. Reprinted by permission.)

brain magnetically, yielding a colorful, moving picture of parts of the brain used to perform a given activity (see Figure 5.5a and b).

Because PET and fMRI require that the participant lie as motionless as possible for an extended time, they are not suitable for infants and young children. A neuroimaging technique that works well in infancy and early childhood is *near infrared spectroscopy (NIRS),* in which infrared (invisible) light is beamed at regions of the cerebral cortex to measure blood flow and oxygen metabolism while the child attends to a stimulus (refer again to Table 5.1). Because the apparatus consists only of thin, flexible optical fibers attached to the scalp using a head cap, a baby can sit on the parent's lap and move during testing—as Figure 5.5c illustrates (Hespos et al., 2010). But unlike PET and fMRI, which map activity changes throughout the brain, NIRS examines only the functioning of the cerebral cortex.

The measures just reviewed are powerful tools for uncovering relationships between the brain and psychological development. But like all research methods, they have limitations. Even though a stimulus produces a consistent pattern of brain activity, investigators cannot be certain that an individual has processed it in a certain way (Kagan, 2013). And a researcher who takes a change in brain activity as an indicator of information processing must make sure that the change was not due instead to hunger, boredom, fatigue, or body movements. Consequently, other methods must be combined with brain-wave and -imaging findings to clarify their meaning (de Haan & Gunnar, 2009). Now let's turn to the developing organization of the cerebral cortex.

Development of the Cerebral Cortex

The **cerebral cortex** surrounds the rest of the brain, resembling half of a shelled walnut. It is the largest brain structure—accounting for 85 percent of the brain's weight and containing the greatest number of neurons and synapses. Because the cerebral cortex is the last part of the brain to stop growing, it is sensitive to environmental influences for a much longer period than any other part of the brain.

REGIONS OF THE CORTEX Figure 5.6 shows specific functions of regions of the cerebral cortex, such as receiving information from the senses, instructing the body to move, and thinking. The order in which cortical regions develop corresponds to the order in which various capacities emerge in the infant and growing child. For example, a burst of synaptic growth occurs in the auditory and visual cortexes and in areas responsible for body movement over the first year—a period of dramatic gains in auditory and visual perception and mastery of motor skills (Gilmore et al., 2012). Language areas are especially active from late infancy through the preschool years, when language development flourishes (Pujol et al., 2006).

The cortical regions with the most extended period of development are the *frontal lobes.* The **prefrontal cortex,** lying in front of areas controlling body movement, is responsible for thought—in particular, consciousness, inhibition of impulses, integration of information, and use of memory, reasoning, planning, and problem-solving strategies. From age 2 months on, the prefrontal cortex functions more effectively. But it undergoes especially rapid myelination and formation and pruning of synapses during the preschool and school years, followed by another period of accelerated growth in adolescence, when it reaches an adult level of synaptic connections (Nelson, 2002; Nelson, Thomas, & de Haan, 2006; Sowell et al., 2002).

LATERALIZATION AND PLASTICITY OF THE CEREBRAL CORTEX

The cerebral cortex has two *hemispheres,* or sides, that differ in their functions. Some tasks are done mostly by the left hemisphere, others by the right. For example, each hemisphere receives sensory information from the side of the body opposite to it and controls only that side.[1] For most of us, the left hemisphere is largely responsible for verbal abilities (such as spoken and written language) and positive emotion (for example, joy). The right hemisphere handles spatial abilities (judging distances, reading maps, and recognizing geometric shapes) and negative emotion (such as distress) (Nelson & Bosquet, 2000). In left-handed people, this pattern may be reversed or, more commonly, the cerebral cortex may be less clearly specialized than in right-handers.

Why does this specialization of the two hemispheres, called **lateralization,** occur? Studies using fMRI reveal that the left hemisphere is better at processing information in a sequential, analytic (piece-by-piece) way, a good approach for dealing with communicative information—both verbal (language) and emotional (a joyful smile). In contrast, the right hemisphere is specialized for processing information in a holistic, integrative manner, ideal for making sense of spatial information and regulating negative emotion. A lateralized brain may have evolved because it enabled humans to cope more successfully with changing environmental demands (Falk, 2005). It permits a wider array of functions to be carried out effectively than if both sides processed information in exactly the same way. However, the popular notion of a "right-brained" or "left-brained" person is an oversimplification. The two hemispheres communicate and work together, doing so more rapidly and effectively with age.

Researchers study the timing of brain lateralization to learn more about **brain plasticity.** A highly *plastic* cerebral cortex, in which many areas are not yet committed to specific functions, has a high capacity for learning. And if a part of the cortex is damaged, other parts can take over the tasks it would have handled. But once the hemispheres lateralize, damage to a specific region means that the abilities it controls cannot be recovered to the same extent or as easily as earlier.

At birth, the hemispheres have already begun to specialize. Most newborns favor the right side of the body in their head position and reflexive reactions (Grattan et al., 1992; Rönnqvist & Hopkins, 1998). Most also show greater activation (detected with either ERP or NIRS) in the left hemisphere while listening to speech sounds or displaying a positive state of arousal. In contrast, the right hemisphere reacts more strongly to nonspeech sounds and to stimuli (such as a sour-tasting fluid) that evoke a negative reaction (Fox & Davidson, 1986; Hespos et al., 2010).

Nevertheless, research on brain-damaged children and adults offers evidence for substantial plasticity in the young brain, summarized in the Biology and Environment box on page 166.

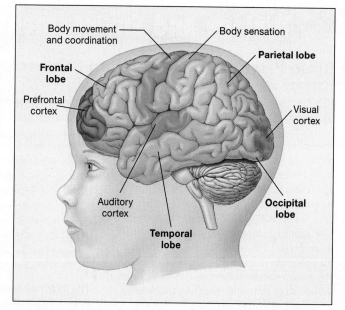

FIGURE 5.6 **The left side of the human brain, showing the cerebral cortex.** The cortex is divided into different lobes, each of which contains a variety of regions with specific functions. Some major regions are labeled here.

---

[1]The eyes are an exception. Messages from the right half of each retina go to the right hemisphere; messages from the left half of each retina go to the left hemisphere. Thus, visual information from *both* eyes is received by *both* hemispheres.

Biology and Environment

Brain Plasticity: Insights from Research on Brain-Damaged Children and Adults

In the first few years of life, the brain is highly plastic. It can reorganize areas committed to specific functions in a way that the mature brain cannot. Adults who suffered injury to a part of the brain in infancy and early childhood usually show fewer cognitive impairments than adults with later-occurring injury (Holland, 2004; Huttenlocher, 2002). Nevertheless, the young brain is not totally plastic. When it is injured, its functioning is compromised. And the more brain tissue destroyed in infancy or early childhood, the poorer the outcomes (Anderson et al., 2006). The extent of plasticity depends on several factors, including age at time of injury, site and severity of damage, skill area, and environmental supports for recovery.

Brain Plasticity in Infancy and Early Childhood

In a large study of children with injuries to the cerebral cortex that occurred around the time of birth or in the first six months of life, language and spatial skills were assessed repeatedly into adolescence (Stiles, Reilly, & Levine, 2012; Stiles et al., 2005, 2008, 2009). All the children had experienced early brain seizures or hemorrhages. Brain-imaging techniques (fMRI and PET) revealed the precise site of damage.

Regardless of whether injury occurred in the left or right cerebral hemisphere, the children showed delays in language development that persisted until about 3½ years of age. That damage to either hemisphere affected early language competence indicates that at first, language functioning is broadly distributed in the brain. But by age 5, the children caught up in vocabulary and grammatical skills. Undamaged areas—in either the left or the right hemisphere—had taken over these language functions.

Compared with language, spatial skills were more impaired after early brain injury. When preschool through adolescent-age youngsters were asked to copy designs, those with early right-hemispheric damage had trouble with holistic processing—accurately representing the overall shape. In contrast, children with left-hemispheric damage captured the basic shape but omitted fine-grained details. Nevertheless, the children showed improvements in their drawings with age—gains that did not occur in brain-injured adults (Stiles, Reilly, & Levine, 2012; Stiles et al., 2003, 2008, 2009).

Clearly, recovery after early brain injury is greater for language than for spatial skills. Why is this so? Researchers speculate that spatial processing is the older of the two capacities in our evolutionary history and, therefore, more lateralized at birth (Stiles et al., 2008). But early brain injury has less impact than later injury on both language and spatial skills, revealing the young brain's plasticity.

The Price of High Plasticity in the Young Brain

Despite impressive recovery of language and (to a lesser extent) spatial skills, children with early brain injuries show deficits in a wide variety of complex mental abilities during the school years. For example, their reading and math progress is slow. In telling stories, they produce simpler narratives than agemates without early brain injuries. And as the demands of daily life increase, they have difficulty managing homework and other responsibilities (Anderson, Spencer-Smith, & Wood, 2011; Stiles, Reilly, & Levine, 2012).

High brain plasticity, researchers explain, comes at a price. When healthy brain regions take over the functions of damaged areas, a "crowding effect" occurs: Multiple tasks must be done by a smaller-than-usual volume of brain tissue (Stiles, 2012). Consequently, the brain processes information less quickly and accurately than it would if it were intact. Complex mental abilities of all kinds suffer into middle childhood, and often longer, because performing them well requires the collaboration of many regions in the cerebral cortex. In sum, the full impact of an early brain injury may not be apparent for many years, until higher-order skills are expected to develop.

Age of Injury and Plasticity

In infancy and childhood, the goal of brain growth is to form neural connections that ensure mastery of essential skills. Animal research reveals that plasticity is greatest while the brain is forming many new synapses; it declines during synaptic pruning (Murphy & Corbett, 2009). At

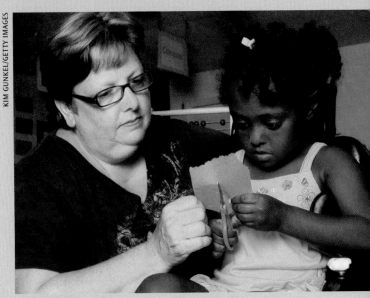

This preschooler, who experienced brain damage in infancy, has been spared massive impairments because of high plasticity of the brain. Here, a teacher encourages her to cut basic shapes to strengthen spatial skills, which remain more impaired than language after early brain injury.

the same time, for as yet unexplained reasons, some young children suffer permanent damage following a localized brain injury (Anderson, Spencer-Smith, & Wood, 2011). Age likely combines with other influences—insult site and severity and environmental factors, such as warm, stimulating parenting and access to intervention services—to affect outcomes.

Furthermore, brain plasticity is not restricted to early childhood. Though far more limited, reorganization in the brain can occur later, even in adulthood. For example, adult stroke victims often display considerable recovery, especially in response to stimulation of language and motor skills. Brain-imaging findings reveal that structures adjacent to the permanently damaged area or in the opposite cerebral hemisphere reorganize to support the impaired ability (Kalra & Ratan, 2007; Murphy & Corbett, 2009). When an individual practices relevant tasks, the brain strengthens existing synapses and generates new ones.

Plasticity seems to be a basic property of the nervous system. Researchers hope to discover how brain plasticity and experience work together throughout life, so they can help people of all ages—with and without brain injuries—develop at their best.

Furthermore, early experience greatly influences the organization of the cerebral cortex. For example, deaf adults who, as infants and children, learned sign language (a spatial skill) depend more than hearing individuals on the right hemisphere for language processing (Neville & Bavelier, 2002). And toddlers who are advanced in language development show greater left-hemispheric specialization for language than their more slowly developing age-mates (Luna et al., 2001; Mills et al., 2005). Apparently, the very process of acquiring language and other skills promotes lateralization.

In sum, the brain is more plastic during the first few years than it will ever be again. An overabundance of synaptic connections supports brain plasticity and, therefore, young children's ability to learn, which is fundamental to their survival. And although the cortex is programmed from the start for hemispheric specialization, experience greatly influences the rate and success of its advancing organization.

Sensitive Periods in Brain Development

Animal studies confirm that early, extreme sensory deprivation results in permanent brain damage and loss of functions—findings that verify the existence of sensitive periods in brain development. For example, early, varied visual experiences must occur for the brain's visual centers to develop normally. If a 1-month-old kitten is deprived of light for just three or four days, these areas of the brain degenerate. If the kitten is kept in the dark during the fourth week of life and beyond, the damage is severe and permanent (Crair, Gillespie, & Stryker, 1998). And the general quality of the early environment affects overall brain growth. When animals reared from birth in physically and socially stimulating surroundings are compared with those reared in isolation, the brains of the stimulated animals are larger and show much denser synaptic connections (Sale, Berardi, & Maffei, 2009).

HUMAN EVIDENCE: VICTIMS OF DEPRIVED EARLY ENVIRONMENTS For ethical reasons, we cannot deliberately deprive some infants of normal rearing experiences and observe the impact on their brains and competencies. Instead, we must turn to natural experiments, in which children were victims of deprived early environments that were later rectified. Such studies have revealed some parallels with the animal evidence just described.

For example, when babies are born with cataracts in both eyes (clouded lenses, preventing clear visual images), those who have corrective surgery within four to six months show rapid improvement in vision, except for subtle aspects of face perception, which require early visual input to the right hemisphere to develop (Maurer & Lewis, 2013; Maurer, Mondloch, & Lewis, 2007). The longer cataract surgery is postponed beyond infancy, the less complete the recovery in visual skills. And if surgery is delayed until adulthood, vision is severely and permanently impaired (Lewis & Maurer, 2005).

Studies of infants placed in orphanages who were later exposed to family rearing confirm the importance of a generally stimulating environment for psychological development. In one investigation, researchers followed the progress of a large sample of children transferred between birth and 3½ years from extremely deprived Romanian orphanages to adoptive families in Great Britain (Beckett et al., 2006; O'Connor et al., 2000; Rutter et al., 1998, 2004, 2010). On arrival, most were impaired in all domains of development. Cognitive catch-up was impressive for children adopted before 6 months, who consistently attained average mental test scores in childhood and adolescence, performing as well as a comparison group of early-adopted British-born children.

But Romanian children who had been institutionalized for more than the first six months showed serious intellectual deficits (see Figure 5.7 on page 168). Although they improved in mental test scores during middle childhood and adolescence, they remained substantially below average. And most displayed at least three serious mental health problems, such as inattention, overactivity, unruly behavior, and autistic-like symptoms (social disinterest, stereotyped behavior) (Kreppner et al., 2007, 2010). A major correlate of both time spent in the institution and poor

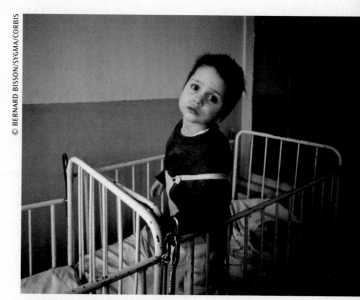

This Romanian orphan receives little adult contact or stimulation. The longer he remains in this barren environment, the greater his risk of brain damage and lasting impairments in all domains of development.

© BERNARD BISSON/SYGMA/CORBIS

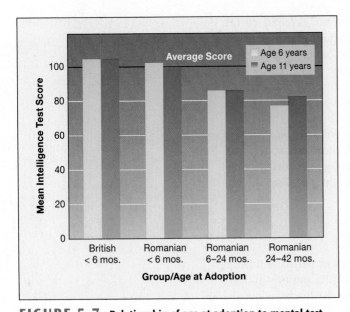

FIGURE 5.7 **Relationship of age at adoption to mental test scores at ages 6 and 11 among British and Romanian adoptees.** Children transferred from Romanian orphanages to British adoptive homes in the first six months of life attained average scores and fared as well as British early-adopted children, suggesting that they had fully recovered from extreme early deprivation. Romanian children adopted after 6 months of age performed well below average. And although those adopted after age 2 improved between ages 6 and 11, they continued to show serious intellectual deficits. (Adapted from Beckett et al., 2006.)

cognitive and emotional functioning was below-average head size, suggesting that early lack of stimulation permanently damaged the brain (Sonuga-Barke, Schlotz, & Kreppner, 2010).

Neurobiological findings indicate that early, prolonged institutionalization leads to a generalized decrease in activity of the cerebral cortex—especially the prefrontal cortex, which governs complex cognition and impulse control. Neural fibers connecting the prefrontal cortex with other brain structures involved in control of emotion are also reduced (Eluvathingal et al., 2006; Nelson, 2007b). And activation of the left cerebral hemisphere, governing positive emotion, is diminished relative to right cerebral activation, governing negative emotion (McLaughlin et al., 2011).

Additional evidence confirms that the chronic stress of early, deprived orphanage rearing disrupts the brain's capacity to manage stress. In another investigation, researchers followed the development of children who had spent their first eight months or more in Romanian institutions and were then adopted into Canadian homes (Gunnar & Cheatham, 2003; Gunnar et al., 2001). Compared with agemates adopted shortly after birth, these children showed extreme stress reactivity, as indicated by high concentrations of the stress hormone *cortisol* in their saliva—a physiological response linked to persistent illness, delayed physical growth, and learning and behavior problems, including deficits in attention and control of anger and other impulses. The longer the children spent in orphanage care, the higher their cortisol levels—even 6½ years after adoption. In other research, orphanage children displayed abnormally low cortisol—a blunted physiological stress response that may be the central nervous system's adaptation to earlier, frequent cortisol elevations (Loman & Gunnar, 2010).

Finally, early deprived rearing may also disrupt the brain's typical response to pleasurable social experiences. After sitting on their mother's lap and playing an enjoyable game, preschoolers adopted, on average, at age 1½ years from Romanian orphanages had abnormally low urine levels of *oxytocin*—a hormone released by the brain that evokes calmness and contentment in the presence of familiar, trusted people (Fries et al., 2005). As we will see in Chapter 7, children who spend their infancy in neglectful institutions often display attachment difficulties.

APPROPRIATE STIMULATION Unlike the orphanage children just described, Grace, whom Monica and Kevin had adopted in Cambodia at 16 months of age, showed favorable progress. Two years earlier, they had adopted Grace's older brother, Eli. When Eli was 2 years old, Monica and Kevin sent a letter and a photo of Eli to his biological mother, describing a bright, happy child. The next day, the Cambodian mother tearfully asked an adoption agency to send her baby daughter to join Eli and his American family.

Although Grace's early environment was very depleted, her biological mother's loving care—holding gently, speaking softly, playfully stimulating, and breastfeeding—may have prevented irreversible damage to her brain. Besides offering gentle, appropriate stimulation, sensitive adult care helps normalize cortisol production in both typically developing and emotionally traumatized infants and young children (Gunnar & Quevedo, 2007; Tarullo & Gunnar, 2006). Good parenting seems to protect the young brain from the potentially damaging effects of both excessive and inadequate stress-hormone exposure.

In the Bucharest Early Intervention Project, 136 institutionalized Romanian babies were randomized into conditions of either care as usual or transfer to high-quality foster families between 6 and 31 months of age. Specially trained social workers provided foster parents with counseling and support. Follow-ups between 2½ and 8 years revealed that the foster-care group exceeded the institutional-care group in intelligence test scores, language skills, emotional responsiveness, social skills, and EEG and ERP assessments of brain development (Fox, Nelson & Zeanah, 2013; Nelson, Fox, & Zeanah, 2014). On all measures, the earlier the foster placement, the better the outcome. But consistent with an early sensitive period, the foster-care group remained behind never-institutionalized agemates living with Bucharest families.

In addition to impoverished environments, ones that overwhelm children with expectations beyond their current capacities interfere with the brain's potential. In recent years, expensive early learning centers have sprung up, in which infants are trained with letter and number flash cards and slightly older toddlers are given a full curriculum of reading, math, science, art, gym, and more. There is no evidence that these programs yield smarter, better "super-babies" (Hirsh-Pasek & Golinkoff, 2003). To the contrary, trying to prime infants with stimulation for which they are not ready can cause them to withdraw, thereby threatening their interest in learning and creating conditions much like stimulus deprivation!

How, then, can we characterize appropriate stimulation during the early years? To answer this question, researchers distinguish between two types of brain development. The first, **experience-expectant brain growth,** refers to the young brain's rapidly developing organization, which depends on ordinary experiences—opportunities to explore the environment, interact with people, and hear language and other sounds. As a result of millions of years of evolution, the brains of all infants, toddlers, and young children *expect* to encounter these experiences and, if they do, grow normally. The second type of brain development, **experience-dependent brain growth,** occurs throughout our lives. It consists of additional growth and the refinement of established brain structures as a result of specific learning experiences that vary widely across individuals and cultures (Greenough & Black, 1992). Reading and writing, playing computer games, weaving an intricate rug, and practicing the violin are examples. The brain of a violinist differs in certain ways from the brain of a poet because each has exercised different brain regions for a long time.

Experience-expectant brain growth occurs naturally, through ordinary, stimulating experiences. This toddler exploring a mossy log engages in the type of activity that best promotes brain development in the early years.

Experience-expectant brain development occurs early and naturally, as caregivers offer babies and preschoolers age-appropriate play materials and engage them in enjoyable daily routines—a shared meal, a game of peekaboo, a bath before bed, a picture book to talk about, or a song to sing. The resulting growth provides the foundation for later-occurring, experience-dependent development (Belsky & de Haan, 2011; Huttenlocher, 2002). No evidence exists for a sensitive period in the first few years of life for mastering skills that depend on extensive training, such as reading, musical performance, or gymnastics (Bruer, 1999). To the contrary, rushing early learning also harms the brain by overwhelming its neural circuits, thereby reducing the brain's sensitivity to the everyday experiences it needs for a healthy start in life.

Changing States of Arousal

Rapid brain growth means that the organization of sleep and wakefulness changes substantially between birth and 2 years, and fussiness and crying also decline. The newborn baby takes round-the-clock naps that total about 16 to 18 hours. Total sleep time declines slowly; the average 2-year-old still needs 12 to 13 hours. But periods of sleep and wakefulness become fewer and longer, and the sleep–wake pattern increasingly conforms to a night–day schedule. Most 6- to 9-month-olds take two daytime naps; by about 18 months, children generally need only one nap (Galland et al., 2012). Finally, between ages 3 and 5, napping subsides.

These changing arousal patterns are due to brain development, but they are also affected by cultural beliefs and practices and parents' needs (Super & Harkness, 2002). Dutch parents, for example, view sleep regularity as far more important than U.S. parents do. And whereas U.S. parents regard a predictable sleep schedule as emerging naturally from within the child, Dutch parents believe that a schedule must be imposed, or the baby's development might suffer (Super & Harkness, 2010; Super et al., 1996). At age 6 months, Dutch babies are put to bed earlier and sleep, on average, 2 hours more per day than their U.S. agemates.

Motivated by demanding work schedules and other needs, many Western parents try to get their babies to sleep through the night as early as 3 to 4 months by offering an evening feeding—a practice that may be at odds with young infants' neurological capacities. Not until

Cultural Influences

Cultural Variation in Infant Sleeping Arrangements

Western child-rearing advice from experts strongly encourages the nighttime separation of baby from parent. For example, the most recent edition of Benjamin Spock's *Baby and Child Care* recommends that babies sleep in their own room by 3 months of age, explaining, "By 6 months, a child who regularly sleeps in her parents' room may feel uneasy sleeping anywhere else" (Spock & Needlman, 2012, p. 62). And the American Academy of Pediatrics (2012b) has issued a controversial warning that parent–infant bedsharing may increase the risk of sudden infant death syndrome (SIDS).

Yet parent–infant "cosleeping" is the norm for approximately 90 percent of the world's population, in cultures as diverse as the Japanese, the rural Guatemalan Maya, the Inuit of northwestern Canada, and the !Kung of Botswana. Japanese and Korean children usually lie next to their mothers throughout infancy and early childhood, and many continue to sleep with a parent or other family member until adolescence (Takahashi, 1990; Yang & Hahn, 2002). Among the Maya, mother–infant bedsharing is interrupted only by the birth of a new baby, when the older child is moved next to the father or to another bed in the same room (Morelli et al., 1992). Bedsharing is also common in U.S. ethnic minority families (McKenna & Volpe, 2007). African-American children, for example, frequently fall asleep with their parents and remain with them for part or all of the night (Buswell & Spatz, 2007).

Cultural values strongly influence infant sleeping arrangements. In one study, researchers interviewed Guatemalan Mayan mothers and American middle-SES mothers about their sleeping practices. Mayan mothers stressed the importance of promoting an *interdependent self,* explaining that cosleeping builds a close parent–child bond, which is necessary for children to learn the ways of people around them. In contrast, American mothers emphasized an *independent self,* mentioning their desire to instill early autonomy, prevent bad habits, and protect their own privacy (Morelli et al., 1992).

Over the past two decades, cosleeping has increased in Western nations. An estimated 11 percent of U.S. infants routinely bedshare, and an additional 30 to 35 percent sometimes do (Buswell & Spatz, 2007; Colson et al., 2013). Proponents of the practice say that it helps infants sleep, makes breastfeeding more convenient, and provides valuable bonding time (McKenna & Volpe, 2007).

During the night, cosleeping babies breastfeed three times longer than infants who sleep alone. Because infants arouse to nurse more often when sleeping next to their mothers, some researchers believe that cosleeping may actually help safeguard babies at risk for SIDS. Consistent with this view, SIDS is rare in Asian cultures where cosleeping is widespread, including Cambodia, China, Japan, Korea, Thailand, and Vietnam (McKenna, 2002; McKenna & McDade, 2005). And contrary to popular belief, cosleeping does not reduce mothers' total sleep time, although they experience more brief awakenings, which permit them to check on their baby (Mao et al., 2004).

Infant sleeping practices affect other aspects of family life. For example, Mayan babies doze off in the midst of ongoing family activities and are carried to bed by their mothers. In contrast, for many North American parents, bedtime often requires a lengthy, elaborate ritual. Perhaps bedtime struggles, so common in Western homes but rare elsewhere in the world, are related to the stress young children feel when they must fall asleep without assistance (Latz, Wolf, & Lozoff, 1999).

Critics warn that bedsharing will promote emotional problems, especially excessive dependency. Yet a longitudinal study following children from the end of pregnancy through age 18 years showed that young people who had bedshared in the early years were no different from others in any aspect of adjustment (Okami, Weisner, & Olmstead, 2002). Another concern is that infants might become trapped under the parent's body or in soft bedding and suffocate. Parents who are obese or who use alcohol, tobacco, or illegal drugs do pose a serious risk

A Vietnamese mother and child sleep together— a practice common in their culture and around the globe. Hard wooden sleeping surfaces protect cosleeping children from entrapment in soft bedding.

to their sleeping babies, as does the use of quilts and comforters or an overly soft mattress (American Academy of Pediatrics, 2012b).

But with appropriate precautions, parents and infants can cosleep safely (Ball & Volpe, 2013). In cultures where cosleeping is widespread, parents and infants usually sleep with light covering on hard surfaces, such as firm mattresses, floor mats, and wooden planks, or infants sleep in a cradle or hammock next to the parents' bed (McKenna, 2001, 2002). And when sharing the same bed, infants typically lie on their back or side facing the mother—positions that promote frequent, easy communication between parent and baby and arousal if breathing is threatened.

Finally, breastfeeding mothers usually assume a distinctive sleeping posture. They face the infant, with knees drawn up under the baby's feet and arm above the baby's head. Besides facilitating feeding, the position prevents the infant from sliding down under covers or up under pillows (Ball, 2006). Because this posture is also seen in female great apes while sharing sleeping nests with their infants, researchers believe it may have evolved to enhance infant safety.

the middle of the first year is the secretion of *melatonin,* a hormone within the brain that promotes drowsiness, much greater at night than during the day (Sadeh, 1997).

Furthermore, as the Cultural Influences box above reveals, isolating infants to promote sleep is rare elsewhere in the world. When babies sleep with their parents, their average sleep period remains constant at three hours from 1 to 8 months of age. Only at the end of the first year, as REM sleep (the state that usually prompts waking) declines, do infants move in the direction of an adultlike sleep–wake schedule (Ficca et al., 1999).

Even after infants sleep through the night, they continue to wake occasionally. When babies begin to crawl and walk, they often show temporary periods of disrupted sleep (Scher, Epstein, & Tirosh, 2004). In studies carried out in Australia, Israel, and the United States, night wakings increased around 6 months and again between 1½ and 2 years and then declined (Armstrong, Quinn, & Dadds, 1994; Scher, Epstein, & Tirosh, 2004; Scher et al., 1995). As Chapter 7 will reveal, around the middle of the first year, infants are forming a clear-cut attachment to their familiar caregiver and begin protesting when he or she leaves. And the challenges of toddlerhood—the ability to range farther from the caregiver and increased awareness of the self as separate from others—often prompt anxiety, evident in disturbed sleep and clinginess. When parents offer comfort, these behaviors subside.

LOOK and LISTEN

Interview a parent of a baby about sleep challenges. What strategies has the parent tried to ease these difficulties? Are the techniques likely to be effective, in view of evidence on infant sleep development?

Ask Yourself

- **REVIEW** How do overproduction of synapses and synaptic pruning support infants' and children's ability to learn?

- **CONNECT** Explain how inappropriate stimulation—either too little or too much—can impair cognitive and emotional development in the early years.

- **APPLY** Which infant enrichment program would you choose: one that emphasizes gentle talking and touching and social games, or one that includes reading and number drills and classical music lessons? Explain.

- **REFLECT** What is your attitude toward parent–infant cosleeping? Is it influenced by your cultural background? Explain.

Influences on Early Physical Growth

5.4 Cite evidence indicating that heredity, nutrition, and parental affection contribute to early physical growth.

Physical growth, like other aspects of development, results from the continuous and complex interplay between genetic and environmental factors. Heredity, nutrition, relative freedom from disease, and emotional well-being all affect early physical growth.

Heredity

Because identical twins are much more alike in body size than fraternal twins, we know that heredity is important in physical growth (Estourgie-van Burk et al., 2006). When diet and health are adequate, height and rate of physical growth are largely determined by heredity. In fact, as long as negative environmental influences such as poor nutrition or illness are not severe, children and adolescents typically show *catch-up growth*—a return to a genetically determined growth path—once conditions improve. After her adoption, Grace grew rapidly until, at age 2, she was nearly average in size by Cambodian standards. Still, the health of the brain, the heart, the digestive system, and many other internal organs may be permanently compromised. (Recall the consequences of inadequate prenatal nutrition for long-term health, discussed on pages 111–112 in Chapter 3.)

Genetic makeup also affects body weight: The weights of adopted children correlate more strongly with those of their biological than of their adoptive parents (Kinnunen, Pietilainen, & Rissanen, 2006). At the same time, environment—in particular, nutrition—plays an especially important role.

Nutrition

Nutrition is especially crucial for development in the first two years because the baby's brain and body are growing so rapidly. Pound for pound, an infant's energy needs are at least twice those of an adult. Twenty-five percent of infants' total caloric intake is devoted to growth, and babies need extra calories to keep rapidly developing organs functioning properly (Meyer, 2009).

Applying What We Know

Reasons to Breastfeed

NUTRITIONAL AND HEALTH ADVANTAGES	EXPLANATION
Provides the correct balance of fat and protein	Compared with the milk of other mammals, human milk is higher in fat and lower in protein. This balance, as well as the unique proteins and fats contained in human milk, is ideal for a rapidly myelinating nervous system.
Ensures nutritional completeness	A mother who breastfeeds need not add other foods to her infant's diet until the baby is 6 months old. The milks of all mammals are low in iron, but the iron contained in breast milk is much more easily absorbed by the baby's system. Consequently, bottle-fed infants need iron-fortified formula.
Helps ensure healthy physical growth	One-year-old breastfed babies are leaner (have a higher percentage of muscle to fat), a growth pattern that persists through the preschool years and that is associated with a reduction in later overweight and obesity.
Protects against many diseases	Breastfeeding transfers antibodies and other infection-fighting agents from mother to baby and enhances functioning of the immune system. Compared with bottle-fed infants, breastfed babies have far fewer allergic reactions and respiratory and intestinal illnesses. Breast milk also has anti-inflammatory effects, which reduce the severity of illness symptoms. Breastfeeding in the first four months (especially when exclusive) is linked to lower blood cholesterol levels in adulthood and, thereby, may help prevent cardiovascular disease.
Protects against faulty jaw development and tooth decay	Sucking the mother's nipple instead of an artificial nipple helps avoid malocclusion, a condition in which the upper and lower jaws do not meet properly. It also protects against tooth decay due to sweet liquid remaining in the mouths of infants who fall asleep while sucking on a bottle.
Ensures digestibility	Because breastfed babies have a different kind of bacteria growing in their intestines than do bottle-fed infants, they rarely suffer from constipation or other gastrointestinal problems.
Smooths the transition to solid foods	Breastfed infants accept new solid foods more easily than do bottle-fed infants, perhaps because of their greater experience with a variety of flavors, which pass from the maternal diet into the mother's milk.

Sources: American Academy of Pediatrics, 2012a; Druet et al., 2012; Ip et al., 2009; Owen et al., 2008.

BREASTFEEDING VERSUS BOTTLE-FEEDING Babies not only need enough food but also the right kind of food. In early infancy, breast milk is ideally suited to their needs, and bottled formulas try to imitate it. Applying What We Know above summarizes major nutritional and health advantages of breastfeeding.

Because of these benefits, breastfed babies in poverty-stricken regions of the world are much less likely to be malnourished and 6 to 14 times more likely to survive the first year of life. The World Health Organization recommends breastfeeding until age 2 years, with solid foods added at 6 months. These practices, if widely followed, would save the lives of more than 800,000 infants annually (World Health Organization, 2012b). Even breastfeeding for just a few weeks offers some protection against respiratory and intestinal infections, which are devastating to young children in developing countries. Also, because a nursing mother is less likely to get pregnant, breastfeeding helps increase spacing among siblings, a major factor in reducing infant and childhood deaths in nations with widespread poverty. (Note, however, that breastfeeding is not a reliable method of birth control.)

Yet many mothers in the developing world do not know about these benefits. In Africa, the Middle East, and Latin America, most babies get some breastfeeding, but fewer than 40 percent are exclusively breastfed for the first six months, and one-third are fully weaned from the breast before 1 year (UNICEF, 2013a). In place of breast milk, mothers give their babies commercial formula or low-grade nutrients, such as rice water or highly diluted cow or goat milk. Contamination of these foods as a result of poor sanitation is common and often leads to illness and infant death. The United Nations has encouraged all hospitals and maternity units in developing countries to promote breastfeeding as long as mothers do not have viral or bacterial infections (such as HIV or tuberculosis) that can be transmitted to the baby. Today, most developing countries have banned the practice of giving free or subsidized formula to new mothers.

Partly as a result of the natural childbirth movement, breastfeeding has become more common in industrialized nations, especially among well-educated women. Today, 77 percent of American mothers begin breastfeeding after birth, but more than one-third stop by 6 months (Centers for Disease Control and Prevention, 2013). And despite the health benefits of breast milk, only 50 percent of preterm infants are breastfed at hospital discharge. Breastfeeding a preterm baby presents special challenges, including maintaining a sufficient milk supply with artificial pumping until the baby is mature enough to suck at the breast and providing the infant with enough sucking experience to learn to feed successfully. Kangaroo care (see page 136 in Chapter 4) and the support of health professionals are helpful.

Breast milk is so easily digestible that a breastfed infant becomes hungry quite often—every 1½ to 2 hours, compared to every 3 or 4 hours for a bottle-fed baby. This makes breastfeeding inconvenient for many employed women. Not surprisingly, mothers who return to work sooner wean their babies from the breast earlier (McCarter-Spaulding, Lucas, & Gore, 2011; Smith & Forrester, 2013). But mothers who cannot be with their babies all the time can still combine breast- and bottle-feeding. The U.S. Department of Health and Human Services (2010a) advises exclusive breastfeeding for the first 6 months and inclusion of breast milk in the baby's diet until at least 1 year.

Women who do not breastfeed sometimes worry that they are depriving their baby of an experience essential for healthy psychological development. Yet breastfed and bottle-fed infants in industrialized nations do not differ in quality of the mother–infant relationship or in later emotional adjustment (Jansen, de Weerth, & Riksen-Walraven, 2008; Lind et al., 2014). Some studies report a slight advantage in intelligence test performance for children and adolescents who were breastfed, after controlling for many factors. Most, however, find no cognitive benefits (Der, Batty, & Deary, 2006).

ARE CHUBBY BABIES AT RISK FOR LATER OVERWEIGHT AND OBESITY? From early infancy, Timmy was an enthusiastic eater who nursed vigorously and gained weight quickly. By 5 months, he began reaching for food on his parents' plates. Vanessa wondered: Was she overfeeding Timmy and increasing his chances of long-term overweight?

Most chubby babies thin out during toddlerhood and the preschool years, as weight gain slows and they become more active. Infants and toddlers can eat nutritious foods freely without risk of becoming overweight. But recent evidence does indicate a strengthening relationship between rapid weight gain in infancy and later obesity (Druet et al., 2012). The trend may be due to the rise in overweight and obesity among adults, who promote unhealthy eating habits in their young children. Interviews with 1,500 U.S. parents of 4- to 24-month-olds revealed that many routinely served older infants and toddlers french fries, pizza, candy, sugary fruit drinks, and soda. On average, infants consumed 20 percent and toddlers 30 percent more calories than they needed (Siega-Riz et al., 2010). At the same time, as many as one-fourth ate no fruits and one-third no vegetables.

How can parents prevent their infants from becoming overweight children and adults? One way is to breastfeed for the first six months, which is associated with slower weight gain over the first year, leaner body build through early childhood, and 10 to 20 percent reduced obesity risk in later life (Gunnarsdottir et al., 2010; Koletzko et al., 2013). Another strategy is for parents to

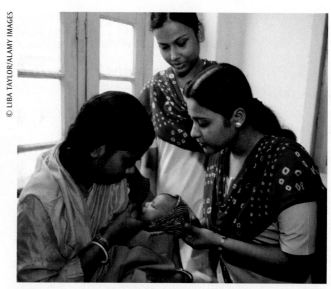

Midwives in India support a mother as she learns to breastfeed her infant. Breastfeeding is especially important in developing countries, where it helps protect babies against life-threatening infections and early death.

LOOK and LISTEN

Ask several parents of 1- to 2-year-olds to keep a diary of all the foods and drinks they offer their toddler over a weekend. How healthy are the toddlers' diets? Did any of the parents report heightened awareness of family nutrition as a result of the diary exercise?

A father supports his toddler's desire to feed himself while also modeling and encouraging healthy eating habits that protect against overweight and obesity.

Social Issues: Health

U.S. Public Policy Changes Improve Infant Feeding Practices in Low-Income Families

In a study in which researchers made periodic home visits to several hundred low-income first-time mothers and their babies, inappropriate feeding practices were pervasive. Rather than a mostly breast-milk diet for the first half-year, the majority of infants were fed formula. And more than 75 percent received solid foods and juices too soon—by age 3 months (Thompson & Bentley, 2013). Inappropriate feeding of solids and liquids in infancy is consistently associated with greater daily caloric intake and excessive weight gain during the first two years (Smith & Forrester, 2013).

The U.S. Special Supplemental Nutrition Program for Women, Infants, and Children (WIC) is a federally funded initiative that provides nutrition education and food to low-income mothers and to their children from birth to age 5. Though not reaching all families in need, WIC serves about half of U.S. infants—2 million annually, two-thirds of whom live in poverty (U.S. Department of Agriculture, 2014).

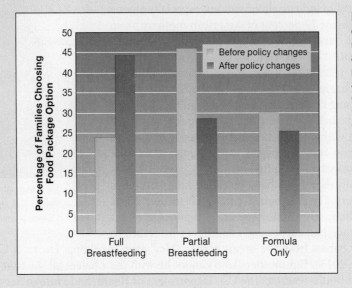

FIGURE 5.8 **Rates of breastfeeding by new mothers at WIC enrollment, as indicated by food package choice, before and after WIC policy changes.** Full breastfeeding nearly doubled after the policy changes, whereas partial breastfeeding and formula-only feeding declined. (Based on Whaley et al., 2012.)

To induce improvements in infant feeding practices, in 2009 WIC strengthened its breast-feeding counseling and educational materials for new mothers. It also offered mothers who breastfeed enhanced food packages for the first 12 months. A "fully breast-feeding package" includes no formula while providing the largest quantity and variety of healthy foods for the mother. A "partially breastfeeding package" includes some formula plus extra healthy foods for the mother, but less than in the fully breastfeeding package. A "formula only package" contains more formula for the baby but only a basic food package for the mother, limited to the first 6 months.

Are WIC's policy changes effective? To find out, researchers first confirmed that maternal food package choice is an accurate indicator of feeding practices at home (Whaley, Koleilat, & Jiang, 2012). Then they examined the distribution of the three types of food packages to 5,000 California families before and after the policy changes. As Figure 5.8 shows, following the new policies, enrollment in the fully breastfeeding option increased sharply—to double its former rate. In contrast, the partially breastfeeding and formula-only package options declined (Whaley et al., 2012). Furthermore, more mothers continued to select the fully breastfeeding packages when their babies reached ages 2 and 6 months, indicating that WIC incentives lengthened the duration of breastfeeding.

Full breastfeeding for the first half-year followed by a healthy infant diet is a WIC priority—part of a national early obesity prevention strategy. The findings just described are particularly impressive, given that the WIC policy changes coincided with the late-2000s recession and a rise in poverty, which is typically linked to reduced breastfeeding and increased unhealthy eating practices.

A WIC counselor meets with breastfeeding mothers to provide nutrition education and enhanced food packages—incentives that increase the number of breastfed babies and the duration of breastfeeding.

avoid giving babies foods loaded with sugar, salt, and saturated fats. As the Social Issues: Health box above illustrates, policy changes directed at low-income families, where breast-feeding rates are lowest and unhealthy feeding practices are highest, are a vital child health measure. And once toddlers learn to walk, climb, and run, parents can also provide plenty of opportunities for energetic play. Finally, as Chapter 11 will reveal, because excessive television viewing is linked to overweight in older children, parents should limit the time very young children spend in front of the TV.

Malnutrition

Osita is an Ethiopian 2-year-old whose mother has never had to worry about his gaining too much weight. When she weaned him at 1 year, he had little to eat besides starchy rice flour cakes. Soon his belly enlarged, his feet swelled, his hair fell out, and a rash appeared on his skin. His bright-eyed curiosity vanished, and he became irritable and listless.

In developing countries and war-torn areas where food resources are limited, malnutrition is widespread. Recent evidence indicates that about one-third of the world's children suffer from malnutrition before age 5 (World Health Organization, 2013b). The 8 percent who are severely affected suffer from two dietary diseases.

Marasmus is a wasted condition of the body caused by a diet low in all essential nutrients. It usually appears in the first year of life when a baby's mother is too malnourished to produce enough breast milk and bottle-feeding is also inadequate. Her starving baby becomes painfully thin and is in danger of dying.

Osita has **kwashiorkor,** caused by an unbalanced diet very low in protein. The disease usually strikes after weaning, between 1 and 3 years of age. It is common in regions where children get just enough calories from starchy foods but little protein. The child's body responds by breaking down its own protein reserves, which causes the swelling and other symptoms that Osita experienced.

Children who survive these extreme forms of malnutrition often grow to be smaller in all body dimensions and suffer from lasting damage to the brain, heart, liver, pancreas, and other organs (Müller & Krawinkel, 2005; Spoelstra et al., 2012). When their diets do improve, they tend to gain excessive weight (Black et al., 2013). A malnourished body protects itself by establishing a low basal metabolism rate, which may endure after nutrition improves. Also, malnutrition may disrupt appetite control centers in the brain, causing the child to overeat when food becomes plentiful.

Learning and behavior are also seriously affected. Animal evidence reveals that a deficient diet permanently reduces brain weight and alters the production of neurotransmitters in the brain—an effect that can disrupt all aspects of development (Bedi, 2003; Haller, 2005). Children who experienced marasmus or kwashiorkor show poor fine-motor coordination, have difficulty paying attention, often display conduct problems, and score low on intelligence tests into adulthood (Galler et al., 1990, 2012; Waber et al., 2014). They also display a more intense stress response to fear-arousing situations, perhaps caused by the constant, gnawing pain of hunger (Fernald & Grantham-McGregor, 1998).

Recall from our discussion of prenatal malnutrition in Chapter 3 that the passivity and irritability of malnourished children worsen the impact of poor diet. These behaviors may appear even when protein-calorie deprivation is only mild to moderate. They also accompany *iron-deficiency anemia,* a condition common among poverty-stricken infants and children that interferes with many central nervous system processes. Withdrawal and listlessness reduce the nutritionally deprived child's ability to pay attention, explore, and evoke sensitive caregiving from parents, whose lives are already disrupted by poverty and stressful living conditions (Corapci, Radan, & Lozoff, 2006; Grantham-McGregor & Ani, 2001). For this reason, interventions for malnourished children must improve the family situation as well as the child's nutrition.

Inadequate nutrition is not confined to developing countries. Because government-supported supplementary food programs do not reach all families in need, an estimated 22 percent of U.S. children suffer from *food insecurity*—uncertain access to enough food for a healthy, active life. Food insecurity is especially high among single-parent families (35 percent) and low-income ethnic minority families—for example, Hispanics and African Americans (23 and 25 percent, respectively) (U.S. Department of Agriculture, 2013b). Although few of these children have marasmus or kwashiorkor, their physical growth and ability to learn are still affected.

The baby on the top, of Niger, Africa, has marasmus, a wasted condition caused by a diet low in all essential nutrients. The swollen abdomen of the toddler on the bottom, also from Niger, is a symptom of kwashiorkor, which results from a diet very low in protein. If these children survive, they are likely to be growth stunted and to suffer from lasting organ damage as well as serious cognitive and emotional impairments.

Emotional Well-Being

We may not think of affection as necessary for healthy physical growth, but it is as vital as food. **Growth faltering** is a term applied to infants whose weight, height, and head circumference are substantially below age-related growth norms and who are withdrawn and apathetic (Black, 2005). In as many as half such cases, a disturbed parent–infant relationship contributes to this failure to grow normally.

Lana, an observant nurse at a public health clinic, became concerned about 8-month-old Melanie, who was 3 pounds lighter than she had been at her last checkup. Lana noted that Melanie kept her eyes on nearby adults, anxiously watching their every move, and rarely smiled at her mother. During feeding and diaper changing, Melanie's mother sometimes appeared depressed and distant, at other times impatient and hostile. Melanie tried to protect herself by tracking her mother's whereabouts and, when she approached, avoiding her gaze.

Often an unhappy marriage and parental psychological disturbance contribute to these serious caregiving problems. And most of the time, the baby is irritable and displays abnormal feeding behaviors, such as poor sucking or vomiting, that both disrupt growth and lead parents to feel anxious and helpless, which stress the parent–infant relationship further (Batchelor, 2008; Linscheid, Budd, & Rasnake, 2005).

In Melanie's case, her alcoholic father was out of work, and her parents argued constantly. Melanie's mother had little energy to meet Melanie's psychological needs. When treated early, by intervening in infant feeding problems, helping parents with their own life challenges, and encouraging sensitive caregiving, babies show quick catch-up growth. But if the disorder is not corrected in infancy, most of these children remain small and show lasting cognitive and emotional difficulties (Black et al., 2007; Crookston et al., 2013).

Ask Yourself

- **REVIEW** Explain why breastfeeding can have lifelong consequences for the development of babies born in poverty-stricken regions of the world.

- **CONNECT** How are bidirectional influences between parent and child involved in the impact of malnutrition on psychological development? After her adoption, how did those influences change for Grace?

- **APPLY** Eight-month-old Shaun is well below average in height and painfully thin. He cries during feedings and is listless and irritable. Shaun's single mother feels overwhelmed and discouraged. Why do Shaun and his mother need intervention quickly? What should health professionals do?

- **REFLECT** Imagine that you are the parent of a newborn baby. Describe feeding practices you would use, and ones you would avoid, to prevent overweight and obesity.

5.5 Describe infant learning capacities, the conditions under which they occur, and the unique value of each.

Learning Capacities

Learning refers to changes in behavior as the result of experience. Babies come into the world with built-in learning capacities that permit them to profit from experience immediately. Infants are capable of two basic forms of learning, which we introduced in Chapter 1: classical and operant conditioning. They also learn through their natural preference for novel stimulation. Finally, shortly after birth, babies learn by observing others; they can imitate the facial expressions and gestures of adults.

Classical Conditioning

Newborn reflexes, discussed in Chapter 4, make **classical conditioning** possible in the young infant. In this form of learning, a neutral stimulus is paired with a stimulus that leads to a reflexive response. Once the baby's nervous system makes the connection between the two stimuli, the neutral stimulus produces the behavior by itself. Classical conditioning helps infants recognize which events usually occur together in the everyday world, so they can anticipate what is about to happen next. As a result, the environment becomes more orderly and predictable. Let's take a closer look at the steps of classical conditioning.

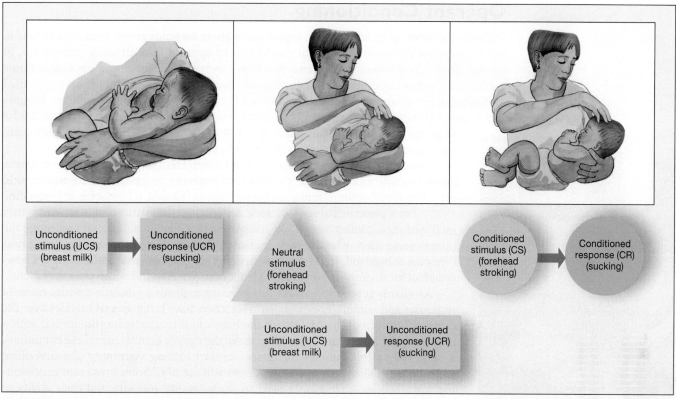

FIGURE 5.9   The steps of classical conditioning. This example shows how a mother classically conditioned her baby to make sucking movements by stroking the baby's forehead at the beginning of feedings.

As Carolyn settled down in the rocking chair to nurse Caitlin, she often stroked Caitlin's forehead. Soon Carolyn noticed that each time she did this, Caitlin made active sucking movements. Caitlin had been classically conditioned. Figure 5.9 shows how it happened:

1. Before learning takes place, an **unconditioned stimulus (UCS)** must consistently produce a *reflexive,* or **unconditioned, response (UCR).** In Caitlin's case, sweet breast milk (UCS) resulted in sucking (UCR).
2. To produce learning, a *neutral stimulus* that does not lead to the reflex is presented just before, or at about the same time as, the UCS. Carolyn stroked Caitlin's forehead as each nursing period began. The stroking (neutral stimulus) was paired with the taste of milk (UCS).
3. If learning has occurred, the neutral stimulus alone produces a response similar to the reflexive response. The neutral stimulus is then called a **conditioned stimulus (CS),** and the response it elicits is called a **conditioned response (CR).** We know that Caitlin has been classically conditioned because stroking her forehead outside the feeding situation (CS) results in sucking (CR).

If the CS is presented alone enough times, without being paired with the UCS, the CR will no longer occur, an outcome called *extinction.* In other words, if Carolyn repeatedly strokes Caitlin's forehead without feeding her, Caitlin will gradually stop sucking in response to stroking.

Young infants can be classically conditioned most easily when the association between two stimuli has survival value. In the example just described, learning which stimuli regularly accompany feeding improves the infant's ability to get food and survive (Blass, Ganchrow, & Steiner, 1984).

In contrast, some responses, such as fear, are very difficult to classically condition in young babies. Until infants have the motor skills to escape unpleasant events, they have no biological need to form these associations. After age 6 months, however, fear is easy to condition. **TAKE A MOMENT...** Return to Chapter 1, page 17, to review John Watson's well-known experiment in which he conditioned Little Albert to withdraw and cry at the sight of a furry white rat. Then test your knowledge of classical conditioning by identifying the UCS, UCR, CS, and CR in Watson's study.

Operant Conditioning

In classical conditioning, babies build expectations about stimulus events in the environment, but they do not influence the stimuli that occur. In **operant conditioning,** infants act, or *operate,* on the environment, and stimuli that follow their behavior change the probability that the behavior will occur again. A stimulus that increases the occurrence of a response is called a **reinforcer.** For example, sweet liquid *reinforces* the sucking response in newborns. Removing a desirable stimulus or presenting an unpleasant one to decrease the occurrence of a response is called **punishment.** A sour-tasting fluid *punishes* newborn babies' sucking response, causing them to purse their lips and stop sucking entirely.

Many stimuli besides food can serve as reinforcers of infant behavior. For example, newborns will suck faster on a nipple that produces interesting sights and sounds, including visual designs, music, or human voices (Floccia, Christophe, & Bertoncini, 1997). Even preterm babies will seek reinforcing stimulation. In one study, they increased their contact with a soft teddy bear that "breathed" at a rate reflecting the infant's respiration, whereas they decreased their contact with a nonbreathing bear (Thoman & Ingersoll, 1993). As these findings suggest, operant conditioning is a powerful tool for finding out what stimuli babies can perceive and which ones they prefer.

As infants get older, operant conditioning expands to include a wider range of responses and stimuli. For example, researchers have hung special mobiles over the cribs of 2- to 6-month-olds. When the baby's foot is attached to the mobile with a long cord, the infant can, by kicking, make the mobile turn. Under these conditions, it takes only a few minutes for infants to start kicking vigorously (Rovee-Collier, 1999; Rovee-Collier & Barr, 2001). As you will see in Chapter 6, operant conditioning with mobiles is frequently used to study infants' memory and their ability to group similar stimuli into categories. Once babies learn the kicking response, researchers see how long and under what conditions they retain it when exposed again to the original mobile or to mobiles with varying features.

Operant conditioning also plays a vital role in the formation of social relationships. As the baby gazes into the adult's eyes, the adult looks and smiles back, and then the infant looks and smiles again. As the behavior of each partner reinforces the other, both continue their pleasurable interaction. In Chapter 7, we will see that this contingent responsiveness contributes to the development of infant–caregiver attachment.

As this baby and father imitate each other's facial expressions, the behavior of each reinforces the other, sustaining their pleasurable interaction.

Habituation

At birth, the human brain is set up to be attracted to novelty. Infants tend to respond more strongly to a new element that has entered their environment, an inclination that ensures that they will continually add to their knowledge base. **Habituation** refers to a gradual reduction in the strength of a response due to repetitive stimulation. Time spent looking at the stimulus, heart rate, respiration rate, and brain activity may all decline, indicating a loss of interest. Once this has occurred, a new stimulus—a change in the environment—causes responsiveness to return to a high level, an increase called **recovery.** For example, when you walk through a familiar space, you notice things that are new and different—a recently hung picture on the wall or a piece of furniture that has been moved. Habituation and recovery promote learning by focusing our attention on those aspects of the environment we know least about.

Researchers studying infants' understanding of the world rely on habituation and recovery more than any other learning capacity. For example, a baby who first *habituates* to a visual pattern (a photo of a baby) and then *recovers* to a new one (a photo of a bald man) appears to remember the first stimulus and perceive the second one as new and different from it. This method of studying infant perception and cognition, illustrated in Figure 5.10, can be used with newborns, including preterm infants (Kavšek & Bornstein, 2010). It has even been used to study the fetus's sensitivity to external stimuli in the third trimester of pregnancy—for example, by measuring changes in fetal heart rate or brain waves when various repeated sounds are presented, followed by a different sound (see page 100 in Chapter 3).

© LAURA DWIGHT PHOTOGRAPHY

Recovery to a new stimulus, or *novelty preference,* assesses infants' *recent memory.* TAKE A MOMENT... Think about what happens when you return to a place you have not seen for a long time. Instead of attending to novelty, you are likely to focus on aspects that are familiar: "I recognize that—I've been here before!" Like adults, infants shift from a novelty preference to a *familiarity preference* as more time intervenes between habituation and test phases in research. That is, babies recover to the familiar stimulus rather than to a novel stimulus (see Figure 5.10) (Colombo, Brez, & Curtindale, 2013; Courage & Howe, 1998; Flom & Bahrick, 2010; Richmond, Colombo, & Hayne, 2007). By focusing on that shift, researchers can also use habituation to assess *remote memory,* or memory for stimuli to which infants were exposed weeks or months earlier.

With age, babies habituate and recover to stimuli more quickly, indicating that they process information more efficiently. Habituation and recovery have been used to assess a wide range of infant perceptual and cognitive capacities—speech perception, musical and visual pattern perception, object perception, categorization, and knowledge of the social world. But despite the strengths of habituation research, its findings are not clear-cut. When looking, sucking, heart rate, or brain activity declines and recovers, what babies actually know about the stimuli to which they responded is uncertain. We will return to this difficulty in Chapter 6.

Imitation

Babies come into the world with a primitive ability to learn through **imitation**—by copying the behavior of another person. For example, Figure 5.11 on page 180 shows a human newborn imitating two adult facial expressions (Meltzoff & Moore, 1977). The newborn's capacity to imitate extends to certain gestures, such as head and index-finger movements, and has been demonstrated in many ethnic groups and cultures (Meltzoff & Kuhl, 1994; Nagy et al., 2005). As the figure reveals, even newborn primates, including chimpanzees (our closest evolutionary relatives), imitate some behaviors (Ferrari et al., 2006; Myowa-Yamakoshi et al., 2004).

Nevertheless, some studies have failed to reproduce the human findings (see, for example, Anisfeld, 2005). And because newborn mouth and tongue movements occur with increased frequency to almost any arousing change in stimulation (such as lively music or flashing lights), some researchers argue that certain newborn "imitative" responses are actually mouthing—a common early exploratory response to interesting stimuli (Jones, 2009). Furthermore, imitation is harder to induce in babies 2 to 3 months old than just after birth. Therefore, skeptics believe that the newborn imitative response is little more than an automatic response that declines with age, much like a reflex (Heyes, 2005).

Others claim that newborns imitate a variety of facial expressions and head movements with effort and determination, even after short delays—when the adult is no longer demonstrating the behavior (Hayne, 2002; Meltzoff & Moore, 1999; Paukner, Ferrari, & Suomi, 2011). Furthermore, these investigators argue that imitation—unlike reflexes—does not decline. Rather, they claim, human babies several months old often do not imitate an adult's behavior right away because they first try to play familiar social games—mutual gazing, cooing, smiling, and waving their arms. But when an adult models a gesture repeatedly, older human infants soon get down to business and imitate (Meltzoff & Moore, 1994). Similarly, imitation declines in baby chimps around 9 weeks of age, when mother–baby mutual gazing and other face-to-face exchanges increase.

According to Andrew Meltzoff, newborns imitate much as older children and adults do—by actively trying to match body movements they *see* with ones they *feel* themselves make

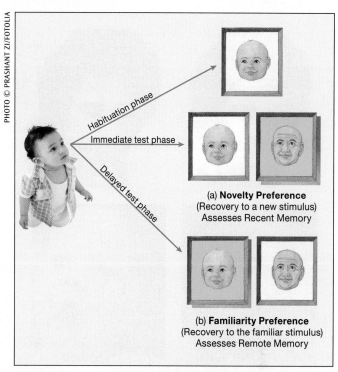

PHOTO © PRASHANT ZI/FOTOLIA

(a) Novelty Preference
(Recovery to a new stimulus)
Assesses Recent Memory

(b) Familiarity Preference
(Recovery to the familiar stimulus)
Assesses Remote Memory

FIGURE 5.10 Using habituation to study infant perception and cognition. In the habituation phase, infants view a photo of a baby until their looking declines. In the test phase, infants are again shown the baby photo, but this time it appears alongside a photo of a bald-headed man. (a) When the test phase occurs soon after the habituation phase (within minutes, hours, or days, depending on the age of the infants), participants who remember the baby face and distinguish it from the man's face show a *novelty preference;* they recover to (spend more time looking at) the new stimulus. (b) When the test phase is delayed for weeks or months, infants who continue to remember the baby face shift to a *familiarity preference;* they recover to the familiar baby face rather than to the novel man's face.

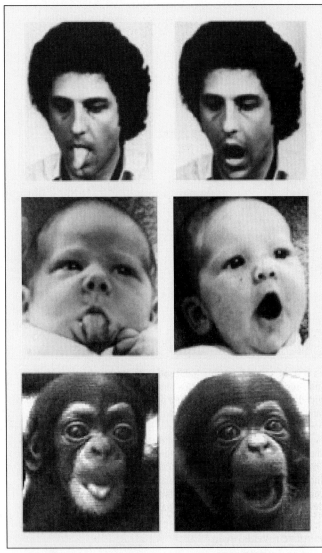

FIGURE 5.11 Imitation by human and chimpanzee newborns. The human infants in the middle row imitating (left) tongue protrusion and (right) mouth opening are 2 to 3 weeks old. The chimpanzee imitating both facial expressions is 2 weeks old. (From A. N. Meltzoff & M. K. Moore, 1977, "Imitation of Facial and Manual Gestures by Human Neonates," *Science, 198*, p. 75. Copyright © 1977 by AAAS. Reprinted by permission of the American Association for the Advancement of Science conveyed through Copyright Clearance Center, Inc., and Dr. Andrew Meltzoff. And from M. Myowa-Yamakoshi et al., 2004, "Imitation in Neonatal Chimpanzees [Pan Troglodytes]." *Developmental Science, 7*, p. 440. Copyright © 2004 by John Wiley and Sons. Reprinted with permission of John Wiley and Sons conveyed through Copyright Clearance Center, Inc.)

(Meltzoff, 2007). Later we will encounter evidence that young babies are remarkably adept at coordinating information across sensory systems.

Scientists have identified specialized cells in motor areas of the cerebral cortex in primates—called **mirror neurons**—that may underlie early imitative capacities (Ferrari & Coudé, 2011). Mirror neurons fire identically when a primate hears or sees an action and when it carries out that action on its own (Rizzolatti & Craighero, 2004). Humans have especially elaborate neural mirroring systems, which enable us to observe another person's behavior (such as smiling or throwing a ball) while simulating the behavior in our own brain. These systems are believed to be the biological basis of a variety of interrelated, complex social abilities, including imitation, empathic sharing of emotions, and understanding others' intentions (Iacoboni, 2009; Schulte-Ruther et al., 2007).

Brain-imaging findings support functioning neural mirroring systems in human infants as early as 6 months of age. Using NIRS, researchers found that the same motor areas of the cerebral cortex were activated in 6-month-olds and in adults when they observed a model engage in a behavior that could be imitated (tapping a box to make a toy pop out) as when they themselves engaged in the motor action (Shimada & Hiraki, 2006). In contrast, when infants and adults observed an object that appeared to move on its own, without human intervention (a ball hanging from the ceiling on a string, swinging like a pendulum), motor areas were not activated.

Still, Meltzoff's view of newborn imitation as a flexible, voluntary capacity remains controversial. Some critics contend that babies learn to imitate gradually through rich social experiences (Ray & Heyes, 2011). And even researchers who believe that newborns can imitate agree that many opportunities to see oneself act, to watch others' responses, and to engage in imitative games with caregivers are required for infants to become proficient imitators (Marshall & Meltzoff, 2011). Consistent with this view, human neural mirroring systems, though possibly functional at birth, undergo an extended period of development (Ferrari et al., 2013; Heyes, 2010). And as we will see in Chapter 6, the capacity to imitate expands greatly over the first two years.

However limited it is at birth, imitation is a powerful means of learning. Using imitation, infants explore their social world, learning from other people. As they notice similarities between their own actions and those of others, they experience other people as "like me" and learn about themselves (Meltzoff, 2007). By tapping into infants' ability to imitate, adults can get infants to exhibit desirable behaviors. Finally, caregivers take great pleasure in a baby who participates in imitative exchanges—a capacity that strengthens the parent–infant bond.

Ask Yourself

- **REVIEW** Provide an example of classical conditioning, of operant conditioning, and of habituation/recovery in young infants. Why is each type of learning useful?

- **CONNECT** Which learning capacities contribute to an infant's first social relationships? Explain, providing examples.

- **APPLY** Nine-month-old Byron has a toy with large, colored push buttons on it. Each time he pushes a button, he hears a nursery tune. Which learning capacity is the manufacturer of this toy taking advantage of? What can Byron's play with the toy reveal about his perception of sound patterns?

Motor Development

5.6 Discuss the general course of motor development during the first two years, along with factors that influence it.

Carolyn, Monica, and Vanessa each kept a baby book, filled with proud notations about when their children held up their heads, reached for objects, sat by themselves, and walked alone. Parents are understandably excited about these new motor skills, which allow babies to master their bodies and the environment in new ways. For example, sitting upright gives infants a new perspective on the world. Reaching permits babies to find out about objects by acting on them. And when infants can move on their own, their opportunities for exploration multiply.

Babies' motor achievements have a powerful effect on their social relationships. When Caitlin crawled at 7½ months, Carolyn and David began to restrict her movements by saying no and expressing mild impatience. When she walked three days after her first birthday, the first "testing of wills" occurred (Biringen et al., 1995). Despite her mother's warnings, she sometimes pulled items from shelves that were off limits. "I said, 'Don't do that!'" Carolyn would repeat firmly, taking Caitlin's hand and redirecting her attention.

At the same time, newly walking babies more actively attend to and initiate social interaction (Clearfield, 2011; Karasik et al., 2011). Caitlin frequently toddled over to her parents to express a greeting, give a hug, or show them an object of interest. Carolyn and David, in turn, increased their verbal responsiveness, expressions of affection, and playful activities. Caitlin's delight as she worked on new motor skills triggered pleasurable reactions in others, which encouraged her efforts further (Mayes & Zigler, 1992). Motor, social, cognitive, and language competencies developed together and supported one another.

The Sequence of Motor Development

Gross-motor development refers to control over actions that help infants get around in the environment, such as crawling, standing, and walking. *Fine-motor development* has to do with smaller movements, such as reaching and grasping. Table 5.2 on page 182 shows the average ages at which U.S. infants and toddlers achieve a variety of gross- and fine-motor skills. It also presents the age range during which most babies accomplish each skill, indicating large individual differences in *rate* of motor progress. Also, a baby who is a late reacher will not necessarily be a late crawler or walker. We would be concerned about a child's development only if many motor skills were seriously delayed.

Historically, researchers assumed that the motor milestones listed in Table 5.2 are separate, innate abilities that emerge in a fixed sequence governed by a built-in maturational timetable. This view has long been discredited. Rather, motor skills are interrelated: Each is a product of earlier motor attainments and a contributor to new ones. And children acquire motor skills in highly individual ways. For example, before her adoption, Grace spent most of her days lying in a hammock. Because she was rarely placed on her tummy and on firm surfaces that enabled her to move on her own, she did not try to crawl. As a result, she pulled to a stand and walked before she crawled! Babies display such skills as rolling, sitting, crawling, and walking in diverse orders rather than in the sequence implied by motor norms (Adolph, Karasik, & Tamis-LeMonda, 2010).

Many influences—both internal and external to the child—join together to support the vast transformations in motor competencies of the first two years. The *dynamic systems perspective,* introduced in Chapter 1 (see pages 29–30), helps us understand how motor development takes place.

Motor Skills as Dynamic Systems

According to the **dynamic systems theory of motor development,** mastery of motor skills involves acquiring increasingly *complex systems of action.* When motor skills work as a system, separate abilities blend together, each cooperating with others to produce more effective ways of exploring and controlling the environment. For example, control of the head and upper chest combine into sitting with support. Kicking, rocking on all fours, and reaching combine

TABLE 5.2	Gross- and Fine-Motor Development in the First Two Years	

MOTOR SKILL	AVERAGE AGE ACHIEVED	AGE RANGE IN WHICH 90 PERCENT OF INFANTS ACHIEVE THE SKILL
When held upright, holds head erect and steady	6 weeks	3 weeks–4 months
When prone, lifts self by arms	2 months	3 weeks–4 months
Rolls from side to back	2 months	3 weeks–5 months
Grasps cube	3 months, 3 weeks	2–7 months
Rolls from back to side	4½ months	2–7 months
Sits alone	7 months	5–9 months
Crawls	7 months	5–11 months
Pulls to stand	8 months	5–12 months
Plays pat-a-cake	9 months, 3 weeks	7–15 months
Stands alone	11 months	9–16 months
Walks alone	11 months, 3 weeks	9–17 months
Builds tower of two cubes	11 months, 3 weeks	10–19 months
Scribbles vigorously	14 months	10–21 months
Walks up stairs with help	16 months	12–23 months
Jumps in place	23 months, 2 weeks	17–30 months
Walks on tiptoe	25 months	16–30 months

Note: These milestones represent overall age trends. Individual differences exist in the precise age at which each milestone is attained.

Sources: Bayley, 1969, 1993, 2005.

to become crawling. Then crawling, standing, and stepping are united into walking (Adolph & Berger, 2006; Thelen & Smith, 1998).

Each new skill is a joint product of the following factors: (1) central nervous system development, (2) the body's movement capacities, (3) the goals the child has in mind, and (4) environmental supports for the skill. Change in any element makes the system less stable, and the child starts to explore and select new, more effective motor patterns. The factors that induce change vary with age. In the early weeks of life, brain and body growth are especially important as infants achieve control over the head, shoulders, and upper torso. Later, the baby's goals (getting a toy or crossing the room) and environmental supports (parental encouragement, objects in the infants' everyday setting) play a greater role.

The broader physical environment also profoundly influences motor skills. Infants with stairs in their home learn to crawl up stairs at an earlier age and also more readily master a back-descent strategy—the safest but also the most challenging position because the baby must turn around at the top, give up visual guidance of her goal, and crawl backward (Berger, Theuring, & Adolph, 2007). And if children were reared on the moon with its reduced gravity, they would prefer jumping to walking or running!

When a skill is first acquired, infants must refine it. For example, in trying to crawl, Caitlin often collapsed on her tummy and moved backward. Soon she figured out how to propel herself forward by alternately pulling with her arms and pushing with her feet, "belly-crawling" in various ways for several weeks. As they attempt a new skill, most babies move back and forth between its presence and absence: An infant might roll over, sit, crawl, or take a few steps but not do so again until the following week. And related, previously mastered skills often become less secure. As the novice walker experiments with balancing the body vertically over two small moving feet, balance during sitting may become temporarily less stable (Chen et al.,

LOOK and LISTEN

Spend an hour observing a newly crawling or walking baby. Note the goals that motivate the baby to move, along with the baby's effort and motor experimentation. Describe parenting behaviors and features of the environment that promote mastery of the skill.

2007). This variability is evidence of loss of stability in the system—in dynamic systems theory, a necessary transition between a less mature and a more mature stable state.

Motor mastery involves intense practice. In learning to walk, for example, toddlers practice six or more hours a day, traveling the length of 29 football fields! They fall, on average, 32 times per hour but rarely cry, returning to motion within a few seconds (Adolph et al., 2012). Gradually their small, unsteady steps change to a longer stride, their feet move closer together, their toes point to the front, and their legs become symmetrically coordinated (Adolph, Vereijken, & Shrout, 2003). As movements are repeated thousands of times, they promote new synaptic connections in the brain that govern motor patterns.

In tackling challenging motor tasks, babies are steadfast problem solvers, taking into account multiple sources of information. They explore ways of adapting to varied surfaces and openings, such as sliding down a steep slope and turning sideways to fit through a narrow doorway (Franchak & Adolph, 2012; Gill, Adolph, & Vereijken, 2009). And when conditions are uncertain—for instance, a ledge that may not be passable—toddlers are more likely to back off when the penalty for error is high (a fall). In these situations, they also place greater weight on caregivers' advice (Adolph et al., 2010). If their mother says "go," they usually proceed; if she says "no," they avoid.

Dynamic systems theory shows us why motor development cannot be genetically determined. Because it is motivated by exploration and the desire to master new tasks and varies with context, heredity can map it out only at a general level. Rather than being *hardwired* into the nervous system, motor behaviors are *softly assembled* from multiple components, allowing for different paths to the same motor skill (Spencer, Perone, & Buss, 2011; Thelen & Smith, 2006).

Dynamic Motor Systems in Action

To find out how infants acquire motor capacities, researchers conduct microgenetic studies (see Chapter 1, page 44), following babies from their first attempts at a skill until it becomes smooth and effortless. Using this strategy, James Galloway and Esther Thelen (2004) held sounding toys alternately in front of infants' hands and feet, from the time they first showed interest until they engaged in well-coordinated reaching and grasping. As Figure 5.12 illustrates, the infants violated the normative sequence of arm and hand control preceding leg and foot control, shown in Table 5.2. They first explored the toys with their feet—as early as 8 weeks of age, at least a month before reaching with their hands!

Why did babies reach "feet first"? Because the hip joint constrains the legs to move less freely than the shoulder joint constrains the arms, infants could more easily control their leg movements. Consequently, foot reaching required far less practice than hand reaching. As these findings confirm, rather than following a strict, predetermined pattern, the order in which motor skills develop depends on the anatomy of the body part being used, the surrounding environment, and the baby's efforts.

Furthermore, in building a more effective dynamic system, babies often use advances in one motor skill to support advances in others. For example, beginning to walk frees the hands for carrying, and new walkers like to fetch distant objects and transport them—often just for the fun of carrying but also to share with their caregivers (Karasik, Tamis-LeMonda, & Adolph, 2011). Observations of new walkers reveal that, surprisingly, they fall less often when carrying objects than when their hands are empty (Karasik et al., 2012). Even though combining walking with carrying is a more attention-demanding task, toddlers integrate object carrying into their emerging "walking system," using it to improve their balance (see Figure 5.13 on page 184).

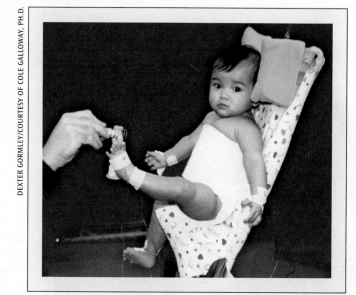

DEXTER GORMLEY/COURTESY OF COLE GALLOWAY, PH.D.

FIGURE 5.12   Reaching "feet first." When sounding toys were held in front of babies' hands and feet, they reached with their feet as early as 8 weeks of age, a month or more before they reached with their hands. This 2½-month-old skillfully explores an object with her foot.

FIGURE 5.13 **New walkers fall less often when carrying objects.** *Left:* When toddlers are first beginning to walk, carrying objects helps them focus attention and steady their balance. *Right:* An empty-handed new walker easily tips over.

Cultural Variations in Motor Development

Cross-cultural research further illustrates how early movement opportunities and a stimulating environment contribute to motor development. Half a century ago, Wayne Dennis (1960) observed infants in Iranian orphanages who were deprived of the tantalizing surroundings that induce infants to acquire motor skills. These babies spent their days lying on their backs in cribs, without toys to play with—conditions far worse than Grace experienced lying in a hammock in her Cambodian home. As a result, most did not move on their own until after 2 years of age. When they finally did move, the constant experience of lying on their backs led them to scoot in a sitting position rather than crawl on their hands and knees. Because babies who scoot come up against furniture with their feet (not their hands), they are far less likely to pull themselves to a standing position in preparation for walking. Indeed, by 3 to 4 years of age, only 15 percent of the Iranian orphans were walking alone.

Cultural variations in infant-rearing practices also affect motor development. **TAKE A MOMENT...** Take a quick survey of several parents you know: Should sitting, crawling, and walking be deliberately encouraged? Answers vary widely from culture to culture. Japanese mothers, for example, believe such efforts are unnecessary (Seymour, 1999). Among the Zinacanteco Indians of southern Mexico and the Gusii of Kenya, rapid motor progress is actively discouraged. Babies who walk before they know enough to keep away from cooking fires and weaving looms are viewed as dangerous to themselves and disruptive to others (Greenfield, 1992).

In contrast, among the Kipsigis of Kenya and the West Indians of Jamaica, babies hold their heads up, sit alone, and walk considerably earlier than North American infants. In both societies, parents emphasize early motor maturity, practicing formal exercises to stimulate particular skills (Adolph, Karasik, & Tamis-LeMonda, 2010). In the first few months, babies are seated in holes dug in the ground, with rolled blankets to keep them upright. Walking is promoted by frequently standing babies in adults' laps, bouncing them on their feet, and exercising the stepping reflex (see page 142 in Chapter 4) (Hopkins & Westra, 1988; Super, 1981). As parents in these cultures support babies in upright postures and rarely put them down on the floor, their infants usually skip crawling—a motor skill regarded as crucial in Western nations!

Finally, because it decreases exposure to "tummy time," the current Western practice of having babies sleep on their backs to protect them from SIDS (see page 145) delays gross-motor milestones of rolling,

The West Indians of Jamaica believe that exercise helps infants grow up strong and physically attractive. This mother "walks" her baby up her body—an activity that contributes to earlier mastery of walking.

sitting, and crawling (Scrutton, 2005). Regularly exposing infants to the tummy-lying position during waking hours prevents these delays.

Fine-Motor Development: Reaching and Grasping

Of all motor skills, reaching may play the greatest role in infant cognitive development. By grasping things, turning them over, and seeing what happens when they are released, infants learn a great deal about the sights, sounds, and feel of objects.

Reaching and grasping, like many other motor skills, start out as gross, diffuse activity and move toward mastery of fine movements. Figure 5.14 illustrates some milestones of reaching over the first nine months. Newborns will actively work to bring their hands into their field of vision: In a dimly lit room, they keep their hand within a narrow beam of light, moving the hand when the light beam moves (van der Meer, 1997). Newborns also make poorly coordinated swipes, called **prereaching,** toward an object in front of them, but because of poor arm and hand control they rarely contact the object. Like newborn reflexes, prereaching drops out around 7 weeks of age, when babies improve in eye movements involved in tracking and fixating on objects, which are essential for accurate reaching (von Hofsten, 2004). Yet these early behaviors suggest that babies are biologically prepared to coordinate hand with eye in the act of exploring.

DEVELOPMENT OF REACHING AND GRASPING At about 3 to 4 months, as infants develop the necessary eye, head, and shoulder control, reaching reappears as purposeful, forward arm movements in the presence of a nearby toy and gradually improves in accuracy (Bhat, Heathcock, & Galloway, 2005). By 5 to 6 months, infants reach for an object in a room that has been darkened during the reach by switching off the lights—a skill that improves over the next few months (Clifton et al., 1994; McCarty & Ashmead, 1999). This indicates that the baby does not need to use vision to guide the arms and hands in reaching. Rather, reaching is largely controlled by *proprioception*—our sense of movement and location in space, arising from stimuli within the body. When vision is freed from the basic act of reaching, it can focus on more complex adjustments, such as fine-tuning actions to fit the distance and shape of objects.

Reaching improves as depth perception advances and as infants gain greater control of body posture and arm and hand movements. Four-month-olds aim their reaches ahead of a moving object so they can catch it (von Hofsten, 1993). Around 5 months, babies reduce their efforts when an object is moved beyond their reach (Robin, Berthier, & Clifton, 1996). By 7 months, the arms become more independent: Infants reach for an object by extending one arm rather than both (Fagard & Pezé, 1997). During the next few months, infants become more efficient at reaching for moving objects—ones that spin, change direction, and move

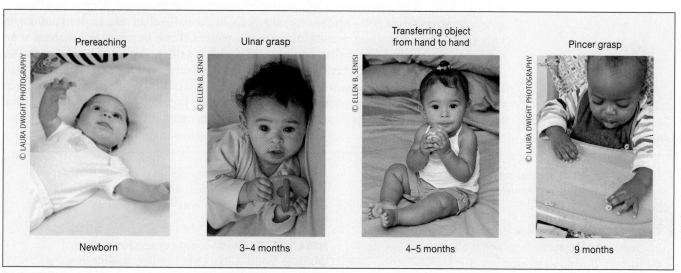

Prereaching   Ulnar grasp   Transferring object from hand to hand   Pincer grasp

Newborn   3–4 months   4–5 months   9 months

FIGURE 5.14 **Some milestones of reaching and grasping.** The average age at which each skill is attained is given. (Ages from Bayley, 1969; Rochat, 1989.)

To explore the surface of this uniquely textured ball, a 6-month-old coordinates both hands—and uses her mouth as well!

sideways, closer, or farther away (Fagard, Spelke, & von Hofsten, 2009; Wentworth, Benson, & Haith, 2000).

Once infants can reach, they increase the quantity and variety of their exploratory behaviors with objects—mouthing, fingering, looking, and combining these actions (Lobo & Galloway, 2013). They also modify their grasp. The newborn's grasp reflex is replaced by the **ulnar grasp,** a clumsy motion in which the young infant's fingers close against the palm. Still, even 4- to 5-month-olds modify their grasp to suit an object's size, shape, and texture (rigid versus soft)—a capacity that improves over the second half-year as infants adjust the hand more precisely and do so in advance of contacting the object (Cicuto et al., 2012; Witherington, 2005). Around 4 to 5 months, when infants begin to sit up, both hands become coordinated in exploring objects. Babies of this age can hold an object in one hand while the other scans it with the tips of the fingers, and they frequently transfer objects from hand to hand (Rochat & Goubet, 1995). By the end of the first year, infants use the thumb and index finger in a well-coordinated **pincer grasp.** Then the ability to manipulate objects greatly expands. The 1-year-old can pick up raisins and blades of grass, turn knobs, and open and close small boxes.

Between 8 and 11 months, reaching and grasping are well-practiced. As a result, attention is released from the motor skill to events that occur before and after obtaining the object. For example, 10-month-olds easily modify their reach to anticipate their next action. They reach for a ball faster when they intend to throw it than when they intend to drop it carefully through a narrow tube (Claxton, Keen, & McCarty, 2003). Around this time, too, infants begin to solve simple problems that involve reaching, such as searching for and finding a hidden toy.

Finally, the capacity to reach for and manipulate an object increases infants' attention to the way an adult reaches for and plays with that same object (Hauf, Aschersleben, & Prinz, 2007). As babies watch what others do, they broaden their understanding of others' behaviors and of the range of actions that can be performed on various objects, gradually incorporating those possibilities into their own object-related behaviors.

EARLY EXPERIENCE AND REACHING   Like other motor milestones, reaching is affected by early experience. In cultures where mothers carry their infants on their hips or in slings for most of the day, babies have rich opportunities to explore with their hands. Among the !Kung of Botswana, infants grasp their mothers' colorful, beaded necklaces to steady themselves while breastfeeding as the mother moves. While riding along, they also frequently swipe at and manipulate their mother's jewelry and other dangling objects (Konner, 1977). As a result, !Kung infants are advanced in development of reaching and grasping. And because babies of Mali and Uganda spend half or more of their day held in sitting or standing positions, which facilitate reaching, they, too, develop manual skills earlier than Western infants, who spend much of their day lying down (Adolph, Karasik, & Tamis-LeMonda, 2010).

Babies' visual surroundings are also influential. In a well-known study, institutionalized infants given a moderate amount of visual stimulation—at first, simple designs and, later, a mobile hung over their crib—reached for objects six weeks earlier than infants given nothing to look at. A third group given massive stimulation—patterned crib bumpers and mobiles at an early age—also reached sooner than unstimulated babies. But this heavy enrichment took its toll. These infants looked away and cried a great deal, and they were less advanced in reaching than the moderately stimulated group (White & Held, 1966). Recall from our discussion of brain development that more stimulation is not necessarily better. Trying to push infants beyond their readiness to handle stimulation can undermine the development of important motor skills.

Ask Yourself

- **REVIEW** Cite evidence that motor development is a joint product of biological, psychological, and environmental factors.

- **CONNECT** Provide several examples of how motor development influences infants' and toddlers' social experiences. How do social experiences, in turn, influence motor development?

- **APPLY** List everyday experiences that support mastery of reaching, grasping, sitting, and crawling. Why should caregivers place young infants in a variety of waking-time body positions?

- **REFLECT** Do you favor early, systematic training of infants in motor skills such as crawling, walking, running, hopping, and stair climbing? Why or why not?

Perceptual Development

In Chapter 4, you learned that the senses of touch, taste, smell, and hearing—but not vision—are remarkably well-developed at birth. Now let's turn to a related question: How does perception change over the first year? Our discussion will address hearing and vision, the focus of almost all research. Unfortunately, little evidence exists on how touch, taste, and smell develop after birth. Also, in Chapter 4 we used the word *sensation* to talk about these capacities. It suggests a fairly passive process—what the baby's receptors detect when exposed to stimulation. Now we use the word *perception,* which is active: When we perceive, we organize and interpret what we see.

As we review the perceptual achievements of infancy, you may find it hard to tell where perception leaves off and thinking begins. The research we are about to discuss provides an excellent bridge to the topic of Chapter 6—cognitive development during the first two years.

Hearing

On Timmy's first birthday, Vanessa bought several CDs of nursery songs, and she turned one on each afternoon at naptime. Soon Timmy let her know his favorite tune. If she put on "Twinkle, Twinkle," he stood up in his crib and whimpered until she replaced it with "Jack and Jill." Timmy's behavior illustrates the greatest change in hearing over the first year of life: Babies start to organize sounds into complex patterns.

Between 4 and 7 months, infants display a sense of musical phrasing. They prefer Mozart minuets with pauses between phrases to those with awkward breaks (Krumhansl & Jusczyk, 1990). Around 6 to 7 months, they can distinguish musical tunes on the basis of variations in rhythmic patterns, including beat structure (duple or triple) and accent structure (emphasis on the first note of every beat unit or at other positions) (Hannon & Johnson, 2004). They are also sensitive to features conveying the purpose of familiar types of songs, preferring to listen to high-pitched playsongs (aimed at entertaining) and low-pitched lullabies (used to soothe) (Tsang & Conrad, 2010). By the end of the first year, infants recognize the same melody when it is played in different keys (Trehub, 2001). As we will see next, 6- to 12-month-olds make comparable discriminations in human speech: They readily detect sound regularities, which will facilitate later language learning.

SPEECH PERCEPTION Recall from Chapter 4 that newborns can distinguish nearly all sounds in human languages and that they prefer listening to speech over nonspeech sounds and to their native tongue rather than a rhythmically distinct foreign language. Brain-imaging evidence reveals that in young infants, discrimination of speech sounds activates *both* auditory and motor areas in the cerebral cortex (Kuhl et al., 2014). Researchers speculate that while perceiving speech sounds, babies also generate internal motor plans that prepare them for producing those sounds.

As infants listen to people talk, they learn to focus on meaningful sound variations. ERP brain-wave recordings reveal that around 5 months, infants become sensitive to syllable stress patterns in their own language (Weber et al., 2004). Between 6 and 8 months, they start to "screen out" sounds not used in their native tongue and, in the case of bilingual infants, in both native languages (Albareda-Castellot, Pons, & Sebastián-Gallés, 2010; Curtin & Werker, 2007). As the Biology and Environment box on page 188 explains, this increased responsiveness to native-language sounds is part of a general "tuning" process in the second half of the first year—a possible sensitive period in which babies acquire a range of perceptual skills for picking up socially important information.

Soon after, infants focus on larger speech units that are critical to figuring out meaning. They recognize familiar words in spoken passages and listen longer to speech with clear clause and phrase boundaries (Johnson & Seidl, 2008; Soderstrom et al., 2003). Around 7 to 9 months, infants extend this sensitivity to speech structure to individual words: They begin to divide the speech stream into wordlike units (Jusczyk, 2002; Saffran, Werker, & Werner, 2006).

5.7 What changes in hearing and in depth, pattern, object, and intermodal perception take place during infancy?

5.8 Explain differentiation theory of perceptual development.

© LAURA DWIGHT PHOTOGRAPHY

A 6-month-old is a remarkable analyzer of the speech stream. While listening to her mother talk, she detects sound patterns, discriminating words and word sequences for which she will later learn meanings.

Biology and Environment

"Tuning in" to Familiar Speech, Faces, and Music: A Sensitive Period for Culture-Specific Learning

To share experiences with members of their family and community, babies must become skilled at making perceptual discriminations that are meaningful in their culture. As we have seen, at first babies are sensitive to virtually all speech sounds but, around 6 months, they narrow their focus, limiting the distinctions they make to the language they hear and will soon learn.

The ability to perceive faces shows a similar **perceptual narrowing effect**—perceptual sensitivity that becomes increasingly attuned with age to information most often encountered. After habituating to one member of each pair of faces in Figure 5.15, 6-month-olds were shown the familiar face and the novel face side by side. For both pairs, they recovered to (looked longer at) the novel face, indicating that they could discriminate the individual faces of both humans and monkeys equally well (Pascalis, de Haan, & Nelson, 2002). But at 9 months, infants no longer showed a novelty preference when viewing the monkey pair. Like adults, they could distinguish only the human faces. Similar findings emerge with sheep faces: Four- to 6-month-olds easily distinguish them, but 9- to 11-month-olds no longer do (Simpson et al., 2011).

This perceptual narrowing effect appears again in musical rhythm perception. Western adults are accustomed to the even-beat pattern of Western music—repetition of the same rhythmic structure in every measure of a tune—and easily notice rhythmic changes that disrupt this familiar beat. But present them with music that does not follow this typical Western rhythmic form—Baltic folk tunes, for example—and they fail to pick up on rhythmic-pattern deviations. In contrast, 6-month-olds can detect such

disruptions in both Western and non-Western melodies. By 12 months, however, after added exposure to Western music, babies are no longer aware of deviations in foreign musical rhythms, although their sensitivity to Western rhythmic structure remains unchanged (Hannon & Trehub, 2005b).

Several weeks of regular interaction with a foreign-language speaker and of daily opportunities to listen to non-Western music fully restore 12-month-olds' sensitivity to wide-ranging speech sounds and music rhythms (Hannon & Trehub, 2005a; Kuhl, Tsao, & Liu, 2003). Similarly, 6-month-olds given three months of training in discriminating individual monkey faces, in which each image is verbally labeled with a distinct name ("Carlos," "Iona") instead of the generic label "monkey," retain their ability to discriminate monkey faces at 9 months (Scott & Monesson, 2009). Adults given similar extensive experiences, by contrast, show little improvement in perceptual sensitivity.

Taken together, these findings suggest a heightened capacity—or sensitive period—in the second half of the first year, when babies are biologically prepared to "zero in" on socially meaningful perceptual distinctions. Notice how,

FIGURE 5.15 **Discrimination of human and monkey faces.** Which of these pairs is easiest for you to tell apart? After habituating to one of the photos in each pair, infants were shown the familiar and the novel face side-by-side. For both pairs, 6-month-olds recovered to (looked longer at) the novel face, indicating that they could discriminate human and monkey faces equally well. By 12 months, babies lost their ability to distinguish the monkey faces. Like adults, they showed a novelty preference only to human stimuli. (From O. Pascalis et al., 2002, "Is Face Processing Species-Specific During the First Year of Life?" *Science, 296,* p. 1322. Copyright © 2002 by AAAS. Republished with permission of American Association for the Advancement of Science conveyed through Copyright Clearance Center, Inc.)

between 6 and 12 months, learning is especially rapid across several domains (speech, faces, and music) and is easily modified by experience. This suggests a broad neurological change—perhaps a special time of experience-expectant brain growth (see page 169) in which babies analyze everyday stimulation of all kinds similarly, in ways that prepare them to participate in their cultural community.

ANALYZING THE SPEECH STREAM How do infants make such rapid progress in perceiving the structure of speech? Research reveals that they have an impressive **statistical learning capacity.** By analyzing the speech stream for patterns—repeatedly occurring sequences of sounds—they acquire a stock of speech structures for which they will later learn meanings, long before they start to talk around age 12 months.

For example, when presented with controlled sequences of nonsense syllables, babies as young as 5 months listened for statistical regularities: They locate words by discriminating syllables that often occur together (indicating that they belong to the same word) from syllables that seldom occur together (indicating a word boundary) (Johnson & Tyler, 2010). Consider the English word sequence *pretty#baby.* After listening to the speech stream for just one minute (about 60 words), babies can distinguish a word-internal syllable pair *(pretty)* from a word-external syllable pair *(ty#ba)*. They prefer to listen to new speech that preserves the word-internal pattern (Saffran, Aslin, & Newport, 1996; Saffran & Thiessen, 2003).

Once infants begin locating words, they focus on the words and discover additional statistical cues that signal word boundaries (Thiessen, Kronstein, & Hufnagle, 2012). For example, 7- to 8-month-olds detect regular syllable-stress patterns—for example, in English and Dutch, that the onset of a strong syllable (*hap*-py, *rab*-bit) often signals a new word (Swingley, 2005; Thiessen & Saffran, 2007). By 10 months, babies can detect words that start with weak syllables, such as "sur*prise,*" by listening for sound regularities before and after the words (Kooijman, Hagoort, & Cutler, 2009).

Clearly, babies have a powerful ability to extract patterns from complex, continuous speech. Their remarkable statistical learning capacity also extends to visual stimuli and is present in the first weeks of life (Aslin & Newport, 2012). Statistical learning seems to be a general capacity that infants use to analyze complex stimulation.

By the middle of the first year, infants also attend to regularities in word sequences. In a study using nonsense words, 7-month-olds distinguished the ABA structure of "ga ti ga" and "li na li" from the ABB structure of "wo fe fe" and "ta la la" (Marcus et al., 1999). They seemed to detect simple word-order rules, a capacity that may eventually help them figure out basic grammar. And as with statistical learning, the capacity to extract ABA and ABB rules also applies to sequences of visual stimuli—and to musical stimuli as well (Dawson & Gerken, 2009; Johnson et al., 2009).

Finally, the more rapidly 10-month-olds detect words within the speech stream (as indicated by ERP recordings), the larger their vocabulary at age 2 years (Junge et al., 2012). Certain features of adults' utterances facilitate such rapid detection. Natural speech, for example, is full of both uninterrupted strings of words and pauses enabling listeners to hear isolated words. Infants exposed to a brief quantity of speech containing both isolated words and the same words embedded in the speech stream ("Doggie!" "See the doggie there?") are better able to discriminate those words when later exposed to fluent speech (Lew-Williams, Pelucchi, & Saffran, 2011). As we will see in Chapter 6, adults' style of communicating with infants greatly facilitates analysis of the structure of speech.

Vision

For exploring the environment, humans depend on vision more than any other sense. Although at first a baby's visual world is fragmented, it undergoes extraordinary changes during the first 7 to 8 months of life.

Visual development is supported by rapid maturation of the eye and visual centers in the cerebral cortex. Recall from Chapter 4 that the newborn baby focuses and perceives color poorly. Around 2 months, infants can focus on objects about as well as adults, and their color vision is adultlike by 4 months (Kellman & Arterberry, 2006). *Visual acuity* (fineness of discrimination) increases steadily throughout the first year, reaching 20/80 by 6 months and an adult level of about 20/20 by 4 years (Slater et al., 2010). Scanning the environment and tracking moving objects also improve over the first half-year as infants see more clearly and better control their eye movements. In addition, as young infants build an organized perceptual world, they scan more thoroughly and systematically, strategically picking up important information (Johnson, Slemmer, & Amso, 2004; von Hofsten & Rosander, 1998). Consequently, scanning enhances perception, and—in bidirectional fashion—perception also enhances scanning.

As babies explore their visual field, they figure out the characteristics of objects and how they are arranged in space. To understand how they do so, let's examine the development of three aspects of vision: depth, pattern, and object perception.

DEPTH PERCEPTION *Depth perception* is the ability to judge the distance of objects from one another and from ourselves. It is important for understanding the layout of the environment and for guiding motor activity.

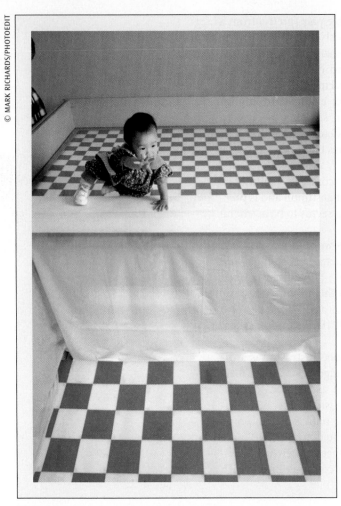

© MARK RICHARDS/PHOTOEDIT

FIGURE 5.16 **The visual cliff.** Plexiglas covers the deep and shallow sides. By refusing to cross the deep side and showing a preference for the shallow side, this infant demonstrates the ability to perceive depth.

Figure 5.16 shows the *visual cliff*, designed by Eleanor Gibson and Richard Walk (1960) and used in the earliest studies of depth perception. It consists of a Plexiglas-covered table with a platform at the center, a "shallow" side with a checkerboard pattern just under the glass, and a "deep" side with a checkerboard several feet below the glass. The researchers found that crawling babies readily crossed the shallow side, but most avoided the deep side. They concluded that around the time infants crawl, most distinguish deep from shallow surfaces and steer clear of drop-offs.

The visual cliff shows that crawling and avoidance of drop-offs are linked, but not how they are related or when depth perception first appears. Recent research has looked at babies' ability to detect specific depth cues, using methods that do not require that they crawl.

Emergence of Depth Perception How do we know when an object is near rather than far away? **TAKE A MOMENT...** Try these exercises to find out. Pick up a small object (such as your cup) and move it toward and away from your face. Did its image grow larger as it approached and smaller as it receded? Next time you take a bike or car ride, notice that nearby objects move past your field of vision more quickly than those far away.

Motion is the first depth cue to which infants are sensitive. Babies 3 to 4 weeks old blink their eyes defensively when an object moves toward their face as though it is going to hit (Nánez & Yonas, 1994). *Binocular depth cues* arise because our two eyes have slightly different views of the visual field. The brain blends these two images, resulting in perception of depth. Research in which two overlapping images are projected before the baby, who wears special goggles to ensure that each eye receives only one image, reveals that sensitivity to binocular cues emerges between 2 and 3 months and improves rapidly over the first year (Birch, 1993; Brown & Miracle, 2003). Finally, beginning at 3 to 4 months and strengthening between 5 and 7 months, babies display sensitivity to *pictorial depth cues*—the ones artists often use to make a painting look three-dimensional. Examples include receding lines that create the illusion of perspective, changes in texture (nearby textures are more detailed than faraway ones), overlapping objects (an object partially hidden by another object is perceived to be more distant), and shadows cast on surfaces (indicating a separation in space between the object and the surface) (Kavšek, Yonas, & Granrud, 2012; Shuwairi, Albert, & Johnson, 2007).

Why does perception of depth cues emerge in the order just described? Researchers speculate that motor development is involved. For example, control of the head during the early weeks of life may help babies notice motion and binocular cues. Around 5 to 6 months, the ability to turn, poke, and feel the surface of objects may promote perception of pictorial cues (Bushnell & Boudreau, 1993; Soska, Adolph, & Johnson, 2010). And as we will see next, one aspect of motor progress—independent movement—plays a vital role in refinement of depth perception.

Independent Movement and Depth Perception At 6 months, Timmy started crawling. "He's fearless!" exclaimed Vanessa. "If I put him down in the middle of the bed, he crawls right over the edge. The same thing happens by the stairs." Will Timmy become wary of the side of the bed and the staircase as he becomes a more experienced crawler? Research suggests that he will. Infants with more crawling experience (regardless of when they started to crawl) are far more likely to refuse to cross the deep side of the visual cliff (Campos et al., 2000).

From extensive everyday experience, babies gradually figure out how to use depth cues to detect the danger of falling. But because the loss of body control that leads to falling differs greatly for each body position, babies must undergo this learning separately for each posture (Adolph & Kretch, 2012). In one study, 9-month-olds, who were experienced sitters but novice crawlers, were placed on the edge of a shallow drop-off that could be widened (Adolph, 2002, 2008). While in the familiar sitting position, infants avoided leaning out for an attractive toy at distances likely to result in falling. But in the unfamiliar crawling position, they headed over the edge, even when the distance was extremely wide! And newly walking babies will step repeatedly over a risky drop-off (Kretch & Adolph, 2013a). They will also careen down slopes and over uneven surfaces without making necessary postural adjustments (Adolph et al., 2008; Joh & Adolph, 2006). Thus, they fall frequently.

Even experienced crawlers and walkers encounter new depth-at-an-edge situations that require additional learning. In one study, researchers encouraged crawling and walking babies to cross bridges varying in width over drop-offs (with an adult following alongside to catch infants if they began to fall). Most avoided crossing impossibly narrow bridges. And the greater their experience, the narrower the bridge both crawlers and walkers attempted to cross. Nevertheless, walkers perceived the likelihood of falling from a narrow bridge more accurately than crawlers. While crossing, crawlers could not easily see and adjust the placement of their hind limbs to prevent falls. In contrast, experienced walkers had figured out how to turn their body to accommodate the narrow passageway (see Figure 5.17) (Kretch & Adolph, 2013b). As infants and toddlers discover how to avoid falling in different postures and situations, their understanding of depth expands.

Independent movement promotes other aspects of three-dimensional understanding. For example, seasoned crawlers are better than their inexperienced agemates at remembering object locations and finding hidden objects (Campos et al., 2000). Why does crawling make such a difference? **TAKE A MOMENT...** Compare your own experience of the environment when you are driven from one place to another with what you experience when you walk or drive yourself. When you move on your own, you are much more aware of landmarks and routes of travel, and you take more careful note of what things look like from different points of view. The same is true for infants. In fact, crawling promotes a new level of brain organization, as indicated by more organized EEG brain-wave activity in the cerebral cortex (Bell & Fox, 1996). Perhaps crawling strengthens certain neural connections, especially those involved in vision and understanding of space.

PATTERN PERCEPTION Even newborns prefer to look at patterned rather than plain stimuli (Fantz, 1961). As they get older, infants prefer more complex patterns. For example, 3-week-olds look longest at black-and-white checkerboards with a few large squares, whereas 8- and 14-week-olds prefer those with many squares (Brennan, Ames, & Moore, 1966).

A general principle, called **contrast sensitivity,** explains early pattern preferences (Banks & Ginsburg, 1985). *Contrast* refers to the difference in the amount of light between adjacent regions in a pattern. If babies are *sensitive to* (can detect) the contrast in two or more

© ELLEN B. SENISI

Infants must learn to use depth cues to detect the danger of falling separately for each posture. When this experienced crawler—who avoids most drop-offs—starts to walk, he will be at risk for stepping off ledges and staircases.

FIGURE 5.17 **An experienced walker crosses a narrow bridge over a drop-off.** This 14-month-old has figured out how to turn his body sideways to accommodate the narrow passageway. (From K. S. Kretch & K. E. Adolph, 2013b, "No Bridge Too High: Infants Decide Whether to Cross Based on the Probability of Falling Not the Severity of the Potential Fall," *Developmental Science, 16,* p. 338. © 2013 Blackwell Publishing Ltd. Reprinted by permission of John Wiley and Sons, Inc., conveyed through Copyright Clearance Center, Inc.)

Bold checkerboard   Complex checkerboard

Appearance of checkerboards to very young infants

FIGURE 5.18 **The way two checkerboards differing in complexity look to infants in the first few weeks of life.** Because of their poor vision, very young infants cannot resolve the fine detail in the *complex checkerboard*. It appears blurred, like a gray field. The large, *bold checkerboard* appears to have more contrast, so babies prefer to look at it. (Adapted from M. S. Banks & P. Salapatek, 1983, "Infant Visual Perception," in M. M. Haith & J. J. Campos (Eds.), *Handbook of Child Psychology: Vol. 2. Infancy and Developmental Psychobiology* [4th ed.], New York: John Wiley & Sons, p. 504. Copyright © 1983 by John Wiley & Sons, Inc. Reproduced with permission of John Wiley & Sons, Inc.)

patterns, they prefer the one with more contrast. To understand this idea, look at the checkerboards in the top row of Figure 5.18. To us, the one with many small squares has more contrasting elements. Now look at the bottom row, which shows how these checkerboards appear to infants in the first few weeks of life. Because of their poor vision, very young babies cannot resolve the small features in more complex patterns, so they prefer to look at the large, bold checkerboard. Around 2 months, when detection of fine-grained detail has improved, infants become sensitive to the contrast in complex patterns and spend more time looking at them (Gwiazda & Birch, 2001).

Combining Pattern Elements In the early weeks of life, infants respond to the separate parts of a pattern. They stare at single high-contrast features, generally on the edges, and have difficulty shifting their gaze away toward other interesting stimuli (Hunnius & Geuze, 2004a, 2004b). At 2 to 3 months, when scanning ability and contrast sensitivity improve, infants thoroughly explore a pattern's internal features, pausing briefly to look at each part (Bronson, 1994).

Once babies can take in all aspects of a pattern, they integrate the parts into a unified whole. Around 4 months, babies are so good at detecting pattern organization that they perceive subjective boundaries that are not really present. For example, they perceive a square in the center of Figure 5.19a, just as you do (Ghim, 1990). And like adults, 3- to 4-month-olds engage in *boundary extension:* When re-exposed to a photo of a natural scene, they remember it as extending beyond its original boundaries. The visual system seems to interpret the photographed scene like a view through a window, which is understood to extend beyond the edges of the window (Quinn & Intraub, 2007).

Older infants carry this sensitivity to subjective form further. For example, 9-month-olds look much longer at an organized series of moving lights that resembles a human being walking than at an upside-down or scrambled version (Proffitt & Bertenthal, 1990). At 12 months, infants can detect familiar objects represented by incomplete drawings, even when as much as two-thirds of the drawing is missing (see Figure 5.19b) (Rose, Jankowski, & Senior, 1997). As these findings reveal, infants' increasing knowledge of objects and actions supports pattern perception.

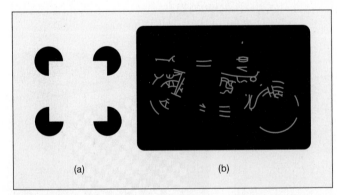

(a)   (b)

FIGURE 5.19 **Subjective boundaries in visual patterns.** (a) Do you perceive a square in the middle of the figure? By 4 months of age, infants do, too. (b) What does the image, missing two-thirds of its outline, look like to you? By 12 months, infants detect a motorcycle. After habituating to the incomplete motorcycle image, they were shown an intact motorcycle figure paired with a novel form. Twelve-month-olds recovered to (looked longer at) the novel figure, indicating that they recognized the motorcycle pattern on the basis of very little visual information. (Adapted from Ghim, 1990; Rose, Jankowski, & Senior, 1997.)

Face Perception Infants' tendency to search for structure in a patterned stimulus applies to face perception. Newborns prefer to look at photos and simplified drawings of faces with features arranged naturally (upright) rather than unnaturally (upside down or sideways) (see Figure 5.20a and b) (Cassia, Turati, & Simion, 2004; Mondloch et al., 1999). They also track a facelike pattern moving across their visual field farther than they track other stimuli (Johnson, 1999). And although they rely more on outer features (hairline and chin) than inner features to distinguish real faces, newborns prefer photos of faces with eyes open and a direct gaze (Farroni et al., 2002; Turati et al., 2006). Yet another amazing capacity is their tendency to look longer at both human and animal faces judged by adults as attractive—a preference that may be the origin of the widespread social bias favoring physically attractive people (Quinn et al., 2008; Slater et al., 2010).

Some researchers claim that these behaviors reflect a built-in capacity to orient toward members of one's own species, just as many newborn animals do (Johnson, 2001; Slater et al., 2011). Others assert that newborns simply prefer any stimulus in which the most

FIGURE 5.20 **Early face perception.** Newborns prefer to look at the photo of a face (a) and the simple pattern resembling a face (b) over the upside-down versions. (c) When the complex drawing of a face on the left and the equally complex, scrambled version on the right are moved across newborns' visual field, they follow the face longer. But if the two stimuli are stationary, infants show no preference for the face until around 2 months of age. (From Cassia, Turati, & Simion, 2004; Johnson, 1999; Mondloch et al., 1999.)

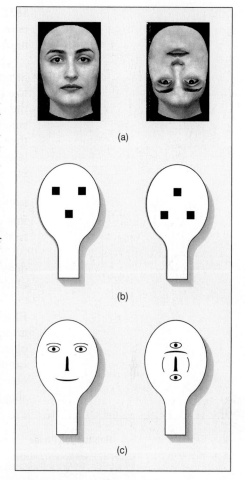

salient elements are arranged horizontally in the upper part of a pattern—like the "eyes" in Figure 5.20b. Indeed, newborns do prefer patterns with these characteristics over other arrangements (Cassia, Turati, & Simion, 2004; Simion et al., 2001). Possibly, however, a bias favoring the facial pattern promotes such preferences. Still other researchers argue that newborns are exposed to faces more often than to other stimuli—early experiences that could quickly "wire" the brain to detect faces and prefer attractive ones (Bukacha, Gauthier, & Tarr, 2006).

Although newborns respond to facelike structures, they cannot discriminate a complex facial pattern from other, equally complex patterns (see Figure 5.20c). But from repeated exposures to their mother's face, they quickly learn to prefer her face to that of an unfamiliar woman, although they mostly attend to its broad outlines. Around 2 months, when they can combine pattern elements into an organized whole, babies prefer a complex drawing of the human face to other equally complex stimulus arrangements (Dannemiller & Stephens, 1988). And they clearly prefer their mother's detailed facial features to those of another woman (Bartrip, Morton, & de Schonen, 2001).

Around 3 months, infants readily make fine distinctions among the features of different faces—for example, between photographs of two strangers, even when the faces are moderately similar (Farroni et al., 2007). At 5 months, infants perceive emotional expressions as meaningful wholes. They treat positive faces (happy and surprised) as different from negative ones (sad and fearful) (Bornstein & Arterberry, 2003). And by 7 months, they discriminate among a wider range of facial expressions, including happiness, surprise, sadness, fearfulness, and anger (Witherington et al., 2010).

Experience influences face processing, leading babies to form group biases at a tender age. As early as 3 months, infants prefer and more easily discriminate among female faces than among male faces (Quinn et al., 2002; Ramsey-Rennels & Langlois, 2006). The greater time infants spend with female adults explains this effect, since babies with a male primary caregiver prefer male faces. Furthermore, 3- to 6-month-olds exposed mostly to members of their own race prefer to look at the faces of members of that race, and between 6 and 9 months their ability to discriminate other-race faces weakens (Kelly et al., 2007, 2009). This own-race bias is absent in babies who have frequent contact with members of other races or who view picture books of other-race faces, and it can be reversed through exposure to racial diversity (Anzures et al., 2013; Heron-Delaney et al., 2011). **TAKE A MOMENT...** Notice how early experience promotes *perceptual narrowing* with respect to gender and racial information in faces, as occurs for species information, discussed in the Biology and Environment box on page 188.

Clearly, extensive face-to-face interaction with caregivers contributes to infants' refinement of face perception. And as babies recognize and respond to the expressive behavior of others, face perception supports their earliest social relationships.

Object Perception

Research on pattern perception involves only two-dimensional stimuli, but our environment is made up of stable, three-dimensional objects. Do young infants perceive a world of independently existing objects—knowledge essential for distinguishing among the self, other people, and things?

Exposure to racial diversity in her child-care center means that this baby is unlikely to have developed a preference for faces of her own race. When infants have limited social experiences, group biases emerge early.

SIZE AND SHAPE CONSTANCY As we move around the environment, the images that objects cast on our retina constantly change in size and shape. To perceive objects as stable and unchanging, we must translate these varying retinal images into a single representation.

Size constancy—perception of an object's size as the same, despite changes in the size of its retinal image—is evident in the first week of life. To test for it, researchers habituated infants to a small cube at varying distances from the eye, in an effort to desensitize them to changes in the cube's retinal image size and direct their attention to the object's actual size. When the small cube was presented together with a new, large cube—but at different distances so that they cast retinal images of the same size—all babies recovered to (looked longer at) the novel large cube, indicating that they distinguished objects on the basis of actual size, not retinal image size (Slater et al., 2010).

Perception of an object's shape as stable, despite changes in the shape projected on the retina, is called **shape constancy.** Habituation research reveals that it, too, is present within the first week of life, long before babies can actively rotate objects with their hands and view them from different angles (Slater & Johnson, 1999).

In sum, both size and shape constancy seem to be built-in capacities that assist babies in detecting a coherent world of objects. Yet they provide only a partial picture of young infants' object perception.

PERCEPTION OF OBJECT IDENTITY At first, babies rely heavily on motion and spatial arrangement to identify objects (Jusczyk et al., 1999; Spelke & Hermer, 1996). When two objects are touching and either move in unison or stand still, babies younger than 4 months cannot distinguish them. Infants, of course, are fascinated by moving objects. As they observe objects' motions, they pick up additional information about objects' boundaries, such as shape, color, and texture.

FIGURE 5.21 **Testing infants' ability to perceive object unity.** (a) Infants were habituated to a rod moving back and forth behind a box against a textured background. Next, they were shown two test displays in alternation: (b) a complete rod and (c) a broken rod with a gap corresponding to the location of the box. Each stimulus was moved back and forth against the textured background, in the same way as the habituation stimulus. Infants 2 months of age and older recovered to (looked longer at) the broken rod than the complete rod. Their novelty preference suggests that they perceive the rod behind the box in the first display as a single unit. (Based on Johnson, 1997.)

For example, as Figure 5.21 reveals, around 2 months, babies realize that a moving rod whose center is hidden behind a box is a complete rod rather than two rod pieces. Motion, a textured background, and a small box (so most of the rod is visible) are necessary for young infants to infer object unity. They need all these cues to heighten the distinction between objects in the display because their ability to scan for salient information is still immature (Amso & Johnson, 2006; Johnson, 2009).

As infants become familiar with many objects and improvements in scanning assist them in integrating each object's features into a unified whole, they rely more on shape, color, and pattern and less on motion (Johnson, 2011; Slater et al., 2010). Babies as young as 4½ months can discriminate two touching objects on the basis of their features in very simple, easy-to-process situations. And prior exposure to one of the test objects enhances 4½-month-olds' ability to discern the boundary between two touching objects—a finding that highlights the role of experience (Dueker, Modi, & Needham, 2003; Needham, 2001).

In everyday life, objects frequently move in and out of sight, so infants must keep track of their disappearance and reappearance to perceive their identity. Habituation research, in which a ball moves back and forth behind a screen, reveals that at age 4 months, infants first perceive the ball's path as continuous (Johnson et al., 2003). Between 4 and 5 months, infants can monitor more intricate paths of objects. As indicated by their future-oriented eye movements (looking ahead to where they expect an object to reappear from behind a barrier), 5-month-olds even keep track of an object that travels on a curvilinear course at varying speeds (Rosander & von Hofsten, 2004). Again, experience—the opportunity to track a moving object along a fully visible path of movement just before testing—enhances young infants' predictive eye tracking (Johnson & Shuwairi, 2009).

From 4 to 11 months, infants increasingly use featural information to detect the identity of an object traveling behind a screen. At first, they need strong featural cues—a change in two features (size and shape, or shape and color)—to signify that a disappearing object is distinct from an emerging object. Later in the first year, change in a single feature is sufficient (Bremner et al., 2013; Wilcox & Woods, 2009). And as before, experience—in particular, physically manipulating the object—boosts older infants' attention to its surface features.

In sum, perception of object identity is mastered gradually over the first year. We will consider a related attainment, infants' understanding of object permanence—awareness that an object still exists when hidden—in Chapter 6.

Intermodal Perception

Our world provides rich, continuous *intermodal stimulation*—simultaneous input from more than one *modality*, or sensory system. In **intermodal perception,** we make sense of these running streams of light, sound, tactile, odor, and taste information, perceiving them as integrated wholes. We know, for example, that an object's shape is the same whether we see it or touch it, that lip movements are closely coordinated with the sound of a voice, and that dropping a rigid object on a hard surface will cause a sharp, banging sound.

Recall that newborns turn in the general direction of a sound and reach for objects in a primitive way. These behaviors suggest that infants expect sight, sound, and touch to go together. Research reveals that babies perceive input from different sensory systems in a unified way by detecting **amodal sensory properties,** information that is not specific to a single modality but that overlaps two or more sensory systems, such as rate, rhythm, duration, intensity, temporal synchrony (for vision and hearing), and texture and shape (for vision and touch). Consider the sight and sound of a bouncing ball or the face and voice of a speaking person. In each event, visual and auditory information are conveyed simultaneously and with the same rate, rhythm, duration, and intensity.

Even newborns are impressive perceivers of amodal properties. After touching an object (such as a cylinder) placed in their palms, they recognize it visually, distinguishing it from a different-shaped object (Sann & Streri, 2007). And they require just one exposure to learn the association between the sight and sound of a toy, such as a rhythmically jangling rattle (Morrongiello, Fenwick, & Chance, 1998).

Within the first half-year, infants master a remarkable range of intermodal relationships. Three- to 5-month-olds can match faces with voices on the basis of lip–voice synchrony, emotional expression, and even age and gender of the speaker. Around 6 months, infants can perceive and remember the unique face–voice pairings of unfamiliar adults (Flom, 2013).

How does intermodal perception develop so quickly? Young infants seem biologically primed to focus on amodal information. Their detection of amodal relations—for example, the common tempo and rhythm in sights and sounds—precedes and provides the basis for detecting more specific intermodal matches, such as the relation between a particular person's face and the sound of her voice or between an object and its verbal label (Bahrick, 2010).

Intermodal sensitivity is crucial for perceptual development. In the first few months, when much stimulation is unfamiliar and confusing, it enables babies to notice meaningful correlations between sensory inputs and rapidly make sense of their surroundings. As a result, inexperienced perceivers notice a unitary event, such as a hammer's tapping, without being distracted by momentarily irrelevant aspects of the situation, such as the hammer's color or orientation (Bahrick, Lickliter, & Flom, 2004).

This toddler exploring a tambourine readily detects amodal relations in the synchronous sounds and visual appearance of its metal jingles.

© LAURA DWIGHT PHOTOGRAPHY

In addition to easing perception of the physical world, intermodal perception facilitates processing of the social world. For example, as 3- to 4-month-olds gaze at an adult's face, they initially require both vocal and visual input to distinguish positive from negative emotional expressions (Flom & Bahrick, 2007; Kahana-Kalman & Walker-Andrews, 2001). Only later do infants discriminate positive from negative emotion in each sensory modality—first in voices (around 5 months), later (from 7 months on) in faces (Bahrick, Hernandez-Reif, & Flom, 2005).

Research suggests that intermodal perception supports diverse aspects of learning. In one study, 3-month-olds were given an operant conditioning task in which kicking their foot made a mobile hung with cylinder-shaped blocks turn. Some babies held in their palms a cylinder, others held a cube, and still others were given no object. Infants given matching amodal information—who viewed the cylinders while holding a cylinder—learned the kicking response fastest (Kraebel, 2012). Those given mismatching information (who held a cube) showed inhibited learning.

Furthermore, because communication is often intermodal (simultaneously verbal, visual, and tactile), infants receive much support from other senses in acquiring language. When parents speak to infants, they often provide temporal synchrony between words, object motions, and touch—for example, saying "doll" while moving a doll and occasionally having the doll touch the infant (Gogate & Bahrick, 1998, 2001). In doing so, caregivers greatly increase the chances that babies will remember the association between the word and the object.

In sum, intermodal stimulation fosters all aspects of psychological development. When caregivers provide many concurrent sights, sounds, and touches, babies process more information and learn faster (Bahrick, 2010). Intermodal perception is yet another fundamental capacity that assists infants in their active efforts to build an orderly, understandable world.

Understanding Perceptual Development

Now that we have reviewed the development of infant perceptual capacities, how can we put together this diverse array of amazing achievements? Widely accepted answers come from the work of Eleanor and James Gibson. According to the Gibsons' **differentiation theory,** infants actively search for *invariant features* of the environment—those that remain stable—in a constantly changing perceptual world. In pattern perception, for example, young babies search for features that stand out and orient toward faces. Soon they explore internal features, noticing *stable relationships* among them. As a result, they detect patterns, such as complex designs and individual faces. Similarly, infants analyze the speech stream for regularities, detecting words, word-order sequences, and—within words—syllable-stress patterns. The development of intermodal perception also reflects this principle (Bahrick & Lickliter, 2012). Babies seek out invariant relationships—first, amodal properties, such as common rate and rhythm, in a voice and face, later more detailed associations, such as unique voice–face matches.

The Gibsons described their theory as *differentiation* (where *differentiate* means "analyze" or "break down") because over time the baby detects finer and finer invariant features among stimuli. In addition to pattern perception and intermodal perception, differentiation applies to depth and object perception: Recall how in each, sensitivity to motion precedes detection of fine-grained features. So one way of understanding perceptual development is to think of it as a built-in tendency to seek order and consistency—a capacity that becomes increasingly fine-tuned with age (Gibson, 1970; Gibson, 1979).

Acting on the environment is vital in perceptual differentiation. According to the Gibsons, perception is guided by the discovery of **affordances**—the action possibilities that a situation offers an organism with certain motor capabilities (Gibson, 2000, 2003). By moving about and exploring the environment, babies figure out which objects can be grasped, squeezed, bounced, or stroked and which surfaces are safe to cross or present the possibility of falling. Sensitivity to affordances means that we spend far less time correcting ineffective actions than we would otherwise: It makes our actions future-oriented and largely successful rather than reactive and blundering.

LOOK and LISTEN

While watching a parent and infant playing, list instances of parental intermodal stimulation and communication. What is the baby likely learning about people, objects, or language from each intermodal experience?

FIGURE 5.22 Acting on the environment plays a major role in perceptual differentiation. Crawling and walking change the way babies perceive a sloping surface. The newly crawling infant on the left plunges headlong down the slope. He has not yet learned that it affords the possibility of falling. The toddler on the right, who has been walking for more than a month, approaches the slope cautiously. Experience in trying to remain upright but frequently tumbling over has made him more aware of the consequences of his movements. He perceives the incline differently than he did at a younger age.

DR. KAREN E. ADOLPH, INFANT ACTION LAB, NEW YORK UNIVERSITY

To illustrate, recall how infants' changing capabilities for independent movement affect their perception. When babies crawl, and again when they walk, they gradually realize that a sloping surface *affords the possibility* of falling (see Figure 5.22). With added weeks of practicing each skill, they hesitate to crawl or walk down a risky incline. Experience in trying to keep their balance on various surfaces makes crawlers and walkers more aware of the consequences of their movements. Crawlers come to detect when surface slant places so much body weight on their arms that they will fall forward, and walkers come to sense when an incline shifts body weight so their legs and feet can no longer hold them upright.

Infants do not transfer their learning about slopes or drop-offs from crawling to walking because the affordances for each posture are different (Adolph, Kretch, & LoBue, 2014). Learning is gradual and effortful because newly crawling and walking babies cross many types of surfaces in their homes each day. As they experiment with balance and postural adjustments to accommodate each, they perceive surfaces in new ways that guide their movements. As a result, they act more competently.

As we conclude this chapter, it is only fair to note that some researchers believe that babies do more than make sense of experience by searching for invariant features and discovering affordances: They also *impose meaning on* what they perceive, constructing categories of objects and events in the surrounding environment. We have seen the glimmerings of this cognitive point of view in this chapter. For example, older babies *interpret* a familiar face as a source of pleasure and affection and a pattern of blinking lights as a moving human being. This cognitive perspective also has merit in understanding the achievements of infancy. In fact, many researchers combine these two positions, regarding infant development as proceeding from a perceptual to a cognitive emphasis over the first year of life.

Ask Yourself

● **REVIEW** Using examples, explain why intermodal stimulation is vital for infants' developing understanding of their physical and social worlds.

● **CONNECT** According to differentiation theory, perceptual development reflects infants' active search for invariant features. Provide examples from research on hearing, pattern perception, and intermodal perception.

● **APPLY** After several weeks of crawling, Ben learned to avoid going headfirst over a drop-off. Now he has started to walk. Can his mother trust him not to step over a risky drop-off? Explain, using the concept of affordances.

● **REFLECT** Are young infants more competent than you thought they were before you read this chapter? List the capacities that most surprised you.

Summary

Body Growth (p. 159)

5.1 Discuss major changes in body size, muscle–fat makeup, body proportions, and variations in rate of physical growth over the first two years.

- Height and weight gains are greater during the first two years than at any other time after birth. Body fat develops quickly during the first nine months, whereas muscle development is slow and gradual.

- Parts of the body grow at different rates, following **cephalocaudal** and **proximodistal trends,** resulting in changing body proportions.

- Girls are ahead of boys in physical maturity, and African-American children tend to be ahead of Caucasian-American children, based on skeletal age.

Brain Development (p. 161)

5.2 Describe brain development during infancy and toddlerhood, current methods of measuring brain functioning, and appropriate stimulation to support the brain's potential.

- Early in development, the brain grows faster than any other organ of the body. Once **neurons** are in place, they rapidly form **synapses** and release **neurotransmitters,** which cross synapses to send messages to other neurons. During the peak period of synaptic growth in any brain area, many surrounding neurons die. Neurons that are seldom stimulated lose their synapses in a process called **synaptic pruning. Glial cells,** responsible for **myelination,** multiply rapidly through the second year, contributing to large gains in brain weight.

- Measures of brain functioning include those that detect changes in electrical activity in the cerebral cortex (EEG, ERPs), neuroimaging techniques (PET, fMRI), and NIRS, which uses infrared light and is suitable for infants and young children.

- The **cerebral cortex** is the largest, most complex brain structure and the last to stop growing. Its regions develop in the general order in which various capacities emerge in the growing child, with the frontal lobes (which contain the **prefrontal cortex**) having the most extended period of development. The hemispheres of the cerebral cortex specialize, a process called **lateralization.** In the first few years of life, there is high **brain plasticity,** with many areas not yet committed to specific functions.

- Both heredity and early experience contribute to brain organization. Stimulation of the brain is essential during sensitive periods—periods in which the brain is developing most rapidly. Prolonged early deprivation, experienced by some babies in orphanages, can disrupt brain growth and interfere with the brain's capacity to manage stress, with long-term physical and psychological consequences.

- Appropriate early stimulation promotes **experience-expectant brain growth** through ordinary experiences. No evidence exists for a sensitive period in the first few years for **experience-dependent brain growth,** which relies on specific learning experiences. In fact, environments that overwhelm children with inappropriately advanced expectations can undermine the brain's potential.

5.3 How does organization of sleep and wakefulness change over the first two years?

- Infants' changing arousal patterns are primarily affected by brain growth, but the social environment also plays a role. Periods of sleep and wakefulness become fewer but longer over the first two years, conforming to a night–day schedule. Most parents in Western nations try to get their babies to sleep through the night much earlier than parents throughout most of the world, who are more likely to sleep with their babies.

Influences on Early Physical Growth (p. 171)

5.4 Cite evidence indicating that heredity, nutrition, and parental affection contribute to early physical growth.

- Twin and adoption studies reveal that heredity contributes to body size and rate of physical growth.

- Breast milk is ideally suited to infants' growth needs. Breastfeeding protects against disease and prevents malnutrition and infant death in poverty-stricken areas of the world.

- Most infants and toddlers can eat nutritious foods freely without risk of becoming overweight. However, the relationship between rapid weight gain in infancy and obesity at older ages is strengthening, perhaps because of a rise in unhealthy early feeding practices, in which babies are given high-fat foods and sugary drinks.

- **Marasmus** and **kwashiorkor** are dietary diseases caused by malnutrition that affect many children in developing countries and, if prolonged, can permanently stunt body growth and brain development. **Growth faltering** illustrates the importance of parental affection and early emotional well-being for normal physical growth.

Learning Capacities (p. 176)

5.5 Describe infant learning capacities, the conditions under which they occur, and the unique value of each.

- **Classical conditioning** is based on the infant's ability to associate events that usually occur together in the everyday world. Infants can be classically conditioned most easily when the pairing of an **unconditioned stimulus (UCS)** and a **conditioned stimulus (CS)** has survival value—for example, learning which stimuli regularly accompany feeding.

- In **operant conditioning,** infants act on their environment and their behavior is followed by either **reinforcers,** which increase the occurrence of a preceding behavior, or **punishment,** which either removes a desirable stimulus or presents an unpleasant one to decrease the occurrence of a response. In young infants, interesting sights and sounds and pleasurable caregiver interaction serve as effective reinforcers.

- **Habituation** and **recovery** reveal that at birth, babies are attracted to novelty. Novelty preference (recovery to a novel stimulus) assesses recent memory, whereas familiarity preference (recovery to the familiar stimulus) assesses remote memory.

- Newborns also have a primitive ability to imitate adults' facial expressions and gestures. **Imitation** is a powerful means of learning, which contributes to the parent–infant bond. Scientists have identified specialized cells called **mirror neurons** that underlie these capacities. However, whether newborn imitation is a voluntary capacity remains controversial.

Motor Development (p. 181)

5.6 *Discuss the general course of motor development during the first two years, along with factors that influence it.*

- According to the **dynamic systems theory of motor development,** children acquire new motor skills by combining existing skills into increasingly complex systems of action. Each new skill is a joint product of central nervous system development, the body's movement possibilities, the child's goals, and environmental supports for the skill.

- Movement opportunities and a stimulating environment profoundly affect motor development, as shown by research on infants reared in deprived institutions. Cultural values and child-rearing customs contribute to the emergence and refinement of early motor skills.

© DON DESPAIR/ALAMY

- During the first year, infants perfect their reaching and grasping. The poorly coordinated **prereaching** of the newborn period drops out. Gradually, reaching becomes more flexible and accurate, and the clumsy **ulnar grasp** is transformed into a refined **pincer grasp** by the end of the first year.

Perceptual Development (p. 187)

5.7 *What changes in hearing and in depth, pattern, object, and intermodal perception take place during infancy?*

- Infants organize sounds into increasingly complex patterns and, in the middle of the first year, become more sensitive to the sounds of their own language. They have an impressive **statistical learning capacity,** which enables them to detect speech regularities for which they will later learn meanings.

- Rapid maturation of the eye and visual centers in the cerebral cortex supports the development of focusing, color discrimination, and visual acuity during the first few months. The ability to scan the environment and track moving objects also improves.

- Research on depth perception reveals that responsiveness to motion develops first, followed by sensitivity to binocular and then to pictorial depth cues. Experience in crawling enhances depth perception, but babies must learn to use depth cues for each body position in order to avoid drop-offs.

- **Contrast sensitivity** accounts for infants' early pattern preferences. At first, babies stare at single, high-contrast features. Over time, they discriminate increasingly complex and meaningful patterns.

- Newborns prefer to look at photos and simplified drawings of faces. Around 2 months, they recognize and prefer their mother's facial features, and at 3 months, they distinguish the features of different faces. From 5 months on, they perceive emotional expressions as meaningful wholes.

- At birth, **size** and **shape constancy** help babies begin to detect a coherent world of objects. At first, infants depend on motion and spatial arrangement to identify objects. After 4 months of age, they rely increasingly on object features, such as distinct shape and surface pattern. Soon they can monitor increasingly intricate paths of objects, and they look for featural information to detect the identity of a moving object.

- From the start, infants are capable of **intermodal perception**—combining information across sensory modalities. Detection of **amodal sensory properties,** such as common rate, rhythm, or intensity, provides the basis for detecting many intermodal matches.

5.8 *Explain differentiation theory of perceptual development.*

- According to **differentiation theory,** perceptual development is a matter of detecting increasingly fine-grained invariant features in a constantly changing perceptual world. Perceptual differentiation is guided by discovery of **affordances**—the action possibilities that a situation offers the individual.

Important Terms and Concepts

affordances (p. 196)
amodal sensory properties (p. 195)
brain plasticity (p. 165)
cephalocaudal trend (p. 161)
cerebral cortex (p. 164)
classical conditioning (p. 176)
conditioned response (CR) (p. 177)
conditioned stimulus (CS) (p. 177)
contrast sensitivity (p. 191)
differentiation theory (p. 196)
dynamic systems theory of motor development (p. 181)
experience-dependent brain growth (p. 169)
experience-expectant brain growth (p. 169)
glial cells (p. 162)

growth faltering (p. 176)
habituation (p. 178)
imitation (p. 179)
intermodal perception (p. 195)
kwashiorkor (p. 175)
lateralization (p. 165)
marasmus (p. 175)
mirror neurons (p. 180)
myelination (p. 162)
neurons (p. 161)
neurotransmitters (p. 161)
operant conditioning (p. 178)
perceptual narrowing effect (p. 188)
pincer grasp (p. 186)
prefrontal cortex (p. 165)

prereaching (p. 185)
proximodistal trend (p. 161)
punishment (p. 178)
recovery (p. 178)
reinforcer (p. 178)
shape constancy (p. 194)
size constancy (p. 194)
statistical learning capacity (p. 188)
synapses (p. 161)
synaptic pruning (p. 162)
ulnar grasp (p. 186)
unconditioned response (UCR) (p. 177)
unconditioned stimulus (UCS) (p. 177)

Cognitive Development in Infancy and Toddlerhood

"My Mother and My Brother"
Maisha Maliha Siddique
8 years, Bangladesh

This toddler delights in his mother's attention and speech as they play. In Chapter 6, you will see that a stimulating environment and the guidance of more mature members of their culture ensure that young children's cognition will develop at its best.

REPRINTED WITH PERMISSION FROM THE INTERNATIONAL MUSEUM OF CHILDREN'S ART, OSLO, NORWAY

When Caitlin, Grace, and Timmy gathered at Ginette's child-care home, the playroom was alive with activity. The three spirited explorers, each nearly 18 months old, were bent on discovery. Grace dropped shapes through holes in a plastic box that Ginette held and adjusted so the harder ones would fall smoothly into place. Once a few shapes were inside, Grace grabbed the box and shook it, squealing with delight as the lid fell open and the shapes scattered around her. The clatter attracted Timmy, who picked up a shape, carried it to the railing at the top of the basement steps, and dropped it overboard, then followed with a teddy bear, a ball, his shoe, and a spoon. Meanwhile, Caitlin pulled open a drawer, unloaded a set of wooden bowls, stacked them in a pile, knocked it over, and then banged two bowls together. With each action, the children seemed to be asking, "How do things work? What makes interesting events happen? Which ones can I control?"

As the toddlers experimented, we could see the beginnings of spoken language—a whole new way of influencing the world. "All gone baw!" Caitlin exclaimed as Timmy tossed the bright red ball down the basement steps. "Bye-bye," Grace chimed in, waving as the ball disappeared from sight. Later that day, Grace revealed the beginnings of make-believe. "Night-night," she said, putting her head down and closing her eyes, ever so pleased that she could decide for herself when and where to go to bed.

Over the first two years, the small, reflexive newborn baby becomes a self-assertive, purposeful being who solves simple problems and starts to master the most amazing human ability: language. Parents wonder, how does all this happen so quickly? This question has also captivated researchers, yielding a wealth of findings along with vigorous debate over how to explain the astonishing pace of infant and toddler cognition.

In this chapter, we take up three perspectives on early cognitive development: Piaget's *cognitive-developmental theory, information processing,* and Vygotsky's *socio-cultural theory*. We also consider the usefulness of tests that measure infants' and toddlers' intellectual progress. Finally, we look at the beginnings of language. We will see how toddlers' first words build on early cognitive achievements and how, very soon, new words and expressions greatly increase the speed and flexibility of their thinking. Throughout development, cognition and language mutually support each other. ■

Piaget's Cognitive-Developmental Theory

Swiss theorist Jan Piaget inspired a vision of children as busy, motivated explorers whose thinking develops as they act directly on the environment. Influenced by his background in biology, Piaget believed that the child's mind forms and modifies psychological structures so they achieve a better fit with external reality. Recall from Chapter 1 that in Piaget's theory, children move through four stages between infancy and adolescence. During these stages, Piaget claimed, all aspects of cognition develop in an integrated fashion, changing in a similar way at about the same time.

Piaget's **sensorimotor stage** spans the first two years of life. Piaget believed that infants and toddlers "think" with their eyes, ears, hands, and other sensorimotor equipment. They cannot yet carry out many activities inside their heads. But by the

6.1 According to Piaget, how do schemes change over the course of development?

6.2 Describe major cognitive attainments of the sensorimotor stage.

6.3 What does follow-up research say about infant cognitive development and the accuracy of Piaget's sensorimotor stage?

end of toddlerhood, children can solve everyday practical problems and represent their experiences in speech, gesture, and play. To appreciate Piaget's view of how these vast changes take place, let's consider some important concepts.

Piaget's Ideas About Cognitive Change

According to Piaget, specific psychological structures—organized ways of making sense of experience called **schemes**—change with age. At first, schemes are sensorimotor action patterns. For example, at 6 months, Timmy dropped objects in a fairly rigid way, simply by letting go of a rattle or teething ring and watching with interest. By 18 months, his "dropping scheme" had become deliberate and creative. In tossing objects down the basement stairs, he threw some in the air, bounced others off walls, released some gently and others forcefully. Soon, instead of just acting on objects, he will show evidence of thinking before he acts. For Piaget, this change marks the transition from sensorimotor to preoperational thought.

In Piaget's theory, two processes, *adaptation* and *organization,* account for changes in schemes.

ADAPTATION **TAKE A MOMENT...** The next time you have a chance, notice how infants and toddlers tirelessly repeat actions that lead to interesting effects. **Adaptation** involves building schemes through direct interaction with the environment. It consists of two complementary activities: *assimilation* and *accommodation.* During **assimilation**, we use our current schemes to interpret the external world. For example, when Timmy dropped objects, he was assimilating them to his sensorimotor "dropping scheme." In **accommodation**, we create new schemes or adjust old ones after noticing that our current ways of thinking do not capture the environment completely. When Timmy dropped objects in different ways, he modified his dropping scheme to take account of the varied properties of objects.

According to Piaget, the balance between assimilation and accommodation varies over time. When children are not changing much, they assimilate more than they accommodate—a steady, comfortable state that Piaget called cognitive *equilibrium.* During times of rapid cognitive change, children are in a state of *disequilibrium,* or cognitive discomfort. Realizing that new information does not match their current schemes, they shift from assimilation to accommodation. After modifying their schemes, they move back toward assimilation, exercising their newly changed structures until they are ready to be modified again.

Each time this back-and-forth movement between equilibrium and disequilibrium occurs, more effective schemes are produced. Because the times of greatest accommodation are the earliest ones, the sensorimotor stage is Piaget's most complex period of development.

ORGANIZATION Schemes also change through **organization**, a process that occurs internally, apart from direct contact with the environment. Once children form new schemes, they rearrange them, linking them with other schemes to create a strongly interconnected cognitive system. For example, eventually Timmy will relate "dropping" to "throwing" and to his developing understanding of "nearness" and "farness." According to Piaget, schemes truly reach equilibrium when they become part of a broad network of structures that can be jointly applied to the surrounding world (Piaget, 1936/1952).

In the following sections, we will first describe infant development as Piaget saw it, noting research that supports his observations. Then we will consider evidence demonstrating that in some ways, babies' cognitive competence is more advanced than Piaget believed.

© LAURA DWIGHT PHOTOGRAPHY

In Piaget's theory, first schemes are sensorimotor action patterns. As this 12-month-old experiments with his dropping scheme, his behavior becomes more deliberate and varied.

The Sensorimotor Stage

The difference between the newborn baby and the 2-year-old child is so vast that Piaget divided the sensorimotor stage into six substages, summarized in Table 6.1. Piaget based this sequence on a very small sample: his own three children. He observed his son and two daughters carefully and also presented them with everyday problems (such as hidden objects) that helped reveal their understanding of the world.

According to Piaget, at birth infants know so little that they cannot explore purposefully. The **circular reaction** provides a special means of adapting their first schemes. It involves stumbling onto a new experience caused by the baby's own motor activity. The reaction is "circular" because, as the infant tries to repeat the event again and again, a sensorimotor response that originally occurred by chance strengthens into a new scheme. Consider Caitlin, who at age 2 months accidentally made a smacking sound after a feeding. Finding this new sound intriguing, she tried to repeat it until, after a few days, she became quite expert at smacking her lips.

The circular reaction initially centers on the infant's own body but later turns outward, toward manipulation of objects. In the second year, it becomes experimental and creative, aimed at producing novel outcomes. Infants' difficulty inhibiting new and interesting behaviors may underlie the circular reaction. This immaturity in inhibition seems to be adaptive, helping to ensure that new skills will not be interrupted before they strengthen (Carey & Markman, 1999). Piaget considered revisions in the circular reaction so important that, as Table 6.1 shows, he named the sensorimotor substages after them.

REPEATING CHANCE BEHAVIORS   Piaget saw newborn reflexes as the building blocks of sensorimotor intelligence. In Substage 1, babies suck, grasp, and look in much the same way, no matter what experiences they encounter.

Around 1 month, as babies enter Substage 2, they start to gain voluntary control over their actions through the *primary circular reaction,* by repeating chance behaviors largely motivated by basic needs. This leads to some simple motor habits, such as sucking their fists or thumbs. Babies of this substage also begin to vary their behavior in response to environmental demands. For example, they open their mouths differently for a nipple than for a spoon. And they start to anticipate events. At age 3 months, when Timmy awoke from his nap, he cried out with hunger. But as soon as Vanessa entered the room, his crying stopped. He knew that feeding time was near.

During Substage 3, from 4 to 8 months, infants sit up and reach for and manipulate objects. These motor achievements strengthen the *secondary circular reaction,* through which babies try to repeat interesting events in the surrounding environment that are caused by their own actions. For example, 4-month-old Caitlin accidentally knocked a toy hung in front of her,

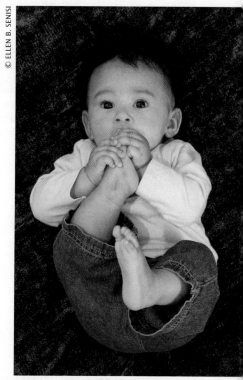

This 3-month-old tries to repeat a newly discovered action—sucking her toes— in a primary circular reaction that helps her gain voluntary control over her behavior.

| TABLE 6.1 | Summary of Piaget's Sensorimotor Stage |

SENSORIMOTOR SUBSTAGE	TYPICAL ADAPTIVE BEHAVIORS
1. Reflexive schemes (birth–1 month)	Newborn reflexes (see Chapter 4, page 142)
2. Primary circular reactions (1–4 months)	Simple motor habits centered around the infant's own body; limited anticipation of events
3. Secondary circular reactions (4–8 months)	Actions aimed at repeating interesting effects in the surrounding world; imitation of familiar behaviors
4. Coordination of secondary circular reactions (8–12 months)	Intentional, or goal-directed, behavior; ability to find a hidden object in the first location in which it is hidden (object permanence); improved anticipation of events; imitation of behaviors slightly different from those the infant usually performs
5. Tertiary circular reactions (12–18 months)	Exploration of the properties of objects by acting on them in novel ways; imitation of novel behaviors; ability to search in several locations for a hidden object (accurate A–B search)
6. Mental representation (18 months–2 years)	Internal depictions of objects and events, as indicated by sudden solutions to problems; ability to find an object that has been moved while out of sight (invisible displacement); deferred imitation; and make-believe play

When this 3-month-old accidentally hits a toy hung in front of her, her action causes it to swing. Using the secondary circular reaction, she tries to recapture this interesting effect. In the process, she forms a new "hitting scheme."

producing a fascinating swinging motion. Over the next three days, Caitlin tried to repeat this effect, gradually forming a new "hitting" scheme. Improved control over their own behavior permits infants to imitate others' behavior more effectively. However, Piaget noted, 4- to 8-month-olds cannot adapt flexibly and quickly enough to imitate novel behaviors. Although they enjoy watching an adult demonstrate a game of pat-a-cake, they are not yet able to participate.

INTENTIONAL BEHAVIOR In Substage 4, 8- to 12-month-olds combine schemes into new, more complex action sequences. As a result, actions that lead to new schemes no longer have a random, hit-or-miss quality—*accidentally* bringing the thumb to the mouth or *happening* to hit the toy. Instead, 8- to 12-month-olds can engage in **intentional, or goal-directed, behavior**, coordinating schemes deliberately to solve simple problems. Consider Piaget's famous object-hiding task, in which he shows the baby an attractive toy and then hides it behind his hand or under a cover. Infants of this substage can find the object by coordinating two schemes—"pushing" aside the obstacle and "grasping" the toy. Piaget regarded these *means–end action sequences* as the foundation for all problem solving.

Retrieving hidden objects reveals that infants have begun to master **object permanence**, the understanding that objects continue to exist when they are out of sight. But this awareness is not yet complete. Babies make the **A-not-B search error**: If they reach several times for an object at a first hiding place (A), then see it moved to a second (B), they still search for it in the first hiding place (A). Consequently, Piaget concluded that they do not have a clear image of the object as persisting when hidden from view.

Infants in Substage 4, who can better anticipate events, sometimes use their capacity for intentional behavior to try to change those events. At 10 months, Timmy crawled after Vanessa when she put on her coat, whimpering to keep her from leaving. Also, babies can now imitate behaviors slightly different from those they usually perform. After watching someone else, they try to stir with a spoon, push a toy car, or drop raisins into a cup (Piaget, 1945/1951).

In Substage 5, from 12 to 18 months, the *tertiary circular reaction,* in which toddlers repeat behaviors with variation, emerges. Recall how Timmy dropped objects over the basement steps, trying this action, then that, then another. This deliberately exploratory approach makes 12- to 18-month-olds better problem solvers. For example, Grace figured out how to fit a shape through a hole in a container by turning and twisting it until it fell through and how to use a stick to get a toy that was out of reach. According to Piaget, this capacity to experiment leads to a more advanced understanding of object permanence. Toddlers look for a hidden toy in several locations, displaying an accurate A–B search. Their more flexible action patterns also permit them to imitate many more behaviors, such as stacking blocks, scribbling on paper, and making funny faces.

To find the toy hidden inside the pot, a 10-month-old engages in intentional, goal-directed behavior—the basis for all problem solving.

Using a tertiary circular reaction, this baby twists, turns, and pushes until a block fits through its matching hole in her shape sorter. Between 12 and 18 months, toddlers take a deliberately experimental approach to problem solving.

MENTAL REPRESENTATION   Substage 6 brings the ability to create **mental representations**—internal depictions of information that the mind can manipulate. Our most powerful mental representations are of two kinds: (1) *images*—mental pictures of objects, people, and spaces; and (2) *concepts*—categories in which similar objects or events are grouped together. We use a mental image to retrace our steps when we've misplaced something or to imitate someone's behavior long after observing it. By thinking in concepts and labeling them (for example, "ball" for all rounded, movable objects used in play), we become more efficient thinkers, organizing our diverse experiences into meaningful, manageable, and memorable units.

Piaget noted that 18- to 24-month-olds arrive at solutions suddenly rather than through trial-and-error behavior. In doing so, they seem to experiment with actions inside their heads—evidence that they can mentally represent their experiences. For example, at 19 months, Grace—after bumping her new push toy against a wall—paused for a moment as if to "think," and then immediately turned the toy in a new direction.

Representation enables older toddlers to solve advanced object permanence problems involving *invisible displacement*—finding a toy moved while out of sight, such as into a small box while under a cover. It also permits **deferred imitation**—the ability to remember and copy the behavior of models who are not present. And it makes possible **make-believe play,** in which children act out everyday and imaginary activities. As the sensorimotor stage draws to a close, mental symbols have become major instruments of thinking.

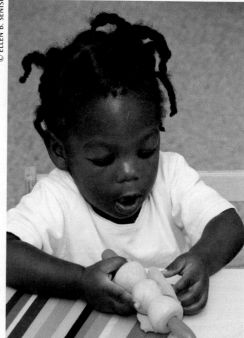

Through deferred imitation, toddlers greatly expand their sensorimotor schemes. While imitating, this 2-year-old encounters a problem faced by all cookie bakers at one time or another.

Follow-Up Research on Infant Cognitive Development

Many studies suggest that infants display a wide array of understandings earlier than Piaget believed. Recall the operant conditioning research reviewed in Chapter 5, in which newborns sucked vigorously on a nipple to gain access to interesting sights and sounds. This behavior, which closely resembles Piaget's secondary circular reaction, shows that babies try to explore and control the external world long before 4 to 8 months. In fact, they do so as soon as they are born.

To discover what infants know about hidden objects and other aspects of physical reality, researchers often use the **violation-of-expectation method.** They may *habituate* babies to a physical event (expose them to the event until their looking declines) to familiarize them with a situation in which their knowledge will be tested. Or they may simply show babies an *expected event* (one that is consistent with reality) and an *unexpected event* (a variation of the first event that violates reality). Heightened attention to the unexpected event suggests that the infant is "surprised" by a deviation from physical reality and, therefore, is aware of that aspect of the physical world.

The violation-of-expectation method is controversial. Some critics believe that it indicates limited, implicit (nonconscious) awareness of physical events—not the full-blown, conscious understanding that was Piaget's focus in requiring infants to act on their surroundings, as in searching for hidden objects (Campos et al., 2008; Munakata, 2001). Others maintain that the method reveals only babies' perceptual preference for novelty, not their knowledge of the physical world (Bremner, 2010; Cohen, 2010; Kagan, 2008). Let's examine this debate in light of recent evidence.

OBJECT PERMANENCE   In a series of studies using the violation-of-expectation method, Renée Baillargeon and her collaborators claimed to have found evidence for object permanence in the first few months of life. Figure 6.1 on page 206 describes and illustrates one of these studies, in which infants exposed to both an expected and an unexpected object-hiding event looked longer at the unexpected event (Aguiar & Baillargeon, 2002; Baillargeon & DeVos, 1991).

Additional violation-of-expectation studies yielded similar results, suggesting that infants look longer at a wide variety of unexpected events involving hidden objects (Newcombe,

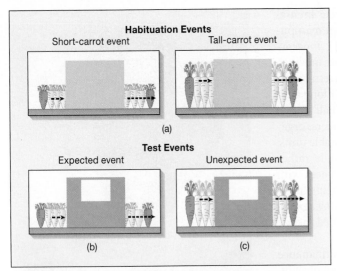

FIGURE 6.1 **Testing young infants for understanding of object permanence using the violation-of-expectation method.** (a) First, infants were habituated to two events: a short carrot and a tall carrot moving behind a yellow screen, on alternate trials. Next, the researchers presented two test events. The color of the screen was changed to help infants notice its window. (b) In the *expected event,* the carrot shorter than the window's lower edge moved behind the blue screen and reappeared on the other side. (c) In the *unexpected event,* the carrot taller than the window's lower edge moved behind the screen and did not appear in the window, but then emerged intact on the other side. Infants as young as 2½ to 3½ months looked longer at the *unexpected event,* suggesting that they had some understanding of object permanence. (Adapted from R. Baillargeon & J. DeVos, 1991, "Object Permanence in Young Infants: Further Evidence," *Child Development, 62,* p. 1230. © 1991, John Wiley and Sons. Reprinted with permission of John Wiley & Sons Ltd. conveyed through Copyright Clearance Center, Inc.)

Sluzenski, & Huttenlocher, 2005; Wang, Baillargeon, & Paterson, 2005). Still, several researchers using similar procedures failed to confirm some of Baillargeon's findings (Cohen & Marks, 2002; Schöner & Thelen, 2006; Sirois & Jackson, 2012). And, as previously noted, critics question what babies' looking preferences tell us about what they actually understand.

But another type of looking behavior suggests that young infants are aware that objects persist when out of view. Four- and 5-month-olds will track a ball's path of movement as it disappears and reappears from behind a barrier, even gazing ahead to where they expect it to emerge. As further support for such awareness, 5- to 9-month-olds more often engaged in such predictive tracking when a ball viewed on a computer screen gradually rolled behind a barrier than when it disappeared instantaneously or imploded (rapidly decreased in size) at the barrier's edge (Bertenthal, Gredebäck, & Boyer, 2013; Bertenthal, Longo, & Kenny, 2007). With age, babies are more likely to fixate on the predicted place of the ball's reappearance and wait for it—evidence of an increasingly secure grasp of object permanence.

If young infants do have some notion of object permanence, how do we explain Piaget's finding that even infants capable of reaching do not try to search for hidden objects before 8 months of age? Compared with looking reactions in violation-of-expectation tasks, searching for a hidden object is far more cognitively demanding: The baby must figure out where the hidden object is. Consistent with this idea, infants solve some object-hiding tasks before others: Eight- to 10-month-olds remove the cover from a partially hidden object before they are able to do so from a fully covered object (Moore & Meltzoff, 2008). And 10-month-olds search for an object placed on a table and covered by a cloth before they search for an object that a hand deposits under a cloth (Moore & Meltzoff, 1999). In the second, more difficult task, infants seem to expect the object to reappear in the hand from which it initially disappeared. When the hand emerges without the object, they conclude that there is no other place the object could be. Not until 14 months can most babies infer that the hand deposited the object under the cloth.

Around this age, toddlers also know that objects continue to exist in their hidden locations after the babies have left the location. After seeing an object hidden in a cupboard, when toddlers returned the next day, they correctly searched for the specific object in its original location (Moore & Meltzoff, 2004). When exposed to a similar cupboard in a new room, the toddlers behaved just as adults do: They saw no reason to search.

SEARCHING FOR OBJECTS HIDDEN IN MORE THAN ONE LOCATION Once 8- to 12-month-olds search for hidden objects, they make the A-not-B search error. Some research suggests that they search at A (where they found the object on previous reaches) instead of B (its most recent location) because they have trouble inhibiting a previously rewarded motor response (Diamond, Cruttenden, & Neiderman, 1994). Another possibility is that after finding the object several times at A, babies do not attend closely when it is hidden at B (Ruffman & Langman, 2002).

A more comprehensive explanation is that a complex, dynamic system of factors—having built a habit of reaching toward A, continuing to look at A, having the hiding place at B appear similar to the one at A, and maintaining a constant body posture—increases the chances that the baby will make the A-not-B search error. Disrupting any one of these factors increases 10-month-olds' accurate searching at B (Thelen et al., 2001). In addition, older infants are still perfecting reaching and grasping (see Chapter 5) (Berger, 2010). If these motor skills are challenging, babies have little attention left to focus on inhibiting their habitual reach toward A.

In sum, mastery of object permanence is a gradual achievement. Babies' understanding becomes increasingly complex with age: They must perceive an object's identity by integrating feature and movement information (see Chapter 5, pages 194–195), distinguish the object from the barrier concealing it and the surface on which it rests, keep track of the object's whereabouts, and use this knowledge to obtain the object (Moore & Meltzoff, 2008). Success at object search tasks coincides with rapid development of the frontal lobes of the cerebral cortex (Bell, 1998). Also crucial are a wide variety of experiences perceiving, acting on, and remembering objects.

MENTAL REPRESENTATION In Piaget's theory, before about 18 months, infants are unable to mentally represent experience. Yet 8- to 10-month-olds' ability to recall the location of hidden objects after delays of more than a minute, and 14-month-olds' recall after delays of a day or more, clearly indicate that babies construct mental representations of objects and their whereabouts (McDonough, 1999; Moore & Meltzoff, 2004). In studies of deferred imitation and problem solving, representational thought is evident even earlier. And toddlers make impressive strides in symbolic understanding, as their grasp of words and photos reveals.

Deferred and Inferred Imitation Piaget studied imitation by noting when his three children demonstrated it in their everyday behavior. Under these conditions, a great deal must be known about the infant's daily life to be sure that deferred imitation—which requires infants to represent a model's past behavior—has occurred.

Laboratory research reveals that deferred imitation is present at 6 weeks of age! Infants who watched an unfamiliar adult's facial expression imitated it when exposed to the same adult the next day (Meltzoff & Moore, 1994). As motor capacities improve, infants copy actions with objects. In one study, adults showed 6- and 9-month-olds a novel series of actions with a puppet: taking its glove off, shaking the glove to ring a bell inside, and replacing the glove. When tested a day later, infants who had seen the novel actions were far more likely to imitate them (see Figure 6.2). And when researchers paired a second, motionless puppet with the first puppet from 1 to 6 days before the demonstration, 6- to 9-month-olds generalized the actions to this new, very different-looking puppet (Barr, Marrott, & Rovee-Collier, 2003; Giles & Rovee-Collier, 2011). Even more impressive, after having seen Puppet A paired with B and

LOOK and LISTEN

Using an attractive toy and cloth, try several object-hiding tasks with 8- to 14-month-olds. Is their search behavior consistent with research findings?

COURTESY OF CAROLYN ROVEE-COLLIER

(a)   (b)

FIGURE 6.2 Testing infants for deferred imitation. After researchers performed a novel series of actions with a puppet, this 6-month-old imitated the actions a day later—(a) removing the glove; (b) shaking the glove to ring a bell inside. With age, gains in recall are evident in deferred imitation of others' behaviors over longer delays.

Puppet B paired with C on successive days, infants transferred modeled actions from A to C and from C to A, although they had not directly observed this pair together (Townsend & Rovee-Collier, 2007). Already, infants can form flexible mental representations that include chains of relevant associations.

Gains in recall, expressed through deferred imitation, are accompanied by changes in brain-wave activity during memory tasks, as measured by ERPs. This suggests that improvements in memory storage in the cerebral cortex contribute to these advances (Bauer et al., 2006). Between 12 and 18 months, toddlers use deferred imitation skillfully to enrich their range of schemes. They retain modeled behaviors for at least several months, copy the actions of peers as well as adults, and imitate across a change in context—for example, enact at home a behavior seen at child care (Meltzoff & Williamson, 2010; Patel, Gaylord, & Fagen, 2013). The ability to recall modeled behaviors in the order they occurred—evident as early as 6 months—also strengthens over the second year (Bauer, 2006; Rovee-Collier & Cuevas, 2009). And when babies imitate in correct sequence, they remember more behaviors (Knopf, Kraus, & Kressley-Mba, 2006).

Older infants and toddlers even imitate rationally, by *inferring* others' intentions! They are more likely to imitate purposeful than accidental or arbitrary behaviors on objects (Hamlin, Hallinan, & Woodward, 2008; Thoermer et al., 2013). And they adapt their imitative acts to a model's goals. If 12-month-olds see an adult perform an unusual action for fun (make a toy dog enter a miniature house by jumping through the chimney, even though its door is wide open), they copy the behavior. But if the adult engages in the odd behavior because she *must* (she makes the dog go through the chimney only after first trying to use the door and finding it locked), 12-month-olds typically imitate the more efficient action (putting the dog through the door) (Schwier et al., 2006).

Between 14 and 18 months, toddlers become increasingly adept at imitating actions an adult *tries* to produce, even if these are not fully realized (Bellagamba, Camaioni, & Colonnesi, 2006; Olineck & Poulin-Dubois, 2009). On one occasion, Ginette attempted to pour some raisins into a small bag but missed, spilling them onto the counter. A moment later, Grace began dropping the raisins into the bag, indicating that she had inferred Ginette's goal.

Though advanced in terms of Piaget's predictions, toddlers' ability to represent others' intentions—a cornerstone of social understanding and communication—has roots in earlier sensorimotor activity (Rosander & von Hofsten, 2011). Infants' skill at engaging in goal-directed actions—reaching for objects at 3 to 4 months, pointing to objects at 9 months—predicts their awareness of an adult's similar behavior as goal-directed (Gerson & Woodward, 2010; Woodward, 2009). And the better 10-month-olds are at detecting the goals of others' gazes and reaches, the more successful they are four months later at inferring an adult's intention from her incomplete actions in an imitation task (Olineck & Poulin-Dubois, 2009).

Problem Solving As Piaget indicated, around 8 months, infants develop intentional means–end action sequences, such as pulling on a cloth to obtain a toy resting on its far end (Willatts, 1999). Out of these explorations of object-to-object relations, the capacity for tool use in problem solving—flexibly manipulating an object as a means to a goal—emerges (Keen, 2011).

For example, 12-month-olds who were repeatedly presented with a spoon oriented so its handle pointed toward their preferred hand (usually the right) adapted their grip when the spoon's handle was presented in the opposite orientation (to the left). As a result, they succeeded in transporting food to their mouths most of the time (McCarty & Keen, 2005). With age, babies increasingly adjusted their grip to fit the spoon's orientation in advance, planning ahead for what they wanted to do with the tool.

By 10 to 12 months, infants can *solve problems by analogy*—apply a solution strategy from one problem to other relevant problems. In one study, babies of this age were given three similar problems, each requiring them to overcome a barrier, grasp a string, and pull it to get an attractive toy. The problems differed in many aspects of their superficial features—texture and color of the string, barrier, and floor mat and type of toy (horse, doll, or car). For the first problem, the parent demonstrated the solution and encouraged the infant to imitate (Chen, Sanchez, & Campbell, 1997). Babies obtained the toy more readily with each additional problem.

These findings suggest that around the end of the first year, infants form flexible mental representations of how to use tools to get objects. They have some ability to move beyond trial-and-error experimentation, represent a solution mentally, and use it in new contexts.

Symbolic Understanding One of the most momentous advances in early development is the realization that words can be used to cue mental images of things not physically present—a symbolic capacity called **displaced reference** that emerges around the first birthday. It greatly expands toddlers' capacity to learn about the world through communicating with others. Observations of 12-month-olds reveal that they respond to the label of an absent toy by looking at and gesturing toward the spot where it usually rests (Saylor, 2004). And on hearing the name of a parent or sibling who has just left the room, most 13-month-olds turn toward the door (DeLoache & Ganea, 2009). The more experience toddlers have with an object and its verbal label, the more likely they are to call up a mental representation when they hear the object's name. As memory and vocabulary improve, skill at displaced reference expands.

But at first, toddlers have difficulty using language to acquire new information about an absent object—an ability that is essential to learn from symbols. In one study, an adult taught 19- and 22-month-olds a name for a stuffed animal—"Lucy" for a frog. Then, with the frog out of sight, the toddler was told that some water had spilled, so "Lucy's all wet!" Finally, the adult showed the toddler three stuffed animals—a wet frog, a dry frog, and a pig—and said, "Get Lucy!" (Ganea et al., 2007). Although all the children remembered that Lucy was a frog, only the 22-month-olds identified the wet frog as Lucy. Nevertheless, older toddlers' reliance on verbal information is fragile. When a verbal message about a toy's new location conflicts with a previously observed location, most 23-month-olds simply go to the initial location. At 30 months, children succeed at finding the toy (Ganea & Harris, 2010). The capacity to use language as a flexible symbolic tool—to modify an existing mental representation—improves from the end of the second into the third year.

A beginning awareness of the symbolic function of pictures emerges in the first year, strengthening in the second. Even newborns perceive a relation between a picture and its referent, as indicated by their preference for looking at a photo of their mother's face (see page 193 in Chapter 5). And by 9 months and perhaps before, the majority of infants recognize that real objects can be grasped while pictures of objects cannot. Most touch, rub, or pat a color photo of an object but rarely try to grasp it (Ziemer, Plumert, & Pick, 2012). These behaviors suggest that 9-month-olds do not mistake a picture for the real thing, though they may not yet comprehend it as a symbol. Manual exploration of pictures declines after 9 months, becoming rare around 18 months (DeLoache & Ganea, 2009).

Around this time, toddlers clearly treat pictures symbolically, as long as pictures strongly resemble real objects. After hearing a novel label ("blicket") applied to a color photo of an unfamiliar object, most 15- to 24-month-olds—when presented with both the real object and its picture and asked to indicate the "blicket"—gave a symbolic response (Ganea et al., 2009). They selected either the real object or both the object and its picture, not the picture alone—a response that strengthened with age.

By the middle of the second year, toddlers often use pictures as vehicles for communicating with others and acquiring new knowledge. They point to, name, and talk about pictures, and they can apply something learned from a book with realistic-looking pictures to real objects, and vice versa (Ganea, Ma, & DeLoache, 2011; Simcock, Garrity, & Barr, 2011).

Picture-rich environments in which caregivers often direct babies' attention to the link between pictures and their referents facilitate pictorial understanding. In non-Western cultures where pictures are rare,

A 17-month-old points to a picture in a book, revealing her beginning awareness of the symbolic function of pictures. But pictures must be highly realistic for toddlers to treat them symbolically.

Social Issues: Education

Baby Learning from TV and Video: The Video Deficit Effect

Children first become TV and video viewers in early infancy, as they are exposed to programs watched by parents and older siblings or to shows aimed at viewers not yet out of diapers, such as the Baby Einstein products. About 40 percent of U.S. 3-month-olds watch regularly, a figure that rises to 90 percent at age 2. During this period, average viewing time increases from just under an hour to 1½ hours a day (Zimmerman, Christakis, & Meltzoff, 2007). Although parents assume that babies learn from TV and videos, research indicates that they cannot take full advantage of them.

Initially, infants respond to videos of people as if viewing people directly—smiling, moving their arms and legs, and (by 6 months) imitating actions of a televised adult (Barr, Muentener, & Garcia, 2007; Marian, Neisser, & Rochat, 1996). But when shown videos of attractive toys, 9-month-olds touch and grab at the screen, suggesting that they confuse the images with the real thing. By the middle of the second year, manual exploration has declined in favor of pointing at the images (Pierroutsakos & Troseth, 2003). Nevertheless, toddlers have difficulty applying what they see on video to real situations.

In a series of studies, some 2-year-olds watched through a window while a live adult hid an object in an adjoining room, while others watched the same event on a video screen. Children in the direct viewing condition retrieved the toy easily; those in the video condition had difficulty (Troseth, 2003; Troseth & DeLoache, 1998). This **video deficit effect**—poorer performance after a video than a live demonstration—has also been found for 2-year-olds' deferred imitation, word learning, and means–end problem solving (Bellagamba et al., 2012; Hayne, Herbert, & Simcock, 2003; Krcmar, Grela, & Linn, 2007).

One explanation is that 2-year-olds typically do not view a video character as offering socially relevant information. After an adult on video announced where she had hidden a toy, few 2-year-olds searched (Schmidt, Crawley-Davis, & Anderson, 2007). In contrast, when the adult uttered the same words while standing in front of the child, 2-year-olds promptly retrieved the object.

Toddlers seem to discount information on video as relevant to their everyday experiences because the people onscreen do not look at and converse with them directly or establish a shared focus on objects, as their caregivers do. In one study, researchers gave some 2-year-olds an interactive video experience (using a two-way, closed-circuit video system). An adult on video interacted with the child for five minutes—calling the child by name, talking about the child's siblings and pets, waiting for the child to respond, and playing interactive games (Troseth, Saylor, & Archer, 2006). Compared with 2-year-olds who viewed the same adult in a noninteractive video, those in the interactive condition were far more successful in using a verbal cue from a person on video to retrieve a toy.

Around age 2½, the video deficit effect declines. Before this age, the American Academy of Pediatrics (2001) recommends against mass media exposure, emphasizing that babies require rich responsive exchanges with caregivers and exploration of their physical surroundings for optimal brain growth and psychological development (see Chapter 5, page 169). In support of

A 2-year-old looks puzzled by a video image. Perhaps she has difficulty grasping its meaning because onscreen characters do not converse with her directly, as adults in real life do.

this advice, amount of TV viewing is negatively related to 8- to 18-month-olds' language progress (Tanimura et al., 2004; Zimmerman, Christakis, & Meltzoff, 2007). And 1- to 3-year-old heavy viewers tend to have attention, memory, and reading difficulties in the early school years (Christakis et al., 2004; Zimmerman & Christakis, 2005).

Toddlers face a complex task in making sense of video: Although they no longer confuse it with reality, they do not know how to mentally represent the relationship between video images and real objects and people. When they do watch TV or video, it is likely to work best as teaching tools when it is rich in social cues (Lauricella et al., 2011). These include use of familiar characters and close-ups in which the character looks directly at the camera, addresses questions to viewers, and pauses to invite a response.

---

symbolic understanding of pictures is delayed (Callaghan et al., 2011). In a study carried out in a village community in Tanzania, Africa, where children receive no exposure to pictures before school entry, an adult taught 1½- to 3-year-olds a new name for an unfamiliar object during a picture-book interaction (Walker, Walker, & Ganea, 2012). When later asked to pick the named object from arrays of pictures and real objects, not until age 3 did the Tanzanian children's performance equal that of U.S. 15-month-olds.

But even after coming to appreciate the symbolic nature of pictures, young children continue to have difficulty grasping the distinction between some pictures (such as line drawings) and their referents, as we will see in Chapter 8. How do infants and toddlers interpret another ever-present, pictorial medium—video? See the Social Issues: Education box above to find out.

Evaluation of the Sensorimotor Stage

Table 6.2 summarizes the remarkable cognitive attainments we have just considered. **TAKE A MOMENT...** Compare this table with Piaget's description of the sensorimotor substages in Table 6.1 on page 203. You will see that infants anticipate events, actively search for hidden objects, master the A–B object search, flexibly vary their sensorimotor schemes, engage in make-believe play, and treat pictures and video images symbolically within Piaget's time frame. Yet other capacities—including secondary circular reactions, understanding of object properties, first signs of object permanence, deferred imitation, problem solving by analogy, and displaced reference of words—emerge earlier than Piaget expected. These findings show that the cognitive attainments of infancy and toddlerhood do not develop together in the neat, stepwise fashion that Piaget predicted.

Recent research raises questions about Piaget's view of how infant development takes place. Consistent with Piaget's ideas, sensorimotor action helps infants construct some forms of knowledge. For example, as we saw in Chapter 5, crawling enhances depth perception and ability to find hidden objects, and handling objects fosters awareness of object properties. Yet we have also seen that infants comprehend a great deal before they are capable of the motor behaviors that Piaget assumed led to those understandings. How can we account for babies' amazing cognitive accomplishments?

ALTERNATIVE EXPLANATIONS Unlike Piaget, who thought babies constructed all mental representations out of sensorimotor activity, most researchers now believe that infants have some built-in cognitive equipment for making sense of experience. But intense disagreement exists over the extent of this initial understanding. As we have seen, much evidence on young infants' cognition rests on the violation-of-expectation method. Researchers who lack confidence in this method argue that babies' cognitive starting point is limited (Campos et al., 2008; Cohen, 2010; Kagan, 2008, 2013c). For example, some believe that newborns begin life with a set of biases for attending to certain information and with general-purpose learning procedures—such as powerful techniques for analyzing complex perceptual information (Bahrick, 2010; Huttenlocher, 2002; Quinn, 2008; Rakison, 2010). Together, these capacities enable infants to construct a wide variety of schemes.

Others, convinced by violation-of-expectation findings, believe that infants start out with impressive understandings. According to this **core knowledge perspective,** babies are born

TABLE 6.2	Some Cognitive Attainments of Infancy and Toddlerhood
AGE	**COGNITIVE ATTAINMENTS**
Birth–1 month	Secondary circular reactions using limited motor skills, such as sucking a nipple to gain access to interesting sights and sounds
1–4 months	Awareness of object permanence, object solidity, and gravity, as suggested by violation-of-expectation findings; deferred imitation of an adult's facial expression over a short delay (one day)
4–8 months	Improved knowledge of object properties and basic numerical knowledge, as suggested by violation-of-expectation findings; deferred imitation of an adult's novel actions on objects over a short delay (one to three days)
8–12 months	Ability to search for a hidden object when covered by a cloth; ability to solve simple problems by analogy to a previous problem
12–18 months	Ability to search in several locations for a hidden object (accurate A–B search); awareness that objects continue to exist in their hidden locations even after the toddler has left the location; deferred imitation of an adult's novel actions on objects after long delays (at least several months) and across a change in situation (from child care to home); rational imitation, inferring the model's intentions; displaced reference of words
18 months–2 years	Ability to find an object moved while out of sight (invisible displacement); deferred imitation of actions an adult tries to produce, even if these are not fully realized; deferred imitation of everyday behaviors in make-believe play; beginning awareness of pictures and video as symbols of reality

TAKE A MOMENT... Which of the capacities listed in this table indicate that mental representation emerges earlier than Piaget believed?

© EDITH HELD/CORBIS

Did this toddler learn to build a block tower by repeatedly acting on objects, as Piaget assumed? Or did he begin life with innate knowledge that helps him understand objects and their relationships quickly, with little hands-on exploration?

with a set of innate knowledge systems, or *core domains of thought.* Each of these prewired understandings permits a ready grasp of new, related information and therefore supports early, rapid development (Carey & Markman, 1999; Leslie, 2004; Spelke & Kinzler, 2007). Core knowledge theorists argue that infants could not make sense of the complex stimulation around them without having been genetically "set up" in the course of evolution to comprehend its crucial aspects.

Researchers have conducted many studies of infants' *physical knowledge,* including object permanence, object solidity (that one object cannot move through another), and gravity (that an object will fall without support). Violation-of-expectation findings suggest that in the first few months, infants have some awareness of all these basic object properties and quickly build on this knowledge (Baillargeon et al., 2009, 2011). Core knowledge theorists also assume that an inherited foundation of *linguistic knowledge* enables swift language acquisition in early childhood—a possibility we will consider later in this chapter. Further, these theorists argue, infants' early orientation toward people initiates rapid development of *psychological knowledge*—in particular, understanding of mental states, such as intentions, emotions, desires, and beliefs, which we will address further in Chapter 7.

Research also suggests that infants have basic *numerical knowledge.* In the best-known study, 5-month-olds saw a screen raised to hide a single toy animal and then watched a hand place a second toy behind the screen. Finally, the screen was removed to reveal either one or two toys. If infants kept track of the two objects (requiring them to add one object to another), then they should look longer at the unexpected, one-toy display—which is what they did (see Figure 6.3)

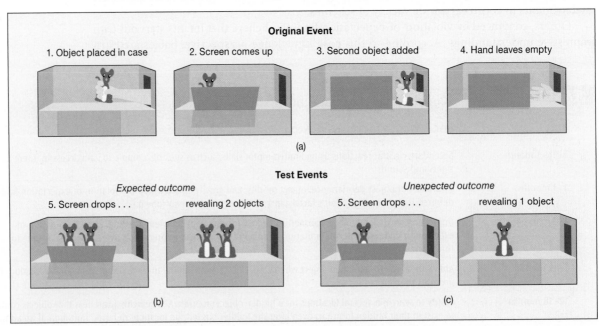

FIGURE 6.3 **Testing infants for basic number concepts.** (a) First, infants saw a screen raised in front of a toy animal. Then an identical toy was added behind the screen. Next, the researchers presented two outcomes. (b) In the *expected outcome,* the screen dropped to reveal two toy animals. (c) In the *unexpected outcome,* the screen dropped to reveal one toy animal. Five-month-olds shown the unexpected outcome looked longer than 5-month-olds shown the expected outcome. The researchers concluded that infants can discriminate the quantities "one" and "two" and use that knowledge to perform simple addition: 1 + 1 = 2. A variation of this procedure suggested that 5-month-olds could also do simple subtraction: 2 − 1 = 1. (From K. Wynn, 1992, "Addition and Subtraction by Human Infants," *Nature, 358,* p. 749. © 1992, Nature Publishing Group. Reprinted by permission from Macmillan Publishers Ltd.)

(Wynn, 1992). These findings and others suggest that babies can discriminate quantities up to three and use that knowledge to perform simple arithmetic—both addition and subtraction (in which two objects are covered and one is removed) (Kobayashi, Hiraki, & Hasegawa, 2005; Kobayashi et al., 2004; Wynn, Bloom, & Chiang, 2002). As further support, ERP brain-wave recordings taken while babies view correct and incorrect simple arithmetic solutions reveal a response pattern identical to the pattern adults show when detecting errors (Berger, Tzur, & Posner, 2006).

Additional evidence suggests that 6-month-olds can distinguish among large sets of items, as long as the difference between those sets is very great—at least a factor of two. For example, they can tell the difference between 8 and 16 dots but not between 8 and 12. At 9 months, babies can discriminate 8 and 12 but not 8 and 10 (Lipton & Spelke, 2003; Xu, Spelke, & Goddard, 2005). Furthermore, research resembling the experiment in Figure 6.3 reveals that 9-month-olds can perform operations on large sets of items, adding and subtracting (McCrink & Wynn, 2004). And by the middle of the first year, babies show distinct ERP brain-wave patterns like those of adults when processing large sets of items (Hyde & Spelke, 2011). As a result, some researchers believe that infants can represent approximate large-number values, and that processing of large-item and small-item sets is governed by different neural networks.

These impressive findings suggest that certain notions of quantity are present in the first year. But like other violation-of-expectation results, the evidence is controversial. Skeptics question whether other aspects of object displays, rather than numerical sensitivity, are responsible for the findings (Cohen & Marks, 2002; Langer, Gillette, & Arriaga, 2003). According to these investigators, claims for infants' knowledge of number concepts are surprising, in view of other research indicating that before 14 to 16 months, toddlers have difficulty making less-than and greater-than comparisons between small sets. And, as we will see in Chapter 9, not until the preschool years do children add and subtract small sets correctly.

Furthermore, critics take issue with the core knowledge assumption, based on violation-of-expectation findings, that infants are endowed with *knowledge* (Bremner, 2010; Cohen, 2009). They argue that young infants' looking behaviors may indicate only a perceptual preference, not the existence of concepts and reasoning. And indisputable evidence for built-in core knowledge requires that it be demonstrated at birth or close to it—in the absence of relevant opportunities to learn (Johnson, 2010). Although tentative support for distinct systems for processing small and large numerical values in newborns has been reported, contrary findings also exist (Coubart et al., 2014; Izard, Dehaene-Lambertz, & Dehaene, 2008; Izard et al., 2009). Thus, much more research is needed.

Finally, the core knowledge perspective, while emphasizing native endowment, acknowledges that experience is essential for children to extend this initial knowledge. But so far, it has said little about which experiences are most important in each core domain and how those experiences advance children's thinking. Despite challenges from critics, core knowledge research has sharpened the field's focus on clarifying the starting point for human cognition and on carefully tracking the changes that build on it.

PIAGET'S LEGACY Follow-up research on Piaget's sensorimotor stage yields broad agreement on two issues. First, many cognitive changes of infancy are gradual and continuous rather than abrupt and stagelike, as Piaget thought (Bjorklund, 2012). Second, rather than developing together, various aspects of infant cognition change unevenly because of the challenges posed by different types of tasks and infants' varying experiences with them. These ideas serve as the basis for another major approach to cognitive development—*information processing*—which we take up next.

Before we turn to this alternative point of view, let's recognize Piaget's enormous contributions. Piaget's work inspired a wealth of research on infant cognition, including studies that challenged his theory. Today, researchers are far from consensus on how to modify or replace his account of infant cognitive development, and some believe that his general approach continues to make sense and fits most of the evidence (Cohen, 2010). Piaget's observations also have been of great practical value. Teachers and caregivers continue to look to the sensorimotor stage for guidelines on how to create developmentally appropriate environments for infants and toddlers.

Applying What We Know

Play Materials That Support Infant and Toddler Cognitive Development

FROM 2 MONTHS	FROM 6 MONTHS	FROM 1 YEAR
Crib mobile	Squeeze toys	Large dolls, toy dishes, toy telephone
Rattles and other handheld sound-making toys, such as a bell on a handle	Nesting cups	Cars and trucks
	Clutch and texture balls	Large blocks, cardboard boxes
Adult-operated music boxes and music recordings with gentle, regular rhythms, songs, and lullabies	Stuffed animals and soft-bodied dolls	Hammer-and-peg toy
	Filling and emptying toys	Pull and push toys, riding toys that can be pushed with feet
	Large and small blocks	Rhythm instruments for shaking and banging, such as bells, cymbals, and drums
	Pots, pans, and spoons from the kitchen	Simple puzzles
	Simple, floating objects for the bath	Sandbox, shovel, and pail
	Picture books with realistic color images	Shallow wading pool and water toys
		Balls of various sizes

TAKE A MOMENT... Now that you are familiar with some milestones of the first two years, what play materials do you think would support the development of sensorimotor and early representational schemes? Prepare a list, justifying it by referring to the cognitive attainments described in the previous sections. Then compare your suggestions to the ones given in Applying What We Know above.

Ask Yourself

- **REVIEW** Using the text discussion on pages 203–210, construct your own summary table of infant and toddler cognitive development. Which entries in your table are consistent with Piaget's sensorimotor stage? Which ones develop earlier than Piaget anticipated?

- **CONNECT** Recall from Chapter 5 (pages 195–196) that around the middle of the first year, infants identify objects by their features and by their paths of movement, even when they cannot observe the entire path. How might these attainments contribute to infants' understanding of object permanence?

- **APPLY** Several times, after her father hid a teething biscuit under a red cup, 12-month-old Mimi retrieved it easily. Then Mimi's father hid the biscuit under a nearby yellow cup. Why did Mimi persist in searching for it under the red cup?

- **REFLECT** What advice would you give the typical U.S. parent about permitting an infant or toddler to watch as much as 1 to 1½ hours of TV or video per day? Explain.

6.4 Describe the information-processing view of cognitive development and the general structure of the information-processing system.

6.5 What changes in attention, memory, and categorization take place over the first two years?

6.6 Describe the strengths and limitations of the information-processing approach to early cognitive development.

Information Processing

Information-processing researchers agree with Piaget that children are active, inquiring beings. But instead of providing a single, unified theory of cognitive development, they focus on many aspects of thinking, from attention, memory, and categorization skills to complex problem solving.

Recall from Chapter 1 that the information-processing approach frequently relies on computer-like flowcharts to describe the human cognitive system. Information-processing theorists are not satisfied with general concepts, such as assimilation and accommodation, to describe how children think. Instead, they want to know exactly what individuals of different ages do when faced with a task or problem (Birney & Sternberg, 2011). The computer model of human thinking is attractive because it is explicit and precise.

A General Model of Information Processing

Most information-processing researchers assume that we hold information in three parts of the mental system for processing: the *sensory register,* the *short-term memory store,* and the *long-term memory store* (see Figure 6.4). As information flows through each, we can use *mental strategies* to operate on and transform it, increasing the chances that we will retain the information, use it efficiently, and think flexibly, adapting it to changing circumstances. To understand this more clearly, let's look at each aspect of the mental system.

First, information enters the **sensory register**, where sights and sounds are represented directly and stored briefly. **TAKE A MOMENT...** Look around you, and then close your eyes. An image of what you saw persists for a few seconds, but then it decays, or disappears, unless you use mental strategies to preserve it. For example, by *attending to* some information more carefully than to other information, you increase the chances that it will transfer to the next step of the information-processing system.

In the second part of the mind, the **short-term memory store**, we retain attended-to information briefly so we can actively "work" on it to reach our goals. One way of looking at the short-term store is in terms of its *basic capacity,* often referred to as *short-term memory:* how many pieces of information can be held at once for a few seconds. But most researchers endorse a contemporary view of the short-term store, which offers a more meaningful indicator of its capacity, called **working memory**—the number of items that can be briefly held in mind while also engaging in some effort to monitor or manipulate those items. Working memory can be thought of as a "mental workspace" that we use to accomplish many activities in daily life. From childhood on, researchers assess changes in its capacity by presenting individuals with lists of items (such as numerical digits or short sentences), asking them to "work on" the items (for example, repeat the digits backward or remember the final word of each sentence in correct order), and seeing how well they do.

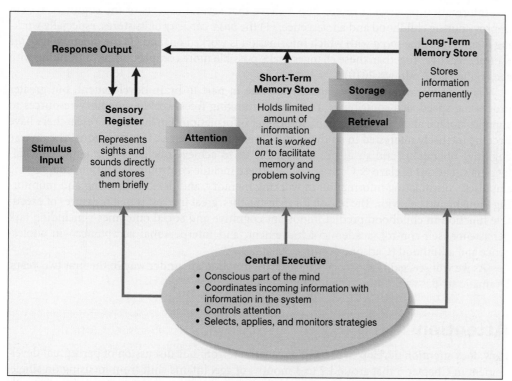

FIGURE 6.4 **Model of the human information-processing system.** Information flows through three parts of the mental system: the *sensory register,* the *short-term memory store,* and the *long-term memory store.* In each, mental strategies can be used to manipulate information, increasing the efficiency and flexibility of thinking and the chances that information will be retained. The *central executive* is the conscious, reflective part of working memory. It coordinates incoming information already in the system, decides what to attend to, and oversees the use of strategies.

The sensory register can take in a wide panorama of information. Short-term and working memory are far more restricted, though their capacity increases steadily from early childhood through adolescence—on a verbatim digit-span task tapping short-term memory, from about 2 to 7 items; and on working-memory tasks, from about 2 to 5 items (Cowan & Alloway, 2009). Still, individual differences are evident at all ages. By engaging in a variety of basic cognitive procedures, such as focusing attention on relevant items and repeating (rehearsing) them rapidly, we increase the chances that information will be retained and accessible to ongoing thinking.

To manage the cognitive system's complex activities, the **central executive** directs the flow of information, implementing the basic procedures just mentioned and also engaging in more sophisticated activities that enable complex, flexible thinking. For example, the central executive coordinates incoming information with information already in the system, and it selects, applies, and monitors strategies that facilitate memory storage, comprehension, reasoning, and problem solving (Pressley & Hilden, 2006). The central executive is the conscious, reflective part of our mental system. It ensures that we think purposefully, to attain our goals.

The more effectively the central executive joins with working memory to process information, the better learned cognitive activities will be and the more *automatically* we can apply them. Consider the richness of your thinking while you automatically drive a car. **Automatic processes** are so well-learned that they require no space in working memory and, therefore, permit us to focus on other information while performing them. Furthermore, the more effectively we process information in working memory, the more likely it will transfer to the third, and largest, storage area—**long-term memory**, our permanent knowledge base, which is unlimited. In fact, we store so much in long-term memory that *retrieval*—getting information back from the system—can be problematic. To aid retrieval, we apply strategies, just as we do in working memory. Information in long-term memory is *categorized* by its contents, much like a library shelving system that enables us to retrieve items by following the same network of associations used to store them in the first place.

Information-processing researchers believe that several aspects of the cognitive system improve during childhood and adolescence: (1) the *basic capacity* of its stores, especially working memory; (2) the *speed* with which information is worked on; and (3) the *functioning of the central executive*. Together, these changes make possible more complex forms of thinking with age (Halford & Andrews, 2010).

Gains in working-memory capacity are due in part to brain development, but greater processing speed also contributes. Fast, fluent thinking frees working-memory resources to support storage and manipulation of additional information. Furthermore, researchers have become intensely interested in studying the development of **executive function**—the diverse cognitive operations and strategies that enable us to achieve our goals in cognitively challenging situations (Zelazo & Carlson, 2012). These include controlling attention, suppressing impulses, coordinating information in working memory, and flexibly directing and monitoring thought and behavior. The reason for investigators' great interest is that measures of executive function in childhood predict important cognitive and social outcomes—including task persistence, self-control, academic achievement, and interpersonal acceptance—in adolescence and adulthood (Carlson, Zelazo, & Faja, 2013).

As we will see, gains in aspects of executive function are under way in the first two years. Dramatic strides will follow in childhood and adolescence.

Attention

How does attention develop in early infancy? Recall from our discussion of perceptual development in Chapter 5 that around 2 to 3 months of age, infants shift from focusing on single, high-contrast features to exploring objects and patterns more thoroughly. Besides attending to more aspects of the environment, infants gradually become more efficient at managing their attention, taking in information more quickly. Habituation research reveals that preterm and newborn babies require a long time—about 3 to 4 minutes—to habituate and recover to novel visual stimuli. But by 4 or 5 months, they need as little as 5 to 10 seconds to take in a complex visual stimulus and recognize it as different from a previous one (Colombo, Kapa, & Curtindale, 2011; Rose, Feldman, & Jankowski, 2001b).

One reason that very young babies' habituation times are so much longer is that they have difficulty disengaging attention from a stimulus (Colombo, 2002). When Carolyn held up a colorful rattle, 2-month-old Caitlin stared intently until, unable to break her gaze, she burst into tears. The ability to shift attention from one stimulus to another improves by 4 months—a change believed to be due to development of structures in the cerebral cortex controlling eye movements (Posner & Rothbart, 2007a).

Over the first year, infants attend to novel and eye-catching events. In the second year, as toddlers become increasingly capable of intentional behavior (refer back to Piaget's Substage 4), attraction to novelty declines (but does not disappear) and *sustained attention* improves, especially when children play with toys. A toddler who engages even in simple goal-directed behavior, such as stacking blocks or putting them in a container, must sustain attention to reach the goal (Ruff & Capozzoli, 2003). As plans and activities gradually become more complex, the duration of attention increases.

Adults can foster sustained attention by encouraging babies' current interest ("Oh, you like that bell!") and prompting the child to stay focused ("See, it makes a noise!"). Consistently helping infants focus attention at 10 months predicts higher intelligence test scores at 18 months (Bono & Stifter, 2003). Also, infants and toddlers gradually become more interested in what others are attending to. Later we will see that this joint attention between caregiver and child is important for language development.

By encouraging her toddler's goal-directed play, this mother promotes sustained attention.

Memory

Methods devised to assess infants' short-term memory, which require keeping in mind an increasingly longer sequence of very briefly presented visual stimuli, reveal that retention increases from 1 item at age 6 months to 2 to 4 items at 12 months (Rose, Feldman, & Janowski, 2001b; Ross-Sheehy, Oakes, & Luck, 2003). Operant conditioning and habituation techniques, which grant babies more extended time to process information, provide windows into early long-term memory. Both methods show that retention of visual events improves greatly with age.

OPERANT CONDITIONING RESEARCH   Using operant conditioning, researchers study infant memory by teaching 2- to 6-month-olds to move a mobile by kicking a foot tied to it with a long cord. Two-month-olds remember how to activate the mobile for 1 to 2 days after training, and 3-month-olds for one week. By 6 months, memory increases to two weeks (Rovee-Collier, 1999; Rovee-Collier & Bhatt, 1993). Around the middle of the first year, babies can manipulate switches or buttons to control stimulation. When 6- to 18-month-olds pressed a lever to make a toy train move around a track, duration of memory continued to increase with age; 13 weeks after training, 18-month-olds still remembered how to press the lever (Hartshorn et al., 1998b). Figure 6.5 on page 218 shows this dramatic rise in retention of operant responses over the first year and a half.

Even after 2- to 6-month-olds forget an operant response, they need only a brief prompt—an adult who shakes the mobile—to reinstate the memory (Hildreth & Rovee-Collier, 2002). And when 6-month-olds are given a chance to reactivate the response themselves for just a couple of minutes—

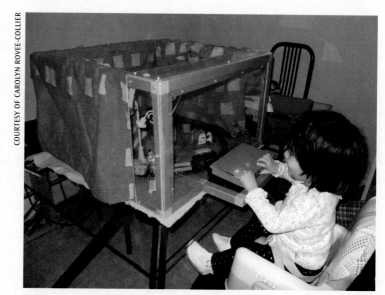

Memory for operant responses improves dramatically over the first 18 months. This 12-month-old has learned to press a lever to make a toy train move around a track—an operant response she is likely to remember when reexposed to the task many weeks later.

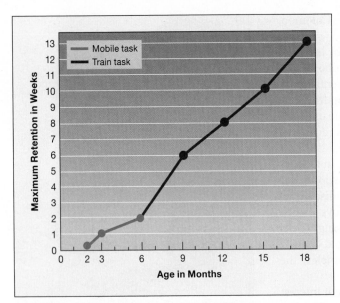

FIGURE 6.5 **Increase in retention in two operant conditioning tasks from 2 to 18 months.** Two- to 6-month-olds were trained to make a kicking response that turned a mobile. Six- to 18-month-olds were trained to press a lever that made a toy train move around a track. Six-month-olds learned both responses and retained them for an identical length of time, indicating that the tasks are comparable. Consequently, researchers could plot a single line of gains in retention from 2 to 18 months. The line shows that memory improves dramatically. (From C. Rovee-Collier & R. Barr, 2001, "Infant Learning and Memory," in G. Bremner & A. Fogel [Eds.], *Blackwell Handbook of Infant Development*, Oxford, U.K.: Blackwell, p. 150. © 2001, 2004 by Blackwell Publishing Ltd. Republished with permission of John Wiley & Sons Ltd. conveyed through Copyright Clearance Center, Inc.)

jiggling the mobile by kicking or moving the train by lever-pressing—their memory not only returns but also extends dramatically, to about 17 weeks (Hildreth, Sweeney, & Rovee-Collier, 2003). Perhaps permitting the baby to generate the previously learned behavior strengthens memory because it reexposes the child to more aspects of the original learning situation. Furthermore, with just five widely spaced adult-provided reminders of the train task extending over 1½ years, babies trained at age 6 months still remembered the response after reaching their second birthday (Hartshorn, 2003).

At first, infants' memory for operant responses is highly *context-dependent*. If 2- to 6-month-olds are not tested in the same situation in which they were trained—with the same mobile and crib bumper and in the same room—they remember poorly (Hayne, 2004). After 9 months, the importance of context declines. Older infants and toddlers remember how to make the toy train move even when its features are altered and testing takes place in a different room (Hartshorn et al., 1998a; Learmonth, Lamberth, & Rovee-Collier, 2004). Crawling is strongly associated with 9-month-olds' formation of an increasingly context-free memory (Herbert, Gross, & Hayne, 2007). As babies move on their own and experience frequent changes in context, they apply learned responses more flexibly, generalizing them to relevant new situations.

HABITUATION RESEARCH   Habituation studies show that infants learn and retain a wide variety of information just by watching objects and events, without being physically active. Sometimes they do so for much longer time spans than in operant conditioning studies. Babies are especially attentive to the movements of objects and people. In one investigation, 5½-month-olds remembered a woman's captivating action (such as blowing bubbles or brushing hair) seven weeks later, as indicated by a *familiarity preference* (see page 179 in Chapter 5) (Bahrick, Gogate, & Ruiz, 2002). The babies were so attentive to the woman's action that they did not remember her face, even when tested 1 minute later for a *novelty preference*.

In Chapter 5, we saw that 3- to 5-month-olds are excellent at discriminating faces. But their memory for the faces of unfamiliar people and for other visual patterns is short-lived—at 3 months, only about 24 hours; at the end of the first year, several days to a few weeks (Fagan, 1973; Pascalis, de Haan, & Nelson, 1998). By contrast, 3-month-olds' memory for the unusual movements of objects (such as a metal nut swinging on the end of a string) persists for at least three months (Bahrick, Hernandez-Reif, & Pickens, 1997).

By 10 to 12 months, infants remember both novel actions and features of objects involved in those actions equally well (Baumgartner & Oakes, 2011). Thus, over the second half-year, sensitivity to object appearance increases. This change, as noted earlier, is fostered by infants' increasing ability to manipulate objects, which helps them learn about objects' observable properties.

Habituation research confirms that infants need not be physically active to acquire new information. Nevertheless, as illustrated by research presented in Chapter 5 on the facilitating role of crawling in finding hidden objects (see page 191), motor activity does promote certain aspects of learning and memory.

RECALL MEMORY   So far, we have discussed only **recognition**—noticing when a stimulus is identical or similar to one previously experienced. It is the simplest form of memory: All babies have to do is indicate (by kicking, pressing a lever, or looking) whether a new experience is identical or similar to a previous one. **Recall** is more challenging because it involves remembering something not present. To recall, you must generate a mental image of the past experience. Can infants engage in recall? By the middle of the first year, they can, as indicated by their ability to find hidden objects and engage in deferred imitation.

Recall memory improves steadily with age. For example, 1-year-olds can retain short sequences of adult-modeled behaviors for up to 3 months, and 1½–year-olds can do so for as long as 12 months. The ability to recall modeled behaviors in the order in which the actions occurred—evident as early as 6 months—strengthens over the second year (Bauer, Larkina, & Deocampo, 2011; Rovee-Collier & Cuevas, 2009). And when toddlers imitate in correct sequence, processing not just separate actions but relations between actions, they remember more (Knopf, Kraus, & Kressley-Mba, 2006).

Long-term recall depends on connections among multiple regions of the cerebral cortex, especially with the prefrontal cortex. During infancy and toddlerhood, these neural circuits develop rapidly (Nelson, Thomas, & de Haan, 2006). The evidence as a whole indicates that infants' memory processing is remarkably similar to that of older children and adults: Babies have distinct short-term and long-term memories and display both recognition and recall. And they acquire information quickly, retain it over time, and apply it flexibly, doing so more effectively with age (Bauer, 2009; Rose et al., 2011). Furthermore, recall assessed through deferred imitation tasks at age 20 months predicts performance on memory tests at age 6, suggesting continuity of memory functions over time (Riggins et al., 2013). Yet a puzzling finding is that older children and adults no longer recall their earliest experiences! See the Biology and Environment box on page 220 for a discussion of *infantile amnesia.*

Categorization

Even young infants can *categorize,* grouping similar objects and events into a single representation. Categorization reduces the enormous amount of new information infants encounter every day, helping them learn and remember (Rakison, 2010).

Creative variations of operant conditioning research with mobiles have been used to find out about infant categorization. One such study, of 3-month-olds, is described and illustrated in Figure 6.6. Similar investigations reveal that in the first few months, babies categorize stimuli on the basis of shape, size, and other physical properties (Wasserman & Rovee-Collier, 2001). By 6 months of age, they can categorize on the basis of two correlated features—for example, the shape and color of an alphabet letter (Bhatt et al., 2004). This ability to categorize using clusters of features prepares babies for acquiring many complex everyday categories.

Habituation has also been used to study infant categorization. Researchers show babies a series of pictures belonging to one category and then see whether they recover to (look longer at) a picture that is not a member of the category (see Figure 6.8 on page 221). Findings reveal that in the second half of the first year, infants group familiar objects into an impressive array of categories—food items, furniture, birds, land animals, air animals, sea animals, plants, vehicles, kitchen utensils, and spatial location ("above" and "below," "on" and "in") (Bornstein, Arterberry, & Mash, 2010; Casasola & Park, 2013; Oakes, Coppage, & Dingel, 1997). Besides organizing the physical world, infants of this age categorize their emotional and social worlds. They sort people and their voices by gender and age, have begun to distinguish emotional expressions, can separate people's natural actions (walking) from other motions, and expect people (but not inanimate objects) to move spontaneously (Spelke, Phillips, & Woodward, 1995; see also Chapter 5, pages 192–193).

Babies' earliest categories are based on similar overall appearance or prominent object parts: legs for animals, wheels for vehicles. But as infants approach their first birthday, more categories appear to be based on subtle sets of features (Cohen, 2003; Mandler, 2004; Quinn, 2008). Older infants can even make categorical distinctions when the perceptual contrast between two categories is minimal (birds versus airplanes).

COURTESY OF CAROLYN ROVEE-COLLIER

FIGURE 6.6 **Investigating infant categorization using operant conditioning.** Three-month-olds were taught to kick to move a mobile that was made of small blocks, all with the letter *A* on them. After a delay, kicking returned to a high level only if the babies were shown a mobile whose blocks were labeled with the same form (the letter *A*). If the form was changed (from *A*s to *2*s), infants no longer kicked vigorously. While making the mobile move, the babies had grouped together its features. They associated the kicking response with the category *A* and, at later testing, distinguished it from the category *2*. (Bhatt, Rovee-Collier, & Weiner, 1994; Hayne, Rovee-Collier, & Perris, 1987)

Biology and Environment

Infantile Amnesia

If infants and toddlers remember many aspects of their everyday lives, how do we explain **infantile amnesia**—that most of us cannot retrieve events that happened to us before age 3? The reason cannot be merely the passage of time because we can recall many personally meaningful one-time events from both the recent and the distant past: the day a sibling was born or a move to a new house—recollections known as **autobiographical memory.**

Several explanations of infantile amnesia exist. One theory credits brain development, pointing to the *hippocampus* (located just under the temporal lobes), which plays a vital role in the formation of new memories. Though its overall structure is formed prenatally, the hippocampus continues to add new neurons well after birth. Integrating those neurons into existing neural circuits is believed to disrupt already stored early memories (Josselyn & Frankland, 2012). In support of this view, the decline in production of hippocampal neurons—in monkeys and rats as well as in humans—coincides with the ability to form stable, long-term memories of unique experiences.

Another conjecture is that older children and adults often use verbal means for storing information, whereas infants' and toddlers' memory processing is largely nonverbal—an incompatibility that may prevent long-term retention of early experiences. To test this idea, researchers sent two adults to the homes of 2- to 4-year-olds with an unusual toy that the children were likely to remember: The Magic Shrinking Machine, shown in Figure 6.7. One adult showed the child how, after inserting an object in an opening on top of the machine and turning a crank that activated flashing lights and musical sounds, the child could retrieve a smaller, identical object (discreetly dropped down a chute by the second adult) from behind a door on the front of the machine.

A day later, the researchers tested the children to see how well they recalled the event. Their nonverbal memory—based on acting out the "shrinking" event and recognizing the "shrunken" objects in photos—was excellent. But even when they had the vocabulary, children younger than age 3 had trouble describing features of the "shrinking" experience. Verbal recall increased sharply between ages 3 and 4—the period during which children "scramble over the amnesia barrier" (Simcock & Hayne, 2003, p. 813). In a follow-up study, which assessed verbal recall 6 years later, only 19 percent—including two children who were younger than age 3— remembered the "shrinking" event (Jack, Simcock, & Hayne, 2012). Those who recalled were more likely to have participated in conversations about the experience with a parent, which could have helped them gain verbal access to the memory.

These findings help us reconcile infants' and toddlers' remarkable memory skills with infantile amnesia. During the first few years, children rely heavily on nonverbal memory techniques, such as visual images and motor actions. As language develops, their ability to use it to refer to preverbal memories requires considerable support in translating the memory into words (Morris & Baker-Ward, 2007). Only after age 3 do children often represent events verbally. As children encode autobiographical events in verbal form, they use language-based cues to retrieve them, increasing the accessibility of memories at later ages (Peterson, Warren, & Short, 2011).

Other findings indicate that the advent of a clear self-image contributes to the end of infantile amnesia (Howe, Courage, & Rooksby, 2009). Toddlers who were advanced in development of a sense of self demonstrated better verbal memories a year later while conversing about past events with their mothers (Harley & Reese, 1999).

Very likely, both neurological change and social experience contribute to the decline of infantile amnesia. Brain development and adult–child interaction may jointly foster self-awareness, language, and improved memory, which enable children to talk with adults about significant past experiences (Bauer, 2007). As a result, preschoolers begin to construct a long-lasting autobiographical narrative of their lives and enter into the history of their family and community.

(a)

(b)

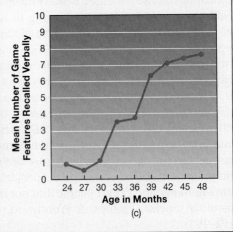
(c)

FIGURE 6.7 **The Magic Shrinking Machine, used to test young children's verbal and nonverbal memory of an unusual event.** After being shown how the machine worked, the child participated in selecting objects from a polka-dot bag, dropping them into the top of the machine (a), and turning a crank, which produced a "shrunken" object (b). When tested the next day, 2- to 4-year-olds' nonverbal memory for the event was excellent. But below 36 months, verbal recall was poor, based on the number of features recalled about the game during an open-ended interview (c). Recall improved between 36 and 48 months, the period during which infantile amnesia subsides. (From G. Simcock & H. Hayne, 2003, "Age-Related Changes in Verbal and Nonverbal Memory During Early Childhood," *Developmental Psychology, 39*, pp. 807, 809. Copyright © 2003 by the American Psychological Association. Reprinted by permission of the American Psychological Association.) *Photos:* Ross Coombes/Courtesy of Harlene Hayne.

As they gain experience in comparing to-be-categorized items in varied ways and their store of verbal labels expands, toddlers start to categorize flexibly: When 14-month-olds are given four balls and four blocks, some made of soft rubber and some of rigid plastic, their sequence of object touching reveals that after classifying by shape, they can switch to classifying by material (soft versus hard) if an adult calls their attention to the new basis for grouping (Ellis & Oakes, 2006).

In addition to touching and sorting, toddlers' categorization skills are evident in their play behaviors. After watching an adult give a toy dog a drink from a cup, most 14-month-olds shown a rabbit and a motorcycle offered the drink only to the rabbit (Mandler & McDonough, 1998). They clearly understood that certain actions are appropriate for some categories of items (animals) but not for others (vehicles).

By the end of the second year, toddlers' grasp of the animate–inanimate distinction expands. Nonlinear motions are typical of animates (a person or a dog jumping), linear motions of inanimates (a car or a table pushed along a surface). At 18 months, toddlers more often imitate a nonlinear motion with a toy that has animate-like parts (legs), even if it represents an inanimate (a bed). At 22 months, displaying a fuller understanding, they imitate a nonlinear motion only with toys in the animate category (a cat but not a bed) (Rakison, 2005). They seem to realize that whereas animates are self-propelled and therefore have varied paths of movement, inanimates move only when acted on, in highly restricted ways.

Researchers disagree on how babies arrive at these impressive attainments. One view holds that older infants and toddlers categorize more effectively because they become increasingly sensitive to fine-grained perceptual features and to stable relations among those features—for example, objects with flapping wings and feathers belong to one category; objects with rigid wings, windows, and a smooth surface belong to another category (Madole, Oakes, & Rakison, 2011; Schultz, 2011). An alternative view is that before the end of the first year, babies undergo a fundamental shift from a perceptual to a conceptual basis for constructing categories, increasingly grouping objects by their common function or behavior (birds versus airplanes, cars versus motorcycles, dogs versus cats) (Mandler, 2004; Träuble & Pauen, 2011).

But all acknowledge that exploration of objects and expanding knowledge of the world contribute (Mash & Bornstein, 2012). In addition, adult labeling of a set of objects with a consistently applied word ("Look at the car!" "Do you see the car?") calls babies' attention to commonalities among objects, fostering categorization as early as 3 to 4 months of age (Ferry, Hespos, & Waxman, 2010). Toddlers' vocabulary growth, in turn, promotes categorization by highlighting new categorical distinctions (Cohen & Brunt, 2009).

Variations among languages lead to cultural differences in development of categories. Korean toddlers, who learn a language in which object names are often omitted from sentences, develop object-sorting skills later than their English-speaking counterparts (Gopnik & Choi, 1990). At the same time, Korean contains a common word, *kkita*, with no English equivalent, referring to a tight fit between objects in contact (a ring on a finger, a cap on a pen). Hearing this label highlights the spatial category "tight-fit" for Korean toddlers, who are advanced in forming it (Choi et al., 1999). After English-speaking 18-month-olds heard the word *tight* while observing several instances of objects fitting together tightly, they readily acquired the tight-fit category (Casasola, Bhagwat, & Burke, 2009). Those who viewed the events without the label did not form the category.

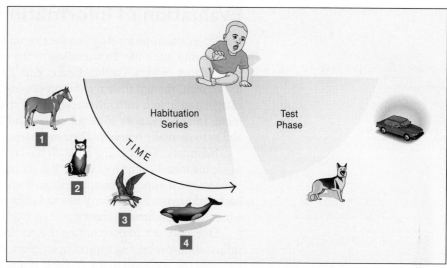

FIGURE 6.8 **Using habituation to study infant categorization.** After habituating to a series of items belonging to one category (in this example, animals), infants are shown two novel items, one that is a member of the category (dog) and one that is not (car). If infants recover to (look longer at or spend more time manipulating) the out-of-category item (car), this indicates that they distinguish it from the set of within-category items (animals). Habituating another group of infants to a series of vehicles and seeing if, when presented with the two test items above, they recover to the dog confirms that babies can distinguish animals from vehicles. This pattern of responding has been found in many infant categorization studies.

LOOK and LISTEN

Observe a toddler playing with a variety of small toys—some representing animals and some representing household objects. What play behaviors reveal the child's ability to categorize?

Evaluation of Information-Processing Findings

The information-processing perspective underscores the continuity of human thinking from infancy into adult life. In attending to the environment, remembering everyday events, and categorizing objects, Caitlin, Grace, and Timmy think in ways that are remarkably similar to our own, though their mental processing is far from proficient. Findings on memory and categorization join with other research in challenging Piaget's view of early cognitive development. Infants' capacity to recall events and to categorize stimuli attests, once again, to their ability to mentally represent their experiences.

Information-processing research has contributed greatly to our view of infants and toddlers as sophisticated cognitive beings. But its central strength—analyzing cognition into its components, such as perception, attention, memory, and categorization—is also its greatest drawback: Information processing has had difficulty putting these components back together into a broad, comprehensive theory.

One approach to overcoming this weakness has been to combine Piaget's theory with the information-processing approach, an effort we will explore in Chapter 12. A more recent trend has been the application of a *dynamic systems view* (see Chapter 1, page 29) to early cognition. In this approach, researchers analyze each cognitive attainment to see how it results from a complex system of prior accomplishments and the child's current goals (Spencer, Perone, & Buss, 2011; Thelen & Smith, 2006). Once these ideas are fully tested, they may move the field closer to a more powerful view of how the minds of infants and children develop.

6.7 How does Vygotsky's concept of the zone of proximal development expand our understanding of early cognitive development?

The Social Context of Early Cognitive Development

Recall the description at the beginning of this chapter of Grace dropping shapes into a container. Notice that she learns about the toy with Ginette's help. With adult support, Grace will gradually become better at matching shapes to openings and dropping them into the container. Then she will be able to perform this and similar activities on her own.

Vygotsky's sociocultural theory emphasizes that children live in rich social and cultural contexts that affect the way their cognitive world is structured (Bodrova & Leong, 2007; Rogoff, 2003). Vygotsky believed that complex mental activities, such as voluntary attention, deliberate memory, categorization, and problem solving, have their origins in social interaction. Through joint activities with more mature members of their society, children master activities and think in ways that have meaning in their culture.

A special Vygotskian concept explains how this happens. The **zone of proximal** (or potential) **development** refers to a range of tasks that the child cannot yet handle alone but can do with the help of more skilled partners. To understand this idea, think about how a sensitive adult (such as Ginette) introduces a child to a new activity. The adult picks a task that the child can master but that is challenging enough that the child cannot do it by herself. Or the adult capitalizes on an activity that the child has chosen. The adult guides and supports, adjusting the level of support offered to fit the child's current level of performance. As the child joins in the interaction and picks up mental strategies, her competence increases, and the adult steps back, permitting the child to take more responsibility for the task. This form of teaching—known as *scaffolding*—promotes learning at all ages, and we will consider it further in Chapter 9.

Vygotsky's ideas have been applied mostly to preschool and school-age children, who are more skilled in language and social communication. Recently, however, his theory has been extended to infancy and toddlerhood. Recall that babies are equipped with capabilities that ensure that caregivers will interact with them (Csibra & Gergely, 2011). Then adults adjust the environment and their communication in ways that promote learning adapted to their cultural circumstances.

A study by Barbara Rogoff and her collaborators (1984) illustrates this process. Placing a jack-in-the-box nearby, the researchers watched how several adults played with Rogoff's son and daughter over the first two years. In the early months, adults tried to focus the baby's attention by working the toy and, as the bunny popped out, saying something like "My, what happened?" By the end of the first year, when cognitive and motor skills had improved, interaction centered on how to use the toy: The adults guided the baby's hand in turning the crank and putting the bunny back in the box. During the second year, adults helped from a distance, using gestures and verbal prompts, such as making a turning motion with the hand near the crank. Research indicates that this fine-tuned support is related to advanced play, language, and problem solving during the second year (Bornstein et al., 1992; Charman et al., 2001; Tamis-LeMonda & Bornstein, 1989).

By bringing the task within his son's zone of proximal development and adjusting his communication to suit the child's needs, the father transfers mental strategies to the child, promoting his cognitive development.

As early as the first year, cultural variations in social experiences affect mental strategies. In the jack-in-the-box example, adults and children focused their attention on a single activity. This strategy, common in Western middle-SES homes, is well-suited to lessons in which children master skills apart from the everyday situations in which they will later use those skills. In contrast, infants and young children in Guatemalan Mayan, Native American, and other indigenous communities often attend to several events at once. For example, one 12-month-old skillfully put objects in a jar while watching a passing truck and blowing into a toy whistle (Chavajay & Rogoff, 1999; Correa-Chavez, Roberts, & Perez, 2011).

Processing several competing events simultaneously may be vital in cultures where children largely learn not through lessons but through keen observation of others' ongoing activities at home, at work, and in public life. In a comparison of 18-month-olds from German middle-SES homes and Nso farming villages in Cameroon, the Nso toddlers copied far fewer experimenter-demonstrated actions on toys than did the German toddlers (Borchert et al., 2013). Nso caregivers rarely create such child-focused teaching situations. Rather, they expect children to imitate observed behaviors without adult prompting. Nso children are motivated to do so because they want to be included in the major activities of their community.

Earlier we saw how infants and toddlers create new schemes by acting on the physical world (Piaget) and how certain skills become better-developed as children represent their experiences more efficiently and meaningfully (information processing). Vygotsky adds a third dimension to our understanding by emphasizing that many aspects of cognitive development are socially prompted and encouraged. The Cultural Influences box on page 224 presents additional evidence for this idea. And we will see even more evidence in the next section, where we look at individual differences in mental development during the first two years.

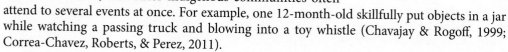

Ask Yourself

- **REVIEW** What impact does toddlers' more advanced play have on the development of attention?

- **CONNECT** List techniques that parents can use to scaffold the development of categorization in infancy and toddlerhood, and explain why each is effective.

- **APPLY** When Timmy was 18 months old, his mother stood behind him, helping him throw a large ball into a box. As his skill improved, she stepped back, letting him try on his own. Using Vygotsky's ideas, explain how Timmy's mother is supporting his cognitive development.

- **REFLECT** Describe your earliest autobiographical memory. How old were you when the event occurred? Do your responses fit with research on infantile amnesia?

Cultural Influences

Social Origins of Make-Believe Play

One of the activities that Ken, your first author's husband, used to do with their two young sons was to bake pineapple upside-down cake, a favorite treat. One Sunday afternoon when a cake was in the making, 21-month-old Peter stood on a chair at the kitchen sink, busily pouring water from one cup to another.

"He's in the way, Dad!" complained 4-year-old David, trying to pull Peter away from the sink.

"Maybe if we let him help, he'll give us room," Ken suggested. As David stirred the batter, Ken poured some into a small bowl for Peter, moved his chair to the side of the sink, and handed him a spoon.

"Here's how you do it, Petey," instructed David, with a superior air. Peter watched as David stirred, then tried to copy his motion. When it was time to pour the batter, Ken helped Peter hold and tip the small bowl.

"Time to bake it," said Ken.

"Bake it, bake it," repeated Peter, watching Ken slip the pan into the oven.

Several hours later, Ken observed one of Peter's earliest instances of make-believe play. He got his pail from the sandbox and, after filling it with a handful of sand, carried it into the kitchen and put it down on the floor in front of the oven. "Bake it, bake it," Peter called to Ken. Together, father and son placed the pretend cake in the oven.

Piaget and his followers concluded that toddlers discover make-believe independently, once they are capable of representational schemes. Vygotsky's theory has challenged this view. He believed that society provides children with opportunities to represent culturally meaningful activities in play. Make-believe, like other complex mental activities, is first learned under the guidance of experts (Meyers & Berk, 2014). In the example just described, Peter extended his capacity to represent daily events when Ken drew him into the baking task and helped him act it out in play.

Current evidence supports the idea that early make-believe is the combined result of children's readiness to engage in it and social experiences that promote it. In Western middle-SES families, play is culturally cultivated by adults, who value it as a developmentally beneficial activity and frequently play with their children (Gaskins, Haight, & Lancy, 2007). In one observational study of U.S. middle-SES toddlers, 75 to 80 percent of make-believe involved mother–child

interaction (Haight & Miller, 1993). At 12 months, make-believe was fairly one-sided: Almost all play episodes were initiated by mothers. But by the end of the second year, half of pretend episodes were initiated by each.

During make-believe, Western mothers offer toddlers a rich array of cues that they are pretending—looking and smiling at the child more, making more exaggerated movements, and using more "we" talk (acknowledging that pretending is a joint endeavor) than they do during the same real-life event (Lillard et al., 2007). These maternal cues encourage toddlers to join in and probably facilitate their ability to distinguish pretend from real acts, which strengthens over the second and third years (Lillard & Witherington, 2004; Ma & Lillard, 2006).

Also, when adults participate, toddlers' make-believe is more elaborate (Keren et al., 2005). They are more likely to combine pretend acts into complex sequences, as Peter did when he put the sand in the bucket (making the batter), carried it into the kitchen, and, with Ken's help, put it in the oven (baking the cake). The more parents pretend with their toddlers, the more time their children devote to make-believe.

In some cultures, such as those of Indonesia and Mexico, where extended-family households and sibling caregiving are common, make-believe is more frequent and more complex with older siblings than with mothers. As early as age 3 to 4, children provide rich, challenging stimulation to their younger brothers and sisters, take these teaching responsibilities seriously, and, with age, become better at them (Zukow-Goldring, 2002). In a study of Zinacanteco Indian children of southern Mexico, by age 8, sibling teachers were highly skilled at showing 2-year-olds how to play at everyday tasks, such as washing and cooking (Maynard, 2002). They often guided toddlers verbally and physically through the task and provided feedback.

In cultures where sibling caregiving is common, make-believe play is more frequent and complex with older siblings than with mothers. These Afghan children play "wedding," dressing the youngest as a bride.

In Western middle-SES families, older siblings less often teach deliberately but still serve as influential models of playful behavior. In New Zealand families of Western European descent, when both a parent and an older sibling were available, toddlers more often imitated the actions of the sibling, especially when siblings engaged in make-believe (Barr & Hayne, 2003).

As we will see in Chapters 9 and 10, make-believe play is a major means through which children extend their cognitive and social skills and learn about important activities in their culture (Nielsen, 2012). Vygotsky's theory, and the findings that support it, tell us that providing a stimulating physical environment is not enough to promote early cognitive development. In addition, toddlers must be invited and encouraged by more skilled members of their culture to participate in the social world around them. Parents and teachers can enhance early make-believe by playing often with toddlers, guiding and elaborating their make-believe themes.

Individual Differences in Early Mental Development

6.8 Describe the mental testing approach, the meaning of intelligence test scores, and the extent to which infant tests predict later performance.

6.9 Discuss environmental influences on early mental development, including home, child care, and early intervention for at-risk infants and toddlers.

Because of Grace's deprived early environment, Kevin and Monica had a child psychologist give her one of many tests available for assessing mental development in infants and toddlers. Worried about Timmy's progress, Vanessa also arranged for him to be tested. At age 22 months, he had only a handful of words in his vocabulary, played in a less mature way than Caitlin and Grace, and seemed restless and overactive.

The cognitive theories we have just discussed try to explain the *process* of development—how children's thinking changes. Mental tests, in contrast, focus on cognitive *products*. Their goal is to measure behaviors that reflect development and to arrive at scores that *predict* future performance, such as later intelligence, school achievement, and adult vocational success. This concern with prediction arose nearly a century ago, when French psychologist Alfred Binet designed the first successful intelligence test, which predicted school achievement (see Chapter 1). It inspired the design of many new tests, including ones that measure intelligence at very early ages.

Infant and Toddler Intelligence Tests

Accurately measuring infants' intelligence is a challenge because young babies cannot answer questions or follow directions. All we can do is present them with stimuli, coax them to respond, and observe their behavior. As a result, most infant tests emphasize perceptual and motor responses. But increasingly, tests are being developed that also tap early language, cognition, and social behavior, especially with older infants and toddlers.

One commonly used test, the *Bayley Scales of Infant and Toddler Development,* is suitable for children between 1 month and 3½ years. The most recent edition, the Bayley-III, has three main subtests: (1) the Cognitive Scale, which includes such items as attention to familiar and unfamiliar objects, looking for a fallen object, and pretend play; (2) the Language Scale, which taps understanding and expressions of language—for example, recognition of objects and people, following simple directions, and naming objects and pictures; and (3) the Motor Scale, which includes gross- and fine-motor skills, such as grasping, sitting, stacking blocks, and climbing stairs (Bayley, 2005).

Two additional Bayley-III scales depend on parental report: (4) the Social-Emotional Scale, which asks caregivers about such behaviors as ease of calming, social responsiveness, and imitation in play; and (5) the Adaptive Behavior Scale, which asks about adaptation to the demands of daily life, including communication, self-control, following rules, and getting along with others.

PHOTO BY STEPHEN AUSMUS/USDA/ARS

A trained examiner administers a test based on the Bayley Scales of Infant Development to a 1-year-old in her mother's lap. Current Bayley-III Cognitive and Language Scales predict preschool mental test performance better than earlier versions.

COMPUTING INTELLIGENCE TEST SCORES Intelligence tests for infants, children, and adults are scored in much the same way—by computing an **intelligence quotient (IQ),** which indicates the extent to which the raw score (number of items passed) deviates from the typical performance of same-age individuals. To make this comparison possible, test designers engage in **standardization**—giving the test to a large, representative sample and using the results as the *standard* for interpreting scores. The standardization sample for the Bayley-III included 1,700 infants, toddlers, and young preschoolers, reflecting the U.S. population in SES and ethnic diversity.

Within the standardization sample, performances at each age level form a **normal distribution,** in which most scores cluster around the mean, or average, with progressively fewer falling toward the extremes (see Figure 6.9 on page 226). This *bell-shaped distribution* results

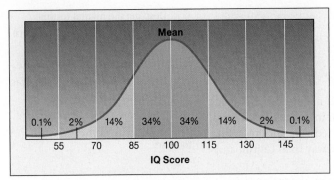

FIGURE 6.9 **Normal distribution of intelligence test scores.** To determine what percentage of same-age individuals in the population a person with a certain IQ outperformed, add the figures to the left of that IQ score. For example, an 8-year-old child with an IQ of 115 scored better than 84 percent of the population of 8-year-olds.

whenever researchers measure individual differences in large samples. When intelligence tests are standardized, the mean IQ is set at 100. An individual's IQ is higher or lower than 100 by an amount that reflects how much his or her test performance deviates from the standardization-sample mean.

The IQ offers a way of finding out whether an individual is ahead, behind, or on time (average) in mental development compared with others of the same age. For example, if Timmy's score is 100, then he did better than 50 percent of his agemates. A child with an IQ of 85 did better than only 16 percent, whereas a child with an IQ of 130 outperformed 98 percent. The IQs of 96 percent of individuals fall between 70 and 130; only a few achieve higher or lower scores.

PREDICTING LATER PERFORMANCE FROM INFANT TESTS

Despite careful construction, most infant tests—including previous editions of the Bayley—predict later intelligence poorly. Infants and toddlers easily become distracted, fatigued, or bored during testing, so their scores often do not reflect their true abilities. And infant perceptual and motor items differ from the tasks given to older children, which increasingly emphasize verbal, conceptual, and problem-solving skills. In contrast, the Bayley-III Cognitive and Language Scales, which better dovetail with childhood tests, are good predictors of preschool mental test performance (Albers & Grieve, 2007). But because most infant test scores do not tap the same dimensions of intelligence measured at older ages, they are conservatively labeled **developmental quotients (DQs)** rather than IQs.

Infant tests are somewhat better at making long-term predictions for extremely low-scoring babies. Today, they are largely used for *screening*—helping to identify for further observation and intervention babies who are likely to have developmental problems.

As an alternative to infant tests, some researchers have turned to information-processing measures, such as habituation, to assess early mental progress. Their findings show that speed of habituation and recovery to novel visual stimuli is among the best available infant predictors of IQ from early childhood to early adulthood, with correlations ranging from the .30s to the .60s (Fagan, Holland, & Wheeler, 2007; Kavšek, 2004). Habituation and recovery seem to be an especially effective early index of intelligence because they assess memory as well as quickness and flexibility of thinking, which underlie intelligent behavior at all ages (Colombo et al., 2004). The consistency of these findings has prompted designers of the Bayley-III to include items that tap such cognitive skills as habituation, object permanence, and categorization.

Early Environment and Mental Development

In Chapter 2, we indicated that intelligence is a complex blend of hereditary and environmental influences. Many studies have examined the relationship of environmental factors to infant and toddler mental test scores. As we consider this evidence, you will encounter findings that highlight the role of heredity as well.

HOME ENVIRONMENT The **Home Observation for Measurement of the Environment (HOME)** is a checklist for gathering information about the quality of children's home lives through observation and parental interview (Caldwell & Bradley, 1994). Applying What We Know on the following page lists the factors measured by the HOME Infant–Toddler Subscales—the most widely used home environment measure during the first three years. A briefer, exclusively observational HOME instrument is also available (Rijlaarsdam et al., 2012).

Each HOME subscale is positively related to toddlers' mental test performance. Regardless of SES and ethnicity, an organized, stimulating physical setting and parental affection, involvement, and encouragement of new skills repeatedly predict better language and IQ scores in toddlerhood and early childhood (Fuligni, Han, & Brooks-Gunn, 2004; Linver, Martin, & Brooks-Gunn, 2004; Tamis-LeMonda et al., 2004; Tong et al., 2007). The extent to which parents converse with infants and toddlers is particularly important. It contributes strongly to

Applying What We Know

Features of a High-Quality Home Life for Infants and Toddlers: The HOME Infant–Toddler Subscales

HOME SUBSCALE	SAMPLE ITEM
Organization of the physical environment	Child's play environment appears safe and free of hazards.
Provision of appropriate play materials	Parent provides toys or interesting activities for child during observer's visit.
Emotional and verbal responsiveness of the parent	Parent caresses or kisses child at least once during observer's visit. Parent spontaneously speaks to child twice or more (excluding scolding) during observer's visit.
Parental acceptance of the child	Parent does not interfere with child's actions or restrict child's movements more than three times during observer's visit.
Parental involvement with the child	Parent tends to keep child within view and to look at child often during observer's visit.
Opportunities for variety in daily stimulation	Child eats at least one meal per day with mother and/or father, according to parental report. Child frequently has a chance to get out of house (for example, accompanies parent on trips to grocery store).

Source: Bradley, 1994; Bradley et al., 2001. A brief, exclusively observational HOME instrument taps the first three subscales only. *See:* Rijlaarsdam et al., 2012.

early language progress, which, in turn, predicts intelligence and academic achievement in elementary school (Hart & Risley, 1995; Hoff, 2013).

Yet we must interpret these correlational findings cautiously. In all the studies, children were reared by their biological parents, with whom they share not just a common environment but also a common heredity. Parents who are genetically more intelligent may provide better experiences while also giving birth to genetically brighter children, who evoke more stimulation from their parents. Research supports this hypothesis, which refers to *genetic–environmental correlation* (see Chapter 2, pages 84–85) (Saudino & Plomin, 1997). But heredity does not account for the entire association between home environment and mental test scores. Family living conditions—both HOME scores and affluence of the surrounding neighborhood—continue to predict children's IQ beyond the contribution of parental IQ and education (Chase-Lansdale et al., 1997; Klebanov et al., 1998).

How can the research summarized so far help us understand Vanessa's concern about Timmy's development? Ben, the psychologist who tested Timmy, found that he scored only slightly below average. Ben talked with Vanessa about her child-rearing practices and watched her play with Timmy. A single parent who worked long hours, Vanessa had little energy for Timmy at the end of the day. Ben also noticed that Vanessa, anxious about Timmy's progress, tended to pressure him, dampening his active behavior and bombarding him with directions: "That's enough ball play. Stack these blocks."

Ben explained that when parents are intrusive in these ways, infants and toddlers are likely to be distractible, play immaturely, and do poorly on mental tests (Bono & Stifter, 2003). He coached Vanessa in how to interact sensitively with Timmy, while assuring her that Timmy's current performance need not forecast his future development. Warm, responsive parenting that builds on toddlers' current capacities is a much better indicator than an early mental test score of how children will do later.

INFANT AND TODDLER CHILD CARE   Today, more than 60 percent of U.S. mothers with a child under age 2 are employed (U.S. Census Bureau, 2014). Child care for infants and toddlers has become common, and its quality—though not as influential as parenting—affects mental development.

© RICK GOMEZ/CORBIS

A mother plays affectionately with her baby. Warm, responsive parental interaction is a better indicator of how a child will do later than early mental test scores.

High-quality child care, with a generous caregiver–child ratio, well-trained caregivers, and developmentally appropriate activities, can be especially beneficial to children from low-SES homes.

Research consistently shows that young children exposed to long hours of mediocre to poor-quality child care—whether they come from middle-class or from low-SES homes—score lower on measures of cognitive, language, academic, and social skills during the preschool, elementary, and secondary school years (Belsky et al., 2007; Dearing, McCartney, & Taylor, 2009; NICHD Early Child Care Research Network, 2000b, 2001, 2003b, 2006; Vandell et al., 2010). In contrast, good child care can reduce the negative impact of a stressed, poverty-stricken home life, and it sustains the benefits of growing up in an economically advantaged family (Lamb & Ahnert, 2006; McCartney et al., 2007; NICHD Early Child Care Research Network, 2003b). As Figure 6.10 illustrates, the Early Childhood Longitudinal Study (see page 42 in Chapter 1), which included a large sample of children diverse in SES and ethnicity followed from birth through the preschool years, confirmed the importance of continuous high-quality child care from infancy through the preschool years (Li et al., 2013).

In contrast to most European countries and to Australia and New Zealand, where child care is nationally regulated and funded to ensure its quality, reports on U.S. child care raise serious concerns. Standards are set by the individual states and vary widely. In studies of quality, only 20 to 25 percent of child-care centers and family child-care homes provided infants and toddlers with sufficiently positive, stimulating experiences to promote healthy psychological development. Most settings offered substandard care (NICHD Early Child Care Research Network, 2000a, 2004). And the cost of child care in the United States is high: On average, full-time center-based care for one infant consumes from 7 to 19 percent of the median income for couples and over 40 percent for single mothers (Child Care Aware, 2013). The cost of a family child-care home is only slightly lower.

Unfortunately, many U.S. children from low-income families experience inadequate child care (NICHD Early Child Care Research Network, 2005; Torquati et al., 2011). But U.S. settings providing the very worst care tend to serve middle-income families. These parents are especially likely to place their children in for-profit centers, where quality tends to be lowest. Economically disadvantaged children more often attend publicly subsidized, nonprofit centers, which are better equipped with learning materials and have smaller group sizes and more favorable teacher–child ratios (Johnson, Ryan, & Brooks-Gunn, 2012), Still, child-care quality for low-income children is often substandard.

See Applying What We Know on the following page for signs of high-quality child care for infants and toddlers, based on standards for **developmentally appropriate practice**. These standards, devised by the U.S. National Association for the Education of Young Children, specify program characteristics that serve young children's developmental and individual needs, based on both current research and consensus among experts. Caitlin, Grace, and Timmy are fortunate to be in family child care that meets these standards.

Child care in the United States is affected by a macrosystem of individualistic values and weak government regulation and funding. Furthermore, many parents think that their children's child-care experiences are better than they really are (Cryer, Tietz, & Wessels, 2002; Torquati et al., 2011). Unable to identify good care or without the financial means to purchase it, they do not demand it. In recent years, recognizing that child care is in a state of crisis, the U.S. federal government and some states have allocated additional funds to subsidize its cost, especially for low-income families (Matthews, 2014). Though far from meeting the need, this increase in resources has had a positive impact on child-care quality and accessibility.

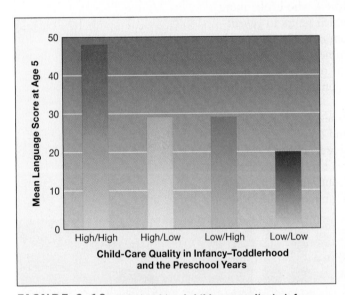

FIGURE 6.10   Relationship of child-care quality in infancy–toddlerhood and the preschool years to language development at age 5. When a nationally representative sample of more than 1,300 children was followed over the first five years, language scores were highest for those experiencing high-quality child care in both infancy–toddlerhood and the preschool years, intermediate for those experiencing high-quality care in just one of these periods, and lowest for those experiencing poor-quality care in both periods. Cognitive, literacy, and math scores also showed this pattern. (Adapted from Weilin Li; George Farkas; Greg J. Duncan; Margaret J. Burchinal & Deborah Lowe Vandell, 2013, "Timing of High-Quality Child Care and Cognitive, Language, and Preacademic Development," *Developmental Psychology*, 49, p. 1448. Copyright © 2013 by the American Psychological Association. Reprinted by permission of the American Psychological Association.)

Applying What We Know

Signs of Developmentally Appropriate Infant and Toddler Child Care

PROGRAM CHARACTERISTIC	SIGNS OF QUALITY
Physical setting	Indoor environment is clean, in good repair, well-lighted, and well-ventilated. Fenced outdoor play space is available. Setting does not appear overcrowded when children are present.
Toys and equipment	Play materials are appropriate for infants and toddlers and are stored on low shelves within easy reach. Cribs, highchairs, infant seats, and child-sized tables and chairs are available. Outdoor equipment includes small riding toys, swings, slide, and sandbox.
Caregiver–child ratio	In child-care centers, caregiver–child ratio is no greater than 1 to 3 for infants and 1 to 6 for toddlers. Group size (number of children in one room) is no greater than 6 infants with 2 caregivers and 12 toddlers with 2 caregivers. In family child-care homes, caregiver is responsible for no more than 6 children; within this group, no more than 2 are infants or toddlers. Staffing is consistent, so infants and toddlers can form relationships with particular caregivers.
Daily activities	Daily schedule includes times for active play, quiet play, naps, snacks, and meals. It is flexible rather than rigid, to meet the needs of individual children. Atmosphere is warm and supportive, and children are never left unsupervised.
Interactions among adults and children	Caregivers respond promptly to infants' and toddlers' distress; hold, talk to, sing, and read to them; and interact with them in a manner that respects the individual child's interests and tolerance for stimulation.
Caregiver qualifications	Caregiver has some training in child development, first aid, and safety.
Relationships with parents	Parents are welcome anytime. Caregivers talk frequently with parents about children's behavior and development.
Licensing and accreditation	Child-care setting, whether a center or a home, is licensed by the state. In the United States, voluntary accreditation by the National Association for the Education of Young Children (www.naeyc.org/accreditation) or the National Association for Family Child Care (www.nafcc.org) is evidence of an especially high-quality program.

Source: Copple & Bredekamp, 2009.

Early Intervention for At-Risk Infants and Toddlers

Children living in persistent poverty are likely to show gradual declines in intelligence test scores and to achieve poorly when they reach school age (Schoon et al., 2012). These problems are largely due to stressful home environments that undermine children's ability to learn and increase the likelihood that they will remain poor as adults (McLoyd, Aikens, & Burton, 2006). A variety of intervention programs have been developed to break this tragic cycle of poverty. Although most begin during the preschool years (we will discuss these in Chapter 9), some start during infancy and continue through early childhood.

In center-based interventions, children attend an organized child-care or preschool program where they receive educational, nutritional, and health services and their parents receive child-rearing and other social service supports. In home-based interventions, a skilled adult visits the home and works with parents, providing social support and teaching them how to stimulate a young child's development. In most programs of either type, participating children score higher than untreated controls on mental tests by age 2. The earlier intervention begins, the longer it lasts, and the greater its scope and intensity (for example, year-round high-quality child care plus generous support services for parents), the better participants' cognitive and academic performance throughout childhood and adolescence (Brooks-Gunn, 2004; Ramey, Ramey, & Lanzi, 2006; Sweet & Appelbaum, 2004).

The Carolina Abecedarian Project illustrates these positive outcomes. In the 1970s, more than 100 infants from poverty-stricken families, ranging in age from 3 weeks to 3 months, were randomly assigned to either a treatment group or a control group. Treatment infants were enrolled in full-time, year-round child care through the preschool years. There they received carefully planned educational experiences aimed at promoting motor, cognitive, language, and social skills and, after age 3, literacy and math concepts. Special emphasis was

LOOK and LISTEN

Ask several employed parents of infants or toddlers to describe what they sought in a child-care setting, along with challenges they faced in finding child care. Are the parents knowledgeable about the ingredients of high-quality care?

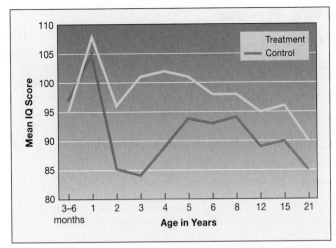

FIGURE 6.11 **IQ scores of treatment and control children from infancy to 21 years in the Carolina Abecedarian Project.** At 1 year, treatment children outperformed controls, an advantage consistently maintained through age 21. The IQ scores of both groups declined gradually during childhood and adolescence—a trend probably due to the damaging impact of poverty on mental development. (Based on Campbell et al., 2001.)

This Early Head Start program provides rich, educational experiences for toddlers plus parent education and family social supports. The most favorable outcomes of Early Head Start result from mixing center- and home-visiting services.

placed on rich, responsive adult–child verbal communication. All children received nutrition and health services; the primary difference between treatment and controls was the intensive child-care experience.

As Figure 6.11 shows, by 12 months of age, the IQs of the two groups diverged. Treatment children sustained an advantage until last tested—at age 21. In addition, throughout their years of schooling, treatment youths achieved considerably higher scores in reading and math. These gains translated into reduced enrollment in special education, more years of schooling completed, higher rates of college enrollment and employment in skilled jobs, and lower rates of drug use and adolescent parenthood (Campbell & Ramey, 2010; Campbell et al., 2001, 2002).

Recognition of the power of intervening as early as possible led the U.S. Congress to provide limited funding for intervention services directed at infants and toddlers who already have serious developmental problems or who are at risk for problems because of poverty. Early Head Start, begun in 1995, currently has 1,000 sites serving about 150,000 low-income children and their families (Schmidt, 2013). It offers an array of coordinated services—child care, educational experiences for infants and toddlers, parenting education, family social support, and health care—delivered through a center-based, home-based, or mixed approach, depending on community needs.

A recent evaluation, conducted when children reached age 3, showed that Early Head Start led to warmer, more stimulating parenting, a reduction in harsh discipline, gains in cognitive and language development, and lessening of child aggression (Love, Chazan-Cohen, & Raikes, 2007; Love et al., 2005; Raikes et al., 2010). The strongest effects occurred at sites mixing center- and home-visiting services.

By age 5, however, the benefits of Early Head Start had declined or disappeared, and a follow-up in fifth grade showed no persisting gains (U.S. Department of Health and Human Services, 2006; Vogel et al., 2010). One speculation is that more intentional educational experiences extending through the preschool years—as in the Abecedarian project—would increase the lasting impact of Early Head Start (Barnett, 2011). Also, some evidence suggests that the cognitive benefits of Early Head Start are greater for certain children—in particular, those who receive little stimulation at home (Bradley, McKelvey, & Whiteside-Mansell, 2011). Although Early Head Start is in need of refinement, it is a promising beginning at providing U.S. infants and toddlers living in poverty with publicly supported intervention.

Ask Yourself

- **REVIEW** What probably accounts for the finding that speed of habituation and recovery to visual stimuli predicts later IQ better than an infant mental test score?

- **CONNECT** Using what you learned about brain development in Chapter 5, explain why it is best to initiate intervention for poverty-stricken children in the first two years rather than later.

- **APPLY** Fifteen-month-old Joey's developmental quotient (DQ) is 115. His mother wants to know exactly what this means and what she should do to support his intellectual development. How would you respond?

- **REFLECT** Suppose you were seeking a child-care setting for your baby. What would you want it to be like, and why?

Language Development

Improvements in perception and cognition during infancy pave the way for an extraordinary human achievement—language. In Chapter 5, we saw that by the second half of the first year, infants make dramatic progress in distinguishing the basic sounds of their language and in segmenting the flow of speech into word and phrase units. They also start to comprehend some word meanings and, around 12 months of age, say their first word. Sometime between 1½ and 2 years, toddlers combine two words (Gleason, 2013). By age 6, children understand the meaning of about 10,000 words, speak in elaborate sentences, and are skilled conversationalists.

To appreciate this awesome task, think about the many abilities involved in your own flexible use of language. When you speak, you must select words that match the underlying concepts you want to convey. To be understood, you must pronounce words correctly. Then you must combine them into phrases and sentences using a complex set of grammatical rules. Finally, you must follow the rules of everyday conversation—taking turns, making comments relevant to what your partner just said, and using an appropriate tone of voice. How do infants and toddlers make such remarkable progress in launching these skills?

Theories of Language Development

In the 1950s, researchers did not take seriously the idea that very young children might be able to figure out important properties of language. Children's regular and rapid attainment of language milestones suggested a process largely governed by maturation, inspiring the nativist perspective on language development. In recent years, new evidence has spawned the interactionist perspective, which emphasizes the joint roles of children's inner capacities and communicative experiences.

THE NATIVIST PERSPECTIVE   According to linguist Noam Chomsky's (1957) *nativist* theory, language is a uniquely human accomplishment, etched into the structure of the brain. Focusing on grammar, Chomsky reasoned that the rules of sentence organization are too complex to be directly taught to or discovered by even a cognitively sophisticated young child. Rather, he proposed that all children have a **language acquisition device (LAD),** an innate system that contains a *universal grammar,* or set of rules common to all languages. It enables children, no matter which language they hear, to understand and speak in a rule-oriented fashion as soon as they pick up enough words.

Are children innately primed to acquire language? Recall from Chapter 4 that newborn babies are remarkably sensitive to speech sounds. And children everywhere reach major language milestones in a similar sequence (Parish-Morris, Golinkoff, & Hirsh-Pasek, 2013). Research reviewed in the Biology and Environment box on page 232, suggesting that children have an impressive ability to invent new language systems, provides some of the most powerful support for the nativist perspective.

Furthermore, the ability to master a grammatically complex language system seems to be unique to humans, as efforts to teach language to nonhuman primates—using either specially devised artificial symbol systems or sign language—have met with limited success. Even after extensive training, chimpanzees (who are closest to humans in terms of evolution) master only a basic vocabulary and short word combinations, and they produce these far less consistently than human preschoolers (Tomasello, Call, & Hare, 2003).

Evidence for specialized language areas in the brain and a sensitive period for language development have also been interpreted as supporting Chomsky's theory. Let's take a closer look at these findings.

6.10 Describe theories of language development, and indicate the emphasis each places on innate abilities and environmental influences.
6.11 Describe major milestones of language development in the first two years, individual differences, and ways adults can support infants' and toddlers' emerging capacities.

Infants communicate from the very beginning of life. How will this child become a fluent speaker of her native language within just a few years? Theorists disagree sharply.

© LAURA DWIGHT PHOTOGRAPHY

Biology and Environment

Deaf Children Invent Language

Can children develop complex, rule-based language systems with minimal language input, or with input so inconsistent that grammatical rules are not readily apparent? If so, such evidence would support Chomsky's idea that the human brain is prewired for language development. Research reveals that deaf children can generate an intricate natural language, even when reared in language-deficient environments.

Minimal Language Input

In a series of studies, researchers tracked the language development of deaf toddlers and pre-schoolers whose parents discouraged signing and addressed them verbally (Goldin-Meadow, 2009). None of the children made progress in acquiring spoken language or used even the most common gestures of their nation's sign language. Nevertheless, in interacting with one another, they spontaneously produced a gestural communication system, called *homesign,* strikingly similar in basic structure to hearing children's verbal language.

The deaf children developed gestural vocabularies with distinct forms for nouns and verbs, similar to the meanings of spoken words. Furthermore, the children combined gestures into novel sentences conforming to basic grammatical rules that were not necessarily those of their parents' spoken language (Goldin-Meadow, Gelman, & Mylander, 2005). For example, to describe a large bubble he had blown, one child first pointed at a bubble jar and then used two open palms with fingers spread to denote the act of "blowing up big."

The children did not pick up their gesture systems from parents, whose gestures were limited—no different from the gestures that hearing speakers produce while talking (Goldin-Meadow, 2003). Rather the children created homesign as they interacted with one another, and they used it for the same diverse purposes as any language—to comment on present and nonpresent objects and events, to ask questions,

to influence others' actions, to tell stories, and to talk about their own and others' signs.

Hearing children acquire a larger vocabulary and a far more complex grammar than children inventing home-sign. This indicates that a rich language environment with partners who "speak" the same language—for deaf children, exposure to adults fluent in an elaborate sign language—fosters typical language development. But without access to conventional language, children generate their own language system.

In Nicaragua, educators brought deaf children and adolescents, each with a unique homesign, together to form a community. Although they had no shared language, in less than two decades they developed Nicaraguan Sign Language, which matches other languages in complexity (Senghas et al., 2005).

Inconsistent Language Input

A study of Simon, a deaf child born to deaf parents who were late learners of American Sign Language (ASL), also illustrates children's remarkable capacity to invent language. As with the deaf children just described, Simon's parent were exposed only to oral language in childhood; only in adolescence did they start to learn ALS. As a result, they had not attained the grammatical competence of native signers, and they used many ASL structures inconsistently. (See the discussion of a sensitive period for language development on page 233.) Simon went to school with hearing teachers and children, so his only ASL input came from his parents.

When Simon was 7, researchers gave him a challenging ASL grammar task, which assessed his knowledge of the verb *to move* (Singleton and Newport, 2004). In ASL, expressing motion requires up to seven grammatical markers, which designate an object's path, orientation, style of movement,

In Nicaragua, educators brought deaf children and adolescents together to form a community. Within two decades, they devised a new language—Nicaraguan Sign Language.

and location, plus a secondary object's features and position relative to the first object and its path. Simon's performance was compared with the performance of several reference groups: his parents, deaf school-age children of deaf native-signing parents, and deaf native-signing adults.

Findings confirmed that Simon's parents' ASL grammar was much weaker than that of native-signing adults. Yet Simon introduced rule usage into his language that greatly exceeded his parents' scores. His performance even surpassed the average score of native-signing deaf children and approached that of native-signing deaf adults. Simon had managed to extract ASL regularities from his parents' imperfect language, arriving at a highly consistent grammar.

Deaf children's remarkable capacity to invent language, despite minimal or inconsistent input, is compatible with the existence of an innate LAD. As we will see, however, other theorists claim that nonlinguistic cognitive capacities, applied to the task of communicating, are responsible.

Language Areas in the Brain Recall from Chapter 5 that for most individuals, language is housed largely in the left hemisphere of the cerebral cortex. Within it are two important language-related structures (see Figure 6.12). To clarify their functions, researchers have, for several decades, studied adults who experienced damage to these structures and display *aphasias,* or communication disorders. *Broca's area,* located in the left frontal lobe, supports grammatical processing and language production. *Wernicke's area,* located in the left temporal lobe, plays a role in comprehending word meaning.

But recent brain-imaging research suggests that the relationship between these brain structures and language functions is complicated. Neither area is solely, or even mainly, responsible for specific language capacities. Rather, the impaired pronunciation and grammar of patients with Broca's aphasia and the meaningless speech streams of patients with Wernicke's aphasia involve the spread of injury to nearby cortical areas and widespread abnormal activity in the left cerebral hemisphere, triggered by the brain damage (Bates et al., 2003; Keller et al., 2009).

The broad association of language functions with left-hemispheric regions is consistent with Chomsky's notion of a brain prepared to process language. But critics point out that at birth, the brain is not fully lateralized; it is highly plastic. Language areas in the cerebral cortex *develop* as children acquire language (Mills & Conboy, 2005). Although the left hemisphere is biased for language processing, if it is injured in the first few years, other regions take over language functions, and most such children eventually attain normal language competence. Thus, left-hemispheric localization, though typical, is not necessary for effective language processing.

Nevertheless, when the young brain allocates language to the right hemisphere—as a result of left-hemispheric damage or learning of sign language (see pages 166–167 in Chapter 5)—it localizes it in roughly the same regions that typically support language in the left hemisphere (Stiles, Reilly, & Levine, 2012). This suggests that those brain structures are uniquely disposed for language processing.

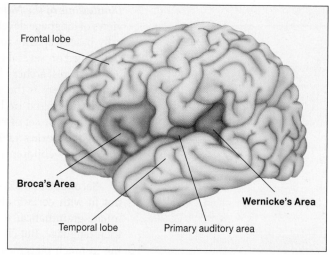

FIGURE 6.12 **Broca's and Wernicke's areas, in the left hemisphere of the cerebral cortex.** Broca's area, located in the frontal lobe, supports grammatical processing and language production. Wernicke's area, located in the temporal lobe, is involved in comprehending word meaning. Contrary to what was once believed, however, neither area is solely or even mainly responsible for these functions.

A Sensitive Period for Language Development Must language be acquired early in life, during an age span in which the brain is particularly responsive to language stimulation? Evidence for a sensitive period that coincides with brain lateralization would support the view that language development has unique biological properties.

To test this idea, researchers have examined the language competence of deaf adults who acquired their first language—American Sign Language (ASL), a gestural system just as complex as any spoken language—at different ages. The later learners, whose parents chose to educate them through the oral method, which relies on speech and lip-reading, did not acquire spoken language because of their profound deafness. Consistent with the sensitive-period notion, those who learned ASL in adolescence or adulthood never became as proficient as those who learned in childhood (Mayberry, 2010; Singleton & Newport, 2004). (Recall from the Biology and Environment box on page 232 that Simon's parents, who acquired ASL in adolescence, scored lower than he did on a test of complex grammar.) However, a precise age cutoff for a decline in first-language competence has not been established.

Is acquiring a second language also harder after a sensitive period has passed? In one study, researchers examined U.S. census data, selecting immigrants from non-English-speaking countries who had resided in the United States for at least ten years. The census form had asked the immigrants to rate how competently they spoke English, from "not at all" to "very well"—self-reports that correlate strongly with objective language measures. As age of immigration increased from infancy and early childhood into adulthood, English proficiency declined (Hakuta, Bialystok, & Wiley, 2003). Furthermore, ERP and fMRI measures of brain activity indicate that second-language processing is less lateralized in older than in younger learners (Neville & Bruer, 2001). But second-language competence does not drop sharply at a certain age. Rather, a continuous, age-related decrease occurs.

In sum, research on both first- and second-language learning reveals a biologically based timeframe for optimum language development. However, the boundaries of this sensitive period remain unclear.

© SYRACUSE NEWSPAPERS/MIKE GREENLAR/THE IMAGE WORKS

Childhood seems to be a sensitive period for optimum language development. This Ethiopian father, attending an English-as-a-second-language class, may never become as proficient an English speaker as his daughter.

Limitations of the Nativist Perspective Chomsky's theory has had a major impact on current views of language development. It is now widely accepted that humans have a unique, biologically based capacity to acquire language. Still, Chomsky's account of development has been challenged on several grounds.

First, researchers have had great difficulty specifying Chomsky's universal grammar. A major problem is the absence of a complete description of these abstract grammatical rules or even an agreed-on list of how many exist or the best examples of them. Chomsky's critics doubt that one set of rules can account for the extraordinary variation in grammatical forms among the world's 5,000 to 8,000 languages (Christiansen & Chater, 2008; Evans & Levinson, 2009). How children manage to link such rules with the strings of words they hear is also unclear.

Second, Chomsky's assumption that grammatical knowledge is innately determined does not fit with certain observations of language development. Once children begin to use an innate grammatical structure, we would expect them to apply it to all relevant instances in their language. But children refine and generalize many grammatical forms gradually, engaging in much piecemeal learning and making errors along the way. For example, one 3-year-old, in grappling with prepositions, initially added *with* to the verb *open* ("You open with scissors") but not to the word *hit* ("He hit me stick") (Tomasello, 2006). As we will see in Chapter 12, complete mastery of some grammatical forms, such as the passive voice, is not achieved until well into middle childhood. This suggests that more experimentation and learning are involved than Chomsky assumed.

THE INTERACTIONIST PERSPECTIVE Recent ideas about language development emphasize *interactions* between inner capacities and environmental influences. One type of interactionist theory applies the information-processing perspective to language development. A second type emphasizes social interaction.

Some information-processing theorists assume that children make sense of their complex language environments by applying powerful cognitive capacities of a general kind (Bates, 2004; Munakata, 2006; Saffran, 2009). These theorists note that regions of the brain housing language also govern similar perceptual and cognitive abilities, such as the capacity to analyze musical and visual patterns (Saygin, Leech, & Dick, 2010; Saygin et al., 2004).

Other theorists blend this information-processing view with Chomsky's nativist perspective. They agree that infants are amazing statistical analyzers of speech and other information (see Chapter 5). But, they argue, these capacities probably are not sufficient to account for mastery of higher-level aspects of language, such as intricate grammatical structures (Aslin & Newport, 2012). They also point out that grammatical competence may depend more on specific brain structures than the other components of language. When 2- to 2½-year-olds and adults listened to short sentences—some grammatically correct, others with phrase-structure violations—both groups showed similarly distinct ERP brain-wave patterns for each sentence type in the left frontal and temporal lobes of the cerebral cortex (Oberecker & Friederici, 2006). This suggests that 2-year-olds process sentence structures using the same neural system as adults do. Furthermore, in studies of older children and adults with left-hemispheric brain damage, grammar is more impaired than other language functions (Curtiss & Schaeffer, 2005).

Still other interactionists emphasize that children's social skills and language experiences are centrally involved in language development. In this *social-interactionist* view, an active child strives to communicate, which cues her caregivers to provide appropriate language experiences, which in turn help her relate the content and structure of language to its social meanings (Bohannon & Bonvillian, 2013; Chapman, 2006).

Among social interactionists, disagreement continues over whether or not children are equipped with specialized language structures (Hsu, Chater, & Vitányi, 2013; Lidz, 2007; Tomasello, 2006). Nevertheless, as we chart the course of language development, we will encounter much support for their central premise—that children's social competencies and language experiences greatly affect their language progress. In reality, native endowment, cognitive-processing strategies, and social experience probably operate in different balances with respect to each aspect of language: pronunciation, vocabulary, grammar, and communication skills. Table 6.3 provides an overview of early language milestones that we will examine in the next few sections.

TABLE 6.3	Milestones of Language Development During the First Two Years

APPROXIMATE AGE	MILESTONE
2 months	Infants coo, making pleasant vowel sounds.
4 months on	Infants observe with interest as the caregiver plays turn-taking games, such as pat-a-cake and peekaboo.
6 months on	Infants babble, adding consonants to their cooing sounds and repeating syllables. By 7 months, babbling starts to include many sounds of spoken languages.
	Infants begin to comprehend a few commonly heard words.
8–12 months	Infants become more accurate at establishing joint attention with the caregiver, who often verbally labels what the baby is looking at.
	Infants actively participate in turn-taking games, trading roles with the caregiver.
	Infants use preverbal gestures, such as showing and pointing, to influence others' goals and behavior and to convey information.
12 months	Babbling includes sound and intonation patterns of the child's language community.
	Speed and accuracy of word comprehension increase rapidly.
	Toddlers say their first recognizable word.
18–24 months	Spoken vocabulary expands from about 50 to 200 to 250 words.
	Toddlers combine two words.

Getting Ready to Talk

Before babies say their first word, they make impressive progress toward understanding and speaking their native tongue. They listen attentively to human speech, and they make speech-like sounds. As adults, we can hardly help but respond.

COOING AND BABBLING   Around 2 months, babies begin to make vowel-like noises, called **cooing** because of their pleasant "oo" quality. Gradually, consonants are added, and around 6 months **babbling** appears, in which infants repeat consonant–vowel combinations, often in long strings, such as "babababababa" or "nanananana."

Babies everywhere (even those who are deaf) start babbling at about the same age and produce a similar range of early sounds. But for babbling to develop further, infants must be able to hear human speech. In hearing-impaired babies, these speechlike sounds are greatly delayed and limited in diversity of sounds (Bass-Ringdahl, 2010). And a deaf infant not exposed to sign language will stop babbling entirely (Oller, 2000).

In one case, a deaf-born 5-month-old received a *cochlear implant*—an electronic device surgically inserted into the ear that converts external sounds into a signal to stimulate the auditory nerve. She showed typical babbling in infancy and resembled her hearing agemates in language development at 3 to 4 years (Schauwers et al., 2004). But if auditory input is not restored until after age 2 (the usual time for cochlear implant surgery), children remain behind in language development. And if implantation occurs after age 4, language delays are severe and persistent (Coene et al., 2011; Svirsky, Teoh, & Neuburger, 2004). These outcomes suggest an early sensitive period for the brain to develop the necessary organization for normal speech processing.

Babies initially produce a limited number of sounds and then expand to a much broader range. Around 7 months, babbling starts to include many sounds of spoken

Even babies who are deaf begin babbling at around 2 months. Those exposed to sign language from birth, as this child has been, babble with their hands, much as hearing babies do through speech.

© KRISTINA KENNEDY/ALAMY

languages. As caregivers respond to infant babbles, older infants modify their babbling to include sound patterns like those in the adult's speech (Goldstein & Schwade, 2008). By 8 to 10 months, babbling reflects the sound and intonation patterns of children's language community, some of which are transferred to their first words (Boysson-Bardies & Vihman, 1991).

TAKE A MOMENT... The next time you hear an older baby babbling, notice how certain sounds appear in particular contexts—for example, when exploring objects, looking at books, or walking upright (Blake & Boysson-Bardies, 1992). Infants seem to be experimenting with the sound system and meaning of language before they speak in conventional ways. Toddlers continue babbling for four or five months after they say their first words.

Deaf infants exposed to sign language from birth babble with their hands much as hearing infants do through speech (Petitto & Marentette, 1991). Furthermore, hearing babies of deaf, signing parents produce babblelike hand motions with the rhythmic patterns of natural sign languages (Petitto et al., 2001, 2004). This sensitivity to language rhythm—evident in both spoken and signed babbling—supports both discovery and production of meaningful language units.

BECOMING A COMMUNICATOR At birth, infants are prepared for some aspects of conversational behavior. For example, newborns initiate interaction through eye contact and terminate it by looking away. By 3 to 4 months, infants start to gaze in the same general direction adults are looking—a skill that becomes more accurate at 10 to 11 months, as babies realize that others' focus offers information about their communicative intentions (to talk about an object) or other goals (to obtain an object) (Brooks & Meltzoff, 2005; Senju, Csibra, & Johnson, 2008). Around their first birthday, infants realize that a person's visual gaze signals a vital connection between the viewer and his or her surroundings, and they want to participate.

This **joint attention,** in which the child attends to the same object or event as the caregiver, who often labels it, contributes greatly to early language development. Infants and toddlers who frequently experience it sustain attention longer, comprehend more language, produce meaningful gestures and words earlier, and show faster vocabulary development through 2 years of age (Brooks & Meltzoff, 2008; Carpenter, Nagel, & Tomasello, 1998; Flom & Pick, 2003; Silvén, 2001). Gains in joint attention at the end of the first year enable babies to establish a "common ground" with the adult, through which they can figure out the meaning of the adult's verbal labels (Tomasello, 2003).

This baby uses a preverbal gesture to draw his caregiver's attention to a picture. The caregiver's verbal response promotes the baby's transition to spoken language.

Around 3 months, interactions between caregivers and babies begin to include *give-and-take*. Infants and mothers mutually imitate the pitch, loudness, and duration of each other's sounds. Mothers take the lead, imitating about twice as often as 3-month-olds, who limit their imitations to a small range of sounds—ones they find easier to produce (Gratier & Devouche, 2011). Between 4 and 6 months, imitation extends to social games, as in pat-a-cake and peekaboo. At first, the parent starts the game and the baby is an amused observer. Gradually, infants join in, and by the end of the first year, they participate actively, trading roles with the caregiver. Through these imitative exchanges, babies practice the turn-taking pattern of human conversation, a vital context for acquiring language and communication skills. Infants' vocalizations and play maturity during games predict advanced language progress during toddlerhood (Rome-Flanders & Cronk, 1995).

At the end of the first year, infants use *preverbal gestures* to direct adults' attention, influence their behavior, and convey helpful information (Tomasello, Carpenter, & Liszkowski, 2007). For example, Caitlin held up a toy to show it, pointed to the cupboard when she wanted a cookie, and pointed at her mother's car keys lying on the floor. Carolyn responded to these gestures and also labeled them ("That's your bear!" "You want a cookie!" "Oh, there are my keys!"). In this way, toddlers learn that using language leads to desired results.

© GERI ENGBERG/THE IMAGE WORKS

Besides using preverbal gestures to serve their own goals, 12-month-olds adapt these gestures to the needs of others. In one study, they pointed more often to an object whose location a searching adult did not know than to an object whose location the adult did know (Liszkowski, Carpenter, & Tomasello, 2008). They also understand what an adult means when she points to the location of a hidden toy (Behne et al., 2012). Already, the cooperative processes essential for effective communication are under way—namely, modifying messages to suit others' intentions and knowledge and recognizing when others have done the same.

The more time caregivers and infants spend in joint activity with objects, the earlier and more often babies use preverbal gestures (Salomo & Liszkowski, 2013). Over time, some of these gestures become explicitly symbolic. For example, a toddler might flap her arms to indicate "butterfly" or raise her palms to signal "all gone." Soon toddlers integrate words with gestures, using the gesture to expand their verbal message, as in pointing to a toy while saying "give" (Capirci et al., 2005). Gradually, gestures recede, and words become dominant. But the greater the number of items toddlers gesture about and the earlier they form word–gesture combinations, the faster their vocabulary growth, the sooner they produce two-word utterances at the end of the second year, and the more complex their sentences are at age 3½ (Huttenlocher et al., 2010; Rowe & Goldin-Meadow, 2009a, 2009b).

First Words

In the middle of the first year, infants begin to understand word meanings. By 5 months, they respond to their own name, preferring to listen to it than to another word matched in stress pattern (Mandel, Jusczyk, & Pisoni, 1995). And when 6-month-olds listened to the words "Mommy" or "Daddy" while viewing side-by-side videos of their parents, they looked longer at the video of the named parent (Tincoff & Jusczyk, 1999). At 9 months, after hearing a word paired with an object, babies looked longer at other objects in the same category than at those in a different category (Balaban & Waxman, 1997).

First spoken words, around 1 year, build on the sensorimotor foundations Piaget described and on categories infants have formed. In a study tracking the first 10 words used by several hundred U.S. and Chinese (both Mandarin- and Cantonese-speaking) babies, important people ("Mama," "Dada"), common objects ("ball," "bread"), and sound effects ("woof-woof," "vroom") were mentioned most often. Action words ("hit," "grab," "hug") and social routines ("hi," "bye"), though also appearing in all three groups, were more often produced by Chinese than U.S. babies—differences we will consider shortly (Tardif et al., 2008). Other investigations concur that earliest words usually include people, objects that move, foods, animals (in families with pets), familiar actions, outcomes of such actions ("hot," "wet"), and social terms (Hart, 2004; Nelson, 1973). In their first 50 words, toddlers rarely name things that just *sit there*, like "table" or "vase."

When young children first learn words, they sometimes apply them too narrowly, an error called **underextension.** At 16 months, Caitlin used "bear" only to refer to the worn and tattered teddy bear she carried nearly constantly. As vocabulary expands, a more common error is **overextension**—applying a word to a wider collection of objects and events than is appropriate. For example, Grace used "car" for buses, trains, trucks, and fire engines. Toddlers' overextensions reflect their sensitivity to categories (MacWhinney, 2005). They apply a new word to a group of similar experiences: "car" to wheeled objects, "open" to opening a door, peeling fruit, and untying shoelaces. This suggests that children often overextend deliberately because they have difficulty recalling or have not acquired a suitable word. And when a word is hard to pronounce, toddlers are likely to substitute a related one they can say (Bloom, 2000). As vocabulary expands and pronunciation improves, overextensions gradually decline.

The Two-Word Utterance Phase

Young toddlers add to their spoken vocabularies at a rate of one to three words a week. Because gains in word production between 18 and 24 months are so impressive (one or two words per day), many researchers concluded that toddlers undergo a *spurt in vocabulary*—a transition

---

LOOK and LISTEN

Observe a toddler for 30 to 60 minutes at home or child care. Jot down preverbal gestures, words, and word–gesture combinations that the baby produces. Do the toddler's language skills fit with research findings?

Toddlers typically utter their first word around 1 year. As their experiences broaden, they label more objects and events, first with single words and then with two-word utterances known as telegraphic speech.

from a slower to a faster learning phase. In actuality, most children show a steady increase in rate of word learning that continues through the preschool years (Ganger & Brent, 2004).

How do toddlers build their vocabularies so quickly? In the second year, they improve in ability to categorize experience, recall words, and grasp others' social cues to meaning, such as eye gaze, pointing, and handling objects (Golinkoff & Hirsh-Pasek, 2006; Liszkowski, Carpenter, & Tomasello, 2007). Furthermore, as toddlers' experiences broaden, they have a wider range of interesting objects and events to label. For example, children approaching age 2 more often mention places to go ("park," "store"). And as they construct a clearer self-image, they add more words that refer to themselves ("me," "mine," "Katy") and to their own and others' bodies and clothing ("eyes," "mouth," "jacket" (Hart, 2004). In Chapter 9, we will consider the diverse strategies young children use to figure out word meanings.

Once toddlers produce 200 to 250 words, they start to combine two words: "Mommy shoe," "go car," "more cookie." These two-word utterances are called **telegraphic speech** because, like a telegram, they focus on high-content words, omitting smaller, less important ones ("can," "the," "to"). Children the world over use them to express an impressive variety of meanings.

Two-word speech consists largely of simple formulas ("more + X," "eat + X"), with different words inserted in the "X" position. Toddlers rarely make gross grammatical errors, such as saying "chair my" instead of "my chair." But their word-order regularities are usually copies of adult word pairings, as when Carolyn remarked to Caitlin, "How about *more sandwich?*" or "Let's see if you can *eat the berries?*" (Tomasello, 2003; Tomasello & Brandt, 2009). When 18- to 23-month-olds were taught noun and verb nonsense words (for example, "meek" for a doll and "gop" for a snapping action), they easily combined the new nouns with words they knew well ("more meek"). But they seldom formed word combinations with the new verbs (Tomasello, 2000; Tomasello et al., 1997). This suggests that they cannot yet flexibly form novel sentences that express subject–verb and verb–object relations, which are the foundation of grammar.

In sum, toddlers are absorbed in figuring out word meanings and using their limited vocabularies in whatever way possible to get their thoughts across. At first, they rely on "concrete pieces of language" they often hear, gradually generalizing from those pieces to word-order and other grammatical rules (Bannard, Lieven, & Tomasello, 2009; Tomasello, 2006). As we will see in Chapter 7, they make steady progress over the preschool years.

Comprehension versus Production

So far, we have focused on language **production**—the words and word combinations children use. What about **comprehension**—the language they understand? At all ages, comprehension develops ahead of production. A five-month lag exists between the time toddlers typically comprehend 50 words (around 13 months) and the time they produce that many (around 18 months) (Menyuk, Liebergott, & Schultz, 1995).

Think back to the distinction made earlier in this chapter between two types of memory—recognition and recall. Comprehension requires only that children *recognize* the meaning of a word. But for production, children must *recall*, or actively retrieve from their memories, not only the word but also the concept for which it stands. Still, the two capacities are related. The speed and accuracy of toddlers' comprehension of spoken language increase dramatically over the second year. And toddlers who are faster and more accurate in comprehension tend to show more rapid growth in words understood and produced over the following year (Fernald & Marchman, 2012). Quick comprehension frees space in working memory for picking up new words and for the more demanding task of using them to communicate.

Individual and Cultural Differences

Although children typically produce their first word around their first birthday, the range is large, from 8 to 18 months—variation due to a complex blend of genetic and environmental influences. Earlier we saw that Timmy's spoken language was delayed, in part because of Vanessa's tense, directive communication with him. But Timmy is also a boy, and research indicates that girls are slightly ahead of boys in early vocabulary growth (Fenson et al., 1994; Van Hulle, Goldsmith, & Lemery, 2004). The most common explanation is girls' faster rate of physical maturation, which is believed to promote earlier development of the left cerebral hemisphere.

Temperament matters, too. Shy toddlers often wait until they understand a great deal before trying to speak. Once they do speak, their vocabularies increase rapidly, although they remain slightly behind their agemates (Spere et al., 2004). Emotionally negative toddlers also acquire language more slowly because their high reactivity diverts them from processing linguistic information (Salley & Dixon, 2007).

Caregiver–child conversation—especially, the richness of adults' vocabularies—also play a strong role (Huttenlocher et al. 2010). Commonly used words for objects appear early in toddlers' speech, and the more often their caregivers use a particular noun, the sooner young children produce it (Goodman, Dale, & Li, 2008). Mothers talk more to toddler-age girls than to boys, and parents converse less often with shy than with sociable children (Leaper, Anderson, & Sanders, 1998; Patterson & Fisher, 2002).

Compared to their higher-SES agemates, children from low-SES homes usually have smaller vocabularies. By 18 to 24 months, they are slower at word comprehension and have acquired 30 percent fewer words (Fernald, Marchman & Weisleder, 2013). Limited parent–child conversation and book reading are major factors. Higher-SES parents typically interact more with their children, using a richer vocabulary, than do low-SES parents (Hoff, 2006). And on average, a middle-SES child is read to for 1,000 hours between 1 and 5 years, a low-SES child for only 25 hours (Neuman, 2003).

Not surprisingly, rate of early vocabulary growth is a strong predictor of low-SES children's vocabulary size at kindergarten entry, which forecasts their later literacy skills and school success (Rowe, Raudenbush, & Goldin-Meadow, 2012). Higher-SES toddlers who lag behind their agemates in word learning have more opportunities to catch up in early childhood.

Young children have distinct styles of early language learning. Caitlin and Grace, like most toddlers, used a **referential style;** their vocabularies consisted mainly of words that referred to objects. A smaller number of toddlers use an **expressive style;** compared to referential children, they produce many more social formulas and pronouns ("thank you," "done," "I want it"). These styles reflect early ideas about the functions of language. Grace, for example, thought words were for naming things. In the week after her adoption, she uttered only a single word in Khmer, her native language. But after two months of listening to English conversation, Grace added words quickly: "Eli," then "doggie," "kitty," "Mama," "Dada," "book," "ball," "car," "cup," "clock," and "chicken"—all within one week. In contrast, expressive-style children believe words are for talking about people's feelings and needs. The vocabularies of referential-style toddlers grow faster because all languages contain many more object labels than social terms (Bates et al., 1994).

What accounts for a toddler's language style? Rapidly developing referential-style children often have an especially active interest in exploring objects. They also eagerly imitate their parents' frequent naming of objects, and their parents imitate back, which helps children remember new labels (Masur & Rodemaker, 1999). Expressive-style children tend to be highly sociable, and their parents more often use verbal routines ("How are you?" "It's no trouble") that support social relationships (Goldfield, 1987).

The two language styles are also linked to culture. Object words (nouns) are particularly common in the vocabularies of English-speaking toddlers, but Chinese, Japanese, and Korean toddlers have more words for actions (verbs) and

© TINA MANLEY/ASIA/ALAMY

This Chinese mother's communication with her toddler probably includes many words for actions and social routines. Her child—like other Chinese children—is likely to display an expressive style, focused on strengthening social relationships.

Applying What We Know

Supporting Early Language Learning

STRATEGY	CONSEQUENCE
Respond to coos and babbles with speech sounds and words.	Encourages experimentation with sounds that can later be blended into first words
	Provides experience with the turn-taking pattern of human conversation
Establish joint attention and comment on what child sees.	Predicts earlier onset of language and faster vocabulary development
Play social games, such as pat-a-cake and peekaboo.	Provides experience with the turn-taking pattern of human conversation
Engage toddlers in joint make-believe play.	Promotes all aspects of conversational dialogue
Engage toddlers in frequent conversations.	Predicts faster early language development and academic success during the school years
Read to toddlers often, engaging them in dialogues about picture books.	Provides exposure to many aspects of language, including vocabulary, grammar, communication skills, and information about written symbols and story structures

social routines. Mothers' speech in each culture reflects this difference (Chan, Brandone, & Tardif, 2009; Chan et al., 2011; Choi & Gopnik, 1995; Fernald & Morikawa, 1993). American mothers frequently label objects when interacting with their babies. Asian mothers, perhaps because of a cultural emphasis on the importance of group membership, emphasize actions and social routines. Also, in Mandarin, sentences often begin with verbs, making action words particularly salient to Mandarin-speaking toddlers.

At what point should parents become concerned if their child talks very little or not at all? If a toddler's development is greatly delayed when compared with the norms in Table 6.3 (page 235), then parents should consult the child's doctor or a speech and language therapist. Late babbling or gesturing may be signs of slow language development that can be prevented with early intervention (Rowe, Raudenbush, & Goldin-Meadow, 2012). Some toddlers who do not follow simple directions or who, after age 2, have difficulty putting their thoughts into words may suffer from a hearing impairment or a language disorder that requires immediate treatment.

Supporting Early Language Development

Consistent with the interactionist view, a rich social environment builds on young children's natural readiness to speak their native tongue. For a summary of how caregivers can consciously support early language learning, see Applying What We Know above. Caregivers also do so unconsciously—through a special style of speech.

Adults in many countries speak to young children in **infant-directed speech (IDS),** a form of communication made up of short sentences with high-pitched, exaggerated expression, clear pronunciation, distinct pauses between speech segments, clear gestures to support verbal meaning, and repetition of new words in a variety of contexts ("See the *ball.*" "The *ball* bounced!") (Fernald et al., 1989; O'Neill et al., 2005). Deaf parents use a similar style of communication when signing to their deaf babies (Masataka, 1996). From birth on, infants prefer IDS over other kinds of adult talk, and by 5 months they are more emotionally responsive to it (Aslin, Jusczyk, & Pisoni, 1998).

IDS builds on several communicative strategies we have already considered: joint attention, turn-taking, and caregivers' sensitivity to toddlers' preverbal gestures. In this example, Carolyn uses IDS with 18-month-old Caitlin:

Caitlin: "Go car."
Carolyn: "Yes, time to go in the car. Where's your jacket?"
Caitlin: [Looks around; walks to the closet.] "Dacket!" [Points to her jacket.]

Carolyn:	"There's that jacket! *[She helps Caitlin into the jacket.]* On it goes! Let's zip up. *[Zips up the jacket.]* Now, say bye-bye to Grace and Timmy."
Caitlin:	"Bye-bye, G-ace. Bye-bye, Te-te."
Carolyn:	"Where's your bear?"
Caitlin:	*[Looks around.]*
Carolyn:	*[Pointing.]* "See? By the sofa." *[Caitlin gets the bear.]*

A mother speaks to her baby in short, clearly pronounced sentences with high-pitched, exaggerated intonation. This form of communication, called infant-directed speech, eases language learning for infants and toddlers.

Notice how Carolyn kept her utterance length just ahead of Caitlin's, creating a sensitive match between language stimulation and Caitlin's current capacities. Parents constantly fine-tune the length and content of their utterances in IDS to fit children's needs—adjustments that enable infants and toddlers to join in and that foster both language comprehension and production (Cameron-Faulkner, Lieven, & Tomasello, 2003; Ma et al., 2011; Rowe, 2008).

As we saw earlier, parent–toddler conversation strongly predicts language development and later academic success. It provides many examples of speech just ahead of the child's current level and a sympathetic environment in which children can try out new skills. Dialogues about picture books are particularly effective. They expose children to great breadth of language and literacy knowledge, from vocabulary, grammar, and communication skills to information about written symbols and story structures. From the end of the first year through early childhood, children who experience regular adult–child book reading are substantially ahead of their agemates in language skills (Karrass & Braungart-Rieker, 2005; Whitehurst & Lonigan, 1998).

Research also reveals that live interaction with a responsive adult is far better suited to spurring early language development than media sources. After a month's regular exposure to a commercial video for babies that labeled common household objects, 12- to 18-month-olds did not add any more words to their vocabulary than nonviewing controls. Rather, toddlers in a comparison group whose parents spent time teaching them the words in everyday activities learned best (DeLoache et al., 2010). Consistent with these findings, a video format that allows an adult to interact responsively with a 2-year-old—as in a Skype session—is an effective context for acquiring new verbs (Roseberry et al., 2014). But viewers younger than age 3 are unable to learn language from TV or video alone—even from programs specially designed for them (Krcmar, Grela, & Lin, 2007; Roseberry et al., 2009). **TAKE A MOMENT...** Return to page 210 to review the *video deficit effect,* noting how these findings illustrate it.

Do social experiences that promote early language development remind you of those that strengthen cognitive development in general? IDS and parent–child conversation create a *zone of proximal development* in which children's language expands. In contrast, adult behaviors that are unresponsive to children's needs or impatient with their efforts to talk result in immature language skills (Baumwell, Tamis-LeMonda, & Bornstein, 1997; Cabrera, Shannon, & Tamis-LeMonda, 2007). In the next chapter, we will see that adult sensitivity supports infants' and toddlers' emotional and social development as well.

Ask Yourself

- **REVIEW** Why is the social-interactionist perspective attractive to many investigators of language development? Cite evidence that supports it.

- **CONNECT** Cognition and language are interrelated. List examples of how cognition fosters language development. Next, list examples of how language fosters cognitive development.

- **APPLY** Fran frequently corrects her 17-month-old son Jeremy's attempts to talk and—fearing that he won't use words—refuses to respond to his gestures. How might Fran be contributing to Jeremy's slow language progress?

- **REFLECT** Find an opportunity to speak to an infant or toddler. Did you use IDS? What features of your speech are likely to promote early language development, and why?

Summary

Piaget's Cognitive-Developmental Theory (p. 201)

6.1 According to Piaget, how do schemes change over the course of development?

- By acting on the environment, children move through four stages in which psychological structures, or **schemes,** achieve a better fit with external reality.

- Schemes change in two ways: through **adaptation,** which is made up of two complementary activities—**assimilation** and **accommodation;** and through **organization,** the internal rearrangement of schemes into a strongly interconnected cognitive system.

6.2 Describe major cognitive attainments of the sensorimotor stage.

- In the **sensorimotor stage,** the **circular reaction** provides a means of adapting first schemes, and the newborn baby's reflexes gradually transform into the more flexible action patterns of the older infant. Around 8 months, infants develop **intentional, or goal-directed, behavior** and begin to understand **object permanence.**

- Twelve- to 18-month-olds engage in more deliberate, varied exploration and no longer make the **A-not-B search error.** Between 18 and 24 months, **mental representation** is evident in sudden solutions to sensorimotor problems, mastery of object-permanence problems involving invisible displacement, **deferred imitation,** and **make-believe play.**

6.3 What does follow-up research say about infant cognitive development and the accuracy of Piaget's sensorimotor stage?

- Many studies suggest that infants display a variety of understandings earlier than Piaget believed. Some awareness of object permanence, as revealed by the **violation-of-expectation method** and object-tracking research, may be evident in the first few months.

- Furthermore, young infants display deferred imitation, and by 10 to 12 months, they solve problems by analogy—attainments that require mental representation. Older infants and toddlers even imitate rationally, by inferring others' intentions.

- A major advance in symbolic understanding, occurring around the first birthday, is **displaced reference**—the realization that words can be used to cue mental images of things not physically present. The capacity to use language to modify mental representations improves from the end of the second into the third year. Awareness of the symbolic function of pictures emerges in the first year and strengthens in the second. Around 2½ years, the **video deficit effect** declines; children grasp the symbolic meaning of video.

- Today, researchers believe that newborns have more built-in equipment for making sense of their world than Piaget assumed, although they disagree on how much initial understanding infants have. According to the **core knowledge perspective,** infants are born with core domains of thought, including physical, psychological, linguistic, and numerical knowledge, that support rapid cognitive development.

© EDITH HELD/CORBIS

- Broad agreement exists that many cognitive changes of infancy are continuous rather than stagelike and that various aspects of cognition develop unevenly, rather than in an integrated fashion.

Information Processing (p. 214)

6.4 Describe the information-processing view of cognitive development and the general structure of the information-processing system.

- Information-processing researchers assume that we hold information in three parts of the mental system: the **sensory register;** the **short-term memory store;** and **long-term memory.** The **central executive** joins with **working memory**—our "mental workspace"—to process information effectively. Well-learned **automatic processes** require no space in working memory, permitting us to focus on other information while performing them.

- Gains in **executive function**—including attention, impulse control, coordinating information in working memory, and flexible thinking—predict important cognitive and social outcomes.

6.5 What changes in attention, memory, and categorization take place over the first two years?

- With age, infants attend to more aspects of the environment and take information in more quickly. In the second year, attention to novelty declines and sustained attention improves.

- Young infants are capable of **recognition** memory. By the middle of the first year, they also engage in **recall.** Both recognition and recall improve steadily with age.

- Infants group stimuli into an expanding array of categories. In the second year, toddlers begin to categorize flexibly, switching their basis of object sorting, and their grasp of the animate–inanimate distinction expands. Babies' exploration of objects, expanding knowledge of the world, and advancing language skills foster categorization.

6.6 Describe the strengths and limitations of the information-processing approach to early cognitive development.

- Information-processing findings challenge Piaget's view of infants as purely sensorimotor beings who cannot mentally represent experiences. But information processing has not yet provided a broad, comprehensive theory of children's thinking.

The Social Context of Early Cognitive Development (p. 222)

6.7 How does Vygotsky's concept of the zone of proximal development expand our understanding of early cognitive development?

- Vygotsky believed that children master tasks within the **zone of proximal development**—ones just ahead of their current capacities—through the support and guidance of more skilled partners. As early as the first year, cultural variations in social experiences affect mental strategies.

© JAMES SHAFFER/PHOTOEDIT

Individual Differences in Early Mental Development (p. 225)

6.8 Describe the mental testing approach, the meaning of intelligence test scores, and the extent to which infant tests predict later performance.

- The mental testing approach measures intellectual development in an effort to predict future performance. Scores are arrived at by computing an **intelligence quotient (IQ),** which compares an individual's performance with that of a **standardization** sample of same-age individuals, whose performances form a **normal distribution.**

- Infant tests consisting largely of perceptual and motor responses predict later intelligence poorly. As a result, scores on infant tests are called **developmental quotients (DQs)**, rather than IQs. Speed of habituation and recovery to visual stimuli is a better predictor of future performance.

6.9 Discuss environmental influences on early mental development, including home, child care, and early intervention for at-risk infants and toddlers.

- Research with the **Home Observation for Measurement of the Environment (HOME)** shows that an organized, stimulating home environment and parental affection, involvement, and encouragement repeatedly predict higher mental test scores. Although the HOME–IQ relationship is partly due to heredity, family living conditions also affect mental development.

© RICK GOMEZ/CORBIS

- Quality of infant and toddler child care influences cognitive, language, academic, and social skills. Standards for **developmentally appropriate practice** specify program characteristics that meet young children's developmental needs.
- Intensive intervention beginning in infancy and extending through early childhood can help prevent the gradual declines in intelligence and the poor academic performance evident in many poverty-stricken children.

Language Development (p. 231)

6.10 Describe theories of language development, and indicate the emphasis each places on innate abilities and environmental influences.

- Chomsky's nativist theory regards children as naturally endowed with a **language acquisition device (LAD)**. Consistent with this perspective, a grammatically complex language system is unique to humans.
- Although language-related structures—Broca's and Wernicke's areas—exist in the left hemisphere of the cerebral cortex, their roles are more complex than previously assumed. But the broad association of language functions with left-hemispheric regions is consistent with Chomsky's notion of a brain prepared to process language. Evidence for a sensitive period for language development also supports this view.
- Recent theories suggest that language development results from *interactions* between inner capacities and environmental influences. Some interactionists apply the information-processing perspective to language development. Others emphasize the importance of children's social skills and language experiences.

6.11 Describe major milestones of language development in the first two years, individual differences, and ways adults can support infants' and toddlers' emerging capacities.

- Infants begin **cooing** at 2 months and **babbling** around 6 months. Around 10 to 11 months, their skill at establishing **joint attention** improves, and soon they use preverbal gestures. Adults can encourage language progress by responding to infants' coos and babbles, playing turn-taking games, establishing joint attention and labeling what babies see, and responding verbally to their preverbal gestures.

- Around 12 months, toddlers say their first word. Young children often make errors of **underextension** and **overextension**. Rate of word learning increases steadily, and once vocabulary reaches about 200 to 250 words, two-word utterances called **telegraphic speech** appear. At all ages, language **comprehension** develops ahead of **production**.

JO UNRUH/GETTY IMAGES

- Girls show faster progress than boys, and both shy and emotionally negative toddlers acquire language more slowly. Low-SES children, who receive less verbal stimulation than higher-SES children, have smaller vocabularies—a strong predictor of later language and literacy skills.
- Most toddlers use a **referential style** of language learning, in which early words consist largely of names for objects. A few use an **expressive style,** in which social formulas and pronouns are common and vocabulary grows more slowly.
- Adults in many cultures speak to young children in **infant-directed speech (IDS),** a simplified form of communication that is well-suited to their learning needs. Parent–toddler conversation is one of the best predictors of early language development and academic competence during the school years.

Important Terms and Concepts

accommodation (p. 202)
adaptation (p. 202)
A-not-B search error (p. 204)
assimilation (p. 202)
autobiographical memory (p. 220)
automatic processes (p. 216)
babbling (p. 235)
central executive (p. 216)
circular reaction (p. 203)
comprehension (p. 238)
cooing (p. 235)
core knowledge perspective (p. 211)
deferred imitation (p. 205)
developmentally appropriate practice (p. 228)
developmental quotient (DQ) (p. 226)
displaced reference (p. 209)

executive function (p. 216)
expressive style (p. 239)
Home Observation for Measurement of the Environment (HOME) (p. 226)
infant-directed speech (IDS) (p. 240)
infantile amnesia (p. 220)
intelligence quotient (IQ) (p. 225)
intentional, or goal-directed, behavior (p. 204)
joint attention (p. 236)
language acquisition device (LAD) (p. 231)
long-term memory (p. 216)
make-believe play (p. 205)
mental representation (p. 205)
normal distribution (p. 225)
object permanence (p. 204)
organization (p. 202)

overextension (p. 237)
production (p. 238)
recall (p. 218)
recognition (p. 218)
referential style (p. 239)
scheme (p. 202)
sensorimotor stage (p. 201)
sensory register (p. 215)
short-term memory store (p. 215)
standardization (p. 225)
telegraphic speech (p. 238)
underextension (p. 237)
video deficit effect (p. 210)
violation-of-expectation method (p. 205)
working memory (p. 215)
zone of proximal development (p. 222)

Emotional and Social Development in Infancy and Toddlerhood

"The Mother and Child"
Ruvini Ariyaranthna
Kahingala
16 years, Sri Lanka

A mutual embrace reflects the strong, affectionate bond between this mother and child. Chapter 7 considers the importance of parental love and sensitivity for infants' and toddlers' feelings of security and competence.

REPRINTED WITH PERMISSION FROM THE INTERNATIONAL MUSEUM OF CHILDREN'S ART, OSLO, NORWAY

As Caitlin reached 8 months of age, her parents noticed that she had become more fearful. One evening, when Carolyn and David left her with a babysitter, she wailed as they headed for the door—an experience she had accepted easily a few weeks earlier. Caitlin and Timmy's caregiver Ginette also observed an increasing wariness of strangers. When she turned to go to another room, both babies dropped their play to crawl after her. At the mail carrier's knock at the door, they clung to Ginette's legs, reaching out to be picked up.

At the same time, each baby seemed more willful. Removing an object from the hand produced little response at 5 months. But at 8 months, when Timmy's mother, Vanessa, took away a table knife he had managed to reach, Timmy burst into angry screams and could not be consoled or distracted.

All Monica and Kevin knew about Grace's first year was that she had been deeply loved by her destitute, homeless mother. Separation from her, followed by a long journey to an unfamiliar home, had left Grace in shock. At first she was extremely sad, turning away when Monica or Kevin picked her up. But as Grace's new parents held her close, spoke gently, and satisfied her craving for food, Grace returned their affection. Two weeks after her arrival, her despondency gave way to a sunny, easygoing disposition. She burst into a wide grin, reached out at the sight of Monica and Kevin, and laughed at her brother Eli's funny faces. Among her first words were the names of family members—"Eli," "Mama," and "Dada." As her second birthday approached, she pointed to herself, exclaiming "Gwace!" and laid claim to treasured possessions. "Gwace's chicken!" she would announce at mealtimes, sucking the marrow from the drumstick, a practice she had brought with her from Cambodia.

Taken together, the children's reactions reflect two related aspects of personality that develop during the first two years: close ties to others and a sense of self. We begin with Erikson's psychosocial theory, which provides an overview of personality development during infancy and toddlerhood. Then, as we chart the course of emotional development, we will discover why fear and anger became more apparent in Caitlin's and Timmy's range of emotions by the end of the first year. Our attention then turns to individual differences in temperament. We will examine biological and environmental contributions to these differences and their consequences for future development.

Next, we take up attachment to the caregiver, the child's first affectionate tie. We will see how the feelings of security that grow out of this important bond support the child's exploration, sense of independence, and expanding social relationships.

Finally, we focus on early self-development. By the end of toddlerhood, Grace recognized herself in mirrors and photographs, labeled herself as a girl, and showed the beginnings of self-control. "Don't touch!" she instructed herself one day as she resisted the desire to pull a lamp cord out of its socket. Cognitive advances combine with social experiences to produce these changes during the second year. ■

7.1 What personality changes take place during Erikson's stages of basic trust versus mistrust and autonomy versus shame and doubt?

Erikson's Theory of Infant and Toddler Personality

Our discussion of major theories in Chapter 1 revealed that psychoanalytic theory is no longer in the mainstream of child development research. But one of its lasting contributions is its ability to capture the essence of personality during each period of development. Recall that although Freud's preoccupation with the channeling of biological drives and his neglect of important experiences beyond infancy and early childhood came to be heavily criticized, the basic outlines of his theory were accepted and elaborated in several subsequent theories. The most influential is Erik Erikson's *psychosocial theory*, also introduced in Chapter 1.

Basic Trust versus Mistrust

Erikson accepted Freud's emphasis on the importance of the parent–infant relationship during feeding, but he expanded and enriched Freud's view. A healthy outcome during infancy, Erikson believed, does not depend on the *amount* of food or oral stimulation offered but rather on the *quality* of caregiving: relieving discomfort promptly and sensitively, holding the infant gently, waiting patiently until the baby has had enough milk, and weaning when the infant shows less interest in breast or bottle.

Erikson recognized that no parent can be perfectly in tune with the baby's needs. Many factors affect parental responsiveness—feelings of personal happiness, current life conditions (for example, additional young children in the family), and culturally valued child-rearing practices. But when the *balance of care* is sympathetic and loving, the psychological conflict of the first year—**basic trust versus mistrust**—is resolved on the positive side. The trusting infant expects the world to be good and gratifying. As a result, he feels confident about venturing out and exploring it, and he emerges from this stage well-prepared for the challenges of toddlerhood. The mistrustful baby cannot count on the kindness and compassion of others, so she protects herself by withdrawing from people and things around her.

On a visit to a science museum, a 2-year-old explores a flight simulator. As the mother supports her toddler's desire to "do it myself," she fosters a healthy sense of autonomy.

© SYRACUSE NEWSPAPERS/S. CANNERELLI/THE IMAGE WORKS

Autonomy versus Shame and Doubt

With the transition to toddlerhood, Freud viewed the parent's manner of toilet training as decisive for psychological health. In Erikson's view, toilet training is only one of many influential experiences. The familiar refrains of newly walking, talking toddlers—"No!" "Do it myself!"—reveal that they have entered a new period of budding selfhood. They want to decide for themselves, not just in toileting but also in other situations. The conflict of toddlerhood, **autonomy versus shame and doubt,** is resolved favorably when parents provide young children with suitable guidance and reasonable choices. A self-confident, secure 2-year-old has parents who do not criticize or attack him when he fails at new skills—using the toilet, eating with a spoon, or putting away toys. And they meet his assertions of independence with tolerance and understanding—for example, by giving him an extra five minutes to finish his play before leaving for the grocery store. In contrast, when parents are over- or undercontrolling, the outcome is a child who feels forced and shamed and who doubts his ability to control his impulses and act competently on his own.

In sum, basic trust and autonomy grow out of warm, sensitive parenting and reasonable expectations for impulse control starting in the second year. If children emerge from the first few years without sufficient trust in caregivers and without a healthy sense of individuality, the seeds are sown for adjustment problems. Adults who have difficulty establishing intimate ties, who are overly dependent on a loved one, or who continually doubt their own ability to meet new challenges may not have fully mastered the tasks of trust and autonomy during infancy and toddlerhood.

Emotional Development

TAKE A MOMENT... Observe several infants and toddlers, noting the emotions each displays, the cues you rely on to interpret the baby's emotional state, and how caregivers respond. Researchers have conducted many such observations to find out how babies convey their emotions and interpret those of others. They have discovered that emotions play powerful roles in organizing the attainments that Erikson regarded as so important: social relationships, exploration of the environment, and discovery of the self (Halle, 2003; Saarni et al., 2006).

Think back to the *dynamic systems perspective* introduced in Chapters 1 and 5. As you read about early emotional development in the sections that follow, notice how emotions are an integral part of young children's dynamic systems of action. Emotions energize development. At the same time, they are an aspect of the system that develops, becoming more varied and complex as children reorganize their behavior to attain new goals (Campos, Frankel, & Camras, 2004; Camras, 2011).

Because infants cannot describe their feelings, determining exactly which emotions they are experiencing is a challenge. Although vocalizations and body movements provide some information, facial expressions offer the most reliable cues. Cross-cultural evidence reveals that people around the world associate photographs of different facial expressions with emotions in the same way (Ekman & Friesen, 1972; Ekman & Matsumoto, 2011). These findings inspired researchers to analyze infants' facial patterns to determine the range of emotions they display at different ages.

Nevertheless, assuming a close correspondence between a pattern of behavior and an underlying emotional state can lead to error. Infants, children, and adults use diverse responses to express a particular emotion. For example, babies on the visual cliff (see page 190 in Chapter 5) generally do not display a fearful facial expression, though they do show signs of avoidance—drawing back and refusing to crawl over the deep side. And the emotional expressions of blind babies, who cannot make eye contact, are muted, prompting parents to withdraw. When therapists show parents how blind infants express emotions through finger movements, parents become more interactive (Fraiberg, 1971; Saarni et al., 2006). Furthermore, the same general response can express several emotions. Depending on the situation, a smile might convey joy, embarrassment, contempt, or a social greeting.

In line with the dynamic systems view, emotional expressions vary with the individual's developing capacities, goals, and context. To infer babies' emotions more accurately, researchers must attend to multiple interacting expressive cues—vocal, facial, and gestural—and see how they vary across situations believed to elicit different emotions (Lewis, 2008). With these ideas in mind, let's chart the course of early emotional development.

Basic Emotions

Basic emotions—happiness, interest, surprise, fear, anger, sadness, and disgust—are universal in humans and other primates and have a long evolutionary history of promoting survival. Do infants come into the world with the ability to express basic emotions? Although signs of some emotions are present, babies' earliest emotional life consists of little more than two global arousal states: attraction to pleasant stimulation and withdrawal from unpleasant stimulation (Camras et al., 2003). Only gradually do emotions become clear, well-organized signals.

The dynamic systems perspective helps us understand how this happens: Children coordinate separate skills into more effective, emotionally expressive systems as the central nervous system develops and the child's goals and experiences change (Camras & Shutter, 2010).

7.2 Describe the development of basic emotions over the first year, noting the adaptive function of each.

7.3 Summarize changes during the first two years in understanding others' emotions, self-conscious emotions, and emotional self-regulation.

Videotaping the facial expressions of her daughter from 6 to 14 weeks, Linda Camras (1992) found that in the early weeks, the baby displayed a fleeting angry face as she was about to cry and a sad face as her crying waned. At first, these expressions appeared on the way to or from full-blown distress and were not clearly linked to the baby's experiences and desires. With age, she was better able to sustain an angry signal when she encountered a blocked goal and a sad signal when she could not overcome an obstacle.

According to one view, sensitive, contingent caregiver communication, in which parents selectively mirror aspects of the baby's diffuse emotional behavior, helps infants construct emotional expressions that more closely resemble those of adults (Gergely & Watson, 1999). With age, face, gaze, voice, and posture form organized patterns that vary meaningfully with environmental events. For example, Caitlin typically responded to her parents' playful interaction with a joyful face, pleasant babbling, and a relaxed posture, as if to say, "This is fun!" In contrast, an unresponsive parent often evokes a sad face, fussy sounds, and a drooping body (sending the message, "I'm despondent") or an angry face, crying, and "pick-me-up" gestures (as if to say, "Change this unpleasant event!") (Weinberg & Tronick, 1994). Gradually, emotional expressions become well-organized and specific—and therefore provide more precise information about the infant's internal state.

Four basic emotions—happiness, anger, sadness, and fear—that have received the most research attention. Let's see how they develop.

HAPPINESS Happiness—expressed first in blissful smiles, later through exuberant laughter—contributes to many aspects of development. When infants achieve new skills, they smile and laugh, displaying delight in motor and cognitive mastery. As the smile encourages caregivers to be affectionate and stimulating, the baby smiles even more (Aksan & Kochanska, 2004). Happiness binds parent and baby into a warm, supportive relationship that fosters the infant's developing competencies.

During the early weeks, newborn babies smile when full, during REM sleep, and in response to gentle touches and sounds, such as stroking of the skin, rocking, and the mother's soft, high-pitched voice. By the end of the first month, infants smile at dynamic, eye-catching sights, such as a bright object jumping suddenly across their field of vision. As infants attend to the parent's face and the parent talks and smiles, babies knit their brows, open their mouths to coo, and move their arms and legs excitedly, gradually becoming more emotionally positive until, between 6 and 10 weeks, the parent's communication evokes a broad grin called the **social smile** (Lavelli & Fogel, 2005; Sroufe & Waters, 1976). These changes parallel the development of infant perceptual capacities—in particular, sensitivity to visual patterns, including the human face (see Chapter 5). And social smiling becomes better-organized and stable as babies learn to use it to evoke and sustain pleasurable face-to-face interaction with the parent.

Development of the social smile, however, varies substantially with culture. The Nso people, a rural farming society of Cameroon, highly value infant calmness, so Nso caregivers discourage emotional expressiveness of all kinds and, instead, emphasize soothing (Keller & Otto, 2009). In contrast, Western middle-SES parents, who value self-expression, enthusiastically promote active social engagement in their babies. In line with these differences, observations of Nso and urban German mother–infant pairs between 6 and 12 weeks revealed that the Nso mothers participated in far fewer face-to-face imitative exchanges, including smiling. As a result, the social smile was considerably delayed in Nso babies (see Figure 7.1) (Wörmann et al., 2012). At 12 weeks, far fewer Nso than German infants smiled during mother–infant mutual gazing.

Laughter, which typically appears around 3 to 4 months, reflects faster processing of information than smiling. But as with smiling, the first laughs occur in response to very active stimuli, such as the parent saying playfully, "I'm gonna get you!" and kissing the baby's tummy. As infants understand more about their world, they laugh at events with subtler elements of surprise, such as a silent game of peekaboo (Sroufe & Wunsch, 1972).

© RADIUS IMAGES/ALAMY IMAGES

This baby's laughter encourages his mother to respond in kind, binding them together in a warm, affectionate relationship that promotes all aspects of development.

Around the middle of the first year, babies smile and laugh more often when interacting with familiar people, a preference that strengthens the parent–child bond. Between 8 and 10 months, infants more often interrupt their play with an interesting toy to relay their delight to an attentive adult (Venezia et al., 2004). And like adults, 10- to 12-month-olds have several smiles, which vary with context— a broad, "cheek-raised" smile in response to a parent's greeting; a reserved, muted smile for a friendly stranger; and a "mouth-open" smile during stimulating play (Bolzani et al., 2002; Messinger & Fogel, 2007). By the end of the first year, the smile has become a deliberate social signal.

ANGER AND SADNESS Newborn babies respond with generalized distress to a variety of unpleasant experiences, including hunger, painful medical procedures, changes in body temperature, and too much or too little stimulation (see Chapter 4). From 4 to 6 months into the second year, angry expressions increase in frequency and intensity (Braungart-Rieker, Hill-Soderlund, & Karrass, 2010). Older infants also react with anger in a wider range of situations—when an interesting object or event is removed, an expected pleasant event does not occur, their arms are restrained, the caregiver leaves for a brief time, or they are put down for a nap (Camras et al., 1992; Stenberg & Campos, 1990; Sullivan & Lewis, 2003).

Why do angry reactions increase with age? As infants become capable of intentional behavior (see Chapter 6), they want to control their own actions and the effects they produce (Mascolo & Fischer, 2007). Furthermore, older infants are better at identifying who caused them pain or removed a toy. Their anger is particularly intense when a caregiver from whom they have come to expect warm behavior causes discomfort. And increased parental limit setting once babies crawl and walk contributes to babies' angry responses (Roben et al., 2012). The rise in anger is also adaptive. Independent movement enables an angry infant to defend herself or overcome an obstacle to obtain a desired object. Finally, anger motivates caregivers to relieve the infant's distress and, in the case of separation, may discourage them from leaving again soon.

Although expressions of sadness also occur in response to pain, removal of an object, and brief separations, they are less common than anger. In contrast, sadness occurs often when infants are deprived of a familiar, loving caregiver (as illustrated by Grace's despondency in the weeks after her adoption) and when parent–infant interaction is seriously disrupted. In several studies, researchers had parents interact with their babies and then, suddenly, assume either a still-faced, unreactive pose or a depressed emotional state. Their 2- to 7-month-olds tried facial expressions, vocalizations, and body movements to get the parent to respond again. When these efforts failed, they turned away, frowned, and cried (Moore, Cohn, & Campbell, 2001; Papousek, 2007). The still-face reaction is identical among American, Canadian, and Chinese babies, suggesting that it is a built-in withdrawal response to caregivers' lack of communication (Kisilevsky et al., 1998; Legerstee & Markova, 2007). Return to Chapter 4, page 153, and note that infants of depressed parents respond this way. When allowed to persist, a sad, vacant outlook disrupts all aspects of early development.

FEAR Like anger, fear rises during the second half of the first year into the second year (Braungart-Rieker, Hill-Soderland, & Karrass, 2010; Brooker et al., 2013). Older infants, for example, look wary, hesitating before playing with a new toy. But the most frequent expression of fear is to unfamiliar adults, a response called **stranger anxiety.** Many infants and toddlers are quite fearful of strangers, although the reaction does not always occur. It depends on several factors: temperament (some babies are generally more fearful), past experiences with strangers, and the current situation. When an unfamiliar adult picks up the infant in a new situation, stranger anxiety is likely. But if the adult sits still while the baby moves around and a parent is nearby, infants often show positive and curious behavior (Horner, 1980). The stranger's style of interaction—expressing warmth, holding out an attractive toy, playing a

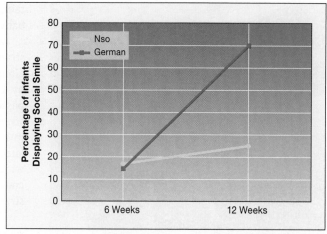

FIGURE 7.1 Development of the social smile in German and Nso infants. At 6 weeks, only a minority of Nso and German infants displayed the social smile during mother–infant mutual gazing. By 12 weeks, the majority of German infants smiled at their mothers. Among Nso infants, whose mothers less often engaged in face-to-face imitative exchanges, social smiling increased only slightly. (Based on Wörmann et al., 2012.)

LOOK and LISTEN

While observing an 8- to 18-month-old with his or her parent, gently approach the baby, offering a toy. Does the baby respond with stranger anxiety? To better understand the baby's behavior, ask the parent to describe his or her temperament and past experiences with strangers.

© CHRISTINA KENNEDY/PHOTOEDIT

When an unfamiliar adult attempts to hold him, this baby makes it clear that he prefers his father. Fear rises during the second half of the first year. Its most frequent expression is stranger anxiety.

familiar game, and approaching slowly rather than abruptly—reduces the baby's fear.

Cross-cultural research reveals that infant-rearing practices can modify stranger anxiety. Among the Efe hunters and gatherers of the Republic of Congo, where the maternal death rate is high, infant survival is safeguarded by a collective caregiving system in which, starting at birth, Efe babies are passed from one adult to another. Consequently, Efe infants show little stranger anxiety (Tronick, Morelli, & Ivey, 1992). In contrast, among infants in Israeli kibbutzim (cooperative agricultural settlements), who live in isolated communities vulnerable to terrorist attacks, wariness of strangers is widespread. By the end of the first year, when infants look to others for cues about how to respond emotionally, kibbutz babies display far greater stranger anxiety than their city-reared counterparts (Saarni et al., 2006).

The rise in fear after 6 months of age keeps newly mobile babies' enthusiasm for exploration in check. Once wariness develops, infants use the familiar caregiver as a **secure base,** or point from which to explore, venturing into the environment and then returning for emotional support. As part of this adaptive system, encounters with strangers lead to two conflicting tendencies: approach (indicated by interest and friendliness) and avoidance (indicated by fear). The infant's behavior is a balance between the two.

As cognitive development permits toddlers to discriminate more effectively between threatening and nonthreatening people and situations, stranger anxiety and other fears of the first two years decline. Fear also wanes as children acquire a wider array of strategies for coping with it, as we will see when we discuss emotional self-regulation.

Understanding and Responding to the Emotions of Others

Infants' emotional expressions are closely tied to their ability to interpret the emotional cues of others. We have seen that in the first few months, babies match the feeling tone of the caregiver in face-to-face communication. Some researchers claim that young babies respond in kind to others' emotions through a built-in, automatic process of *emotional contagion* (Stern, 1985). Others believe that infants acquire these emotional contingencies through operant conditioning—for example, learning that a smile generally triggers caregiver responsiveness and that distress prompts a comforting response (Saarni et al., 2006).

Around 3 months, infants become sensitive to the structure and timing of face-to-face interactions (see Chapter 6, page 236). When they gaze, smile, or vocalize, they now expect their social partner to respond in kind, and they reply with positive vocal and emotional reactions (Markova & Legerstee, 2006). Within these exchanges, babies become increasingly aware of the range of emotional expressions (Montague & Walker-Andrews, 2001). According to some researchers, out of this early imitative communication, infants start to view others as "like me," which lays the foundation for understanding others' thoughts and feelings (Meltzoff, 2013).

By 4 to 5 months, infants distinguish positive from negative emotion in voices, and soon after, they do so in facial expressions, gradually discriminating a wider range of emotions (see Chapter 5). Around the middle of the first year, they match specific facial and vocal displays of emotion. Infants look longer at an appropriate face–voice pairing (such as a happy face with a happy voice) than at an inappropriate one (a happy face with an angry voice) (de Haan & Matheson, 2009; Vaillant-Molina, Bahrick, & Flom, 2013).

Responding to emotional expressions as organized wholes indicates that these signals are becoming meaningful to babies. From 7 months on, ERPs recorded while infants attend to facial expressions reveal reorganized brain-wave patterns resembling those of adults, suggesting enhanced processing of emotional cues (Grossmann, Striano, & Friederici, 2007). As skill at establishing joint attention improves (see Chapter 6), infants realize that an emotional expression not only has meaning but is also a meaningful reaction to a specific object or event (Moses et al., 2001).

Once these understandings are in place, beginning at 8 to 10 months, infants engage in **social referencing**—actively seeking emotional information from a trusted person in an uncertain situation (Mumme et al., 2007). Many studies show that a caregiver's emotional expression (happy, angry, or fearful) influences whether a 1-year-old will be wary of strangers, play with an unfamiliar toy, or cross the deep side of the visual cliff (de Rosnay et al., 2006; Stenberg, 2003; Striano & Rochat, 2000). The adult's voice—either alone or combined with a facial expression—is more effective than a facial expression alone (Kim, Walden, & Knieps, 2010; Vaish & Striano, 2004). The voice conveys both emotional and verbal information, and the baby need not turn toward the adult but, instead, can focus on evaluating the novel event.

As toddlers start to appreciate that others' emotional reactions may differ from their own, social referencing allows them to compare their own and others' assessments of events. In one study, an adult showed 14- and 18-month-olds broccoli and crackers. In one condition, she acted delighted with the taste of broccoli but disgusted with the taste of crackers. In the other condition, she showed the reverse preference. When asked to share the food, 14-month-olds offered only the type of food they themselves preferred—usually crackers. In contrast, 18-month-olds gave the adult whichever food she appeared to like, regardless of their own preferences (Repacholi & Gopnik, 1997).

In sum, in social referencing, toddlers use others' emotional messages to evaluate the safety and security of their surroundings, to guide their own actions, and to gather information about others' intentions and preferences. These experiences, along with cognitive and language development, probably help toddlers refine the meanings of emotions of the same valence—for example, happiness versus surprise, anger versus fear—during the second year (Gendler, Witherington, & Edwards, 2008; Saarni et al., 2006).

LOOK and LISTEN

Observe a toddler and parent at a playground, park, or shopping mall, noting circumstances that trigger social referencing. How does the parent convey emotional information? How does the toddler respond?

Emergence of Self-Conscious Emotions

Besides basic emotions, humans are capable of a second, higher-order set of feelings, including guilt, shame, embarrassment, envy, and pride. These are called **self-conscious emotions** because each involves injury to or enhancement of our sense of self. We feel guilt when we know that we have harmed someone and want to correct the wrongdoing. Envy arises when we desire something that another possesses, so we try to restore our sense of self-worth by securing that possession. When we are ashamed or embarrassed, we have negative feelings about our behavior, and we want to retreat so others will no longer notice our failings. In contrast, pride reflects delight in the self's achievements, and we are inclined to tell others what we have accomplished and to take on further challenges (Lewis, 2014).

Self-conscious emotions appear in the middle of the second year, as 18- to 24-month-olds become firmly aware of the self as a separate, unique individual. Toddlers show shame and embarrassment by lowering their eyes, hanging their heads, and hiding their faces with their hands. They show guiltlike reactions, too. After noticing Grace's unhappiness, 22-month-old Caitlin returned a toy she had grabbed and patted her upset playmate. Pride and envy also emerge around age 2 (Barrett, 2005; Garner, 2003; Lewis, 2014).

Besides self-awareness, self-conscious emotions require an additional ingredient: adult instruction in *when* to feel proud, ashamed, or guilty. Parents begin this tutoring early when they say, "Look how far you can throw that ball!" or "You should feel ashamed for grabbing that toy!" Self-conscious emotions play important roles in children's achievement-related and moral behaviors. The situations in which adults encourage these feelings vary from culture to culture. In Western nations, most children are taught to feel pride over personal achievement—throwing a ball the farthest, winning a game, and (later on) getting good grades. In cultures such as China and Japan, which promote an interdependent self, calling attention to individual success

A mother praises her 2-year-old's success at tower-building. To experience the self-conscious emotion of pride, young children need self-awareness as well as adult instruction in when to feel proud of an accomplishment.

© LAURA DWIGHT PHOTOGRAPHY

evokes embarrassment and self-effacement. And violating cultural standards by failing to show concern for others—a parent, a teacher, or an employer—sparks intense shame (Akimoto & Sanbinmatsu, 1999; Lewis, 1992).

Beginnings of Emotional Self-Regulation

Besides expressing a wider range of emotions, infants and toddlers begin to manage their emotional experiences. **Emotional self-regulation** refers to the strategies we use to adjust our emotional state to a comfortable level of intensity so we can accomplish our goals (Eisenberg, 2006; Thompson & Goodvin, 2007). When you remind yourself that an anxiety-provoking event will be over soon, suppress your anger at a friend's behavior, or decide not to see a scary horror film, you are engaging in emotional self-regulation.

Emotional self-regulation requires voluntary, effortful management of emotions. This capacity for *effortful control* improves rapidly in early childhood, as the result of development of the prefrontal cortex and a history of support from caregivers, who help children manage intense emotion and teach them strategies for doing so (Rothbart, Posner, & Kieras, 2006). Individual differences in control of emotion are already evident in infancy and, by early childhood, play such a vital role in adjustment that—as we will see later—effortful control is regarded as a major dimension of temperament. A good start in regulating emotion during the first two years contributes greatly to autonomy and mastery of cognitive and social skills. Poorly regulated toddlers, by contrast, are at risk for long-lasting adjustment difficulties (Eisenberg et al., 2004; Lawson & Ruff, 2004).

In the early months, infants have only a limited capacity to regulate their emotional states. When their feelings get too intense, they are easily overwhelmed. They depend on the soothing interventions of caregivers for distraction and reorienting of attention—being lifted to the shoulder, rocked, gently stroked, and talked to softly.

More effective functioning of the prefrontal cortex increases the baby's tolerance for stimulation. Between 2 and 4 months, caregivers build on this capacity by initiating face-to-face play and attention to objects. In these interactions, parents arouse pleasure in the baby while adjusting the pace of their own behavior so the infant does not become overwhelmed and distressed (Kopp & Neufeld, 2003). As a result, the baby's tolerance for stimulation increases further.

By 4 to 6 months, the ability to shift attention away from unpleasant events and to engage in self-soothing helps infants control emotion. In the second half-year, they become better at communicating their need for help in regulating emotion by gesturing and vocalizing to the caregiver (Stifter & Braungart, 1995). And crawling and walking, which permit babies to approach or retreat from various situations, foster more effective self-regulation. Also, further gains in attention permit older infants and toddlers to sustain interest in their surroundings and in play activities for a longer time (Rothbart & Bates, 2006).

As caregivers help infants regulate their emotional states, they contribute to the child's style of emotional self-regulation. Infants whose parents "read" and respond contingently and sympathetically to their emotional cues tend to be less fussy, to express more pleasurable emotion, to be more interested in exploration, and to be easier to soothe (Braungart-Rieker, Hill-Soderlund, & Karrass, 2010; Crockenberg & Leerkes, 2004). In contrast, parents who respond impatiently or angrily or who wait to intervene until the infant has become extremely agitated reinforce the baby's rapid rise to intense distress. This makes it harder for parents to soothe the baby in the future—and for the baby to learn to calm herself. When caregivers fail to regulate stressful experiences for infants who cannot yet regulate them for themselves, brain structures that buffer stress may fail to develop properly, resulting in an anxious, reactive child who has a reduced capacity for managing emotional problems (Blair & Raver, 2012; Little & Carter, 2005).

Caregivers also provide lessons in socially approved ways of expressing feelings. Beginning in the first few months, parents encourage infants to suppress negative emotion by imitating their expressions of interest, happiness, and surprise more often than their expressions of anger and sadness. Boys get more of this training than girls, in part because boys have a harder time regulating negative emotion (Else-Quest, 2006; Malatesta et al., 1986). As a result, the well-known sex difference—females as emotionally expressive and males as emotionally

controlled—is fostered at a tender age. Cultures that highly value social harmony place particular emphasis on socially appropriate emotional behavior. Compared with North Americans, Japanese and Chinese adults discourage the expression of strong emotion in babies (Camras, Kolmodin, & Chen, 2008; Friedlmeier, Corapci, & Cole, 2011). By the end of the first year, Chinese and Japanese infants smile, laugh, and cry less than American babies (Camras et al., 1998; Gartstein et al., 2010).

In the second year, growth in representation and language leads to new ways of regulating emotions. A vocabulary for talking about feelings—"happy," "love," "surprised," "scary," "yucky," "mad"—develops rapidly after 18 months, but toddlers are not yet good at using language to manage their emotions. Temper tantrums tend to occur because toddlers cannot control the intense anger that often arises when an adult rejects their demands, particularly when they are fatigued or hungry (Mascolo & Fischer, 2007). Toddlers whose parents are emotionally sympathetic but set limits (by not giving in to tantrums), who distract the child by offering acceptable alternatives, and who later suggest better ways to handle adult refusals display more effective anger-regulation strategies and social skills during the preschool years (Lecuyer & Houck, 2006).

Patient, sensitive parents also talk about emotions and encourage toddlers to describe their internal states. Then, when 2-year-olds feel distressed, they can guide caregivers in helping them (Cole, Armstrong, & Pemberton, 2010). For example, while listening to a story about monsters, Grace whimpered, "Mommy, scary." Monica put the book down and gave Grace a comforting hug.

Chinese and Japanese adults discourage the expression of strong emotion in infants. This baby's calm demeanor is typical of Chinese infants, who tend to smile and cry less than American babies.

Ask Yourself

● **REVIEW** Why do many infants show stranger anxiety in the second half of the first year? What factors can increase or decrease wariness of strangers?

● **CONNECT** Why do children of depressed parents have difficulty regulating emotion (see page 153 in Chapter 4)? What implications do their weak self-regulatory skills have for their response to cognitive and social challenges?

● **APPLY** At age 14 months, Reggie built a block tower and gleefully knocked it down. But at age 2, he called to his mother and pointed proudly to his tall block tower. What explains this change in Reggie's emotional behavior?

● **REFLECT** Describe several recent instances illustrating how you typically manage negative emotion. How might your early experiences, gender, and cultural background have influenced your style of emotional self-regulation?

Temperament and Development

From early infancy, Caitlin's sociability was unmistakable. She smiled and laughed while interacting with adults and, in her second year, readily approached other children. Meanwhile, Monica marveled at Grace's calm, relaxed disposition. At 19 months, she sat contentedly in a highchair through a two-hour family celebration at a restaurant. In contrast, Timmy was active and distractible. Vanessa found herself chasing him as he dropped one toy, moved on to the next, and climbed on chairs and tables.

When we describe one person as cheerful and upbeat, another as active and energetic, and still others as calm, cautious, or prone to angry outbursts, we are referring to **temperament**— early-appearing, stable individual differences in reactivity and self-regulation. *Reactivity* refers to quickness and intensity of emotional arousal, attention, and motor activity. *Self-regulation,* as we have seen, refers to strategies that modify that reactivity (Rothbart, 2011; Rothbart & Bates, 2006). The psychological traits that make up temperament are believed to form the cornerstone of the adult personality.

7.4 What is temperament, and how is it measured?

7.5 Discuss the roles of heredity and environment in the stability of temperament, including the goodness-of-fit model.

In 1956, Alexander Thomas and Stella Chess initiated the New York Longitudinal Study, a groundbreaking investigation of the development of temperament that followed 141 children from early infancy well into adulthood. Results showed that temperament can increase a child's chances of experiencing psychological problems or, alternatively, protect a child from the negative effects of a highly stressful home life. At the same time, Thomas and Chess (1977) discovered that parenting practices can modify children's emotional styles considerably.

These findings stimulated a growing body of research on temperament, including its stability, biological roots, and interaction with child-rearing experiences. Let's begin to explore these issues by looking at the structure, or makeup, of temperament and how it is measured.

The Structure of Temperament

Thomas and Chess's model of temperament inspired all others that followed. When detailed descriptions of infants' and children's behavior obtained from parental interviews were rated on nine dimensions of temperament, certain characteristics clustered together, yielding three types of children:

- The **easy child** (40 percent of the sample) quickly establishes regular routines in infancy, is generally cheerful, and adapts easily to new experiences.
- The **difficult child** (10 percent of the sample) is irregular in daily routines, is slow to accept new experiences, and tends to react negatively and intensely.
- The **slow-to-warm-up child** (15 percent of the sample) is inactive, shows mild, low-key reactions to environmental stimuli, is negative in mood, and adjusts slowly to new experiences.

Note that 35 percent of the children did not fit any of these categories. Instead, they showed unique blends of temperamental characteristics.

The difficult pattern has sparked the most interest because it places children at high risk for adjustment problems—both anxious withdrawal and aggressive behavior in early and middle childhood (Bates, Wachs, & Emde, 1994; Ramos et al., 2005). Compared with difficult children, slow-to-warm-up children present fewer problems initially. However, they tend to show excessive fearfulness and slow, constricted behavior in the late preschool and school years, when they are expected to respond actively and quickly in classrooms and peer groups (Chess & Thomas, 1984; Schmitz et al., 1999).

Today, the most influential model of temperament is Mary Rothbart's, described in Table 7.1. It combines related traits proposed by Thomas and Chess and other researchers, yielding a concise list of just six dimensions. For example, distractibility and persistence are considered opposite ends of the same dimension, which is labeled "attention span/persistence." A unique feature of Rothbart's model is inclusion of both "fearful distress" and "irritable distress," which distinguish between reactivity triggered by fear and reactivity due to frustration. And the model deletes overly broad dimensions such as regularity of body functions and intensity of reaction (Rothbart, 2011; Rothbart, Ahadi, & Evans, 2000). A child who is regular in sleeping is not necessarily regular in eating or bowel habits. And a child who smiles and laughs intensely is not necessarily intense in fear, irritability, or motor activity.

Rothbart's dimensions represent the three underlying components included in the definition of temperament: (1) *emotion* ("fearful distress," "irritable distress," "positive affect"), (2) *attention* ("attention span/persistence"), and (3) *action* ("activity level"). According to Rothbart, individuals differ not just in their reactivity on each dimension but also in the self-regulatory dimension of temperament, **effortful control**—the capacity to voluntarily suppress a dominant response in order

On a visit to a playground, this toddler reacts with irritable distress when he sees he must wait for a turn to use a swing. Patient, supportive parenting can help him modify his biologically based temperament and better manage his reactivity.

© ERIC FOWKE/PHOTOEDIT

TABLE 7.1	Rothbart's Model of Temperament
DIMENSION	**DESCRIPTION**
Reactivity	
Activity level	Level of gross-motor activity
Attention span/persistence	Duration of orienting or interest
Fearful distress	Wariness and distress in response to intense or novel stimuli, including time to adjust to new situations
Irritable distress	Extent of fussing, crying, and distress when desires are frustrated
Positive affect	Frequency of expression of happiness and pleasure
Self-Regulation	
Effortful control	Capacity to voluntarily suppress a dominant, reactive response in order to plan and execute a more adaptive response
	In the first two years, called *orienting/regulation,* which refers to the capacity to engage in self-soothing, shift attention from unpleasant events, and sustain interest for an extended time

to plan and execute a more adaptive response (Rothbart, 2003; Rothbart & Bates, 2006). Variations in effortful control are evident in how effectively a child can focus and shift attention, inhibit impulses, and manage negative emotion.

Beginning in early childhood, capacity for effortful control predicts favorable development and adjustment in cultures as diverse as China and the United States (Zhou, Lengua, & Wang, 2009). Outcomes include persistence, task mastery, academic achievement, moral maturity (such as concern about wrongdoing and willingness to apologize), and social behaviors of cooperation, sharing, and helpfulness, which contribute to positive relationships with adults and peers (Eisenberg, 2010; Kochanska & Aksan, 2006; Posner & Rothbart, 2007b; Valiente, Lemery-Chalfant, & Swanson, 2010).

Measuring Temperament

Temperament is often assessed through interviews or questionnaires given to parents. Behavior ratings by pediatricians, teachers, and others familiar with the child and laboratory observations by researchers have also been used. Parental reports are convenient and take advantage of parents' depth of knowledge about their child across many situations (Gartstein & Rothbart, 2003). Although information from parents has been criticized as being biased, parental reports are moderately related to researchers' observations of children's behavior (Majdandžić & van den Boom, 2007; Mangelsdorf, Schoppe, & Buur, 2000). And parent perceptions are vital for understanding how parents view and respond to their child.

Observations by researchers in the home or laboratory avoid the subjectivity of parent reports but can lead to other inaccuracies. In homes, observers find it hard to capture rare but important events, such as infants' response to frustration. And in the unfamiliar lab setting, fearful children who calmly avoid certain experiences at home may become too upset to complete the session (Rothbart, 2011). Still, researchers can better control children's experiences in the lab. And they can conveniently combine observations of behavior with neurobiological measures to gain insight into the biological basis of temperament.

Most neurobiological research has focused on children who fall at opposite extremes of the positive-affect and fearful-distress dimensions of temperament: **inhibited,** or **shy, children,** who react negatively to and withdraw from novel stimuli, and **uninhibited,** or **sociable, children,** who display positive emotion and approach novel stimuli. As the Biology and Environment box on page 256 reveals, biologically based reactivity—evident in heart rate, hormone levels, and measures of brain activity—differentiates children with inhibited and uninhibited temperaments.

Biology and Environment

Development of Shyness and Sociability

wo 4-month-old babies, Larry and Mitch, visited the laboratory of Jerome Kagan, who observed their reactions to a variety of unfamiliar experiences. When exposed to new sights and sounds, such as a moving mobile decorated with colorful toys, Larry tensed his muscles, moved his arms and legs with agitation, and began to cry. In contrast, Mitch remained relaxed and quiet, smiling and cooing at the excitement around him.

As toddlers, Larry and Mitch returned to the laboratory, where they experienced a variety of procedures designed to induce uncertainty. Electrodes were placed on their bodies and blood pressure cuffs on their arms to measure heart rate; toy robots, animals, and puppets moved before their eyes; and unfamiliar people entered and behaved in unexpected ways or wore novel costumes. While Larry whimpered and quickly withdrew, Mitch watched with interest, laughed at the strange sights, and approached the toys and strangers.

On a third visit, at age 4½, Larry barely talked or smiled during an interview with an unfamiliar adult. In contrast, Mitch asked questions and communicated his pleasure at each new activity. In a playroom with two unfamiliar peers, Larry pulled back and watched, while Mitch made friends quickly.

In longitudinal research on several hundred Caucasian infants followed into adolescence, Kagan found that about 20 percent of 4-month-olds were, like Larry, easily upset by novelty; another 40 percent, like Mitch, were comfortable, even delighted, with new experiences. About 20 to 25 percent of these extreme groups retained their temperamental styles as they grew older (Kagan, 2003, 2013d; Kagan et al., 2007). But most children's dispositions became less extreme over time. Genetic makeup and child-rearing experiences jointly influenced stability and change in temperament.

Neurobiological Correlates of Shyness and Sociability

Individual differences in arousal of the *amygdala,* an inner brain structure devoted to processing of novelty and emotional information, contribute to these contrasting temperaments. In shy, inhibited children, novel stimuli easily excite the amygdala and its connections to the cerebral cortex and sympathetic nervous system, which prepares the body to act in the face of threat. In sociable, uninhibited children, the same level of stimulation

evokes minimal neural excitation (Kagan, 2013d). In support of this theory, while viewing photos of unfamiliar faces, adults who had been classified as inhibited in the second year of life showed greater fMRI activity in the amygdala than adults who had been uninhibited as toddlers (Schwartz et al., 2012). And additional neurobiological responses known to be mediated by the amygdala distinguish these two emotional styles:

- *Heart rate.* From the first few weeks of life, the heart rates of shy children are consistently higher than those of sociable children, and they speed up further in response to unfamiliar events (Schmidt et al., 2007; Snidman et al., 1995).
- *Cortisol.* Saliva concentrations of the stress hormone cortisol tend to be higher, and to rise more in response to a stressful event, in shy than in sociable children (Schmidt et al., 1997, 1999; Zimmermann & Stansbury, 2004).
- *Pupil dilation, blood pressure, and skin surface temperature.* Compared with sociable children, shy children show greater pupil dilation, rise in blood pressure, and cooling of the fingertips when faced with novelty (Kagan et al., 1999, 2007).

Another physiological correlate of approach–withdrawal to people and objects is the pattern of brain waves in the frontal lobes of the cerebral cortex. Shy infants and preschoolers show greater EEG activity in the right frontal lobe, which is associated with negative emotional reactivity; sociable children show the opposite pattern (Fox et al., 2008; Kagan et al., 2007). Inhibited children also show a stronger ERP brain-wave response to unfamiliar visual scenes (Kagan, 2013d). Neural activity in the amygdala, which is transmitted to the frontal lobes, probably contributes to these differences.

Child-Rearing Practices

According to Kagan, most extremely shy or sociable children inherit a physiology that biases them toward a particular temperamental style. Yet heritability research indicates that genes contribute only modestly to shyness and sociability (Kagan, 2013d). Experience has a profound impact.

Child-rearing practices affect the chances that an emotionally reactive baby will become a fearful child. Warm, supportive parenting reduces shy infants' and preschoolers' intense physiological

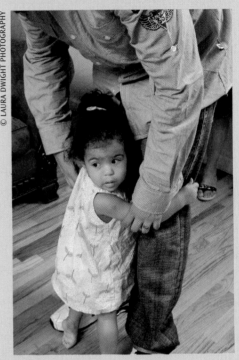

A strong physiological response to uncertain situations prompts this child to cling to her father. With patient, insistent encouragement, her parents can help her overcome the urge to retreat from unfamiliar events.

reaction to novelty, whereas cold, intrusive parenting that punishes or denies children's feelings heightens anxiety (Coplan & Arbeau, 2008; Davis & Buss, 2012). And if parents overprotect infants and young children who dislike novelty, they make it harder for the child to overcome an urge to retreat. Parents who make appropriate demands for their child to approach new experiences help shy youngsters overcome fear (Rubin & Burgess, 2002).

When inhibition persists, it leads to excessive cautiousness, low self-esteem, and loneliness (Fordham & Stevenson-Hinde, 1999; Rubin, Stewart, & Coplan, 1995). In adolescence, persistent shyness increases the risk of severe anxiety, depression, and other internalizing problems, including unrealistic worries about harm, illness, and criticism for mistakes as well as social phobia—intense fear of being humiliated in social situations (Kagan, 2013d; Karevold et al., 2012). For inhibited children to acquire effective social skills, parenting must be tailored to their temperaments—a theme we will encounter again in this and later chapters.

Stability of Temperament

Young children who score low or high on attention span, irritability, sociability, shyness, or effortful control tend to respond similarly when assessed again several months to a few years later and, occasionally, even into the adult years (Casalin et al., 2012; Caspi et al., 2003; Kochanska & Knaack, 2003; Majdandžić & van den Boom, 2007; van den Akker et al., 2010). However, the overall stability of temperament is low in infancy and toddlerhood and only moderate from the preschool years on (Putnam, Samson, & Rothbart, 2000). Some children remain the same, but many others change.

Why isn't temperament more stable? A major reason is that temperament itself develops with age. To illustrate, let's look at irritability and activity level. Recall from Chapter 4 that the early months are a period of fussing and crying for most babies. As infants better regulate their attention and emotions, many who initially seemed irritable become calm and content. In the case of activity level, the meaning of the behavior changes. At first, an active, wriggling infant tends to be highly aroused and uncomfortable, whereas an inactive baby is often alert and attentive. Once infants move on their own, the reverse is so! An active crawler is usually alert and interested in exploration, whereas an inactive baby may be fearful and withdrawn.

These discrepancies help us understand why long-term prediction from early temperament is best achieved after age 3, when children's styles of responding are better established (Roberts & DelVecchio, 2000). In line with this idea, between ages 2½ and 3, children improve substantially and also perform more consistently across a wide range of tasks requiring effortful control, such as waiting for a reward, lowering their voice to a whisper, succeeding at games like "Simon Says," and selectively attending to one stimulus while ignoring competing stimuli (Kochanska, Murray, & Harlan, 2000; Li-Grining, 2007). Researchers believe that around this time, areas in the prefrontal cortex involved in suppressing impulses develop rapidly (Rothbart, 2011).

Nevertheless, the ease with which children manage their reactivity in early childhood depends on the type and strength of the reactive emotion involved. Preschoolers who were highly fearful as toddlers score slightly better than their agemates in effortful control. In contrast, angry, irritable toddlers tend to be less effective at effortful control at later ages (Bridgett et al., 2009; Kochanska & Knaack, 2003). Other evidence confirms that child rearing plays an important role in modifying temperamental traits. Toddlers and young preschoolers who have fearful or negative, irritable temperaments but experience patient, supportive parenting gain most in capacity to manage their reactivity (Kim & Kochanska, 2012; Warren & Simmens, 2005). But if exposed to insensitive or unresponsive parenting, these emotionally negative children are especially likely to score low in effortful control, placing them at risk for adjustment problems.

In sum, many factors affect the extent to which a child's temperament remains stable, including development of the biological systems on which temperament is based, the child's capacity for effortful control, and the success of her efforts, which depend on the quality and intensity of her emotional reactivity. When we consider the evidence as a whole, the low to moderate stability of temperament makes sense. It also confirms that child rearing can modify biologically based temperamental traits considerably and that children with certain traits, such as negative emotionality, are especially susceptible to the influence of parenting—a finding we will return to shortly. With these ideas in mind, let's take a closer look at genetic and environmental contributions to temperament and personality.

Genetic and Environmental Influences

The word *temperament* implies a genetic foundation for individual differences in personality. Identical twins are more similar than fraternal twins across a wide range of temperamental traits (activity level, attention span, shyness/sociability, irritability, and effortful control) and personality measures (introversion/extroversion, anxiety, agreeableness, curiosity and imaginativeness, and impulsivity) (Bouchard, 2004; Caspi & Shiner, 2006; Krueger & Johnson, 2008; Roisman & Fraley, 2006). In Chapter 2, we noted that heritability estimates derived from twin studies suggest a moderate role for genetic factors in temperament and personality: About half of individual differences have been attributed to differences in genetic makeup.

Although genetic influences on temperament are clear, environment is also powerful. Recall from Chapter 5 that children exposed to severe malnutrition in infancy remain more distractible and fearful than their agemates, even after dietary improvement. And infants reared in deprived orphanages are easily overwhelmed by stressful events. Their poor regulation of emotion results in inattention and weak impulse control, including frequent expressions of anger (see pages 168 and 175).

Furthermore, heredity and environment often jointly contribute to temperament, since a child's initial approach to the world can be intensified or lessened by experience. To illustrate, let's begin by looking closely at ethnic and gender differences in temperament.

ETHNIC AND GENDER DIFFERENCES   Compared with North American Caucasian infants, Chinese and Japanese babies tend to be less active, irritable, and vocal; more easily soothed when upset; and better at quieting themselves (Kagan, 2013d; Lewis, Ramsay, & Kawakami, 1993). Grace's capacity to remain contentedly seated in her highchair through a long family dinner certainly fits with this evidence. Chinese and Japanese babies are also more fearful and inhibited, remaining closer to their mothers in an unfamiliar playroom and displaying more anxiety when interacting with a stranger (Chen, Wang, & DeSouza, 2006).

These variations may have genetic roots, but they are supported by cultural beliefs and practices, yielding a possible *gene–environment correlation.* Japanese mothers usually say that babies come into the world as independent beings who must learn to rely on their parents through close physical contact. American mothers, in contrast, typically believe that they must wean the baby away from dependency toward autonomy. Consistent with these beliefs, Asian mothers interact gently, soothingly, and gesturally with their infants, whereas Caucasian mothers use a more active, stimulating, verbal approach (Kagan, 2010; Rothbaum et al., 2000). Also, recall from our discussion of emotional self-regulation that Chinese and Japanese adults discourage babies from expressing strong emotion, which contributes further to their infants' tranquility.

Similarly, gender differences in temperament are evident in infancy, suggesting a genetic foundation. Boys are more active and daring, more irritable when frustrated, more likely to express high-intensity pleasure in play, and slightly more impulsive than girls—factors that contribute to boys' higher injury rates throughout childhood and adolescence. Girls, in contrast, tend to be more anxious and timid. And girls' large advantage in effortful control undoubtedly contributes to their greater cooperativeness, better school performance, and lower incidence of behavior problems (Else-Quest, 2012; Else-Quest et al., 2006). At the same time, parents more often encourage their young sons to be physically active and their daughters to seek help and physical closeness—through activities they encourage and through more positive reactions when their child exhibits temperamental traits consistent with gender stereotypes (Bryan & Dix, 2009; Ruble, Martin, & Berenbaum, 2006).

Gender differences in temperament are evident in children's play styles. Boys tend to engage in more active, high-intensity play. And girls' large advantage in effortful control helps explain their greater cooperativeness.

DIFFERENTIAL SUSCEPTIBILITY TO REARING EXPERIENCES
Earlier we discussed findings indicating that emotionally reactive toddlers function worse than other children when exposed to inept parenting, yet benefit most from good parenting. Researchers have become increasingly interested in temperamental differences in children's susceptibility (or responsiveness) to environmental influences (Pluess & Belsky, 2011). Using molecular genetic analyses, they are clarifying how these *gene–environment interactions* operate.

In one study, 2-year-olds with a chromosome 7 gene containing a certain repetition of DNA base pairs, called short 5-HTTLPR—which interferes with functioning of the inhibitory neurotransmitter serotonin and, thus, greatly increases the risk of negative mood, fear of the unfamiliar, and self-regulation difficulties—became increasingly irritable as their mothers' anxiety about parenting increased (Ivorra et al., 2010). Maternal anxiety, however, had little impact on children without this gene. In another investigation, toddlers with the short 5-HTTLPR gene responded especially favorably to effective parenting (Kochanska, Philibert, & Barry, 2009; Kochanska et al. 2011). With maternal warmth and support in mastering new skills, their capacity for self-regulation improved during the preschool years, equaling that of agemates with a low-risk genotype. They were also advantaged in academic and social skills compared to their counterparts with less responsive mothers.

Consistently, the short 5-HTTLPR genotype combined with maladaptive parenting leads to externalizing problems, including defiance and aggression (van IJzendoorn, Belsky, & Bakermans-Kranenburg, 2012). Why is this so? A two-year follow-up of 1-year-olds from poverty-stricken families revealed that parenting quality had little impact on children with a low-risk genotype. In contrast, toddlers with a high-risk genotype became increasingly reactive emotionally to their mother's insensitive, hostile, and rejecting behavior, responding with distress, anger, and uncontrolled screaming (see Figure 7.2) (Davies & Cicchetti, 2014). Negative emotionality, in turn, predicted a sharp rise in aggression and defiance over the preschool years—externalizing difficulties that often persist.

As these outcomes reveal, children with the short 5-HTTLPR gene show unusually high early *plasticity* (see page 9 in Chapter 1 to review). They are particularly susceptible to the effects of both good and poor parenting. Because young children with this "susceptibility attribute" fare better than other children when parenting is supportive, they are likely to respond especially well to interventions aimed at reducing parental stress and promoting responsive child rearing.

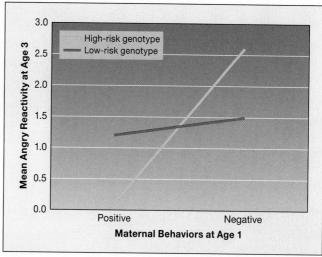

FIGURE 7.2 **Angry reactivity at age 3 in response to positive and negative maternal behaviors for children with and without the short 5-HTTLPR gene.** Children with a low-risk genotype (without the gene) responded little to quality of maternal behavior. Those with a high-risk genotype (with the gene), in contrast, were highly susceptible to parenting quality—both good and bad. They displayed little anger when exposed to maternal affection and encouragement but high anger to maternal insensitivity and hostility. (Adapted from P. T. Davies and D. Cicchetti, 2014, "How and Why Does the 5-HTTLPR Gene Moderate Associations Between Maternal Unresponsiveness and Children's Disruptive Problems?" *Child Development, 85,* p. 494. Copyright © 2013 Society for Research in Child Development, Inc., and The Authors. Reprinted with permission of John Wiley and Sons, Inc., conveyed through Copyright Clearance Center, Inc.)

SIBLINGS' UNIQUE EXPERIENCES   In families with several children, another influence on temperament is at work. Parents often look for differences between siblings: "She's a lot more active." "He's more sociable." "She's far more persistent." As a result, parents often view siblings as more distinct than other observers do.

In a large study of 1- to 3-year-old twin pairs, parents rated identical twins as less alike in temperament than researchers' ratings indicated. And whereas researchers rated fraternal twins as moderately similar, parents viewed them as somewhat opposite in temperament—one shy and the other sociable, one active and the other restrained, one persistent and the other distractible (Saudino, 2003). This tendency to emphasize each child's unique qualities affects parenting practices. Each child, in turn, evokes responses from caregivers that are consistent with parental beliefs and with the child's developing temperament.

Besides different experiences within the family, siblings have distinct experiences with teachers, peers, and others in their community that affect development. And as we will see in Chapter 13, in middle childhood and adolescence, siblings often seek ways to differ from one another. In sum, temperament and personality can be understood only in terms of complex interdependencies between genetic and environmental factors.

LOOK and LISTEN

Ask several parents of siblings to describe their children's temperaments, along with child-rearing practices they use with each. Do the parents tend to emphasize differences? Are their child-rearing practices responsive to their views of each child's unique qualities?

Temperament and Child Rearing: The Goodness-of-Fit Model

If a child's disposition interferes with learning or getting along with others, adults must gently but consistently counteract the child's maladaptive style. Thomas and Chess (1977) proposed a **goodness-of-fit model** to explain how temperament and environment can together produce favorable outcomes. Goodness of fit involves creating child-rearing environments

This parent's firm but affectionate approach to discipline is "a good fit" with his son's difficult temperament, helping the toddler gain in effortful control and manage negative emotion.

that recognize each child's temperament while simultaneously encouraging more adaptive functioning.

Goodness of fit helps explain why difficult children (who withdraw from new experiences and react negatively and intensely) frequently experience parenting that fits poorly with their dispositions. As infants, they are less likely to receive sensitive caregiving. By the second year, their parents tend to resort to angry, punitive discipline, which undermines the development of effortful control. As the child reacts with defiance and disobedience, parents become increasingly stressed (Bridgett et al., 2009; Paulussen-Hoogeboom et al., 2007). As a result, they continue their coercive tactics and also discipline inconsistently, sometimes rewarding the child's noncompliance by giving in to it (Pesonen et al., 2008; van Aken et al., 2007). These practices sustain and even increase the child's irritable, conflict-ridden style.

In contrast, when parents are positive and sensitive, which helps infants and toddlers—especially those who are emotionally reactive—regulate emotion, difficultness declines by age 2 or 3 (Raikes et al., 2007). In toddlerhood and childhood, parental sensitivity, support, clear expectations, and limits foster effortful control, reducing the likelihood that difficultness will persist and lead to emotional and social difficulties (Cipriano & Stifter, 2010; Jaffari-Bimmel et al., 2006).

Effective parenting of difficult children, however, also depends on life conditions—good parental mental health, marital happiness, and favorable economic conditions (Schoppe-Sullivan et al., 2007). In a comparison of the temperaments of Russian and U.S. babies, Russian infants were more emotionally negative, fearful, and upset when frustrated (Gartstein, Slobodskaya, & Kinsht, 2003). At the time of the study, Russian parents faced a severely depressed national economy. Because of financial worries and longer work hours, Russian parents may have lacked time and energy for patient parenting.

Cultural values also affect the fit between parenting and child temperament, as research in China illustrates. In the past, high valuing of social harmony, which discourages self-assertion, led Chinese adults to evaluate shy children positively. Chinese children of two decades ago appeared well-adjusted, both academically and socially (Chen, Rubin, & Li, 1995; Chen et al., 1998). But rapid expansion of a market economy in China, which requires assertiveness and sociability for success, may be responsible for a change in Chinese parents' and teachers' attitudes toward childhood shyness (Chen, Wang, & DeSouza, 2006; Yu, 2002). In an investigation of Shanghai fourth graders, the association between shyness and adjustment also changed over time. Whereas shyness was positively correlated with teacher-rated competence, peer acceptance, leadership, and academic achievement in 1990, these relationships weakened in 1998 and reversed in 2002, when they mirrored findings of Western research (Chen et al., 2005). But in rural areas of China, positive valuing of shyness persists, and shy children continue to enjoy high social status and are well-adjusted (Chen, Wang, & Cao, 2011). Cultural context makes a difference in whether shy children receive support or disapproval and whether they adjust well or poorly.

An effective match between rearing conditions and child temperament is best accomplished early, before unfavorable temperament–environment relationships produce maladjustment. Recall from Chapter 6 that Vanessa often behaved in an overly directive way with Timmy in an effort to contain his high activity level. A poor fit between her intrusive parenting and Timmy's active temperament may have contributed to his tendency to move from one activity to the next with little involvement.

The goodness-of-fit model reminds us that babies have unique dispositions that adults must accept. Parents can neither take full credit for their children's virtues nor be blamed for all their faults. But parents can turn an environment that exaggerates a child's problems into one that builds on the child's strengths. As we will see, goodness of fit is also at the heart of infant–caregiver attachment. This first intimate relationship grows out of interaction between parent and baby, to which the emotional styles of both partners contribute.

Ask Yourself

● **REVIEW** Describe emotionally reactive and easy-going children's differential susceptibility to rearing experiences. Why are emotionally reactive children who receive warm, supportive parenting at especially low risk for self-regulation difficulties?

● **CONNECT** Explain how findings on ethnic and gender differences in temperament illustrate gene–environment correlation, discussed on page 84 in Chapter 2.

● **APPLY** Mandy and Jeff are parents of 2-year-old inhibited Sam and 3-year-old emotionally reactive Maria. Explain the importance of effortful control to Mandy and Jeff, and suggest ways they can strengthen it in each of their children.

● **REFLECT** How would you describe your temperament as a young child? Do you think it has remained stable, or has it changed? What factors might be involved?

Development of Attachment

Attachment is the strong affectionate tie we have with special people in our lives that leads us to experience pleasure and joy when we interact with them and to be comforted by their nearness in times of stress. By the second half-year, infants have become attached to familiar people who have responded to their needs. **TAKE A MOMENT...** Watch how babies of this age single out their parents for special attention: When the parent enters the room, the baby breaks into a broad, friendly smile. When she picks him up, he pats her face, explores her hair, and snuggles against her. When he feels anxious or afraid, he crawls into her lap and clings closely.

Freud first suggested that the infant's emotional tie to the mother is the foundation for all later relationships. Contemporary research indicates that—although the infant–parent bond is vitally important—later development is influenced not just by early attachment experiences but also by the continuing quality of the parent–child relationship.

Attachment has also been the subject of intense theoretical debate. Recall that the *psychoanalytic perspective* regards feeding as the central context in which caregivers and babies build this close emotional bond. *Behaviorism,* too, emphasizes the importance of feeding but for different reasons. According to a well-known behaviorist account, infants learn to prefer the mother's soft caresses, warm smiles, and tender words because these events are paired with tension relief as she satisfies the baby's hunger.

Although feeding is an important context for building a close relationship, attachment does not depend on hunger satisfaction. In the 1950s, a famous experiment showed that rhesus monkeys reared with terry-cloth and wire-mesh "surrogate mothers" clung to the soft terry-cloth substitute, even though the wire-mesh "mother" held the bottle and infants had to climb onto it to be fed (Harlow & Zimmerman, 1959). Human infants, too, become attached to family members who seldom feed them, including fathers, siblings, and grandparents. And toddlers in Western cultures who sleep alone and experience frequent daytime separations from their parents sometimes develop strong emotional ties to cuddly objects, such as blankets and teddy bears, that play no role in infant feeding!

Both psychoanalytic and behaviorist accounts of attachment have another problem: They emphasize the caregiver's contribution to the attachment relationship but pay little attention to the importance of the infant's characteristics.

Bowlby's Ethological Theory

Today, **ethological theory of attachment,** which recognizes the infant's emotional tie to the caregiver as an evolved response that promotes survival, is the most widely accepted view. John Bowlby (1969), who first applied this perspective to the infant–caregiver bond, retained the psychoanalytic idea that quality of attachment to the caregiver has profound implications for the child's feelings of security and capacity to form trusting relationships.

7.6 What are the unique features of ethological theory of attachment?

7.7 Cite the four attachment patterns assessed by the Strange Situation and the Attachment Q-Sort, and discuss factors that affect attachment security.

7.8 Discuss infants' formation of multiple attachments, and indicate how attachment paves the way for early peer sociability.

7.9 Describe and interpret the relationship between secure attachment in infancy and psychological development in childhood.

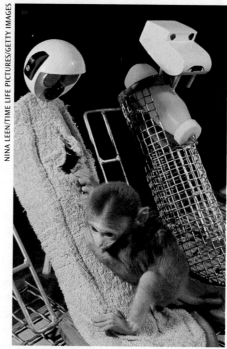

NINA LEEN/TIME LIFE PICTURES/GETTY IMAGES

Baby monkeys reared with "surrogate mothers" preferred to cling to a soft terry-cloth "mother" instead of a wire-mesh "mother" that held a bottle. These findings contradict the drive-reduction explanation of attachment, which assumes that the parent–infant relationship is based on feeding.

LOOK and LISTEN

Watch an 8- to 18-month-old at play for 20 to 30 minutes. Describe the baby's use of the parent or other familiar caregiver as a secure base from which to explore.

At the same time, Bowlby was inspired by Konrad Lorenz's studies of imprinting in baby geese (see Chapter 1). Bowlby believed that the human infant, like the young of other animal species, is endowed with a set of built-in behaviors that keep the parent nearby to protect the infant from danger and to provide support for exploring and mastering the environment. Contact with the parent also ensures that the baby will be fed, but Bowlby pointed out that feeding is not the basis for attachment. Rather, attachment can best be understood in an evolutionary context in which survival of the species—through ensuring both safety and competence—is of utmost importance.

According to Bowlby, the infant's relationship with the parent begins as a set of innate signals that call the adult to the baby's side. Over time, a true affectionate bond forms, supported by new cognitive and emotional capacities as well as by a history of warm, sensitive care. Attachment develops in four phases:

1. *Preattachment phase* (birth to 6 weeks). Built-in signals—grasping, smiling, crying, and gazing into the adult's eyes—help bring newborn babies into close contact with other humans, who comfort them. Babies of this age recognize their own mother's smell, voice, and face (see Chapter 4). But they are not yet attached to her, since they do not mind being left with an unfamiliar adult.

2. *"Attachment in the making" phase* (6 weeks to 6–8 months). During this phase, infants respond differently to a familiar caregiver than to a stranger. For example, at 4 months, Timmy smiled, laughed, and babbled more freely when interacting with his mother and quieted more quickly when she picked him up. As infants learn that their own actions affect the behavior of those around them, they begin to develop a *sense of trust*—the expectation that the caregiver will respond when signaled—but they still do not protest when separated from her.

3. *"Clear-cut" attachment phase* (6–8 months to 18 months–2 years). Now attachment to the familiar caregiver is evident. Babies display **separation anxiety,** becoming upset when their trusted caregiver leaves. Like stranger anxiety (see page 249), separation anxiety does not always occur; it depends on infant temperament and the current situation. But in many cultures, separation anxiety increases between 6 and 15 months, suggesting that infants have developed a clear understanding that the caregiver continues to exist when not in view. Besides protesting the parent's departure, older infants and toddlers try hard to maintain her presence. They approach, follow, and climb on her in preference to others. And they use the familiar caregiver as a secure base from which to explore.

4. *Formation of a reciprocal relationship* (18 months to 2 years and on). By the end of the second year, rapid growth in representation and language enables toddlers to understand some of the factors that influence the parent's coming and going and to predict her return. As a result, separation protest declines. Now children negotiate with the caregiver, using requests and persuasion to alter her goals. For example, at age 2, Caitlin asked Carolyn and David to read her a story before leaving her with a babysitter. The extra time with her parents, along with a better understanding of where they were going ("to have dinner with Uncle Sean") and when they would be back ("right after you go to sleep"), helped Caitlin withstand her parents' absence.

With her teacher's enticement to play and an explanation that her mother will be back soon, this 2-year-old is likely separate without tears. Her language and representational skills enable her to predict her mother's return, so separation anxiety declines.

According to Bowlby (1980), out of their experiences during these four phases, children construct an enduring affectionate tie to the caregiver that they can use as a secure base in the parent's absence. This image serves as an **internal working model,** or set of expectations about the availability of attachment figures, their likelihood of providing support during times of stress, and the self's interaction with those figures. The internal working model becomes a vital part of personality, serving as a guide for all future close relationships (Bretherton & Munholland, 2008).

Consistent with these ideas, as early as the second year, toddlers form attachment-related expectations about parental comfort and support. In one study, securely attached 12- to 16-month-olds looked longer at a video of an unresponsive caregiver (inconsistent with their expectations) than a video of a responsive caregiver. Insecurely attached toddlers, in contrast,

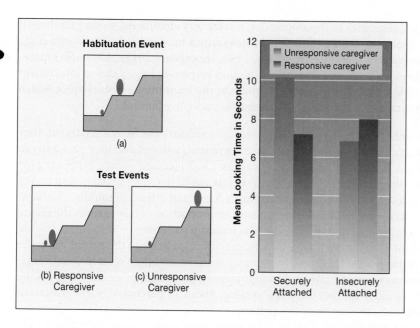

FIGURE 7.3 **Testing toddlers for internal working models of attachment.** (a) First, 12- to 16-month-olds were habituated to a video of two animated shapes, one large (the "caregiver") and one small (the "child"). The caregiver traveled halfway up an incline to a plateau, and the child began to "cry," depicted by pulsing and bouncing paired with an infant cry. Next the researchers presented two test events: (b) In the *responsive caregiver outcome,* the caregiver returned to the child. (c) In the *unresponsive caregiver outcome,* the caregiver continued up the slope away from the child. Securely attached toddlers looked longer at the unresponsive outcome, depicting caregiver behavior inconsistent with their expectations. Insecurely attached toddlers did not differentiate between the two test events. (Based on Johnson, Dweck, & Chen, 2007.)

did not distinguish between the two (see Figure 7.3) (Johnson, Dweck, & Chen, 2007; Johnson et al., 2010). With age, children continually revise and expand their internal working model as their cognitive, emotional, and social capacities increase and as they interact with parents and form other close bonds with adults, siblings, and friends.

Measuring the Security of Attachment

Although all family-reared babies become attached to a familiar caregiver by the second year, the quality of this relationship differs from child to child. Some infants appear relaxed and secure in the presence of the caregiver; they know they can count on her for protection and support. Others seem anxious and uncertain.

A widely used laboratory technique for assessing the quality of attachment between 1 and 2 years of age is the **Strange Situation.** In designing it, Mary Ainsworth and her colleagues reasoned that securely attached infants and toddlers should use the parent as a secure base from which to explore in an unfamiliar playroom. In addition, when the parent leaves, an unfamiliar adult should be less comforting than the parent. The Strange Situation takes the baby through eight short episodes in which brief separations from and reunions with the parent occur (see Table 7.2).

TABLE 7.2	Episodes in the Strange Situation	
EPISODE	**EVENTS**	**ATTACHMENT BEHAVIOR OBSERVED**
1	Researcher introduces parent and baby to playroom and then leaves.	
2	Parent is seated while baby plays with toys.	Parent as a secure base
3	Stranger enters, is seated, and talks to parent.	Reaction to unfamiliar adult
4	Parent leaves room. Stranger responds to baby and offers comfort if baby is upset.	Separation anxiety
5	Parent returns, greets baby, and offers comfort if necessary. Stranger leaves room.	Reaction to reunion
6	Parent leaves room.	Separation anxiety
7	Stranger enters room and offers comfort.	Ability to be soothed by stranger
8	Parent returns, greets baby, offers comfort if necessary, and tries to reinterest baby in toys.	Reaction to reunion

Note: Episode 1 lasts about 30 seconds; each of the remaining episodes lasts about 3 minutes. Separation episodes are cut short if the baby becomes very upset. Reunion episodes are extended if the baby needs more time to calm down and return to play.

Source: Ainsworth et al., 1978.

Observing infants' responses to these episodes, researchers identified a secure attachment pattern and three patterns of insecurity; a few babies cannot be classified (Ainsworth et al., 1978; Barnett & Vondra, 1999; Main & Solomon, 1990; Thompson, 2013). Although separation anxiety varies among the groups, the baby's reunion responses largely define attachment quality. **TAKE A MOMENT...** From the description at the beginning of this chapter, which pattern do you think Grace displayed after adjusting to her adoptive family?

- **Secure attachment.** These infants use the parent as a secure base. When separated, they may or may not cry, but if they do, it is because the parent is absent and they prefer her to the stranger. When the parent returns, they express clear pleasure—some expressing joy from a distance, others asking to be held until settling down to return to play—and crying is reduced immediately. About 60 percent of North American infants in middle-SES families show this pattern. (In low-SES families, a smaller proportion of babies show the secure pattern, with higher proportions falling into the insecure patterns.)
- **Insecure–avoidant attachment.** These infants seem unresponsive to the parent when she is present. When she leaves, they usually are not distressed, and they react to the stranger in much the same way as to the parent. During reunion, they avoid or are slow to greet the parent, and when picked up, they often fail to cling. About 15 percent of North American infants in middle-SES families show this pattern.
- **Insecure–resistant attachment.** Before separation, these infants seek closeness to the parent and often fail to explore. When the parent leaves, they are usually distressed, and on her return they combine clinginess with angry, resistive behavior (struggling when held, hitting and pushing) or with an anxious focus on the parent. Many continue to cry after being picked up and cannot be comforted easily. About 10 percent of North American infants in middle-SES families show this pattern.
- **Disorganized/disoriented attachment.** This pattern reflects the greatest insecurity. At reunion, these infants show confused, contradictory behaviors—for example, looking away while the parent is holding them or approaching the parent with flat, depressed emotion. Most display a dazed facial expression, and a few cry out unexpectedly after having calmed down or display odd, frozen postures. About 15 percent of North American infants in middle-SES families show this pattern.

An alternative method, the **Attachment Q-Sort,** suitable for children between 1 and 5 years, depends on home observations (Waters et al., 1995). Either the parent or a highly trained observer sorts 90 behaviors—such as "Child greets mother with a big smile when she enters the room," "If mother moves very far, child follows along," and "Child uses mother's facial expressions as a good source of information when something looks risky or threatening"—into nine categories ranging from "highly descriptive" to "not at all descriptive" of the child. Then a score, ranging from high to low in security, is computed.

Because the Q-Sort taps a wider array of attachment-related behaviors than the Strange Situation, it may better reflect the parent–infant relationship in everyday life. However, the Q-Sort method is time-consuming, requiring a nonparent informant to spend several hours observing the child before sorting the descriptors, and it does not differentiate between types of insecurity. The Q-Sort responses of expert observers correspond well with babies' secure-base behavior in the Strange Situation, but parents' Q-Sorts do not (van IJzendoorn et al., 2004). Parents of insecure children, especially, may have difficulty accurately reporting their child's attachment behaviors.

Stability of Attachment

Research on the stability of attachment patterns between 1 and 2 years of age yields a wide range of findings. In some studies, as many as 70 to 90 percent of children remain the same in their reactions to parents; in others, only 30 to 40 percent do (Thompson, 2006, 2013). A close look at which babies stay the same and which ones change yields a more consistent picture. Quality of attachment is usually secure and stable for middle-SES babies experiencing favorable life conditions. And infants who move from insecurity to security typically have well-adjusted mothers with positive family and friendship ties. Perhaps many became parents before they were psychologically ready but, with social support, grew into the role.

In contrast, in low-SES families with many daily stresses, attachment generally moves away from security or changes from one insecure pattern to another (Fish, 2004; Levendosky et al., 2011; Vondra et al., 2001). And in a long-term follow-up from infancy to early adulthood, child maltreatment, maternal depression, and poor family functioning were associated with shifts from security to insecurity (Weinfield, Sroufe, & Egeland, 2000; Weinfield, Whaley, & Egeland, 2004).

These findings indicate that securely attached babies more often maintain their attachment status than insecure babies, whose relationship with the caregiver is, by definition, fragile and uncertain. The exception is disorganized/disoriented attachment, an insecure pattern that is either highly stable or that consistently predicts insecurity of another type in adolescence and early adulthood (Aikens, Howes, & Hamilton, 2009; Hesse & Main, 2000; Weinfeld, Whaley, & Egeland, 2004). As you will soon see, many disorganized/disoriented infants experience extremely negative caregiving, which may disrupt emotional self-regulation so severely that confused, ambivalent feelings toward parents persist.

Cultural Variations

Cross-cultural evidence indicates that attachment patterns may have to be interpreted differently in certain cultures. For example, as Figure 7.4 reveals, German infants show considerably more avoidant attachment than American babies do. But German parents value independence and encourage their infants to be nonclingy, so the baby's behavior may be an intended outcome of cultural beliefs and practices (Grossmann et al., 1985). In contrast, a study of infants of the Dogon people of Mali, Africa, revealed that none showed avoidant attachment to their mothers (True, Pisani, & Oumar, 2001). Even when grandmothers are primary caregivers (as they are with firstborn sons), Dogon mothers remain available to their babies, holding them close and nursing them promptly in response to hunger and distress.

Japanese infants, as well, rarely show avoidant attachment (refer again to Figure 7.4). Rather, many are resistantly attached, but this reaction may not represent true insecurity. Japanese mothers rarely leave their babies in others' care, so the Strange Situation probably induces greater stress in them than in infants who frequently experience maternal separations (Takahashi, 1990). Also, Japanese parents view the attention seeking that is part of resistant attachment as a normal indicator of infants' efforts to satisfy dependency and security needs (Rothbaum et al., 2007). Likewise, infants in Israeli kibbutzim frequently show resistant attachment. For these babies, who can sense the fear of unfamiliar people that is pervasive in their communities (see page 250), the Strange Situation probably induces unusual distress (van IJzendoorn & Sagi, 1999). Despite these and other cultural variations, the secure pattern is still the most common attachment quality in all societies studied to date (van IJzendoorn & Sagi-Schwartz, 2008).

Factors That Affect Attachment Security

What factors might influence attachment security? Researchers have looked closely at four important influences: (1) early availability of a consistent caregiver, (2) quality of caregiving, (3) the baby's characteristics, and (4) family context, including parents' internal working models.

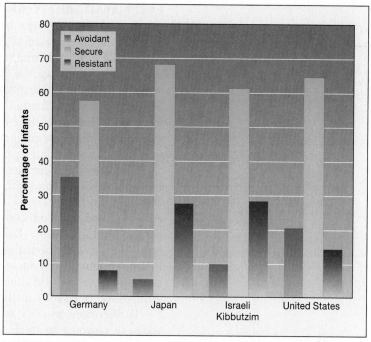

FIGURE 7.4 **A cross-cultural comparison of infants' reactions in the Strange Situation.** A high percentage of German babies seem avoidantly attached, whereas a substantial number of Japanese and Israeli kibbutz infants appear resistantly attached. Note that these responses may not reflect true insecurity. Instead, they are probably due to cultural differences in child-rearing practices. (Based on van IJzendoorn & Kroonenberg, 1988; van IJzendoorn & Sagi-Schwartz, 2008.)

Dogon mothers of Mali, West Africa, stay close to their babies and respond promptly and gently to infant hunger and distress. With their mothers consistently available, none of the Dogon babies show avoidant attachment.

EARLY AVAILABILITY OF A CONSISTENT CAREGIVER What happens when a baby does not have the opportunity to establish a close tie to a caregiver? To find out, researchers followed the development of infants in an institution with a good caregiver–child ratio and a rich selection of books and toys. However, staff turnover was so rapid that the average child had 50 caregivers by age 4½. Many of these children became "late adoptees" who were placed in homes after age 4. Most developed deep ties with their adoptive parents, indicating that a first attachment can develop as late as 4 to 6 years of age (Hodges & Tizard, 1989; Tizard & Rees, 1975). But these children were more likely to display attachment difficulties, including an excessive desire for adult attention, "overfriendliness" to unfamiliar adults and peers, failure to check back with the parent in anxiety-arousing situations, and few friendships.

Children who spent their first year or more in deprived Eastern European orphanages—though also able to bond with their adoptive parents—show elevated rates of attachment insecurity (van den Dries et al., 2009; Smyke et al., 2010). And they, too, are at high risk for emotional and social difficulties. Whereas many are indiscriminately friendly, others are sad, anxious, and withdrawn (Bakermans-Kranenberg et al., 2011; O'Connor et al., 2003). These symptoms typically persist and are associated with wide-ranging mental health problems in middle childhood and adolescence, including cognitive impairments, inattention and over-activity, depression, and either social avoidance or aggressive behavior (Kreppner et al., 2007, 2010; Rutter et al., 2007, 2010; Zeanah, 2000).

Furthermore, as early as 7 months, institutionalized children show reduced ERP brain waves in response to facial expressions of emotion and have trouble discriminating such expressions—outcomes that suggest disrupted formation of neural structures involved in "reading" emotions (Parker et al., 2005). These problems are still evident in preschoolers adopted during the second year, who find it hard to match appropriate facial expressions with situations in stories (Fries & Pollak, 2004). Consistent with these findings, in adopted children with longer institutional stays, the volume of the *amygdala* (see page 256) is atypically large (Tottenham et al., 2011). The larger the amygdala, the worse adopted children perform on tasks assessing understanding of emotion and the poorer their emotional self-regulation. Overall, the evidence indicates that fully normal emotional development depends on establishing a close tie with a caregiver early in life.

QUALITY OF CAREGIVING Dozens of studies report that **sensitive caregiving**—responding promptly, consistently, and appropriately to infants and holding them tenderly and carefully—is moderately related to attachment security in both biological and adoptive mother–infant pairs and in diverse cultures and SES groups (Belsky & Fearon, 2008; De Wolff & van IJzendoorn, 1997; van IJzendoorn et al., 2004). Mothers of securely attached babies also frequently refer to their infants' mental states and motives: "You really *like* that swing!" "Do you *remember* Grandma?" This tendency to treat the baby as a person with inner thoughts and feelings seems to promote sensitive caregiving (Meins et al., 2001, 2003). In contrast, insecurely attached infants tend to have mothers who engage in less physical contact, handle them awkwardly or in a "routine" manner, and are sometimes resentful and rejecting, particularly in response to infant distress (Ainsworth et al., 1978; Isabella, 1993; McElwain & Booth-LaForce, 2006; Pederson & Moran, 1996).

Also, in studies of Western babies, a special form of communication called **interactional synchrony** separates the experiences of secure from insecure babies. It is best described as a sensitively tuned "emotional dance," in which the caregiver responds to infant signals in a well-timed, rhythmic, appropriate fashion. In addition, both partners match emotional states, especially the positive ones (Bigelow et al., 2010; Isabella & Belsky, 1991; Nievar & Becker, 2008). For example, when Caitlin excitedly shook a rattle, Carolyn responded with a broad smile and an enthusiastic "That-a-girl!" In return, Caitlin smiled and cooed. And when Caitlin fussed and cried, Carolyn soothed with gentle touches and soft, sympathetic words.

Earlier we saw that sensitive face-to-face play, in which interactional synchrony occurs, increases babies' responsiveness to others' emotional

A father and baby engage in a sensitively tuned form of communication called interactional synchrony, in which they match emotional states, especially positive ones. Among Western infants, this style of communication predicts secure attachment.

© CHAD SPRINGER/CULTURA/CORBIS

messages and helps them regulate emotion. But moderate adult–infant coordination is a better predictor of attachment security than "tight" coordination, in which the adult responds to most infant cues (Jaffee et al., 2001). Perhaps warm, sensitive caregivers use a relaxed, flexible style of communication in which they comfortably accept and repair emotional mismatches, returning to a synchronous state.

Cultures vary in their view of sensitivity toward infants. Among the Gusii people of Kenya, mothers rarely cuddle, hug, or interact playfully with their babies, although they are very responsive to their babies' needs. Yet most Gusii infants appear securely attached (LeVine et al., 1994). This suggests that security depends on attentive caregiving, not necessarily on moment-by-moment contingent interaction. Puerto Rican mothers, who highly value obedience and socially appropriate behavior, often physically direct and limit their babies' actions—a caregiving style linked to attachment security in Puerto Rican culture (Carlson & Harwood, 2003). Yet in many Western cultures, such physical control and restriction of exploration are viewed as intrusive and predict insecurity (Belsky & Fearon, 2008; Whipple, Bernier, & Mageau, 2011).

Compared with securely attached infants, avoidant babies tend to receive overstimulating, intrusive care. Their mothers might, for example, talk energetically to them while they are looking away or falling asleep. By avoiding the mother, these infants appear to be escaping from overwhelming interaction. Resistant infants often experience inconsistent care. Their mothers are unresponsive to infant signals. Yet when the baby begins to explore, these mothers interfere, shifting the infant's attention back to themselves. As a result, the baby is overly dependent as well as angry at the mother's lack of involvement (Cassidy & Berlin, 1994; Isabella & Belsky, 1991).

Highly inadequate caregiving is a powerful predictor of disruptions in attachment. Child abuse and neglect (topics we will consider in Chapter 10) are associated with all three forms of attachment insecurity. Among maltreated infants, disorganized/disoriented attachment is especially high (Cyr et al., 2010). Persistently depressed mothers, mothers with very low marital satisfaction, and parents suffering from a traumatic event, such as serious illness or loss of a loved one, also tend to promote the uncertain behaviors of this pattern (Campbell et al., 2004; Madigan et al., 2006; Moss et al., 2005). And some mothers of disorganized/disoriented infants engage in frightening, contradictory, and unpleasant behaviors, such as looking scared, teasing the baby, holding the baby stiffly at a distance, roughly pulling the baby by the arm, or seeking reassurance from the upset child (Lyons-Ruth, Bronfman, & Parsons, 1999; Moran et al., 2008; Solomon & George, 2011). Perhaps the baby's disorganized behavior reflects a conflicted reaction to the parent, who sometimes comforts but at other times arouses fear.

INFANT CHARACTERISTICS   Because attachment is the result of a *relationship* between two partners, infant characteristics should affect how easily it is established. In Chapters 3 and 4 we saw that prematurity, birth complications, and newborn illness make caregiving more taxing. In families under stress, these difficulties are linked to attachment insecurity. In one study, the *combination* of preterm birth with either socioeconomic risk (poverty, single parenthood, high-school dropout) or maternal psychological risk (depression, high emotional stress)—but not preterm birth alone—reduced maternal sensitivity, which predicted insecure attachment at 12 months (Candelaria, Teti, & Black, 2011). Infants with special needs probably require greater parental sensitivity, which stressed parents often cannot provide. But at-risk newborns whose parents have adequate time and patience to care for them fare quite well in attachment security (Brisch et al., 2005; Cox, Hopkins, & Hans, 2000).

With respect to temperament, babies who are emotionally reactive are more likely to develop later insecure attachments (van IJzendoorn et al., 2004; Vaughn, Bost, & Van IJzendoorn, 2008). And disorganized newborn behavior, evident in scores on the Neonatal Behavioral Assessment Scale (NBAS, see Chapter 4), increases the risk of disorganized/disoriented attachment at the end of the first year (Spangler, Fremmer-Bomik, & Grossmann, 1996).

Again, however, evidence highlighting gene–environment interactions suggests that parental mental health and caregiving are involved. For example, babies with the short 5-HTTLPR gene, which is associated with emotional reactivity (see pages 258–259), are more likely than infants with a low-risk genotype to exhibit disorganized-disoriented attachment, but only when their mothers display low responsiveness or other negative parenting characteristics

(Spangler et al., 2009). In other research, mothers' experience of unresolved loss of a loved one or other trauma was associated with attachment disorganization, but only in infants with a chromosome-11 gene having a certain repetition of DNA base pairs (called DRD4 7-repeat), which is linked to impulsive, overactive behavior (Gervai, 2009; van IJzendoorn & Bakermans-Kranenburg, 2006). Babies with this genetic marker, who face special self-regulation challenges, were more susceptible to the negative impact of maternal adjustment problems.

If children's temperaments alone determined attachment quality, we would expect attachment, like temperament, to be at least moderately heritable. Yet twin comparisons reveal that the heritability of attachment is virtually nil (O'Connor & Croft, 2001; Roisman & Fraley, 2008). Rather, babies with certain genotypes are at increased risk for attachment insecurity when they also experience insensitive parenting. Consistent with this conclusion, about two-thirds of siblings establish similar attachment patterns with their parents, although the siblings often differ in temperament (Cole, 2006; Dozier et al., 2001). This suggests that most parents try to adjust their caregiving to each child's individual needs.

Interventions that teach parents to interact sensitively with difficult-to-care-for infants and toddlers enhance both sensitive care and attachment security (Velderman et al., 2006). One program that focused on both maternal sensitivity and effective discipline was particularly effective in reducing stress reactivity (as indicated by lower cortisol levels) and disruptive behavior among toddlers with the DRD4 7-repeat gene (Bakermans-Kranenburg & van IJzendoorn, 2011; Bakermans-Kranenburg et al., 2008a, 2008b). These findings suggest that the DRD4 7-repeat—like the short 5-HTTLPR gene—makes children more susceptible to the effects of both negative and positive parenting.

FAMILY CIRCUMSTANCES Shortly after Timmy's birth, his parents divorced, and his father moved to a distant city. Anxious and distracted, Vanessa placed 2-month-old Timmy in Ginette's child-care home and began working 50-hour weeks to make ends meet. On days Vanessa stayed late at the office, a babysitter picked Timmy up, gave him dinner, and put him to bed. Once or twice a week, Vanessa went to get Timmy from child care. As he neared his first birthday, Vanessa noticed that, unlike the other children, who reached out, crawled, or ran to their parents, Timmy ignored her.

Timmy's behavior reflects a repeated finding: Job loss, a failing marriage, financial difficulties, or parental psychological problems (such as anxiety or depression) can undermine attachment indirectly by interfering with parental sensitivity. These stressors can also affect babies' sense of security directly by altering the emotional climate of the family (for example, exposing them to angry adult interactions) or by disrupting familiar daily routines (Finger et al., 2009; Thompson, 2013). By reducing parental stress and improving the quality of parent–child communication, social support fosters attachment security (Moss et al., 2005). Ginette's sensitivity toward Timmy was helpful, as was the parenting advice Vanessa received from Ben, a psychologist. As Timmy turned 2, his relationship with his mother seemed warmer.

Family circumstances are linked to attachment quality. Observing her parents' heated quarrels may undermine this child's sense of emotional security.

PARENTS' INTERNAL WORKING MODELS Parents bring to the family context their own history of attachment experiences, from which they construct internal working models that they apply to the bonds they establish with their babies. Monica, who recalled her mother as tense and preoccupied, expressed regret that they had not had a closer relationship. Is her image of parenthood likely to affect Grace's attachment security?

To assess parents' internal working models, researchers ask them to evaluate childhood memories of attachment experiences (Main & Goldwyn, 1998). Parents who discuss their childhoods with objectivity and balance, regardless of whether their experiences were positive or negative, tend to have securely attached infants and to behave sensitively toward them. In contrast, parents who dismiss the importance of early relationships or describe them in angry, confused ways usually have insecurely attached children and are less warm, sensitive, and encouraging of learning and mastery (Behrens, Hesse, & Main, 2007; Coyl, Newland, & Freeman, 2010; McFarland-Piazza et al., 2012; Steele, Steele, & Fonagy, 1996).

© IMAGEBROKER/ALAMY

But we must not assume any direct transfer of parents' childhood experiences to quality of attachment with their own children. Internal working models are *reconstructed memories* affected by many factors, including relationship experiences over the life course, personality, and current life satisfaction. Longitudinal research reveals that negative life events can weaken the link between an individual's own attachment security in infancy and a secure internal working model in adulthood. And insecurely attached babies who become adults with insecure internal working models often have lives that, based on self-reports in adulthood, are filled with family crises (Waters et al., 2000; Weinfield, Sroufe, & Egeland, 2000).

In sum, our early rearing experiences do not destine us to become either sensitive or insensitive parents. Rather, the way we *view* our childhoods—our ability to come to terms with negative events, to integrate new information into our working models, and to look back on our own parents in an understanding, forgiving way—is far more influential in how we rear our children than the actual history of care we received (Bretherton & Munholland, 2008).

ATTACHMENT IN CONTEXT   Carolyn and Vanessa returned to work when their babies were 2 to 3 months old. Monica did the same a few weeks after Grace's adoption. When parents divide their time between work and parenting and place their infants and toddlers in child care, is quality of attachment and child adjustment affected? See the Social Issues: Health box on page 270 for research that addresses this issue.

After reading the box, consider each factor that influences the development of attachment—infant and parent characteristics, parents' relationship with each other, outside-the-family stressors, the availability of social supports, parents' views of their attachment history, and child-care arrangements. Although attachment builds within the warmth and intimacy of caregiver–infant interaction, it can be fully understood only from an ecological systems perspective. **TAKE A MOMENT...** Return to Chapter 1, pages 26–29, to review Bronfenbrenner's ecological systems theory. Notice how research confirms the importance of each level of the environment for attachment security.

Multiple Attachments

As we have indicated, babies develop attachments to a variety of familiar people—not just mothers, but also fathers, grandparents, siblings, and professional caregivers. Although Bowlby (1969) believed that infants are predisposed to direct their attachment behaviors to a single special person, especially when they are distressed, his theory allows for these multiple attachments.

FATHERS   An anxious, unhappy 1-year-old who is permitted to choose between the mother and the father as a source of comfort and security will usually choose the mother. But this preference typically declines over the second year. And when babies are not distressed, they approach, vocalize to, and smile equally often at both parents, who in turn are equally responsive to their infant's social bids (Bornstein, 2006; Parke, 2002).

Fathers' sensitive caregiving predicts infant attachment security, though somewhat less strongly than mothers' (Brown, Mangelsdorf, & Neff, 2012; Lucassen et al., 2011). At the same time, interventions aimed at increasing parental sensitivity and attachment security, though successful with both mothers and fathers, appear more effective with fathers (Bakermans-Kranenburg, Van IJzendoorn, & Juffer, 2003). As infancy progresses, mothers and fathers in many cultures, including Australia, Canada, Germany, India, Israel, Italy, Japan, and the United States, tend to interact differently with their babies: Mothers devote more time to physical care and expressing affection, fathers to playful interaction (Freeman & Newland, 2010; Roopnarine et al., 1990).

Also, mothers and fathers tend to play differently. Mothers more often provide toys, talk to infants, and gently play conventional games like pat-a-cake and peekaboo. In contrast, fathers—especially with their infant sons—tend to engage in highly stimulating physical play with bursts of excitement and surprise that increase as play progresses (Feldman, 2003). As long as fathers are also sensitive, this stimulating, startling play style helps babies regulate

LOOK *and* **LISTEN**

Observe parents at play with infants at home or a family gathering, describing both similarities and differences in mothers' and fathers' behaviors. Are your observations consistent with research findings?

Social Issues: Health

Does Child Care Threaten Attachment Security and Later Adjustment?

A re infants who experience daily separations from their employed parents and early placement in child care at risk for attachment insecurity and developmental problems? Some researchers think so, but others disagree. Let's look closely at the evidence.

Attachment Quality

Some studies suggest that babies placed in full-time child care before 12 months of age are more likely to display insecure attachment in the Strange Situation (Belsky, 2001, 2005). But the best current evidence—from the U.S. National Institute of Child Health and Development (NICHD) Study of Early Child Care, the largest longitudinal investigation to date, including more than 1,300 infants and their families—confirms that use of nonparental care by itself does not affect attachment quality (NICHD Early Child Care Research Network, 1997, 2001). Rather, the relationship between child care and emotional well-being depends on both family and child-care experiences.

Family Circumstances

We have seen that family conditions affect children's attachment security and later adjustment. Findings of the NICHD Study confirmed that parenting quality, assessed using a combination of maternal sensitivity and HOME scores (see page 227 in Chapter 6), exerted a more powerful impact on children's adjustment than did exposure to child care (NICHD Early Childhood Research Network, 1998; Watamura et al., 2011).

For employed parents, balancing work and caregiving can be stressful. Mothers who are fatigued and anxious because they feel overloaded by work and family pressures may respond less sensitively to their babies, thereby risking the infant's security. And as paternal involvement in caregiving has risen (see page 271), many more U.S. fathers in dual-earner families also report work–family life conflict (Galinsky, Aumann, & Bond, 2009).

Quality and Extent of Child Care

Nevertheless, poor-quality child care may contribute to a higher rate of insecure attachment. In the NICHD Study, when babies were exposed to combined home and child-care risk factors— insensitive caregiving at home along with insensitive caregiving in child care, long hours in child care, or more than one child-care arrangement— the rate of insecurity increased. Overall, mother–child interaction was more favorable when

children attended higher-quality child care and also spent fewer hours in child care (NICHD Early Child Care Research Network, 1997, 1999).

Furthermore, when these children reached age 3, a history of higher-quality child care predicted better social skills (NICHD Early Child Care Research Network, 2002b). However, at age 4½ to 5, children averaging more than 30 child-care hours per week displayed more externalizing problems, especially defiance, disobedience, and aggression. For those who had been in child-care centers as opposed to family child-care homes, this outcome persisted through elementary school (Belsky et al., 2007; NICHD Early Child Care Research Network, 2003a, 2006).

But these findings do not necessarily mean that child care causes behavior problems. Rather, heavy exposure to substandard care, which is widespread in the United States, may promote these difficulties, especially when combined with family risk factors. A closer look at the NICHD participants during the preschool years revealed that those in both poor-quality home and child-care environments fared worst in social skills and problem behaviors, whereas those in both high-quality home and child-care environments fared best. In between were preschoolers in high-quality child care but poor-quality homes (Watamura et al., 2011). These children benefited from the *protective influence* of high-quality child care.

Evidence from other industrialized nations confirms that full-time child care need not harm children's development. For example, amount of time spent in child care in Australia and Norway, which also offer high-quality, government-subsidized center-based care, is unrelated to children's behavior problems (Love et al., 2003; Zachrisson et al. 2013).

Still, some children may be particularly stressed by long child-care hours. Many infants, toddlers, and preschoolers attending child-care centers for full days show a mild increase in saliva concentrations of the stress hormone cortisol across the day—a pattern that does not occur on days they spend at home. In one study, children rated as highly fearful by their caregivers experienced an especially sharp increase in cortisol levels (Watamura et al., 2003). Inhibited children may find the constant company of large numbers of peers particularly stressful. Nevertheless, a secure attachment to a professional caregiver is protective (Badanes, Dmitrieva & Watamura, 2012). It is associated with falling cortisol levels across the child-care day.

© ELLEN B. SENISI

High-quality child care, with generous caregiver–child ratios, small group sizes, and knowledgeable caregivers, can be part of a system that promotes all aspects of development, including attachment security.

Conclusions

Taken together, research suggests that some infants may be at risk for attachment insecurity and adjustment problems due to inadequate child care, long hours in such care, and the joint pressures their parents experience from full-time employment and parenthood. But it is inappropriate to use these findings to justify a reduction in child-care services. When family incomes are limited or mothers who want to work are forced to stay at home, children's emotional security is not promoted.

Instead, it makes sense to increase the availability of high-quality child care and to relieve work–family-life conflict by providing parents with paid employment leave (see page 139 in Chapter 4) and opportunities for part-time work. In the NICHD study, part-time (as opposed to full-time) employment during the baby's first year was associated with greater maternal sensitivity and a higher-quality home environment, which yielded more favorable development in early childhood (Brooks-Gunn, Han, & Waldfogel, 2010).

Finally, the professional caregiver's relationship with the baby is vital. When caregiver–child ratios are generous, group sizes are small, and caregivers are educated about child development, caregivers' interactions are more positive, their attachments to babies are more secure, and children develop more favorably—cognitively, emotionally, and socially (Biringen et al., 2012; NICHD Early Child Care Research Network, 2000b, 2002a, 2006). Child care with these characteristics can become part of an ecological system that relieves parental and child stress, thereby promoting healthy attachment and development.

emotion in intensely arousing situations and may prepare them to venture confidently into active, unpredictable contexts, including novel physical environments and play with peers (Cabrera et al., 2007; Hazen et al., 2010). In a German study, fathers' sensitive, challenging play with preschoolers predicted favorable emotional and social adjustment from kindergarten to early adulthood (Grossmann et al, 2008).

Play is a vital context in which fathers build secure attachments (Newland, Coyl, & Freeman, 2008). It may be especially influential in cultures where long work hours prevent most fathers from sharing in infant caregiving, such as Japan (Hewlett, 2004; Shwalb et al., 2004). In many Western nations, however, a strict division of parental roles—mother as caregiver, father as playmate—has changed over the past several decades in response to women's workforce participation and to cultural valuing of gender equality.

A U.S. national survey of several thousand employed workers indicated that U.S. fathers under age 29 devote about 85 percent as much time as mothers do to children—on average, just over 4 hours per workday, nearly double the hours young fathers reported three decades ago. Although fathers age 29 to 42 spend somewhat less time with children, their involvement has also increased substantially (see Figure 7.5). Today, nearly one-third of U.S. employed women say that their spouse or partner shares equally in or takes most responsibility for childcare tasks (Galinsky, Aumann, & Bond, 2009). Paternal availability to children is fairly similar across SES and ethnic groups, with one exception: Hispanic fathers spend more time engaged, probably because of the particularly high value that Hispanic cultures place on family involvement (Cabrera & García Coll, 2004; Parke et al., 2004a).

A warm marital bond and supportive coparenting (see page 69 in Chapter 2) promote both parents' sensitivity and involvement and children's attachment security, but they are especially important for fathers (Brown et al., 2010; Lamb & Lewis, 2004; Laurent, Kim, & Capaldi, 2008). See the Cultural Influences box on page 272 for cross-cultural evidence documenting this conclusion—and also highlighting the powerful role of paternal warmth in children's development.

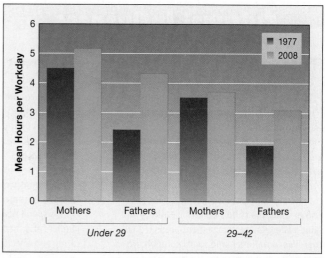

FIGURE 7.5 **Average amount of time per workday U.S. employed mothers and fathers reported spending with their children (age 12 and younger) in 1977 and 2008.** In national surveys of several thousand employed parents, mothers' time with children remained fairly stable from 1977 to 2008; fathers' time increased substantially. (Based on Galinsky, Aumann, & Bond, 2009.)

GRANDPARENT PRIMARY CAREGIVERS Nearly 2.4 million U.S. children—4 to 5 percent of the child population—live with their grandparents but apart from parents, in so-called *skipped-generation families* (U.S. Census Bureau, 2014b). The number of grandparents rearing grandchildren has increased over the past two decades. The arrangement occurs in all ethnic groups, though more often in African-American, Hispanic, and Native-American families than in Caucasian families. Although grandparent caregivers are more likely to be women than men, many grandfathers participate (Fuller-Thomson & Minkler, 2005, 2007; Minkler & Fuller-Thomson, 2005). Grandparents generally step in when parents' troubled lives—as a result of substance abuse, child abuse and neglect, mental illness, or adolescent parenthood—threaten children's well-being (Langosch, 2012). Often these families take in two or more children.

As a result, grandparents usually assume the parenting role under highly stressful life circumstances. Unfavorable child-rearing experiences have left their mark on children, who show high rates of learning difficulties, depression, and antisocial behavior. Absent parents' adjustment difficulties strain family relationships. Parents may interfere by violating the grandparents' behavioral limits, taking grandchildren away without permission, or making promises to children that they do not keep. These youngsters also introduce financial burdens into households

Despite stressful family conditions, grandparents who provide long-term physical and emotional care form deep attachments with their grandchildren.

Cultural Influences

The Powerful Role of Paternal Warmth in Development

Research in diverse cultures demonstrates that fathers' warmth contributes greatly to children's long-term favorable development. In studies of many societies and ethnic groups around the world, researchers coded paternal expressions of love and nurturance—evident in such behaviors as cuddling, hugging, comforting, playing, verbally expressing love, and praising the child's behavior. Fathers' sustained affectionate involvement predicted later cognitive, emotional, and social competence as strongly as did mothers' warmth—and occasionally more strongly (Rohner & Veneziano, 2001; Veneziano, 2003). And in Western cultures, paternal warmth and secure attachment are associated with children's mature social behavior and a reduction in a wide range of difficulties, including childhood emotional and behavior problems and adolescent substance abuse and delinquency (Lamb & Lewis, 2013; Michiels et al., 2010; Nelson & Coyne, 2009; Tacon & Caldera, 2001).

Fathers who devote little time to physical caregiving express warmth through play. In a German study, fathers' play sensitivity—accepting toddlers' play initiatives, adapting play behaviors to toddlers' capacities, and responding appropriately to toddlers' expressions of emotion—predicted children's secure internal working models of attachment during middle childhood and adolescence (Grossmann et al., 2002). Through play, fathers seemed to transfer to young children

a sense of confidence about parental support, which may strengthen their capacity to master many later challenges.

What factors promote paternal warmth? Cross-cultural research reveals a consistent association between the amount of time fathers spend near infants and toddlers and their expressions of caring and affection (Rohner & Veneziano, 2001). Consider the Aka hunters and gatherers of Central Africa, where fathers spend more time in physical proximity to their babies than in any other known society. Observations reveal that Aka fathers are within arm's reach of infants more than half the day. They pick up, cuddle, and play with their babies at least five times as often as fathers in other hunting-and-gathering societies. Why are Aka fathers so involved? The bond between Aka husband and wife is unusually cooperative and intimate. Throughout the day, couples share hunting, food preparation, and social and leisure activities (Hewlett, 1992). The more Aka parents are together, the greater the father's loving interaction with his baby.

In Western cultures as well, happily married fathers whose partners coparent effectively with

In both Western and non-Western nations, paternal warmth predicts long-term favorable cognitive, emotional, and social development.

them spend more time with and interact more effectively with their infants. In contrast, marital dissatisfaction is associated with insensitive paternal care (Brown et al., 2010; Lundy, 2002; Sevigny & Loutzenhiser, 2010). Clearly, fathers' warm relationships with their partners and with their babies are closely linked. Evidence for the power of fathers' affection, reported in virtually every culture and ethnic group studied, is reason to encourage more men to engage in nurturing care of young children.

that often are already low-income (Mills, Gomez-Smith, & De Leon, 2005; Williamson, Softas-Nall, & Miller, 2003). And grandparent caregivers, at a time when they anticipated having more time for spouses, friends, and leisure, instead have less. Many report feeling emotionally drained, depressed, and worried about what will happen to the children if their own health fails (Hayslip & Kaminski, 2005; Langosch, 2012).

Nevertheless, because they provide physical and emotional care for an extended time and are invested in the child's well-being, grandparent caregivers forge significant attachment relationships with their grandchildren (Poehlmann, 2003). Warm grandparent–grandchild bonds help protect children from worsening adjustment problems, even under conditions of great hardship (Hicks & Goedereis, 2009). Still, grandparent caregivers have a tremendous need for social and financial support and intervention services for their at-risk grandchildren.

SIBLINGS Despite declines in family size, 80 percent of North American and European children grow up with at least one sibling (Dunn, 2004). The arrival of a new baby is a difficult experience for most preschoolers, who—realizing that they must now share their parents' attention and affection—often become demanding, clingy, deliberately naughty, and less affectionate with their parents for a time. Attachment security also typically declines, especially for children over age 2 (old enough to feel threatened and displaced) and for those with mothers under stress (Teti et al., 1996; Volling, 2012).

Applying What We Know

Encouraging Affectionate Ties Between Infants and Their Preschool Siblings

SUGGESTION	DESCRIPTION
Spend extra time with the older child.	Parents can minimize the older child's feelings of being deprived of affection and attention by setting aside time to spend with her. Fathers can be especially helpful, planning special outings with the preschooler and taking over care of the baby so the mother can be with the older child.
Handle sibling misbehavior with patience.	When parents respond patiently to the older sibling's misbehavior and demands for attention, these reactions are usually temporary. Parents can give the preschooler opportunities to feel proud of being more grown-up than the baby—for example, by encouraging the older child to assist with feeding, bathing, dressing, and offering toys, and showing appreciation for these efforts.
Discuss the baby's wants and needs.	By helping the older sibling understand the baby's point of view, parents can promote friendly, considerate behavior. They can say, for example, "He's so little that he just can't wait to be fed" or "He's trying to reach his rattle, and he can't."
Express positive emotion toward your partner and engage in joint problem solving.	When parents mutually support each other's parenting behavior, their good communication helps the older sibling cope adaptively with jealousy and conflict.

Yet resentment is only one feature of the rich emotional relationship that starts to build between siblings after a baby's birth. Older children also show affection and concern—kissing and patting the baby and calling out, "Mom, he needs you," when the infant cries. By the end of the first year, babies typically spend much time with older siblings and are comforted by the presence of a preschool-age brother or sister during short parental absences. Throughout childhood, children continue to treat older siblings as attachment figures, turning to them for comfort in stressful situations when parents are unavailable (Seibert & Kerns, 2009). And in the second year, as toddlers imitate and join in play with their brothers and sisters, siblings start to become gratifying sources of companionship (Barr & Hayne, 2003).

Nevertheless, individual differences in sibling relationships emerge soon after the new baby's arrival. Temperament plays an important role. For example, conflict is greater when one sibling is emotionally intense or highly active (Brody, Stoneman, & McCoy, 1994; Dunn, 1994). And maternal warmth toward both children is related to positive sibling interaction and to preschoolers' support of a distressed younger sibling (Volling, 2001; Volling & Belsky, 1992). Mothers who frequently play with their children and explain the toddler's wants and needs to the preschool sibling foster sibling cooperation. In contrast, maternal harshness and lack of involvement are linked to antagonistic sibling relationships (Howe, Aquan-Assee, & Bukowski, 2001).

Finally, a good marriage is correlated with older preschool siblings' capacity to cope adaptively with jealousy and conflict (Volling, McElwain, & Miller, 2002). Perhaps good communication between parents serves as a model of effective problem solving. It may also foster a generally happy family environment, giving children less reason to feel jealous.

Refer to Applying What We Know above for ways to promote positive relationships between babies and their preschool siblings. Siblings offer a rich social context in which children learn and practice a wide range of skills, including affectionate caring, conflict resolution, and control of hostile and envious feelings.

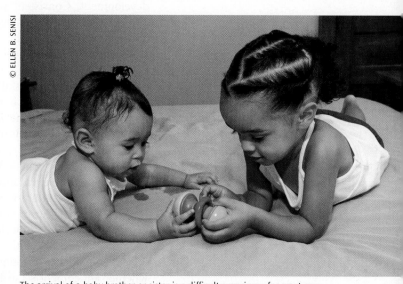

The arrival of a baby brother or sister is a difficult experience for most preschoolers. Maternal warmth toward both children assures the older sibling of continuing parental love, models affectionate caring, and is related to positive sibling interaction.

Advances in peer sociability during the second year are evident in toddlers' coordinated interaction, mostly in the form of mutual imitation.

From Attachment to Peer Sociability

In cultures where agemates have regular contact during the first year of life, peer sociability begins early. By age 6 months, Caitlin and Timmy occasionally looked, reached, smiled, and babbled when they saw each other. These isolated social acts increased until, by the end of the first year, an occasional reciprocal exchange occurred in which the children grinned, gestured, or otherwise imitated a playmate's behavior (Vandell & Mueller, 1995).

Between 1 and 2 years, as toddlers appreciate that others have intentions, desires, and emotions distinct from their own, they increasingly view one another as playmates (Brownell & Kopp, 2007). As a result, coordinated interaction occurs more often, largely in the form of offering each other objects, sharing positive emotions, and mutual imitation involving jumping, chasing, or banging a toy (Vandell et al., 2006; Williams, Mastergeorge, & Ontai, 2010). These exchanges promote peer engagement and create joint understandings that aid verbal communication.

Around age 2, toddlers use words to talk about and influence a peer's behavior, as when Caitlin said to Grace, "Let's play chase," and after the game got going, "Hey, good running!" (Eckerman & Peterman, 2001). Reciprocal play and positive emotion are especially frequent in toddlers' interactions with familiar agemates, suggesting that they are building true peer relationships (Ross et al., 1992).

Though limited, peer sociability is present in the first two years and is promoted by the early caregiver–child bond. From interacting with sensitive adults, babies learn how to send and interpret emotional signals in their first peer associations (Trevarthen, 2003). Toddlers who have a warm parental relationship or who attend high-quality child care with a small group size and a generous caregiver–child ratio—features that promote warm, stimulating caregiving and gentle support for engaging with peers—display more positive and extended peer exchanges. These children, in turn, display more socially competent behavior as preschoolers (Deynoot-Schaub & Riksen-Walraven, 2006a, 2006b; Howes & Matheson, 1992; Williams, Mastergeorge, & Ontai, 2010).

Attachment and Later Development

According to psychoanalytic and ethological theories, the inner feelings of affection and security that result from a healthy attachment relationship support all aspects of psychological development. Consistent with this view, an extended longitudinal study found that preschoolers who had been securely attached as babies were rated by their teachers as higher in self-esteem, social skills, and empathy than were their insecurely attached counterparts, who displayed more behavior problems. When studied again at age 11 in summer camp, children who had been secure infants had more favorable relationships with peers, closer friendships, and better social skills, as judged by camp counselors. And as these well-functioning school-age children became adolescents and young adults, they continued to benefit from more supportive social networks, formed more stable and gratifying romantic relationships, and attained higher levels of education (Elicker, Englund, & Sroufe, 1992; Sroufe, 2002; Sroufe et al., 2005).

For some researchers, these findings indicate that secure attachment in infancy causes improved cognitive, emotional, and social competence in later years. Yet contrary evidence exists. In other longitudinal studies, secure infants generally fared better than insecure infants, but not always (Fearon et al., 2010; McCartney et al., 2004; Schneider, Atkinson, & Tardif, 2001; Stams, Juffer, & van IJzendoorn, 2002).

What accounts for the inconsistency in research findings on the consequences of early attachment quality? Mounting evidence indicates that *continuity of caregiving* determines whether attachment security is linked to later development (Lamb et al., 1985; Thompson, 2013). Children whose parents respond sensitively not just in infancy but also in later years are likely to develop favorably. In contrast, children whose parents react insensitively or who, over a long period, are exposed to a negative family climate tend to establish lasting patterns of avoidant, resistant, or disorganized behavior and are at greater risk for developmental difficulties.

A close look at the relationship between parenting and children's adjustment in the first few years supports this emphasis on continuity of caregiving. Disorganized/disoriented attachment, a pattern associated with serious parental psychological problems and highly maladaptive caregiving, is strongly linked to internalizing and externalizing difficulties in childhood (Lyons-Ruth, Bronfman, & Parsons, 1999; Moss, Cyr, & Dubois-Comtois, 2004; Moss et al., 2006). And when a large sample of children were tracked from age 1 to 3 years, those with histories of secure attachment followed by sensitive parenting scored highest in cognitive, emotional, and social outcomes. Those with histories of insecure attachment followed by insensitive parenting scored lowest, while those with mixed histories of attachment and maternal sensitivity scored in between (Belsky & Fearon, 2002). Specifically, insecurely attached infants whose mothers became more positive and supportive in early childhood showed signs of developmental recovery.

Does this trend remind you of our discussion of *resilience* in Chapter 1? A child whose parental caregiving improves or who has other compensating affectionate ties can bounce back from adversity. In contrast, a child who experiences tender care in infancy but lacks sympathetic ties later on is at risk for problems.

Although a secure attachment in infancy does not guarantee continued good parenting, it does launch the parent–child relationship on a positive path. An early warm, positive parent–child tie, sustained over time, promotes many aspects of children's development: a more confident and complex self-concept, more advanced emotional understanding, better emotional self-regulation, more effective social skills, a stronger sense of moral responsibility, and higher motivation to achieve in school (Drake, Belsky, & Fearon, 2014; Groh et al., 2014; Thompson, 2013). But the effects of early attachment security are *conditional*—dependent on the quality of the baby's future relationships. Finally, as we will see again in future chapters, attachment is just one of the complex influences on children's psychological development.

Ask Yourself

- **REVIEW** What factors explain stability in attachment pattern for some children and change for others? Are these factors also involved in the link between attachment in infancy and later development? Explain.

- **CONNECT** Review research on emotional self-regulation on pages 252–253. How do the caregiving experiences of securely attached infants promote the development of emotional self-regulation?

- **APPLY** What attachment pattern did Timmy display when Vanessa picked him up from child care, and what factors probably contributed to it?

- **REFLECT** How would you characterize your internal working model? What factors, in addition to your early relationship with your parents, might have influenced it?

Self-Development

Infancy is a rich formative period for the development of physical and social understanding. In Chapter 6, you learned that infants develop an appreciation of the permanence of objects. And in this chapter, we have seen that over the first year, infants recognize and respond appropriately to others' emotions and distinguish familiar from unfamiliar people. That both objects and people achieve an independent, stable existence for the infant implies that knowledge of the self as a separate, permanent entity is also emerging.

7.10 Describe the development of self-awareness in infancy and toddlerhood, along with the emotional and social capacities it supports.

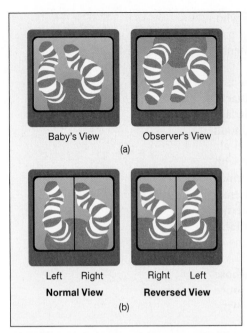

FIGURE 7.6 **Three-month-olds' emerging self-awareness, as indicated by reactions to video images.** (a) When shown two side-by-side views of their kicking legs, babies looked longer at the novel, observer's view than at their own view. (b) When shown a normal view of their leg positions alongside a reversed view, infants looked longer at the novel, reversed view. (Based on Rochat, 1998.)

This 18-month-old makes silly faces in a mirror, a playful response to her reflection that indicates she is aware of herself as a separate being and recognizes her unique physical features.

Self-Awareness

After Caitlin's bath, Carolyn often held her in front of the bathroom mirror. As early as the first few months, Caitlin smiled and returned friendly behaviors to her image. At what age did she realize that the charming baby gazing and grinning back was herself?

BEGINNINGS OF SELF-AWARENESS At birth, infants sense that they are physically distinct from their surroundings. For example, newborns display a stronger rooting reflex in response to external stimulation (an adult's finger touching their cheek) than to self-stimulation (their own hand contacting their cheek) (Rochat & Hespos, 1997). Newborns' remarkable capacity for intermodal perception (see page 195 in Chapter 5) supports the beginnings of self-awareness (Rochat, 2013). As they feel their own touch, feel and watch their limbs move, and feel and hear themselves cry, babies experience intermodal matches that differentiate their own body from surrounding bodies and objects.

Over the first few months, infants distinguish their own visual image from other stimuli, but their self-awareness is limited—expressed only in perception and action. When shown two side-by-side video images of their kicking legs, one from their own perspective (camera behind the baby) and one from an observer's perspective (camera in front of the baby), 3-month-olds looked longer at the observer's view (see Figure 7.6a). In another video-image comparison, they looked longer at a reversal of their leg positions than at a normal view (see Figure 7.6b) (Rochat, 1998). This suggests that young babies have a sense of their own body as a distinct entity, since they have habituated to it, as indicated by their interest in novel views of the body. By 4 months, infants look and smile more at video images of others than video images of themselves (Rochat & Striano, 2002). This indicates that they distinguish between the two and treat another person (as opposed to the self) as a potential social partner.

This discrimination of one's own limb and facial movements from those of others in real-time video presentations reflects an *implicit sense of self–world differentiation.* Implicit self-awareness is also evident in young infants' social expectations—for example, in protest or withdrawal when face-to-face interaction with a responsive adult is disrupted (see page 249). As early as 2 months, infants display a sense of their own agency in relation to other people. These early signs of self-experience serve as the foundation for development of *explicit self-awareness:* an objective understanding that the self is a unique object in a world of objects, which includes representations of one's own physical features and body dimensions.

EXPLICIT SELF-AWARENESS During the second year, toddlers become consciously aware of the self's physical features. In several studies, 9- to 28-month-olds were placed in front of a mirror. Then, under the pretext of wiping the baby's face, each mother rubbed red dye on her child's nose or forehead. Younger babies touched the mirror as if the red mark had nothing to do with them. But the majority of those older than 18 to 20 months touched or rubbed their strange-looking noses or foreheads, a response indicating clear awareness of their unique facial appearance (Bard et al., 2006; Lewis & Brooks-Gunn, 1979). And some toddlers act silly or coy in front of the mirror, playfully experimenting with the way the self looks (Bullock & Lutkenhaus, 1990).

Around age 2, *self-recognition*—identification of the self as a physically unique being—is well under way. Children point to themselves in photos and refer to themselves by name or with a personal pronoun ("I" or "me") (Lewis & Ramsay, 2004). And soon they will identify themselves in images with less detail and fidelity than mirrors. Around age 2½, most reach for a sticker surreptitiously placed on top of their heads when shown themselves in a live video, and around age 3 most recognize their own shadow (Cameron & Gallup, 1988; Suddendorf, Simcock, & Nielsen, 2007).

As self-recognition takes shape, older toddlers also construct an explicit *body self-awareness*. At the end of the second year, they realize that their own body can serve as an obstacle. When asked to push a shopping cart while standing on a mat attached to its rear axle, most 18- to 21-month-olds (but not younger children) figured out how to remove themselves from the mat so the cart would move—an ability that improved with age (Moore et al., 2007).

Nevertheless, toddlers make **scale errors,** attempting to do things that their body size makes impossible. For example, they will try to put on dolls' clothes, sit in a doll-sized chair or walk through a doorway too narrow for them to pass through (Brownell, Zerwas, & Ramani, 2007; DeLoache, Uttal, & Rosengren, 2004). They are amazingly persistent, even seeking an adult's help after they repeatedly do not succeed! Possibly, toddlers lack an accurate understanding of their own body dimensions. Alternatively, they may simply be exploring the consequences of squeezing into restricted spaces, as they are far less likely to try when the risk of harming themselves is high (for example, if the too-narrow doorway is next to a ledge where they could fall) (Franchak & Adolph, 2012). Scale errors decline between ages 2 and 3½. Young preschoolers are still learning to process physical information when acting with their own bodies.

INFLUENCES ON SELF-AWARENESS What experiences contribute to gains in self-awareness? During the first year, as infants act on the environment, they probably notice effects that help them sort out self, other people, and objects (Nadel, Prepin, & Okanda, 2005; Rochat, 2001). For example, batting a mobile and seeing it swing in a pattern different from the infant's own actions gives the baby information about the relation between self and physical world. Smiling and vocalizing at a caregiver who smiles and vocalizes back helps specify the relation between self and social world. And watching the movements of one's own hands and feet provides still another kind of feedback—one under much more direct control than the movements of other people or objects. The contrast between these experiences helps infants sense that they are separate from external reality.

Researchers do not yet know exactly how toddlers acquire the various aspects of explicit self-awareness. But sensitive caregiving seems to play a role. Compared to their insecurely attached agemates, securely attached toddlers display more complex self-related actions during play, such as making a doll labeled as the self take a drink or kiss a teddy bear. They also show greater knowledge of their own physical features—for example, in labeling body parts (Pipp, Easterbrooks, & Brown, 1993; Pipp, Easterbrooks, & Harmon, 1992). And 18-month-olds who often establish joint attention with their caregivers are advanced in mirror self-recognition (Nichols, Fox, & Mundy, 2005). Joint attention offers toddlers many opportunities to engage in social referencing—to compare their own and others' reactions to objects and events—which may enhance toddlers' awareness of their own physical uniqueness.

Cultural variations exist in early self-development. In one investigation, urban middle-SES German and East Indian toddlers attained mirror self-recognition earlier than toddlers of non-Western farming communities, such as the Nso people of rural Cameroon and rural families of East India (see Figure 7.7) (Kärtner et al., 2012). Urban German and, to a lesser extent, urban East Indian mothers placed considerable emphasis on *autonomous child-rearing goals,* including promoting personal talents and interests and expressing one's own preferences, which strongly predicted earlier mirror self-recognition. In contrast, Nso and East Indian rural mothers valued *relational child rearing goals*—doing what parents say and sharing with others. In related research, Nso toddlers, though delayed in mirror self-recognition, displayed an earlier capacity to comply with adult requests than did middle-SES urban Greek toddlers, whose mothers encouraged child autonomy (Keller et al., 2004).

LOOK and LISTEN

Ask several parents of 1½- to 3-year-olds if they have observed any instances of scale errors. Have the parent hand the toddler doll-sized clothing (hat, jacket, or shoe) or furniture (table, slide, or car) and watch for scale errors.

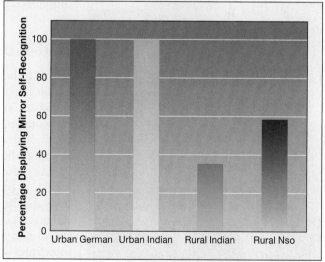

FIGURE 7.7 **Mirror self-recognition at 19 months in four cultures.** Urban middle-SES German and East Indian toddlers attained mirror self-recognition earlier than Nso toddlers of rural Cameroon and toddlers of rural East India—a finding that held even after toddlers were provided considerable experience in seeing themselves in mirrors. Urban German and East Indian mothers emphasized autonomous child-rearing goals, which strongly predicted earlier self-recognition. In contrast, rural Nso and East Indian mothers valued relational child-rearing goals. (Based on Kärtner et al., 2012.)

SELF-AWARENESS AND EARLY EMOTIONAL AND SOCIAL DEVELOPMENT Self-awareness quickly becomes a central part of children's emotional and social lives. Recall that self-conscious emotions depend on a strengthening sense of self. Self-awareness also leads to first efforts to understand another's perspective. We have seen that toddlers increasingly appreciate others' intentions, feelings, and desires. Older toddlers who have experienced sensitive caregiving and emotionally available parents draw on their advancing capacity to distinguish what happens to oneself from what happens to others to express first signs of **empathy**—the ability to understand another's emotional state and feel with that person, or respond emotionally in a similar way. For example, they communicate concern when others are distressed and may offer what they themselves find comforting—a hug, a reassuring comment, or a favorite doll or blanket (Hoffman, 2000; Moreno, Klute, & Robinson, 2008).

At the same time, toddlers demonstrate clearer awareness of how to upset others. One 18-month-old heard her mother talking to another adult about an older sibling: "Anny is really frightened of spiders. In fact, there's a particular toy spider that we've got that she just hates" (Dunn, 1989, p. 107). The innocent-looking toddler ran to the bedroom, returned with the toy spider, and pushed it in front of Anny's face!

Categorizing the Self

By the end of the second year, language becomes a powerful tool in self-development. Between 18 and 30 months, children develop a **categorical self** as they classify themselves and others on the basis of age ("baby," "boy," or "man"), sex ("boy" or "girl"), physical characteristics ("big," "strong"), and even goodness and badness ("I good girl." "Tommy mean!"). They also start to refer to the self's competencies ("Did it!" "I can't") (Stipek, Gralinski, & Kopp, 1990).

Toddlers use their limited understanding of these social categories to organize their own behavior. As early as 17 months, children select and play in a more involved way with toys that are stereotyped for their own gender—dolls and tea sets for girls, trucks and cars for boys. Their ability to label their own gender predicts a sharp rise in these play preferences over the next few months (Zosuls et al., 2009). Then parents encourage gender-typed behavior by responding more positively when toddlers display it (Ruble, Martin, & Berenbaum, 2006). As we will see in Chapter 10, gender typing increases dramatically during early childhood.

This father encourages compliance and the beginnings of self-control. The toddler joins in the task with an eager, willing spirit, which suggests he is adopting the adult's directive as his own.

Self-Control

Self-awareness also contributes to *effortful control,* the extent to which children can inhibit impulses, manage negative emotion, and behave in socially acceptable ways. To behave in a self-controlled fashion, children must think of themselves as separate, autonomous beings who can direct their own actions. And they must have the representational and memory capacities to recall a caregiver's directive ("Caitlin, don't touch that light socket!") and apply it to their own behavior.

As these capacities emerge between 12 and 18 months, toddlers first become capable of **compliance:** They show clear awareness of caregivers' wishes and expectations and can obey simple requests and commands. And, as every parent knows, they can also decide to do just the opposite! Although defiance in preschoolers is associated with negative parent–child relationships and poor adjustment, toddlers who sometimes strongly resist parental demands tend to have sensitive, supportive parents with whom they interact positively. These parents recognize the young child's need for self-assertion and autonomy (Dix et al., 2007).

Indeed, active resistance in toddlerhood does not predict later, persisting defiance. Rather, for most toddlers, assertiveness and opposition occur alongside compliance with an eager, willing spirit, which suggests that the child is beginning to adopt the adult's directives as his own (Kochanska, Murray, & Harlan, 2000). Compliance quickly leads to toddlers' first consciencelike verbalizations—for example, correcting the self by saying "No, can't" before reaching for a treat or jumping on the sofa.

Applying What We Know

Helping Toddlers Develop Compliance and Self-Control

SUGGESTION	RATIONALE
Respond to the toddler with sensitivity and encouragement.	Toddlers whose parents are sensitive and supportive at times actively resist, but they are also are more compliant and self-controlled.
Provide advance notice when the toddler must stop an enjoyable activity.	Toddlers find it more difficult to stop a pleasant activity that is already under way than to wait before engaging in a desired action.
Offer many prompts and reminders.	Toddlers' ability to remember and comply with rules is limited; they need continuous adult oversight and patient assistance.
Respond to self-controlled behavior with verbal and physical approval.	Praise and hugs reinforce appropriate behavior, increasing the likelihood that it will occur again.
Encourage selective and sustained attention (see Chapter 6, page 217).	Development of attention is related to self-control. Children who can shift attention from a captivating stimulus and focus on a less attractive alternative are better at controlling their impulses.
Support language development (see Chapter 6, pages 240–241).	Early language development is related to self-control. In the second year, children begin to use language to remind themselves of adult expectations and to delay gratification.
Gradually increase rules in a manner consistent with the toddler's developing capacities.	As cognition and language improve, toddlers can follow more rules related to safety, respect for people and property, family routines, manners, and simple chores.

Researchers often study the early emergence of self-control by giving children tasks that, like the situations just mentioned, require **delay of gratification**—waiting for an appropriate time and place to engage in a tempting act. Between ages 1½ and 4, children show an increasing capacity to wait before eating a treat, opening a present, or playing with a toy (Cole, LeDonne, & Tan, 2013; Vaughn, Kopp, & Krakow, 1984). Children who are advanced in development of attention, language, and suppressing negative emotion tend to be better at delaying gratification—findings that help explain why girls are typically more self-controlled than boys (Else-Quest et al., 2012). Some toddlers already use verbal and other attention-diverting techniques—talking to themselves, singing, or looking away—to keep from engaging in prohibited acts.

Like effortful control in general, young children's capacity to delay gratification is influenced by both temperament and quality of caregiving (Kochanska & Aksan, 2006; Kochanska & Knaack, 2003). Inhibited children find it easier to wait than angry, irritable children do. But toddlers and preschoolers who experience parental warmth and gentle encouragement are more likely to be cooperative and to resist temptation. Such parenting—which encourages and models patient, nonimpulsive behavior—is particularly important for temperamentally reactive babies and preschoolers (Kochanska, Aksan, & Carlson, 2005; Kochanska & Kim, 2013). TAKE A MOMENT... Turn back to page 260, and note how these findings provide yet another example of the importance of goodness of fit between temperament and child rearing.

As self-control improves, parents gradually expand the rules they expect toddlers to follow, from safety and respect for property and people to family routines, manners, and simple chores (Gralinski & Kopp, 1993). Still, toddlers' control over their own actions depends on constant parental oversight and reminders. Several prompts ("Remember, we're going to go in just a minute") and gentle insistence were usually necessary to get Caitlin to stop playing so that she and her parents could go on an errand. Applying What We Know above summarizes ways to help toddlers develop compliance and self-control.

As the second year of life drew to a close, Carolyn, Monica, and Vanessa were delighted at their children's readiness to learn the rules of social life. As we will see in Chapter 10, advances in cognition and language, along with parental warmth and reasonable demands for maturity, lead preschoolers to make tremendous strides in this area.

Ask Yourself

- **REVIEW** Why is insisting that infants comply with parental directives inappropriate? What competencies are necessary for the emergence of compliance and self-control?

- **CONNECT** What type of early parenting fosters the development of emotional self-regulation, secure attachment, and self-control? Why, in each instance, is it effective?

- **APPLY** Len, a caregiver of 1- and 2-year-olds, wonders whether toddlers recognize themselves. List signs of self-recognition in the second year that Len can observe. What behaviors reveal that toddlers are still forming objective representations of their own physical features?

- **REFLECT** In view of research on toddlers' compliance, active resistance, and budding capacity to delay gratification, do you think that "the terrible twos," a commonly used expression to characterize typical toddler behavior, is an apt description? Explain.

Summary

Erikson's Theory of Infant and Toddler Personality (p. 246)

7.1 What personality changes take place during Erikson's stages of basic trust versus mistrust and autonomy versus shame and doubt?

- Warm, responsive caregiving leads infants to resolve Erikson's psychological conflict of **basic trust versus mistrust** on the positive side. During toddlerhood, **autonomy versus shame and doubt** is resolved favorably when parents provide appropriate guidance and reasonable choices. If children emerge from the first few years without sufficient trust and autonomy, the seeds are sown for adjustment problems.

© SYRACUSE NEWSPAPERS/ S. CANNERELLI/THE IMAGE WORKS

Emotional Development (p. 247)

7.2 Describe the development of basic emotions over the first year, noting the adaptive function of each.

- During the first half-year, **basic emotions** gradually become clear, well-organized signals. The **social smile** appears between 6 and 10 weeks, laughter around 3 to 4 months. Happiness strengthens the parent–child bond and reflects as well as supports physical and cognitive mastery.

- Anger and fear, especially in the form of **stranger anxiety,** increase in the second half of the first year as infants' cognitive and motor capacities improve. Newly mobile babies use the familiar caregiver as a **secure base** from which to explore.

7.3 Summarize changes during the first two years in understanding others' emotions, self-conscious emotions, and emotional self-regulation.

- The ability to understand others' emotional expressions expands over the first year. Beginning at 8 to 10 months, infants engage in **social referencing.** By the middle of the second year, infants become aware that others' emotional reactions may differ from their own.

- During toddlerhood, self-awareness and adult instruction provide the foundation for **self-conscious emotions:** guilt, shame, embarrassment, envy, and pride. **Emotional self-regulation** emerges as the prefrontal cortex functions more effectively and as caregivers sensitively assist infants in adjusting their emotional reactions. In the second year, growth in representation and language leads to more effective ways of regulating emotion.

Temperament and Development (p. 253)

7.4 What is temperament, and how is it measured?

- Children differ greatly in **temperament**—early appearing, stable individual differences in reactivity and self-regulation. The New York Longitudinal Study identified three patterns: the **easy child,** the **difficult child,** and the **slow-to-warm-up child.** The most influential model of temperament, devised by Mary Rothbart, includes dimensions representing emotion, attention, and action, along with **effortful control,** the ability to regulate one's reactivity.

© ERIC FOWKE/PHOTOEDIT

- Temperament is assessed through parental reports, behavior ratings by others familiar with the child, and laboratory observations. Most neurobiological research has focused on distinguishing **inhibited, or shy, children** from **uninhibited, or sociable, children.**

7.5 Discuss the roles of heredity and environment in the stability of temperament, including the goodness-of-fit model.

- Temperament has low to moderate stability: It develops with age and can be modified by experience. Long-term prediction from early temperament is best achieved after age 3, when children improve substantially in effortful control.

- Temperament has a genetic foundation, but child rearing and cultural beliefs and practices have much to do with maintaining or changing it. Children with the short 5-HTTLPR gene, which heightens risk of negative mood, fearfulness, and self-regulation difficulties, are more susceptible to the effects of rearing experiences: They function worse than other children when exposed to inept parenting but benefit most from good parenting. Parents tend to emphasize temperamental differences between siblings.

- According to the **goodness-of-fit model,** parenting practices that fit well with the child's temperament help children achieve more adaptive functioning.

Development of Attachment

(p. 261)

7.6 What are the unique features of ethological theory of attachment?

- **Ethological theory,** the most widely accepted perspective on **attachment,** recognizes the infant's emotional tie to the caregiver as an evolved response that promotes survival. In early infancy, a set of built-in behaviors encourages the parent to remain close to the baby.

- Around 6 to 8 months, **separation anxiety** and use of the parent as a secure base indicate the existence of a true attachment bond. As representation and language develop, separation anxiety declines. From early caregiving experiences, children construct an **internal working model** that guides future close relationships.

7.7 Cite the four attachment patterns assessed by the Strange Situation and the Attachment Q-Sort, and discuss factors that affect attachment security.

- Using the **Strange Situation,** a laboratory technique for measuring the quality of attachment between 1 and 2 years of age, researchers have identified four attachment patterns: **secure, insecure-avoidant, insecure-resistant,** and **disorganized/disoriented attachment.** The **Attachment Q-Sort,** based on home observations of children between ages 1 and 5, yields a score ranging from low to high security.

- Securely attached babies in middle-SES families with favorable life conditions more often maintain their attachment pattern than insecure babies. However, the disorganized/disoriented pattern is highly stable. Cultural conditions must be considered in interpreting the meaning of attachment patterns.

- Attachment security is influenced by early availability of a consistent caregiver, quality of caregiving, the fit between the baby's temperament and parenting practices, and family circumstances. **Sensitive caregiving** is moderately related to secure attachment. In Western cultures, **interactional synchrony** characterizes the experiences of securely attached babies.

- Parents' internal working models are good predictors of infant attachment patterns. However, parents' childhood experiences do not transfer directly to quality of attachment with their own children.

7.8 Discuss infants' formation of multiple attachments, and indicate how attachment paves the way for early peer sociability.

- Infants develop strong affectionate ties to fathers, who tend to engage in more exciting, physical play than do mothers. Especially in cultures where fathers devote little time to infant care, play is a vital context in which fathers and babies build secure attachments, predicting favorable emotional and social adjustment.

© CHAD SPRINGER/CULTURA/CORBIS

- Grandparents who serve as primary caregivers for grandchildren forge significant attachment ties that help protect children with troubled family lives from adjustment problems.

- Early in the first year, infants start to form rich emotional relationships with siblings that combine rivalry and resentment with affection and sympathetic concern. Individual differences in quality of sibling relationships are influenced by temperament, parenting, and marital quality.

- Peer sociability begins in infancy with isolated social acts, followed by reciprocal exchanges (largely in the form of mutual imitation) in the second year of life. A warm caregiver-child bond promotes peer sociability.

7.9 Describe and interpret the relationship between secure attachment in infancy and psychological development in childhood.

- Continuity of caregiving determines whether attachment security is linked to later development. If caregiving improves, children can recover from an insecure attachment history.

Self-Development (p. 275)

7.10 Describe the development of self-awareness in infancy and toddlerhood, along with the emotional and social capacities it supports.

- At birth, infants sense that they are physically distinct from their surroundings, an implicit self-awareness that expands over the early months and serves as the foundation for explicit self-awareness. In the middle of the second year, self-recognition emerges as toddlers become consciously aware of the self's physical features. However, toddlers make **scale errors,** attempting to do things their body size makes impossible.

- Self-awareness leads to toddlers' first efforts to appreciate others' perspectives, including early signs of **empathy.** Between 18 and 30 months, as language develops, children develop a **categorical self,** classifying themselves and others on the basis of age, sex, physical characteristics, and competencies.

- Self-awareness also contributes to gains in self-control. **Compliance** emerges between 12 and 18 months, followed by **delay of gratification,** which strengthens between 1½ and 4 years. Toddlers who experience parental warmth and gentle encouragement are likely to be advanced in self-control.

Important Terms and Concepts

attachment (p. 261)
Attachment Q-Sort (p. 264)
autonomy versus shame and doubt (p. 246)
basic emotions (p. 247)
basic trust versus mistrust (p. 246)
categorical self (p. 278)
compliance (p. 278)
delay of gratification (p. 279)
difficult child (p. 254)
disorganized/disoriented attachment (p. 264)
easy child (p. 254)
effortful control (p. 254)

emotional self-regulation (p. 252)
empathy (p. 278)
ethological theory of attachment (p. 261)
goodness-of-fit model (p. 259)
inhibited, or shy, child (p. 255)
insecure-avoidant attachment (p. 264)
insecure-resistant attachment (p. 264)
interactional synchrony (p. 266)
internal working model (p. 262)
scale errors (p. 277)
secure attachment (p. 264)
secure base (p. 250)

self-conscious emotions (p. 251)
sensitive caregiving (p. 266)
separation anxiety (p. 262)
slow-to-warm-up child (p. 254)
social referencing (p. 251)
social smile (p. 248)
stranger anxiety (p. 249)
Strange Situation (p. 263)
temperament (p. 253)
uninhibited, or sociable, child (p. 255)

MILESTONES
Development in Infancy and Toddlerhood

ARIEL SKELLY/BLEND IMAGES/GETTY IMAGES

PHYSICAL

- Height and weight increase rapidly. (159–160)
- Newborn reflexes decline. (143)
- Distinguishes basic tastes and odors; shows preference for sweet-tasting foods. (148)
- Responses can be classically and operantly conditioned. (176–178)
- Habituates to unchanging stimuli; recovers to novel stimuli. (178–179)
- Sleep is increasingly organized into a night–day schedule. (169)
- Holds head up, rolls over, and grasps objects. (182)
- Shows sensitivity to motion, then binocular, and finally pictorial depth cues. (189–190)
- Recognizes and prefers human facial pattern; recognizes features of mother's face. (192–193)
- Perceives auditory and visual stimuli as organized patterns. (187, 195)
- Moves from relying on motion and spatial arrangement to using featural information—shape, color, and pattern—to visually detect the identity of an object. (194)
- Masters a wide range of intermodal (visual, auditory, and tactile) relationships. (195–196)

COGNITIVE

- Engages in immediate and deferred imitation of adults' facial expressions. (207)
- Repeats chance behaviors that lead to pleasurable and interesting results. (203–204)
- Has some awareness of many physical properties (including object permanence) and basic numerical knowledge. (205–206)
- Attention becomes more efficient and flexible. (216–217)
- Recognition memory for visual events improves. (217–218)
- Forms categories based on objects' similar physical properties. (219)

LANGUAGE

- Coos and, by the end of this period, babbles. (235)
- Begins to establish joint attention with caregiver, who labels objects and events. (236)

EMOTIONAL/SOCIAL

- Social smile and laughter emerge. (248)
- Matches feeling tone of caregiver in face-to-face communication; later, expects matched responses. (250)
- Distinguishes positive from negative emotion in voices and facial expressions. (250)
- Emotional expressions become well organized and meaningfully related to environmental events (250)

© TETRA IMAGES/ALAMY

- Regulates emotion by shifting attention and self-soothing. (252)
- Smiles, laughs, and babbles more to caregiver than to a stranger. (262)
- Awareness of self as physically distinct from surroundings increases. (276)

PHYSICAL

- Approaches adultlike sleep–wake schedule. (169)
- Sits alone, crawls, and walks. (182)

© LAURA DWIGHT PHOTOGRAPHY

- Reaching and grasping improve in flexibility and accuracy; shows refined pincer grasp. (185–186)

- "Screens out" sounds not used in own language; perceives meaningful speech. (187–189)
- Increasingly uses featural information to detect the identity of an object. (194–195)
- Intermodal perception continues to improve. (196)

COGNITIVE

- Engages in intentional, or goal-directed, behavior. (204)
- Finds an object hidden in an initial location. (204)

© LAURA DWIGHT PHOTOGRAPHY

- Recall memory improves, as indicated by gains in deferred imitation of adults' actions with objects. (207–208)
- Solves simple problems by analogy to a previous problem. (208)
- Categorizes objects on the basis of subtle sets of features, even when the perceptual contrast between categories is minimal. (219)

LANGUAGE

- Babbling expands to include many sounds of spoken languages and patterns of the child's language community. (235–236)
- Joint attention with caregiver becomes more accurate. (236)
- Takes turns in games, such as pat-a-cake and peekaboo. (236)

© ELLEN B. SENISI

- Uses preverbal gestures (showing, pointing) to influence others' goals and behavior and to convey information. (236)
- Comprehends some word meanings. (237)
- Around end of this period, understands displaced reference of words and says first words. (237)

Note: Numbers in parentheses indicate the page or pages on which each milestone is discussed.

EMOTIONAL/SOCIAL

- Smiling and laughter increase in frequency and expressiveness. (249)
- Anger and fear increase in frequency and intensity. (249–250)
- Stranger anxiety and separation anxiety appear. (250, 262)
- Uses caregiver as a secure base for exploration. (250)
- Shows "clear-cut" attachment to a familiar caregiver. (262)
- Increasingly detects the meaning of others' emotional expressions and engages in social referencing. (250–251)
- Regulates emotion by approaching and retreating from stimulation. (252)

13–18 MONTHS

PHYSICAL

- Height and weight gain are rapid, but not as great as in first year; toddlers slim down. (159–160)
- Walking is better coordinated (182)
- Manipulates small objects with improved coordination. (186, 204)

COGNITIVE

- Explores the properties of objects by acting on them in novel ways. (203)
- Searches in several locations for a hidden object. (206)
- Engages in deferred imitation of adults' actions with objects over longer delays and across a change in context—for example, from child care to home. (208)
- Sustained attention improves. (217)
- Recall memory improves further. (219)
- Sorts objects into categories. (221)
- Realizes that pictures can symbolize real objects. (209)

LANGUAGE

- Steadily adds to vocabulary. (237)
- By end of this period, produces 50 words. (235)

EMOTIONAL/SOCIAL

- Joins in play with familiar adults, siblings, and peers. (273–274)

- Realizes that others' emotional reactions may differ from one's own. (251)
- Complies with simple directives. (278)

19–24 MONTHS

PHYSICAL

- Jumps, walks on tiptoe, runs, and climbs. (182)

- Manipulates small objects with good coordination. (186, 204)

COGNITIVE

- Solves simple problems suddenly, through representation. (205)
- Finds a hidden object that has been moved while out of sight. (205)
- Engages in make-believe play, using simple actions experienced in everyday life. (205)

- Engages in deferred imitation of actions an adult tries to produce, even if not fully realized. (208)
- Categorizes objects conceptually, on the basis of common function or behavior. (221)
- Begins to use language as a flexible symbolic tool, to modify existing mental representations. (209)

LANGUAGE

- Produces 200 to 250 words. (235)
- Combines two words. (238)

EMOTIONAL/SOCIAL

- Self-conscious emotions (shame, embarrassment, guilt, envy, and pride) emerge. (251)
- Acquires a vocabulary for talking about feelings. (253)
- Begins to use language to assist with emotional self-regulation. (253)
- Begins to tolerate caregiver's absences more easily; separation anxiety declines. (262)
- Recognizes image of self and, by end of this period, uses own name or personal pronoun to refer to self. (276)

- Less often makes scale errors. (276–277)
- Shows signs of empathy. (278)
- Categorizes self and others on the basis of age, sex, physical characteristics, goodness and badness, and competencies. (278)
- Shows gender-stereotyped toy preferences. (278)
- Self-control, as indicated by delay of gratification, emerges. (279)
- Starts to use words to influence a playmate's behavior. (274)

Physical Development in Early Childhood

REPRINTED WITH PERMISSION FROM THE INTERNATIONAL MUSEUM OF CHILDREN'S ART, OSLO, NORWAY

"My Strength Is Greater Than Yours"
Gao Ao
4 years, China

As this boy grows larger and stronger, he eagerly demonstrates his newly acquired arm-wrestling skills with his father. Chapter 8 highlights the close link between physical growth and other aspects of development in early childhood.

For more than a decade, our fourth-floor office windows have overlooked the preschool and kindergarten play yard of our university laboratory school. On mild fall and spring mornings, classroom doors swing open, and sand table, easels, and large blocks spill out into a small courtyard. Alongside the building is a grassy area with jungle gyms, swings, a playhouse, and a flower garden planted by the children; beyond it, a circular path lined with tricycles and wagons. Each day, the setting is alive with activity.

Even from our distant vantage points, the physical changes of early childhood are evident. Children's bodies are longer and leaner than they were a year or two earlier. The awkward gait of toddlerhood has disappeared in favor of more refined movements that include running, climbing, jumping, galloping, and skipping. Children scale the jungle gym, race across the lawn, turn somersaults, and vigorously pedal tricycles. Just as impressive as these gross-motor achievements are gains in fine-motor skills. At the sand table, children build hills, valleys, caves, and roads and prepare trays of pretend cookies and cupcakes. And as they grew older, their paintings at the outdoor easels took on greater structure and detail as family members, houses, trees, birds, sky, monsters, and letterlike forms appeared in the colorful creations.

The years from 2 to 6 are often called "the play years"—aptly so, since play blossoms during this time and supports every aspect of development. Our discussion of early childhood opens with the physical achievements of this period—growth in body size, improvements in motor coordination, and refinements in perception. We pay special attention to genetic and environmental factors that support these changes, as well as to their intimate connection with other domains of development. The children we came to know well, first by watching from our office windows and later by observing at close range in their classrooms, will provide many examples of developmental trends and individual differences. ■

Body Growth

In early childhood, the rapid increase in body size of the first two years tapers off into a slower growth pattern. On average, children add 2 to 3 inches in height and about 5 pounds in weight each year. Boys continue to be slightly larger than girls. As the "baby fat" that began to decline in toddlerhood drops off further, children gradually become thinner, although girls retain somewhat more body fat than boys, who are slightly more muscular. As the torso lengthens and widens, internal organs tuck neatly inside, and the spine straightens. As Figure 8.1 on page 286 shows, by age 5 the top-heavy, bowlegged, potbellied toddler has become a more streamlined, flat-tummied, longer-legged child with body proportions similar to those of adults. Consequently, posture and balance improve—changes that foster gains in motor coordination.

Individual differences in body size are even more apparent during early childhood than in infancy and toddlerhood. Speeding around the bike path in the play yard, 5-year-old Darryl—at 48 inches tall and 55 pounds—towered over his kindergarten classmates. (The average North American 5-year-old boy is 43 inches tall and weighs 42 pounds.) Priti, an Asian-Indian child, was unusually small because of genetic factors linked to her cultural ancestry. And Lynette and Hal, two Caucasian children with impoverished home lives, were well below average for reasons we will discuss shortly.

8.1 Describe changes in body size, proportions, and skeletal maturity during early childhood.

8.2 Describe brain development in early childhood.

The existence of these variations in body size reminds us that growth norms for one population are not good standards for children elsewhere in the world. Consider the Efe of the Republic of Congo, whose typical adult height is less than 5 feet. For genetic reasons, the impact of hormones controlling body size is reduced in Efe children (Meazza, Pagani, & Bozzola, 2011). By age 5, the average Efe child is shorter than more than 97 percent of North American and European 5-year-olds, and Efe children reach puberty and stop growing at an earlier age than U.S. comparison children. Researchers disagree on why the Efe's small size evolved. Some suggest that it reduces their caloric requirements in the face of food scarcity in the rain forests of Central Africa, others that it permits easy movement through the dense forest underbrush, and still others that it enables earlier childbearing to compensate for the Efe's extremely high mortality rate (Migliano, Vinicius, & Lahr, 2007; Perry & Dominy, 2009). Efe children's short stature is not a sign of growth or health problems. But for other children, such as Lynette and Hal, extremely slow growth is cause for concern.

PHOTOS OF WILSON: DIAHANNE LUCAS; PHOTOS OF MARIEL: © JIM WEST PHOTOGRAPHY

Wilson at 3 years

Wilson at 3½ years

Wilson at 4½ years

Wilson at 5 years

Mariel at 2½ years

Mariel at 4 years

Mariel at 4½ years

Mariel at 5 years

FIGURE 8.1   Body growth during early childhood. During the preschool years, children grow more slowly than in infancy and toddlerhood. Wilson and Mariel's bodies became more streamlined, flat-tummied, and longer-legged. Boys continue to be slightly taller, heavier, and more muscular than girls. But generally, the two sexes are similar in body proportions and physical capacities.

Skeletal Growth

The skeletal changes of infancy continue throughout early childhood. Between ages 2 and 6, approximately 45 new *epiphyses,* or growth centers in which cartilage hardens into bone, emerge in various parts of the skeleton. Other epiphyses will appear in middle childhood. X-rays of these growth centers enable doctors to estimate children's *skeletal age,* or progress toward physical maturity (see page 161 in Chapter 5)—information helpful in diagnosing growth disorders.

By the end of the preschool years, children start to lose their primary, or "baby," teeth. The age at which they do so is heavily influenced by genetic factors. For example, girls, who are ahead of boys in physical development, lose their primary teeth sooner. Cultural ancestry also makes a difference. North American children typically get their first secondary (permanent) tooth at 6½ years, children in Ghana at just over 5 years, and children in Hong Kong around the sixth birthday (Burns, 2000). But nutritional factors also influence dental development. Prolonged malnutrition delays the appearance of permanent teeth, whereas overweight and obesity accelerate it (Costacurta et al., 2012; Heinrich-Weltzien et al., 2013).

Diseased baby teeth can affect the health of permanent teeth, so preventing decay in primary teeth is essential—by brushing consistently, avoiding sugary foods, drinking fluoridated water, and getting topical fluoride treatments and sealants (plastic coatings that protect tooth surfaces). Another factor is exposure to tobacco smoke, which suppresses children's immune system, including the ability to fight bacteria responsible for tooth decay. The risk associated with this suppression is greatest in infancy and early childhood, when the immune system is not yet fully mature (Aligne et al., 2003). Young children in homes with regular smokers are at increased risk for decayed teeth (Hanioka et al., 2011).

Unfortunately, an estimated 28 percent of U.S. preschoolers have tooth decay, a figure that rises to 50 percent in middle childhood and 60 percent by age 18. Causes include poor diet and inadequate health care—factors that are more likely to affect low-SES children. About 30 percent of U.S. children living in poverty have untreated dental caries (National Institutes of Health, 2011).

During early childhood, body fat declines, the torso enlarges to better accommodate the internal organs, and the spine straightens. This 5-year-old appears more streamlined than his younger playmate.

Brain Development

Between ages 2 and 6, the brain increases from 70 percent of its adult weight to 90 percent. At the same time, preschoolers improve in a wide variety of skills—physical coordination, perception, attention, memory, language, logical thinking, and imagination.

In addition to increasing in weight, the brain undergoes much reshaping and refining. By age 4 to 5, many parts of the cerebral cortex have overproduced synapses. In some regions, such as the prefrontal cortex, the number of synapses is nearly double the adult value. Together, synaptic growth and myelination of neural fibers result in a high energy need. In fact, fMRI evidence reveals that energy metabolism in the cerebral cortex reaches a peak around this age (Huttenlocher, 2002; Nelson, Thomas, & de Haan, 2006).

Recall from Chapter 5 that overabundance of synaptic connections supports *plasticity* of the young brain, helping to ensure that the child will acquire certain abilities even if some areas are damaged. *Synaptic pruning* follows: Neurons that are seldom stimulated lose their connective fibers, and the number of synapses is reduced (see page 162). As the structures of stimulated neurons become more elaborate and require more space, surrounding neurons die, and brain plasticity declines. By age 8 to 10, energy consumption of most cortical regions diminishes to near-adult levels (Lebel & Beaulieu, 2011; Nelson, 2002). In addition, cognitive functions are no longer as widely distributed in the cerebral cortex. Rather, they increasingly localize in distinct neural systems that become better integrated, reflecting a developmental shift toward a more fine-tuned, efficient neural organization (Bathelt et al., 2013; Markant & Thomas, 2013).

EEG, NIRS, and fMRI measures of neural activity reveal especially rapid growth from early to middle childhood in prefrontal-cortical areas devoted to various aspects of executive

A 5-year-old illustrates gains in executive function, supported by rapid growth of the prefrontal cortex, as she engages in an activity that challenges her capacity to attend, remember, and plan.

function. These include inhibition of impulses, attention, working memory, and planning and organizing behavior—capacities that advance markedly during the preschool years (Bunge & Wright, 2007; Durston & Casey, 2006). Furthermore, for most children, the left cerebral hemisphere is especially active between 3 and 6 years and then levels off. In contrast, activity in the right hemisphere increases steadily throughout early and middle childhood, with a slight spurt between ages 8 and 10 (Thatcher, Walker, & Giudice, 1987; Thompson et al., 2000).

These findings fit nicely with what we know about several aspects of cognitive development. Early childhood is a time of marked gains on tasks that depend on the prefrontal cortex—ones that require suppression of impulses in favor of thoughtful responses (Rothbart, 2011). Further, language skills (typically housed in the left hemisphere) increase at an astonishing pace in early childhood, and they support children's increasing control over behavior, also mediated by the prefrontal cortex. In contrast, spatial skills (usually located in the right hemisphere), such as giving directions, drawing pictures, and recognizing geometric shapes, develop gradually over childhood and adolescence.

Differences in rate of development between the two hemispheres suggest that they are continuing to *lateralize* (specialize in functions). Let's take a closer look at brain lateralization during early childhood by focusing on handedness.

HANDEDNESS   On a visit to the preschool, we watched 3-year-old Moira as she drew pictures, worked puzzles, ate a snack, and played outside. Unlike most of her classmates, Moira does most things—drawing, eating, and zipping her jacket—with her left hand. But she uses her right hand for a few activities, such as throwing a ball. Research on handedness, along with other evidence covered in Chapter 5, supports the joint contribution of nature and nurture to brain lateralization.

As early as the tenth prenatal week, most fetuses show a right-hand preference during thumb-sucking (Hepper, McCartney, & Shannon, 1998). And by age 6 months, infants typically display a smoother, more efficient movement when reaching with their right than their left arm. These early tendencies may contribute to the right-handed bias of most children by the end of the first year (Nelson, Campbell, & Michel, 2013; Rönnqvist & Domellöf, 2006). During toddlerhood and early childhood, handedness gradually extends to a wider range of skills.

Handedness reflects the greater capacity of one side of the brain—the individual's **dominant cerebral hemisphere**—to carry out skilled motor action. Other important abilities are generally located on the dominant side as well. For right-handed people—in Western nations, 90 percent of the population—language is housed in the left hemisphere with hand control. For the left-handed 10 percent, language is occasionally located in the right hemisphere or, more often, shared between the hemispheres (Szaflarski et al., 2012). This indicates that the brains of left-handers tend to be less strongly lateralized than those of right-handers. Consistent with this idea, many left-handed individuals (like Moira) are also *ambidextrous*. Although they prefer their left hand, they sometimes use their right hand skillfully as well.

Left-handed parents show only a weak tendency to have left-handed children (Vuoksimaa et al., 2009). One genetic theory proposes that most children inherit a gene that *biases* them for right-handedness and a left-dominant cerebral hemisphere. But that bias is not strong enough to overcome experiences that might sway children toward a left-hand preference (Annett, 2002). Even prenatal events may profoundly affect handedness. Both identical and fraternal twins are more likely than ordinary siblings to differ in hand preference, probably because twins usually lie in opposite orientations in the uterus (Derom et al., 1996). The orientation of most singleton fetuses—facing toward the left—is believed to promote greater control over movements on the body's right side (Previc, 1991).

Handedness also involves practice. Newborns' bias in head position causes them to spend more time looking at and using one hand, which contributes to greater skillfulness of that hand

Twins are more likely than ordinary siblings to differ in hand preference, perhaps because twins usually lie in opposite orientations in the uterus.

(Hinojosa, Sheu, & Michael, 2003). Handedness is strongest for complex skills requiring extensive training, such as eating with utensils, writing, and engaging in athletic activities. Also, wide cultural differences exist in rates of left-handedness. For example, in tribal and village cultures, the rate of left-handedness is relatively high. But in a study of one such society in New Guinea, individuals who had attended school in childhood were far more likely to be extremely right-handed—findings that highlight the role of experience (Geuze et al., 2012).

Although rates of left-handedness are elevated among people with intellectual disabilities and mental illness, atypical brain lateralization is probably not responsible for these individuals' problems. Rather, early damage to the left hemisphere may have caused their disabilities while also leading to a shift in handedness. In support of this idea, left-handedness is associated with prenatal and birth difficulties that can result in brain damage, including maternal stress, prolonged labor, prematurity, Rh incompatibility, and breech delivery (Domellöf, Johansson, & Rönnqvist, 2011; Kurganskaya, 2011).

Most left-handers, however, have no developmental problems—in fact, unusual lateralization may have certain advantages. Left- and mixed-handed young people are slightly advantaged in speed and flexibility of thinking, and they are more likely than their right-handed agemates to develop outstanding verbal and mathematical talents (Beratis et al., 2013; Noroozian et al., 2012). More even distribution of cognitive functions across both hemispheres may be responsible.

OTHER ADVANCES IN BRAIN DEVELOPMENT   Besides the cerebral cortex, several other areas of the brain make strides during early childhood (see Figure 8.2). All of these changes involve establishing links between parts of the brain, increasing the coordinated functioning of the central nervous system.

At the rear and base of the brain is the **cerebellum,** a structure that aids in balance and control of body movement. Fibers linking the cerebellum to the cerebral cortex grow and myelinate from birth through the preschool years. This change contributes to dramatic gains in motor coordination: By the end of the preschool years, children can play hopscotch, throw a ball with well-coordinated movements, and print letters of the alphabet. Connections between the cerebellum and the cerebral cortex also support thinking. Children with damage to the cerebellum usually display both motor and cognitive deficits, including problems with memory, planning, and language (Noterdaeme et al., 2002; Riva & Giorgi, 2000).

The **reticular formation,** a structure in the brain stem that maintains alertness and consciousness, generates synapses and myelinates throughout early childhood and into adolescence. Neurons in the reticular formation send out fibers to other areas of the brain. Many go to the prefrontal cortex, contributing to improvements in sustained, controlled attention.

An inner-brain structure called the **hippocampus,** which plays a vital role in memory and in images of space that help us find our way, undergoes rapid synapse formation and myelination in the second half of the first year, when recall memory and independent movement emerge. Over the preschool and elementary school years, the hippocampus and surrounding areas of the cerebral cortex continue to develop swiftly, establishing connections with one another and with the prefrontal cortex and lateralizing toward greater right-sided activation (Hopf et al., 2013; Nelson, Thomas, & de Haan, 2006). These changes make possible the

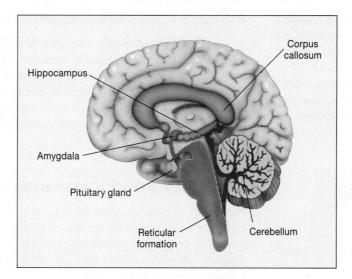

FIGURE 8.2 **Cross-section of the human brain, showing the location of the cerebellum, the reticular formation, the hippocampus, the amygdala, and the corpus callosum.** These structures undergo considerable development during early childhood. Also shown is the pituitary gland, which secretes hormones that control body growth (see page 290).

Continued growth of the corpus callosum in early childhood contributes to improved motor coordination, enabling this child to keep his balance while hopping across a path of circles.

dramatic gains in memory and spatial understanding of early and middle childhood—ability to use strategies to store and retrieve information, expansion of autobiographical memory (which brings an end to infantile amnesia), and drawing and reading of maps (which we will take up in Chapter 9).

Also located in the inner brain, adjacent to the hippocampus, is the **amygdala,** a structure that plays a central role in processing of novelty and emotional information. The amygdala is sensitive to facial emotional expressions, especially fear (Adolphs, 2010). It also enhances memory for emotionally salient events, thereby ensuring that information relevant for survival—stimuli that evoke fear or signify safety—will be retrieved on future occasions. This capacity for emotional learning seems to emerge in early childhood: Damage to the amygdala in the first few years leads to loss of ability to learn about fear and safety signals and wide-ranging socially inappropriate behaviors (Shaw, Brierley, & David, 2005). Throughout childhood and adolescence, connections between the amygdala and the prefrontal cortex, which governs regulation of emotion, form and myelinate (Tottenham, Hare, & Casey, 2009). Recall from Chapter 7 that in socially anxious children, the amygdala is overly reactive to threatening situations (see page 256).

The **corpus callosum** is a large bundle of fibers connecting the two cerebral hemispheres. Production of synapses and myelination of the corpus callosum increase at 1 year, peak between 3 and 6 years, then continue at a slower pace through middle childhood and adolescence (Thompson et al., 2000). The corpus callosum supports smooth coordination of movements on both sides of the body and integration of many aspects of thinking, including perception, attention, memory, language, and problem solving. The more complex the task, the more essential communication is between the hemispheres.

Ask Yourself

- **REVIEW** What aspects of brain development support the tremendous gains in language, thinking, and motor control of early childhood?

- **CONNECT** What stand on the nature–nurture issue do findings on development of handedness support? Explain, using research findings.

- **APPLY** Dental checkups revealed a high incidence of untreated tooth decay in a U.S. preschool program serving low-income children. Using findings presented in this and previous chapters, list possible contributing factors.

- **REFLECT** How early, and to what extent, did you experience tooth decay in childhood? What factors might have been responsible?

8.3 Explain how heredity influences physical growth.

8.4 Describe the effects of emotional well-being, restful sleep, nutrition, and infectious disease on physical growth and health in early childhood.

8.5 What factors increase the risk of unintentional injuries, and how can childhood injuries be prevented?

Influences on Physical Growth and Health

As we consider factors affecting growth and health in early childhood, you will encounter some familiar themes. Heredity remains important, but environmental factors—including emotional well-being, good nutrition, relative freedom from disease, and physical safety—are also essential. And as the Biology and Environment box on the following page illustrates, environmental pollutants can threaten children's healthy development. The extent to which low-level lead—one of the most common—undermines children's mental and emotional functioning is the focus of intensive research.

Heredity and Hormones

The impact of heredity on physical growth is evident throughout childhood. Children's physical size and rate of growth are related to those of their parents (Bogin, 2001). Genes influence growth by controlling the body's production of hormones. Figure 8.2 on page 289 shows the **pituitary gland,** located at the base of the brain, which plays a critical role by releasing two hormones that induce growth.

Biology and Environment

Low-Level Lead Exposure and Children's Development

ead is a highly toxic element that, at blood levels exceeding 60 μg/dL (micrograms per deciliter), causes brain swelling, hemorrhaging, disrupted functioning of neurons, and widespread cell death. Before 1980, exposure to lead resulted from use of lead-based paints for the interiors of residences (infants and young children often ate paint flakes) and from use of leaded gasoline (car exhaust resulted in a highly breathable form of lead). Laws limiting the lead content of paint and mandating lead-free gasoline led to a sharp decline in children's lead levels, from an average of 15 μg/dL in 1980 to 1.3 μg/dL today (Kennedy et al., 2014).

But in areas near airports with significant burning of jet fuel, near industries using lead production processes, or where lead-based paint remains in older homes, children's blood levels are still markedly elevated. In some areas, water-pipe corrosion has caused lead to rise in drinking water. Contaminated soil and imported consumer products, such as toys made of leaded plastic, are additional sources of exposure (Cole & Winsler, 2010). Today, about 5 percent of U.S. children have blood-lead levels exceeding 5 μg/dL—the level deemed high enough by the U.S. government to warrant immediate efforts to reduce exposure (Centers for Disease Control and Prevention, 2014c). Most live in large central cities and come from low-SES ethnic minority families.

Does lead contamination, even in small quantities, impair children's cognitive functioning?

Until recently, answers were unclear. Studies reporting a negative relationship between children's current lead levels and intelligence test performance had serious limitations. Researchers knew nothing about children's history of lead exposure and often failed to control for factors associated with both blood-lead levels and mental test scores (such as SES, home environmental quality, and nutrition) that might account for the findings.

Over the past quarter century, eight longitudinal studies of the developmental consequences of lead have been conducted in multiple countries, including the United States, Australia, Mexico, and Yugoslavia. Some focused on inner-city, low-SES minority children, others on middle- and upper-middle-SES suburban children, and one on children living close to a lead smelter. Each tracked children's lead exposure over an extended time and included relevant controls.

All but one site reported negative relationships between lead exposure and children's IQs (Canfield et al., 2003; Hubbs-Tait et al., 2005; Lanphear et al., 2005). Higher blood levels were also associated with deficits in verbal and visual-motor skills and with distractibility, overactivity, poor organization, and behavior problems. And an array of additional findings suggested that persistent childhood lead exposure contributes to antisocial behavior in adolescence (Needleman et al., 2002; Nevin, 2006; Stretesky & Lynch, 2004).

The investigations did not agree on an age period of greatest vulnerability. In some, relationships were strongest in toddlerhood and early childhood; in others, in middle childhood, suggesting cumulative effects over time. Still other studies reported similar lead-related cognitive deficits from infancy through adolescence. Overall, poorer intelligence test scores associated with lead exposure seemed to be permanent. Children given drugs to induce excretion of lead (chelation) did not improve

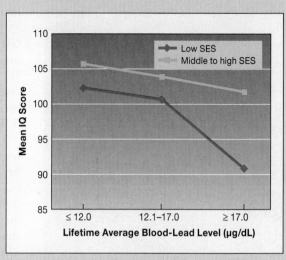

FIGURE 8.3 **Relationship of lifetime average lead exposure to 11-to-13-year-olds' IQ by SES.** In this study, conducted in the lead-smelting city of Port Pirie, Australia, blood-lead levels of 375 children were measured repeatedly from birth to age 11 to 13. The lead-exposure-related drop in IQ was much greater for low-SES than higher-SES children. (Based on Tong, McMichael, & Baghurst, 2000.)

(Dietrich et al., 2004; Rogan et al., 2001). Negative cognitive consequences were evident at all levels of lead exposure, with one study reporting persisting effects into early adulthood (Canfield et al., 2003; Lanphear et al., 2005; Mazumdar et al., 2011; Wright et al., 2008).

Furthermore, in several investigations, cognitive consequences were much greater for low-SES than middle- and higher-SES children (see, for example, Figure 8.3) (Bellinger, Leviton, & Sloman, 1990; Ris et al., 2004; Tong, McMichael, & Baghurst, 2000). A stressed, disorganized home life seems to heighten lead-induced damage. Dietary factors can also magnify lead's toxic effects. Iron and zinc deficiencies, especially common in low-SES children, increase lead concentration in the blood (Noonan et al., 2003; Wolf, Jimenez, & Lozoff, 2003; Wright et al., 2003).

In sum, lead impairs cognitive development and contributes to behavior problems. Low-SES children are more likely both to live in lead-contaminated areas and to experience additional risks that magnify lead-induced damage. Because lead is a stable element, its release into the air and soil is difficult to reverse. Therefore, in addition to laws that control lead pollution, interventions that reduce the negative impact of lead—through involved parenting, dietary enrichment, better schools, and public education about lead hazards—are vital.

These children play near a smelting factory in Copsa Mica, Romania, which ranks among the world's most polluted cities in levels of lead and other toxins. Longitudinal studies consistently show lasting negative effects of lead exposure, including learning impairments and behavior problems.

© TRINITY MIRROR/MIRRORPIX/ALAMY

These preschoolers are the same age but different greatly in body size. Early treatment of growth hormone (GH) deficiency leads to substantial gains in height, but little justification exists for intervention with normal-GH children whose short stature simply reflects human diversity.

The first, **growth hormone (GH),** is necessary from birth on for development of almost all body tissues. GH acts directly but also accomplishes its task with the help of an intermediary. It stimulates the liver and epiphyses of the skeleton to release another hormone called *insulin-like growth factor 1 (IGF-1),* which triggers cell duplication throughout the body, especially the skeleton, muscles, nerves, bone marrow (origin of blood cells), liver, kidney, skin, and lungs.

About 2 percent of children suffer from inherited conditions that cause either GH deficiency or IGF-1 deficiency (in which GH fails to stimulate IGF-1). Without medical intervention, such children reach an average mature height of only 4 to 4½ feet. When treated early with injections of GH or IGF-1 (depending on the disorder), such children show catch-up growth and then grow at a normal rate, becoming much taller than they would have without treatment (Bright, Mendoza, & Rosenfeld, 2009; Saenger, 2003).

The availability of synthetic GH has also made it possible to treat short, normal-GH children with hormone injections, in hopes of increasing their final height. Thousands of parents, concerned that their children will suffer social stigma because of their shortness, have sought this GH therapy. But most normal-GH children given GH treatment grow only slightly taller than their previously predicted mature height (Rosenbloom, 2009). And contrary to popular belief, normal-GH short children are not deficient in self-esteem or other aspects of psychological adjustment (Gardner & Sandberg, 2011). So despite the existence of "heightism" in Western cultures, little justification exists for medically intervening in short stature that is merely the result of biologically normal human diversity.

A second pituitary hormone, **thyroid-stimulating hormone (TSH),** prompts the thyroid gland in the neck to release *thyroxine,* which is necessary for brain development and for GH to have its full impact on body size. Infants born with inadequate thyroxine must receive it at once, or they will be intellectually disabled. Once the most rapid period of brain development is complete, children with too little thyroxine grow at a below-average rate, but the central nervous system is no longer affected (Donaldson & Jones, 2013). With prompt treatment, such children catch up in body growth and eventually reach normal size.

Emotional Well-Being

In childhood as in infancy, emotional well-being can profoundly affect growth and health. Preschoolers with very stressful home lives (due to divorce, financial difficulties, or parental job loss) suffer more respiratory and intestinal illnesses and more unintentional injuries than others (Kemeny, 2003).

In addition, high stress suppresses the release of GH (Deltondo et al., 2008). Consequently, extreme emotional deprivation can lead to **psychosocial dwarfism,** a growth disorder that appears between ages 2 and 15. Typical characteristics include decreased secretion of GH and *melatonin,* a hormone within the brain that promotes sleep (during which GH is released), very short stature, and immature skeletal age. Also, these children display serious adjustment problems, which help distinguish psychosocial dwarfism from normal shortness (Muños-Hoyos et al., 2011; Tarren-Sweeney, 2006). Lynette, the 4-year-old mentioned earlier in this chapter, was diagnosed with this condition. She was placed in foster care after child welfare authorities discovered that she spent most of the day at home alone, unsupervised, and also might have been physically abused. When children like Lynette are removed from their emotionally inadequate environments, their GH levels quickly return to normal, and they grow rapidly. But if treatment is delayed, the dwarfism can be permanent.

Sleep Habits and Problems

Because GH is released during the child's sleeping hours, sleep contributes to body growth. And a well-rested child is better able to play, learn, and contribute positively to family functioning. Many studies confirm that sleep difficulties are associated with impaired cognitive performance, including decreased attention, speed of thinking, working memory, and intelligence and achievement test scores, as well as with internalizing and externalizing problems. The impact of disrupted sleep on cognitive functioning and emotional adjustment is more pronounced for low-SES children. Perhaps insufficient sleep heightens the impact of other environmental stressors prevalent in their daily lives (Buckhalt et al., 2009; El-Sheikh et al., 2010, 2013; Goodnight et al., 2007). Also, children who sleep poorly disturb their parents' sleep, which can generate significant family stress—a major reason that sleep difficulties are among the most frequent concerns parents raise with their preschooler's doctor.

Total sleep declines in early childhood; on average, 2- and 3-year-olds sleep 11 to 12 hours, 4- to 6-year-olds 10 to 11 hours. But substantial variability exists, with lesser- or greater-than-average sleep remaining fairly stable over time (Jenni & Carskadon, 2012). Younger preschoolers typically take a 1- to 2-hour nap in the early afternoon, although day-time sleep need also varies widely. Some continue to take two naps, as they did in toddlerhood; others give up napping entirely. Most Caucasian-American children stop napping between ages 3 and 4, although a quiet rest period after lunch helps them rejuvenate for the rest of the day. Perhaps because of greater cultural acceptance, napping remains common among African-American, Asian, and Hispanic children throughout early childhood, balanced by a tendency to go to bed later and to sleep less at night (Crosby, LeBourgeois, & Harsh, 2005; Mindell et al., 2013). And napping at preschool enhances memories acquired earlier in the day, especially for children who nap regularly at home (Kurdziel, Duclos, & Spencer, 2013). Consequently, replacing nap opportunities with additional learning activities in early childhood programs may be counterproductive.

The majority of Western parents engage in bedtime routines with their preschoolers, though in the United States this is slightly more common among white than African-American and Hispanic parents. As Figure 8.4 shows, Caucasian preschoolers are less likely to cosleep with their parents than their African-American and Hispanic agemates. White children more often go to bed with a security object, which may help them adjust to feelings of uneasiness at being left by themselves in a darkened room. African-American preschoolers are especially likely to share a bedroom with siblings (Milan, Snow, & Belay, 2007). In most cases, parent–child cosleeping is not associated with problems during the preschool years, other than more frequent night wakings by parents due to children's movements (Gaylor et al., 2005; Worthman, 2011). Western cosleeping children generally ask to sleep in their own bed by age 6 or 7.

Difficulty falling asleep—calling to the parent or asking for another drink of water—is common in early childhood, occurring in about one-third of preschoolers. But Caucasian parents more often express concern about their child falling asleep at a regular time than do African-American parents (Milan, Snow, & Belay, 2007). Perhaps Caucasian parents more highly value a scheduled bedtime and tend to view falling asleep without protest as a sign of maturity—expectations likely to be unmet at least occasionally.

Sleep problems frequently result from inadequate parental control over young children's TV, computer, and video game use, which is linked to later bedtimes, longer delay in falling asleep, and greater number of night wakings (Mindell et al., 2013). Sleep difficulties may also stem from a mismatch between parental demands and children's biology. The parent may step up pressure on the child, who vigorously resists because of a lower-than-average need for sleep. Consequently, sleep interventions should include parent education about individual differences in young children's sleep requirements (Johnson & Mindell, 2011). Intense bedtime struggles sometimes result from family turmoil, as children worry about how their parents

© BLEND IMAGES/ALAMY

Compared with their Caucasian peers, African-American preschoolers are more likely to share a bedroom with siblings or cosleep with parents. As a result, they less often depend on a security object to reduce the discomfort of being left alone in a darkened room.

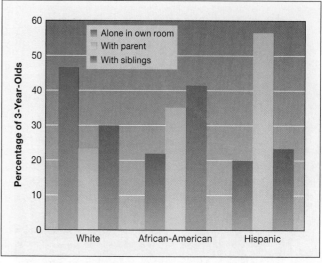

FIGURE 8.4 Sleeping arrangements of U.S. 3-year-olds by ethnicity. A survey of several thousand mothers who were asked about their 3-year-old's typical sleep location revealed that white preschoolers were far more likely to sleep alone in their own bedroom than African-American and Hispanic preschoolers. Among minority children, more Hispanic preschoolers slept with a parent, more African-American preschoolers with siblings. (Based on Milan, Snow, & Belay, 2007.)

may get along when they are asleep and not available to distract them. In these cases, addressing family stress and conflict is key to improving children's sleep.

Finally, most children waken during the night from time to time, and those who cannot return to sleep on their own may suffer from a sleep disorder. Because young children have vivid imaginations and difficulty separating fantasy from reality, *nightmares* are common; half of 3- to 6-year-olds experience them from time to time. And about 4 percent of children are frequent *sleepwalkers,* who are unaware of their wanderings during the night. Gently awakening and returning the child to bed helps avoid self-injury. *Sleep terrors,* which affect 3 percent of young children, are perhaps the most upsetting sleep problem to parents. In these panic-stricken arousals from deep sleep, the child may scream, thrash, speak incoherently, show a sharp rise in heart rate and breathing, and initially be unresponsive to parents' attempts to comfort. Sleepwalking and sleep terrors tend to run in families, suggesting a genetic influence (Guilleminault et al., 2003; Moore & Mindell, 2012). But they can also be triggered by stress or extreme fatigue.

Fortunately, sleep disorders of early childhood usually subside without treatment. In the few cases that persist, children require a medical and psychological evaluation. Their disturbed sleep may be a sign of neurological or emotional difficulties.

Nutrition

With the transition to early childhood, many children become unpredictable, picky eaters. One father we know wistfully recalled how his son, as a toddler, eagerly sampled Chinese food: "He ate rice, chicken chow mein, egg rolls—and now, at age 3, the only thing he'll try is the ice cream!"

Preschoolers' appetites decline because their growth has slowed. Their wariness of new foods is also adaptive: If they stick to familiar foods, they are less likely to swallow dangerous substances when adults are not around to protect them (Birch & Fisher, 1995). Parents need not worry about variations in amount eaten from meal to meal. Over the course of a day, preschoolers compensate for eating little at one meal by eating more at a later one (Hursti, 1999).

Though they eat less, preschoolers need a high-quality diet, including the same foods adults need, but in smaller amounts. These include milk and milk products, meat or meat alternatives (such as eggs, dried peas or beans, and peanut butter), vegetables and fruits, and breads and cereals. Fats, oils, and salt are best kept to a minimum because of their link to high blood pressure and heart disease in adulthood. And foods high in sugar should be eaten only in small amounts to prevent tooth decay and protect against overweight and obesity—a topic we will take up in Chapter 11.

Children tend to imitate the food choices and eating practices of people they admire, both adults and peers. For example, mothers who drink milk or soft drinks tend to have 5-year-old daughters with a similar beverage preference (Fisher et al., 2001). In Mexico, where children see family members delighting in the taste of peppery foods, preschoolers enthusiastically eat chili peppers, whereas most U.S. children reject them (Birch, Zimmerman, & Hind, 1980).

Repeated, unpressured exposure to a new food also increases acceptance (Fuller et al., 2005). In one study, preschoolers were given one of three versions of a food they had never eaten before (sweet, salty, or plain tofu). After 8 to 15 exposures, they readily ate the food. But they preferred the version they had already tasted. For example, children in the "sweet" condition liked sweet tofu best, and those in the "plain" condition liked plain tofu best (Sullivan & Birch, 1990). These findings reveal that adding sugar or salt in hopes of increasing a young child's willingness to eat healthy foods simply strengthens the child's desire for a sugary or salty taste. Similarly, offering children sweet fruit drinks or soft drinks promotes "milk avoidance." Compared to their milk-drinking agemates, milk-avoiders are shorter in

© ADAM HESTER/CORBIS

This Mexican 3-year-old helps his mother prepare refried beans for dinner. Children tend to imitate the food preferences of those they admire—both adults and peers.

Applying What We Know

Encouraging Good Nutrition in Early Childhood

SUGGESTION	DESCRIPTION
Offer a varied, healthy diet.	Provide a well-balanced variety of nutritious foods that are colorful and attractively served. Avoid including sweets and "junk" foods in the child's regular food environment.
Offer predictable meals as well as several snacks each day.	Preschoolers' stomachs are small, and they may not be able to eat enough in three meals to satisfy their energy requirements. They benefit from extra opportunities to eat.
Offer small portions, and permit the child to serve him- or herself and to ask for seconds.	When too much food is put on the plate, preschoolers (like adults) often overeat, increasing the risk of obesity. On average, preschoolers consume 25 percent less at a meal when permitted to serve themselves.
Offer healthy new foods early in a meal and repeatedly at subsequent meals, and respond with patience if the child rejects the food.	Introduce healthy new foods before the child's appetite is satisfied. Let children see you eat and enjoy the new food. If the child rejects it, accept the refusal and serve it again at another meal. As foods become more familiar, they are more readily accepted.
Keep mealtimes pleasant, include the child in mealtime conversations, and refrain from coercing the child to eat.	A pleasant, relaxed eating environment helps children develop positive attitudes about food. Refrain from constantly offering food, pressuring the child to eat, or engaging in confrontations over disliked foods and table manners—practices associated with children's refusal to eat.
Avoid using food as a reward and restricting access to certain foods.	Saying "No dessert until you clean your plate" tells children that they must eat even if they are not hungry and that dessert is the best part of the meal. Restricting access to a food increases children's valuing of that food and efforts to obtain it.

Sources: Fisher, Rolls, & Birch, 2003; Jansen et al., 2012.

stature and have a lower bone density—a condition that leads to a lifelong reduction in strength and to increased risk of bone fractures (Black et al., 2002).

The emotional climate at mealtimes has a powerful impact on children's eating habits. When parents are worried about how well their preschoolers are eating, meals can become unpleasant and stressful. Coercing children to eat—for example, by offering bribes, such as "Finish your vegetables, and you get an extra cookie"—causes children to like the healthy food less and the treat more (Birch, Fisher, & Davison, 2003). Similarly, restricting access to tasty foods focuses children's attention on those foods and increases their desire to eat them. In a study of nearly 5,000 Dutch 4-year-olds, maternal feeding practices were strongly associated with children's unhealthy weight, in both directions. The more mothers reported pressuring their child to eat, the greater the likelihood of an underweight child. And the more mothers reported restricting their child's eating, the greater the chances of an overweight or obese child (see Figure 8.5) (Jansen et al., 2012). Too much parental control over eating seems to interfere with children's responsiveness to hunger cues, resulting either in withdrawal from food or in excessive eating.

Children's healthy eating depends on a healthy food environment, but too much adult control limits their opportunities to develop self-control, thereby promoting overeating. For ways to encourage healthy, varied eating in young children, refer to Applying What We Know above.

Finally, as indicated in earlier chapters, many children in the United States and in developing countries lack access to sufficient high-quality food to support healthy growth. Five-year-old Hal rode a bus from a poor neighborhood to our laboratory preschool. His mother's paycheck barely covered her rent, let alone food. Hal's diet was deficient in protein and in essential vitamins and minerals—iron

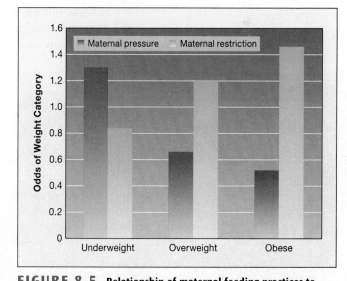

FIGURE 8.5 Relationship of maternal feeding practices to preschoolers' risk of underweight, overweight, and obesity. In a Dutch study of nearly 5,000 four-year-olds, mothers who pressured their child to eat were more likely to have an underweight child. Mothers who restricted their child's eating increased their chances of having an overweight or obese child. These relationships held even after controlling for many factors that could have influenced maternal feeding practices and preschoolers' weight gain, including parents' SES, ethnicity, height, and weight and children's enjoyment of eating. (Based on Jansen et al., 2012.)

LOOK and LISTEN

Arrange to join a family with at least one preschooler for a meal, and closely observe parental mealtime practices. Are they likely to promote healthy eating habits? Explain.

(to prevent anemia), calcium (to support development of bones and teeth), zinc (to support immune system functioning, neural communication, and cell duplication), vitamin A (to help maintain eyes, skin, and a variety of internal organs), and vitamin C (to facilitate iron absorption and wound healing). These are the most common dietary deficiencies of the preschool years (Yousafzai, Yakoob, & Bhutta, 2013).

Hal was small for his age, pale, inattentive, and unruly at preschool. By the school years, low-SES U.S. children are, on average, about ½ to 1 inch shorter than their economically advantaged counterparts (Cecil et al., 2005). And throughout childhood and adolescence, a nutritionally deficient diet is associated with attention and memory difficulties, poorer intelligence and achievement test scores, and behavior problems—especially hyperactivity and aggression—even after family factors that might account for these relationships (such as stressors, parental psychological health, education, warmth, and stimulation of the child) are controlled (Liu et al., 2004; Lukowski et al., 2010; Slack & Yoo, 2005).

Infectious Disease

One day, we noticed that Hal had been absent from the play yard for several weeks, so we asked Leslie, his preschool teacher, what was wrong. "Hal's been hospitalized with the measles," she explained. "He's had difficulty recovering—lost weight when there wasn't much to lose in the first place." In well-nourished children, ordinary childhood illnesses have no effect on physical growth. But when children are undernourished, disease interacts with malnutrition in a vicious spiral, with potentially severe consequences.

INFECTIOUS DISEASE AND MALNUTRITION   Hal's reaction to the measles is commonplace in developing nations, where a large proportion of the population lives in poverty and children do not receive routine immunizations. Illnesses such as measles and chicken pox, which typically do not appear until after age 3 in industrialized nations, occur much earlier. Poor diet depresses the body's immune system, making children far more susceptible to disease. Of the 6.6 million annual deaths of children under age 5 worldwide, 98 percent are in developing countries, and 65 percent are due to infectious diseases (World Health Organization, 2012a, 2013a).

Disease, in turn, is a major contributor to malnutrition, hindering both physical growth and cognitive development. Illness reduces appetite and limits the body's ability to absorb foods, especially in children with intestinal infections. In developing countries, widespread diarrhea, resulting from unsafe water and contaminated foods, leads to growth stunting and an estimated one million childhood deaths each year (Unger et al., 2014). Studies carried out in the slums and shantytowns of Brazil and Peru reveal that the more persistent diarrhea is in early childhood, the shorter children are in height and the lower their intelligence test scores during the school years (Checkley et al., 2003; Niehaus et al., 2002).

Most developmental impairments and deaths due to diarrhea can be prevented with nearly cost-free *oral rehydration therapy (ORT),* in which sick children are given a glucose, salt, and water solution that quickly replaces fluids the body loses. Since 1990, public health workers have taught nearly half the families in the developing world how to administer ORT. Also, supplements of zinc (essential for immune system functioning), which cost only 25 cents for a ten-day supply, substantially reduce the incidence of severe and prolonged diarrhea, especially when combined with ORT (Galvao et al., 2013). Through these interventions, the lives of millions of children are saved each year.

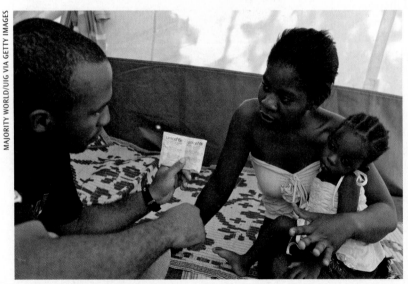

A public health worker teaches a Haitian mother how to prepare an oral rehydration therapy (ORT) packet for her child, who is suffering from diarrhea. This nearly cost-free treatment saves the lives of millions of children in developing countries each year.

MAJORITY WORLD/UIG VIA GETTY IMAGES

IMMUNIZATION In industrialized nations, childhood diseases have declined dramatically during the past half century, largely as a result of widespread immunization of infants and young children. Hal got the measles because, unlike his classmates from more advantaged homes, he did not receive a full program of immunizations.

In the United States, routine childhood immunizations have prevented an estimated 322 million illnesses and 700,000 deaths over the past two decades (Whitney et al., 2014). Yet about 20 percent of U.S. infants and toddlers are not fully immunized. Of the 80 percent who receive a complete schedule of vaccinations in the first two years, some do not receive the immunizations they need later, in early childhood. Overall, 17 percent of U.S. preschoolers lack essential immunizations. The rate rises to 22 percent for poverty-stricken children, many of whom do not receive full protection until age 5 or 6, when it is required for school entry (Centers for Disease Control and Prevention, 2013b). In contrast, fewer than 10 percent of preschoolers lack immunizations in Australia, Denmark,

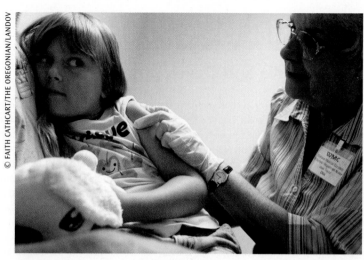

Although routine childhood immunizations prevent illness and death, fewer preschoolers in the United States receive timely essential vaccinations than do their counterparts in many Western nations.

and Norway, and fewer than 5 percent in Canada, the Netherlands, Sweden, and the United Kingdom (World Health Organization, 2014a).

Why does the United States lag behind these countries in immunization? Although the U.S. Affordable Care act greatly improved health insurance coverage for American children, many low-income children remain without coverage (return to pages 79–80 in Chapter 2 to review) and, therefore, may not receive timely vaccinations. In 1994, all U.S. children whose parents are unable to pay were guaranteed free immunizations, a program that has led to gains in vaccination rates.

But inability to pay for vaccines is not the only cause of U.S. inadequate immunization. Parents with little education and with stressful daily lives often fail to schedule vaccination appointments, and those without a primary-care physician do not want to endure long waits in crowded U.S. public health clinics (Falagas & Zarkadoulia, 2008). Some parents have been influenced by media reports—now widely discredited—suggesting a link between a mercury-based preservative used for decades in vaccines and a rise in the number of children diagnosed with autism. In fact, large-scale studies show no association with autism and no consistent effects on cognitive performance (Hensley & Briars, 2010; Richler et al., 2006; Stehr-Green et al., 2003; Thompson et al., 2007). Still, as a precautionary measure, mercury-free versions of childhood vaccines are now available. Other parents have religious or philosophical objections—for example, the belief that children should develop immunities naturally.

In areas where many parents refuse to immunize their children, disease outbreaks of whooping cough and rubella have occurred, with life-threatening consequences (Kennedy & Gust, 2008). Public education programs directed at increasing parental knowledge about the importance and safety of timely immunizations, and convenient opportunities to obtain them free or at low cost, are badly needed. The Netherlands achieves its high child immunization rate by giving parents of every newborn baby a written schedule that shows exactly when and where the child should be immunized (Lernout et al., 2013). If a parent does not bring the child at the specified time, a public health nurse calls the family. When appointments are missed repeatedly, the nurse goes to the home to ensure that the child receives the recommended vaccines.

A final point regarding communicable disease in early childhood deserves mention. Childhood illness rises with child-care attendance. On average, an infant or toddler in child care becomes sick 9 to 10 times a year, a preschooler 6 to 7 times. The diseases that spread most rapidly are those most frequently suffered by young children—diarrhea and respiratory infections. The risk that a respiratory infection will result in *otitis media*, or middle ear infection, is greatly elevated. To learn about the consequences of otitis media and how to prevent it, consult the Social Issues: Health box on page 298.

Social Issues: Health

Otitis Media and Development

During his first year in child care, 2-year-old Alex caught five colds, had the flu on two occasions, and experienced repeated *otitis media* (middle ear infection). Alex is not unusual. By age 3, 75 percent of U.S. children have had respiratory illnesses that resulted in at least one bout of otitis media; nearly half of these have had three or more bouts (Aronson & Henderson, 2006). Although antibiotics eliminate the bacteria responsible for otitis media, they do not reduce fluid buildup in the middle ear, which causes mild to moderate hearing loss that can last for weeks or months.

The incidence of otitis media is greatest between 6 months and 3 years, when children are first acquiring language. Frequent infections predict delayed language progress in early childhood and poorer academic performance, including reading deficits, after school entry (Racanello & McCabe, 2010).

How might otitis media disrupt language and academic progress? Difficulties in perceiving and processing speech sounds, particularly in noisy settings, may be responsible. Children with many bouts are less attentive to others' speech and less persistent at tasks (Asbjornsen et al., 2005; Polka & Rvachew, 2005). Their distractibility may result from an inability to make out what people around them are saying—which, in turn, may reduce the quality of others' interactions with them.

Because otitis media is so widespread, current evidence argues strongly in favor of early prevention. Crowded living conditions and exposure to cigarette smoke and other pollutants are linked to the disease, probably accounting for its high incidence among low-SES children. And compared with children remaining at home, rates of otitis media nearly double in children who attend child-care centers, where severe, antibacterial-resistant strains of respiratory infections can easily develop and spread. Risk increases further with the number of daily child-care settings a child experiences, which magnifies the number of peers with whom the child comes in contact (Morrissey, 2013).

Early otitis media can be prevented in the following ways:

Otitis media is widespread among children who attend child-care centers, where close contact leads to rapid spread of respiratory infection.

- *Frequent screening for the disease, followed by prompt medical intervention.* Plastic tubes that drain the narrow Eustachian tubes of the middle ear often are used to treat chronic otitis media in children, although their effectiveness has been disputed.
- *Child-care settings that control infection.* Because infants and young children often put toys in their mouths, these objects should be rinsed frequently with a disinfectant. Pacifier use has also been linked to a greater risk of otitis media (Rovers et al., 2008). Spacious, well-ventilated rooms and small group sizes help limit spread of the disease.
- *Verbally stimulating adult–child interaction.* Developmental problems associated with otitis media are reduced or eliminated in high-quality child-care centers. When caregivers are verbally stimulating and keep noise to a minimum, children have more opportunities to hear, and benefit from, spoken language (Vernon-Feagans et al., 2007).
- *Vaccines.* Many cases of otitis media are associated with influenza infection, making regular flu vaccination a helpful preventive measure (Principi, Baggi, & Esposito, 2012).

Childhood Injuries

More than any other child in the preschool classroom, 3-year-old Tommy had trouble sitting still and paying attention. Instead, he darted from one place and activity to another. One day, he narrowly escaped serious injury when he put his mother's car in gear while she was outside scraping ice from its windows. The vehicle rolled through a guardrail and over the side of a 10-foot concrete underpass, where it hung until rescue workers arrived. Police charged Tommy's mother with failing to use a restraint seat for a child younger than age 8.

Unintentional injuries are the leading cause of childhood mortality in industrialized nations. Although U.S. childhood injury fatalities have declined steadily over the past 35 years due to state laws and community policies aimed at improving child safety, the United States nevertheless ranks poorly in these largely preventable events, as Figure 8.6 reveals. About 35 percent of U.S. childhood deaths and 50 percent of adolescent deaths result from injuries, causing over 8,000 children to die annually (Child Trends, 2014c). And among the hundreds of thousands of injured children and youths who survive, many suffer pain, brain damage, and permanent physical disabilities.

FIGURE 8.6 International death rates due to unintentional injury among 1- to 14-year-olds. Compared with other industrialized nations, the United States has a high injury death rate, largely because of widespread childhood poverty and shortages of high-quality child care. Injury death rates are many times higher in developing nations, where poverty, rapid population growth, overcrowding in cities, and inadequate safety measures endanger children's lives. (Based on World Health Organization, 2008.)

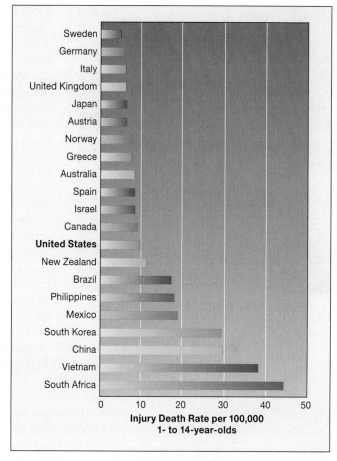

Injury Death Rate per 100,000
1- to 14-year-olds

Auto and traffic accidents, drownings, and burns are the most common childhood injuries (Safe Kids Worldwide, 2013). Motor vehicle collisions are by far the most frequent source of injury. They rank as the second leading U.S. cause of death from birth to age 5 (after suffocation among infants and drowning among toddlers and preschoolers) and as the leading cause of death among school-age children and adolescents.

FACTORS RELATED TO CHILDHOOD INJURIES The common view of childhood injuries as "accidental" suggests that they are due to chance and cannot be prevented. In fact, these injuries occur within a complex *ecological system* of individual, family, community, and societal influences—and we can do something about them.

As Tommy's case suggests, individual differences exist in the safety of children's behaviors. Because of their higher activity level and greater impulsivity and risk taking, boys are nearly twice as likely as girls to be injured, and their injuries are more severe (Child Trends, 2014c). Parents realize that they need to take more steps to protect their young sons than daughters from injury, and most do so. Still, mothers judge the chances of preventing injury in sons to be lower (Morrongiello & Kiriakou, 2004; Morrongiello, Ondejko, & Littlejohn, 2004). This belief may keep parents from sufficiently monitoring the most injury-prone boys.

Children with certain temperamental characteristics—inattentiveness, overactivity, irritability, defiance, and aggression—are also at greater risk for injury (Ordonana, Caspi, & Moffitt, 2008; Schwebel & Gaines, 2007). As we saw in Chapter 7, these children present child-rearing challenges. They are likely to protest when placed in auto seat restraints, to refuse to take a companion's hand when crossing the street, and to disobey after repeated instruction and discipline.

Poverty, single parenthood, and low parental education are also strongly associated with injury (Dudani, Macpherson, & Tamim, 2010; Schwebel & Brezausek, 2007). Parents who must cope with many daily stresses often have little time or energy to monitor the safety of their children. And their homes and neighborhoods are likely to be noisy, crowded, and rundown, posing further risks.

Broad societal conditions also affect childhood injury. In developing countries, the rate of death from injury before age 15 is five times as high as in developed nations and soon may exceed disease as the leading cause of childhood mortality (refer again to Figure 8.6). Rapid population growth, overcrowding in cities, and heavy road traffic combined with weak safety measures are major causes. Safety devices, such as car safety seats and bicycle helmets, are neither readily available nor affordable.

Childhood injury rates are high in the United States because of extensive poverty, shortages of high-quality child care (to supervise children in their parents' absence), and a high rate of births to teenagers, who are neither psychologically nor financially ready for parenthood (Child Trends, 2014c; Ekéus, Christensson, & Hjern, 2003). But U.S. children from advantaged families are also at considerably greater risk for injury than children in Western Europe. This indicates that besides reducing poverty and teenage pregnancy and upgrading the status of child care, additional steps are needed to ensure children's safety.

GARY S. CHAPMAN/GETTY IMAGES

Boys' higher activity level and greater impulsivity and risk taking explain why they are more likely to be injured and to suffer severe injuries than girls.

Parental attention to simple precautions—such as wearing bicycle helmets—can substantially reduce childhood injury rates.

PREVENTING CHILDHOOD INJURIES Childhood injuries have many causes, so a variety of approaches are needed to control them. Laws prevent many injuries by requiring car safety seats, child-resistant caps on medicine bottles, flameproof clothing, and fencing around backyard swimming pools—the site of 50 percent of early childhood drownings. Communities can help by modifying their physical environments. Providing inexpensive and widely available public transportation can reduce the amount of time that children spend in cars. Playgrounds, a common site of injury, can be covered with protective surfaces. Free, easily installed window guards can be given to families in high-rise apartment buildings to prevent falls. And media campaigns can inform parents and children about safety issues.

But even though they know better, many parents and children behave in ways that compromise safety. During the past several decades, U.S. parents have changed very little in how much they do to protect their children, citing such reasons as "the chances of serious injury are slim," taking necessary steps "is a hassle," and (among low-income families) safety devices (such as home fire extinguishers and bicycle helmets) "cost too much." For example, 27 percent of U.S. parents (like Tommy's mother) fail to place their children in car safety seats, and 84 percent of infant seats and 40 percent of child booster seats are improperly used. Yet research confirms that young children properly restrained in car safety seats have an 80 percent reduced risk of fatal injury (Safe Kids Worldwide, 2008, 2011). American parents, especially, seem willing to ignore familiar safety practices, perhaps because of the high value they place on individual rights and personal freedom.

Furthermore, many parents overestimate young children's knowledge of safety rules, relying on such assumed knowledge rather than monitoring and controlling access to hazards—a premature transition associated with a rise in home injuries. When parents teach safety rules to preschoolers, they often do so as a reaction to unsafe behaviors, rather than as an advance preventive. And they frequently fail to explain the basis for the rules—despite evidence that explanations enhance children's retention, understanding, and compliance (Morrongiello, Ondejko, & Littlejohn, 2004; Morrongiello et al., 2014). Even with well-learned rules, preschoolers need supervision to ensure that they comply (Morrongiello, Midgett, & Shields, 2001).

Interventions aimed at parents that highlight risk factors and that model and reinforce safety practices are effective in reducing home hazards and childhood injuries (Kendrick et al., 2008). Attention must also be paid to family conditions that can prevent childhood injury: relieving crowding in the home, providing social supports to ease parental stress, and teaching parents to use effective discipline—a topic we will take up in Chapter 10. Positive parenting—an affectionate, supportive relationship with the child; consistent, reasonable expectations for maturity; and oversight to ensure safety-rule compliance—substantially reduces injury rates, especially in overactive, emotionally reactive, and impulsive children (Schwebel & Gaines, 2007). But to implement these strategies, parents must have ample time and emotional resources as well as relevant knowledge and skills. Refer to Applying What We Know on the following page for ways to minimize unintentional injuries in early childhood.

Ask Yourself

- **REVIEW** Describe factors that contribute to sleep problems during the preschool years.

- **CONNECT** Using research on malnutrition or on unintentional injuries, show how physical growth and health in early childhood result from a continuous, complex interplay between heredity and environment.

- **APPLY** One day, Leslie prepared a new snack to serve at preschool: celery stuffed with ricotta cheese and pineapple. The first time she served it, few children touched it. How can Leslie encourage her students to accept the snack? What tactics should she avoid?

- **REFLECT** Ask a parent or other family member whether, as a preschooler, you were a picky eater, suffered from many infectious diseases, or sustained any serious injuries. In each instance, what factors might have been responsible?

Applying What We Know

Reducing Unintentional Injuries in Early Childhood

SUGGESTION	DESCRIPTION
Provide age-appropriate supervision and safety instruction.	Despite gains in understanding and self-control, preschoolers need nearly constant supervision. To encourage children to remember and obey safety rules, establish the rules, explain the reasons behind them, consistently enforce them, and praise children for following them.
Know the child's temperament.	Children who are unusually active, distractible, negative, or curious have more than their share of injuries and need extra monitoring.
Eliminate the most serious dangers from the home.	Examine all spaces for safety. For example, in the kitchen, store dangerous products in high cabinets out of sight, and keep sharp implements in a latched drawer. Remove guns; if that is impossible, store them unloaded in a locked cabinet. Always accompany young preschoolers to the bathroom, and keep all medicines in containers with safety caps.
During automobile travel, always restrain the child properly in the back seat of the car.	Use an age-appropriate, properly installed car safety seat or booster seat up to age 8 or until the child is 4 feet 9 inches tall, and strap the child in correctly every time. Children should always ride in the back seat; passenger-side air bags in the front seat deploy so forcefully that they can cause injury or death to a child. Never leave a child alone in a car, even on a cool, sunny day; a child's core body temperature increases 3 to 5 times faster than an adult's, with risk of permanent injury or death.
Select safe playground equipment and sites.	Make sure sand, wood chips, or rubberized matting has been placed under swings, see-saws, and jungle gyms. Check yards for dangerous plants. Always supervise outdoor play.
Be extra cautious around water.	Constantly observe children during water play; even shallow, inflatable pools are frequent sites of drownings. While they are swimming, young children's heads should not be immersed in water; they may swallow so much that they develop water intoxication, which can lead to convulsions and death.
Practice safety around animals.	Wait to get a pet until the child is mature enough to handle and help care for it—usually around age 5 or 6. Never leave a young child alone with an animal; bites often occur during playful roughhousing. Model and teach humane pet treatment.

Source: Safe Kids Worldwide, 2008.

Motor Development

8.6 Cite major milestones of gross- and fine-motor development in early childhood.

8.7 Describe individual differences in preschoolers' motor skills and ways to enhance motor development in early childhood.

TAKE A MOMENT... Observe several 2- to 6-year-olds at play in a neighborhood park, preschool, or child-care center. You will see that an explosion of new motor skills occurs in early childhood, each of which builds on the simpler movement patterns of toddlerhood.

During the preschool years, children continue to integrate previously acquired skills into more complex, *dynamic systems.* Then they revise each new skill as their bodies grow larger and stronger, their central nervous systems develop, their environments present new challenges, and they set new goals, aided by gains in perceptual and cognitive capacities.

Gross-Motor Development

As children's bodies become more streamlined and less top-heavy, their center of gravity shifts downward, toward the trunk. As a result, balance improves greatly, paving the way for new motor skills involving large muscles of the body. By age 2, preschoolers' gaits become smooth and rhythmic—secure enough that soon they leave the ground, at first by running and later by jumping, hopping, galloping, and skipping.

As children become steadier on their feet, their arms and torsos are freed to experiment with new skills—throwing and catching balls, steering tricycles, and swinging on horizontal bars and rings. Then upper- and lower-body skills combine into more refined actions. Five- and 6-year-olds simultaneously steer and pedal a tricycle and flexibly move their whole body when throwing, catching, hopping, and jumping. By the end of the preschool years, all skills

TABLE 8.1	Changes in Gross- and Fine-Motor Skills During Early Childhood	
AGE	**GROSS-MOTOR SKILLS**	**FINE-MOTOR SKILLS**
2–3 years	Walks more rhythmically; hurried walk changes to run Jumps, hops, throws, and catches with rigid upper body Pushes riding toy with feet; little steering	Puts on and removes simple items of clothing Zips and unzips large zippers Uses spoon effectively
3–4 years	Walks up stairs, alternating feet, and down stairs, leading with one foot Jumps and hops, flexing upper body Throws and catches with slight involvement of upper body; still catches by trapping ball against chest Pedals and steers tricycle	Fastens and unfastens large buttons Serves self food without assistance Uses scissors Copies vertical line and circle Draws first picture of person, using tadpole image
4–5 years	Walks down stairs, alternating feet Runs more smoothly Gallops and skips with one foot Throws ball with increased body rotation and transfer of weight from one foot to the other; catches ball with hands Rides tricycle rapidly, steers smoothly	Uses fork effectively Cuts with scissors following line Copies triangle, cross, and some letters
5–6 years	Increases running speed to 12 feet per second Gallops more smoothly; engages in true skipping Displays mature throwing and catching pattern Rides bicycle with training wheels	Uses knife to cut soft food Ties shoes Draws person with six parts Copies some numbers and simple words

Sources: Cratty, 1986; Haywood & Getchell, 2014.

are performed with greater speed and endurance. Table 8.1 provides a closer look at gross-motor development in early childhood.

Changes in ball skills provide an excellent illustration of preschoolers' gross-motor progress. Young preschoolers stand still, facing the target, throwing with their arm thrust forward (see Figure 8.7a). Catching is equally awkward. Two-year-olds extend their arms and hands rigidly, using them as a single unit to trap the ball. By age 3, children flex their elbows enough to trap the ball against the chest. But if the ball arrives too quickly, they cannot adapt, and it may bounce off the body (Haywood & Getchell, 2014).

Gradually, children call on the shoulders, torso, trunk, and legs to support throwing and catching. By age 4, children rotate the body and take a step forward to add force to their throw.

Throwing style typical of young preschoolers

(a)

Throwing style typical of older children

(b)

FIGURE 8.7 **Changes in throwing during early childhood.** At age 2 to 3, children stand still, simply bringing the hand back and throwing rigidly without taking a step. Gradually, they involve the entire body. By age 5 to 6, they typically engage in arm, leg, and trunk rotation and preparatory action before executing the throw. Integrated throwing movements become increasingly refined and adapted to the throwing situation during middle childhood. (Adapted figures drawn from film tracings taken in the Motor Development and Child Study Laboratory, University of Wisconsin–Madison and now available from the Motor Development Film Collection, Kinesiology Division, Bowling Green State University. © Mary Ann Roberton. Reprinted by permission of Mary Ann Roberton.).

Around 5 to 6 years, they begin by shifting their weight to a rear foot in a preparatory backswing and then shift forward, rotating the trunk and stepping into the throw as they release the ball (see Figure 8.7b). As a result, the ball travels faster and farther. When the ball is returned, older preschoolers predict its place of landing by moving forward, backward, or sideways. Soon, they can catch the ball with their hands and fingers, "giving" with arms and body to absorb the force of the ball.

LOOK and **LISTEN**

Play a game of catch with a 2- to 3-year-old, then with a 4- to 6-year-old. What differences in movement and coordination are evident?

Fine-Motor Development

Like gross-motor development, fine-motor skills take a giant leap forward in the preschool years. As control of the hands and fingers improves, young children put puzzles together, build with small blocks, cut and paste, and string beads. To parents, fine-motor progress is most apparent in two areas: (1) children's care of their own bodies, and (2) the drawings and paintings that fill the walls at home, child care, and preschool.

SELF-HELP SKILLS   As Table 8.1 shows, young children gradually become self-sufficient at dressing and feeding. Two-year-olds put on and take off simple items of clothing. By age 3, children can dress and undress well enough to take care of toileting needs by themselves. Between ages 4 and 5, children can dress and undress without supervision. At mealtimes, young preschoolers use a spoon well, and they can serve themselves. By age 4 they are adept with a fork, and around 5 to 6 years they can use a knife to cut soft foods. Roomy clothing with large buttons and zippers and child-sized eating utensils help children master these skills.

Preschoolers get great satisfaction from managing their own bodies. They are proud of their independence, and their new skills also make life easier for adults. But parents must be patient about these abilities: When tired and in a hurry, young children often revert to eating with their fingers. And the 3-year-old who dresses himself in the morning sometimes ends up with his shirt on inside out, his pants on backward, and his left snow boot on his right foot! Perhaps the most complex self-help skill of early childhood is shoe tying, mastered around age 6. Success requires a longer attention span, memory for an intricate series of hand movements, and the dexterity to perform them. Shoe tying illustrates the close connection between motor and cognitive development, as do two other skills: drawing and writing.

DRAWING   When given crayon and paper, even toddlers scribble in imitation of others. As the young child's ability to mentally represent the world expands, marks on the page take on meaning. A variety of factors combine with fine-motor control in the development of children's artful representations (Golomb, 2004). These include the realization that pictures can serve as symbols, improved planning and spatial understanding, and the emphasis that the child's culture places on artistic expression.

Typically, drawing progresses through the following sequence:

Preschoolers gradually become more proficient at self-help skills of dressing and feeding themselves. Most master shoe tying, the most complex self-help skill, around age 6.

1. *Scribbles.* Western children begin to draw during the second year. At first, the intended representation is contained in gestures rather than in the resulting marks on the page. For example, one 18-month-old made her crayon hop and, as it produced a series of dots, explained, "Rabbit goes hop-hop" (Winner, 1986).

   Recall from Chapter 6 that 2-year-olds treat realistic-looking pictures symbolically, but they have difficulty interpreting line drawings. When an adult held up a drawing indicating which of two objects preschoolers should drop down a chute, 3-year-olds used the drawing as a symbol to guide their behavior, but 2-year-olds did not (Callaghan, 1999).
2. *First representational forms.* Around age 3, children's scribbles start to become pictures. Often children make a gesture with the crayon, notice that they have drawn a recognizable shape, and then label it. In one case, a 2-year-old made some random marks on a page and then, realizing the resemblance between his scribbles and noodles, named the creation "chicken pie and noodles" (Winner, 1986).

LOOK *and* **LISTEN**

Visit a preschool or child-care center where artwork by 3- to 5-year-olds is plentiful. Note developmental progress in drawings of human and animal figures and in the complexity of children's pictures.

Few 3-year-olds spontaneously draw so others can tell what their picture represents. However, after an adult demonstrated how drawings can be used to stand for objects in a game, more 3-year-olds drew recognizable forms (Callaghan & Rankin, 2002). Western parents and teachers spend much time promoting 2- and 3-year-olds' language and make-believe play but relatively little time showing them how they can use drawings to represent their world (Cohn, 2014). When adults draw with children and point out resemblances between drawings and objects, preschoolers' pictures become more comprehensible and detailed (Braswell & Callanan, 2003).

A major milestone in drawing occurs when children use lines to represent the boundaries of objects. This enables 3- and 4-year-olds to draw their first picture of a person. Fine-motor and cognitive limitations lead the preschooler to reduce the figure to the simplest form that still looks human—the universal "tadpole" image, a circular shape with lines attached, shown on the left in Figure 8.8. Four-year-olds add features, such as eyes, nose, mouth, hair, fingers, and feet, as the tadpole drawings illustrate.

3. *More realistic drawings.* Five- and 6-year-olds create more complex drawings, like the one on the right in Figure 8.8, containing more conventional human and animal figures, with the head and body differentiated. Older preschoolers' drawings still contain perceptual distortions because they have just begun to represent depth. Use of depth cues, such as overlapping objects, smaller size for distant than for near objects, diagonal placement, and converging lines, increases during middle childhood (Nicholls & Kennedy, 1992).

Realism in drawings appears gradually, as perception, language (ability to describe visual details), sustained attention, memory, and fine-motor capacities improve (Riggs, Jolley, & Simpson, 2013; Toomela, 2002). Drawing of geometric objects follows the steps illustrated in Figure 8.9. (1) Three- to 7-year olds draw a single unit to stand for an object. To represent a cube, they draw a square; to represent a cylinder, they draw a circle, an oval, or a rectangle. (2) During the late preschool and school years, children represent salient object parts. They draw several squares to stand for a cube's sides and draw two circles and some lines to represent a cylinder. However, the parts are not joined properly. (3) Older school-age children and adolescents integrate object parts into a realistic whole (Toomela, 1999).

FIGURE 8.8 **Examples of young children's drawings.** The universal tadpolelike shape that children use to draw their first picture of a person is shown on the left. The tadpole soon becomes an anchor for greater detail as arms, fingers, toes, and facial features sprout from the basic shape. By the end of the preschool years, children produce more complex, differentiated pictures like the one on the right, drawn by a 6-year-old child. (*Left:* From H. Gardner, 1980, *Artful Scribbles: The Significance of Children's Drawing*, New York: Basic Books, p. 64. Copyright © 1980 by Howard Gardner. Reprinted by permission of Basic Books, a member of the Perseus Books, conveyed through Copyright Clearance Center. *Right:* From E. Winner, "Where Pelicans Kiss Seals," *Psychology Today*, 20[8], August 1986, p. 35. Reprinted by permission from the collection of Ellen Winner.)

Drawing Category and Approximate Age Range	Cube	Cylinder
Single Units (3 to 7 years)		
Object Parts (4 to 13 years)		
Integrated Whole (8 years and older)		

FIGURE 8.9 **Development of children's drawings of geometric objects—a cube and a cylinder.** As these examples show, drawings change from single units to representation of object parts. Then the parts are integrated into a realistic whole. (Based on Toomela, 1999.)

Cultural Influences

Why Are Children from Asian Cultures Advanced in Drawing Skills?

Return to the elaborate, expressive drawing, by a Chinese artist just 4 years old, on the opening page of this chapter. Observations of young children's drawings in Asian cultures, such as China, Japan, Korea, the Philippines, Taiwan, and Vietnam, reveal skills that are remarkably advanced over those of their Western agemates. What explains such early artistic ability?

To answer this question, researchers have examined cultural influences on children's drawings, comparing China to the United States. Artistic models offered by the culture, teaching strategies, valuing of the visual arts, and expectations for children's artistic development can have a notable impact on the art that children produce.

In China's 4,000-year-old artistic tradition, adults showed children how to draw, encouraging them to master the precise steps required to depict people, butterflies, fish, birds, and other images. When taught to paint, Chinese children follow prescribed brush strokes, at first copying their teacher's model. To learn to write, they must concentrate hard on the unique details of each Chinese character—a requirement that likely augments their drawing ability. Chinese parents and teachers believe that children can be creative only after they have acquired a foundation of artistic knowledge and technique (Golomb, 2004). To that end, China has devised a national art curriculum with standards and teaching materials extending from age 3 through secondary school.

The United States, as well, has a rich artistic tradition, but its styles and conventions are enormously diverse compared with those of Asian cultures. Children everywhere try to imitate the art around them as a way to acquire their culture's "visual language." But American children face a

daunting imitative task, much like a child growing up in a context where each person speaks a different language (Cohn, 2014). Furthermore, U.S. art education emphasizes independence—finding one's own style. American teachers typically assume that copying others' drawings stifles creativity, so they discourage children from doing so (Copple & Bredekamp, 2009). Rather than promoting correct ways to draw, U.S. teachers emphasize imagination and self-expression.

Does the Chinese method of teaching drawing skills beginning in the preschool years interfere with children's creativity? To find out, researchers followed a group of Chinese-American children of immigrant parents and a group of Caucasian-American children, all from middle-SES two-parent families, from ages 5 to 9. At two-year intervals, the children's human-figure drawings were rated for maturity and originality—inclusion of novel elements (Huntsinger et al., 2011). Findings revealed that on each occasion, the Chinese-American children's drawings were more advanced and also more creative.

Interviews revealed that Caucasian-American parents more often mentioned providing their children with a rich variety of art materials, whereas Chinese-American parents more often reported enrolling their children in art lessons, rating the development of artistic competence as more important. The Chinese-American children also spent more time as preschoolers and kindergartners in focused practice of fine-motor

TAO IMAGES RM/GETTY IMAGES

The complex drawings of these kindergartners in Shanghai, China, benefit from adult expectations that young children learn to draw well, careful teaching of artistic knowledge and technique, and the rich artistic tradition of Chinese culture.

tasks, including drawing. And the more time they spent, especially when their parents taught and modeled drawing at home, the more mature their drawing skills. At the same time, Chinese-American children's artistic creativity flourished under this systematic approach to promoting artistic maturity.

In sum, even though young Chinese children are taught how to draw, their artistic products are original. Once they succeed at drawing basic forms, they spontaneously add unusual details of their own. Although Western children may come up with rich ideas about what to draw, until they acquire the necessary skills, they cannot implement those ideas. Cross-cultural research indicates that children benefit from adult guidance in learning to draw, just as they do in learning to talk.

CULTURAL VARIATIONS IN DEVELOPMENT OF DRAWING   In cultures that have rich artistic traditions and that highly value artistic competence, children create elaborate drawings that reflect the conventions of their culture. Adults encourage young children by guiding them in mastering basic drawing skills, modeling ways to draw, and discussing their pictures. Peers, as well, talk about one another's drawings and copy from one another's work (Boyatzis, 2000; Braswell, 2006). All of these practices enhance young children's drawing progress. And as the Cultural Influences box above reveals, they help explain why, from an early age, children in Asian cultures are advanced over Western children in drawing skills.

In cultures with little interest in art, even older children and adolescents produce simple forms. In the Jimi Valley, a remote region of Papua New Guinea with no indigenous pictorial

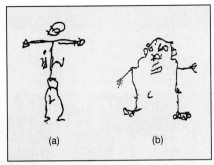

FIGURE 8.10 Human figure drawings produced by nonschooled 10- to 15-year-olds of the Jimi Valley of Papua New Guinea. Many produced (a) "stick" figures or (b) "contour" figures, which resemble the tadpole form of young preschoolers. (From M. Martlew & K. J. Connolly, 1996, "Human Figure Drawings by Schooled and Unschooled Children in Papua New Guinea," *Child Development, 67,* pp. 2750–2751. © The Society for Research in Child Development. Adapted with permission of John Wiley and Sons, Inc., conveyed through Copyright Clearance Center, Inc.)

Gains in fine-motor control and perception, along with experience with written materials, contribute to this 5-year-old's skill at printing.

FIGURE 8.11 Variations in 3-year-olds' pencil grip. Through experimenting with different grips, preschoolers gradually discover an adult grip with one or two fingers on top of the pencil, which maximizes writing stability and efficiency. (Based on Greer & Lockman, 1998.)

art, many children do not go to school and therefore have little opportunity to develop drawing skills. When a Western researcher asked nonschooled Jimi 10- to 15-year-olds to draw a human figure for the first time, most produced nonrepresentational scribbles and shapes or simple "stick" or "contour" images (see Figure 8.10) (Martlew & Connolly, 1996). These forms, which resemble those of preschoolers, seem to be a universal beginning in drawing. Once children realize that lines must evoke human features, they find solutions to figure drawing that vary somewhat from culture to culture but, overall, follow the sequence described earlier.

EARLY PRINTING When preschoolers first try to write, they scribble, making no distinction between writing and drawing. As they experiment with lines and shapes, notice print in storybooks, and observe people writing, they attempt to print letters and, later, words. Around age 4, children's writing shows some distinctive features of print, such as separate forms arranged in a line on the page. But children often include picturelike devices. For example, they might use a circular shape to write "sun." Or they might call a large scribble the word *lion,* a small scribble the word *caterpillar,* and a red scribble the word *apple* (Ehri & Roberts, 2006; Levin & Bus, 2003). Applying their understanding of the symbolic function of drawings, 4-year-olds asked to write typically make a "drawing of print." Only gradually, as they learn to name the letters of the alphabet and to link them with language sounds, do preschoolers realize that writing stands for language.

Preschoolers' first attempts to print often involve their name, generally using a single letter. "How do you make a *D?*" your first author's older son David asked at age 3½. When his mother printed a large uppercase *D,* he tried to copy. "*D* for David," he proclaimed, quite satisfied with his backward, imperfect creation. A year later, David added several letters, and around age 5, he printed his name clearly enough that others could read it.

Between ages 3 and 5, children acquire skill in gripping a pencil. As Figure 8.11 shows, 3-year-olds display diverse grip patterns and pencil angles, varying their grip depending on the direction and location of the marks they want to make. By trying out different forms of pencil-holding, they discover the grip and angle that maximize stability and writing efficiency (Greer & Lockman, 1998). By age 5, most children use an adult grip pattern and a fairly constant pencil angle across a range of drawing and writing conditions.

In addition to gains in fine-motor control, advances in perception contribute to the ability to print. Like many children, David continued to reverse letters until well into second grade. Once preschoolers distinguish writing from nonwriting around age 4, they make progress in identifying individual letters. Many preschoolers confuse letter pairs that are alike in shape with subtle distinctive features, such as *C* and *G, E* and *F,* and *M* and *W* (Bornstein & Arterberry, 1999). Mirror-image letter pairs (*b* and *d, p* and *q*) are especially hard to discriminate. Until children start to read, they do not find it especially useful to notice the difference between these forms.

The ability to tune in to mirror images and to scan a printed line from left to right improves as children gain experience with written materials (Casey, 1986). The more parents and teachers assist preschoolers in their efforts to print, the more advanced children are in writing and other aspects of literacy development (Aram & Levin, 2011). We will consider early childhood literacy in greater detail in Chapter 9.

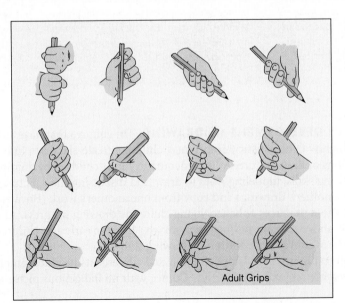

Adult Grips

Individual Differences in Motor Skills

Wide individual differences exist in the ages at which children reach motor milestones. A child with a tall, muscular body tends to move more quickly and to acquire certain skills earlier than a short, stocky youngster. And as in other domains, parents and teachers probably provide more encouragement to children with biologically based motor-skill advantages.

Sex differences in motor skills are evident in early childhood. Boys are ahead of girls in skills that emphasize force and power. By age 5, they can broad-jump slightly farther, run slightly faster, and throw a ball about 5 feet farther. Girls have an edge in fine-motor skills and in certain gross-motor skills that require a combination of good balance and foot movement, such as hopping and skipping (Fischman, Moore, & Steele, 1992; Haywood & Getchell, 2014). Boys' greater muscle mass and, in the case of throwing, slightly longer forearms contribute to their skill advantages. And girls' greater overall physical maturity may be partly responsible for their better balance and precision of movement.

From an early age, boys and girls are usually channeled into different physical activities. For example, fathers are more likely to play catch with their sons than with their daughters. Baseballs and footballs are purchased for boys, jump ropes and sewing materials for girls. Sex differences in motor skills increase with age, but they remain small throughout childhood (Greendorfer, Lewko, & Rosengren, 1996). This suggests that social pressures for boys to be active and physically skilled and for girls to play quietly at fine-motor activities exaggerate small genetically based sex differences. In support of this view, boys can throw a ball much farther than girls only when using their dominant hand. When they use their nondominant hand, the sex difference is minimal (Williams, Haywood, & Painter, 1996). Boys' superior throwing largely results from practice.

Sex differences in motor development are already apparent in early childhood. Girls have an edge in skills that require balance and precision of movement, like jumping rope, but boys benefit from greater encouragement to improve their skill levels in throwing, catching, and running.

Enhancing Early Childhood Motor Development

Many Western parents provide preschoolers with early training in gymnastics, tumbling, dance, soccer, and other movement skills through organized classes. These experiences can offer excellent opportunities for exercise and social interaction. But aside from throwing (where direct instruction is helpful), formal lessons during the preschool years have little added impact on gross-motor progress. Rather, children master the gross-motor skills of early childhood through everyday play.

Nevertheless, the physical environment in which play takes place can affect mastery of complex motor skills. The National Association for Sport and Physical Education (2009) recommends that preschoolers engage in at least 60 minutes of adult-planned physical experiences in which parents and teachers provide enjoyable games and other playful activities, and up to several hours of child-directed physical activity, every day. When children have play spaces and equipment appropriate for running, climbing, jumping, and throwing and are encouraged to use them, they respond eagerly to these challenges. But if balls are too large and heavy to be properly grasped and thrown, or jungle gyms, ladders, and horizontal bars are suitable for only the largest and strongest children, then preschoolers cannot easily acquire new motor skills. Playgrounds must offer a range of equipment to meet the diverse needs of individual children.

Similarly, development of fine-motor skills can be supported through daily routines, such as dressing and pouring juice, and through richly equipped early childhood environments that include puzzles, construction sets, drawing, painting, sculpting, cutting, and pasting. And as the Cultural Influences box on page 305 revealed, adults who guide and support children in acquiring drawing skills foster artistic development.

When play spaces are properly designed and equipped, young children respond eagerly to motor challenges and develop new skills through informal play.

Finally, the social climate created by adults can enhance or dampen preschoolers' motor development. When parents and teachers criticize a child's performance, push specific motor skills, or promote a competitive attitude, they risk undermining children's self-confidence and, in turn, their motor progress (Berk, 2006). Adult involvement in young children's motor activities should focus on fun rather than on winning or perfecting the "correct" technique.

Ask Yourself

- **REVIEW** Describe typical changes in children's drawings in early childhood, along with factors that contribute to those changes. Why are children from Asian cultures advanced in drawing skills?

- **CONNECT** How are experiences that best support preschoolers' gross-motor development consistent with experience-expectant brain growth of the early years? (Return to page 169 in Chapter 5 to review.)

- **APPLY** Mabel and Chad want to do everything they can to support their 3-year-old daughter's athletic development. What advice would you give them?

- **REFLECT** Do you think American children should be provided with systematic instruction in drawing skills beginning in early childhood, similar to the direct teaching Chinese children receive? Explain.

Summary

Body Growth (p. 285)

8.1 Describe changes in body size, proportions, and skeletal maturity during early childhood.

- Gains in body size taper off in early childhood as children become longer and leaner, and individual differences in body size and rate of growth are more apparent. In various parts of the skeleton, new epiphyses emerge, where cartilage hardens into bone.

LAYLAND MASUDA/MOMENT OPEN/GETTY IMAGES

- By the end of the preschool years, children start to lose their primary teeth. Care of primary teeth is essential because diseased baby teeth can affect the health of permanent teeth. Childhood tooth decay remains common, especially among low-SES children.

8.2 Describe brain development in early childhood.

- Neural fibers in the brain continue to form synapses and myelinate. By this time, many parts of the cerebral cortex have overproduced synapses, and *synaptic pruning* occurs. To make room for the connective structures of stimulated neurons, many surrounding neurons die, leading to reduced brain plasticity.

- Prefrontal-cortical areas devoted to various aspects of executive function show rapid growth from early to middle childhood. In addition, for most children, the left cerebral hemisphere develops ahead of the right, supporting rapidly expanding language skills.

- Hand preference, which reflects an individual's **dominant cerebral hemisphere,** strengthens during early childhood. Research on handedness supports the joint contribution of nature and nurture to brain lateralization.

- During early childhood, connections are established between brain structures. Fibers linking the **cerebellum** to the cerebral cortex grow and myelinate, enhancing motor coordination and cognition. The **reticular formation,** responsible for alertness and consciousness; the **hippocampus,** which plays a vital role in memory and understanding of space; the **amygdala,** which plays a central role in processing novelty and emotional information; and the **corpus callosum,** which connects the two cortical hemispheres, also form synapses and myelinate.

Influences on Physical Growth and Health (p. 290)

8.3 Explain how heredity influences physical growth.

- Heredity influences physical growth by controlling production and release of two vital hormones from the **pituitary gland: growth hormone (GH),** which affects the development of almost all body tissues, and **thyroid-stimulating hormone (TSH),** which affects brain growth and body size.

8.4 Describe the effects of emotional well-being, restful sleep, nutrition, and infectious disease on physical growth and health in early childhood.

- Emotional well-being continues to influence growth and health. Extreme emotional deprivation can lead to **psychosocial dwarfism.**

- Restful sleep contributes to body growth, since GH is released during the child's sleeping hours. Sleep difficulties impair cognitive functioning and emotional adjustment, especially for low-SES children. Although total sleep need declines, substantial variability exists.

- Sleep problems sometimes stem from inadequate parental control over young children's use of electronic devices, as well as a mismatch between parental demands and children's sleep needs. Many preschoolers have difficulty falling asleep, and most awaken occasionally at night. A few children suffer from sleep disorders, such as sleepwalking or sleep terrors, which run in families, suggesting a genetic influence. These problems can also be triggered by stress or extreme fatigue. Most subside with age.

- As growth rate slows, preschoolers' appetites decline, and they often become wary of new foods. Modeling by others, repeated exposure to new foods, and a positive emotional climate at mealtimes can promote healthy, varied eating.

- Dietary deficiencies—most commonly in protein, vitamins, and minerals—are associated with attention and memory difficulties, academic and behavior problems, and greater susceptibility to infectious diseases. Disease also contributes to malnutrition, especially when intestinal infections cause persistent diarrhea. In developing countries, inexpensive oral rehydration therapy (ORT) and supplements of zinc can prevent most developmental impairments and deaths due to diarrhea.

- Immunization rates are lower in the United States than in other industrialized nations because many economically disadvantaged children lack access to necessary health care. Parental stress and misconceptions about vaccine safety also contribute.

8.5 What factors increase the risk of unintentional injuries, and how can childhood injuries be prevented?

- Unintentional injuries are the leading cause of childhood mortality in industrialized nations. Injury victims are more likely to be boys; to be temperamentally irritable, inattentive, overactive, and aggressive; and to live in stressed, poverty-stricken, crowded family environments.

- Effective injury prevention includes passing laws that promote child safety; creating safer home, travel, and play environments; relieving sources of family stress; improving public education; and changing parent and child behaviors.

Motor Development (p. 301)

8.6 Cite major milestones of gross- and fine-motor development in early childhood.

- As the child's center of gravity shifts toward the trunk, balance improves, paving the way for new gross-motor achievements. Preschoolers' gaits become smooth and rhythmic; they run, jump, hop, gallop; eventually skip, throw, and catch; and generally become better coordinated.

- Increasing control of the hands and fingers leads to dramatic improvements in fine-motor skills. Preschoolers gradually dress themselves and use a fork and knife.

- By age 3, children's scribbles become pictures. As perceptual, cognitive, and fine-motor capacities improve, children's drawings increase in complexity and realism. Children's drawings are also influenced by their culture's artistic traditions.

- Between 3 and 5 years, children experiment with pencil grip; by age 5, most use an adultlike grip that maximizes stability and writing efficiency.

- Advances in perception and exposure to written materials contribute to progress in discriminating and accurately printing individual letters. When parents and teachers support children's efforts to print, preschoolers are more advanced in writing and other aspects of literacy development.

8.7 Describe individual differences in preschoolers' motor skills and ways to enhance motor development in early childhood.

- Body build and opportunity for physical play affect early childhood motor development. Sex differences that favor boys in skills requiring force and power and girls in skills requiring good balance and fine movements are partly genetic, but social pressures exaggerate them.

- Children master the motor skills of early childhood through informal play experiences, with little benefit from exposure to formal training. Richly equipped play environments that accommodate a wide range of physical abilities are important. Emphasizing pleasure in motor activities is the best way to foster motor development during the preschool years.

Important Terms and Concepts

amygdala (p. 290)
cerebellum (p. 289)
corpus callosum (p. 290)
dominant cerebral hemisphere (p. 288)

growth hormone (GH) (p. 292)
hippocampus (p. 289)
pituitary gland (p. 290)
psychosocial dwarfism (p. 292)

reticular formation (p. 289)
thyroid-stimulating hormone (TSH) (p. 292)

chapter 9

Cognitive Development in Early Childhood

REPRINTED WITH PERMISSION FROM THE INTERNATIONAL MUSEUM OF CHILDREN'S ART, OSLO, NORWAY

Untitled
Bermain Samil Belajar
6 years, Indonesia

Storybooks expose these children to a wealth of language and literacy experiences and encourage discovery of the wider world. Mental representation blossoms in early childhood, contributing greatly to cognitive and language development.

One rainy morning, as we observed in our laboratory preschool, Leslie, the children's teacher, joined us at the back of the room for a moment. "Preschoolers' minds are such a curious blend of logic, fantasy, and faulty reasoning," Leslie reflected. "Every day, I'm startled by the maturity and originality of what they say and do. Yet at other times, their thinking seems limited and inflexible."

Leslie's comments sum up the puzzling contradictions of early childhood cognition. That day, for example, 3-year-old Sammy looked up, startled, after a loud crash of thunder outside. "A magic man turned on the thunder!" he pronounced. Even when Leslie patiently explained that thunder is caused by lightning, not by a person turning it on or off, Sammy persisted: "Then a magic lady did it."

In other respects, Sammy's thinking was surprisingly advanced. At snack time, he accurately counted, "One, two, three, four!" and then got four cartons of milk, one for each child at his table. Sammy's keen memory and ability to categorize were also evident. He could recite by heart *The Very Hungry Caterpillar,* a story he had heard many times. And he could name and classify dozens of animals.

But when his snack group included more than four children, Sammy's counting broke down. And some of his notions about quantity seemed as fantastic as his understanding of thunder. After Priti dumped out her raisins, scattering them in front of her, Sammy asked, "How come you got lots, and I only got this little bit?" He didn't realize that he had just as many raisins; his were simply all bunched up in a tiny red box. While Priti was washing her hands after snack, Sammy put her remaining raisins in her cubby. When Priti returned and looked for her raisins, Sammy pronounced, "You know where they are!" He failed to grasp that Priti, who hadn't seen him move the raisins, would expect them to be where she had left them.

In this chapter, we explore early childhood cognition, drawing on three theories with which you are already familiar. To understand Sammy's reasoning, we turn first to Piaget's and Vygotsky's theories along with evidence highlighting the strengths and limitations of each. Then we examine additional research on young children's cognition inspired by the information-processing perspective. Next, we address factors that contribute to individual differences in mental development—the home environment, the quality of preschool and child care, and the many hours young children spend with electronic media. Our chapter concludes with the dramatic expansion of language in early childhood. ◾

Piaget's Theory: The Preoperational Stage

As children move from the sensorimotor to the **preoperational stage,** which spans the years 2 to 7, the most obvious change is an extraordinary increase in representational, or symbolic, activity. Recall that infants and toddlers have considerable ability to mentally represent their world. In early childhood, this capacity blossoms.

9.1 Describe advances in mental representation, and limitations of thinking, during the preoperational stage.

9.2 What does follow-up research imply about the accuracy of Piaget's preoperational stage?

9.3 What educational principles can be derived from Piaget's theory?

Advances in Mental Representation

Piaget acknowledged that language is our most flexible means of mental representation. By detaching thought from action, it permits far more efficient thinking than was possible earlier. When we think in words, we overcome the limits of our momentary experiences. We can deal with past, present, and future at once and combine concepts in unique ways, as when we imagine a hungry caterpillar eating bananas or monsters flying through the forest at night.

But Piaget did not regard language as a primary ingredient in childhood cognitive change. Instead, he believed that sensorimotor activity leads to internal images of experience, which children then label with words (Piaget, 1936/1952). In support of Piaget's view, recall from Chapter 6 that children's first words have a strong sensorimotor basis. And toddlers acquire an impressive range of categories long before they use words to label them (see page 219). But as we will see, Piaget underestimated the power of language to spur children's cognition.

Make-Believe Play

Make-believe play is another excellent example of the development of representation in early childhood. Piaget believed that through pretending, young children practice and strengthen newly acquired representational schemes. Drawing on his ideas, several investigators have traced changes in make-believe play during the preschool years.

DEVELOPMENT OF MAKE-BELIEVE   One day, Sammy's 20-month-old brother, Dwayne, visited the classroom. Dwayne wandered around, picked up a toy telephone receiver, eyed his mother, said, "Hi, Mommy," and then dropped it. Next, he found a cup, pretended to drink, and then toddled off again. Meanwhile, Sammy joined Vance and Lynette in the block area for a space shuttle launch.

"That can be our control tower," Sammy suggested, pointing to a corner by a bookshelf. "Countdown!" he announced, speaking into his "walkie-talkie"—a small wooden block. "Five, six, two, four, one, blastoff!" Lynette made a doll push a pretend button, and the rocket was off!

Comparing Dwayne's pretend play with Sammy's, we see three important changes that reflect the preschool child's growing symbolic mastery:

- *Play detaches from the real-life conditions associated with it.* In early pretending, toddlers use only realistic objects—a toy telephone to talk into or a cup to drink from. Their earliest pretend acts usually imitate adults' actions and are not yet flexible. Children younger than age 2, for example, will pretend to drink from a cup but refuse to pretend a cup is a hat (Rakoczy, Tomasello, & Striano, 2005). They have trouble using an object (cup) that already has an obvious use as a symbol of another object (hat).

  After age 2, children pretend with less realistic toys—for example, a block for a telephone receiver. Gradually, they can imagine objects and events without any support from the real world, as Sammy's imaginary control tower illustrates (O'Reilly, 1995; Striano, Tomasello, & Rochat, 2001). And by age 3, they flexibly understand that an object (a yellow stick) may take on one fictional identity (a toothbrush) in one pretend game and another fictional identity (a carrot) in a different pretend game (Wyman, Rakoczy, & Tomasello, 2009).
- *Play becomes less self-centered.* At first, make-believe is directed toward the self. For example, Dwayne pretends to feed only himself. Soon, children begin to direct pretend actions toward objects, as when a child feeds a doll. Early in the third year, they become detached participants, making a doll feed itself or pushing a button to launch a rocket (McCune, 1993). Make-believe becomes less self-centered as children realize that agents and recipients of pretend actions can be independent of themselves.
- *Play includes more complex combinations of schemes.* Dwayne can pretend to drink from a cup, but he does not yet combine drinking with pouring. Later, children combine schemes with those of peers in **sociodramatic play,** the make-believe with others that is under way by the end of the second year and that increases rapidly in complexity during early childhood (Kavanaugh, 2006a). Already, Sammy and his classmates can create and coordinate several roles in an elaborate plot. By the end of the preschool years, children have a sophisticated understanding of role relationships and story lines.

LOOK and LISTEN

Observe the make-believe play of several 2- to 4-year-olds at home or in a preschool or child-care center. Describe pretend acts that exemplify important developmental changes.

Children as young as age 2 display awareness that make-believe is a representational activity. They distinguish make-believe from real experiences and grasp that pretending is a deliberate effort to act out imaginary ideas— an understanding that strengthens over early childhood (Rakoczy, Tomasello, & Striano, 2004; Sobel, 2006). **TAKE A MOMENT...** Listen closely to preschoolers as they assign roles and negotiate plans in sociodramatic play: "*You pretend to be* the astronaut, *I'll act like* I'm operating the control tower!*" *"Wait, *I gotta set up* the spaceship." In communicating about pretend, children think about their own and others' fanciful representations—evidence that they have begun to reason about people's mental activities, a topic we will return to later in this chapter.

BENEFITS OF MAKE-BELIEVE   Today, Piaget's view of make-believe as mere practice of representational schemes is regarded as too limited. Play not only reflects but also contributes to children's cognitive and social skills. Socio-dramatic play has been studied most thoroughly. Compared with social nonpretend activities (such as drawing

Make-believe play increases in sophistication during the preschool years. Children increasingly coordinate make-believe roles and pretend with less realistic toys. These children "drive," using plastic flower plates as steering wheels.

or putting puzzles together), during sociodramatic play preschoolers' interactions last longer, show more involvement, draw more children into the activity, and are more cooperative (Creasey, Jarvis, & Berk, 1998).

It is not surprising, then, that preschoolers who spend more time in sociodramatic play are rated by observers as more socially competent a year later (Lindsey & Colwell, 2013). And many studies reveal that make-believe strengthens a wide variety of cognitive capacities: sustained attention, inhibiting impulses, memory, logical reasoning, language and literacy (including story comprehension and storytelling skills), imagination, creativity, and the ability to reflect on one's own thinking, regulate one's own behavior, and take another's perspective (Berk & Meyers, 2013; Buchsbaum et al., 2012; Carlson & White, 2013; Mottweiler & Taylor, 2014; Nicolopoulou & Ilgaz, 2013; Roskos & Christie, 2013).

Between 25 and 45 percent of preschoolers and young school-age children spend much time in solitary make-believe, creating *imaginary companions*—special fantasized friends endowed with humanlike qualities. For example, one preschooler created Nutsy and Nutsy, a pair of boisterous birds who lived outside her bedroom window and often went along on family outings (Gleason, Sebanc, & Hartup, 2000; Taylor et al., 2004). Imaginary companions were once viewed as a sign of maladjustment, but research challenges this assumption. Children with an invisible playmate typically treat it with care and affection and say it offers caring, comfort, and good company, just as their real friendships do (Gleason & Hohmann, 2006; Hoff, 2005). Such children also display more complex and imaginative pretend play, are advanced in understanding others' viewpoints and emotions, and are more sociable with peers (Bouldin, 2006; Gleason, 2013; Taylor & Carlson, 1997; Trionfi & Reese, 2009).

Applying What We Know on page 314 lists ways to enhance preschoolers' make-believe. Later we will return to the origins and consequences of make-believe from an alternative perspective—that of Vygotsky.

Symbol–Real-World Relations

In a corner of the classroom, Leslie set up a dollhouse, replete with tiny furnishings. Sammy liked to arrange the furniture to match his real-world living room, kitchen, and bedroom. Representations of reality, like Sammy's, are powerful cognitive tools. When we understand that a picture, model, or map corresponds to something specific in everyday life, we can use these tools to find out about objects and places we have not experienced.

In Chapter 6, we saw that by the middle of the second year, children grasp the symbolic function of realistic-looking pictures (such as photos). When do children comprehend scale

Applying What We Know

Enhancing Make-Believe Play in Early Childhood

STRATEGY	DESCRIPTION
Provide sufficient space and play materials.	Generous space and materials allow for many play options and reduce conflict.
Encourage children's play without controlling it.	Model, guide, and build on young preschoolers' play themes. Provide open-ended suggestions (for example, "Would the animals like a train ride?"), and talk with the child about the thoughts, motivations, and emotions of play characters. These forms of adult support lead to more elaborate pretending. Refrain from directing the child's play; excessive adult control destroys the creativity and pleasure of make-believe.
Offer a variety of both realistic materials and materials without clear functions.	Children use realistic materials, such as trucks, dolls, tea sets, dress-up clothes, and toy scenes (house, farm, garage, airport) to act out everyday roles in their culture. Materials without clear functions (such as blocks, cardboard cylinders, paper bags, and sand) inspire fantastic role play, such as "pirate" and "creature from outer space."
Ensure that children have many rich, real-world experiences to inspire positive fantasy play.	Opportunities to participate in real-world activities with adults and to observe adult roles in the community provide children with rich social knowledge to integrate into make-believe. Restricting television viewing, especially programs with violent content, limits the degree to which violent themes and aggressive behavior become part of children's play. (See Chapter 10, pages 381–383.)
Help children solve social conflicts constructively.	Cooperation is essential for sociodramatic play. Guide children toward positive relationships with agemates by helping them resolve disagreements constructively. For example, ask, "What could you do if you want a turn?" If the child cannot think of possibilities, suggest options, and assist the child in implementing them.

Sources: Nielsen & Christie, 2008; Weisberg et al., 2013.

models as symbols for real-world spaces? In one study, 2½- and 3-year-olds watched an adult hide a small toy (Little Snoopy) in a scale model of a room and then were asked to retrieve it. Next, they had to find a larger toy (Big Snoopy) hidden in the room that the model represented. Not until age 3 could most children use the model as a guide to finding Big Snoopy in the real room (DeLoache, 1987). The 2½-year-olds did not realize that the model could be both *a toy room* and *a symbol of another room*. They had trouble with **dual representation**—viewing a symbolic object as both an object in its own right and a symbol.

In support of this interpretation, when researchers made the model room less prominent as an object, by placing it behind a window and preventing children from touching it, more 2½-year-olds succeeded at the search task (DeLoache, 2002). Recall, also, that in make-believe play, 1½- to 2-year-olds cannot use an object that has an obvious use (cup) to stand for another object (hat). Likewise, most 2-year-olds do not yet grasp that a line drawing—an object in its own right—also represents real-world objects (see page 304 in Chapter 8).

Similarly, when presented with objects disguised in various ways and asked what each "looks like" and what each "is really and truly," preschoolers have difficulty. For example, when asked whether a stone painted to look like an egg is "really and truly" an egg, children younger than age 6 often responded "yes" (Flavell, Green, & Flavell, 1987). But simplify these *appearance–reality tasks* by permitting children to solve them nonverbally, by selecting from an

Children who experience a variety of symbols come to understand dual representation—for example, that this dollhouse is both an object in its own right and can stand for another, a full-sized house that people live in.

array of objects the one that "really" has a particular identity, and most 3-year-olds perform well (Deák, Ray, & Brenneman, 2003). They realize that an object can be one thing (a stone) while symbolizing another (an egg).

How do children grasp the dual representation of symbolic objects? When adults point out similarities between models and real-world spaces, 2½-year-olds perform better on the find-Snoopy task (Peralta de Mendoza & Salsa, 2003). Also, insight into one type of symbol–real-world relation helps preschoolers master others. For example, children regard realistic-looking pictures as symbols early, around 1½ to 2 years, because a picture's primary purpose is to stand for something; it is not an interesting object in its own right (Simcock & DeLoache, 2006). And 3-year-olds who can use a model of a room to locate Big Snoopy readily transfer their understanding to a simple map (Marzolf & DeLoache, 1994).

In sum, exposing young children to diverse symbols—picture books, photographs, drawings, make-believe, and maps—helps them appreciate that one object can stand for another. With age, children come to understand a wide range of symbols that have little physical similarity to what they represent (Liben, 2009). As a result, doors open to vast realms of knowledge.

Limitations of Preoperational Thought

Aside from gains in representation, Piaget described preschoolers in terms of what they *cannot* understand. As the term *preoperational* suggests, he compared them to older, more competent children who have reached the concrete operational stage. According to Piaget, young children are not capable of *operations*—mental representations of actions that obey logical rules. Rather, their thinking is rigid, limited to one aspect of a situation at a time, and strongly influenced by the way things appear at the moment.

EGOCENTRIC AND ANIMISTIC THINKING For Piaget, the most fundamental deficiency of preoperational thinking is **egocentrism**—failure to distinguish the symbolic viewpoints of others from one's own. He believed that when children first mentally represent the world, they tend to focus on their own viewpoint and assume that others perceive, think, and feel the same way they do.

Piaget's most convincing demonstration of egocentrism involves his *three-mountains problem,* described in Figure 9.1. He also regarded egocentrism as responsible for preoperational children's **animistic thinking**—the belief that inanimate objects have lifelike qualities, such as thoughts, wishes, feelings, and intentions (Piaget, 1926/1930). Recall Sammy's insistence that someone must have turned on the thunder. According to Piaget, because young children egocentrically assign human purposes to physical events, magical thinking is common during the preschool years.

Piaget argued that preschoolers' egocentric bias prevents them from *accommodating,* or reflecting on and revising their faulty reasoning in response to their physical and social worlds. To understand this shortcoming, let's consider some additional tasks that Piaget gave to children.

INABILITY TO CONSERVE Piaget's famous conservation tasks reveal several deficiencies of preoperational thinking. **Conservation** refers to the idea that certain physical characteristics of objects remain the same, even when their outward appearance changes. At snack time, Sammy and Priti had identical boxes of raisins, but when Priti spread her raisins out on the table, Sammy was convinced that she had more.

In another conservation task involving liquid, the child is shown two identical tall glasses of water and asked if they contain equal

FIGURE 9.1 Piaget's three-mountains problem. Each mountain is distinguished by its color and by its summit. One has a red cross, another a small house, and the third a snow-capped peak. Children at the preoperational stage respond egocentrically. They cannot select a picture that shows the mountains from the doll's perspective. Instead, they simply choose the photo that reflects their own vantage point.

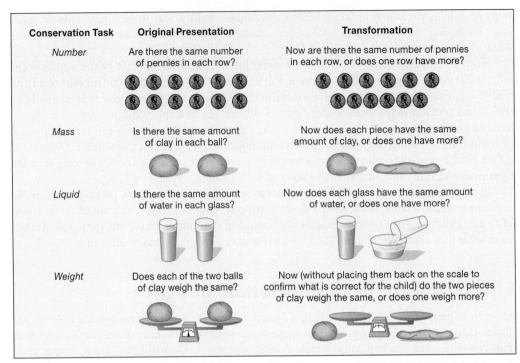

Conservation Task	Original Presentation	Transformation
Number	Are there the same number of pennies in each row?	Now are there the same number of pennies in each row, or does one row have more?
Mass	Is there the same amount of clay in each ball?	Now does each piece have the same amount of clay, or does one have more?
Liquid	Is there the same amount of water in each glass?	Now does each glass have the same amount of water, or does one have more?
Weight	Does each of the two balls of clay weigh the same?	Now (without placing them back on the scale to confirm what is correct for the child) do the two pieces of clay weigh the same, or does one weigh more?

FIGURE 9.2 **Some Piagetian conservation tasks.** Children at the preoperational stage cannot yet conserve. These tasks are mastered gradually over the concrete operational stage. Children in Western nations typically acquire conservation of number, mass, and liquid sometime between 5 and 7 years and conservation of weight between 8 and 10 years.

amounts. Once the child agrees, the water in one glass is poured into a short, wide container, changing its appearance but not its amount. Then the child is asked whether the amount of water is the same or has changed. Preoperational children think the quantity has changed. They explain, "There is less now because the water is way down here" (that is, its level is so low) or, "There is more now because it is all spread out." Figure 9.2 illustrates other conservation tasks that you can try with children.

The inability to conserve highlights several related aspects of preoperational children's thinking. First, their understanding is *centered*, or characterized by **centration.** They focus on one aspect of a situation, neglecting other important features. In conservation of liquid, the child *centers* on the height of the water, failing to realize that changes in width compensate for the changes in height. Second, children are easily distracted by the *perceptual appearance* of objects. Third, children treat the initial and final *states* of the water as unrelated events, ignoring the *dynamic transformation* (pouring of water) between them.

The most important illogical feature of preoperational thought is its **irreversibility**—an inability to mentally go through a series of steps in a problem and then reverse direction, returning to the starting point. *Reversibility* is part of every logical operation. After Priti spills her raisins, Sammy cannot reverse by thinking, "I know Priti doesn't have more raisins than I do. If we put them back in that little box, her raisins and mine would look just the same."

LACK OF HIERARCHICAL CLASSIFICATION Preoperational children have difficulty with **hierarchical classification**—the organization of objects into classes and subclasses on the basis of similarities and differences. Piaget's famous *class inclusion problem*, illustrated in Figure 9.3, demonstrates this limitation. Preoperational children *center* on the overriding feature, red. They do not think reversibly, moving from the whole class (flowers) to the parts (red and blue) and back again.

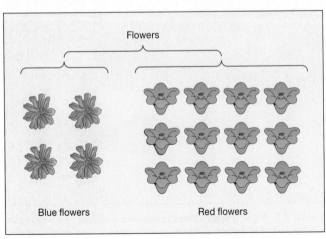

FIGURE 9.3 **A Piagetian class inclusion problem.** Children are shown 16 flowers, 4 of which are blue and 12 of which are red. Asked, "Are there more red flowers or flowers?" the preoperational child responds, "More red flowers," failing to realize that both red and blue flowers are included in the category "flowers."

Follow-Up Research on Preoperational Thought

Over the past three decades, researchers have challenged Piaget's view of preschoolers as cognitively deficient. Because many Piagetian problems contain unfamiliar elements or too many pieces of information for young children to handle at once, preschoolers' responses often do not reflect their true abilities. Piaget also missed many naturally occurring instances of effective reasoning by preschoolers. Let's look at some examples.

EGOCENTRIC, ANIMISTIC, AND MAGICAL THINKING Do young children really believe that a person standing elsewhere in a room sees exactly what they see? When researchers use simplified tasks with familiar objects, 3-year-olds show clear awareness of others' vantage points, such as recognizing how something looks to another person who is looking at it through a color filter (Moll & Meltzoff, 2011). Even 2-year-olds realize that what they see sometimes differs from what another person sees. When asked to help an adult look for a lost object, 24-month-olds (but not 18-month-olds) handed her a toy resting behind a bucket that was within their line of sight but not the adult's (Moll & Tomasello, 2006).

Nonegocentric responses also appear in young children's conversations. For example, preschoolers adapt their speech to fit the needs of their listeners. Four-year-olds use shorter, simpler expressions when talking to 2-year-olds than to agemates or adults (Gelman & Shatz, 1978). And in describing objects, children do not use such words as "big" and "little" in a rigid, egocentric fashion. Instead, they *adjust* their descriptions to allow for context. By age 3, children judge a 2-inch shoe as little when seen by itself (because it is much smaller than most shoes) but as big for a tiny 5-inch-tall doll (Ebeling & Gelman, 1994).

In previous chapters, we saw that toddlers have already begun to infer others' intentions and perspectives. And in his later writings, Piaget (1945/1951) did describe preschoolers' egocentrism as a *tendency* rather than an inability. As we revisit the topic of perspective taking, we will see that it develops gradually throughout childhood and adolescence.

Piaget also overestimated preschoolers' animistic beliefs. Even infants have begun to distinguish animate from inanimate, as indicated by their remarkable categorical distinctions among living and nonliving things (see Chapter 6, page 219). By age 2½, children give psychological explanations ("he likes to" or "she wants to") for people and other animals but rarely for objects (Hickling & Wellman, 2001). And 3- to 5-year-olds asked whether a variety of animals and objects can eat, grow, talk, think, remember, see, or feel mostly attribute these capacities to animals, not objects. In addition, they rarely attribute biological properties (like eating and growing) to robots, indicating that they are well aware that even a self-moving object with lifelike features is not alive. But unlike adults, preschoolers often say that robots have perceptual and psychological capacities—for example, seeing, thinking, and remembering (Jipson & Gelman, 2007; Subrahmanyam, Gelman, & Lafosse, 2002). These responses result from incomplete knowledge about certain objects, and they decline with age.

Similarly, preschoolers think that magic accounts for events they otherwise cannot explain, as in Sammy's magical explanation of thunder in the opening to this chapter. But their notions of magic are flexible and appropriate. For example, older 3-year-olds and 4-year-olds think that violations of physical laws (walking through a wall) and mental laws (turning on the TV just by thinking about it) require magic more than violations of social conventions (taking a bath with shoes on) (Browne & Woolley, 2004). And they are more likely to say that a magical process—wishing—caused an event (an object to appear in a box) when a person made the wish before the event occurred, the event was consistent with the wish (the wished-for object rather than another object appeared in the box), and no alternative causes

Three- to 5-year-olds distinguish between animate and inanimate and realize, for example, that a robot with lifelike features cannot eat or grow. But because of incomplete knowledge, they often claim that robots have perceptual and psychological capacities, such as seeing, thinking, and remembering.

© TATSUYUKI TAYAMA/FUJIFOTOS/THE IMAGE WORKS

were apparent (Woolley, Browne, & Boerger, 2006). These features of causality are the same ones preschoolers rely on in ordinary situations.

Between ages 4 and 8, as children gain familiarity with physical events and principles, their magical beliefs decline. They figure out who is really behind Santa Claus and the Tooth Fairy, and they realize that magicians' feats are due to trickery (Woolley & Cornelius, 2013). And increasingly, children say that events in fantastical stories couldn't really happen and that characters in such stories aren't real (Woolley & Cox, 2007). Still, because children entertain the possibility that something they imagine might materialize, they may react with anxiety to scary stories, TV shows, and nightmares.

Religion and culture play a role in children's fantastic and supernatural ideas. For example, Jewish children are more likely than their Christian agemates to express disbelief in Santa Claus and the Tooth Fairy. Having heard at home that Santa is imaginary, they seem to generalize this attitude to other unseen agents (Woolley, 1997). And cultural myths about wishing—for example, the custom of making a wish before blowing out birthday candles—probably underlie the conviction of most 3- to 6-year-olds that by wishing, you can sometimes make your desires come true (Woolley, 2000).

In actuality, both children and adults endorse natural and supernatural accounts of hard-to-explain events, with these types of explanations coexisting. Children, however, prefer natural over supernatural explanations, even in cultures that strongly endorse supernatural beliefs (Woolley, Cornelius, & Lacey, 2011). In one study, researchers asked 5- to 15-year-olds living in South African communities where witchcraft beliefs were widespread to explain why certain people got AIDS (Legare & Gelman, 2008). Children of all ages—even 5-year-olds—more often gave biological explanations (contact with a sick person, exposure to germs) than bewitchment explanations (a neighbor cast a spell). Bewitchment accounts increased in middle childhood, as children acquired their culture's belief system, but they did not replace biological explanations. And children mentioned witchcraft as a cause of serious illness far less often than did adults!

LOGICAL THOUGHT   Many studies show that when preschoolers are given tasks that are simplified and made relevant to their everyday lives, they do not display the illogical characteristics that Piaget saw in the preoperational stage. For example, when a conservation-of-number task is scaled down to include only three items instead of six or seven, 3-year-olds perform well (Gelman, 1972). And when preschoolers are asked carefully worded questions about what happens to substances (such as sugar) after they are dissolved in water, they give accurate explanations. Most 3- to 5-year-olds know that the substance is conserved—that it continues to exist, can be tasted, and makes the liquid heavier, even though it is invisible in the water (Au, Sidle, & Rollins, 1993; Rosen & Rozin, 1993).

Preschoolers' ability to reason about transformations is evident on other problems. They can engage in impressive *reasoning by analogy* about physical changes. When presented with the picture-matching problem "Play dough is to cut-up play dough as apple is to . . .?," even 3-year-olds choose the correct answer (a cut-up apple) from a set of alternatives, several of which (a bitten apple, a cut-up loaf of bread) share physical features with the right choice (Goswami, 1996). These findings indicate that in familiar contexts, preschoolers can overcome appearances and think logically about cause and effect.

Finally, even without detailed biological or mechanical knowledge, preschoolers realize that the insides of animals are responsible for certain cause–effect sequences (such as willing oneself to move) that are impossible for nonliving things, such as machines (Gelman, 2003; Keil & Lockhart, 1999). Preschoolers seem to use illogical reasoning only when they must grapple with unfamiliar topics, too much information, or contradictory facts that they cannot reconcile.

CATEGORIZATION   Despite their difficulty with Piagetian class inclusion tasks, preschoolers organize their everyday knowledge into nested categories at an early age. By the beginning of early childhood, children's categories include objects that go together because of their common function, behavior, or natural kind (animate versus inanimate), challenging Piaget's assumption that preschoolers' thinking is wholly governed by perceptual appearances.

LOOK and LISTEN

Try the conservation of number and mass tasks in Figure 9.2 with a 3- or 4-year-old. Next, simplify conservation of number by reducing the number of pennies, and relate conservation of mass to the child's experience by pretending the clay is baking dough and transforming it into cupcakes. Did the child perform more competently?

Indeed, 2- to 5-year-olds readily draw appropriate inferences about non-observable characteristics shared by category members. For example, after being told that a bird has warm blood and that a stegosaurus (dinosaur) has cold blood, preschoolers infer that a pterodactyl (labeled a dinosaur) has cold blood, even though it closely resembles a bird (Gopnik & Nazzi, 2003). And when shown a set of three characters—two of whom look different but share an inner trait ("outgoing") and two of whom look similar but have different inner traits (one "shy," one "outgoing")—preschoolers rely on the trait category, not physical appearance, to predict similar preferred activities (Heyman & Gelman, 2000).

Nevertheless, when most instances of a category have a certain perceptual property (such as long ears), preschoolers readily categorize on the basis of perceptual features. This indicates that they flexibly use different types of information to classify, depending on the situation (Rakison & Lawson, 2013). And past experiences influence which information they decide to use. When Native-American 5-year-olds growing up on the Menominee Reservation in northern Wisconsin were compared with 5-year-olds growing up in Boston, the Menominee children often used relations in the natural world to categorize animals. For example, they grouped together wolves and eagles because of their shared forest habitat (Ross et al., 2003). The Boston children, in contrast, mostly relied on common features of the animals.

During the second and third years, and perhaps earlier, children's categories differentiate. They form many *basic-level categories*—ones at an intermediate level of generality, such as "chairs," "tables," and "beds." By the third year, children easily move back and forth between basic-level categories and *general categories,* such as "furniture." And they break down basic-level categories into *subcategories,* such as "rocking chairs" and "desk chairs."

Preschoolers' rapidly expanding vocabularies and general knowledge support their impressive skill at categorizing, and they benefit greatly from conversations with adults, who frequently label and explain categories to young children. When adults use the word *bird* for hummingbirds, turkeys, and swans, they signal to children that something other than physical similarity binds these instances together (Gelman, 2003, 2006; Gelman & Kalish, 2006). Picture-book reading is an especially rich context for understanding categories. In conversing about books with their preschoolers, parents provide information that guides children's inferences about the structure of categories: "Penguins live at the South Pole, swim, catch fish, and have thick layers of fat and feathers that help them stay warm." Furthermore, as the Social Issues: Education box on page 320 indicates, young children ask many questions about their world and generally get informative answers, which are particularly well-suited to advancing their conceptual understanding.

In sum, although preschoolers' category systems are less complex than those of older children and adults, they already have the capacity to classify hierarchically and on the basis of nonobvious properties. And they use logical, causal reasoning to identify the features that form the basis of a category and to classify new members.

These 4-year-olds understand that a category ("dinosaurs") can be based on underlying characteristics ("cold-blooded"), not just on perceptual features such as upright posture and scaly skin.

Evaluation of the Preoperational Stage

Table 9.1 on page 321 provides an overview of the cognitive attainments of early childhood just considered. **TAKE A MOMENT...** Compare them with Piaget's description of the preoperational child on pages 315–316. The evidence as a whole indicates that Piaget was partly wrong and partly right about young children's cognitive capacities. When given simplified tasks based on familiar experiences, preschoolers show the beginnings of logical thinking. How can we make sense of the contradictions between Piaget's conclusions and the findings of recent research?

That preschoolers have some logical understandings that strengthen with age indicates that they attain logical operations gradually. Over time, children rely on increasingly effective mental (as opposed to perceptual) approaches to solving problems. For example, children who

Social Issues: Education

Children's Questions: Catalyst for Cognitive Development

"Dad, what's that?" asked 4-year-old Emily as her father chopped vegetables for dinner.

"It's an onion," her father said.

"Is an onion a fruit?" Emily asked.

"It's a vegetable," her father replied. "A root vegetable because it grows underground."

Emily wrinkled her nose. "Why does it smell yucky?"

"I don't know," her father admitted. "But after dinner we can look it up online and find out."

When young children converse with adults, they ask, on average, more than one question per minute! Do inquisitive children like Emily really want answers to their many questions? Or are they—as their parents sometimes conclude—merely clamoring for attention?

An analysis of diaries that parents diverse in SES and ethnicity kept of their children's questions and of audio recordings of parent–child interactions revealed that at every age between 1 and 5 years, 70 to 90 percent of children's questions were information-seeking ("What's that [pointing to a crawfish]?") as opposed to non-information-seeking ("Can I have a cookie?") (Chouinard, 2007). And from age 2 on, children increasingly built on their fact-oriented questions with follow-up questions that asked for causes and explanations ("What do crawfish eat?" "Why does it have claws?"). By age 3½, these sets of "building questions" made up about half of children's questions, confirming that preschoolers ask questions purposefully, to obtain clarifying information about things that puzzle them.

Answers to children's questions provide them with the precise knowledge they need at the precise moment they need it. Even before children can talk, they ask questions by gesturing at objects in their environment. A pointing gesture, for example, might lead a parent to say, "That's a ball. See, it bounces!" And the content

of children's questions is related to their cognitive development. At a time when vocabulary is advancing rapidly, about 60 percent of 1½- to 2-year-olds' questions ask for names of objects. With age, preschoolers increasingly ask about function ("What's it do?"), activity ("What's he doing?"), state ("Is she hungry?"), and theory of mind ("How does the pilot *know* where to fly?").

Context also makes a difference. Compared with everyday situations, a visit to a zoo elicits many more questions about biological information from 2- to 4-year-olds: "Why is the lion sleeping?" "Is he dead?" "What do bats eat?" "Will the baby lion grow bigger?" Biological questions calling for explanations increased with age as 3- and 4-year-olds tried to make sense of such processes as growth, life, illness, and death—concepts they are currently grappling with and that will soon advance (see page 418 in Chapter 11).

The usefulness of children's questions depends on adults' answers. Most of the time, parents respond informatively. If they do not, preschoolers often express dissatisfaction (Frazier, Gelman, & Wellman, 2009). And they can be amazingly persistent, asking again until they get the information they want. Especially for 1- and 2-year-olds, parents often respond with additional relevant knowledge aimed at enhancing children's understanding and guiding further thinking. Parents also adjust the complexity of their answers to fit their children's maturity (Callanan & Oakes, 1992). To a question like "Why does the light come on?" 3-year-olds typically get simpler, "prior cause" explanations ("I turned on the switch"). Slightly older children

Preschoolers' questions are often purposeful efforts to understand things that puzzle them. Because adults' answers provide the precise knowledge children need at the precise moment they need it, question-asking is a powerful source of cognitive development.

frequently get "mechanism" explanations ("The switch allows electricity to reach the light bulb").

In non-Western village cultures, young children engage in question asking just as often as their Western counterparts, but they rarely ask why-questions, aimed at getting explanations. As we will see later in this chapter, preschoolers in village societies are included in nearly all aspects of family and community life, reducing their need to ask adults to explain (Gauvain, Munroe, & Beebe, 2012). In contrast, Western children's explanatory questions are important for acquiring the wide-ranging knowledge needed to make sense of their complex world, much of which children cannot directly experience.

Clearly, asking questions is a major means through which Western children strive to attain adultlike understandings. Children's questions offer parents and teachers a fascinating window into their factual and conceptual knowledge, along with a wealth of opportunities to help them learn.

cannot use counting to compare two sets of items do not conserve number. Rather, they rely on perceptual cues to compare the amounts in two sets of items (Rouselle, Palmers, & Noël, 2004). Once preschoolers can count, they apply this skill to conservation-of-number tasks involving just a few items. As counting improves, they extend the strategy to problems with more items. By age 6, they understand that number remains the same after a transformation in the length and spacing of a set of items as long as nothing is added or taken away (Halford & Andrews, 2011). Consequently, they no longer need to count to verify their answer.

Evidence that preschool children can be trained to perform well on Piagetian problems also supports the idea that operational thought is not absent at one point in time and present at another (Ping & Goldin-Meadow, 2008; Siegler & Svetina, 2006). Children who possess some understanding would naturally benefit from training, unlike those with no understanding at

TABLE 9.1	Some Cognitive Attainments of Early Childhood

APPROXIMATE AGE		COGNITIVE ATTAINMENTS
2–4 years	© ELLEN B. SENISI/THE IMAGE WORKS	Shows a dramatic increase in representational activity, as reflected in the development of language, make-believe play, understanding of dual representation, and categorization
		Takes the perspective of others in simplified, familiar situations and in everyday, face-to-face communication
		Distinguishes animate beings from inanimate objects; prefers natural over supernatural explanations for events
		Grasps conservation, notices transformations, reverses thinking, and understands many cause-and-effect relationships in simplified, familiar situations
		Categorizes objects on the basis of common function, behavior, and natural kind as well as perceptual features, depending on context; uses inner causal features to categorize objects varying widely in external appearance
		Sorts familiar objects into hierarchically organized categories
4–7 years	RYAN McVAY/ PHOTODISC/GETTY IMAGES	Becomes increasingly aware that make-believe (and other thought processes) are representational activities
		Replaces beliefs in magical creatures and events with plausible explanations
		Passes Piaget's conservation of number, mass, and liquid problems

all. The gradual development of logical operations poses a serious challenge to Piaget's assumption of abrupt change toward logical reasoning around age 6 or 7. Does a preoperational stage really exist? Some no longer think so. Recall from Chapter 6 that according to the information-processing perspective, children work out their understanding of each type of task separately, and their thought processes are basically the same at all ages—just present to a greater or lesser extent.

Other experts think that the stage concept is still valid, with modifications. For example, some *neo-Piagetian theorists* combine Piaget's stage approach with the information-processing emphasis on task-specific change (Case, 1998; Halford & Andrews, 2011). They believe that Piaget's strict stage definition must be transformed into a less tightly knit concept, one in which a related set of competencies develops over an extended period, depending on brain development and specific experiences. These investigators point to findings indicating that as long as the complexity of tasks and children's exposure to them are carefully controlled, children approach those tasks in similar, stage-consistent ways (Andrews & Halford, 2002; Case & Okamoto, 1996). For example, in drawing pictures, preschoolers depict objects separately, ignoring their spatial arrangement (return to the drawing in Figure 8.9 on page 304 for an example). In understanding stories, they grasp a single story line but have trouble with a main plot plus one or more subplots.

This flexible stage notion recognizes the unique qualities of early childhood thinking. At the same time, it provides a better account of why, as Leslie put it, "Preschoolers' minds are such a blend of logic, fantasy, and faulty reasoning."

Piaget and Education

Three educational principles derived from Piaget's theory continue to influence teacher training and classroom practices, especially during early childhood:

- *Discovery learning.* In a Piagetian classroom, children are encouraged to discover for themselves through spontaneous interaction with the environment. Instead of presenting ready-made knowledge verbally, teachers provide a rich variety of activities designed to promote exploration and discovery, including art, puzzles, table games, dress-up clothing, building blocks, books, measuring tools, natural science tasks, and musical instruments.

- *Sensitivity to children's readiness to learn.* In a Piagetian classroom, teachers introduce activities that build on children's current thinking, challenging their incorrect ways of viewing the world. But they do not try to speed up development by imposing new skills before children indicate they are interested and ready.
- *Acceptance of individual differences.* Piaget's theory assumes that all children go through the same sequence of development, but at different rates. Therefore, teachers must plan activities for individual children and small groups, not just for the whole class. In addition, teachers evaluate each child's educational progress in relation to the child's previous development, rather than on the basis of normative standards, or average performance of same-age peers.

Like his stages, educational applications of Piaget's theory have met with criticism, especially his insistence that young children learn primarily through acting on the environment (Brainerd, 2003). As we have already seen, children also use language-based routes to knowledge—a point emphasized by Vygotsky's sociocultural theory, to which we now turn. Nevertheless, Piaget's influence on education has been powerful. He gave teachers new ways to observe, understand, and enhance young children's development and offered strong theoretical justification for child-oriented approaches to classroom teaching and learning.

Ask Yourself

- **REVIEW** Select two of the following features of preoperational thought: egocentrism, a focus on perceptual appearances, difficulty reasoning about transformations, and lack of hierarchical classification. Present evidence indicating that preschoolers are more capable thinkers than Piaget assumed.

- **CONNECT** Make-believe play promotes both cognitive and social development (see page 313). Explain why this is so.

- **APPLY** Three-year-old Will understands that his tricycle isn't alive and can't feel or move on its own. But at the beach, while watching the sun dip below the horizon, Will exclaimed, "The sun is tired. It's going to sleep!" What explains this apparent contradiction in Will's reasoning?

- **REFLECT** Did you have an imaginary companion as a young child? If so, what was your companion like, and why did you create it? Were your parents aware of your companion? What was their attitude toward it?

9.4 Describe Vygotsky's perspective on the social origins and significance of children's private speech.

9.5 Describe applications of Vygotsky's theory to education, and evaluate his major ideas.

Vygotsky's Sociocultural Theory

Piaget's de-emphasis on language as a source of cognitive development brought on yet another challenge, this time from Vygotsky's sociocultural theory, which stresses the social context of cognitive development. In Vygotsky's view, the child and the social environment collaborate to mold cognition in culturally adaptive ways. During early childhood, rapid growth of language broadens preschoolers' participation in social dialogues with more knowledgeable individuals, who encourage them to master culturally important tasks. Soon children start to communicate with themselves in much the same way they converse with others. This greatly enhances the complexity of their thinking and their ability to control their own behavior. Let's see how this happens.

Private Speech

TAKE A MOMENT... Watch preschoolers as they play and explore the environment, and you will see that they frequently talk out loud to themselves. For example, as Sammy worked a puzzle, he said, "Where's the red piece? I need the red one. Now, a blue one. No, it doesn't fit. Try it here."

Piaget (1923/1926) called these utterances *egocentric speech,* reflecting his belief that young children have difficulty taking the perspectives of others. Their talk, he said, is often "talk for self" in which they express thoughts in whatever form they happen to occur, regardless of whether a listener can understand. Piaget believed that cognitive development and certain social experiences eventually bring an end to egocentric speech. Specifically, through disagreements with peers, children see that others hold viewpoints different from their own. As a result, egocentric speech declines in favor of social speech, in which children adapt what they say to their listeners.

Vygotsky (1934/1987) disagreed strongly with Piaget's conclusions. Because language helps children think about their mental activities and behavior and select courses of action, Vygotsky saw it as the foundation for all higher cognitive processes, including controlled attention, deliberate memorization and recall, categorization, planning, problem solving, and self-reflection. In Vygotsky's view, children speak to themselves for self-guidance. As they get older and find tasks easier, their self-directed speech is internalized as silent, *inner speech*—the internal verbal dialogues we carry on while thinking and acting in everyday situations.

A 4-year-old talks to herself as she draws. Research supports Vygotsky's theory that children use private speech to guide their thinking and behavior.

Over the past three decades, almost all studies have supported Vygotsky's perspective (Berk & Harris, 2003; Winsler, 2009). As a result, children's self-directed speech is now called **private speech** instead of egocentric speech. Research shows that children use more of it when tasks are appropriately challenging—neither too easy nor too hard but within their *zone of proximal development,* or range of mastery (see page 222 in Chapter 6). For example, Figure 9.4 shows how 5- and 6-year-olds' private speech increased as researchers made a problem-solving task moderately difficult, then decreased as the task became very difficult (Fernyhough & Fradley, 2005).

With age, as Vygotsky predicted, private speech goes underground, changing into whispers and silent lip movements. Furthermore, children who freely use private speech during a challenging activity are more attentive and involved and show better task performance than their less talkative agemates (Al-Namlah, Fernyhough, & Meins, 2006; Benigno et al., 2011; Lidstone, Meins, & Fernyhough, 2010).

Finally, compared with their agemates, children with learning and behavior problems engage in more private speech over a longer period of development (Berk, 2001b; Bono & Bizri, 2014; Winsler et al., 2007). They seem to use private speech to help compensate for impairments in attention and cognitive processing that make many tasks more difficult for them.

Social Origins of Early Childhood Cognition

Where does private speech come from? Recall from Chapter 6 that Vygotsky believed children's learning takes place within the *zone of proximal development*—a range of tasks too difficult for the child to do alone but possible with the help of others. Consider the joint activity of Sammy and his mother, who helps him put together a difficult puzzle:

Sammy: "I can't get this one in." *[Tries to insert a piece in the wrong place.]*

Mother: "Which piece might go down here?" *[Points to the bottom of the puzzle.]*

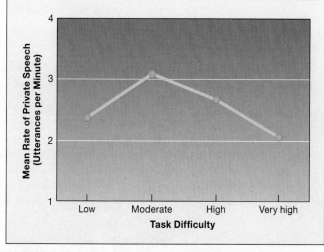

FIGURE 9.4 **Relationship of private speech to task difficulty among 5- and 6-year-olds.** Researchers increased the difficulty of a problem-solving task. Private speech rose as the task became moderately difficult, then declined as it became highly difficult. Children are more likely to use private speech for self-guidance when tasks are within their zone of proximal development, or range of mastery. (Adapted from Fernyhough & Fradley, 2005.)

Sammy: "His shoes." *[Looks for a piece resembling the clown's shoes but tries the wrong one.]*

Mother: "Well, what piece looks like this shape?" *[Pointing again to the bottom of the puzzle.]*

Sammy: "The brown one." *[Tries it, and it fits; then attempts another piece and looks at his mother.]*

Mother: "Try turning it just a little." *[Gestures to show him.]*

Sammy: "There!" *[Puts in several more pieces while his mother watches.]*

By questioning, prompting, and suggesting strategies, Sammy's mother keeps the puzzle within his zone of proximal development, at a manageable level of difficulty.

EFFECTIVE SOCIAL INTERACTION   To promote cognitive development, social interaction must have two vital features. The first is **intersubjectivity,** the process by which two participants who begin a task with different understandings arrive at a shared understanding (Newson & Newson, 1975). Intersubjectivity creates a common ground for communication, as each partner adjusts to the other's perspective. Adults try to promote it when they translate their own insights in ways that are within the child's grasp. As the child stretches to understand the adult, she is drawn into a more mature approach to the situation.

The capacity for intersubjectivity is present early, in parent–infant mutual gaze, exchange of vocal and emotional signals, imitation, and joint play with objects; and in toddlers' capacity to infer others' intentions (Csibra, 2010; Feldman, 2007c). Later, language facilitates intersubjectivity. As conversational skills improve, preschoolers increasingly seek others' help and direct that assistance to ensure that it is beneficial. Between ages 3 and 5, children strive for intersubjectivity in dialogues with peers, as when they affirm a playmate's message, add new ideas, and make contributions to ongoing play to sustain it. They can also be heard saying, "I think [this way]. What do you think?"—evidence of a willingness to share viewpoints (Berk, 2001b). In these ways, children create zones of proximal development for one another.

A second important feature of social experience is **scaffolding**—adjusting the support offered during a teaching session to fit the child's current level of performance. When the child has little notion of how to proceed, the adult uses direct instruction, breaking the task into manageable units, suggesting strategies, and offering rationales for using them. As the child's competence increases, effective scaffolders—like Sammy's mother—gradually and sensitively withdraw support, turning over responsibility to the child. Then children take the language of these dialogues, make it part of their private speech, and use this speech to organize their independent efforts. Although preschoolers freely use private speech when alone or when others are nearby, they use more in the presence of others (McGonigle-Chalmers, Slater, & Smith, 2014). This suggests that some private speech retains a social purpose, perhaps as an indirect appeal for renewed scaffolding should the child need additional help.

Scaffolding captures the form of teaching interaction that occurs as children work on school or school-like tasks, such as puzzles, model building, picture matching, and (later) academic assignments. It may not apply to other contexts that are equally vital for cognitive development—for example, play or everyday activities, during which adults usually support children's efforts without deliberately teaching. To encompass children's diverse opportunities to learn through involvement with others, Barbara Rogoff (1998, 2003) suggests the term **guided participation,** a broader concept than scaffolding. It refers to shared endeavors between more expert and less expert participants, without specifying the precise features of communication. Consequently, it allows for variations across situations and cultures.

LOOK and LISTEN

Ask a preschooler to join you in working a difficult puzzle or another challenging task. How did you scaffold the child's progress? Did the child display any self-guiding private speech?

© LAURA DWIGHT PHOTOGRAPHY

A grandfather engages in scaffolding by breaking a challenging construction task into manageable units, suggesting strategies, and gradually turning over responsibility to his 3-year-old grandchild.

RESEARCH ON SOCIAL INTERACTION AND COGNITIVE DEVELOPMENT What evidence supports Vygotsky's ideas on the social origins of cognitive development? In previous chapters, we reviewed evidence indicating that when adults establish intersubjectivity by being stimulating, responsive, and supportive, they foster many competencies—attention, language, complex play, and understanding of others' perspectives. In several studies, children whose parents were effective scaffolders used more private speech, were more successful when attempting difficult tasks on their own, and were advanced in overall cognitive development (Berk & Spuhl, 1995; Conner & Cross, 2003; Mulvaney et al., 2006).

Nevertheless, effective scaffolding can take different forms in different cultures. In an investigation of Hmong families who had emigrated from Southeast Asia to the United States, once again, parental cognitive support was associated with children's advanced reasoning skills. But unlike Caucasian-American parents, who emphasize independence by encouraging their children to think of ways to approach a task, Hmong parents—who highly value interdependence and child obedience—frequently tell their children what to do (for example, "put this block piece here, then this piece on top of it") (Stright, Herr, & Neitzel, 2009). Among Caucasian-American children, such directive scaffolding is associated with kindergartners' lack of self-control and behavior problems (Neitzel & Stright, 2003). Among the Hmong children, however, it predicted capacity to follow rules, be organized, and finish assignments.

Vygotsky and Early Childhood Education

Both Piagetian and Vygotskian classrooms emphasize active participation and acceptance of individual differences. But a Vygotskian classroom goes beyond independent discovery to promote *assisted discovery.* Teachers guide children's learning with explanations, demonstrations, and verbal prompts, tailoring their interventions to each child's zone of proximal development. Assisted discovery is aided by *peer collaboration,* as children with varying abilities work in groups, teaching and helping one another.

Vygotsky (1935/1978) saw make-believe play as the ideal social context for fostering cognitive development in early childhood. As children create imaginary situations, they learn to follow internal ideas and social rules rather than their immediate impulses. For example, a child pretending to go to sleep follows the rules of bedtime behavior. A child imagining himself as a father and a doll as a child conforms to the rules of parental behavior (Meyers & Berk, 2014). According to Vygotsky, make-believe play is a unique, broadly influential zone of proximal development in which children try out a wide variety of challenging activities and acquire many new competencies.

Turn back to page 313 to review findings that make-believe play enhances a diverse array of cognitive and social skills. Pretending is also rich in private speech—a finding that supports its role in helping children bring action under the control of thought (Krafft & Berk, 1998). Preschoolers who spend more time engaged in sociodramatic play are better at inhibiting impulses, regulating emotion, and taking personal responsibility for following classroom rules (Kelly & Hammond, 2011; Lemche et al., 2003; Ogan & Berk, 2009). These findings support the role of make-believe in children's increasing self-control.

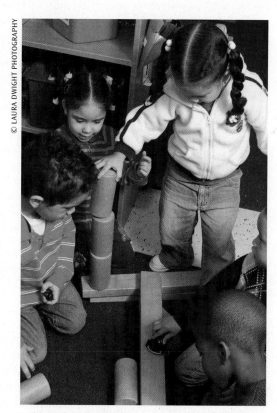

© LAURA DWIGHT PHOTOGRAPHY

In this Vygotksy-inspired classroom, preschoolers benefit from peer collaboration as they jointly create an elaborate block structure.

Evaluation of Vygotsky's Theory

In granting social experience a fundamental role in cognitive development, Vygotsky's theory underscores the vital role of teaching and helps us understand the wide cultural variation in children's cognitive skills. Nevertheless, it has not gone unchallenged. In some cultures, verbal dialogues are not the only—or even the most important—means through which children learn. When Western parents scaffold their young children's mastery of challenging tasks, they

Cultural Influences

Children in Village and Tribal Cultures Observe and Participate in Adult Work

In Western societies, children are largely excluded from participating in adult work, which generally takes place outside the home. The role of equipping children with the skills they need to become competent workers is assigned to school. In early childhood, middle-SES parents' interactions with children emphasize child-focused activities designed to prepare children to succeed academically—especially adult–child conversations and play that enhance language, literacy, and other school-related knowledge. In village and tribal cultures, children receive little or no schooling, spend their days in contact with or participating in adult work, and start to assume mature responsibilities in early childhood (Gaskins, 2013a). Consequently, parents have little need to rely on conversation and play to teach children.

A study comparing 2- and 3-year-olds' daily lives in four cultures—two U.S. middle-SES suburbs, the Efe hunters and gatherers of the Republic of Congo, and a Mayan agricultural town in Guatemala—documented these differences (Morelli, Rogoff, & Angelillo, 2003). In the U.S. communities, young children had little access to adult work and spent much time conversing and playing with adults. In contrast, the Efe and Mayan children rarely engaged in these child-focused activities. Instead, they spent their days close to—and frequently observing—adult work, which often took place in or near the Efe campsite or the Mayan family home.

An ethnography of a remote Mayan village in Yucatán, Mexico, shows that when young children

are legitimate onlookers and participants in a daily life structured around adult work, their competencies differ from those of Western preschoolers (Gaskins, 1999; Gaskins, Haight, & Lancy, 2007). Yucatec Mayan adults are subsistence farmers. Men tend cornfields, aided by sons age 8 and older. Women prepare meals, wash clothes, and care for the livestock and garden, assisted by daughters and by sons too young to work in the fields. Children join in these activities from the second year on. When not participating, they are expected to be self-sufficient. Young children make many nonwork decisions for themselves—how much to sleep and eat, what to wear, when to take their daily bath, and even when to start school. As a result, Yucatec Mayan preschoolers are highly competent at self-care. In contrast, their make-believe play is limited; when it occurs, they usually imitate adult work. Otherwise, they watch others—for hours each day.

Yucatec Mayan parents rarely converse or play with preschoolers or scaffold their learning. Rather, when children imitate adult tasks, parents conclude that they are ready for more responsibility. Then they assign chores, selecting tasks the child can do with little help so that adult work is not disturbed. If a child cannot do a task, the adult takes over and the child observes, reengaging when able to contribute.

A Mayan 3-year-old imitates her mother in balancing a basket of laundry on her head. Children in Guatemalan Mayan culture observe and participate in the work of their community from an early age.

Expected to be autonomous and helpful, Yucatec Mayan children seldom display attention-getting behaviors or ask others for something interesting to do. From an early age, they can sit quietly for long periods—through a lengthy religious service or a three-hour truck ride. And when an adult interrupts their activity and directs them to do a chore, they respond eagerly to the type of command that Western children frequently avoid or resent. By age 5, Yucatec Mayan children spontaneously take responsibility for tasks beyond those assigned.

assume much responsibility for children's motivation by frequently giving verbal instructions and conversing with the child. Their communication resembles the teaching that occurs in school, where their children will spend years preparing for adult life. But in cultures that place less emphasis on schooling and literacy, parents often expect children to take greater responsibility for acquiring new skills through keen observation and participation in community activities (Rogoff, 2003; Rogoff, Correa-Chavez, & Silva, 2011). See the Cultural Influences box above for research illustrating this difference.

Vygotsky's theory has also been criticized for saying little about how basic motor, perceptual, attention, memory, and problem-solving skills, discussed in Chapters 5 and 6, contribute to socially transmitted higher cognitive processes. For example, his theory does not address how these elementary capacities spark changes in children's social experiences, from which more advanced cognition springs (Daniels, 2011; Miller, 2009). Piaget paid far more attention than Vygotsky to the development of basic cognitive processes. It is intriguing to speculate about the broader theory that might exist today had Piaget and Vygotsky—the two twentieth-century giants of cognitive development—had a chance to meet and weave together their extraordinary accomplishments.

Ask Yourself

● **REVIEW** Describe features of social interaction that support children's cognitive development. How does such interaction create a zone of proximal development?

● **CONNECT** Explain how Piaget's and Vygotsky's theories complement each other. How would classroom practices inspired by these theories be similar? How would they differ?

● **APPLY** Tanisha sees her 5-year-old son Toby talking aloud to himself as he plays. She wonders whether she should discourage this behavior. Use Vygotsky's theory to explain why Toby talks to himself. How would you advise Tanisha?

● **REFLECT** When do you use private speech? Does it serve a self-guiding function for you, as it does for children? Explain.

Information Processing

9.6 How do attention, memory, and problem solving change during early childhood?

9.7 Describe the young child's theory of mind.

9.8 Summarize children's literacy and mathematical knowledge during early childhood.

Return to the model of information processing discussed on pages 215–216 in Chapter 6. Recall that information processing focuses on cognitive operations and mental strategies that children use to transform stimuli flowing into their mental systems. As we have already seen, early childhood is a period of dramatic strides in mental representation. And the various components of executive function that enable children to succeed in cognitively challenging situations—attention, impulse control, working memory, and planning—show impressive gains, leading to more efficient and flexible ways of manipulating information and solving problems (Carlson, Zelazo, & Faja, 2013). Preschoolers also become more aware of their own mental life and begin to acquire academically relevant knowledge important for school success.

Attention

As parents and teachers know, preschoolers—compared with school-age children—spend shorter times involved in tasks and are more easily distracted. But recall from Chapter 6 that sustained attention improves in toddlerhood, a trend that continues during early childhood.

INHIBITION   A major reason is a steady gain in children's ability to inhibit impulses and keep their mind on a competing goal. Consider a task in which the child must tap once when the adult taps twice and tap twice when the adult taps once, or must say "night" to a picture of the sun and "day" to a picture of the moon with stars. As Figure 9.5 shows, 3- and 4-year-olds make many errors. But by age 6 to 7, children find such tasks easy (Kirkham, Cruess, & Diamond, 2003; Zelazo et al., 2003). They can resist the "pull" of their attention toward a dominant stimulus—a skill that, as early as age 3 to 5, predicts social maturity as well as subsequent reading and math achievement from kindergarten through high school (Blair & Razza, 2007; Duncan et al., 2007; Rhoades, Greenberg, & Domitrovich, 2009). Simultaneously, ERP and fMRI measures reveal a steady age-related increase in activation of the prefrontal cortex while children engage in activities requiring suppression of inappropriate responses (Bartgis, Lilly, & Thomas, 2003; Luna et al., 2001).

Gains in working memory, enabling preschoolers to hold in mind and manipulate more information at once (see page 215 in Chapter 6), contribute to the development of attention. A larger working memory permits preschoolers to generate increasingly complex play and problem-solving goals, which require concentration to attain (Senn, Espy, & Kaufmann, 2004). Greater working-memory capacity

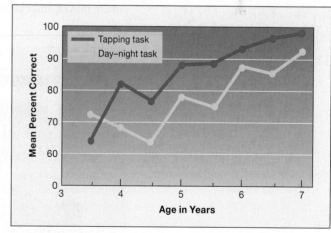

FIGURE 9.5 **Gains between ages 3 and 7 in performance on tasks requiring children to inhibit an impulse and focus on a competing goal.** In the tapping task, children had to tap once when the adult tapped twice and tap twice when the adult tapped once. In the day–night task, children had to say "night" to a picture of the sun and "day" to a picture of the moon with stars. (From A. Diamond, 2004, "Normal Development of Prefrontal Cortex from Birth to Young Adulthood: Cognitive Functions, Anatomy, and Biochemistry," as appeared in D. T. Stuss & R. T. Knight, [Eds.], *Principles of Frontal Lobe Function*, New York: Oxford University Press, p. 474. Reprinted by permission of Adele Diamond.)

Playing Simon Says requires inhibition—refraining from acting when the teacher's command omits "Simon says." These 3- and 4-year-olds find the game challenging. By the end of early childhood, it will be easy.

also eases effort in inhibiting incorrect responses, thereby improving performance.

Adult scaffolding of attention also makes a difference. Preschoolers whose parents offer suggestions, questions, and comments that help the child overcome frustration and sustain direction on a challenging task are more mature, cognitively and socially, when reassessed a year or two later (Bono & Stifter, 2003). In one study, parents' effective scaffolding of 2- and 3-year-olds while solving a complex puzzle predicted higher scores on diverse executive function tasks at age 4, including measures of inhibition and working memory (which, as noted earlier, contributes to attention) (Hammond et al., 2012). Among the 2-year-olds, effective scaffolding was associated with gains in language, which in turn fostered improved executive function, likely by augmenting children's ability to verbally regulate their own behavior through private speech.

PLANNING During early childhood, children also become better at **planning**—thinking out a sequence of acts ahead of time and allocating attention accordingly to reach a goal. As long as tasks are familiar and not too complex, older preschoolers can follow a plan.

Consider a task, devised to resemble real-world planning, in which 3- to 5-year-olds were shown a doll named Molly, a camera, and a miniature zoo with a path, along which were three animal cages. The first and third cages had storage lockers next to them; the middle cage, with no locker, housed a kangaroo (see Figure 9.6). The children were told that Molly could follow the path only once and that she wanted to take a picture of the kangaroo. Then they were asked, "What locker could you leave the camera in so Molly can get it and take a photo of the kangaroo?" (McColgan & McCormack, 2008). Not until age 5 children were children able to plan effectively, selecting the locker at the first cage. On this and other planning tasks, younger preschoolers seem to have difficulty postponing action in favor of mapping out a sequence of future moves and evaluating the consequences of each (McCormack & Atance, 2011; Russell,

FIGURE 9.6 **Miniature zoo used to assess children's planning.** After having been told that Molly wanted to take a picture of the kangaroo but could follow the path only once, preschoolers were asked which locker the camera should be left in so Molly could get it and take the photo. Not until age 5 did children plan, more often selecting the first locker. (Based on McColgan & McCormack, 2008.)

Alexis, & Clayton, 2010). These procedures require inhibition and increased working memory, in addition to planning skill.

Children learn much from cultural tools that support planning—directions for playing games, patterns for construction, recipes for cooking—especially when they collaborate with more expert planners. When 4- to 7-year-olds were observed jointly constructing a toy with their mothers, the mothers provided basic information about the usefulness of plans and how to implement specific steps: "Do you want to look at the picture and see what goes where? What piece do you need first?" After working with their mothers, younger children more often referred to the plan when building on their own (Gauvain, 2004; Gauvain, de la Ossa, & Hurtado-Ortiz, 2001). When parents encourage planning in everyday activities, from loading the dishwasher to packing for a vacation, they help children plan more effectively.

Memory

Unlike infants and toddlers, preschoolers have the language skills to describe what they remember, and they can follow directions on simple memory tasks. As a result, memory becomes easier to study in early childhood.

RECOGNITION AND RECALL TAKE A MOMENT... Show a young child a set of 10 pictures or toys. Then mix them up with some unfamiliar items, and ask the child to point to the ones in the original set. You will find that preschoolers' *recognition* memory—ability to tell whether a stimulus is the same as or similar to one they have seen before—is remarkably good. In fact, 4- and 5-year-olds perform nearly perfectly.

Now keep the items out of view, and ask the child to name the ones she saw. This more demanding task requires *recall*—generating a mental image of an absent stimulus. Young children's recall is much poorer than their recognition. At age 2, they can recall no more than one or two items, and at age 4 only about three or four (Perlmutter, 1984).

Of course, recognition is much easier than recall for adults as well, but in comparison to adults, children's recall is quite deficient. Improvement in recall over the preschool years is strongly associated with language development, which greatly enhances long-lasting representations of both lists of items and past experiences (Melby-Lervag & Hulme, 2010; Ornstein, Haden, & Elischberger, 2006). But even preschoolers with good language skills recall poorly because they are not skilled at using **memory strategies,** deliberate mental activities that improve our chances of remembering. For example, to retain information, you may *rehearse,* repeating the items over and over, or *organize,* intentionally grouping items that are alike so that you can easily retrieve them by thinking of their similar characteristics.

Why do young children seldom use memory strategies? One reason is that strategies tax their limited working memories. Preschoolers have difficulty holding on to pieces of information and applying a strategy at the same time.

MEMORY FOR EVERYDAY EXPERIENCES Think about the difference between your recall of listlike information and your memory for everyday experiences—what researchers call **episodic memory.** In remembering lists, you recall isolated bits, reproducing them exactly as you originally learned them. In remembering everyday experiences, you recall complex, meaningful information. Between 3 and 6 years, children improve sharply in memory for relations among stimuli. For example, in a set of photos, they remember not just the animals they saw but also their contexts, such as a bear emerging from a tunnel or a zebra tied to a tree on a city street (Lloyd, Doydum, & Newcombe, 2009). The capacity to *bind together stimuli* when encoding and retrieving them supports the development of an increasingly rich event memory during early childhood.

Memory for Familiar Events. Like adults, preschoolers remember familiar, repeated events—what you do when you go to child care or have dinner—in terms of **scripts,** general descriptions of what occurs and when it occurs in a particular situation. Young children's scripts begin as a structure of main acts. For example, when asked to tell what happens at a restaurant, a 3-year-old might say, "You go in, get the food, eat, and then pay." Although children's first

Like adults, preschoolers remember familiar, repeated events, such as brushing teeth, in terms of scripts. Over time, children construct more elaborate scripts: "You squeeze out the toothpaste and brush your teeth. You rinse your mouth and then your toothbrush."

scripts contain only a few acts, as long as events in a situation take place in logical order, they are almost always recalled in correct sequence (Bauer, 2002, 2006). With age, scripts become more spontaneous and elaborate, as in this 5-year-old's account of going to a restaurant: "You go in. You can sit in a booth or at a table. Then you tell the waitress what you want. You eat. If you want dessert, you can have some. Then you pay and go home" (Hudson, Fivush, & Kuebli, 1992).

Scripts help children organize, interpret, and predict everyday experiences. Once formed, they can be used to predict what will happen on similar occasions in the future. Children rely on scripts to assist recall when listening to and telling stories. They also act out scripts in make-believe play as they pretend to put the baby to bed, go on a trip, or play school. And scripts support children's earliest efforts at planning by helping them represent sequences of actions that lead to desired goals (Hudson & Mayhew, 2009).

Memory for One-Time Events. In Chapter 6, we considered a second type of episodic memory—*autobiographical memory,* or representations of personally meaningful, one-time events. As 3- to 6-year-olds' cognitive and conversational skills improve, their descriptions of special events become better organized in time, more detailed, enriched with a personal perspective, and related to the larger context of their lives. A young preschooler simply reports, "I went camping." Older preschoolers include specifics: where and when the event happened and who was present. And with age, preschoolers increasingly include subjective information—why, for example, an event was exciting, funny, sad, or made them feel proud or embarrassed—that explains the event's personal significance (Bauer, 2013; Fivush, 2001; Pathman et al., 2013). For example, they might say, "I loved sleeping all night in the tent!"

Adults use two styles to elicit children's autobiographical narratives. In the *elaborative style,* they follow the child's lead, ask varied questions, add information to the child's statements, and volunteer their own recollections and evaluations of events. For example, after a field trip to the zoo, Leslie asked, "What was the first thing we did? Why weren't the parrots in their cages? I thought the roaring lion was scary. What did you think?" In this way, she helped the children reestablish and reorganize their memory of the field trip. In contrast, adults who use the *repetitive style* provide little information and keep repeating the same questions, regardless of the child's interest: "Do you remember the zoo? What did we do at the zoo? What did we do there?"

Preschoolers who experience the elaborative style recall more information about past events and also produce more organized and detailed personal stories when followed up one to two years later (Cleveland & Reese, 2005; Farrant & Reese, 2000). Parents can be trained to use an elaborative style, which also enhances the richness of preschoolers' event memories (Reese & Newcombe, 2007).

As children converse with adults about the past, they not only improve their autobiographical memory but also create a shared history that strengthens close relationships and self-understanding. Parents and preschoolers with secure attachment bonds engage in more elaborate reminiscing (Bost et al., 2006; Reese, Newcombe, & Bird, 2006). And 5- and 6-year-olds of elaborative-style parents describe themselves in clearer, more consistent ways (Bird & Reese, 2006).

Girls tend to have more organized and detailed narratives about past events than boys (Bauer et al., 2007). And compared with Asian children, Western children produce narratives with more talk about their own thoughts and emotions—knowledge that contributes to an appreciation of the personal meaning of events and, therefore, to better recall (Wang, 2008). These differences fit with variations in parent–child conversations. Parents

As this toddler talks about past experiences, his mother responds in an elaborative style, asking varied questions and contributing her own recollections and evaluations of events. Through such conversations, she enriches his autobiographical memory.

reminisce in more detail and talk more about the emotional significance of events with daughters (Fivush, 2009). And cultural valuing of interdependence leads many Asian parents to discourage children from talking about themselves. Chinese parents, for example, engage in less detailed and evaluative past-event dialogues with their preschoolers (Fivush & Wang, 2005; Wang, 2006a).

Consistent with these early experiences, women report an earlier age of first memory and more vivid early memories than men. And Western adults' autobiographical memories include earlier, more detailed events that focus more on their own roles than do the memories of Asians, who tend to highlight the roles of others (Wang, 2006b).

Problem Solving

How do preschoolers use their cognitive competencies to discover new problem-solving strategies? To find out, let's look in on 5-year-old Darryl as he adds marbles tucked into pairs of small bags that Leslie set out on a table.

As Darryl deals with adding each pair, his strategies vary. Sometimes he guesses, without applying any strategy. At other times, he counts from one on his fingers. For example, for bags containing 2 + 4 marbles, his fingers pop up one by one as he exclaims, "One, two, three, four, five, six!" On still other occasions, he starts with the lower digit, 2, and "counts on" ("two, three, four, five, six"). Or he begins with the higher digit, 4, and "counts on" ("four, five, six")— a strategy called *min* because it minimizes the work. Sometimes, he simply retrieves the answer from memory.

To study children's problem solving, Robert Siegler (1996, 2006) used the microgenetic research design (see Chapter 1, page 44), presenting children with many problems over an extended time. He found that children experiment with diverse strategies on many types of problems—basic math facts, numerical estimation, conservation, memory for lists of items, reading first words, spelling, even tic-tac-toe. And their strategy use follows the overlapping-waves pattern shown in Figure 9.7. According to **overlapping-waves theory,** when given challenging problems, children try out various strategies and observe which work best, which work less well, and which are ineffective. Gradually, they select strategies on the basis of two criteria: *accuracy* and *speed*—for basic addition, the *min* strategy. As children home in on effective strategies for solving the problems at hand, correct solutions become more strongly associated with problems, and children display the most efficient strategy—automatic retrieval of the answer.

How do children move from less to more effective strategies? Often they discover faster, more accurate strategies by using more time-consuming techniques. For example, by repeatedly counting on fingers, Darryl began to recognize the number of fingers he held up. Also, certain problems dramatize the need for a better strategy. When Darryl opened a pair of bags, one containing ten marbles and the other with only two, he realized that *min* would be best. Teaching children to reason logically with concepts relevant to the problems is also helpful (Alibali, Phillips, & Fischer, 2009; Siegler & Svetina, 2006). Once Darryl understood that he got the same result regardless of the order in which he combined two sets (3 + 6 = 9 and 6 + 3 = 9), he more often used *min* and arrived at correct answers. Finally, a large improvement in the accuracy of a newly discovered strategy over previous strategies generally leads to rapid adoption of the new approach (Siegler, 2006).

As children transition to automatic retrieval, fMRI evidence reveals reorganized and better integrated activity in networks of brain regions involved in memory-based problem solving (Cho et al.,

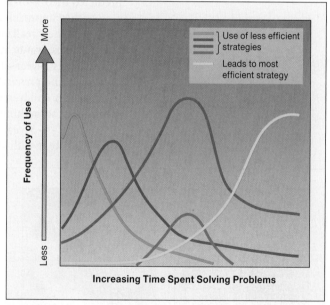

FIGURE 9.7 **Overlapping-waves pattern of strategy use in problem solving.** When given challenging problems, a child generates a variety of strategies, each represented by a wave. The waves overlap because the child tries several different strategies at the same time. Use of each strategy, depicted by the height of the wave, is constantly changing. As the child observes which strategies work best, which work less well, and which are ineffective, the strategy that results in the most rapid, accurate solutions wins out. (From R. S. Siegler, *Emerging Minds: The Process of Change in Children's Thinking.* Copyright © 1996 by Oxford University Press, Inc. Adapted by permission of Oxford University Press, Inc.)

2011). These include the prefrontal cortex, the hippocampus, and other areas in the cerebral cortex known to support long-term retention. Augmented brain functioning, in turn, likely enhances future problem solving.

Many factors, including practice, reasoning, tasks with new challenges, and adult assistance, contribute to gains in problem solving. And experimenting with less mature strategies lets children see the limitations of those techniques. In sum, overlapping-waves theory emphasizes that trying many strategies is vital for developing new, more effective solution techniques. The overlapping-waves pattern characterizes problem solving across a wide range of ages. And in the tradition of the information-processing approach, the theory views development as occurring gradually, rather than in discontinuous stages.

The Young Child's Theory of Mind

As representation of the world, memory, and problem solving improve, children start to reflect on their own thought processes. They begin to construct a *theory of mind*, or coherent set of ideas about mental activities. This understanding is also called **metacognition,** or "thinking about thought" (the prefix *meta-* means "beyond" or "higher"). As adults, we have a complex appreciation of our inner mental worlds, which we use to interpret our own and others' behavior and to improve our performance on various tasks. How early are children aware of their mental lives, and how complete and accurate is their knowledge?

AWARENESS OF MENTAL LIFE   At the end of the first year, babies view people as intentional beings who can share and influence one another's mental states, a milestone that opens the door to new forms of communication—joint attention, social referencing, preverbal gestures, and spoken language. These early milestones serve as the foundation for later mental understandings. In longitudinal research, 10-month-olds' ability to discern others' intentions predicted theory-of-mind competence at age 4 (Wellman et al., 2008).

As they approach age 2, children display a clearer grasp of others' emotions and desires, evident in their realization that people often differ from one another and from themselves in likes, dislikes, wants, needs, and wishes ("Mommy like broccoli. Daddy like carrots. I no like carrots."). As 2-year-olds' vocabularies expand, their first verbs include such words as *think, remember,* and *pretend* (Wellman, 2002).

By age 3, children realize that thinking takes place inside their heads and that a person can think about something without seeing, touching, or talking about it (Flavell, Green, & Flavell, 1995). But 2- to 3-year-olds' verbal responses indicate that they think people always behave in ways consistent with their *desires;* they do not understand that less obvious, more interpretive mental states, such as *beliefs,* also affect behavior. Between ages 3 and 4, children use *think* and *know* to refer to their own and others' thoughts and beliefs (Wellman, 2011). And from age 4 on, they realize that both *beliefs* and *desires* determine behavior.

Dramatic evidence for this advance comes from games that test whether preschoolers realize that *false beliefs*—ones that do not represent reality accurately—can guide people's behavior. **TAKE A MOMENT...** For example, show a child two small closed boxes—a familiar Band-Aid box and a plain, unmarked box (see Figure 9.8). Then say, "Pick the box you think has the Band-Aids in it." Children usually pick the marked container. Next, open the boxes and show the child that, contrary to her own belief, the marked one is empty, and the unmarked one contains the Band-Aids. Finally, introduce the child to a hand puppet and explain, "Here's Pam. She has a cut, see? Where do you think she'll look for Band-Aids? Why would she look in there? Before you looked inside, did you think that the plain box contained the Band-Aids? Why?" (Bartsch & Wellman, 1995). Only a handful of 3-year-olds can explain Pam's—and their own—false beliefs, but many 4-year-olds can.

FIGURE 9.8   Example of a false-belief task. (a) An adult shows a child the contents of a Band-Aid box and of an unmarked box. The Band-Aids are in the unmarked container. (b) The adult introduces the child to a hand puppet named Pam and asks the child to predict where Pam would look for the Band-Aids and to explain Pam's behavior. The task reveals whether children understand that without having seen that the Band-Aids are in the unmarked container, Pam will hold a false belief.

Some researchers claim that the procedures just described, which require verbal responses, grossly underestimate younger children's ability to attribute false beliefs to others. Relying on the violation-of-expectation method (which depends on looking behavior), these investigators assert that children comprehend others' false beliefs by age 15 months (Baillargeon, Scott, & He, 2010). But like other violation-of-expectation evidence, this conclusion is controversial (see page 206 in Chapter 6) (Sirios & Jackson, 2007). Yet in a study relying on active behavior (helping), most 18-month-olds—after observing an adult reach for a box previously used for blocks that now contained a spoon—based their choice of how to help her on her false belief about the contents of the box: They gave her a block rather than a spoon (Buttelmann et al., 2014). This suggests that toddlers *implicitly* understand that people's actions can be guided by false beliefs, though more evidence is needed to confirm this conclusion (Astington & Hughes, 2013). Researchers cannot yet explain the striking contrast between toddlers' success on nonverbal tasks and 3-year-olds' consistent failure on verbal assessments.

Among children of diverse cultural and SES backgrounds, *explicit* false-belief understanding, assessed with verbal tasks, strengthens after age 3½, becoming more secure between ages 4 and 6 (Wellman, 2012). During that time, it becomes a powerful tool for reflecting on the thoughts and emotions of oneself and others and a good predictor of social skills (Hughes, Ensor, & Marks, 2010). Understanding the mind contributes to *selective trust*—the realization that some people are more credible sources of information than others. For example, preschooler's developing grasp of mental states, including false belief, predicts greater willingness to follow the advice of a helpful person as opposed to a trickster, which emerges around age 5 (Vanderbilt, Liu, & Heyman, 2011).

Finally, mastery of false belief is associated with early reading ability, probably because it helps children comprehend story narratives (Astington & Pelletier, 2005). To follow a story line, children generally must link plot actions with characters' motives and beliefs.

FACTORS CONTRIBUTING TO PRESCHOOLERS' THEORY OF MIND   How do children develop a theory of mind beginning at such a young age? Research indicates that language, executive function, make-believe play, and social experiences all contribute.

Language and Verbal Reasoning.   The prefrontal cortex seems to play a crucial role in theory-of-mind development. ERP brain-wave recordings obtained while 4- to 6-year-olds reasoned about others' beliefs revealed that children who pass false-belief tasks (as opposed to those who fail) display a distinct pattern of activity in the left prefrontal cortex (Liu et al., 2009). This left-prefrontal ERP pattern also appears when adults reason verbally about mental concepts.

Understanding the mind requires the ability to reflect on thoughts, which language makes possible. Many studies indicate that language ability strongly predicts preschoolers' grasp of false belief (Milligan, Astington, & Dack, 2007). Children who spontaneously use, or who are trained to use, complex sentences with mental-state words are especially likely to pass false-belief tasks (de Villiers & de Villiers, 2000; Hale & Tager-Flusberg, 2003). The Quechua village people of the Peruvian highlands refer to mental states such as "think" and "believe" indirectly, because their language lacks mental-state terms. Quechua children have difficulty with false-belief tasks for years after children in industrialized nations have mastered them (Vinden, 1996).

Executive Function.   Several aspects of preschoolers' executive function—ability to inhibit inappropriate responses, think flexibly, and plan—predict mastery of false-belief (Benson et al., 2013; Hughes & Ensor, 2007). Like language, these cognitive skills enhance children's ability to reflect on experiences and mental states. Gains in inhibition are strongly related to mastery of false belief, perhaps because false-belief tasks require suppression of an irrelevant response—the tendency to assume that others' knowledge and beliefs are the same as one's own (Birch & Bloom, 2003; Carlson, Moses, & Claxton, 2004).

Make-Believe Play.   Make-believe offers a rich context for thinking about the mind. As children act out roles, they often express the thoughts and emotions of the characters they portray and then reason about their implications (Kavanaugh, 2006b). These experiences may increase children's awareness that belief influences behavior. In support of this idea, preschoolers who engage in extensive fantasy play or who have imaginary companions—and, thus, are deeply absorbed in creating make-believe characters—are advanced in understanding false belief and other aspects of the mind (Astington & Jenkins, 1995; Lalonde & Chandler, 1995).

Social Interaction. Social experiences also promote understanding of the mind. In longitudinal research, mothers of securely attached babies were more likely to comment appropriately on their infants' mental states: "Do you *remember* Grandma?" "You really *like* that swing!" These mothers continued to describe their children, when they reached preschool age, in terms of mental characteristics: "She's got *a mind of her own!*" This maternal "mind-mindedness" was positively associated with later performance on false-belief and other theory-of-mind tasks (Laranjo et al., 2010; Meins et al., 2003; Ruffman et al., 2006). As we saw earlier, secure attachment is related to more elaborative parent–child narratives, which often include discussions of mental states (Ontai & Thompson, 2008; Taumoepeau & Ruffman, 2006). These conversations expose preschoolers to concepts and language that help them think about their own and others' mental lives.

Interaction with siblings, especially older siblings, contributes to preschoolers' awareness of others' perspectives and, therefore, promotes understanding of false belief.

Also, preschoolers with siblings who are children (but not infants)—especially those with older siblings or two or more siblings—tend to be more aware of false belief. Children with older siblings close in age, and those with more siblings, are exposed to and participate in more family talk about varying thoughts, beliefs, and emotions (Hughes et al., 2010; McAlister & Peterson, 2006, 2007). Similarly, preschool friends who often engage in mental-state talk are advanced in false-belief and other mental-state understandings (de Rosnay & Hughes, 2006; Hughes & Dunn, 1998). These social experiences offer extra opportunities to observe different viewpoints and talk about inner states.

Children from interdependent cultural backgrounds, where talk about one's own opinions and emotions is discouraged, are delayed in passing false-belief tasks in relation to Western children. Preschoolers growing up in China and Iran, for example, attain a grasp of explicit false-belief somewhat later than their Australian and American agemates (Shahaeian et al., 2011; Wellman et al., 2006). Both Chinese and Iranian parents teach children to respect their elders' authority and to avoid disagreeing with the viewpoints of parents and other family members.

Core knowledge theorists (see Chapter 6, pages 211–213) believe that to profit from the social experiences just described, children must be biologically prepared to develop a theory of mind. They claim that children with *autism,* for whom mastery of false belief is either greatly delayed or absent, are deficient in the brain mechanism that enables humans to detect mental states. See the Biology and Environment box on the following page to find out more about the biological basis of reasoning about the mind.

LIMITATIONS OF THE YOUNG CHILD'S THEORY OF MIND Though surprisingly advanced, preschoolers' awareness of mental activities is far from complete. For example, 3- and 4-year-olds are unaware that people continue to think while they wait, look at pictures, listen to stories, or read books—that is, when there are no obvious cues that they are thinking. Preschoolers also do not realize that when two people view the same object, their trains of thought will differ because of variations in their knowledge and other characteristics (Eisbach, 2004; Flavell, Green, & Flavell, 1995; Flavell et al., 1997).

A major reason for these findings is that children younger than age 6 pay little attention to the *process* of thinking. When asked about subtle distinctions between mental states, such as *know* and *forget,* they express confusion (Lyon & Flavell, 1994). And they often insist that they have always known information they just learned (Taylor, Esbenson, & Bennett, 1994). Finally, they believe that all events must be directly observed to be known. They do not understand that *mental inferences* can be a source of knowledge (Miller, Hardin, & Montgomery, 2003).

RONNIE KAUFMAN/LARRY HIRSHOWITZ/GETTY IMAGES

Biology and Environment

Autism and Theory of Mind

Michael stood at the water table in Leslie's classroom, repeatedly filling a plastic cup and dumping out its contents—dip-splash, dip-splash—until Leslie came over and redirected his actions. Without looking at Leslie's face, Michael moved to a new repetitive pursuit: pouring water from one cup into another and back again. As other children entered the play space and conversed, Michael hardly noticed. He rarely spoke, and when he did, he usually used words to get things he wanted, not to exchange ideas.

Michael has *autism*, a term meaning "absorbed in the self." Autism varies in severity along a continuum, called *autistic spectrum disorder*. Michael's difficulties are substantial. Like other similarly affected children, by age 3 he displayed deficits in three core areas of functioning. First, he had only limited ability to engage in nonverbal behaviors required for successful social interaction, such as eye gaze, facial expressions, gestures, imitation, and give-and-take. Second, his language was delayed and stereotyped. He used words to echo what others said and to get things he wanted, not to exchange ideas. Third, he engaged in much less make-believe play than other children (American Psychiatric Association, 2013; Walenski, Tager-Flusberg, & Ullman, 2006). And Michael showed another typical feature of autism: His interests were narrow and overly intense. For example, one day he sat for more than an hour spinning a toy Ferris wheel.

Researchers agree that autism stems from abnormal brain functioning, usually due to genetic or prenatal environmental causes. Beginning in the first year, children with the disorder have larger-than-average brains, with the greatest excess in brain-region volume occurring in the prefrontal cortex (Courchesne et al., 2011). This brain overgrowth is believed to result from lack of synaptic pruning, which accompanies typical development of cognitive, language, and communication skills.

The amygdala, especially, grows abnormally large in childhood, followed by a greater than average reduction in size in adolescence and adulthood. This deviant growth pattern is believed to contribute to deficits in emotion processing and social interaction involved in the disorder (Allely, Gillberg, & Wilson, 2014; Hobson et al., 2013). fMRI studies also reveal that autism is associated with reduced activity in areas of the cerebral cortex involved in emotional and social responsiveness and with weaker connections between the amygdala and the temporal lobes (important for processing facial expressions) (Monk et al., 2010).

Furthermore, brain-imaging evidence reveals that preschoolers with autism show a deficient left-hemispheric response to speech sounds (Eyler, Pierce, & Courchesne, 2012). Failure of the left hemisphere of the cerebral cortex to lateralize for language may underlie these children's language deficits.

Mounting evidence reveals that children with autism are impaired in theory of mind. Long after they reach the intellectual level of an average 4-year-old, they have great difficulty with false belief. Most find it hard to attribute mental states to themselves or others (Steele, Joseph, & Tager-Flusberg, 2003). They rarely use mental-state words such as *believe, think, know, feel,* and *pretend.*

As early as the second year, children with autism show deficits in emotional and social capacities believed to contribute to an understanding of mental life. Compared with other children, they less often establish eye contact, have difficulty distinguishing facial expressions, and seldom engage in social referencing or imitate an adult's novel behaviors (Chawarska, Macari, & Shic, 2013; Vivanti et al., 2008). Furthermore, they are relatively insensitive to eye gaze as a cue to what a speaker is talking about. Instead, they often assume that another person's language refers to what they themselves are looking at—a possible reason for their frequent nonsensical expressions.

Do these findings indicate that autism is due to impairment in an innate, core brain function that leaves the child unable to detect others' mental states and therefore deficient in human sociability? Some researchers think so (Baron-Cohen, 2011; Baron-Cohen & Belmonte, 2005). But others point out that individuals with general intellectual disability but not autism also do poorly on tasks assessing mental understanding

This child, who has autism, is barely aware of his teacher and classmates. Researchers disagree on whether the deficient emotional and social capacities accompanying autism result from a basic impairment in ability to detect others' mental states, a deficit in executive function, or a style of information processing that focuses on parts rather than patterns and coherent wholes.

(Yirmiya et al., 1998). This suggests that cognitive deficits are largely responsible.

One conjecture is that children with autism are impaired in executive function. This leaves them deficient in skills involved in flexible, goal-oriented thinking, including shifting attention to address relevant aspects of a situation, inhibiting irrelevant responses, applying strategies, and generating plans (Joseph & Tager-Flusberg, 2004; Robinson et al., 2009). Another possibility is that children with autism display a peculiar style of information processing, preferring to process the parts of stimuli over patterns and coherent wholes (Happé & Frith, 2006). Deficits in thinking flexibly and in holistic processing of stimuli would each interfere with understanding the social world because social interaction requires quick integration of information from various sources and evaluation of alternative possibilities.

It is not clear which of these hypotheses is correct. Some research suggests that impairments in social awareness, flexible thinking, processing coherent wholes, and verbal ability contribute independently to autism (Pellicano et al., 2006). Perhaps several biologically based deficits underlie the tragic social isolation of children like Michael.

These findings suggest that preschoolers view the mind as a passive container of information. Consequently, they greatly underestimate the amount of mental activity that people engage in and are poor at inferring what people know or are thinking about (Wellman, 2002). In contrast, older children view the mind as an active, constructive agent that selects and interprets information—a change we will consider in Chapter 12.

Early Literacy and Mathematical Development

Researchers are studying how children's information-processing capacities affect the development of basic reading, writing, and mathematical skills that prepare them for school. The way preschoolers begin to master these complex activities gives us additional information about their cognitive strengths and limitations—knowledge we can use to foster early literacy and mathematical development.

LITERACY   One week, Leslie's students created a make-believe grocery store. They brought empty food boxes from home, placed them on shelves in the classroom, labeled items with prices, made shopping lists, and wrote checks at the cash register. A sign at the entrance announced the daily specials: "APLS BNS 5¢" ("apples bananas 5¢").

As such play reveals, preschoolers understand a great deal about written language long before they learn to read or write in conventional ways. This is not surprising: Children in industrialized nations live in a world filled with written symbols. Each day, they observe and participate in activities involving storybooks, calendars, lists, and signs. Children's active efforts to construct literacy knowledge through informal experiences are called **emergent literacy.**

Young preschoolers search for units of written language as they "read" memorized versions of stories and recognize familiar signs ("PIZZA"). But they do not yet understand the symbolic function of the elements of print (Bialystok & Martin, 2003). Many preschoolers think that a single letter stands for a whole word or that each letter in a person's signature represents a separate name. Initially, as we noted in Chapter 8, preschoolers do not distinguish between drawing and writing but often believe that letters (like pictures) resemble the meanings they represent. For example, one child explained that the word *sun* begins with the letter *O* because that letter is shaped like the sun; to demonstrate, he drew an *O* surrounded with rays to produce a picture of the sun.

Children revise these ideas as their perceptual and cognitive capacities improve, as they encounter writing in many contexts, and as adults help them with written communication. Gradually preschoolers notice more features of written language and depict writing that varies in function, as in the "story" and "grocery list" in Figure 9.9.

Eventually children figure out that letters are parts of words and are linked to sounds in systematic ways, as 5- to 7-year-olds' invented spellings illustrate. At first, children rely on sounds in the names of letters: "ADE LAFWTS KRMD NTU A LAVATR" ("eighty elephants crammed into a[n] elevator"). Over time, they grasp sound–letter correspondences and learn that some letters have more than one common sound and that context affects their use (*a* is pronounced differently in "cat" than in "table") (McGee & Richgels, 2012).

Literacy development builds on a broad foundation of spoken language and knowledge about the world (Dickinson, Golinkoff, & Hirsh-Pasek, 2010). **Phonological awareness**—the ability to reflect on and manipulate the sound structures of spoken language, as indicated by sensitivity to changes in sounds within words, to rhyming, and to incorrect pronunciation—is a strong predictor of emergent literacy and later reading and spelling achievement (Dickinson et al., 2003; Paris & Paris, 2006). When combined with sound–letter knowledge, it enables children to isolate speech segments and link them with their written symbols. Vocabulary

© LAURA DWIGHT PHOTOGRAPHY

Preschoolers acquire literacy knowledge informally by participating in everyday activities involving written symbols. These young chefs "write down" orders they need to fill.

and grammatical knowledge are also influential. And preschoolers' narrative competence, assessed through having them retell stories, fosters diverse language skills essential for literacy progress, including phonological awareness (Hipfner-Boucher et al., 2014). Coherent storytelling requires attention to large language structures, such as character, setting, problem, and resolution. It seems to support the smaller-scale analysis involved in awareness of sound structures.

The more informal literacy experiences young children have, the better their language and emergent literacy development and their later reading skills (Dickinson & McCabe, 2001; Speece et al., 2004). Pointing out letter–sound correspondences and playing language–sound games enhance children's awareness of the sound structures of language and how they are represented in print (Ehri & Roberts, 2006; Foy & Mann, 2003). *Interactive reading*, in which adults discuss storybook content with preschoolers, promotes many aspects of language and literacy development. And adult-supported writing activities that focus on narrative, such as preparing a letter or a story, also have wide-ranging benefits (Purcell-Gates, 1996; Wasik & Bond, 2001). In longitudinal research, each of these literacy experiences is linked to improved reading achievement in middle childhood (Hood, Conlon, & Andrews, 2008; Senechal & LeFevre, 2002; Storch & Whitehurst, 2001).

Preschoolers from low-SES families have fewer home and preschool language and literacy learning opportunities—a major reason that they are behind in emergent literacy skills and in reading achievement throughout the school years (Foster & Miller, 2007; Turnbull et al., 2009). Age-appropriate books, for example, are scarce in their environments. In one survey of four middle- and low-income communities, the middle-income neighborhoods averaged 13 books per child, the low-income neighborhoods just 1 book for every 300 children (Neuman & Celano, 2001).

On average, a low-SES child is read to for a total of 25 hours during the preschool years, a higher-SES child for 1,000 hours. The SES gap in early literacy experiences translates into large differences in knowledge and skills that are vital for reading readiness at kindergarten entry (see Figure 9.10). Kindergartners who are behind in emergent literacy development tend to remain behind, performing poorly in reading in the early grades (National Early Literacy Panel, 2008). Over time, skilled readers acquire wide-ranging knowledge more efficiently, progressing more rapidly than poor readers in all achievement areas (Neuman, 2006). In this way, literacy deficiencies at the start of school contribute to widening achievement disparities between economically advantaged and disadvantaged children that often persist into high school.

High-quality intervention can reduce the SES gap in early literacy development substantially. Providing low-SES parents with children's books, along with guidance in how to stimulate emergent literacy, greatly enhances literacy activities in the home (High et al., 2000; Huebner & Payne, 2010). And when teachers are shown how to engage in effective early childhood instruction of diverse literacy skills, low-SES preschoolers gain in emergent literacy components included in their classroom experiences (Hilbert & Eis, 2014; Lonigan et al., 2013). For ways to support early childhood literacy development, refer to Applying What We Know on page 338.

MATHEMATICAL REASONING   Mathematical reasoning, like literacy, builds on informal knowledge. Between 14 and 16 months, toddlers display a beginning grasp of **ordinality,** or order relationships between quantities—for example, that 3 is more than 2, and 2 is more than 1. In the early preschool years, children attach verbal labels *(lots, little, big, small)* to

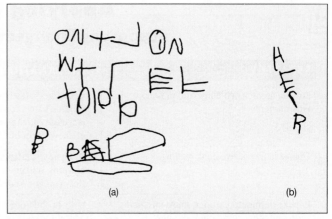

FIGURE 9.9   **A story (a) and a grocery list (b) written by a 4-year-old child.** This child's writing has many features of real print. It also reveals an awareness of different kinds of written expression. (From McGee, Lea M.; Richgels, Donald J., *Literacy's Beginnings: Supporting Young Readers and Writers,* 4th Ed., © 2004. Reprinted and Electronically reproduced by permission of Pearson Education, Inc., Upper Saddle River, New Jersey.)

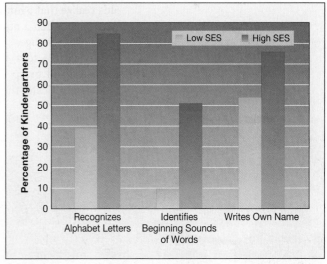

FIGURE 9.10   **Some reading readiness skills at kindergarten entry by SES.** The SES gap in emergent literacy development is large. (Adapted from Lee & Burkham, 2002.)

Applying What We Know

Supporting Emergent Literacy in Early Childhood

STRATEGY	EXPLANATION
Provide literacy-rich home and preschool environments.	Homes and preschools with abundant reading and writing materials—including a wide variety of children's storybooks, some relevant to children's ethnic backgrounds—open the door to a wealth of language and literacy experiences. Make-believe play in which children have many opportunities to use newly acquired literacy skills in meaningful ways spurs literacy development.
Engage in interactive book reading.	When adults discuss story content, ask open-ended questions about story events, explain the meaning of words, and point out features of print, they promote language development, comprehension of story content, knowledge of story structure, and awareness of units of written language.
Provide outings to libraries, museums, parks, zoos, and other community settings.	Visits to child-oriented community settings enhance children's general knowledge and offer many opportunities to see how written language is used in everyday life. They also provide personally meaningful topics for narrative conversation, which promote many language skills essential for literacy development.
Point out letter–sound correspondences, play rhyming and other language–sound games, and read rhyming poems and stories.	Experiences that help children isolate the sounds in words foster *phonological awareness*—a powerful predictor of early childhood literacy knowledge and later reading and spelling achievement.
Support children's efforts at writing, especially narrative products.	Assisting children in their efforts to write—especially letters, stories, and other narratives—fosters many language and literacy skills.
Model literacy activities.	When children see adults engaged in reading and writing activities, they better understand the diverse everyday functions of literacy skills and the knowledge and pleasure that literacy brings. As a result, children's motivation to become literate is strengthened.

Sources: McGee & Richgels, 2012; Neuman, 2006.

amounts and sizes. Sometime in the third year, they begin to count. By the time children turn 3, most can count rows of about five objects, although they do not yet know what the words mean. For example, when asked for *one,* they give one item, but when asked for *two, three, four,* or *five,* they usually give a larger, but incorrect, amount. Nevertheless, 2½- to 3½-year-olds realize that a number word refers to a unique quantity (Sarnecka & Gelman, 2004). They know that when a number label changes (for example, from *five* to *six*), the number of items should also change.

By age 3½ to 4, most children have mastered the meaning of numbers up to *ten,* count correctly, and grasp the vital principle of **cardinality**—that the last number in a counting sequence indicates the quantity of items in the set (Sarnecka & Wright, 2013). In the preschool scene described in the opening of this chapter, Sammy showed an understanding of cardinality when he counted four children at his snack table and then retrieved four milk cartons. Mastery of cardinality increases the efficiency of counting. By age 4, children use counting to solve simple arithmetic problems. At first, their strategies are tied to the order of numbers presented; when given 2 + 4, they count on from 2 (Bryant & Nunes, 2002). But soon they experiment with other strategies and master the *min* strategy, a more efficient approach (see page 331). Around this time, children realize that subtraction cancels out addition. Knowing, for example, that 4 + 3 = 7, they infer without counting that 7 − 3 = 4 (Rasmussen, Ho, & Bisanz, 2003). Grasping basic arithmetic rules greatly facilitates rapid, accurate computation.

© ELLEN B. SENISI

Preschoolers "hop" a toy frog along a number line, measuring the length of each jump. Through informal exploration of number concepts, they construct basic understandings essential for learning math skills later on.

Understanding basic arithmetic makes possible beginning *estimation*—the ability to generate approximate answers, which are useful for evaluating the accuracy of exact answers. After watching several doughnuts being added to or removed from a plate of four to ten doughnuts, 3- and 4-year-olds make sensible predictions about how many are on the plate (Zur & Gelman, 2004). Still, children can estimate only just beyond their calculation competence. For example, preschoolers who can solve addition problems with sums up to 10 can estimate answers with sums up to about 20 (Dowker, 2003). And as with arithmetic operations, children try out diverse estimation strategies, gradually moving to more efficient, accurate techniques.

The arithmetic knowledge just described emerges universally around the world. But when adults provide many occasions for counting, comparing quantities, and talking about number concepts, children acquire these understandings sooner (Ginsburg, Lee, & Boyd, 2008). Math proficiency at kindergarten entry strongly predicts math achievement years later, in elementary and secondary school (Duncan et al., 2007; Geary, 2006).

As with emergent literacy, children from low-SES families begin kindergarten with considerably less math knowledge than their higher-SES agemates—a gap due to differences in environmental supports. Just a few sessions devoted to playing a number board game with an adult (see Figure 9.11) led to a dramatic improvement in low-SES 4-year-olds' number concepts and proficiency at counting from 1 to 10 (Siegler, 2009). And in an early childhood math curriculum called *Building Blocks,* materials that promote math concepts and skills through three types of media—computers, manipulatives, and print—enable teachers to weave math into many preschool daily activities, from building blocks to art and stories (Clements et al., 2011). Compared with agemates randomly assigned to other preschool programs, low-SES preschoolers experiencing Building Blocks showed substantially greater year-end gains in math concepts and skills, including counting, sequencing, arithmetic computation, and geometric shapes.

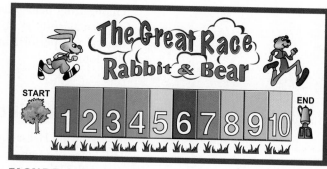

FIGURE 9.11 A number board game. An adult and child took turns using a spinner with a "1" section and a "2" section, which indicated how far to move a token on each turn. Children were asked to say the number spun and the numbers on the spaces as they moved. For example, a child on 5 who spun 2 would say "6, 7." Compared with agemates who played a color version of the game (it had only colored spaces on the board and a spinner with matching color sections), low-SES 4-year-olds who played the number board game showed large gains in number concepts and counting proficiency from 1 to 10. (From R. S. Siegler, 2009, "Improving Preschoolers' Number Sense Using Information-Processing Theory," in O. A. Barbarin & B. H. Wasik, eds., *Handbook of Child Development and Early Education.* New York: Guilford, p. 438. Reprinted by permission of Guilford Publications, Inc.)

LOOK and **LISTEN**

Ask several parents of preschoolers what they routinely do to help their children learn about math. Then ask what they do to support literacy. Do the parents promote math as much as literacy learning?

Ask Yourself

- **REVIEW** Describe a typical 4-year-old's understanding of mental activities, noting both strengths and limitations.

- **CONNECT** Cite evidence on the development of preschoolers' memory, theory of mind, and literacy and mathematical understanding that is consistent with Vygotsky's sociocultural theory.

- **APPLY** Lena wonders why her 4-year-old son Gregor's teacher provides extensive playtime in learning centers during each preschool day. Explain to Lena how adult-supported play can promote literacy and math skills essential for academic success.

- **REFLECT** Describe informal experiences important for literacy and math development that you experienced while growing up.

Individual Differences in Mental Development

Psychologists and educators typically measure how well preschoolers are developing mentally by giving them intelligence tests. Scores are computed in the same way as they are for infants and toddlers (return to Chapter 6, pages 225–226, to review). But instead of

9.9 Describe the content of early childhood intelligence tests and the impact of home, preschool and kindergarten programs, child care, and educational media on mental development.

emphasizing perceptual and motor responses, tests for preschoolers sample a wide range of mental abilities. Understanding the link between early childhood experiences and mental test performance highlights ways to intervene in support of children's cognitive development.

Early Childhood Intelligence Tests

Five-year-old Hal sat in a small, unfamiliar testing room while Sarah gave him an intelligence test. Some of Sarah's questions were *verbal*. For example, she showed Hal a picture of a shovel and said, "Tell me what this is"—an item measuring vocabulary. She tested Hal's memory by asking him to repeat sentences and lists of numbers back to her. She probed his quantitative knowledge and problem solving by seeing if he could count and solve simple addition and subtraction problems. Finally, to assess Hal's spatial reasoning, Sarah used *nonverbal* tasks: Hal copied designs with special blocks, figured out the pattern in a series of shapes, and indicated what a piece of paper folded and cut would look like when unfolded (Roid, 2003; Wechsler, 2002).

Sarah knew that Hal came from an economically disadvantaged family. When low-SES and certain ethnic minority preschoolers are bombarded with questions by an unfamiliar adult, they sometimes react with anxiety. Also, such children may not define the testing situation in achievement terms (Ford, Kozey, & Negreiros, 2012). Instead, they may look for attention and approval from the adult and may settle for lower performance than their abilities allow. Sarah spent time playing with Hal before she began testing and encouraged him while the test was in progress. Under these conditions, low-SES preschoolers improve in performance (Bracken, 2000).

The questions Sarah asked Hal tap knowledge and skills that not all children have had an equal opportunity to learn. In Chapter 12, we will take up the hotly debated issue of *cultural bias* in mental testing. For now, keep in mind that intelligence tests do not sample all human abilities, and performance is affected by cultural and situational factors. Nevertheless, test scores remain important: By age 6 to 7, they are good predictors of later IQ and academic achievement, which are related to vocational success in industrialized societies. Let's see how the environments in which children spend their days—home, preschool, and child care—affect mental test performance.

Home Environment and Mental Development

A special version of the *Home Observation for Measurement of the Environment (HOME)*, covered in Chapter 6, assesses aspects of 3- to 6-year-olds' home lives that foster intellectual growth (see Applying What We Know on the following page). Preschoolers who develop well intellectually have homes rich in educational toys and books. Their parents are warm and affectionate, stimulate language and academic knowledge, and arrange interesting outings. They also make reasonable demands for socially mature behavior—for example, that the child perform simple chores and behave courteously toward others. And these parents resolve conflicts with reason instead of physical force and punishment (Bradley & Caldwell, 1982; Espy, Molfese, & DiLalla, 2001; Roberts, Burchinal, & Durham, 1999).

As we saw in Chapter 2, these characteristics are less often seen in low-SES families. When parents manage, despite low education and income, to obtain high HOME scores, their preschoolers do substantially better on intelligence tests and measures of language and emergent literacy skills (Berger, Paxson, & Waldfogel, 2009; Mistry et al., 2008). In a study of African-American 3- and 4-year-olds from low-income families, HOME cognitive stimulation and emotional support subscales predicted reading achievement four years later (Zaslow et al., 2006). These findings (along with others we will discuss in Chapter 12) indicate that the home plays a major role in the generally poorer intellectual performance of low-SES children compared to their higher-SES peers.

Applying What We Know

Features of a High-Quality Home Life for Preschoolers: The HOME Early Childhood Subscales

HOME SUBSCALE	SAMPLE ITEMS
Cognitive stimulation through toys, games, and reading material	Home includes toys that teach colors, sizes, and shapes.
Language stimulation	Parent converses with child at least twice during observer's visit.
Organization of the physical environment	All visible rooms are reasonably clean and minimally cluttered.
Emotional support; parental pride, affection, and warmth	Parent spontaneously praises child's qualities or behavior twice during observer's visit. Parent caresses, kisses, or hugs child at least once during observer's visit.
Stimulation of academic behavior	Child is encouraged to learn colors.
Parental modeling and encouragement of social maturity	Parent introduces interviewer to child.
Opportunities for variety in daily stimulation	Family member takes child on one outing (picnic, shopping) at least every other week.
Avoidance of physical punishment	Parent neither slaps nor spanks child during observer's visit.

Sources: Bradley, 1994; Bradley et al., 2001.

Preschool, Kindergarten, and Child Care

Children between ages 2 and 6 spend even more time away from their homes and parents than infants and toddlers do. Largely because of the rise in maternal employment, over the past several decades the number of young children enrolled in preschool or child care has steadily increased, to more than 60 percent in the United States (U.S. Census Bureau, 2014b).

A *preschool* is a program with planned educational experiences aimed at enhancing the development of 2- to 5-year-olds. In contrast, *child care* refers to a variety of arrangements for supervising children of employed parents, ranging from care in the caregiver's or the child's home to some type of center-based program. The line between preschool and child care is fuzzy. Parents often select a preschool as a child-care option. And in response to the needs of employed parents, many U.S. preschools, as well as most public school kindergartens, have increased their hours from half to full days (Child Trends, 2013).

With age, preschoolers tend to shift from home-based to center-based early childhood programs. In the United States, children of higher-income parents and children of very low-income parents are especially likely to be in preschools or child-care centers (Federal Interagency Forum on Child and Family Statistics, 2013). Many low-income working parents rely on care by relatives because they are not eligible for public preschool or government-subsidized child-care centers. A few states offer government-funded prekindergarten programs located within public schools to all 4-year-olds (Barnett et al., 2013). The goal of these universal prekindergartens is to ensure that as many children as possible, from all SES levels, enter kindergarten prepared to succeed.

TYPES OF PRESCHOOL AND KINDERGARTEN   Preschool and kindergarten programs range along a continuum from child-centered to teacher-directed. In **child-centered programs,** teachers provide activities from which children select, and much learning takes place through play. In contrast, in **academic programs,** teachers structure children's learning, teaching letters, numbers, colors, shapes, and other academic skills through formal lessons, often using repetition and drill.

Despite evidence that formal academic training undermines young children's motivation and emotional well-being, early childhood teachers have felt increased pressure to take this approach. Preschoolers and kindergartners who spend much time in large-group

Five-year-olds in a Montessori classroom benefit cognitively and socially from materials designed to promote exploration and discovery and ample time for both individual and small-group learning.

teacher-directed academic instruction and completing worksheets—as opposed to being actively engaged in learning centers by warm, responsive teachers—display more stress behaviors (such as wiggling and rocking), have less confidence in their abilities, prefer less challenging tasks, and are less advanced in motor, academic, language, and social skills at the end of the school year (Stipek, 2011; Stipek et al., 1995). Follow-ups reveal lasting effects through elementary school in poorer study habits and lower achievement test scores (Burts et al., 1992; Hart et al., 1998, 2003). These outcomes are strongest for low-SES children, with whom teachers more often use a directive, academic approach—a disturbing trend in view of its negative impact on motivation and learning (Stipek, 2004).

Although government spending for universal prekindergarten is controversial in the United States, in Western Europe such programs are widespread and child-centered in their daily activities. Enrolled preschoolers of all SES backgrounds show gains in cognitive and social development still evident in elementary and secondary school (Rindermann & Ceci, 2008; Waldfogel & Zhai, 2008). Findings on some U.S universal prekindergarten programs that meet rigorous state standards of quality—especially, provision of rich teacher–child interactions and stimulating learning activities—reveal up to a one-year advantage in kindergarten and first-grade language, literacy, and math scores relative to those of children not enrolled (Gormley & Phillips, 2009; Weiland & Yoshikawa, 2013). Children from low-SES families benefit most.

A special type of child-centered approach is *Montessori education,* devised more than a century ago by Italian physician and child development researcher Maria Montessori, who originally applied her method to poverty-stricken children. Features of Montessori schooling include multiage classrooms, teaching materials specially designed to promote exploration and discovery, long time periods for individual and small-group learning in child-chosen activities, and equal emphasis on academic and social development (Lillard, 2007). In an evaluation of public preschools serving mostly urban minority children in Milwaukee, researchers compared students randomly assigned to either Montessori or other classrooms (Lillard & Else-Quest, 2006). Five-year-olds who had completed two years of Montessori education outperformed controls in literacy and math skills, cognitive flexibility, false-belief understanding, concern with fairness in solving conflicts with peers, and cooperative play with agemates.

As for the dramatic rise in U.S. full-day kindergartens, the longer school day is associated with better academic achievement in the early elementary grades. But benefits for social development are mixed (Cooper et al., 2010). Some evidence suggests that kindergartners in full-day as opposed to half-day classrooms have more behavior problems.

EARLY INTERVENTION FOR AT-RISK PRESCHOOLERS In the 1960s, as part of the "War on Poverty" in the United States, many intervention programs for low-SES preschoolers were initiated, in an effort to address learning problems prior to school entry. The most extensive of these federal programs, **Project Head Start,** began in 1965. A typical Head Start center provides children with a year or two of preschool, along with nutritional and health services. Parent involvement is central to the Head Start philosophy. Parents serve on policy councils, contribute to program planning, work directly with children in classrooms, attend special programs on parenting and child development, and receive services directed at their own emotional, social, and vocational needs. Currently, Head Start serves about 904,000 children and their families across the nation (Office of Head Start, 2014).

Benefits of Preschool Intervention. More than two decades of research have established the long-term benefits of preschool intervention. The most extensive of these studies combined data from seven interventions implemented by universities or research foundations. Results showed that poverty-stricken children who attended programs scored higher in IQ and achievement than controls during the first two to three years of elementary school. After that, differences declined (Lazar & Darlington, 1982). But on real-life measures of school adjustment, children and adolescents who had received intervention remained ahead. They were less likely to be placed in special education or retained in grade, and a greater number graduated from high school.

A separate report on one program—the High/Scope Perry Preschool Project—revealed benefits lasting well into adulthood. Two years' exposure to cognitively enriching preschool was associated with increased employment and reduced pregnancy and delinquency rates in adolescence. At age 27, those who had attended preschool were more likely than their no-preschool counterparts to have graduated from high school and college, have higher earnings, be married, and own their own home—and less likely to have been involved with the criminal justice system (see Figure 9.12) (Weikart, 1998). In the most recent follow-up, at age 40, the intervention group sustained its advantage on all measures of life success, including education, income, family life, and law-abiding behavior (Schweinhart, 2010; Schweinhart et al., 2005).

Do effects on school adjustment of these excellent interventions generalize to Head Start and other community-based preschool interventions? Gains are similar, though not as strong. Head Start preschoolers, who are more economically disadvantaged than children in university-based programs, have more severe learning and behavior problems. And quality of Head Start—though better than in most preschool programs serving low-SES children—often does not equal that of model university-based programs (Resnick, 2010; U.S. Department of Health and Human Services, 2010b). But community-based interventions of documented high quality are associated with diverse life-success outcomes, including higher rates of high school graduation and college enrollment and lower rates of adolescent drug use and delinquency (Yoshikawa et al., 2013).

A consistent finding is that gains in IQ and achievement test scores from attending Head Start and other interventions quickly dissolve. In the Head Start Impact Study, a nationally representative sample of 5,000 Head Start–eligible 3- and 4-year-olds was randomly assigned to one year of Head Start or to a control group that could attend other types of preschool programs (Puma et al., 2012; U.S. Department of Health and Human Services, 2010b). By year's end, Head Start 3-year-olds had gained relative to controls in vocabulary, emergent literacy, and math skills; 4-year-olds in vocabulary, emergent literacy, and color identification. Head Start 3-year-olds also benefited socially, displaying declines in overactivity and withdrawn behavior. But except for language skills, academic test-score advantages were no longer evident by the end of first grade. And Head Start graduates did not differ from controls on any achievement measures at the end of third grade.

What explains these disappointing outcomes? Head Start children typically enter inferior public schools in poverty-stricken neighborhoods, which undermine the

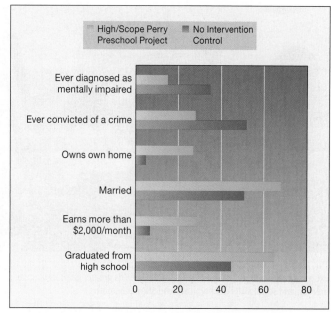

FIGURE 9.12 **Some outcomes of the High/Scope Perry Preschool Project on follow-up at age 27.** Although two years of a cognitively enriching preschool program did not eradicate the effects of growing up in poverty, children who received intervention were advantaged over no-intervention controls on all measures of life success when they reached adulthood. (Adapted from Schweinhart, 2010; Schweinhart et al., 2005.)

Project Head Start provides children from poverty-stricken families with preschool education and nutritional and health services. High-quality early educational intervention has benefits lasting into adulthood.

This teacher integrates Head Start REDI into her preschool classroom. By delivering extra educational enrichment, Head Start REDI yields greater gains in language, literacy, and social skills than typical Head Start classrooms.

benefits of preschool education (Brooks-Gunn, 2003; Ramey, Ramey, & Lanzi, 2006). An exception is the Chicago Child–Parent Centers—a program emphasizing literacy intervention and parent involvement that began at age 3 and continued through third grade—in which gains in academic achievement were still evident in middle school (Reynolds & Temple, 1998). And recall from Chapter 6 that when intensive intervention persists from infancy through early childhood, IQ gains are more likely to endure into adulthood (see pages 229–230).

Still, the improved school adjustment that results from attending a one- or two-year Head Start program is impressive. Program effects on parents may contribute: The more involved parents are in Head Start, the better their child-rearing practices and the more stimulating their home learning environments. These factors are positively related to preschoolers' independence, task persistence in the classroom, and year-end academic, language, and social skills (Bulotsky-Shearer et al., 2012; Marcon, 1999; McLoyd, Aikens, & Burton, 2006).

Strengthening Preschool Intervention. A few supplementary programs have responded to the need to intensify preschool intervention to augment its impact. One of the most widely implemented is *Head Start REDI* (Research-based Developmentally Informed), an enrichment curriculum designed for integration into existing Head Start classrooms. Before school begins, Head Start teachers—60 percent of whom do not have teaching certificates—take workshops in which they learn research-based strategies for enhancing language, literacy, and social skills. Throughout the school year, they receive one-to-one mentoring from master teachers, aimed at ensuring effective delivery of REDI.

Relative to typical Head Start classrooms, Head Start plus REDI yields higher year-end language, literacy, and social development scores. These advantages are still evident at the end of kindergarten, with stronger effects in elementary schools with many poorly achieving students (Bierman et al., 2008, 2014). REDI's powerful impact on teaching quality is believed to be responsible. Teachers trained in REDI converse with preschoolers in more cognitively complex ways and more often use management strategies that prevent disruptive behavior (Domitrovich et al., 2009).

Head Start is highly cost-effective when compared with the price of providing special education, treating criminal behavior, and supporting unemployed adults. Economists estimate a lifetime return to society of more than $300,000 to $500,000 on an investment of about $17,000 per preschool child—a potential savings of many billions of dollars if every poverty-stricken preschooler in the United States were enrolled (Heckman et al., 2010). Because of limited funding, however, only 60 percent of 3- and 4-year-olds living in poverty attend some type of preschool program, with Head Start serving just half of these children (Magnuson & Shager, 2010).

CHILD CARE We have seen that high-quality early intervention can enhance the development of economically disadvantaged children. As noted in Chapter 6, however, much U.S. child care lacks quality. Preschoolers exposed to substandard child care, particularly for long hours, score lower in cognitive and social skills and display more behavior problems (Lamb & Ahnert, 2006; NICHD Early Child Care Research Network, 2003b, 2006). Externalizing difficulties

Ingredients of high-quality child care include small group size, generous caregiver–child ratios, richly equipped activity areas, and well-educated caregivers. Child care that meets these criteria enhances development, especially for low-SES preschoolers.

Applying What We Know

Signs of Developmentally Appropriate Early Childhood Programs

PROGRAM CHARACTERISTIC	SIGNS OF QUALITY
Physical setting	Indoor environment is clean, in good repair, and well-ventilated. Classroom space is divided into richly equipped activity areas, including make-believe play, blocks, science, math, games and puzzles, books, art, and music. Fenced outdoor play space is equipped with swings, climbing equipment, tricycles, and sandbox.
Group size	In preschools and child-care centers, group size is no greater than 18 to 20 children with two teachers.
Teacher–child ratio	In preschools and child-care centers, teacher is responsible for no more than 8 to 10 children. In family child-care homes, caregiver is responsible for no more than 6 children.
Daily activities	Children select many of their own activities and learn through experiences relevant to their own lives, mainly in small groups or individually. Teachers facilitate children's involvement, accept individual differences, and adjust expectations to children's developing capacities.
Interactions between adults and children	Teachers move among groups and individuals, asking questions, offering suggestions, and adding more complex ideas. Teachers use positive guidance techniques, such as modeling and encouraging expected behavior and redirecting children to more acceptable activities.
Teacher qualifications	Teachers have college-level specialized preparation in early childhood development, early childhood education, or a related field.
Relationships with parents	Parents are encouraged to observe and participate. Teachers talk frequently with parents about children's behavior and development.
Licensing and accreditation	Preschool and child-care programs are licensed by the state. Voluntary accreditation by the National Association for the Education of Young Children *(www.naeyc.org/academy)* or the National Association for Family Child Care *(www.nafcc.org)* is evidence of an especially high-quality program.

Sources: Copple & Bredekamp, 2009.

are especially likely to endure into the school years after extensive exposure to mediocre care (Belsky et al., 2007; Vandell et al., 2010). Psychological well-being also declines when children experience the instability of several child-care settings. The emotional problems of temperamentally difficult preschoolers worsen considerably (De Schipper, van IJzendoorn, & Tavecchio, 2004; De Schipper et al., 2004).

In contrast, good child care enhances language, cognitive, and social development, especially for low-SES children—effects that persist into elementary school and, for academic achievement in one investigation, adolescence (Burchinal, Vandergrift, & Pianta, 2010; Dearing, McCartney, & Taylor, 2009; Vandell et al., 2010). Center-based care is more strongly associated with cognitive gains than are other child-care arrangements (Abner et al., 2013). Good-quality child-care centers are more likely than family child-care homes to provide a systematic educational program.

What are the ingredients of high-quality early childhood education? Large-scale studies identify several important factors: group size (number of children in a single space), teacher–child ratio, teachers' educational preparation, and teachers' personal commitment to learning about and caring for children. When these characteristics are favorable, adults are more verbally stimulating and sensitive to children's developmental needs (Lamb & Ahnert, 2006).

Applying What We Know above summarizes characteristics of high-quality early childhood programs, based on standards for developmentally appropriate practice devised by the U.S. National Association for the Education of Young Children. These standards offer a set of worthy goals as the United States strives to upgrade child-care, preschool, and kindergarten services for young children.

LOOK and LISTEN

Arrange to observe at a child-care center and to talk to its director. Jot down signs of quality, referring to Applying What We Know above. How would you rate the center's overall quality?

Educational Media

Besides home and preschool, young children spend much time in another learning environment: screen media, including both television and computers. In the industrialized world, nearly all homes have at least one television set, and most have two or more. And more than 90 percent of U.S. children live in homes with one or more computers, 80 percent of which have an Internet connection, usually a high-speed link (Rideout, Foehr, & Roberts, 2010; U.S. Census Bureau, 2014).

EDUCATIONAL TELEVISION   Sammy's favorite TV program, *Sesame Street,* uses lively visual and sound effects to stress basic literacy and number concepts and presents engaging puppet and human characters to teach general knowledge, emotional and social understanding, and social skills. Today, *Sesame Street* is broadcast in more than 140 countries, making it the most widely viewed children's program in the world (Sesame Workshop, 2014).

Time devoted to watching children's educational programs, including *Sesame Street,* is associated with gains in early literacy and math skills and with academic progress in elementary school (Ennemoser & Schneider, 2007; Mares & Pan, 2013). One study reported a link between preschool viewing of *Sesame Street* (and similar educational programs) and getting higher grades, reading more books, and placing more value on achievement in high school (Anderson et al., 2001).

Sesame Street has modified its previous rapid-paced format in favor of more leisurely episodes with a clear story line. Programs with slow-paced action and easy-to-follow narratives, such as *Arthur* and *The Magic School Bus,* are associated with improved executive function, greater recall of program content, gains in vocabulary and reading skills, and more elaborate make-believe play than programs presenting quick, disconnected bits of information (Lillard & Peterson, 2011; Linebarger & Piotrowski, 2010; Singer & Singer, 2005). Narratively structured educational TV eases processing demands, facilitating sustained attention and freeing up space in working memory for applying program content to real-life situations.

Despite the spread of computers, television remains the dominant form of youth media, with children first becoming viewers in early infancy. About 40 percent of U.S. 3-month-olds regularly watch either TV or videos, a figure that rises to 90 percent by age 2 (Zimmerman, Christakis, & Meltzoff, 2007). The average U.S. 2- to 6-year-old watches TV programs and videos from 1½ to 2⅔ hours a day. In middle childhood, viewing time increases to an average of 3½ hours a day, then declines slightly in adolescence (Common Sense Media, 2013; Rideout, Foehr, & Roberts, 2010).

Low-SES children are more frequent TV viewers, perhaps because few alternative forms of entertainment are available in their neighborhoods or affordable for their parents. On the positive side, preschoolers in low-SES families watch as much educational television as their economically advantaged agemates (Common Sense Media, 2013). But parents with limited education are more likely to engage in practices that heighten TV viewing of all kinds, including leaving the TV on all day and eating family meals in front of it (Rideout, Foehr, & Roberts, 2010).

The average U.S. child, from infancy to middle childhood, experiences nearly 4 hours of background television a day (Lapierre, Piotrowski, & Klinebarger, 2012). Background TV impairs young children's sustained attention to play activities and reduces the quantity and quality of parent–child interaction (Courage & Howe, 2010; Kirkorian et al., 2009). Kindergartners and first graders in families where the TV is on nearly constantly are far less likely than their agemates to have acquired beginning reading skills (Vandewater et al., 2005).

About 35 percent of U.S. preschoolers and 45 percent of school-age children have a TV set in their bedroom. These children are exposed to even more background TV than their agemates and spend from 40 to 90 minutes more per day watching programs, usually with no parental restrictions on what they view (Common Sense Media, 2013; Rideout & Hamel, 2006).

Does extensive TV viewing take children away from worthwhile activities? The more preschool and school-age children watch prime-time shows and cartoons, the less time they spend reading and interacting with others and the poorer their academic skills (Ennemoser &

Schneider, 2007; Huston et al., 1999; Wright et al., 2001). Whereas educational programs can be beneficial, watching entertainment TV—especially heavy viewing—detracts from children's school success and social experiences.

LEARNING WITH COMPUTERS   The majority of 2- to 4-year-olds have used a computer at one time or another, with more than one-third doing so regularly—from once a week to every day. But although almost all young children from higher-income families have access to a computer at home, only about half of those from low-income families do (Common Sense Media, 2013; Fletcher et al., 2014).

Because computers can have rich educational benefits, most early childhood classrooms include computer-learning centers. Computer literacy and math programs, including online storybooks, expand children's general knowledge and encourage diverse language, literacy, and arithmetic skills (Karemaker, Pitchford, & O'Malley, 2010; Li, Atkins, & Stanton, 2006). Turning over control of the mouse to preschoolers, allowing them to interact directly with the activity, enhances attention and interest (Calvert, Strong, & Gallagher, 2005). Kindergartners who use computers to draw or write produce more elaborate pictures and text, make fewer writing errors, and edit their work much as older children do.

Simplified computer languages that children can use to make designs or build structures introduce them to programming skills. As long as adults support children's efforts, these activities promote problem solving and metacognition (awareness of thought processes) because children must plan and reflect on their thinking to get their programs to work. Furthermore, while programming, children are especially likely to help one another and to persist in the face of challenge (Resnick & Silverman, 2005; Tran & Subrahmanyam, 2013). Small groups often gather around classroom computers, and children more often collaborate than in other pursuits.

In a classroom computer-learning center, preschoolers play a game in which they construct an imaginary landscape of mountains, lakes, rivers, and roads in an on-screen sandbox. The game is designed to support their developing understanding of symbol–real-world relations.

As with television, children spend much time using computers and other screen media for entertainment, especially game playing. Parental reports suggest that about half of U.S. preschoolers play electronic games at least occasionally. In addition to computers, many use mobile devices, including smart phones and tablets, where parents have downloaded game apps for them. Still, preschoolers typically spend little time playing electronic games—on average, just 12 minutes per day (Common Sense Media, 2013). Time devoted to doing so rises sharply in middle childhood and adolescence, when—as we will see in Chapter 12—a large sex difference favoring boys emerges.

Games designed for young children generally have specific educational goals, including literacy, math, science, colors, and other concepts. But on the whole, TV and game media are rife with gender stereotypes and violence. We will consider the impact of screen media on emotional and social development in the next chapter.

Ask Yourself

- **REVIEW** What findings indicate that child-centered rather than academic preschools and kindergartens are better suited to fostering academic development?

- **CONNECT** Compare outcomes resulting from preschool intervention programs with those from interventions beginning in infancy (see pages 229–230 in Chapter 6). Which are more likely to lead to lasting cognitive gains? Explain.

- **APPLY** Your senator has heard that IQ gains resulting from Head Start do not last, so he plans to vote against additional funding. Write a letter explaining why he should support Head Start.

- **REFLECT** How much and what kinds of TV viewing and computer use did you engage in as a child? How do you think your home media environment influenced your development?

9.10 Trace the development of vocabulary, grammar, and conversational skills in early childhood.

9.11 Cite factors that support language learning in early childhood.

Language Development

Language is intimately related to virtually all the cognitive changes discussed in this chapter. Between ages 2 and 6, children make momentous advances in language. Their remarkable achievements, as well as their mistakes along the way, reveal their active, rule-oriented approach to mastering their native tongue.

Vocabulary

At age 2, Sammy had a spoken vocabulary of 250 words. By age 6, he will have acquired around 10,000 words (Byrnes & Wasik, 2009). To accomplish this feat, Sammy will learn about five new words each day. How do children build their vocabularies so quickly? Research shows that they can connect new words with their underlying concepts after only a brief encounter, a process called **fast-mapping.** Even toddlers comprehend new labels remarkably quickly, but they need more repetitions of the word's use across several situations than preschoolers, who process speech-based information faster and are better able to categorize and recall it (Akhtar & Montague, 1999; Fernald, Perfors, & Marchman, 2006). Still, fast-mapping does not imply that children immediately acquired adultlike word meanings.

TYPES OF WORDS   One day, Leslie announced to the children that they would soon take a field trip. That night, Sammy excitedly told his mother, "We're going on a field trip!" When she asked where the class would go, Sammy responded matter-of-factly, "To a field!" Sammy's error suggests that young children fast-map some words more easily than others.

Children in many Western and non-Western language communities fast-map labels for objects especially rapidly because these refer to concepts that are easy to perceive (McDonough et al., 2011; Parish-Morris et al., 2010). When adults point to, label, and talk about an object, they help the child figure out the word's meaning (Gershoff-Stowe & Hahn, 2007). Soon children add verbs *(go, run, broke),* which require understandings of relationships between objects and actions. Because learning verbs is more cognitively challenging, preschoolers speaking quite different languages take longer to extend a new verb ("*push* the bike") to other instances of the same action ("*push* the box") than they do to extend a novel noun to other objects in the same category (Imai et al., 2008; Scott & Fisher, 2012). In mastering verb meanings, they benefit from multiple examples of the same verb used in a consistent manner in different contexts.

Nevertheless, young children learning Chinese, Japanese, and Korean—languages in which nouns are often omitted from adults' sentences, while verbs are stressed—acquire verbs much sooner (early in the second year) and more readily than their English-speaking agemates (Chan et al., 2011; Tardif, 2006). Besides increased exposure to verbs, Chinese-speaking children hear a greater variety of verbs denoting physical actions, which are visually obvious and therefore easiest to master (Ma et al., 2009). For example, Mandarin Chinese has several verbs for *carry,* each referring to a different way of carrying, such as on one's back, in one's arms, or with one's hands.

As young children acquire verbs, they also add modifiers *(red, round, sad).* First they make general distinctions *(big–small),* then more specific ones *(tall–short, high–low, wide–narrow)* (Stevenson & Pollitt, 1987).

STRATEGIES FOR WORD LEARNING   Children figure out the meanings of words by contrasting them with words they already know and assigning the new label to a gap in their vocabulary. On hearing a new word, 2-year-olds repeat the word or acknowledge it with "yeah" or "uh-huh" in their next verbalization 60 percent of the time (Clark, 2007). This suggests that they assign the word a preliminary meaning and often start to use it right away. Over time, they refine its meaning, striving to match its conventional use in their language community.

When learning a new noun, toddlers and preschoolers acquiring diverse languages tend to assume it refers to an object category at the basic level—an intermediate level of generality (see page 319). This preference helps young children narrow the range of possible meanings.

Once they acquire a basic-level name *(dog)*, they add names at other hierarchical levels—both more general *(animal)* and more specific *(beagle, greyhound)* (Imai & Haryu, 2004; Waxman & Lidz, 2006).

How do children discover which concept each word picks out? This process is not yet fully understood. One speculation is that early in vocabulary growth, children adopt a **mutual exclusivity bias**—the assumption that words refer to entirely separate (nonoverlapping) categories (Markman, 1992). Two-year-olds seem to rely on mutual exclusivity when the objects named are perceptually distinct—for example, differ clearly in shape. After hearing the labels for two distinct novel objects (for example, *clip* and *horn*), they assign each word correctly, to the whole object, not just a part of it (Waxman & Senghas, 1992).

Indeed, children's first several hundred nouns refer mostly to objects well-organized by shape. In a study in which toddlers repeatedly played with and heard names for novel objects of different shapes ("That's a *wif*") over a nine-week period, they soon formed the generalization that only similar-shaped objects have the same name (Smith et al., 2002; Yoshida & Smith, 2003). Toddlers with this training added more than three times as many object names to their vocabularies outside the laboratory as did untrained controls. Because shape is a perceptual property relevant to most object categories for which they have already learned names, this *shape bias* helps preschoolers master additional names of objects, and vocabulary accelerates.

To engage in effective verbal communication, preschoolers must master and combine principles of word meaning, grammar, and everyday conversation. How they accomplish this feat so rapidly is the focus of intensive research and debate.

Once the name of a whole object is familiar, on hearing a new name for the object, 2- and 3-year-olds set aside the mutual exclusivity assumption. For example, if the object *(bottle)* has a part that stands out *(spout)*, children readily apply the new label to it (Hansen & Markman, 2009). In these instances, mutual exclusivity helps limit the possibilities the child must consider. Still, mutual exclusivity and object shape cannot account for preschoolers' remarkably flexible responses when objects have more than one name.

By age 3, preschoolers' memory, categorization, and language skills have expanded, and they assign multiple labels to many objects (Deák, Yen, & Pettit, 2001). For example, they refer to a sticker of a gray goose as "sticker," "goose," and "gray." In these instances, children often call on other aspects of language. According to one proposal, preschoolers discover many word meanings by observing how words are used in syntax, or the structure of sentences—a strategy called **syntactic bootstrapping** (Gleitman et al., 2005; Naigles & Swenson, 2007). Consider an adult who says, "This is a *citron* one," while showing the child a yellow car. Two- and 3-year-olds conclude that a new word used as an adjective for a familiar object (car) refers to a property of that object (Imai & Haryu, 2004). As children hear the word in various sentence structures ("That lemon is bright *citron*"), they use syntactic information to refine the word's meaning and generalize it to other categories. Preschoolers' capacity to use syntactic cues to discern word meanings predicts vocabulary growth in diverse languages (McBride-Chang et al., 2008).

Young children also take advantage of the rich social information that adults frequently provide when they introduce new words. In one study, an adult performed an action on an object and then used a new label while looking back and forth between the child and the object, as if inviting the child to play. Two-year-olds concluded that the label referred to the action, not the object (Tomasello & Akhtar, 1995). And when an adult first designates the whole object ("The bird has something . . .") and then points to a part of it ("in its beak"), 3-year-olds realize that *beak* is a certain part, not the whole bird (Saylor, Sabbagh, & Baldwin, 2002).

Adults also inform children directly about word meanings. Parents commonly highlight the meaning of adjectives by using the new label with several objects (a "red car," a "red truck")—information that helps children infer that the word refers to an object property (Hall, Burns, & Pawluski, 2003). And adults often explain which of two or more words to use, by saying, for example, "You can call it a sea creature, but it's better to say *dolphin*" (Callanan & Sabbagh, 2004). In these situations, preschoolers often call on their expanding theory of mind to facilitate word learning. For example, by age 3 they can use a speaker's recently expressed

Young children rely on any useful information available to add to their vocabularies. As he makes a bird feeder, this preschooler attends to a variety of perceptual, social, and linguistic cues to grasp the meanings of unfamiliar words, such as *pine cone, spread, dip, bird seed,* and *munching sparrow.*

desire ("I really want to play with the *riff* ") to figure out the label belonging to one of two novel objects (Saylor & Troseth, 2006).

Furthermore, to fill in for words they have not yet learned, children as young as age 3 coin new words using ones they already know—for example, "plant-man" for a gardener or "crayoner" for a child using crayons. Preschoolers also extend language meanings through metaphor—like the 3-year-old who described a stomachache as a "fire engine in my tummy" (Winner, 1988). Young preschoolers' metaphors involve concrete sensory comparisons: "Clouds are pillows," "Leaves are dancers." As their vocabulary and general knowledge expand, they appreciate nonsensory comparisons: "Friends are like magnets," "Time flies by" (Keil, 1986; Özçalişkan, 2005). Metaphors permit young children to communicate in amazingly vivid and memorable ways.

EXPLAINING VOCABULARY DEVELOPMENT Children acquire vocabulary so efficiently and accurately that some theorists believe that they are innately biased to induce word meanings using certain principles, such as mutual exclusivity and syntactic bootstrapping (Lidz, Gleitman, & Gleitman, 2004). But critics observe that a small set of built-in, fixed principles cannot account for the varied, flexible manner in which children master vocabulary (Parish-Morris, Golinkoff, & Hirsh-Pasek, 2013). And many word-learning strategies cannot be innate because children acquiring different languages use different approaches to mastering the same meanings.

An alternative view is that vocabulary growth is governed by the same cognitive strategies that children apply to nonlinguistic information. According to one account, children draw on a *coalition* of cues—perceptual, social, and linguistic—which shift in importance with age (Golinkoff & Hirsh-Pasek, 2006, 2008). Infants rely solely on perceptual features. Toddlers and young preschoolers, while still sensitive to perceptual features (such as object shape and physical action), increasingly attend to social cues—the speaker's direction of gaze, gestures, expressions of intention and desire, and soon the speaker's knowledge (Hollich, Hirsh-Pasek, & Golinkoff, 2000; Pruden et al., 2006). And as language develops further, linguistic cues—sentence structure and intonation (stress, pitch, and loudness)—play larger roles.

Preschoolers are most successful at figuring out new word meanings when several kinds of information are available (Parish-Morris, Golinkoff, & Hirsh-Pasek, 2013). Researchers have just begun to study the multiple cues that children use for different kinds of words and how their combined strategies change with development.

Grammar

Grammar refers to the way we combine words into meaningful phrases and sentences. Between ages 2 and 3, English-speaking children use simple sentences that follow a subject–verb–object word order. Children learning other languages adopt the word orders of the adult speech to which they are exposed.

BASIC RULES Toddlers' greater looking times at scenes that match sentences they hear reveal that they comprehend the meaning of basic grammatical structures that they cannot yet produce, such as "Big Bird is tickling Cookie Monster" or "What did the ball hit?" (Seidl, Hollich, & Jusczyk, 2003). First use of grammatical rules, however, is piecemeal—limited to just a few verbs. As children listen for familiar verbs in adults' speech, they expand their own utterances containing those verbs, relying on adult speech as their model (Gathercole, Sebastián, & Soto, 1999). Sammy, for example, added the preposition *with* to the verb *open* ("You open with scissors") but not to the word *hit* ("He hit me stick").

To test preschoolers' ability to generate novel sentences that conform to basic English grammar, researchers had them use a new verb in the subject–verb–object form after hearing it in a different construction, such as passive: "Ernie is getting *gorped* by the dog." When

© ELLEN B. SENISI

children were asked what the dog was doing, the percentage who could respond, "He's *gorping* Ernie," rose steadily with age. But not until age 3½ to 4 could the majority of children apply the fundamental subject–verb–object structure broadly, to newly acquired verbs (Chan et al., 2010; Tomasello, 2003, 2006).

As these examples suggest, once children form three-word sentences, they also make small additions and changes in words that enable speakers to express meanings flexibly and efficiently. For example, they add *-ing* for ongoing actions *(playing)*, *-s* for plural *(cats)*, use prepositions *(in* and *on)*, and form various tenses of the verb *to be (is, are, were, has been, will)*. All English-speaking children master these grammatical markers in a regular sequence, from the simplest meanings and structures *(-ing, in* and *on, -s)* to the most complex (tenses of the verb *to be)* (Brown, 1973). As with basic word order, comprehension of these small units proceeds ahead of production (Soderstrom, 2008; Wood, Kouider, & Carey, 2009). Even 1½- to 2-year-olds can discriminate an adult's correct from incorrect application of the plural *-s* months in advance of using it themselves.

Once children acquire these markers, they sometimes overextend the rules to words that are exceptions, a type of error called **overregularization.** "We each got two *foots*" and "My toy car *breaked*" are expressions that appear between ages 2 and 3 and persist into middle childhood (Maratsos, 2000; Marcus, 1995). Children less often make this error on frequently used irregular verbs, such as the past tense of *go (went)* and *say (said)*, which they hear often enough to learn by rote. For rarely used verbs such as *grow* and *sing*, children alternate for months—or even several years—between overregularized forms *(growed, singed)* and correct forms, until the irregular form eventually wins out. Overregularization provides evidence that children apply grammatical rules creatively.

COMPLEX STRUCTURES   Gradually, preschoolers master more complex grammatical structures, although they make errors along the way. In first creating questions, 2- and 3-year-olds use many formulas: "Where's *X?*" "Can I *X?*" (Dabrowska, 2000; Tomasello, 2003). Question asking remains variable for the next couple of years. An analysis of one child's questions revealed that he inverted the subject and verb when asking certain questions but not others ("What she will do?" "Why he can go?"). The correct expressions were the ones he heard most often in his mother's speech (Rowland & Pine, 2000). And sometimes children produce errors in subject–verb agreement ("Where does the dogs play?") and subject case ("Where can me sit?") (Rowland, 2007).

Similarly, children have trouble with some passive sentences. When told, "The car is pushed by the truck," young preschoolers often make a toy car push a truck. By age 4½, they understand such expressions, whether they contain familiar or novel verbs (Dittmar et al., 2014). Nevertheless, full mastery of the passive form is not complete until the end of middle childhood.

Though grammatical development takes place gradually, preschoolers' grasp of language structures is remarkable. By age 4 to 5, they form embedded sentences ("I think *he will come*"), tag questions ("Dad's going to be home soon, *isn't he?*"), and indirect objects ("He showed *his friend* the present") (Zukowski, 2013). As the preschool years draw to a close, children use most of the grammatical constructions of their language competently.

EXPLAINING GRAMMATICAL DEVELOPMENT   Evidence that grammatical development is an extended process has raised questions about Chomsky's *language acquisition device (LAD)*, which assumes that children have innate knowledge of grammatical rules (see Chapter 6, page 231). Some experts believe that grammar is a product of general cognitive development—children's tendency to search the environment for consistencies and patterns of all sorts (Bloom, 1999; Chang, Dell, & Bock, 2006; Tomasello, 2003). Yet among these theorists, debate continues over just how children master grammar.

According to one view, young children rely on *semantics,* or word meanings, to figure out grammatical rules—an approach called **semantic bootstrapping.** For example, children might begin by grouping together words with "agent qualities" (things that cause actions) as *subjects* and words with "action qualities" as *verbs*. Then they merge these categories with observations of how words are used in sentences (Bates & MacWhinney, 1987; Braine, 1994).

Others believe that children master grammar through direct observation of the structure of language: They notice which words appear in the same positions in sentences and are combined in the same way with other words. Over time, they group words into grammatical categories and use them appropriately in sentences (Bannard, Lieven, & Tomasello, 2009; Chang, Dell, & Bock, 2006; Tomasello, 2011).

Still other theorists agree with the essence of Chomsky's theory. One idea accepts semantic bootstrapping but proposes that the grammatical categories into which children group word meanings are innate—present at the outset (Pinker, 1999; Tien, 2013). Critics, however, point out that toddlers' two-word utterances do not reflect a flexible grasp of grammar (return to Chapter 6, page 238, to review). In sum, controversy persists over whether a universal, built-in language-processing device exists or whether children draw on general cognitive-processing procedures, devising unique strategies adapted to the specific language that they hear (Howell & Becker, 2013; Lidz, 2007).

Conversation

Besides acquiring vocabulary and grammar, children must learn to engage in effective and appropriate communication—by taking turns, staying on the same topic, stating their messages clearly, and conforming to cultural rules for social interaction. This practical, social side of language is called **pragmatics,** and preschoolers make considerable headway in mastering it.

As early as age 2, children are skilled conversationalists. In face-to-face interaction, they take turns and respond appropriately to their partner's remarks (Pan & Snow, 1999). With age, the number of turns over which children can sustain interaction, ability to maintain a topic over time, and responsiveness to queries requesting clarifications increase (Comeau, Genesee, & Mendelson, 2010; Snow et al., 1996). By age 3, children can infer a speaker's intention when the speaker expresses it indirectly. For example, most know that an adult who, in response to an offer of cereal, says, "We have no milk," is declining the cereal (Schulze, Grassmann, & Tomasello, 2013). These surprisingly advanced abilities probably grow out of early interactive experiences (see Chapter 6).

Indeed, the presence of a sibling seems to be especially conducive to acquiring the pragmatics of language. Preschoolers closely monitor conversations between their twin or older siblings and parents, and they often try to join in. When they do, these verbal exchanges last longer, with each participant taking more turns (Barton & Strosberg, 1997; Barton & Tomasello, 1991). As they listen to these conversations, young language learners pick up important skills, such as use of personal pronouns (*I* versus *you*), which are more common in the early vocabularies of later-born than of firstborn siblings (Pine, 1995). Furthermore, older siblings' remarks to a younger brother or sister often focus on regulating interaction: "Do you like Kermit?" "OK, your turn" (Oshima-Takane & Robbins, 2003). This emphasis probably contributes to younger siblings' conversational skills.

These preschoolers likely use more assertive language when speaking for a male puppet than they would if speaking for a female puppet. In doing so, they reveal their early grasp of stereotypic features of social roles in their culture.

By age 4, children adapt their language to social expectations. For example, in acting out roles with hand puppets, they show that they understand the stereotypic features of different social positions. They use more commands when playing socially dominant and male roles (teacher, doctor, father) but speak more politely and use more indirect requests when playing less dominant and female roles (student, patient, mother) (Andersen, 2000).

Preschoolers' conversational skills occasionally do break down—for example, when talking on the phone. Here is an excerpt from one 4-year-old's phone conversation with his grandfather:

Grandfather: "How old will you be?"
John: "Dis many." *[Holding up four fingers.]*
Grandfather: "Huh?"
John: "Dis many." *[Again holding up four fingers.]* (Warren & Tate, 1992, pp. 259–260)

© LAURA DWIGHT PHOTOGRAPHY

Young children's conversations appear less mature in highly demanding situations in which they cannot see their listeners' reactions or rely on typical conversational aids, such as gestures and objects to talk about. But when asked to tell a listener how to solve a simple puzzle, 3- to 6-year-olds give more specific directions over the phone than in person, indicating that they realize that more verbal description is necessary on the phone (Cameron & Lee, 1997). Between ages 4 and 8, both conversing and giving directions over the phone improve greatly.

Supporting Language Learning in Early Childhood

How can adults foster preschoolers' language development? As in toddlerhood, interaction with more skilled speakers remains vital in early childhood. Conversational give-and-take with adults, either at home or in preschool, is consistently related to

Adults can support preschoolers' grammatical learning through indirect feedback, including recasts and expansions, which model grammatical alternatives to incorrect constructions.

language progress (Hart & Risley, 1995; Hoff, 2006; Huttenlocher et al, 2010). Furthermore, recall that language learning and literacy development are closely linked. Return to Applying What We Know on page 338, and notice how each strategy for supporting emergent literacy also fosters language progress.

Sensitive, caring adults use additional techniques that promote language skills. When children use words incorrectly or communicate unclearly, they give helpful, explicit feedback: "I can't tell which ball you want. Do you mean a large or small one or a red or green one?" But they do not overcorrect, especially when children make grammatical mistakes. Criticism discourages children from freely using language in ways that lead to new skills.

Instead, adults often provide indirect feedback about grammar by using two strategies, often in combination: **recasts**—restructuring inaccurate speech into correct form, and **expansions**—elaborating on children's speech, increasing its complexity (Bohannon & Stanowicz, 1988; Chouinard & Clark, 2003). For example, if a child says, "I gotted new red shoes," the parent might respond, "Yes, you got a pair of new red shoes." In one study, after such corrective input, 2- to 4-year-olds often shifted to correct forms—improvements still evident several months later (Saxton, Backley, & Gallaway, 2005). However, the impact of such feedback has been challenged. The techniques are not used in all cultures and, in a few investigations, had no impact on children's grammar (Strapp & Federico, 2000; Valian, 1999). Rather than eliminating errors, perhaps expansions and recasts model grammatical alternatives and encourage children to experiment with them.

In language, as in other aspects of cognitive development, parents and teachers gently prompt young children to take the next developmental step forward. Children strive to master language because they want to connect with other people. Adults, in turn, respond to children's desire to become competent speakers by listening attentively, elaborating on what children say, modeling correct usage, and stimulating children to talk further. In the next chapter, we will see that this combination of warmth and encouragement of mature behavior is at the heart of early childhood emotional and social development as well.

LOOK and LISTEN

Observe a parent conversing with a 2- or 3-year-old child during play or picture-book reading. List examples of how the parent promotes the child's vocabulary, grammar, and pragmatic skills. Do the findings just described remind you once again of Vygotsky's theory?

Ask Yourself

● **REVIEW** Provide a list of recommendations for promoting language development in early childhood, noting research that supports each.

● **CONNECT** Explain how children's strategies for word learning support the interactionist perspective on language development, described on page 234 in Chapter 6.

● **APPLY** Sammy's mother explained to him that the family would take a vacation in Miami. The next morning, Sammy announced, "I gotted my bags packed. When are we going to Your-ami?" What explains Sammy's errors?

Summary

Piaget's Theory: The Preoperational Stage (p. 311)

9.1 Describe advances in mental representation, and limitations of thinking, during the preoperational stage.

- Rapid advances in mental representation, notably language and make-believe play, mark the beginning of Piaget's **preoperational stage.** With age, make-believe becomes increasingly complex, evident in **sociodramatic play** with peers. Make-believe supports many aspects of cognitive and social development. **Dual representation** improves rapidly over the third year of life as children realize that models, drawings, and simple maps correspond to circumstances in the real world.

© ELLEN B. SENISI

- Aside from representation, Piaget described preschoolers in terms of deficits rather than strengths. Because **egocentrism** prevents them from reflecting on their own thinking and accommodating, it contributes to **animistic thinking, centration,** and **irreversibility.** These difficulties cause preschoolers to fail **conservation** and **hierarchical classification** tasks.

9.2 What does follow-up research imply about the accuracy of Piaget's preoperational stage?

- When young children are given familiar and simplified problems, their performance appears more mature than Piaget assumed. Preschoolers recognize differing perspectives, distinguish animate from inanimate objects, have flexible and appropriate notions of magic, and notice and reason about transformations and cause-and-effect relations. They also show impressive skill at flexibly categorizing on the basis of both perceptually apparent and nonobservable characteristics, depending on the situation.

- Rather than being absent in the preschool years, operational thinking develops gradually. These findings challenge Piaget's concept of stage.

9.3 What educational principles can be derived from Piaget's theory?

- A Piagetian classroom promotes discovery learning, sensitivity to children's readiness to learn, and acceptance of individual differences.

Vygotsky's Sociocultural Theory (p. 322)

9.4 Describe Vygotsky's perspective on the social origins and significance of children's private speech.

- In contrast to Piaget, Vygotsky regarded language as the foundation for all higher cognitive processes. According to Vygotsky, **private speech,** or language used for self-guidance, emerges out of social communication as adults and more skilled peers help children master challenging tasks within the zone of proximal development. Eventually, private speech is internalized as inner, verbal thought.

- **Intersubjectivity** and **scaffolding** are two features of social interaction that promote transfer of cognitive processes to children. **Guided participation** recognizes situational and cultural variations in adult support of children's efforts.

9.5 Describe applications of Vygotsky's theory to education, and evaluate his major ideas.

- A Vygotskian classroom emphasizes assisted discovery, in which both teacher guidance and peer collaboration are vitally important. Make-believe play is a unique, broadly influential zone of proximal development in early childhood.

- Vygotsky's theory helps us understand the wide cultural variation in cognitive skills. In some cultures, verbal communication is not the only means—or even the most important means—through which children learn. Vygotsky said little about how basic cognitive and motor capacities, which develop in infancy, contribute to socially transmitted higher cognitive processes.

Information Processing (p. 327)

9.6 How do attention, memory, and problem solving change during early childhood?

- Preschoolers' executive function shows impressive gains. Sustained attention increases sharply, due to gains in inhibition and in working memory, which allows more complex play and problem-solving goals. Adult scaffolding supports gains in attention, and **planning** also improves.

- Young children's recognition memory is remarkably accurate. But their recall of listlike information is poor because they use **memory strategies** less effectively than older children.

- **Episodic memory,** or memory for everyday experiences, improves greatly in early childhood. Like adults, preschoolers remember recurring events as **scripts,** which become more elaborate with age.

- As cognitive and conversational skills improve, children's autobiographical memories become more organized, detailed, and related to the larger context of their lives, especially when adults use an elaborative style to talk about the past.

- According to **overlapping-waves theory,** children try out various strategies to solve challenging problems, gradually selecting those that result in rapid, accurate solutions. Practice with strategies, reasoning, tasks with new challenges, and adult assistance contribute to improved problem solving.

9.7 Describe the young child's theory of mind.

- Preschoolers begin to construct a theory of mind, indicating that they are capable of **metacognition,** or thinking about thought. From age 4 on, they realize that both beliefs and desires can influence behavior, in that they pass verbal false-belief tasks. False-belief understanding enhances children's capacity to reflect on the thoughts and emotions of oneself and others.

- Language, executive function, make-believe play, and mental-state talk with adults, older siblings, and friends contribute to young children's awareness of false belief and other mental-state understandings.

RONNIE KAUFMAN/LARRY HIRSHOWITZ/GETTY IMAGES

- Preschoolers regard the mind as a passive container of information. As a result, they have difficulty inferring what people know or are thinking about.

9.8 Summarize children's literacy and mathematical knowledge during early childhood.

- Young children's **emergent literacy** reveals that they understand a great deal about written language before they read and write in conventional ways. Preschoolers gradually revise incorrect ideas about the meaning of written symbols as their perceptual and cognitive capacities improve, as they encounter writing in many contexts, and as adults help them make sense of written information.

- Literacy development builds on a foundation of spoken language and knowledge about the world. **Phonological awareness** strongly predicts emergent literacy and later reading and spelling achievement. Preschoolers' vocabulary, grammatical knowledge, and narrative competence are also influential. Informal literacy experiences, including adult–child interactive storybook reading, foster literacy development.

- Mathematical reasoning also builds on informal knowledge. Toddlers' beginning grasp of **ordinality** serves as the basis for more complex understandings. By age 3½ to 4, they grasp the principle of **cardinality,** which increases the efficiency of counting. Soon children experiment with diverse strategies to solve simple arithmetic problems. When adults provide many occasions for counting and comparing quantities, children construct basic numerical concepts sooner.

Individual Differences in Mental Development (p. 339)

9.9 *Describe the content of early childhood intelligence tests and the impact of home, preschool and kindergarten programs, child care, and educational media on mental development.*

- Intelligence tests in early childhood sample a range of verbal and nonverbal skills, including vocabulary, memory, quantitative knowledge, problem solving, and spatial reasoning. By age 6 to 7, scores are good predictors of later IQ and academic achievement.

- A warm, stimulating home and parental reasonable demands for mature behavior promotes children's intellectual development. Home environment plays a major role in the poorer intellectual performance of low-SES children in comparison to their higher-SES peers.

- Preschools and kindergartens range along a continuum from **child-centered programs,** in which much learning occurs through play, to **academic programs,** in which teachers structure children's learning, often using repetition and drill. Emphasizing formal academic training undermines children's motivation and negatively influences later achievement.

© ELLEN B. SENISI

- **Project Head Start** is the most extensive federally funded preschool program for low-income children in the United States. High-quality preschool intervention results in immediate IQ and achievement gains and long-term improvements in school adjustment, educational attainment, and life success. Parental involvement in Head Start, and the implementation of Head Start REDI, yield higher year-end academic, language, and social skills.

- Poor-quality child care undermines preschoolers' cognitive and social skills. In contrast, good child care enhances cognitive, language, and social development, especially for low-SES children.

- Children pick up academic knowledge from educational television and computer software. TV programs with slow-paced action and easy-to-follow narratives help preschoolers comprehend program content. Introducing children to computer programming skills promotes problem solving and metacognition. But heavy exposure to prime-time TV, cartoons, and inappropriate electronic games reduces time spent reading and interacting with others and is associated with poorer academic skills.

Language Development (p. 348)

9.10 *Trace the development of vocabulary, grammar, and conversational skills in early childhood.*

- Supported by **fast-mapping,** preschoolers' vocabularies increase dramatically. According to one view, children are innately biased to induce word meanings using a **mutual exclusivity bias** and **syntactic bootstrapping.** Another proposal is that children use the same cognitive strategies they apply to nonlinguistic information. An alternative perspective is that preschoolers figure out word meanings from a coalition of cues—perceptual, social, and linguistic—which shift in importance with age.

- Between ages 2 and 3, children adopt the word order of their language. As they master grammatical constructions, they sometimes **overregularize,** applying the rules to words that are exceptions. By the end of the preschool years, children have acquired a wide variety of complex grammatical forms.

- Some experts believe that grammar is a product of general cognitive development. According to one view, children engage in **semantic bootstrapping,** relying on word meanings to figure out grammatical rules. Others agree with the essence of Chomsky's theory that children's brains are innately tuned for acquiring grammar.

- **Pragmatics** refers to the practical, social side of language. In face-to-face interaction with peers, young preschoolers are already skilled conversationalists. By age 4, they adapt their language to social expectations.

9.11 *Cite factors that support language learning in early childhood.*

- Conversational give-and-take with more skilled speakers fosters preschoolers' language skills. Adults provide both explicit feedback on the clarity of children's utterances and indirect feedback about grammar through **recasts** and **expansions.** However, the impact of these strategies, which are not used in all cultures, has been challenged.

Important Terms and Concepts

academic programs (p. 341)

animistic thinking (p. 315)

cardinality (p. 338)

centration (p. 316)

child-centered programs (p. 341)

conservation (p. 315)

dual representation (p. 314)

egocentrism (p. 315)

emergent literacy (p. 336)

episodic memory (p. 329)

expansions (p. 353)

fast-mapping (p. 348)

guided participation (p. 324)

hierarchical classification (p. 316)

intersubjectivity (p. 324)

irreversibility (p. 316)

memory strategies (p. 329)

metacognition (p. 332)

mutual exclusivity bias (p. 349)

ordinality (p. 337)

overlapping-waves theory (p. 331)

overregularization (p. 351)

phonological awareness (p. 336)

planning (p. 328)

pragmatics (p. 352)

preoperational stage (p. 311)

private speech (p. 323)

Project Head Start (p. 342)

recasts (p. 353)

scaffolding (p. 324)

scripts (p. 329)

semantic bootstrapping (p. 351)

sociodramatic play (p. 312)

syntactic bootstrapping (p. 349)

Emotional and Social Development in Early Childhood

REPRINTED WITH PERMISSION FROM THE INTERNATIONAL MUSEUM OF CHILDREN'S ART, OSLO, NORWAY

"My Wonderful Birthday"
Anonymous
7 years, India

First friendships serve as important contexts for acquiring emotional and social skills, including understanding of emotion, capacity to solve social problems, and morality. Chapter 10 considers these and other facets of emotional and social development in early childhood.

As the children in Leslie's classroom moved through the preschool years, their personalities took on clearer definition. By age 3, they voiced firm likes and dislikes as well as new ideas about themselves. "Stop bothering me," Sammy said to Mark, who had reached for Sammy's beanbag as Sammy aimed it toward the mouth of a large clown face. "See, I'm great at this game," Sammy announced with confidence, an attitude that kept him trying, even though he missed most of the throws.

The children's conversations also revealed their first notions about morality. Often they combined statements about right and wrong with forceful attempts to defend their own desires. "You're 'posed to share," stated Mark, grabbing the beanbag out of Sammy's hand.

"I was here first! Gimme it back," demanded Sammy, pushing Mark. The two boys struggled for the beanbag until Leslie intervened, provided an extra set of beanbags, and showed them how they could both play.

As the interaction between Sammy and Mark reveals, preschoolers quickly become complex social beings. Young children argue, grab, and push, but cooperative exchanges are far more frequent. Between ages 2 and 6, first friendships form, in which children converse, act out complementary roles, and learn that their own desires for companionship and toys are best met when they consider others' needs and interests.

The children's developing understanding of their social world was especially apparent in their growing attention to the dividing line between male and female. While Lynette and Karen cared for a sick baby doll in the housekeeping area, Sammy, Vance, and Mark transformed the block corner into a busy intersection. "Green light, go!" shouted police officer Sammy as Vance and Mark pushed large wooden cars and trucks across the floor. Already, the children preferred peers of their own gender, and their play themes mirrored their culture's gender stereotypes.

This chapter is devoted to the many facets of early childhood emotional and social development. We begin with Erik Erikson's theory, which provides an overview of personality change in the preschool years. Then we consider children's concepts of themselves, their insights into their social and moral worlds, their gender typing, and their increasing ability to manage their emotional and social behaviors. Finally, we ask, What is effective child rearing? And we consider the complex conditions that support good parenting or lead it to break down, including the serious and widespread problems of child abuse and neglect. ■

Erikson's Theory: Initiative versus Guilt

Erikson (1950) described early childhood as a period of "vigorous unfolding." Once children have a sense of autonomy, they become less contrary than they were as toddlers. Their energies are freed for tackling the psychological conflict of the preschool years: **initiative versus guilt.** As the word *initiative* suggests, young children have a

10.1 What personality changes take place during Erikson's stage of initiative versus guilt?

A Guatemalan 3-year-old pretends to shell corn. By acting out family scenes and adult occupations, young children around the world develop a sense of initiative, gaining insight into what they can do and become in their culture.

new sense of purposefulness. They are eager to tackle new tasks, join in activities with peers, and discover what they can do with the help of adults. They also make strides in conscience development.

Erikson regarded play as a means through which young children learn about themselves and their social world. Play permits preschoolers to try new skills with little risk of criticism and failure. It also creates a small social organization of children who must cooperate to achieve common goals. Around the world, children act out family scenes and highly visible occupations—police officer, doctor, and nurse in Western societies, rabbit hunter and potter among the Hopi Indians, hut builder and spear maker among the Baka of West Africa (Gaskins, 2013).

Recall that Erikson's theory builds on Freud's psychosexual stages (see Chapter 1, page 15). In Freud's Oedipus and Electra conflicts, to avoid punishment and maintain the affection of parents, children form a *superego*, or conscience, by *identifying* with the same-sex parent. As a result, they adopt the moral and gender-role standards of their society. For Erikson, the negative outcome of early childhood is an overly strict superego that causes children to feel too much guilt because they have been threatened, criticized, and punished excessively by adults. When this happens, preschoolers' exuberant play and bold efforts to master new tasks break down.

Although Freud's ideas are no longer accepted as satisfactory explanations of conscience development, Erikson's image of initiative captures the diverse changes in young children's emotional and social lives. Early childhood is, indeed, a time when children develop a confident self-image, more effective control over their emotions, new social skills, the foundations of morality, and a clear sense of themselves as boy or girl. Now let's look closely at each of these aspects of development.

10.2 Describe the development of self-concept and self-esteem in early childhood.

Self-Understanding

As we saw in Chapter 7, infants and toddlers make strides in acquiring *body self-awareness*. *Psychological self-awareness* emerges in early childhood, as language development enables children to talk about their own subjective experience of being. In Chapter 9, we noted that preschoolers acquire a vocabulary for talking about their inner mental lives and refine their understanding of mental states. As self-awareness strengthens, children focus more intently on qualities that make the self unique. They begin to develop a **self-concept,** the set of attributes, abilities, attitudes, and values that an individual believes defines who he or she is. This mental representation of the self has profound implications for children's emotional and social lives, influencing their preferences for activities and social partners and their vulnerability to stress.

Foundations of Self-Concept

Ask a 3- to 5-year-old to tell you about him- or herself, and you are likely to hear something like this: "I'm Tommy. I'm 4 years old. I can wash my hair all by myself. I have a new Tinkertoy set, and I made this big, big tower." Preschoolers' self-concepts largely consist of observable characteristics, such as their name, physical appearance, possessions, and everyday behaviors (Harter, 2012a; Watson, 1990).

By age 3½, children also describe themselves in terms of typical emotions and attitudes ("I'm happy when I play with my friends"; "I don't like scary TV programs"; "I usually do what Mommy says"), suggesting a beginning understanding of their unique psychological characteristics (Eder & Mangelsdorf, 1997). And by age 5, children's degree of agreement with a battery of such statements coincides with maternal reports of their personality traits, indicating that older preschoolers have a sense of their own timidity, agreeableness, and positive or negative affect (Brown et al., 2008). As further support for this emerging grasp of personality, when given a trait label ("shy," "mean"), 4-year-olds infer appropriate motives and feelings. For example, they know that a shy person doesn't like to be with unfamiliar people (Heyman & Gelman, 1999). But most preschoolers do not yet say "I'm helpful" or "I'm shy." Direct references to personality traits must wait for greater cognitive maturity.

A warm, sensitive parent–child relationship seems to foster a more positive, coherent early self-concept. In one study, 4-year-olds with a secure attachment to their mothers were more likely than their insecurely attached agemates to describe themselves in favorable terms at age 5—with statements reflecting agreeableness and positive affect (Goodvin et al., 2008). Also, recall from Chapter 9 that securely attached preschoolers participate in more elaborative parent–child conversations about personally experienced events, which help them understand themselves (see page 330). When, in past-event conversations, a child discovers that she finds swimming, getting together with friends, and going to the zoo fun, she can begin to connect these specific experiences into a general understanding of "what I enjoy." The result is a clearer image of herself (Fivush, 2011).

Elaborative reminiscing that focuses on young children's *internal states*—their thoughts, feelings, and subjective experiences—plays an especially important role in early self-concept development. Although preschoolers rarely describe themselves with reference to personality traits, they are more likely to mention traits ("I'm smart," "I'm really strong!") and typical emotions ("My brother makes me feel cranky") if their parents talk to them about causes and consequences of internal states ("Tell mommy why you were crying") (Wang, Doan, & Song, 2010). Also, 4- and 5-year-olds describe their emotional tendencies more favorably—"I'm not scared, not me!"—if their parents reminisce with them about times when they successfully resolved upsetting feelings (Goodvin & Romdall, 2013). By emphasizing the personal meaning of past events, conversations about internal states facilitate development of self-knowledge.

As early as age 2, parents use narratives of past events to impart rules, standards for behavior, and evaluative information about the child: "You added the milk when we made the mashed potatoes. That's a very important job!" (Nelson, 2003). As the Cultural Influences box on page 360 reveals, these self-evaluative narratives are a major means through which caregivers imbue the young child's self-concept with cultural values.

As they talk about personally significant events and as their cognitive skills advance, preschoolers gradually come to view themselves as persisting over time. Around age 4, children first become certain that a video image of themselves replayed shortly after it was filmed is still "me" (Povinelli, 2001). Similarly, when researchers asked 3- to 5-year-olds to imagine a future event (walking next to a waterfall) and to envision a future personal state by choosing from three items (a raincoat, money, a blanket) the one they need to bring with them, performance—along with future-state justifications ("I'm gonna get wet")—increased sharply from age 3 to 4 (Atance & Meltzoff, 2005).

When asked to tell about themselves, preschoolers typically mention observable characteristics—physical appearance, possessions, and everyday behaviors and skills, such as "I can tie my own shoes." They also have an emerging grasp of their unique psychological characteristics—for this 5-year-old, persistence and determination!

Emergence of Self-Esteem

Another aspect of self-concept emerges in early childhood: **self-esteem,** the judgments we make about our own worth and the feelings associated with those judgments. TAKE A MOMENT... Make a list of your own self-judgments. Notice that, besides a global appraisal of your worth as a person, you have a variety of separate self-evaluations concerning different activities. These evaluations are among the most important aspects of self-development because they affect our emotional experiences, future behavior, and long-term psychological adjustment.

Cultural Influences

Cultural Variations in Personal Storytelling: Implications for Early Self-Concept

Preschoolers of many cultural backgrounds participate in personal storytelling with their parents. Striking cultural differences exist in parents' selection and interpretation of events in these narratives, affecting the way children view themselves.

In one study, researchers spent hundreds of hours over a two-year period studying the storytelling practices of six middle-SES Irish-American families in Chicago and six middle-SES Chinese families in Taiwan. From extensive videotapes of adults' conversations with the children from age 2½ to 4, the investigators identified personal stories and coded them for content, quality of their endings, and evaluation of the child (Miller, Fung, & Mintz, 1996; Miller et al., 1997, 2012).

Parents in both cultures discussed pleasurable holidays and family excursions in similar ways and with similar frequency. But five times more often than the Irish-American parents, the Chinese parents told long stories about their preschoolers' previous misdeeds—using impolite language, writing on the wall, or playing in an overly rowdy way. These narratives, often sparked by a current misdeed, were conveyed with warmth and caring, stressed the impact of misbehavior on others ("You made Mama lose face"), and often ended with direct teaching of proper behavior

("Saying dirty words is not good"). By contrast, in the few instances in which Irish-American stories referred to transgressions, parents downplayed their seriousness, attributing them to the child's spunk and assertiveness.

Early narratives about the child launch preschoolers' self-concepts on culturally distinct paths (Miller, Fung, & Koven, 2007). Influenced by Confucian traditions of strict discipline and social obligations, Chinese parents integrated these values into their stories, affirming the importance of not disgracing the family and explicitly conveying expectations in the story's conclusion. Although Irish-American parents disciplined their children, they rarely dwelt on misdeeds in storytelling. Rather, they cast the child's shortcomings in a positive light, perhaps to promote self-esteem.

Whereas most Americans believe that favorable self-esteem is crucial for healthy development, Chinese adults generally see it as unimportant or even negative—as impeding the child's willingness to listen and be corrected (Miller et al., 2002). Consistent with this view, the Chinese parents did little to cultivate their child's individuality. Instead, they used storytelling to guide the child toward socially responsible behavior. Hence, by the end of the preschool years, the Chinese

A Chinese mother speaks gently to her child about proper behavior. Chinese parents often use storytelling to point out how their child's misdeeds affect others. The Chinese child's self-concept, in turn, emphasizes social obligations.

child's self-image emphasizes a sense of belonging and obligations to others ("I belong to the Lee family"; "I like to help my mom wash dishes"), whereas the American child's is more autonomous, consisting largely of personal descriptions ("I do lots of puzzles"; "I like hockey") (Wang, 2004; Wang, Doan, & Song, 2010).

After creating a "camera" and "flash," this preschooler pretends to take pictures. Her high self-esteem contributes greatly to her initiative in mastering many new skills.

By age 4, preschoolers have several self-judgments—for example, about learning things well in school, making friends, getting along with parents, and treating others kindly (Marsh, Ellis, & Craven, 2002). But young children lack the cognitive maturity necessary to develop a global sense of self-esteem. They are not yet able to assimilate the judgments of other people, and they cannot combine information about their competencies in different domains. Thus, their self-appraisals are fragmented. Also, because they have difficulty distinguishing between their desired and their actual competence, they usually rate their own ability as extremely high and often underestimate task difficulty, as Sammy did when he asserted, despite his many misses, that he was great at beanbag throwing (Harter, 2012a).

High self-esteem contributes greatly to preschoolers' initiative during a period in which they must master many new skills. By age 3, children whose parents patiently encourage while offering information about how to succeed are enthusiastic and highly motivated. In contrast, children with a history of parental criticism of their worth and performance give up easily when faced with challenges and express shame and despondency after failing (Kelley, Brownell, & Campbell, 2000). When preschool nonpersisters use dolls to act out an adult's reaction to failure, they anticipate disapproval—saying, for example, "He's punished because he can't do the puzzle" (Burhans & Dweck, 1995). They are also likely to report that their parents berate them for making small mistakes (Heyman, Dweck, & Cain, 1992). Adults can avoid promoting these self-defeating reactions by adjusting their expectations to children's capacities, scaffolding children's attempts at difficult tasks (see Chapter 9, page 324), and pointing out effort and improvement in children's work or behavior.

Ask Yourself

- **REVIEW** Why is self-esteem typically extremely high in early childhood?

- **APPLY** Joshua wants to know how he can help his 3-year-old daughter build a positive self-concept. Provide several recommendations.

- **REFLECT** When you were a child, did your parents actively promote your self-esteem? How did their efforts reflect your family's cultural background? Explain.

Emotional Development

Gains in representation, language, and self-concept support emotional development in early childhood. Between ages 2 and 6, children make strides in the emotional abilities that, collectively, researchers refer to as *emotional competence* (Denham et al., 2011; Saarni et al., 2006). First, preschoolers gain in emotional understanding, becoming better able to talk about feelings and to respond appropriately to others' emotional signals. Second, they become better at emotional self-regulation—in particular, at coping with intense negative emotion. Finally, preschoolers more often experience *self-conscious emotions* and *empathy*, which contribute to their developing sense of morality.

Parenting strongly influences preschoolers' emotional competence. Emotional competence, in turn, is vital for successful peer relationships and overall mental health.

10.3 Identify changes in understanding and expressing emotion during early childhood, citing factors that influence those changes.

Understanding Emotion

Preschoolers' vocabulary for talking about emotion expands rapidly, and they use it skillfully to reflect on their own and others' behavior. Here are some excerpts from conversations in which 2-year-olds and 6-year-olds commented on emotionally charged experiences:

> *Two-year-old: [After father shouted at child, she became angry, shouting back.]* "I'm mad at you, Daddy. I'm going away. Good-bye."
>
> *Two-year-old: [Commenting on another child who refused to nap and cried.]* "Mom, Annie cry. Annie sad."
>
> *Six-year-old: [In response to mother's comment, "It's hard to hear the baby crying."]* "Well, it's not as hard for me as it is for you." [*When mother asked why*] "Well, you like Johnny better than I do! I like him a little, and you like him a lot, so I think it's harder for you to hear him cry."
>
> *Six-year-old: [Trying to comfort a small boy in church whose mother had gone up to communion.]* "Aw, that's all right. She'll be right back. Don't be afraid. I'm here." (Bretherton et al., 1986, pp. 536, 540, 541)

COGNITIVE DEVELOPMENT AND EMOTIONAL UNDERSTANDING   As these examples show, young preschoolers refer to causes, consequences, and behavioral signs of emotion, and over time their understanding becomes more accurate and complex (Thompson, Winer, & Goodvin, 2011). By age 4 to 5, they correctly judge the causes of many basic emotions ("He's happy because he's swinging very high"; "He's sad because he misses his mother"). Preschoolers' explanations tend to emphasize external factors over internal states, a balance that changes with age (Rieffe, Terwogt, & Cowan, 2005). In Chapter 9, we saw that after age 4, children appreciate that both desires and beliefs motivate behavior. Once these understandings are secure, children's grasp of how internal factors can trigger emotion expands.

Preschoolers are good at inferring how others are feeling based on their behavior. For example, they can tell that a child who jumps up and down and claps his hands is probably happy, and one who is tearful and withdrawn is sad (Widen & Russell, 2011). And they are beginning to realize that thinking and feeling are interconnected—that a person reminded of a

This child's carefree gestures and humorous words suggest to her playmates that she feels joyful, and they respond in kind with laughter.

previous sad experience is likely to feel sad and that unpleasant feelings can be eased by changing one's thoughts (Davis et al., 2010; Lagattuta, Wellman, & Flavell, 1997; Sayfan & Lagattuta, 2009). Furthermore, they come up with effective ways to relieve others' negative emotions, such as hugging to reduce sadness (Fabes et al., 1988). Overall, preschoolers have an impressive ability to interpret, predict, and change others' feelings.

At the same time, preschoolers have difficulty interpreting situations that offer conflicting cues about how a person is feeling. When shown a picture of a happy-faced child with a broken bicycle, 4- and 5-year-olds tended to rely only on the emotional expression: "He's happy because he likes to ride his bike." Older children more often reconciled the two cues: "He's happy because his father promised to help fix his broken bike" (Gnepp, 1983; Hoffner & Badzinski, 1989). As in their approach to Piagetian tasks, young children focus on the most obvious aspect of a complex emotional situation to the neglect of other relevant information.

SOCIAL EXPERIENCE AND EMOTIONAL UNDERSTANDING   The more parents label emotions, explain them, and express warmth and enthusiasm when conversing with preschoolers, the more "emotion words" children use and the better developed their emotional understanding (Fivush & Haden, 2005; Laible & Song, 2006). Discussions focusing on negative experiences or involving disagreements are particularly helpful.

In one study, mothers engaged in more detailed dialogues about causes of emotion and more often validated their preschoolers' feelings when discussing negative (as opposed to positive) topics. And the more elaborative the discussions, the higher the children scored in emotional understanding (Laible, 2011). In another study, when mothers explained feelings, negotiated, and compromised during conflicts with their 2½-year-olds, their children, at age 3, were advanced in emotional understanding and used similar strategies to resolve disagreements (Laible & Thompson, 2002). Such dialogues seem to help children reflect on the causes and consequences of emotion while also modeling mature communication skills. Furthermore, preschoolers who are securely attached better understand emotion (Thompson, 2011). Attachment security, as we have seen, is related to more elaborative parent–child narratives, including discussions of feelings that highlight the emotional significance of past events.

Knowledge about emotion helps children in their efforts to get along with others. As early as 3 to 5 years of age, it is related to friendly, considerate behavior, constructive responses to disputes with agemates, and perspective-taking ability (Garner & Estep, 2001; Hughes & Ensor, 2010; O'Brien at al., 2011). As children learn about emotion from interacting with adults, they engage in more emotion talk with siblings and friends (Hughes & Dunn, 1998). And preschoolers who refer to feelings when interacting with playmates are better liked by their peers (Fabes et al., 2001). Children seem to recognize that acknowledging others' emotions and explaining their own enhance the quality of relationships.

Emotional Self-Regulation

Language also contributes to preschoolers' improved *emotional self-regulation,* or ability to manage the experience and expression of emotion (Cole, Armstrong, & Pemberton, 2010). By age 3 to 4, children verbalize a variety of strategies for adjusting their emotional arousal to a more comfortable level (Thompson & Goodvin, 2007). For example, they know they can blunt emotions by restricting sensory input (covering their eyes or ears to block out a scary sight or sound), talking to themselves ("Mommy said she'll be back soon"), or changing their goals (deciding that they don't want to play anyway after being excluded from a game).

As children use these strategies, emotional outbursts decline. *Effortful control*—in particular, inhibiting impulses and shifting attention—is vital in managing emotion in early childhood. Three-year-olds who can distract themselves when frustrated tend to become

Applying What We Know

Helping Children Manage Common Fears of Early Childhood

FEAR	SUGGESTION
Monsters, ghosts, and darkness	Reduce exposure to frightening stories and TV programs until the child is better able to distinguish appearance from reality. "Search" the child's room for monsters, showing him that none are there. Use a night-light, sit by the child's bed until he falls asleep, and tuck in a favorite toy for protection.
Preschool or child care	If the child resists going to preschool but seems content once there, the fear is probably separation. Provide warmth and caring while gently encouraging independence. If the child fears being at preschool, try to find out why—the teacher, the children, or a crowded, noisy environment. Provide support by accompanying the child and gradually lessening the amount of time you stay.
Animals	Do not force the child to approach a dog, cat, or other animal that arouses fear. Let the child move at her own pace. Demonstrate how to hold and pet the animal, showing that when treated gently, the animal is friendly. If the child is larger than the animal, emphasize this: "You're so big. That kitty is probably afraid of *you!*"
Intense fears	If a child's fear is intense, persists for a long time, interferes with daily activities, and cannot be reduced in any of the ways just suggested, it has reached the level of a *phobia.* Some phobias are linked to family problems and require counseling. Other phobias diminish without treatment as the child's emotional self-regulation improves.

cooperative school-age children with few problem behaviors (Gilliom et al., 2002). By age 3, effortful control predicts children's skill at portraying an emotion they do not feel—for example, reacting cheerfully after receiving an undesirable gift (Kieras et al., 2005). These emotional "masks" are largely limited to the positive feelings of happiness and surprise. Children of all ages (and adults as well) find it harder to act sad, angry, or disgusted than pleased (Denham, 1998). To promote good social relations, most cultures teach children to communicate positive feelings and inhibit unpleasant ones.

Temperament affects the development of emotional self-regulation. Children who experience negative emotion intensely find it harder to inhibit feelings and shift attention away from disturbing events. They are more likely to be anxious and fearful, respond with irritation to others' distress, react angrily or aggressively when frustrated, and get along poorly with teachers and peers (Eisenberg, Smith, & Spinrad, 2011; Raikes et al., 2007).

To avoid social difficulties, emotionally reactive children must develop effective emotion-regulation strategies. By watching parents manage their feelings, children learn strategies for regulating their own. Parents who are in tune with their own emotional experiences tend to be supportive and patient with their preschoolers, offering suggestions and explanations of emotion-regulation strategies that strengthen children's capacity to handle stress (Meyer et al., 2014; Morris et al., 2011). In contrast, when parents rarely express positive emotion, dismiss children's feelings as unimportant, and fail to control their own anger, children's emotion management and psychological adjustment suffer (Hill et al., 2006; Thompson & Meyer, 2007). And because emotionally reactive children become increasingly difficult to rear, they are often targets of ineffective parenting, which compounds their poor self-regulation.

Adult–child conversations that prepare children for difficult experiences also foster emotional self-regulation (Thompson & Goodman, 2010). Parents who discuss what to expect and ways to handle anxiety offer coping strategies that children can apply. Nevertheless, preschoolers' vivid imaginations and incomplete grasp of the distinction between appearance and reality make fears common in early childhood. Consult Applying What We Know above for ways adults can help young children manage fears.

Self-Conscious Emotions

One morning in Leslie's classroom, a group of children crowded around for a bread-baking activity. Leslie asked them to wait patiently while she got a baking pan. But Sammy reached over to feel the dough, and the bowl tumbled off the table. When Leslie returned, Sammy looked at her, then covered his eyes with his hands, and said, "I did something bad." He felt ashamed and guilty.

As their self-concepts develop, preschoolers become increasingly sensitive to praise and blame or (as Sammy did) to the possibility of such feedback. As a result, they more often experience *self-conscious emotions*—feelings that involve injury to or enhancement of their sense of self (see Chapter 7). By age 3, self-conscious emotions are clearly linked to self-evaluation (Lagattuta & Thompson, 2007; Lewis, 1995). But because preschoolers are still developing standards of excellence and conduct, they depend on messages from parents, teachers, and others who matter to them to know *when* to feel proud, ashamed, or guilty, often viewing adult expectations as obligatory rules ("Dad said you're 'posed to take turns") (Thompson, Meyer, & McGinley, 2006).

When parents repeatedly comment on the worth of the child and her performance ("That's a bad job! I thought you were a good girl"), children experience self-conscious emotions intensely—more shame after failure, more pride after success. In contrast, when parents focus on how to improve performance ("You did it this way; now try doing it that way"), they induce moderate, more adaptive levels of shame and pride and greater persistence on difficult tasks (Kelley, Brownell, & Campbell, 2000; Lewis, 1998).

Among Western children, intense shame is associated with feelings of personal inadequacy ("I'm stupid"; "I'm a terrible person") and with maladjustment—withdrawal and depression as well as intense anger and aggression toward those who participated in the shame-evoking situation (Lindsay-Hartz, de Rivera, & Mascolo, 1995; Mills, 2005). In contrast, guilt—when it occurs in appropriate circumstances and is neither excessive nor accompanied by shame—is related to good adjustment. Guilt helps children resist harmful impulses, and it motivates a misbehaving child to repair the damage and behave more considerately (Mascolo & Fischer, 2007; Tangney, Stuewig, & Mashek, 2007). But overwhelming guilt—involving such high emotional distress that the child cannot make amends—is linked to depressive symptoms as early as age 3 (Luby et al., 2009).

Finally, the consequences of shame for children's adjustment may vary across cultures. As illustrated in the Cultural Influences box on page 360, people in Asian societies, who tend to define themselves in relation to their social group, view shame as an adaptive reminder of an interdependent self and of the importance of others' judgments (Friedlmeier, Corapci, & Cole, 2011).

Empathy and Sympathy

Empathy is another emotional capacity that becomes more common in early childhood. It serves as a motivator of **prosocial, or altruistic, behavior**—actions that benefit another person without any expected reward for the self (Spinrad & Eisenberg, 2009). Compared with toddlers, preschoolers rely more on words to communicate empathic feelings, a change that indicates a more reflective level of empathy. When a 4-year-old received a Christmas gift that she hadn't included on her list for Santa, she assumed it belonged to another little girl and pleaded with her parents, "We've got to give it back—Santa's made a big mistake. I think the girl's crying 'cause she didn't get her present!" As the ability to take the perspective of others improves, empathic responding increases.

Yet empathy—*feeling with* another person and responding emotionally in a similar way—does not always yield acts of kindness and helpfulness. For some children, empathizing with an upset adult or peer escalates into *personal distress*. In trying to reduce these feelings, the child focuses on her own anxiety rather than on the person in need. As a result, empathy does not lead to **sympathy**—feelings of concern or sorrow for another's plight.

Temperament plays a role in whether empathy prompts sympathetic, prosocial behavior or a personally distressed, self-focused response. Children who are sociable, assertive, and good at regulating emotion are more likely to help, share, and comfort others in distress. But poor emotion regulators less often display sympathetic concern and prosocial behavior (Eisenberg, Fabes, & Spinrad, 2006; Eisenberg et al., 1998). When faced with someone in need, they react with behavioral and physiological distress—frowning, lip biting, thumb sucking, comfort seeking, a rise in heart rate, and a sharp increase in EEG brain-wave activity in the right cerebral hemisphere, which houses negative emotion—indications that they are overwhelmed by their feelings (Liew et al., 2010; Pickens, Field, & Nawrocki, 2001).

Preschoolers develop empathic concern in the context of secure parent–child attachment relationships (Murphy & Laible, 2013). When parents are warm, encourage emotional expressiveness, and show sensitive, empathic concern for their preschoolers' feelings, children react with concern to others' distress—a response that persists into adolescence and young adulthood (Michalik et al., 2007; Strayer & Roberts, 2004; Taylor et al., 2013). Besides modeling sympathy, parents can teach children the importance of kindness and can intervene when they display inappropriate emotion—strategies that predict high levels of sympathetic responding (Eisenberg, 2003).

In contrast, angry, punitive parenting disrupts the development of empathy at an early age—particularly among children who are poor emotion regulators and who therefore respond to parental hostility with especially high personal distress (Valiente et al., 2004). In one study, physically abused preschoolers at a child-care center rarely expressed concern at a peer's unhappiness but, rather, reacted with fear, anger, and physical attacks (Klimes-Dougan & Kistner, 1990). The children's behavior resembled their parents' insensitive responses to the suffering of others.

As children's language skills and ability to take the perspective of others improve, empathy also increases, motivating prosocial, or altruistic, behavior.

Ask Yourself

- **REVIEW** What do preschoolers understand about emotion, and how do cognition and social experience contribute to their understanding?

- **CONNECT** Cite ways that parenting contributes to preschoolers' self-concept, self-esteem, emotional understanding, emotional self-regulation, self-conscious emotions, and empathy and sympathy. Do you see any patterns? Explain.

- **APPLY** On a hike with his family, 5-year-old Ryan became frightened when he reached a very steep section of the trail. His father gently helped him climb up while saying, "Can you be brave? Being brave is when you feel scared but you do it anyway." What aspect of emotional development is Ryan's father trying to promote, and why is his intervention likely to help Ryan?

Peer Relations

10.4 Describe peer sociability, friendship, and social problem solving in early childhood, along with cultural and parental influences on early peer relations.

As children become increasingly self-aware and better at communicating and understanding the thoughts and feelings of others, their skill at interacting with peers improves rapidly. Peers provide young children with learning experiences they can get in no other way. Because peers interact on an equal footing, they must keep a conversation going, cooperate, and set goals in play. With peers, children form friendships—special relationships marked by attachment and common interests. Let's look at how peer interaction changes over the preschool years.

Advances in Peer Sociability

Mildred Parten (1932), one of the first to study peer sociability among 2- to 5-year-olds, noticed a dramatic rise with age in joint, interactive play. She concluded that social development proceeds in a three-step sequence. It begins with **nonsocial activity**—unoccupied, onlooker behavior and solitary play. Then it shifts to **parallel play,** a limited form of social participation in which a child plays near other children with similar materials but does not try to influence their behavior. At the highest level are two forms of true social interaction. In **associative play,** children engage in separate activities but exchange toys and comment on one another's behavior. Finally, in **cooperative play,** a more advanced type of interaction, children orient toward a common goal, such as acting out a make-believe theme.

FOLLOW-UP RESEARCH ON PEER SOCIABILITY   Longitudinal evidence indicates that these play forms emerge in the order Parten suggested but that later-appearing ones do not replace earlier ones in a developmental sequence (Rubin, Bukowski, & Parker, 2006). Rather, all types coexist in early childhood.

TAKE A MOMENT... Watch preschool children move from one type of play to another in a play group or classroom. You will see that they often transition from onlooker to parallel to cooperative play and back again (Robinson et al., 2003). Preschoolers seem to use parallel play as a way station. To successfully join the ongoing play of peers, they often first engage in parallel play nearby, easing into the group's activities—a strategy that increases the likelihood of being accepted. Later, they may return to parallel play as a respite from the high demands of complex social interaction and as a crossroad to new activities.

Although nonsocial activity declines with age, it is still the most frequent form among 3- to 4-year-olds. Even among kindergartners it continues to occupy about one-third of children's free-play time. Both solitary and parallel play remain fairly stable from 3 to 6 years, accounting for as much of the young child's play as highly social, cooperative interaction (Rubin, Fein, & Vandenberg, 1983).

We now understand it is the *type,* not the amount, of solitary and parallel play that changes during early childhood. In studies of preschoolers' play in Taiwan and the United States, researchers rated the *cognitive maturity* of nonsocial, parallel, and cooperative play by applying the categories shown in Table 10.1. Within each of Parten's play types, older children displayed more cognitively mature behavior than younger children (Pan, 1994; Rubin, Watson, & Jambor, 1978).

Often parents wonder whether a preschooler who spends large amounts of time playing alone is developing normally. But only *certain types* of nonsocial activity—aimless wandering, hovering near peers, and functional play involving immature, repetitive motor action—are cause for concern. Children who behave reticently, by watching peers without playing, are usually temperamentally inhibited—high in social fearfulness (Coplan & Ooi, 2014). Their parents frequently overprotect them, criticize their social awkwardness, and unnecessarily control their play activities instead of patiently encouraging them to approach other children and helping them form at least one rewarding friendship, which protects against persisting

LOOK *and* **LISTEN**

Observe several 3- to 5-year-olds during a free-play period in a preschool or child-care program. How much time does each child devote to nonsocial activity, parallel play, and socially interactive play? Do children seem to use parallel play as a way station between activities?

Four-year-olds *(left)* engage in parallel play. Cooperative play *(right)* develops later than parallel play, but preschoolers continue to move back and forth between the two types of sociability. They often use parallel play as a respite from the complex demands of cooperation.

TABLE 10.1	Developmental Sequence of Cognitive Play Categories	
PLAY CATEGORY	**DESCRIPTION**	**EXAMPLES**
Functional play	Simple, repetitive motor movements with or without objects, especially common during the first two years	Running around a room, rolling a car back and forth, kneading clay with no intent to make something
Constructive play	Creating or constructing something, especially common between 3 and 6 years	Making a house out of toy blocks, drawing a picture, putting together a puzzle
Make-believe play	Acting out everyday and imaginary roles, especially common between 2 and 6 years	Playing house, school, or police officer; acting out storybook or television characters

Source: Rubin, Fein, & Vandenberg, 1983.

adjustment problems (Guimond et al., 2012; Rubin, Bukowski, & Parker, 2006; Rubin, Burgess, & Hastings, 2002). And preschoolers who engage in solitary, repetitive behavior (banging blocks, making a doll jump up and down) tend to be immature, impulsive children who find it difficult to regulate anger and aggression (Coplan et al., 2001). In the classroom, both reticent and impulsive children experience peer ostracism, with boys at greater risk for rejection than girls (Coplan & Arbeau, 2008).

But other preschoolers with low rates of peer interaction are not socially anxious or impulsive. They simply prefer to play alone, and their solitary activities are positive and constructive. Teachers encourage such play by setting out art materials, books, puzzles, and building toys. Children who spend much time at these activities are usually well-adjusted, and when they do play with peers, they show socially skilled behavior (Coplan & Armer, 2007). Still, a few preschoolers who engage in age-appropriate solitary play—again, more often boys—are rebuffed by peers (Coplan et al., 2001, 2004). Perhaps because quiet play is inconsistent with the "masculine" gender role, boys who engage in it are at risk for negative reactions from both parents and peers and, eventually, for adjustment problems.

As noted in Chapter 9, *sociodramatic play*—an advanced form of cooperative play—becomes especially common over the preschool years and supports cognitive, emotional, and social development. In joint make-believe, preschoolers act out and respond to one another's pretend feelings. They also explore and gain control of fear-arousing experiences when they play doctor or pretend to search for monsters in a magical forest. As a result, they can better understand others' feelings and regulate their own (Meyers & Berk, 2014). Finally, preschoolers spend much time negotiating roles and rules in sociodramatic play. To create and manage complex plots, they must resolve disputes through discussion and compromise.

When researchers observed free-play periods in preschools, they found that girls participated more in sociodramatic play, whereas boys participated more in friendly, vigorous interactions called *rough-and-tumble play*. Each type of play was associated with gains in emotional competence one year later (Lindsey & Colwell, 2013). Both sociodramatic play and rough-and-tumble play require children to understand emotions, exercise self-control, and respond to other children's verbal and nonverbal cues. We will return to the topic of rough-and-tumble play in Chapter 11.

CULTURAL VARIATIONS   Peer sociability takes different forms, depending on the relative importance cultures place on group harmony as opposed to individual autonomy (Chen, 2012). For example, children in India generally play in large groups. Much of their behavior is imitative, occurs in unison, and involves close physical contact—a play style requiring high levels of cooperation. In a game called Bhatto Bhatto, children act out a script about a trip to the market, touching one another's elbows and hands as they pretend to cut and share a tasty vegetable (Roopnarine et al., 1994).

As another example, young Chinese children—unlike their North American agemates, who tend to reject reticent peers—are typically accepting of passive, reticent behaviors among their playmates (Chen et al., 2006; French et al., 2011). In Chapter 7, we saw that until recently, cultural values that discourage self-assertion led to positive evaluations of shyness in China

Agta village children in the Philippines play a tug-of-war game. Large group, highly cooperative play occurs more often in societies that value group harmony rather than individual autonomy.

(see page 260). Apparently, this benevolent attitude is still evident in the play behaviors of young Chinese children.

Cultural beliefs about the importance of play also affect early peer associations. Caregivers who view play as mere entertainment are less likely to provide props or to encourage pretend than those who value its cognitive and social benefits (Gaskins, 2014). Recall the description of children's daily lives in village and tribal cultures, described on page 326 in Chapter 9. Mayan parents, for example, do not promote children's play—yet Mayan children are socially competent. When Mayan children do pretend, their play themes are *interpretive* of daily life—involving a limited number of scripts that reflect everyday roles and experiences. Children in industrialized, urban contexts more often engage in *inventive* play, generating make-believe scenarios unconstrained by actual experience (Gaskins, 2013). Perhaps Western-style sociodramatic play, with its elaborate materials and wide-ranging imaginative themes, is particularly important for social development in societies where the worlds of adults and children are distinct. It may be less crucial in village cultures where children participate in adult activities from an early age.

First Friendships

As preschoolers interact, first friendships form that serve as important contexts for emotional and social development. **TAKE A MOMENT...** Jot down a description of what *friendship* means to you. You probably pictured a mutual relationship involving companionship, sharing, understanding of thoughts and feelings, and caring for and comforting one another in times of need. In addition, mature friendships endure over time and survive occasional conflicts.

Preschoolers understand something about the uniqueness of friendship. They say that a friend is someone "who likes you" and with whom you spend a lot of time playing. Yet their ideas about friendship are far from mature. Four- to 7-year-olds regard friendship as pleasurable play and sharing of toys. But friendship does not yet have a long-term, enduring quality based on mutual trust (Damon, 1988; Hartup, 2006). "Mark's my best friend," Sammy would declare on days when the boys got along well. But when a dispute arose, he would reverse himself: "Mark, you're not my friend!" When researchers asked preschoolers to identify their best friends—the children they most liked to play with—less than one-third mentioned the same best friend one year later, and only about one-fourth identified playmates who reciprocally named them as best friends (Eivers et al., 2012).

Nevertheless, interactions between young friends are unique. Preschoolers give twice as much reinforcement—greetings, praise, and compliance—to children they identify as friends, and they also receive more from them. Friends play together in more complex ways and are more cooperative and emotionally expressive—talking, laughing, and looking at each other more often than nonfriends do (Hartup, 2006; Vaughn et al., 2001). And early childhood friendships offer social support: Children who begin kindergarten with friends in their class or readily make new friends adjust to school more favorably (Ladd, Birch, & Buhs, 1999; Proulx & Poulin, 2013). Perhaps the company of friends serves as a secure base from which to develop new relationships, enhancing children's feelings of comfort in the new classroom.

Peer Relations and School Readiness

The ease with which kindergartners make new friends and are accepted by classmates predicts cooperative participation in classroom activities and self-directed completion of learning tasks. These behaviors, in turn, promote gains in achievement (Ladd, Birch, & Buhs, 1999;

Ladd, Buhs, & Seid, 2000). Of course, kindergartners with friendly, prosocial behavioral styles make new friends easily, whereas those with weak emotional self-regulation skills and argumentative, aggressive, or peer-avoidant styles establish poor-quality relationships and make few friends.

In Chapter 7, we indicated that certain genetically influenced temperamental traits—negative mood, emotional reactivity, and weak effortful control—place children at risk for adjustment problems, including peer difficulties (Boivin et al., 2013). But recall, also, that environment—in particular, parenting quality—contributes profoundly to outcomes for these children. Early childhood classroom contexts also make a difference. In research in which identical-twin pair members' kindergarten experiences differed, those encountering peer rejection or conflict-ridden teacher relationships performed less well academically in first grade than their twin counterparts with more favorable classroom social experiences (Vitaro et al. 2012).

The capacity to form mutually rewarding friendships, cooperate with peers, and build positive ties with teachers enables young children to integrate themselves into classroom environments in ways that foster both academic and social competence. Socially competent preschoolers are more motivated and persistent, consistently exceeding their less socially skilled peers in language, literacy, and math scores in the early school grades (Walker & Henderson, 2012; Ziv, 2013). Because social maturity in early childhood contributes to later academic performance, readiness for kindergarten must be assessed in terms of not only academic skills but also social skills.

Positive peer interactions among young children occur most often in unstructured situations such as free play, making it important for preschools to provide space, time, materials, and adult scaffolding to support child-directed activities (Booren, Downer, & Vitiello, 2012). Warm, responsive teacher–child interaction is also vital, especially for shy, impulsive, emotionally negative, and aggressive children, who are at high risk for social difficulties (Brendgen et al., 2011; McClelland et al., 2007). In studies involving several thousand 4-year-olds in public preschools in six states, teacher sensitivity and emotional support were potent predictors of children's social competence during preschool and in a follow-up after kindergarten entry (Curby et al., 2009; Mashburn et al., 2008). Along with excellent teacher preparation, other indicators of program quality—small group sizes, generous teacher–child ratios, and developmentally appropriate daily activities (see page 345)—create classroom conditions that make positive teacher and peer relationships more likely.

In evaluating readiness for school, children's capacity for friendly, cooperative interaction is just as important as their academic skills.

Social Problem Solving

As noted earlier, children, even those who are best friends, come into conflict—events that provide invaluable learning experiences in resolving disputes constructively. Preschoolers' disagreements only rarely result in hostile encounters. Although friends argue more than other peers do, they are also more likely to work out their differences through negotiation and to continue interacting (Rubin et al., 2011).

TAKE A MOMENT... At your next opportunity, observe preschoolers' play, noting disputes over objects ("That's mine!" "I had it first!"), entry into and control over play activities ("I'm on your team, Jerry." "No, you're not!"), and disagreements over facts, ideas, and beliefs ("I'm taller than he is." "No, you aren't!"). Children take these matters quite seriously. Social conflicts provide repeated occasions for **social problem solving**—generating and applying strategies that prevent or resolve disagreements, resulting in outcomes that are both acceptable to others and beneficial to the self. To engage in social problem solving, children must bring together diverse social understandings.

FIGURE 10.1 **An information-processing model of social problem solving.** The model is circular because children often engage in several information-processing activities at once—for example, interpreting information as they notice it and continuing to consider the meaning of another's behavior while they generate and evaluate problem-solving strategies. The model also takes into account the impact of mental state on social information processing—in particular, children's knowledge of social rules, their representations of past social experiences, and their expectations for future experiences. Peer evaluations and responses to enacted strategies are also important factors in social problem solving. (Adapted from N. R. Crick & K. A. Dodge, 1994, "A Review and Reformulation of Social Information-Processing Mechanisms in Children's Social Adjustment," *Psychological Bulletin, 115,* 74–101, Figure 2 [adapted], p. 76. Copyright © 1994 by the American Psychological Association. Reprinted with permission of the American Psychological Association.)

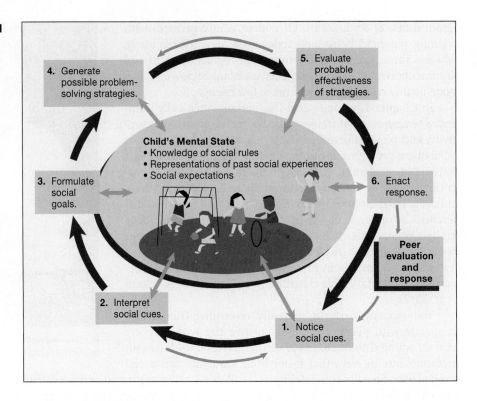

THE SOCIAL PROBLEM-SOLVING PROCESS Nicki Crick and Kenneth Dodge (1994) organize the steps of social problem solving into the circular model shown in Figure 10.1. Notice how this flowchart takes an *information-processing approach,* clarifying exactly what a child must do to grapple with and solve a social problem. It enables identification of processing deficits, so intervention can be tailored to meet individual needs.

Social problem solving profoundly affects peer relations. Children who get along well with agemates interpret social cues accurately, formulate goals (helping or cooperating with peers) that enhance relationships, and have a repertoire of effective problem-solving strategies—for example, politely asking to play, requesting an explanation when they do not understand a peer's behavior, and working out a compromise when faced with peer disagreement. In contrast, children with peer difficulties often hold biased social expectations. Consequently, they attend selectively to social cues (such as hostile acts) and misinterpret others' behavior (view an unintentional jostle as hostile). Their social goals (satisfying an impulse, getting even with or avoiding a peer) often lead to strategies that damage relationships (Dodge, Coie, & Lynam, 2006; Meece & Mize, 2011). They might barge into a play group without asking, use threats and physical force, or fearfully hover around peers' activities.

Children improve greatly in social problem solving over the preschool and early school years. Between ages 2 and 4, they increasingly display positive emotion and sociable behavior when negotiating with peers (Walker et al., 2013). Five- to 7-year-olds tend to rely on persuasion and compromise, to think of alternative strategies when an initial one does not work, and to resolve disagreements without adult intervention (Mayeux & Cillessen, 2003). Sometimes they suggest creating new, mutual goals, reflecting awareness that how they solve current problems will influence the future of the relationship (Yeates, Schultz, & Selman, 1991). By kindergarten, the accuracy and effectiveness of each component of social problem solving are related to socially competent behavior (Dodge et al., 1986).

ENHANCING SOCIAL PROBLEM SOLVING Intervening with children who have weak social problem-solving skills can foster development in several ways. Besides improving peer relations, effective social problem solving offers children a sense of mastery in the face of stressful life events. It reduces the risk of adjustment difficulties in children from low-SES and troubled families (Goodman, Gravitt, & Kaslow, 1995).

In one intervention—the *Promoting Alternative Thinking Strategies (PATHS)* curriculum for preschool children—teachers provide children with weekly lessons in the ingredients of social problem solving. Using stories, puppet characters, discussion, and role-play demonstrations, they teach such skills as detecting others' feelings, planning sequences of action, generating effective strategies, and anticipating probable outcomes. In evaluations of PATHS, preschoolers who completed 30 lessons in their Head Start classrooms scored higher than no-intervention controls in accurately "reading" others' emotions, inferring how others are likely to feel based on situational cues, selecting competent solutions to social conflicts, and cooperating and communicating with peers (Bierman et al., 2008; Domitrovich, Cortes, & Greenberg, 2007).

Parental Influences on Early Peer Relations

Children first acquire skills for interacting with peers within the family. Parents influence children's peer sociability both *directly,* through attempts to influence children's peer relations, and *indirectly,* through their child-rearing practices and play.

DIRECT PARENTAL INFLUENCES Outside preschool, child care, and kindergarten, young children depend on parents to help them establish rewarding peer associations. Preschoolers whose parents frequently arrange informal peer play activities tend to have larger peer networks and to be more socially skilled (Ladd, LeSieur, & Profilet, 1993). In providing play opportunities, parents show children how to initiate peer contacts and encourage them to be good "hosts" who consider their playmates' needs.

Parents also influence children's peer interaction skills by offering guidance on how to act toward others. Their skillful suggestions for managing conflict, discouraging teasing, and entering a play group are associated with preschoolers' social competence and peer acceptance (Mize & Pettit, 2010; Parke et al., 2004b).

INDIRECT PARENTAL INFLUENCES Many parenting behaviors not directly aimed at promoting peer sociability nevertheless influence it. For example, secure attachments to parents are linked to more responsive, harmonious peer interactions; larger peer networks; and warmer, more supportive friendships throughout childhood and adolescence (Laible, 2007; Lucas-Thompson & Clarke-Stewart, 2007; Wood, Emmerson, & Cowan, 2004). The sensitive, emotionally expressive communication that contributes to attachment security may be responsible. In several studies, highly involved, emotionally positive parent–child conversations and play predicted prosocial behavior and positive peer relations in preschool children (Clark & Ladd, 2000; Lindsey & Mize, 2000).

Parent–child play seems particularly effective for promoting peer interaction skills. During play, parents interact with their child on a "level playing field," much as peers do. And perhaps because parents play more with children of their own sex, mothers' play is more strongly linked to daughters' competence, fathers' play to sons' competence (Lindsey & Mize, 2000; Pettit et al., 1998).

As we have seen, some preschoolers already have great difficulty with peer relations. In Leslie's classroom, Robbie was one of them. Wherever he happened to be, comments like "Robbie ruined our block tower" and "Robbie hit me for no reason" could be heard. As we take up moral development in the next section, you will learn more about how parenting contributed to Robbie's peer problems.

Parents' play with young children, especially same-sex children, is linked to social competence. By playing with his father as he would with a peer, this child acquires social skills that facilitate peer interaction.

Ask Yourself

- **REVIEW** How is social competence related to children's school readiness, and what can early childhood teachers do to promote positive peer relations?

- **CONNECT** Illustrate the influence of temperament on social problem solving by explaining how an impulsive child and a shy child might respond at each social problem-solving step in Figure 10.1 on page 370.

- **APPLY** Three-year-old Ben lives in the country, with no other preschoolers nearby. His parents wonder whether it is worth driving Ben into town once a week to participate in a peer play group. What advice would you give Ben's parents, and why?

- **REFLECT** What forms of play do you recall engaging in as a young child? In what ways might those early experiences reflect your gender, culture, and family background?

10.5 What are the central features of psychoanalytic, social learning, and cognitive-developmental approaches to moral development?

10.6 Describe the development of aggression in early childhood, including family and media influences.

Foundations of Morality

Young children's behavior provides many examples of their budding moral sense. In Chapter 4, we noted that newborn (and older) infants often cry in response to the cries of other babies, a possible precursor of empathy. And after watching scenes in which one puppet helps another by returning a dropped ball while a second takes the ball away, babies as young as 3 months overwhelmingly preferred (looked longer at) the helpful character over the hinderer (Hamlin & Wynn, 2011). They seem implicitly drawn to the "nice" guy and repelled by the "mean" guy.

By the middle of the second year, toddlers expect others to act fairly, by dividing resources equally among recipients (Geraci & Surian, 2011). As children reach age 2, they often use language to evaluate their own and others' actions: "I naughty. I wrote on the wall" or (after being hit by another child) "Connie not nice." And we have seen that children of this age share toys, help others, and cooperate in games—early indicators of considerate, responsible, prosocial attitudes.

Adults everywhere take note of this developing capacity to distinguish right from wrong and to accommodate the needs of others. Some cultures have special terms for it. The Utku Indians of Hudson Bay say the child develops *ihuma* (reason). The Fijians believe that *vakayalo* (sense) appears. In response, parents hold children more responsible for their actions (Dunn, 2005). By the end of early childhood, children can state many moral rules: "Don't take someone's things without asking." "Tell the truth!" In addition, they argue over matters of justice: "You sat there last time, so it's my turn." "It's not fair. He got more!"

All theories of moral development recognize that conscience begins to take shape in early childhood. And most agree that at first, the child's morality is *externally controlled* by adults. Gradually, it becomes regulated by *inner standards*. Truly moral individuals do not do the right thing just to conform to others' expectations. Rather, they have developed compassionate concerns and principles of good conduct, which they follow in many situations.

Each major theory of development emphasizes a different aspect of morality. Psychoanalytic theory stresses the *emotional side* of conscience development—in particular, identification and guilt as motivators of good conduct. Social learning theory focuses on how *moral behavior* is learned through reinforcement and modeling. Finally, the cognitive-developmental perspective emphasizes *thinking*—children's ability to reason about justice and fairness.

The Psychoanalytic Perspective

Recall that according to Freud, young children form a *superego*, or conscience, by *identifying* with the same-sex parent, whose moral standards they adopt. Children obey the superego to avoid *guilt,* a painful emotion that arises each time they are tempted to misbehave. Moral development, Freud believed, is largely complete by 5 to 6 years of age.

Today, most researchers disagree with Freud's view of conscience development. In his theory (see page 16 in Chapter 1), fear of punishment and loss of parental love motivate conscience formation and moral behavior. Yet children whose parents frequently use threats, commands, or physical force tend to violate standards often and feel little guilt, whereas parental warmth and responsiveness predict greater guilt following transgressions (Kochanska et al., 2005, 2008). And if a parent withdraws love after misbehavior—for example, refuses to speak to or states a dislike for the child—children often respond with high levels of self-blame, thinking, "I'm no good," or "Nobody loves me." Eventually, to protect themselves from overwhelming guilt, these children may deny the emotion and, as a result, also develop a weak conscience (Kochanska, 1991; Zahn-Waxler et al., 1990).

INDUCTIVE DISCIPLINE In contrast, conscience formation is promoted by a type of discipline called **induction,** in which an adult helps make the child aware of feelings by pointing out the effects of the child's misbehavior on others, especially noting their distress and making clear that the child caused it. For example, a parent might say, "If you keep pushing him, he'll fall down and cry" or "She's crying because you won't give back her doll" (Hoffman, 2000). When generally warm parents provide explanations that match the child's capacity to understand, while firmly insisting that the child listen and comply, induction is effective as early as age 2. Preschoolers whose parents use it are more likely to refrain from wrongdoing, confess and repair damages after misdeeds, and display prosocial behavior (Choe, Olson, & Sameroff, 2013; Volling, Mahoney, & Rauer, 2009).

The success of induction may lie in its power to motivate children's active commitment to moral standards, in the following ways:

This teacher uses inductive discipline to explain to a child how her misbehavior affects others. She indicates how the child should behave, encouraging empathy and sympathetic concern.

- Induction gives children information about how to behave that they can use in future situations.
- By emphasizing the impact of the child's actions on others, induction encourages empathy and sympathetic concern, which motivate prosocial behavior.
- Giving children reasons for changing their behavior encourages them to adopt moral standards because those standards make sense.
- Children who consistently experience induction may form a *script* for the negative emotional consequences of harming others: Child causes harm, inductive message points out harm, child feels empathy for victim, child makes amends (Hoffman, 2000). The script deters future transgressions.

In contrast, discipline that relies too heavily on threats of punishment or withdrawal of love makes children so anxious and frightened that they cannot think clearly enough to figure out what they should do. As a result, these practices do not get children to internalize moral rules and—as noted earlier—also interfere with empathy and prosocial responding (Eisenberg, Fabes, & Spinrad, 2006; Padilla-Walker, 2008). Nevertheless, warnings, disapproval, and commands are sometimes necessary to get an unruly child to listen to an inductive message (Grusec, 2006).

THE CHILD'S CONTRIBUTION Although good discipline is crucial, children's characteristics also affect the success of parenting techniques. Twin studies suggest a modest genetic contribution to empathy (Knafo et al., 2009). More empathic children require less power assertion and are more responsive to induction.

Temperament is also influential. Mild, patient tactics—requests, suggestions, and explanations—are sufficient to prompt guilt reactions and conscience development in anxious, fearful preschoolers (Kochanska et al., 2002). But with fearless, impulsive children, gentle discipline has little impact. As a result, parents of preschoolers high in externalizing behavior are unlikely to use induction, relying instead on power assertive methods including physical punishment. But power assertion also works poorly. It undermines the child's capacity for effortful control, which strongly predicts good conduct, empathy, sympathy, and prosocial behavior (Kochanska & Aksan, 2006). Parents of impulsive children can foster conscience development by ensuring a warm, harmonious relationship and combining firm correction of misbehavior with induction (Kim et al., 2014; Kochanska & Kim, 2014). When children are so low in anxiety that parental disapproval causes them little discomfort, a close parent–child bond provides an alternative foundation for morality. It motivates children to listen to parents as a means of preserving an affectionate, supportive relationship.

In sum, to foster early moral development, parents must tailor their disciplinary strategies to their child's personality. Does this remind you of *goodness of fit,* discussed in Chapter 7? Return to page 259 to review this idea.

THE ROLE OF GUILT   Although little support exists for Freudian ideas about conscience development, Freud was correct that guilt motivates moral action. By the end of toddlerhood, guilt reactions are evident, and preschoolers' assertions reveal that they have internalized the parent's moral voice: "Didn't you hear my mommy? We'd better not play with these toys."

Inducing *empathy-based* guilt (expressions of personal responsibility and regret, such as "I'm sorry I hurt him") by explaining that the child is causing someone distress and has disappointed the parent is a means of influencing children without using coercion. Empathy-based guilt reactions are associated with stopping harmful actions, repairing damage caused by misdeeds, and engaging in future prosocial behavior (Eisenberg, Eggum, & Edwards, 2010). At the same time, parents must help children deal with guilt feelings constructively—by guiding them to make up for immoral behavior rather than minimizing or excusing it (Bybee, Merisca, & Velasco, 1998).

But contrary to what Freud believed, guilt is not the only force that compels us to act morally. Nor is moral development complete by the end of early childhood. Rather, it is a gradual process that extends into adulthood, building on foundations that emerge during early childhood.

When children are impulsive and low in anxiety, a secure attachment relationship motivates conscience development. This preschooler wants to follow parental rules to preserve an affectionate, supportive relationship with her father.

Social Learning Theory

According to social learning theory, morality does not have a unique course of development. Rather, moral behavior is acquired just like any other set of responses: through reinforcement and modeling.

IMPORTANCE OF MODELING   *Operant conditioning*—reinforcement for good behavior, in the form of approval, affection, and other rewards—is not enough for children to acquire moral responses. For a behavior to be reinforced, it must first occur spontaneously. Yet many prosocial acts—sharing, helping, comforting an unhappy playmate—occur so rarely at first that reinforcement cannot explain their rapid development in early childhood. Rather, social learning theorists believe that children learn to behave morally largely through *modeling*—by observing and imitating people who demonstrate appropriate behavior (Grusec, 1988). Once children acquire a moral response, such as sharing or telling the truth, reinforcement in the form of praise for the act ("That was a very nice thing to do") and for the child's character ("You're a very kind and considerate boy") increases its frequency (Mills & Grusec, 1989).

Nevertheless, certain characteristics of models affect children's willingness to imitate:

- *Warmth and responsiveness.* Preschoolers are more likely to copy prosocial actions of warm, responsive (as opposed to cold, distant) adults (Yarrow, Scott, & Waxler, 1973). Warmth seems to make children more attentive and receptive to the model and is itself an example of a prosocial response.

- *Competence and power.* Children admire and therefore tend to imitate competent, powerful models—especially older peers and adults (Bandura, 1977).
- *Consistency between assertions and behavior.* When models say one thing and do another—for example, announce that "it's important to help others" but rarely engage in helpful acts—children generally choose the most lenient standard of behavior (Mischel & Liebert, 1966).

Models are most influential in the early years. In one study, toddlers' eager, willing imitation of their mothers' behavior predicted moral conduct (not cheating in a game) and guilt following transgressions at age 3 (Forman, Aksan, & Kochanska, 2004). At the end of the preschool years, children who have had consistent exposure to caring adults tend to behave prosocially whether or not a model is present (Mussen & Eisenberg-Berg, 1977). They have internalized prosocial rules from repeated observations and encouragement by others.

EFFECTS OF PUNISHMENT   Many parents realize that angrily yelling at, slapping, and spanking children are ineffective disciplinary tactics. A sharp reprimand or physical force to restrain or move a child is justified when immediate obedience is necessary—for example, when a 3-year-old is about to run into the street. In fact, parents are most likely to use forceful methods under these conditions. But to foster long-term goals, such as acting kindly toward others, they tend to rely on warmth and reasoning (Kuczynski, 1984; Lansford et al., 2012). And in response to serious transgressions, such as lying or stealing, they often combine power assertion with reasoning (Grusec, 2006).

Frequent punishment promotes immediate compliance but not lasting changes in behavior. For example, Robbie's parents often punished by hitting, shouting, and criticizing. But as soon as they were out of sight, Robbie usually engaged in the unacceptable behavior again. The more harsh threats, angry physical control, and physical punishment children experience, the more likely they are to develop serious, lasting problems. These include weak internalization of moral rules; depression, aggression, antisocial behavior, and poor academic performance in childhood and adolescence; and depression, alcohol abuse, criminality, physical health problems, and family violence in adulthood (Afifi et al., 2006, 2013; Bender et al., 2007; Kochanska, Aksan, & Nichols, 2003; Lynch et al., 2006).

Repeated harsh punishment has several undesirable side effects:

- Parents often spank in response to children's aggression. Yet the punishment itself models aggression!
- Harshly treated children react with anger, resentment, and a chronic sense of being personally threatened, which prompts a focus on the self's distress rather than a sympathetic orientation to others' needs.
- Children who are frequently punished develop a more conflict-ridden and less supportive parent–child relationship and also learn to avoid the punitive parent (McLoyd & Smith, 2002; Shaw, Lacourse, & Nagin, 2005). Consequently, the parent's effectiveness at teaching desirable behaviors is substantially reduced.
- By stopping children's misbehavior temporarily, harsh punishment gives adults immediate relief, reinforcing them for using coercive discipline. For this reason, a punitive adult is likely to punish with greater frequency over time, a course of action that can spiral into serious abuse.
- Children, adolescents, and adults whose parents used *corporal punishment*—physical force that inflicts pain but not injury—are more accepting of such discipline (Deater-Deckard et al., 2003; Vitrup & Holden, 2010). In this way, use of physical punishment may transfer to the next generation.

Although corporal punishment spans the SES spectrum, its frequency and harshness are elevated among less educated, economically disadvantaged parents (Giles-Sims, Strauss, & Sugarman, 1995; Lansford et al., 2009). And consistently, parents with conflict-ridden marriages and with mental health problems (who are emotionally reactive, depressed, or aggressive) are more likely to be punitive and also to have hard-to-manage children, whose disobedience evokes more parental harshness (Erath et al., 2006; Knafo & Plomin, 2006). But even after

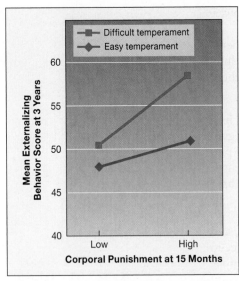

FIGURE 10.2 Relationship of parental corporal punishment at age 15 months to externalizing behavior, by child temperament. Corporal punishment was associated with increased externalizing behavior (anger and aggression) for both easy and difficult children, even after controlling for family and parenting characteristics. The rise in externalizing behavior was greater for difficult children—a difference also evident in a follow-up during first grade. (From M. K. Mulvaney & C. J. Mebert, 2007, "Parental Corporal Punishment Predicts Behavior Problems in Early Childhood," *Journal of Family Psychology, 21,* p. 394. Copyright © 2007 by the American Psychological Association. Reprinted with permission of the American Psychological Association.)

controlling for child, parenting, and family characteristics that might otherwise account for the relationship, longitudinal findings reveal a link between physical punishment and later child and adolescent aggression (Lansford et al., 2011; Lee et al., 2013; MacKenzie et al., 2013; Taylor et al., 2010).

On average, the negative effects of physical punishment are small after controlling for the factors just mentioned (Ferguson, 2013). But physical punishment affects children with vulnerable temperaments more negatively than others. For example, in a longitudinal study extending from 15 months to 3 years, early corporal punishment predicted externalizing behavior problems in preschoolers of diverse temperaments, but negative outcomes were more pronounced among temperamentally difficult children (see Figure 10.2) (Mulvaney & Mebert, 2007). Similar findings emerged from a twin study in which physical punishment was most detrimental for children at high genetic risk for behavior problems (Boutwell et al., 2011). **TAKE A MOMENT...** Return to page 85 in Chapter 2 to review findings indicating that good parenting can shield children genetically at risk for aggression and antisocial activity from developing those behaviors.

In view of these findings, the widespread use of corporal punishment by American parents is cause for concern. Surveys of nationally representative samples of U.S. households reveal that although corporal punishment increases from infancy to age 5 and then declines, it is high at all ages (see Figure 10.3) (Gershoff et al., 2012; Straus & Stewart, 1999). Furthermore, over the past 40 years, the prevalence of physical punishment has remained stable among preschoolers and declined only slightly (remaining high) among school-age children (Zolotor et al., 2011). And more than one-fourth of physically punishing U.S. parents report having used a hard object, such as a brush or a belt (Gershoff, 2002).

A prevailing American belief is that corporal punishment, if implemented by caring parents, is harmless, perhaps even beneficial. In one opinion poll, 72 percent of adults agreed that it is "OK to spank a child" (Survey USA, 2005). But as the Cultural Influences box on the following page reveals, this assumption is valid only under conditions of limited use in certain social contexts.

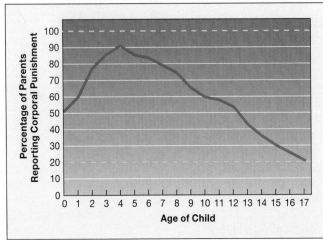

FIGURE 10.3 Prevalence of corporal punishment by child's age. Estimates are based on the percentage of parents in a nationally representative U.S. sample of nearly 1,000 reporting one or more instances of spanking, slapping, pinching, shaking, or hitting with a hard object in the past year. Physical punishment increases sharply during early childhood and then declines, but it is high at all ages. (Adapted from M. A. Straus & J. H. Stewart, 1999, "Corporal Punishment by American Parents: National Data on Prevalence, Chronicity, Severity, and Duration in Relation to Child and Family Characteristics," *Clinical Child and Family Psychology Review, 2,* p. 59. Reprinted with permission from Springer Science+Business Media conveyed through Copyright Clearance Center, Inc.)

ALTERNATIVES TO HARSH PUNISHMENT Alternatives to criticism, slaps, and spankings can reduce the side effects of punishment. A technique called **time out** involves removing children from the immediate setting—for example, by sending them to their rooms—until they are ready to act appropriately. When a child is out of control, a few minutes in time out can be enough to change behavior while also giving angry parents time to cool off (Morawska & Sanders, 2011). Another approach is *withdrawal of privileges,* such as playing outside or watching a favorite TV program. Like time out, removing privileges allows parents to avoid using harsh techniques that can easily intensify into violence.

When parents do decide to use punishment, they can increase its effectiveness in three ways:

- *Consistency.* Permitting children to act inappropriately on some occasions but scolding them on others confuses children, and the unacceptable act persists (Acker & O'Leary, 1996).
- *A warm parent–child relationship.* Children of involved, caring parents find the interruption in parental affection that accompanies punishment especially unpleasant. They want to regain parental warmth and approval as quickly as possible.
- *Explanations.* Providing reasons for mild punishment helps children relate the misdeed to expectations for future behavior. This approach leads to far greater reduction in misbehavior than using punishment alone (Larzelere et al., 1996).

Cultural Influences

Ethnic Differences in the Consequences of Physical Punishment

In an African-American community, six elders, all of whom had volunteered to serve as mentors for parents facing child-rearing challenges, met to discuss parenting issues at a social service agency. Their attitudes toward discipline were strikingly different from those of the white social workers who had brought them together. Each elder argued that successful child rearing required appropriate physical tactics. At the same time, they voiced strong disapproval of screaming or cursing at children, calling such out-of-control parental behavior "abusive." Ruth, the oldest and most respected member of the group, characterized good parenting as a complex combination of warmth, teaching, talking nicely, and disciplining physically. She related how an older neighbor advised her to handle her own children when she was a young parent:

> She said to me says, don't scream . . . you talk to them real nice and sweet and when they do something ugly . . . she say you get a nice little switch and you won't have any trouble with them and from that day that's the way I raised 'em. (Mosby et al., 1999, pp. 511–512)

In several studies, corporal punishment predicted externalizing problems similarly among white, black, Hispanic, and Asian children (Gershoff et al., 2012; MacKenzie et al., 2013). But other studies point to ethnic variations. In one longitudinal investigation, researchers followed several hundred families, collecting information from mothers on disciplinary strategies and from teachers on children's problem behaviors from kindergarten through fourth grade. Regardless of ethnicity, reasoning was the most common approach to discipline, spanking the least common. But predictors and outcomes

of spanking varied, depending on family ethnicity.

Among white families, externalizing behavior in kindergarten predicted parental physical punishment in first through third grades, which in turn led to more externalizing behavior by fourth grade. In contrast, among African-American families, kindergarten externalizing behavior was unrelated to later physical punishment, and physical punishment did not augment externalizing behavior (Lansford et al., 2012). The investigators concluded that white parents more often use physical discipline in reaction to challenging behaviors, causing those behaviors to escalate. African-American parents, in contrast, seem to use physical punishment to prevent child difficulties, thereby reducing its negative consequences.

Consistent with this interpretation, African-American and Caucasian-American parents report meting out physical punishment differently. In black families, such discipline is typically culturally approved, mild, delivered in a context of parental warmth, accompanied by verbal teaching, and aimed at helping children become responsible adults. White parents, in contrast, usually consider physical punishment to be wrong, so when they resort to it, they are often highly agitated and rejecting of the child (Dodge, McLoyd, & Lansford, 2006; LeCuyer et al., 2011). As a result, most black children may view spanking as a practice carried out with their best interests in mind, whereas white children may regard it as an act of aggression.

In support of this view, when several thousand ethnically diverse children were followed from the preschool through the early school

© ELLEN B. SENISI

In African-American families, physical discipline is often culturally approved, generally mild, and delivered in a context of parental warmth. As a result, children may view it as an effort to encourage maturity, not as an act of aggression.

years, spanking was associated with a rise in behavior problems if parents were cold and rejecting but not if they were warm and supportive (McLoyd & Smith, 2002). In another study, spanking predicted depressive symptoms only among a small number of African-American children whose mothers disapproved of the practice and, as a result, tended to use it when they were highly angry and frustrated (McLoyd et al., 2007).

These findings are not an endorsement of physical punishment. Other forms of discipline, such as time out, and the positive parenting strategies listed on page 378, are far more effective (Simons, Simons, & Su, 2013). But it is noteworthy that the meaning and impact of physical discipline vary sharply with its intensity, context of warmth and support, and cultural approval.

POSITIVE RELATIONSHIPS, POSITIVE PARENTING The most effective forms of discipline encourage good conduct—by building a mutually respectful bond with the child, letting the child know ahead of time how to act, and praising mature behavior. When sensitivity, cooperation, and shared positive emotion are evident in joint activities between parents and preschoolers, children show firmer conscience development—expressing empathy after transgressions, behaving responsibly, playing fairly in games, and considering others' welfare (Kochanska et al., 2005, 2008). Parent–child closeness leads children to heed parental demands because children feel a sense of commitment to the relationship.

Consult Applying What We Know on page 378 for ways to parent positively. Parents who use these strategies focus on long-term social and life skills—cooperation, problem solving, and consideration for others. As a result, they greatly reduce the need for punishment.

Applying What We Know

Positive Parenting

STRATEGY	EXPLANATION
Use transgressions as opportunities to teach.	When a child engages in harmful or unsafe behavior, intervene firmly, and then use induction, which motivates children to make amends and behave prosocially.
Reduce opportunities for misbehavior.	On long car trips, bring back-seat activities that relieve children's restlessness. At the supermarket, converse with children, and let them help with shopping. Children then learn to occupy themselves constructively when options are limited.
Provide reasons for rules.	When children appreciate that rules are fair to all concerned, not arbitrary, they strive to follow the rules because they are reasonable and rational.
Arrange for children to participate in family routines and duties.	By joining with adults in preparing a meal, washing dishes, or raking leaves, children develop a sense of responsible participation in family and community life and acquire many practical skills.
When children are obstinate, try compromising and problem solving.	When a child refuses to obey, express understanding of the child's feelings ("I know it's not fun to clean up"), suggest a compromise ("You put those away, I'll take care of these"), and help the child think of ways to avoid the problem in the future. Responding firmly but kindly and respectfully increases the likelihood of willing cooperation.
Encourage mature behavior.	Express confidence in children's capacity to learn and appreciation for effort and cooperation, as in "You gave that your best!" "Thanks for helping!" Adult encouragement fosters pride and satisfaction in succeeding, thereby inspiring children to improve further.
Be sensitive to children's physical and emotional resources.	When children are tired, ill, or bored, they are likely to engage in attention-getting, disorganized, or otherwise improper behavior as a reaction to discomfort. In these instances, meeting the child's needs makes more sense than disciplining.

Sources: Berk, 2001a; Grusec, 2006.

The Cognitive-Developmental Perspective

The psychoanalytic and behaviorist approaches to morality focus on how children acquire ready-made standards of good conduct from adults. In contrast, the cognitive-developmental perspective regards children as *active thinkers* about social rules. As early as the preschool years, children make moral judgments, deciding what is right or wrong on the basis of concepts they construct about justice and fairness (Gibbs, 2010; Helwig & Turiel, 2011).

PRESCHOOLERS' MORAL UNDERSTANDING Young children have some well-developed ideas about morality. As long as researchers emphasize people's intentions, 3-year-olds say that a person with bad intentions—someone who deliberately frightens, embarrasses, or otherwise hurts another—is more deserving of punishment than a well-intentioned person. They also protest when they see one person harming another (Helwig, Zelazo, & Wilson, 2001; Vaish, Missana, & Tomasello, 2011). Around age 4, children know that a person who expresses an insincere intention—saying, "I'll come over and help you rake leaves"—while not intending to do so—is lying (Maas, 2008). And 4-year-olds approve of telling the truth and disapprove of lying, even when a lie remains undetected (Bussey, 1992).

Furthermore, preschoolers in diverse cultures distinguish **moral imperatives,** which protect people's rights and welfare, from two other types of rules and expectations: **social conventions,** customs determined solely by consensus, such as table manners and politeness rituals (saying "please" and "thank you"); and **matters of personal choice,** such as choice of friends, hairstyle, and leisure activities, which do not violate rights and are up to the individual (Killen, Margie, & Sinno, 2006; Nucci & Gingo, 2011; Smetana, 2006). Interviews with 3- and 4-year-olds reveal that they consider moral violations (unprovoked hitting, stealing an apple) as more wrong than violations of social conventions (eating ice cream with your fingers). They also say that moral violations would still be wrong even if an adult did not see them and no rules existed to prohibit them because they harm others (Smetana et al, 2012). And preschoolers' concern with personal choice, conveyed through statements like "I'm gonna wear *this* shirt," serves as the springboard for moral concepts of individual rights, which will expand greatly in middle childhood and adolescence.

Young children's moral reasoning tends to be *rigid,* emphasizing salient features and consequences while neglecting other important information. For example, they have difficulty distinguishing between accidental and intentional transgressions (Killen et al. 2011). And they are more likely than older children to claim that stealing and lying are always wrong, even when a person has a morally sound reason for engaging in these acts (Lourenço, 2003; Poplinger et al., 2011). Furthermore, their explanations for why hitting others is wrong are simplistic and centered on physical harm: "When you get hit, it hurts, and you start to cry" (Nucci, 2008).

Still, preschoolers' ability to distinguish moral imperatives from social conventions is impressive. How do they do so? According to cognitive-developmental theorists, they *actively make sense* of their experiences (Helwig & Turiel, 2011). They observe that after a moral offense, peers respond with strong negative emotion, describe their own injury or loss, tell another child to stop, or retaliate. And an adult who intervenes is likely to call attention to the rights and feelings of the victim. In contrast, violations of social convention elicit less intense peer reactions. And in these situations, adults usually demand obedience without explanation or point to the importance of keeping order.

This preschooler understands that his choice of a toy is a matter of personal choice, distinct from moral imperatives and social conventions.

SOCIAL EXPERIENCE AND MORAL UNDERSTANDING Cognition and language support preschoolers' moral understanding, but social experiences are vital. Disputes with siblings and peers over rights, possessions, and property allow preschoolers to negotiate, compromise, and work out their first ideas about justice and fairness. Children also learn from warm, sensitive parental communication and from observing how adults handle rule violations (Turiel & Killen, 2010). And they benefit greatly from adult–child discussions of moral issues. Children who are advanced in moral thinking tend to have parents who adapt their communications about fighting, honesty, and ownership to what their children can understand, tell stories with moral implications, encourage prosocial behavior, and gently stimulate the child to think further, without being hostile or critical (Janssens & Deković, 1997; Walker & Taylor, 1991).

Preschoolers who verbally and physically assault others, often with little or no provocation, are already delayed in moral reasoning (Helwig & Turiel, 2004). Without special help, such children show long-term disruptions in moral development, deficits in self-control, and ultimately an antisocial lifestyle.

The Other Side of Morality: Development of Aggression

Beginning in late infancy, all children display aggression from time to time, and as opportunities to interact with siblings and peers increase, aggressive outbursts occur more often (Dodge, Coie, & Lynam, 2006; Nærde et al. 2014). By the second year, aggressive acts with two distinct purposes emerge. Initially, the most common is **proactive** (or *instrumental*) **aggression,** in which children act to fulfill a need or desire—to obtain an object, privilege, space, or social reward, such as adult or peer attention—and unemotionally attack a person to achieve their goal. The other type, **reactive** (or *hostile*) **aggression,** is an angry, defensive response to provocation or a blocked goal and is meant to hurt another person (Dodge, Coie, & Lynam, 2006; Vitaro & Brendgen, 2012).

Proactive and reactive aggression come in three forms, which are the focus of most research:

- **Physical aggression** harms others through physical injury—pushing, hitting, kicking, or punching others, or destroying another's property.
- **Verbal aggression** harms others through threats of physical aggression, name-calling, or hostile teasing.

These preschoolers display proactive aggression, pushing and grabbing as they argue over a game. Proactive aggression declines with age as children learn to compromise and share, and as their capacity to delay gratification improves.

- **Relational aggression** damages another's peer relationships through social exclusion, malicious gossip, or friendship manipulation.

Although verbal aggression is always direct, physical and relational aggression can be either *direct* or *indirect*. For example, hitting injures a person directly, whereas destroying property indirectly inflicts physical harm. Similarly, saying, "Do what I say, or I won't be your friend," conveys relational aggression directly, while spreading rumors, refusing to talk to a peer, or manipulating friendship by saying behind someone's back, "Don't play with her; she's a nerd," does so indirectly.

In early childhood, verbal aggression gradually replaces physical aggression as language develops and adults and peers react negatively and strongly to physical attacks (Alink et al., 2006; Vitaro & Brendgen, 2012). And proactive aggression declines as preschoolers' improved capacity to delay gratification enables them to resist grabbing others' possessions. But reactive aggression in verbal and relational forms tends to rise over early and middle childhood (Côté et al., 2007; Tremblay, 2000). Older children are better able to recognize malicious intentions and, as a result, more often retaliate in hostile ways.

By age 17 months, boys are more physically aggressive than girls—a difference found throughout childhood in many cultures (Baillargeon et al., 2007; Card et al., 2008; Lussier, Corrado, & Tzoumakis, 2012). The sex difference is due in part to biology—in particular, to male sex hormones (androgens) and temperamental traits (activity level, irritability, impulsivity) on which boys score higher. Gender-role conformity is also important. For example, parents respond far more negatively to physical fighting in girls (Arnold, McWilliams, & Harvey-Arnold, 1998).

Although girls have a reputation for being both verbally and relationally more aggressive than boys, the sex difference is small (Crick, Ostrov, & Werner, 2006; Crick et al., 2006). Beginning in the preschool years, girls concentrate most of their aggressive acts in the relational category. Boys inflict harm in more variable ways. Physically and verbally aggressive boys also tend to be relationally aggressive (Card et al., 2008). Therefore, boys display overall rates of aggression that are much higher than girls'.

At the same time, girls more often use indirect relational tactics that—in disrupting intimate bonds especially important to girls—can be particularly mean. Whereas physical attacks are usually brief, acts of indirect relational aggression may extend for hours, weeks, or even months (Nelson, Robinson, & Hart, 2005; Underwood, 2003). In one instance, a 6-year-old girl formed a "pretty-girls club" and—for nearly an entire school year—convinced its members to exclude several classmates by saying they were "dirty and smelly."

An occasional aggressive exchange between preschoolers is normal. Children sometimes assert their sense of self through these encounters, which become important learning experiences as adults intervene and teach social problem solving (Vaughn et al., 2003). But some children—especially those who are emotionally negative, impulsive, and disobedient—are at risk for early, high rates of physical or relational aggression (or both) that can persist. Persistent aggression, in turn, predicts later internalizing and externalizing difficulties and social skills deficits, including loneliness, anxiety, depression, peer relationship problems, and antisocial activity in middle childhood and adolescence (Côté et al., 2007; Crick, Ostrov, & Werner, 2006; Ostrov et al., 2013).

THE FAMILY AS TRAINING GROUND FOR AGGRESSIVE BEHAVIOR "I can't control him; he's impossible," Robbie's mother, Nadine, complained to Leslie one day. When Leslie asked if Robbie might be troubled by something happening at home, she discovered that his parents fought constantly and resorted to harsh, inconsistent discipline. The same child-rearing practices that undermine moral internalization—love withdrawal, power assertion, physical punishment, negative comments and emotions, and inconsistency—are linked to aggression from early childhood through adolescence, in children of both sexes and in many cultures, with most of these practices predicting both physical and relational forms (Côté et al., 2007; Gershoff et al., 2010; Kuppens et al., 2013; Nelson et al., 2013; Olson et al. 2011).

In families like Robbie's, anger and punitiveness quickly create a conflict-ridden family atmosphere and an "out-of-control" child. The pattern begins with forceful discipline, which occurs more often with stressful life experiences (such as economic hardship or an unhappy marriage), a parent with an unstable personality, or a temperamentally difficult child (Dodge, Coie, & Lynam, 2006). Typically, the parent threatens, criticizes, and punishes, and the child whines, yells, and refuses until the parent "gives in." At the end of each exchange, both parent and child get relief from stopping the unpleasant behavior of the other, so the behaviors repeat and escalate.

As these cycles become more frequent, they generate anxiety and irritability among other family members, who soon join in the hostile interactions. Compared with siblings in typical families, preschool siblings who have critical, punitive parents are more aggressive toward one another. Physically, verbally, and relationally destructive sibling conflict, in turn, quickly spreads to peer relationships, contributing to poor impulse control and antisocial behavior by the early school years (Garcia et al., 2000; Miller et al., 2012; Ostrov, Crick, & Stauffacher, 2006).

Boys are more likely than girls to be targets of harsh, inconsistent discipline because they are more active and impulsive and therefore harder to control. When children who are extreme in these characteristics are exposed to emotionally negative, inept parenting, their capacity for emotional self-regulation, empathic responding, and guilt after transgressions is severely disrupted (Eisenberg, Eggum, & Edwards, 2010). Consequently, they lash out when disappointed, frustrated, or faced with a sad or fearful victim.

SOCIAL INFORMATION-PROCESSING DEFICITS Children who are products of these family processes soon acquire a distorted view of the social world. Those who are high in reactive aggression often see hostile intent where it does not exist—in situations where peers' intentions are unclear, where harm is accidental, and even where peers are trying to be helpful (Lochman & Dodge, 1998; Orobio de Castro et al., 2002). When such children feel threatened (for example, a researcher tells them that a peer they will work with is in a bad mood and might pick a fight), they are especially likely to interpret accidental mishaps as hostile (Williams et al., 2003). As a result, they make many unprovoked attacks, which trigger aggressive retaliations.

Children high in proactive aggression have different deficits in social information processing. Compared with agemates, they believe there are more benefits and fewer costs for engaging in destructive acts (Arsenio, 2010; Dodge et al., 1997). And they are more likely to think that aggression "works," producing material rewards and reducing others' unpleasant behaviors (Arsenio & Lemerise, 2001; Goldstein & Tisak, 2004). Thus, they callously use aggression to advance their own goals and are relatively unconcerned about causing suffering in others—an aggressive style associated with later, more severe conduct problems, violent behavior, and delinquency (Marsee & Frick, 2010).

TAKE A MOMENT... Return to the information-processing model of social problem solving on page 370. Notice how reactive aggression is linked to deficiencies in recognizing and interpreting social cues. In contrast, proactive aggression is associated with deficiencies in formulating social goals (caring more about satisfying one's own needs than getting along with others) and generating and evaluating strategies (engaging in aggression and evaluating it favorably) (Arsenio, 2010). A substantial number of aggressive children engage in both reactive and proactive acts, while others largely display one type (Fite et al., 2008).

Highly aggressive children tend to be rejected by peers, to fail in school, and (by adolescence) to seek out deviant peers. Together, these factors contribute to the long-term stability of aggression.

MEDIA AND AGGRESSION In the United States, 57 percent of TV programs between 6 A.M. and 11 P.M. contain violent scenes, often portraying repeated aggressive acts that go unpunished. TV victims of violence are rarely shown experiencing serious harm, and few programs condemn violence or depict other ways of solving problems (Center for Communication and Social Policy, 1998). Verbally and relationally aggressive acts are particularly frequent in reality

© CHRISTINA KENNEDY/ALAMY

TV violence increases the likelihood of hostile thoughts and emotions and tolerance of real-world aggression. Playing violent video and computer games has similar effects.

TV shows (Coyne, Robinson, & Nelson, 2010). And violent content is 9 percent above average in children's programming, with cartoons being the most violent.

Reviewers of thousands of studies—using a wide variety of research designs, methods, and participants from diverse cultures—have concluded that TV violence increases the likelihood of hostile thoughts and emotions and of verbally, physically, and relationally aggressive behavior (Bushman & Huesmann, 2012; Comstock & Scharrer, 2006). A growing number of studies show that playing violent video and computer games has similar effects (Anderson et al., 2010; Hofferth, 2010). Although young people of all ages are susceptible, preschool and young school-age children are especially likely to imitate TV violence because they believe that much TV fiction is real and accept what they see uncritically.

Violent programming not only creates short-term difficulties in parent and peer relations but also has lasting negative consequences. In several longitudinal studies, time spent watching TV in childhood and adolescence predicted aggressive behavior in early adulthood, after other factors linked to TV viewing (such as prior child and parent aggression, IQ, parent education, family income, and neighborhood crime) were controlled (see Figure 10.4) (Graber et al., 2006; Huesmann et al., 2003; Johnson et al., 2002). Aggressive children and adolescents have a greater appetite for violent media fare. And boys devote more time to violent media than girls, in part because of male-oriented themes of conquest and adventure and use of males as lead characters. But even in nonaggressive children, violent TV sparks hostile thoughts and behavior; its impact is simply less intense.

Furthermore, media violence "hardens" children to aggression, making them more willing to tolerate it in others (Anderson et al., 2003, 2010). Viewers quickly habituate, responding with reduced arousal and greater acceptance when exposed to real-world instances.

Preschoolers, as we saw in Chapter 9, spend much time watching educational programs for young children. Although beneficial for cognitive and academic progress, high exposure to educational programs is associated with a rise in relational aggression in young children (Ostrov, Gentile, & Mullins, 2013). The likely reason is that these programs often present social-conflict scenes, in a well-intentioned effort to model social problem solving. But preschoolers have difficulty connecting characters' relational conflicts to their eventual favorable resolutions, so they readily imitate the relationally aggressive acts they see. When brief explanations are inserted, alerting young viewers to an educational program's prosocial message, they more often respond as intended (Mares & Acosta, 2010).

The ease with which screen media can manipulate children's beliefs and behavior has led to strong public pressure to improve its content. In Canada, a nationwide broadcasting code bans from children's shows realistic scenes of violence that minimize consequences and cartoons with violence as the central theme. Further, violent programming intended for adults cannot be shown on Canadian channels before 9 P.M. In the United States, however, the First Amendment right to free speech has hampered efforts to regulate TV broadcasting (and many Canadian children have access to violent TV fare on U.S. channels).

As a result, parents bear most responsibility for regulating their children's exposure to media violence and other inappropriate content. In the United States, TV programs are rated for violent and sexual content, and since 2000 new TV sets have been required to contain the V-chip, which allows parents to block undesired material. And parents can control children's Internet access by using filters or programs that monitor website visits.

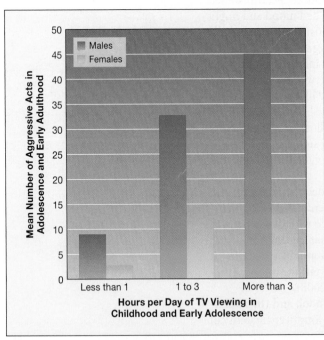

FIGURE 10.4   Relationship of television viewing in childhood and early adolescence to aggressive acts in adolescence and early adulthood. Interviews with more than 700 parents and youths revealed that the more TV watched in childhood and early adolescence, the greater the annual number of aggressive acts committed by the young person, as reported in follow-up interviews at ages 16 and 22. (Based on Johnson et al., 2002.)

Applying What We Know

Regulating Screen Media Use

STRATEGY	EXPLANATION
Limit TV viewing and computer and tablet use.	Parents should provide clear rules limiting children's TV viewing and computer and tablet use and should stick to the rules. The TV or computer should not be used as a babysitter. Placing a TV or a computer in a child's bedroom substantially increases use and makes the child's activity hard to monitor.
Avoid using screen media as a reward.	When media access is used as a reward or withheld as punishment, children become increasingly attracted to it.
When possible, watch TV and view online content with children, helping them understand what they see.	By raising questions about realism in media depictions, expressing disapproval of on-screen behavior, and encouraging discussion, adults help children understand and critically evaluate TV and online content.
Link TV and online content to everyday learning experiences.	Parents can extend TV and online learning in ways that encourage children to engage actively with their surroundings. For example, a program on animals might spark a trip to the zoo, a visit to the library for books about animals, or new ways of observing and caring for the family pet.
Model good media practices.	Parents' media behavior influences children's behavior. Parents should avoid excessive TV and computer use, limit their own exposure to harmful media content, and limit mobile device use during family interactions.
Use a warm, rational approach to child rearing.	Children of warm parents who make reasonable demands for mature behavior prefer media experiences with educational and prosocial content and are less attracted to violent programming.

Yet surveys of U.S. parents indicate that 20 to 30 percent of preschoolers and 40 percent of school-age children experience no limits on TV or computer use at home. Some children begin visiting websites without parental supervision as early as age 4 (Rideout & Hamel, 2006; Roberts, Foehr, & Rideout, 2005; Varnhagen, 2007). Also, parents often model excessive, inappropriate screen media use. In a naturalistic study of adults with children in fast food restaurants, almost one-third of the adults spent the entire meal absorbed with mobile devices instead of engaging with the children in their care (Radesky et al., 2014).

To help parents improve their children's "media diet," one group of researchers devised a 12-month intervention in which they guided parents in replacing violent programs with age-appropriate prosocial programs. Compared to a control group, children in intervention families displayed lower rates of externalizing behavior and improved social competence (Christakis et al., 2013). Applying What We Know above lists strategies parents can use to regulate children's screen media use.

HELPING CHILDREN AND PARENTS CONTROL AGGRESSION Treatment for aggressive children must begin early, before their antisocial behavior becomes well-practiced and difficult to change. Breaking the cycle of hostilities between family members and promoting effective ways of relating to others is crucial. The coercive cycles of punitive parents and aggressive children are so persistent that these children often are punished when they do behave appropriately!

Leslie suggested that Robbie's parents see a family therapist, who observed their ineffective practices and coached them in alternatives. They learned not to give in to Robbie, to pair commands with reasons, and to replace verbal insults and spankings with more effective punishments, such as time out and withdrawal of privileges. The therapist also encouraged Robbie's parents to be warmer and to give him attention and approval for prosocial acts. Finally, she helped them with their marital problems. This, in addition to their improved ability to manage Robbie's behavior, greatly reduced tension and conflict in the household.

Parent training programs based on social learning theory have been devised to improve parenting in families like Robbie's. In one highly effective approach called *Incredible Years*, parents complete 18 weekly group sessions facilitated by two professionals, who teach parenting techniques for promoting children's academic, emotional, and social skills and for managing disruptive behaviors. Sessions include coaching, modeling, and practicing effective

LOOK and LISTEN

Watch a half-hour of children's cartoons and a prime-time movie on TV, and tally the number of violent acts, including those that go unpunished. How often did violence occur in each type of program? What do young viewers learn about the consequences of violence?

parenting behaviors—experiences aimed at interrupting parent–child destructive interaction while promoting positive relationships and competencies (Webster-Stratton & Reid, 2010). A special focus is positive parenting, including attention, encouragement, and praise for pro-social behaviors.

Evaluations in which families with aggressive children were randomly assigned to either Incredible Years or control groups reveal that the program is highly effective at improving parenting and reducing child behavior problems. And the effects endure. In one 8- to 12- year follow-up, 75 percent of young children with serious conduct problems whose parents participated in Incredible Years were well-adjusted as teenagers (Webster-Stratton, Rinaldi, & Reid, 2011).

At preschool, Leslie began teaching Robbie more successful ways of relating to peers, had him practice these skills, and praised him for using them. As opportunities arose, she encouraged Robbie to talk about a playmate's feelings and to express his own. As he increasingly took the perspective of others, empathized, and felt sympathetic concern, his lashing out at peers declined (Izard et al., 2008). Robbie participated in a social problem-solving intervention as well (return to pages 370–371 to review).

Finally, relieving stressors that stem from poverty and neighborhood disorganization and providing families with social supports help prevent childhood aggression (Boyle & Lipman, 2002; Bugental, Corpuz, & Schwartz, 2012). When parents better cope with difficulties in their own lives, interventions aimed at reducing children's aggression are even more effective.

Ask Yourself

- **REVIEW** What experiences help preschoolers differentiate moral imperatives, social conventions, and matters of personal choice?

- **CONNECT** What must parents do to foster conscience development in fearless, impulsive children? How does this illustrate the concept of goodness of fit (see pages 259–260 in Chapter 7)?

- **APPLY** Alice and Wayne want their two young children to become morally mature, caring individuals. List some parenting practices they should use and some they should avoid.

- **REFLECT** Which types of punishment for a misbehaving preschooler do you endorse, and which types do you reject? Why?

10.7 Discuss biological and environmental influences on preschoolers' gender-stereotyped beliefs and behavior.

10.8 Describe and evaluate major theories that explain the emergence of gender identity.

Gender Typing

Gender typing refers to any association of objects, activities, roles, or traits with one sex or the other in ways that conform to cultural stereotypes (Blakemore, Berenbaum, & Liben, 2009). In Leslie's classroom, girls spent more time in the housekeeping, art, and reading corners, while boys gathered more often in spaces devoted to blocks, woodworking, and active play. Already, the children had acquired many gender-linked beliefs and preferences and tended to play with peers of their own sex.

The same theories that provide accounts of morality have been used to explain children's gender typing: *social learning theory,* with its emphasis on modeling and reinforcement, and *cognitive-developmental theory,* with its focus on children as active thinkers about their social world. As we will see, neither is adequate by itself. *Gender schema theory,* a third perspective that combines elements of both, has gained favor. In the following sections, we consider the early development of gender typing.

Gender-Stereotyped Beliefs and Behaviors

Even before children can label their own sex consistently, they have begun to acquire subtle associations with gender that most of us hold—men as rough and sharp, women as soft and round. In one study, 18-month-olds linked such items as fir trees and hammers with males, although they had not yet learned comparable feminine associations (Eichstedt et al., 2002). Recall from Chapter 7 that around age 2, children use such words as *boy, girl, lady,* and *man* appropriately. As soon as gender categories are established, children sort out what they mean in terms of activities and behaviors.

Preschoolers associate toys, clothing, tools, household items, games, occupations, colors (pink and blue), and behaviors (physical and relational aggression) with one sex or the other (Banse et al., 2010; Giles & Heyman, 2005; Poulin-Dubois et al., 2002). And their actions reflect their beliefs, not only in play preferences but in personality traits as well. As we have seen, boys tend to be more active, impulsive, assertive, and physically aggressive. Girls tend to be more fearful, dependent, emotionally sensitive, compliant, advanced in effortful control, and skilled at understanding self-conscious emotions and at inflicting indirect relational aggression (Bosacki & Moore, 2004; Else-Quest, 2012; Underwood, 2003).

Between ages 3 and 4, gender-stereotyped beliefs strengthen—so much so that many children apply them as blanket rules rather than flexible guidelines (Halim, Ruble, & Tamis-LeMonda, 2013). When children were asked whether gender stereotypes could be violated, half or more of 3- and 4-year-olds answered "no" to clothing, hairstyle, certain play styles (girls playing roughly), and play with certain toys (Barbie dolls and G.I. Joes) (Blakemore, 2003). Furthermore, most 3- to 6-year-olds are firm about not wanting to be friends with a child who violates a gender stereotype (a boy who wears nail polish, a girl who plays with trucks) or to attend a school where such violations are allowed (Ruble et al., 2007).

The rigidity of preschoolers' gender stereotypes helps us understand some commonly observed everyday behaviors. When Leslie showed her class a picture of a Scottish bagpiper wearing a kilt, the children insisted, "Men don't wear skirts!" During free play, they often exclaimed that girls can't be police officers and boys don't take care of babies. These one-sided judgments are a joint product of gender stereotyping in the environment and young children's cognitive limitations—in particular, their difficulty coordinating conflicting sources of information (Trautner et al., 2005). Most preschoolers do not yet realize that characteristics *associated with* one's sex—activities, toys, occupations, hairstyle, and clothing—do not *determine* whether a person is male or female. They have trouble understanding that males and females can be different in terms of their bodies but similar in many other ways.

Gender typing is well under way in the preschool years. Girls tend to play with girls and are drawn to toys and activities that emphasize nurturance, cooperation, and physical attractiveness.

Biological Influences on Gender Typing

The sex differences in play and personality traits just described appear in many cultures around the world (Munroe & Romney, 2006; Whiting & Edwards, 1988). Certain ones—male activity level and physical aggression, female emotional sensitivity, and a preference for same-sex playmates—are widespread among mammalian species (de Waal, 1993, 2001). According to an evolutionary perspective, the adult life of our male ancestors was oriented toward competing for mates, that of our female ancestors toward rearing children. Therefore, males became genetically primed for dominance and females for intimacy, responsiveness, and cooperativeness. Evolutionary theorists claim that family and cultural forces can influence the intensity of genetically based sex differences, leading some individuals to be more gender-typed than others. But experience cannot eradicate those aspects of gender typing that served adaptive functions in human history (Konner, 2010; Maccoby, 2002).

Experiments with animals reveal that prenatally administered androgens increase active play and suppress maternal caregiving in both male and female mammals (Sato et al., 2004). Research with humans reveals similar patterns. Girls exposed prenatally to high levels of androgens (due to normal variation in hormone levels or to a genetic defect) show more "masculine" behaviors—a preference for trucks and blocks over dolls, for active over quiet play, and for boys as playmates—even when their parents encourage them to engage in gender-typical play (Berenbaum & Beltz, 2011; Cohen-Bendahan, van de Beek, & Berenbaum, 2005). Maternal stress during pregnancy—such as unemployment, divorce, or death of a close relative—may influence prenatal hormones, and it has been linked to "masculine" behaviors among preschool girls (Barrett et al., 2014). Similarly, boys with reduced prenatal androgen exposure (due to hereditary defects or maternal contact with industrial chemicals that interfere with androgen production) tend to engage in "feminine" behaviors, including toy choices, play behaviors, and preference for girl playmates (Jürgensen et al., 2007; Swan et al., 2010).

Eleanor Maccoby (1998) argues that biologically based sex differences, which affect children's play styles, lead children to choose same-sex playmates whose interests and behaviors are compatible with their own. Preschool girls like to play in pairs with other girls because they share a preference for quieter activities involving cooperative roles. Boys prefer larger-group play with other boys, who desire to run, climb, play-fight, compete, and build up and knock down (Fabes, Martin, & Hanish, 2003). At age 4, children spend three times as much time with same-sex as with other-sex playmates. By age 6, this ratio has climbed to 11 to 1 (Martin & Fabes, 2001).

Environmental Influences on Gender Typing

In a study following almost 14,000 British children from ages 2½ to 13, gender-typed behavior rose steadily over early childhood and persisted into early adolescence, with the most gender-typed young preschoolers showing the sharpest increase (Golombok et al., 2008; 2012). A wealth of evidence reveals that environmental forces—at home, at school, and in the community—build on genetic influences to promote vigorous gender typing in early childhood.

THE FAMILY Beginning at birth, parents have different expectations of sons than of daughters (see Chapter 7). Many parents prefer that their children play with "gender-appropriate" toys (Blakemore & Hill, 2008). They tend to describe achievement, competition, and control of emotion as important for sons and warmth, polite behavior, and closely supervised activities as important for daughters (Brody, 1999; Turner & Gervai, 1995).

Actual parenting practices reflect these beliefs. Parents give their sons toys that stress action and competition (guns, cars, tools, and footballs) and their daughters toys that emphasize nurturance, cooperation, and physical attractiveness (dolls, tea sets, and jewelry) (Leaper, 1994; Leaper & Friedman, 2007). Fathers of preschoolers report more physical interactions—chasing, playing ball, playing outdoors—with sons, and more literacy activities—singing, reading, storytelling—with daughters (Leavell et al., 2011). Parents also tend to react more positively when a son plays with cars and trucks, demands attention, runs and climbs, or tries to take toys from others. When interacting with daughters, they more often direct play activities, provide help, encourage participation in household tasks, make supportive statements (approval, praise, and agreement), and refer to emotions (Clearfield & Nelson, 2006; Fagot & Hagan, 1991; Leaper, 2000). For example, when playing housekeeping, mothers engage in high rates of supportive emotion talk with girls.

As these findings suggest, language is a powerful indirect means for teaching children about gender stereotypes. Earlier we saw that most young children hold rigid beliefs about gender. Although their strict views are due in part to cognitive limitations, they also draw on relevant social experiences to construct these beliefs. Even parents who believe strongly in gender equality unconsciously use language that highlights gender

Of the two sexes, boys are more gender-typed. Fathers, especially, promote "masculine" behavior in their preschool sons through activities that stress action and competition.

CAVAN IMAGES/GETTY IMAGES

distinctions and informs children about traditional gender roles (see the Social Issues box on pages 388–389).

Of the two sexes, boys are more gender-typed. Fathers, especially, tend to insist that boys conform to gender roles. They place more pressure to achieve on sons than on daughters and are less tolerant of "cross-gender" behavior in sons—more concerned when a boy acts like a "sissy" than when a girl acts like a "tomboy" (Blakemore & Hill, 2008; Wood, Desmarais, & Gugula, 2002). Yet some parents have more flexible views. Recognizing the negative effects of restrictive norms for males, they want their sons to be comfortable expressing feelings. As one father explained: "I'm more reserved than my wife emotionally. I realize that it is better to have our son be more open emotionally. . . . So, that's a challenge. You want him to open up, and you have to do the same thing. I'm not used to doing that" (Parker et al., 2012, p. 61).

Parents who hold nonstereotyped values and behave accordingly have children who are less gender-typed (Brody, 1997; Tenenbaum & Leaper, 2002). Young children with gay or lesbian parents are less gender-typed than agemates with heterosexual parents, perhaps because of their parents' more egalitarian gender norms (Fulcher, Sutfin, & Patterson, 2008; Goldberg, Kashy, & Smith, 2012).

Other family members may also reduce gender typing. For example, children with older, other-sex siblings have many more opportunities to imitate and participate in "cross-gender" activities and, as a result, are less gender-typed in play preferences, attitudes, and personality traits (McHale et al., 2001; Rust et al., 2000).

TEACHERS   Teachers often act in ways that extend gender-role learning. Several times, Leslie caught herself emphasizing gender distinctions when she called out, "Will the girls line up on one side and the boys on the other?" or pleaded "Boys, I wish you'd quiet down like the girls!"

Like parents, preschool teachers encourage girls to participate in adult-structured activities. Girls frequently cluster around the teacher, following directions, while boys are attracted to play areas where adults are minimally involved (Campbell, Shirley, & Candy, 2004). As a result, boys and girls engage in different social behaviors. Compliance and bids for help occur more often in adult-structured contexts; assertiveness, leadership, and creative use of materials in unstructured pursuits.

As early as kindergarten, teachers give more overall attention (both positive and negative) to boys than to girls—a difference evident in diverse countries, including China, England, and the United States. They praise boys more for their academic knowledge but also use more disapproval and controlling discipline with them (Chen & Rao, 2011; Davies, 2008; Swinson & Harrop, 2009). Teachers seem to expect boys to misbehave more often—a belief based partly on boys' actual behavior and partly on gender stereotypes.

PEERS   Children's same-sex peer associations make the peer context an especially potent source of gender-role learning. The more preschoolers play with same-sex partners, the more their behavior becomes gender-typed—in toy choices, activity level, aggression, and adult involvement (Martin et al., 2011, 2013).

By age 3, same-sex peers positively reinforce one another for gender-typed play by praising, imitating, or joining in. In contrast, when preschoolers engage in "cross-gender" activities—for example, when boys play with dolls or girls with cars and trucks—peers criticize them. Boys are especially intolerant of cross-gender play in other boys (Thorne, 1993). A boy who frequently crosses gender lines is likely to be ignored by other boys, even when he does engage in "masculine" activities!

Children also develop different styles of social influence in gender-segregated peer groups. To get their way in large-group play, boys often rely on commands, threats, and physical force. Girls' preference for playing in pairs leads to greater concern with a partner's needs, evident in girls' use of polite requests, persuasion, and acceptance. When girls communicate assertively with commands, other girls tend to respond with aggression (Hanish et al., 2012).

LOOK and LISTEN

While observing 3- to 5-year-olds during a free-play period in a preschool or child-care program, note the extent of gender segregation and gender-typed play. Did styles of social influence differ in boys' and girls' gender-segregated groups? Jot down examples.

Children develop different styles of interaction in gender-segregated play. Boys more often use commands and physical force to get their way. Girls, out of greater concern for their playmate's feelings, rely on polite requests and persuasion.

Social Issues: Education

Children Learn About Gender Through Mother–Child Conversations

In an investigation of the power of language to shape children's beliefs and expectations about gender, mothers were asked to converse with their 2- to 6-year-olds about picture books containing images of male and female children and adults engaged in various activities, half consistent and half inconsistent with gender stereotypes. Each picture was accompanied by the question, "Who can X?" where X was the activity on the page.

One mother, who believed in gender equality, turned to a picture of a boy driving a boat and asked, "Who's driving the boat?"

Her 4-year-old son replied, "A sail-man."

The mother affirmed, "A sail-man. Yup, a sailor." Then she asked, "Who can be a sailor? Boys and girls?"

"Boys," the child replied.

"Boys . . . OK," the mother again affirmed. The child stated more decisively, "Only boys."

Again the mother agreed, "Only boys," and turned the page (Gelman, Taylor, & Nguyen, 2004, p. 104).

A detailed analysis of picture-book conversations revealed that mothers' directly expressed attitudes about gender stereotypes were neutral, largely because, like this mother, they typically posed questions to their children. But by age 4,

children often voiced stereotypes, and—nearly one-third of the time—mothers affirmed them! Some mothers either moved on with the conversation or repeated the question, as in the conversation above, but rarely—just 2 percent of the time—did they explicitly counter a child's stereotype, and usually only when the book itself included stereotype-inconsistent pictures.

Although the researchers did not ask mothers to discuss gender, the mothers called attention to it even when they did not need to do so. In the English language, many nouns referring to people convey age-related information *(kid, baby, 2-year-old, preschooler, teenager, grownup, senior),* whereas only a few encode gender *(male, female, sister, brother, aunt, uncle).* Yet when using a noun to refer to a person, mothers explicitly called attention to gender more than half the time, even though the people shown in the books varied as much in age (children versus adults) as in gender. Mothers labeled gender, either with nouns or with pronouns (which in English always refer to gender), especially often when conversing with 2-year-olds: "Is that a he or a she?" "That's a boy." "There's a girl." Such statements encourage toddlers to sort their social world into gender categories, even when the statements themselves do not explicitly convey stereotypes.

© LAURA DWIGHT PHOTOGRAPHY

While reading, this mother may unconsciously teach her child to see the world in gender-linked terms—by referring to gender unnecessarily or by making generic gender statements ("Most girls prefer X"; "Boys usually don't like X").

Furthermore, both mothers and children frequently expressed *generic utterances*—ones that were broad in scope, referring to many, or nearly all, males and females: "Boys can be

---

LOOK and LISTEN

Observe a parent discussing a picture book with a 3- to 6-year-old. How many times did the parent make generic statements about gender? How about the child? Did the parent accept or correct the child's generic utterances?

Girls soon find that gentle tactics succeed with other girls but not with boys, who ignore their courteous overtures (Leaper, 1994). Boys' unresponsiveness gives girls another reason to stop interacting with them.

Over time, children come to believe in the "correctness" of gender-segregated play and to perceive themselves as more similar to same-sex than other-sex peers, which further strengthen gender segregation and gender-stereotyped activities (Martin et al., 1999, 2011). As boys and girls separate, *in-group favoritism*—more positive evaluations of members of one's own gender—becomes another factor that sustains the separate social worlds of boys and girls, resulting in "two distinct subcultures" of shared knowledge, beliefs, interests, and behaviors (Maccoby, 2002; Ruble, Martin, & Berenbaum, 2006).

THE BROADER SOCIAL ENVIRONMENT   Although children's everyday environments have changed to some degree, they continue to present many examples of gender typing—in occupations, leisure activities, media portrayals, and achievements of men and women. For example, although today's TV programs include more career-oriented women than in the past, female characters continue to be young, attractive, caring, emotional, and victimized and to be seen in romantic and family contexts. In contrast, male characters are usually dominant and powerful. Stereotypes are especially prevalent in cartoons and computer games. These media depictions contribute to young children's biased beliefs about roles and behaviors suitable for males and females (Halim, Ruble, & Tamis-LeMonda, 2013; Leaper, 2013).

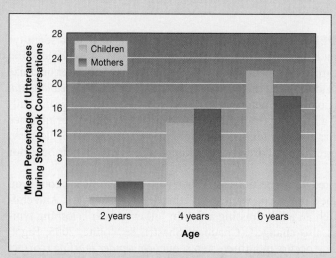

FIGURE 10.5 Mothers' and children's use of generic references to gender during storybook conversations. Generic utterances were broad in scope, in that they referred to many, or nearly all, males and females. Mothers' and children's use of generics increased dramatically between ages 2 and 6. At age 2, mothers produced more generics than children. By age 6, children produced more generics than mothers. (From S. A. Gelman, M. G. Taylor, & S. P. Nguyen, "Mother–Child Conversations About Gender," *Monographs of the Society for Research in Child Development,* 69[1, Serial No. 275], p. 46. © 2004 The Society for Research in Child Development, Inc. Republished with permission of John Wiley and Sons, Inc., conveyed through Copyright Clearance Center, Inc.)

sailors." "Most girls don't like trucks." Even generics that were gender-neutral ("Lots of girls in this book") or denied a stereotype ("Boys can be ballet dancers, too") prompted children to view individuals of the same gender as alike and to ignore exceptions. As we will see later in this chapter, generics promote gender-role conformity. Statements such as "This toy is for girls" induce children to prefer the toy labeled for their own sex and to avoid the toy labeled for the other sex.

Mothers' and children's use of generics increased sharply between ages 2 and 6, a period in which gender stereotyping and gender-role conformity rise dramatically (See Figure 10.5). Initially, mothers led the way in generic talk; at age 2 they introduced these category-wide generalizations nearly three times as often as children. By age 6, however, children were producing generics more often than mothers. In addition, mother–child pairs produced more generics about males than about females, and generics were especially common in speech to and from boys, who are the more gender typed of the two sexes.

Even though these mothers overwhelmingly believed in gender equality, they did little to instill those ideas in their children. To the contrary, their most common response to children's stereotypical comments was to affirm them! In this way, even without directly teaching stereotypes, parents—through language—provide a wealth of implicit cues that enable children to readily construct them.

Adults can combat stereotypical thinking in children through concerted efforts to avoid gendered language. Here are some suggestions:

- Refrain from labeling gender when it is unnecessary, substituting *child, friend, adult,* or *person,* for *boy, girl, man,* or *woman.*
- Substitute references to individuals ("That person wants to be a firefighter") for generic expressions, or use qualifiers ("Some boys and some girls want to be firefighters"). Experimental research confirms that generic statements strongly induce in preschoolers social biases of all kinds—gender, ethnic, and racial (Rhodes, Leslie, & Tworek, 2012).
- Monitor your own inclination to affirm children's stereotypical claims, countering these as often as possible.
- Discuss gender biases in language with children, pointing out how words can shape inappropriate beliefs and expectations and asking children to avoid using gender labels and generics.

As we will see next, children do more than imitate the many gender-linked responses they observe. They soon come to view not just their social surroundings but also themselves through a "gender-biased lens"—a perspective that can seriously restrict their interests and learning opportunities.

Gender Identity

As adults, each of us has a **gender identity**—an image of oneself as relatively masculine or feminine in characteristics. By middle childhood, researchers can measure gender identity by asking children to rate themselves on personality traits. A child or adult with a "masculine" identity scores high on traditionally masculine items (such as *ambitious, competitive,* and *self-sufficient*) and low on traditionally feminine items (such as *affectionate, cheerful,* and *soft-spoken*). Someone with a "feminine" identity does the reverse. And a substantial minority (especially females) have a gender identity called **androgyny,** scoring high on both masculine and feminine personality characteristics.

Gender identity is a good predictor of psychological adjustment. "Masculine" and androgynous children and adults have higher self-esteem than "feminine" individuals, perhaps because many typically feminine traits are not highly valued by society (DiDonato & Berenbaum, 2011; Harter, 2012a). Also, androgynous individuals are more adaptable—able to show masculine independence or feminine sensitivity, depending on the situation (Huyck, 1996; Taylor &

Hall, 1982). The existence of an androgynous identity demonstrates that children can acquire a mixture of positive qualities traditionally associated with each gender—an orientation that may best help them realize their potential.

EMERGENCE OF GENDER IDENTITY   How do children develop a gender identity? According to *social learning theory,* behavior comes before self-perceptions. Preschoolers first acquire gender-typed responses through modeling and reinforcement and only later organize these behaviors into gender-linked ideas about themselves. In contrast, *cognitive-developmental theory* maintains that self-perceptions come before behavior. Over the preschool years, children acquire **gender constancy**—a full understanding of the biologically based permanence of their gender, including the realization that sex remains the same over time, even if clothing, hairstyle, and play activities change. Then children use this knowledge to guide their behavior (Kohlberg, 1966).

When 3- to 5-year-olds are asked such questions as "When you (a girl) grow up, could you ever be a daddy?" or "Could you be a boy if you wanted to?" they freely answer yes. And children younger than age 6 who watch an adult dressing a doll in "other-gender" clothing typically insist that the doll's sex has also changed (Chauhan, Shastri, & Mohite, 2005; Fagot, 1985). Mastery of gender constancy occurs in a three-step sequence: *gender labeling* (correct naming of one's own and others' sex), *gender stability* (understanding that gender remains the same over time), and *gender consistency* (realization that gender is not altered by superficial changes in clothing or activities). Full attainment of gender constancy is strongly related to ability to pass Piagetian conservation and verbal appearance–reality tasks (see page 314 in Chapter 9) (De Lisi & Gallagher, 1991; Trautner, Gervai, & Nemeth, 2003). Indeed, gender constancy tasks can be considered a type of appearance–reality problem, in that children must distinguish what a person looks like from who he or she really is.

Is cognitive-developmental theory correct that gender constancy is responsible for children's gender-typed behavior? Evidence for this assumption is weak. Although outcomes are not entirely consistent, some evidence suggests that gender constancy actually contributes to the emergence of more flexible gender-role attitudes during the school years (Ruble et al., 2007). But overall, the impact of gender constancy on gender typing is not great. As research in the following section reveals, gender-role adoption is more powerfully affected by children's beliefs about how close the connection must be between their own gender and their behavior.

GENDER SCHEMA THEORY   **Gender schema theory** is an information-processing approach to gender typing that combines social learning and cognitive-developmental features. It explains how environmental pressures and children's cognitions work together to shape gender-role development (Martin & Halverson, 1987; Martin, Ruble, & Szkrybalo, 2002). Young children pick up gender-stereotyped preferences and behaviors from others. At the same time, they organize their experiences into *gender schemas,* or masculine and feminine categories, that they use to interpret their world. As soon as preschoolers can label their own gender, they select gender schemas consistent with it ("Only boys can be doctors" or "Cooking is a girl's job") and apply those categories to themselves.

We have seen that individual differences exist in the extent to which children endorse gender-typed views. Figure 10.6 shows different cognitive pathways for children who often apply gender schemas to their experiences and those who rarely do (Liben & Bigler, 2002). Consider Billy, who encounters a doll. If Billy is a *gender-schematic child,* his *gender-salience filter* immediately makes gender highly relevant. Drawing on his prior learning, he asks himself, "Should boys play with dolls?" If he answers "yes" and the toy interests him, he will approach it, explore it, and learn more about it. If he answers "no," he will respond by avoiding the "gender-inappropriate" toy. But if Billy is a *gender-aschematic child*—one who seldom views the world in gender-linked terms—he simply asks himself, "Do I like this toy?" and responds on the basis of his interests.

To examine the consequences of gender-schematic processing, researchers showed 4- and 5-year-olds gender-neutral toys that varied in attractiveness. An adult labeled some as boys' toys and others as girls' toys, leaving a third group unlabeled. Most children engaged

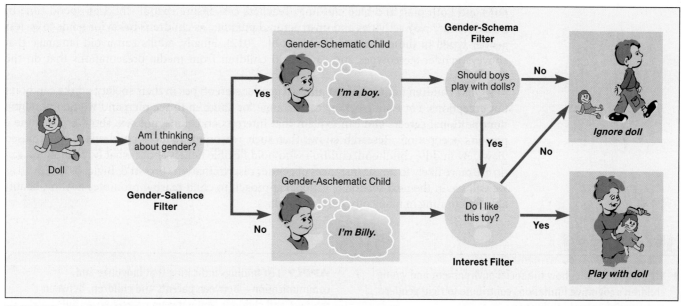

FIGURE 10.6 **Cognitive pathways for gender-schematic and gender-aschematic children.** In *gender-schematic children,* the gender-salience filter immediately makes gender highly relevant: Billy sees a doll and thinks, "I'm a boy. Should boys play with dolls?" Drawing on his experiences, he answers "yes" or "no." If he answers "yes" and the doll interests him, he plays with the doll. If he answers "no," he avoids the "gender-inappropriate" toy. *Gender-aschematic children* rarely view the world in gender-linked terms. Billy simply asks, "Do I like this toy?" and responds on the basis of his interests. (Reprinted by permission of Rebecca Bigler.)

in gender-schematic reasoning, preferring toys labeled for their gender and predicting that same-sex peers would also like those toys (Martin, Eisenbud, & Rose, 1995). Highly attractive toys, especially, lost their appeal when they were labeled as for the other gender.

Gender-schematic thinking is so powerful that when children see others behaving in "gender-inconsistent" ways, they often distort their memory to make it "gender-consistent." For example, when shown a picture of a male nurse, they may remember him as a doctor (Martin & Ruble, 2004). And, because gender-schematic preschoolers typically conclude, "What I like, children of my own sex will also like," they often use their own preferences to add to their gender biases (Liben & Bigler, 2002). For example, a girl who dislikes oysters may declare, "Only boys like oysters!" even though she has never actually been given information supporting such a stereotype. At least partly for this reason, young children's gender schemas contain both culturally standard and nonstandard ideas (Tenenbaum et al., 2010). Not until well into the school years do children's gender schemas fully resemble those of adults.

Reducing Gender Stereotyping in Young Children

How can we help young children avoid rigid gender schemas that restrict their behavior and learning opportunities? No easy recipe exists. Biology clearly affects children's gender typing, channeling boys, on average, toward active, competitive play and girls toward quieter, more intimate interaction. But most aspects of gender typing are not built into human nature (Ruble, Martin, & Berenbaum, 2006).

Because young children's cognitive limitations lead them to assume that cultural practices determine gender, parents and teachers are wise to delay preschoolers' exposure to gender-stereotyped messages. Adults can begin by limiting traditional gender roles in their own behavior and provide children with nontraditional alternatives. For example, parents can take turns making dinner, bathing children, and driving the family car, and they can give their sons and daughters both trucks and

Parents and teachers can reduce preschoolers' gender stereotyping by modeling nonstereotyped behaviors and providing nontraditional alternatives. For this boy, making cookies is not "for girls." It's an activity he and his mother enjoy together.

dolls and both pink and blue clothing. Teachers can ensure that all children spend time in mixed-gender play activities and unstructured pursuits, as children's behavior tends to be less gender-typed in these contexts (Goble et al., 2012). Finally, adults can avoid language that conveys gender stereotypes and can shield children from media presentations that do the same.

Once children notice the vast array of gender stereotypes in their society, adults can point out exceptions. For example, they can arrange for children to see men and women pursuing nontraditional careers and can explain that interests and skills, not sex, should determine a person's occupation. Research shows that such reasoning reduces children's gender-biased views. By middle childhood, children who hold flexible beliefs about what boys and girls can do are more likely to notice instances of gender discrimination (Brown & Bigler, 2004). And as we will see in the next section, a rational approach to child rearing promotes healthy, adaptable functioning in many other areas as well.

Ask Yourself

- **REVIEW** Explain how the social environment and young children's cognitive limitations contribute to rigid gender stereotyping in early childhood.

- **CONNECT** In addition to gender-stereotyped beliefs, what other aspects of young children's social understanding tend to be rigid and one-sided in early childhood?

- **APPLY** List findings indicating that language and communication—between parents and children, between teachers and children, and between peers—powerfully affect children's gender typing. What recommendations would you make to counteract these influences?

- **REFLECT** Would you describe your own gender identity as "masculine," "feminine," or "androgynous"? What biological and social factors might have influenced your gender identity?

10.9 Describe the impact of child-rearing styles on development, and explain why authoritative parenting is effective.

10.10 Discuss the multiple origins of child maltreatment, its consequences for development, and prevention strategies.

Child Rearing and Emotional and Social Development

In this and previous chapters, we have seen how parents can foster children's competence—by building a parent–child relationship based on affection and cooperation, by modeling and reinforcing mature behavior, by using reasoning and inductive discipline, and by guiding and encouraging mastery of new skills. Now let's put these practices together into an overall view of effective parenting.

Styles of Child Rearing

Child-rearing styles are combinations of parenting behaviors that occur over a wide range of situations, creating an enduring child-rearing climate. In a landmark series of studies, Diana Baumrind gathered information on child rearing by watching parents interact with their preschoolers (Baumrind, 1971). Her findings, and those of others who have extended her work, reveal three features that consistently differentiate an effective style from less effective ones: (1) acceptance and involvement, (2) control, and (3) autonomy granting (Gray & Steinberg, 1999; Hart, Newell, & Olsen, 2003). Table 10.2 shows how child-rearing styles differ in these features. Let's discuss each style in turn.

AUTHORITATIVE CHILD REARING The **authoritative child-rearing style**—the most successful approach—involves high acceptance and involvement, adaptive control techniques, and appropriate autonomy granting. Authoritative parents are warm, attentive, and sensitive

TABLE 10.2   Features of Child-Rearing Styles

CHILD-REARING STYLE	ACCEPTANCE AND INVOLVEMENT	CONTROL	AUTONOMY GRANTING
Authoritative	Is warm, responsive, attentive, and sensitive to the child's needs	Engages in confrontive behavioral control: Makes reasonable demands for mature behavior and consistently enforces and explains them	Permits the child to make decisions in accord with readiness. Encourages the child to express thoughts, feelings, and desires. When parent and child disagree, engages in joint decision making when possible
Authoritarian	Is cold and rejecting and frequently degrades the child	Engages in coercive behavioral control: Makes excessive demands for mature behavior, uses force and punishment. Often uses psychological control, withdrawing love and manipulating and intruding on the child's individuality and attachment to parents	Makes decisions for the child. Rarely listens to the child's point of view
Permissive	Is warm but overindulgent or inattentive	Is lax in behavioral control: Makes few or no demands for mature behavior	Permits the child to make many decisions before the child is ready
Uninvolved	Is emotionally detached and withdrawn	Is lax in behavioral control: Makes few or no demands for mature behavior	Is indifferent to the child's decision making and point of view

to their child's needs. They establish an enjoyable, emotionally fulfilling parent–child relationship that draws the child into close connection. When necessary, authoritative parents exercise firm, reasonable control called *confrontive control*: They insist on mature behavior, give reasons for their expectations, and use disciplinary encounters as "teaching moments" to promote the child's self-regulation. They avoid using *coercive control*, which is arbitrary, rigid, intrusive, and punitive. Finally, authoritative parents engage in gradual, appropriate *autonomy granting*, allowing the child to make decisions in areas where he is ready to do so (Baumrind, 2013; Kuczynski & Lollis, 2002; Russell, Mize, & Bissaker, 2004).

Throughout childhood and adolescence, authoritative parenting is linked to many aspects of competence—an upbeat mood, self-control, task persistence, cooperativeness, high self-esteem, social and moral maturity, and favorable school performance (Amato & Fowler, 2002; Aunola, Stattin, & Nurmi, 2000; Gonzalez & Wolters, 2006; Mackey, Arnold, & Pratt, 2001; Milevsky et al., 2007; Steinberg, Darling, & Fletcher, 1995).

AUTHORITARIAN CHILD REARING

The **authoritarian child-rearing style** is low in acceptance and involvement, high in coercive control, and low in autonomy granting. Authoritarian parents appear cold and rejecting. To exert control, they yell, command, criticize, and threaten. "Do it because I said so!" is their attitude. They make decisions for their child and expect their child to accept their word unquestioningly. If the child resists, authoritarian parents resort to force and punishment.

Children of authoritarian parents are more likely to be anxious, unhappy, and low in self-esteem and self-reliance. When frustrated, they tend to react with hostility and, like their parents, use force to get their way. Boys, especially, show high rates of anger and defiance. Although girls also engage in acting-out behavior, they are more likely to be dependent, lacking interest in exploration, and overwhelmed by challenging tasks (Hart, Newell, & Olsen, 2003; Kakihara et al., 2010; Thompson, Hollis, & Richards, 2003). Children and adolescents exposed to the authoritarian style typically do poorly in school. However, because of their parents' concern with control, they tend to achieve better and to commit fewer antisocial acts than peers with undemanding parents—that is, those whose parents use one of the two styles we will consider next (Steinberg, Blatt-Eisengart, & Cauffman, 2006).

In addition to unwarranted direct control, authoritarian parents engage in a more subtle type called **psychological control**, in which they attempt to take advantage of children's psychological needs by intruding on and manipulating their verbal expressions, individuality, and attachments to parents. These parents frequently interrupt or put down the child's ideas, decisions, and choice of friends. When they are dissatisfied, they withdraw love, making their affection contingent on the child's compliance. Children subjected to psychological control exhibit adjustment problems involving both anxious, withdrawn behavior and defiance and aggression—especially the relational form, which (like parental psychological control) damages relationships through manipulation and exclusion (Barber, Stolz, & Olsen, 2005; Barber & Xia, 2013; Kuppens et al., 2013).

PERMISSIVE CHILD REARING   The **permissive child-rearing style** is warm and accepting but uninvolved. Permissive parents are either overindulgent or inattentive and, thus, engage in little control. Instead of gradually granting autonomy, they allow children to make many of their own decisions at an age when they are not yet capable of doing so. Their children can eat meals and go to bed when they feel like it and watch as much television as they want. They do not have to learn good manners or do household chores. Although some permissive parents truly believe in this approach, many others simply lack confidence in their ability to influence their child's behavior (Oyserman et al., 2005).

Children of permissive parents are impulsive, disobedient, and rebellious. They are also overly demanding and dependent on adults, and they show less persistence on tasks, poorer school achievement, and more antisocial behavior. The link between permissive parenting and dependent, nonachieving, rebellious behavior is especially strong for boys (Barber & Olsen, 1997; Steinberg, Blatt-Eisengart, & Cauffman, 2006).

UNINVOLVED CHILD REARING   The **uninvolved child-rearing style** combines low acceptance and involvement with little control and general indifference to issues of autonomy. Often these parents are emotionally detached and depressed and so overwhelmed by life stress that they have little time and energy for children. At its extreme, uninvolved parenting is a form of child maltreatment called *neglect*. Especially when it begins early, it disrupts virtually all aspects of development (see Chapter 4, page 153). Even with less extreme parental disengagement, children and adolescents display many problems—poor emotional self-regulation, school achievement difficulties, and antisocial behavior (Aunola, Stattin, & Nurmi, 2000; Schroeder et al., 2010).

What Makes Authoritative Child Rearing Effective?

Like other correlational findings, the association between authoritative parenting and children's competence is open to interpretation. Perhaps parents of well-adjusted children are authoritative because their youngsters have especially cooperative dispositions. But although temperamentally fearless, impulsive children and emotionally negative children are more likely to evoke coercive, inconsistent discipline, extra warmth and firm control succeed in modifying these children's maladaptive styles (Cipriano & Stifter, 2010; Kochanska, Philibert, & Barry, 2009; Larzelere, Cox, & Mandara, 2013). With fearful, inhibited children, parents must suppress their tendency to overprotect and take over solving the child's social problems. Instead, inhibited children benefit from extra encouragement to be assertive and express their autonomy (Nelson et al., 2006; Rubin & Burgess, 2002).

Longitudinal research indicates that among children of diverse temperaments, authoritative child rearing in the preschool years predicts maturity and adjustment in adolescence, whereas authoritarian or permissive child rearing predicts adolescent immaturity and adjustment difficulties. And a variant of authoritativeness in which parents exert strong control over the child's behavior—becoming directive but not coercive—yields just as favorable long-term outcomes as a more democratic approach (Baumrind, Larzelere, & Owens, 2010). Indeed, some children, because of their dispositions, require "heavier doses" of certain authoritative features.

In sum, authoritative child rearing seems to create a positive emotional context for parental influence in the following ways:

- Warm, involved parents who are secure in the standards they hold for their children model caring concern as well as confident, self-controlled behavior.
- Children are far more likely to comply with and internalize control that appears fair and reasonable, not arbitrary.
- By adjusting demands and autonomy granting to children's capacities, authoritative parents convey to children that they are competent and can do things successfully for themselves. In this way, parents foster favorable self-esteem and cognitive and social maturity.
- Supportive aspects of the authoritative style, including parental acceptance, involvement, and rational control, are a powerful source of *resilience*, protecting children from the negative effects of family stress and poverty (Beyers et al., 2003).

Cultural Variations

Although authoritative parenting is broadly advantageous, ethnic minority parents often have distinct child-rearing beliefs and practices reflecting cultural values. Let's look at some examples.

Compared with Western parents, Chinese parents describe their parenting as more controlling. They are more directive in teaching and scheduling their children's time, as a way of fostering self-control and high achievement. Chinese parents may appear less warm than Western parents because they withhold praise, which they believe results in self-satisfied, poorly motivated children (Cheah & Li, 2010; Ng, Pomerantz, & Deng, 2014). High control reflects the Confucian belief in strict discipline, respect for elders, and socially desirable behavior, taught by deeply involved parents. Chinese parents report expressing affection and concern and using induction and other reasoning-oriented discipline as much as American parents do, but they more often shame a misbehaving child, withdraw love, and use physical punishment (Cheah et al., 2009; Shwalb et al., 2004). When these practices become excessive, resulting in an authoritarian style high in psychological or coercive control, Chinese children display the same negative outcomes as Western children: poor academic achievement, anxiety, depression, impaired self-regulation, and aggressive behavior (Chan, 2010; Lee et al., 2012; Pomerantz & Wang, 2009; Pong, Johnston, & Chen, 2010; Sorkhabi & Mandara, 2013).

In Hispanic families, Asian Pacific Island families, and Caribbean families of African and East Indian origin, firm insistence on respect for parental authority is paired with high parental warmth—a combination suited to promoting cognitive and social competence and family loyalty (Halgunseth, Ispa, & Rudy, 2006; Harrison et al., 1994; Roopnarine & Evans, 2007). Hispanic fathers typically spend much time with their children and are warm and sensitive (Cabrera & Bradley, 2012). In Caribbean families that immigrated to the United States, fathers' authoritativeness—but not mothers'—predicted preschoolers' literacy and math skills, probably because Caribbean fathers take a larger role in guiding their children's academic progress (Roopnarine et al., 2006).

Although wide variation exists, low-SES African-American parents tend to expect immediate obedience. They believe strict parenting fosters self-control and vigilance in risky surroundings. African-American parents who use controlling strategies tend to have cognitively and socially competent children who view parental control as a sign of love and concern (Mason et al., 2004). Recall, also, that a history of mild physical punishment is associated with a reduction in antisocial behavior among African-American youths but with an increase among Caucasian Americans (refer to the Cultural Influences box on page 377). Most African-American parents who use strict, "no-nonsense" discipline use physical punishment sparingly and combine it with warmth and reasoning.

These cultural variations remind us that child-rearing styles must be viewed in their larger context. As we have seen, many factors contribute to good parenting:

LOOK *and* **LISTEN**

Ask several parents to explain their style of child rearing, inquiring about acceptance and involvement, control, and autonomy granting. Look, especially, for variations in amount and type of control over children's behavior along with parents' rationales.

In Caribbean families of African origins, respect for parental authority is paired with high parental warmth—a combination that promotes competence and family loyalty.

personal characteristics of the child and parent, SES, extended family and community supports, cultural values and practices, and public policies.

As we turn to the topic of child maltreatment, our discussion will underscore, once again, that effective child rearing is sustained not just by the desire of mothers and fathers to be good parents. Almost all want to be. Unfortunately, when vital supports for parenting break down, children—as well as parents—can suffer terribly.

Child Maltreatment

Child maltreatment is as old as human history, but only in recent decades has the problem been widely acknowledged and studied. Perhaps public concern has increased because child maltreatment is especially common in large industrialized nations. In the most recently reported year, nearly 700,000 U.S. children (9 out of every 1,000) were identified as victims (U.S. Department of Health and Human Services, 2013). Because most cases go unreported, the true figures are much higher.

Child maltreatment takes the following forms:

- *Physical abuse:* Assaults, such as kicking, biting, shaking, punching, or stabbing, that inflict physical injury
- *Sexual abuse:* Fondling, intercourse, exhibitionism, commercial exploitation through prostitution or production of pornography, and other forms of sexual exploitation
- *Neglect:* Failure to meet a child's basic needs for food, clothing, medical attention, education, or supervision
- *Emotional abuse:* Acts that could cause serious emotional harm, including social isolation, repeated unreasonable demands, ridicule, humiliation, intimidation, or terrorizing

Neglect accounts for about 78 percent of reported cases, physical abuse for 18 percent, emotional abuse for 9 percent, and sexual abuse for 9 percent (U.S. Department of Health and Human Services, 2013). But these figures are only approximate, as many children experience more than one form.

Parents commit more than 80 percent of abusive incidents. Other relatives account for about 6 percent, and the remainder are perpetrated by parents' unmarried partners, school personnel, camp counselors, and other adults. Infants, toddlers, and preschoolers are at greatest risk for neglect, physical abuse, and emotional abuse. Sexual abuse is perpetrated more often against school-age and early adolescent children. But each type occurs at every age (Trocmé & Wolfe, 2002; U.S. Department of Health and Human Services, 2013). Because many sexual abuse victims are identified in middle childhood, we will pay special attention to this form of maltreatment in Chapter 13.

ORIGINS OF CHILD MALTREATMENT Early findings suggested that child maltreatment was rooted in adult psychological disturbance (Kempe et al., 1962). But although child maltreatment is more common among disturbed parents, it soon became clear that a single "abusive personality type" does not exist. Parents who were abused as children do not necessarily become abusers (Jaffee et al., 2013). And sometimes even "normal" parents harm their children!

For help in understanding child maltreatment, researchers turned to *ecological systems theory* (see Chapters 1 and 2). They discovered that many interacting variables—at the family, community, and cultural levels—contribute. The more risks present, the greater the likelihood that abuse or neglect will occur. Table 10.3 summarizes factors associated with child maltreatment.

The Family. Within the family, children whose characteristics make them more challenging to rear are more likely to become targets of abuse. These include premature or very sick babies and children who are temperamentally difficult, are inattentive and overactive, or have other developmental problems. Child factors, however, only slightly increase the risk of abuse (Jaudes & Mackey-Bilaver, 2008; Sidebotham et al., 2003). Whether such children are maltreated largely depends on parents' characteristics.

TABLE 10.3	Factors Related to Child Maltreatment
FACTOR	**DESCRIPTION**
Parent characteristics	Psychological disturbance; alcohol and drug abuse; history of abuse as a child; belief in harsh physical discipline; desire to satisfy unmet emotional needs through the child; unreasonable expectations for child behavior; young age (most under 30); low educational level; lack of parenting skills
Child characteristics	Premature or very sick baby; difficult temperament; inattentiveness and overactivity; other developmental problems
Family characteristics	Low income or poverty; homelessness; marital instability; social isolation; partner abuse; frequent moves; large families with closely spaced children; overcrowded living conditions; nonbiological caregivers present; disorganized household; lack of steady employment; other signs of high life stress
Community	Characterized by violence and social isolation; few parks, child-care centers, preschool programs, recreation centers, or religious institutions to serve as family supports
Culture	Approval of physical force and violence as ways to solve problems

Sources: Centers for Disease Control and Prevention, 2014d; Wekerle & Wolfe, 2003; Whipple, 2006.

Maltreating parents are less skillful than other parents in handling discipline confrontations and getting children to cooperate in working toward common goals. They also suffer from biased thinking about their child. For example, they often attribute their baby's crying or their child's misdeeds to a stubborn or bad disposition, evaluate children's transgressions as worse than they are, and feel powerless in parenting—perspectives that lead them to move quickly toward physical force (Bugental & Happaney, 2004; Crouch et al., 2008).

Most parents have enough self-control not to respond to their children's misbehavior or developmental problems with abuse. Other factors combine with these conditions to prompt an extreme response. Unmanageable parental stress is strongly associated with maltreatment. Abusive parents respond to stressful situations with high emotional arousal. And low income, low education (less than a high school diploma), unemployment, alcohol and drug use, marital conflict, overcrowded living conditions, frequent moves, and extreme household disorganization are common in abusive homes (Dakil et al., 2012; Wulczyn, 2009). These conditions increase the chances that parents will be too overwhelmed to meet basic child-rearing responsibilities or will vent their frustrations by lashing out at their children.

The Community. The majority of abusive and neglectful parents are isolated from both formal and informal social supports. Because of their life histories, many have learned to mistrust and avoid others and are poorly skilled at establishing and maintaining positive relationships. Also, maltreating parents are more likely to live in unstable, rundown neighborhoods that provide few links between family and community, such as parks, recreation centers, and religious institutions (Guterman et al., 2009; Tomyr, Ouimet, & Ugnat, 2012). These parents lack "lifelines" to others and have no one to turn to for help during stressful times.

The Larger Culture. Cultural values, laws, and customs profoundly affect the chances that child maltreatment will occur when parents feel overburdened. Societies that view violence as an appropriate way to solve problems set the stage for child abuse.

Although the United States has laws to protect children from maltreatment, widespread support exists for use of physical force with children (refer back to page 376). Many countries—including Austria, Croatia, Cyprus, Denmark, Finland, Germany, Israel, Latvia, Norway, Spain, Sweden, and Uruguay—have outlawed corporal

© JEFF GREENBERG/PHOTOEDIT

High parental stress, low income and education, and extreme household disorganization are often associated with child maltreatment. Abusive parents are more likely to live in rundown neighborhoods that offer few sources of social support.

punishment, a measure that dampens both physical discipline and abuse (Zolotor & Puzia, 2010). Furthermore, all industrialized nations except the United States prohibit corporal punishment in schools. The U.S. Supreme Court has twice upheld the right of school officials to use corporal punishment. Fortunately, 31 U.S. states and the District of Columbia have passed laws that ban it.

CONSEQUENCES OF CHILD MALTREATMENT The family circumstances of maltreated children impair the development of attachment security, emotional self-regulation, empathy and sympathy, self-concept, social skills, and academic motivation. Over time, these youngsters show serious adjustment problems—cognitive deficits including impaired executive function, school failure, severe depression, aggressive behavior, peer difficulties, substance abuse, and violent crime (Gould et al., 2010; Kaplow & Widom, 2007; Nikulina & Widom, 2013; Stronach et al., 2011).

How do these damaging consequences occur? Recall our earlier discussion of hostile cycles of parent–child interaction. For abused children, these are especially severe. Also, a family characteristic strongly associated with child abuse is partner abuse (Graham-Bermann & Howell, 2011). Clearly, the home lives of abused children overflow with adult conduct that leads to profound distress, including emotional insecurity (see page 69 in Chapter 2), and to aggression as a way of solving problems.

Furthermore, demeaning parental messages, in which children are ridiculed, humiliated, rejected, or terrorized, result in low self-esteem, high anxiety, self-blame, and efforts to escape from extreme psychological pain—at times severe enough to lead to attempted suicide in adolescence. At school, maltreated children present serious discipline problems (Wolfe, 2005). Their noncompliance, poor motivation, and cognitive immaturity interfere with academic achievement, further undermining their chances for life success.

Finally, repeated abuse is associated with central nervous system damage, including abnormal EEG brain-wave activity; fMRI-detected reduced size and impaired functioning of the cerebral cortex, corpus callosum, cerebellum, and hippocampus; and atypical production of the stress hormone cortisol—initially too high but, after months of abuse, often too low. Over time, the massive trauma of persistent abuse seems to blunt children's normal physiological response to stress (Cicchetti, 2007; Hart & Rubia, 2012; Jaffee & Christian, 2014). These effects increase the chances that cognitive and emotional problems will endure.

PREVENTING CHILD MALTREATMENT Because child maltreatment is embedded in families, communities, and society as a whole, efforts to prevent it must be directed at each of these levels. Many approaches have been suggested, including teaching high-risk parents effective child-rearing strategies, providing direct experience with children in high school child development courses, and developing broad social programs aimed at improving economic conditions and community services.

We have seen that providing social supports to families is effective in easing parental stress. This approach sharply reduces child maltreatment as well. A trusting relationship with another person is the most important factor in preventing mothers with childhood histories of abuse from repeating the cycle with their own children (Egeland, Jacobvitz, & Sroufe, 1988). Parents Anonymous, a U.S. organization with affiliate programs around the world, helps child-abusing parents learn constructive parenting practices, largely through social supports. Its local chapters offer self-help group meetings, daily phone calls, and regular home visits to relieve social isolation and teach responsible child-rearing skills.

Early intervention aimed at strengthening both child and parent competencies can improve parenting practices, thereby preventing child maltreatment (Howard & Brooks-Gunn, 2009). Healthy Families America, a program that

Each year, fourth to sixth graders across Los Angeles County enter a poster contest to celebrate Child Abuse Prevention Month. This recent winner appeals to parents to treat children with warmth and caring. (Katrina Weng, 4th Grade, Ya Ya Fine Art, Arcadia, CA. Courtesy ICAN Associates, Los Angeles County InterAgency Council on Child Abuse & Neglect, *ican4kids.org*.)

began in Hawaii and has spread to 430 sites across the United States and Canada, identifies families at risk for maltreatment during pregnancy or at birth. Each receives three years of home visitation, in which a trained worker helps parents manage crises, encourages effective child rearing, and puts parents in touch with community services to meet their own and their children's needs (Healthy Families America, 2011). In an evaluation in which over 600 families were randomly assigned to intervention and control groups, Healthy Families home visitation alone reduced only neglect, not abuse (Duggan et al., 2004). But adding a *cognitive component* dramatically increased its impact. When home visitors helped parents change negative appraisals of their children—by countering inaccurate interpretations (for example, that the baby is behaving with malicious intent) and by working on solving child-rearing problems—physical punishment and abuse dropped sharply after one year of intervention (see Figure 10.7) (Bugental et al., 2002). Another home-visiting program shown to reduce child abuse and neglect is the Nurse–Family Partnership, discussed on page 114 in Chapter 3 (Olds et al., 2009).

Still, many experts believe that child maltreatment cannot be eliminated as long as violence is widespread and harsh physical punishment is regarded as acceptable. In addition, combating poverty and its diverse correlates—family stress and disorganization, inadequate food and medical care, teenage parenthood, low-birth-weight babies, and parental hopelessness—would protect many children.

Although more cases reach the courts than in decades past, child maltreatment is difficult to prove. Usually, the only witnesses are the child victims or other loyal family members. And even when the evidence is strong, judges hesitate to impose the ultimate safeguard against further harm: permanently removing the child from the family. There are several reasons for their reluctance. First, in the United States, government intervention into family life is viewed as a last resort. Second, despite destructive family relationships, maltreated children and their parents usually are attached to one another, and neither desires separation. Finally, the U.S. legal system tends to regard children as parental property rather than as human beings in their own right, and this also has stood in the way of court-ordered protection.

Even with intensive treatment, some adults persist in their abusive acts. An estimated 1,600 U.S. children, most of them infants and preschoolers, die from maltreatment annually. Nearly half suffered from physical abuse, including beatings, drownings, suffocation, or *shaken baby syndrome,* in which shaking an infant or young child inflicts brain and neck injuries. About 70 percent were neglected, some so severely that it caused their deaths (U.S. Department of Health and Human Services, 2013). When parents are unlikely to change their behavior, the drastic step of separating parent from child and legally terminating parental rights is the only justifiable course of action.

Child maltreatment is a sad note on which to end our discussion of a period of childhood that is so full of excitement, awakening, and discovery. But there is reason to be optimistic. Great strides have been made over the past several decades in understanding and preventing child maltreatment.

FIGURE 10.7 **Impact of a home visitation program with a cognitive component on preventing physical abuse of young children.** In an enhanced home visitation condition, home visitors not only provided social support, encouraged effective child rearing, and connected families with community resources but also helped at-risk parents change their negative appraisals of their babies and solve child-rearing problems. After one year of intervention, this cognitive component sharply reduced physical abuse of babies (hitting, shaking, beating, kicking, biting) compared with an unenhanced home visitation condition and a no-intervention control. (Adapted from Bugental et al., 2002.)

Ask Yourself

- **REVIEW** Summarize findings on ethnic variations in child-rearing styles. Is the concept of authoritative parenting useful for understanding effective parenting across cultures? Explain.

- **CONNECT** Which child-rearing style is most likely to be associated with inductive discipline, and why?

- **APPLY** Chandra heard a news report about 10 severely neglected children, living in squalor in an inner-city tenement. She wondered, "Why would parents so mistreat their children?" How would you answer Chandra?

- **REFLECT** How would you classify your parents' child-rearing styles? What factors might have influenced their approach to parenting?

Summary

Erikson's Theory: Initiative versus Guilt (p. 357)

10.1 What personality changes take place during Erikson's stage of initiative versus guilt?

- Preschoolers develop a new sense of purposefulness as they grapple with Erikson's psychological conflict of **initiative versus guilt.** A healthy sense of initiative depends on exploring the social world and trying new skills through play and experiencing supportive child rearing that fosters a secure (but not overly strict) conscience.

Self-Understanding (p. 358)

10.2 Describe the development of self-concept and self-esteem in early childhood.

- As preschoolers think more intently about themselves, they construct a **self-concept** that consists largely of observable characteristics and typical emotions and attitudes. Older preschoolers also have an emerging grasp of their own personalities.

- Securely attached preschoolers have a more positive, coherent self-concept. More elaborative parent–child conversations about past events contribute to a clearer self-image, and conversations about internal states facilitate self-knowledge.

- Preschoolers' **self-esteem** consists of several self-judgments. Their high self-esteem contributes to a mastery-oriented approach to the environment.

Emotional Development (p. 361)

10.3 Identify changes in understanding and expressing emotion during early childhood, citing factors that influence those changes.

- Preschoolers have an impressive understanding of the causes, consequences, and behavioral signs of basic emotions, which is supported by cognitive development, secure attachment, and conversations about feelings.

- By age 3 to 4, children are aware of various strategies for emotional self-regulation. Temperament, parental modeling, and parental communication about coping strategies influence preschoolers' capacity to handle negative emotion.

- As their self-concepts become better developed, preschoolers experience self-conscious emotions, such as pride, shame, and guilt, more often. However, they depend on parental feedback to know when to feel these emotions.

- Empathy also becomes more common in early childhood. The extent to which empathy leads to **sympathy** and results in **prosocial, or altruistic, behavior** depends on temperament and parenting.

Peer Relations (p. 365)

10.4 Describe peer sociability, friendship, and social problem solving in early childhood, along with cultural and parental influences on early peer relations.

- During early childhood, peer interaction increases as children move from **nonsocial activity** to **parallel play** and then to **associative** and **cooperative play.** Nevertheless, both solitary and parallel play remain common.

- With age, sociodramatic play occurs more often, supporting cognitive, emotional, and social development. Cultural valuing of group harmony versus individual autonomy influences play, as do beliefs about the importance of play.

- Preschoolers view friendship in concrete, activity-based terms. Compared to other peer interactions, those with friends are more cooperative and emotionally expressive. Early childhood friendship and peer acceptance contribute to academic and social adjustment in kindergarten.

© GAETANO IMAGES INC./ALAMY

- Social conflicts offer occasions for **social problem solving,** which improves over the preschool and early school years. By kindergarten, each of its information-processing components is related to socially competent behavior.

- Parents influence early peer relations both directly, through attempts to influence their child's interactions with peers, and indirectly, through their child-rearing practices.

Foundations of Morality (p. 372)

10.5 What are the central features of psychoanalytic, social learning, and cognitive-developmental approaches to moral development?

- The psychoanalytic perspective emphasizes the emotional side of moral development. Although guilt is an important motivator of moral action, contrary to Freud's theory, discipline promoting fear of punishment and loss of parental love does not foster conscience development. **Induction** is far more effective.

- Social learning theory focuses on how children learn moral behavior through reinforcement and modeling. Effective adult models of morality are warm, powerful, and consistent in what they say and do.

- Alternatives such as **time out** and withdrawal of privileges can help parents avoid the undesirable side effects of harsh punishment. When parents use punishment, they can increase its effectiveness by being consistent, maintaining a warm parent–child relationship, and offering explanations. The most effective discipline encourages good conduct by building a mutually respectful bond with the child.

- The cognitive-developmental perspective views children as active thinkers about social rules. By age 4, children consider intentions in making moral judgments and distinguish truthfulness from lying. Preschoolers also distinguish **moral imperatives** from **social conventions** and **matters of personal choice,** but they tend to reason rigidly about morality.

- Through sibling and peer interaction, children work out their first ideas about justice and fairness. Parents who discuss moral issues with their children help them reason about morality.

10.6 Describe the development of aggression in early childhood, including family and media influences.

- During early childhood, **proactive aggression** declines while **reactive aggression** increases. Proactive and reactive aggression come in three forms: **physical aggression** (more common in boys), **verbal aggression,** and **relational aggression** (where girls' aggression tends to concentrate).

- Ineffective discipline and a conflict-ridden family atmosphere promote children's aggression. Children high in reactive aggression see hostility where it does not exist, making many unprovoked attacks. Those high in proactive aggression callously use it to advance their own goals—a style that predicts severe conduct problems. Media violence also triggers aggression.

- Teaching parents effective child-rearing practices, intervening to enhance children's emotional and social skills, relieving family stress through social supports, and shielding children from violent media reduce aggressive behavior.

Gender Typing (p. 384)

10.7 Discuss biological and environmental influences on preschoolers' gender-stereotyped beliefs and behavior.

- **Gender typing** is well under way in early childhood. Preschoolers acquire a wide range of gender-stereotyped beliefs, which operate as blanket rules rather than flexible guidelines for behavior.

- Prenatal hormones contribute to boys' higher activity level and rowdier play and to children's preference for same-sex playmates. But parents, same-sex older siblings, teachers, peers, and the broader social environment encourage many gender-typed responses. Parents apply more pressure for gender-role conformity to sons, and boys are more gender-typed than girls.

10.8 Describe and evaluate major theories that explain the emergence of gender identity.

- Although most people have a traditional **gender identity,** some are **androgynous,** combining both masculine and feminine characteristics. Masculine and androgynous identities are linked to better psychological adjustment.

- According to social learning theory, preschoolers first acquire gender-typed responses through modeling and reinforcement, then organize these into gender-linked ideas about themselves. Cognitive-developmental theory suggests that **gender constancy** must be mastered before children develop gender-typed behavior, but evidence for this assumption is weak.

- **Gender schema theory** combines features of social learning and cognitive-developmental perspectives. As children acquire gender-stereotyped preferences and behaviors, they form masculine and feminine categories, or gender schemas, that they apply to themselves and their world.

Child Rearing and Emotional and Social Development (p. 392)

10.9 Describe the impact of child-rearing styles on development, and explain why authoritative parenting is effective.

- Three features distinguish the major **child-rearing styles:** (1) acceptance and involvement, (2) control, and (3) autonomy granting. Compared with the **authoritarian, permissive,** and **uninvolved styles,** the **authoritative style** promotes cognitive, emotional, and social competence. Warmth, confrontive rather than coercive control, and gradual autonomy granting account for the effectiveness of the authoritative style. **Psychological control** is associated with authoritarian parenting and contributes to adjustment problems.

- Certain ethnic groups, including Chinese, Hispanic, Asian Pacific Island, and African-American, combine parental warmth with high levels of control. But when control becomes harsh and excessive, it impairs academic and social competence.

10.10 Discuss the multiple origins of child maltreatment, its consequences for development, and prevention strategies.

- Child maltreatment is related to factors within the family, community, and larger culture. Maltreating parents use ineffective discipline and hold a negatively biased view of their child. Unmanageable parental stress and social isolation greatly increase the chances that abuse and neglect will occur. When a society approves of force and violence as a means for solving problems, child abuse is promoted.

- Maltreated children are impaired in attachment security, emotional self-regulation, empathy and sympathy, self-concept, social skills, and academic motivation. They are also likely to suffer central nervous system damage. Successful prevention of child maltreatment requires efforts at the family, community, and societal levels.

Important Terms and Concepts

androgyny (p. 389)
associative play (p. 366)
authoritarian child-rearing style (p. 393)
authoritative child-rearing style (p. 392)
child-rearing styles (p. 392)
cooperative play (p. 366)
gender constancy (p. 390)
gender identity (p. 389)
gender schema theory (p. 390)
gender typing (p. 384)
induction (p. 373)

initiative versus guilt (p. 357)
matters of personal choice (p. 378)
moral imperatives (p. 378)
nonsocial activity (p. 365)
parallel play (p. 366)
permissive child-rearing style (p. 394)
physical aggression (p. 379)
proactive aggression (p. 379)
prosocial, or altruistic, behavior (p. 364)
psychological control (p. 394)
reactive aggression (p. 379)

relational aggression (p. 380)
self-concept (p. 358)
self-esteem (p. 359)
social conventions (p. 378)
social problem solving (p. 369)
sympathy (p. 364)
time out (p. 376)
uninvolved child-rearing style (p. 394)
verbal aggression (p. 379)

MILESTONES
Development in Early Childhood

---

2 YEARS

PHYSICAL

- Throughout early childhood, height and weight increase more slowly than in toddlerhood. (285)
- Balance improves; walking becomes smooth and rhythmic; running emerges. (301–302)

- Jumps, hops, throws, and catches with rigid upper body. (302)
- Puts on and removes simple items of clothing. (302–303)
- Uses spoon effectively. (302)
- First drawings are gestural scribbles. (303)

COGNITIVE

- Increasingly uses language as a flexible symbolic tool, to modify existing mental representations. (312)
- Make-believe becomes less dependent on realistic objects, less self-centered, and more complex; sociodramatic play increases. (312)
- Takes the perspective of others in simplified, familiar situations and in face-to-face communication. (317, 332)
- Recognition memory is well developed. (329)
- Shows awareness of the difference between inner mental and outer physical events. (332)
- Begins to count. (338)

LANGUAGE

- Vocabulary increases rapidly. (348)
- Uses a coalition of cues—perceptual and, increasingly, social and linguistic—to figure out word meanings. (350)
- Speaks in simple sentences that follow basic word order of native language. (350)
- Adds grammatical markers. (351)
- Displays effective conversational skills. (352)

EMOTIONAL/SOCIAL

- Understands causes, consequences, and behavioral signs of basic emotions. (361)
- Begins to develop self-concept and self-esteem. (358–360)
- Shows early signs of developing moral sense—verbal evaluations of own and others' actions and distress at harmful behaviors. (372, 378)
- May display proactive (or instrumental) aggression. (379)
- Gender-stereotyped beliefs and behavior increase. (385)

3–4 YEARS

PHYSICAL

- May no longer need a daytime nap. (293)
- Running, jumping, hopping, throwing, and catching become more refined, with flexible upper body. (302)
- Galloping and one-foot skipping appear. (302)
- Pedals and steers tricycle. (302)

- Uses scissors. (302)
- Uses fork effectively. (302)
- Draws first picture of a person, using tadpole image. (304)
- Distinguishes writing from nonwriting. (306)

COGNITIVE

- Understands the symbolic function of drawings and of models of real-world spaces. (303–304, 314–315)
- Grasps conservation, reasons about transformations, reverses thinking, and understands cause-and-effect relationships in simplified, familiar situations. (318)
- Sorts familiar objects into hierarchically organized categories. (319)
- Distinguishes appearance from reality. (314–315)
- Uses private speech to guide behavior during challenging tasks. (323)
- Improves in sustained attention. (327–328)
- Uses scripts to recall familiar events. (329)
- Understands that both beliefs and desires determine behavior. (332)
- Knows meaning of numbers up to ten, counts correctly, and grasps cardinality. (338)

Note: Numbers in parentheses indicate the page or pages on which each milestone is discussed.

LANGUAGE

- Aware of some meaningful features of written language. (336)
- Coins new words based on known words; extends language meanings through metaphor. (350)

- Masters increasingly complex grammatical structures, occasionally overextending grammatical rules to exceptions. (351)
- Adjusts speech to fit the age, sex, and social status of listeners. (317, 352)

EMOTIONAL/SOCIAL

- Describes self in terms of observable characteristics and typical emotions and attitudes. (358)
- Has several self-esteems, such as learning things in school, making friends, and getting along with parents. (360)
- Emotional self-regulation improves. (362)
- Experiences self-conscious emotions more often. (364)
- Relies more on language to express empathy. (364)
- Engages in associative and cooperative play with peers, in addition to parallel play. (366)

- Proactive aggression declines, while reactive aggression (verbal and relational) increases. (380)
- Forms first friendships, based on pleasurable play and sharing of toys. (368)
- Distinguishes moral imperatives from social conventions and matters of personal choices. (378)
- Preference for same-sex playmates strengthens. (386)

5–6 YEARS

PHYSICAL

- Starts to lose primary teeth. (287)
- Increases running speed, gallops more smoothly, and engages in true skipping. (302)
- Displays mature, flexible throwing and catching patterns. (302)
- Uses knife to cut soft foods. (302, 303)
- Ties shoes. (302, 303)
- Draws more complex pictures. (304)

- Uses an adult pencil grip, writes name, copies some numbers and simple words, and discriminates letters of the alphabet. (302, 306)

COGNITIVE

- Replaces beliefs in magical creatures and events with natural, plausible explanations. (318)
- Improves in ability to distinguish appearance from reality. (314–315)
- Passes Piaget's conservation of number, mass, and liquid problems. (316)
- Continues to improve in sustained attention; begins to plan effectively. (327–329)

- Improves in recognition, recall, scripted memory, and autobiographical memory. (329–330)

- Understanding of false belief strengthens. (333)

LANGUAGE

- Understands that letters and sounds are linked in systematic ways. (336)
- Uses invented spellings. (336)
- By age 6, has acquired a vocabulary of about 10,000 words. (348)
- Uses most grammatical constructions competently. (351)

EMOTIONAL/SOCIAL

- Improves in emotional understanding (ability to interpret, predict, and influence others' emotional reactions). (361–362)

- Becomes better at social problem solving. (370)
- Has acquired many morally relevant rules and behaviors. (372)
- Gender-stereotyped beliefs and behavior, and preference for same-sex playmates, continue to strengthen. (387)
- Understands gender constancy. (390)

Note: Numbers in parentheses indicate the page or pages on which each milestone is discussed.

Physical Development in Middle Childhood

REPRINTED WITH PERMISSION FROM THE INTERNATIONAL CHILD ART FOUNDATION, WASHINGTON, DC

"My Favorite Sport"
Su Degirmenci & Miray Celik
9 years, Turkey

This confident swimmer's exploration of the undersea world is aided by gains in strength, agility, and flexibility. Chapter 11 takes up the diverse physical attainments of middle childhood and their close connection with other domains of development.

"I'm on my way, Mom!" hollered 10-year-old Joey as he stuffed the last bite of toast into his mouth, slung his book bag over his shoulder, dashed out the door, jumped on his bike, and headed down the street for school. Joey's 8-year-old sister Lizzie followed, kissing her mother goodbye and pedaling furiously until she caught up with Joey. Rena, the children's mother and one of our colleagues at the university, watched from the front porch as her son and daughter disappeared in the distance.

"They're branching out," Rena commented over lunch that day, as she described the children's expanding activities and relationships. Homework, household chores, soccer teams, music lessons, scouting, friends at school and in the neighborhood, and Joey's new paper route were all part of the children's routine. "It seems as if the basics are all there; I don't have to monitor Joey and Lizzie so constantly anymore. Being a parent is still very challenging, but it's more a matter of refinements—helping them become independent, competent, and productive individuals."

Joey and Lizzie have entered middle childhood—the years from 6 to 11. Around the world, children of this age are assigned new responsibilities. For children in industrialized nations, like Joey and Lizzie, middle childhood is often called the "school years" because its onset is marked by the start of formal schooling. In village and tribal cultures, the school may be a field or a jungle. But universally, mature members of society guide children of this age period toward real-world tasks that increasingly resemble those they will perform as adults.

This chapter focuses on physical growth in middle childhood—changes less spectacular than those of earlier years. By age 6, the brain has reached 90 percent of its adult weight, and the body continues to grow slowly. In this way, nature gives school-age children the mental powers to master challenging tasks as well as added time—before reaching physical maturity—to acquire the knowledge and skills essential for life in a complex social world.

We begin by reviewing typical growth trends and special health concerns. Then we turn to rapid gains in motor abilities, which support practical everyday activities, athletic skills, and participation in organized games. We will see that each of these achievements is affected by and also contributes to cognitive, emotional, and social development. Our discussion will echo a familiar theme—that all domains are interrelated. ■

Body Growth

Physical growth during the school years continues at the slow, regular pace of early childhood. At age 6, the average North American child weighs about 45 pounds and is 3½ feet tall. Over the next few years, children will add about 2 to 3 inches in height and 5 pounds in weight each year (see Figure 11.1 on page 407). Between ages 6 and 8, girls are slightly shorter and lighter than boys. By age 9, this trend reverses. Already, Rena noticed, Lizzie was starting to catch up with Joey in physical size as she approached the dramatic adolescent growth spurt, which occurs two years earlier in girls than in boys.

Because the lower portion of the body is growing fastest, Joey and Lizzie appeared longer-legged than they had in early childhood. They grew out of their jeans more quickly than their jackets and frequently needed larger shoes. As in early childhood,

11.1 Describe changes in body size, proportions, and skeletal maturity during middle childhood.

11.2 Describe brain development in middle childhood.

girls have slightly more body fat and boys more muscle. After age 8, girls begin accumulating fat at a faster rate, and they will add even more during adolescence (Hauspie & Roelants, 2012).

Worldwide Variations in Body Size

TAKE A MOMENT... Glance into any elementary school classroom, and you will see wide individual differences in body growth. Diversity in physical size is especially apparent when we travel to different nations. Worldwide, a 9-inch gap exists between the smallest and the largest 8-year-olds. The shortest children, found in South America, Asia, the Pacific Islands, and parts of Africa, include such ethnic groups as Colombian, Burmese, Thai, Vietnamese, Ethiopian, and Bantu. The tallest children—living in Australia, northern and central Europe, Canada, and the United States—come from Czech, Dutch, Latvian, Norwegian, Swiss, and African populations (Meredith, 1978; Ruff, 2002). These findings remind us that *growth norms* (age-related averages for height and weight) must be applied cautiously, especially in countries with high immigration rates and many ethnic minorities.

What accounts for these vast differences in physical size? Both heredity and environment are involved. Body size sometimes reflects evolutionary adaptations to a particular climate. Long, lean physiques are typical in hot, tropical regions and short, stocky ones in cold, Arctic areas (Katzmarzyk & Leonard, 1998). Also, children who grow tallest usually live in developed countries, where food is plentiful and infectious diseases are largely controlled. Physically small children tend to live in less developed regions, where poverty, hunger, and disease are common (Steckel, 2012). When families move from poor to wealthy nations, their children not only grow taller but also change to a longer-legged body shape. (Recall that during childhood, the legs are growing fastest.) For example, U.S.-born school-age children of immigrant Guatemalan Mayan parents are, on average, 4½ inches taller, with legs nearly 3 inches longer, than their agemates in Guatemalan Mayan villages (Bogin et al., 2002; Varela-Silva et al., 2007).

Body size sometimes results from evolutionary adaptations to a particular climate. These Tanzanian boys live on the hot African plains. Their long, lean physiques permit their bodies to cool easily.

Secular Trends in Physical Growth

Over the past 150 years, **secular trends in physical growth**—changes in body size from one generation to the next—have occurred in industrialized nations. Joey and Lizzie are taller and heavier than their parents and grandparents were as children. These trends have been found in Australia, Canada, Japan, New Zealand, the United States, and nearly all European countries (Ong, Ahmed, & Dunger, 2006). The secular gain appears early in life, increases over childhood and early adolescence, then declines as mature body size is reached. This pattern suggests that the larger size of today's children is mostly due to a faster rate of physical development.

Once again, improved health and nutrition are largely responsible for these growth gains. As developing nations make socioeconomic progress, they also show secular gains (Ji & Chen, 2008). Secular increases are smaller for low-income children, who have poorer diets and are more likely to suffer from growth-stunting illnesses. And in regions with widespread poverty, famine, and disease, either no secular change or a secular decrease in body size has occurred (Bogin, 2013; Cole, 2000). In most industrialized nations, the secular gain in height has slowed in recent decades. Weight gain, however, is continuing. As we will see later, overweight and obesity have reached epic proportions.

Although varying considerably in physical size, these second graders are taller and heavier than previous generations were at the same age. Improved health and nutrition account for this secular trend throughout the industrialized world.

Skeletal Growth

During middle childhood, the bones of the body lengthen and broaden. However, ligaments are not yet firmly attached to bones. This, combined with increasing muscle strength, gives children

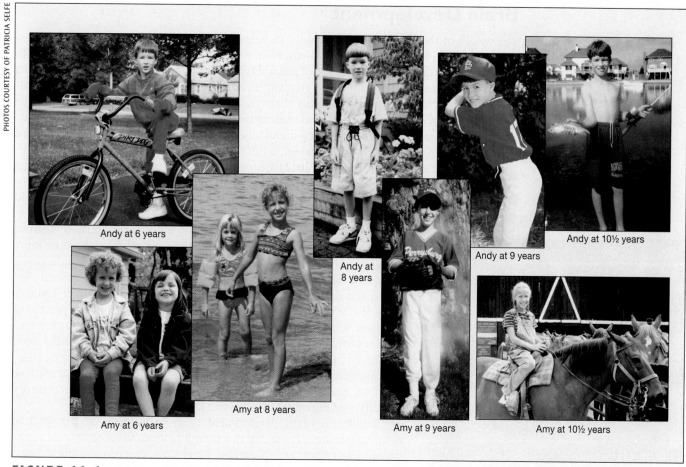

PHOTOS COURTESY OF PATRICIA SELFE

Andy at 6 years

Andy at 8 years

Andy at 9 years

Andy at 10½ years

Amy at 6 years

Amy at 8 years

Amy at 9 years

Amy at 10½ years

FIGURE 11.1 **Body growth during middle childhood.** Andy and Amy continued the slow, regular pattern of growth that they showed in early childhood (see Chapter 8, page 286). But around age 9, Amy began to grow at a faster rate than Andy. At age 10½, she was taller, heavier, and more mature-looking.

unusual flexibility of movement. School-age children often seem like "physical contortionists," turning cartwheels and doing splits and handstands. As their bodies become stronger, many children experience a greater desire for physical exercise. Nighttime "growing pains"—stiffness and aches in the legs—are common (Uziel et al., 2012). These subside as bones strengthen to accommodate increased physical activity and as muscles adapt to an enlarging skeleton.

Between ages 6 and 12, all 20 primary teeth are lost and replaced by permanent ones, with girls losing their teeth slightly earlier than boys. The first teeth to go are the lower and then upper front teeth, giving many first and second graders a "toothless" smile. For a while, the permanent teeth seem much too large. Gradually, growth of the facial bones, especially those of the jaw and chin, causes the child's face to lengthen and the mouth to widen, accommodating the newly erupting teeth.

Care of the teeth is essential during the school years because dental health affects the child's appearance, speech, and ability to chew properly. Parents need to remind children to brush their teeth thoroughly, and most children need help with flossing until about 9 years of age. More than 50 percent of U.S. school-age children have at least some tooth decay. Low-SES children have especially high levels, with about 30 percent untreated (National Institutes of Health, 2011). As decay progresses, they experience pain, embarrassment at damaged teeth, distraction from play and learning, and school absences due to dental-related illnesses.

Malocclusion, a condition in which the upper and lower teeth do not meet properly, occurs in one-third of school-age children. In about 14 percent of cases, serious difficulties in biting and chewing result. Malocclusion can be caused by thumb sucking after permanent teeth erupt. School-age children who continue to engage in the habit may require gentle but persistent encouragement to give it up (Garde et al., 2014). A more frequent cause of malocclusion is crowding of permanent teeth. In some children, this problem clears up as the jaw grows. Others need braces, a common sight by the end of elementary school.

Brain Development

The weight of the brain increases by only 10 percent during middle childhood and adolescence. Nevertheless, considerable growth occurs in certain brain structures. Using fMRI, researchers can detect the volume of two general types of brain tissue: *white matter,* consisting largely of myelinated nerve fibers, and *gray matter,* consisting mostly of neurons and supportive material. White matter rises steadily throughout childhood and adolescence, especially in the prefrontal cortex (responsible for consciousness, impulse control, integration of information, and strategic thinking), in the parietal lobes (supporting spatial abilities), and in the corpus callosum (leading to more efficient communication between the two cortical hemispheres) (Giedd et al., 2009; Smit et al., 2012). Because interconnectivity among distant regions of the cerebral cortex increases, the prefrontal cortex becomes a more effective "executive"— coordinating integrated functioning of various areas, yielding more complex, flexible, and adaptive behavior.

In middle childhood, the prefrontal cortex becomes a more effective "executive," coordinating integrated functioning of various brain regions. These changes support more complex, flexible abilities, such as this kayaker's deft maneuvering.

SKIP BROWN/LIFESIZE/GETTY IMAGES

As children acquire more complex abilities, stimulated neurons increase in synaptic connections, and their neural fibers become more elaborate and myelinated. As a result, gray matter peaks in middle childhood and then declines as synaptic pruning (reduction of unused synapses) and death of surrounding neurons proceed (Markant & Thomas, 2013; Silk & Wood, 2011). Recall from Chapter 5 that about 40 percent of synapses are pruned over childhood and adolescence. Pruning and accompanying reorganization and selection of brain circuits lead to more optimized functioning of specific brain regions and, thus, to more effective information processing. In particular, children gain in executive function, including sustained attention, inhibition, working memory capacity, and organized, flexible thinking.

Additional brain development likely takes place at the level of neurotransmitters, chemicals that permit neurons to communicate across synapses (see Chapter 5, page 161). Over time, neurons become increasingly selective, responding only to certain chemical messages. This change may add to school-age children's more efficient thinking. Secretions of particular neurotransmitters are related to cognitive performance, social and emotional adjustment, and ability to withstand stress. When neurotransmitters are not present in appropriate balances, children may suffer serious developmental problems, such as inattention and overactivity, emotional disturbance, and epilepsy (an illness involving brain seizures and loss of motor control) (Brooks et al., 2006; Kurian et al., 2011; Weller, Kloos, & Weller, 2006).

Researchers also believe that brain functioning may change in middle childhood because of the influence of hormones. Around age 7 to 8, an increase in androgens (male sex hormones), secreted by the adrenal glands (located on top of the kidneys), occurs in children of both sexes. Androgens will rise further among boys at puberty, when the testes release them in large amounts. Androgens affect brain organization and behavior in many animal species, including humans. Recall from Chapter 10 that androgens contribute to boys' higher activity level and physical aggression. They may also promote social dominance and play-fighting, topics we will take up at the end of this chapter (Azurmendi et al., 2006).

Ask Yourself

● **REVIEW** What aspects of physical growth account for the long-legged appearance of many 8- to 12-year-olds?

● **CONNECT** Relate secular trends in physical growth to the concept of cohort effects, discussed on page 41 in Chapter 1.

● **APPLY** Joey complained to his mother that it wasn't fair that his younger sister Lizzie was almost as tall as he was. He worried that he wasn't growing fast enough. How should Rena respond to Joey's concern?

● **REFLECT** How does your height compare with that of your parents and grandparents when they were your age? Do your observations illustrate secular trends?

Common Health Problems

Children from economically advantaged homes, like Joey and Lizzie, are at their healthiest in middle childhood, full of energy and play. Growth in lung size permits more air to be exchanged with each breath, so children are better able to exercise vigorously without tiring. The cumulative effects of good nutrition, combined with rapid development of the body's immune system, offer greater protection against disease. In fact, children who spent much time in child-care centers during the preschool years, and therefore experienced frequent respiratory and ear infections, are sick less often than their agemates after reaching elementary school (Côté et al., 2010). Their increased immunity may grant them a learning advantage, as they miss fewer days of school.

Not surprisingly, poverty continues to be a powerful predictor of poor health during middle childhood. Because economically disadvantaged U.S. children often lack health insurance and, if they are publicly insured, generally receive a lower standard of care (see Chapter 8, page 297), many do not have regular access to a doctor. A substantial number also lack such basic necessities as a comfortable home and regular meals.

Nutrition

Children need a well-balanced, plentiful diet to provide energy for successful learning in school and increased physical activity. With their increasing focus on play, friendships, and new activities, many children spend little time at the table. Joey's hurried breakfast, described at the beginning of this chapter, is a common event in middle childhood. The percentage of children who eat meals with their families drops sharply between ages 9 and 14. Family dinnertimes have waned in general over the past two decades. Yet eating an evening meal with parents leads to a diet higher in fruits, vegetables, grains, and milk products and lower in soft drinks and fast foods (Burgess-Champoux et al., 2009; Hammons & Fiese, 2011).

School-age children report that they "feel better" and "focus better" after eating healthy foods and that they feel sluggish, "like a blob," after eating junk foods. In a longitudinal study of nearly 14,000 U.S. children, a parent-reported diet high in sugar, fat, and processed food in early childhood predicted slightly lower IQ at age 8, after many factors that might otherwise account for this association were controlled (Northstone et al., 2012). Even mild nutritional deficits can affect cognitive functioning. Among school-age children from middle- to high-SES families, insufficient dietary iron and folate are related to poorer concentration and mental test performance (Arija et al., 2006; Low et al., 2013). Children say that a major barrier to healthy eating is the ready availability of unhealthy options, even in their homes. As one sixth grader commented, "When I get home from school, I think, 'I should eat some fruit,' but then I see the chips" (O'Dea, 2003, p. 498).

Recall from Chapter 8 that food familiarity and food preferences are strongly linked: Children like best foods they have eaten repeatedly in the past. Readily available, healthy between-meal snacks—such as cheese, fruit, raw vegetables, and peanut butter—can help meet school-age children's nutritional needs and increase their liking for healthy foods.

As we have seen in earlier chapters, many poverty-stricken children in developing countries and in the United States suffer from serious and prolonged malnutrition. By middle childhood, the effects are apparent in delayed physical growth, impaired motor coordination, inattention, and low IQ. The negative impact of malnutrition on learning and behavior may intensify as children encounter new academic and social challenges at school. First, as in earlier years, growth-stunted school-age children show greater stress reactivity, as indicated by a sharper rise in heart rate and in saliva levels of the stress hormone cortisol (Fernald & Grantham-McGregor, 1998). Second, animal evidence reveals that a deficient diet alters the production of neurotransmitters in the brain—an effect that can disrupt all aspects of psychological functioning (Haller, 2005).

Unfortunately, malnutrition that persists from infancy or early childhood into the school years usually results in permanent physical and mental damage (Grantham-McGregor, Walker, & Chang, 2000; Liu et al., 2003). Government-sponsored supplementary food programs from the early years through adolescence can prevent these effects.

11.3 Describe the causes and consequences of serious nutritional problems in middle childhood, giving special attention to obesity.

11.4 What factors contribute to myopia, otitis media, nocturnal enuresis, and asthma, and how can these health problems be reduced?

11.5 Describe changes in the occurrence of unintentional injuries during middle childhood, and cite effective interventions.

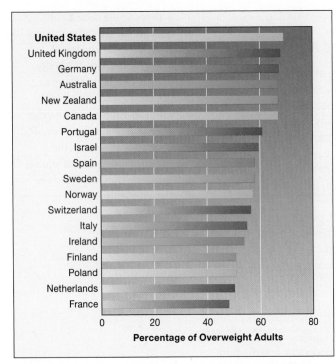

FIGURE 11.2 **Overweight adults in eighteen industrialized nations.** The United States outranks all other developed nations in pervasiveness of overweight in the adult population, defined here according to the widely accepted adult standard of a BMI greater than 25. (Based on World Health Organization, 2014c.)

Overweight and Obesity

Mona, a very heavy child in Lizzie's class, often watched from the sidelines during recess. When she did join in games, she was slow and clumsy, the target of unkind comments: "Move it, Tubs!" Although Mona was a good student, the other children rejected her in the classroom as well. When they chose partners for special activities, Mona was among the last to be selected. Most afternoons, she walked home alone while her schoolmates gathered in groups, talking, laughing, and chasing. At home, Mona sought comfort in high-calorie snacks.

Mona suffers from **obesity,** a greater-than-20-percent increase over healthy weight, based on *body mass index (BMI)*—a ratio of weight to height associated with body fat. A BMI above the 85th percentile for a child's age and sex is considered *overweight,* a BMI above the 95th percentile *obese.* During the past several decades, a rise in overweight and obesity has occurred in many Western nations (see Figure 11.2), with large increases in Canada, Germany, Israel, Greece, Ireland, New Zealand, United Kingdom, and the United States. Today, 32 percent of U.S. children and adolescents are overweight, more than half of them extremely so: 17 percent are obese (Ogden et al., 2014; World Health Organization, 2014d). Smaller increases have occurred in other industrialized nations, including Finland, the Netherlands, Norway, and Sweden.

Obesity rates have also risen in developing countries, as urbanization shifts the population toward sedentary lifestyles and diets high in meats and energy-dense refined foods (World Health Organization, 2014d). In China, for example, where obesity was nearly nonexistent a generation ago, today 20 percent of urban children are overweight and 8 percent obese—a fortyfold increase over the past 25 years, with obesity affecting twice as many boys as girls (Sun et al., 2014). In addition to lifestyle changes, a prevailing belief in Chinese culture that excess body fat represents prosperity and health—carried over from a half-century ago, when famine caused millions of deaths—has contributed to this alarming upsurge. High valuing of sons may induce Chinese parents to offer boys especially generous portions of meat, dairy products, and other energy-dense foods that were once scarce but are now widely available.

Overweight rises with age, from 23 percent among U.S. preschoolers to 35 percent among school-age children and adolescents to an astronomical 69 percent among adults (Ogden et al., 2014). In a longitudinal study of more than 1,000 U.S. children, overweight preschoolers were five times more likely than their normal-weight peers to be overweight at age 12 (Nader et al., 2006). And few young people who are persistently overweight in adolescence attain a normal weight in adulthood (Patton et al., 2011).

Besides serious emotional and social difficulties, obese children are at risk for lifelong health problems. Symptoms that begin to appear in the early school years—high blood pressure, high cholesterol levels, respiratory abnormalities, insulin resistance, and inflammatory reactions—are powerful predictors of heart disease, circulatory difficulties, type 2 diabetes, gallbladder disease, sleep and digestive disorders, many forms of cancer, and early death. Furthermore, obesity has caused a dramatic rise in cases of diabetes in children, sometimes leading to early, severe complications, including stroke, kidney failure, and circulatory problems that heighten the risk of eventual blindness and leg amputation (Biro & Wien, 2010; Lakshman, Elks, & Ong, 2012). As you can see from Table 11.1, childhood obesity is a complex physical disorder with multiple causes.

CAUSES OF OBESITY Not all children are equally at risk for excessive weight gain. Overweight children tend to have overweight parents, and identical twins are more likely to share the disorder than fraternal twins. But heredity accounts for only a *tendency* to gain weight (Kral & Faith, 2009). The importance of environment is evident in the consistent relationship of low SES to overweight and obesity in industrialized nations, especially among ethnic

TABLE 11.1   Factors Contributing to Childhood Obesity

FACTOR	DESCRIPTION
Heredity	Obese children are likely to have at least one obese parent, and identical twins are more likely than fraternal twins to share the disorder.
Socioeconomic status	Obesity is more common in low-SES families.
Early growth pattern	Infants who gain weight rapidly are at greater risk for obesity, probably because their parents promote unhealthy eating habits (see Chapter 5).
Family eating habits	When parents purchase high-calorie fast foods, treats, and junk food; use them as rewards; anxiously overfeed; or control their children's intake, their children are more likely to be obese.
Responsiveness to food cues	Obese children often decide when to eat on the basis of external cues, such as taste, smell, sight, time of day, and food-related words, rather than hunger.
Physical activity	Obese children are less physically active than their normal-weight peers.
Television viewing	Children who spend many hours watching television are more likely to become obese.
Early malnutrition	Early, severe malnutrition that results in growth stunting increases the risk of later obesity.

minorities—in the United States, African-American, Hispanic, and Native-American children and adults (Martinson, McLanahan, & Brooks-Gunn, 2012; Ogden et al., 2014). Factors responsible include lack of knowledge about healthy diet; a tendency to buy high-fat, low-cost foods; neighborhoods that lack convenient access to affordable, healthy foods in grocery stores and restaurants; and family stress, which can prompt overeating.

Furthermore, children who were undernourished in their early years are at risk for later excessive weight gain. Studies in many poverty-stricken regions of the world reveal that growth-stunted children are more likely to be overweight than their nonstunted agemates (Branca & Ferrari, 2002). In industrialized nations, many studies confirm that children whose mothers smoked during pregnancy and who therefore are often born underweight (see Chapter 3) are at elevated risk for later overweight and obesity (Rogers, 2009). A malnourished body protects itself by establishing a low basal metabolism rate, which may endure after nutrition improves. Also, malnutrition may disrupt appetite control centers in the brain, causing the child to overeat when food becomes plentiful. Nevertheless, in the developing world (unlike in industrialized countries), obesity risk is greatest for individuals living in economically well-off households, probably because of greater food availability and reduced activity levels (Subramanian et al., 2011).

Parental feeding practices also contribute to childhood obesity. Overweight children are more likely to eat larger quantities of high-calorie sugary and fatty foods, perhaps because these foods are plentiful in the diets offered by their parents, who also tend to be overweight (Kit, Ogden, & Flegal, 2014). Frequent eating out—which increases parents' and children's consumption of high-calorie fast foods—is linked to overweight. And it likely plays a major role in the consistent relationship between mothers' employment hours and elevated BMI among school-age children (Morrissey, Dunifon, & Kalil, 2011). Demanding work schedules reduce the time parents have for healthy meal preparation.

Furthermore, some parents anxiously overfeed, interpreting almost all their child's discomforts as a desire for food—a practice common among immigrant parents and grandparents who, as children themselves, survived deadly famines or periods of food deprivation due to poverty. Still other parents are overly controlling, restricting when, what, and how much their child eats and worrying about weight gain (Jansen et al., 2012). In each case, parents undermine children's ability to regulate their own food intake. Also, parents of overweight

ROLF BRUDERER/BLEND IMAGES/GETTY IMAGES

Frequent eating out, which increases both parents' and children's consumption of high-calorie fast foods, contributes to excessive weight gain.

Social Issues: Health

Family Stressors and Childhood Obesity

In response to chronic stress, many adults and children increase their food consumption—especially foods high in sugar and fat—and gain excessive weight. How can a stressful daily life prompt overeating?

One route is through elevated stress hormones, including cortisol, which signal the body to increase energy expenditure and the brain, in turn, to boost caloric intake (Zellner et al., 2006). In a second pathway, chronic stress triggers insulin resistance—a prediabetic condition that frequently induces a raging appetite (Dallman et al., 2003).

Furthermore, the effort required to manage persistent stress can easily strain self-regulatory capacity, leaving the individual unable to limit excessive eating (Blair, 2010). In several studies, the greater the number of home-life stressors in school-age children's lives, the poorer their regulation of negative emotion and behavior (Evans, 2003; Evans et al., 2005). Impaired self-regulation, then, might be a major intervening factor in the link between childhood chronic stress and obesity.

To find out, researchers followed several hundred children from economically disadvantaged families, assessing family stressors and self-regulatory ability at age 9 and change in BMI four years later, at age 13 (Evans et al., 2012). Number of stressors experienced—including poverty, single-parent household, residential crowding, noise, household clutter, lack of books and play materials, child separation from the family, and exposure to violence—strongly predicted impaired self-regulation, as indicated by children's delay of gratification (ability to wait for a reward). Poor self-regulation, in turn, largely accounted for the relationship between family stressors and gain in BMI over time.

In obesity prevention programs, children given self-regulation training—instructions to "stop and think" in eating situations—show beneficial outcomes in terms of improved eating behaviors and weight

This 9-year-old, living in shelter housing with her mother, is at high risk for obesity. Home-life stressors, including poverty, single-parenthood, noise, crowding, and clutter, contribute to overeating by impairing children's self-regulation.

loss (Johnson, 2000). But such training is likely to be fully effective only when stressors in children's family lives are manageable, not overwhelming.

LOOK and LISTEN

Observe in the check-out area of a supermarket for an hour on a weekend, recording the percentage of families with children whose carts contain large quantities of high-calorie processed foods and soft drinks. In how many of these families are parents and children overweight?

children often use high-fat, sugary foods to reinforce other behaviors, leading children to attach great value to treats (Sherry et al., 2004).

Because of these experiences, obese children soon develop maladaptive eating habits. They are more responsive than normal-weight individuals to external stimuli associated with food—taste, sight, smell, time of day, and food-related words—and less responsive to internal hunger cues (Jansen et al., 2003; Temple et al., 2007). Furthermore, a stressful family life contributes to children's diminished self-regulatory capacity, amplifying uncontrolled eating (see the Social Issues: Health box above).

Another factor implicated in weight gain is insufficient sleep (Nielsen, Danielsen, & Sørensen, 2011). A follow-up of more than 2,000 U.S. 3- to 12-year-olds revealed that children who got less nightly sleep were more likely to be overweight five years later (Snell, Adam, & Duncan, 2007). Reduced sleep may increase time available for eating, leave children too fatigued for physical activity, or disrupt the brain's regulation of hunger and metabolism.

Overweight children are less physically active than their normal-weight peers. Inactivity is both cause and consequence of excessive weight gain. Research reveals that the rise in childhood obesity is due in part to the many hours U.S. children spend watching television. In a study that tracked children's TV viewing from ages 4 to 11, the more TV children watched, the more body fat they added. Children who devoted more than 3 hours per day to TV accumulated 40 percent more fat than those devoting less than 1¾ hours (see Figure 11.3) (Proctor et al., 2003). Watching TV reduces time devoted to physical exercise, and TV ads encourage children to eat fattening, unhealthy snacks. Children permitted to have a TV in their bedroom—a practice linked to especially high TV viewing—are at even further risk for overweight (de Jong et al., 2013).

Finally, the broader food environment affects the incidence of obesity. The Pima Indians of Arizona, who two decades ago changed from a traditional diet of plant foods to a high-fat, typically American diet, have one of the world's highest obesity rates. Compared with descendants of their ancestors living in the remote Sierra Madre region of Mexico, the Arizona Pima have body weights 50 percent greater. Half the population has diabetes (8 times the national average), with many in their twenties and thirties already disabled by the disease—blind, in wheelchairs, and on kidney dialysis. The Pima have a genetic susceptibility to overweight, but it emerges only under Western dietary conditions. U.S. Pima children who are obese display double the rate of illness-related premature deaths after they reach adulthood as their normal-weight peers (Franks et al., 2010; Traurig et al., 2009). Other ethnic groups with a hereditary tendency to gain weight include Pacific Islanders, including native Hawaiians and Samoans (Furusawa et al., 2010). Many now eat an Americanized diet of high-calorie processed and fast foods, and over 80 percent are overweight.

CONSEQUENCES OF OBESITY Unfortunately, physical attractiveness is a powerful predictor of social acceptance. In Western societies, both children and adults rate obese youngsters as unlikable, stereotyping them as lazy, sloppy, dirty, ugly, stupid, and deceitful (Penny & Haddock, 2007; Tiggemann & Anesbury, 2000). In school, obese children and adolescents are often socially isolated. They report more emotional, social, and school difficulties, including peer teasing, rejection, and consequent low self-esteem (van Grieken et al., 2013; Zeller & Modi, 2006). They also tend to achieve less well than their healthy-weight agemates (Datar & Sturm, 2006).

Because unhappiness and overeating contribute to each other, the child remains overweight. Persistent obesity from childhood into adolescence predicts serious behavior problems, including defiance, aggression, severe depression, and suicidal thoughts and behavior (Puhl & Latner, 2007; Young-Hyman et al., 2006). Furthermore, overweight girls are more likely to reach puberty early, increasing their risk for early sexual activity and other adjustment problems.

The psychological consequences of obesity combine with continuing discrimination to result in reduced life chances. Overweight adults are less likely than their normal-weight agemates to receive financial aid for college, be rented apartments, find mates, and be offered jobs. And they report frequent mistreatment by family members, peers, co-workers, and health-care professionals, which intensifies physical and psychological health problems (Carr & Friedman, 2005; Puhl, Heuer, & Brownell, 2010).

TREATING OBESITY Childhood obesity is difficult to treat because it is a family disorder. In Mona's case, the school nurse suggested that Mona and her obese mother enter a weight-loss program together. But Mona's mother, unhappily married for many years, had her own reasons for overeating. She rejected this idea, claiming that Mona would eventually decide to lose weight on her own. In one study, only one-fourth of overweight parents judged their overweight children to have a weight problem (Jeffrey, 2004). Consistent with these findings, fewer than 20 percent of obese children get any treatment. Although many try to slim down in adolescence, they often go on crash diets that make matters worse. Temporary starvation leads to physical stress, discomfort, and fatigue. Soon the child returns to old eating patterns, and weight rebounds to a higher level. Then, to protect itself, the body burns calories more slowly and becomes more resistant to future weight loss.

The most effective interventions are family-based and focus on changing behaviors (Oude et al., 2009). In one program, both parent and child revised eating patterns, exercised daily, and reinforced each other with praise and points for progress, which they exchanged for special activities and times together. The more weight parents lost, the more their children lost (Wrotniak et al., 2004). Follow-ups after five and ten years showed that children maintained their weight loss more effectively than adults—a finding that underscores the importance of

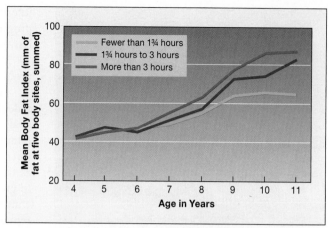

FIGURE 11.3 **Relationship of television viewing to gains in body fat from ages 4 to 11.** Researchers followed more than 100 children from ages 4 to 11, collecting information on hours per day of television viewing and on body fat, measured in millimeters of skinfold thickness at five body sites (upper arms, shoulders, abdomen, trunk, and thighs). The more TV children watched, the greater the gain in body fat. At ages 10 to 11, the difference between children watching fewer than 1¾ hours and those watching more than 3 hours had become large. (Adapted from M. H. Proctor et al., 2003, "Television Viewing and Change in Body Fat from Preschool to Early Adolescence: The Framingham Children's Study," *International Journal of Obesity, 27,* p. 831. Reprinted by permission from Macmillan Publishers Ltd.)

ARIEL SKELLEY/BLEND IMAGES/GETTY IMAGES

This mother and son reinforce each other's efforts to lose weight and get in shape. The most effective interventions for childhood obesity focus on changing the whole family's behaviors, emphasizing fitness and healthy eating.

intervening at an early age (Epstein, Roemmich, & Raynor, 2001). Treatment programs that focus on both diet and lifestyle can yield substantial, long-lasting weight reduction among children and adolescents (Nemet et al., 2005). But these interventions work best when parents' and children's weight problems are not severe.

Getting obese children to exercise is challenging because they find being sedentary pleasurable. Approaches that encourage setting personal exercise goals and keeping a record of success at meeting those goals are helpful (Staniford, Breckon, & Copeland, 2012). One successful technique is to reinforce obese children for spending less time inactive. Providing rewards (such as tickets to the zoo or a baseball game) for reducing sedentary time leads to greater liking for physical activity and more weight loss than reinforcing children directly for exercising or punishing them (by loss of privileges) for remaining inactive (Epstein et al., 1997). Rewarding children for giving up inactivity seems to increase their sense of personal control over exercising—a factor linked to sustained physical activity.

Children consume one-third of their daily energy intake at school. Therefore, schools can help reduce obesity by serving healthier meals and ensuring regular physical activity (Lakshman, Elks, & Ong, 2012). Because obesity is expected to rise further without broad prevention strategies, many U.S. states and cities have passed obesity-reduction legislation. Among measures taken are weight-related school screenings for all children, improved nutrition standards and limited vending machine access in schools, additional recess time in the elementary grades and physical education time in all grades, and obesity awareness and weight-reduction programs as part of school curricula. A review of school-based efforts reported impressive benefits (Waters et al., 2011). Obesity prevention in schools was more successful in reducing 6- to 12-year-olds' BMIs than programs delivered in other community settings, perhaps because schools are better able to provide long-term, comprehensive intervention.

Finally, obesity prevention and reduction are becoming U.S. national priorities. The *Let's Move* campaign, launched by First Lady Michelle Obama in 2010, aims to create partnerships among federal and state governments, communities, businesses, schools, and health organizations to solve the childhood obesity problem within a generation. Among its goals are:

- increased public education about healthy eating and physical activity, including limiting time devoted to TV viewing
- greater access to healthy, affordable foods in low-income neighborhoods, where overweight and obesity are highest
- laws mandating improved labels on foods and menus specifying nutritional content and calories
- improved quality of government-supported school breakfasts and lunches
- expanded opportunities for physical activity in schools as well as in communities, by building more parks, recreation centers, and walking and bike paths

For more information, visit *www.letsmove.gov.*

LOOK *and* **LISTEN**

Contact your state and city governments to find out about their childhood obesity prevention legislation. Can policies be improved?

Vision and Hearing

The most common vision problem in middle childhood is *myopia,* or nearsightedness. By the end of the school years, it affects nearly 25 percent of children—a rate that rises to 60 percent by early adulthood (Rahi, Cumberland, & Peckham, 2011).

Heredity plays a role: Identical twins are more likely than fraternal twins to share the condition (Pacella et al., 1999). And compared to children with no myopic parents, those with one myopic parent have twice the risk, and those with two myopic parents two to five times the risk, of becoming myopic themselves. Worldwide, myopia occurs far more frequently in Asian than in Caucasian populations (Morgan, Ohno-Matsui, & Saw, 2012). Early biological trauma can also induce myopia. School-age children with low birth weights show an especially high rate, believed to result from immaturity of visual structures, slower eye growth, and a greater incidence of eye disease (Molloy et al., 2013).

When parents warn their children not to read in dim light or sit too close to the TV or computer screen, their concern ("You'll ruin your eyes!") is well-founded. In diverse cultures, the more time children spend reading, writing, using the computer, and doing other close work, the more likely they are to be myopic. Conversely, the incidence of myopia is reduced in school-age children who spend more time playing outdoors (Pan, Ramamurthy, & Saw, 2012; Russo et al., 2014). Myopia is one of the few health conditions to increase with SES, and it has become more prevalent in recent generations. Fortunately, myopia can be overcome easily with corrective lenses.

During middle childhood, the Eustachian tube (canal that runs from the inner ear to the throat) becomes longer, narrower, and more slanted, preventing fluid and bacteria from traveling so easily from the mouth to the ear. As a result, *otitis media* (middle ear infection), common in infancy and early childhood (see Chapter 8), becomes less frequent. Still, about 3 to 4 percent of the school-age population, and as many as 20 percent of low-SES children, develop some hearing loss as a result of repeated infections (Ryding et al., 2002). With regular screening for both vision and hearing, defects can be corrected before they lead to serious learning difficulties.

Bedwetting

One Friday afternoon, Terry called Joey to see if he could sleep over, but Joey refused. "I can't," said Joey anxiously, without offering an explanation.

"Why not? We can take our sleeping bags out in the backyard. Come on, it'll be cool!"

"My mom won't let me," Joey responded, unconvincingly. "I mean, well, I think we're busy. We're doing something tonight."

"Gosh, Joey, this is the third time you've said no. See if I'll ask you again!" snapped Terry as he hung up the phone.

Joey is one of 10 percent of U.S. school-age children who suffer from **nocturnal enuresis,** or bedwetting during the night. At all ages, more boys than girls are affected. In the overwhelming majority of cases, the problem has biological roots. Heredity is a major contributing factor: Parents with a history of bedwetting are far more likely to have a child with the problem, and identical twins are more likely than fraternal twins to share it (von Gontard, Heron, & Joinson, 2011). Most often, enuresis is caused by a failure of muscular responses that inhibit urination or by a hormonal imbalance that permits too much urine to accumulate during the night. Some children also have difficulty awakening to the sensation of a full bladder (Becker, 2013). Punishing a school-age child for wetting is only likely to make matters worse.

To treat enuresis, doctors often prescribe a synthetic hormone called desmopressin, which reduces the amount of urine produced. Although medication is a short-term solution for children attending camp or visiting a friend's house, once children stop taking it, they typically begin wetting again (Kwak et al., 2010). The most effective treatment is a urine alarm that wakes the child at the first sign of dampness and works according to conditioning principles. Success rates of about 55 to 75 percent occur after four to six months of treatment (Glazener, Evans, & Petro, 2005). The few children who relapse achieve dryness after trying the alarm a second time.

Although a decade ago, only a minority of U.S. school-age children with nocturnal enuresis saw a health professional about the problem, today increasing numbers of parents seek treatment (Kushnir, Kushnir, & Sadeh, 2013). Doing so has immediate, positive psychological consequences. It leads to gains in restful sleep, parents' evaluation of their child's behavior, and children's self-esteem (Longstaffe, Moffatt, & Whalen, 2000). Although many children outgrow enuresis without intervention, this generally takes years.

Illnesses

Children experience a somewhat higher rate of illness during the first two years of elementary school than later, because of exposure to sick children and an immune system that is still developing. Typically, illness causes children to miss from 1 to 5 days of school per year (National Survey of Children's Health, 2012). Longer absences usually can be traced to a few students with chronic health problems.

About 20 to 25 percent of U.S. children living at home have chronic diseases and conditions (including physical disabilities) (Compas et al., 2012). By far the most common—accounting for about one-third of childhood chronic illness and the most frequent cause of school absence and childhood hospitalization—is *asthma,* in which the bronchial tubes (passages that connect the throat and lungs) are highly sensitive (Basinger, 2013). In response to a variety of stimuli, such as cold weather, infection, exercise, allergies, and emotional stress, they fill with mucus and contract, leading to coughing, wheezing, and serious breathing difficulties.

The prevalence of asthma in the United States has increased steadily over the past several decades. It is now at its highest level, with nearly 10 percent of children affected. Although heredity contributes to asthma, researchers believe that environmental factors are necessary to spark the illness. Boys, African-American children, and children who were born underweight, whose parents smoke, and who live in poverty are at greatest risk (Centers for Disease Control and Prevention, 2012; Pearlman et al., 2006). The higher rate and greater severity of asthma among African-American and poverty-stricken children may be the result of pollution in inner-city areas (which triggers allergic reactions), stressful home lives, and lack of access to good health care. Childhood obesity is also related to asthma (Hampton, 2014). High levels of blood-circulating inflammatory substances associated with body fat and the pressure of excess weight on the chest wall may be responsible.

These children, who live in an inner-city community where asthma is common, use a meter to measure the daily concentration of air pollutants. The device will warn them when pollution reaches a level likely to trigger asthma attacks.

PAT GREENHOUSE/THE BOSTON GLOBE VIA GETTY IMAGES

About 2 percent of U.S. children have more severe chronic illnesses, such as sickle cell anemia, cystic fibrosis, diabetes, arthritis, cancer, and acquired immune deficiency syndrome (AIDS). Painful medical treatments, physical discomfort, and changes in appearance often disrupt the sick child's daily life, making it difficult to concentrate in school and separating the child from peers. As the illness worsens, family and child stress increases (Marin et al., 2009; Rodriguez, Dunn, & Compas, 2012). For these reasons, chronically ill children are at risk for academic, emotional, and social difficulties. In adolescence, they are more likely than their agemates to suffer from low self-esteem and depression and report more often smoking cigarettes, using illegal drugs, and thinking about and attempting suicide (Erickson et al., 2005).

A strong link exists between good family functioning and child well-being for chronically ill children, just as it does for physically healthy children (Compas et al., 2012). Interventions that foster positive family relationships help parent and child cope effectively with the disease and improve adjustment. These include:

- Health education, in which parents and children learn about the illness and get training in how to manage it
- Home visits by health professionals, who offer counseling and social support to enhance parents' and children's strategies for managing the stress of chronic illness
- Schools that accommodate children's special health and education needs
- Disease-specific summer camps, which teach children self-help skills and give parents time off from the demands of caring for an ill youngster
- Parent and peer support groups

Unintentional Injuries

As we conclude our discussion of threats to school-age children's health, let's return to the topic of unintentional injuries (discussed in detail in Chapter 8). As Figure 11.4 shows, injury fatalities increase from middle childhood into adolescence, with rates for boys rising considerably above those for girls. Poverty and either rural or inner-city residence—factors associated with dangerous environments and reduced parental monitoring of children—are also linked to high injury rates (Birken et al., 2006; Schwebel et al., 2004).

Motor vehicle accidents, involving children as passengers or pedestrians, continue to be the leading cause of injury, followed by bicycle accidents (Bailar-Heath & Valley-Gray, 2010). Pedestrian injuries most often result from midblock dart-outs, bicycle accidents from disobeying traffic signals and rules. When many stimuli impinge on them at once, young school-age children often fail to think before they act. They need frequent reminders, supervision, and prohibitions against venturing into busy traffic on their own. Yet a study that tracked routine supervision provided to middle-SES 7- to 10-year-olds at home revealed that the children were unsupervised 35 percent of the time (Morrongiello, Kane, Zdzieborski, 2011). Both nonsupervision and indirect supervision (parent checking on the child intermittently) were associated with increased injuries.

As children range farther from home, safety education related to their widening world becomes important. Effective school- and community-based prevention programs use extensive modeling and rehearsal of safety practices, give children feedback about their performance along with praise and tangible rewards for acquiring safety skills, and provide occasional booster sessions. Targeting specific injury risks (such as traffic safety) rather than many risks at once yields longer-lasting results (Nauta et al., 2014). As part of these programs, parents, who often overestimate their child's safety knowledge and physical abilities, must be educated about children's age-related safety capacities (Schwebel & Bounds, 2003).

One vital safety measure is legally requiring that children wear protective helmets while bicycling, in-line skating, skateboarding, or using scooters. This precaution leads to a 9 percent reduction in head injuries, a leading cause of permanent physical disability and death in school-age children (Karkhaneh et al., 2013). Combining helmet use with preventive education and other community-based prevention strategies is especially effective. In the Harlem Hospital Injury Prevention Program, inner-city children attended bicycle safety clinics, during which helmets were distributed. They also received traffic safety education in their classrooms and in a simulated traffic environment. In addition, existing playgrounds were improved and new ones constructed to provide expanded off-street play areas, and more community-sponsored, supervised recreational activities were offered (Durkin et al., 1999). As a result, motor vehicle and bicycle injuries declined by 36 percent.

Not all children respond to efforts to increase their safety. By middle childhood, the greatest risk-takers tend to be those whose parents do not act as safety-conscious models, rarely supervise their children's activities, or use punitive or inconsistent discipline to enforce rules (Rowe, Maughan, & Goodman, 2004; Tuchfarber, Zins, & Jason, 1997). These child-rearing tactics, as we saw in Chapter 10, spark children's defiance, reduce their willingness to comply, and actually promote high-risk behavior.

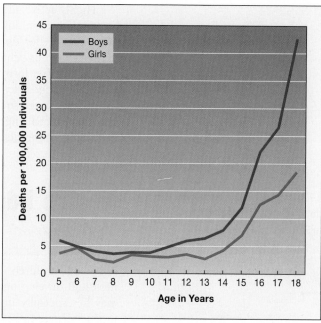

FIGURE 11.4 **U.S. rates of injury mortality from middle childhood to adolescence.** Injury fatalities increase with age, and the gap between boys and girls expands. Motor vehicle (passenger and pedestrian) accidents are the leading cause, with bicycle injuries next in line. (Based on National Center for Injury Prevention and Control, 2013.)

These Oglala children of South Dakota risk serious injury when they don't wear helmets while riding bikes and horses. Head injuries are a leading cause of permanent disability and death in school-age children.

Highly active, impulsive children, many of whom are boys, remain particularly susceptible to injury in middle childhood. Although they have just as much safety knowledge as their peers, they are far less likely to implement it. Parents tend to be particularly lax in intervening in the dangerous behaviors of such children, especially under conditions of persistent marital conflict or other forms of distress (Schwebel et al., 2011, 2012). Furthermore, compared with girls, boys judge risky play activities as less likely to result in injury, and they pay less attention to injury risk cues, such as a peer who looks hesitant or fearful (Morrongiello & Rennie, 1998). The greatest challenge for injury-control programs is reaching these children, altering high-risk factors in their families, and reducing the dangers to which they are exposed.

11.6 What can parents and teachers do to encourage good health practices in school-age children?

Health Education

Psychologists, educators, and pediatricians are intensely interested in finding ways to help school-age children understand their bodies, acquire mature conceptions of health and illness, and develop behaviors that foster good health throughout life. The school-age period may be especially important for fostering healthy lifestyles because of the child's growing independence, increasing cognitive capacities, and rapidly developing self-concept, which includes a sense of physical well-being.

During middle childhood, children can comprehend a wide range of health information—about the structure and functioning of their bodies, about good nutrition, and about the causes and consequences of physical injuries and diseases. When given scientific facts, they build on basic biological concepts acquired during the preschool years, and their understanding advances. For example, a 5-year-old is likely to say, "You get a cold when your friend sneezes and gives you her germs" (Legare, Zhu, & Wellman, 2013). A 10-year-old, in contrast, offers a deeper, more detailed explanation: "You get a cold when your sinuses fill with mucus. Sometimes your lungs do, too, and you get a cough. Colds come from viruses. They get into the bloodstream and make your platelet count go down" (Myant & Williams, 2005).

Without effective teaching, however, school-age children readily generalize their knowledge of familiar health conditions to less familiar ones. As a result, they may conclude that risk factors for colds (getting sneezed on, sharing a Coke) can cause AIDS or that cancer (like a cold) is contagious (González-Rivera & Bauermeister, 2007). Furthermore, supernatural accounts of illness widespread in certain cultures—such as "Maybe his sickness is punishment for bad behavior"—must be gently countered with scientific facts (Raman & Gelman, 2004). Otherwise, these incorrect ideas can lead to unnecessary anxiety about getting a serious disease.

A visiting doctor discusses biological information about the human body with fifth graders. When school-age children are provided with scientific facts, they gain in understanding of health and illness.

Nevertheless, most efforts to impart health information to school-age children have little impact on behavior (Tinsley, 2003). Several related reasons underlie this gap between knowledge and practice:

- Health is seldom an important goal for children, who feel good most of the time. They are far more concerned about schoolwork, friends, and play.
- Children do not yet have an adultlike time perspective that relates past, present, and future. They cannot see the connection between engaging in preventive behaviors now and experiencing later health consequences.
- Much health information given to children is contradicted by other sources, such as television advertising and the examples of adults and peers.

Consequently, teaching school-age children health-related facts, though important, must be supplemented by other efforts. As we have seen, a powerful means of fostering children's

Applying What We Know

Strategies for Fostering Healthy Lifestyles in School-Age Children

STRATEGY	DESCRIPTION
Increase health-related knowledge and encourage healthy behaviors.	Provide health education that imparts scientific information about health concepts and healthy lifestyles and that includes modeling, role playing, rehearsal, and reinforcement of good health practices.
Involve parents in supporting health education.	Communicate with parents about health education goals in school, encouraging them to extend these efforts at home. Teach parents about unhealthy dietary practices and how to create healthy food environments at home. Promote proper parental supervision by providing information on children's age-related safety capacities.
Provide healthy environments in schools.	Ask school administrators to ensure that school breakfasts and lunches follow widely accepted dietary guidelines. Limit access to vending machines with junk food. Work for daily recess periods in elementary school and mandatory daily physical education at all grade levels.
Make voluntary screening for risk factors available as part of health education.	Offer periodic measures of height, weight, body mass, blood pressure, and adequacy of diet. Educate children about the meaning of each index, and encourage improvement.
Promote pleasurable physical activity.	Provide opportunities for regular, vigorous physical exercise through activities that de-emphasize competition and stress skill building and personal and social enjoyment.
Teach children to be critical of media advertising.	Besides teaching children to be skeptical of ads for unhealthy foods on TV and other screen media, reduce such advertising in schools—for example, on sports scoreboards.
Work for safer, healthier community environments for children.	Form community action groups to improve child safety, school nutrition, and play environments, and initiate community programs that foster healthy physical activity.

health is to reduce hazards, such as pollution, an unhealthy diet, and inadequate medical and dental care. At the same time, because environments will never be totally free of health risks, parents and teachers must coach children in good health practices and must model and reinforce these behaviors. Refer to Applying What We Know above for ways to foster healthy lifestyles in school-age children.

Ask Yourself

- **REVIEW** Select one of the following health problems of middle childhood: obesity, myopia, bedwetting, asthma, or unintentional injuries. Explain how both genetic and environmental factors contribute to it.

- **CONNECT** Children who were undernourished in the early years are more likely to become overweight when their food environments improve. Explain how this finding illustrates epigenesis, described on page 86 in Chapter 2.

- **APPLY** Nine-year-old Talia is afraid to hug and kiss her grandmother, who has cancer. What explains Talia's mistaken belief that the same behaviors that cause colds to spread might lead her to catch cancer? What would you do to change her thinking?

- **REFLECT** List unintentional injuries that you experienced as a child. Were you injury-prone? Why or why not?

Motor Development and Play

TAKE A MOMENT... Visit a park on a pleasant weekend afternoon, and watch several preschool and school-age children at play. You will see that gains in body size and muscle strength support improved motor coordination during middle childhood. And greater cognitive and social maturity enables older children to use their new motor skills in more complex ways. A major change in children's play takes place at this time.

11.7 Cite major changes in gross- and fine-motor development during middle childhood.

11.8 Describe individual differences in motor performance during middle childhood.

11.9 What qualities of children's play are evident in middle childhood?

11.10 What steps can schools take to promote physical fitness in middle childhood?

Improved physical flexibility, balance, agility, and force, along with more efficient information processing, promote gains in school-age children's gross-motor skills.

Gross-Motor Development

During the school years, running, jumping, hopping, and ball skills become more refined. At Joey and Lizzie's school, we watched during the third to sixth graders' recess. Children burst into sprints as they raced across the playground, jumped quickly over rotating ropes, engaged in intricate hopscotch patterns, kicked and dribbled soccer balls, batted at balls pitched by their classmates, and balanced adeptly as they walked heel-to-toe across narrow ledges. Table 11.2 summarizes gross-motor achievements between 6 and 12 years of age. These diverse skills reflect gains in four basic motor capacities:

- *Flexibility.* Compared with preschoolers, school-age children are physically more pliable and elastic, a difference evident as they swing bats, kick balls, jump over hurdles, and execute tumbling routines.
- *Balance.* Improved balance supports many athletic skills, including running, hopping, skipping, throwing, kicking, and the rapid changes of direction required in many team sports.
- *Agility.* Quicker and more accurate movements are evident in the fancy footwork of dance and cheerleading and in the forward, backward, and sideways motions used to dodge opponents in tag and soccer.
- *Force.* Older children can throw and kick a ball harder and propel themselves farther off the ground when running and jumping than they could at earlier ages (Haywood & Getchell, 2014).

Along with body growth, more efficient information processing plays a vital role in improved motor performance. Younger children often have difficulty with skills that require rapid responding, such as dribbling and batting. During middle childhood, the capacity to react only to relevant information increases. And steady gains in reaction time occur, including anticipatory

TABLE 11.2	**Changes in Gross-Motor Skills During Middle Childhood**	
	SKILL	**DEVELOPMENTAL CHANGE**
	Running	Running speed increases from 12 feet per second at age 6 to over 18 feet per second at age 12.
	Other gait variations	Skipping improves. Sideways stepping appears around age 6 and becomes more continuous and fluid with age.
	Vertical jump	Height jumped increases from 4 inches at age 6 to 12 inches at age 12.
	Standing broad jump	Distance jumped increases from 3 feet at age 6 to over 5 feet at age 12.
	Precision jumping and hopping (on a mat divided into squares)	By age 7, children can accurately jump and hop from square to square, a performance that improves until age 9 and then levels off.
	Throwing	Throwing speed, distance, and accuracy increase for both sexes, but much more for boys than for girls. At age 6, a ball thrown by a boy travels 39 feet per second, one by a girl 29 feet per second. At age 12, a ball thrown by a boy travels 78 feet per second, one by a girl 56 feet per second.
	Catching	Ability to catch small balls thrown over greater distances improves with age.
	Kicking	Kicking speed and accuracy improve, with boys considerably ahead of girls. At age 6, a ball kicked by a boy travels 21 feet per second, one by a girl 13 feet per second. At age 12, a ball kicked by a boy travels 34 feet per second, one by a girl 26 feet per second.
	Batting	Batting motions become more effective with age, increasing in speed and accuracy and involving the entire body.
	Dribbling	Style of hand dribbling gradually changes, from awkward slapping of the ball to continuous, relaxed, even stroking.

Sources: Haywood & Getchell, 2014; Malina & Bouchard, 1991.

responding to repeated visual stimuli, such as a thrown ball in a game of catch or a turning rope in a game of jump rope: Ten-year-olds react twice as quickly as 5-year-olds (Debrabant et al., 2012; Kail, 2003). These differences in speed of reaction have practical implications for physical education. Because 5- to 7-year-olds are seldom successful at batting a thrown ball, T-ball is more appropriate for them than baseball. Similarly, handball, four-square, and kickball should precede instruction in tennis, basketball, and football.

Fine-Motor Development

Fine-motor development also improves over the school years. On rainy afternoons, Joey and Lizzie experimented with yo-yos, built model airplanes, and wove potholders on small looms. Like many children, they took up musical instruments, which demand considerable fine-motor control. And gains in fine-motor skill are especially evident in children's writing and drawing.

By age 6, most children can print the alphabet, their first and last names, and the numbers from 1 to 10 with reasonable clarity. Their writing is large, however, because they make strokes using the entire arm rather than just the wrist and fingers. Children usually master uppercase letters first because their horizontal and vertical motions are easier to control than the small curves of the lowercase alphabet. Legibility of writing gradually increases as children produce more accurate letters with uniform height and spacing.

Children's drawings show dramatic gains in organization, detail, and representation of depth during middle childhood. By the end of the preschool years, children can accurately copy many two-dimensional shapes, and they integrate these into their drawings. Some depth cues have also begun to appear, such as making distant objects smaller than near ones (Braine et al., 1993). Yet recall from Chapter 8 that before age 8, children have trouble accurately copying a three-dimensional form, such as a cube or cylinder (see page 304). Around 9 to 10 years, the third dimension is clearly evident through overlapping objects, diagonal placement, and converging lines. Furthermore, as Figure 11.5 shows, school-age children not only depict objects in considerable detail but also relate them to one another as part of an organized whole (Case, 1998; Case & Okamoto, 1996).

INTERNATIONAL COLLECTION OF CHILD ART, MILNER LIBRARY, ILLINOIS STATE UNIVERSITY, NORMAL, IL

FIGURE 11.5 Increase in organization, detail, and depth cues in school-age children's drawings. TAKE A MOMENT... Compare both drawings to the one by a 6-year-old in Figure 8.8 on page 304. In the drawing by an 8-year-old on the top, notice how all parts are depicted in relation to one another and with greater detail. Integration of depth cues increases dramatically over the school years, as shown in the drawing on the bottom by an 11-year-old. Here, depth is indicated by overlapping objects, diagonal placement, and converging lines, as well as by making distant objects smaller than near ones.

Individual Differences in Motor Skills

As at younger ages, school-age children show marked individual differences in motor capacities that are influenced by both heredity and environment. Body build is one factor: Taller, more muscular children excel at many motor tasks. And children whose parents encourage physical exercise tend to enjoy it more and also to be more skilled.

Family income affects children's access to lessons needed to develop abilities in areas such as ballet, tennis, gymnastics, and instrumental music. For low-SES children, school and community provisions for nurturing athletics and other motor skills by making lessons, equipment, and opportunities for regular practice available and affordable are crucial. When these experiences combine with parental encouragement, many low-SES children become highly skilled.

Sex differences in motor skills that appeared during the preschool years extend into middle childhood and, in some instances, become more pronounced. Girls have an edge in fine-motor skills of handwriting and drawing and in gross-motor capacities that depend on balance and agility, such as hopping and skipping (Haywood & Getchell, 2014). But boys out-perform girls on all other skills listed in Table 11.2, especially throwing and kicking.

School-age boys' genetic advantage in muscle mass is not large enough to account for their gross-motor superiority. Rather, the social environment plays a larger role. Research confirms that parents hold higher expectations for boys' athletic performance, and children readily absorb these messages. From first through twelfth grades, girls are less positive than boys about the value of sports and their own sports ability—differences explained in part by parental beliefs (Fredricks & Eccles, 2002; Gentile et al., 2009). The more strongly girls believe that females are incompetent at sports (such as hockey or soccer), the lower they judge their own ability and the poorer they actually perform (Belcher et al., 2003; Chalabaev, Sarrazin, & Fontayne, 2009). But girls and older school-age children regard boys' advantage in sports as unjust. They indicate, for example, that coaches should spend equal time with children of each sex and that female sports should command just as much media attention as male sports (Solomon & Bredemeier, 1999).

Educating parents about the minimal differences between school-age boys' and girls' physical capacities and sensitizing them to unfair biases against promotion of girls' athletic ability may help increase girls' self-confidence and participation in athletics. Greater emphasis on skill training for girls, along with increased attention to their athletic achievements, is also likely to help. As a positive sign, compared with a generation ago, many more girls now participate in individual and team sports such as gymnastics and soccer, though their involvement continues to lag behind boys' (Kanters et al., 2013; Sabo & Veliz, 2011). Middle childhood is a crucial time to encourage girls' sports participation because during this period, children start to discover what they are good at and make some definite skill commitments.

Games with Rules

The physical activities of school-age children reflect an important advance in quality of play: Games with rules become common. Children around the world engage in an enormous variety of informally organized games, including variants on popular sports such as soccer, baseball, and basketball. In addition to the best-known childhood games, such as tag, jacks, and hopscotch, children have also invented hundreds of other games, including red rover, statues, leapfrog, kick the can, and prisoner's base.

Gains in perspective taking—in particular, the ability to understand the roles of several players in a game—permit this transition to rule-oriented games. These play experiences, in turn, contribute greatly to emotional and social development. Child-invented games usually rely on simple physical skills and a sizable element of luck. As a result, they rarely become contests of individual ability. Instead, they permit children to try out different styles of cooperating, competing, winning, and losing with little personal risk. Also, in their efforts to organize a game, children discover why rules are necessary and which ones work well. In fact, they often spend as much time working out the details of how a game should proceed as they do playing the game! As we will see in Chapter 13, these experiences help children form more mature concepts of fairness and justice.

Compared with past generations, children today spend less time gathering informally on sidewalks and in playgrounds. In part, this change reflects parental concern about neighborhood safety, as well as competition for children's time from TV, video games, and the Internet. Another factor is the rise in adult-organized sports, such as Little League baseball and soccer and hockey leagues, which fill many hours that children from economically advantaged families used to devote to spontaneous play.

Still, in village societies in developing countries and in many low-SES communities in industrialized nations, children's informal sports and games remain common. In an ethnographic study

A group of boys gather in their school yard for a pick-up game of basketball. Unlike their economically advantaged agemates, children in low-SES communities often play child-organized games, which serve as rich contexts for social learning.

© ELIZABETH CREWS/THE IMAGE WORKS

in two communities—one a refugee camp in Angola, Africa, the other a Chicago public housing complex—the overwhelming majority of 6- to 12-year-olds engaged in child-organized games at least once a week, and half or more did so nearly every day. Play in each context reflected distinct cultural values (Guest, 2013). In the Angolan community, games emphasized imitation of social roles—soccer moves of admired professional players, the intricate operation of a cooking spice shop. Games in Chicago, in contrast, were competitive and individualistic. In ballgames, for example, children often made sure peers noticed when they batted or fielded balls particularly well.

Adult-Organized Youth Sports

About half of U.S. children—60 percent of boys and 37 percent of girls—participate in organized sports outside of school hours at some time between ages 5 and 18 (National Council of Youth Sports, 2008; SFIA, 2013). Children in low-SES communities, however, are profoundly underserved, with girls and ethnic minorities having especially limited opportunities. In a comparison of two neighborhoods in Oakland, Calfornia, 67 percent of teenage girls in a well-to-do area were members of athletic teams (Team Up for Youth, 2014). But just a few miles away, in a poverty-stricken, largely minority part of the city, a mere 11 percent were involved in organized sports.

For most children, joining community athletic teams is associated with increased self-esteem and social skills (Daniels & Leaper, 2006; Fletcher, Nickerson, & Wright, 2003). Among shy children, sports participation seems to play a protective role, fostering self-confidence and a decline in social anxiety, perhaps because it provides a sense of group belonging and a basis for communicating with peers (Findlay & Coplan, 2008). And children who view themselves as good at sports are more likely to continue playing on teams in adolescence, which predicts greater participation in sports and other physical fitness activities in early adulthood (Kjønniksen, Anderssen, & Wold, 2009; Marsh et al., 2007).

With their coach's encouragement, these young softball players are likely to view themselves as good at sports and to continue playing. In contrast, coaches who criticize and overemphasize competition promote early athletic dropout.

In some cases, though, the arguments of critics—that youth sports overemphasize competition and substitute adult control for children's natural experimentation with rules and strategies—are valid. When coaches make winning paramount, weaker performers generally experience social ostracism, with boys—for whom competence at sports is linked to peer admiration—affected more than girls (Stryer, Tofler, & Lapchick, 1998). And children who join teams so early that the necessary skills are beyond their abilities soon lose interest.

Parents, even more than coaches, influence children's athletic attitudes and abilities. At the extreme are parents who value sports so highly that they punish their child for making mistakes, insist that the child keep playing after injury, hold the child back in school to ensure a physical advantage, or even seek medical interventions to improve the child's performance (Wall & Côté, 2007). High parental pressure sets the stage for emotional difficulties and early athletic dropout, not elite performance.

In most organized youth sports, health and safety rules help ensure that injuries are infrequent and mild. An exception is football, which has a high incidence of serious injury. Eight- to 12-year-old boys in tackle football leagues experience rates of concussion—brain injuries resulting from a blow to the head or body—that equal those of high school and college players (Kontos et al., 2013). And in any sport, frequent, intense practice can lead to painful "overuse" injuries that, in extreme cases, cause stress-related fractures resulting in impaired physical growth (Frank et al., 2007). On highly competitive teams with year-round training, overuse injuries are common.

When parents and coaches emphasize effort, improvement, participation, and teamwork, young athletes enjoy sports more, exert greater effort to improve their skills, and perceive themselves as more competent at their chosen sport (Ullrich-French & Smith, 2006). See Applying What We Know on page 424 for ways to ensure that athletic leagues provide children with positive learning experiences.

LOOK and **LISTEN**

Observe a youth athletic-league game, such as soccer, baseball, or hockey. Do coaches and parents encourage children's effort and skill gains, or are they overly focused on winning? Cite examples of adult and child behaviors.

Applying What We Know

Providing Developmentally Appropriate Organized Sports in Middle Childhood

STRATEGY	DESCRIPTION
Build on children's interests.	Permit children to select from among appropriate activities the ones that suit them best. Do not push children into sports they do not enjoy.
Teach age-appropriate skills.	For children younger than age 9, emphasize basic skills, such as kicking, throwing, and batting, and simplified games that grant all participants adequate playing time.
Emphasize enjoyment.	Permit children to progress at their own pace and to play for the fun of it, whether or not they become expert athletes.
Limit the frequency and length of practices.	Adjust practice time to children's attention spans and need for unstructured time with peers, with family, and for homework. Two practices a week, each no longer than 30 minutes for younger school-age children and 60 minutes for older school-age children, are sufficient.
Focus on personal and team improvement.	Emphasize effort, skill gains, and teamwork rather than winning. Avoid criticism for errors and defeat, which promotes anxiety and avoidance of athletics.
Discourage unhealthy competition.	Avoid all-star games and championship ceremonies that recognize individuals. Instead, acknowledge all participants.
Permit children to contribute to rules and strategies.	Involve children in decisions aimed at ensuring fair play and teamwork. To strengthen desirable responses, reinforce compliance rather than punishing noncompliance.

Shadows of Our Evolutionary Past

TAKE A MOMENT... While watching children in your neighborhood park, notice how they occasionally wrestle, roll, hit, and run after one another, alternating roles while smiling and laughing. This friendly chasing and play-fighting is called **rough-and-tumble play.** It emerges in the preschool years and peaks in middle childhood, and children in many cultures engage in it with peers whom they like especially well (Pellegrini, 2004). After a rough-and-tumble episode, children continue interacting rather than separating, as they do after an aggressive encounter.

Children's rough-and-tumble play resembles the social behavior of many other young mammals. It seems to originate in parents' physical play with babies, especially fathers' play with sons (see page 269 in Chapter 7). And it is more common among boys, probably because prenatal exposure to androgens predisposes boys toward active play (see Chapter 10, page 385). Boys' rough-and-tumble largely consists of playful wrestling and hitting, whereas girls tend to engage in running and chasing, with only brief physical contact.

In middle childhood, rough-and-tumble accounts for as much as 10 percent of free-play behavior, before declining in adolescence. In our evolutionary past, it may have been important for developing fighting skill. It also helps children form a **dominance hierarchy**—a stable ordering of group members that predicts who will win when conflict arises. Observations of arguments, threats, and physical attacks between children reveal a consistent lineup of winners and losers that becomes increasingly stable in middle childhood and adolescence, especially among boys. Once school-age children establish a dominance hierarchy, hostility is rare. Children seem to use play-fighting as a safe context to assess the strength of a peer before challenging that peer's dominance (Fry, 2014; Roseth et al., 2007). Rough-and-tumble play offers lessons in how to handle combative interactions with restraint.

As children reach puberty, individual differences in strength become apparent, and rough-and-tumble play declines. When it does occur, its meaning changes: Adolescent boys' rough-and-tumble is linked to aggression (Pellegrini, 2003). Unlike children, teenage rough-and-tumble players "cheat," hurting their opponent. In explanation, boys often say that they are retaliating, apparently to reestablish dominance. Thus, a play behavior that limits aggression in childhood becomes a context for hostility in adolescence.

© CLEVE BRYANT/PHOTOEDIT

In our evolutionary past, rough-and-tumble play—which can be distinguished from aggression by its friendly quality—may have been important for developing fighting skill and establishing dominance hierarchies.

Social Issues: Education

School Recess—A Time to Play, a Time to Learn

When 7-year-old Whitney's family moved to a new city, she left a school with three daily recess periods for one with just a single 15-minute break per day, which her second-grade teacher canceled if any child misbehaved. Whitney, who had previously enjoyed school, complained daily of headaches and an upset stomach. Her mother, Jill, thought, "My child is stressing out because she can't move all day!" After Jill and other parents successfully appealed to the school board to add a second recess period, Whitney's symptoms vanished (Rauber, 2006).

In recent years, recess—along with its rich opportunities for child-organized play and peer interaction—has diminished or disappeared in many U.S. schools (American Academy of Pediatrics, 2013). Under the assumption that extra time for academics will translate into achievement gains, 80 percent of school districts no longer require daily recess for elementary school students. Among districts that do, fewer than half mandate at least 20 minutes of recess per day (Centers for Disease Control and Prevention, 2014b).

Yet rather than subtracting from classroom learning, recess periods boost it! Research dating back more than 100 years confirms that distributing cognitively demanding tasks over a longer time by introducing regular breaks, rather than consolidating intensive effort within one period, enhances attention and performance at all ages. Such breaks are particularly important for young children.

In a series of studies, school-age children were more attentive in the classroom after recess than before it—an effect that was greater for second than fourth graders (Pellegrini, Huberty, & Jones, 1995). And relative to nonparticipating agemates, second and third graders randomly assigned to a program of 10-minute periods of physical activity distributed across the school day scored substantially higher in academic achievement at a three-year follow-up (Donnelly et al., 2009). Teacher ratings of classroom disruptive behavior also decline for children who have more than 15 minutes of recess a day (Barros, Silver, & Stein, 2009).

In another investigation, kindergartners' and first graders' engagement in peer conversation and games during recess positively predicted later academic achievement, even after other factors that might explain the relationship (such as previous achievement) were controlled (Pellegrini et al., 2002). Recall from Chapter 10 that children's social maturity contributes substantially to early academic competence. Recess is one of the few remaining contexts devoted to child-organized games that provide practice in vital social skills—cooperation, leadership, followership, and inhibition of aggression—under adult supervision rather than direction. As children transfer these skills to the classroom, they may join in discussions, collaborate, follow rules, and enjoy academic pursuits more—factors that enhance motivation and achievement.

Finally, children are even more physically active during recess than in gym class (U.S.

© BILL ARON/PHOTO EDIT

School-age children, especially girls, are even more physically active during recess than in gym class. By providing regular opportunities for unstructured play and games, recess promotes physical, academic, and social competence.

Department of Education, 2006). School-age girls, especially, engage in more moderate-to-vigorous exercise during recess than at other times of the day (Mota et al., 2005). In sum, regular, unstructured recess fosters children's health and competence—physically, academically, and socially.

Physical Education

Physical activity supports many aspects of children's development—their health, their sense of self-worth as physically active and capable beings, and the cognitive and social skills necessary for getting along with others. A large body of evidence links school-based physical activity to improved academic achievement (Centers for Disease Control and Prevention, 2010). Yet to devote more time to academic instruction, U.S. elementary schools have cut back on recess (see the Social Issues: Education box above).

Similarly, although most U.S. states require some physical education, only six require it in every grade, and only one mandates at least 30 minutes per school day in elementary school and 45 minutes in middle and high school. Nearly half of U.S elementary and secondary school students do not attend any physical education classes during a typical school week. Not surprisingly, physical inactivity among children and adolescents is

© RICK WILKING/REUTERS/CORBIS

These children participate in a friendly running race where finishing—not winning—is the goal. Many experts believe that physical education classes should emphasize informal games, individual exercise, and personal progress rather than competitive sports.

pervasive. Fewer than one-third of 6- to 17-year-olds engage in at least moderate-intensity activity for 60 minutes per day, including some vigorous activity (involving breathing hard and sweating) on three of those days—the U.S. government recommendations for good health (National Association for Sport and Physical Education, 2012). With the transition to adolescence, physical activity declines, more for girls than for boys.

Many experts believe that schools should not only offer more frequent physical education classes but also change the content of these programs. Training in competitive sports, often a high priority, is unlikely to reach the least physically fit youngsters, who avoid activities demanding a high level of skill. Instead, programs should emphasize enjoyable, informal games and individual exercise (walking, running, jumping, tumbling, and climbing)—pursuits most likely to endure. Furthermore, children of varying skill levels are more likely to sustain physical activity when teachers focus on each child's personal progress and contribution to team accomplishment (Connor, 2003). Then physical education fosters a healthy sense of self while satisfying school-age children's need to participate with others.

Physically fit children take great pleasure in their rapidly developing motor skills. As a result, they develop rewarding interests in physical activity and sports and are more likely to become active adolescents and adults who reap many benefits (Kjønniksen, Torsheim, & Wold, 2008). These include greater physical strength, resistance to many illnesses (from colds and flu to cancer, diabetes, and heart disease), enhanced psychological well-being, and a longer life.

Ask Yourself

- **REVIEW** Explain the adaptive value of rough-and-tumble play and dominance hierarchies.

- **CONNECT** On Saturdays, 10-year-old Billy gathers with friends on the driveway of his house to play basketball. Besides improved ball skills, what else is he learning?

- **APPLY** Nine-year-old Allison thinks she isn't good at sports, and she doesn't like physical education class. Suggest some strategies her teacher can use to improve her pleasure and involvement in physical activity.

- **REFLECT** Did you participate in adult-organized sports as a child? If so, what kind of climate for learning did coaches and parents create? What impact do you think your experiences had on your development?

Summary

Body Growth (p. 405)

11.1 Describe changes in body size, proportions, and skeletal maturity during middle childhood.

- School-age children's growth is slow and regular, though large individual and ethnic variations exist in physical growth. On average, they add about 2 to 3 inches in height and 5 pounds in weight each year. By age 9, girls overtake boys in physical size.

- **Secular trends in physical growth** have occurred in industrialized nations. Because of improved health and nutrition, many children are growing larger and reaching physical maturity earlier than their ancestors.

- Bones continue to lengthen and broaden, and permanent teeth replace primary teeth. Tooth decay affects over half of U.S. school-age children, with especially high levels among low-SES children. One-third of school-age children suffer from **malocclusion,** making braces common by the end of elementary school.

11.2 Describe brain development in middle childhood.

- Only a small gain in brain size occurs during middle childhood. White matter (myelinated nerve fibers) rises steadily. As interconnectivity among distant areas of the cerebral cortex increases, the prefrontal cortex becomes a more effective "executive." Gray matter (neurons and supportive material) peaks and then declines as a result of synaptic pruning. Accompanying reorganization and selection of brain circuits lead to more effective information processing, especially executive function.

Common Health Problems (p. 409)

11.3 Describe the causes and consequences of serious nutritional problems in middle childhood, giving special attention to obesity.

- Poverty-stricken children in developing countries and in the United States continue to suffer from serious and prolonged malnutrition, which can permanently impair physical and mental development.

ZACK WITTMAN FOR THE BOSTON GLOBE VIA GETTY IMAGES

- Overweight and **obesity** have increased dramatically in both industrialized and developing nations. Although heredity contributes to obesity, parental feeding practices, maladaptive eating habits, reduced sleep, lack of exercise, and Western high-fat diets are more powerful influences. Obese children are often socially rejected, are more likely to report feeling depressed, and display more behavior problems than their normal-weight peers.

- Family-based interventions aimed at changing parents' and children's eating patterns and lifestyles are the most effective approaches to treating childhood obesity. Rewarding obese children for reducing sedentary time is effective in getting them to enjoy and engage in more physical activity. Schools can help by ensuring regular physical activity and serving healthier meals.

11.4 What factors contribute to myopia, otitis media, nocturnal enuresis, and asthma, and how can these health problems be reduced?

- The most common vision problem, myopia, is influenced by heredity, early biological trauma, and time spent reading and doing other close work. It is one of the few health conditions that increases with family education and income. Although ear infections decline during the school years, many low-SES children experience some hearing loss because of chronic, untreated otitis media.

- Heredity is responsible for most cases of **nocturnal enuresis,** through a failure of muscular responses that inhibit urination or a hormonal imbalance that permits too much urine to accumulate. The most effective treatment is a urine alarm that works according to conditioning principles.

- Asthma is the most frequent cause of school absence and hospitalization in U.S. children. It occurs more often among African-American and poverty-stricken children, perhaps because of inner-city pollution, stressful home lives, and lack of access to good health care. Childhood obesity is also a factor.

- Children with severe chronic illnesses are at risk for academic, emotional, and social difficulties, but positive family interactions improve adjustment.

11.5 Describe changes in the occurrence of unintentional injuries during middle childhood, and cite effective interventions.

- Unintentional injuries increase over middle childhood and adolescence, especially for boys, with motor vehicle and bicycle accidents accounting for most of the rise. Parental supervision is key to preventing such injuries.

- Effective school- and community-based safety education programs use modeling and rehearsal of safety practices and reward children for good performance. Parents also must be educated about children's age-related safety capacities. One vital safety measure is insisting that children wear protective bicycle helmets, which dramatically reduces the risk of serious head injury.

Health Education (p. 418)

11.6 What can parents and teachers do to encourage good health practices in school-age children?

- Besides providing health-related information, adults must reduce health hazards in children's environments, coach children in good health practices, and model and reinforce these behaviors.

Motor Development and Play (p. 419)

11.7 Cite major changes in gross- and fine-motor development during middle childhood.

- Gross-motor improvements in flexibility, balance, agility, and force occur, and gains in responding only to relevant information and in reaction time also contribute to athletic performance.

- Fine-motor development also improves. Handwriting becomes more legible, and children's drawings show dramatic increases in organization, detail, and representation of depth.

11.8 Describe individual differences in motor performance during middle childhood.

- Wide individual differences in children's motor capacities are influenced by both heredity and environment, including such factors as body build, parental encouragement, and opportunities to take lessons.

- Gender stereotypes, which affect parental expectations for children's athletic performance, largely account for school-age boys' superiority on a wide range of gross-motor skills. Greater emphasis on skill training for girls and attention to their athletic achievements can help increase their involvement and performance.

11.9 What qualities of children's play are evident in middle childhood?

- Games with rules become common during the school years, contributing to emotional and social development. Expansion of adult-organized youth sports programs is associated with increased self-esteem and social competence in most players, but such programs are less available to low SES children. For some children, adult overemphasis on competition promotes undue anxiety and avoidance of sports. Encouraging effort, improvement, participation, and teamwork makes organized sports enjoyable and beneficial for self-esteem.

- Some features of children's physical activity reflect our evolutionary past. **Rough-and-tumble play** may once have been important for the development of fighting skill and may help children establish a **dominance hierarchy.** In middle childhood, dominance hierarchies become increasingly stable, especially among boys, and serve the adaptive function of limiting aggression among group members.

11.10 What steps can schools take to promote physical fitness in middle childhood?

- In addition to providing an opportunity for physical activity, school recess is a rich context for child-organized games and social interaction.

- Despite cutbacks in U.S. elementary schools, regular physical education classes help ensure that all children have access to the physical, cognitive, and social benefits of exercise and play, which translate into lifelong psychological and physical health benefits.

Important Terms and Concepts

dominance hierarchy (p. 424)
malocclusion (p. 407)

nocturnal enuresis (p. 415)
obesity (p. 410)

rough-and-tumble play (p. 424)
secular trends in physical growth (p. 406)

chapter 12

Cognitive Development in Middle Childhood

REPRINTED WITH PERMISSION FROM THE WORLD AWARENESS CHILDREN'S MUSEUM, GLENS FALLS, NEW YORK

"Game of Sanga"
Florence Faure
10 years, Gabon

Middle childhood brings dramatic gains in attention, memory, categorization, reasoning, and problem solving. These children use their advancing cognitive skills to play a popular game.

"Finally!" 6-year-old Lizzie exclaimed the day Rena enrolled her in elementary school. "Now I get to go to real school just like Joey!" Lizzie confidently walked into a combined kindergarten–first-grade class in her neighborhood school, pencils, crayons, and writing pad in hand, ready for a more disciplined approach to learning than she had experienced previously. As a preschooler, Lizzie had loved playing school, giving assignments as the "teacher" and pretending to read and write as the "student." Now she was eager to master the tasks that had sparked her imagination as a 4- and 5-year-old.

Lizzie had entered a whole new world of challenging activities. In a single morning, she and her classmates met in reading groups, wrote in journals, worked on addition and subtraction, and sorted leaves gathered for a science project. As Lizzie and Joey moved through the elementary school grades, they tackled increasingly complex projects and became more accomplished at reading, writing, math skills, and general knowledge of the world.

To understand the cognitive attainments of middle childhood, we turn to research inspired by Piaget's theory and the information-processing approach. And we look at expanding definitions of intelligence that help us appreciate individual differences in mental development. We also examine the genetic and environmental roots of IQ scores, which often influence important educational decisions. Our discussion continues with language, which blossoms further in these years. Finally, we consider the role of schools in children's development. ■

Piaget's Theory: The Concrete Operational Stage

When Lizzie was 4, Piaget's conservation problems confused her (see Chapter 9, page 316). For example, when water was poured from a tall, narrow container into a short, wide one, she insisted that the amount of water had changed. Three years later, when one of our child development students interviewed her, she found this task easy. "Of course it's the same!" she exclaimed. "The water's shorter, but it's also wider. Pour it back," she instructed. "You'll see, it's the same amount!"

Attainments of the Concrete Operational Stage

Lizzie has entered Piaget's **concrete operational stage,** which extends from about 7 to 11 years. Compared with early childhood, thought is more logical, flexible, and organized.

CONSERVATION The ability to pass *conservation tasks* provides clear evidence of *operations*—mental actions that obey logical rules. Notice how Lizzie is capable of **decentration,** focusing on several aspects of a problem and relating them, rather than centering on just one. She also demonstrates **reversibility,** the capacity to think through a series of steps and then mentally reverse direction, returning to the starting point. Recall from Chapter 9 that reversibility is part of every logical operation. It is solidly achieved in middle childhood.

12.1 What are the major characteristics of concrete operational thought?

12.2 Discuss follow-up research on concrete operational thought.

An improved ability to categorize underlies children's interest in collecting objects during middle childhood. Here, a 9-year-old sorts and organizes her extensive shell collection.

CLASSIFICATION Between ages 7 and 10, children pass Piaget's *class inclusion problem* (see page 316). This indicates that they are more aware of classification hierarchies and can focus on relations between a general category and two specific categories at the same time—on three relations at once. Children of this age are better able to inhibit their habitual strategy of perceptually comparing the two specific categories (blue flowers and yellow flowers) in favor of relating each specific category to its less-obvious general category (flowers) (Borst et al., 2013; Ni, 1998). School-age children's enhanced classification skills are evident in their enthusiasm for collecting treasured objects. At age 10, Joey spent hours sorting and resorting his baseball cards, grouping them first by league and team, then by playing position and batting average. He could separate the players into a variety of classes and subclasses and easily rearrange them.

SERIATION The ability to order items along a quantitative dimension, such as length or weight, is called **seriation.** To test for it, Piaget asked children to arrange sticks of different lengths from shortest to longest. Older preschoolers can put the sticks in a row to create the series, but they do so haphazardly, making many errors. In contrast, 6- to 7-year-olds create the series efficiently, moving in an orderly sequence from the smallest stick, to the next largest, and so on.

The concrete operational child can also seriate mentally, an ability called **transitive inference.** In a well-known transitive inference problem, Piaget showed children pairings of sticks of different colors. From observing that stick *A* is longer than stick *B* and that stick *B* is longer than stick *C,* children must infer that *A* is longer than *C.* Like Piaget's class inclusion task, transitive inference requires children to integrate three relations at once—in this instance, *A–B, B–C,* and *A–C.* As long as they receive help in remembering the premises (*A–B* and *B–C*), 7- to 8-year-olds can grasp transitive inference (Wright, 2006). And when the task is made relevant to children's everyday experiences—for example, based on winners of races between pairs of cartoon characters—6-year-olds perform well (Wright, Robertson, & Hadfield, 2011).

SPATIAL REASONING Piaget found that school-age children's understanding of space is more accurate than that of preschoolers. To illustrate, let's consider children's **cognitive maps**—their mental representations of spaces, such as a classroom, school, or neighborhood. Drawing or reading a map of a large-scale space (school or neighborhood) requires considerable perspective-taking skill. Because the entire space cannot be seen at once, children must infer its overall layout by relating its separate parts.

Preschoolers and young school-age children include *landmarks* on maps they draw of a single room, but their arrangement is not always accurate. They do better when asked to place stickers showing the location of furniture and people on a map of the room. But if the map is rotated to a position other than the room's orientation, they have difficulty (Liben & Downs, 1993). In identifying landmarks on a rotated map, 7-year-olds are aided by the opportunity to walk through the room (Lehnung et al., 2003). Actively exploring it permits them to experience landmarks from different vantage points, which fosters a more flexible mental representation.

With respect to large-scale outdoor environments, not until age 9 can many children accurately place stickers on a map to indicate the location of landmarks. Children who spontaneously use strategies that help them align the map with their current location in the space—rotating the map or tracing their route on it—show better performance (Liben et al., 2013). Around this age, the maps children draw of large-scale spaces become better organized, showing landmarks along an *organized route of travel.* At the same time, children are able to give clear, well-organized instructions for getting from one place to another by using a "mental walk" strategy—imagining another person's movements along a route (Gauvain & Rogoff, 1989b).

At the end of middle childhood, most children can form an accurate *overall view of a large-scale space.* And they readily draw and read maps, even when the orientation of the map and the space it represents do not match (Liben, 2009). Ten- to 12-year-olds also grasp the notion of *scale*—the proportional relation between a space and its map representation (Liben, 2006). And they appreciate that in interpreting map symbols, a mapmaker's assigned meaning supersedes physical resemblance—for example, that green dots (not red dots) may indicate where red fire trucks are located (Myers & Liben, 2008).

Map-related experiences greatly improve children's map skills. When teachers asked fourth graders to write down the clues they used to decide where stickers (signifying landmark locations) should go on a map of an outdoor space, the accuracy of children's performance improved (Kastens & Liben, 2007). Such self-generated explanations seem to induce learners to reflect on and revise their own thinking, sparking gains in many types of problem solving among students from elementary school through college. And a computer-based curriculum called *Where Are We,* consisting of 12 map-reading and map-making lessons, led to substantial improvements in second to fourth graders' performance on diverse mapping tasks (Liben, Kastens, & Stevenson, 2001).

Cultural frameworks influence children's map making. In many non-Western communities, people rarely use maps for way finding but rely on information from neighbors, street vendors, and shopkeepers. Also, compared to their Western agemates, non-Western children less often ride in cars and more often walk, which results in intimate neighborhood knowledge. When a researcher had 12-year-olds in small cities in India and in the United States draw maps of their neighborhoods, the Indian children represented a rich array of landmarks and aspects of social life, such as people and vehicles, in a small area surrounding their home. The U.S children, in contrast, drew a more formal, extended space, highlighting main streets and key directions (north–south, east–west) but including few landmarks (see Figure 12.1) (Parameswaran, 2003). Although the U.S. children's maps scored higher in cognitive maturity, this difference reflected cultural interpretations of the task: When asked to create a map to "help people find their way," the Indian children drew spaces as far-reaching and organized as the U.S. children's.

Third graders locate landmarks on a trail map of a nearby park. Map-related classroom experiences support their advancing mental representations of large-scale spaces.

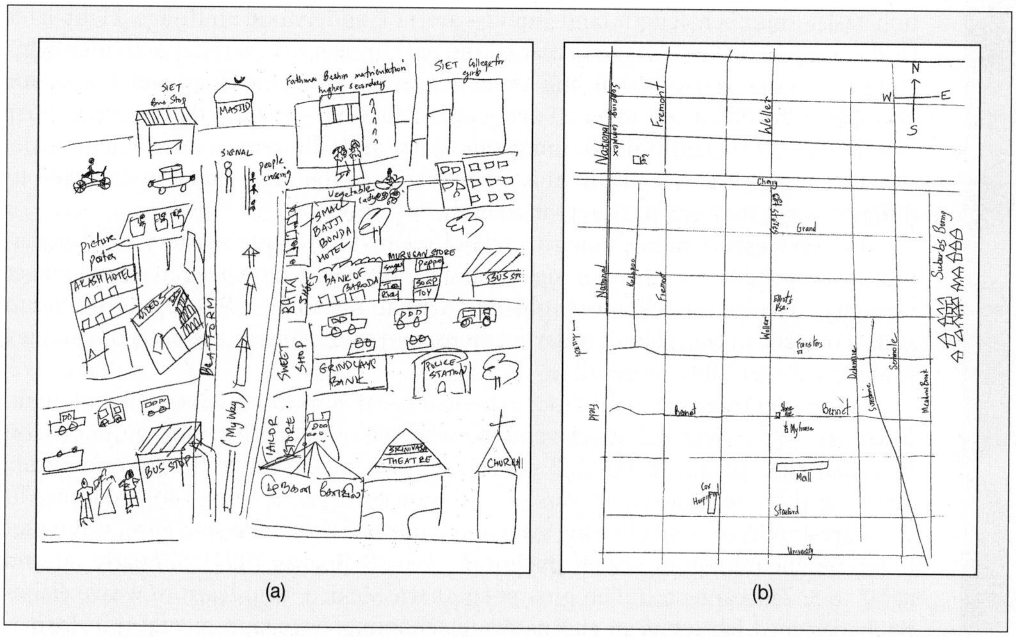

FIGURE 12.1 **Maps drawn by older school-age children from India and the United States.** (a) The Indian child depicted many landmarks and features of social life in a small area near her home. (b) The U.S. child drew a more extended space and highlighted main streets and key directions. (From G. Parameswaran, 2003, "Experimenter Instructions as a Mediator in the Effects of Culture on Mapping One's Neighborhood," *Journal of Environmental Psychology, 23,* pp. 415–416. Copyright © 2003, reprinted with permission from Elsevier, Ltd., conveyed through Copyright Clearance Center, Inc.)

LOOK and LISTEN

Ask a 6- to 8-year-old and a 9- to 12-year-old to draw a neighborhood map showing important landmarks, such as the school, a friend's house, or a shopping area. In what ways do the children's maps differ?

Limitations of Concrete Operational Thought

As the name of this stage suggests, concrete operational thinking suffers from one important limitation: Children think in an organized, logical fashion only when dealing with concrete information they can perceive directly. Their mental operations work poorly with abstract ideas—ones not apparent in the real world. Consider children's solutions to transitive inference problems. When shown pairs of sticks of unequal length, Lizzie easily engaged in transitive inference. But she had great difficulty with a hypothetical version of this task: "Susan is taller than Sally, and Sally is taller than Mary. Who is the tallest?" Not until age 11 or 12 can children typically solve this problem.

That logical thought is at first tied to immediate situations helps account for a special feature of concrete operational reasoning. Children master concrete operational tasks step by step, not all at once. For example, they usually grasp conservation of number first, followed by length, liquid, and mass, and then weight. This *continuum of acquisition* (or gradual mastery) of logical concepts is another indication of the limitations of concrete operational thinking (Fischer & Bidell, 1991). Rather than coming up with general logical principles that they apply to all relevant situations, children seem to work out the logic of each problem separately.

Follow-Up Research on Concrete Operational Thought

According to Piaget, brain development combined with experience in a rich and varied external world should lead children everywhere to reach the concrete operational stage. Yet recent evidence indicates that cultural and school practices have much to do with mastery of Piagetian tasks (Rogoff, 2003). And information-processing research helps explain the gradual mastery of logical concepts in middle childhood.

This Brazilian street vendor might not perform well on Piagetian class inclusion tasks, but he is likely to understand versions relevant to street vending—for example, that "all the chewing gum" represents a larger quantity than the amount of any one flavor.

THE IMPACT OF CULTURE AND SCHOOLING   In village societies, conservation is often delayed. For example, among the Hausa of Nigeria, who live in small agricultural settlements and rarely send their children to school, even basic conservation tasks—number, length, and liquid—are not understood until age 11 or later (Fahrmeier, 1978). This suggests that taking part in relevant everyday activities helps children master conservation and other Piagetian problems. Joey and Lizzie, for example, think of fairness in terms of equal distribution—a value emphasized in their culture. They frequently divide materials, such as Halloween treats or lemonade, equally among their friends. Because they often see the same quantity arranged in different ways, they grasp conservation early.

The very experience of going to school seems to promote mastery of Piagetian tasks. When children of the same age are tested, those who have been in school longer do better on transitive inference problems (Artman & Cahan, 1993). Opportunities to seriate objects, to learn about order relations, and to remember the parts of complex problems are probably responsible.

Yet certain informal, nonschool experiences can also foster operational thought. Brazilian 6- to 9-year-old street vendors, who seldom attend school, do poorly on Piagetian class inclusion tasks. But they perform much better than economically advantaged schoolchildren on versions relevant to street vending—for example, "If you have 4 units of mint chewing gum and 2 units of grape chewing gum, is it better to sell me the mint gum or [all] the gum?" (Ceci & Roazzi, 1994). Similarly, around age 7 to 8, Zinacanteco Indian girls of southern Mexico, who learn to weave elaborately designed fabrics as an alternative to schooling, engage in mental transformations to figure out how a warp strung on a loom will turn out as woven cloth—reasoning expected at the concrete operational stage (Maynard & Greenfield, 2003). North American children of the same age, who do much better than Zinacanteco children on Piagetian tasks, have great difficulty with these weaving problems.

On the basis of such findings, some investigators have concluded that the forms of logic required by Piagetian tasks do not emerge spontaneously in children but, rather, are heavily influenced by training, context, and cultural conditions. Does this view remind you of Vygotsky's sociocultural theory, which we discussed in earlier chapters?

AN INFORMATION-PROCESSING VIEW OF CONCRETE OPERATIONAL THOUGHT

As we saw in Chapter 9, preschoolers show the beginnings of logical thinking on simplified and familiar tasks. The gradual mastery of logical concepts in middle childhood raises a familiar question about Piaget's theory: Is an abrupt stagewise transition to logical thought the best way to describe cognitive development in middle childhood?

Some *neo-Piagetian theorists* argue that the development of operational thinking can best be understood in terms of expansion of information-processing capacity rather than a sudden shift to a new stage. For example, Robbie Case (1996, 1998) proposed that change within each Piagetian stage, and movement from one stage to the next, are largely due to gains in the efficiency with which children use their limited working memories. According to Case, with practice, cognitive schemes demand less attention and are applied more rapidly, becoming automatic. This frees up space in working memory (see Chapter 6, page 216) so children can focus on combining old schemes and generating new ones. For instance, a child who sees water poured from one container to another recognizes that the height of the liquid changes. As this understanding becomes routine, the child notices that the width of the water changes as well. Soon children coordinate these observations, and they grasp conservation of liquid. Then, as this logical idea becomes well-practiced, the child transfer it to more demanding situations, such as weight.

Once the schemes of a Piagetian stage are sufficiently automatic, enough working memory is available to integrate them into an improved representation. As a result, children acquire *central conceptual structures*—networks of concepts and relations that permit them to think more effectively in a wide range of situations. The central conceptual structures that emerge from integrating concrete operational schemes are broadly applicable principles that result in increasingly complex, systematic reasoning of Piaget's formal operational stage.

As this child pours milk from one container to another, he recognizes the change first in height and then, as this observation becomes automatic, in width. Eventually he coordinates these observations and grasps conservation of liquid.

Case and his colleagues—along with other information processing researchers—have examined children's performance on a wide variety of Piagetian and other tasks. In each, preschoolers typically focus on only one or two dimensions. In understanding stories, for example, they grasp only a single story line. In drawing pictures, they depict objects separately. By the early school years, children coordinate two or three dimensions—two story lines in a single plot, and drawings that show both the features of objects and their relationships. Around 9 to 11 years, children integrate multiple dimensions (Case, 1998; Halford & Andrews, 2006). They tell coherent stories with a main plot and several subplots. And their drawings follow a set of rules for representing perspective and, therefore, include several points of reference, such as near, midway, and far.

Case's theory, along with other similar neo-Piagetian perspectives, helps explain why many understandings appear in specific situations at different times rather than being mastered all at once (Barrouillet & Gaillard, 2011a). First, different forms of the same logical insight, such as the various conservation tasks, vary in their processing demands, with those acquired later requiring more space in working memory. Second, children's experiences vary widely. A child who often listens to and tells stories but rarely draws pictures displays more advanced central conceptual structures in storytelling than in drawing. Compared with Piaget's theory, neoPiagetian approaches better account for unevenness in cognitive development (Andrews & Halford, 2011). When tasks make similar processing demands, such as Piaget's class inclusion and transitive inference problems (each of which requires children to consider three relations at once), children with relevant experiences master those tasks at about the same time.

Evaluation of the Concrete Operational Stage

Piaget was correct that school-age children approach many problems in more organized, rational ways than preschoolers. But disagreement continues over whether this difference occurs because of *continuous* improvement in logical skills or *discontinuous* restructuring of children's thinking (as Piaget's stage idea assumes). Many researchers think that both types of change may be involved (Andrews & Halford, 2011; Barrouillet & Gaillard, 2011b; Case, 1998; Fischer & Bidell, 2006).

During the school years, children apply logical schemes to many more tasks. In the process, their thought seems to change qualitatively—toward a more comprehensive grasp of the underlying principles of logical thought. Piaget himself seems to have recognized this possibility in evidence for gradual mastery of conservation and other tasks. So perhaps some blend of Piagetian and information-processing ideas holds the greatest promise for explaining cognitive development in middle childhood.

Ask Yourself

- **REVIEW** Children's performance on conservation tasks illustrates a continuum of acquisition of logical concepts. Review the preceding sections, and list additional examples of gradual development of operational reasoning.

- **CONNECT** Explain how advances in perspective taking contribute to school-age children's improved ability to draw and use maps.

- **APPLY** Nine-year-old Adrienne spends many hours helping her father build furniture in his woodworking shop. How might this experience facilitate Adrienne's advanced performance on Piagetian seriation problems?

- **REFLECT** Which aspects of Piaget's description of the concrete operational child do you accept? Which do you doubt? Explain, citing research evidence.

12.3 Cite basic changes in information processing, and describe the development of attention and memory in middle childhood.

12.4 Describe the school-age child's theory of mind and capacity to engage in self-regulation.

12.5 Discuss current perspectives on teaching reading and mathematics to elementary school children.

Information Processing

In contrast to Piaget's focus on overall cognitive change, the information-processing perspective examines separate aspects of thinking. As noted in our discussion of Case's theory, capacity of working memory continues to increase in middle childhood, as does speed of thinking. And school-age children make strides in other facets of executive function, including attention, planning, strategic memory, and self-regulation. Each contributes vitally to academic learning.

Executive Function

During the school years, a time of continued development of the prefrontal cortex, executive function undergoes marked improvement, and its various aspects become more strongly interrelated (Xu et al., 2013). Children handle increasingly difficult tasks that require the integration of working memory, inhibition, and flexible thinking, which, in turn, support gains in planning, strategic thinking, and self-monitoring and self-correction of behavior.

Heritability evidence suggests substantial genetic influence on various aspects of executive function, including combining information in working memory, controlling attention, and inhibiting inappropriate responses (Hansell et al., 2001; Polderman et al., 2009; Young et al., 2009) And molecular genetic analyses are identifying specific genes related to severely deficient function of executive components, such as attention and inhibition, which (as we will soon see) contribute to learning and behavior disorders, such as attention-deficit hyperactivity disorder (ADHD).

But in both typically and atypically developing children, heredity combines with environmental factors to influence executive function. In Chapter 3, we reviewed evidence indicating that prenatal teratogens can impair impulse control, attention, planning, and other executive processes. And poverty and stressful living conditions can undermine executive function, with powerfully negative consequences for academic achievement and social competence (Blair & Raver, 2012). As we turn now to the development of an array of executive processes, our discussion will confirm once more that supportive home and school experiences are essential for their optimal development.

Middle childhood is a period of marked gains in executive function. In this science project on how flood plains are formed, fifth graders must plan, flexibly implement strategies, and monitor their progress, redirecting unsuccessful efforts.

Working-Memory Capacity

Gains in working-memory capacity, like other aspects of executive function, are supported by brain development (Cowan et al., 2011). And as Case's theory emphasizes, working memory benefits from increased efficiency of thinking. Time needed to process information on a wide variety of cognitive tasks declines rapidly between ages 6 and 12 in diverse cultures, likely due to myelination and synaptic pruning in the cerebral cortex (Kail & Ferrer, 2007; Kail et al., 2013). A faster thinker can hold on to and operate on more information at once. Still, individual differences in working-memory capacity exist, and they are of particular concern because they predict intelligence test scores and academic achievement in many subjects (DeMarie & Lopez, 2014).

Many studies confirm that children with persistent learning difficulties in reading and math are often deficient in working memory (Alloway, 2009; Alloway et al., 2009). Observations of elementary school children with limited working memories revealed that they often failed at school assignments that made heavy memory demands (Gathercole, Lamont, & Alloway, 2006). They could not follow complex instructions, lost their place in tasks with multiple steps, and frequently gave up before finishing their work. The children struggled because they could not hold in mind sufficient information to complete assignments.

Compared to their economically advantaged agemates, children from poverty-stricken families are more likely to score low on working-memory tasks. In one study, years of childhood spent in poverty predicted reduced working memory in early adulthood (Evans & Schamberg, 2009). Childhood neurobiological measures of stress (elevated blood pressure and stress hormone levels, including cortisol) largely explained this poverty–working-memory association. Chronic stress, as we saw in Chapter 5, can impair brain structure and function, especially in the prefrontal cortex and its connections with the hippocampus, which govern working-memory capacity.

About 15 percent of children have very low working-memory scores, the majority of whom struggle in school (Holmes, Gathercole, & Dunning, 2010). Interventions are needed to reduce memory loads so these children can learn. Effective approaches include communicating in short sentences with familiar vocabulary, repeating task instructions, breaking complex tasks into manageable parts, and encouraging children to use external memory aids (such as lists of useful spellings when writing or number lines when doing math).

In addition, direct training with working-memory tasks is effective. In one study, researchers embedded such training in interactive computer games. Ten-year-olds with learning difficulties were randomly assigned to low-frequency training (once a week), high-frequency training (four times a week), or a no-training control (Alloway, Bibile, & Lau, 2013). Compared with the other groups, students experiencing high-frequency training improved substantially in working-memory capacity, IQ, and spelling achievement—gains still evident 8 months after training had ended.

Attention

During middle childhood, gains in sustained attention continue. In addition, attention becomes more selective, flexible, and planful.

SELECTIVITY AND FLEXIBILITY   As Joey and Lizzie moved through elementary school, they became better at deliberately attending to relevant aspects of a task and inhibiting irrelevant responses. One way researchers study this increasing selectivity of attention is by introducing irrelevant stimuli into a task and seeing how well children attend to its central elements. For example, they might present a stream of numbers on a computer screen and ask children to press a button whenever a particular two-digit sequence (such as "1" followed by "9") appears. Findings show that selective attention improves sharply between ages 6 and 10, with gains continuing through adolescence (Gomez-Perez & Ostrosky-Solis, 2006; Tabibi & Pfeffer, 2007; Vakil et al., 2009).

Older children also flexibly adapt their attention to situational requirements. For example, when asked to sort cards with pictures that vary in both color and shape, children age 5 and older readily switch their basis of sorting from color to shape when asked to do so; younger children have difficulty (Brooks et al., 2003; Zelazo, Carlson, & Kesek, 2008). Notice how this task requires working memory to retain relevant sorting rules (color and shape), inhibition of the irrelevant rule, and cognitive flexibility in responding to a rule switch by updating working memory and inhibition accordingly.

Over middle childhood, selectivity and flexibility of attention become better controlled and more efficient (Carlson, Zelazo, & Faja, 2013). Children can focus and adapt their attention in the face of increasingly complex distractors—skills that contribute to more organized, strategic, and planful approaches to challenging tasks with age.

PLANNING   Planning on multistep tasks improves over the school years. When 5- to 9-year-olds were given lists of items to obtain from a play grocery store, older children more often took time to scan the store before shopping, figuring out the best sequence in which to gather the items. They also paused more often to look for each item before moving to get it (Gauvain & Rogoff, 1989a; Szepkouski, Gauvain, & Carberry, 1994). Consequently, they followed shorter routes through the aisles.

Effective planning often goes beyond implementing a sequence of moves: In many instances, children must evaluate the entire sequence *in advance* to see if it will get them to their goal. To assess both sequential and advance planning, 4- to 10-year-olds were presented with the paddle-box illustrated in Figure 12.2. On each trial, they had to get a small item from the paddle on which an adult placed it to the open goal at the bottom of the box. The paddles

FIGURE 12.2 **Examples of sequential- and advance-planning solutions using the paddle box.** An adult placed a small item on one of the horizontal paddles within the box, visible to the child through its transparent cover. Children had to get the item to the open goal at the bottom of the box. The paddles could be rotated to three positions—flat, diagonal, or left—using handles extending out the front of the box. (a) In sequential planning, rotating the start paddle first, without presetting other paddles, leads to success. (b) In advance planning, children must preset at least one other paddle before rotating the start paddle. (From E. C. Tecwyn, S. K. S. Thorpe, & J. Chappell, 2014, "Development of Planning in 4- to 10-Year-Old Children: Reducing Inhibitory Demands Does Not Improve Performance," *Journal of Experimental Child Psychology, 125,* p. 92. Copyright © 2014 with permission from Elsevier, Ltd., conveyed through Copyright Clearance Center, Inc.)

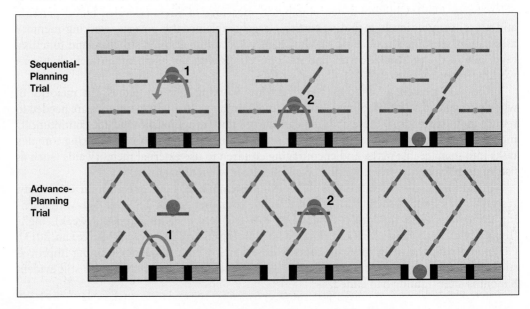

could be rotated to three positions: flat, diagonal left, or diagonal right. On sequential trials, children could rotate the start paddle first and still succeed. On advance-planning trials, to prevent the object from being trapped, children needed to preset one or two other paddles before rotating the start paddle (Tecwyn, Thorpe, & Chappell, 2014). Many of the youngest children succeeded at sequential planning, but advance planning was difficult: Not until age 9 to 10 did children consistently perform well.

The development of planning illustrates how attention becomes coordinated with other cognitive processes. Children must postpone action in favor of weighing alternatives, organizing an efficient sequence of steps, and remembering the steps so they can attend to each one. Along the way, they must monitor how well the plan works and revise it if necessary.

As Chapter 9 revealed, children learn much about planning by collaborating with more expert planners. With age, they take more responsibility in these joint endeavors, such as suggesting planning strategies and organizing task materials. The demands of school tasks—and teachers' explanations of how to plan—also contribute to gains in planning.

But adult-controlled activities may rob children of opportunities to plan. In one study, researchers videotaped small groups of first and second graders devising plays that they would perform for their class (Baker-Sennett, Matusov, & Rogoff, 2008). Some groups were child-led; others were led by adult volunteers. Child-led groups engaged in extensive planning—brainstorming themes and working out the details of their improvisations. But when adults planned the play in advance, the children spent most of their time in nonplanning pursuits, such as rehearsing lines and making play props. The adults missed a rich opportunity to scaffold learning (see page 324 in Chapter 9) by turning over responsibility for play planning to the children and guiding and supporting, as needed.

The attentional and planning strategies just considered are crucial for success in school. Unfortunately, some children have great difficulty paying attention. See the Biology and Environment box on pages 438–439 for a discussion of the serious learning and behavior problems of children with attention-deficit hyperactivity disorder.

Memory Strategies

As attention improves, so do *memory strategies,* the deliberate mental activities we use to store and retain information. When Lizzie had a list of things to learn, such as the capitals of the United States or the names of geometric shapes, she immediately used **rehearsal**—repeating the information to herself. Language proficiency predicts the emergence of rehearsal in the early grade school years, perhaps because a certain vocabulary size and ability to automatically name items is necessary for children to use the strategy (Bebko et al., 2014). Soon after, a second strategy becomes common: **organization**—grouping related items together (for example, all state capitals in the same part of the country), an approach that greatly improves recall (Schneider, 2002).

Perfecting memory strategies requires time and effort. For example, 8-year-old Lizzie rehearsed in a piecemeal fashion. After being given the word *cat* in a list of words, she said, "Cat, cat, cat." But 10-year-old Joey combined previous words with each new item, saying, "Desk, man, yard, cat, cat." This active, cumulative approach, in which neighboring words create contexts for each other that trigger recall, yields much better memory (Lehman & Hasselhorn, 2007, 2012). Furthermore, whereas Lizzy often organized by everyday association (hat–head, carrot–rabbit), Joey grouped items *taxonomically,* based on common properties (clothing, food, animals) and, thus, into fewer categories—an efficient procedure yielding dramatic memory gains (Bjorklund et al., 1994). And Joey used organization in a wide range of memory tasks, whereas Lizzie used it only when categorical relations among items were obvious.

As children gain in familiarity with strategies and in working-memory capacity, they combine several strategies—for example, organizing items, stating the category names, and finally rehearsing. The more strategies children apply simultaneously, the better they remember (DeMarie et al., 2004; Schwenck, Bjorklund, & Schneider, 2007). Younger children often try out various memory strategies but use them less systematically and successfully than older children. Still, their tendency to experiment allows them to discover which strategies work best and how to combine them effectively. Recall from *overlapping-waves theory,* discussed in Chapter 9,

Biology and Environment

Children with Attention-Deficit Hyperactivity Disorder

While the other fifth graders worked quietly at their desks, Calvin squirmed, dropped his pencil, looked out the window, fiddled with his shoelaces, and talked aloud. "Hey Joey," he yelled across the room, "wanna play ball after school?" But the other children weren't eager to play with Calvin, who was physically awkward and failed to follow the rules of the game. He had trouble taking turns at bat. In the outfield, he tossed his mitt up in the air and looked elsewhere when the ball came his way. Calvin's desk was a chaotic mess. He often lost pencils, books, and other school materials, and he had difficulty remembering assignments and due dates.

Symptoms of ADHD

Calvin is one of 3 to 7 percent of U.S. school-age children with **attention-deficit hyperactivity disorder (ADHD),** which involves inattention, impulsivity, and excessive motor activity resulting in academic and social problems (American Psychiatric Association, 2013; Goldstein, 2011). Boys are diagnosed three to nine times as often as girls. However, many girls with ADHD seem to be overlooked, either because their symptoms are less flagrant or because of a gender bias:

A difficult, disruptive boy is more likely to be referred for treatment (Faraone, Biederman, & Mick, 2006).

Children with ADHD cannot stay focused on a task that requires mental effort for more than a few minutes. They often act impulsively, ignoring social rules and lashing out with hostility when frustrated. Many, though not all, are *hyperactive,* exhausting parents and teachers and irritating other children with their excessive motor activity. For a child to be diagnosed with ADHD, these symptoms must have appeared before age 12 as a persistent problem.

Because of their difficulty concentrating, ADHD children score lower in IQ than other children, though the difference is mostly accounted for by a small subgroup with substantially below-average scores (Biederman et al., 2012). Researchers agree that deficient executive function underlies ADHD symptoms. According to one view, children with ADHD are impaired in capacity to inhibit action in favor of thought— a basic difficulty that results in wide-ranging inadequacies in executive processing and, therefore, in impulsive, disorganized behavior (Barkley, 2003a). Another hypothesis is that ADHD is the direct result of a cluster of executive-processing

problems that interfere with ability to guide one's own actions (Brown, 2006). Research confirms that children with ADHD do poorly on tasks requiring sustained attention; find it hard to ignore irrelevant information; have difficulty with memory, planning, reasoning, and problem solving in academic and social situations; and often fail to manage frustration and intense emotion (Barkley, 2003b, 2006).

Origins of ADHD

ADHD runs in families and is highly heritable. Identical twins share it more often than fraternal twins (Freitag et al., 2010; Rasmussen et al., 2004). Children with ADHD show abnormal brain functioning, including reduced electrical and blood-flow activity and structural abnormalities in the prefrontal cortex and in other areas involved in attention, inhibition of behavior, and other aspects of motor control (Mackie et al., 2007). Also, the brains of children with ADHD grow more slowly and are about 3 percent smaller in overall volume, with a thinner cerebral cortex, than the brains of unaffected agemates (Narr et al., 2009; Shaw et al., 2007). Several genes that disrupt functioning of the neurotransmitters serotonin (involved in

---

that children experiment with strategies when faced with many cognitive challenges—an approach that enables them to gradually "home in" on the most effective techniques.

By the end of middle childhood, children start to use **elaboration**—creating a relationship, or shared meaning, between two or more pieces of information that are not members of the same category. For example, to learn the words *fish* and *pipe,* you might generate the verbal statement or mental image, "The fish is smoking a pipe." This highly effective memory technique, which requires considerable effort and space in working memory, becomes increasingly common in adolescence and early adulthood (Schneider & Pressley, 1997).

Because organization and elaboration combine items into *meaningful chunks,* they permit children to hold onto much more information and, as a result, further expand working memory. In addition, when children link a new item to information they already know, they can *retrieve* it easily by thinking of other items associated with it. As we will see, this also contributes to improved memory during the school years.

Knowledge and Memory Performance

During middle childhood, the long-term knowledge base grows larger and becomes organized into increasingly elaborate, hierarchically structured networks. This rapid growth of knowledge helps children use strategies and remember (Schneider, 2002). In other words, knowing more about a topic makes new information more meaningful and familiar, so it is easier to store and retrieve.

inhibition and self-control) and dopamine (required for effective cognitive processing) have been implicated in the disorder (Akutagava-Martins et al., 2013).

At the same time, ADHD is associated with environmental factors. Prenatal teratogens—such as tobacco, alcohol, illegal drugs, and environmental pollutants—are linked to inattention and hyperactivity (see Chapter 3). And they can combine with certain genotypes to greatly increase risk of the disorder (see page 87 in Chapter 2). Furthermore, children with ADHD are more likely to have parents with psychological disorders and to come from homes where family stress is high (Law et al., 2014). These circumstances often intensify the child's preexisting difficulties.

Treating ADHD

Calvin's doctor eventually prescribed stimulant medication, the most common treatment for ADHD. As long as dosage is carefully regulated, these drugs reduce impulsivity and hyperactivity and improve attention for about 70 percent of children who take them (Greenhill, Halperin, & Abikoff, 1999). Stimulant medication seems to increase activity in the prefrontal cortex, thereby improving the child's capacity to sustain attention and to inhibit off-task and self-stimulating behavior. However, if stimulant treatment is

initiated late, after age 9 or 10, it does not reduce the decline in academic performance associated with ADHD (Zoëga et al., 2012).

By itself, drug treatment is insufficient for helping children compensate for inattention and impulsivity in everyday situations. So far, the most effective treatments combine medication with interventions that model and reinforce appropriate academic and social behaviors (Smith, Barkley, & Shapiro, 2006). New approaches that provide children with adult-guided activities designed to augment executive-function skills yield improved performance on attention, working memory, cognitive flexibility, and planning tasks (Miranda et al., 2013; Tamm, Nakonezny, & Hughes, 2014). But more research is needed on the extent to which these gains generalize to the classroom.

Family intervention is also vital. Inattentive, hyperactive children strain the patience of parents, who are likely to react punitively and inconsistently—a child-rearing style that strengthens defiant, aggressive behavior. In fact, in 50 to 75 percent of cases, these two sets of

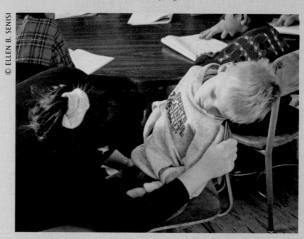

This child frequently engages in disruptive behavior at school. Children with ADHD have great difficulty staying on task and often act impulsively, ignoring social rules.

behavior problems occur together (Goldstein, 2011).

ADHD is usually a lifelong disorder. Affected individuals are at risk for persistent antisocial behavior, depression, alcohol and drug abuse, and other problems (Kessler et al., 2005, 2006). Adults with ADHD continue to need help in structuring their environments, regulating negative emotion, selecting appropriate careers, and understanding their condition as a biological deficit rather than a character flaw.

To investigate this idea, school-age children who were expert chess players were tested on how well they could remember complex chessboard arrangements. Then their performance was compared with that of adults who knew how to play chess but were not especially knowledgeable. The children's expert knowledge enabled them to reproduce the chessboard configurations considerably better than the adults could (Bédard & Chi, 1992).

In another study, researchers classified fourth graders as either experts or novices in knowledge of soccer and then gave both groups lists of soccer and nonsoccer items to learn. Experts remembered far more items on the soccer list (but not on the nonsoccer list) than novices. And during recall, the experts' listing of items was better organized, as indicated by clustering of items into categories (Schneider & Bjorklund, 1992). This superior organization at retrieval suggests that highly knowledgeable children organize information in their area of expertise with little or no effort—by rapidly associating new items with the large number they already know (Bjorklund & Douglas, 1997). Consequently, experts can devote more working-memory resources to using recalled information to reason and solve problems.

But knowledge is not the only important factor in children's strategic memory processing. Children who are expert in an area are usually highly motivated. As a result, they not only acquire knowledge more quickly but also *actively use what they know* to add more. In contrast, academically unsuccessful children often fail to ask how previously stored information can clarify new material. This, in turn, interferes with the development of a broad knowledge base (Schneider & Bjorklund, 1998). So extensive knowledge and use of memory strategies support one another.

Children in a shanty town on the outskirts of Lima use laptops provided by the Peruvian government. Societal modernization—access to contemporary resources for communication and literacy—is broadly associated with improved cognitive performance.

Culture, Schooling, and Memory Strategies

Rehearsal, organization, and elaboration are techniques that children and adults usually use when they need to remember information for its own sake. On many other occasions, memory occurs as a natural byproduct of participation in daily activities. For example, Joey can spout a wealth of facts about baseball teams and players—information he picked up from watching ball games, discussing the game, and trading baseball cards with his friends. And without prior rehearsal, he can recount the story line of an exciting movie or novel—narrative material that is already meaningfully organized.

A repeated finding is that people in village cultures who have little formal schooling do not use or benefit from instruction in memory strategies because they see no practical reason to use these techniques (Rogoff, 2003). Tasks requiring children to engage in isolated recall, which are common in classrooms, strongly motivate memory strategies. In fact, children in developed nations get so much practice with this type of learning that they do not refine techniques that rely on cues available in everyday life, such as spatial location and arrangement of objects. For example, Guatemalan Mayan 9-year-olds do slightly better than their U.S. agemates when told to remember the placement of 40 familiar objects in a play scene (Rogoff & Waddell, 1982). U.S. children often rehearse object names when it would be more effective to keep track of spatial relations.

Societal *modernization,* as indicated by the presence of communication, literacy, and other economically advantageous resources in homes—such as books, writing tablets, electricity, radio, TV, and car ownership—is broadly associated with performance on cognitive tasks commonly administered to children in industrialized nations. In an investigation in which researchers rated towns in Belize, Kenya, Nepal, and American Samoa for degree of modernization, Belize and American Samoa exceeded Kenya and Nepal (Gauvain & Munroe, 2009). Modernity predicted both extent of schooling and 5- to 9-year-olds' cognitive scores—on a memory test plus an array of other measures.

In sum, the development of memory strategies and other cognitive skills valued in complex societies is not just a product of a more competent information-processing system. It also depends on task demands, schooling, and cultural circumstances.

The School-Age Child's Theory of Mind

During middle childhood, children's *theory of mind,* or set of beliefs about mental activities, becomes much more elaborate and refined. Recall from Chapter 9 that this awareness of thought is often called *metacognition.* Children's improved ability to reflect on their own mental life is another reason that their thinking and problem solving advance.

KNOWLEDGE OF COGNITIVE CAPACITIES Unlike preschoolers, who view the mind as a passive container of information, older children regard it as an active, constructive agent that selects and transforms information (Astington & Hughes, 2013). Consequently, they have a much better understanding of cognitive processes and the impact of psychological factors on performance. For example, with age, elementary school children become increasingly aware of effective memory strategies and why they work (Alexander et al., 2003). And they gradually grasp relationships between mental activities—for example, that remembering is crucial for understanding and that understanding strengthens memory (Schwanenflugel, Henderson, & Fabricius, 1998).

Furthermore, school-age children's understanding of sources of knowledge expands. They are aware that people can extend their knowledge not only by directly observing events and talking to others but also by making *mental inferences* (Miller, Hardin, & Montgomery,

2003). This grasp of inference enables knowledge of false belief to expand. In several studies, researchers told children complex stories involving one character's belief about a second character's belief. Then the children answered questions about what the first character thought the second character would do (see Figure 12.3). By age 6 to 7, children were aware that people form beliefs about other people's beliefs and that these *second-order beliefs* can be wrong!

Appreciation of *second-order false belief* enables children to pinpoint the reasons that another person arrived at a certain belief (Astington, Pelletier, & Homer, 2002; Miller, 2009; Naito & Seki, 2009). Notice how it requires the ability to view a situation from at least two perspectives—that is, to reason simultaneously about what two or more people are thinking, a form of perspective taking called **recursive thought.** We think recursively when we make such statements as, "*Lisa believes* that *Jason believes* the letter is under his pillow, but that's *not what Jason really believes; he knows* the letter is in the desk."

The capacity for recursive thought greatly assists children in appreciating that people can harbor quite different interpretations of the same situation. For example, 6- to 7-year-olds realize that when two people view the same object, their trains of thought will differ because of variations in their knowledge, experiences, or other characteristics (Eisbach, 2004). Children of this age also understand that two people can make sense of the same event—such as an ambiguous fragment taken from a larger drawing they have never seen—quite differently, no matter what beliefs or biases they bring to the situation (Lalonde & Chandler, 2002). They recognize that the same reality can legitimately be construed in multiple ways. Indeed, school-age children's newfound awareness of varying viewpoints is so powerful that, at first, they overextend it (Lagattuta, Sayfan, & Blattman, 2010). Six- and 7-year-olds are especially likely to overlook the fact that people with differing past experiences sometimes agree!

ERP and fMRI evidence reveals that from age 6 to 11, children become increasingly selective in the brain regions they recruit when thinking about another's mental states (Bowman et al., 2012; Gweon et al., 2012). In addition to the prefrontal cortex, they activate an area connecting the right temporal and parietal lobes (known to play a crucial role in theory-of-mind processes), just as adults do.

As with other cognitive attainments, schooling contributes to a more reflective, process-oriented view of the mind. In a study of rural children of Cameroon, Africa, those who attended school performed much better on theory-of-mind tasks (Vinden, 2002). In school, teachers often call attention to the workings of the mind when they remind children to pay attention, remember mental steps, share points of view with peers, and evaluate their own and others' reasoning. As recursive perspective taking becomes more secure, children more often use persuasive strategies to try to change others' viewpoints (Bartsch, London, & Campbell,

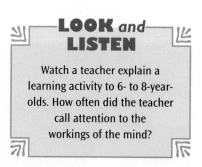

LOOK and LISTEN

Watch a teacher explain a learning activity to 6- to 8-year-olds. How often did the teacher call attention to the workings of the mind?

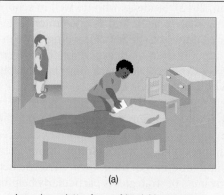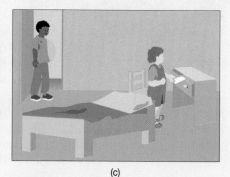

(a)	(b)	(c)
Jason has a letter from a friend. Lisa wants to read the letter, but Jason doesn't want her to. Jason puts the letter under his pillow.	Jason leaves the room to help his mother.	While Jason is gone, Lisa takes the letter and reads it. Jason returns and watches Lisa, but Lisa doesn't see Jason. Then Lisa puts the letter in Jason's desk.

FIGURE 12.3   A second-order false belief task. After relating the story in the sequence of pictures, the researcher asks a second-order false-belief question: "Where does Lisa think Jason will look for the letter? Why?" Around age 7, children answer correctly—that Lisa thinks Jason will look under his pillow because Lisa doesn't know that Jason saw her put the letter in the desk. (Adapted from Astington, Pelletier, & Homer, 2002.)

2007). They also grasp complex, recursive verbal expressions, such as irony and sarcasm, as we will see later when we address language development.

KNOWLEDGE OF STRATEGIES Consistent with their more active view of the mind, school-age children are far more conscious of mental strategies than preschoolers. When shown video clips depicting two children using different recall strategies and asked which one is likely to produce better memory, kindergarten and young elementary school children knew that rehearsing or organizing is better than looking or naming (Justice, 1986; Schneider, 1986). Older children were aware of more subtle differences—that organizing is better than rehearsing.

Between third and fifth grade, children develop a much better appreciation of how and why strategies work (Alexander et al., 2003). Consequently, fifth graders are considerably better than younger children at discriminating good from bad reasoning. When given examples varying in quality, fifth graders consistently rated "good" reasoning as based on weighing of possibilities (rather than jumping to conclusions) and gathering of evidence (rather than ignoring important facts), even if such reasoning led to an unfavorable result (Amsterlaw, 2006).

Cognitive Self-Regulation

Although metacognition expands, school-age children frequently have difficulty putting what they know about thinking into action. They are not yet good at **cognitive self-regulation,** the process of continuously monitoring progress toward a goal, checking outcomes, and redirecting unsuccessful efforts. For example, Lizzie is aware that she should attend closely to her teacher's directions, group items when memorizing, reread a complicated paragraph to make sure she understands it, and relate new information to what she already knows. But she does not always engage in these activities.

This fifth grader's capacity for cognitive self-regulation is evident in the convenient way she organizes materials, making sure her textbook glossary and dictionary are handy. When she encounters an unfamiliar word, she can quickly look up its definition.

To study cognitive self-regulation, researchers sometimes look at the impact of children's awareness of memory strategies on how well they remember. By second grade, the more children know about memory strategies, the more they recall—a relationship that strengthens over middle childhood (DeMarie et al., 2004). And when children apply a strategy consistently, their knowledge of strategies strengthens, resulting in a bidirectional relationship between metacognition and strategic processing that enhances self-regulation (Schlagmüller & Schneider, 2002).

Why does cognitive self-regulation develop gradually? Monitoring learning outcomes is cognitively demanding, requiring constant evaluation of effort and progress. Throughout elementary and secondary school, self-regulation predicts academic success (Zimmerman & Labuhn, 2012). Students who do well in school know when their learning is going well and when it is not. If they encounter obstacles, they take steps to address them—for example, organize the learning environment, review confusing material, or seek support from more expert adults or peers (Schunk & Zimmerman, 2013). This active, purposeful approach contrasts sharply with the passive orientation of students who achieve poorly.

Parents and teachers can foster self-regulation. In one study, researchers observed parents instructing their children on a problem-solving task during the summer before third grade. Parents who patiently pointed out important features of the task and suggested strategies had children who, in the classroom, more often discussed ways to approach problems and monitored their own performance (Stright et al., 2002). Explaining the effectiveness of strategies is particularly helpful because it provides a rationale for future action.

Children who acquire effective self-regulatory skills develop a sense of *academic self-efficacy*—confidence in their own ability, which supports future self-regulation (Schunk & Pajares, 2005). Unfortunately, some children receive messages from parents and teachers that seriously undermine their academic self-esteem and self-regulatory skills. We will consider these *learned-helpless* students, along with ways to help them, in Chapter 13.

Applications of Information Processing to Academic Learning

When Joey completed kindergarten, he recognized some familiar written words, used what he knew about letter–sound relations to decode simple words, predicted what might happen next in a beginning-reader story, and could retell its main events in sequence. In second grade, he read grade-level books independently, used story context to help identify unfamiliar words, and read aloud with expression. By fourth grade, he was a proficient reader who understood different types of texts, including biographies, fiction, and poetry.

In math, as a new first grader Joey counted to 100 by ones and tens, perform one-digit addition and subtraction with ease, and could decompose the numbers from 11 to 19 to determine, "How many more than 10" as the foundation for understanding place value. In third grade, he used his grasp of place value to perform two-digit arithmetic, multiplied and divided within 100, and had begun to master fractions and percentages.

Fundamental discoveries about the development of information processing have been applied to children's learning of reading and mathematics. Researchers are identifying the cognitive ingredients of skilled performance, tracing their development, and distinguishing good from poor learners by pinpointing differences in cognitive skills. They hope, as a result, to design teaching methods that will improve children's learning.

READING   Reading makes use of many skills at once, taxing all aspects of our information-processing systems. We must perceive single letters and letter combinations, translate them into speech sounds, recognize the visual appearance of many common words, hold chunks of text in working memory while interpreting their meaning, and combine the meanings of various parts of a text passage into an understandable whole. And because reading is so demanding, most or all of these skills must be done automatically. If one or more are poorly developed, they will compete for resources in our limited working memories, and reading performance will decline.

© ELLEN B. SENISI

In this second-grade classroom, teaching of phonics is embedded in captivating stories. Combining instruction in basic skills with whole-language teaching is more effective in promoting children's reading progress than either approach alone.

As children make the transition from emergent literacy to conventional reading, *phonological awareness*—the ability to reflect on and manipulate the sound structure of spoken language—continues to facilitate their progress (see page 336 in Chapter 9). Other information-processing skills also contribute. Gains in processing speed foster children's rapid conversion of visual symbols into sounds (Moll et al., 2014). Visual scanning and discrimination play important roles and improve with reading experience (Rayner, Pollatsek, & Starr, 2003). Performing all these skills efficiently releases working memory for higher-level activities involved in comprehending the text's meaning.

Until recently, researchers were involved in an intense debate over how to teach beginning reading. Those who took a **whole-language approach** argued that from the beginning, children should be exposed to text in its complete form—stories, poems, letters, posters, and lists—so that they can appreciate the communicative function of written language. According to this view, as long as reading is kept meaningful, children will be motivated to discover the specific skills they need (Goodman, 2005). Other experts advocated a **phonics approach,** believing that children should first be coached on *phonics*—the basic rules for translating written symbols into sounds. Only after mastering these skills should they get complex reading material (Adams, 2002).

Many studies show that children learn best with a mixture of both approaches. In kindergarten, first, and second grades, teaching that includes phonics boosts reading scores, especially for children who lag behind in reading progress (Block, 2012; Brady, 2011). And when teachers combine real reading and writing with teaching of phonics and engage in other excellent teaching practices—encouraging children to tackle reading challenges and integrating reading into all school subjects—first graders show far greater literacy progress (Pressley et al., 2002).

TABLE 12.1	Sequence of Reading Development
GRADE/AGE	**DEVELOPMENT**
Preschool 2–5 years	"Pretends" to read; recognizes some familiar signs ("ON," "OFF," "PIZZA"); "pretends" to write; prints own name and other words
Kindergarten 5–6 years	Knows the most frequent letter–sound correspondences; recognizes some familiar written words; decodes simple, one-syllable words; retells story main events in sequence
Grades 1 and 2 6–7 years	Knows letter–sound correspondences for common double consonants; decodes regularly spelled one-syllable words; recognizes some irregularly spelled words; reads grade-level texts with increasing accuracy on repeated readings
Grades 2 and 3 7–8 years	Reads grade-level stories more fluently; knows letter–sound correspondences for common vowel combinations; decodes multisyllable words and an increasing number of irregularly spelled words; reads grade-level stories more fluently and expressively, while also comprehending
Grades 4 to 9 9–15 years	Reads to acquire new knowledge, usually without questioning the reading material; understands different types of texts, including biographies, fiction, and poetry
Grades 10 to 12 15–18 years	Reads more widely, tapping materials with diverse viewpoints

Source: Chall, 1983; Common Core, 2010.

Why might combining phonics with whole language work best? Learning the relationships between letters and sounds enables children to *decode,* or decipher, words they have never seen before. Children who enter school low in phonological awareness make far better reading progress when given training in phonics (Casalis & Cole, 2009). Soon they detect new letter–sound relations while reading on their own, and as their fluency in decoding words increases, they are freer to attend to text meaning. Without early phonics training, such children (many of whom come from poverty-stricken families) are substantially behind their age-mates in text comprehension skills by third grade (Foster & Miller, 2007).

Yet too much emphasis on basic skills may cause children to lose sight of the goal of reading: understanding. Children who read aloud fluently without registering meaning know little about effective reading strategies—for example, that they must read more carefully if they will be tested than if they are reading for pleasure, that relating ideas in the text to personal experiences and general knowledge will deepen understanding, and that explaining a passage in one's own words is a good way to assess comprehension. Teaching aimed at increasing awareness and use of reading strategies enhances reading performance from third grade on (Paris & Paris, 2006).

Table 12.1 charts the general sequence of reading development. Notice the major shift, around age 7 to 8, from "learning to read" to "reading to learn" (Melzi & Schick, 2013). As decoding and comprehension skills reach a high level of efficiency, older readers become actively engaged with the text. They adjust the way they read to fit their current purpose—sometimes seeking new facts and ideas, sometimes questioning, agreeing with, or disagreeing with the writer's viewpoint.

MATHEMATICS Mathematics teaching in elementary school builds on and greatly enriches children's informal knowledge of number concepts and counting. Written notation systems and formal computational techniques enhance children's ability to represent numbers and compute. Over the early elementary school years, children acquire basic math facts through a combination of frequent practice, experimentation with diverse computational procedures (through which they discover faster, more accurate techniques), reasoning about number concepts, and teaching that conveys effective strategies. (Return to Chapter 9, page 339, for research supporting the importance of both extended practice and a grasp of concepts.) Eventually children retrieve answers automatically and apply this basic knowledge to more complex problems.

Arguments about how to teach mathematics resemble those about reading, pitting drill in computing against "number sense," or understanding. Again, a blend of both approaches is most beneficial (Fuson, 2009). In learning basic math, poorly performing students use cumbersome, error-prone techniques or try to retrieve answers from memory too soon. They have not sufficiently experimented with strategies to see which are most effective and to reorganize their observations in logical, efficient ways—for example, noticing that multiplication problems involving 2 (2 × 8) are equivalent to addition doubles (8 + 8). On tasks assessing their grasp of math concepts, their performance is weak (Clements & Sarama, 2012). This suggests that encouraging students to apply strategies and making sure they know why certain strategies work well are essential for solid mastery of basic math.

A similar picture emerges for more complex skills, such as carrying in addition, borrowing in subtraction, and operating with decimals and fractions. Children taught by rote cannot apply the procedure to new problems. Instead, they persistently make mistakes, following a "math rule" that they recall incorrectly because they do not understand it (Carpenter et al., 1999). Look at the following subtraction errors:

$$
\begin{array}{r}
427 \\
-138 \\
\hline
311
\end{array}
\qquad
\begin{array}{r}
7002 \\
-5445 \\
\hline
1447
\end{array}
$$

In the first problem, the child consistently subtracts a smaller from a larger digit, regardless of which is on top. In the second, the child skips columns with zeros in a borrowing operation and, whenever there is a zero on top, writes the bottom digit as the answer.

Children who are given rich opportunities to experiment with problem solving, to appreciate the reasons behind strategies, and to evaluate solution techniques seldom make such errors. In one study, second graders who were taught in these ways not only mastered correct procedures but even invented their own successful strategies, some of which were superior to standard, school-taught methods! Consider this solution:

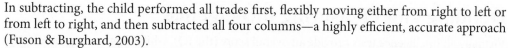

In subtracting, the child performed all trades first, flexibly moving either from right to left or from left to right, and then subtracted all four columns—a highly efficient, accurate approach (Fuson & Burghard, 2003).

In a German study, the more teachers emphasized conceptual knowledge, by having children actively construct meanings in word problems before practicing computation and memorizing math facts, the more children gained in math achievement from second to third grade (Staub & Stern, 2002). Children taught in this way draw on their solid knowledge of relationships between operations (for example, that the inverse of division is multiplication) to generate efficient, flexible procedures: To solve the division problem 360/9, they might multiply 9 × 40 = 360. And because such children have been encouraged to estimate answers, if they go down the wrong track in computation, they are usually self-correcting. Furthermore, they appreciate connections between math operations and problem contexts. They can solve a word problem ("Jesse spent $3.45 for bananas, $2.62 for bread, and $3.55 for peanut butter. Can he pay for it all with a $10 bill?") quickly through estimation instead of exact calculation (De Corte & Verschaffel, 2006).

In Asian countries, students receive a variety of supports for acquiring mathematical knowledge and often excel at math computation and reasoning. Use of the metric system helps Asian children grasp place value. The consistent structure of number words in Asian languages (*ten-two* for 12, *ten-three* for 13) also makes this idea clear (Miura & Okamoto, 2003). And because Asian number words are shorter and more quickly pronounced, more digits can be held in working memory at once, increasing speed of thinking. Furthermore, Chinese parents provide their children with extensive everyday practice in counting and

© LAURA DWIGHT PHOTOGRAPHY

This fourth grader uses paper cut in different sizes to clarify the concept of fractions. The most effective math teaching combines frequent practice with instruction emphasizing conceptual understanding.

computation—experiences that contribute to the superiority of Chinese over U.S. children's math knowledge, even before school entry (Siegler & Mu, 2008; Zhou et al., 2006). Finally, as we will see later in this chapter, compared with lessons in the United States, those in Asian classrooms devote more time to exploring math concepts and less to drill and repetition.

Ask Yourself

- **REVIEW** Cite evidence indicating that school-age children view the mind as an active, constructive agent.

- **APPLY** After viewing a slide show on endangered species, second and fifth graders in Lizzie and Joey's school were asked to remember as many animals as they could. Explain why fifth graders recalled much more than second graders.

- **APPLY** Lizzie knows that if you have difficulty learning part of a task, you should devote extra attention to that part. But she plays each of her piano pieces from beginning to end instead of practicing the hard parts. Explain why Lizzie does not engage in cognitive self-regulation.

- **REFLECT** In your elementary school math education, how much emphasis was placed on computational drill and how much on understanding concepts? How do you think that balance affected your interest and performance in math?

12.6 Describe major approaches to defining intelligence.

12.7 Describe evidence indicating that both heredity and environment contribute to intelligence.

Individual Differences in Mental Development

Around age 6, IQ becomes more stable than it was at earlier ages, and it correlates moderately well with academic achievement, typically around .50 to .60. And children with higher IQs are more likely when they grow up to attain higher levels of education and enter more prestigious occupations (Brody, 1997; Deary et al., 2007). Because IQ predicts school performance and educational attainment, it often enters into educational decisions. Do intelligence tests accurately assess the school-age child's ability to profit from academic instruction? Let's look closely at this controversial issue.

Defining and Measuring Intelligence

Virtually all intelligence tests provide an overall score (the IQ), which represents *general intelligence* or reasoning ability, along with an array of separate scores measuring specific mental abilities. But intelligence is a collection of many capacities, not all of which are included on currently available tests (Carroll, 2005; Sternberg, 2008). Test designers use a complicated statistical technique called *factor analysis* to identify the various abilities that intelligence tests measure. It identifies which sets of test items cluster together, meaning that test-takers who do well on one item in the cluster tend to do well on the others. Distinct clusters are called *factors*, each of which represents an ability. See Figure 12.4 for items typically included in intelligence tests for children.

The intelligence tests given from time to time in classrooms are *group-administered tests*. They permit large numbers of students to be tested at once and are useful for instructional planning and for identifying children who require more extensive evaluation with *individually administered tests*. Unlike group tests, which teachers can give with minimal training, individually administered tests demand considerable training and experience to give well. The examiner not only considers the child's answers but also observes the child's behavior, noting such reactions as attention to and interest in the tasks and wariness of the adult. These observations provide insight into whether the test score accurately reflects the child's abilities. Two individual tests—the Stanford-Binet and the Wechsler—are often used to identify highly intelligent children and to diagnose children with learning problems.

The contemporary descendent of Alfred Binet's first successful intelligence test is the *Stanford-Binet Intelligence Scales*, Fifth Edition, for individuals from age 2 to adulthood. In addition to general intelligence, it assesses five intellectual factors: general knowledge, quantitative reasoning, visual–spatial processing, working memory, and basic information processing (such as speed of analyzing information). Each factor includes both a verbal mode and a nonverbal mode of testing, yielding 10 subtests in all (Roid, 2003; Roid & Pomplun, 2012). The nonverbal subtests, which do not require spoken language, are especially useful when assessing individuals with limited English, hearing impairments, or communication disorders. The knowledge and quantitative reasoning factors emphasize culturally loaded, fact-oriented information, such as vocabulary and arithmetic problems. In contrast, the visual–spatial processing, working-memory, and basic information-processing factors are assumed to be less culturally biased because they require little specific information (see the spatial visualization item in Figure 12.4).

The *Wechsler Intelligence Scale for Children–IV (WISC–IV)* is the fourth edition of a widely used test for 6- through 16-year-olds. A downward extension of it, the *Wechsler Preschool and Primary Scale of Intelligence–Revised (WPPSI–III),* is appropriate for children 2 years 6 months through 7 years 3 months (Wechsler, 2002, 2003). The Wechsler tests offered both a measure of general intelligence and a variety of factor scores long before the Stanford-Binet. As a result, many psychologists and educators came to prefer them. The WISC–IV has four broad intellectual factors: verbal reasoning, perceptual (or visual–spatial) reasoning, working memory, and processing speed. Each factor is made up of two or three subtests, yielding 10 separate scores in all. The WISC-IV was designed to downplay culture-dependent information, which is emphasized on only one factor (verbal reasoning). According to the test designers, the result is the most "culture-fair" intelligence test available (Williams, Weiss, & Rolfhus, 2003). The WISC was also the first test to be standardized on children representing the total population of the United States, including ethnic minorities.

Recent Efforts to Define Intelligence

As we have seen, intelligence tests now tap important aspects of information processing. In line with this trend, some researchers have combined the mental-testing approach to defining intelligence with the information-processing approach. They believe that once we identify the processing skills that separate individuals who test well from those who test poorly, we will know more about how to intervene to improve performance. These investigators conduct *componential analyses* of children's test scores. This means that they look for relationships between aspects (or components) of information processing and children's intelligence test scores.

Processing speed, measured in terms of reaction time on diverse cognitive tasks, is moderately related to IQ (Coyle, 2013; Li et al., 2004). Individuals whose nervous systems function more efficiently, permitting them to take in more information and manipulate it quickly, appear to have an edge in intellectual skills. In support of this interpretation, fast, strong ERPs (EEG brain waves in response to stimulation) predict both speedy cognitive processing and higher mental test scores (Rijsdijk & Boomsma, 1997; Schmid, Tirsch, & Scherb, 2002). And measures of working-memory capacity, to which processing speed contributes, correlate well with IQ (Giofré, Mammarella, & Cornoldi, 2013; Swanson, 2011).

But other factors, including flexible attention, memory, and reasoning strategies, are as important as efficient thinking in predicting IQ, and they explain some of the association between response speed and good test performance (Lohman, 2000). Children who apply

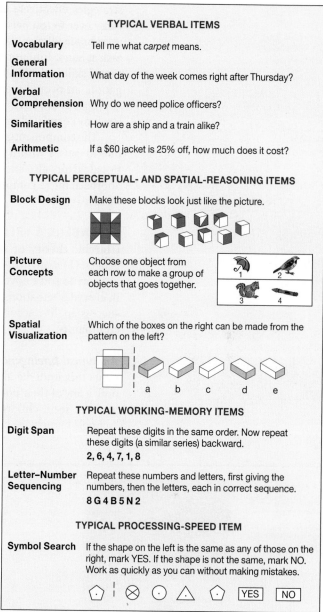

FIGURE 12.4 Test items like those on commonly used intelligence tests for children. The verbal items emphasize culturally loaded, fact-oriented information. The perceptual- and spatial-reasoning, working-memory, and processing-speed items emphasize aspects of information processing and are assumed to assess more biologically based skills.

strategies effectively acquire more knowledge and can retrieve it rapidly—advantages that carry over to test performance. Similarly, recall from page 436 that available space in working memory facilitates effective inhibition—keeping irrelevant information from intruding on the task at hand. Inhibition and sustained and selective attention are among a wide array of attentional skills related to IQ (Schweizer, Moosbrugger, & Goldhammer, 2006). In one investigation, an overall measure of executive function predicted intelligence in 7- to 9-year-olds (Brydges et al., 2012). Recall from page 434 that aspects of executive function become more strongly correlated in middle childhood: They unify into a single factor.

The componential approach has one major shortcoming: It regards intelligence as entirely due to causes within the child. Throughout this book, we have seen how cultural and situational factors also affect children's thinking. Robert Sternberg has expanded the componential approach into a comprehensive theory that regards intelligence as a product of inner and outer forces.

STERNBERG'S TRIARCHIC THEORY   As Figure 12.5 shows, Sternberg's (2005, 2008, 2013) **triarchic theory of successful intelligence** is made up of three broad, interacting intelligences: (1) *analytical intelligence,* or information-processing skills; (2) *creative intelligence,* the capacity to solve novel problems; and (3) *practical intelligence,* application of intellectual skills in everyday situations. Intelligent behavior involves balancing all three intelligences to achieve success in life according to one's personal goals and the requirements of one's cultural community.

Analytical Intelligence.   *Analytical intelligence* consists of the information-processing components that underlie all intelligent acts. But on intelligence tests, processing skills are used in only a few of their potential ways, resulting in far too narrow a view of intelligent behavior. As we have seen, children in village societies do not necessarily perform well on measures of "school" knowledge but thrive when processing information in out-of-school situations.

Creative Intelligence.   In any context, success depends not only on processing familiar information but also on generating useful solutions to new problems. People who are *creative* think more skillfully than others when faced with novelty. Given a new task, they apply their information-processing skills in exceptionally effective ways, rapidly making these skills automatic so that working memory is freed for more complex aspects of the situation. Consequently, they quickly move to high-level performance. Although all of us are capable of some creativity, only a few individuals excel at generating novel solutions.

Practical Intelligence.   Finally, intelligence is a *practical,* goal-oriented activity aimed at *adapting to, shaping,* or *selecting environments.* Intelligent people skillfully *adapt* their thinking to fit with both their desires and the demands of their everyday worlds. When they cannot adapt to a situation, they try to *shape,* or change, it to meet their needs. If they cannot shape it, they *select* new contexts that better match their skills, values, or goals. Practical intelligence reminds us that intelligent behavior is never culture-free. Children with certain life histories do well at the behaviors required for success on intelligence tests and adapt easily to the testing conditions and tasks. Others, with different backgrounds, may misinterpret or reject the testing context. Yet such children often display sophisticated abilities in daily life—for example, telling stories, engaging in complex artistic activities, or interacting skillfully with other people.

The triarchic theory emphasizes the complexity of intelligent behavior and the limitations of current intelligence tests in assessing

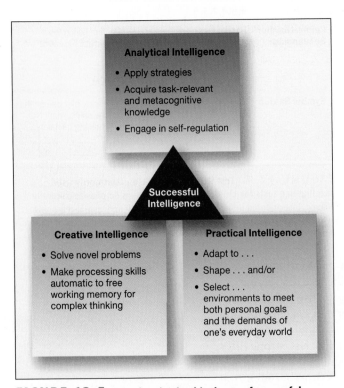

FIGURE 12.5   Sternberg's triarchic theory of successful intelligence. People who behave intelligently balance three interrelated intelligences—analytical, creative, and practical—to achieve success in life, defined by their personal goals and the requirements of their cultural communities.

that complexity. For example, out-of-school, practical forms of intelligence are vital for life success and help explain why cultures vary widely in the behaviors they regard as intelligent (Sternberg, 2011). When researchers asked ethnically diverse parents for their idea of an intelligent first grader, Caucasian Americans mentioned cognitive traits. In contrast, ethnic minorities (Cambodian, Filipino, Vietnamese, and Mexican immigrants) saw noncognitive capacities—motivation, self-management, and social skills—as particularly important (Okagaki & Sternberg, 1993). According to Sternberg, intelligence tests can easily underestimate, and even overlook, the cognitive strengths of some children, especially ethnic minorities.

GARDNER'S THEORY OF MULTIPLE INTELLIGENCES

In yet another view of how information-processing skills underlie intelligence behavior, Howard Gardner's (1983, 1993, 2011) **theory of multiple intelligences** defines intelligence in terms of distinct sets of processing operations that permit individuals to engage in a wide range of culturally valued activities. Dismissing the idea of general intelligence, Gardner proposes at least eight independent intelligences (see Table 12.2).

According to Gardner, people are capable of at least eight distinct intelligences. Through a project aimed at improving sea turtle nesting habitats, these children expand and enrich their naturalist intelligence.

Gardner believes that each intelligence has a unique neurological basis, a distinct course of development, and different expert, or "end-state," performances. At the same time, he emphasizes that a lengthy process of education is required to transform any raw potential into a mature social role (Gardner, 2011). Cultural values and learning opportunities affect the extent to which a child's intellectual strengths are realized and the way they are expressed.

Gardner's list of abilities has yet to be firmly grounded in research. Neurological evidence for the independence of his abilities is weak. Some exceptionally gifted individuals have abilities that are broad rather than limited to a particular domain (Piirto, 2007). And research with mental tests suggests that several of Gardner's intelligences (linguistic, logico-mathematical, and spatial) have at least some features in common. Nevertheless, Gardner calls attention to several intelligences not tapped by IQ scores.

TABLE 12.2	Gardner's Multiple Intelligences	
INTELLIGENCE	**PROCESSING OPERATIONS**	**END-STATE PERFORMANCE POSSIBILITIES**
Linguistic	Sensitivity to the sounds, rhythms, and meaning of words and the functions of language	Poet, journalist
Logico-mathematical	Sensitivity to, and capacity to detect, logical or numerical patterns; ability to handle long chains of logical reasoning	Mathematician
Musical	Ability to produce and appreciate pitch, rhythm (or melody), and aesthetic quality of the forms of musical expressiveness	Instrumentalist, composer
Spatial	Ability to perceive the visual–spatial world accurately, to perform transformations on those perceptions, and to re-create aspects of visual experience in the absence of relevant stimuli	Sculptor, navigator
Bodily-kinesthetic	Ability to use the body skillfully for expressive as well as goal-directed purposes; ability to handle objects skillfully	Dancer, athlete
Naturalist	Ability to recognize and classify all varieties of animals, minerals, and plants	Biologist
Interpersonal	Ability to detect and respond appropriately to the moods, temperaments, motivations, and intentions of others	Therapist, salesperson
Intrapersonal	Ability to discriminate complex inner feelings and to use them to guide one's own behavior; knowledge of one's own strengths, weaknesses, desires, and intelligences	Person with detailed, accurate self-knowledge

Sources: Gardner, 1983, 1993, 2011.

For example, Gardner's interpersonal and intrapersonal intelligences include a set of skills for accurately perceiving, reasoning about, and regulating emotion that has become known as *emotional intelligence*. Among school-age children and adolescents, measures of emotional intelligence are positively associated with self-esteem, empathy, prosocial behavior, cooperation, leadership skills, and academic performance and negatively associated with internalizing and externalizing problems (Brackett, Rivers, & Salovey, 2011; Ferrando et al., 2011). These findings have increased teachers' awareness that providing classroom lessons that coach students in emotional abilities can improve their adjustment.

TAKE A MOMENT... Review the *core knowledge perspective*, discussed on page 211 in Chapter 6, and compare it with Gardner's view. Gardner also accepts the existence of innately specified, core domains of thought, present at birth or emerging early in life. Then, as children respond to the demands of their culture, they transform those intelligences to fit the activities they are called on to perform. Gardner's multiple intelligences have been helpful in efforts to understand and nurture children's special talents, a topic we will take up at the end of this chapter.

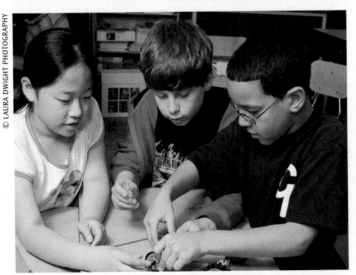

© LAURA DWIGHT PHOTOGRAPHY

In this fifth-grade class at an urban elementary school, IQ scores may vary with ethnicity and SES. Research aimed at explaining these differences has generated heated controversy.

Explaining Individual and Group Differences in IQ

When we compare individuals in terms of academic achievement, years of education, and occupational status, it is clear that certain sectors of the population are advantaged over others. In trying to explain these differences, researchers have compared the IQ scores of ethnic and SES groups. American black children and adolescents score, on average, 10 to 12 IQ points below American white children. Although the difference has been shrinking over the past several decades, a substantial gap remains (Flynn, 2007; Nisbett, 2009; Nisbett et al., 2012). Hispanic children fall midway between black and white children, and Asian Americans score slightly higher than their white counterparts—about 3 points (Ceci, Rosenblum, & Kumpf, 1998).

The IQ gap between middle-SES and low-SES children—about 9 points—accounts for some of the ethnic differences in IQ, but not all (Brooks-Gunn et al., 2003). Of course, IQ varies greatly *within* each ethnic and SES group, and minority top performers are typically indistinguishable from top performers in the white majority. Still, these group differences are large enough and of serious enough consequence that they cannot be ignored.

In the 1970s, the IQ nature–nurture controversy escalated after psychologist Arthur Jensen (1969) published a controversial monograph entitled, "How Much Can We Boost IQ and Scholastic Achievement?" Jensen's answer was "not much." He claimed—and still maintains—that heredity is largely responsible for individual, ethnic, and SES variations in intelligence (Jensen, 1998, 2001; Rushton & Jensen, 2006, 2010). Jensen's work prompted an outpouring of research studies and responses, including ethical challenges reflecting deep concern that his conclusions would fuel social prejudices. Richard Herrnstein and Charles Murray rekindled the controversy with *The Bell Curve* (1994). Like Jensen, they argued that heredity contributes substantially to individual and SES differences in IQ, and they implied that heredity plays a sizable role in the black–white IQ gap. Let's look closely at some important evidence.

NATURE VERSUS NURTURE In Chapter 2 we introduced the *heritability estimate*. Recall that heritabilities are obtained from *kinship studies*, which compare family members. The most powerful evidence on the heritability of IQ involves twin comparisons. The IQ scores of identical twins (who share all their genes) are more similar than those of fraternal twins (who are genetically no more alike than ordinary siblings). On the basis of this and other kinship evidence, researchers estimate that about half the differences in IQ among children can be traced to their genetic makeup.

Recall, however, that heritabilities risk overestimating genetic influences and underestimating environmental influences. Although these measures offer convincing evidence that genes contribute to IQ, disagreement persists over how large a role heredity plays. As we saw in Chapter 2, the heritability of children's intelligence rises with parental education and income—conditions that enable children to realize their genetic potential. And heritability estimates do not reveal the complex processes through which genes and experiences influence intelligence as children develop. So far, little progress has been made in identifying genetic markers associated with typical variation in IQ (Butcher et al., 2008; Nisbett et al., 2012). Among the few markers found, relationships with intellectual ability are weak and inconsistent.

Compared with heritability evidence, adoption studies offer a wider range of information. Findings consistently reveal that when young children are adopted into caring, stimulating homes, their IQs rise substantially compared with the IQs of nonadopted children who remain in economically deprived families (Hunt, 2011; van IJzendoorn, Juffer, & Poelhuis, 2005). But adopted children benefit to varying degrees. In one investigation, children of two extreme groups of biological mothers—those with IQs below 95 and those with IQs above 120—were adopted at birth by parents who were well above average in income and education. During the school years, the children of the low-IQ biological mothers scored above average in IQ, indicating that test performance can be greatly improved by an advantaged home life. But they did not do as well as children of high-IQ biological mothers placed in similar adoptive families (Loehlin, Horn, & Willerman, 1997). Adoption research confirms that heredity and environment jointly contribute to IQ.

Adoption studies also shed light on the black–white IQ gap. In two investigations, African-American children adopted into economically well-off white homes during the first year of life scored high on intelligence tests, attaining mean IQs of 110 and 117 by middle childhood—20 to 30 points higher than the typical scores of children growing up in low-income black communities (Moore, 1986; Scarr & Weinberg, 1983). IQ gains of black children "reared in the culture of the tests and schools" are consistent with a wealth of evidence that poverty severely depresses the intelligence of ethnic minority children (Nisbett et al., 2012).

Dramatic gains in IQ from one generation to the next offer additional support for the conclusion that, given new experiences and opportunities, members of oppressed groups can move far beyond their current test performance. See the Cultural Influences box on page 452 to learn about the *Flynn effect*.

CULTURAL INFLUENCES   A controversial question raised about ethnic differences in IQ has to do with whether they result from *test bias*. If a test samples knowledge and skills that not all groups of children have had equal opportunity to learn, or if the testing situation impairs the performance of some groups but not others, the resulting score is a biased, or unfair, measure.

Some experts reject the idea that intelligence tests are biased, claiming that they are intended to represent success in the common culture. According to this view, because IQ predicts academic achievement equally well for majority and minority children, IQ tests are fair to both groups (Edwards & Oakland, 2006; Jensen, 2002). Others believe that lack of exposure to certain communication styles and knowledge, along with negative stereotypes about the test-taker's ethnic group, can undermine children's performance (McKown, 2013; Sternberg, 2005). Let's look at the evidence.

Language and Communication Styles. Ethnic minority families often foster unique language skills that do not match the expectations of most classrooms and testing situations. African-American English is a complex, rule-governed dialect used by most African Americans in the United States (Craig & Washington, 2006). Nevertheless, it is often inaccurately viewed as a deficient form of standard American English rather than as different from it, and as a low-status dialect associated with poverty.

The majority of African-American children entering school speak African-American English, though they vary greatly in the extent to which they use it. Greater users tend to come from low-SES families, who quickly learn that the language they bring from home is devalued in school, whereas standard American English is respected. Teachers

© LAURA DWIGHT PHOTOGRAPHY

Many African-Amercan children enter school speaking African-American English. Their home discourse differs from standard English, on which school learning is based.

Cultural Influences

The Flynn Effect: Massive Generational Gains in IQ

After gathering IQ scores from diverse nations that had either military mental testing or frequent testing of other large, representative samples, James Flynn (1999, 2007) reported a finding so consistent and intriguing that it became known as the **Flynn effect:** IQs have increased steadily from one generation to the next. Evidence for the Flynn effect now exists for 30 nations (Nisbett et al., 2012). This dramatic *secular trend* in intelligence test performance holds for industrialized and developing nations, both genders, and individuals varying in ethnicity and SES (Ang, Rodgers, & Wänström, 2010; Rodgers & Wänström, 2007.) Gains are greatest on tests of spatial reasoning—tasks often assumed to be "culture-fair" and, therefore, mostly genetically based.

The amount of increase depends on extent of societal modernization (see page 440 to review). Among European and North American nations that modernized by the early twentieth century, IQ gains have been about 3 points per decade (Flynn, 2007). IQ has continued to increment at that pace in England and the United States, but gains have slowed in certain nations with especially favorable economic and social conditions, such as Norway and Sweden (Schneider, 2006; Sundet, Barlaug, & Torjussen, 2004).

Among nations that modernized later, around the mid-twentieth century (such as Argentina), IQ gains tend to be larger, as much as 5 to 6 points per decade (Flynn & Rossi-Casé, 2011). And nations that began to modernize in the late-twentieth century (Caribbean countries, Kenya, Sudan) show even greater increments, especially in spatial reasoning (Daley et al., 2003; Khaleefa, Sulman, & Lynn, 2009). The degree of societal modernity possible today is far greater than it was a century ago.

Diverse aspects of modernization probably underlie the better reasoning ability of each successive generation. These include improved education, health, and technology (TV, computers, the Internet); more cognitively demanding jobs and leisure activities (reading, chess, video games); a generally more stimulating world; and greater test-taking motivation.

As developing nations continue to advance in IQ, they are projected to catch up with the industrialized world by the end of the twenty-first century (Nisbett et al., 2012). Large, environmentally induced gains in IQ over time present a major challenge to the assumption that black–white and other ethnic variations in IQ are genetic.

Dramatic generational gains in IQ may result, in part, from greater participation by each successive generation in cognitively stimulating leisure activities.

frequently try to "correct" or eliminate their use of African-American English forms, replacing them with standard English (Washington & Thomas-Tate, 2009). Because their home discourse is distinctly different from the linguistic knowledge required to learn to read, children who speak mostly African-American English in school generally progress slowly in reading and achieve poorly (Charity, Scarborough, & Griffin, 2004).

Many African-American children learn to flexibly shift between African-American English and standard English by third grade. But those who continue to speak mostly their African-American dialect through the later grades—the majority of whom live in poverty and therefore have few opportunities outside of school for exposure to standard English—fall further behind in reading and in overall achievement (Washington & Thomas-Tate, 2009). These children have a special need for school programs that facilitate mastery of standard English while respecting and accommodating their home language in the classroom.

Research also reveals that many ethnic minority parents without extensive education prefer a *collaborative style of communication* when completing tasks with children. They work together in a coordinated, fluid way, each focused on the same aspect of the problem. This pattern of adult–child engagement has been observed in Native-American, Canadian Inuit, Hispanic, and Guatemalan Mayan cultures (Chavajay & Rogoff, 2002; Crago, Annahatak, & Ningiuruvik, 1993; Paradise & Rogoff, 2009). With increasing education, parents establish a *hierarchical style of communication,* like that of classrooms and tests. The parent directs each child to carry out an aspect of the task, and children work independently (Greenfield, Suzuki, & Rothstein-Fish, 2006). This sharp discontinuity between home and school communication practices likely contributes to low-SES minority children's lower IQ and school performance.

Knowledge. Many researchers argue that IQ scores are affected by specific information acquired as part of majority-culture upbringing. Consistent with this view, low-SES African-American children often miss vocabulary words on intelligence tests that have alternative meanings in their cultural community—for example, interpreting the word *frame* as "physique" or *wrapping* as "rapping," referring to the style of music (Champion, 2003).

Knowledge affects ability to reason effectively. When researchers assessed black and white community college students' familiarity with vocabulary taken from items on an intelligence test, the whites had considerably more knowledge (Fagan & Holland, 2007). But the African-American students were just as capable at learning new words, either from dictionary definitions or from their use in sentences. When verbal comprehension, similarities, and analogies test items depended on words and concepts that the white students knew better, the whites scored higher than the blacks. But when the same types of items involved words and concepts that the two groups knew equally well, the two groups did not differ. Prior knowledge, not reasoning ability, fully explained ethnic differences in performance.

Even nonverbal test items, such as spatial reasoning, depend on learning opportunities. For example, among children, adolescents, and adults alike, playing video games that require fast responding and mental rotation of visual images increases success on spatial test items (Uttal et al., 2013). Low-income minority children, who often grow up in more "people-oriented" than "object-oriented" homes, may lack opportunities to use games and objects that promote certain intellectual skills.

Furthermore, the sheer amount of time a child spends in school predicts IQ. In comparisons of children of the same age who are in different grades, those who have been in school longer score higher in verbal intelligence—a difference that increases as the children advance further in school (Bedard & Dhuey, 2006). Similarly, the earlier young people leave school, the greater their loss of IQ points (Ceci, 1999). And over the summer months, IQ and academic skills decline for low-SES children but rise for higher-SES children, who have greater access to educational activities (Burkam et al., 2004). Taken together, these findings indicate that children's exposure to the knowledge and ways of thinking valued in classrooms has a sizable impact on their intelligence test performance.

Stereotypes. **TAKE A MOMENT...** Imagine trying to succeed at an activity when the prevailing attitude is that members of your group are incompetent. What might you be feeling? **Stereotype threat**—the fear of being judged on the basis of a negative stereotype—can trigger anxiety that interferes with performance. Mounting evidence confirms that stereotype threat undermines test taking in children and adults (McKown & Strambler, 2009). For example, researchers gave African-American, Hispanic-American, and Caucasian-American 6- to 10-year-olds verbal tasks. Some children were told that the tasks were "not a test." Others were told that they were "a test of how good children are at school problems"—a statement designed to induce stereotype threat in the ethnic minority children. Among children who were aware of ethnic stereotypes (such as "black people aren't smart"), African Americans and Hispanics performed far worse in the "test" condition than in the "not a test" condition (McKown & Weinstein, 2003). Caucasian children, in contrast, performed similarly in both conditions.

From third grade on, children become increasingly conscious of ethnic stereotypes, and those from stigmatized groups are especially mindful of them. When confronted with stereotype threat, they well up with anxiety, which reduces mental resources available for doing well on challenging tasks. By early adolescence, many low-SES minority students start to devalue doing well in school, saying it is not important to them (Cooper & Huh, 2008; Killen, Rutland, & Ruck, 2011). Self-protective disengagement, sparked by stereotype threat, may be responsible. This weakening of motivation can have serious long-term consequences. Research shows that self-discipline—effort and delay of gratification—predicts changes in school performance, as measured by report card grades, better than IQ does (Duckworth, Quinn, & Tsukayama, 2012).

© ELLEN B. SENISI

School-age children become increasingly conscious of ethnic stereotypes, and those from stigmatized groups are especially mindful of them. Fear of being judged on the basis of a negative stereotype may undermine this Hispanic fourth grader's performance on a spelling test.

Reducing Cultural Bias in Testing

Although not all experts agree, many acknowledge that IQ scores can underestimate the intelligence of children from ethnic minority groups. A special concern exists about incorrectly labeling minority children as slow learners and assigning them to remedial classes, which are far less stimulating than regular school experiences. Because of this danger, test scores need to be combined with assessments of children's adaptive behavior—their ability to cope with the demands of their everyday environments. The child who does poorly on an IQ test yet plays a complex game on the playground or figures out how to rewire a broken TV is unlikely to be intellectually deficient.

In addition, flexible testing procedures enhance minority children's performance. In an approach called **dynamic assessment,** an innovation consistent with Vygotsky's zone of proximal development, the adult introduces purposeful teaching into the testing situation to find out what the child can attain with social support (Lidz, 2001; Robinson-Zañartu & Carlson, 2013). While intervening, the adult seeks the teaching style best suited to the individual child and communicates strategies that the child can apply in new situations.

Research shows that "static" assessments, such as IQ scores, frequently underestimate how well children do on test items after adult assistance. Children's receptivity to teaching and their capacity to transfer what they have learned to novel problems add considerably to the prediction of future performance (Haywood & Lidz, 2007; Sternberg & Grigorenko, 2002). In one study, first graders diverse in SES and ethnicity participated in two dynamic assessment sessions in which they were asked to solve a series of unfamiliar math equations that increased in difficulty, such as __+1 = 4 (easier) and 3 + 6 = 5 + __ (difficult). When a child could not solve an equation, an adult provided increasingly explicit teaching until the child either succeeded or still had trouble, in which case the session ended. Over and above static IQ-like measures of children's verbal, math, and reasoning abilities, performance during dynamic assessment strongly predicted end-of-year scores on a test of math story problems, which children usually find highly challenging (Seethaler et al., 2012). Dynamic assessment seemed to evoke reasoning skills and conceptual understandings that children readily transferred to a very different and demanding type of math.

Cultural bias in testing can also be reduced by countering the negative impact of stereotype threat. A variety of brief, school-based interventions are effective. Persuading students that their intelligence depends heavily on effort, not on a stereotype of native endowment, is helpful (Blackwell, Trzesniewski, & Dweck, 2007). Another approach is to encourage minority students to affirm their self-worth by writing a short essay about their most important values (for example, a close friendship or a self-defining skill). This self-affirmation intervention was just as successful in boosting end-of-term grades of poorly performing middle school students as it was for students doing moderately well in school (see Figure 12.6) (Cohen, Garcia, & Master, 2006).

In view of its many problems, should intelligence testing in schools be suspended? Most experts regard this solution as unacceptable. Without testing, important educational decisions would be based only on subjective impressions, perhaps increasing discriminatory placement of minority children. Intelligence tests are useful when interpreted carefully by examiners who are sensitive to cultural influences on test performance. And despite their limitations, IQ scores continue to be valid measures of school learning potential for the majority of Western children.

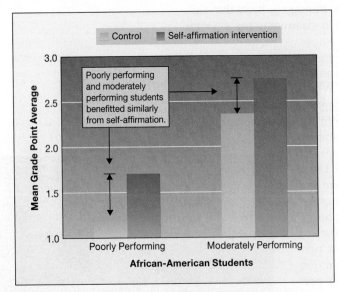

FIGURE 12.6 **Impact of a self-affirmation intervention on African-American middle school students' end-of-term grade-point average.** Early in the fall term, several hundred middle-school students were randomly assigned to either a self-affirmation intervention, in which they wrote brief essays about why their most important values were important to them, or a control condition, in which they wrote essays about why their least important values might be important to someone else. African-American students experiencing the self-affirmation condition attained substantially higher end-of-term course grades than did controls; poorly performing and moderately performing students benefited similarly. White students' grades (not shown) were unaffected, indicating that the treatment succeeded by lessening the negative impact of stereotype threat on African Americans. (Based on Cohen, Garcia, & Master, 2006.)

Ask Yourself

- **REVIEW** Using Sternberg's triarchic theory and Gardner's theory of multiple intelligences, explain the limitations of current mental tests in assessing the diversity of human intelligence.

- **CONNECT** Explain how dynamic assessment is consistent with Vygotsky's zone of proximal development and with scaffolding (see Chapter 9, pages 323–324).

- **APPLY** Josefina, a Hispanic fourth grader, does well on homework assignments. But when her teacher announces, "It's time for a test to see how much you've learned," Josefina usually does poorly. How might stereotype threat explain this inconsistency?

- **REFLECT** Do you think that intelligence tests are culturally biased? What observations and evidence influenced your conclusion?

Language Development

12.8 Describe changes in metalinguistic awareness, vocabulary, grammar, and pragmatics during middle childhood.

12.9 Describe bilingual development, along with advantages of bilingualism in childhood.

Vocabulary, grammar, and pragmatics continue to develop in middle childhood, though less obviously than at earlier ages. In addition, children's attitude toward language undergoes a fundamental shift. They develop **metalinguistic awareness,** the ability to think about language as a system.

Schooling contributes greatly to these language competencies. Reflecting on language is extremely common during reading instruction. And fluent reading is a major new source of language learning (Ravid & Tolchinsky, 2002). As we will see, an improved ability to reflect on language grows out of literacy and supports many complex language skills.

Vocabulary

During the elementary school years, vocabulary increases fourfold, eventually exceeding comprehension of 40,000 words. On average, children learn about 20 new words each day—a rate of growth greater than in early childhood. In addition to the word-learning strategies discussed in Chapter 9, school-age children enlarge their vocabularies by analyzing the structure of complex words. From *happy* and *decide,* they quickly derive the meanings of *happiness* and *decision* (Larsen & Nippold, 2007). They also figure out many more word meanings from context.

As at earlier ages, children benefit from conversations with more expert speakers, especially when their partners use and explain complex words (Weizman & Snow, 2001). But because written language contains a far more diverse and complex vocabulary than spoken language, reading contributes enormously to vocabulary growth. Avid readers are exposed to more than 4 million words per year, average readers to 600,000 words. But children who rarely read encounter only about 50,000 words (Anderson, Wilson, & Fielding, 1988). By second to third grade, reading comprehension and reading habits are strongly predict later vocabulary size into high school (Cain & Oakhill, 2011).

As their knowledge becomes better organized, older school-age children think about and use words more precisely: In addition to the verb *fall,* for example, they also use *topple, tumble,* and *plummet* (Berman, 2007). Word definitions also illustrate this change. Five- and 6-year-olds offer concrete descriptions referring to functions or appearance—*knife:* "when you're cutting carrots"; *bicycle:* "it's got wheels, a chain, and handlebars." By the end of elementary school, synonyms and explanations of categorical relationships appear—for example, *knife:* "something you could cut with. A saw is like a knife. It could also be a weapon" (Uccelli & Pan, 2013; Wehren, De Lisi, & Arnold, 1981). This advance reflects older children's ability to deal with word meanings on an entirely verbal plane. They can add new words to their vocabulary simply by being given a definition.

© ELLEN B. SENISI

A fifth grader encounters new words with complex meanings in a current events article. Stimulating reading experiences contribute greatly to vocabulary growth.

LOOK and LISTEN

Record examples of 8- to 10-year-olds' humor, or examine storybooks for humor aimed at second through fourth graders. Does it require a grasp of the multiple meanings of words?

School-age children's more reflective and analytical approach to language permits them to appreciate the multiple meanings of words—to recognize, for example, that many words, such as *cool* or *neat,* have psychological as well as physical meanings: "Cool shirt!" or "That movie was really neat!" This grasp of double meanings permits 8- to 10-year-olds to comprehend subtle metaphors, such as "sharp as a tack" and "spilling the beans" (Nippold, Taylor, & Baker, 1996; Wellman & Hickling, 1994). It also leads to a change in children's humor. Riddles and puns that alternate between different meanings of a key word are common: "Hey, did you take a bath?" "Why, is one missing?"

Grammar

During the school years, mastery of complex grammatical constructions improves. For example, English-speaking children use the passive voice more frequently, and they more often extend it from an abbreviated structure ("It broke") into full statements ("The glass was broken by Mary") (Israel, Johnson, & Brooks, 2000; Tomasello, 2006). Older children also apply their grasp of the passive voice to a wider range of nouns and verbs. Preschoolers comprehend the passive best when the subject of the sentence is an animate being and the verb is an action word: "The boy is *kissed* by the girl." School-age children extend the passive to inanimate subjects *(drum, hat)* and include experiential verbs *(like, know)* (Lempert, 1989; Pinker, Lebeaux, & Frost, 1987). Although the passive form is challenging, language input makes a difference. When adults speak a language that emphasizes full passives, such as Inuktitut (spoken by the Inuit people of Arctic Canada), children produce them earlier (Allen & Crago, 1996).

Another grammatical achievement of middle childhood is advanced understanding of infinitive phrases—the difference between "John is eager to please" and "John is easy to please" (Berman, 2007; Chomsky, 1969). Like gains in vocabulary, appreciation of these subtle grammatical distinctions is supported by improved ability to analyze and reflect on language.

Pragmatics

The school years also bring dramatic gains in *pragmatics,* the communicative side of language. Opportunities to communicate in many situations with a variety of people help children refine these skills.

COMMUNICATING CLEARLY   In middle childhood, children can adapt to the needs of listeners in challenging communicative situations, such as describing one object among a group of very similar objects. Whereas preschoolers tend to give ambiguous descriptions ("the red one"), school-age children are precise: "the round red one with stripes on it" (Deutsch & Pechmann, 1982). Because peers challenge unclear messages that adults accept, peer interaction probably contributes greatly to this aspect of conversational competence.

The ability to evaluate the clarity of others' messages improves as well, and children become better at resolving inconsistencies. Consider the instruction, "Put the frog on the book in the box." Preschoolers cannot make sense of the ambiguity, even though they use similar embedded phrases in their own speech. They respond by attending only to the first prepositional phrase ("on the book") and place a toy frog on a book. School-age children, in contrast, can attend to and integrate two competing representations ("on the book" and "in the box") (Hurewitz et al., 2000). They quickly figure out the speaker's meaning and pick up a toy frog resting on a book and place it in a box.

Furthermore, a more advanced theory of mind—in particular, the capacity for recursive thought—enables children to detect increasingly subtle, indirect expressions of meaning with age (Lee, Torrance, & Olson, 2001). Seven-year-old Lizzie often avoided her daily garbage-disposal chore, so she knew that her mother's comment, "The garbage is beginning to smell," really meant, "Take that garbage out!" Around age 8, children begin to grasp irony and sarcasm (Glenright & Pexman, 2010). After Rena prepared a dish for dinner that Joey didn't like, he quipped sarcastically, "Oh boy, my favorite!" Notice how these remarks require the speaker to consider at least two perspectives simultaneously—in Joey's case, his mother's desire to serve a particular dish despite his objection, expressed through a critical comment with a double meaning.

NARRATIVES As a result of improved memory, ability to take the perspective of listeners, and conversations with adults about past experiences, children's narratives increase in organization, detail, and expressiveness. A typical 4- or 5-year-old's narrative states what happened: "We went to the lake. We fished and waited. Paul caught a huge catfish!" Six- and 7-year-olds add orienting information (time, place, participants) and connectives ("next," "then," "so," "finally") that lend coherence to the story. Gradually, narratives lengthen into a *classic form* in which events not only build to a high point but resolve: "After Paul reeled in the catfish, Dad cleaned and cooked it. Then we ate it all up!" And evaluative comments rise dramatically, becoming common by age 8 to 9: "The catfish tasted great. Paul was so proud!" (Melzi & Schick, 2013; Ukrainetz et al., 2005).

Children's narratives vary widely across cultures, reflecting the styles of significant adults in their lives. African-American children like this second grader tend to tell longer, more complex stories than white children.

Because children pick up the narrative styles of significant adults in their lives, their narratives vary widely across cultures. For example, instead of the *topic-focused style* of most American school-age children, who describe an experience from beginning to end, African-American children often use a *topic-associating style* in which they blend several similar experiences. One 9-year-old related having a tooth pulled, then described seeing her sister's tooth pulled, next told how she had removed one of her baby teeth, and concluded, "I'm a pullin-teeth expert . . . call me, and I'll be over" (McCabe, 1997, p. 164). Like adults in their families and communities, African-American children are more attuned to keeping their listeners interested than relating a linear sequence of story events. They often embellish their narratives by including fictional elements and many references to characters' motives and intentions (Gorman et al., 2011). As a result, African-American children's narratives are usually longer and more complex than those of white children.

The ability to generate clear oral narratives enhances reading comprehension and prepares children for producing longer, more explicit written narratives. In families who regularly eat meals together, children are advanced in language and literacy development, perhaps because mealtimes offer many opportunities to relate personal stories (Snow & Beals, 2006).

Learning Two Languages

Joey and Lizzie speak only one language—English, their native tongue. Yet throughout the world, many children grow up *bilingual,* learning two languages and sometimes more than two. An estimated 22 percent of U.S. children—11 million in all—speak a language other than English at home (U.S. Census Bureau, 2014b).

BILINGUAL DEVELOPMENT Children can become bilingual in two ways: (1) by acquiring both languages at the same time in early childhood or (2) by learning a second language after mastering the first. Children of bilingual parents who teach them both languages in infancy and early childhood separate the language systems early on and attain early language milestones according to a typical timetable (Hoff et al., 2012; Weikum et al., 2007). Preschoolers acquire normal native ability in the language of their surrounding community and good-to-native ability in the second language, depending on their exposure to it (Serratrice, 2013). When school-age children acquire a second language, they generally take 5 to 7 years to attain speaking and writing skills on a par with those of native-speaking agemates (Paradis, 2007).

Like many bilingual adults, bilingual children sometimes engage in *code switching*—producing an utterance in one language that contains one or more "guest" words from the other—without violating the grammar of either language. Rather than a sign of confusion, code switching is adaptive, reflecting deliberate control of the two languages (Bhatt & Bolonyai, 2011). Children may engage in code switching because they lack the vocabulary to convey a particular thought in one language, so they use the other. And children who code-switch the most are those whose parents often do so. Bilingual adults frequently code-switch to express cultural identity, and children may follow suit—as when a Korean child speaking English switches to Korean on mentioning her piano teacher, as a sign of respect for authority (Chung, 2006). Opportunities to listen to code switching may facilitate bilingual development. For example, a child accustomed to hearing French sentences with English guest words may rely on sentence-level cues to figure out English word meanings.

Recall from Chapter 6 that, just as with first-language development, a *sensitive period* for second-language development exists. Although mastery must begin sometime in childhood for full development to occur, a precise age cutoff for a decline in second-language learning has not been established (see page 233).

Children who become fluent in two languages develop denser gray matter (neurons and connective fibers) in areas of the left hemisphere devoted to language. And compared to monolinguals, bilinguals show greater activity in these areas and in the prefrontal cortex during linguistic tasks, likely due to the high executive-processing demands of controlling two languages (Costa & Sebastián-Gallés, 2014). Because both languages are always active, bilingual speakers must continuously decide which one to use in particular social situations, resisting attention to the other.

This increase in executive processing has diverse cognitive benefits as bilinguals acquire more efficient executive-function skills and apply those to other tasks (Bialystok, 2011). Bilingual children and adults outperform others on tests of sustained and selective attention, inhibition of irrelevant information, flexible thinking, analytical reasoning, concept formation, and false-belief (Bialystok, Craik, & Luk, 2012; Carlson & Meltzoff, 2008). They are also advanced in certain aspects of metalinguistic awareness, such as detection of errors in grammar, meaning, and conventions of conversation (responding politely, relevantly, and informatively). And children transfer their phonological awareness skills in one language to the other, especially if their two languages share phonological features and letter–sound correspondences, as Spanish and English do (Bialystok, 2013; Siegal, Iozzi, & Surian, 2009). These capacities enhance reading achievement.

BILINGUAL EDUCATION The advantages of bilingualism provide strong justification for bilingual education programs in schools. In Canada, about 7 percent of elementary school students are enrolled in *language immersion programs,* in which English-speaking children typically are taught entirely in French from kindergarten through second grade. Gradually, English is introduced as a subject in third grade, though French continues to be the main classroom language. This strategy succeeds in developing children who are proficient in both languages. Though initial delays in English literacy achievement are common, by grade 6 immersion students achieve as well in reading, writing, and math as their counterparts in the regular English program (Genesee & Jared, 2008; Lyster & Genesee, 2012).

In the United States, fierce disagreement exists over the question of how best to educate ethnic minority children with limited English proficiency. Some believe that time spent communicating in the child's native tongue detracts from English-language achievement, which is crucial for success in the worlds of school and work. Other educators, committed to developing minority children's native language while fostering mastery of English, note that providing instruction in the native tongue lets minority children know that their heritage is respected. It also prevents inadequate proficiency in both languages. Minority children who gradually lose their first language as a result of being taught the second end up limited in both languages for a time (McCabe et al., 2013). This circumstance leads to serious academic difficulties and is believed to contribute to the high rates of school failure and dropout among low-SES Hispanic youngsters, who make up over 60 percent of the U.S. language-minority population.

At present, public opinion and educational practice favor English-only instruction. Many U.S. states have passed laws declaring English to be their official language, creating conditions in which schools have no obligation to teach minority students in languages other than English. Where bilingual education exists, its goal is to transition students to English-only instruction as soon as possible (Wright, 2013). Yet in classrooms where both languages are integrated into the curriculum, minority children are more involved in learning, participate more actively in class discussions,

The child on the left, a native Spanish speaker, benefits from an English–Spanish bilingual classroom, which sustains her native language while she masters English. And her native-English-speaking classmate has the opportunity to begin learning Spanish!

© CHRISTINA KENNEDY/PHOTOEDIT

and acquire the second language more easily—gains that predict better academic achievement (Guglielmi, 2008). In contrast, when teachers speak only in a language that children can barely understand, minority children display frustration, boredom, and withdrawal. Under these conditions, U.S. kindergartners with limited English proficiency quickly fall behind their English-proficient counterparts in oral language and reading skills and are likely to struggle academically throughout their school years (Paradis, Genesee, & Crago 2011). This downward spiral in achievement is greatest in high-poverty schools, where resources to support the needs of language-minority children are especially scarce.

Supporters of U.S. English-only education often point to the success of Canadian language immersion programs, in which classroom lessons are conducted in the second language. But Canadian parents enroll their children in immersion classrooms voluntarily, and students in those programs are native speakers of the dominant language of their region. Furthermore, teaching in the child's native language is merely delayed, not ruled out. For U.S. non-English-speaking minority children, whose native languages are not valued by the larger society, a different strategy is necessary: one that promotes children's native-language and literacy skills while they learn English.

Ask Yourself

- **REVIEW** Cite examples of how metalinguistic awareness fosters school-age children's language progress.

- **CONNECT** How can bilingual education promote ethnic minority children's cognitive and academic development?

- **APPLY** After soccer practice, 10-year-old Shana remarked, "I'm wiped out!" Megan, her 5-year-old sister, responded, "What did'ya wipe out?" Explain Shana's and Megan's different understandings.

- **REFLECT** Considering research on bilingualism, what changes would you make in your own second-language learning, and why?

Children's Learning in School

Evidence cited throughout this chapter indicates that schools are vital forces in children's cognitive development. How do schools exert such a powerful influence? Research looking at schools as complex social systems—class size, educational philosophies, teacher–student relationships, and larger cultural context—provides important insights. As you read about these topics, refer to Applying What We Know on page 460, which summarizes characteristics of high-quality education in elementary school.

Class Size

As each school year began, Rena telephoned the principal's office to ask, "How large will Joey's and Lizzie's classes be?" Her concern is well-founded. In a large field experiment, more than 6,000 Tennessee kindergartners were randomly assigned to three class types: "small" (13 to 17 students), "regular" (22 to 25 students) with only a teacher, and regular with a teacher plus a full-time teacher's aide. These arrangements continued into third grade. Small-class students scored higher in reading and math achievement each year (Mosteller, 1995). Placing teacher's aides in regular-size classes had no impact. Rather, experiencing small classes from kindergarten through third grade predicted substantially higher achievement from fourth through ninth grades, after children had returned to regular-size classes. It also predicted greater likelihood of graduating from high school, particularly for low-SES students (Finn, Gerber, & Boyd-Zaharias, 2005; Nye, Hedges, & Konstantopoulos, 2001).

Small class size, especially if introduced at school entry, is associated with better academic progress even after diverse measures of teacher quality have been controlled (Brühweiler &

12.10 Describe the impact of class size and educational philosophies on children's motivation and academic achievement.

12.11 Discuss the role of teacher–student interaction and grouping practices in academic achievement.

12.12 Describe benefits of, as well as concerns about, educational media.

12.13 Under what conditions is placement of children with mild intellectual disability or learning disabilities in regular classrooms successful?

12.14 Describe the characteristics of gifted children and efforts to meet their educational needs.

12.15 How well-educated are U.S. children compared with children in other industrialized nations?

Applying What We Know

Signs of High-Quality Education in Elementary School

CLASSROOM CHARACTERISTICS	SIGNS OF QUALITY
Class size	Optimum class size is no larger than 18 to 20 children.
Physical setting	Space is divided into richly equipped activity centers—for reading, writing, playing math or language games, exploring science, working on construction projects, using computers, and engaging in other academic pursuits. Spaces are used flexibly for individual and small-group activities and whole-class gatherings.
Curriculum	The curriculum helps children both achieve academic standards and make sense of their learning. Subjects are integrated so that children apply knowledge in one area to others. The curriculum is implemented through activities responsive to children's interests, ideas, and everyday lives, including their cultural backgrounds.
Daily activities	Teachers provide challenging activities that include opportunities for small-group and independent work. Groupings vary in size and makeup of children, depending on the activity and on children's learning needs. Teachers encourage cooperative learning and guide children in attaining it.
Interactions between teachers and children	Teachers foster each child's progress and use intellectually engaging strategies, including posing problems, asking thought-provoking questions, discussing ideas, and adding complexity to tasks. They also demonstrate, explain, coach, and assist in other ways, depending on each child's learning needs.
Evaluations of progress	Teachers regularly evaluate children's progress through written observations and work samples, which they use to enhance and individualize teaching. They help children reflect on their work and decide how to improve it. They also seek information and perspectives from parents on how well children are learning and include parents' views in evaluations.
Relationship with parents	Teachers forge partnerships with parents. They hold periodic conferences and encourage parents to visit the classroom anytime, to observe and volunteer.

Source: Copple & Bredekamp, 2009.

Blatchford, 2011). Why is it beneficial? With fewer children, teachers spend less time disciplining and more time teaching and giving individual attention. Also, children who learn in smaller groups show better concentration, higher-quality class participation, and more favorable attitudes toward school (Blatchford, 2012; Blatchford, Bassett, & Brown, 2005, 2011).

Educational Philosophies

Each teacher brings to the classroom an educational philosophy that plays a major role in children's learning. Two philosophical approaches have received the most research attention. They differ in what children are taught, in the way they are believed to learn, and in how their progress is evaluated.

TRADITIONAL VERSUS CONSTRUCTIVIST CLASSROOMS   In a **traditional classroom,** the teacher is the sole authority for knowledge, rules, and decision making and does most of the talking. Students are relatively passive—listening, responding when called on, and completing teacher-assigned tasks. Their progress is evaluated by how well they keep pace with a uniform set of standards for their grade.

A **constructivist classroom,** in contrast, encourages students to *construct* their own knowledge. Although constructivist approaches vary, many are grounded in Piaget's theory, which views children as active agents who reflect on and coordinate their own thoughts, rather than absorbing those of others. A glance inside a constructivist classroom reveals richly equipped learning centers, small groups and individuals solving self-chosen problems, and a teacher who guides and supports in response to children's needs. Students are evaluated by considering their progress in relation to their own prior development.

In the United States, the pendulum has swung back and forth between these two views. In the 1960s and early 1970s, constructivist classrooms gained in popularity. Then, as concern arose over the academic progress of children and youths, a "back-to-basics" movement arose, and classrooms returned to traditional instruction. This style, still prevalent today, has become increasingly pronounced as a result of the U.S. No Child Left Behind Act, signed into law in 2001 (Darling-Hammond, 2010; Kew et al., 2012). Because it places heavy pressure on teachers and school administrators to improve achievement test scores, it has narrowed the curricular focus in many schools to preparing students to take such tests.

Although older elementary school children in traditional classrooms have a slight edge in achievement test scores, constructivist settings are associated with many other benefits—gains in critical thinking, greater social and moral maturity, and more positive attitudes toward school (DeVries, 2001; Rathunde & Csikszentmihalyi, 2005; Walberg, 1986). And as noted in Chapter 9, when teacher-directed instruction is emphasized in preschool and kindergarten, it actually undermines academic motivation and achievement, especially in low-SES children.

The emphasis on knowledge absorption in many kindergarten and primary classrooms has contributed to a trend among parents to delay their child's school entry—especially among higher-SES families and if the child is a boy with a birth date close to the cutoff for kindergarten enrollment. But research reveals no long-term academic or social benefits (Bassok & Reardon, 2013; Lincove & Painter, 2006). To the contrary, younger first graders reap achievement gains from on-time enrollment, outperforming same-age children a year behind them (Stipek & Byler, 2001). An alternative perspective is that school readiness can be cultivated through classroom experiences that foster children's individual progress.

NEW PHILOSOPHICAL DIRECTIONS   New approaches to education, grounded in Vygotsky's sociocultural theory, capitalize on the rich social context of the classroom to spur children's learning. In these **social-constructivist classrooms,** children participate in a wide range of challenging activities with teachers and peers, with whom they jointly construct understandings. As children *appropriate* (take for themselves) the knowledge and strategies generated through working together, they become competent, contributing members of their classroom community and advance in cognitive and social development (Bodrova & Leong, 2007; Lourenço, 2012). Vygotsky's emphasis on the social origins of complex mental activities has inspired the following educational themes:

- *Teachers and children as partners in learning.* A classroom rich in both teacher–child and child–child collaboration transfers culturally valued ways of thinking to children.
- *Experience with many types of symbolic communication in meaningful activities.* As children master reading, writing, and mathematics, they become aware of their culture's communication systems, reflect on their own thinking, and bring it under voluntary control. **TAKE A MOMENT...** Can you identify research presented earlier in this chapter that supports this theme?
- *Teaching adapted to each child's zone of proximal development.* Assistance that both responds to current understandings and encourages children to take the next step helps ensure that each child makes the best progress possible.

Let's look at two examples of a growing number of programs that have translated these ideas into action.

Reciprocal Teaching.   Originally designed to improve reading comprehension in poorly achieving students, this Vygotsky-inspired teaching method has been extended to other subjects and all schoolchildren (Palincsar & Herrenkohl, 1999). In **reciprocal teaching,** a teacher and two to four students form a cooperative group and take turns leading dialogues on the content of a text passage. Within the dialogues, group members apply four cognitive strategies: questioning, summarizing, clarifying, and predicting.

The dialogue leader (at first a teacher, later a student) begins by *asking questions* about the content of the text passage. Students offer answers, raise additional questions, and, in case of disagreement, reread the original text. Next, the leader *summarizes* the passage, and children discuss the summary and *clarify* unfamiliar ideas. Finally, the leader encourages students to *predict* upcoming content based on clues in the passage.

Elementary and middle school students exposed to reciprocal teaching show impressive gains in reading comprehension compared to controls taught in other ways (Schunemann, Sporer, & Brunstein, 2013; Sporer, Brunstein, & Kieschke, 2009). Notice how reciprocal teaching creates a zone of proximal development in which children learn to scaffold one another's

LOOK and LISTEN

Ask an elementary school teacher to sum up his or her educational philosophy. Is it closest to a traditional, constructivist, or social-constructivist view? Has the teacher encountered any obstacles to implementing that philosophy? Explain.

progress and assume more responsibility for comprehending text passages. Also, by collaborating with others, children forge group expectations for high-level thinking, more often apply their metacognitive knowledge, and acquire skills vital for learning and success in everyday life.

Communities of Learners. Recognizing that collaboration requires a supportive context to be most effective, another Vygotsky-based innovation makes it a schoolwide value. Classrooms become **communities of learners** where teachers guide the overall process of learning but no other distinction is made between adult and child contributors: All participate in joint endeavors and have the authority to define and resolve problems. This approach is based on the assumption that different people have different expertises that can benefit the community and that students, too, may become experts (Sewell, St George, & Cullen, 2013). Classroom activities are often long-term projects addressing complex, real-world problems. In working toward project goals, children and teachers draw on the expertises of one another and of others within and outside the school.

A teacher and students form a community of learners to plan, plant, and track the growth of a vegetable garden. During this complex, long-term project, all participants—adults as well as children—may become experts who share knowledge, teaching one another.

In one classroom, students studied animal–habitat relationships in order to design an animal of the future, suited to environmental changes. The class formed small research groups, each of which selected a subtopic—for example, defense against predators, protection from the elements, reproduction, or food getting. Each group member assumed responsibility for part of the subtopic, consulting diverse experts and preparing teaching materials. Then group members taught one another, assembled their contributions, and brought them to the community as a whole so the knowledge gathered could be used to solve the problem (Brown, 1997; Stone, 2005). The result was a multifaceted understanding of the topic that would have been too difficult and time-consuming for any learner to accomplish alone.

In communities of learners, collaboration is created from within by teachers and children and supported from without by the culture of the school (Sullivan & Glanz, 2006). As a result, the approach broadens Vygotsky's concept of the zone of proximal development, from a child in collaboration with a more expert partner (adult or peer) to multiple, interrelated zones.

Teacher–Student Interaction

Elementary and secondary school students describe good teachers as caring, helpful, and stimulating—behaviors associated with gains in motivation, achievement, and positive peer relations (Hughes & Kwok, 2006, 2007; Hughes, Zhang, & Hill, 2006; O'Connor & McCartney, 2007). But too many U.S. teachers—especially those in schools with many students from low-income families—emphasize repetitive drill over higher-level thinking, such as grappling with ideas and applying knowledge to new situations (Valli, Croninger, & Buese, 2012). This focus on low-level skills becomes increasingly pronounced over the school year as state-mandated achievement testing draws nearer.

Of course, teachers do not interact in the same way with all children. Well-behaved, high-achieving students typically get more support and praise, whereas unruly students have more conflicts with teachers and receive more criticism (Henricsson & Rydell, 2004). Warm, low-conflict teacher–student relationships have an especially strong impact on academic self-esteem, achievement, and social behavior of low-SES minority students and other children at risk for learning difficulties (Hughes, 2011; Hughes et al., 2012; Spilt et al., 2012). But overall, higher-SES students—who tend to be higher-achieving and to have fewer learning and behavior problems—have more sensitive and supportive relationships with teachers (Jerome, Hamre, & Pianta, 2008).

Unfortunately, once teachers' attitudes toward students are established, they can become more extreme than is warranted by children's behavior. Of special concern are **educational self-fulfilling prophecies:** Children may adopt teachers' positive or negative views and start to live up to them. This effect is particularly strong when teachers emphasize competition and publicly compare children, regularly favoring the best students (Weinstein, 2002).

ALISTAIR BERG/DIGITAL VISION/GETTY IMAGES

Teacher expectations have a greater impact on low-achieving than high-achieving students (McKown, Gregory, & Weinstein, 2010). When a teacher is critical, high achievers can fall back on their history of success. Low-achieving students' sensitivity to self-fulfilling prophecies can be beneficial when teachers believe in them. But biased teacher judgments are usually slanted in a negative direction.

Furthermore, much evidence confirms that academic stereotypes about ethnic minority students have self-fulfilling effects on their behavior (Madon et al., 2011). In one study, African-American and Hispanic elementary school students taught by high-bias teachers (who expected them to do poorly) showed substantially lower end-of-year achievement than their counterparts taught by low-bias teachers (McKown & Weinstein, 2008). Recall our discussion of *stereotype threat.* A child in the position of confirming a negative stereotype may respond with especially intense anxiety and reduced motivation, amplifying a negative self-fulfilling prophecy.

Grouping Practices

In many schools, students are assigned to *homogeneous* groups or classes, in which children of similar ability levels are taught together. Homogeneous grouping can be a potent source of self-fulfilling prophecies. Low-group students—who as early as first grade are more likely to be low-SES, minority, and male—get more drill on basic facts and skills, engage in less discussion, and progress at a slower pace. Gradually, they decline in self-esteem and motivation and fall further behind in achievement (Lleras & Rangel, 2009; Worthy, Hungerford-Kresser, & Hampton, 2009).

Unfortunately, widespread SES and ethnic segregation in U.S. schools consigns large numbers of low-SES, minority students to a form of school-wide, deleterious homogeneous grouping. Refer to the Social Issues: Education box on page 464 to find out how magnet schools foster heterogeneous learning contexts, thereby reducing achievement differences between SES and ethnic minority groups.

However, small, heterogeneous groups of students working together often engage in poorer-quality interaction (less accurate explanations and answers) than homogeneous groups of above-average students (Webb, Nemer, & Chizhik, 1998). For collaboration between heterogeneous peers to succeed, children need extensive training and guidance in **cooperative learning,** in which small groups of classmates work toward common goals—by considering one another's ideas, appropriately challenging one another, providing sufficient explanations to correct misunderstandings, and resolving differences of opinion on the basis of reasons and evidence. When teachers prompt, explain, model, and have children role-play how to work together effectively, cooperative learning among heterogeneous peers results in more complex reasoning, greater enjoyment of learning, and achievement gains across a wide range of subjects (Gillies, 2003; Jadallah et al., 2011; Webb et al., 2008).

Consider an investigation in which teachers taught heterogeneous groups of fourth graders to collaborate in reasoning about controversial issues, such as whether zoos are good places for animals. Over 10 group sessions, the students increasingly engaged in more advanced reasoning by analogy—comparisons that moved beyond surface features ("In a zoo it would be just like being in jail") to higher-order relations ("Pretend this classroom is like a cage. And who would rather be here or recess?"). During discussions, use of analogies "snowballed." When one student introduced an analogy, other students often elaborated on it and contributed new analogies ("Cause it's like your mom locking you in your room for a week") (Lin et al., 2012). Together, students used analogy as a powerfully persuasive tool, capitalizing on it to introduce new information and perspectives.

Educational Media

Virtually all public schools in industrialized nations have integrated computers into their instructional programs and can access the Internet. And, as noted in Chapter 9, most U.S. children have access to a home computer, usually with an Internet connection. Although the

Fourth graders work together to complete an assignment. Successful cooperative learning enhances children's enjoyment of learning and academic achievement.

Social Issues: Education

Magnet Schools: Equal Access to High-Quality Education

Each school-day morning, Emma leaves her affluent suburban neighborhood, riding a school bus 20 miles to a magnet school in an impoverished, mostly Hispanic inner-city neighborhood. In her fifth-grade class, she settles into a science project with her friend Maricela, who lives in the local neighborhood. For the first hour of the day, the girls use a thermometer, ice water, and a stopwatch to determine which of several materials is the best insulator, recording and graphing their data. Throughout the school, which specializes in innovative math and science teaching, students diverse in SES and ethnicity learn side-by-side.

Despite the 1954 U.S. Supreme Court *Brown v. Board of Education* decision ordering schools to desegregate, school integration receded over the 1990s as federal courts canceled their integration orders and returned this authority to states and cities. Since 2000, the racial divide in American education has improved only modestly (Stroub & Richards, 2013). When minority students attend ethnically mixed schools, they typically do so with other minorities.

U.S. schools in inner-city, low-income neighborhoods are vastly disadvantaged in funding and therefore in educational opportunities, largely because public education is primarily supported by local property taxes. Federal and state grants-in-aid are not sufficient to close this funding gap between rich and poor districts. Consequently, in inner-city segregated neighborhoods, dilapidated school buildings; inexperienced teachers; outdated, poor-quality educational resources; and school cultures that fail to encourage strong teaching are widespread (Condron, 2013). The negative impact on student achievement is severe.

A promising solution is the establishment of magnet schools. In addition to the usual curriculum, they emphasize a specific area of interest—such as performing arts, math and science, or technology. Families outside the school neighborhood are attracted to magnet schools (hence the name) by their rich academic offerings. Often magnets are located in low-income, minority areas, where they serve the neighborhood student population. Other students, who apply and are admitted by lottery, are bussed in—many from well-to-do city and suburban neighborhoods. In another model, all students—including those in the surrounding neighborhood—must apply. In either case, magnet schools are voluntarily desegregated.

Do magnet schools enhance minority student achievement? A Connecticut study comparing students enrolled in magnet middle schools with those whose lottery numbers were not drawn and who therefore attended other city schools confirmed that the magnets served a far more diverse student population. Although magnet-

A magnet-school teacher receives hugs from her first-grade students at a party celebrating news that she is a finalist for Texas Elementary Teacher of the Year. Magnet schools typically attract students diverse in ethnicity and SES because of their rich academic offerings and innovative teaching.

school enrollees and nonadmitted applicants were similar in ethnicity, SES, and prior academic achievement, magnet students showed greater gains in reading and math achievement over a two-year period—outcomes especially pronounced for low-SES, ethnic minority students (Bifulco, Cobb, & Bell, 2009).

By high school, the higher-achieving peer environments of ethnically diverse schools encourage more students to pursue higher education (Franklin, 2012). In sum, magnet schools are a promising approach for overcoming the negative forces of SES and ethnic isolation in American schools.

---

overwhelming majority of higher-SES homes have computers and Internet, more than 70 percent of U.S. low-SES families with school-age children and adolescents now have them (Common Sense Media, 2013; U.S. Census Bureau, 2014b).

Computer use is associated with academic progress. Word processing, for example, enables children to write freely, without having to struggle with handwriting. Because they can revise their text's meaning and style and also check their spelling, they worry less about making mistakes. As a result, their written products tend to be longer and of higher quality (Clements & Sarama, 2003). And as in early childhood, computer programming projects promote problem solving and metacognition and are common classroom contexts for peer collaboration (see page 346 in Chapter 9).

As children get older, they increasingly use screen media for schoolwork, mostly to search the Web for information and to prepare written assignments—activities linked to improved problem-solving skills and academic achievement (Judge, Puckett, & Bell, 2006; Tran & Subrahmanyam, 2013). The more low-SES middle school students use the Internet for information gathering (either for school or for personal interests), the better their subsequent reading achievement and school grades (Jackson et al., 2011). Perhaps those who use the Web to find information also devote more time to reading, given that many Web pages are heavily text-based.

With age, video game play rises dramatically: two-thirds of U.S. 6- to 8-year-olds, and the overwhelming majority of 8- to 18-year-olds, have played at one time or another. Young school-age children, on average, devote 20 minutes per day to gaming, older school-age children and adolescents 73 minutes. Boys are two to three times more likely than girls to be daily players (Common Sense Media, 2013; Rideout, Foehr, & Roberts, 2010).

Although video games with violent content are harmful (see Chapter 10), game play is also rich in cognitive benefits. These include gains in eye-and-hand coordination, visual processing speed, attention, strategic thinking, and spatial reasoning (see page 453) (Tran & Subrahmanyam, 2013). Games emphasizing academic skills, such as reading or math, succeed in teaching their intended content (Murphy et al., 2002). And because adventure games typically involve substantial cognitive challenge—navigating a series of worlds and manipulating variables to overcome obstacles—successful play requires strategic thinking, planning, self-regulation, problem solving, and (in fantasy role-play games) imagination (Boyan & Sherry, 2011; Valkenburg & Calvert, 2012). These cognitive demands usually increase as games progress. Furthermore, playing video games collaboratively with peers can promote cooperative skills, which may transfer to other contexts.

The learning advantages of screen media raise concerns about a "digital divide" between SES and gender groups. Computers and Internet connections are less prevalent in low-SES than in middle-SES homes, and the SES gap in access to tablets and educational apps is even larger (Common Sense Media, 2013; Lenhart et al., 2010). Boys spend more time with screen media than girls and use them somewhat differently. Boys, as mentioned earlier, play games far more often, and they also devote more time to downloading music, creating Web pages, writing computer programs, and using graphics programs. Girls emphasize information gathering and social communication (Lenhart et al., 2010; Looker & Thiessen, 2003; Rideout, Foehr, & Roberts, 2010). Schools need to ensure that girls and economically disadvantaged students have many opportunities to benefit from the diverse, cognitively enriching aspects of screen-media technology.

Because children find mastering complex game elements highly motivating, designing video games to teach academic content is likely to boost achievement for all children. But devoting too much time to computer use—especially playing entertainment video games, even those with nonviolent content—is linked to poorer school performance (Gentile, 2011; Hofferth, 2010). Like entertainment TV (see Chapter 10), excessive game play detracts from time devoted to homework, reading, and other activities that have greater educational benefits.

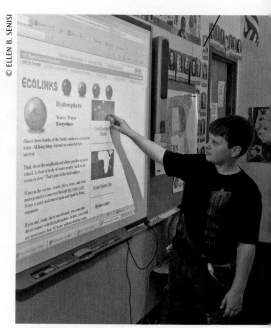

This fifth grader uses a digital whiteboard to interact with an environmental education website. Using the Internet to search for information is linked to better reading achievement and school grades.

Teaching Children with Special Needs

We have seen that effective teachers flexibly adjust their teaching strategies to accommodate students with a wide range of abilities and characteristics. But such adjustments are increasingly difficult at the very low and high ends of the ability distribution. How do schools serve children with special learning needs?

CHILDREN WITH LEARNING DIFFICULTIES   U.S. legislation mandates that schools place children who require special supports for learning in the "least restrictive" (as close to normal as possible) environments that meet their educational needs. In **inclusive classrooms,** students with learning difficulties learn alongside typical students in the regular educational setting for part or all of the school day—a practice designed to prepare them for participation in society and to combat prejudices against individuals with disabilities. Largely as the result of parental pressures, an increasing number of students experience *full inclusion*—full-time placement in regular classrooms.

Students with mild intellectual disability are sometimes integrated into inclusive classrooms. Typically, their IQs fall between 55 and 70, and they also show problems in adaptive behavior, or skills of everyday living (American Psychiatric Association, 2013). But the largest number designated for inclusion—5 to 10 percent of school-age children—have **learning disabilities,** great difficulty with one or more aspects of learning, usually reading. As a result,

In this inclusive classroom, children with special needs learn alongside typical students. Such arrangements can be beneficial, but some students with disabilities are overwhelmed by the academic and social demands of a regular classroom.

their achievement is considerably behind what would be expected on the basis of their IQ. Sometimes, deficits express themselves in other ways—for example, as severe inattention (see page 438), which depresses both intelligence and achievement test scores. The problems of students with learning disabilities cannot be traced to any obvious physical or emotional difficulty or to environmental disadvantage. Instead, deficits in brain functioning are involved (Waber, 2010). Some learning disabilities run in families, and in certain cases, specific genes have been identified that contribute to the problem (Goldstein, 2011). In many instances, the cause is unknown.

Although some students benefit academically from inclusion, many do not. Achievement gains depend on both the severity of the disability and the support services available (Downing, 2010). Furthermore, children with disabilities often are rejected by regular-classroom peers. Students with intellectual disability are overwhelmed by the social skills of their classmates; they cannot interact adeptly in a conversation or game. And the processing deficits of some students with learning disabilities lead to problems in social awareness and responsiveness (Lohrmann & Bambara, 2006; Nowicki, Brown, & Stepien, 2014).

Does this mean that students with special needs cannot be served in regular classrooms? Not necessarily. Often these children do best when they receive instruction in a resource room for part of the day and in the regular classroom for the remainder (McLeskey & Waldron, 2011). In the resource room, a special education teacher works with students on an individual and small-group basis. Then, depending on their progress, children join typically developing classmates for different subjects and amounts of time.

Special steps must be taken to promote positive peer relations in inclusive classrooms. Peer tutoring experiences in which teachers guide typical students in supporting the academic progress of classmates with learning difficulties lead to friendly interaction, improved peer acceptance, and achievement gains (Mastropieri et al., 2013). Teachers can also prepare their class for the arrival of a student with special needs. Under these conditions, inclusion may foster emotional sensitivity and prosocial behavior among regular classmates.

GIFTED CHILDREN In Joey and Lizzie's school, some children were **gifted,** displaying exceptional intellectual strengths. One or two students in every grade have IQ scores above 130, the standard definition of giftedness based on intelligence test performance (Pfeiffer & Yermish, 2014). High-IQ children, as we have seen, have keen memories and an exceptional capacity to solve challenging academic problems. Yet recognition that intelligence tests do not sample the entire range of human cognitive skills, as noted earlier in this chapter, has led to an expanded conception of giftedness.

As sixth graders rehearse a play they have written, they gain experience in generating original ideas, evaluating those ideas, and choosing the most promising—vital ingredients of creativity.

Creativity and Talent. **Creativity** is the ability to produce work that is *original* yet *appropriate*—something that others have not thought of that is useful in some way (Lubart, 2003). A child with high potential for creativity can be designated as gifted. Tests of creative capacity tap **divergent thinking**—the generation of multiple and unusual possibilities when faced with a task or problem. Divergent thinking contrasts sharply with **convergent thinking,** which involves arriving at a single correct answer and is emphasized on intelligence tests (Guilford, 1985).

Because highly creative children (like high-IQ children) are often better at some types of tasks than others, a variety of tests of divergent thinking are available (Runco, 1992; Torrance, 1988). A verbal measure might ask children to name uses for common objects (such as a newspaper). A figural measure might ask them to come up with drawings based on a circular motif (see Figure 12.7). A "real-world problem" measure requires students to suggest solutions to everyday problems. Responses can be scored for the number of ideas generated and their originality.

Yet critics point out that these measures are poor predictors of creative accomplishment in everyday life because they tap only one of the complex cognitive contributions to creativity (Plucker & Makel, 2010). Also involved are defining new and important problems, evaluating divergent ideas, choosing the most promising, and calling on relevant knowledge to understand and solve problems (Lubart, Georgsdottir, & Besançon, 2009).

Consider these ingredients, and you will see why people usually demonstrate expertise and creativity in only one or a few related areas. Even individuals designated as gifted by virtue of their high IQ often show uneven ability across academic subjects. Partly for this reason, definitions of giftedness have been extended to include **talent**—outstanding performance in a specific field. Case studies reveal that excellence in such endeavors as creative writing, mathematics, science, music, visual arts, athletics, and leadership have roots in specialized skills that first appear in childhood (Moran & Gardner, 2006). Highly talented children are biologically prepared to master their domain of interest, and they display a passion for doing so.

But talent must be nurtured. Studies of the backgrounds of talented children and highly accomplished adults often reveal parents who are warm and sensitive, provide a stimulating home life, are devoted to developing their child's abilities, and provide models of hard work and high achievement. These parents are reasonably demanding but not driving or overambitious (Winner, 2000). They arrange for caring teachers while the child is young and for more rigorous master teachers as the child's talent develops.

FIGURE 12.7 **Responses of an 8-year-old who scored high on a figural measure of divergent thinking.** This child was asked to make as many pictures as she could from the circles on the page. The titles she gave her drawings, from left to right, are as follows: "Dracula," "one-eyed monster," "pumpkin," "Hula-Hoop," "poster," "wheelchair," "earth," "stoplight," "planet," "movie camera," "sad face," "picture," "beach ball," "the letter *O*," "car," "glasses." Tests of divergent thinking tap only one of the complex cognitive contributions to creativity. (Reprinted by permission of Laura E. Berk.)

Although most are well-adjusted, gifted children and adolescents are more likely than their typical classmates to experience social isolation, partly because their highly driven, independent styles leave them out of step with peers and partly because they enjoy solitude, which is necessary to develop their talents (Pfeiffer & Yermish, 2014). Still, gifted children desire gratifying peer relationships, and some—more often girls than boys—try to become better-liked by hiding their abilities (Reis, 2004).

Finally, whereas many talented youths become experts in their fields and solve problems in new ways, few become highly creative. Rapidly mastering an existing field and thinking flexibly within it require different skills than innovating in that field. Gifted individuals who are restless with the status quo and daring about changing it are rare. And before these individuals become creative masters, they typically spend a decade or more becoming proficient in their field of interest (Simonton, 2009). The world, however, needs both experts and creators.

Educating the Gifted. Gifted children thrive in learning environments that permit them to choose topics for extended projects, take intellectual risks, reflect on ideas, and interact with like-minded peers. When not sufficiently challenged, they sometimes lose their drive to excel. And when parents and teachers push them too hard, by adolescence they are likely to ask, "Who am I doing this for?" If the answer is not "myself," they may decide not to pursue their gift (Winner, 2000, p. 166).

Although many schools offer programs for the gifted, debate about their effectiveness usually focuses on factors irrelevant to giftedness—whether to provide enrichment in regular classrooms, to pull children out for special instruction (the most common practice), or to advance brighter students to a higher grade. Overall, gifted children fare well within each of these models, as long as special activities promote problem solving, critical thinking, and creativity (Guignard & Lubart, 2007).

Gardner's theory of multiple intelligences has inspired several model programs that provide enrichment to all students in diverse subjects, so any child capable of high-level performance can manifest it. Meaningful activities, each tapping a specific intelligence or set of intelligences, serve as contexts for assessing strengths and weaknesses and, on that basis, teaching new knowledge and original thinking (Gardner, 2000; Hoerr, 2004). For example, linguistic intelligence might be fostered through storytelling or playwriting; spatial intelligence through drawing, sculpting, or taking apart and reassembling objects; and kinesthetic intelligence through dance or pantomime.

Evidence is still needed on how effectively these programs nurture children's talents and creativity. But they have already succeeded in one way—by highlighting the strengths of some students who previously had been considered unexceptional or even at risk for school failure (Ford, 2012). Consequently, they may be especially useful in identifying talented low-SES, ethnic minority children, who are often underrepresented in programs for the gifted.

How Well-Educated Are U.S. Children?

Our discussion of schooling has largely focused on how teachers can support the education of children. Yet we have also seen that many factors—both within and outside schools—affect children's learning. Societal values, school resources, quality of teaching, and parental encouragement all play important roles. These multiple influences are especially apparent when schooling is examined in cross-cultural perspective.

In international studies of reading, mathematics, and science achievement, young people in China, Korea, and Japan are consistently top performers. Among Western nations, Canada, Finland, the Netherlands, and Switzerland are also in the top tier. But U.S. students typically perform at or below the international averages (see Figure 12.8) (Programme for International Student Assessment, 2012).

Why do U.S. students fall behind in academic accomplishments? According to international comparisons, instruction in the United States is less challenging, more focused on absorbing facts, and less focused on high-level reasoning and critical thinking than in other countries. A growing number of experts believe that the U.S. No Child Left Behind Act has contributed to these trends because it mandates severe sanctions for schools whose students do not meet targeted goals on achievement tests—initially, student transfers to higher-performing schools; and ultimately, staff firing, closure, state takeover, or other restructuring (Darling-Hammond, 2010; Kew et al., 2012; Ravitch, 2010).

Furthermore, countries with large socioeconomic inequalities (such as the United States) rank lower in achievement, in part because low-SES children tend to live in less favorable families and neighborhoods (Condron, 2013). But the United States is also far less equitable than top achieving countries in the quality of education it provides its low-SES and ethnic minority students. U.S. teachers, for example, vary much more in training, salaries, and teaching conditions.

Finland is a case in point. In the 1980s, it abandoned a national testing system used to ability-group students and replaced it with curricula, teaching practices, and assessments aimed at cultivating initiative, problem solving, and creativity—vital abilities needed for success in the twenty-first century. Finnish teachers are highly trained: They must complete several years of graduate-level education at government expense (Ripley, 2013). And Finnish education is grounded in equal opportunity for all—a policy that has nearly eliminated SES variations in achievement, despite an influx of immigrant students from low-income families into Finnish schools over the past decade.

	Country	Average Math Achievement Score
High-Performing Nations	China (Shanghai)	613
	Singapore	573
	China (Hong Kong)	561
	Taiwan	560
	Korea	554
	China (Macao)	538
	Japan	536
	Switzerland	531
	Netherlands	523
	Estonia	521
	Finland	519
	Canada	518
	Poland	518
	Belgium	515
	Germany	514
Intermediate-Performing Nations	Austria	506
	Australia	504
	Ireland	501
	Slovenia	501
	Denmark	500
	New Zealand	500
	Czech Republic	499
	France	495
International Average = 494	United Kingdom	494
	Iceland	493
	Luxembourg	490
	Norway	489
	Portugal	487
	Italy	485
	Spain	484
	Russian Federation	482
	United States	**481**
	Sweden	478
	Hungary	477
Low-Performing Nations	Israel	466
	Greece	453
	Turkey	448
	Romania	445

FIGURE 12.8 **Average mathematics scores of 15-year-olds by country.** The Programme for International Student Assessment measured achievement in many nations around the world. In recent comparisons of countries' performance, the United States performed below the international average in math; in reading and science, its performance was about average. (Adapted from Programme for International Student Assessment, 2012.)

In-depth research on learning environments in Asian nations, such as Japan, Korea, and Taiwan, also highlights social forces that foster strong student learning. Among these is cultural valuing of effort. Whereas American parents and teachers tend to regard native ability as the key to academic success, Japanese, Korean, and Taiwanese parents and teachers believe that all children can succeed academically as long as they try hard. Asian parents devote many more hours to helping their children with homework (Stevenson, Lee, & Mu, 2000). And Asian children, influenced by interdependent values, typically view striving to do well in school as a moral obligation—part of their responsibility to family and community (Hau & Ho, 2010).

As in Finland, all students in Japan, Korea, and Taiwan receive the same nationally mandated, high-quality instruction, delivered by teachers who are well-prepared, highly respected in their society, and far better paid than U.S. teachers (Kang & Hong, 2008; U.S. Department of Education, 2014). Academic lessons are particularly well-organized and presented in ways that capture children's attention and encourage high-level thinking (Grow-Maienza, Hahn, & Joo, 2001). And Japanese teachers are three times as likely as U.S. teachers to work outside class with students who need extra help (Woodward & Ono, 2004).

Finnish students explain the results of a static electricity experiment. Their country's education system—designed to cultivate initiative, problem solving, and creativity in all students—has nearly eliminated SES variations in achievement.

The Finnish and Asian examples underscore the need for American families, schools, and the larger society to work together to upgrade education. Over the past fifteen years, U.S. international rankings in reading, math, and science achievement have declined. And although the U.S. National Assessment of Educational Progress—in which challenging achievement tests are given to nationally representative samples of 9-, 13-, and 17-year-olds—has shown slight gains in reading and moderate gains in math since 1990, the increments have not been sufficient to catch up internationally (U.S. Department of Education, 2014).

These disappointing achievement outcomes underscore the need for "a broader, bolder approach to U.S. education." Recommended strategies, verified by research, include:

- supporting parents in attaining economic security, creating stimulating home learning environments, monitoring their children's academic progress, and communicating often with teachers
- investing in high-quality preschool education, so every child arrives at school ready to learn
- strengthening teacher education
- providing intellectually challenging, relevant instruction with real-world applications
- vigorously pursuing school improvements that reduce the large inequities in quality of education between SES and ethnic groups.

Ask Yourself

- **REVIEW** List some teaching practices that foster children's academic achievement and some that undermine it. For each practice, explain why it is or is not effective.

- **CONNECT** Review research on child-rearing styles on pages 392–394 in Chapter 10. What style do gifted children who realize their potential typically experience? Explain.

- **APPLY** Sandy wonders why her daughter Mira's teacher often has students work on assignments in small, cooperative groups. Explain the benefits of this approach to Sandy. What must Mira's teacher do to ensure that cooperative learning succeeds?

- **REFLECT** What grouping practices were used in your elementary education—homogeneous, heterogeneous, or a combination? What impact do you think those practices had on your motivation and achievement?

Summary

Piaget's Theory: The Concrete Operational Stage (p. 429)

12.1 What are the major characteristics of concrete operational thought?

- In the **concrete operational stage,** children's thought becomes more logical, flexible, and organized. Mastery of conservation requires **decentration** and **reversibility** in thinking.

- School-age children are also better at hierarchical classification and **seriation,** including **transitive inference,** the ability to seriate mentally. Their spatial reasoning improves, as illustrated by their understanding of **cognitive maps.** By the end of middle childhood, they form accurate overall views of large-scale spaces and grasp the meaning of scale and map symbols.

12.2 Discuss follow-up research on concrete operational thought.

- Concrete operational children think logically only when dealing with concrete, tangible information, and mastery of concrete operational tasks occurs gradually. Specific cultural practices, especially those associated with schooling, promote mastery of Piagetian tasks.

- Some researchers attribute the gradual development of operational thought to expansion of information-processing capacity. Case's neo-Piagetian theory proposes that gains in working-memory efficiency explain cognitive change, within and between stages. With practice, cognitive schemes become more automatic, freeing up space in working memory for combining old schemes and generating new ones. Eventually, children consolidate schemes into central conceptual structures and are increasingly able to coordinate multiple dimensions.

Information Processing (p. 434)

12.3 Cite basic changes in information processing, and describe the development of attention and memory in middle childhood.

- Marked improvement in executive function enables school-age children to handle increasingly complex tasks that require integration of working memory, inhibition, and flexible thinking. Heredity and environment combine to influence various executive processes.

- Increased speed of thinking supports gains in working-memory capacity. Children with working-memory deficits suffer from persistent learning difficulties in school.

- During middle childhood, attention becomes more sustained, selective, and flexible. Deficits in executive processing and inhibition may underlie symptoms of **attention-deficit hyperactivity disorder (ADHD),** which leads to serious academic and social problems.

- Children become better at planning, particularly when adults turn over responsibility to them and guide and support them as needed.

- Memory strategies also improve. **Rehearsal** appears first, followed by **organization** and then **elaboration.** With age, children use several memory strategies at once.

- Development of the long-term knowledge base facilitates strategic memory processing, as does children's motivation to use what they know. Memory strategies are not used by children in village cultures who have no formal schooling. Societal modernization is broadly associated with improved cognitive performance.

12.4 Describe the school-age child's theory of mind and capacity to engage in self-regulation.

- Metacognition expands as school-age children view the mind as an active, constructive agent. Consequently, they better understand cognitive processes and factors that influence them. Awareness of the role of mental inferences enables mastery of second-order false belief and promotes **recursive thought.** School-age children also become increasingly conscious of how and why mental strategies work and able to discriminate good from bad reasoning.

- **Cognitive self-regulation** develops gradually. It improves with adult instruction in effective strategy use and predicts academic success.

12.5 Discuss current perspectives on teaching reading and mathematics to elementary school children.

- Skilled reading draws on all aspects of the information-processing system. A combination of **whole-language** and **phonics** is most effective for teaching beginning reading.

- Teaching that combines practice in basic skills with conceptual understanding also is best in mathematics. Students benefit from extensive opportunities to experiment with strategies and reason about number concepts.

Individual Differences in Mental Development (p. 446)

12.6 Describe major approaches to defining intelligence.

- During the school years, IQ becomes more stable and correlates moderately with academic achievement. Most intelligence tests yield an overall score as well as scores for separate intellectual factors. The *Stanford-Binet Intelligence Scales,* Fifth Edition, and the *Wechsler Intelligence Scale for Children–IV (WISC–IV)* are widely used individually administered intelligence tests.

- The componential approach to defining intelligence seeks to identify the inner, information-processing skills that contribute to mental test performance. Speed of thinking, working-memory capacity, flexible attention, and memory and reasoning strategies are positively related to IQ.

- Sternberg's **triarchic theory of successful intelligence** views intelligence as an interaction of analytical intelligence (information-processing skills), creative intelligence (ability to solve novel problems), and practical intelligence (application of intellectual skills in everyday situations).

- Gardner's **theory of multiple intelligences** identifies at least eight mental abilities, each with a distinct biological basis and course of development. It has been helpful in stimulating efforts to define, measure, and foster emotional intelligence.

12.7 Describe evidence indicating that both heredity and environment contribute to intelligence.

- Heritability estimates and adoption research reveal that intelligence is a product of both heredity and environment. Adoption studies along with the **Flynn effect**—dramatic generational gains in IQ—suggest that environmental factors account for the black–white IQ gap.

- IQ scores are affected by culturally influenced language and communication styles, knowledge, and sheer amount of time spent in school. **Stereotype threat** can trigger anxiety that impairs test performance. **Dynamic assessment** helps many minority children perform more competently on mental tests.

Language Development (p. 455)

12.8 Describe changes in metalinguistic awareness, vocabulary, grammar, and pragmatics during middle childhood.

- Schooling, especially reading, contributes greatly to **metalinguistic awareness** and other complex language competencies. Vocabulary continues to grow rapidly, and children have a more precise and flexible understanding of word meanings. They also use more complex grammatical constructions and conversational strategies, and their narratives increase in organization, detail, and expressiveness.

12.9 Describe bilingual development, along with advantages of bilingualism in childhood.

- Children who learn two languages in early childhood acquire each according to a typical timetable. When school-age children acquire a second language, they typically take 5 to 7 years to attain the competence of native-speaking agemates.
- Bilingual children are better at diverse executive-function skills and certain aspects of metalinguistic awareness. They transfer their phonological awareness skills in one language to the other, which enhances reading achievement.
- In Canada, language immersion programs succeed in developing children who are proficient in both English and French. In the United States, bilingual education that combines instruction in the native language and in English supports academic learning in children with limited English proficiency.

Children's Learning in School
(p. 459)

12.10 Describe the impact of class size and educational philosophies on children's motivation and academic achievement.

- As class size declines, academic achievement improves. Older students in **traditional classrooms** have a slight edge in academic achievement over those in **constructivist classrooms,** who gain in academic motivation, critical thinking, and social and moral maturity.
- Vygotsky-inspired **social-constructivist classrooms** use the rich social context of the classroom to promote learning, often employing such methods as **reciprocal teaching** and **communities of learners.** Students benefit from working collaboratively and from teaching adapted to each child's zone of proximal development.

ALISTAIR BERG/DIGITAL VISION/ GETTY IMAGES

12.11 Discuss the role of teacher–student interaction and grouping practices in academic achievement.

- Caring, helpful, and stimulating teaching fosters children's motivation and academic achievement. **Educational self-fulfilling prophecies** have a greater impact on low achievers and are most likely to occur in homogenous classrooms and ones that emphasize competition and public evaluation.
- To benefit from collaboration with heterogeneous peers, children need extensive training in **cooperative learning.** Ethnically diverse magnet schools are also associated with higher achievement.

12.12 Describe benefits of, as well as concerns about, educational media.

- Using screen media for schoolwork, including searching for information, preparing assignments, and playing academic and nonviolent adventure games, has cognitive benefits and is linked to improved achievement. Low-SES children are disadvantaged in computer and Internet use, and boys tend to be more skilled at complex computer activities than girls.

12.13 Under what conditions is placement of children with mild intellectual disability or learning disabilities in regular classrooms successful?

- Students with mild intellectual disability and **learning disabilities** are often placed in **inclusive classrooms** where they learn alongside typical students. Success depends on meeting individual academic needs and promoting positive peer relations.

12.14 Describe the characteristics of gifted children and efforts to meet their educational needs.

- **Giftedness** includes high IQ, **creativity,** and **talent.** Tests of creativity that tap **divergent thinking** rather than **convergent thinking** focus on only one of the complex cognitive ingredients of creativity. Gifted children are more likely than their peers to experience social isolation.
- Gifted children who thrive have parents and teachers who nurture their extraordinary abilities and make reasonable demands. They are best served by educational programs that build on their special strengths.

12.15 How well-educated are U.S. children compared with children in other industrialized nations?

- In international studies, U.S. students typically display average or below-average performance. Compared with education in top-achieving nations, U.S. instruction is less focused on high-level reasoning and critical thinking. Whereas high-achieving nations emphasize equal opportunity for all, U.S. low-income and ethnic minority students typically attend inferior-quality schools.

Important Terms and Concepts

attention-deficit hyperactivity disorder (ADHD) (p. 438)
cognitive maps (p. 430)
cognitive self-regulation (p. 442)
communities of learners (p. 462)
concrete operational stage (p. 429)
constructivist classroom (p. 460)
convergent thinking (p. 466)
cooperative learning (p. 463)
creativity (p. 466)
decentration (p. 429)
divergent thinking (p. 466)

dynamic assessment (p. 454)
educational self-fulfilling prophecies (p. 462)
elaboration (p. 438)
Flynn effect (p. 452)
gifted (p. 466)
inclusive classrooms (p. 465)
learning disabilities (p. 465)
metalinguistic awareness (p. 455)
organization (p. 437)
phonics approach (p. 443)
reciprocal teaching (p. 461)
recursive thought (p. 441)

rehearsal (p. 437)
reversibility (p. 429)
seriation (p. 430)
social-constructivist classroom (p. 461)
stereotype threat (p. 453)
talent (p. 467)
theory of multiple intelligences (p. 449)
traditional classroom (p. 460)
transitive inference (p. 430)
triarchic theory of successful intelligence (p. 448)
whole-language approach (p. 443)

chapter 13

Emotional and Social Development in Middle Childhood

REPRINTED WITH PERMISSION FROM THE INTERNATIONAL MUSEUM OF CHILDREN'S ART, OSLO, NORWAY

"Our Multiracial and Multireligious Society"
Tay Xue Er
9 years, Singapore

As this artist's colorful portrayal of ethnic and religious diversity suggests, school-age children become capable of viewing themselves and others from multiple perspectives. This change contributes to improved self-understanding, a more flexible grasp of moral obligations, declining racial and ethnic prejudices, and deepening friendships.

One afternoon as school dismissed, Joey urgently tapped his best friend Terry on the shoulder. "Gotta talk to you," Joey pleaded. "Everything was going great until I got that word—*porcupine*," Joey went on, referring to the fifth-grade spelling bee that day. "Just my luck! *P-o-r-k*, that's how I spelled it! I can't believe it. Maybe I'm not so good at social studies," Joey confided, "but I *know* I'm better at spelling than that stuck-up Belinda Brown. I knocked myself out studying those spelling lists. Then *she* got all the easy words. If I *had* to lose, why couldn't it be to a nice person?"

Joey's conversation reflects new emotional and social capacities. By entering the spelling bee, he shows *industriousness,* the energetic pursuit of meaningful achievement in his culture—a major change of middle childhood. Joey's social understanding has also expanded. He can size up strengths, weaknesses, and personality characteristics. Furthermore, friendship means something different to Joey than it did earlier: He counts on his best friend, Terry, for understanding and emotional support.

For an overview of the personality changes of middle childhood, we return to Erikson's theory. Then we look at children's views of themselves and of others, their moral understanding, and their peer relationships. Each increases in complexity as children reason more effectively and spend more time in school and with agemates.

Despite changing parent–child relationships, the family remains powerfully influential in middle childhood. Today, family lifestyles are more diverse than ever before. Through Joey's and his younger sister Lizzie's experiences with parental divorce, we will see that family functioning is far more important than family structure in ensuring children's well-being. Finally, we look at some common emotional problems of middle childhood. ■

Erikson's Theory: Industry versus Inferiority

According to Erikson (1950), children whose previous experiences have been positive enter middle childhood prepared to redirect their energies from the make-believe of early childhood into realistic accomplishment. Erikson believed that the combination of adult expectations and children's drive toward mastery sets the stage for the psychological conflict of middle childhood: **industry versus inferiority,** which is resolved positively when experiences lead children to develop a sense of competence at useful skills and tasks.

In cultures everywhere, adults respond to children's improved physical and cognitive capacities by making new demands, and children are ready to benefit from those challenges. Among the Baka hunters and gatherers of Cameroon, 5- to 7-year-olds fetch and carry water, bathe and mind younger siblings, and accompany adults on food-gathering missions. In a miniature village behind the main camp, children practice hut building, spear shaping, and fire making (Avis & Harris, 1991). The Ngoni of Malawi, Central Africa, believe that when children shed their first teeth,

13.1 What personality changes take place during Erikson's stage of industry versus inferiority?

they are mature enough for intensive skill training. Six and 7-year-old boys move out of family huts into dormitories, where they enter a system of male domination and instruction (Rogoff, 1996). All children of this age are expected to show independence and are held accountable for irresponsible and disrespectful behavior.

In industrialized nations, the beginning of formal schooling marks the transition to middle childhood. With it comes literacy training, which prepares children for a vast array of specialized careers. In school, children discover their own and others' unique capacities, learn the value of division of labor, and develop a sense of moral commitment and responsibility. The danger at this stage is *inferiority,* reflected in the pessimism of children who have little confidence in their ability to do things well. This sense of inadequacy can develop when family life has not prepared children for school life or when teachers and peers destroy children's feelings of competence and mastery with negative responses.

Erikson's sense of industry combines several developments of middle childhood: a positive but realistic self-concept, pride in accomplishment, moral responsibility, and cooperative participation with agemates. How do these aspects of self and social relationships change over the school years?

The industriousness of middle childhood involves responding to new expectations for realistic accomplishment. In the informal, encouraging atmosphere of this classroom in India, children come to view themselves as responsible, capable, and cooperative.

13.2 Describe school-age children's self-concept and self-esteem, and discuss factors that affect their achievement-related attributions.

Self-Understanding

In middle childhood, children become able to describe themselves in terms of psychological traits, to compare their own characteristics with those of their peers, and to speculate about the causes of their strengths and weaknesses. These transformations in self-understanding have a major impact on children's self-esteem.

Self-Concept

During the school years, children refine their self-concept, organizing their observations of behaviors and internal states into general dispositions. A major change takes place between ages 8 and 11, as the following self-description by an 11-year-old illustrates:

> My name is A. I'm a human being. I'm a girl. I'm a truthful person. I'm not pretty. I do so-so in my studies. I'm a very good cellist. I'm a very good pianist. I'm a little bit tall for my age. I like several boys. I like several girls. I'm old-fashioned. I play tennis. I am a very good swimmer. I try to be helpful. I'm always ready to be friends with anybody. Mostly I'm good, but I lose my temper. I'm not well liked by some girls and boys. I don't know if I'm liked by boys or not. (Montemayor & Eisen, 1977, pp. 317–318)

Instead of specific behaviors, this child emphasizes competencies: "a very good cellist," "so-so in my studies" (Damon & Hart, 1988). She also describes her personality, mentioning both positive and negative traits: "truthful" but short-tempered. Older school-age children are far less likely than younger children to describe themselves in extreme, all-or-none ways (Harter, 2012a).

These evaluative self-descriptions result from school-age children's frequent **social comparisons**—judgments of their appearance, abilities, and behavior in relation to those of others. For example, Joey observed that he was "better at spelling" than his peers but "not so good at social studies." Whereas 4- to 6-year-olds can compare their own performance to that of a single peer, older children can compare multiple individuals, including themselves (Butler, 1998; Harter, 2012a).

Cognitive, Social, and Cultural Influences on Self-Concept

What factors account for these revisions in self-concept? Cognitive development affects the changing *structure* of the self. School-age children, as we saw in Chapter 12, can better coordinate several aspects of a situation in reasoning about their physical world. Similarly, in the social realm, they combine typical experiences and behaviors into stable psychological dispositions, blend positive and negative characteristics, and compare their own characteristics with those of many peers (Harter, 2012a). In middle childhood, children also gain a clearer understanding that traits are linked to specific desires (a "generous" person *wants* to share) and, therefore, are causes of behavior (Yuill & Pearson, 1998).

The changing *content* of self-concept is a product of both cognitive capacities and feedback from others. Sociologist George Herbert Mead (1934) proposed that a well-organized psychological self emerges when children adopt a view of the self that resembles others' attitudes toward the child. Mead's ideas indicate that *perspective-taking skills*—in particular, an improved ability to infer what other people are thinking and to distinguish those viewpoints from one's own—are crucial for developing a self-concept based on personality traits. As we saw in Chapter 12, middle childhood brings the capacity for recursive thought, which enables school-age children to "read" others' messages more accurately and internalize their expectations. As they do so, they form an *ideal self* that they use to evaluate their real self. As we will see, a large discrepancy between the two can greatly undermine self-esteem, leading to sadness, hopelessness, and depression.

As school-age children enter a wider range of settings beyond the family, their self-concepts include frequent reference to social groups. When asked about themselves, these baseball players are likely to mention being a member of a Little League team.

Parental support for self-development continues to be vitally important. School-age children with a history of elaborative parent–child conversations about past experiences construct a rich, positive narrative about the self and thus have more complex, favorable, and coherent self-concepts (Harter, 2012a). Children also look to more people beyond the family for information about themselves as they enter a wider range of settings in school and community. And self-descriptions now include frequent reference to social groups: "I'm a Boy Scout, a paper boy, and a Prairie City soccer player," said Joey. As children move into adolescence, their sources of self-definition become more selective. Although parents and other adults remain influential, self-concept is increasingly vested in feedback from close friends (Oosterwegel & Oppenheimer, 1993).

But recall that the content of self-concept varies from culture to culture. In earlier chapters, we noted that Asian parents stress harmonious interdependence, whereas Western parents emphasize independence and self-assertion. When asked to recall personally significant past experiences (their last birthday, a time their parent scolded them), U.S. school-age children gave longer accounts including more personal preferences, interests, skills, and opinions. Chinese children, in contrast, more often referred to social interactions and to others rather than themselves. Similarly, in their self-descriptions, U.S. children listed more personal attributes ("I'm smart," "I like hockey"), Chinese children more attributes involving group membership and relationships with others ("I'm in second grade," "My friends are crazy about me") (Wang, 2006b; Wang, Shao, & Li, 2010).

LOOK and **LISTEN**

Ask several 8- to 11-year-old children to tell you about themselves. Do their self-descriptions include personality traits (both positive and negative), social comparisons, and references to social groups, as is typical in middle childhood?

Self-Esteem

Recall that most preschoolers have extremely high self-esteem. But as children enter school and receive much more feedback about how well they perform compared with their peers, self-esteem differentiates and also adjusts to a more realistic level.

To study school-age children's self-esteem, researchers ask them to indicate the extent to which statements such as "I'm good at reading" or "I'm usually the one chosen for games" are true of themselves. By age 6 to 7, children in diverse Western cultures have formed at least four

PHOTOS FROM LEFT TO RIGHT: © ELLEN B. SENISI; © TIM PANNELL/CORBIS; © MITCH WOJNAROWICZ/THE IMAGE WORKS; © RADIUS IMAGES/PHOTOLIBRARY

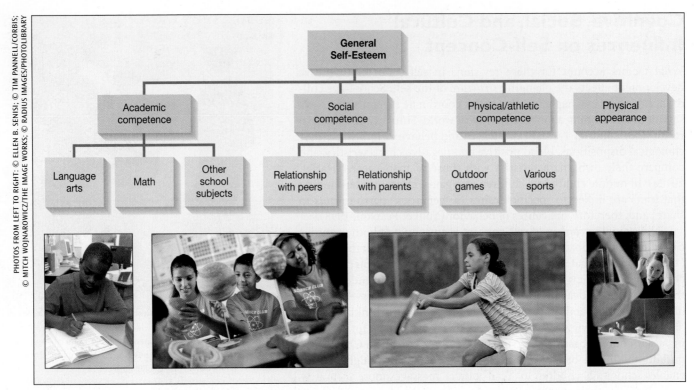

FIGURE 13.1 **Hierarchical structure of self-esteem in the mid-elementary school years.** From their experiences in different settings, children form at least four separate self-esteems: academic competence, social competence, physical/athletic competence, and physical appearance. These differentiate into additional self-evaluations and combine to form a general sense of self-esteem.

broad self-evaluations: academic competence, social competence, physical/athletic competence, and physical appearance. Within these are more refined categories that become increasingly distinct with age (Marsh, 1990; Marsh & Ayotte, 2003; Van den Bergh & De Rycke, 2003). Furthermore, the capacity to view the self in terms of stable dispositions permits school-age children to combine their separate self-evaluations into a general psychological image of themselves—an overall sense of self-esteem (Harter, 2012a). As a result, self-esteem takes on the hierarchical structure shown in Figure 13.1.

Children attach greater importance to certain self-evaluations than to others. Although individual differences exist, during childhood and adolescence perceived physical appearance correlates more strongly with overall self-worth than does any other self-esteem factor (O'Dea, 2012; Shapka & Keating, 2005). Emphasis on appearance—in the media, by parents and peers, and in society—has major implications for young people's overall satisfaction with themselves.

Self-esteem generally remains high during elementary school but becomes more realistic and nuanced as children evaluate themselves in various areas (Marsh, Craven, & Debus, 1998; Wigfield et al., 1997). These changes occur as children receive more competence-related feedback, as their performances are increasingly judged in relation to those of others, and as they become cognitively capable of social comparison (Harter, 2012a).

Influences on Self-Esteem

From middle childhood on, individual differences in self-esteem become increasingly stable (Trzesniewski, Donnellan, & Robins, 2003). And positive relationships among self-esteem, valuing of various activities, and success at those activities emerge and strengthen with age. Academic self-esteem predicts how important, useful, and enjoyable children judge school subjects to be, their willingness to try hard, and their achievement (Denissen, Zarrett, & Eccles, 2007; Valentine, DuBois, & Cooper, 2004; Whitesell et al., 2009). Children with high social self-esteem are consistently better-liked by classmates (Jacobs et al., 2002). And as we saw in Chapter 11, sense of athletic competence is positively associated with investment in and performance at sports.

Furthermore, across age, sex, SES, and ethnic groups, individuals with favorable self-esteem tend to be well-adjusted, sociable, and conscientious. In contrast, a profile of low self-esteem in all areas is linked to anxiety, depression, and antisocial behavior (DuBois et al., 1999; Robins et al., 2001; Sowislo & Orth, 2013).

CULTURE AND GENDER   Cultural forces profoundly affect self-esteem. An especially strong emphasis on social comparison in school may explain why Chinese and Japanese children, despite their higher academic achievement, score lower than U.S. children in self-esteem— a difference that widens with age (Harter, 2012a; Twenge & Crocker, 2002). At the same time, because their culture values modesty and social harmony, Asian children rely less on social comparisons to promote their own self-esteem. Rather, they tend to be reserved in positive self-judgments but generous in praise of others (Falbo et al., 1997).

Gender-stereotyped beliefs also affect self-esteem. In one study, the more 5- to 8-year-old girls talked with friends about the way people look, watched TV shows focusing on physical appearance, and perceived their friends as valuing thinness, the greater their dissatisfaction with their physical self and the lower their overall self-esteem a year later (Dohnt & Tiggemann, 2006). And in an investigation of third-graders, being overweight was more strongly linked to negative body image for girls than boys (Shriver et al., 2013). By the end of middle childhood, girls feel less confident than boys about their physical appearance and athletic abilities. With respect to academic self-esteem, boys, again, are somewhat advantaged: Whereas girls score higher in language-arts self-esteem, boys have higher math and science self-esteem—even when children of equal skill levels are compared (Jacobs et al., 2002; Kurtz-Costes et al., 2008). At the same time, girls exceed boys in self-esteem dimensions of close friendship and social acceptance.

Children learn African drumming skills at a community center during Kwanzaa, a holiday honoring their African heritage. A stronger sense of ethnic pride may contribute to slightly higher self-esteem among African-American children compared with their Caucasian agemates.

Compared with their Caucasian agemates, African-American children tend to have slightly higher self-esteem, perhaps because of warm extended families and a stronger sense of ethnic pride (Gray-Little & Hafdahl, 2000; Harter, 2012a). But media exposure has the opposite effect: The more TV African-American children watch, the lower their self-esteem—an association that also applies to Caucasian girls. In contrast, TV viewing predicts higher self-esteem among Caucasian boys (Martins & Harrison, 2012). Ethnic and gender stereotypes in TV programs may explain these findings. Finally, children and adolescents who attend schools or live in neighborhoods where their SES and ethnic groups are well-represented feel a stronger sense of belonging and have fewer self-esteem problems (Gray-Little & Carels, 1997).

CHILD-REARING PRACTICES   Children whose parents use an *authoritative* child-rearing style (see Chapter 10) feel especially good about themselves (Lindsey et al, 2008; McKinney, Donnelly, & Renk, 2008). Warm, positive parenting lets children know that they are accepted as competent and worthwhile. And firm but appropriate expectations, backed up with explanations, help them evaluate their own behavior against reasonable standards.

Controlling parents—those who too often help or make decisions for their child—communicate a sense of inadequacy to children. Having parents who are repeatedly disapproving and insulting is also linked to low self-esteem (Kernis, 2002; Pomerantz & Eaton, 2000). Children subjected to such parenting need constant reassurance, and many rely heavily on peers to affirm their self-worth—a risk factor for adjustment difficulties, including aggression and antisocial behavior (Donnellan et al., 2005). In contrast, indulgent parenting is associated with unrealistically high self-esteem, which also undermines development. These children—whom researchers label *narcissistic* because they combine an inflated sense of superiority with obsessive worry about what others think of them—are vulnerable to temporary, sharp drops in self-esteem when their overblown self-images are challenged (Thomaes et al., 2013). They tend to lash out at peers who express disapproval and display adjustment problems, including meanness and aggression (Hughes, Cavell, & Grossman, 1997; Thomaes et al., 2008).

American cultural values have increasingly emphasized a focus on the self that may lead parents to indulge children and boost their self-esteem too much. The self-esteem of U.S. youths has risen sharply in recent decades—a period in which parenting literature, educational policies, and social programs have advised promoting children's self-esteem (Gentile, Twenge, & Campbell, 2010). Research, however, confirms that children do not benefit from compliments ("You're terrific") that have no basis in real accomplishment (Wentzel & Brophy, 2014). Rather, the best way to foster a positive, secure self-image is to encourage children to strive for worthwhile goals. Over time, a bidirectional relationship emerges: Achievement fosters self-esteem, which contributes to further effort and gains in performance (Marsh et al., 2005).

What can adults do to promote, and to avoid undermining, this mutually supportive relationship between motivation and self-esteem? Some answers come from research on the precise content of adults' messages to children in achievement situations. Let's look first at the meanings children assign to their successes and failures.

ACHIEVEMENT-RELATED ATTRIBUTIONS   *Attributions* are our common, everyday explanations for the causes of behavior. Notice how Joey, in talking about the spelling bee at the beginning of this chapter, attributes his disappointing performance to *luck* (Belinda got all the easy words) and his usual success to *ability* (he *knows* he's a better speller than Belinda). Joey also appreciates that *effort* matters: "I knocked myself out studying those spelling lists."

The combination of improved reasoning skills and frequent evaluative feedback permits 10- to 12-year-olds to separate all these variables in explaining performance (Dweck, 2002). Those who are high in academic self-esteem and motivation make **mastery-oriented attributions,** crediting their successes to ability—a characteristic they can improve by trying hard and can count on when faced with new challenges. This *incremental view of ability*—that it can increase through effort—influences the way mastery-oriented children interpret negative events. They attribute failure to factors that can be changed and controlled, such as insufficient effort or a difficult task (Dweck & Molden, 2013). So whether these children succeed or fail, they take an industrious, persistent approach to learning.

In contrast, children who develop **learned helplessness** attribute their failures, not their successes, to ability. When they succeed, they are likely to conclude that external factors, such as luck, are responsible. Unlike their mastery-oriented counterparts, they hold a *fixed view of ability*—that it cannot be improved by trying hard (Dweck & Molden, 2013). When a task is difficult, these children experience an anxious loss of control—in Erikson's terms, a pervasive sense of inferiority. They give up without really trying.

Children's attributions affect their goals. Mastery-oriented children focus on *learning goals*—seeking information on how best to increase their ability through effort. Hence, their performance improves over time (Dweck & Molden, 2013). In contrast, learned-helpless children focus on *performance goals*—obtaining positive and avoiding negative evaluations of their fragile sense of ability. Gradually their ability ceases to predict how well they do. In one study, the more fourth to sixth graders held self-critical attributions, the lower they rated their competence, the less they knew about effective study strategies, the more they avoided challenge, and the poorer their academic performance. These outcomes strengthened their fixed view of ability (Pomerantz & Saxon, 2001). Because learned-helpless children fail to connect effort with success, they do not develop the metacognitive and self-regulatory skills necessary for high achievement (see Chapter 12). Lack of effective learning strategies, reduced persistence, and a sense of loss of control sustain one another in a vicious cycle.

INFLUENCES ON ACHIEVEMENT-RELATED ATTRIBUTIONS   What accounts for the different attributions of mastery-oriented and learned-helpless children? Adult communication plays a key role. When parents hold a fixed view of ability, their perceptions of children's academic competence tend to act as self-fulfilling prophecies (see page 462 in Chapter 12). Their children's self-evaluations and school grades conform more closely to parental ability judgments than do those of children whose parents deny that ability is fixed (Pomerantz & Dong, 2006). Parents who believe little can be done to improve ability may ignore information that is inconsistent with their perceptions, giving their child little opportunity to counteract a negative parental evaluation. Indeed, children with a learned-helpless style often have parents who believe their child is not very capable and must work much harder than others to succeed.

When the child fails, the parent might say, "You can't do that, can you? It's OK if you quit" (Hokoda & Fincham, 1995).

When a child succeeds, adults can offer **person praise,** which emphasizes the child's traits ("You're so smart"; "you're very artistic"), or **process praise,** which emphasizes behavior and effort ("you worked really hard"; "you figured it out"). Research indicates that adults use more person praise with children low in self-esteem and more process praise with children high in self-esteem. Perhaps they believe that any positive messages about children's characteristics can help raise self-esteem. But children—especially those with low self-esteem—respond unfavorably to person praise. They feel more shame following failure if they previously received person praise, less shame if they previously received process praise or no praise at all (Brummelman et al., 2014). Consistent with a learned-helpless orientation, person praise teaches children that abilities are fixed, which leads them to question their competence in the face of failure and retreat from challenges (Pomerantz & Kempner, 2013; Skipper & Douglas, 2012). In contrast, process praise implies that competence develops through persistence and hard work, consistent with a mastery orientation (Pomerantz, Grolnick, & Price, 2013).

When adults offer process praise emphasizing behavior and effort, children learn that persistence and hard work build competence. Teacher remarks such as, "You found a good way to solve that problem!" will foster a mastery-oriented approach in this student.

Teachers' messages also affect children's attributions. Teachers who are caring and helpful and who emphasize learning over getting good grades tend to have mastery-oriented students (Anderman et al., 2001). In a study of third to eighth graders, students who viewed their teachers as providing positive, supportive learning conditions worked harder and participated more in class—factors that predicted high achievement, which sustained children's belief in the role of effort. In contrast, students with unsupportive teachers regarded their performance as externally controlled (by their teachers or by luck). This attitude predicted withdrawal from learning activities and declining achievement—outcomes that led children to doubt their ability (Skinner, Zimmer-Gembeck, & Connell, 1998).

For some children, performance is especially likely to be undermined by adult feedback. Despite their higher achievement, girls more often than boys attribute poor performance to lack of ability. When girls do not do well, they tend to receive messages from teachers and parents that their ability is at fault, and negative stereotypes (for example, that girls are weak at math) undermine their interest and performance (Gunderson et al., 2012; Tomasetto, Alparone, & Cadinu, 2011). And as Chapter 12 revealed, low-SES ethnic minority students often receive less favorable feedback from teachers, especially when assigned to homogeneous groups of poorly achieving students—conditions that result in a drop in academic self-esteem and achievement (Harris & Graham, 2007).

Cognitive development also affects attributions. Five- and 6-year-olds tend to believe, optimistically, that undesirable traits such as messiness, clumsiness, attention problems, or learning difficulties will improve greatly with age. In contrast, 7- to 10-year-olds' views are more realistic. They recognize that negative traits can change but expect only moderate improvement, and they understand that such change requires effort. Still, they are more optimistic than adults about the possibility of altering undesirable characteristics (Lockhart, Chang, & Story, 2002; Lockhart et al., 2008). This positive but realistic outlook is adaptive for school-age children, who must exert effort to develop competence and behave responsibly.

Finally, cultural values influence children's views about success and failure. Asian parents and teachers are more likely than their American counterparts to hold an incremental view of ability (see page 469 in Chapter 12) and to view effort as key to success and also as a moral responsibility—messages they transmit to children (Mok, Kennedy, & Moore, 2011; Pomerantz, Ng, & Wang, 2008). Asians also attend more to failure than to success because failure indicates where corrective action is needed. Americans, in contrast, focus more on success because it enhances self-esteem. Observations of U.S. and Chinese mothers' responses to their fourth and fifth graders' puzzle solutions revealed that the U.S. mothers offered more praise after success, whereas the Chinese mothers more often pointed out the child's inadequate performance. And regardless of success or failure, Chinese mothers made more task-relevant

LOOK and **LISTEN**

Observe a school-age child working on a challenging homework assignment under the guidance of a parent or other adult. What features of the adult's communication likely foster mastery-oriented attributions? How about learned helplessness? Explain.

Applying What We Know

Fostering a Mastery-Oriented Approach to Learning

CONTEXT	DESCRIPTION
Provision of tasks	Select tasks that are meaningful, responsive to a diversity of student interests, and appropriately matched to current competence so that the child is challenged but not overwhelmed.
Parent and teacher encouragement	Communicate warmth, confidence in the child's abilities, the value of achievement, and the importance of effort in success. Resist the urge to praise children's personal qualities; focus instead on their competent behavior, sustained effort, and successful strategies. Model high effort in overcoming failure. (For teachers) Communicate often with parents, suggesting ways to foster children's effort and progress. (For parents) Monitor schoolwork; provide scaffolded assistance that promotes knowledge of effective strategies and self-regulation.
Performance evaluations	Make evaluations private; avoid publicizing success or failure through wall posters, stars, privileges to "smart" children, and prizes for "best" performance. Emphasize individual progress and self-improvement. Provide accurate, constructive feedback to children about their performance.
School environment	Offer small classes, which permit teachers to provide individualized support for mastery. Provide for cooperative learning (see page 463 in Chapter 12), in which children assist one another; avoid ability grouping, which makes evaluations of children's progress public. Accommodate individual and cultural differences in styles of learning. Create an atmosphere that sends a clear message that all students can learn.

Sources: Hilt, 2004; Wentzel & Brophy, 2014; Wigfield et al., 2006.

statements aimed at ensuring that children exerted sufficient effort to do well ("You concentrated on it"; "You only got 6 out of 12") (see Figure 13.2). When children continued with the task after mothers left the room, the Chinese children showed greater gains in performance (Ng, Pomerantz, & Lam, 2007).

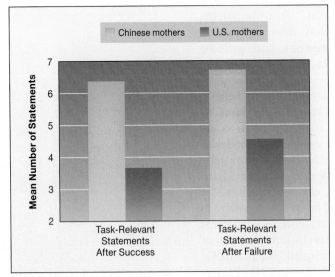

FIGURE 13.2 Chinese and U.S. mothers' task-relevant statements in response to their fourth-grade child's success or failure on puzzle tasks. Observations revealed that regardless of whether their child had just succeeded or failed, Chinese mothers were more likely than U.S. mothers to make task-relevant statements aimed at ensuring that the child exerted high effort. (Based on Ng, Pomerantz, & Lam, 2007.)

FOSTERING A MASTERY-ORIENTED APPROACH An intervention called **attribution retraining** encourages learned-helpless children to believe they can overcome failure by exerting more effort and using more effective strategies. Children are given tasks difficult enough that they will experience some failure, followed by repeated feedback that helps them revise their attributions: "You can do it if you try harder." After they succeed, children are given process praise—"Your strategies worked"; "You really tried hard on that one"—so that they attribute their success to both effort and effective strategies, not chance. Another approach is to encourage low-effort children to focus less on grades, more on mastering a task for its own sake, and more on individual performance improvement than on comparisons with classmates (Horner & Gaither, 2004; Wentzel & Brophy, 2014). Instruction in effective strategies and self-regulation is also vital, to compensate for development lost in this area and to ensure that renewed effort pays off (Berkeley, Mastropieri, & Scruggs, 2011; Wigfield et al., 2006).

Attribution retraining is best begun in middle childhood, before children's views of themselves become hard to change. An even better approach is to prevent learned helplessness, using the techniques summarized in Applying What We Know above.

Ask Yourself

- **REVIEW** How do cultural values, parent and teacher communication, and attribution styles affect self-esteem in middle childhood?

- **CONNECT** What cognitive changes, described in Chapter 12 (pages 440–441), support the transition to a self-concept emphasizing competencies, personality traits, and social comparisons?

- **APPLY** Should parents try to promote children's self-esteem by telling them they're "smart" or "wonderful"? Are children harmed if they do not feel good about everything they do? Explain.

- **REFLECT** Recall your own attributions for academic successes and failures when you were in elementary school. What are those attributions like now? What messages from others may have contributed to your attributions?

Emotional Development

13.3 Cite changes in the expression and understanding of emotion in middle childhood.

Greater self-awareness and social sensitivity support advances in emotional competence in middle childhood. Gains take place in experience of self-conscious emotions, emotional understanding, and emotional self-regulation.

Self-Conscious Emotions

As children integrate social expectations into their self-concepts, self-conscious emotions of pride and guilt become clearly governed by personal responsibility. Unlike preschoolers, school-age children experience pride in a new accomplishment and guilt over a transgression even when no adult is present (Harter, 2012a). Also, children no longer report guilt for any mishap, as they did earlier, but only for intentional wrongdoing, such as ignoring responsibilities, cheating, or lying (Ferguson, Stegge, & Damhuis, 1991). These changes reflect the older child's more mature sense of morality, a topic addressed later in this chapter.

When school-age children feel pride or guilt, they connect success or failure to specific aspects of the self: "I tried hard on that difficult task, and it paid off" (pride) or "I made a mistake, and now I have to deal with it" (guilt). They tend to feel shame when their violation of a standard is not under their control (Lewis & Ramsay, 2002; Saarni et al., 2006). For example, Lizzie felt ashamed when she dropped a spoonful of spaghetti and had a large spot on her shirt for the rest of the school day. But as children develop an overall sense of self-esteem, they may also experience shame after a controllable breach of standards if someone blames them for it (Harter, 2012a; Mascolo & Fischer, 1995). For example, the child whose teacher or parent reprimands him following poor performance ("Everyone else can do it! Why can't you?") may hang his head in shame, repeating to himself, "I'm stupid! I'm a terrible kid!"

Pride motivates children to take on further challenges, whereas guilt prompts them to make amends and to strive for self-improvement. But profound feelings of shame (as noted in Chapter 10) are particularly destructive. A sharp, shame-induced drop in self-esteem can trigger withdrawal and depression or intense anger at those who participated in the shame-evoking situation, followed by lashing out with aggression (Mills, 2005). A summary of findings from many studies confirmed that children and adolescents who experience guilt after transgressions tend to be well-adjusted—unlikely to react with depression, anger, or aggression. In contrast, those who experience shame are prone to these adjustment problems (Muris & Meesters, 2014).

If this child reacts with guilt to wrongdoing, he is likely to make amends. But adult blame and criticism may cause him to experience intense shame, leading to depression, anger, and a sharp drop in self-esteem.

© ELLEN B. SENISI

Third graders help prepare meal packages to be sent to Africa to feed children in need. Gains in emotional understanding and perspective taking in middle childhood enable children to respond with empathy to people's general life condition.

Emotional Understanding

School-age children's understanding of mental activity means that, unlike preschoolers, they are likely to explain emotion by referring to internal states, such as happy or sad thoughts, rather than to external events (Flavell, Flavell, & Green, 2001). Also, between ages 6 and 12, children become more aware of circumstances likely to spark mixed emotions, each of which may be positive or negative and may differ in intensity, and they increasingly report experiencing more than one emotion at a time (Pons et al., 2003; Zadjel et al., 2013). For example, recalling the birthday present he received from his grandmother, Joey reflected, "I was very happy I got something but a little sad that I didn't get just what I wanted."

Appreciating mixed emotions helps children realize that people's expressions may not reflect their true feelings (Misailidi, 2006). It also fosters awareness of self-conscious emotions. For example, between ages 6 and 7, children improve sharply in ability to distinguish pride from happiness and surprise (Tracy, Robins, & Lagattuta, 2005). And 8- and 9-year-olds understand that pride combines two sources of happiness—joy in accomplishment and joy that a significant person recognized that accomplishment (Harter, 1999).

Furthermore, children of this age can reconcile contradictory facial and situational cues in figuring out another's feelings. And they can use information about "what might have happened" to predict how people will feel in a new situation—realizing, for example, that someone will feel a sense of relief when an actual outcome is more favorable than what might have occurred (Guttentag & Ferrell, 2004).

As with self-understanding, gains in emotional understanding are supported by cognitive development and social experiences, especially adults' sensitivity to children's feelings and willingness to discuss emotions. Together, these factors contribute to a rise in empathy as well. As children move closer to adolescence, advances in recursive perspective taking permit an empathic response not just to people's immediate distress but also to their general life condition (Hoffman, 2000). As at early ages, emotional understanding and empathy are linked to favorable social relationships and prosocial behavior (Eisenberg, Spinrad, & Morris, 2013). As Joey and Lizzie imagined how people who are chronically ill or hungry feel and evoked those emotions in themselves, they gave part of their allowance to charity and joined in fundraising projects through school, community center, and scouting.

Emotional Self-Regulation

In Chapter 10, we saw that emotional understanding and effortful control, along with parents' modeling and teaching of emotion-regulation strategies, contribute to young children's ability to manage emotions. These factors continue to play important roles during middle childhood, a period of rapid gains in emotional self-regulation (Morris et al., 2007; Zalewski et al., 2011).

By age 10, most children shift adaptively between two general strategies for managing emotion. In **problem-centered coping,** they appraise the situation as changeable, identify the difficulty, and decide what to do about it. If problem solving does not work, they engage in **emotion-centered coping,** which is internal, private, and aimed at controlling distress when little can be done about an outcome (Kliewer, Fearnow, & Miller, 1996; Lazarus & Lazarus, 1994). For example, when faced with an anxiety-provoking test or an angry friend, older school-age children view problem solving and seeking social support as the best strategies. But when outcomes are beyond their control—after receiving a bad grade—they opt for distraction or try to redefine the situation in ways that help them accept it: "Things could be worse. There'll be another test." School-age children's improved ability to appraise situations and reflect on thoughts and feelings means that, compared with preschoolers, they more often use these internal strategies to manage emotion (Brenner & Salovey, 1997).

Cognitive development and a wider range of social experiences permit children to flexibly vary their coping strategies (Zimmer-Gembeck & Skinner, 2011). Furthermore, through interacting with parents, teachers, and peers, school-age children become more knowledgeable about socially approved ways to display negative emotion. With age, they increasingly prefer verbal expression ("Please stop pushing and wait your turn") to crying, sulking, or aggression (Shipman et al., 2003; Waters & Thompson, 2014). Young school-age children justify these more mature displays of emotion by mentioning avoidance of punishment or disapproval, but by third grade, they begin to emphasize concern for others' feelings. Children with this awareness are rated as especially helpful, cooperative, and socially responsive by teachers and as better-liked by peers (Garner, 1996; McDowell & Parke, 2000).

When emotional self-regulation has developed well, school-age children acquire a sense of *emotional self-efficacy*—a feeling of being in control of their emotional experience (Saarni, 2000; Thompson & Goodman, 2010). This fosters a favorable self-image and an optimistic outlook, which further help children face emotional challenges. As at younger ages, children whose parents respond sensitively and helpfully when the child is distressed are emotionally well-regulated—generally upbeat in mood and also empathic and prosocial (Abraham & Kerns, 2013; Vinik, Almas, & Grusec, 2011). When mothers supported their 5-year-olds' emotional development in this way, children demonstrated more effective emotional self-regulation at age 7, which in turn predicted better quality friendships at age 10 (Blair et al., 2014). In contrast, poorly regulated children often experience hostile, dismissive parental reactions to distress (Morris et al., 2007). These children are overwhelmed by negative emotion, a response that interferes with empathy and prosocial behavior.

Finally, culture influences emotional self-regulation. In a striking illustration, researchers studied children in two subcultures in rural Nepal. In response to stories about emotionally charged situations (such as peer aggression or an unjust parental punishment), Hindu children more often said they would feel angry but would try to mask their feelings. Buddhist children, in contrast, interpreted the situation so that they felt "just OK" rather than angry. "Why be angry?" they explained. "The event already happened." Accordingly, Hindu mothers reported that they often teach their children how to control their emotional behavior, whereas Buddhist mothers pointed to the value their religion places on a calm, peaceful disposition (Cole & Tamang, 1998; Cole, Tamang, & Shrestha, 2006). Compared to both Nepalese groups, U.S. children preferred conveying anger verbally in these situations; for example, to an unjust punishment, they answered, "If I say I'm angry, he'll stop hurting me!" (Cole, Bruschi, & Tamang, 2002). Notice how this response fits with the Western emphasis on personal rights and self-expression.

Through interacting with adults and peers, school-age children acquire socially approved ways to express negative emotion. These friends use words rather than crying, sulking, or aggression to confront a disagreement.

LOOK and LISTEN

Ask several school-age children how they would manage their emotions in the following situations: (1) a friend is angry with them, and (2) they receive a bad grade on an important test. Do their responses reflect flexible, adaptive coping?

Moral Development

13.4 Describe changes in moral understanding during middle childhood, including children's understanding of diversity and inequality.

Recall from Chapter 10 that preschoolers pick up many morally relevant behaviors through modeling and reinforcement. By middle childhood, they have had time to internalize rules for good conduct: "It's good to help others in trouble" or "It's wrong to take something that doesn't belong to you." This change leads children to become considerably more independent and trustworthy.

In Chapter 10, we also saw that children do not just copy their morality from others. As the cognitive-developmental approach emphasizes, they actively think about right and wrong. An expanding social world, the capacity to consider more information when reasoning, and gains in recursive perspective taking lead moral understanding to advance greatly in middle childhood.

School-age children recognize that certain social conventions have a clear purpose—such as separating recyclables from trash to reduce waste. They regard violations of these types of conventions as closer to moral transgressions.

Moral and Social-Conventional Understanding

During middle childhood, children construct a flexible appreciation of moral rules. They take into account an increasing number of variables, including both an actor's intentions and the context of his behavior in terms of harm done to others. For example, between ages 7 and 11, children increasingly say it is acceptable to hit another child in certain situations—in self-defense, to protect someone else from serious bodily injury, or to prevent the other child from hurting herself (Jambon & Smetana, 2014). Older children focus less on the actor's transgression (hitting) and more on the positive aim of his actions (trying to prevent harm).

Similarly, by age 7 to 8, children no longer say truth telling is always good and lying is always bad but also consider prosocial and antisocial intentions and the context of the behavior. They evaluate certain types of truthfulness very negatively— for example, blunt statements, particularly when made in public contexts where they are especially likely to have negative social consequences (telling a friend that you don't like her drawing) (Ma et al., 2011).

Although both Chinese and Canadian schoolchildren consider lying about antisocial acts "very naughty," Chinese children more often rate lying favorably when the intention is modesty, as when a student who has thoughtfully picked up litter from the playground says, "I didn't do it" (Cameron et al., 2012; Lee et al., 2001). Similarly, Chinese children are more likely to favor lying to support the group at the expense of the individual (claiming you're sick so, as a poor singer, you won't harm your class's chances of winning a singing competition). In contrast, Canadian children more often favor lying to support the individual at the expense of the group (asserting that a friend who is a poor speller is actually a good speller because the friend wants to participate in a spelling competition) (Fu et al., 2007; Lau et al., 2012). These judgments reflect school-age children's increasingly sophisticated understanding of different reasons for deception (Mills, 2013). They realize that people may convey inaccurate information because they are biased, trying to be persuasive, or concerned about how others will react.

As children construct more advanced ideas about justice, they clarify and link moral imperatives and social conventions. School-age children distinguish social conventions with a clear *purpose* (not running in school hallways to prevent injuries) from ones with no obvious justification (crossing a "forbidden" line on the playground). They regard violations of purposeful conventions as closer to moral transgressions (Buchanan-Barrow & Barrett, 1998).

Furthermore, as with moral rules, older children realize that people's intentions and the context of their actions affect the moral implications of violating a social convention. In one study, 8- to 10-year-olds judged that because of a flag's symbolic value, burning it to express disapproval of a country or to start a cooking fire is worse than burning it accidentally. They also stated that public flag burning is worse than private flag burning because it inflicts emotional harm on others. But they recognized that flag burning is a form of freedom of expression, and most agreed it would be acceptable in a country that treated its citizens unfairly (Helwig & Prencipe, 1999).

In middle childhood, children also realize that people whose *knowledge* differs may not be equally responsible for moral transgressions. Many 7-year-olds tolerate a teacher's decision to give more snack to girls than to boys because she thinks (incorrectly) that girls need more food. But when a teacher gives girls more snack because she holds an *immoral belief* ("it's all right to be nicer to girls than boys"), almost all children judge her actions negatively (Wainryb & Ford, 1998).

Understanding Individual Rights

When children challenge adult authority, they typically do so within the personal domain. As their grasp of moral imperatives and social conventions strengthens, so does their conviction that certain choices, such as hairstyle, friends, and leisure activities, are up to the individual (Nucci, 2005).

Notions of personal choice, in turn, enhance children's moral understanding. As early as age 6, children view freedom of speech and religion as individual rights, even if laws exist that deny those rights (Helwig, 2006). And they regard laws that discriminate against individuals—for example, denying certain people access to medical care or education—as wrong and worthy of violating (Helwig & Jasiobedzka, 2001). In justifying their responses, children appeal to personal privileges and, by the end of middle childhood, to the importance of individual rights for maintaining a fair society.

At the same time, older school-age children place limits on individual choice. Fourth graders faced with conflicting moral and personal concerns—such as whether or not to befriend a classmate of a different race or gender—typically decide in favor of kindness and fairness (Killen et al., 2002). Partly for this reason, prejudice generally declines in middle childhood.

Culture and Moral Understanding

Children and adolescents in diverse cultures use similar criteria to reason about moral, social-conventional, and personal concerns (Neff & Helwig, 2002; Nucci, 2005, 2008). For example, Chinese young people, whose culture places a high value on respect for and deference to adult authority, nevertheless say that adults have no right to interfere in children's personal matters, such as how they spend free time (Hasebe, Nucci, & Nucci, 2004). A Colombian child illustrated this passionate defense of personal control when asked if a teacher had the right to tell a student where to sit during circle time. In the absence of a moral reason from the teacher, the child declared, "She should be able to sit wherever she wants" (Ardila-Rey & Killen, 2001, p. 249).

Furthermore, American and Korean children alike claim that a child with no position of authority should be obeyed when she gives a directive that is fair and caring, such as telling others to share candy or to return lost money to its owner. And even in Korean culture, which places a high value on deference to authority, 7- to 11-year-olds evaluate negatively an adult's order to engage in immoral acts, such as stealing or refusing to share—a response that strengthens with age (Kim, 1998). In sum, children everywhere seem to realize that higher principles, independent of rule and authority, must prevail when people's personal rights and welfare are at stake.

Understanding Diversity and Inequality

By the early school years, children absorb prevailing societal attitudes, associating power and privilege with white people and poverty and inferior status with people of color. They do not necessarily acquire these views directly from parents or friends, whose attitudes often differ from their own (Aboud & Doyle, 1996). Perhaps white parents are reluctant to discuss their racial and ethnic views with children, and friends also say little. Given limited or ambiguous information, children may fill in the gaps with information they encounter in the media and elsewhere in their environments.

Consistent with this idea, research indicates that children pick up much information about group status from implicit messages in their surroundings. In one investigation, 7- to 12-year-olds attending a summer school were randomly assigned to social groups, identified by colored T-shirts (yellow or blue) that the children wore. The researchers hung posters in the classroom depicting yellow-group members as having higher status—for example, as having won more athletic and spelling competitions. When teachers used the groups as the basis for seating arrangements, assignments, and bulletin-board displays, the children in the high-status group evaluated their own group more favorably than the other group, and the children in the low-status group viewed their own group less favorably (Bigler, Brown, & Markell, 2001). But when teachers ignored the social groupings, no prejudice emerged.

These findings indicate that children do not necessarily form stereotypes even when some basis for them exists—in this instance, information on wall posters. But when an authority figure behaves in ways that endorse group status distinctions, children form biased attitudes.

Fourth graders participate in a nature walk during a school lunch break. Around age 7 or 8, voicing of negative attitudes toward minorities declines, and most children judge exclusion based on skin color to be unfair.

IN-GROUP AND OUT-GROUP BIASES: DEVELOPMENT OF PREJUDICE Studies in diverse Western nations confirm that by age 5 to 6, white children generally evaluate their own racial group favorably and other racial groups less favorably or negatively (Aboud, 2003; Bennett et al., 2004; Nesdale et al., 2004). Many minority children of this age, in a reverse pattern, assign positive characteristics to the privileged white majority and negative characteristics to their own group (Corenblum, 2003; Newheiser et al., 2014).

But recall that with age, children pay more attention to inner traits. The capacity to classify the social world in multiple ways enables school-age children to understand that people can be both "the same" and "different"—those who look different need not think, feel, or act differently. Consequently, voicing of negative attitudes toward minorities declines after age 7 or 8 (Aboud, 2008; Raabe & Beelman, 2011). Around this time, both majority and minority children express *in-group favoritism,* and white children's prejudice against *out-group* members often weakens (Nesdale et al., 2005; Ruble et al., 2004). Most school-age children and adolescents are also quick to verbalize that it is wrong to exclude others from peer-group and learning activities on the basis of skin color—discrimination they evaluate as unfair (Killen et al., 2002).

Yet even in children aware of the injustice of discrimination, prejudice often operates unintentionally and without awareness—as it does in many adults (Dunham, Baron, & Banaji, 2006). Consider a study in which U.S. children and adults were shown pictures of computer-generated racially ambiguous faces displaying happy and angry expressions and asked to classify them by race. White participants more often categorized happy faces as white and angry faces as African American or Asian. These implicit biases were evident across all ages tested—as early as 3 or 4. In contrast, African-American participants did not show any racial biases in their responses (Dunham, Chen, & Banaji, 2013). The absence of any in-group favoritism (classifying happy faces as black) suggests an early emerging, implicit sensitivity to prevailing racial attitudes among African Americans.

These findings raise the question of whether the decline in white children's explicit racial bias during middle childhood is a true decrease, or whether it reflects their growing awareness of widely held standards that deem prejudice to be inappropriate—or both. Around age 10, white children start to avoid talking about race in order to appear unbiased, just as many adults do (Apfelbaum et al., 2008). At least to some degree, then, older school-age children's desire to present themselves in a socially acceptable light may contribute to reduced explicit out-group prejudice, while implicit racial bias persists.

Nevertheless, the extent to which children hold racial and ethnic biases varies, depending on the following personal and situational factors:

- *A fixed view of personality traits.* Children who believe personality traits are fixed rather than changeable often judge others as either "good" or "bad." Ignoring motives and circumstances, they readily form prejudices based on limited information. For example, they might infer that "a new child at school who tells a lie to get other kids to like her" is simply a bad person (Levy & Dweck, 1999).
- *Overly high self-esteem.* Children (and adults) with very high self-esteem are more likely to hold racial and ethnic prejudices (Baumeister et al., 2003; Bigler, Brown, & Markell, 2001). These individuals seem to belittle disadvantaged individuals or groups to justify their own extremely favorable self-evaluation. Children who say their own ethnicity makes them feel especially "good"—and thus perhaps socially superior—are more likely to display in-group favoritism and out-group prejudice (Pfeifer et al., 2007).
- *A social world in which people are sorted into groups.* The more adults highlight group distinctions for children and the less interracial contact children experience, the more likely white children will express in-group favoritism and out-group prejudice (Killen et al., 2010).

© SYRACUSE NEWSPAPERS/MIKE GREENLAR/THE IMAGE WORKS

REDUCING PREJUDICE   Research confirms that an effective way to reduce prejudice is through intergroup contact, in which racially and ethnically different children have equal status, work toward common goals, and become personally acquainted, and in which authority figures (such as parents and teachers) expect them to engage in such interaction. Children assigned to cooperative learning groups with peers of diverse backgrounds show low levels of prejudice in their expressions of likability and in their behavior. For example, they form more cross-race friendships (Pettigrew & Tropp, 2006). Sharing thoughts and feelings with close, cross-race friends, in turn, reduces even subtle, unintentional prejudices (Turner, Hewstone, & Voci, 2007). But positive effects seem not to generalize to out-group members who are not part of these learning teams.

Third graders perform a traditional Chinese dance at their culturally diverse school. Opportunities to work together toward common goals can reduce even subtle, unintentional prejudices as racially and ethnically different children get to know one another.

Long-term contact and collaboration among neighborhood, school, and community groups may be the best way to reduce prejudice (Rutland, Killen, & Abrams, 2010). School environments that expose children to broad ethnic diversity, teach them to understand and value those differences, directly address the damage caused by prejudice, and encourage perspective taking and empathy both prevent children from forming negative biases and reduce already acquired biases (Dweck, 2009). Unfortunately, as noted in Chapter 12, segregation is widespread in U.S. schools, which seldom offer exposure to the diversity necessary for countering negative racial and ethnic biases. Return to page 464 to review efforts of magnet schools to reduce this racial divide.

Finally, inducing children to view others' traits as changeable, by discussing with them the many possible influences on those traits, is helpful. The more children believe that people can change their personalities, the more they report liking, wanting to spend time with, and perceiving themselves as similar to members of disadvantaged out-groups. Furthermore, children who believe that human attributes are changeable spend more time volunteering to help people in need—for example, by serving meals to homeless people or reading to poverty-stricken preschoolers (Karafantis & Levy, 2004). Volunteering may, in turn, promote a view of others as changeable by helping children take the perspective of the underprivileged and appreciate the social conditions that lead to disadvantage.

Ask Yourself

● **REVIEW** How does emotional self-regulation improve in middle childhood? What implications do these advances have for children's self-esteem?

● **CONNECT** Cite examples of how older children's capacity to take more information into account enhances their emotional understanding, perspective taking, and moral understanding.

● **APPLY** Ten-year-old Marla says her classmate Bernadette will never get good grades because she's lazy. Jane believes that Bernadette tries but can't concentrate because her parents are divorcing. Why is Marla more likely than Jane to develop prejudices?

● **REFLECT** Did you attend an integrated elementary school? Why is school integration vital for reducing racial and ethnic prejudice?

Peer Relations

In middle childhood, the society of peers becomes an increasingly important context for development. Advances in recursive perspective taking permit more sophisticated understanding of self and others. These developments, in turn, enhance peer interaction. Compared with preschoolers, school-age children resolve conflicts more effectively, using persuasion and

13.5 How do peer sociability and friendship change in middle childhood?

13.6 Describe major categories of peer acceptance and ways to help rejected children.

compromise (Mayeux & Cillessen, 2003). Sharing, helping, and other prosocial acts also increase. In line with these changes, aggression declines. But the drop is greatest for physical attacks (Côté et al., 2007; Tremblay, 2000). As we will see, verbal and relational aggression continue as children form peer groups.

Peer Groups

TAKE A MOMENT... Watch children in the schoolyard or neighborhood, and notice how they often gather in groups of three to a dozen or more. In what ways are members of the same group noticeably alike?

By the end of middle childhood, children display a strong desire for group belonging. They form **peer groups,** collectives that generate unique values and standards for behavior and a social structure of leaders and followers. Peer groups organize on the basis of proximity (being in the same classroom) and similarity in sex, ethnicity, academic achievement, popularity, and aggression (Rubin et al., 2013). When groups are tracked for 3 to 6 weeks, membership changes very little. When they are followed for a year or longer, substantial change can occur, depending on whether children are reshuffled into different classrooms. For children who remain together, 50 to 70 percent of groups consist mostly of the same children from year to year (Cairns, Xie, & Leung, 1998).

The practices of these informal groups lead to a "peer culture" that typically involves a specialized vocabulary, dress code, and place to "hang out." Joey and three other boys formed a club whose "uniform" was T-shirts, jeans, and sneakers. They met at recess and on Saturdays in the tree house in Joey's backyard. Calling themselves "the pack," the boys devised a secret handshake and chose Joey as their leader. Their activities included improving the clubhouse, trading baseball cards, playing basketball and video games, and—just as important—keeping unwanted peers and adults out!

As children develop these exclusive associations, the codes of dress and behavior that grow out of them become more broadly influential. Peers who deviate—by "kissing up" to teachers, wearing the wrong clothes, or tattling on classmates—are often rebuffed, becoming targets of critical glances and comments. These customs bind peers together, creating a sense of group identity. Within the group, children acquire many social skills—cooperation, leadership, followership, and loyalty to collective goals. Through these experiences, children experiment with and learn about social organizations.

As with other aspects of social reasoning, children evaluate a group's decision to exclude a peer in complex ways. Most view exclusion as wrong, even when they see themselves as different from the excluded child. And with age, children are less likely to endorse excluding someone because of unconventional appearance or behavior. Girls, especially, regard exclusion as unjust, perhaps because they experience it more often than boys (Killen, Crystal, & Watanabe, 2002). But when a peer threatens group functioning, by acting disruptively or by lacking skills to participate in a valued group activity (such as sports), both boys and girls say that exclusion is justified—a perspective that strengthens with age (Killen & Stangor, 2001).

Despite these sophisticated understandings, children do exclude unjustly, often using relationally aggressive tactics. Peer groups—at the instigation of their leaders, who can be skillfully aggressive—frequently oust no longer "respected" children. Some of these castouts, whose own previous hostility toward outsiders reduces their chances of being included elsewhere, turn to other low-status peers with poor social skills (Farmer et al., 2010). Socially anxious children, when ousted, often become increasingly peer-avoidant and thus more isolated (Buhs, Ladd, & Herald-Brown, 2010). In either case, opportunities to acquire socially competent behavior diminish.

School-age children's desire for group belonging can also be satisfied through formal group ties such as scouting, 4-H, and religious

© BJARKI REYR MR/ALAMY

Peer groups first form in middle childhood. These boys have probably established a social structure of leaders and followers as they gather for a soccer game. Their relaxed body language and similar dress suggest a strong sense of group belonging.

youth groups. Adult involvement holds in check the negative behaviors associated with children's informal peer groups. And through working on joint projects and helping in their communities, children gain in social and moral maturity (Vandell & Shumow, 1999).

Friendships

Whereas peer groups provide children with insight into larger social structures, friendships contribute to the development of trust and sensitivity. During the school years, friendship becomes more complex and psychologically based. Consider the following 8-year-old's ideas:

> *Why is Shelly your best friend?* Because she helps me when I'm sad, and she shares. . . . *What makes Shelly so special?* I've known her longer, I sit next to her and got to know her better. . . . *How come you like Shelly better than anyone else?* She's done the most for me. She never disagrees, she never eats in front of me, she never walks away when I'm crying, and she helps me on my homework. . . . *How do you get someone to like you?* . . . If you're nice to [your friends], they'll be nice to you. (Damon, 1988, pp. 80–81)

As these responses show, friendship has become a mutually agreed-on relationship in which children like each other's personal qualities and respond to one another's needs and desires. And once a friendship forms, *trust* becomes its defining feature. School-age children state that a good friendship is based on acts of kindness, signifying that each person can be counted on to support the other (Hartup & Abecassis, 2004). Consequently, older children regard violations of trust, such as not helping when others need help, breaking promises, and gossiping behind the other's back, as serious breaches of friendship.

Because of these features, school-age children's friendships are more selective. Whereas preschoolers say they have lots of friends, by age 8 or 9 children name only a handful of good friends. Girls, who demand greater closeness than boys, are more exclusive in their friendships. In addition, children tend to select friends similar to themselves in age, sex, race, ethnicity, and SES. Friends also resemble one another in personality (sociability, inattention/hyperactivity, aggression, depression), peer popularity, academic achievement, and prosocial behavior (Hartup, 2006; Rubin et al., 2013). But friendship opportunities offered by children's environments also affect their choices. As noted earlier, in integrated classrooms with mixed-race collaborative learning groups, students form more cross-race friendships.

Over middle childhood, high-quality friendships remain fairly stable: About 50 to 70 percent endure over a school year, and some last for several years (Berndt, 2004). Friendships spanning several contexts—such as school, religious institution, and children of parents' friends—are more enduring (Troutman & Fletcher, 2010). Through friendships, children learn the importance of emotional commitment. They come to realize that close relationships can survive disagreements if friends are secure in their liking for each other (Hartup, 2006). Friendship provides an important context in which children learn to tolerate criticism and resolve disputes in ways that meet both partners' needs.

Yet the impact of friendships on children's development depends on the nature of their friends. Children who bring kindness and compassion to their friendships strengthen each other's prosocial tendencies. But when aggressive children make friends, the relationship is often riddled with hostile interaction and is at risk for breakup, especially when just one member of the pair is aggressive (Ellis & Zarbatany, 2007). Aggressive girls' friendships are high in exchange of private feelings but also full of relational hostility, including jealousy, conflict, and betrayal. Aggressive boys' friendships involve frequent expressions of anger, coercive statements, physical attacks, and enticements to rule breaking (Bagwell & Coie, 2004; Rubin et al., 2013; Werner & Crick, 2004). These findings indicate that the social problems of aggressive children operate within their closest peer ties. As we will see next, these children often acquire negative reputations in the wider world of peers.

LOOK and LISTEN

Ask an 8- to 11-year-old to tell you what he or she looks for in a best friend. Is *trust* centrally important? Does the child mention personality traits, just as school-age children do in describing themselves (see page 474)?

© ELLEN B. SENISI

During middle childhood, concepts of friendship become more psychologically based. School-age friendships are more selective than those of younger children, and girls demand greater friendship closeness than do boys.

Peer Acceptance

Peer acceptance refers to likability—the extent to which a child is viewed by a group of age-mates, such as classmates, as a worthy social partner. Unlike friendship, peer acceptance is not a mutual relationship but a one-sided perspective, involving the group's view of an individual. Nevertheless, better-accepted children tend to be socially competent and, thus, to have more friends and more positive relationships with them (Mayeux, Houser, & Dyches, 2011).

To assess peer acceptance, researchers usually use self-reports that measure *social preferences*—for example, asking children to identify classmates whom they "like most" or "like least" (Cillessen, 2009). These self-reports yield five general categories of peer acceptance:

- **Popular children,** who get many positive votes (are well-liked)
- **Rejected children,** who get many negative votes (are disliked)
- **Controversial children,** who receive many votes, both positive and negative (are both liked and disliked)
- **Neglected children,** who are seldom mentioned, either positively or negatively
- **Average children,** who receive average numbers of positive and negative votes

Another approach assesses *perceived popularity*—children's judgments of whom most of their classmates admire. Only moderate correspondence exists between the classmates children perceive as popular (believe are admired by many others) and those classified as popular based on peer preferences (receive many "like most" ratings) (Mayeux, Houser, & Dyches, 2011).

Peer acceptance is a powerful predictor of current as well as later psychological adjustment. Rejected children, especially, are anxious, unhappy, disruptive, and low in self-esteem. Both teachers and parents rate them as having a wide range of emotional and social problems. Peer rejection in middle childhood is also strongly associated with poor school performance, absenteeism, dropping out, substance use, depression, antisocial behavior, and delinquency in adolescence and with criminality in adulthood (Ladd, 2005; Rubin, et al., 2013).

However, earlier influences—children's characteristics combined with parenting practices—may largely explain the link between peer acceptance and adjustment. School-age children with peer-relationship problems are more likely to have preexisting, weak emotional self-regulation skills and to have experienced family stress due to low income, insensitive child rearing, and coercive discipline (Blair et al., 2014; Trentacosta & Shaw, 2009). Nevertheless, as we will see, rejected children evoke reactions from peers that contribute to their unfavorable development.

DETERMINANTS OF PEER ACCEPTANCE Why is one child liked while another is rejected? A wealth of research reveals that social behavior plays a powerful role.

Peers gather around a popular classmate. Most popular children are prosocial—academically successful, socially sensitive, and cooperative. But some are antisocial, admired for their skill at controlling peer relationships through relational aggression.

Popular Children. Socially successful children include those who are well-liked (socially accepted) and those who are admired (high in perceived popularity). **Popular-prosocial children,** who are both socially accepted and admired, combine academic and social competence. They perform well in school, communicate with peers in friendly and cooperative ways, and solve social problems constructively (Cillessen & Bellmore, 2004; Mayeux, Houser, & Dyches, 2011).

But other popular children are admired for their socially adept yet belligerent behavior. **Popular-antisocial children** include "tough" boys—athletically skilled but poor students who cause trouble and defy adult authority—and relationally aggressive boys and girls who enhance their own status by ignoring, excluding, and spreading rumors about other children (Rose, Swenson, & Waller, 2004; Vaillancourt & Hymel, 2006). Despite their aggressiveness, peers often view these youths as "cool," perhaps because of their athletic abilities and sophisticated but devious social skills.

Although peer admiration gives these children some protection against lasting adjustment difficulties, their antisocial acts require intervention (Rodkin et al., 2006). With age, peers like these high-status, aggressive youths less and less, a trend that is stronger for relationally aggressive girls. The more socially prominent and controlling these girls become, the more they engage in relational aggression (Mayeux, Houser, & Dyches, 2011). Eventually peers condemn their nasty tactics and reject them.

Rejected Children. Rejected children display a wide range of negative social behaviors. The largest subtype, **rejected-aggressive children,** show high rates of conflict, physical and relational aggression, and hyperactive, inattentive, and impulsive behavior. They are usually deficient in perspective taking, and they tend to misinterpret innocent behaviors of peers as hostile and to blame others for their social difficulties (Dodge, Coie, & Lynam, 2006; Rubin et al., 2013). Compared with popular-antisocial children, they are more extremely antagonistic.

In contrast, **rejected-withdrawn children** are passive and socially awkward. Overwhelmed by social anxiety, they hold negative expectations about interactions with peers and worry about being scorned and attacked. Like their aggressive counterparts, they typically feel like retaliating rather than compromising when conflicts arise, although they less often act on those feelings (Hart et al., 2000; Rubin et al., 2013; Troop-Gordon & Asher, 2005).

Rejected children are excluded by peers as early as kindergarten. Rejection, in turn, further impairs biased social information processing, heightening hostility (Lansford et al., 2010). Soon their classroom participation declines, their feelings of loneliness rise, their academic achievement falters, and they want to avoid school (Buhs, Ladd, & Herald-Brown, 2010; Gooren et al., 2011). Most have few friends, and some have none—a circumstance linked to low self-esteem, mistrust of peers, and severe adjustment difficulties (Ladd et al., 2011; Pedersen et al., 2007).

Both types of rejected children are at risk for peer harassment. But as the Biology and Environment box on page 492 reveals, rejected-aggressive children also act as bullies, and rejected-withdrawn children are especially likely to be victimized (Putallaz et al., 2007).

Controversial and Neglected Children. Consistent with the mixed peer opinion they engender, controversial children display a blend of positive and negative social behaviors. They are hostile and disruptive, but they also engage in positive, prosocial acts. Even though some peers dislike them, they have qualities that protect them from exclusion. They have many friends and are happy with their peer relationships (de Bruyn & Cillessen, 2006). But like their popular-antisocial counterparts, they often bully others and engage in calculated relational aggression to sustain their dominance (Putallaz et al., 2007).

Perhaps the most surprising finding on peer acceptance is that neglected children, once thought to be in need of treatment, are usually well-adjusted. Although they engage in low rates of interaction and are considered shy by their classmates, most are just as socially skilled as average children and do not report feeling unhappy about their social life. When they want to, they can break away from their usual, preferred pattern of playing alone, cooperating well with peers and forming positive, stable friendships (Ladd & Burgess, 1999; Ladd et al., 2011). Consequently, neglected status (like controversial status) is often temporary. Neglected, socially competent children remind us that an outgoing, gregarious personality style is not the only path to emotional well-being. Nevertheless, a few neglected children are socially anxious and poorly skilled and, thus, at risk for peer rejection.

HELPING REJECTED CHILDREN A variety of interventions exist to improve the peer relations and psychological adjustment of rejected children. Most involve coaching, modeling, and reinforcing positive social skills, such as how to initiate interaction with a peer, cooperate in play, and respond to another child with friendly emotion and approval. Several of these programs have produced gains in social competence and peer acceptance still present from several weeks to a year later (Asher & Rose, 1997; DeRosier, 2007).

Combining social-skills training with other treatments increases its effectiveness. Rejected children are often poor students, whose low academic self-esteem magnifies their negative interactions with teachers and classmates. Intensive academic tutoring improves both school achievement and social acceptance (O'Neil et al., 1997).

Still another approach focuses on training in perspective taking and social problem solving. But many rejected-aggressive children are unaware of their poor social skills and do not take responsibility for their social failures (Mrug, Hoza, & Gerdes, 2001). Rejected-withdrawn

Biology and Environment

Bullies and Their Victims

Follow the activities of aggressive children over a school day, and you will see that they reserve their hostilities for certain peers. A highly destructive form of interaction is **peer victimization,** in which particular children become targets of verbal and physical attacks or other forms of abuse. What sustains these repeated assault–retreat cycles between pairs of children?

Almost 20 percent of children are bullies, while 25 percent are repeatedly victimized. Most bullies who engage in face-to-face physical and verbal attacks are boys, but a considerable number of girls have bombarded vulnerable classmates with verbal and relational hostility (Cook et al., 2010).

As bullies move into adolescence, an increasing number attack through electronic means. About 20 to 40 percent of youths have experienced "cyberbullying" through text messages, e-mail, chat rooms, or other electronic tools (Kowalski & Limber, 2013). Compared with face-to-face bullying, gender differences in cyberbullying are less pronounced; the indirectness of online aggression may lead girls to prefer it (Menesini & Spiel, 2012). Girls more often use text messages, e-mail, or chat rooms to cyberbully, whereas boys more often distribute embarrassing photos or videos (Menesini, Nicocenti, & Calussi, 2011).

"Traditional" bullying and cyberbullying frequently co-occur: Bullies and victims in one context are frequently involved in the other. But electronic bullying is not always an extension of traditional bullying (Smith et al., 2008). And victims are far less likely to report cyberbullying to parents or adults at school. Most of the time, the cyberbully's identity is unknown to the victim and audience.

Many bullies are disliked, or become so, because of their cruelty. But a substantial number are socially prominent, powerful youngsters who are broadly admired for their physical attractiveness, leadership, or athletic abilities (Vaillancourt et al., 2010b). To preserve their high social status, bullies often target already peer-rejected children, whom classmates are unlikely to defend (Veenstra et al., 2010). This helps explain why peers rarely intervene to help victims, and why about 20 to 30 percent of onlookers encourage bullies, even joining in (Salmivalli & Voeten, 2004). Bullying occurs more often in schools where teachers are viewed as unfair and uncaring and where many students judge bullying behaviors to be "OK" (Guerra, Williams, & Sadek, 2011).

Indeed, bullies, and the peers who assist them, typically display social-cognitive deficits, including overly high self-esteem, pride in their acts, and indifference to harm done to their victims (Hymel et al., 2010).

Depression and other internalizing difficulties increase children's risk of both real-life and cyber victimization (Kochel, Ladd, & Rudolph, 2012; Vaillancourt et al., 2013). Biologically based traits—an inhibited temperament and a frail physical appearance—contribute. But victims also have histories of resistant attachment, overly controlling child rearing, and maternal overprotection—parenting that prompts anxiety, low self-esteem, and dependency, resulting in a fearful demeanor that marks these children and youths as vulnerable (Snyder et al., 2003).

Other adjustment problems associated with victimization include loneliness, low peer acceptance, poor school performance, disruptive behavior, and school avoidance (Kochel, Ladd, & Rudolph, 2012; Paul & Cillessen, 2003). And like persistent child abuse, victimization is linked to impaired production of cortisol, suggesting a chronically disrupted physiological response to stress (Vaillancourt, Hymel, & McDougall, 2013).

As instances of traditional bullying and cyberbullying accumulate, victims report substantial interference with daily functioning. Both forms of victimization are related to rising anxiety, depression, and suicidal thoughts (Menesini, Calussi, & Nocentini, 2012; van den Eijnden et al., 2014). Repeated cyberattacks directed at widespread damage to the victim's reputation—for example, circulating malicious videos on cell phones or social networking sites—magnify these effects.

Aggression and victimization are not polar opposites. One-third to one-half of victims are also aggressive, meeting out physical, relational, or cyberhostilities. Bullies usually respond by abusing them again—a cycle that sustains their victim status. Among rejected children, these bully/victims are the most despised. They often have histories of extremely maladaptive parenting, including child abuse. This combination of highly negative home and peer experiences places them at severe risk for maladjustment (Kowalski, Limber, & Agatston, 2008).

Interventions that change victimized children's negative opinions of themselves and that teach them to respond in nonreinforcing ways to their attackers are helpful. Another way to assist victimized children is to help them acquire the social skills needed to form and maintain a

Many bullies are socially prominent, admired youngsters who target peer-rejected children as a means of preserving their high social status. Classmates are unlikely to defend these victims, and some join in the verbal and physical attacks.

gratifying friendship. When children have a close friend to whom they can turn for help, bullying episodes typically end quickly. Anxious, withdrawn children with a close friend have fewer adjustment problems than those with no friends (Fox & Boulton, 2006; Laursen et al., 2007).

Although modifying victimized children's behavior can help, the best way to reduce bullying is to change youth environments (including school, sports programs, recreation centers, and neighborhoods), promoting prosocial attitudes and behaviors. Effective approaches include developing school and community codes against both traditional bullying and cyberbullying; teaching child bystanders to intervene; strengthening parental oversight of children and youths' use of cell phones, computers, and the Internet; and increasing adult supervision of high-bullying areas in schools, such as hallways, lunchroom, and schoolyard (Kiriakidis & Kavoura, 2010; Vaillancourt et al., 2010a).

The U.S. Department of Health and Human Services manages an antibullying website, *www.stopbullying.gov,* which raises awareness of the harmfulness of bullying and provides parents, teachers, and students with information on prevention.

children, in contrast, are likely to develop a *learned-helpless* approach to peer acceptance—concluding, after repeated rebuffs, that they will never be liked (Wichmann, Coplan, & Daniels, 2004). Both types of rejected children need help attributing their peer difficulties to internal, changeable causes.

As rejected children gain in social skills, teachers must encourage peers to alter their negative opinions. Accepted children often selectively recall their negative acts while overlooking their positive ones (Mikami, Lerner, & Lun, 2010). Consequently, even in the face of contrary evidence, rejected children's negative reputations tend to persist. Teachers' praise and expressions of liking, along with classroom expectations for social acceptance, can modify peer judgments (De Laet at al., 2014; Mikami et al., 2013).

Finally, because rejected children's socially incompetent behaviors often originate in a poor fit between the child's temperament and parenting practices, interventions focusing on the child may not be sufficient (Bierman & Powers, 2009). Without improving the quality of parent–child interaction, rejected children will continue to practice poor interpersonal skills at home and, as a result, may soon return to their old behavior patterns.

LOOK *and* LISTEN

Contact a nearby elementary school or a school district office to find out what practices are in place to prevent bullying. Inquire about a written antibullying policy, and request a copy.

Gender Typing

Children's understanding of gender roles broadens in middle childhood, and their gender identities (views of themselves as relatively masculine or feminine) change as well. We will see how gender stereotypes influence children's attitudes, behaviors, peer relations, and self-perceptions.

13.7 What changes in gender-stereotyped beliefs and gender identity occur during middle childhood?

Gender-Stereotyped Beliefs

By age 5, gender stereotyping of activities and occupations is well-established. During the school years, knowledge of stereotypes increases in the less obvious areas of personality traits and achievement.

PERSONALITY TRAITS   Research in many cultures reveals that stereotyping of personality traits increases steadily in middle childhood, becoming adultlike around age 11 (Best, 2001; Heyman & Legare, 2004). For example, children regard "tough," "aggressive," "rational," and "dominant" as masculine and "gentle," "affectionate," and "dependent" as feminine.

Children derive these distinctions from observing sex differences in behavior as well as from adult treatment. When helping a child with a task, for example, parents (especially fathers) behave in a more mastery-oriented fashion with sons, setting higher standards, explaining concepts, and pointing out important features of tasks—particularly during gender-typed pursuits, such as science activities (Tenenbaum & Leaper, 2003; Tenenbaum et al., 2005). Furthermore, parents less often encourage girls to make their own decisions. And both parents and teachers more often praise boys for knowledge and accomplishment, girls for obedience (Good & Brophy, 2003; Pomerantz & Ruble, 1998).

ACHIEVEMENT AREAS   Shortly after entering elementary school, school-age children figure out which academic subjects and skill areas are "masculine" and which are "feminine." They often regard reading, spelling, art, and music as more for girls and mathematics, athletics, and mechanical skills as more for boys (Cvencek, Meltzoff, & Greenwald, 2011; Eccles, Jacobs, & Harold, 1990). These stereotypes—and the attitudes and behaviors of parents and teachers that promote them—influence children's preferences for and sense of competence at certain subjects. As we saw in our discussion of self-esteem, boys tend to feel more competent than girls at math, science, and athletics, whereas girls feel more competent than boys at language arts (see page 477).

Adults' gender-typed judgments of children's competence can have lasting consequences. In one study, mothers' early perceptions of their children's competence at math continued to predict daughters' self-perceptions and also career choices in their mid-twenties. Young

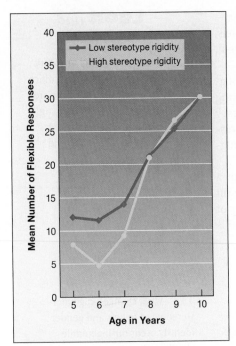

FIGURE 13.3 **Changes in gender-stereotype flexibility between ages 5 and 10.** German schoolchildren responded annually to a questionnaire assessing the flexibility of their gender-stereotyped beliefs (whether they thought both genders could display a personality trait or engage in an activity). Children differing in degree of gender-stereotype rigidity at age 5 eventually became equally flexible. Findings support the powerful role of cognitive changes in inducing flexibility, since early individual differences in rigidity were not sustained. (From H. M. Trautner et al., 2005, "Rigidity and Flexibility of Gender Stereotypes in Childhood: Developmental or Differential?," *Infant and Child Development, 14,* p. 371. Copyright © 2005 John Wiley & Sons Limited. Reprinted by permission of John Wiley and Sons, Ltd., conveyed through Copyright Clearance Center, Inc.)

women whose mothers had regarded them as highly capable at math were far more likely to choose a physical science career (Bleeker & Jacobs, 2004). Yet mothers rarely made such optimistic judgments about girls.

An encouraging sign is that some gender-stereotyped beliefs about achievement may be changing. In several recent investigations carried out in Canada, France, and the United States, a majority of elementary and secondary students disagreed with the idea that math is a "masculine" subject (Martinot, Bagès, & Désert, 2012; Martinot & Désert, 2007; Plante, Théoret, & Favreau, 2009; Rowley et al., 2007). And when Canadian students were given the option of rating math as a "feminine" subject (not offered in previous studies), an impressive number—though more girls than boys—expressed the view that it is predominantly feminine. The overwhelming majority of these young people, however, continued to view language arts traditionally—as largely "feminine." And they still perceived girls to do better in language arts than in math.

TOWARD GREATER FLEXIBILITY Although school-age children are aware of many gender stereotypes, they also develop a more flexible, open-minded view of what males and females *can do,* a trend that continues into adolescence.

In studying gender stereotyping, researchers usually ask children whether or not both genders can display a personality trait or engage in an activity—responses that measure **gender-stereotype flexibility,** or overlap in the characteristics of males and females. In a German study that followed children from ages 5 to 10, regardless of the degree of early gender-stereotype rigidity, flexibility increased dramatically from age 7 on (see Figure 13.3) (Trautner et al., 2005). As they develop the capacity to integrate conflicting social cues, children realize that a person's sex is not a certain predictor of his or her personality traits, activities, and behaviors (Halim & Ruble, 2010). Similarly, by the end of the school years, most children regard gender typing as socially rather than biologically influenced (Taylor, Rhodes, & Gelman, 2009).

But acknowledging that people *can* cross gender lines does not mean that children always *approve* of doing so. In one longitudinal study, between ages 7 and 13, children generally became more open-minded about girls being offered the same opportunities as boys (Crouter et al., 2007). But the change was less pronounced for boys than girls, and for children whose parents held more traditional gender attitudes.

Furthermore, many school-age children take a harsh view of certain violations—boys playing with dolls and wearing girls' clothing, girls acting noisily and roughly. They are especially intolerant when boys engage in these "cross-gender" acts, which children regard as nearly as bad as moral transgressions (Blakemore, 2003; Levy, Taylor, & Gelman, 1995). When asked for open-ended descriptions of boys and girls, children most often mention girls' physical appearance ("is pretty," "wears dresses") and boys' activities and personality traits ("likes trucks," "is rough") (Miller et al., 2009). The salience of these stereotypes helps explain why, when children of the other sex display the behaviors just mentioned, they are likely to experience severe peer disapproval.

Nevertheless, school-age children do extend more flexible gender attitudes to the peer context to some degree. As with ethnicity, the majority regard excluding an agemate from peer group activities on the basis of gender as unfair. But between fourth and seventh grades, more young people—again, especially boys—say it is OK to exclude on the basis of gender than ethnicity (see Figure 13.4). They

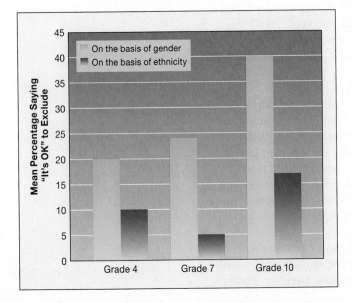

FIGURE 13.4 **Percentage of children and adolescents saying "It's OK" to exclude an agemate from a peer-group activity on the basis of gender and ethnicity.** When asked about excluding an other-sex or other-ethnicity peer from a peer-group activity (a music club in which members trade CDs), many more young people said that it is OK to do so on the basis of gender than on the basis of ethnicity. Willingness to exclude on the basis of gender increased with age, with many participants justifying their decision by pointing to sex differences in interests and communication styles. (Based on Killen et al., 2002.)

point to concerns about group functioning related to sex differences in interests and communication styles—boys' preference for active pursuits and commanding forceful behavior, girls' preference for quiet activities, politeness, and compromise (Killen et al., 2002, p. 56). Indeed, sex-segregated peer associations strengthen during middle childhood and continue to contribute powerfully to gender typing (see Chapter 10, page 386).

Gender Identity and Behavior

Children who were more strongly gender-typed relative to their agemates in early childhood usually remain so in middle childhood (Golombok et al., 2008). Nevertheless, overall changes do occur, with boys' and girls' gender identities following different paths.

From third to sixth grade, boys tend to strengthen their identification with "masculine" personality traits, whereas girls' identification with "feminine" traits declines. Girls often describe themselves as having some "other-gender" characteristics (Serbin, Powlishta, & Gulko, 1993). And whereas boys usually stick to "masculine" pursuits, many girls experiment with a wider range of options—from cooking and sewing to sports and science projects—and more often consider traditionally male future work roles, such as firefighter or astronomer (Liben & Bigler, 2002).

These changes reflect a mixture of cognitive and social forces. School-age children of both sexes are aware that society attaches greater prestige to "masculine" characteristics. For example, they rate "masculine" occupations as having higher status than "feminine" occupations, and an unfamiliar job as higher in status when portrayed with a male worker than a female worker (Liben, Bigler, & Krogh, 2001; Weisgram, Bigler, & Liben, 2010). Messages from adults and peers are also influential. In Chapter 10, we saw that parents (especially fathers) are especially disapproving when sons, as opposed to daughters, cross gender lines. Similarly, a tomboyish girl can interact with boys without losing the approval of her female peers, but a boy who hangs out with girls is likely to be ridiculed and rejected.

As school-age children make social comparisons and characterize themselves in terms of stable dispositions, their gender identity expands to include the following self-evaluations, which greatly affect their adjustment:

- *Gender typicality*—the degree to which the child feels similar to others of the same gender. Although children need not be highly gender typed to view themselves as gender-typical, their psychological well-being depends, to some degree, on feeling that they "fit in" with their same-sex peers.
- *Gender contentedness*—the degree to which the child feels comfortable with his or her gender assignment, which also promotes happiness.
- *Felt pressure to conform to gender roles*—the degree to which the child feels parents and peers disapprove of his or her gender-related traits. Because such pressure reduces the likelihood that children will explore options related to their interests and talents, children who feel strong gender-typed pressure are often distressed.

In a longitudinal study of third through seventh graders, *gender-typical* and *gender-contented* children gained in self-esteem over the following year. In contrast, children who were *gender-atypical* and *gender-discontented* declined in self-worth. Furthermore, gender-atypical children who reported *intense pressure to conform to gender roles* experienced serious difficulties—withdrawal, sadness, disappointment, and anxiety (Yunger, Carver, & Perry, 2004). Clearly, how children feel about themselves in relation to their gender group becomes vitally important in middle childhood and adolescence, and those who experience rejection because of their gender-atypical traits suffer profoundly.

Researchers and therapists are debating how best to help children who feel gender-atypical (Byne et al., 2012). Some favor providing therapy that reinforces traditional gender-role activities, to increase compatibility with same-sex peers (Zucker, 2006). Others oppose this approach on grounds that it is likely to heighten felt pressure to conform (which predicts maladjustment) and—for children who

An 8-year-old launches the rocket she made in her school's Young Astronaut Club. Whereas school-age boys usually stick to "masculine" pursuits, girls experiment with a wider range of options.

fail to change—may result in parental rejection. These experts advocate intervening with parents and peers to help them become more accepting of children's gender-atypical interests and behaviors (Bigler, 2007; Hill et al., 2010). **TAKE A MOMENT...** In view of what you have learned about the development of children's gender typing in Chapter 10 and this chapter, which approach do you think would be more successful, and why?

Ask Yourself

- **REVIEW** Return to page 389 in Chapter 10, and review the concept of *androgyny*. Which of the two sexes is more androygynous in middle childhood, and why?

- **CONNECT** Describe similarities in development of self-concept, attitudes toward racial and ethnic minorities, and gender-stereotyped beliefs in middle childhood.

- **APPLY** What changes in parent–child and teacher–child relationships are likely to help rejected children?

- **REFLECT** As a school-age child, did you have classmates you would classify as popular-antisocial? What were they like, and why do you think peers admired them?

13.8 How do parent–child communication and sibling relationships change in middle childhood?

13.9 How do children fare in lesbian and gay families and in never-married, single-parent families?

13.10 What factors influence children's adjustment to divorce and blended family arrangements?

13.11 How do maternal employment and life in dual-earner families affect children's development?

Family Influences

As children move into school, peer, and community contexts, the parent–child relationship changes. At the same time, children's well-being continues to depend on the quality of family interaction. In the following sections, we will see that contemporary diversity in family life—fewer births per family unit, more lesbian and gay parents who are open about their sexual orientation, more never-married parents, and continuing high rates of divorce, remarriage, and maternal employment—have reshaped the family system. **TAKE A MOMENT...** As you consider this array of family forms, note how children's well-being, in each instance, depends on the quality of family interaction, which is sustained by supportive ties to kin and community and by favorable public policies.

Parent–Child Relationships

In middle childhood, the amount of time children spend with parents declines dramatically. Children's growing independence means that parents must deal with new issues. "I've struggled with how many chores to assign, how much allowance to give, whether their friends are good influences, and what to do about problems at school," Rena remarked. "And then there's the challenge of keeping track of them when they're out—or even when they're home and I'm not there to see what's going on."

Despite these new concerns, child rearing becomes easier for parents who established an authoritative style during the early years. Reasoning is more effective with school-age children because of their greater capacity for logical thinking and their increased respect for parents' expert knowledge (Collins, Madsen, & Susman-Stillman, 2002). And children of parents who engage in joint decision making when possible are more likely to listen to parents' perspectives in situations where compliance is vital (Kuczynski & Lollis, 2002; Russell, Mize, & Bissaker, 2004).

As children demonstrate that they can manage daily activities and responsibilities, effective parents gradually shift control from adult to child. They do not let go entirely but, rather, engage in **coregulation,** a form of supervision in which they exercise general oversight while letting children take charge of moment-by-moment decision making (Maccoby, 1984). Coregulation grows out of a warm, cooperative relationship between parent and child based on give-and-take and mutual respect. Parents must guide and monitor from a distance and effectively communicate expectations when they are with their children. And children must inform parents of their whereabouts, activities, and problems so parents can intervene when necessary (Collins, Madsen, & Susman-Stillman, 2002). Coregulation supports and protects children while preparing them for adolescence, when they will make many important decisions themselves.

As at younger ages, mothers spend more time than fathers with school-age children and know more about children's everyday activities, although many fathers are highly involved (see page 271 in Chapter 7). Both parents, however, tend to devote more time to children of their own sex (Lam, McHale, & Crouter, 2012). In parents' separate activities with children, mothers are more concerned with caregiving and ensuring that children meet responsibilities for homework, after-school lessons, and chores. Fathers, especially those with sons, focus on achievement-related and recreational pursuits (Collins & Russell, 1991). But when both parents are present, fathers engage in as much caregiving as mothers.

Although children often press for greater independence, they also know how much they need their parents' support. In one study, fifth and sixth graders described parents as the most influential people in their lives, often turning to them for affection, advice, enhancement of self-worth, and assistance with everyday problems (Furman & Buhrmester, 1992). A strong sense of attachment security to at least one parent is positively related to school-age children's academic and social self-esteem and negatively related to depression (Diener et al., 2008; Kerns, Brumariu, & Seibert, 2011). And in a longitudinal survey of more than 13,000 nationally representative U.S. parents, those who were warm and involved, monitored their child's activities, and avoided coercive discipline were more likely to have academically and socially competent children. Using these authoritative strategies in middle childhood predicted reduced engagement in antisocial behavior when children reached adolescence (Amato & Fowler, 2002).

Siblings

In addition to parents and friends, siblings continue to be important sources of support. Yet sibling rivalry tends to increase in middle childhood. As children participate in a wider range of activities, parents often compare siblings' traits and accomplishments. The child who gets less parental affection, more disapproval, or fewer material resources is likely to be resentful and show poorer adjustment (Dunn, 2004; McHale, Updegraff, & Whiteman, 2012).

For same-sex siblings who are close in age, parental comparisons are more frequent, resulting in more quarreling and antagonism. This effect is particularly strong when parents are under stress as a result of financial worries, marital conflict, single parenthood, or child negativity (Jenkins, Rasbash, & O'Connor, 2003). Parents whose energies are drained become less careful about being fair. Perhaps because fathers, overall, spend less time with children than mothers, children react especially intensely when fathers prefer one child: Jealousy over attention from fathers predicts sibling conflict (Kolak & Volling, 2011).

To reduce rivalry, siblings often strive to be different from one another (McHale, Updegraff, & Whiteman, 2012). For example, two brothers we know deliberately selected different athletic pursuits and musical instruments. If the older one did especially well at an activity, the younger one did not want to try it. Parents can limit these effects by making an effort not to compare children, but some feedback about their competencies is inevitable. As siblings attempt to win recognition for their own uniqueness, they shape important aspects of each other's development.

Although conflict rises, many siblings continue to rely on each other for companionship, assistance, and emotional support (Siebert & Kerns, 2009). When researchers asked siblings about shared daily activities, children mentioned that older siblings often helped younger siblings with academic and peer challenges. And both offered each other help with family issues (Tucker, McHale, & Crouter, 2001). But for siblings to reap these benefits, parental encouragement of warm, considerate sibling ties is vital. Providing parents with training in mediation—how to get siblings to lay down ground rules, clarify their points of disagreement and common ground, and discuss possible solutions—increases siblings' awareness of each other's perspectives and reduces animosity (Smith & Ross, 2007).

© SHEHZAD NOORANI/DRIK/MAJORITY WORLD/THE IMAGE WORKS

An older sister helps her 6-year-old brother with homework. Although sibling rivalry tends to increase in middle childhood, siblings also provide each other with emotional support and help with difficult tasks.

When siblings get along well, the older sibling's academic and social competence tends to "rub off on" the younger sibling, fostering more favorable achievement and peer relations (Brody & Murry, 2001; Lamarche et al., 2006). But destructive sibling conflict in middle childhood is associated with detrimental outcomes, including conflict-ridden peer relationships, anxiety, depressed mood, and later substance use and delinquency, even after other family-relationship factors are controlled (Kim et al., 2007; Ostrov, Crick, & Stauffacher, 2006).

Only Children

Although sibling relationships bring many benefits, they are not essential for normal development. Contrary to popular belief, only children are not spoiled, and, in some respects, they are advantaged. U.S. children growing up in one-child and multichild families do not differ in self-rated personality traits (Mottus, Indus, & Allik, 2008). And compared to children with siblings, only children are higher in self-esteem and achievement motivation, do better in school, and attain higher levels of education. One reason may be that only children have somewhat closer relationships with parents, who may exert more pressure for mastery and accomplishment and can invest more time in their child's educational experiences (Falbo, 2012). Furthermore, only children have just as many close, high-quality friends as children with siblings. However, they tend to be less well-accepted in the peer group, perhaps because they have not had opportunities to learn effective conflict-resolution strategies through sibling interaction (Kitzmann, Cohen, & Lockwood, 2002).

Favorable development also characterizes only children in China, where a one-child family policy was strictly enforced in densely populated urban areas for more than three decades to control population growth. (In 2013, China relaxed the policy, permitting couples to have two children if one parent is an only child.) Compared with agemates who have siblings, Chinese only children are advanced in cognitive development and academic achievement. They also feel more emotionally secure, perhaps because government disapproval promotes tension in families with more than one child (Falbo, 2012; Jiao, Ji, & Jing, 1996; Yang et al., 1995). Chinese mothers usually ensure that their children have regular contact with first cousins, who are considered siblings. Perhaps as a result, Chinese only children do not differ from agemates with siblings in social skills and peer acceptance (Hart, Newell, & Olsen, 2003).

Lesbian and Gay Families

According to recent estimates, about 20 to 35 percent of lesbian couples and 5 to 15 percent of gay couples are parents, most through previous heterosexual marriages, some through adoption, and a growing number through reproductive technologies (Brewster, Tillman, & Jokinen-Gordon, 2014; Gates, 2013). In the past, because of laws assuming that gay men and lesbians could not be adequate parents, those who divorced a heterosexual partner lost custody of their children. Today, the majority of U.S. states hold that sexual orientation is irrelevant to custody or adoption—a change likely spurred by the increasing acceptance of same-sex marriage, now legal in the majority of states. Custody and adoption by lesbian and gay parents are also legal in many other industrialized nations.

Most research on families headed by same-sex couples is limited to volunteer samples. Findings indicate that lesbian and gay parents are as committed to and effective at child rearing as heterosexual parents and sometimes more so (Bos, 2013). Also, whether born to or adopted by their parents or conceived through donor insemination, children in lesbian and gay families do not differ from the children of heterosexual parents in mental health, peer relations, gender-role behavior, or quality of life (Bos & Sandfort, 2010; Farr, Forssell, & Patterson, 2010; Goldberg, 2010; van Gelderen et al., 2012).

To surmount the potential bias associated with volunteer samples, some researchers take advantage of large, nationally representative

JENS KALAENE/PICTURE-ALLIANCE/DPA/AP IMAGES

Lesbian and gay parents are as committed to and as effective at child rearing as heterosexual parents. And their children do not differ in mental health, peer relations, gender-role behavior, or quality of life.

data banks to study lesbian and gay families. Findings confirm that children with same-sex and opposite-sex parents develop similarly, and that children's adjustment is linked to factors other than parental sexual orientation (Moore & Stambolis-Ruhstorfer, 2013). For example, close parent–child relationships predict better peer relations and a reduction in adolescent delinquency, whereas family transitions (such as parental divorce and remarriage) are related to academic difficulties, regardless of family form (Potter, 2012; Russell & Muraco, 2013).

The large majority of children of lesbian and gay parents identify as heterosexual (Patterson, 2013). But some evidence suggests that more adolescents from lesbian and gay families experiment for a time with partners of both sexes, perhaps as a result of being reared in families and communities especially tolerant of nonconformity and difference (Bos, van Balen, & van den Boom, 2004; Gartrell, Bos, & Goldberg, 2011). In support of this interpretation, a Dutch investigation found that 8- to 12-year-old children of lesbian parents felt slightly less parental pressure to conform to gender roles than did children of heterosexual parents. The two groups were similar in other aspects of gender identity (gender typicality and gender contentedness; see page 495). At the same time, the children of lesbian parents reported greater sexual questioning—less certainty about future heterosexual attractions and relationships, though the group difference was mild (see Figure 13.5) (Bos & Sandfort, 2010).

A major concern of lesbian and gay parents is that their children will be stigmatized by their parents' sexual orientation. Peer teasing and disapproval are problems for some children of same-sex parents, but close parent–child relationships, supportive school environments, and connections with other lesbian and gay families protect children from the negative effects of these experiences (Bos, 2013). Overall, children of lesbian and gay parents can be distinguished from other children mainly by issues related to living in discriminatory contexts.

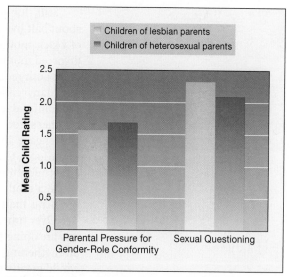

FIGURE 13.5 **Reports of parental pressure for gender-role conformity and of sexual questioning by 8- to 12-year-olds of lesbian and heterosexual parents.** Compared with children of heterosexual parents, children of lesbian parents rated parental pressure slightly lower and sexual questioning higher. Neither group expressed strong parental pressure or sexual questioning (participants rated each on a 4-point scale, and mean ratings ranged from 1.5 to 2.3). (Based on Bos & Sandfort, 2010.)

Never-Married Single-Parent Families

Over the past several decades, births to unmarried mothers in industrialized nations have increased dramatically. Today, about 40 percent of U.S. births are to single mothers, more than double the percentage in 1980 (Martin et al., 2013). Whereas teenage parenthood has declined steadily since 1990, births to single adult women have increased, with a particularly sharp rise during the first decade of the twenty-first century (Curtin, Ventura, & Martinez, 2014).

A growing number of nonmarital births are planned and occur to cohabiting couples. But these relationships—common among young adults with low education—are often unstable (Cherlin, 2010; Gibson-Davis & Rackin, 2014). And despite this trend, more than 12 percent of U.S. children live with a single parent who has never married and does not have a partner. Of these parents, about 90 percent are mothers, 10 percent fathers (Curtin, Ventura, & Martinez, 2014; U.S. Census Bureau, 2014b).

Single motherhood is especially prevalent among African-American young women, who are considerably more likely than white women to give birth outside of marriage and less likely to live with the baby's father. As a result, more than half of births to black mothers in their twenties are to women without a partner, compared with about 14 percent of births to white women (Child Trends, 2014a; Hamilton et al., 2014). Job loss, persisting unemployment, and consequent inability of many black men to support a family have contributed to the number of African-American never-married, single-mother families.

Never-married African-American mothers often receive child-rearing support from extended family, especially their own mothers and sometimes male relatives (Anderson, 2012). Compared with their white counterparts, low-SES African-American women tend to marry later—within a decade after birth of the first child—but not necessarily to the child's biological father (Dixon, 2009; Wu, Bumpass, & Musick, 2001).

Still, for low-SES women, single parenthood generally increases financial hardship; about half live in poverty (Mather, 2010). Nearly 50 percent of white mothers and 60 percent of black mothers have a second child while unmarried. And they are far less likely than divorced mothers to receive paternal child support payments, although child support enforcement both reduces financial stress and increases father involvement (Huang, 2006).

Many children in single-mother homes display adjustment problems associated with economic adversity (Lamb, 2012). Furthermore, children of never-married mothers who lack a father's consistent warmth and involvement show less favorable cognitive development and engage in more antisocial behavior than children in low-SES, first-marriage families (Waldfogel, Craigie, & Brooks-Gunn, 2010). But marriage to the child's biological father benefits children only when the father is a reliable source of economic and emotional support. When a mother pairs up with an antisocial father, her child is at far greater risk for conduct problems than if she had reared the child alone (Jaffee et al., 2003).

Over time, most unmarried fathers—who usually have no more than a modest education and are doing poorly financially—spend less and less time with their children (Lerman, 2010). Strengthening social support, education, and employment opportunities for low-SES parents would greatly enhance the well-being of single mothers and their children.

Divorce

Children's interactions with parents and siblings are affected by other aspects of family life. Joey and Lizzie's relationship had been particularly negative only a few years before. Joey pushed, hit, taunted, and called Lizzie names. Although she tried to retaliate, Lizzie was no match for Joey's larger size. The arguments usually ended with Lizzie running in tears to her mother. Joey and Lizzie's fighting coincided with their parents' growing marital unhappiness. When Joey was 8 and Lizzie 5, their father, Drake, moved out.

Between 1960 and 1985, divorce rates in Western nations rose dramatically before stabilizing in most countries. The United States has experienced a decline in divorces over the past fifteen years, largely due to a rise in age at first marriage (couples marrying at older ages have a lower divorce rate). Nevertheless, the United States continues to have the highest divorce rate in the world (see Figure 13.6). Of the 45 percent of American marriages that end in divorce, half involve children. More than one-fourth of U.S. children live in divorced, single-parent households. Although most reside with their mothers, the percentage in father-headed households has increased steadily, to about 14 percent (U.S. Census Bureau, 2014b).

Children of divorce spend an average of five years in a single-parent home—almost a third of childhood. For many, divorce leads to new family relationships. About two-thirds of divorced parents marry again. Half their children eventually experience a third major change—the end of their parent's second marriage (Hetherington & Kelly, 2002).

These figures reveal that divorce is not a single event in the lives of parents and children. Instead, it is a transition that leads to a variety of new living arrangements, accompanied by changes in housing, income, and family roles and responsibilities. Although divorce is stressful for children and increases their risk of adjustment problems, most adjust favorably (Greene et al., 2012; Lamb, 2012). How well children fare depends on many factors: the custodial parent's psychological health, the child's characteristics, and social supports within the family and surrounding community.

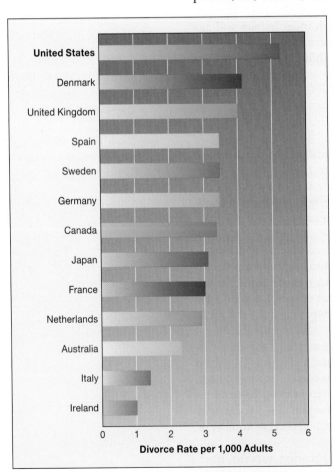

FIGURE 13.6 **Divorce rates in 13 industrialized nations.**
The U.S. divorce rate is the highest in the world, far exceeding divorce rates in other countries. (Based on U.S. Census Bureau, 2014b.)

IMMEDIATE CONSEQUENCES "Things were worst after Drake and I decided to separate," Rena reflected. "We fought over division of our belongings and custody of the children, and the kids suffered. Sobbing, Lizzie told me she was 'sorry she made Daddy go away.' Joey kicked and threw things at home and didn't do his work at school. In the midst of everything, I could hardly deal with their problems. We had to sell the house; I couldn't afford it alone. And I needed a better-paying job."

Family conflict often rises in newly divorced households as parents try to settle disputes over children and possessions. Once one parent moves out, additional events threaten supportive interactions between parents and children. Mother-headed households typically experience a sharp drop in income. In the United States, 28 percent of divorced mothers with young children live in poverty and many more are low-income, getting less than the full amount of child support from the absent father or none at all (U.S. Census Bureau, 2011). They often have to move to lower-cost housing, reducing supportive ties to neighbors and friends.

The transition from marriage to divorce typically leads to high maternal stress, depression, and anxiety and to a disorganized family life. Declines in well-being are greatest for mothers of young children

When parents divorce, young children often blame themselves and respond with both fear and anger. This father's soothing words help his daughter understand that she is not responsible for the marital breakup.

(Williams & Dunne-Bryant, 2006). "Meals and bedtimes were at all hours, the house didn't get cleaned, and I stopped taking Joey and Lizzie on weekend outings," said Rena. As children react with distress and anger to their less secure home lives, discipline may become harsh and inconsistent. Over time, contact with noncustodial fathers—and the quality of the father–child relationship—often decreases, particularly when parental conflict is high (Troilo & Coleman, 2012). Fathers who see their children only occasionally are inclined to be permissive and indulgent, making the mother's task of managing the child even more difficult.

The more parents argue and fail to provide children with warmth, involvement, and consistent guidance, the poorer children's adjustment (Lamb, 2012). About 20 to 25 percent of children in divorced families display severe problems, compared with about 10 percent in nondivorced families (Greene et al., 2012; Lansford, 2009). At the same time, reactions vary with children's age, temperament, and sex.

Children's Age. Five-year-old Lizzie's fear that she had caused her father to leave home is not unusual. Preschool and young school-age children often blame themselves for a marital breakup and fear that both parents may abandon them (Lansford et al., 2006). Hence, they are more likely to display both anxious, fearful and angry, defiant reactions than older children and adolescents with the cognitive maturity to understand that they are not responsible for their parents' divorce.

Still, many school-age and adolescent youngsters also react strongly, experiencing depressed mood, declining in school performance, becoming unruly, and escaping into undesirable peer activities, such as running away, truancy, substance use, and early sexual activity, particularly when family conflict is high and parental supervision is low (Arkes, 2013; Kleinsorge & Covitz, 2012; Lansford et al., 2006). Some older children—especially the oldest child in the family—display more mature behavior, willingly taking on extra household tasks, care of younger siblings, and emotional support of a depressed, anxious mother. But if these demands are too great, these children may eventually become resentful, withdraw from the family, and engage in angry, acting-out behavior (Hetherington & Kelly, 2002).

Children's Temperament and Sex. Exposure to stressful life events and inadequate parenting magnifies the problems of temperamentally difficult children (see Chapter 7). In contrast, easy children are less often targets of parental anger and also cope more effectively with adversity.

These findings help explain sex differences in response to divorce. Girls sometimes respond as Lizzie did, with internalizing reactions such as crying, self-criticism, and withdrawal. More often, children of both sexes show demanding, attention-getting behavior. But in mother-custody families, boys are at slightly greater risk for serious adjustment problems (Amato, 2010). Recall from Chapter 10 that boys are more active and noncompliant—behaviors that increase with exposure to parental conflict and inconsistent discipline. Research reveals that long before the marital breakup, sons of divorcing couples display higher rates of impulsivity, defiance, and aggression—behaviors that may have been caused by their parents' marital problems while also contributing to them (Shaw, Winslow, & Flanagan, 1999; Strohschein, 2005). As a result, more boys enter the period of turmoil surrounding divorce with reduced capacity to cope with family stress.

Perhaps because their behavior is more unruly, boys of divorcing parents receive less emotional support from mothers, teachers, and peers. And as Joey's behavior toward Lizzie illustrates, the cycles of coercive interaction between distressed children and their divorced mothers soon spread to sibling relations (Sheehan et al., 2004). After divorce, children who are challenging to rear generally get worse.

LONG-TERM CONSEQUENCES Rena eventually found better-paying work and gained control over the daily operation of the household. Her own feelings of anger and rejection also declined. And after several meetings with a counselor, Rena and Drake realized the harmful impact of their quarreling on Joey and Lizzie. Drake visited regularly and handled Joey's disruptiveness with firmness and consistency. Soon Joey's school performance improved, his behavior problems subsided, and both children seemed calmer and happier.

Most children show improved adjustment by two years after divorce. Yet overall, children and adolescents of divorced parents continue to score slightly lower than children of continuously married parents in academic achievement, self-esteem, social competence, and emotional and behavioral adjustment (Lansford, 2009). Children with difficult temperaments are more likely to drop out of school, to be depressed, and to engage in antisocial behavior in adolescence. And divorce is linked to problems with adolescent sexuality and development of intimate ties. Young people who experienced parental divorce—especially more than once—display higher rates of early sexual activity and adolescent parenthood. Some experience other lasting difficulties—reduced educational attainment, troubled romantic relationships and marriages, divorce in adulthood, and unsatisfying parent–child relationships (Amato, 2006, 2010; Lansford, 2009). Thus, divorce can have consequences for subsequent generations.

The overriding factor in positive adjustment is effective parenting—how well the custodial parent handles stress and shields the child from family conflict, and the extent to which each parent uses authoritative child rearing (Lamb, 2012). Parent-training programs can help custodial parents support their children's development. For example, when researchers randomly assigned divorced mothers with children to parent training and control conditions, training improved mother–child relationships and increased children's coping skills, with effects persisting for six years (Velez et al., 2011).

Where the custodial parent is the mother, regular contact with fathers is also important. But only about one-third of children today experience at least weekly visits (Amato & Dorius, 2010). The more paternal contact and the warmer the relationship, the less children react with defiance and aggression (Dunn et al., 2004). For girls, a good father–child relationship protects against early sexual activity and unhappy romantic involvements. For boys, it seems to affect overall psychological well-being. In fact, some studies report that outcomes for sons are better when the father is the custodial parent (Clarke-Stewart & Hayward, 1996; McLanahan, 1999). Fathers' greater economic security and image of authority seem to help them engage in effective parenting with sons. And boys in father-custody families may benefit from greater involvement of both parents because noncustodial mothers participate more in their children's lives than noncustodial fathers.

Although divorce is painful for children, remaining in an intact but high-conflict family is much worse than making the transition to

© BURGER/PHANIE/THE IMAGE WORKS

Regular contact with both parents and effective coparenting—supporting each other in their child-rearing roles—greatly improve adjustment in children of divorce.

a low-conflict, single-parent household (Lamb, 2012; Strohschein, 2005). However, more parents today are divorcing because they are moderately (rather than extremely) dissatisfied with their relationship. Research suggests that children in these low-discord homes are especially puzzled and upset. Perhaps these youngsters' inability to understand the marital breakup and grief over the loss of a seemingly happy home life explain why the adjustment problems of children of divorce have intensified over time (Amato, 2001; Lansford, 2009).

Regardless of the extent of their friction, parents who set aside their disagreements and engage in effective coparenting (see page 69 in Chapter 2), supporting each other in their child-rearing roles, greatly improve their children's chances of growing up competent, stable, and happy (Lamb, 2012). Caring extended-family members, teachers, siblings, and friends also reduce the likelihood that divorce will result in long-term difficulties (Hetherington, 2003).

DIVORCE MEDIATION, JOINT CUSTODY, AND CHILD SUPPORT   Awareness that divorce is highly stressful for children and families has led to community-based services aimed at helping them through this difficult time. One such service is **divorce mediation,** a series of meetings between divorcing adults and a trained professional aimed at reducing family conflict, including legal battles over property division and child custody. Mediation increases out-of-court settlements, cooperation and involvement of both parents in child rearing, and parents' and children's feelings of well-being (Douglas, 2006; Emery, Sbarra, & Grover, 2005).

To further encourage parents to resolve their disputes, parent education programs are becoming common. During several sessions, professionals teach parents about the positive impact of constructive conflict resolution and of respectful, cooperative coparenting on children's well-being (Braver et al., 2005; Cookston et al., 2006; Wolchik et al., 2002). Because of the demonstrated impact of parent education on parental cooperation, courts in many U.S. states may require parents to attend a program.

Joint custody, which grants each parent an equal say in important decisions about the child's upbringing, is becoming increasingly common. Children usually reside with one parent and see the other on a fixed schedule, similar to the typical sole-custody situation. In other cases, parents share physical custody, and children move between homes and sometimes between schools and peer groups. These transitions can be especially hard on some children. Joint-custody parents usually report little conflict—fortunately so, since the success of the arrangement depends on effective coparenting (Bauserman, 2012). And their children, regardless of living arrangements, tend to be better-adjusted than children in sole-maternal-custody homes (Bauserman, 2002).

Finally, many single-parent families depend on child support from the absent parent to relieve financial strain. All U.S. states have procedures for withholding wages from parents who fail to make these payments. Although child support is usually not enough to lift a single-parent family out of poverty, it can ease its burdens substantially. Noncustodial fathers who have generous visitation schedules and see their children often are more likely to pay child support regularly (Amato & Sobolewski, 2004). And increases in contact with the child and in child support over time predict better coparenting relationships (Hofferth, Forry, & Peters, 2010). Applying What We Know on page 504 summarizes ways to help children adjust to their parents' divorce.

Blended Families

"If you get married to Wendell and Daddy gets married to Carol," Lizzie wondered aloud to Rena, "then I'll have two sisters and one more brother. And let's see, how many grandmothers and grandfathers? A lot!" exclaimed Lizzie.

About 60 percent of divorced parents remarry within a few years. Others *cohabit,* or share a sexual relationship and a residence with a partner outside of marriage. Parent, stepparent, and children form a new family structure called a **blended, or reconstituted, family.** For some children, this expanded family network is positive, bringing greater adult attention. But children in blended families usually have more adjustment problems—including internalizing and externalizing symptoms and poor school performance—than children in stable,

Applying What We Know

Helping Children Adjust to Their Parents' Divorce

SUGGESTION	EXPLANATION
Shield children from conflict.	Witnessing intense parental conflict is very damaging to children. If one parent insists on expressing hostility, children fare better if the other parent does not respond in kind.
Provide children with as much continuity, familiarity, and predictability as possible.	Children adjust better during the period surrounding divorce when their lives have some stability—for example, the same school, bedroom, babysitter, playmates, and daily schedule.
Explain the divorce and tell children what to expect.	Children may develop fears of abandonment if they are not prepared for their parents' separation. They should be told that their parents will not be living together anymore, which parent will be moving out, and when they will be able to see that parent. If possible, parents should explain the divorce together, providing a reason that each child can understand and assuring children that they are not to blame.
Emphasize the permanence of the divorce.	Fantasies of parents getting back together can prevent children from accepting the reality of their current life. Children should be told that the divorce is final and that they cannot change this fact.
Respond sympathetically to children's feelings.	Children need supportive, understanding responses to their feelings of sadness, fear, and anger. For children to adjust well, their painful emotions must be acknowledged, not denied or avoided.
Engage in authoritative parenting.	Parents who engage in authoritative parenting—providing affection and acceptance, reasonable demands for mature behavior, and consistent, rational discipline—greatly reduce their children's risk of maladjustment following divorce.
Promote continuing relationships with both parents.	When parents disentangle their lingering hostility toward the former spouse from the child's need for a continuing relationship with the other parent, children adjust well. Grandparents and other extended-family members can help by not taking sides.

Source: Teyber, 2001.

first-marriage families (Anderson & Greene, 2013; Pryor, 2014). Switching to stepparents' new rules and expectations can be stressful, and children often view steprelatives as intruders. How well they adapt is, again, related to the quality of family functioning (Hetherington & Kelly, 2002). This depends on which parent forms a new relationship, the child's age and sex, and the complexity of blended-family relationships. As we will see, older children and girls seem to have the hardest time.

MOTHER–STEPFATHER FAMILIES Because mothers generally retain custody of children, the most common form of blended family is a mother–stepfather arrangement. Boys tend to adjust quickly, welcoming a stepfather who is warm, who refrains from exerting his authority too quickly, and who offers relief from coercive cycles of mother–son interaction. Mothers' friction with sons also declines as a result of greater economic security, another adult to share household tasks, and an end to loneliness (Visher, Visher, & Pasley, 2003). Stepfathers who marry rather than cohabit are more involved in parenting, perhaps because men who choose to marry a mother with children are more interested in and skilled at child rearing (Hofferth & Anderson, 2003). Girls, however, often have difficulty with their custodial mother's remarriage. Stepfathers disrupt the close ties many girls have established with their mothers, and girls often react with sulky, resistant behavior (Pryor, 2014).

But age affects these findings. Older school-age children and adolescents of both sexes display more irresponsible, acting-out behavior than their peers not in stepfamilies (Hetherington & Stanley-Hagan, 2000; Robertson, 2008). If parents are warmer and more involved with their biological children than with their stepchildren, older children are more likely to notice and challenge unfair treatment. And adolescents often view the new stepparent as a threat to their freedom, especially

© KAYTE DEIOMA/PHOTOEDIT

When stepparents move into their new roles gradually, first building warm relationships with stepchildren, they ease adjustment to life in a blended family.

if they experienced little parental monitoring in the single-parent family. But when teenagers have affectionate, cooperative relationships with their mothers, many develop good relationships with stepfathers—a circumstance linked to more favorable adolescent well-being (King, 2009; Pryor, 2014).

FATHER–STEPMOTHER FAMILIES   Remarriage of noncustodial fathers often leads to reduced contact with their biological children, especially when fathers remarry quickly, before they have established postdivorce parent–child routines (Dunn, 2002; Juby et al., 2007). When fathers have custody, children typically react negatively to remarriage. One reason is that children living with fathers often start out with more problems. Perhaps the biological mother could no longer handle the difficult child (usually a boy), so the father and his new partner are faced with a youngster who has behavior problems. In other instances, the father has custody because of a very close relationship with the child, and his remarriage disrupts this bond (Buchanan, Maccoby, & Dornbusch, 1996).

Girls, especially, have a hard time getting along with their stepmothers, either because the remarriage threatens the girl's bond with her father or because she becomes entangled in loyalty conflicts between the two mother figures. But the longer children live in father–stepmother households, the closer they feel to their stepmothers and the more positive their interaction with them becomes (King, 2007). With time and patience, children of both genders benefit from the support of a second mother figure.

SUPPORT FOR BLENDED FAMILIES   Parenting education and couples counseling can help parents and children adapt to the complexities of blended families. Effective approaches encourage stepparents to move into their new roles gradually by first building a warm relationship with the child, which makes more active parenting possible (Pasley & Garneau, 2012; Pryor, 2014). Counselors can offer couples guidance in coparenting to limit loyalty conflicts and provide consistency in child rearing. And tempering parents' unrealistic expectations for children's rapid adjustment—by pointing out that building a unified blended family often takes years—makes it easier for families to endure the transition and succeed.

Unfortunately, the divorce rate for second marriages is even higher than for first marriages. Parents with antisocial tendencies and poor child-rearing skills are particularly likely to have several divorces and remarriages. The more marital transitions children experience, the greater their adjustment difficulties (Amato, 2010). These families usually require prolonged, intensive therapy.

Maternal Employment and Dual-Earner Families

Today, U.S. single and married mothers are in the labor market in nearly equal proportions, and more than three-fourths of those with school-age children are employed (U.S. Census Bureau, 2014b). In Chapter 7, we saw that the impact of maternal employment on early development depends on the quality of child care and the continuing parent–child relationship. The same is true in middle childhood.

MATERNAL EMPLOYMENT AND CHILD DEVELOPMENT   When mothers enjoy their work and remain committed to parenting, children show favorable adjustment—higher self-esteem, more positive family and peer relations, less gender-stereotyped beliefs, and better grades in school. Girls, especially, profit from the image of female competence. Regardless of SES, daughters of employed mothers perceive women's roles as involving more freedom of choice and satisfaction and are more achievement- and career-oriented (Hoffman, 2000).

Parenting practices contribute to these benefits. Employed mothers who value their parenting role are more likely to use authoritative child rearing and coregulation. Also, children in dual-earner households devote more daily hours to doing homework under parental guidance and participate more in household chores. And maternal employment often leads fathers—especially those who believe in the importance of the paternal role and who feel successful at parenting—to take on greater child-rearing responsibilities, with a small but

Employed mothers who enjoy their work while also valuing the parenting role tend to have children who show higher self-esteem, more positive family and peer relations, less gender-stereotyped beliefs, and better school performance.

increasing number staying home full-time (Gottfried, Gottfried, & Bathurst, 2002; Jacobs & Kelley, 2006). Paternal involvement is associated in childhood and adolescence with higher intelligence and achievement, more mature social behavior, and a flexible view of gender roles; and in adulthood with generally better mental health (Coltrane, 1996; Pleck & Masciadrelli, 2004).

But when employment places heavy demands on parents' schedules or is stressful for other reasons, children are at risk for ineffective parenting (Strazdins et al., 2013). Working many hours, working a nonstandard schedule (such as night or weekend shifts), or experiencing a negative workplace atmosphere is associated with lower quality parenting, fewer joint parent–child activities, poorer cognitive development, and increased behavior problems throughout childhood and adolescence (Li et al., 2014; Strazdins et al., 2006).

Negative consequences are magnified when low-SES mothers spend long days at low-paying, physically exhausting jobs—conditions linked to maternal depression and to harsh, inconsistent discipline (Raver, 2003). In contrast, part-time employment and flexible work schedules are associated with good child adjustment (Hill et al., 2006; Youn, Leon, & Lee, 2012). By preventing role overload, these arrangements help parents meet children's needs.

SUPPORT FOR EMPLOYED PARENTS AND THEIR FAMILIES In dual-earner families, the father's willingness to share responsibilities is crucial. If he helps little or not at all, the mother carries a double load, at home and at work, leading to fatigue, distress, and little time and energy for children. Fortunately, compared to three decades ago, today's U.S. fathers are far more involved in child care. But their increased participation has resulted in a growing number of fathers who also report role overload (Galinsky, Aumann, & Bond, 2009). In an Australian study, children (especially sons) of fathers who worked long hours were at higher risk for behavior problems (Johnson et al., 2013).

Employed parents need assistance from work settings and communities in their child-rearing roles. Part-time employment, flexible schedules, job sharing, on-site child care, and paid leave when children are ill help parents juggle the demands of work and child rearing (Butts, Casper, & Yang, 2013). Equal pay and employment opportunities for women are also important. Because these policies enhance financial status and morale, they improve the way parents feel and behave when they arrive home at the end of the working day.

CHILD CARE FOR SCHOOL-AGE CHILDREN High-quality child care is vital for parents' peace of mind and children's well-being, even during middle childhood. An estimated 4.5 million 5- to 14-year-olds in the United States are **self-care children,** who regularly look after themselves for some period of time during after-school hours (Laughlin, 2013). Self-care increases with age and also with SES, perhaps because of the greater safety of higher-income neighborhoods. But when lower-SES parents lack alternatives to self-care, their children spend more hours on their own (Casper & Smith, 2002).

The implications of self-care for development depend on children's maturity and the way they spend their time. Among younger school-age children, those who spend more hours alone have more adjustment difficulties (Vandell & Posner, 1999). As children become old enough to look after themselves, those who have a history of authoritative child rearing, are monitored by parental telephone calls, and have regular after-school chores appear responsible and well-adjusted. In contrast, children left to their own devices are more likely to bend to peer pressures and engage in antisocial behavior (Coley, Morris, & Hernandez, 2004; Vandell et al., 2006).

Before age 8 or 9, most children need supervision because they are not yet competent to handle emergencies (Galambos & Maggs, 1991). But

Attending high-quality after-school programs that include enrichment activities is linked to good school performance and emotional and social adjustment, particularly for low-SES children.

throughout middle childhood and early adolescence, attending after-school programs with well-trained and supportive staffs, generous adult–child ratios, and skill-building activities is linked to good school performance and emotional and social adjustment (Durlak, Weissberg, & Pachan, 2010; Kantaoka & Vandell, 2013). Low-SES children who participate in "after-care" programs offering academic assistance and enrichment activities (scouting, music and art lessons, clubs) show special benefits. They exceed their self-care counterparts in classroom work habits, academic achievement, and prosocial behavior and display fewer behavior problems (Lauer et al., 2006; Vandell et al., 2006).

Unfortunately, good after-care is in especially short supply in low-income neighborhoods. Ethnic minority children, immigrant children, and children from economically disadvantaged families are least likely to be enrolled (Greenberg, 2013). A special need exists for well-planned programs in poverty-stricken areas—ones that provide safe environments, warm relationships with adults, and enjoyable, goal-oriented activities.

LOOK and LISTEN

In your community, what school-based after-care programs are available, and how plentiful are they in low-income neighborhoods? If possible, visit a program, observing for supportive adult involvement, academic assistance, and enrichment activities.

Ask Yourself

- **REVIEW** Describe and explain changes in sibling relationships during middle childhood.

- **CONNECT** How does each level in Bronfenbrenner's ecological systems theory—microsystem, mesosystem, exosystem, and macrosystem—contribute to effects of parents' employment on children's development?

- **APPLY** Steve and Marissa are in the midst of an acrimonious divorce. Their 9-year-old son Dennis has become hostile and defiant. How can Steve and Marissa help Dennis adjust?

- **REFLECT** What after-school child-care arrangements did you experience in elementary school? How do you think they influenced your development?

Some Common Problems of Development

We have considered a variety of stressful experiences that place children at risk for future problems. Next, we address two more areas of concern: school-age children's fears and anxieties and the consequences of child sexual abuse. Finally, we sum up factors that help school-age children cope effectively with stress.

13.12 Cite common fears and anxieties in middle childhood.

13.13 Discuss factors related to child sexual abuse, its consequences for children's development, and its prevention and treatment.

13.14 Cite factors that foster resilience in middle childhood.

Fears and Anxieties

Although fears of the dark, thunder and lightning, and supernatural beings persist into middle childhood, older children's anxieties are also directed toward new concerns. As children begin to understand the realities of the wider world, the possibility of personal harm (being robbed, stabbed, or shot) and media events (war and disasters) often trouble them. Other common worries include academic failure, separation from parents, parents' health, physical injuries, the possibility of dying, and peer rejection (Muris & Field, 2011; Weems & Costa, 2005). Because children often mull over frightening thoughts at bedtime, nighttime fears actually increase between ages 7 and 9 (Muris et al., 2001).

As long as fears are not too intense, most children handle them constructively, using the more sophisticated emotional self-regulation strategies that develop in middle childhood. Consequently, overall number of fears declines with age, especially for girls, who express more fears than boys throughout childhood and adolescence (Gullone, 2000; Muris & Field, 2011). But about 5 percent of school-age children develop an intense, unmanageable fear, called a **phobia.** Children with inhibited temperaments are at high risk, displaying phobias five to six times as often as other children (Ollendick, King, & Muris, 2002).

Some children with phobias and other anxieties develop *school refusal*—severe apprehension about attending school, often accompanied by physical complaints such as dizziness, nausea, stomachaches, and vomiting (Wimmer, 2013). About one-third of children with school

Some children develop school refusal—severe apprehension about attending school. For many younger children, the real fear is maternal separation, often due to parental overprotection.

refusal are 5- to 7-year-olds for whom the real fear is maternal separation. Family therapy helps these children, whose difficulty can often be traced to parental overprotection (Elliott, 1999).

Most cases of school refusal appear around age 11 to 13, in children who usually find a particular aspect of school frightening—an overcritical teacher, a school bully, or too much parental pressure to achieve. A change in school environment or parenting practices may be needed. Firm insistence that the child return to school, along with training in how to manage anxiety and cope with difficult situations, is also helpful (Kearney, Spear, & Mihalas, 2014).

Severe childhood anxieties may also arise from harsh living conditions. In inner-city ghettos and in war-torn areas of the world, many children live in the midst of constant danger, chaos, and deprivation. As the Cultural Influences box on the following page reveals, they are at risk for long-term emotional distress and behavior problems. Finally, as we saw in our discussion of child abuse in Chapter 10, too often violence and other destructive acts become part of adult–child relationships. During middle childhood, child sexual abuse increases.

Child Sexual Abuse

Until recently, child sexual abuse was considered rare, and adults often dismissed children's claims of abuse. In the 1970s, efforts by professionals and media attention led to recognition of child sexual abuse as a serious and widespread problem. About 63,000 cases in the United States were confirmed in the most recently reported year (U.S. Department of Health and Human Services, 2013). But this figure greatly underestimates the extent of sexual abuse, since most victims either delay disclosure for a long time or remain silent (Martin & Silverstone, 2013).

CHARACTERISTICS OF ABUSERS AND VICTIMS   Globally, an estimated 18 percent of girls and 8 percent of boys are sexually abused during childhood or adolescence (Stoltenborgh et al., 2011). Most cases are reported in middle childhood, but for some victims, abuse begins early in life and continues for many years (Collin-Vézina, Daigneault, & Hébert, 2013; Trickett, Noll, & Putnam, 2011).

In the vast majority of cases, the abuser is a male, often a parent or someone the parent knows well—a father, stepfather, live-in boyfriend, uncle, or older brother (Olafson, 2011). If the abuser is a nonrelative, the person is usually someone the child has come to know and trust, such as a teacher, caregiver, clergy member, or family friend (Sullivan et al., 2011). The Internet and mobile phones have become avenues through which some perpetrators commit sexual abuse—for example, by exposing children and adolescents to pornography and online sexual advances as a way of "grooming" them for sexual acts offline (Kloess, Beech, & Harkins, 2014). Sadly, a substantial number of abusers are themselves children or adolescents, many of whom are also victims of sexual abuse or other forms of maltreatment (Vizard, 2013).

Abusers make the child comply in a variety of distasteful ways, including deception, bribery, verbal intimidation, and physical force. You may wonder how any adult—especially a parent or close relative—could violate a child sexually. Many offenders deny their own responsibility, blaming the abuse on the willing participation of a seductive youngster. Yet children are not capable of making a deliberate, informed decision to enter into a sexual relationship! Even older children and adolescents are not free to say yes

Miami schoolchildren participate in a candlelight vigil sponsored by Amigos For Kids, a nonprofit organization dedicated to preventing child abuse and neglect. Adjustment problems resulting from child abuse, including sexual abuse, are often severe and persistent.

Cultural Influences

Impact of Ethnic and Political Violence on Children

Around the world, many children live with armed conflict, terrorism, and other acts of violence stemming from ethnic and political tensions. Some children participate in fighting, either because they are forced or because they want to please adults. Others are kidnapped, assaulted, and tortured. Child bystanders often come under direct fire and may be killed or physically maimed. And many watch in horror as family members, friends, and neighbors flee, are wounded, or die. In the past decade, wars have left 6 million children physically disabled, 20 million homeless, and more than 1 million separated from their parents (UNICEF, 2011).

When war and social crises are temporary, most children can be comforted and do not show long-term emotional difficulties. But chronic danger requires children to make substantial adjustments that can seriously impair their psychological functioning. Those who react with maladaptive thoughts about themselves ("I must be going crazy" or "I don't feel like myself anymore") and the world ("bad things always happen" or "other people cannot be trusted") are at heightened risk of experiencing posttraumatic stress symptoms—extreme fear and anxiety that persists, even after they are no longer in danger (Palosaari et al., 2013).

Many children of war lose their sense of safety, become desensitized to violence, are haunted by terrifying intrusive memories, display immature moral reasoning, and build a pessimistic view of the future. Anxiety and depression increase, as do aggression and antisocial behavior (Eisenberg & Silver, 2011; Klingman, 2006). These outcomes appear to be culturally universal, emerging among children in every war zone studied—from Bosnia, Rwanda, and the Sudan to the West Bank, Gaza, Iraq, Afghanistan, and Syria.

Parental affection and reassurance are the best protection against lasting problems. When parents offer security, discuss traumatic experiences with children sympathetically, and serve as role models of calm emotional strength, most children can withstand even extreme war-related violence (Gewirtz, Forgatch, & Wieling, 2008). Children who are separated from parents must rely on help from their communities. Orphans in Eritrea who were placed in residential settings where they could form close emotional ties with an adult showed less emotional stress five years later than orphans placed in impersonal settings (Wolff & Fesseha, 1999). Education and recreation programs are powerful safeguards, too, providing children with consistency in their lives along with teacher and peer supports.

With the September 11, 2001, terrorist attacks on the World Trade Center, some U.S. children experienced extreme wartime violence firsthand. Most children, however, learned about the attacks indirectly—from the media or from caregivers or peers. Both direct and indirect exposure triggered child and adolescent distress, but extended exposure—having a family member affected or repeatedly witnessing the attacks on TV—resulted in more severe symptoms (Agronick et al., 2007; Rosen & Cohen, 2010). During the following months, distress reactions declined, though more slowly for children with conflict-ridden parent–child relationships or preexisting adjustment problems.

Unlike many war-traumatized children in the developing world, students in New York's Public

KHALIL MAZRAAWI/AFP/GETTY IMAGES

At a refugee camp in Jordan, Syrian children wearing facemasks to protect against blowing sand play games with a caring adult. Most have witnessed violent atrocities and lost family members in Syria's civil war. Sensitive adult support can help them regain a sense of safety.

School 31, who watched from their classrooms as the towers collapsed, received immediate intervention—a "trauma curriculum" in which they expressed emotions through writing, drawing, and discussion and participated in experiences aimed at restoring trust and tolerance (Lagnado, 2001). Older children learned about the feelings of their Muslim classmates, the dire condition of children in Afghanistan, and ways to help victims as a means of overcoming a sense of helplessness.

When wartime drains families and communities of resources, international organizations must step in and help children. The Children and War Foundation, *www.childrenandwar.org,* offers programs and manuals that train local personnel in how to promote children's adaptive coping (Yule et al., 2013). Efforts to preserve children's physical, psychological, and educational well-being may be the best way to stop the transmission of violence to the next generation.

---

or no. Rather, the responsibility lies with abusers, who tend to have characteristics that predispose them toward sexual exploitation of children. They have great difficulty controlling their impulses and may suffer from psychological disorders, including alcohol and drug abuse. Often they pick out children who are unlikely to defend themselves or to be believed—those who are physically weak, emotionally deprived, socially isolated, or affected by disabilities (Collin-Vézina, Daigneault, & Hébert, 2013).

Reported cases of child sexual abuse are linked to poverty, marital instability, and resulting weakening of family ties. Children who live in homes with a constantly changing cast of characters—repeated marriages, separations, and new partners—are especially vulnerable. But children in economically advantaged, stable homes are also victims, although their abuse is more likely to escape detection (Murray, Nguyen, & Cohen, 2014).

© 2015 BY CHILD LURES, LTD. ALL RIGHTS RESERVED.

Teaching children to recognize inappropriate sexual advances and where to turn for help reduces the risk of abuse. Few schools include such programs, however, because any education about sex or sexual abuse is controversial.

CONSEQUENCES OF SEXUAL ABUSE The adjustment problems of child sexual abuse victims—including anxiety, depression, low self-esteem, mistrust of adults, and anger and hostility—are often severe and can persist for years after the abusive episodes. Younger children frequently react with sleep difficulties, loss of appetite, and generalized fearfulness. Adolescents may run away and show suicidal reactions, substance abuse, and delinquency. Longitudinal research suggests that rates of obesity and other physical and mental health problems are elevated among survivors of child sexual abuse. At all ages, persistent abuse accompanied by force, violence, and a close relationship to the perpetrator (incest) has a more severe impact. And sexual abuse, like physical abuse, is associated with central nervous system damage (Trickett, Noll, & Putnam, 2011; Wolfe, 2006).

Sexually abused children frequently display precocious sexual knowledge and behavior. In adolescence, abused young people often become promiscuous, increasing the risk of teenage pregnancy. As adults, they show elevated arrest rates for sex crimes (mostly against children) and prostitution. Furthermore, women who were sexually abused are likely to choose partners who abuse them and their children. As mothers, they often engage in irresponsible and coercive parenting, including child abuse and neglect (Collin-Vézina, Daigneault, & Hébert, 2013; Salter et al., 2003; Trickett, Noll, & Putnam, 2011). In these ways, the harmful impact of sexual abuse is transmitted to the next generation.

PREVENTION AND TREATMENT Treating child sexual abuse is difficult. The reactions of family members—anxiety about harm to the child, anger toward the abuser, and sometimes hostility toward the victim for telling—can increase children's distress. Because sexual abuse typically appears in the midst of other serious family problems, specialized trauma-focused therapy with both children and parents is usually needed (Olafson, 2011). The best way to reduce the suffering of victims is to prevent sexual abuse from continuing. Today, courts are prosecuting abusers more vigorously and taking children's testimony more seriously (see the Social Issues: Health box on the following page).

Educational programs that teach children to recognize inappropriate sexual advances and whom to turn to for help reduce the risk of abuse (Finkelhor, 2009). Yet because of controversies over educating children about sexual abuse, few schools offer these interventions. New Zealand is the only country with a national, school-based prevention program targeting sexual abuse. In Keeping Ourselves Safe, children and adolescents learn that abusers are rarely strangers. Parent involvement ensures that home and school collaborate in teaching children self-protection skills. Evaluations reveal that virtually all New Zealand parents and children support the program and that it has helped many children avoid or report abuse (Sanders, 2006).

Fostering Resilience in Middle Childhood

Throughout middle childhood—and other periods of development—children are confronted with challenging and sometimes threatening situations that require them to cope with psychological stress. In this trio of chapters, we have considered such topics as chronic illness, learning disabilities, achievement expectations, divorce, harsh living conditions and wartime trauma, and sexual abuse. Each taxes children's coping resources, creating serious risks for development.

Nevertheless, only a modest relationship exists between stressful life experiences and psychological disturbance in childhood (Masten, 2014). In our discussion in Chapter 4 of the long-term consequences of birth complications, we noted that some children manage to overcome the combined effects of birth trauma, poverty, and a troubled family life. The same is true for school difficulties, family transitions, the experience of war, and child maltreatment.

Social Issues: Health

Children's Eyewitness Testimony

Increasingly, children are being called on to testify in court cases involving child abuse and neglect, child custody, and other matters. The experience can be difficult and traumatic, requiring children to report on highly stressful events and sometimes to speak against a parent or other relative to whom they feel loyal. In some family disputes, they may fear punishment for telling the truth. In addition, child witnesses are faced with an unfamiliar situation—at the very least an interview in the judge's chambers and at most an open courtroom with judge, jury, spectators, and the possibility of unsympathetic cross-examination. Not surprisingly, these conditions can compromise the accuracy of children's recall.

Age Differences

Until recently, children younger than age 5 were rarely asked to testify, and not until age 10 were they assumed fully competent to do so. As a result of societal reactions to rising rates of child abuse and the difficulty of prosecuting perpetrators, legal requirements for child testimony have been relaxed in the United States (Brainerd & Reyna, 2012; Klemfuss & Ceci, 2012). Children as young as age 3 frequently serve as witnesses.

Compared with preschoolers, school-age children are better at giving accurate, detailed narrative accounts of past experiences and correctly inferring others' motives and intentions. Older children are also generally more resistant to misleading questions that attorneys may ask when probing for more information or, in cross-examination, trying to influence the child's response (Zajac, O'Neill, & Hayne, 2012). Inhibition (ability to suppress impulses and focus on a competing goal), which improves from early to middle childhood, predicts children's resistance to suggestion (Melinder, Endestad, & Magnussen, 2006).

Nevertheless, when properly questioned, even 3-year-olds can recall recent events accurately (Peterson & Rideout, 1998). And in the face of biased interviewing, adolescents and adults often form elaborate, false memories of events (Ceci et al., 2007).

Suggestibility

Court testimony often involves repeated questioning—a procedure that, by itself, negatively affects children's response consistency and accuracy (Kräenbühl, Blades, & Eiser, 2009). When adults lead witnesses by suggesting incorrect "facts," interrupt their denials, reinforce them for giving desired answers, ask complex and confusing

questions, or use a confrontational style, they further increase the likelihood of incorrect reporting by children and adolescents alike (Sparling et al., 2011; Zajac, O'Neill, & Hayne, 2012).

In one study, 4- to 8-year-olds were asked to recall details about a visitor who had come to their classroom a week earlier. Half the children received a low-pressure interview containing leading questions that implied abuse ("He took your clothes off, didn't he?"). The other half received a high-pressure interview in which an adult told the child that her friends had said "yes" to the leading questions, praised the child for agreeing ("You're doing great"), and, if the child did not agree, repeated the question. Children were far more likely to give false information—even fabricating quite fantastic events—in the high-pressure condition (Finnilä et al., 2003).

By the time children appear in court, weeks, months, or even years have passed since the target events. When a long delay is combined with biased interviewing and with stereotyping of the accused ("He's in jail because he's been bad"), children can easily be misled into giving false information (Quas et al., 2007). The more distinctive and personally relevant an event is, the more likely children are to recall it accurately over time. For example, a year later, even when exposed to misleading information, children correctly reported details of an injury that required emergency room treatment (Peterson, Parsons, & Dean, 2004). Children's memories of these experiences remain remarkably intact for as long as five years (Peterson, 2012).

In many sexual abuse cases, anatomically correct dolls or body diagrams are used to prompt children's recall. Although these methods may help older children provide more detail, they increase the suggestibility of preschoolers, who report physical and sexual contact that never happened (Poole & Bruck, 2012). Props are confusing to very young witnesses because they require dual representation of the doll or drawing as both an object and a symbol—understandings that are still emerging during the preschool years (see Chapter 9, page 314).

School-age eyewitnesses are better able than preschoolers to give accurate, detailed descriptions and correctly infer others' motives and intentions. This juvenile court judge can promote accurate recall by using a warm, supportive tone and avoiding leading questions.

Interventions

Adults must prepare child witnesses so they understand the courtroom process and know what to expect. In some places, "court schools" take children through the setting and give them an opportunity to role-play court activities. Practice interviews—in which children learn to provide the most accurate, detailed information possible and to admit not knowing rather than agreeing or guessing—are helpful (Zajac, O'Neill & Hayne, 2012).

At the same time, legal professionals must use interviewing procedures that increase children's accurate reporting. Unbiased, open-ended questions that prompt children to disclose details— "Tell me what happened" or "You said there was a man; tell me about the man"—reduce suggestibility (Steele, 2012). Also, a warm, supportive interview tone fosters accurate recall, perhaps by easing children's anxiety so they feel freer to counter an interviewer's false suggestions (Ceci, Bruck, & Battin, 2000).

If children are likely to experience emotional trauma or later punishment (as in a family dispute), courtroom procedures are sometimes adapted to protect them. For example, children can testify over closed-circuit TV so they do not have to face an abuser. When it is not wise for a child to participate directly, impartial expert witnesses can provide testimony that reports on the child's psychological condition and includes important elements of the child's story.

Applying What We Know

Resources That Foster Resilience in Middle Childhood

TYPE OF RESOURCE	DESCRIPTION
Personal	• Easygoing, sociable temperament • Above-average intelligence • Favorable self-esteem • Persistence in the face of challenge and pleasure in mastery • Good emotional self-regulation and flexible coping strategies
Family	• Warm, trusting relationship with at least one parent • Authoritative child-rearing style • Positive discipline, avoidance of coercive tactics • Warm, supportive sibling relationships
School	• Teachers who are warm, helpful, and stimulating; who encourage students to collaborate; and who emphasize effort and self-improvement • Lessons in tolerance and respect and codes against bullying, which promote positive peer relationships and gratifying friendships • Extracurricular activities, including sports and social service pursuits, that strengthen physical, cognitive, and social skills
Community	• High-quality after-school programs that protect children's safety and offer stimulating, skill-building activities • An adult—such as an extended-family member, teacher, or neighbor—who provides warmth and social support and is a positive coping model • Stability of neighborhood residents and services—safe outdoor play areas, community centers, and religious organizations—that relieve parental stress and encourage families and neighbors to share leisure time • Youth groups—scouting, clubs, religious youth groups, and other organized activities—that promote positive peer relationships and prosocial behavior

Note: One or a few resources may be sufficient to foster resilience, since each resource strengthens others.
Sources: Commission on Children at Risk, 2008; Wright & Masten, 2005.

Refer to Applying What We Know above for an overview of factors that promote *resilience*—the capacity to overcome adversity—during middle childhood.

Often just one or a few of these ingredients account for why one child is "stress-resilient" and another is not. Usually, however, personal and environmental factors are interconnected: Each resource favoring resilience strengthens others in a *developmental cascade* (Masten & Cicchetti, 2010). For example, safe, stable neighborhoods with family-friendly community services reduce parents' daily hassles and stress, thereby promoting good parenting (Chen, Howard, & Brooks-Gunn, 2011). Unfavorable home and neighborhood experiences can also cascade, increasing the chances that children will act in ways that expose them to further hardship. When negative conditions pile up, such as marital discord, poverty, crowded living conditions, neighborhood violence, and abuse and neglect, the rate of maladjustment multiplies (Wright & Masten, 2005).

Of great concern are children's violent acts. Violence committed in schools and communities by U.S. children and adolescents with troubled lives has at times reached the level of atrocities—maimings and murders of adults and peers. Because children spend a great deal of time in school, the quality of their relationships with teachers and classmates strongly influences their development, academically and socially (Elias, Parker, & Rosenblatt, 2005; Hughes, 2011).

Several highly effective school-based *social and emotional learning programs* reduce violence (including bullying and gang involvement) and other antisocial acts and increase academic motivation by fostering social competence and supportive relationships (CASEL, 2013; Durlak et al., 2011). Among these is the 4Rs (Reading, Writing, Respect, and Resolution) Program, which provides elementary school students with weekly lessons in emotional and social understanding and skills (Aber et al., 2011). Topics include handling anger, developing empathy, being assertive, resolving social conflicts, cooperating, appreciating diversity, and identifying and standing up against prejudice and bullying. The program is integrated with language arts: High-quality children's literature, selected for relevance to program themes, complements each lesson. Discussion, writing, and role play of the stories deepen students' understanding of conflict, emotions, relationships, and community.

To evaluate the effectiveness of 4Rs, researchers randomly assigned 18 elementary schools in New York City to the program or a control condition. Teachers in 4Rs schools used more supportive instructional techniques—encouraging discussion, making concepts relevant to students' everyday lives, and providing feedback that acknowledges effort. And children who received 4Rs instruction became less depressed and less likely to misinterpret others' acts as hostile. After a second year of intervention, the benefits spread to other related outcomes: Teachers rated 4Rs children as less aggressive, more attentive, and more socially competent compared to children in control schools (Aber et al., 2011). In unsafe neighborhoods, 4Rs transforms schools into places of safety and mutual respect, where learning can occur.

Programs like 4Rs recognize that resilience is not a preexisting attribute but rather a capacity that *develops*, enabling children to use internal and external resources to cope with adversity (Dessel, 2010). Throughout our discussion, we have seen how families, schools, communities, and society as a whole can enhance or undermine the school-age child's developing sense of competence. Young people whose childhood experiences helped them learn to control impulses, overcome obstacles, strive for self-direction, and respond considerately and sympathetically to others meet the challenges of the next period—adolescence—quite well.

Fifth graders in a social and emotional learning program role play stories emphasizing honesty, empathy, and resolving social conflicts. In the skit shown here, the two students on the left, after being caught shoplifting, are questioned by the store manager.

Ask Yourself

- **REVIEW** When children must testify in court cases, what factors increase the chances of accurate reporting?

- **CONNECT** Explain how results of the 4Rs program illustrate the concept of developmental cascade.

- **APPLY** Claire told her 6-year-old daughter to be very careful never to talk to or take candy from strangers. Why is Claire's warning unlikely to protect her daughter from sexual abuse?

- **REFLECT** Describe a challenging time during your childhood. What aspects of the experience increased stress? What resources helped you cope with adversity?

Summary

Erikson's Theory: Industry versus Inferiority (p. 473)

13.1 What personality changes take place during Erikson's stage of industry versus inferiority?

- According to Erikson, children who successfully resolve the psychological conflict of **industry versus inferiority** develop a sense of competence at useful skills and tasks, learn the value of division of labor, and develop a sense of moral commitment and responsibility.

Self-Understanding (p. 474)

13.2 Describe school-age children's self-concept and self-esteem, and discuss factors that affect their achievement-related attributions.

- During middle childhood, children's self-concepts include personality traits (both positive and negative), competencies, and **social comparisons.** Self-esteem differentiates further and becomes hierarchically organized and more realistic as children receive more competence-related feedback and compare their performance to that of others.

- Cultural forces and child-rearing practices affect self-esteem. Gender stereotypes contribute to sex differences in physical, academic, and social self-esteem. Warm extended families and strong ethnic pride may contribute to the slight self-esteem advantage of African-American over Caucasian children. The authoritative child-rearing style is linked to favorable self-esteem.

- Children with **mastery-oriented attributions** hold an incremental view of ability, believing that it can be improved by trying hard, and attribute failure to insufficient effort. In contrast, children with **learned helplessness** attribute success to external factors, such as luck, and hold a fixed view of ability. They believe their failures are due to low ability, which cannot be modified.

- Supportive parents and teachers and cultural valuing of effort increase the likelihood of a mastery-oriented approach. By teaching children that abilities are fixed, **person praise** promotes learned helplessness. In contrast, **process praise** by focusing on behavior and effort, fosters a mastery orientation. **Attribution retraining** encourages learned-helpless children to believe they can overcome failure by exerting more effort.

Emotional Development (p. 481)

13.3 *Cite changes in the expression and understanding of emotion in middle childhood.*

- Self-conscious emotions of pride and guilt become clearly governed by personal responsibility. Intense shame can shatter self-esteem.

- School-age children recognize that people can experience more than one emotion at a time and that emotional expressions may not reflect people's true feelings. They also reconcile contradictory cues in interpreting another's feelings. Empathy increases and includes sensitivity to people's immediate distress and their general life condition.

- By age 10, most children can shift adaptively between **problem-centered** and **emotion-centered coping** in regulating emotion. Emotionally well-regulated children develop a sense of emotional self-efficacy and are optimistic, prosocial, and well-liked by peers.

AP IMAGES/THE EVANSVILLE COURIER & PRESS, JASON CLARK

Moral Development (p. 483)

13.4 *Describe changes in moral understanding during middle childhood, including children's understanding of diversity and inequality.*

- During middle childhood, children construct a flexible appreciation of moral rules. They clarify and link moral imperatives and social conventions, considering the purpose of the rule; people's intentions, knowledge, and beliefs; and the context of their actions. They also better understand individual rights. When moral and personal concerns conflict, older school-age children typically emphasize fairness. Children in diverse cultures use similar criteria to reason about moral, social-conventional, and personal concerns.

- Children pick up prevailing societal attitudes about race and ethnicity. With age, school-age children understand that people who look different need not think, feel, or act differently and that prejudice violates widely held social standards. Consequently, explicit prejudice typically declines, although prejudice often continues to operate implicitly. Children most likely to hold racial and ethnic biases are those who believe that personality traits are fixed, who have overly high self-esteem, and who live among adults who highlight group differences. Long-term, intergroup contact may be most effective at reducing prejudice.

Peer Relations (p. 487)

13.5 *How do peer sociability and friendship change in middle childhood?*

- Peer interaction becomes more prosocial, and physical aggression declines. By the end of middle childhood, children organize themselves into **peer groups.**

- Friendships develop into mutual relationships based on trust and become more selective. Children tend to choose friends who resemble themselves in age, sex, race, ethnicity, SES, personality, popularity, academic achievement, and prosocial behavior. Girls form closer, more exclusive friendships than boys.

13.6 *Describe major categories of peer acceptance and ways to help rejected children.*

- On measures of **peer acceptance, popular children** are well-liked by many agemates; **rejected children** are mostly disliked; **controversial children** are both liked and disliked; **neglected children** arouse little reaction, positive or negative, but are usually well-adjusted; and **average children** receive average numbers of positive and negative reactions.

- **Popular-prosocial children** are academically and socially competent, while **popular-antisocial children** are aggressive but admired, perhaps for their athletic ability and sophisticated but devious social skills. Rejected children also divide into two subtypes: **rejected-aggressive children,** who are especially high in conflict and hostility, and **rejected-withdrawn children,** who are passive, socially awkward, and frequent targets of **peer victimization.**

- Coaching in social skills, academic tutoring, and training in perspective taking and social problem solving have been used to help rejected youngsters. To produce lasting change, intervening in parent–child interaction is often necessary.

Gender Typing (p. 493)

13.7 *What changes in gender-stereotyped beliefs and gender identity occur during middle childhood?*

- School-age children extend their awareness of gender stereotypes to personality traits and academic subjects. But they also develop **gender-stereotype flexibility**—a more open-minded view of what males and females can do.

- Boys strengthen their identification with the masculine role, whereas girls feel free to experiment with "cross-gender" activities. Gender identity includes self-evaluations of gender typicality, contentedness, and felt pressure to conform to gender roles—each of which affects adjustment.

Family Influences (p. 496)

13.8 *How do parent–child communication and sibling relationships change in middle childhood?*

- Despite declines in time spent with parents, **coregulation** allows parents to exercise general oversight of children, who increasingly make their own decisions.

- Sibling rivalry tends to increase with greater participation in diverse activities and more frequent parental comparisons. Siblings often try to reduce this rivalry by striving to be different from one another. Only children do not differ from children with siblings in self-rated personality traits and are higher in self-esteem, school performance, and educational attainment.

13.9 *How do children fare in lesbian and gay families and in never-married, single-parent families?*

- Lesbian and gay parents are as committed to and effective at child rearing as heterosexual parents. Their children do not differ from the children of heterosexual parents in adjustment and gender identity, except in feeling slightly less parental pressure to conform to gender roles.

© SHEHZAD NOORANI/DRIK/ MAJORITY WORLD/THE IMAGE WORKS

- Never-married parenthood generally increases financial hardship for low-SES mothers and their children. Children of never-married mothers who lack a father's warmth and involvement achieve less well in school and engage in more antisocial behavior than children in low-SES, first-marriage families.

13.10 What factors influence children's adjustment to divorce and blended family arrangements?

- Although marital breakup is stressful for children, individual differences exist based on parental psychological health, child characteristics (age, temperament, and sex), and social supports. Children with difficult temperaments are at greater risk for adjustment problems. In both sexes, divorce is linked to early sexual activity, adolescent parenthood, and long-term relationship difficulties.

- The overriding factor in positive adjustment following divorce is effective parenting. Positive father–child relationships have protective value, as do caring extended family members, teachers, siblings, and friends.

- **Divorce mediation** and parent education programs can foster parental conflict resolution and cooperation in the period surrounding divorce. The success of joint custody depends on effective coparenting.

- When divorced parents enter new relationships and form **blended, or reconstituted, families**, girls, older children, and children in father–stepmother families tend to have more adjustment problems. Stepparents can help children adjust by moving into their roles gradually.

13.11 How do maternal employment and life in dual-earner families affect children's development?

- When employed mothers enjoy their work and remain committed to parenting, their children benefit from higher self-esteem, more positive family and peer relations, less gender-stereotyped beliefs, and better school grades. In dual-earner families, the father's willingness to share household responsibilities is linked to many positive child outcomes. Workplace supports help parents meet the demands of work and child rearing.

- Authoritative child rearing, parental monitoring, and regular after-school chores lead **self-care children** to be responsible and well-adjusted. Good "after-care" programs also aid school performance and emotional and social adjustment, with low-SES children showing special benefits.

Some Common Problems of Development (p. 507)

13.12 Cite common fears and anxieties in middle childhood.

- School-age children's fears are directed toward new concerns, including personal harm, media events, academic failure, parents' health, and peer rejection. Children with inhibited temperaments are at high risk for developing **phobias.** Harsh living conditions, presenting constant danger, chaos, and deprivation, can result in long-term emotional stress and behavior problems.

13.13 Discuss factors related to child sexual abuse, its consequences for children's development, and its prevention and treatment.

- Child sexual abuse is generally committed by male family members, more often against girls than against boys. Abusers have characteristics that predispose them toward sexual exploitation of children. Reported cases are strongly associated with poverty and marital instability.

- Abused children often have severe, persisting adjustment problems. Treatment typically requires specialized trauma-focused therapy with both children and parents. Educational programs that teach children to recognize inappropriate sexual advances and whom to turn to for help reduce the risk of sexual abuse.

13.14 Cite factors that foster resilience in middle childhood.

- Only a modest relationship exists between stressful life experiences and psychological disturbance in childhood. Children's personal characteristics, a warm family life that includes authoritative parenting, and school and community resources predict resilience. Each resource favoring resilience usually strengthens others, in a developmental cascade.

Important Terms and Concepts

attribution retraining (p. 480)
average children (p. 490)
blended, or reconstituted, family (p. 503)
controversial children (p. 490)
coregulation (p. 496)
divorce mediation (p. 503)
emotion-centered coping (p. 482)
gender-stereotype flexibility (p. 494)
industry versus inferiority (p. 473)

learned helplessness (p. 478)
mastery-oriented attributions (p. 478)
neglected children (p. 490)
peer acceptance (p. 490)
peer groups (p. 488)
peer victimization (p. 492)
person praise (p. 479)
phobia (p. 507)
popular children (p. 490)

popular-antisocial children (p. 490)
popular-prosocial children (p. 490)
problem-centered coping (p. 482)
process praise (p. 479)
rejected children (p. 490)
rejected-aggressive children (p. 491)
rejected-withdrawn children (p. 491)
self-care children (p. 506)
social comparisons (p. 474)

MILESTONES

Development in Middle Childhood

6–8 YEARS

PHYSICAL

- Slow gains in height and weight continue until adolescent growth spurt. (405)
- Permanent teeth gradually replace primary teeth. (407)
- Legibility of writing increases. (421)
- Drawings become more organized and detailed and include some depth cues. (421)
- Games with rules and rough-and-tumble play become common. (422, 424)

COGNITIVE

- Thought becomes more logical, as shown by the ability to pass Piagetian conservation, class inclusion, and seriation problems. (429–430)

- Attention becomes more selective, flexible, and planful. (436–437)
- Uses memory strategies of rehearsal and then organization. (437)
- Awareness of mental activities, of the impact of psychological factors (such as applying memory strategies) on task performance, and of sources of knowledge (including mental inferences) expands. (440–441)
- Views situations from at least two perspectives, as indicated by appreciation of second-order false beliefs. (441)
- Uses informal knowledge of number concepts and counting to master more complex mathematical skills. (444–445)

LANGUAGE

- Vocabulary increases rapidly as children learn about 20 new words each day. (455)
- Word definitions are concrete, referring to functions and appearance. (455)
- Transitions from "learning to read" to "reading to learn." (444)

- Metalinguistic awareness improves. (455, 458)
- Communicates with increasing clarity, adapting to listeners' needs. (456)
- Grasps increasingly subtle, indirect expressions of language meaning, including irony and sarcasm. (456)
- Narratives increase in organization, detail, and expressiveness. (457)

EMOTIONAL/SOCIAL

- Self-concept includes personality traits and social comparisons. (474)
- Self-esteem differentiates, is hierarchically organized, and becomes more realistic. (475–476)
- Self-conscious emotions of pride and guilt are governed by personal responsibility. (481)
- Recognizes that people can experience more than one emotion at a time and that their expressions may not reflect their true feelings. (482)

- Empathy increases. (482)
- Reconciles contradictory facial and situational cues in understanding another's feelings. (482)
- Becomes more independent and trustworthy. (483)
- Constructs a flexible appreciation of moral rules, taking prosocial and antisocial intentions and the context of behavior into account. (484)
- Resolves conflicts more effectively; sharing, helping, and other prosocial acts increase. (488)
- Physical aggression declines; verbal and relational aggression continue. (487–488)

Note: Numbers in parentheses indicate the page or pages on which each milestone is discussed.

9–11 YEARS

PHYSICAL

- Adolescent growth spurt begins two years earlier in girls than in boys. (405)
- Executes gross motor skills of running, jumping, throwing, catching, kicking, batting, and dribbling more quickly and with better coordination. (420–421)

- Steady gains in attention and reaction time contribute to improved motor performance. (420–421)
- Representation of depth in drawings expands. (421)
- Dominance hierarchies become more stable, especially among boys. (424)

COGNITIVE

- Continues to master Piagetian tasks in a step-by-step fashion. (432)
- Spatial reasoning improves, as illustrated by more sophisticated map-reading and map-drawing skills, including an overall view of space and understanding of scale. (430–431)

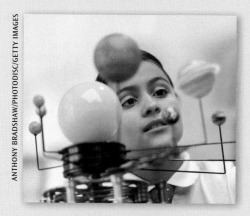

- Selective attention and planning improve further. (436–437)
- Uses memory strategies of rehearsal and organization more effectively. (437)
- Applies several memory strategies simultaneously; begins to use elaboration. (437–438)
- Long-term knowledge base grows larger and becomes better organized. (438)
- Awareness of mental activities, including effective memory strategies and reasoning, becomes more elaborate and refined. (442)
- Cognitive self-regulation improves. (442)

LANGUAGE

- Thinks about and uses words more precisely; word definitions emphasize synonyms and categorical relations. (455)
- By the end of elementary school, has acquired a vocabulary of about 40,000 words. (455)
- Continues to master complex grammatical constructions, such as passive voice and infinitive phrases. (456)
- Continues to improve in understanding of subtle, indirect expressions of language meaning. (456)

- Narratives lengthen and increase in organization, detail, and expressiveness. (457)

EMOTIONAL/SOCIAL

- Continues to refine self-concept to include competencies, positive and negative personality traits, and more sophisticated social comparisons. (474)
- Distinguishes ability, effort, and luck in attributions for success and failure. (478–479)
- Empathic responding extends to general life conditions. (482)

- Shifts adaptively between problem-centered and emotion-centered strategies in regulating emotion. (482)
- Clarifies and links moral imperatives and social conventions. (484)
- Convictions about matters of personal choice strengthen, and understanding of individual rights expands. (484–485)
- Friendships become more selective and are based on mutual trust. (489)
- Peer groups emerge. (488)

- Becomes aware of a wider range of gender stereotypes, including personality traits and achievement areas, but has a flexible appreciation of what males and females can do. (493–494)
- Gender identity expands to include self-evaluations of typicality, contentedness, and pressure to conform. (494–495)
- Sibling rivalry tends to increase. (497)

Note: Numbers in parentheses indicate the page or pages on which each milestone is discussed.

Glossary

A

academic programs Preschool and kindergarten programs in which teachers structure children's learning, teaching academic skills through formal lessons that often involve repetition and drill. Distinguished from *child-centered programs*. (p. 341)

accommodation In Piaget's theory, that part of adaptation in which new schemes are created and old ones adjusted to produce a better fit with the environment. Distinguished from *assimilation*. (p. 202)

adaptation In Piaget's theory, the process of building schemes through direct interaction with the environment. Consists of two complementary activities: *assimilation* and *accommodation*. (p. 202)

affordances The action possibilities that a situation offers an organism with certain motor capabilities. Discovering affordances plays a major role in perceptual differentiation. (p. 196)

age of viability The age at which the fetus can first survive if born early. Occurs sometime between 22 and 26 weeks. (p. 99)

alcohol-related neurodevelopmental disorder (ARND) The least severe form of fetal alcohol spectrum disorder, involving impairment in at least three areas of mental functioning but with typical physical growth and absence of facial abnormalities. Distinguished from *fetal alcohol syndrome (FAS)* and *partial fetal alcohol syndrome (p-FAS)*. (p. 107)

allele Each of two or more forms of a gene, one inherited from the mother and one from the father, located at the same place on corresponding pairs of chromosomes. (p. 55)

amnion The inner membrane that forms a protective covering around the prenatal organism. (p. 97)

amniotic fluid The fluid that fills the amnion, which helps keep temperature constant and provides a cushion against jolts caused by the woman's movements. (p. 97)

amodal sensory properties Information that overlaps two or more sensory systems, such as rate, rhythm, duration, intensity, and temporal synchrony in visual and auditory input. (p. 195)

amygdala An inner-brain structure that plays a central role in processing of novelty and emotional information. (p. 290)

androgyny The gender identity held by individuals who score high on both traditionally masculine and traditionally feminine personality characteristics. (p. 389)

animistic thinking The belief that inanimate objects have lifelike qualities, such as thoughts, wishes, feelings, and intentions. (p. 315)

A-not-B search error The error made by 8- to 12-month-olds who, after reaching several times for an object at one hiding place (A), then seeing it moved to second (B), still search for it in the first hiding place (A). (p. 204)

anoxia Inadequate oxygen supply. (p. 133)

Apgar Scale A rating system on each of five characteristics—heart rate, respiratory effort, reflex irritability, muscle tone, and color—used to assess the newborn baby's physical condition immediately after birth. (p. 126)

applied behavior analysis Observations of relationships between behavior and environmental events, followed by systematic changes in those events based on procedures of conditioning and modeling. The goal is to eliminate undesirable behaviors and increase desirable responses. (p. 18)

assimilation That part of adaptation in which the external world is interpreted in terms of current schemes. Distinguished from *accommodation*. (p. 202)

associative play A form of true social interaction in which children engage in separate activities but exchange toys and comment on one another's behavior. Distinguished from *nonsocial activity, parallel play,* and *cooperative play*. (p. 366)

attachment The strong affectionate tie that humans have with special people in their lives, which leads them to experience pleasure and joy when interacting with them and to be comforted by their nearness in times of stress. (p. 261)

Attachment Q-Sort A method of assessing attac from high to low, in children between 1 and 5 ye observations of a variety of attachment-related behaviors. (p. 264)

attention-deficit hyperactivity disorder (ADHD) A disorder involving inattention, impulsivity, and excessive motor activity, resulting in academic and social problems. (p. 438)

attribution retraining An intervention that encourages learned-helpless children to believe they can overcome failure by exerting more effort and using more effective strategies. (p. 480)

authoritarian child-rearing style A child-rearing style that is low in acceptance and involvement, high in coercive and psychological control, and low in autonomy granting. Distinguished from *authoritative, permissive,* and *uninvolved child-rearing styles*. (p. 393)

authoritative child-rearing style A child-rearing style that is high in acceptance and involvement, adaptive control techniques, and appropriate autonomy granting. Distinguished from *authoritarian, permissive,* and *uninvolved child-rearing styles*. (p. 392)

autobiographical memory Long-lasting representations of personally meaningful one-time events from both the recent and the distant past. (p. 220)

automatic processes Cognitive activities that are so well-learned that they require no space in working memory and, therefore, permit an individual to focus on other information while performing them. (p. 216)

autonomy versus shame and doubt In Erikson's theory, the psychological conflict of toddlerhood, which is resolved favorably when parents provide young children with suitable guidance and reasonable choices. (p. 246)

autosomes The 22 matching chromosome pairs in each human cell. (p. 53)

average children Children who receive average numbers of positive and negative votes on self-report measures of social preferences. Distinguished from *popular, rejected, controversial,* and *neglected children*. (p. 490)

B

babbling Repetition of consonant–vowel combinations in long strings, beginning around 6 months of age. (p. 235)

basic emotions Emotions such as happiness, interest, surprise, fear, anger, sadness, and disgust that are universal in humans and other primates and have a long evolutionary history of promoting survival. (p. 247)

basic trust versus mistrust In Erikson's theory, the psychological conflict of infancy, which is resolved positively when the balance of care is sympathetic and loving. (p. 246)

behavioral genetics A field devoted to uncovering the contributions of nature and nurture to the diversity in human traits and abilities. (p. 82)

behaviorism An approach that regards directly observable events—stimuli and responses—as the appropriate focus of study and views the development of behavior as taking place through classical and operant conditioning. (p. 17)

blastocyst The prenatal cell mass four days after fertilization, when 60 to 70 cells exist that form a hollow, fluid-filled ball. (p. 97)

blended, or **reconstituted, family** A family structure formed through cohabitation or remarriage that includes parent, stepparent, and children. (p. 503)

bonding Parents' feelings of affection and concern for the newborn baby. (p. 141)

brain plasticity The capacity of various parts of the cerebral cortex to take over functions of damaged regions. Declines as hemispheres of the cerebral cortex lateralize. (p. 165)

breech position A position of the baby in the uterus that would cause the buttocks or feet to be delivered first. (p. 132)

C

cardinality The mathematical principle stating that the last number in a counting sequence indicates the quantity of items in the set. (p. 338)

orical self Classification of the self according to prominent ways in which people differ, such as age sex, physical characteristics, and goodness and badness. Develops between 18 and 30 months. (p. 278)

carrier A heterozygous individual who can pass a recessive trait to his or her children. (p. 55)

central executive In information processing, the conscious, reflective part of the mental system that directs the flow of information by deciding what to attend to, coordinating incoming information with information already in the system, and selecting, applying, and monitoring strategies that facilitate memory storage, comprehension, reasoning, and problem solving. (p. 216)

centration In Piaget's theory, the tendency of preoperational children to focus on one aspect of a situation while neglecting other important features. Distinguished from *decentration*. (p. 316)

cephalocaudal trend An organized pattern of physical growth in which the head develops more rapidly than the lower part of the body ("head to tail"). Distinguished from *proximodistal trend*. (p. 161)

cerebellum A structure at the rear and base of the brain that aids in balance and control of body movement. (p. 289)

cerebral cortex The largest, most complex structure of the human brain, containing the greatest number of neurons and synapses, which accounts for the highly developed intelligence of the human species. (p. 164)

cesarean delivery A surgical birth in which the doctor makes an incision in the mother's abdomen and lifts the baby out of the uterus. (p. 131)

child-centered programs Preschool and kindergarten programs in which teachers provide a variety of activities from which children select, and much learning takes place through play. Distinguished from *academic programs*. (p. 341)

child development An area of study devoted to understanding constancy and change from conception through adolescence. (p. 4)

child-rearing styles Combinations of parenting behaviors that occur over a wide range of situations, creating an enduring child-rearing climate. (p. 392)

chorion The outer membrane that forms a protective covering around the prenatal organism. It sends out tiny hairlike villi, from which the placenta begins to develop. (p. 97)

chromosomes Rodlike structures in the cell nucleus that store and transmit genetic information. (p. 51)

chronosystem In ecological systems theory, temporal changes in environments, either externally imposed or arising from within the child, that produce new conditions affecting development. Distinguished from *microsystem, mesosystem, exosystem,* and *macrosystem*. (p. 29)

circular reaction In Piaget's theory, a means of building schemes in which infants try to repeat a chance event caused by their own motor activity. (p. 203)

classical conditioning A form of learning that involves associating a neutral stimulus with a stimulus that leads to a reflexive response. Once the nervous system makes the connection between the two stimuli, the neutral stimulus produces the behavior by itself. (p. 176)

clinical interview An interview method in which the researcher uses a flexible, conversational style to probe for the participant's point of view. Distinguished from *structured interview*. (p. 34)

clinical, or **case study, method** A research method in which the aim is to obtain as complete a picture as possible of one individual's psychological functioning by bringing together a wide range of information, including interview data, observations, and sometimes test scores. (p. 35)

cognitive-developmental theory An approach introduced by Piaget that views children as actively constructing knowledge as they manipulate and explore their world, and in which cognitive development takes place in stages. (p. 19)

cognitive maps Mental representations of spaces, such as classroom, school, or neighborhood. (p. 430)

cognitive self-regulation The process of continuously monitoring progress toward a goal, checking outcomes, and redirecting unsuccessful efforts. (p. 442)

cohort effects The effects of cultural-historical change on the accuracy of longitudinal and cross-sectional research findings. Results based on one cohort—individuals developing in the same time period, who are influenced by particular historical and cultural conditions—may not apply to other cohorts. (p. 41)

communities of learners An educational approach inspired by Vygotsky's theory, in which teachers guide the overall process of learning, but otherwise, no distinction is made between adult and child contributors: All participate in joint endeavors, and students have the authority to define and resolve problems as they work toward project goals, which often address complex real-world issues. (p. 462)

compliance Obedience to requests and commands. (p. 278)

comprehension In language development, the words and word combinations that children understand. Distinguished from *production*. (p. 238)

concrete operational stage Piaget's third stage, extending from about 7 to 11 years of age, during which thought becomes logical, flexible, and organized in its application to concrete information, but the capacity for abstract thinking is not yet present. (p. 429)

conditioned response (CR) In classical conditioning, a new response produced by a conditioned stimulus (CS) that is similar to the unconditioned, or reflexive, response (UCR). (p. 177)

conditioned stimulus (CS) In classical conditioning, a neutral stimulus that, through pairing with an unconditioned stimulus (UCS), leads to a new, conditioned response (CR). Distinguished from *unconditioned stimulus*. (p. 177)

conservation The understanding that certain physical characteristics of objects remain the same, even when their outward appearance changes. (p. 315)

constructivist classroom A classroom grounded in Piaget's view of children as active learners who construct their own knowledge. Features include richly equipped learning centers, small groups and individuals solving self-chosen problems, a teacher who guides and supports in response to children's needs, and evaluation based on individual students' progress in relation to their own prior development. Distinguished from *traditional classroom* and *social-constructivist classroom*. (p. 460)

contexts Unique combinations of personal and environmental circumstances that can result in different paths of development. (p. 8)

continuous development The view that development is a process of gradually adding more of the same types of skills that were there to begin with. Distinguished from *discontinuous development*. (p. 7)

contrast sensitivity A general principle accounting for early visual pattern preferences, which states that if babies can detect a difference in contrast between two patterns, they prefer the pattern with more contrast. (pp. 191–192)

controversial children Children who receive many votes, both positive and negative, on self-report measures of social preferences, indicating that they are both liked and disliked. Distinguished from *popular, rejected, neglected,* and *average children*. (p. 490)

convergent thinking The type of thinking emphasized on intelligence tests, which involves arriving at a single correct answer to a problem. Distinguished from *divergent thinking*. (p. 466)

cooing Pleasant vowel-like noises made by infants, beginning around 2 months of age. (p. 235)

cooperative learning Collaboration on a task by a small group of classmates who work toward common goals by considering one another's ideas, appropriately challenging one another, providing sufficient explanations to correct misunderstandings, and resolving differences of opinion on the basis of reasons and evidence. (p. 463)

cooperative play A form of social interaction in which children orient toward a common goal, such as acting out a make-believe theme. Distinguished from *nonsocial activity, parallel play,* and *associative play*. (p. 366)

coparenting The extent to which parents mutually support each other's parenting behaviors. (p. 69)

coregulation A form of supervision in which parents exercise general oversight while permitting children to take charge of moment-by-moment decision making. (p. 496)

core knowledge perspective A perspective that states that infants are born with a set of innate knowledge systems, or core domains of thought, each of which permits a ready grasp of new, related information and therefore supports early, rapid development of certain aspects of cognition. (p. 211)

corpus callosum The large bundle of fibers connecting the two hemispheres of the cerebral cortex. Supports smooth coordination of movements on both sides of the body and integration of many aspects of thinking. (p. 290)

correlational design A research design in which the investigator gathers information on individuals without altering their experiences and then examines relationships between participants' characteristics and their behavior or development. Does not permit inferences about cause and effect. (p. 38)

correlation coefficient A number, ranging from +1.00 to −1.00, that describes the strength and direction of the relationship between two variables. (p. 38)

creativity The ability to produce work that is original yet appropriate—something others have not thought of that is useful in some way. (p. 466)

cross-sectional design A research design in which groups of participants of different ages are studied at the same point in time. Distinguished from *longitudinal design*. (p. 42)

D

decentration In Piaget's theory, the capacity of concrete operational children to focus on several aspects of a problem and related them. Distinguished from *centration*. (p. 429)

deferred imitation The ability to remember and copy the behavior of models who are not present. (p. 205)

delay of gratification The ability to wait for an appropriate time and place to engage in a tempting act. (p. 279)

deoxyribonucleic acid (DNA) Long, double-stranded molecules that make up chromosomes. (p. 52)

dependent variable In an experiment, the variable the investigator expects to be influenced by the independent variable. Distinguished from *independent variable*. (pp. 38–39)

developmental cognitive neuroscience An area of investigation that brings together researchers from psychology, biology, neuroscience, and medicine to study the relationship between changes in the brain and the developing child's cognitive processing and behavior patterns. (p. 23)

developmental social neuroscience An area of investigation that brings together researchers from psychology, biology, neuroscience, and medicine to study the relationship between changes in the brain and emotional and social development. (p. 23)

developmentally appropriate practice A set of standards, devised by the U.S. National Association for the Education of Young Children, specifying program characteristics that meet young children's developmental and individual needs, based on current research and the consensus of experts. (p. 228)

developmental quotient (DQ) A score on an infant intelligence test, computed in the same manner as an IQ but labeled more conservatively because it does not tap the same dimensions of intelligence measured in older children. (p. 226)

developmental science An interdisciplinary field devoted to the study of all changes humans experience throughout the lifespan. (p. 4)

differentiation theory The view that perceptual development involves the detection of increasingly finer, invariant features in the environment. (p. 196)

difficult child A child whose temperament is characterized by irregular daily routines, slow acceptance of new experiences, and a tendency to react negatively and intensely. Distinguished from *easy child* and *slow-to-warm-up child*. (p. 254)

dilation and effacement of the cervix Widening and thinning of the cervix, as uterine contractions become more frequent and powerful, during the first stage of labor. (p. 125)

discontinuous development A view of development as a process in which new ways of understanding and responding to the world emerge at specific times. Distinguished from *continuous development*. (p. 8)

disorganized/disoriented attachment The attachment pattern reflecting the greatest insecurity, characterizing infants who show confused, contradictory behaviors when reunited with the parent after a separation. Distinguished from secure, *insecure–avoidant*, and *insecure–resistant attachment*. (p. 264)

displaced reference The realization that words can be used to cue mental images of things not physically present. (p. 209)

divergent thinking The type of thinking associated with creativity, which involves generating multiple and unusual possibilities when faced with a task or problem. Distinguished from *convergent thinking*. (p. 466)

divorce mediation A series of meetings between divorcing adults and a trained professional that are aimed at reducing family conflict, including legal battles over property division and child custody. (p. 503)

dominance hierarchy A stable ordering of group members that predicts who will win when conflict arises. (p. 424)

dominant cerebral hemisphere The hemisphere of the cerebral cortex responsible for skilled motor action and other important abilities. In right-handed individuals, the left hemisphere is dominant; in left-handed individuals, motor and language skills are often shared between the hemispheres. (p. 288)

dominant–recessive inheritance A pattern of inheritance in which, under heterozygous conditions, the influence of only one allele is apparent. (p. 55)

dual representation The ability to view a symbolic object as both an object in its own right and a symbol. (p. 314)

dynamic assessment An innovative approach to testing consistent with Vygotsky's zone of proximal development, in which an adult introduces purposeful teaching into the testing situation to find out what the child can attain with social support. (p. 454)

dynamic systems perspective A view that regards the child's mind, body, and physical and social worlds as a dynamic, integrated system. A change in any part of the system leads the child to reorganize his or her behavior so the various components of the system work together again but in a more complex, effective way. (p. 29)

dynamic systems theory of motor development A theory that views new motor skills as reorganizations of previously mastered skills, which lead to more effective ways of exploring and controlling the environment. Each new skill is a joint product of central nervous system development, the body's movement capacities, the goals the child has in mind, and environmental supports for the skill. (p. 181)

E

easy child A child whose temperament is characterized by establishment of regular routines in infancy, general cheerfulness, and easy adaptation to new experiences. Distinguished from *difficult child* and *slow-to-warm-up child*. (p. 254)

ecological systems theory Bronfenbrenner's approach, which views the child as developing within a complex system of relationships affected by multiple levels of the surrounding environment, from immediate settings of family and school to broad cultural values, laws, customs, and resources. (p. 26)

educational self-fulfilling prophecies Teachers' positive or negative views of individual children, who tend to adopt and start to live up to those views. (p. 462)

effortful control The self-regulatory dimension of temperament, involving voluntary suppression of a dominant response in order to plan and execute a more adaptive response. (pp. 254–255)

egocentrism Failure to distinguish the symbolic viewpoints of others from one's own. (p. 315)

elaboration A memory strategy that involves creating a relationship, or shared meaning, between two or more items of information that are not members of the same category. (p. 438)

embryo The prenatal organism from 2 to 8 weeks after conception—the period when the groundwork is laid for all body structures and internal organs. (p. 98)

embryonic disk Cluster of cells on the inside of the blastocyst, from which the new organism will develop. (p. 97)

emergent literacy Children's active efforts to construct literacy knowledge through informal experiences. (p. 336)

emotional self-regulation Strategies for adjusting our emotional state to a comfortable level of intensity so we can accomplish our goals. (p. 252)

emotion-centered coping A strategy for managing emotion that is internal, private, and aimed at controlling distress when little can be done about an outcome. Distinguished from *problem-centered coping*. (p. 482)

empathy The ability to understand another's emotional state and to feel with that person, or respond emotionally in a similar way. (p. 278)

epigenesis Development resulting from ongoing, bidirectional exchanges between heredity and all levels of the environment. (p. 86)

episodic memory Memory for everyday experiences. (p. 329)

ethnography A research method in which an investigator attempts to understand the unique values and social processes of a culture or a distinct social group through participant observation—spending months and sometimes years in the cultural community, gathering field notes. (p. 36)

ethological theory of attachment Bowlby's theory, the most widely accepted view of attachment, which recognizes the infant's emotional tie to the caregiver as an evolved response that promotes survival. (p. 261)

ethology An approach concerned with the adaptive, or survival, value of behavior and its evolutionary history. (p. 24)

evolutionary developmental psychology An approach that seeks to understand the adaptive value of species-wide cognitive, emotional, and social competencies as those competencies change with age. (p. 25)

executive function The diverse cognitive operations and strategies that enable us to achieve our goals in cognitively challenging situations. Includes controlling attention, suppressing impulses, coordinating information in working memory, and flexibly directing and monitoring thought and behavior. (p. 216)

exosystem In ecological systems theory, social settings that do not contain children but nevertheless affect children's experiences—for example, parents' workplaces, their religious institutions, health and welfare services in the community, and parents' social networks. Distinguished from *microsystem, mesosystem, macrosystem,* and *chronosystem*. (p. 27)

expansions Adult responses that elaborate on children's speech, increasing its complexity. (p. 353)

experience-dependent brain growth Growth and refinement of established brain structures as a result of specific learning experiences that vary widely across individuals and cultures. Distinguished from *experience-expectant brain growth*. (p. 169)

experience-expectant brain growth The young brain's rapidly developing organization, which depends on ordinary experiences—opportunities to explore the environment, interact with people, and hear language and other sounds. Distinguished from *experience-dependent brain growth*. (p. 169)

experimental design A research design in which the investigator randomly assigns participants to two or more treatment conditions and studies the effect that manipulating an independent variable has on a dependent variable. Permits inferences about cause and effect. (p. 38)

expressive style A style of early language learning in which toddlers use language mainly to talk about people's feelings and needs, producing many social formulas and pronouns. Distinguished from *referential style*. (p. 239)

extended-family household A household in which parent and child live with one or more adult relatives. (p. 78)

F

fast mapping Children's ability to connect new words with their underlying concepts after only a brief encounter. (p. 348)

fetal alcohol spectrum disorder (FASD) A range of physical, mental, and behavioral outcomes caused by prenatal alcohol exposure, including *fetal alcohol syndrome (FAS), partial fetal alcohol syndrome (p-FAS),* and *alcohol-related neurodevelopmental disorder (ARND).* (p. 106)

fetal alcohol syndrome (FAS) The most severe form of fetal alcohol spectrum disorder, distinguished by slow physical growth, facial abnormalities, and brain injury. Usually affects children whose mothers drank heavily throughout pregnancy. Distinguished from *partial fetal alcohol syndrome (p-FAS)* and *alcohol-related neurodevelopmental disorder (ARND).* (p. 106)

fetal monitors Electronic instruments that track the baby's heart rate during labor. (p. 130)

fetus The prenatal organism from the ninth week to the end of pregnancy—the period during which body structures are completed and rapid growth in size occurs. (p. 99)

Flynn effect The steady increase in IQ from one generation to the next. (p. 452)

fraternal, or **dizygotic, twins** Twins resulting from the release and fertilization of two ova. Genetically, they are no more alike than ordinary siblings. Distinguished from *identical,* or *monozygotic, twins.* (p. 53)

G

gametes Sex cells, or sperm and ova, which contain half as many chromosomes as regular body cells. (p. 53)

gender constancy A full understanding of the biologically based permanence of one's gender, including the realization that sex remains the same over time, even if clothing, hairstyle, and play activities change. (p. 390)

gender identity An image of oneself as relatively masculine or feminine in characteristics. (p. 389)

gender schema theory An information-processing approach to gender typing that explains how environmental pressures and children's cognitions work together to shape gender-role development. (p. 390)

gender-stereotype flexibility The belief that both males and females can display a gender-stereotyped personality trait or activity—that overlap exists in the characteristics of males and females. (p. 494)

gender typing Any association of objects, activities, roles, or traits with one sex or the other in ways that conform to cultural stereotypes. (p. 384)

gene A segment of a DNA molecule that contains instructions for producing various proteins that contribute to the body's growth and functioning. (p. 52)

genetic counseling A communication process designed to help couples assess their chances of giving birth to a baby with a hereditary disorder and choose the best course of action in view of risks and family goals. (p. 61)

gene–environment correlation The view that heredity influences the environments to which individuals are exposed. (p. 84)

gene–environment interaction The view that because of their genetic makeup, individuals differ in their responsiveness to qualities of the environment. (p. 83)

genomic imprinting A pattern of inheritance in which alleles are imprinted, or chemically marked, in such a way that one pair member is activated, regardless of its makeup. (p. 58)

genotype An individual's genetic makeup. Distinguished from *phenotype*. (p. 51)

gifted Displaying exceptional intellectual strengths, such as high IQ, creativity, or specialized talent. (p. 466)

glial cells Cells that are responsible for myelination of neural fibers, improving the efficiency of message transfer and, in certain instances, also participate directly in neural communication. (p. 162)

goodness-of-fit model A model that describes how favorable adjustment depends on an effective match, or good fit, between a child's temperament and child-rearing environment. (pp. 259–260)

growth faltering Failure of an infant to grow normally, characterized by weight, height, and head circumference substantially below age-related norms and by withdrawn, apathetic behavior, with a disturbed parent–infant relationship often a contributing factor. (p. 176)

growth hormone (GH) A pituitary hormone that affects the development of almost all body tissues. (p. 292)

guided participation Shared endeavors between more expert and less expert participants, without specifying the precise features of communication, thereby allowing for variations across situations and cultures. A broader concept than *scaffolding*. (p. 324)

H

habituation A gradual reduction in the strength of a response due to repetitive stimulation. (p. 178)

heritability estimate A measure of the extent to which individual differences in complex traits, such as intelligence or personality, in a specific population are due to genetic factors. (p. 82)

heterozygous Having two different alleles at the same place on a pair of chromosomes. Distinguished from *homozygous*. (p. 55)

hierarchical classification The organization of objects into classes and subclasses on the basis of similarities and differences. (p. 316)

hippocampus An inner-brain structure that plays a vital role in memory and in images of space we use to help us find our way. (p. 289)

Home Observation for Measurement of the Environment (HOME) A checklist for gathering information about the quality of children's home lives through observation and parental interview. (p. 226)

homozygous Having two identical alleles at the same place on a pair of chromosomes. Distinguished from *heterozygous*. (p. 55)

I

identical, or **monozygotic, twins** Twins that result when a zygote, during early cell duplication, separates into two clusters of cells that have the same genetic makeup. Distinguished from *fraternal,* or *dizygotic, twins.* (p. 54)

imitation Learning by copying the behavior of another person. Also known as *modeling* or *observational learning.* (p. 179)

implantation Attachment of the blastocyst to the uterine lining, which occurs 7 to 9 days after fertilization. (p. 97)

inclusive classrooms Classrooms in which students with learning difficulties learn alongside typical students in a regular educational setting for part or all of the school day. (p. 465)

incomplete dominance A pattern of inheritance in which both alleles are expressed in the phenotype, resulting in a combined trait, or one that is intermediate between the two. (p. 57)

independent variable In an experiment, the variable the researcher expects to cause changes in another variable and that the researcher manipulates by randomly assigning participants to treatment conditions. Distinguished from *dependent variable.* (p. 38)

induced labor A labor started artificially by breaking the amnion and giving the mother a hormone that stimulates contractions. (p. 131)

induction A type of discipline in which an adult helps the child notice feelings by pointing out the effects of the child's misbehavior on others. (p. 373)

industry versus inferiority In Erikson's theory, the psychological conflict of middle childhood, which is resolved positively when experiences lead children to develop a sense of competence at useful skills and tasks. (p. 473)

infantile amnesia The inability of most people to remember events that happened to them before age 3. (p. 220)

infant-directed speech (IDS) A form of communication used by adults to speak to infants and toddlers, consisting of short sentences with high-pitched, exaggerated expression, clear pronunciation, distinct pauses between speech segments, clear gestures to support verbal meaning, and repetition of new words in a variety of contexts. (p. 240)

infant mortality The number of deaths in the first year of life per 1,000 live births. An index used around the world to assess the overall health of a nation's children. (p. 138)

information processing An approach that views the human mind as a symbol-manipulating system through which information flows and that regards cognitive development as a continuous process. (p. 21)

inhibited, or **shy, child** A child whose temperament is such that he or she reacts negatively to and withdraws from novel stimuli. Distinguished from *uninhibited,* or *sociable, child.* (p. 255)

initiative versus guilt In Erikson's theory, the psychological conflict of early childhood, which is resolved positively through play experiences that foster a healthy sense of purposefulness and through development of a superego, or conscience, that is not overly strict or guilt-ridden. (p. 357)

insecure–avoidant attachment The attachment pattern characterizing infants who seem unresponsive to the parent when she is present, are usually not distressed by parental separation, and avoid or are slow to greet the parent when she returns. Distinguished from *secure, insecure–resistant,* and *disorganized/disoriented attachment.* (p. 264)

insecure–resistant attachment The attachment pattern characterizing infants who seek closeness to the parent before her departure, are usually distressed when she leaves, and combine clinginess with angry, resistive behavior or with an anxious focus on the parent when she returns. Distinguished from *secure, insecure–avoidant,* and *disorganized/disoriented attachment.* (p. 264)

intelligence quotient (IQ) A score that permits an individual's performance on an intelligence test to be compared to the performances of same-age individuals. (p. 225)

intentional, or **goal-directed, behavior** A sequence of actions in which schemes are deliberately coordinated to solve simple problems. (p. 204)

interactional synchrony A form of communication in which the caregiver responds to infant signals in a well-timed, rhythmic, appropriate fashion and both partners match emotional states, especially positive ones. (p. 266)

intermodal perception Perception that combines information from more than one modality, or sensory system, resulting in an integrated whole. (p. 195)

internal working model A set of expectations, derived from early caregiving experiences, about the availability of attachment figures, their likelihood of providing support during times of stress, and the self's interaction with those figures. Becomes a vital part of personality, serving as a guide for all future close relationships. (p. 262)

intersubjectivity The process by which two participants who begin a task with different understandings arrive at a shared understanding. (p. 324)

irreversibility The inability to mentally go through a series of steps in a problem and then reverse direction, returning to the starting point. Distinguished from *reversibility.* (p. 316)

J

joint attention A state in which the child and caregiver attend to the same object or event and the caregiver labels what the child sees. Contributes greatly to early language development. (p. 236)

K

kinship studies Studies comparing the characteristics of family members to determine the importance of heredity in complex human characteristics. (p. 82)

kwashiorkor A disease caused by an unbalanced diet very low in protein, which usually appears after weaning, between 1 and 3 years of age. Symptoms include an enlarged belly, swollen feet, hair loss, skin rash, and irritable, listless behavior. (p. 175)

L

language acquisition device (LAD) In Chomsky's theory, an innate system containing a universal grammar, or set of rules common to all languages, that enables children, no matter which language they hear, to understand

and speak in a rule-oriented fashion as soon as they have learned enough words. (p. 231)

lanugo White, downy hair that covers the entire body of the fetus, helping the vernix stick to the skin. (p. 99)

lateralization Specialization of functions in the two hemispheres of the cerebral cortex. (p. 165)

learned helplessness Attribution of success to external factors such as luck, and failure to low ability, which cannot be improved through effort. Distinguished from *mastery-oriented attributions*. (p. 478)

learning disability Great difficulty with one or more aspects of learning, usually reading, resulting in achievement considerably behind what would be expected on the basis of a child's IQ. (p. 465)

longitudinal design A research design in which participants are studied repeatedly at different ages, and changes are noted as they get older. Distinguished from *cross-sectional design*. (p. 41)

long-term memory In information processing, the largest storage area in the mental system, containing our permanent knowledge base. (p. 216)

M

macrosystem In ecological systems theory, cultural values, laws, customs, and resources that influence experiences and interactions at inner levels of the environment. Distinguished from *microsystem, mesosystem, exosystem,* and *chronosystem*. (p. 27)

make-believe play A type of play in which children act out everyday and imaginary activities. (p. 205)

malocclusion A condition in which the upper and lower teeth do not meet properly. (p. 407)

marasmus A disease caused by a diet low in all essential nutrients that usually appears in the first year of life and leads to a wasted condition of the body. (p. 175)

mastery-oriented attributions Attributions that credit success to ability, which can be improved by trying hard, and failure to insufficient effort. Distinguished from *learned helplessness*. (p. 478)

matters of personal choice Concerns that do not violate the rights of others and, therefore, are up to each individual, such as choice of friends, hairstyle, and leisure activities. Distinguished from *moral imperatives* and *social conventions*. (p. 378)

maturation A genetically determined, naturally unfolding course of growth. (p. 13)

meiosis The process of cell division through which gametes are formed and in which the number of chromosomes in each cell is halved. (p. 53)

memory strategies Deliberate mental activities that improve the likelihood of remembering. (p. 329)

mental representation An internal depiction of information that the mind can manipulate. (p. 205)

mesosystem In ecological systems theory, connections between children's microsystems, or immediate settings. Distinguished from *microsystem, exosystem, macrosystem,* and *chronosystem*. (p. 27)

metacognition Thinking about thought; awareness of mental activities. (p. 332)

metalinguistic awareness The ability to think about language as a system. (p. 455)

methylation A biochemical process triggered by certain experiences, in which a set of chemical compounds (called a methyl group) lands on top of a gene and changes its impact, reducing or silencing its expression. (p. 86)

microgenetic design An adaptation of the longitudinal design, in which investigators present children with a novel task and follow their mastery over a series of closely spaced sessions to observe how change occurs. (p. 44)

microsystem In ecological systems theory, the innermost level of the environment, consisting of activities and interaction patterns in the child's immediate surroundings. Distinguished from *mesosystem, exosystem, macrosystem,* and *chronosystem*. (p. 26)

mirror neurons Specialized cells in many areas of the cerebral cortex in primates that underlie the ability to imitate by firing identically when a primate hears or sees an action and when it carries out that action on its own. (p. 180)

moral imperatives Rules and expectations that protect people's rights and welfare. Distinguished from *social conventions* and *matters of personal choice*. (p. 378)

mutation A sudden but permanent change in a segment of DNA. (p. 58)

mutual exclusivity bias Early in vocabulary growth, children's assumption that words refer to entirely separate (nonoverlapping) categories. (p. 349)

myelination The coating of neural fibers with *myelin,* an insulating fatty sheath that improves the efficiency of message transfer. (p. 162)

N

naturalistic observation A research method in which the researcher goes into the natural environment to observe the behavior of interest. Distinguished from *structured observation*. (p. 32)

natural, or **prepared, childbirth** A group of techniques aimed at reducing pain and medical intervention and making childbirth a rewarding experience. (p. 128)

nature–nurture controversy Debate among theorists about whether genetic or environmental factors are more important influences on development. (p. 9)

neglected children Children who are seldom mentioned, either positively or negatively, on self-report measures of social preferences. Distinguished from *popular, controversial, rejected,* and *average children*. (p. 490)

Neonatal Behavioral Assessment Scale (NBAS) A test developed to assess a newborn infant's behavior in terms of reflexes, muscle tone, state changes, responsiveness to physical and social stimuli, and other reactions. (p. 150)

neonatal mortality The number of deaths in the first month of life per 1,000 live births. (p. 138)

neural tube During the period of the embryo, the primitive spinal cord that develops from the ectoderm, the top of which swells to form the brain. (p. 98)

neurons Nerve cells that store and transmit information. (p. 161)

neurotransmitters Chemicals released by neurons that cross the synapse to send messages to other neurons. (p. 161)

niche-picking A type of gene–environment correlation in which individuals actively choose environments that complement their heredity. (p. 85)

nocturnal enuresis Bedwetting during the night. (p. 415)

non-rapid-eye-movement (NREM) sleep A regular sleep state in which the body is almost motionless and heart rate, breathing, and brain-wave activity are slow and even. Distinguished from *rapid-eye-movement (REM) sleep*. (p. 144)

nonsocial activity Unoccupied, onlooker behavior and solitary play. Distinguished from *parallel play, associative play,* and *cooperative play*. (pp. 365–366)

normal distribution The bell-shaped distribution that results when individual differences are measured in large samples. Most scores cluster around the mean, or average, with progressively fewer falling toward the extremes. (pp. 225–226)

normative approach An approach to development in which measures of behavior are taken on large numbers of individuals and age-related averages are computed to represent typical development. (pp. 13–14)

O

obesity A greater-than-20-percent increase over healthy weight, based on body mass index (BMI)—a ratio of weight to height associated with body fat. (p. 410)

object permanence The understanding that objects continue to exist when they are out of sight. (p. 204)

operant conditioning A form of learning in which a spontaneous behavior is followed by a stimulus that changes the probability that the behavior will occur again. (p. 178)

ordinality The mathematical principle specifying order relationships (more than and less than) between quantities. (p. 337)

organization In Piaget's theory, the internal rearrangement and linking together of schemes so that they form a strongly interconnected cognitive system. In information processing, a memory strategy that involves grouping related items together to improve recall. (pp. 202, 437)

overextension An early vocabulary error in which a word is applied to a wider collection of objects and events than is appropriate. Distinguished from *underextension*. (p. 237)

overlapping-waves theory A theory of problem solving, which states that when given challenging problems, children try out various strategies and gradually select those that are fastest and most accurate. (p. 331)

overregularization Extension of regular grammatical rules to words that are exceptions. (p. 351)

P

parallel play A limited form of social participation in which a child plays near other children with similar materials but does not interact with them. Distinguished from *nonsocial activity, associative play,* and *cooperative play.* (p. 366)

partial fetal alcohol syndrome (p-FAS) A form of fetal alcohol spectrum disorder characterized by facial abnormalities and brain injury, but less severe than fetal alcohol syndrome. Usually affects children whose mothers drank alcohol in smaller quantities during pregnancy. Distinguished from fetal alcohol syndrome (FAS) and alcohol-related neurodevelopmental disorder (ARND). (pp. 106–107)

peer acceptance Likability, or the extent to which a child is viewed by a group of agemates, such as classmates, as a worthy social partner. (p. 490)

peer groups Collectives of peers who generate unique values and standards for behavior and a social structure of leaders and followers. (p. 488)

peer victimization A destructive form of peer interaction in which particular children become targets of verbal and physical attacks or other forms of abuse. (p. 492)

perceptual narrowing effect Perceptual sensitivity that becomes increasingly attuned with age to information most often encountered. (p. 188)

permissive child-rearing style A child-rearing style that is high in acceptance but either overindulgent or inattentive, low in control, and inappropriately lenient in autonomy granting. Distinguished from *authoritative, authoritarian,* and *uninvolved child-rearing styles.* (p. 394)

person praise Praise from an adult that emphasizes the child's traits, as in "you're so smart"; "you're very artistic." Distinguished from *process praise.* (p. 479)

phenotype An individual's directly observable physical and behavioral characteristics, which are determined by both genetic and environmental factors. Distinguished from *genotype.* (p. 51)

phobia An intense, unmanageable fear. (p. 507)

phonics approach An approach to beginning reading instruction that emphasizes coaching children on phonics—the basic rules for translating written symbols into sounds—before exposing them to complex reading material. Distinguished from *whole-language approach.* (p. 443)

phonological awareness The ability to reflect on and manipulate the sound structures of spoken language, as indicated by sensitivity to changes in sounds within words, to rhyming, and to incorrect pronunciation. A strong predictor of emergent literacy. (p. 336)

physical aggression A form of aggression that harms others through physical injury to themselves or their property. Distinguished from *verbal aggression* and *relational aggression.* (p. 379)

pincer grasp The well-coordinated grasp that emerges at the end of the first year, involving thumb and index finger opposition. (p. 186)

pituitary gland A gland located at the base of the brain that releases hormones that induce physical growth. (p. 290)

placenta The organ that permits exchange of nutrients and waste products between the bloodstreams of the mother and the embryo, while also preventing the mother's and embryo's blood from mixing directly. (p. 97)

planning Thinking out a sequence of acts ahead of time and allocating attention accordingly to reach a goal. (p. 328)

plasticity Openness of human development to change in response to influential experiences. (p. 9)

polygenic inheritance A pattern of inheritance in which many genes affect the characteristic in question. (p. 59)

popular-antisocial children A subtype of popular children who are admired for their socially adept yet belligerent behavior. Includes "tough" boys who are athletically skilled but poor students who cause trouble and defy adult authority, and relationally aggressive boys and girls. Distinguished from *popular-prosocial children.* (p. 490)

popular children Children who receive many positive votes on self-report measures of social preferences, indicating they are well-liked. Distinguished from *rejected, controversial, neglected,* and *average children.* (p. 490)

popular-prosocial children A subtype of popular children who are both socially accepted and admired and who combine academic and social competence. Distinguished from *popular-antisocial children.* (p. 490)

pragmatics The practical, social side of language, concerned with how to engage in effective and appropriate communication. (p. 352)

prefrontal cortex The region of the cerebral cortex, lying in front of areas controlling body movement, that is responsible for thought—in particular, for consciousness, inhibition of impulses, integration of information, and use of memory, reasoning, planning, and problem-solving strategies. (p. 165)

prenatal diagnostic methods Medical procedures that permit detection of developmental problems before birth. (p. 64)

preoperational stage Piaget's second stage, extending from about 2 to 7 years of age, in which children undergo an extraordinary increase in representational, or symbolic, activity, although thought is not yet logical. (p. 311)

prereaching The poorly coordinated swipes toward objects of newborn babies. (p. 185)

preterm infants Infants born several weeks or more before their due date. (p. 135)

private speech Self-directed speech that children use to plan and guide their own behavior. (p. 323)

proactive aggression A type of aggression in which children act to fulfill a need or desire—to obtain an object, privilege, space, or social reward, such as adult or peer attention—and unemotionally attack a person to achieve their goal. Also called *instrumental aggression.* Distinguished from *reactive aggression.* (p. 379)

problem-centered coping A strategy for managing emotion in which the individual appraises the situation as changeable, identifies the difficulty, and decides what to do about it. Distinguished from *emotion-centered coping.* (p. 482)

process praise Praise from an adult that emphasizes the child's behavior and effort, such as "you worked really hard" or "you figured it out." Distinguished from *person praise.* (p. 479)

production In language development, the words and word combinations that children use. Distinguished from *comprehension.* (p. 238)

Project Head Start The most extensive U.S. federally funded preschool intervention program, which provides low-SES children with a year or two of preschool education, along with nutritional and health services, and encourages parent involvement in children's learning and development. (p. 342)

prosocial, or **altruistic, behavior** Actions that benefit another person without any expected reward for the self. (p. 364)

protein-coding genes Genes that directly affect the body's characteristics. Distinguished from *regulator genes.* (p. 52)

proximodistal trend An organized pattern of physical growth that proceeds from the center of the body outward. Distinguished from *cephalocaudal trend.* (p. 161)

psychoanalytic perspective An approach to personality development introduced by Freud that assumes children move through a series of stages in which they confront conflicts between biological drives and social expectations. How these conflicts are resolved determines the person's ability to learn, to get along with others, and to cope with anxiety. (p. 15)

psychological control Parental control that attempts to take advantage of children's psychological needs by intruding on and manipulating children's verbal expressions, individuality, and attachments to parents. (p. 394)

psychosexual theory Freud's theory, which emphasizes that how parents manage children's sexual and aggressive drives in the first few years of life is crucial for healthy personality development. (p. 15)

psychosocial dwarfism A growth disorder, usually appearing between 2 and 15 years of age, caused by extreme emotional deprivation. It is characterized by decreased GH secretion, very short stature, immature skeletal age, and serious adjustment problems, which help distinguish it from normal shortness. (p. 292)

psychosocial theory Erikson's theory, which emphasizes that at each Freudian stage, individuals not only develop a unique personality but also acquire attitudes and skills that help them become active, contributing members of society. (p. 15)

public policies Laws and government programs designed to improve current conditions. (p. 79)

punishment In operant conditioning, removal of a desirable stimulus or presentation of an unpleasant stimulus, either of which decreases the occurrence of a response. (p. 178)

R

random assignment An unbiased procedure for assigning participants to treatment conditions in an experiment, such as drawing numbers out of a hat or flipping a coin. It increases the chances that participants' characteristics will be equally distributed across treatment groups. (p. 39)

rapid-eye-movement (REM) sleep An irregular sleep state in which brain-wave activity is similar to that of the waking state. Distinguished from *non-rapid-eye-movement (NREM) sleep*. (p. 144)

reactive aggression An angry, defensive response to provocation or a blocked goal that is intended to hurt another person. Also called *hostile aggression*. Distinguished from *proactive aggression*. (p. 379)

recall The form of memory that involves remembering something not present, by generating a mental image of a past experience. Distinguished from *recognition*. (p. 218)

recasts Adult responses that restructure children's grammatically inaccurate speech into correct form. (p. 353)

reciprocal teaching A teaching method in which a teacher and two to four students form a cooperative group and take turns leading dialogues, creating a zone of proximal development in which children scaffold one another's progress. (p. 461)

recognition The form of memory that involves noticing whether a stimulus is identical or similar to one previously experienced. Distinguished from *recall*. (p. 218)

recovery Following habituation, an increase in responsiveness to a new stimulus. (p. 178)

recursive thought A form of perspective taking that requires the ability to view a situation from at least two perspectives—that is, to reason simultaneously about what two or more people are thinking. (p. 441)

referential style A style of early language learning in which toddlers use language mainly to label objects. Distinguished from *expressive style*. (p. 239)

reflex An inborn, automatic response to a particular form of stimulation. (p. 141)

regulator genes Genes that modify the instructions given by *protein coding genes*, greatly complicating their impact. (p. 52)

rehearsal A memory strategy that involves repeating information to oneself to improve recall. (p. 437)

reinforcer In operant conditioning, a stimulus that increases the occurrence of a response. (p. 178)

rejected-aggressive children A subtype of rejected children who show high rates of conflict, physical and relational aggression, and hyperactive, inattentive, and impulsive behavior. Distinguished from *rejected-withdrawn children*. (p. 491)

rejected children Children who receive many negative votes on self-report measures of social preferences, indicating they are disliked. Distinguished from *popular, controversial, neglected,* and *average children*. (p. 490)

rejected-withdrawn children A subtype of rejected children who are passive, socially awkward, and overwhelmed by social anxiety. Distinguished from *rejected-aggressive children*. (p. 491)

relational aggression A form of aggression that damages another's peer relationships through social exclusion, malicious gossip, or friendship manipulation. Distinguished from *physical aggression* and *verbal aggression*. (p. 380)

resilience The ability to adapt effectively in the face of threats to development. (p. 10)

reticular formation A structure in the brain stem that maintains alertness and consciousness. (p. 289)

reversibility The capacity to think through a series of steps in a problem and then mentally reverse direction, returning to the starting point. Distinguished from *irreversibility*. (p. 429)

Rh factor incompatibility A condition that arises when the Rh protein is present in the fetus's blood but not in the mother's, causing the mother to build up antibodies to the foreign Rh protein. If these enter the fetus's system, they destroy red blood cells, reducing the oxygen supply to organs and tissues. (p. 113)

rooming in An arrangement in which the newborn baby stays in the mother's hospital room all or most of the time. (p. 141)

rough-and-tumble play A form of peer interaction involving friendly chasing and play-fighting that emerges in the preschool years and peaks in middle childhood. In our evolutionary past, it may have been important for the development of fighting skill. (p. 424)

S

scaffolding Adjusting the support offered during a teaching session to fit the child's current level of performance. As competence increases, the adult gradually and sensitively withdraws support, turning responsibility over to the child. (p. 324)

scale errors Toddlers' attempts to do things that their body size makes impossible, such as trying to put on dolls' clothes, sit in a doll-sized chair, or walk through a door too narrow to pass through. (p. 277)

scheme In Piaget's theory, a specific psychological structure, or organized way of making sense of experience, that changes with age. (p. 202)

scripts General descriptions of what occurs and when it occurs in a particular situation, used to organize, interpret, and predict everyday experiences. (p. 329)

secular trends in physical growth Changes in body size from one generation to the next. (p. 406)

secure attachment The attachment pattern characterizing infants who use the parent as a secure base from which to explore and may be distressed by parental separation but actively seek contact and are easily comforted by the parent when she returns. Distinguished from *insecure–avoidant, insecure–resistant,* and *disorganized/disoriented attachment*. (p. 264)

secure base Role of the familiar caregiver as a point from which the infant explores, venturing into the environment and then returning for emotional support. (p. 250)

self-care children Children who regularly look after themselves for some period of time during after-school hours. (p. 506)

self-concept The set of attributes, abilities, attitudes, and values that an individual believes defines who he or she is. (p. 358)

self-conscious emotions Emotions involving injury to or enhancement of the sense of self, such as guilt, shame, embarrassment, envy, and pride. (p. 251)

self-esteem An aspect of self-concept that involves judgments about one's own worth and the feelings associated with those judgments. (p. 359)

semantic bootstrapping Using semantics, or word meanings, to figure out grammatical rules. (p. 351)

sensitive caregiving Caregiving that involves responding promptly, consistently, and appropriately to infants and holding them tenderly and carefully. (p. 266)

sensitive period A time that is biologically optimal for certain capacities to emerge because the individual is especially responsive to environmental influences. (p. 24)

sensorimotor stage Piaget's first stage, spanning the first two years of life, during which infants and toddlers "think" with their eyes, ears, hands, and other sensorimotor equipment. (p. 201)

sensory register In information processing, the part of the mental system in which sights and sounds are represented directly and stored briefly before they either decay or are transferred to working memory. (p. 215)

separation anxiety An infant's distressed reaction to the departure of their trusted caregiver. (p. 262)

sequential design A research design in which several similar cross-sectional or longitudinal studies (called sequences) are conducted at varying times. (p. 43)

seriation The ability to order items along a quantitative dimension, such as length or weight. (p. 430)

sex chromosomes The twenty-third pair of chromosomes—called XX in females, XY in males—which determines the sex of the individual. (p. 53)

shape constancy Perception of an object's shape as the same, despite changes in the shape projected on the retina. (p. 194)

short-term memory store That part of the mind in which attended-to information is retained briefly so that we can actively "work" on it to achieve our goals. (p. 215)

size constancy Perception of an object's size as the same, despite changes in the size of its retinal image. (p. 194)

slow-to-warm-up child A child whose temperament is characterized by inactivity; mild, low-key reactions to environmental stimuli; negative mood; and slow adjustment to new experiences. Distinguished from *easy child* and *difficult child*. (p. 254)

small-for-date infants Infants whose birth weight is below their expected weight considering length of the pregnancy. (p. 135)

social comparisons Judgments of one's own appearance, abilities, and behavior in relation to those of others. (p. 474)

social-constructivist classroom A classroom grounded in Vygotsky's sociocultural theory, in which children participate in a wide range of challenging activities with teachers and peers, with whom they jointly construct understandings. Distinguished from *traditional classroom* and *constructivist classroom*. (p. 461)

social conventions Customs determined by consensus, such as table manners and politeness rituals. Distinguished from *moral imperatives* and *matters of personal choice*. (p. 378)

social learning theory An approach that emphasizes the role of modeling, also known as imitation or observational learning, in the development of behavior. (p. 17)

social problem solving Generating and applying strategies that prevent or resolve disagreements, resulting in outcomes that are both acceptable to others and beneficial to the self. (p. 369)

social referencing Actively seeking emotional information from a trusted person in an uncertain situation. (p. 251)

social smile The infant's broad grin evoked by the parent's communication, first appearing between 6 and 10 weeks of age. (p. 248)

sociocultural theory Vygotsky's perspective, which focuses on how children acquire the ways of thinking and behaving that make up a community's culture through social interaction, especially cooperative dialogues with more knowledgeable members of society. (p. 25)

sociodramatic play The make-believe play with others that is under way by the end of the second year and that increases rapidly in complexity during early childhood. (p. 312)

socioeconomic status (SES) A measure of an individual's social position and economic well-being that combines three related variables: years of education, the prestige of one's job and the skill it requires, and income. (p. 70)

stage A qualitative change in thinking, feeling, and behaving that characterizes a specific period of development. (p. 8)

standardization The practice of giving an intelligence test to a large, representative sample and using the results as the standard for interpreting individual scores. (p. 225)

states of arousal Degrees of sleep and wakefulness. (p. 143)

statistical learning capacity The capacity to analyze the speech stream for repeatedly occurring sequences of sounds, through which infants acquire a stock of speech structures for which they will later learn meanings. (p. 188)

stereotype threat The fear of being judged on the basis of a negative stereotype, which can trigger anxiety that interferes with performance. (p. 453)

stranger anxiety The infant's expression of fear in response to unfamiliar adults, which appears in many babies in the second half of the first year. (p. 249)

Strange Situation A laboratory procedure used to assess the quality of attachment between 1 and 2 years of age by observing the baby's responses to eight short episodes involving brief separations from and reunions with the caregiver in an unfamiliar playroom. (p. 263)

structured interview An interview method in which each participant is asked the same questions in the same way. Distinguished from *clinical interview*. (p. 35)

structured observation A research method in which the investigator sets up a laboratory situation that evokes the behavior of interest so that every participant has an equal opportunity to display the response. Distinguished from *naturalistic observation*. (p. 33)

subculture A group of people with beliefs and customs that differ from those of the larger culture. (p. 78)

sudden infant death syndrome (SIDS) The unexpected death, usually during the night, of an infant under 1 year of age that remains unexplained after thorough investigation. (p. 145)

sympathy Feelings of concern or sorrow for another's plight. (p. 364)

synapses The gaps between neurons, across which chemical messages are sent. (p. 161)

synaptic pruning Loss of synapses by seldom-stimulated neurons, a process that returns neurons not needed at the moment to an uncommitted state so they can support future development. (p. 162)

syntactic bootstrapping Figuring out word meanings by observing how words are used in syntax, or the structure of sentences. (p. 349)

T

talent Outstanding performance in a specific field. (p. 467)

telegraphic speech Toddlers' two-word utterances that, like a telegram, focus on high-content words while omitting smaller, less important ones. (p. 238)

temperament Early-appearing, stable individual differences in reactivity (quickness and intensity of emotional arousal, attention, and motor activity) and self-regulation (strategies that modify reactivity). (p. 253)

teratogen Any environmental agent that causes damage during the prenatal period. (p. 101)

theory An orderly, integrated set of statements that describes, explains, and predicts behavior. (p. 7)

theory of multiple intelligences Gardner's theory, which proposes at least eight independent intelligences, defined in terms of distinct sets of processing operations that permit individuals to engage in a wide range of culturally valued activities. (p. 449)

thyroid-stimulating hormone (TSH) A pituitary hormone that stimulates the thyroid gland to release thyroxine, which is necessary for brain development and for growth hormone to have its full impact on body size. (p. 292)

time out A form of mild punishment in which children are removed from the immediate setting until they are ready to act appropriately. (p. 376)

traditional classroom A classroom in which the teacher is the sole authority for knowledge, rules, and decision making and students are relatively passive learners who are evaluated in relation to a uniform set of standards for their grade. Distinguished from *constructivist classroom* and *social-constructivist classroom*. (p. 460)

transition Climax of the first stage of labor, in which the frequency and strength of contractions are at their peak and the cervix opens completely. (p. 125)

transitive inference The ability to seriate, or order items along a quantitative dimension, mentally. (p. 430)

triarchic theory of successful intelligence Sternberg's theory, which identifies three broad, interacting intelligences—analytical, creative, and practical—that must be balanced to achieve success according to one's personal goals and the requirements of one's cultural community. (p. 448)

trimesters Three equal time periods, each lasting three months, into which prenatal development is divided. (p. 99)

trophoblast The thin outer ring of cells of the blastocyst, which will become the structures that provide protective covering and nourishment to the new organism. (p. 97)

U

ulnar grasp The clumsy grasp of the young infant, in which the fingers close against the palm. (p. 186)

umbilical cord The long cord connecting the prenatal organism to the placenta that delivers nutrients and removes waste products. (p. 98)

unconditioned response (UCR) In classical conditioning, a reflexive response that is produced by an unconditioned stimulus (UCS). Distinguished from *conditioned response*. (p. 177)

unconditioned stimulus (UCS) In classical conditioning, a stimulus that leads to a reflexive response. Distinguished from *conditioned stimulus*. (p. 177)

underextension An early vocabulary error in which young children apply a word too narrowly, to a smaller number of objects and events than is appropriate. Distinguished from *overextension*. (p. 237)

uninhibited, or sociable, child A child whose temperament is such that he or she displays positive emotion to and approaches novel stimuli. Distinguished from *inhibited, or shy, child*. (p. 255)

uninvolved child-rearing style A child-rearing style that combines low acceptance and involvement with little control and general indifference to issues of autonomy. Distinguished from *authoritative, authoritarian, and permissive child-rearing styles*. (p. 394)

V

verbal aggression A form of aggression that harms others through threats of physical aggression, name-calling, or hostile teasing. Distinguished from *physical* and *relational aggression*. (p. 379)

vernix A white, cheeselike substance that covers the fetus, protecting the skin from chapping due to constant exposure to amniotic fluid. (p. 99)

video deficit effect In toddlers, poorer performance on tasks after watching a video than a live demonstration. (p. 210)

violation-of-expectation method A method in which researchers show babies an expected event (one that is consistent with reality) and an unexpected event (a variation of the first event that violates reality). Heightened attention to the unexpected event suggests that the infant is "surprised" by a deviation from physical reality and, therefore, is aware of that aspect of the physical world. (p. 205)

visual acuity Fineness of visual discrimination. (p. 150)

W

whole-language approach An approach to beginning reading instruction in which children are exposed to text in its complete form, using reading materials that are whole and meaningful to promote appreciation of the communicative function of written language. Distinguished from *phonics approach*. (p. 443)

working memory The number of items that can be briefly held in mind while also engaging in some effort to monitor or manipulate those items—a "mental workspace" that we use to accomplish many activities in daily life. A contemporary view of the short-term memory store. (p. 215)

X

X-linked inheritance A pattern of inheritance in which a recessive gene is carried on the X chromosome, resulting in males being more likely than females to be affected because the male's sex chromosomes do not match. (p. 57)

Z

zone of proximal development In Vygotsky's theory, a range of tasks too difficult for a child to do alone but that the child can do with the help of more skilled partners. (p. 222)

zygote The newly fertilized cell formed by the union of sperm and ovum at conception. (p. 53)

A

Aarnoudse-Moens, C. S., Weisglas-Kuperus, N., & van Goudoever, J. B. (2009). Meta-analysis of neurobehavioral outcomes in very preterm and/or very low birth weight children. *Pediatrics, 124,* 717–728.

Aber, L., Brown, J. L., Jones, S. M., Berg, J., & Torrente, C. (2011). School-based strategies to prevent violence, trauma, and psychopathology: The challenges of going to scale. *Development and Psychopathology, 23,* 411–421.

Abner, K. S., Gordon, R. A., Kaestner, R., & Korenman, S. (2013). Does child-care quality mediate associations between type of care and development? *Journal of Marriage and Family, 75,* 1203–1217.

Aboud, F. E. (2003). The formation of in-group favoritism and out-group prejudice in young children: Are they distinct attitudes? *Developmental Psychology, 39,* 48–60.

Aboud, F. E. (2008). A social-cognitive developmental theory of prejudice. In S. M. Quintana & C. McKown (Eds.), *Handbook of race, racism, and the developing child* (pp. 55–71). Hoboken, NJ: Wiley.

Aboud, F. E., & Doyle, A. (1996). Parental and peer influences on children's racial attitudes. *International Journal of Intercultural Relations, 20,* 371–383.

Abraham, M. M., & Kerns, K. A. (2013). Positive and negative emotions and coping as mediators of mother–child attachment and peer relationships. *Merrill-Palmer Quarterly, 59,* 399–425.

Achenbach, T. M., Howell C. T., & Aoki, M. F. (1993). Nine-year outcome of the Vermont Intervention Program for low-birthweight infants, *Pediatrics, 91,* 45–55.

Acker, M. M., & O'Leary, S. G. (1996). Inconsistency of mothers' feedback and toddlers' misbehavior and negative affect. *Journal of Abnormal Child Psychology, 24,* 703–714.

Ackerman, J. P., Riggins, T., & Black, M M. (2010). A review of the effects of prenatal cocaine exposure among school-aged children. *Pediatrics, 125,* 554–565.

Adam, E. K., Snell, E. K., & Pendry, P. (2007). Sleep timing and quantity in ecological and family context: A nationally representative time-diary study. *Journal of Family Psychology, 21,* 4–19.

Adams, M. J. (2002). Alphabetic anxiety and explicit, systemic phonics instruction. In S. B. Neuman & D. K. Dickinson (Eds.), *Handbook of early literacy research* (Vol. 1, pp. 66–80). New York: Guilford.

Adolph, K. E. (2002). Learning to keep balance. In R. V. Kail (Ed.), *Advances in child development and behavior* (Vol. 30, pp. 1–40). Boston: Academic Press.

Adolph, K. E. (2008). Learning to move. *Current Directions in Psychological Science, 17,* 213–218.

Adolph, K. E., & Berger, S. E. (2006). Motor development. In D. Kuhn & R. Siegler (Eds.), *Handbook of child psychology: Vol. 2. Cognition, perception, and language* (6th ed., pp. 161–213). Hoboken, NJ: Wiley.

Adolph, K. E., Cole, W. G., Komati, M., Garciaguirre, J. S., Badaly, D., Lingeman, J. M., et al. (2012). How do you learn to walk? Thousands of steps and hundreds of falls per day. *Psychological Science, 23,* 1387–1394.

Adolph, K. E., Karasik, L. B., & Tamis-LeMonda, C. S. (2010). Motor skill. In M. H. Bornstein (Ed.), *Handbook of cultural developmental science* (pp. 61–88). New York: Psychology Press.

Adolph, K. E., & Kretch, K. S. (2012). Infants on the edge: Beyond the visual cliff. In A. Slater & P. Quinn (Eds.), *Developmental psychology: Revisiting the classic studies* (pp. 36–55). London: Sage.

Adolph, K. E., Kretch, K. S., & LoBue, V. (2014). Fear of heights in infants? *Current Directions in Psychological Science, 23,* 60–66.

Adolph, K. E., Tamis-LeMonda, C. S., Ishak, S., Karasik, L. B., & Lobo, S. A. (2008). Locomotor experience and use of social information are posture specific. *Developmental Psychology, 44,* 1705–1714.

Adolph, K. E., Vereijken, B., & Shrout, P. E. (2003). What changes in infant walking and why. *Child Development, 74,* 475–497.

Adolphs, R. (2010). What does the amygdala contribute to social cognition? *Annals of the New York Academy of Sciences, 119,* 42–61.

Adzick, N. S. (2013). Prospects for fetal surgery. *Early Human Development, 89,* 881–886.

Afifi, T. O., Brownridge, D. A., Cox, B. J., & Sareen J. (2006). Physical punishment, childhood abuse and psychiatric disorders. *Child Abuse and Neglect, 30,* 1093–1103.

Afifi, T. O., Mota, M., MacMillan, H. L., & Sareen, J. (2013). Harsh physical punishment in childhood and adult physical health. *Pediatrics, 132,* e333–e340.

Agronick, G., Stueve, A., Vargo, S., & O'Donnell, L. (2007). New York City young adults' psychological reactions to 9/11: Findings from the Reach for Health longitudinal study. *American Journal of Community Psychology, 39,* 79–90.

Aguiar, A., & Baillargeon, R. (2002). Developments in young infants' reasoning about occluded objects. *Cognitive Psychology, 45,* 267–336.

Ahmadlou, M., Gharib, M., Hemmti, S., Vameghi, R., & Sajedi, F. (2013). Disrupted small-world brain network in children with Down syndrome. *Clinical Neurophysiology, 124,* 1755–1764.

Aikens, J. W., Howes, C., & Hamilton, C. (2009). Attachment stability and the emergence of unresolved representations in adolescence. *Attachment and Human Development, 11,* 491–512.

Ainsworth, M. D. S., Blehar, M. C., Waters, E., & Wall, S. (1978). *Patterns of attachment.* Hillsdale, NJ: Erlbaum.

Akhtar, N., & Montague, L. (1999). Early lexical acquisition: The role of cross-situational learning. *First Language, 19,* 347–358.

Akimoto, S. A., & Sanbinmatsu, D. M. (1999). Differences in self-effacing behavior between European and Japanese Americans: Effect on competence evaluations. *Journal of Cross-Cultural Psychology, 30,* 159–177.

Aksan, N., & Kochanska, G. (2004). Heterogeneity of joy in infancy. *Infancy, 6,* 79–94.

Akutagava-Martins, G. C., Salatino-Liveira, A., Kieling, C. C., Rohde, A., & Hutz, M. H. (2013). Genetics of attention-deficit/hyperactivity disorder: Current findings and future directions. *Expert Review of Neurotherapeutics, 13,* 435–445.

Alati, R., Smith, G. D., Lewis, S. J., Sayal, K., Draper, E. S., Golding, J., et al. (2013). Effect of prenatal alcohol exposure on childhood academic outcomes: Contrasting maternal and paternal associations in the ALSPAC Study. *PLOS ONE, 8*(10), e74844.

Albareda-Castellot, B., Pons, F., & Sebastián-Gallés, N. (2010). The acquisition of phonetic categories in bilingual infants: New data from an anticipatory eye movement paradigm. *Developmental Science, 14,* 395–401.

Albers, C. A., & Grieve, A. J. (2007). Test review: Bayley, N. (2006). Bayley Scales of Infant and Toddler Development—Third Edition. San Antonio, TX: Harcourt Assessment. *Journal of Psychoeducational Assessment, 25,* 180–190.

Aldridge, M. A., Stillman, R. D., & Bower, T. G. R. (2001). Newborn categorization of vowel-like sounds. *Developmental Science, 4,* 220–232.

Alexander, J. M., Fabricius, W. V., Fleming, V. M., Zwahr, M., & Brown, S. A. (2003). The development of metacognitive causal explanations. *Learning and Individual Differences, 13,* 227–238.

Alhusen, J. L. (2008). A literature update on maternal–fetal attachment. *Journal of Obstetric, Gynecologic, and Neonatal Nursing, 37,* 315–328.

Alibali, M. W., Phillips, K. M. O., & Fischer, A. D. (2009). Learning new problem-solving strategies leads to changes in problem representation. *Cognitive Development, 24,* 89–101.

Aligne, C. A., Moss, M. E., Auinger, P., & Weitzman, M. (2003). Association of pediatric dental caries with passive smoking. *Journal of the American Medical Association, 289,* 1258–1264.

Alink, L. R. A., Mesman, J., van Zeijl, J., Stolk, M. N., Juffer, F., & Koot, H. M. (2006). The early childhood aggression curve: Development of physical aggression in 10- to 50-month-old children. *Child Development, 77,* 954–966.

Allely, C. S., Gillberg, C., & Wilson, P. (2014). Neurobiological abnormalities in the first few years of life in individuals later diagnosed with autism spectrum disorder: A review of recent data. *Behavioural Neurology.* Retrieved from www.hindawi.com/journals/bn/2014/210780/

Allen, K. A. (2014). Moderate hypothermia: Is selective head cooling or whole body cooling better? *Advances in Neonatal Care, 14,* 113–118.

Allen, S. E. M., & Crago, M. B. (1996). Early passive acquisition in Inukitut. *Journal of Child Language, 23,* 129–156.

Alloway, T. P. (2009). Working memory, but not IQ, predicts subsequent learning in children with learning difficulties. *European Journal of Psychological Assessment, 25,* 92–98.

Alloway, T. P., Bibile, V., & Lau, G. (2013). Computerized working memory training: Can it lead to gains in cognitive skills in students? *Computers in Human Behavior, 29,* 632–638.

Alloway, T. P., Gathercole, S. E., Kirkwood, H., & Elliott, J. (2009). The cognitive and behavioral characteristics of children with low working memory. *Child Development, 80,* 606–621.

Al-Namlah, A. S., Fernyhough, C., & Meins, E. (2006). Sociocultural influences on the development of verbal mediation: Private speech and phonological recoding in Saudi Arabian and British samples. *Developmental Psychology, 42,* 117–131.

Amato, P. R. (2001). Children of divorce in the 1990s: An update of the Amato and Keith (1991) meta-analysis. *Journal of Family Psychology, 15,* 355–370.

Amato, P. R. (2006). Marital discord, divorce, and children's well-being: Results from a 20-year longitudinal study of two generation. In A. Clarke-Stewart & J. Dunn (Eds.), *Families count: Effects on child and adolescent development* (pp. 179–202). New York: Cambridge University Press.

Amato, P. R. (2010). Research on divorce: Continuing trends and new developments. *Journal of Marriage and Family, 72,* 650–666.

Amato, P. R., & Dorius, C. (2010). Fathers, children, and divorce. In M. E. Lamb (Ed.), *The role of the father in child development* (5th ed., pp. 177–200). Hoboken, NJ: Wiley.

Amato, P. R., & Fowler, F. (2002). Parenting practices, child adjustment, and family diversity. *Journal of Marriage and the Family, 64,* 703–716.

Amato, P. R., & Sobolewski, J. M. (2004). The effects of divorce on fathers and children: Nonresidential fathers and stepfathers. In M. E. Lamb (Ed.), *The role of the father in child development* (4th ed., pp. 341–367). Hoboken, NJ: Wiley.

American Academy of Pediatrics. (2001). Committee on Public Education: Children, adolescents, and television. *Pediatrics, 104,* 341–343.

American Academy of Pediatrics. (2012a). Breastfeeding and the use of human milk. *Pediatrics, 129,* e827–e841.

American Academy of Pediatrics. (2012b). SIDS and other sleep-related infant deaths: Expansion of recommendations for a safe sleep environment *Pediatrics, 128,* e1341.

American Academy of Pediatrics. (2013). The crucial role of recess in school. *Pediatrics, 131,* 183–188.

American Association of Birth Centers. (2014). *Position statement: Immersion in water during labor and birth.* Retrieved from www.birthcenters.org/webfm_send/145

American Diabetes Association. (2014). *Statistics about diabetes.* Retrieved from www.diabetes.org/diabetes-basics/statistics

American Psychiatric Association. (2013). *Diagnostic and statistical manual of mental disorders* (5th ed.). Arlington, VA: Author.

American Psychological Association. (2010). Ethical principles of psychologists and code of conduct. Retrieved from www.apa.org/ethics/code/index.aspx

Amso, D., & Johnson, S. P. (2006). Learning by selection: Visual search and object perception in young infants. *Developmental Psychology, 42,* 1236–1245.

Amsterlaw, J. (2006). Children's beliefs about everyday reasoning. *Child Development, 77,* 443–464.

Ananth, C. V., Chauhan, S. P., Chen, H.-Y., & D'Alton, M. E. (2013). Electronic fetal monitoring in the United States:

Temporal trends and adverse perinatal outcomes. *Obstetrics and Gynecology, 121,* 927–933.

Ananth, C. V., Friedman, A. M., & Gyamfi-Bannerman, C. (2013). Epidemiology of moderate preterm, late preterm and early term delivery. *Clinics in Perinatology, 40,* 601–610.

Anderman, E. M., Eccles, J. S., Yoon, K. S., Roeser, R., Wigfield, A., & Blumenfeld, P. (2001). Learning to value mathematics and reading: Relations to mastery and performance-oriented instructional practices. *Contemporary Educational Psychology, 26,* 76–95.

Andersen, E. (2000). Exploring register knowledge: The value of "controlled improvisation." In L. Menn & N. B. Ratner (Eds.), *Methods for studying language production* (pp. 225–248). Mahwah, NJ: Erlbaum.

Anderson, C. A., Berkowitz, L., Donnerstein, E., Huesmann, R., Johnson, J. D., Linz, D., Malamuth, N. M., & Wartella, E. (2003). The influence of media violence on youth. *Psychological Science in the Public Interest, 4*(3), 81–106.

Anderson, C. A., Shibuya, A., Ihori, N., Swing, E. L., Bushman, B. J., Sakamoto, A., et al. (2010). Violent video game effects on aggression, empathy, and prosocial behavior in Eastern and Western countries: A meta-analytic review. *Psychological Bulletin, 136,* 151–173.

Anderson, C. M. (2012). The diversity, strengths, and challenges of single-parent households. In F. Walsh (Ed.), *Normal family processes: Growing diversity and complexity* (4th ed., pp. 128–148). New York: Guilford.

Anderson, D. M., Huston, A. C., Schmitt, K. L., Linebarger, D. L., & Wright, J. C. (2001). Early childhood television viewing and adolescent behavior. *Monographs of the Society for Research in Child Development, 66*(1, Serial No. 264).

Anderson, E. R., & Greene, S. M. (2013). Beyond divorce: Research on children in repartnered and remarried families. *Family Court Review, 51,* 119–130.

Anderson, R. C., Wilson, P. T., & Fielding, L. G. (1988). Growth in reading and how children spend their time outside of school. *Reading Research Quarterly, 23,* 285–303.

Anderson, V., & Beauchamp, M. H. (2013). A theoretical model of developmental social neuroscience. In V. Anderson & M. H. Beauchamp (Eds.), *Developmental social neuroscience and childhood brain insult: Theory and practice* (pp. 3–20). New York: Guilford.

Anderson, V., Spencer-Smith, M., & Wood, A. (2011). Do children really recover better? Neurobehavioural plasticity after early brain insult. *Brain, 134,* 2197–2221.

Anderson, V. A., Catroppa, C., Dudgeon, P., Morse, S. A., Haritou, F., & Rosenfeld, J. V. (2006). Understanding predictors of functional recovery and outcome 30 months following early childhood head injury. *Neuropsychology, 20,* 42–57.

Andrews, G., & Halford, G. S. (2002). A cognitive complexity metric applied to cognitive development. *Cognitive Psychology, 45,* 475–506.

Andrews, G., & Halford, G. (2011). Recent advances in relational complexity theory and its application to cognitive development. In P. Barrouillet & V. Gaillard (Eds.), *Cognitive development and working memory* (pp. 47–68). Hove, UK: Psychology Press.

Ang, S., Rodgers, J. L., & Wänström, L. (2010). The Flynn effect within subgroups in the U.S.: Gender, race, income, education, and urbanization differences in the NLSY-Children data. *Intelligence, 38,* 367–384.

Anisfeld, M. (2005). No compelling evidence to dispute Piaget's timetable of the development of representational imitation in infancy. In S. Hurley & N. Chater (Eds.), *Perspectives on imitation: From neuroscience to social science: Vol. 2. Imitation, human development, and culture* (pp. 107–131). Cambridge, MA: MIT Press.

Annett, M. (2002). *Handedness and brain asymmetry: The right shift theory.* Hove, UK: Psychology Press.

Anzures, G., Quinn, P. C., Pascalis, O., Slater, A. M., Tanaka, J. W., & Lee, K. (2013). Developmental origins of the other-race effect. *Current Directions in Psychological Science, 22,* 173–178.

Apfelbaum, E. P., Pauker, K., Ambady, N., Sommers, S. R., & Norton, M. I. (2008). Learning (not) to talk about race: When older children underperform in social categorization. *Developmental Psychology, 44,* 1513–1518.

Apgar, V. (1953). A proposal for a new method of evaluation in the newborn infant. *Current Research in Anesthesia and Analgesia, 32,* 260–267.

Aram, D., & Levin, I. (2011). Home support of children in the writing process. In S. B. Neuman & D. K. Dickinson (Eds.), *Handbook of early literacy research* (Vol. 3, pp. 189–199). New York: Guilford.

Arcus, D., & Chambers, P. (2008). Childhood risks associated with adoption. In T. P. Gullotta & G. M. Blau (Eds.), *Family influences on childhood behavior and development* (pp. 117–142). New York: Routledge.

Ardila-Rey, A., & Killen, M. (2001). Middle-class Colombian children's evaluations of personal, moral, and social-conventional interactions in the classroom. *International Journal of Behavioral Development, 25,* 246–255.

Arija, V., Esparó, G., Fernández-Ballart, J., Murphy, M. M., Biarnés, E., & Canals, J. (2006). Nutritional status and performance in test of verbal and nonverbal intelligence in 6 year old children. *Intelligence, 34,* 141–149.

Arkes, J. (2013). The temporal effects of parental divorce on youth substance use. *Substance Use and Misuse, 48,* 290–297.

Armstrong, K. L., Quinn, R. A., & Dadds, M. R. (1994). The sleep patterns of normal children. *Medical Journal of Australia, 161,* 202–206.

Arnett, J. J. (2007). Emerging adulthood: What is it and what is it good for? *Child Development Perspectives, 1,* 68–73.

Arnett, J. J. (2011). Emerging adulthood(s): The cultural psychology of a new life stage. In L. E. Jensen (Ed.), *Bridging cultural and developmental approaches to psychology: New syntheses in theory, research, and policy* (pp. 255–275). New York: Oxford University Press.

Arnold, D. H., McWilliams, L., & Harvey-Arnold, E. (1998). Teacher discipline and child misbehavior in daycare: Untangling causality with correlational data. *Developmental Psychology, 34,* 276–287.

Arnon, S., Shapsa, A., Forman, L., Regev, R., Bauer, S., & Litmanovitz, I. (2006). Live music is beneficial to preterm infants in the neonatal intensive care unit. *Birth, 33,* 131–136.

Aronson, A. A., & Henderson, S. O. (2006). Pediatrics, otitis media. *eMedicine Specialties, Pediatrics.* Retrieved from www.emedicine.com/emerg/topic393.htm

Arsenio, W. F. (2010). Integrating emotion attributions, morality, and aggression: Research and theoretical foundations. In W. F. Arsenio & E. A. Lemerise (Eds.), *Emotions, aggression, and morality in children: Bridging development and psychopathology* (pp. 75–94). Washington, DC: American Psychological Association.

Arsenio, W. F., & Lemerise, E. A. (2001). Varieties of childhood bullying: Values, emotion processes, and social competence. *Social Development, 10,* 59–73.

Artman, L., & Cahan, S. (1993). Schooling and the development of transitive inference. *Developmental Psychology, 29,* 753–759.

Asbjornsen, A. E., Obrzut, J. E., Boliek, C. A., Myking, E., Holmefjord, A., & Reisaeter, S. (2005). Impaired auditory attention skills following middle-ear infections. *Child Neuropsychology, 11,* 121–133.

Asher, S. R., & Rose, A. J. (1997). Promoting children's social-emotional adjustment with peers. In P. Salovey & D. J. Sluyter (Eds.), *Emotional development and emotional intelligence* (pp. 193–195). New York: Basic Books.

Aslin, R. N., Jusczyk, P. W., & Pisoni, D. B. (1998). Speech and auditory processing during infancy: Constraints on and precursors to language. In D. Kuhn & R. S. Siegler (Eds.), *Handbook of child psychology: Vol. 2. Cognition, perception, and language* (5th ed., pp. 147–198). New York: Wiley.

Aslin, R. N., & Newport, E. L. (2012). Statistical learning: From acquiring specific items to forming general rules. *Psychological Science, 21,* 170–176.

Astington, J. W., & Hughes, C. (2013). Theory of mind: Self-reflection and social understanding. In S. M. Carlson, P. D. Zelazo, & S. Faja (Eds.), *Oxford handbook of developmental psychology: Vol. 2. Self and other* (pp. 398–424). New York: Oxford University Press.

Astington, J. W., & Jenkins, J. M. (1995). Theory of mind development and social understanding. *Cognition and Emotion, 9,* 151–165.

Astington, J. W., & Pelletier, J. (2005). Theory of mind, language, and learning in the early years: Developmental origins of school readiness. In B. D. Homer & C. S. Tamis-LeMonda (Eds.), *The development of social cognition and communication* (pp. 205–230). Mahwah, NJ: Erlbaum.

Astington, J. W., Pelletier, J., & Homer, B. (2002). Theory of mind and epistemological development: The relation between children's second-order false belief understanding and their ability to reason about evidence. *New Ideas in Psychology, 20,* 131–144.

Atance, C. M., & Meltzoff, A. N. (2005). My future self: Young children's ability to anticipate and explain future states. *Cognitive Development, 20,* 341–361.

Au, T. K., Sidle, A. L., & Rollins, K. B. (1993). Developing an intuitive understanding of conservation and contamination: Invisible particles as a plausible mechanism. *Developmental Psychology, 29,* 286–299.

Aunola, K., Stattin, H., & Nurmi, J.-E. (2000). Parenting styles and adolescents' achievement strategies. *Journal of Adolescence, 23,* 205–222.

Avis, J., & Harris, P. L. (1991). Belief–desire reasoning among Baka children: Evidence for a universal conception of mind. *Child Development, 62,* 460–467.

Axelin, A., Salantera, S., & Lehtonen, L. (2006). "Facilitated tucking by parents" in pain management of preterm infants—a randomized crossover trial. *Early Human Development, 82,* 241–247.

Azurmendi, A., Braza, F., Garcia, A., Braza, P., Munoz, J. M., & Sanchez-Martin, J. R. (2006). Aggression, dominance, and affiliation: Their relationships with androgen levels and intelligence in 5-year-old children. *Hormones and Behavior, 50,* 132–140.

B

Bacallao, M. L., & Smokowski, P. R. (2007). The costs of getting ahead: Mexican family system changes after immigration. *Family Relations, 56,* 52–66.

Badanes, L. S., Dmitrieva, J., & Watamura, S. E. (2012). Understanding cortisol reactivity across the day at child care: The potential buffering role of secure attachments to caregivers. *Early Childhood Research Quarterly, 27,* 156–165.

Badiee, Z., Asghari, M., & Mohammadizadeh, M. (2013). The calming effect of maternal breast milk odor on premature infants. *Pediatrics and Neonatology, 54,* 322–325.

Baer, J. (2002). Is family cohesion a risk or protective factor during adolescent development? *Journal of Marriage and Family, 64,* 668–675.

Bagwell, C. L., & Coie, J. D. (2004). The best friendships of aggressive boys: Relationship quality, conflict management, and rule-breaking behavior. *Journal of Experimental Child Psychology, 88,* 5–24.

Bahrick, L. E. (2010). Intermodal perception and selective attention to intersensory redundancy: Implications for typical social development and autism. In G. Bremner & T. D. Wachs (Eds.), *Wiley-Blackwell handbook of infant development: Vol. 1* (2nd ed., pp. 120–166). Malden, MA: Blackwell.

Bahrick, L. E., Gogate, L. J., & Ruiz, I. (2002). Attention and memory for faces and actions in infancy: The salience of actions over faces in dynamic events. *Child Development, 73,* 1629–1643.

Bahrick, L. E., Hernandez-Reif, M., & Flom, R. (2005). The development of infant learning about specific face–voice relations. *Developmental Psychology, 41,* 541–552.

Bahrick, L. E., Hernandez-Reif, M., & Pickens, J. N. (1997). The effect of retrieval cues on visual preferences and memory in infancy: Evidence for a four-phase attention function. *Journal of Experimental Child Psychology, 67,* 1–20.

Bahrick, L. E., & Lickliter, R. (2012). The role of intersensory redundancy in early perceptual, cognitive, and social development. In A. J. Bremner, D. J. Lewkowicz, & C. Spence (Eds.), *Multisensory development* (183–206). Oxford, UK: Oxford University Press.

Bahrick, L. E., Lickliter, R., & Flom, R. (2004). Intersensory redundancy guides the development of selective attention, perception, and cognition in infancy. *Current Directions in Psychological Science, 13,* 99–102.

Bailar-Heath, M., & Valley-Gray, S. (2010). Accident prevention. In P. C. McCabe & S. R. Shaw (Eds.), *Pediatric disorders* (pp. 123–132). Thousand Oaks, CA; Corwin Press.

Baillargeon, R., & DeVos, J. (1991). Object permanence in young infants: Further evidence. *Child Development, 62,* 1227–1246.

Baillargeon, R., Li, J., Gertner, Y., & Wu, D. (2011). How do infants reason about physical events? In U. Goswami (Ed.), *Wiley-Blackwell handbook of childhood cognitive development* (2nd ed., pp. 11–48). Chichester, UK: Wiley-Blackwell.

Baillargeon, R., Li, J., Ng, W., & Yuan, S. (2009). An account of infants' physical reasoning. In A. Woodward & A. Needham (Eds.), *Learning and the infant mind* (pp. 66–116). New York: Oxford University Press.

Baillargeon, R., Scott, R. M., & He, Z. (2010). False-belief understanding in infants. *Trends in Cognitive Sciences, 14,* 110–118.

Baillargeon, R. H., Zoccolillo, M., Keenan, K., Côté, S., Pérusse, D., Wu, H.-X., & Boivin, M. (2007). Gender differences in physical aggression: A prospective population-based survey of children before and after 2 years of age. *Developmental Psychology, 43,* 13–26.

Bakermans-Kranenburg, M. J., Steele, H., Zeanah, C. H., Muhamedrahimov, R. J, Vorria, P., & Dobrova-Krol, N. A. (2011). Attachment and emotional development in institutional care: Characteristics and catch up. In R. B. McCall, M. H. van IJzendoorn, F. Juffer, C. J. Groark, & V. K. Groza (Eds), *Children without permanent parents: Research, practice, and policy. Monographs of the Society for Research in Child Development, 76*(4, Serial No. 301), 62–91.

Bakermans-Kranenburg, M. J., & van IJzendoorn, M. H. (2011). Differential susceptibility to rearing environment depending on dopamine-related genes: New evidence and a meta-analysis. *Development and Psychopathology, 23,* 39–52.

Bakermans-Kranenburg, M. J., van IJzendoorn, M. H., & Juffer, F. (2003). Less is more: Meta-analyses of sensitivity and attachment interventions in early childhood. *Psychological Bulletin, 129,* 195–215.

Bakermans-Kranenburg, M. J., van IJzendoorn, M. H., Mesman, J., Alink, L. R. A., & Juffer, F. (2008a). Effects of an attachment-based intervention on daily cortisol moderated by dopamine receptor D4: A randomized control trial on 1-to 3-year-olds screened for externalizing behavior. *Development and Psychopathology, 20,* 805–820.

Bakermans-Kranenburg, M. J., van IJzendoorn, M. H., Pijlman, F. T. A., Mesman, J., & Juffer, F. (2008b). Experimental evidence for differential sensitivity: Dopamine D4 receptor polymorphism (DRD4 VNTR) moderates intervention effects on toddlers' externalizing behavior in a randomized control trial. *Developmental Psychology, 44,* 293–300.

Baker-Sennett, J., Matusov, E., & Rogoff, B. (2008). Children's planning of classroom plays with adult or child direction. *Social Development, 17,* 998–1018.

Balaban, M. T., & Waxman, S. R. (1997). Do words facilitate object categorization in 9-month-old infants? *Journal of Experimental Child Psychology, 64,* 3–26.

Ball, H. (2006). Parent–infant bed-sharing behavior: Effects of feeding type and presence of father. *Human Nature, 17,* 301–318.

Ball, H. L., & Volpe, L. E. (2013). Sudden infant death syndrome (SIDS) risk reduction and infant sleep location—moving the discussion forward. *Social Science and Medicine, 79,* 84–91.

Baltes, P. B., Lindenberger, U., & Staudinger, U. M. (2006). Life span theory in developmental psychology. In R. M. Lerner & W. Damon (Eds.), *Handbook of child psychology: Vol. 1. Theoretical models of human development* (6th ed., pp. 569–664). Hoboken, N. J.: Wiley.

Bandstra, E. S., Morrow, C. E., Mansoor, E., & Accornero, V. H. (2010). Prenatal drug exposure: Infant and toddler outcomes. *Journal of Addictive Diseases, 29,* 245–258.

Bandura, A. (1977). *Social learning theory.* Englewood Cliffs, NJ: Prentice-Hall.

Bandura, A. (1992). Perceived self-efficacy in cognitive development and functioning. *Educational Psychologist, 28,* 117–118.

Bandura, A. (2001). Social cognitive theory: An agentic perspective. *Annual Review of Psychology, 52,* 1–26.

Bandura, A. (2011). Social cognitive theory. In P. A. M. Van Lange, A. W. Kruglanski, & E. T. Higgins (Eds.), *Handbook of theories of social psychology* (Vol. 1, pp. 349–373). Thousand Oaks, CA: Sage.

Bang, H. G. (2011). What makes it easy or hard for you to do your homework? An account of newcomer immigrant youths' afterschool academic lives. *Current Issues in Education, 14*(3), 1–26.

Banks, M. S. (1980). The development of visual accommodation during early infancy. *Child Development, 51,* 157–173.

Banks, M. S., & Ginsburg, A. P. (1985). Early visual preferences: A review and new theoretical treatment. In

H. W. Reese (Ed.), *Advances in child development and behavior* (Vol. 19, pp. 207–246). New York: Academic Press.

Bannard, C., Lieven, E., & Tomasello, M. (2009). Modeling children's early grammatical knowledge. *Proceedings of the National Academy of Sciences, 106,* 17284–17289.

Banse, R., Gawronski, B., Rebetez, C., Gutt, H., & Morton, J. B. (2010). The development of spontaneous gender stereotyping in childhood: Relations to stereotype knowledge and stereotype flexibility. *Developmental Science, 13,* 298–306.

Barber, B. K., & Olsen, J. A. (1997). Socialization in context: Connection, regulation, and autonomy in the family, school, and neighborhood, and with peers. *Journal of Adolescent Research, 12,* 287–315.

Barber, B. K., Stolz, H. E., & Olsen, J. A. (2005). Parental support, psychological control, and behavioral control: Assessing relevance across time, culture, and method. *Monographs of the Society for Research in Child Development, 70*(4, Serial No. 282).

Barber, B. K., & Xia, M. (2013). The centrality of control to parenting and its effects. In R. E. Larzelere, A. S. Morris, & A. W. Harrist (Eds.), *Authoritative parenting: Synthesizing nurturance and discipline for optimal child development* (pp. 61–88). Washington, DC: American Psychological Association.

Bard, K. A., Todd, B. K., Bernier, C., Love, J., & Leavens, D. A. (2006). Self-awareness in human and chimpanzee infants: What is measured and what is meant by the mark and mirror test? *Infancy, 9,* 191–219.

Bar-Haim, Y., Ziv, T., Lamy, D., & Hodes, R. M. (2006). Nature and nurture in own-race face processing. *Psychological Science, 17,* 159–163.

Barker, D. J., Osmond, C., Thornburg, K. L., Kajantie, E., Forsen, T., & Eriksson, J. G. (2008). A possible link between the pubertal growth of girls and breast cancer in their daughters. *American Journal of Human Biology, 20,* 127–131.

Barker, D. J., & Thornberg, K. L. (2013). Placental programming of chronic diseases, cancer and lifespan: A review. *Placenta, 34,* 841–845.

Barker, D. J. P. (2009). Growth and chronic disease: Findings in the Helsinki Birth Cohort. *Annals of Human Biology, 36,* 445–458.

Barkley, R. A. (2003a). Attention-deficit/hyperactivity disorder. In E. J. Mash & R. A. Barkley (Eds.), *Child psychopathology* (2nd ed., pp. 75–143). New York: Guilford.

Barkley, R. A. (2003b). Issues in the diagnosis of attention-deficit hyperactivity disorder in children. *Brain and Development, 25,* 77–83.

Barkley, R. A. (2006). Attention-deficit/hyperactivity disorder. In R. A. Barkley, D. A. Wolfe, & E. J. Mash (Eds.), *Behavioral and emotional disorders in adolescents: Nature, assessment, and treatment* (pp. 91–152). New York: Guilford.

Barnes, G. M., Hoffman, J. H., Welte, J. W., Farrell, M. P., & Dintcheff, B. A. (2007). Adolescents' time use: Effects on substance use, delinquency and sexual activity. *Journal of Youth and Adolescence, 36,* 697–710.

Barnett, D., & Vondra, J. I. (1999). Atypical patterns of early attachment: Theory, research, and current directions. In J. I. Vondra & D. Barnett (Eds.), *Atypical attachment in infancy and early childhood among children at developmental risk. Monographs of the Society for Research in Child Development, 64*(3, Serial No. 258), pp. 1–24.

Barnett, W. S. (2011). Effectiveness of early educational intervention. *Science, 333,* 975–978.

Barnett, W. S., Carolan, M. E., Squires, J. H., & Brown, K. C. (2013). *The state of preschool 2013.* Newark, NJ: National Institute for Early Education Research, Rutgers University.

Baron, I. S., & Rey-Casserly, C. (2010). Extremely preterm birth outcome: A review of four decades of cognitive research. *Neuropsychology Review, 20,* 430–452.

Baron-Cohen, S. (2011). What is theory of mind, and is it impaired in ASC? In S. Bolte & J. Hallmayer (Eds.). *Autism spectrum conditions: FAQs on autism, Asperger syndrome, and atypical autism answered by international experts* (pp. 136–138). Cambridge, MA: Hogrefe Publishing.

Baron-Cohen, S., & Belmonte, M. K. (2005). Autism: A window onto the development of the social and the

analytic brain. *Annual Review of Neuroscience, 28,* 109–126.

Barr, H. M., Streissguth, A. P., Darby, B. L., & Sampson, P. D. (1990). Prenatal exposure to alcohol, caffeine, tobacco, and aspirin: Effects on fine and gross motor performance in 4-year-old children. *Developmental Psychology, 26,* 339–348.

Barr, R., & Hayne, H. (2003). It's not what you know, it's who you know: Older siblings facilitate imitation during infancy. *International Journal of Early Years Education, 11,* 7–21.

Barr, R., Marrott, H., & Rovee-Collier, C. (2003). The role of sensory preconditioning in memory retrieval by preverbal infants. *Learning and Behavior, 31,* 111–123.

Barr, R., Muentener, P., & Garcia, A. (2007). Age-related changes in deferred imitation from television by 6- to 18-month-olds. *Developmental Science, 10,* 910–921.

Barr, R. G. (2001). "Colic" is something infants do, rather than a condition they "have": A developmental approach to crying phenomena patterns, pacification and (patho) genesis. In R. G. Barr, I. St James-Roberts, & M. R. Keefe (Eds.), *New evidence on unexplained infant crying* (pp. 87–104). St. Louis: Johnson & Johnson Pediatric Institute.

Barr, R. G., Paterson, J. A., MacMartin, L. M., & Lehtonen, L. (2005). Prolonged and unsoothable crying bouts in infants with and without colic. *Journal of Developmental and Behavioral Pediatrics, 26,* 14–23.

Barrett, E. S., Redmon, J. B., Wang, C., Sparks, A., & Swan, S. H. (2014). Exposure to prenatal life events stress is associated with masculinized play behavior in girls. *NeuroToxicology, 41,* 20–27.

Barrett, K. C. (2005). The origins of social emotions and self-regulation in toddlerhood: New evidence. *Cognition and Emotion, 19,* 953–979.

Barros, R. M., Silver, E. J., & Stein, R. E. K. (2009). School recess and group classroom behavior. *Pediatrics, 123,* 431–436.

Barrouillet, P., & Gaillard, V. (2011a). Advances and issues: Some thoughts about controversial questions. In P. Barrouillet & V. Gaillard (Eds.), *Cognitive development and working memory* (pp. 263–271). Hove, UK: Psychology Press.

Barrouillet, P., & Gaillard, V. (2011b). (Eds.). *Cognitive development and working memory: A dialogue between neo-Piagetian and cognitive approaches.* Hove, UK: Psychology Press.

Bartgis, J., Lilly, A. R., & Thomas, D. G. (2003). Event-related potential and behavioral measures of attention in 5-, 7-, and 9-year-olds. *Journal of General Psychology, 130,* 311–335.

Barthell, J. E., & Mrozek, J. D. (2013). Neonatal drug withdrawal. *Minnesota Medicine, 96,* 48–50.

Bartocci, M., Berggvist, L. L., Lagercrantz, H., & Anand, K. J. (2006). Pain activates cortical areas in the preterm newborn brain. *Pain, 122,* 109–117.

Barton, M. E., & Strosberg, R. (1997). Conversational patterns of two-year-old twins in mother–twin–twin triads. *Journal of Child Language, 24,* 257–269.

Barton, M. E., & Tomasello, M. (1991). Joint attention and conversation in mother–infant–sibling triads. *Child Development, 62,* 517–529.

Bartrip, J., Morton, J., & de Schonen, S. (2001). Responses to mother's face in 3-week to 3-month-old infants. *British Journal of Developmental Psychology, 19,* 219–232.

Bartsch, K., London, K., & Campbell, M. D. (2007). Children's attention to beliefs in interactive persuasion tasks. *Developmental Psychology, 43,* 111–120.

Bartsch, K., & Wellman, H. M. (1995). *Children talk about the mind.* New York: Oxford University Press.

Basinger, B. (2013). Low-income and minority children with asthma. In L. Rubin & J. Merrick (Eds.), *Environmental health disparities with children: Asthma, obesity and food* (pp. 61–72). Hauppauge, NY: Nova Science.

Bass, J. L., Corwin, M., Gozal, D., Moore, C., Nishida, H., Parker, S., Schonwald, A., Wilker, R. E., Stehle, S., & Kinane, T. B. (2004). The effect of chronic or intermittent hypoxia on cognition in childhood: A review of the evidence. *Pediatrics, 114,* 805–816.

Bassok, D., & Reardon, S. F. (2013). "Academic redshirting" in kindergarten: Prevalence, patterns, and implications. *Educational Evaluation and Policy Analysis, 35,* 283–297.

Bass-Ringdahl, S. M. (2010). The relationship of audibility and the development of canonical babbling in young children with hearing impairment. *Journal of Deaf Studies and Deaf Education, 15,* 287–310.

Batchelor, J. (2008). "Failure to thrive" revisited. *Child Abuse Review, 17,* 147–159.

Bates, E. (2004). Explaining and interpreting deficits in language development across clinical groups: Where do we go from here? *Brain and Language, 88,* 248–253.

Bates, E., & MacWhinney, B. (1987). Competition, variation, and language learning. In B. MacWhinney (Ed.), *Mechanisms of language acquisition* (pp. 157–193). Hillsdale, NJ: Erlbaum.

Bates, E., Marchman, V., Thal, D., Fenson, L., Dale, P., Reznick, J. S., Reilly, J., & Hartung, J. (1994). Developmental and stylistic variation in the composition of early vocabulary. *Journal of Child Language, 21,* 85–123.

Bates, E., Wilson, S. M., Saygin, A. P., Dick, F., Sereno, M. I., Knight, R. T., & Dronkers, N. F. (2003). Voxel-based lesion-symptom mapping. *Nature Neuroscience, 6,* 448–450.

Bates, J. E., Wachs, T. D., & Emde, R. N. (1994). Toward practical uses for biological concepts. In J. E. Bates & T. D. Wachs (Eds.), *Temperament: Individual differences at the interface of biology and behavior* (pp. 275–306). Washington, DC: American Psychological Association.

Bathelt, J., O'Reilly, H., Clayden, J. D., Cross, J. H., & de Haan, M. (2013). Functional brain network organization of children between 2 and 5 years derived from reconstructed activity of cortical sources of high-density EEG recordings. *NeuroImage, 82,* 595–604.

Bauer, P. A. (2013). Memory. In S. M. Carlson, P. D. Zelazo, & S. Faja (Eds.), *Oxford handbook of developmental psychology: Vol. 1. Body and mind* (pp. 505–541). New York: Oxford University Press.

Bauer, P. J. (2002). Early memory development. In U. Goswami (Ed.), *Blackwell handbook of child cognitive development* (pp. 127–150). Malden, MA: Blackwell.

Bauer, P. J. (2006). Event memory. In D. Kuhn & R. Siegler (Eds.), *Handbook of child psychology: Vol. 2. Cognition, perception, and language* (6th ed., pp. 373–425). Hoboken, NJ: Wiley.

Bauer, P. J. (2007). Recall in infancy: A neurodevelopmental account. *Current Directions in Psychological Science, 16,* 142–146.

Bauer, P. J. (2009). Learning and memory: Like a horse and carriage. In A. Woodward & A. Needham (Eds.), *Learning and the infant mind* (pp. 3–28). New York: Oxford University Press.

Bauer, P. J., Bruch, M. M., Scholin, S. E., & Gulin, O. E. (2007). Using cue words to investigate the distribution of autobiographical memories in childhood. *Psychological Science, 18,* 910–916.

Bauer, P. J., Larkina, M., & Deocampo, J. (2011). Early memory development. In U. Goswami (Ed.), *Wiley-Blackwell handbook of childhood cognitive development* (2nd ed., pp. 153–179). Chichester, UK: Wiley-Blackwell.

Bauer, P. J., Wiebe, S. A., Carver, L. J., Lukowski, A. F., Haight, J. C., Waters, J. M., & Nelson, C. A. (2006). Electrophysiological indexes of encoding and behavioral indexes of recall: Examining relations and developmental change late in the first year of life. *Developmental Neuropsychology, 29,* 293–320.

Baumeister, R. F., Campbell, J. D., Krueger, J. I., & Vohs, K. D. (2003). Does high self-esteem cause better performance, interpersonal success, happiness, or healthier lifestyles? *Psychological Science in the Public Interest, 4*(1), 1–44.

Baumgartner, H. A., & Oakes, L. M. (2011). Infants' developing sensitivity to object function: Attention to features and feature correlations. *Journal of Cognition and Development, 12,* 275–298.

Baumrind, D. (1971). Current patterns of parental authority. *Developmental Psychology Monograph, 4* (No. 1, Pt. 2).

Baumrind, D. (2013). Authoritative parenting revisited: History and current status. In R. E. Larzelere, A. S. Morris, & A. W. Harrist (Eds.), *Authoritative parenting: Synthesizing nurturance and discipline for optimal child development* (pp. 11–34). Washington, DC: American Psychological Association.

Baumrind, D., Larzelere, R. E., & Owens, E. B. (2010). Effects of preschool parents' power assertive patterns and practices on adolescent development. *Parenting, 10,* 157–201.

Baumwell, L., Tamis-LeMonda, C. S., & Bornstein, M. H. (1997). Maternal verbal sensitivity and child language comprehension. *Infant Behavior and Development, 20,* 247–258.

Bauserman, R. (2002). Child adjustment in joint-custody versus sole-custody arrangements: A meta-analytic review. *Journal of Family Psychology, 16,* 91–102.

Bauserman, R. (2012). A meta-analysis of parental satisfaction, adjustment, and conflict in joint custody and sole custody following divorce. *Journal of Divorce & Remarriage, 53,* 464–488.

Bayley, N. (1969). *Bayley Scales of Infant Development.* New York: Psychological Corporation.

Bayley, N. (1993). *Bayley Scales of Infant Development* (2nd ed.). New York: Psychological Corporation.

Bayley, N. (2005). *Bayley Scales of Infant and Toddler Development* (3rd ed.). (Bayley III). San Antonio, TX: Harcourt Assessment.

Beauchamp, G. K., & Mennella, J. A. (2011). Flavor perception in human infants: Development and functional significance. *Digestion, 83*(Suppl. 1), 1–6.

Bebko, J. M., McMorris, C. A., Metcalfe, A., Ricciuti, C., & Goldstein, G. (2014). Language proficiency and metacognition as predictors of spontaneous rehearsal in children. *Canadian Journal of Experimental Psychology, 68,* 46–58.

Becker, K., El-Faddagh, M., Schmidt, M. H., Esser, G., & Laucht, M. (2008). Interaction of dopamine transporter genotype with prenatal smoke exposure on ADHD symptoms. *Journal of Pediatrics, 152,* 263–269.

Becker, R. E. (2013). Nocturnal enuresis. In S. V. Kothare & A. Ivanenko (Eds.), *Parasomnias: Clinical characteristics and treatment* (pp. 293–301). New York: Springer Science + Media.

Beckett, C., Maughan, B., Rutter, M., Castle, J., Colvert, E., & Groothues, C. (2006). Do the effects of early severe deprivation on cognition persist into early adolescence? Findings from the English and Romanian adoptees study. *Child Development, 77,* 696–711.

Bédard, J., & Chi, M. T. (1992). Expertise. *Current Directions in Psychological Science, 1,* 135–139.

Bedard, K., & Dhuey, E. (2006). The persistence of early childhood maturity: International evidence of long-run age effects. *The Quarterly Journal of Economics, 121,* 1437–1472.

Bedi, K. S. (2003). Nutritional effects on neuron numbers. *Nutritional Neuroscience, 6,* 141–152.

Behm, I., Zubair, Connolly, G. N., & Alpert, H. R. (2012). Increasing prevalence of smoke-free homes and decreasing rates of sudden infant death syndrome in the United States: An ecological association study. *Tobacco Control, 21,* 6–11.

Behne, T., Liszkowski, U., Carpenter, M., & Tomasello, M. (2012). Twelve-month-olds' comprehension and production of pointing. *British Journal of Developmental Psychology, 30,* 359–375.

Behnke, M., & Smith, V. C. (2013). Prenatal substance abuse: Short- and long-term effects on the exposed fetus. *Pediatrics, 131,* e1009–e1024.

Behrens, K. Y., Hesse, E., & Main, M. (2007). Mothers' attachment status as determined by the Adult Attachment Interview predicts their 6-year-olds' reunion responses: A study conducted in Japan. *Developmental Psychology, 43*(6), 1553–1567.

Belcher, D., Lee, A., Solmon, M., & Harrison, L. (2003). The influence of gender-related beliefs and conceptions of ability on women learning the hockey wrist shot. *Research Quarterly for Exercise and Sport, 74,* 183–192.

Bell, M. A. (1998). Frontal lobe function during infancy: Implications for the development of cognition and attention. In J. E. Richards (Ed.), *Cognitive neuroscience of attention: A developmental perspective* (pp. 327–362). Mahwah, NJ: Erlbaum.

Bell, M. A., & Fox, N. A. (1996). Crawling experience is related to changes in cortical organization during infancy: Evidence from EEG coherence. *Developmental Psychobiology, 29,* 551–561.

Bellagamba, F., Camaioni, L., & Colonnesi, C. (2006). Change in children's understanding of others' intentional actions. *Developmental Science, 9,* 182–188.

Bellagamba, F., Laghi, F., Lonigro, A., & Pace, C. S. (2012). Re-enactment of intended acts from a video presentation by 18- and 24-month-old children. *Cognitive Processes, 13,* 381–386.

Bellinger, D. C., Leviton, A., & Sloman, J. (1990). Antecedents and correlates of improved cognitive performance in children exposed in utero to low levels of lead. *Environmental Health Perspectives, 89,* 5–11.

Belsky, J. (2001). Emanuel Miller Lecture: Developmental risks (still) associated with early child care. *Journal of Child Psychology and Psychiatry, 42,* 845–859.

Belsky, J. (2005). Attachment theory and research in ecological perspective: Insights from the Pennsylvania Infant and Family Development Project and the NICHD Study of Early Child Care. In K. E. Grossmann, K. Grossmann, & E. Waters (Eds.), *Attachment from infancy to adulthood: The major longitudinal studies* (pp. 71–97). New York: Guilford.

Belsky, J., & de Haan, M. (2011). Parenting and children's brain development: The end of the beginning. *Journal of Child Psychology and Psychiatry, 52,* 409–428.

Belsky, J., & Fearon, R. M. P. (2002). Early attachment security, subsequent maternal sensitivity, and later child development: Does continuity in development depend on caregiving? *Attachment and Human Development, 4,* 361–387.

Belsky, J., & Fearon, R. M. P. (2008). Precursors of attachment security. In J. Cassidy & P. R. Shaver (Eds.), *Handbook of attachment* (2nd ed., pp. 295–316). New York: Guilford.

Belsky, J., Schlomer, G. L., & Ellis, B. J. (2012). Beyond cumulative risk: Distinguishing harshness and unpredictability as determinants of parenting and early life history strategy. *Developmental Psychology, 48,* 662–673.

Belsky, J., Vandell, D. L., Burchinal, M., Clarke-Stewart, K. A., McCartney, K., & Owen, M. T. (2007). Are there long-term effects of early child care? *Child Development, 78,* 681–701.

Bemmels, H. R., Burt, A., Legrand, L. N., Iacono, W. G., & McGue, M. (2008). The heritability of life events: An adolescent twin and adoption study. *Twin Research and Human Genetics, 11,* 257–265.

Bender, H. L., Allen, J. P., McElhaney, K. B., Antonishak, J., Moore, C. M., Kelly, H. L., & Davis, S. M. (2007). Use of harsh physical discipline and developmental outcomes in adolescence. *Development and Psychopathology, 19,* 227–242.

Benigno, J. P., Byrd, D. L., McNamara, P. H., Berg, W. K., & Farrar, M. J. (2011). Talking through transitions: Microgenetic changes in preschoolers' private speech. *Child Language Teaching and Therapy, 27,* 269–285.

Bennett, M., Barrett, M., Karakozov, R., Kipiani, G., Lyons, E., Pavlenko, V., & Riazanova, T. (2004). Young children's evaluations of the ingroup and outgroups: A multinational study. *Social Development, 13,* 124–141.

Benson, J. E., Sabbagh, M. A., Carlson, S. M., & Zelazo, P. D. (2013). Individual differences in executive functioning predict preschoolers' improvement from theory-of-mind training. *Developmental Psychology, 49,* 1615–1627.

Benson, P. L., Scales, P. C., Hamilton, S. F., & Sesma, A., Jr. (2006). Positive youth development: Theory, research, and applications. In R. M. Lerner (Ed.), *Handbook of child psychology: Vol. 1. Theoretical models of human development* (6th ed., pp. 894–941). Hoboken, NJ: Wiley.

Bera, A., Ghosh, J., Singh, A. K., Hazra, A., Mukherjee, S., & Mukherjee, R. (2014). Effect of kangaroo mother care on growth and development of low birthweight babies up to 12 months of age: A controlled clinical trial. *Acta Paediatrica, 103,* 643–650.

Beratis, I. N., Rabavilas, A. D., Kyprianou, M., Papadimitriou, G. N., & Papageorgiou, C. (2013). Investigation of the link between higher order cognitive functions and handedness. *Journal of Clinical and Experimental Neuropsychology, 35,* 393–403.

Berenbaum, S. A., & Beltz, A. M. (2011). Sexual differentiation in human behavior: Effects of prenatal and pubertal organizational hormones. *Frontiers in Neuroendocrinology, 32,* 183–200.

Berger, A., Tzur, G., & Posner, M. I. (2006). Infant brains detect arithmetic errors. *Proceedings of the National Academy of Sciences, 103,* 12649–12653.

Berger, L. M., Paxson, C., & Waldfogel, J. (2009). Income and child development. *Children and Youth Services Review, 31,* 978–989.

Berger, S. E. (2010). Locomotor expertise predicts infants' perseverative errors. *Developmental Psychology, 46,* 326–336.

Berger, S. E., Theuring, C., & Adolph, K. E. (2007). How and when infants learn to climb stairs. *Infant Behavior and Development, 30*, 36–49.

Berk, L. E. (2001a). *Awakening children's minds: How parents and teachers can make a difference.* New York: Oxford University Press.

Berk, L. E. (2001b). Private speech and self-regulation in children with impulse-control difficulties: Implications for research and practice. *Journal of Cognitive Education and Psychology, 2*(1), 1–21.

Berk, L. E. (2006). Looking at kindergarten children. In D. Gullo (Ed.), *K today: Teaching and learning in the kindergarten year* (pp. 11–25). Washington, DC: National Association for the Education of Young Children.

Berk, L. E., & Harris, S. (2003). Vygotsky, Lev. In L. Nadel (Ed.), *Encyclopedia of cognitive science.* London: Macmillan.

Berk, L. E., & Meyers, A. M. (2013). The role of make-believe play in the development of executive function: Status of research and future directions. *American Journal of Play, 6*, 98–110.

Berk, L. E., & Spuhl, S. T. (1995). Maternal interaction, private speech, and task performance in preschool children. *Early Childhood Research Quarterly, 10*, 145–169.

Berkeley, S., Mastropieri, M. A., & Scruggs, T. E. (2011). Reading comprehension strategy instruction and attribution retraining for secondary students with learning and other mild disabilities. *Journal of Learning Disabilities, 44*, 18–31.

Berkowitz, R. L., Roberts, J., & Minkoff, H. (2006). Challenging the strategy of maternal age-based prenatal genetic counseling. *Journal of the American Medical Association, 295*, 1446–1448.

Berman, R. A. (2007). Developing linguistic knowledge and language use across adolescence. In K. Hirsh-Pasek & R. M. Golinkoff (Eds.), *Action meets word: How children learn verbs* (pp. 347–367). New York: Oxford University Press.

Berndt, T. J. (2004). Children's friendships: Shifts over a half-century in perspectives on their development and effects. *Merrill-Palmer Quarterly, 50*, 206–223.

Bertenthal, B. I., Gredebäck, G., & Boyer, T. W. (2013). Differential contributions of development and learning to infants' knowledge of object continuity and discontinuity. *Child Development, 84*, 413–421.

Bertenthal, B. I., Longo, M. R., & Kenny, S. (2007). Phenomenal permanence and the development of predictive tracking in infancy. *Child Development, 78*, 350–363.

Bertrand, J., & Dang, E. P. (2012). Fetal alcohol spectrum disorders: Review of teratogenicity, diagnosis and treatment issues. In D. Hollar (Ed.), *Handbook of children with special health care needs* (pp. 231–258). New York: Springer Science + Business Media.

Best, D. (2009). From the American Academy of Pediatrics: Technical report—Secondhand and prenatal tobacco smoke exposure. *Pediatrics, 124*, e1017–1044.

Best, D. L. (2001). Gender concepts: Convergence in cross-cultural research and methodologies. *Cross-cultural Research: The Journal of Comparative Social Science, 35*, 23–43.

Beyers, J. M., Bates, J. E., Pettit, G. S., & Dodge, K. A. (2003). Neighborhood structure, parenting processes, and the development of youths' externalizing behaviors: A multilevel analysis. *American Journal of Community Psychology, 31*, 35–53.

Bhat, A., Heathcock, J., & Galloway, J. C. (2005). Toy-oriented changes in hand and joint kinematics during the emergence of purposeful reaching. *Infant Behavior and Development, 28*, 445–465.

Bhatt, R. M., & Bolonyai, A. (2011). Code-switching and the optimal grammar of bilingual language use. *Bilingualism: Language and Cognition, 14*, 522–546.

Bhatt, R. S., Rovee-Collier, C., & Weiner, S. (1994). Developmental changes in the interface between perception and memory retrieval. *Developmental Psychology, 30*, 151–162.

Bhatt, R. S., Wilk, A., Hill, D., & Rovee-Collier, C. (2004). Correlated attributes and categorization in the first half-year of life. *Developmental Psychobiology, 44*, 103–115.

Bialystok, E. (2011). Reshaping the mind: The benefits of bilingualism. *Canadian Journal of Experimental Psychology, 65*, 229–235.

Bialystok, E. (2013). The impact of bilingualism on language and literacy development. In T. K. Bhatia & W. C. Ritchie (Eds.), *Handbook of bilingualism and multilingualism* (pp. 624–648). Chichester, UK: Wiley-Blackwell.

Bialystok, E., & Craik, F. I. M., & Luk, G. (2012). Bilingualism: Consequences for mind and brain. *Trends in Cognitive Sciences, 16*, 240–250.

Bialystok, E., & Martin, M. M. (2003). Notation to symbol: Development in children's understanding of print. *Journal of Experimental Child Psychology, 86*, 223–243.

Bianchi, D. W. (2012). From prenatal genomic diagnosis to fetal personalized medicine: Progress and challenges. *Nature Medicine, 18*, 1041–1051.

Bianchi, S. M., & Raley, S. B. (2005). Time allocation in families. In S. M. Bianchi, L. M. Casper, & R. B. King (Eds.), *Work, family, health, and well-being* (pp. 21–48). Mahwah, NJ: Erlbaum.

Bianco, A., Stone, J., Lynch, L., Lapinski, R., Berkowitz, G., & Berkowitz, R. L. (1996). Pregnancy outcome at age 40 and older. *Obstetrics and Gynecology, 87*, 917–922.

Bick, J., Dozier, M., Bernard, K., Grasso, D., & Simons, R. (2013). Foster mother–infant bonding: Associations between foster mothers' oxytocin production, electrophysiological brain activity, feelings of commitment, and caregiving quality. *Child Development, 84*, 826–840.

Biederman, J., Fried, R., Petty, C., Mahoney, L., & Faraone, S. V. (2012). An examination of the impact of attention-deficit hyperactivity disorder on IQ: A large controlled family-based analysis. *Canadian Journal of Psychiatry, 57*, 608–616.

Bielawska-Batorowicz, E., & Kossakowska-Petrycka, K. (2006). Depressive mood in men after the birth of their offspring in relation to a partner's depression, social support, fathers' personality and prenatal expectations. *Journal of Reproductive and Infant Psychology, 24*, 21–29.

Bierman, K. L., Domitrovich, C. E., Nix, R. L., Gest, S. D., Welsh, J. A., Greenberg, M. T., et al. (2008). Promoting academic and social-emotional school readiness: The Head Start REDI program. *Child Development, 79*, 1802–1817.

Bierman, K. L., Nix, R. L., Heinrichs, B. S., Domitrovich, C. E., Gest, S. D., Welsh, J. A., et al. (2014). Effects of Head Start REDI on children's outcomes 1 year later in different kindergarten contexts. *Child Development, 85*, 140–159.

Bierman, K. L., & Powers, C. J. (2009). Social skills training to improve peer relations. In K. H. Rubin, W. M. Bukowski, & B. Laursen (Eds.), *Handbook of peer interactions, relationships, and groups* (pp. 603–621). New York: Guilford.

Bifulco, R., Cobb, C. D., & Bell, C. (2009). Can interdistrict choice boost student achievement? The case of Connecticut's interdistrict magnet school program. *Educational Evaluation and Policy Analysis, 31*, 323–345.

Bigelow, A. E., MacLean, K., Proctor, J., Myatt, T., Gillis, R., & Power, M. (2010). Maternal sensitivity throughout infancy: Continuity and relation to attachment security. *Infant Behavior and Development, 33*, 50–60.

Bigler, R. S. (2007, June). Personal communication.

Bigler, R. S., Brown, C. S., & Markell, M. (2001). When groups are not created equal: Effects of group status on the formation of intergroup attitudes in children. *Child Development, 72*, 1151–1162.

Birch, E. E. (1993). Stereopsis in infants and its developmental relation to visual acuity. In K. Simons (Ed.), *Early visual development: Normal and abnormal* (pp. 224–236). New York: Oxford University Press.

Birch, L. L., & Fisher, J. A. (1995). Appetite and eating behavior in children. *Pediatric Clinics of North America, 42*, 931–953.

Birch, L. L., Fisher, J. O., & Davison, K. K. (2003). Learning to overeat: Maternal use of restrictive feeding practices promotes girls' eating in the absence of hunger. *American Journal of Clinical Nutrition, 78*, 215–220.

Birch, L. L., Zimmerman, S., & Hind, H. (1980). The influence of social-affective context on preschool children's food preferences. *Child Development, 51*, 856–861.

Birch, S. A. J., & Bloom, P. (2003). Children are cursed: An asymmetric bias in mental-state attribution. *Psychological Science, 14*, 283–285.

Bird, A., & Reese, E. (2006). Emotional reminiscing and the development of an autobiographical self. *Developmental Psychology, 42*, 613–626.

Biringen, Z., Altenhofen, S., Aberle, J., Baker, M., Brosal, A., Bennett, S., et al. (2012). Emotional availability, attachment, and intervention in center-based child care for infants and toddlers. *Development and Psychopathology, 24*, 23–34.

Biringen, Z., Emde, R. N., Campos, J. J., & Appelbaum, M. I. (1995). Affective reorganization in the infant, the mother, and the dyad: The role of upright locomotion and its timing. *Child Development, 66*, 499–514.

Birken, C. S., Parkin, P. C., To, T., & Macarthur, C. (2006). Trends in rates of death from unintentional injury among Canadian children in urban areas: Influence of socioeconomic status. *Canadian Medical Association Journal, 175*, 867–868.

Birney, D. P., & Sternberg, R. J. (2011). The development of cognitive abilities. In M. H. Bornstein & M. E. Lamb (Eds.), *Developmental science: An advanced textbook* (6th ed., pp. 353–388). New York: Psychology Press.

Biro, F. M., & Wien, M. (2010). Childhood obesity and adult morbidities. *American Journal of Clinical Nutrition, 91*, 1499S–1505S.

Bjorklund, D. F. (2012). *Children's thinking* (5th ed.). Belmont, CA: Cengage Learning.

Bjorklund, D. F., Causey, K., & Periss, V. (2009). The evolution and development of human social cognition. In P. Kappeler & J. Silk (Eds.), *Mind the gap: Racing the origins of human universals* (pp. 351–371). Berlin: Springer Verlag.

Bjorklund, D. F., & Douglas, R. N. (1997). The development of memory strategies. In N. Cowan (Ed.), *The development of memory in childhood* (pp. 83–111). Hove, UK: Psychology Press.

Bjorklund, D. F., Schneider, W., Cassel, W. S., & Ashley, E. (1994). Training and extension of a memory strategy: Evidence for utilization deficiencies in high- and low-IQ children. *Child Development, 65*, 951–965.

Black, M. M. (2005). Failure to thrive. In M. C. Roberts (Ed.), *Handbook of pediatric psychology and psychiatry* (3rd ed., pp. 499–511). New York: Guilford.

Black, M. M., Dubowitz, H., Krishnakumar, A., & Starr, R. H., Jr. (2007). Early intervention and recovery among children with failure to thrive: Follow-up at age 8. *Pediatrics, 120*, 59–69.

Black, R. E., Victora, C. G., Walker, S. P., Bhutta, Z. A., Christian, P., de Onis, M. et al. (2013). Maternal and child undernutrition and overweight in low-income and middle-income countries. *Lancet, 382*, 427–451.

Black, R. E., Williams, S. M., Jones, I. E., & Goulding, A. (2002). Children who avoid drinking cow's milk have low dietary calcium intakes and poor bone health. *American Journal of Clinical Nutrition, 76*, 675–680.

Blackwell, L. S., Trzesniewski, K. H., & Dweck, C. S. (2007). Implicit theories of intelligence predict achievement across an adolescent transition: A longitudinal study and an intervention. *Child Development, 78*, 246–263.

Blair, B. L., Perry, N. B., O'Brien, M., Calkins, S. D., Keane, S. P., & Shanahan, L. (2014). The indirect effects of maternal emotion socialization on friendship quality in middle childhood. *Developmental Psychology, 50*, 566–576.

Blair, C. (2010). Stress and the development of self-regulation in context. *Child Development Perspectives, 4*, 181–188.

Blair, C., & Raver, C. C. (2012). Child development in the context of adversity: Experiential canalization of brain and behavior. *American Psychologist, 67*, 309–318.

Blair, C., & Razza, R. P. (2007). Relating effortful control, executive function, and false belief understanding to emerging math and literacy ability in kindergarten. *Developmental Psychology, 78*, 647–663.

Blake, J., & Boysson-Bardies, B. de (1992). Patterns in babbling: A cross-linguistic study. *Journal of Child Language, 19*, 51–74.

Blakemore, J. E. O. (2003). Children's beliefs about violating gender norms: Boys shouldn't look like girls, and girls shouldn't act like boys. *Sex Roles, 48*, 411–419.

Blakemore, J. E. O., Berenbaum, S. A., & Liben, L. S. (2009). *Gender development.* New York: Psychology Press.

Blakemore, J. E. O., & Hill, C. A. (2008). The Child Gender Socialization Scale: A measure to compare traditional and feminist parents. *Sex Roles, 58*, 192–207.

Blakemore, S.-J., Dahl, R. E., Frith, U., & Pine, D. S. (2011). Developmental cognitive neuroscience. *Developmental Cognitive Neuroscience, 1*, 3–6.

Blasi, C. H., & Bjorklund, D. F. (2003). Evolutionary developmental psychology: A new tool for better understanding human ontogeny. *Human Development, 46,* 259–281.

Blass, E. M., Ganchrow, J. R., & Steiner, J. E. (1984). Classical conditioning in newborn humans 2–48 hours of age. *Infant Behavior and Development, 7,* 223–235.

Blatchford, P. (2012). Three generations of research on class-size effects. In K. R. Harris (Ed.), *APA educational psychology handbook: Vol. 2. Individual differences and cultural and contextual factors* (pp. 530–554). Washington, DC: American Psychological Association.

Blatchford, P., Bassett, P., & Brown, P. (2005). Teachers' and pupils' behavior in large and small classes: A systematic observation study of pupils aged 10 and 11 years. *Journal of Educational Psychology, 97,* 454–467.

Blatchford, P., Bassett, P., & Brown, P. (2011). Examining the effect of class size on classroom engagement and teacher–pupil interaction: Differences in relation to pupil prior attainment and primary vs. secondary schools. *Learning and Instruction, 21,* 715–730.

Bleeker, M. M., & Jacobs, J. E. (2004). Achievement in math and science: Do mothers' beliefs matter 12 years later? *Journal of Educational Psychology, 96,* 97–109.

Block, C. C. (2012). Proven and promising reading instruction. In J. S. Carlson & J. R. Levin (Eds.), *Instructional strategies for improving students' learning* (pp. 3–41). Charlotte, NC: Information Age Publishing.

Blood-Siegfried, J. (2009). The role of infection and inflammation in sudden infant death syndrome. *Immunopharmacology and Immunotoxicology, 31,* 516– 23.

Bloom, L. (2000). The intentionality model of language development: How to learn a word, any word. In R. Golinkoff, K. Hirsh-Pasek, N. Akhtar, L. Bloom, G. Hollich, L. Smith, M. Tomasello, & A. Woodward (Eds.), *Becoming a word learner: A debate on lexical acquisition.* New York: Oxford University Press.

Bloom, P. (1999). The role of semantics in solving the bootstrapping problem. In R. Jackendoff & P. Bloom (Eds.), *Language, logic, and concepts* (pp. 285–309). Cambridge, MA: MIT Press.

Bloom, T., Glass, N., Curry, M. A., Hernandez, R., & Houck, G. (2013). Maternal stress exposures, reactions, and priorities for stress reduction among low-income, urban women. *Journal of Midwifery and Women's Health, 58,* 167–174.

Blumenfeld, P. C., Marx, R. W., & Harris, C. J. (2006). Learning environments. In K. A. Renninger & I. E. Sigel (Eds.), *Handbook of child psychology: Vol. 4. Child psychology in practice* (6th ed., pp. 297–342). Hoboken, NJ: Wiley.

Bodrova, E., & Leong, D. J. (2007). *Tools of the mind: The Vygotskian approach to early childhood education* (2nd ed.). Upper Saddle River, NJ: Merrill Prentice Hall.

Bogin, B. (2001). *The growth of humanity.* New York: Wiley-Liss.

Bogin, B. (2013). Recent advances in growth research: Nutritional, molecular, and endocrine perspectives. In M. W. Gillman, P. D. Gluckman, & R. G. Rosenfeld (Eds.), *Recent advances in growth research: Nutritional, molecular and endocrine perspectives* (Vol. 71, pp. 115–126). Basel, Switzerland: Karger.

Bogin, B., Smith, P., Orden, A. B., Varela, S., & Loucky, J. (2002). Rapid change in height and body proportions of Maya American children. *American Journal of Human Biology, 14,* 753–761.

Bohannon, J. N., III, & Bonvillian, J. D. (2013). Theoretical approaches to language acquisition. In J. B. Gleason & N. B. Ratner (Eds.), *The development of language* (8th ed., pp. 190–240). Upper Saddle River, NJ: Pearson.

Bohannon, J. N., III, & Stanowicz, L. (1988). The issue of negative evidence: Adult responses to children's language errors. *Developmental Psychology, 24,* 684–689.

Boivin, M., Brendgen, M., Vitaro, F., Dionne, G., Girard, A., Pérusse, D., & Tremblay, R. E. (2013). Strong genetic contribution to peer relationship difficulties at school entry: Findings from a longitudinal twin study. *Child Development, 84,* 1098–1114.

Bolisetty, S., Bajuk, B., Me, A.-L., Vincent, T., Sutton, L., & Lui, K. (2006). Preterm outcome table (POT): A simple tool to aid counselling parents of very preterm infants. *Australian and New Zealand Journal of Obstetrics and Gynaecology, 46,* 189–192.

Bolzani, L. H., Messinger, D. S., Yale, M., & Dondi, M. (2002). Smiling in infancy. In M. H. Abel (Ed.), *An empirical reflection on the smile* (pp. 111–136). Lewiston, NY: Edwin Mellen Press.

Bono, K. E., & Bizri, R. (2014). The role of language and private speech in preschoolers' self-regulation. *Early Child Development and Care, 184,* 658–670.

Bono, M. A., & Stifter, C. A. (2003). Maternal attention-directing strategies and infant focused attention during problem solving. *Infancy, 4,* 235–250.

Booren, L. M., Downer, J. T., & Vitiello, V. E. (2012). Observations of children's interactions with teachers, peers, and tasks across preschool classroom activity settings. *Early Education and Development, 23,* 517–538.

Borchert, S., Lamm, B., Graf, F., & Knopf, M. (2013). Deferred imitation in 18-month-olds from two cultural contexts: The case of Cameroonian Nso farmer and German-middle class infants. *Infant Behavior and Development, 36,* 717–727.

Bornstein, M. H. (1989). Sensitive periods in development: Structural characteristics and causal interpretations. *Psychological Bulletin, 105,* 179–197.

Bornstein, M. H. (2006). Parenting science and practice. In K. Renninger & I. E. Sigel (Eds.), *Handbook of child psychology: Vol. 4. Child psychology in practice* (6th ed., pp. 893–949). Hoboken, NJ: Wiley.

Bornstein, M. H., & Arterberry, M. E. (1999). Perceptual development. In M. H. Bornstein & M. E. Lamb (Eds.), *Developmental psychology: An advanced textbook* (pp. 231–274). Mahwah, NJ: Erlbaum.

Bornstein, M. H., & Arterberry, M. E. (2003). Recognition, discrimination, and categorization of smiling by 5-month-old infants. *Developmental Science, 6,* 585–599.

Bornstein, M. H., Arterberry, M. E., & Mash, C. (2010). Infant object categorization transcends object–context relations. *Infant Behavior and Development, 33,* 7–15.

Bornstein, M. H., & Sawyer, J. (2006). Family systems. In K. McCartney & D. Phillips (Eds.), *Blackwell handbook of early childhood development* (pp. 381–398). Malden, MA: Blackwell.

Bornstein, M. H., Vibbert, M., Tal, J., & O'Donnell, K. (1992). Toddler language and play in the second year: Stability, covariation, and influences of parenting. *First Language, 12,* 323–338.

Borst, C. G. (1995). *Catching babies: The professionalization of childbirth, 1870–1920.* Cambridge, MA: Harvard University Press.

Borst, G., Poirel, N., Pineau, A., Cassotti, M., & Houdé, O. (2013). Inhibitory control efficiency in a Piaget-like class-inclusion task in school-age children and adults: A developmental negative priming study. *Developmental Psychology, 49,* 1366–1374.

Bos, H. (2013). Lesbian-mother families formed through donor insemination. In A. E. Goldberg & K. R. Allen (Eds.), *LGBT-parent families: Innovations in research and implications for practice* (pp. 21–37). New York: Springer.

Bos, H., & Sandfort, T. G. M. (2010). Children's gender identity in lesbian and heterosexual two-parent families. *Sex Roles, 62,* 114–126.

Bos, H. M. W., van Balen, F., & van den Boom, D. C. (2004). Experience of parenthood, couple relationship, social support, and child-rearing goals in planned lesbian mother families. *Journal of Child Psychology and Psychiatry, 25,* 755–764.

Bosacki, S. L., & Moore, C. (2004). Preschoolers' understanding of simple and complex emotions: Links with gender and language. *Sex Roles, 50,* 659–675.

Bost, K. K., Shin, N., McBride, B. A., Brown, G. L., Vaughn, B. E., & Coppola, G. (2006). Maternal secure base scripts, children's attachment security, and mother–child narrative styles. *Attachment and Human Development, 8,* 241–260.

Bouchard, G. (2011). The role of psychosocial variables in prenatal attachment: An examination of moderational effects. *Journal of Reproductive and Infant Psychology, 29,* 197–207.

Bouchard, T. J. (2004). Genetic influence on human psychological traits: A survey. *Current Directions in Psychological Science, 13,* 148–151.

Boucher, O., Bastien, C. H., Saint-Amour, D., Dewailly, E., Ayotte, P., Jacobson, J. L., Jacobson, et al. (2010). Prenatal exposure to methylmercury and PCBs affects distinct stages of information processing: An event-related potential study with Inuit children. *Neurotoxicology, 31,* 373–384.

Boucher, O., Muckle, G., & Bastien, C. H. (2009). Prenatal exposure to polychlorinated biphenyls: A neuropsychologic analysis. *Environmental Health Perspectives, 117,* 7–16.

Bouldin, P. (2006). An investigation of the fantasy predisposition and fantasy style of children with imaginary companions. *Journal of Genetic Psychology, 167,* 17–29.

Boutwell, B. B., Franklin, C. A., Barnes, J. C., & Beaver, K. M. (2011). Physical punishment and childhood aggression: The role of gender and gene–environment interplay. *Aggressive Behavior, 37,* 559–568.

Bowlby, J. (1969). *Attachment and loss: Vol. 1. Attachment.* New York: Basic Books.

Bowlby, J. (1980). *Attachment and loss: Vol. 3. Loss.* New York: Basic Books.

Bowman, L. C., Liu, D., Meltzoff, A. N., & Wellman, H. M. (2012). Neural correlates of belief–desire reasoning in 7- and 8-year-old children: An event-related potential study. *Developmental Science, 15,* 618–632.

Boyan, A., & Sherry, J. L. (2011). The challenge in creating games for education: Aligning mental models with game models. *Child Development Perspectives, 5,* 82–87.

Boyatzis, C. J. (2000). The artistic evolution of mommy: A longitudinal case study of symbolic and social processes. In C. J. Boyatzis & M. W. Watson (Eds.), *Symbolic and social constraints on the development of children's artistic style* (pp. 5–29). San Francisco: Jossey-Bass.

Boyd-Franklin, N. (2006). *Black families in therapy* (2nd ed.). New York: Guilford.

Boyle, M. H., & Lipman, E. L. (2002). Do places matter? Socioeconomic disadvantage and behavioral problems of children in Canada. *Journal of Consulting and Clinical Psychology, 70,* 378–389.

Boysson-Bardies, B. de, & Vihman, M. M. (1991). Adaptation to language: Evidence from babbling and first words in four languages. *Language, 67,* 297–319.

Bracken, B. A. (2000). *The psychoeducational assessment of preschool children.* Boston: Allyn and Bacon.

Brackett, M. A., Rivers, S. E., & Salovey, P. (2011). Emotional intelligence: Implications for personal, social, academic, and workplace success. *Social and Personality Compass, 5,* 88–103.

Bradley, R. H. (1994). The HOME Inventory: Review and reflections. In H. W. Reese (Ed.), *Advances in child development and behavior* (Vol. 25, pp. 241–288). San Diego: Academic Press.

Bradley, R. H., & Caldwell, B. M. (1982). The consistency of the home environment and its relation to child development. *International Journal of Behavioral Development, 5,* 445–465.

Bradley, R. H., & Corwyn, R. F. (2003). Age and ethnic variations in family process mediators of SES. In M. H. Bornstein & R. H. Bradley (Eds.), *Socioeconomic status, parenting, and child development* (pp. 161–188). Mahwah, NJ: Erlbaum.

Bradley, R. H., Corwyn, R. F., McAdoo, H. P., & García Coll, C. (2001). The home environments of children in the United States. Part I: Variations by age, ethnicity, and poverty status. *Child Development, 72,* 1844–1867.

Bradley, R. H., McKelvy, L. M., & Whiteside-Mansell, L. (2011). Does the quality of stimulation and support in the home environment moderate the effect of early education programs? *Child Development, 82,* 2110–2122.

Bradley, R. H., Whiteside, L., Mundfrom, D. J., Casey, P. H., Kelleher, K. J.,& Pope, S. K. (1994). Contribution of early intervention and early caregiving experiences to resilience in low-birthweight, premature children living in poverty. *Journal of Clinical Child Psychology, 23,* 425–434.

Brady, S. A. (2011). Efficacy of phonics teaching for reading outcomes: Indications from post-NRP research. In S. A. Brady, D. Braze, & C. A. Fowler (Eds.), *Explaining individual differences in reading: Theory and evidence* (pp. 69–96). New York: Psychology Press.

Braine, L. G., Schauble, L., Kugelmass, S., & Winter, A. (1993). Representation of depth by children: Spatial strategies and lateral biases. *Developmental Psychology, 29,* 466–479.

Braine, M. D. S. (1994). Is nativism sufficient? *Journal of Child Language, 21,* 1–23.

Brainerd, C. J. (2003). Jean Piaget, learning, research, and American education. In B. J. Zimmerman (Ed.), *Educational psychology: A century of contributions* (pp. 251–287). Mahwah, NJ: Erlbaum.

Brainerd, C. J., & Reyna, V. F. (2012). Reliability of children's testimony in the era of developmental reversals. *Developmental Review, 32,* 224–267.

Branca, F., & Ferrari, M. (2002). Impact of micronutrient deficiencies on growth: The stunting syndrome. *Annals of Nutrition and Metabolism, 46*(Suppl. 1), 8–17.

Branje, S. J. T., van Lieshout, C. F. M., van Aken, M. A. G., & Haselager, G. J. T. (2004). Perceived support in sibling relationships and adolescent adjustment. *Journal of Child Psychology and Psychiatry, 45*, 1385–1396.

Braswell, G. S. (2006). Sociocultural contexts for the early development of semiotic production. *Psychological Bulletin, 132*, 877–894.

Braswell, G. S., & Callanan, M. A. (2003). Learning to draw recognizable graphic representations during mother–child interactions. *Merrill-Palmer Quarterly, 49*, 471–494.

Braungart-Rieker, J. M., Hill-Soderlund, A. L., & Karrass, J. (2010). Fear and anger reactivity trajectories from 4 to 16 months: The roles of temperament, regulation, and maternal sensitivity. *Developmental Psychology, 46*, 791–804.

Braver, S. L., Griffin, W. A., Cookston, J. T., Sandler, I. N., & Williams, J. (2005). Promoting better fathering among divorced non-resident fathers. In W. M. Pinsof & J. Lebow (Eds.), *Family psychology: The art of the science* (pp. 295–325). New York: Oxford University Press.

Bray, S., Dunkin, B., Hong, D. S., & Reiss, A. I. (2011). Reduced functional connectivity during working memory in Turner syndrome. *Cerebral Cortex, 21*, 2471–2481.

Brazelton, T. B., Koslowski, B., & Tronick, E. (1976). Neonatal behavior among urban Zambians and Americans. *Journal of the American Academy of Child Psychiatry, 15*, 97–107.

Brazelton, T. B., & Nugent, J. K. (2011). *Neonatal Behavioral Assessment Scale* (4th ed.). London: Mac Keith Press.

Brazelton, T. B., Nugent, J. K., & Lester, B. M. (1987). Neonatal Behavioral Assessment Scale. In J. D. Osofsky (Ed.), *Handbook of infant development* (2nd ed., pp. 780–817). New York: Wiley.

Bremner, J. G. (2010). Cognitive development: Knowledge of the physical world. In J. G. Bremner & T. D. Wachs (Eds.), *Wiley-Blackwell handbook of infant development: Vol. 1. Basic research* (2nd ed., pp. 204–242). Oxford, UK: Wiley.

Bremner, J. G., Slater, A. M., Mason, U. C., Spring, J., & Johnson, S. P. (2013). Trajectory perception and object continuity: Effects of shape and color change on 4-month-olds' perception of object identity. *Developmental Psychology, 49*, 1021–1026.

Brendgen, M., Boivin, M., Dionne, G., Barker, E. D., Vitaro, F., Girard, A., Tremblay, R., & Pérusse, D. (2011). Gene-environment processes linking aggression, peer victimization, and the teacher–child relationship. *Child Development, 82*, 2021–2036.

Brennan, L. M., Shelleby, E. C., Shaw, D. S., Gardner, F., Dishion, T. J., & Wilson, M. (2013). Indirect effects of the family check-up on school-age academic achievement through improvements in parenting in early childhood. *Journal of Educational Psychology, 105*, 762–773.

Brennan, W. M., Ames, E. W., & Moore, R. W. (1966). Age differences in infants' attention to patterns of different complexities. *Science, 151*, 354–356.

Brenner, E., & Salovey, P. (1997). Emotional regulation during childhood: Developmental, interpersonal, and individual considerations. In P. Salovey & D. Sluyter (Eds.), *Emotional literacy and emotional development* (pp. 168–192). New York: Basic Books.

Bretherton, I., Fritz, J., Zahn-Waxler, C., & Ridgeway, D. (1986). Learning to talk about emotions: A functionalist perspective. *Child Development, 57*, 529–548.

Bretherton, I., & Munholland, K. A. (2008). Internal working models in attachment relationships. In J. Cassidy & P. R. Shaver (Eds.), *Handbook of attachment: Theory, research, and clinical applications* (2nd ed., pp. 102–127). New York: Guilford.

Brewster, K. L., Tillman, K. H., & Jokinen-Gordon, H. (2014). Demographic characteristics of lesbian parents in the United States. *Population Research and Policy Review, 33*, 485–502.

Bridgett, D. J., Gartstein, M. A., Putnam, S. P., McKay, T., Iddins, R., Robertson, C., et al. (2009). Maternal and contextual influences and the effect of temperament development during infancy on parenting in toddlerhood. *Infant Behavior and Development, 32*, 103–116.

Bright, G. M., Mendoza, J. R., & Rosenfeld, R. G. (2009). Recombinant human insulin-like growth factor-1 treatment: Ready for primetime. *Endocrinology and Metabolism Clinics of North America, 38*, 625–638.

Brisch, K. H., Bechinger, D., Betzler, S., Heineman, H., Kachele, H., Pohlandt, F., et al. (2005). Attachment quality in very low-birthweight premature infants in relation to maternal attachment representations and neurological development. *Parenting: Science and Practice, 5*, 11–32.

Brody, G. H., & Murry, V. M. (2001). Sibling socialization of competence in rural, single-parent African American families. *Journal of Marriage and the Family, 63*, 996–1008.

Brody, G. H., Stoneman, Z., & McCoy, J. K. (1994). Forecasting sibling relationships in early adolescence from child temperament and family processes in middle childhood. *Child Development, 65*, 771–784.

Brody, L. (1999). *Gender, emotion, and the family*. Cambridge, MA: Harvard University Press.

Brody, L. R. (1997). Gender and emotion: Beyond stereotypes. *Journal of Social Issues, 53*, 369–393.

Brody, N. (1997). Intelligence, schooling, and society. *American Psychologist, 52*, 1046–1050.

Brodzinsky, D. M. (2011). Children's understanding of adoption: Developmental and clinical implications. *Professional Psychology: Research and Practice, 42*, 200–207.

Bronfenbrenner, U. (Ed.). (2005). *Making human beings human*. Thousand Oaks, CA: Sage.

Bronfenbrenner, U., & Morris, P. A. (2006). The bioecological model of human development. In R. M. Lerner (Ed.), *Handbook of child psychology: Vol. 1. Theoretical models of human development* (6th ed., pp. 793–828). Hoboken, NJ: Wiley.

Bronson, G. W. (1994). Infants' transitions toward adult-like scanning. *Child Development, 65*, 1243–1261.

Brooker, R. J., Buss, K. A., Lemery-Chalfant, K., Aksan, N., Davidson, R. J., & Goldsmith, H. H. (2013). The development of stranger fear in infancy and toddlerhood: Normative development, individual differences, antecedents, and outcomes. *Developmental Science, 16*, 864–878.

Brooks, K., Xu, X., Chen, W., Zhou, K., Neale, B., & Lowe, N. (2006). The analysis of 51 genes in DSM-IV combined type attention deficit hyperactivity disorder: Association signals in DRD4, DAT1, and 16 other genes. *Molecular Psychiatry, 11*, 935–953.

Brooks, P. J., Hanauere, J. B., Padowska, B., & Rosman, H. (2003). The role of selective attention in preschoolers' rule use in a novel dimensional card sort. *Cognitive Development, 18*, 195–215.

Brooks, R., & Meltzoff, A. N. (2005). The development of gaze following and its relation to language. *Developmental Science, 8*, 535–543.

Brooks, R., & Meltzoff, A. N. (2008). Infant gaze following and pointing predict accelerated vocabulary growth through two years of age: A longitudinal, growth curve modeling study. *Journal of Child Language, 35*, 207–220.

Brooks-Gunn, J. (2003). Do you believe in magic? What we can expect from early childhood intervention programs. *Social Policy Report of the Society for Research in Child Development, 27*(1).

Brooks-Gunn, J. (2004). Intervention and policy as change agents for young children. In P. L. Chase-Lansdale, K. Kiernan, & R. J. Friedman (Eds.), *Human development across lives and generations: The potential for change* (pp. 293–340). New York: Cambridge University Press.

Brooks-Gunn, J., Han, W.-J., & Waldfogel, J. (2010). First-year maternal employment and child development in the first 7 years. *Monographs of the Society for Research in Child Development, 75*(No. 2, Serial No. 296).

Brooks-Gunn, J., Klebanov, P. K., Smith, J., Duncan, G. J., & Lee, K. (2003). The black–white test score gap in young children. Contributions of test and family characteristics. *Applied Developmental Science, 7*, 239–252.

Brown, A. L. (1997). Transforming schools into communities of thinking and learning about serious matters. *American Psychologist, 52*, 399–413.

Brown, A. M., & Miracle, J. A. (2003). Early binocular vision in human infants: Limitations on the generality of the Superposition Hypothesis. *Vision Research, 43*, 1563–1574.

Brown, C. S., & Bigler, R. S. (2004). Children's perceptions of gender discrimination. *Developmental Psychology, 40*, 714–726.

Brown, G. L., Mangelsdorf, S. C., Agathen, J. M., & Ho, M.-H. (2008). Young children's psychological selves: Convergence with maternal reports of child personality. *Social Development, 17*, 161–182.

Brown, G. L., Mangelsdorf, S. C., & Neff, C. (2012). Father involvement, paternal sensitivity, and father–child attachment security in the first 3 years. *Journal of Family Psychology, 26*, 421–430.

Brown, G. L., Schoppe-Sullivan, S. J., Mangelsdorf, S. C., & Neff, C. (2010). Observed and reported supportive coparenting as predictors of infant–mother and infant–father attachment security. *Early Child Development and Care, 180*, 121–137.

Brown, R. W. (1973). *A first language: The early stages*. Cambridge, MA: Harvard University Press.

Brown, T. E. (2006). Executive functions and attention deficit hyperactivity disorder: Implications of two conflicting views. *International Journal of Disability, Development and Education, 53*, 35–46.

Browne, C. A., & Woolley, J. D. (2004). Preschoolers' magical explanations for violations of physical, social, and mental laws. *Journal of Cognition and Development, 5*, 239–260.

Browne, J. V., & Talmi, A. (2005). Family-based intervention to enhance infant–parent relationships in the neonatal intensive care unit. *Journal of Pediatric Psychology, 30*, 667–677.

Brownell, C. A., & Kopp, C. B. (2007). Transitions in toddler socioemotional development: Behavior, understanding, relationships. In C. A. Brownell & C. B. Kopp (Eds.), *Socioemotional development in the toddler years: Transitions and transformations* (pp. 1–40). New York: Guilford.

Brownell, C. A., Zerwas, S., & Ramani, G. B. (2007). "So big": The development of body self-awareness in toddlers. *Child Development, 78*, 1426–1440.

Bruer, J. T. (1999). *The myth of the first three years*. New York: Free Press.

Brühwiler, C., & Blatchford, P. (2011). Effects of class size and adaptive teaching competency on classroom processes and academic outcome. *Learning and Instruction, 21*, 95–108.

Brummelman, E., Thomaes, S., Overbeek, G., Orobio de Castro, B., van den Hout, M. A., & Bushman, B. J. (2014). On feeding those hungry for praise: Person praise backfires in children with low self-esteem. *Journal of Experimental Psychology: General, 143*, 9–14.

Bruschweiler-Stern, N. (2004). A multifocal neonatal intervention. In A. J. Sameroff, S. C. McDonough, & K. L. Rosenblum (Eds.), *Treating parent–infant relationship problems* (pp. 188–212). New York: Guilford.

Bruzzese, J., & Fisher, C. B. (2003). Assessing and enhancing the research consent capacity of children and youth. *Applied Developmental Science, 7*, 13–26.

Bryan, A. E., & Dix, T. (2009). Mothers' emotions and behavioral support during interactions with toddlers: The role of child temperament. *Social Development, 18*, 647–670.

Bryant, D. M., Hoeft, F., Lai, S., Lackey, J., Roeltgen, D., Ross, J., et al. (2012). Sex chromosomes and the brain: A study of neuroanatomy in XYY syndrome. *Developmental Medicine and Child Neurology, 54*, 1149–1156.

Bryant, P., & Nunes, T. (2002). Children's understanding of mathematics. In U. Goswami (Ed.), *Blackwell handbook of childhood cognitive development* (pp. 412–439). Malden, MA: Blackwell.

Brydges, C. R., Reid, C. L., Fox, A. M., & Anderson, M. (2012). A unitary executive function predicts intelligence in children. *Intelligence, 40*, 458–469.

Bryk, R. L., & Fisher, P. A. (2012). Training the brain: Practical applications of neural plasticity from the intersection of cognitive neuroscience, developmental psychology, and prevention science. *American Psychologist, 67*, 87–100.

Buchanan, C. M., Maccoby, E. E., & Dornbusch, S. M. (1996). *Adolescents after divorce*. Cambridge, MA: Harvard University Press.

Buchanan-Barrow, E., & Barrett, M. (1998). Children's rule discrimination within the context of the school. *British Journal of Developmental Psychology, 16*, 539–551.

Buchsbaum, D., Dridgers, S., Weisberg, D. S., & Gopnik, A. (2012). The power of possibility: Causal learning, counterfactual reasoning, and pretend play. *Philosophical Transactions of the Royal Society B, 367*, 2202–2212.

Buckhalt, J. A., El-Sheikh, M., Keller, P. S., & Kelly, R. J. (2009). Concurrent and longitudinal relations between children's sleep and cognitive functioning: The moderating role of parent education. *Child Development, 80*, 875–892.

Buckingham-Howes, S., Berger, S., Shafer, S., Scaletti, L. A., & Black, M. M. (2013). Systematic review of prenatal cocaine exposure and adolescent development. *Pediatrics, 13,* e1917–e1936.

Bugental, D. B., Corpuz, R., & Schwartz, A. (2012). Preventing children's aggression: Outcomes of an early intervention. *Developmental Psychology, 48,* 1443–1449.

Bugental, D. B., Ellerson, P. C., Lin, E. K., Rainey, B., & Kokotovic, A. (2002). A cognitive approach to child abuse prevention. *Journal of Family Psychology, 16,* 243–258.

Bugental, D. B., & Happaney, K. (2004). Predicting infant maltreatment in low-income families: The interactive effects of maternal attributions and child status at birth. *Developmental Psychology, 40,* 234–243.

Buhrmester, D., & Furman, W. (1990). Perceptions of sibling relationships during middle childhood and adolescence. *Child Development, 61,* 1387–1398.

Buhs, E. S., Ladd, G. W., & Herald-Brown, S. L. (2010). Victimization and exclusion: Links to peer rejection, classroom engagement, and achievement. In S. R. Jimerson, S. M. Swearer, & D. L. Espelage (Eds.), *Handbook of bullying in schools: An international perspective* (pp. 163–172). New York: Routledge.

Bukacha, C. M., Gauthier, S., & Tarr, M. J. (2006). Beyond faces and modularity: The power of an expertise framework. *Trends in Cognitive Sciences, 10,* 159–166.

Bullock, M., & Lutkenhaus, P. (1990). Who am I? The development of self-understanding in toddlers. *Merrill-Palmer Quarterly, 36,* 217–238.

Bulotsky-Shearer, R. J., Wen, X., Faria, A.-M., Hahs-Vaughn, D. L., & Korfmacher, J. (2012). National profiles of classroom quality and family involvement: A multilevel examination of proximal influences on Head Start children's school readiness. *Early Childhood Research Quarterly, 27,* 627–639.

Bunge, S. A., & Wright, S. B. (2007). Neurodevelopmental changes in working memory and cognitive control. *Current Opinion in Neurobiology, 17,* 243–250.

Burchinal, M., Vandergrift, N., & Pianta, R. (2010). Threshold analysis of association between child care quality and child outcomes for low-income children in pre-kindergarten programs. *Early Childhood Research Quarterly, 25,* 166–176.

Burden, M. J., Jacobson, S. W., & Jacobson, J. L. (2005). Relation of prenatal alcohol exposure to cognitive processing speed and efficiency in childhood. *Alcoholism: Clinical and Experimental Research, 29,* 1473–1483.

Burgess-Champoux, T. L., Larson, N., Neumark-Sztainer, D., Hannan, P. J., & Story, M. (2009). Are family meal patterns associated with overall diet quality during the transition from early to middle adolescence? *Journal of Nutrition Education and Behavior, 41,* 79–86.

Burhans, K. K., & Dweck, C. S. (1995). Helplessness in early childhood: The role of contingent worth. *Child Development, 66,* 1719–1738.

Burkam, D. T., Ready, D. D., Lee, V. E., & LoGerfo, L. F. (2004). Social-class differences in summer learning between kindergarten and first grade: Model specification and estimation. *Sociology of Education, 77,* 1–31.

Burns, C. E. (2000). *Pediatric primary care: A handbook for nurse practitioners.* Philadelphia: Saunders.

Burts, D. C., Hart, C. H., Charlesworth, R., Fleege, P. O., Mosley, J., & Thomasson, R. H. (1992). Observed activities and stress behaviors of children in developmentally appropriate and inappropriate kindergarten classrooms. *Early Childhood Research Quarterly, 7,* 297–318.

Bush, K. R., & Peterson, G. W. (2008). Family influences on child development. In T. P. Gullotta & G. M. Blau (Eds.), *Handbook of child behavioral issues: Evidence-based approaches to prevention and treatment* (pp. 43–67). New York: Routledge.

Bushman, B. J., & Huesmann, L. R. (2012). Effects of violent media on aggression. In Singer, D. G. & Singer, J. L. (Eds.), *Handbook of Children and the Media* (2nd ed., pp. 231–248). Thousand Oaks, CA: Sage.

Bushnell, E. W., & Boudreau, J. P. (1993). Motor development and the mind: The potential role of motor abilities as a determinant of aspects of perceptual development. *Child Development, 64,* 1005–1021.

Bussey, K. (1992). Lying and truthfulness: Children's definitions, standards, and evaluative reactions. *Child Development, 63,* 129–137.

Buswell, S. D., & Spatz, D. L. (2007). Parent–infant co-sleeping and its relationship to breastfeeding. *Journal of Pediatric Health Care, 21,* 22–28.

Butcher, L. M., Davis, O. S. P., Craig, I. W., & Plomin, R. (2008). Genome-wide quantitative trait locus association scan of general cognitive ability using pooled DNA and 500K single nucleotide polymorphism microarrays. *Genes, Brains and Behavior, 7,* 435–446.

Butler, M. G., & Meaney, J. (Eds.). (2005). *Genetics of developmental disabilities.* Boca Raton, FL: Taylor & Francis.

Butler, M. G. (2009). Genomic imprinting disorders in humans: A mini-review. *Journal of Assisted Reproduction and Genetics, 26,* 477–486.

Butler, R. (1998). Age trends in the use of social and temporal comparison for self-evaluation: Examination of a novel developmental hypothesis. *Child Development, 69,* 1054–1073.

Buttelmann, D., Over, H., Carpenter, M., & Tomasello, M. (2014). Eighteen-month-olds false beliefs in an unexpected-contents task. *Journal of Experimental Child Psychology, 119,* 120–126.

Butts, M. M., Casper, W. J., & Yang, T. S. (2013). How important are work–family support policies? A meta-analytic investigation of their effects on employee outcomes. *Journal of Applied Psychology, 98,* 1–25.

Bybee, J., Merisca, R., & Velasco, R. (1998). The development of reactions to guilt-producing events. In J. Bybee (Ed.), *Guilt and children* (pp. 185–213). San Diego: Academic Press.

Byne, W., Bradley, S. J., Coleman, E., Eyler, A. E., Green, R., Menvielle, E. J., et al. (2012). Report of the American Psychiatric Association Task Force on Treatment of Gender Identity Disorder. *Archives of Sexual Behavior, 41,* 759–796.

Byrnes, J. P., & Wasik, B. A. (2009). *Language and literacy development: What educators need to know.* New York: Guilford.

C

Cabrera, N. J., & Bradley, R. H. (2012). Latino fathers and their children. *Child Development Perspectives, 6,* 232–238.

Cabrera, N. J., Fitzgerald, H. E., Bradley, R. H., & Roggman, L. (2007). Modeling the dynamics of paternal influence on children over the life course. *Applied Developmental Science, 11,* 185–189.

Cabrera, N. J., & García Coll, C. (2004). Latino fathers: Uncharted territory in need of much exploration. In M. E. Lamb (Ed.), *The role of the father in child development* (4th ed., pp. 98–120). Hoboken, NJ: Wiley.

Cabrera, N. J., Shannon, J. D., & Tamis-LeMonda, C. (2007). Fathers' influence on their children's cognitive and emotional development: From toddlers to pre-K. *Applied Developmental Science, 11,* 208–213.

Cain, K., & Oakhill, J. (2011). Matthew effects in young readers: Reading comprehension and reading experience aid vocabulary development. *Journal of Learning Disabilities, 44,* 431–443.

Cain, M. A., Bornick, P., & Whiteman, V. (2013). The maternal, fetal, and neonatal effects of cocaine exposure in pregnancy. *Clinical Obstetrics and Gynecology, 56,* 124–132.

Cairns, R. B., & Cairns, B. D. (2006). The making of developmental psychology. In R. M. Lerner (Ed.), *Handbook of child psychology: Vol. 1. Theoretical models of human development* (6th ed., pp. 89–165). Hoboken, NJ: Wiley.

Cairns, R. B., Xie, H., & Leung, M.-C. (1998). The popularity of friendship and the neglect of social networks: Toward a new balance. In W. M. Bukowski & A. H. Cillessen (Eds.), *Sociometry then and now: Building on six decades of measuring children's experiences with the peer group* (pp. 25–53). San Francisco: Jossey-Bass.

Caldera, Y. M., & Lindsey, E. W. (2006). Coparenting, mother–infant interaction, and infant–parent attachment relationships in two-parent families. *Journal of Family Psychology, 20,* 275–283.

Caldwell, B. M., & Bradley, R. H. (1994). Environmental issues in developmental follow-up research. In S. L. Friedman & H. C. Haywood (Eds.), *Developmental follow-up* (pp. 235–256). San Diego: Academic Press.

Calaff, K. P. (2008). Supportive schooling: Practices that support culturally and linguistically diverse students' preparation for college. *NASSP Bulletin, 92,* 95–110.

Callaghan, T. C. (1999). Early understanding and production of graphic symbols. *Child Development, 70,* 1314–1324.

Callaghan, T. C., Moll, H., Rakoczy, H., Warneken, F., Lizkowski, U., Behne, T., & Tomasello, M. (2011). Early social cognition in three cultural contexts. *Monographs of the Society for Research in Child Development, 76*(2, Serial No. 299).

Callaghan, T. C., & Rankin, M. P. (2002). Emergence of graphic symbol functioning and the question of domain specificity: A longitudinal training study. *Child Development, 73,* 359–376.

Callanan, M. A., & Oakes, L. M. (1992). Preschoolers' questions and parents' explanations: Causal thinking in everyday activity. *Cognitive Development, 7,* 213–233.

Callanan, M. A., & Sabbagh, M. A. (2004). Multiple labels for objects in conversations with young children: Parents' language and children's developing expectations about word meanings. *Developmental Psychology, 40,* 746–763.

Calvert, S. L., Strong, B. L., & Gallagher, L. (2005). Control as an engagement feature for young children's attention to, and learning of, computer content. *American Behavioral Scientist, 48,* 578–589.

Cameron, C. A., Lau, C., Fu, G., & Lee, K. (2012). Development of children's moral evaluations of modesty and self-promotion in diverse cultural settings. *Journal of Moral Education, 41,* 61–78.

Cameron, C. A., & Lee, K. (1997). The development of children's telephone communication. *Journal of Applied Developmental Psychology, 18,* 55–70.

Cameron, P. A., & Gallup, G. G. (1988). Shadow recognition in human infants. *Infant Behavior and Development, 11,* 465–471.

Cameron-Faulkner, T., Lieven, E., & Tomasello, M. (2003). A construction based analysis of child directed speech. *Cognitive Science, 27,* 843–873.

Campbell, A., Shirley, L., & Candy, J. (2004). A longitudinal study of gender-related cognition and behaviour. *Developmental Science, 7,* 1–9.

Campbell, D., Scott, K. D., Klaus, M. H., & Falk, M. (2007). Female relatives or friends trained as labor doulas: Outcomes at 6 to 8 weeks postpartum. *Birth, 34,* 220–227.

Campbell, D. A., Lake, M. F., Falk, M., & Backstrand, J. R. (2006). A randomized control trial of continuous support in labor by a lay doula. *Journal of Obstetrics and Gynecology and Neonatal Nursing, 35,* 456–464.

Campbell, F. A., Pungello, E. P., Miller-Johnson, S., Burchinal, M., & Ramey, C. T. (2001). The development of cognitive and academic abilities: Growth curves from an early childhood educational experiment. *Developmental Psychology, 37,* 231–242.

Campbell, F. A., & Ramey, C. T. (2010). Carolina Abecedarian Project. In A. Reynolds, A. J. Rolick, M. M. Englund, & J. A. Temple (Eds.), *Childhood programs and practices in the first decade of life: A human capital integration* (pp. 76–98). New York: Cambridge University Press.

Campbell, F. A., Ramey, C. T., Pungello, E., Sparling, J., & Miller-Johnson, S. (2002). Early childhood education: Young adult outcomes from the Abecedarian Project. *Applied Developmental Science, 6,* 42–57.

Campbell, S. B., Brownell, C. A., Hungerford, A., Spieker, S. J., Mohan, R., & Blessing, J. S. (2004). The course of maternal depressive symptoms and maternal sensitivity as predictors of attachment security at 36 months. *Development and Psychopathology, 16,* 231–252.

Campos, J. J., Anderson, D. I., Barbu-Roth, M. A., Hubbard, E. M., Hertenstein, J. J., & Witherington, D. (2000). Travel broadens the mind. *Infancy, 1,* 149–219.

Campos, J. J., Frankel, C. B., & Camras, L. (2004). On the nature of emotion regulation. *Child Development, 75,* 377–394.

Campos, J. J., Witherington, D., Anderson, D. I., Frankel, C. I., Uchiyama, I., & Barbu-Roth, M. (2008). Rediscovering development in infancy. *Child Development, 79,* 1625–1632.

Campos, R. G. (1989). Soothing pain-elicited distress in infants with swaddling and pacifiers. *Child Development, 60,* 781–792.

Camras, L. (2011). Differentiation, dynamical integration and functional emotional development. *Emotion Review, 3,* 138–146.

Camras, L., Kolmodin, K., & Chen, Y. (2008). Mothers' self-reported emotional expression in mainland Chinese,

Chinese American and European American families. *International Journal of Behavioral Development, 32,* 459–463.

Camras, L. A. (1992). Expressive development and basic emotions. *Cognition and Emotion, 6,* 267–283.

Camras, L. A., Oster, H., Campos, J. J., & Bakeman, R. (2003). Emotional facial expressions in European-American, Japanese, and Chinese infants. *Annals of the New York Academy of Sciences, 1000,* 1–17.

Camras, L. A., Oster, H., Campos, J. J., Campos, R., Ujie, T., Miyake, K., Wang, L., & Meng, Z. (1998). Production of emotional and facial expressions in European-American, Japanese, and Chinese infants. *Developmental Psychology, 34,* 616–628.

Camras, L. A., Oster, H., Campos, J. J., Miyake, K., & Bradshaw, D. (1992). Japanese and American infants' responses to arm restraint. *Developmental Psychology, 28,* 578–583.

Camras, L. A., & Shutter, J. M. (2010). Emotional facial expressions in infancy. *Emotion Review, 2,* 120–129.

Candelaria, M., Teti, D. M., & Black, M. M. (2011). Multi-risk infants: Predicting attachment security from sociodemographic, psychosocial, and health risk among African-American preterm infants. *Journal of Child Psychology and Psychiatry, 52,* 870–877.

Canfield, R., Henderson, C., Cory-Slechta, D., Cox, C., Jusko, T., & Lanphear, B. (2003). Intellectual impairment in children with blood lead concentrations below 10 µg per deciliter. *New England Journal of Medicine, 348,* 1517–1526.

Capirci, O., Contaldo, A., Caselli, M. C., & Volterra, V. (2005). From action to language through gesture. *Gesture, 5,* 155–177.

Card, N. A., Stucky, B. D., Sawalani, G. M., & Little, T. D. (2008). Direct and indirect aggression during childhood and adolescence: A meta-analytic review of gender differences, intercorrelations, and relations to maladjustment. *Child Development, 79,* 1185–1229.

Carey, S., & Markman, E. M. (1999). Cognitive development. In B. M. Bly & D. E. Rumelhart (Eds.), *Cognitive science* (pp. 201–254). San Diego: Academic Press.

Carlson, S. M., & Meltzoff, A. N. (2008). Bilingual experience and executive functioning in young children. *Developmental Science, 11,* 282–298.

Carlson, S. M., Moses, L. J., & Claxton, S. J. (2004). Individual differences in executive functioning and theory of mind: An investigation of inhibitory control and planning ability. *Journal of Experimental Child Psychology, 87,* 299–319.

Carlson, S. M., & White, R. E. (2013). Executive function, pretend play, and imagination. In R. E. White & S. M. Carlson (Eds.), *Oxford handbook of the development of imagination* (pp. 161–174). New York: Oxford University Press.

Carlson, S. M., & Zelazo, P. D., & Faja, S. (2013). Executive function. In P. D. Zelazo (Ed.), *Oxford handbook of developmental psychology, Vol. 1: Body and mind* (pp. 706–743). New York: Oxford University Press.

Carlson, V. J., & Harwood, R. L. (2003). Attachment, culture, and the caregiving system: The cultural patterning of everyday experiences among Anglo and Puerto Rican mother–infant pairs. *Infant Mental Health Journal, 24,* 53–73.

Carpenter, M., Nagel, K., & Tomasello, M. (1998). Social cognition, joint attention, and communicative competence. *Monographs of the Society for Research in Child Development, 63*(4, Serial No. 255).

Carpenter, T. P., Fennema, E., Fuson, K., Hiebert, J., Human, P., & Murray, H. (1999). Learning basic number concepts and skills as problem solving. In E. Fennema & T. A. Romberg (Eds.), *Mathematics classrooms that promote understanding: Studies in mathematical thinking and learning series* (pp. 45–61). Mahwah, NJ: Erlbaum.

Carr, D., & Friedman, M. A. (2005). Is obesity stigmatizing? Body weight, perceived discrimination, and psychological well-being in the United States. *Journal of Health and Social Behavior, 46,* 244–256.

Carr, J. (2002). Down syndrome. In P. Howlin & O. Udwin (Eds.), *Outcomes in neurodevelopmental and genetic disorders* (pp. 169–197). New York: Cambridge University Press.

Carroll, J. B. (2005). The three-stratum theory of cognitive abilities. In D. P. Flanagan & P. L. Harrison (Eds.),

Contemporary intellectual assessment: Theories, tests, and issues (2nd ed., pp. 69–76). New York: Guilford.

CASA. (2006). *The importance of family dinners III.* New York: National Center on Addiction and Substance Abuse, Columbia University.

Casalin, S., Luyten, P., Vliegen, N., & Meurs, P. (2012). The structure and stability of temperament from infancy to toddlerhood: A one-year prospective study. *Infant Behavior and Development, 35,* 94–108.

Casalis, S., & Cole, P. (2009). On the relationship between morphological and phonological awareness: Effects of training in kindergarten and in first-grade reading. *First Language, 29,* 113–142.

Casasola, M., Bhagwat, J., & Burke, A. S. (2009). Learning to form a spatial category of tight-fit relations: How experience with a label can give a boost. *Developmental Psychology, 45,* 711–723.

Casasola, M., & Park, Y. (2013). Developmental changes in infant spatial categorization: When more is best and when less is enough. *Child Development, 84,* 1004–1019.

Case, R. (1996). Introduction: Reconceptualizing the nature of children's conceptual structures and their development in middle childhood. In R. Case & Y. Okamoto (Eds.), The role of central conceptual structures in the development of children's thought. *Monographs of the Society for Research in Child Development, 246*(61, Serial No. 246), pp. 1–26.

Case, R. (1998). The development of conceptual structures. In D. Kuhn & R. S. Siegler (Eds.), *Handbook of child psychology: Vol. 2. Cognition, perception, and language* (pp. 745–800). New York: Wiley.

Case, R., & Okamoto, Y. (Eds.). (1996). The role of central conceptual structures in the development of children's thought. *Monographs of the Society for Research in Child Development, 61*(1–2, Serial No. 246).

CASEL (Collaborative for Academic, Social, and Emotional Learning). (2013). *CASEL guide: Effective social and emotional learning programs (Preschool and elementary school edition).* Chicago, IL: Author.

Caserta, D., Graziano, A., Lo Monte, G., Bordi, G., & Moscarini, M. (2013). Heavy metals and placental fetal–maternal barrier: A mini-review on the major concerns. *European Review for Medical and Pharmacological Sciences, 17,* 2198–2206.

Casey, B. M. (1986). Individual differences in selective attention among prereaders: A key to mirror-image confusions. *Developmental Psychology, 22,* 824–831.

Casper, L. M., & Smith, K. E. (2002). Dispelling the myths: Self-care, class, and race. *Journal of Family Issues, 23,* 716–727.

Caspi, A., Elder, G. H., Jr., & Bem, D. J. (1987). Moving against the world: Life-course patterns of explosive children. *Developmental Psychology, 23,* 308–313.

Caspi, A., Elder, G. H., Jr., & Bem, D. J. (1988). Moving away from the world: Life-course patterns of shy children. *Developmental Psychology, 24,* 824–831.

Caspi, A., Harrington, H., Milne, B., Amell, J. W., Theodore, R. F., & Moffitt, T. E. (2003). Children's behavioral styles at age 3 are linked to their adult personality traits at age 26. *Journal of Personality, 71,* 495–513.

Caspi, A., McClay, J., Moffitt, T. E., Mill, J., Martin, J., & Craig, I. W. (2002). Role of genotype in the cycle of violence in maltreated children. *Science, 297,* 851–854.

Caspi, A., Moffitt, T. E., Morgan, J., Rutter, M., Taylor, A., Kim-Cohen, J., & Polo-Tomas, M. (2004). Maternal expressed emotion predicts children's antisocial behavior problems: Using monozygotic-twin differences to identify environmental effects on behavioral development. *Developmental Psychology, 40,* 149–161.

Caspi, A., & Roberts, B. W. (2001). Personality development across the life course: The argument for change and continuity. *Psychological Inquiry, 12,* 49–66.

Caspi, A., & Shiner, L. (2006). Personality development. In N. Eisenberg (Ed.), *Handbook of child psychology: Vol. 3. Social, emotional, and personality development* (6th ed., pp. 300–365). Hoboken, NJ: Wiley.

Cassia, V. M., Turati, C., & Simion, F. (2004). Can a nonspecific bias toward top-heavy patterns explain newborns' face preference? *Psychological Science, 15,* 379–383.

Cassidy, J., & Berlin, L. J. (1994). The insecure/ambivalent pattern of attachment: Theory and research. *Child Development, 65,* 971–991.

Catalano, R., Ahern, J., Bruckner, T., Anderson, E., & Saxton, K. (2009). Gender-specific selection in utero among contemporary human birth cohorts. *Paediatric and Perinatal Epidemiology, 23,* 273–278.

Catalano, R., Zilko, C. E., Saxton, K. B., & Bruckner, T. (2010). Selection in utero: A biological response to mass layoffs. *American Journal of Human Biology, 22,* 396–400.

Caton, D., Corry, M. P., Frigoletto, F. D., Hopkins, D. P., Liberman, E., & Mayberry, L. (2002). The nature and management of labor pain: Executive summary. *American Journal of Obstetrics and Gynecology, 186,* S1–S15.

Caughey, R. W., & Michels, K. B. (2009). Birth weight and childhood leukemia: A meta-analysis and review of the current evidence. *International Journal of Cancer, 124,* 2658–2670.

Ceci, S. J. (1999). Schooling and intelligence. In S. J. Ceci & W. M. Williams (Eds.), *The nature–nurture debate: The essential readings* (pp. 168–175). Oxford, UK: Blackwell.

Ceci, S. J., Bruck, M., & Battin, D. (2000). The suggestibility of children's testimony. In Bjorklund, D. (Ed), *False-memory creation in children and adults* (pp. 169–201). Mahwah, NJ: Erlbaum.

Ceci, S. J., Kulkofsky, S., Klemfuss, J. Z., Sweeney, C. D., & Bruck, M. (2007). Unwarranted assumptions about children's testimonial accuracy. *Annual Review of Clinical Psychology, 3,* 311–328.

Ceci, S. J., & Roazzi, A. (1994). The effects of context on cognition: Postcards from Brazil. In R. J. Sternberg (Ed.), *Mind in context* (pp. 74–101). New York: Cambridge University Press.

Ceci, S. J., Rosenblum, T. B., & Kumpf, M. (1998). The shrinking gap between high- and low-scoring groups: Current trends and possible causes. In U. Neisser (Ed.), *The rising curve: Long-term gains in IQ and related measures* (pp. 287–302). Washington, DC: American Psychological Association.

Cecil, J. E., Watt, P., Murrie, I. S. L., Wrieden, W., Wallis, D. J., Hetherington, M. M., Bolton-Smith, C., & Palmer, C. N. A. (2005). Childhood obesity and socioeconomic status: A novel role for height growth limitation. *International Journal of Obesity, 29,* 1199–1203.

Center for Communication and Social Policy (Ed.). (1998). *National Television Violence Study* (Vol. 2). Newbury Park, CA: Sage.

Centers for Disease Control and Prevention. (2010). *The association between school-based physical activity, including physical education, and academic performance.* Retrieved from www.cdc.gov/healthyyouth/health_and_academics/pdf/pape_executive_summary.pdf

Centers for Disease Control and Prevention. (2012). *Trends in asthma prevalence, health care use, and mortality in the United States, 2001–2010.* Retrieved from www.cdc.gov/nchs/data/databriefs/db94.htm

Centers for Disease Control and Prevention. (2013). Breastfeeding report card: United States 2013. Retrieved from www.cdc.gov/breastfeeding/pdf/2013breastfeedingreportcard.pdf

Centers for Disease Control and Prevention. (2014a). Assisted reproductive technology (ART). Retrieved from www.cdc.gov/art/ARTReports.htm

Centers for Disease Control and Prevention. (2014b). *Bridging the Gap Research Program: Supporting recess in elementary schools.* Atlanta, GA: U.S. Department of Health and Human Services.

Centers for Disease Control and Prevention. (2014c). CDC's healthy homes and lead program: What do parents need to know to protect their children? Retrieved from www.cdc.gov/nceh/lead/acclpp/blood_lead_levels.htm

Centers for Disease Control and Prevention. (2014d). *Child maltreatment: Risk and protective factors.* Retrieved from www.cdc.gov/violenceprevention/childmaltreatment/riskprotectivefactors.html

Centers for Disease Control and Prevention. (2014e). National, state, and selected local area vaccination coverage among children aged 19–35 months—United States, 2013. *Morbidity and Mortality Weekly Report, 63,* 741–748.

Centers for Disease Control and Prevention. (2014f). Tobacco use and pregnancy. Retrieved from www.cdc.gov/Reproductivehealth/TobaccoUsePregnancy/index.htm

Cernoch, J. M., & Porter, R. H. (1985). Recognition of maternal axillary odors by infants. *Child Development, 56,* 1593–1598.

Cetinkaya, M. B., Siano, L. J., & Benadiva, C. (2013). Reproductive outcome of women 43 years and beyond undergoing ART treatment with their own oocytes in two Connecticut university programs. *Journal of Assisted Reproductive Genetics, 30,* 673–678.

Chalabaev, A., Sarrazin, P., & Fontayne, P. (2009). Stereotype endorsement and perceived ability as mediators of the girls' gender orientation–soccer performance relationship. *Psychology of Sport and Exercise, 10,* 297–299.

Chall, J. S. (1983). *Stages of reading development.* New York: McGraw-Hill.

Champion, T. B. (2003). "A matter of vocabulary": Performances of low-income African-American Head Start children on the Peabody Picture Vocabulary Test. *Communication Disorders Quarterly, 24,* 121–127.

Chan, A., Meints, K., Lieven, E., & Tomasello, M. (2010). Young children's comprehension of English SVO word order revisited: Testing the same children in act-out and intermodal preferential looking tasks. *Cognitive Development, 25,* 30–45.

Chan, C. C. Y., Brandone, A. C., & Tardif, T. (2009). Culture, context, or behavioral control? English- and Mandarin-speaking mothers' use of nouns and verbs in joint book reading. *Journal of Cross-Cultural Psychology, 40,* 584–602.

Chan, C. C. Y., Tardif, T., Chen, J., Pulverman, R. B., Zhu, L., & Meng, X. (2011). English- and Chinese-learning infants map novel labels to objects and actions differently. *Developmental Psychology, 47,* 1459–1471.

Chan, S. M. (2010). Aggressive behaviour in early elementary school children: Relations to authoritarian parenting, children's negative emotionality and coping strategies. *Early Child Development and Care, 180,* 1253–1269.

Chandra, A., Copen, C. E., & Stephen, E. H. (2013). *Infertility and impaired fecundity in the United States, 1982–2010: Data from the National Survey of Family Growth.* Hyattsville, MD: Centers for Disease Control and Prevention. Retrieved from www.cdc.gov/nchs/data/nhsr/nhsr067.pdf

Chandra, R. K. (1991). Interactions between early nutrition and the immune system. In *Ciba Foundation Symposium No. 156* (pp. 77–92). Chichester, UK: Wiley.

Chang, F., Dell, G. S., & Bock, K. (2006). Becoming syntactic. *Psychological Review, 113,* 234–272.

Chapman, R. S. (2006). Children's language learning: An interactionist perspective. In R. Paul (Ed.), *Language disorders from a developmental perspective* (pp. 1–53). Mahwah, NJ: Erlbaum.

Charity, A. H., Scarborough, H. S., & Griffin, D. M. (2004). Familiarity with school English in African American children and its relation to early reading achievement. *Child Development, 75,* 1340–1356.

Charman, T., Baron-Cohen, S., Swettenham, J., Baird, G., Cox, A., & Drew, A. (2001). Testing joint attention, imitation, and play as infancy precursors to language and theory of mind. *Cognitive Development, 15,* 481–49.

Chase-Lansdale, P. L., Gordon, R., Brooks-Gunn, J., & Klebanov, P. K. (1997). Neighborhood and family influences on the intellectual and behavioral competence of preschool and early school-age children. In J. Brooks-Gunn, G. Duncan, & J. L. Aber (Eds.), *Neighborhood poverty: Context and consequences for development* (pp. 79–118). New York: Russell Sage Foundation.

Chauhan, G. S., Shastri, J., & Mohite, P. (2005). Development of gender constancy in preschoolers. *Psychological Studies, 50,* 62–71.

Chavajay, P., & Rogoff, B. (1999). Cultural variation in management of attention by children and their caregivers. *Developmental Psychology, 35,* 1079–1090.

Chavajay, P., & Rogoff, B. (2002). Schooling and traditional collaborative social organization of problem solving by Mayan mothers and children. *Developmental Psychology, 38,* 55–66.

Chawarska, K., Macari, S., & Shic, F. (2013). Decreased spontaneous attention to social scenes in 6-month-old infants later diagnosed with autism spectrum disorders. *Biological Psychiatry, 74,* 195–203.

Cheah, C. S. L., Leung, C. Y. Y., Tahseen, M., & Schultz, D. (2009). Authoritative parenting among immigrant Chinese mothers of preschoolers. *Journal of Family Psychology, 23,* 311–320.

Cheah, C. S. L. & Li, J. (2010). Parenting of young immigrant Chinese children: Challenges facing their social-emotional and intellectual development. In

E. L. Grigorenko & R. Takanishi (Eds.), *Immigration, diversity, and education* (pp. 225–241). New York: Routledge.

Checkley, W., Epstein, L. D., Gilman, R. H., Cabrera, L., & Black, R. E. (2003). Effects of acute diarrhea on linear growth in Peruvian children. *American Journal of Epidemiology, 157,* 166–175.

Chen, E. S. L., & Rao, N. (2011). Gender socialization in Chinese kindergartens: Teachers' contributions. *Sex Roles, 64,* 103–116.

Chen, J. J., Howard, K. S., & Brooks-Gunn, J. (2011). How do neighborhoods matter across the life span? In K. L. Fingerman, C. A. Berg, J. Smith, & T. C. Antonucci (Eds.), *Handbook of life-span development* (pp. 805–836). New York: Springer.

Chen, L.-C., Metcalfe, J. S., Jeka, J. J., & Clark, J. E. (2007). Two steps forward and one back: Learning to walk affects infants' sitting posture. *Infant Behavior and Development, 30,* 16–25.

Chen, X. (2012). Culture, peer interaction, and socioemotional development. *Child Development Perspectives, 6,* 27–34.

Chen, X., Cen, G., Li, D., & He, Y. (2005). Social functioning and adjustment in Chinese children: The imprint of historical time. *Child Development, 76,* 182–195.

Chen, X., DeSouza, A. T., Chen, H., & Wang, L. (2006). Reticent behavior and experiences in peer interactions in Chinese and Canadian children. *Developmental Psychology, 42,* 656–665.

Chen, X., & Eisenberg, N. (2012). Understanding cultural issues in child development: Introduction. *Child Development Perspectives, 6,* 1–14.

Chen, X., Hastings, P. D., Rubin, K. H., Chen, H., Cen, G., & Stewart, S. L. (1998). Child-rearing attitudes and behavioral inhibition in Chinese and Canadian toddlers: A cross-cultural study. *Developmental Psychology, 34,* 677–686.

Chen, X., Rubin, K. H., & Li, Z. (1995). Social functioning and adjustment in Chinese children: A longitudinal study. *Developmental Psychology, 31,* 531–539.

Chen, X., Wang, L., & Cao, R. (2011). Shyness-sensitivity and unsociability in rural Chinese children: Relations with social, school, and psychological adjustment. *Child Development, 82,* 1531–1543.

Chen, X., Wang, L., & DeSouza, A. (2006). Temperament, socioemotional functioning, and peer relationships in Chinese and North American children. In X. Chen, D. C. French, & B. H. Schneider (Eds.), *Peer relationships in cultural context* (pp. 123–147). New York: Cambridge University Press.

Chen, Y., Li, H., & Meng, L. (2013). Prenatal sex selection and missing girls in China: Evidence from the diffusion of diagnostic ultrasound. *Journal of Human Resources, 48,* 36–70.

Chen, Y.-C., Yu, M.-L., Rogan, W., Gladen, B., & Hsu, C.-C. (1994). A 6-year follow-up of behavior and activity disorders in the Taiwan Yu-cheng children. *American Journal of Public Health, 84,* 415–421.

Chen, Y.-J., & Hsu, C.-C. (1994). Effects of prenatal exposure to PCBs on the neurological function of children: A neuropsychological and neuro-physiological study. *Developmental Medicine and Child Neurology, 36,* 312–320.

Chen, Z., Sanchez, R. P., & Campbell, T. (1997). From beyond to within their grasp: The rudiments of analogical problem solving in 10- to 13-month-olds. *Developmental Psychology, 33,* 790–801.

Cherlin, A. J. (2010). Demographic trends in the United States: A review of research in the 2000s. *Journal of Marriage and Family, 72,* 403–419.

Chess, S., & Thomas, A. (1984). *Origins and evolution of behavior disorders.* New York: Brunner/Mazel.

Chiang, T., Schultz, R. M., & Lampson, M. A. (2012). Meiotic origins of maternal age-related aneuploidy. *Biology of Reproduction, 86,* 1–7.

Child Care Aware. (2013). *Parents and the high cost of child care: 2013 report.* Arlington, VA: Author.

Child Health USA. (2013). *SIDS/SUID.* Retrieved from www.mchb.hrsa.gov/chusa13/perinatal-health-status-indicators/p/SIDS-SUID.html

Child Trends. (2013). *Full-day kindergarten: Indicators on children and youth.* Retrieved from www.childtrends.org/wp-content/uploads/2013/06/102_Full-day-kindergarten.pdf

Child Trends. (2014a). *Births to unmarried women.* Retrieved from www.childtrends.org/?indicators=births-to-unmarried-women

Child Trends. (2014b). *Late or no prenatal care: Indicators on children and youth.* Retrieved from www.childtrends.org/wp-content/uploads/2012/11/25_Prenatal_Care.pdf

Child Trends. (2014c). *Unintentional injuries: Indicators on children and youth.* Retrieved from www.childtrends.org/wp-content/uploads/2014/10/122_Unintentional_Injuries.pdf

Cho, S., Ryali, S., Geary, D. C., & Menon, V. (2011). How does a child solve 7 + 8? Decoding brain activity patterns associated with counting and retrieval strategies. *Developmental Science, 14,* 989–1001.

Choe, D. E., Olson, S. L., & Sameroff, A. J. (2013). The interplay of externalizing problems and physical discipline and inductive discipline during childhood. *Developmental Psychology, 49,* 2029–2039.

Choi, S., & Gopnik, A. (1995). Early acquisition of verbs in Korean: A cross-linguistic study. *Journal of Child Language, 22,* 497–529.

Choi, S., McDonough, L., Bowerman, M., & Mandler, J. M. (1999). Early sensitivity to language-specific spatial categories in English and Korean. *Cognitive Development, 14,* 241–268.

Chomsky, C. (1969). *The acquisition of syntax in children from five to ten.* Cambridge, MA: MIT Press.

Chomsky, N. (1957). *Syntactic structures.* The Hague: Mouton.

Chouinard, M. M. (2007). Children's questions: A mechanism for cognitive development. *Monographs of the Society for Research in Child Development, 72*(1, Serial No. 286).

Chouinard, M. M., & Clark, E. V. (2003). Adult reformulations of child errors as negative evidence. *Journal of Child Language, 30,* 637–669.

Christakis, D. A., Garrison, M. M., Herrenkohl, T., Haggerty, K, Rivara, F. P., Zhou, C., & Liekweg, K. (2013). Modifying media content for preschool children: A randomized controlled trial. *Pediatrics, 131,* 431–438.

Christakis, D. A., Zimmerman, F. J., DiGiuseppe, D. L., & McCarty, C. A. (2004). Early television exposure and subsequent attentional problems in children. *Pediatrics, 113,* 708–713.

Christiansen, M. H., & Chater, N. (2008). Language as shaped by the brain. *Behavioral and Brain Sciences, 31,* 489–558.

Christoffersen, M. N. (2012). A study of adopted children, their environment, and development: A systematic review. *Adoption Quarterly, 15,* 220–237.

Chung, H. H. (2006). Code switching as a communicative strategy: A case study of Korean–English bilinguals. *Bilingual Research Journal, 30,* 293–307.

Cicchetti, D. (2007). Intervention and policy implications of research on neurobiological functioning in maltreated children. In J. L. Aber, S. J. Bishop-Josef, S. M. Jones, K. T. McLearn, & D. A. Phillips (Eds.), *Child development and social policy* (pp. 167–184). Washington, DC: American Psychological Association.

Cicuto, N. A., Rocha, F., de Campos, A. C., & Silva, F. P. dos Santos. (2012). Adaptive actions of young infants in the task of reaching for objects. *Developmental Psychobiology, 55,* 275–282.

Cillessen, A. H. N. (2009). Sociometric methods. In K. H. Rubin & W. M. Bukowski (Eds.), *Handbook of peer interactions, relationships, and groups* (pp. 82–99). New York: Guilford.

Cillessen, A. H. N., & Bellmore, A. D. (2004). Social skills and interpersonal perception in early and middle childhood. In P. K. Smith & C. H. Hart (Eds.), *Blackwell handbook of childhood social development* (pp. 355–374). Malden, MA: Blackwell.

Cipriano, E. A., & Stifter, C. A. (2010). Predicting preschool effortful control from toddler temperament and parenting behavior. *Journal of Applied Developmental Psychology, 31,* 221–230.

Clapp, J. F., III, Kim, H., Burciu, B., Schmidt, S., Petry, K., & Lopez, B. (2002). Continuing regular exercise during pregnancy: Effect of exercise volume on fetoplacental growth. *American Journal of Obstetrics and Gynecology, 186,* 142–147.

Clark, E. V. (2007). Young children's uptake of new words in conversation. *Language in Society, 36,* 157–182.

Clark, K. E., & Ladd, G. W. (2000). Connectedness and autonomy support in parent–child relationships: Links to children's socioemotional orientation and peer relationships. *Developmental Psychology, 36,* 485–498.

Clark, S. M., Ghulmiyyah, L. M., & Hankins, G. D. (2008). Antenatal antecedents and the impact of obstetric care in the etiology of cerebral palsy. *Clinical Obstetrics and Gynecology, 51,* 775–786.

Clarke-Stewart, K. A. (1998). Historical shifts and underlying themes in ideas about rearing young children in the United States: Where have we been? Where are we going? *Early Development and Parenting, 7,* 101–117.

Clarke-Stewart, K. A., & Hayward, C. (1996). Advantages of father custody and contact for the psychological well-being of school-age children. *Journal of Applied Developmental Psychology, 17,* 239–270.

Claxton, L. J., Keen, R., & McCarty, M. E. (2003). Evidence of motor planning in infant reaching behavior. *Psychological Science, 14,* 354–356.

Clearfield, M. W. (2011). Learning to walk changes infants' social interactions. *Infant Behavior and Development, 34,* 15–25.

Clearfield, M. W., & Nelson, N. M. (2006). Sex differences in mothers' speech and play behavior with 6-, 9-, and 14-month-old infants. *Sex Roles, 54,* 127–137.

Clements, D. H., & Sarama, J. (2003). Young children and technology: What does the research say? *Young Children, 58*(6), 34–40.

Clements, D. H., & Sarama, J. (2012). Learning and teaching early and elementary mathematics. In J. S. Carlson & J. R. Levin (Eds.), *Instructional strategies for improving students' learning* (pp. 205–212). Charlotte, NC: Information Age Publishing.

Clements, D. H., Sarama, J., Spitler, M. E., Lange, A. A., & Wolfe, C. B. (2011). Mathematics learned by young children in an intervention based on learning trajectories: A large-scale cluster randomized trial. *Journal for Research in Mathematics Education, 42,* 127–166.

Cleveland, E. S., & Reese, E. (2005). Maternal structure and autonomy support in conversations about the past: Contributions to children's autobiographical memory. *Developmental Psychology, 41,* 376–388.

Clifton, R. K., Rochat, P., Robin, D. J., & Berthier, N. E. (1994). Multimodal perception in the control of infant reaching. *Journal of Experimental Psychology: Human Perception and Performance, 20,* 876–886.

Cluett, E. R., & Burns, E. (2013). Immersion in water in labour and birth. *São Paulo Medical Journal, 131,* 364.

Cnattingius, S., Lundberg, F., Sandin, S., Grönberg, H., & Iliadou, A. (2009). Birth characteristics and risk of prostate cancer: The contribution of genetic factors. *Cancer Epidemiology, 18,* 2422–2466.

Coene, M., Schauwers, K., Gillis, S., Rooryck, J., & Govaerts, P. J. (2011). Genetic predisposition and sensory experience in language development: Evidence from cochlear-implanted children. *Language and Cognitive Processes, 26,* 1083–1101.

Cohen, G. L., Garcia, J., & Master, A. (2006). Reducing the racial achievement gap: A social-psychological intervention. *Science, 313,* 1307–1310.

Cohen, L. B. (2003). Commentary on Part I: Unresolved issues in infant categorization. In D. H. Rakison & L. M. Oakes (Eds.), *Early category and concept development: Making sense of the blooming, buzzing confusion* (pp. 193–209). New York: Oxford University Press.

Cohen, L. B. (2009). The evolution of infant cognition: A personal account. *Infancy, 14,* 403–413.

Cohen, L. B. (2010). A bottom-up approach to infant perception and cognition: A summary of evidence and discussion of issues. In S. P. Johnson (Ed.), *Neoconstructivism: The new science of cognitive development* (pp. 335–346). New York: Oxford University Press.

Cohen, L. B., & Brunt, J. (2009). Early word learning and categorization: Methodological issues and recent empirical evidence. In J. Colombo, P. McCardle, & L. Freund (Eds.), *Infant pathways to language: Methods, models, and research disorders* (pp. 245–266). New York: Psychology Press.

Cohen, L. B., & Marks, K. S. (2002). How infants process addition and subtraction events. *Developmental Science, 5,* 186–201.

Cohen-Bendahan, C. C., van de Beek, C., & Berenbaum, S. A. (2005). Prenatal sex hormone effects on child and adult sex-typed behavior: Methods and findings. *Neuroscience and Biobehavioral Reviews, 29,* 353–384.

Cohn, N. (2014). Framing "I can't draw": The influence of cultural frames on the development of drawing. *Culture and Psychology, 20,* 102–117.

Coldwell, J., Pike, A., & Dunn, J. (2008). Maternal differential treatment and child adjustment: A multi-informant approach. *Social Development, 17,* 596–612.

Cole, C., & Winsler, A. (2010). Protecting children from exposure to lead: Old problem, new data, and new policy needs. *Social Policy Report of the Society for Research in Child Development, 24*(1).

Cole, M. (2006). Culture and cognitive development in phylogenetic, historical, and ontogenetic perspective. In D. Kuhn & R. S. Siegler (Eds.), *Handbook of child psychology: Vol. 2. Cognition, perception, and language* (6th ed., pp. 636–685). Hoboken, NJ: Wiley.

Cole, P. M., Armstrong, L. M., & Pemberton, C. K. (2010). The role of language in the development of emotion regulation. In S. D. Calkins & M. A. Bell (Eds.), *Child development at the intersection of emotion and cognition* (pp. 59–77). Washington, DC: American Psychological Association.

Cole, P. M., Bruschi, C. J., & Tamang, B. L. (2002). Cultural differences in children's emotional reactions to difficult situations. *Child Development, 73,* 983–996.

Cole, P. M., LeDonne, E. N., & Tan, P. Z. (2013). A longitudinal examination of maternal emotions in relation to young children's developing self-regulation. *Parenting: Science and Practice, 13,* 113–132.

Cole, P. M., & Tamang, B. L. (1998). Nepali children's ideas about emotional displays in hypothetical challenges. *Developmental Psychology, 34,* 640–648.

Cole, P. M., Tamang, B. L., & Shrestha, S. (2006). Cultural variations in the socialization of young children's anger and shame. *Child Development, 77,* 1237–1251.

Cole, T. J. (2000). Secular trends in growth. *Proceedings of the Nutrition Society, 59,* 317–324.

Coles, C. D., Goldstein, F. C., Lynch, M. E., Chen, X., Kable, J. A., Johnson, K. C., et al. (2011). Memory and brain volume in adults prenatally exposed to alcohol. *Brain and Cognition, 75,* 67–77.

Coley, R. L., Morris, J. E., & Hernandez, D. (2004). Out-of-school care and problem behavior trajectories among low-income adolescents: Individual, family, and neighborhood characteristics as added risks. *Child Development, 75,* 948–965.

Collins, J. W., Rankin, K. M., & David, R. J. (2011). Low birth weight across generations: The effect of economic environment. *Maternal and Child Health Journal, 15,* 438–445.

Collins, W. A., & Hartup, W. W. (2013). History of research in developmental psychology. In P. D. Zelazo (Ed.), *Oxford handbook of developmental psychology* (pp. 13–34). New York: Oxford University Press.

Collins, W. A., Madsen, S. D., & Susman-Stillman, A. (2002). Parenting during middle childhood. In M. H. Bornstein (Ed.), *Handbook of parenting: Vol. 1. Children and parenting* (2nd ed., pp. 73–101). Mahwah, NJ: Erlbaum.

Collins, W. A., & Russell, G. (1991). Mother–child and father–child interactions in middle childhood and adolescence. *Developmental Review, 11,* 99–136.

Collin-Vézina, D., Daigneault, I., & Hébert, M. (2013). Lessons learned from child sexual abuse research: Prevalence, outcomes, and preventive strategies. *Child and Adolescent Psychiatry and Mental Health, 7,* 1–9.

Colman, L. L., & Colman, A. D. (1991). *Pregnancy: The psychological experience.* New York: Noonday Press.

Colombo, J. (2002). Infant attention grows up: The emergence of a developmental cognitive neuroscience perspective. *Current Directions in Psychological Science, 11,* 196–199.

Colombo, J., Brez, C. C., & Curtindale, L. M. (2013). Infant perception and cognition. In R. M. Lerner, M. A. Easterbrooks, & J. Mistry (Eds.), *Handbook of psychology: Vol. 6. Developmental psychology* (pp. 61–89). Hoboken, NJ: Wiley.

Colombo, J., Kapa, L., & Curtindale, L. (2011). Varieties of attention in infancy. In L. M. Oakes, C. H. Cashon, M. Casasola, & D. Rakison (Eds.), *Infant perception and cognition* (3–25). New York: Oxford University Press.

Colombo, J., Shaddy, D. J., Richman, W. A., Maikranz, J. M., & Blaga, O. M. (2004). The developmental course of habituation in infancy and preschool outcome. *Infancy, 5,* 1–38.

Colson, E. R., Rybin, D. R., Smith, L. A., Colton, T., Lister, G., & Corwin, M. J. (2009). Trends and factors associated with infant sleeping position: The National Infant Sleep Position Study, 1993–2007. *Archives of Pediatric and Adolescent Medicine, 163,* 1122–1128.

Colson, E. R., Willinger, M., Rybin, D., Heeren, T., Smith, L. A., Lister, G., et al. (2013). Trends and factors associated with infant bed sharing, 1993–2010. The National Infant Sleep Position Study. *JAMA Pediatrics, 167,* 1032–1037.

Coltrane, S. (1996). *Family man.* New York: Oxford University Press.

Comeau, L., Genessee, F., & Mendelson, M. (2012). A comparison of bilingual and monolingual children's conversational repairs. *First Language, 30,* 354–374.

Commission on Children at Risk. (2008). Hardwired to connect: The new scientific case for authoritative communities. In K. K. Kline (Ed.), *Authoritative communities: The scientific case for nurturing the whole child* (pp. 3–68). New York: Springer.

Common Core. (2010). *Common Core state standards for English language arts & literacy in history/social science, and technical subjects.* Retrieved from www.corestandards.org/ELA-Literacy

Common Sense Media. (2013). *Zero to eight: Children's media use in America 2013.* San Francisco, CA: Author. Retrieved from www.commonsensemedia.org/research/zero-to-eight-childrens-media-use-in-america-2013

Compas, B. E., Jaser, S. S., Dunn, M. J., & Rodriguez, E. M. (2012). Coping with chronic illness in childhood and adolescence. *Annual Review of Clinical Psychology, 8,* 455–480.

Comstock, G., & Scharrer, E. (2006). Media and popular culture. In K. A. Renninger & I. E. Sigel (Eds.), *Handbook of child psychology: Vol. 4. Child psychology in practice* (6th ed., pp. 817–863). Hoboken, NJ: Wiley.

Conde-Agudelo, A., Belizan, J. M., & Diaz-Rossello, J. (2011). Kangaroo mother care to reduce morbidity and mortality in low birthweight infants. *Cochrane Database of Systematic Reviews, Issue 3*(Art. No. CD002771).

Condron, D. J. (2013). Affluence, inequality, and educational achievement: A structural analysis of 97 jurisdictions, across the globe. *Sociological Spectrum, 33,* 73–97.

Conger, R. D., & Donnellan, M. B. (2007). An interactionist perspective on the socioeconomic context of human development. *Annual Review of Psychology, 58,* 175–199.

Conner, D. B., & Cross, D. R. (2003). Longitudinal analysis of the presence, efficacy, and stability of maternal scaffolding during informal problem-solving interactions. *British Journal of Developmental Psychology, 21,* 315–334.

Connor, J. M. (2003). Physical activity and well-being. In M. H. Bornstein, L. Davidson, C. L. M. Keyes, K. A. Moore, & the Center for Child Well-Being (Eds.), *Well-being: Positive development across the life course* (pp. 65–79). Mahwah, NJ: Erlbaum.

Cook, C. R., Williams, K. R., Guerra, N. G., & Kim, T. E. (2010). Variability in the prevalence of bullying and victimization: A cross-national and methodological analysis. In S. R. Jimerson, S. M. Swearer, & D. L. Espelage (Eds.), *Handbook of bullying in schools: An international perspective* (pp. 347–362). New York: Routledge.

Cookston, J. T., Braver, S. L., Griffin, W. A., De Lusé, S. R., & Miles, J. C. (2006). Effects of the Dads for Life intervention on interparental conflict and coparenting in the two years after divorce. *Family Process, 46,* 123–137.

Cooper, H., Batts, A., Patall, E. A., & Dent, A. L. (2010). Effects of full-day kindergarten on academic achievement and social development. *Review of Educational Research, 80,* 54–70.

Cooper, R., & Huh, C. R. (2008). Improving academic possibilities of students of color during the middle school to high school transition: Conceptual and strategic considerations in a U.S. context. In J. K. Asamen, M. L. Ellis, & G. L. Berry (Eds.), *Sage handbook of child development, multiculturalism, and media* (pp. 143–162). Thousand Oaks, CA: Sage.

Coplan, R. J., & Arbeau, K. A. (2008). The stresses of a "brave new world": Shyness and school adjustment in kindergarten. *Journal of Research in Childhood Education, 22,* 377–389.

Coplan, R. J., & Armer, M. (2007). A "multitude" of solitude: A closer look at social withdrawal and nonsocial play in early childhood. *Child Development Perspectives, 1,* 26–32.

Coplan, R. J., Gavinsky-Molina, M. H., Lagace-Seguin, D., & Wichmann, C. (2001). When girls versus boys play alone: Nonsocial play and adjustment in kindergarten. *Developmental Psychology, 37,* 464–474.

Coplan, R. J., & Ooi, L. (2014). The causes and consequences of "playing alone" in childhood. In R. J. Coplan & J. C. Bowker (Eds.), *The handbook of solitude: Psychological perspectives on social isolation, social withdrawal, and being alone* (pp. 111–128). Chichester, UK: Wiley-Blackwell.

Coplan, R. J., Prakash, K., O'Neil, K., & Armer, M. (2004). Do you "want" to play? Distinguishing between conflicted shyness and social disinterest in early childhood. *Developmental Psychology, 40*, 244–258.

Copple, C., & Bredekamp, S. (2009). *Developmentally appropriate practice in early childhood programs* (3rd ed.). Washington, DC: National Association for the Education of Young Children.

Corapci, F., Radan, A. E., & Lozoff, B. (2006). Iron deficiency in infancy and mother–child interaction at 5 years. *Journal of Developmental and Behavioral Pediatrics, 27*, 371–378.

Corenblum, B. (2003). What children remember about ingroup and outgroup peers: Effects of stereotypes on children's processing of information about group members. *Journal of Experimental Child Psychology, 86*, 32–66.

Cornwell, A. C., & Feigenbaum, P. (2006). Sleep biological rhythms in normal infants and those at high risk for SIDS. *Chronobiology International, 23*, 935–961.

Correa-Chavez, M., Roberts, A. L. D., & Perez, M. M. (2011). Cultural patterns in children's learning through keen observation and participation in their communities. In J. B. Benson (Ed.), *Advances in child development and behavior* (Vol. 40, pp. 209–241). San Diego, CA: Elsevier Academic Press.

Costa, A., & Sebastián-Gallés, N. (2014). How does the bilingual experience sculpt the brain? *Nature Reviews Neuroscience, 15*, 336–345.

Costacurta, M., Sicuro, L., Di Renzo, L., & Condo, R. (2012). Childhood obesity and skeletal-dental maturity. *European Journal of Paediatric Dentistry, 13*, 128–132.

Côté, S. M., Petitclerc, A., Raynault, M.-F., Falissard, B., Boivin, M., & Tremblay, R. E. (2010). Short- and long-term risk of infections as a function of group child care attendance: An 8-year population-based study. *Archives of Pediatric and Adolescent Medicine, 164*, 1132–1137.

Côté, S. M., Vaillancourt, T., Barker, E. D., Nagin, D., & Tremblay, R. E. (2007). The joint development of physical and indirect aggression: Predictors of continuity and change during childhood. *Development and Psychopathology, 19*, 37–55.

Coubart, A., Izard, V., Spelke, E. S., Marie, J., & Streri, A. (2014). Dissociation between small and large numerosities in newborn infants. *Developmental Science, 17*, 11–22.

Coulton, C. J., Crampton, D. S., Irwin, M., Spilsbury, J. C., & Korbin, J. E. (2007). How neighborhoods influence child maltreatment: A review of the literature and alternative pathways. *Child Abuse and Neglect, 31*, 1117–1142.

Courage, M. L., & Howe, M. L. (1998). The ebb and flow of infant attentional preferences: Evidence for longterm recognition memory in 3-month-olds. *Journal of Experimental Child Psychology, 18*, 98–106.

Courage, M. L., & Howe, M. L. (2010). To watch or not to watch: Infants and toddlers in a brave new electronic world. *Developmental Review, 30*, 101–115.

Courchesne, E., Mouton, P. R., Calhoun, M. E., Semendeferi, K., Ahrens-Barbeau, C., Hallet, M. J., et al. (2011). Neuron number and size in prefrontal cortex of children with autism. *Journal of the American Medical Association, 306*, 2001–2010.

Cowan, C. P., & Cowan, P. A. (1997). Working with couples during stressful transitions. In S. Dreman (Ed.), *The family on the threshold of the 21st century* (pp. 17–47). Mahwah, NJ: Erlbaum.

Cowan, N., & Alloway, T. (2009). Development of working memory in childhood. In M. L. Courage & N. Cowan (Eds.), *Development of memory in infancy and childhood* (pp. 303–342). Hove, UK: Psychology Press.

Cowan, N., Morey, C. C., AuBuchon, A. M., Zwilling, C. E., Gilchrist, A. L., & Saults, J. S. (2011). New insights into an old problem: Distinguishing storage from processing in the development of working memory. In P. Barrouillet & V. Gaillard (Eds.), *Cognitive development and working memory* (pp. 137–150). Hove, UK: Psychology Press.

Cox, S. M., Hopkins, J., & Hans, S. L. (2000). Attachment in preterm infants and their mothers: Neonatal risk status and maternal representations. *Infant Mental Health Journal, 21*, 464–480.

Coyl, D. D., Newland, L. A., & Freeman, H. (2010). Predicting preschoolers' attachment security from parenting behaviours, parents' attachment relationships and their use of social support. *Early Child Development and Care, 180*, 499–512.

Coyle, T. R. (2013). Effects of processing speed on intelligence may be underestimated: Comment on Demetriou et al. (2013). *Intelligence, 41*, 732–734.

Coyne, S. M., Robinson, S. L., & Nelson, D. A. (2010). Does reality backbite? Verbal and relational aggression in reality television programs. *Journal of Broadcasting and Electronic Media, 54*, 282–298.

Crago, M. B., Annahatak, B., & Ningiuruvik, L. (1993). Changing patterns of language socialization in Inuit homes. *Anthropology and Education Quarterly, 24*, 205–223.

Craig, C. M., & Lee, D. N. (1999). Neonatal control of sucking pressure: Evidence for an intrinsic τ-guide. *Experimental Brain Research, 124*, 371–382.

Craig, H. K., & Washington, J. A. (2006). *Malik goes to school: Examining the language skills of African American students from preschool–5th grade.* Mahwah, NJ: Erlbaum.

Craig, W. M., Pepler, D., & Atlas, R. (2000). Observations of bullying in the playground and in the classroom. *School Psychology International, 21*, 22–36.

Crain, W. (2010). *Theories of development: Concepts and applications* (6th ed.). Upper Saddle River, NJ: Pearson.

Crair, M. C., Gillespie, D. C., & Stryker, M. P. (1998). The role of visual experience in the development of columns in the cat visual cortex. *Science, 279*, 566–570.

Cratty, B. J. (1986). *Perceptual and motor development in infants and children* (3rd ed.). Englewood Cliffs, NJ: Prentice-Hall.

Creasey, G. L., Jarvis, P. A., & Berk, L. E. (1998). Play and social competence. In O. N. Saracho & B. Spodek (Eds.), *Multiple perspectives on play in early childhood education* (pp. 116–143). Albany: State University of New York Press.

Crick, N. R., & Dodge, K. A. (1994). A review and reformulation of social information-processing mechanisms in children's social adjustment. *Psychological Bulletin, 115*, 74–101.

Crick, N. R., Ostrov, J. M., Burr, J. E., Cullerton-Sen, C., Jansen-Yeh, E., & Ralston, P. (2006). A longitudinal study of relational and physical aggression in preschool. *Journal of Applied Developmental Psychology, 27*, 254–268.

Crick, N. R., Ostrov, J. M., & Werner, N. E. (2006). A longitudinal study of relational aggression, physical aggression, and social-psychological adjustment. *Journal of Abnormal Child Psychology, 34*, 131–142.

Crockenberg. S. C., & Leerkes, E. M. (2003). Parental acceptance, postpartum depression, and maternal sensitivity: Mediating and moderating processes. *Journal of Family Psychology, 17*, 80–93.

Crockenberg, S. C., & Leerkes, E. M. (2004). Infant and maternal behaviors regulate infant reactivity to novelty at 6 months. *Developmental Psychology, 40*, 1123–1132.

Crookston, B. T., Schott, W., Cueto, S., Dearden, K. A., Engle, P., Georgiadis, A., et al. (2013). Postinfancy growth, schooling, and cognitive achievement: Young lives. *American Journal of Clinical Nutrition, 98*, 1555–1563.

Crosby, B., LeBourgeois, M. K., & Harsh, J. (2005). Racial differences in reported napping and nocturnal sleep in 2- to 8-year-old children. *Pediatrics, 115*, 225–232.

Crouch, J. L., Skowronski, J. J., Milner, J. S., & Harris, B. (2008). Parental responses to infant crying: The influence of child physical abuse risk and hostile priming. *Child Abuse and Neglect, 32*, 702–710.

Crouter, A. C., Whiteman, S. D., McHale, S. M., & Osgood, D. W. (2007). Development of gender attitude traditionality across middle childhood and adolescence. *Child Development, 78*, 911–926.

Cryer, D., Tietze, W., & Wessels, H. (2002). Parents' perceptions of their children's child care: A cross-national comparison. *Early Childhood Research Quarterly, 17*, 259–277.

Csibra, G. (2010). Recognizing communicative intentions in infancy. *Mind and Language, 25*, 141–168.

Csibra, G., & Gergely, G. (2011). Natural pedagogy as evolutionary adaptation. *Philosophical Transactions of the Royal Society B, 366*, 1149–1157.

Cummings, E. M., & Davies, P. T. (2010). *Children, emotional security and marital conflict.* New York: Guilford.

Cummings, E. M., Goeke-Morey, M. C., & Papp, L. M. (2004). Everyday marital conflict and child aggression. *Journal of Abnormal Child Psychology, 32*, 191–202.

Curby, T. W., LoCasale-Crouch, J., Konold, T. R., Pianta, R. C., Howes, C., Burchinal, M., et al. (2009). The relations of observed pre-K classroom quality profiles to children's achievement and social competence. *Early Education and Development, 20*, 346–372.

Curran, M., Hazen, N., Jacobvitz, D., & Feldman, A. (2005). Representations of early family relationships predict marital maintenance during the transition to parenthood. *Journal of Family Psychology, 19*, 189–197.

Curtin, S., & Werker, J. F. (2007). The perceptual foundations of phonological development. In G. Gaskell (Ed.), *Oxford handbook of psycholinguistics* (pp. 579–599). Oxford, UK: Oxford University Press.

Curtin, S. C., Ventura, S. J., & Martinez, G. M. (2014). Recent declines in nonmarital childbearing in the United States. *NCHS data brief, no. 162.* Hyattsville, MD: National Center for Health Statistics. Retrieved from www.cdc.gov/nchs/data/databriefs/db162.pdf

Curtiss, S., & Schaeffer, J. (2005). Syntactic development in children with hemispherectomy: The I-, D-, and C-systems. *Brain and Language, 94*, 147–166.

Cutuli, J. J., Herbers, J. E., Rinaldi, M., Masten, A. S., & Oberg, C. N. (2010). Asthma and behavior in homeless 4- to 7-year-olds. *Pediatrics, 125*, e145-e151.

Cvencek, D., Meltzoff, A. N., & Greenwald, A. G. (2011). Math–gender stereotypes in elementary school children. *Child Development, 82*, 766–779.

Cyr, C., Euser, E. M., Bakermans-Kranenburg, M. J., & van IJzendoorn, M. H. (2010). Attachment security and disorganization in maltreating and high-risk families: Implications for developmental theory. *Development and Psychopathology, 14*, 843–860.

D

Dabrowska, E. (2000). From formula to schema: The acquisition of English questions. *Cognitive Linguistics, 11*, 1–20.

Dakil, S. R., Cox, M., Lin, H., & Flores, G. (2012). Physical abuse in U.S. children: Risk factors and deficiencies in referrals to support services. *Journal of Aggression, Maltreatment, and Trauma, 21*, 555–569.

Daley, T. C., Whaley, S. E., Sigman, M. D., Espinosa, M. P., & Neumann, C. (2003). IQ on the rise: The Flynn effect in rural Kenyan children. *Psychological Science, 14*, 215–219.

Dallman, M. F., Pecoraro, N., Akana, S. F., la Fleur, S. E., Gomez, F., Houshyar, H., et al. (2003). Chronic stress and obesity: A new view of "comfort food." *Proceedings of the National Academy of Sciences, 100*, 11696–11701.

Damon, W. (1988). *The moral child.* New York: Free Press.

Damon, W., & Hart, D. (1988). *Self-understanding in childhood and adolescence.* New York: Cambridge University Press.

Daniels, E., & Leaper, C. (2006). A longitudinal investigation of sport participation, peer acceptance, and self-esteem among adolescent girls and boys. *Sex Roles, 55*, 875–880.

Daniels, H. (2011). Vygotsky and psychology. In U. Goswami (Ed.), *The Wiley-Blackwell handbook of childhood cognitive development* (2nd ed., pp. 673-696). Malden, MA: Wiley-Blackwell.

Dannemiller, J. L., & Stephens, B. R. (1988). A critical test of infant pattern preference models. *Child Development, 59*, 210–216.

Danzer, E., & Johnson, M. P. (2014). Fetal surgery for neural tube defects. *Seminars in Fetal and Neonatal Medicine, 19*, 2–8.

Darling, N., & Steinberg, L. (1997). Community influences on adolescent achievement and deviance. In J. Brooks-Gunn, G. Duncan, & L. Aber (Eds.), *Neighborhood poverty: Context and consequences for children: Conceptual, ethological, and policy approaches to studying neighborhoods* (Vol. 2, pp. 120–131). New York: Russell Sage Foundation.

Darling-Hammond, L. (2010). *The flat world and education: How America's commitment to equity will determine our future.* New York: Teachers College Press.

Darwin, C. (2003). *The origin of species: 150th anniversary edition.* New York: Signet Classics. (Original work published 1859)

Das, D. A., Grimmer, D. A., Sparnon, A. L., McRae, S. E., & Thomas, B. H. (2005). The efficacy of playing a virtual reality game in modulating pain for children with acute burn injuries: A randomized controlled trial. *BMC Pediatrics, 5*(1), 1–10.

Datar, A., & Sturm, R. (2006). Childhood overweight and elementary school outcomes. *International Journal of Obesity, 30,* 1449–1460.

Davies, J. (2008). Differential teacher positive and negative interactions with male and female pupils in the primary school setting. *Educational and Child Psychology, 25,* 17–26.

Davies, P. T., & Cichetti, D. (2014). How and why does the 5-HTTLPR gender moderate associations between maternal unresponsiveness and children's disruptive problems? *Child Development, 85,* 484–500.

Davis, A. S., & Escobar, L. F. (2013). Early childhood disorders: Down syndrome. In A. S. Davis (Ed.), *Psychopathology of childhood and adolescence: A neuropsychological approach* (pp. 569–580). New York: Springer.

Davis, E. L., & Buss, K. A. (2012). Moderators of the relation between shyness and behavior with peers: Cortisol dysregulation and maternal emotion socialization. *Social Development, 21,* 801–820.

Davis, E. L., Levine, L. J., Lench, H. C., & Quas, J. A. (2010). Metacognitive emotion regulation: Children's awareness that changing thoughts and goals can alleviate negative emotions. *Emotion, 10,* 498–510.

Davis, K. F., Parker, K. P., & Montgomery, G. L. (2004). Sleep in infants and young children. Part 1: Normal sleep. *Journal of Pediatric Health Care, 18,* 65–71.

Dawley, K., Loch, J., & Bindrich, I. (2007). The Nurse–Family Partnership. *American Journal of Nursing, 107,* 60–67.

Dawson, C., & Gerken, L. A. (2009). From domain-generality to domain-sensitivity: 4-month-olds learn an abstract repetition rule in music that 7-month-olds do not. *Cognition, 111,* 378–382.

Deák, G. O., Ray, S. D., & Brenneman, K. (2003). Children's perseverative appearance–reality errors are related to emerging language skills. *Child Development, 74,* 944–964.

Deák, G. O., Yen, L., & Pettit, J. (2001). By any other name: When will preschoolers produce several labels for a reference? *Journal of Child Language, 28,* 787–804.

Dearing, E., McCartney, K., & Taylor, B. A. (2009). Does higher quality early child care promote low-income children's math and reading achievement in middle childhood? *Child Development, 80,* 1329–1349.

Dearing, E., Wimer, C., Simpkins, S. D., Lund, T., Bouffard, S. M., Caronongan, P., & Kreider, H. (2009). Do neighborhood and home contexts help explain why low-income children miss opportunities to participate in activities outside of school? *Developmental Psychology, 45,* 1545–1562.

Deary, I. J., Strand, S., Smith, P., & Fernandes, C. (2007). Intelligence and educational achievement. *Intelligence, 35,* 13–21.

Deater-Deckard, K., Lansford, J. E., Dodge, K. A., Pettit, G. S., & Bates, J. E. (2003). The development of attitudes about physical punishment: An 8-year longitudinal study. *Journal of Family Psychology, 17,* 351–360.

Debes, F., Budtz-Jorgensen, E., Weihe, P., White, R. F., & Grandjean, P. (2006). Impact of prenatal methylmercury exposure on neurobehavioral function at age 14 years. *Neurotoxicology and Teratology, 28,* 363–375.

DeBoer, T., Scott, L. S., & Nelson, C. A. (2007). Methods for acquiring and analyzing infant event-related potentials. In M. de Haan (Ed.), *Infant EEG and event-related potentials* (pp. 5–37). New York: Psychology Press.

Debrabant, J., Gheysen, F., Vingerhoets, G., & Van Waelvelde, H. (2012). Age-related differences in predictive response timing in children: Evidence from regularly relative to irregularly paced reaction time performance. *Human Movement Science, 31,* 801–810.

de Bruyn, E. H., & Cillessen, A. H. N. (2006). Popularity in early adolescence: Prosocial and antisocial subtypes. *Journal of Adolescent Research, 21,* 607–627.

DeCasper, A. J., & Spence, M. J. (1986). Prenatal maternal speech influences newborns' perception of speech sounds. *Infant Behavior and Development, 9,* 133–150.

De Corte, E., & Verschaffel, L. (2006). Mathematical thinking and learning. In K. A. Renninger & I. E. Sigel (Eds.), *Handbook of child psychology: Vol. 4. Child psychology in practice* (6th ed., pp. 103–152). Hoboken, NJ: Wiley.

de Haan, M., & Gunnar, M. R. (2009). The brain in a social environment: Why study development? In M. de Haan & M. R. Gunnar (Eds.), *Handbook of developmental social neuroscience* (pp. 3–12). New York: Guilford.

de Haan, M., & Matheson, A. (2009). The development and neural bases of processing emotion in faces and voices. In M. de Haan & M. R. Gunnar (Eds.), *Handbook of developmental social science* (pp. 107–121). New York: Guilford.

de Jong, E., Visscher, T. L. S., HiraSing, R. A., Heymans, M. W., Seidell, J. C., & Renders, C. M. (2013). Association between TV viewing, computer use and overweight, determinants and competing activities of screen time in 4- to 13-year-old children. *International Journal of Obesity, 37,* 47–53.

De Laet, S. Doumen, S., Vervoort, E., Colpin, H., Van Leeuwen, K., Goossens, L., & Verschueren, K. (2014). Transactional links between teacher–child relationship quality and perceived versus sociometric popularity: A three-wave longitudinal study. *Child Development, 85,* 1647–1662.

Delahunty, K. M., McKay, D. W., Noseworthy, D. E., & Storey, A. E. (2007). Prolactin responses to infant cues in men and women: Effects of parental experience and recent infant contact. *Hormones and Behavior, 51,* 213–220.

De Lisi, R., & Gallagher, A. M. (1991). Understanding gender stability and constancy in Argentinean children. *Merrill-Palmer Quarterly, 37,* 483–502.

DeLoache, J. S. (1987). Rapid change in symbolic functioning of very young children. *Science, 238,* 1556–1557.

DeLoache, J. S. (2002). The symbol-mindedness of young children. In W. Hartup & R. A. Weinberg (Eds.), *Minnesota symposia on child psychology* (Vol. 32, pp. 73–101). Mahwah, NJ: Erlbaum.

DeLoache, J. S., Chiong, C., Sherman, K., Islam, N., Vanderborght, M., Troseth, G. L., et al. (2010). Do babies learn from baby media? *Psychological Science, 21,* 1570–1574.

DeLoache, J. S., & Ganea, P. A. (2009). Symbol-based learning in infancy. In A. Woodward & A. Needham (Eds.), *Learning and the infant mind* (pp. 263–285). New York: Oxford University Press.

DeLoache, J. S., Uttal, D., & Rosengren, K. (2004). Scale errors offer evidence for a perception–action dissociation early in life. *Science, 304,* 1027–1029.

Deltondo, J., Por, I., Hu, W., Merchenthaler, I., Semeniken, K., Jojart, J., & Dudas, B. (2008). Associations between the human growth hormone-releasing hormone and neuropeptide-Y-immunoreactive systems in the human diencephalons: A possible morphological substrate of the impact of stress on growth. *Neuroscience, 153,* 1146–1152.

DeMarie, D., & Lopez, L. M. (2014). Memory in schools. In P. J. Bauer & R. Fivush (Eds.), *Wiley handbook on the development of children's memory* (Vol. 2, pp. 836–864). Malden, MA: Wiley-Blackwell.

DeMarie, D., Miller, P. H., Ferron, J., & Cunningham, W. R. (2004). Path analysis tests of theoretical models of children's memory performance. *Journal of Cognition and Development, 5,* 461–492.

DeNavas-Walt, C., Proctor, B. D., & Smith, J. C. (2011). Income, poverty, and health insurance coverage in the United States: 2010. *U.S. Census Bureau, Current Population Reports,* P60–P239. Washington, DC: U.S. Government Printing Office.

Denham, S. (1998). *Emotional development in young children.* New York: Guilford.

Denham, S., Warren, H., von Salisch, M., Benga, O., Chin, J., & Geangu, E. (2011). Emotions and social development in childhood. In P. K. Smith & C. H. Hart (Eds.). *Wiley-Blackwell handbook of childhood social development* (2nd ed., pp. 413–433). Chichester, UK: Wiley-Blackwell.

Denissen, J. J. A., Zarrett, N. R., & Eccles, J. S. (2007). I like to do it, I'm able, and I know I am: Longitudinal couplings between domain-specific achievement, self-concept, and interest. *Child Development, 78,* 430–447.

Dennis, W. (1960). Causes of retardation among institutionalized children: Iran. *Journal of Genetic Psychology, 96,* 47–59.

Deprest, J. A., Devlieger, R., Srisupundit, K., Beck, V., Sandaite, I., Rusconi, S., et al. (2010). Fetal surgery is a clinical reality. *Seminars in Fetal & Neonatal Medicine, 15,* 58–67.

Der, G., Batty, G. D., & Deary, I. J. (2006). Effect of breastfeeding on intelligence in children: Prospective study, sibling pairs analysis, and meta-analysis. *British Medical Journal, 333,* 945.

DeRoche, K., & Welsh, M. (2008). Twenty-five years of research on neurocognitive outcomes in early-treated phenylketonuria: Intelligence and executive function. *Developmental Neuropsychology, 33,* 474–504.

Derom, C., Thiery, E., Vlietinck, R., Loos, R., & Derom, R. (1996). Handedness in twins according to zygosity and chorion type: A preliminary report. *Behavior Genetics, 26,* 407–408.

DeRose, L. M., & Brooks-Gunn, J. (2006). Transition into adolescence: The role of pubertal processes. In L. Balter & C. S. Tamis-LeMonda (Eds.), *Child psychology: A handbook of contemporary issues* (2nd ed., pp. 385–414). New York: Psychology Press.

DeRosier, M. E. (2007). Peer-rejected and bullied children: A safe schools initiative for elementary school students. In J. E. Zins, M. J. Elias, & C. A. Maher (Eds.), *Bullying, victimization, and peer harassment* (pp. 257–276). New York: Haworth.

de Rosnay, M., Copper, P. J., Tsigaras, N., & Murray, L. (2006). Transmission of social anxiety from mother to infant: An experimental study using a social referencing paradigm. *Behavior Research and Therapy, 44,* 1165–1175.

de Rosnay, M., & Hughes, C. (2006). Conversation and theory of mind: Do children talk their way to socio-cognitive understanding? *British Journal of Developmental Psychology, 24,* 7–37.

De Schipper, J. C., Tavecchio, L. W. C., van IJzendoorn, M. H., & van Zeijl, J. (2004). Goodness-of-fit in center day care: Relations of temperament, stability, and quality of care with the child's adjustment. *Early Childhood Research Quarterly, 19,* 257–272.

De Schipper, J. C., van IJzendoorn, M. H., & Tavecchio, L. W. C. (2004). Stability in center day care: Relations with children's well-being and problem behavior in day care. *Social Development, 13,* 531–550.

De Souza, E., Alberman, E., & Morris, J. K. (2009). Down syndrome and paternal age, a new analysis of case-control data collected in the 1960s. *American Journal of Medical Genetics, 149A,* 1205–1208.

Dessel, A. (2010). Prejudice in schools: Promotion of an inclusive culture and climate. *Education and Urban Society, 42,* 407–429.

Deutsch, F. M., Ruble, D. N., Fleming, A., Brooks-Gunn, J., & Stangor, C. (1988). Information-seeking and maternal self-definition during the transition to motherhood. *Journal of Personality and Social Psychology, 55,* 420–431.

Deutsch, W., & Pechmann, T. (1982). Social interaction and the development of definite descriptions. *Cognition, 11,* 159–184.

Devi, N. P. G., Shenbagvalli, R., Ramesh, K., & Rathinam, S. N. (2009). Rapid progression of HIV infection in infancy. *Indian Pediatrics, 46,* 53–56.

de Villiers, J. G., & de Villiers, P. A. (2000). Linguistic determinism and the understanding of false beliefs. In P. Mitchell & K. J. Riggs (Eds.), *Children's reasoning and the mind* (pp. 87–99). Hove, UK: Psychology Press.

Devlin, A. M., Brain, U., Austin, J., & Oberlander, T. F. (2010). Prenatal exposure to maternal depressed mood and the MTHFR C677T variant affect SLC6A4 methlation in infants at birth. *PLOS ONE, 5,* e12201.

DeVries, R. (2001). Constructivist education in preschool and elementary school: The sociomoral atmosphere as the first educational goal. In S. L. Golbeck (Ed.), *Psychological perspectives on early childhood education* (pp. 153–180). Mahwah, NJ: Erlbaum.

de Waal, F. B. M. (1993). Sex differences in chimpanzee (and human) behavior: A matter of social values? In M. Hechter, L. Nadel, & R. E. Michod (Eds.), *The origin of values* (pp. 285–303). New York: Aldine de Gruyter.

de Waal, F. B. M. (2001). *Tree of origin.* Cambridge, MA: Harvard University Press.

de Weerd, A. W., & van den Bossche, A. S. (2003). The development of sleep during the first months of life. *Sleep Medicine Reviews, 7,* 179–191.

De Wolff, M. S., & van IJzendoorn, M. H. (1997). Sensitivity and attachment: A meta-analysis on parental antecedents of infant attachment. *Child Development, 68,* 571–591.

Deynoot-Schaub, M. J. G., & Riksen-Walraven, J. M. (2006a). Peer contacts of 15-month-olds in childcare: Links with child temperament, parent—child interaction and quality of childcare. *Social Development 15*, 709–729.

Deynoot-Schaub, M. J. G., & Riksen-Walraven, J. M. (2006b). Peer interaction in child care centres at 15 and 23 months: Stability and links with children's socioemotional adjustment. *Infant Behavior and Development, 29*, 276–288.

Diamond, A. (2009). The interplay of biology and the environment broadly defined. *Developmental Psychology, 45*, 1–8.

Diamond, A., Cruttenden, L., & Neiderman, D. (1994). AB with multiple wells: 1. Why are multiple wells sometimes easier than two wells? 2. Memory or memory + inhibition. *Developmental Psychology, 30*, 192–205.

Diav-Citrin, O. (2011). Prenatal exposures associated with neurodevelopmental delay and disabilities. *Developmental Disabilities, 17*, 71–84.

Dickinson, D. K., Golinkoff, R. M., & Hirsh-Pasek, K. (2010). Speaking out for language: Why language is central to reading development. *Educational Researcher, 39*, 305–310.

Dickinson, D. K., & McCabe, A. (2001). Bringing it all together: The multiple origins, skills, and environmental supports of early literacy. *Learning Disabilities Research and Practice, 16*, 186–202.

Dickinson, D. K., McCabe, A., Anastasopoulos, L., Peisner-Feinberg, E. S., & Poe, M. D. (2003). The comprehensive language approach to early literacy: The interrelationships among vocabulary, phonological sensitivity, and print knowledge among preschool-age children. *Journal of Educational Psychology, 95*, 465–481.

Dick-Read, G. (1959). *Childbirth without fear*. New York: Harper & Brothers.

DiDonato, M. D., & Berenbaum, S. A. (2011). The benefits and drawbacks of gender typing: How different dimensions are related to psychological adjustment. *Archives of Sexual Behavior, 40*, 457–463.

Diener, M. L., Isabella, R., Behunin, M. G., & Wong, M. S. (2008). Attachment to mothers and fathers during middle childhood: Associations with child gender, grade, and competence. *Social Development, 17*, 84–101.

Dietrich, K. N., Ware, J. H., Salganik, M., Radcliffe, J., Rogan, W. J., & Rhoads, G. C. (2004). Effect of chelation therapy on the neuropsychological and behavioral development of lead-exposed children after school entry. *Pediatrics, 114*, 19–26.

Dildy, G. A., Jackson, G. M., Fowers, G. K., Oshiro, B. T., Varner, M. W., & Clark, S. L. (1996). Very advanced maternal age: Pregnancy after age 45. *American Journal of Obstetrics and Gynecology, 175*, 668–674.

DiPietro, J. A., Bornstein, M. H., Costigan, K. A., Pressman, E. K., Hahn, C.-S., & Painter, K. (2002). What does fetal movement predict about behavior during the first two years of life? *Developmental Psychobiology, 40*, 358–371.

DiPietro, J. A., Hodgson, D. M., Costigan, K. A., & Hilton, S. C. (1996). Fetal neurobehavioral development. *Child Development, 67*, 2553–2567.

DiPietro, J. A., Novak, M. F. S. X., Costigan, K. A., Atella, L. D., & Reusing, S. P. (2006). Maternal psychological distress during pregnancy in relation to child development at age two. *Child Development, 77*, 573–587.

Dishion, T. J., Shaw, D., Connell, A., Gardner, F., Weaver, C., & Wilson, M. (2008). The family checkup with high-risk indigent families: Preventing problem behavior by increasing parents' positive behavior support in early childhood. *Child Development, 79*, 1395–1414.

Dittmar, M., Abbot-Smith, K., Lieven, E., & Tomasello, M. (2014). Familiar verbs are not always easier than novel verbs: How German preschool children comprehend active and passive sentences. *Cognitive Science, 38*, 128–151.

Dix, T., Stewart, A. D., Gershoff, E. T., & Day, W. H. (2007). Autonomy and children's reactions to being controlled: Evidence that both compliance and defiance may be positive markers in early development. *Child Development, 78*, 1204–1221.

Dixon, P. (2009). Marriage among African Americans: What does the research reveal? *Journal of African American Studies, 13*, 29–46.

Dodd, V. L. (2005). Implications of kangaroo care for growth and development in preterm infants. *JOGNN, 34*, 218–232.

Dodge, K. A., Coie, J. D., & Lynam, D. (2006). Aggression and antisocial behavior in youth. In N. Eisenberg (Ed.), *Handbook of child psychology: Vol. 3. Social, emotional, and personality development* (6th ed., pp. 719–788). Hoboken, NJ: Wiley.

Dodge, K. A., Lochman, J. E., Harnish, J. D., Bates, J. E., & Pettit, G. S. (1997). Reactive and proactive aggression in school children and psychiatrically impaired chronically assaultive youth. *Journal of Abnormal Psychology, 106*, 37–51.

Dodge, K. A., McLoyd, V. C., & Lansford, J. E. (2006). The cultural context of physically disciplining children. In V. C. McLoyd, N. E. Hill, & K. A. Dodge (Eds.), *African-American family life: Ecological and cultural diversity* (pp. 245–263). New York: Guilford.

Dodge, K. A., Pettit, G. S., McClaskey, C. L., & Brown, M. M. (1986). Social competence in children. *Monographs of the Society for Research in Child Development, 51*(2, Serial No. 213).

Dohnt, H., & Tiggemann, M. (2006). The contribution of peer and media influences to the development of body satisfaction and self-esteem in young girls: A prospective study. *Developmental Psychology, 42*, 929–936.

Domellöf, E., Johansson, A., & Rönnqvist, L. (2011). Handedness in preterm born children: A systematic review and meta-analysis. *Neuropsychologia, 49*, 2299–2310.

Domitrovich, C. E., Cortes, R. C., & Greenberg, M. T. (2007). Improving young children's social and emotional competence: A randomized trial of the preschool "PATHS" curriculum. *The Journal of Primary Prevention, 28*, 67–91.

Domitrovich, C. E., Gest, S. D., Gill, S., Bierman, K. L., Welsh, J. A., & Jones, D. (2009). Fostering high-quality teaching with an enriched curriculum and professional development support: The Head Start REDI program. *American Educational Research Journal, 46*, 567–597.

Donaldson, M., & Jones, J. (2013). Optimising outcome in congenital hypothyroidism: Current opinions on best practice in initial assessment and subsequent management. *Journal of Clinical Research in Pediatric Endocrinology, 5*(Suppl. 12), 13–22.

Dondi, M., Simion, F., & Caltran, G. (1999). Can newborns discriminate between their own cry and the cry of another newborn infant? *Developmental Psychology, 35*, 418–426.

Donnellan, M. B., Trzesniewski, K. H., Robins, R. W., Moffitt, T. E., & Caspi, A. (2005). Low self-esteem is related to aggression, antisocial behavior, and delinquency. *Psychological Science, 16*, 328–335.

Donnelly, J. E., Greene, J. L., Gibson, C. A., Smith, B. K., Washburn, R. A., Sullivan, D. K., DuBose, K., et al. (2009). Physical activity across the curriculum (PAAC): A randomized controlled trial to promote physical activity and diminish overweight and obesity in elementary school children. *Preventive Medicine, 49*, 336–341.

Dorris, M. (1989). *The broken cord*. New York: Harper & Row.

Dorwie, F. M., & Pacquiao, D. F. (2014). Practices of traditional birth attendants in Sierra Leone and perceptions by mothers and health professionals familiar with their care. *Journal of Transcultural Nursing, 25*, 33–41.

Doss, B. D., Rhoades, G. K., Stanley, S. M., & Markman, H. J. (2009). The effect of the transition to parenthood on relationship quality: An 8-year prospective study. *Journal of Personality and Social Psychology, 96*, 601–619.

dos Santos Silva, I., De Stavola, B. L., Hardy, R. J., Kuh, D. J., McCormack, V. A., & Wadsworth, M. E. J. (2004). Is the association of birth weight with premenopausal breast cancer risk mediated through childhood growth? *British Journal of Cancer, 91*, 519–524.

Double, E. B., Mabuchi, K., Cullings, H. M., Preston, D. L., Kodama, K., Shimizu, Y., et al. (2011). Long-term radiation-related health effects in a unique human population: Lessons learned from the atomic bomb survivors of Hiroshima and Nagasaki. *Disaster Medicine and Public Health Preparedness, 5*(Suppl. 1), S122–S133.

Douglas, E. M. (2006). *Mending broken families: Social policies for divorced families*. Lanham, MD: Rowman & Littlefield.

Dowker, A. (2003). Younger children's estimates for addition: The zone of partial knowledge and understanding. In A. J. Baroody & A. Dowker (Eds.), *The development of arithmetic concepts and skills: Constructing adaptive expertise* (pp. 243–265). Mahwah, NJ: Erlbaum.

Downe, S., Finlayson, K., Walsh, D., & Lavender, T. (2009). "Weighing up and balancing out": A meta-synthesis of barriers to antenatal care for marginalized women in high-income countries. *BJOG, 116*, 518–529.

Downing, J. E. (2010). *Academic instruction for students with moderate and severe intellectual disabilities*. Thousand Oaks, CA: Corwin.

Dozier, M., Stovall, K. C., Albus, K. E., & Bates, B. (2001). Attachment for infants in foster care: The role of caregiver state of mind. *Child Development, 72*, 1467–1477.

Drake, K., Belsky, J., & Fearon, R. M. P. (2014). From early attachment to engagement with learning in school: The role of self-regulation and persistence. *Developmental Psychology, 50*, 1350–1361.

Driscoll, M. C. (2007). Sickle cell disease. *Pediatrics in Review, 28*, 259–268.

Driver, J., Tabares, A., Shapiro, A. F., & Gottman, J. M. (2012). Couple interaction in happy and unhappy marriages: Gottman Laboratory studies. In F. Walsh (Ed.), *Normal family processes: Growing diversity and complexity* (pp. 57–77). New York: Guilford.

Druet, C., Stettler, N., Sharp, S., Simmons, R. K., Cooper, C., Smith, G. D., et al. (2012). Prediction of childhood obesity by infancy weight gain: An individual-level meta-analysis. *Paediatric and Perinatal Epidemiology, 26*, 19–26.

DuBois, D. L., Felner, R. D., Brand, S., & George, G. R. (1999). Profiles of self-esteem in early adolescence: Identification and investigation of adaptive correlates. *American Journal of Community Psychology, 27*, 899–932.

Duckworth, A. L., Quinn, P. D., & Tsukayama, E. (2012). What No Child Left Behind leaves behind: The roles of IQ and self-control in predicting standardized achievement test scores and report card grades. *Journal of Educational Psychology, 104*, 439–451.

Dudani, A., Macpherson, A., & Tamim, H. (2010). Childhood behavior problems and unintentional injury: A longitudinal, population-based study. *Journal of Developmental and Behavioral Pediatrics, 31*, 276–285.

Dueker, G. L., Modi, A., & Needham, A. (2003). 4.5-month-old infants' learning, retention and use of object boundary information. *Infant Behavior and Development, 26*, 588–605.

Duggan, A., McFarlane, E., Fuddy, L., Burrell, L., Higman, S. M., Windham, A., & Sia, C. (2004). Randomized trial of a statewide home visiting program: Impact in preventing child abuse and neglect. *Child Abuse and Neglect, 28*, 597–622.

Duncan, G. J., & Magnuson, K. A. (2003). Off with Hollingshead: Socioeconomic resources, parenting, and child development. In M. H. Bornstein & R. H. Bradley (Eds.), *Socioeconomic status, parenting, and child development* (pp. 83–106). Mahwah, NJ: Erlbaum.

Duncan, G. J., Dowsett, C. J., Claessens, A., Magnuson, K., Huston, A. C., Klebanov, P., et al. (2007). School readiness and later achievement. *Developmental Psychology, 43*, 1428–1446.

Duncan, L. E., Pollastri, A. R., & Smoller, J. W. (2014). Mind the gap: Why many geneticists and psychological scientists have discrepant views about gene–environment interaction (GXE) research. *American Psychologist, 69*, 249–268.

Duncan, S. R., Paterson, D. S., Hoffman, J. M., Mokler, D. J., et al. (2010). Brainstem serotonergic deficiency in sudden infant death syndrome. *Journal of the American Medical Association, 303*, 430–437.

Dundek, L. H. (2006) Establishment of a Somali doula program at a large metropolitan hospital. *Journal of Perinatal and Neonatal Nursing, 20*, 128–137.

Dunham, Y., Baron, A. S., & Banaji, M. R. (2006). From American city to Japanese village: A cross-cultural investigation of implicit race attitudes. *Child Development, 77*, 1129–1520.

Dunham, Y., Chen, E. E., & Banaji, M. R. (2013). Two signatures of implicit intergroup attitudes: Developmental invariance and early enculturation. *Psychological Science, 24*, 860–868.

Dunifon, R., Kalil, A., & Danziger, S. K. (2003). Maternal work behavior under welfare reform: How does the transition from welfare to work affect child development? *Children and Youth Services Review, 25*, 55–82.

Dunkel-Schetter, C. (2011). Psychological science on pregnancy: Stress processes, biopsychosocial models, and emerging research issues. *Annual Review of Psychology, 62*, 531–558.

Dunkel-Shetter, C., & Lobel, M. (2012). Pregnancy and birth: A multilevel analysis of stress and birth weight. In

T. A. Revenson, A. Baum, & J., Singer (Eds.), *Handbook of Health Psychology* (2nd ed., pp. 431–463). London: Psychology Press.

Dunn, J. (1989). Siblings and the development of social understanding in early childhood. In P. G. Zukow (Ed.), *Sibling interaction across cultures* (pp. 106–116). New York: Springer-Verlag.

Dunn, J. (1994). Temperament, siblings, and the development of relationships. In W. B. Carey & S. C. McDevitt (Eds.), *Prevention and early intervention* (pp. 50–58). New York: Brunner/Mazel.

Dunn, J. (2002). The adjustment of children in stepfamilies: Lessons from community studies. *Child and Adolescent Mental Health, 7,* 154–161.

Dunn, J. (2004). Sibling relationships. In P. K. Smith & C. H. Hart (Eds.), *Handbook of childhood social development* (pp. 223–237). Malden, MA: Blackwell.

Dunn, J. (2005). Moral development in early childhood and social interaction in the family. In M. Killen & J. G. Smetana (Eds.), *Handbook of moral development* (pp. 331–350). Mahwah, NJ: Erlbaum.

Dunn, J., Cheng, H., O'Connor, T. G., & Bridges, L. (2004). Children's perspectives on their relationships with their nonresident fathers: Influences, outcomes and implications. *Journal of Child Psychology and Psychiatry, 45,* 553–566.

Durkin, M. S., Laraque, D., Lubman, I., & Barlow, B. (1999). Epidemiology and prevention of traffic injuries to urban children and adolescents. *Pediatrics, 103,* e74.

Durlak, J. A., Weissberg, R. P., Dymnicki, A. B., Taylor, R. D., & Schellinger, K. B. (2011). The impact of enhancing students' social and emotional learning: A meta-analysis of school-based universal interventions. *Child Development, 82,* 405–432.

Durlak, J. A., Weissberg, R. P., & Pachan, M. (2010). A meta-analysis of after-school programs that seek to promote personal and social skills in children and adolescents. *American Journal of Community Psychology, 45,* 294–309.

Durston, S., & Casey, B. J. (2006). What have we learned about cognitive development from neuroimaging? *Neuropsychologia, 44,* 2149–2157.

Duszak, R. S. (2009). Congenital rubella syndrome—major review. *Optometry, 80,* 36–43.

Dweck, C. S. (2002). Messages that motivate: How praise molds students' beliefs, motivation, and performance (in surprising ways). In J. Aronson (Ed.), *Improving academic achievement: Impact of psychological factors on education* (pp. 37–60). San Diego, CA: Academic Press.

Dweck, C. S. (2009). Prejudice: How it develops and how it can be undone. *Human Development, 52,* 371–376.

Dweck, C. S., & Molden, D. C. (2013). Self-theories: Their impact on competence motivation and acquisition. In A. J. Elliott & C. J. Dweck (Eds.), *Handbook of confidence and motivation* (pp. 122–140). New York: Guilford.

Dynarski, M., James-Burdumy, S., Moore, M., Rosenberg, L., Deke, J., & Mansfield, W. (2004). *When schools stay open late: The national evaluation of the 21st Century Community Learning Centers Program: New findings.* Washington DC: U.S. Department of Education.

Dyrdal, G. M., & Lucas, R. E. (2013). Reaction and adaptation to the birth of a child: A couple-level analysis. *Developmental Psychology, 49,* 749–761.

Dzurova, D., & Pikhart, H. (2005). Down syndrome, paternal age and education: Comparison of California and the Czech Republic. *BMC Public Health, 5,* 69.

E

Ebeling, K. S., & Gelman, S. A. (1994). Children's use of context in interpreting "big" and "little." *Child Development, 65,* 1178–1192.

Eccles, J. S., Jacobs, J., & Harold, R. D. (1990). Gender-role stereotypes, expectancy effects, and parents' role in the socialization of gender differences in self-perceptions and skill acquisition. *Journal of Social Issues, 46,* 183–201.

Eckerman, C. O., & Peterman, K. (2001). Peers and infant social/communicative development. In G. Bremner & A. Fogel (Eds.), *Blackwell handbook of infant development* (pp. 326–350). Malden, MA: Blackwell.

Eder, R. A., & Mangelsdorf, S. C. (1997). The emotional basis of early personality development: Implications for the emergent self-concept. In R. Hogan, J. Johnson, & S. Briggs (Eds.), *Handbook of personality psychology* (pp. 209–240). San Diego, CA: Academic Press.

Edwards, O. W., & Oakland, T. D. (2006). Factorial invariance of Woodcock-Johnson III scores for African Americans and Caucasian Americans. *Journal of Psychoeducational Assessment, 24,* 358–366.

Egeland, B., Jacobvitz, D., & Sroufe, L. A. (1988). Breaking the cycle of abuse. *Child Development, 59,* 1080–1088.

Ehri, L. C., & Roberts, T. (2006). The roots of learning to read and write: Acquisition of letters and phonemic awareness. In D. K. Dickinson & S. B. Neuman (Eds.), *Handbook of early literacy research* (Vol. 2, pp. 113–131). New York: Guilford.

Eichstedt, J. A., Serbin, L. A., Poulin-Dubois, D., & Sen, M. G. (2002). Of bears and men: Infants' knowledge of conventional and metaphorical gender stereotypes. *Infant Behavior and Development, 25,* 296–310.

Einspieler, C., Marschik, P. B., & Prechtl, H. F. R. (2008). Human motor behavior: Prenatal origin and early postnatal development. *Zeitschrift für Psychologie, 216,* 147–153.

Eisbach, A. O. (2004). Children's developing awareness of diversity in people's trains of thought. *Child Development, 75,* 1694–1707.

Eisenberg, N. (2003). Prosocial behavior, empathy, and sympathy. In M. H. Bornstein & L. Davidson (Eds.), *Well-being: Positive development across the life course* (pp. 253–265). Mahwah, NJ: Erlbaum.

Eisenberg, N. (2006). Emotion-related regulation. In H. E. Fitzgerald, B. M. Lester., & B. Zuckerman (Eds.), *The crisis in youth mental health: Critical issues and effective programs, Vol. 1: Childhood disorders* (pp. 133–155). Westport, CT: Praeger.

Eisenberg, N. (2010). Empathy-related responding: Links with self-regulation, moral judgment, and moral behavior. In M. Mikulincer & P. R. Shaver (Eds.), *Prosocial motives, emotions, and behavior: The better angels of our nature* (pp. 129–148). Washington, DC: American Psychological Association.

Eisenberg, N., Eggum, N. D., & Edwards, A. (2010). Empathy-related responding and moral development. In W. F. Arsenio & E. A. Lemerise (Eds.), *Emotions, aggression, and morality in children: Bridging development and psychopathology* (pp. 115–135). Washington, DC: American Psychological Association.

Eisenberg, N., Fabes, R. A., Shepard, S. A., Murphy, B. C., Jones, S., & Guthrie, I. K. (1998). Contemporaneous and longitudinal prediction of children's sympathy from dispositional regulation and emotionality. *Developmental Psychology, 34,* 910–924.

Eisenberg, N., Fabes, R. A., & Spinrad, T. L. (2006). Prosocial development. In N. Eisenberg (Ed.), *Handbook of child psychology: Vol. 3. Social, emotional, and personality development* (6th ed., pp. 646–718). Hoboken, NJ: Wiley.

Eisenberg, N., & Silver, R. C. (2011). Growing up in the shadow of terrorism. *American Psychologist, 66,* 468–481.

Eisenberg, N., Smith, C. L., & Spinrad, T. L. (2011). Effortful control: Relations with emotion regulation, adjustment, and socialization in childhood. In K. D. Vohs & R. F. Baumeister (Eds.), *Handbook of self-regulation: Research, theory, and applications* (2nd ed., pp. 263–283). New York: Guilford.

Eisenberg, N., Spinrad, T., Fabes, R., Reiser, M., Cumberland, A., & Shepard, S. (2004). The relations of effortful control and impulsivity to children's resiliency and adjustment. *Child Development, 75,* 25–46.

Eisenberg, N., Spinrad, T. L., & Morris, A. S. (2013). Prosocial Development. In P. D. Zelazo (Ed.), *Oxford handbook of developmental psychology, Vol. 2: Self and other* (pp. 300–325). New York: Oxford University Press.

Eivers, A. R., Brendgen, M., Vitaro, F., & Borge, A. I. H. (2012). Concurrent and longitudinal links between children's and their friends' antisocial and prosocial behavior in preschool. *Early Childhood Research Quarterly, 27,* 137–146.

Ekéus, C., Christensson, K., & Hjern, A. (2003). Unintentional and violent injuries among preschool children of teenage mothers in Sweden: A national cohort study. *Journal of Epidemiology and Community Health, 58,* 680–685.

Ekéus, C., Högberg, U., & Norman, M. (2014). Vacuum assisted birth and risk for cerebral complications in term newborn infants: A population-based cohort study. *BMC Pregnancy and Childbirth, 14,* 36.

Ekman, P., & Friesen, W. (1972). Constants across culture in the face and emotion. *Journal of Personality and Social Psychology, 17,* 124–129.

Ekman, P., & Matsumoto, D. (2011). Reading faces: The universality of emotional expression. In M. A. Gernsbacher, R W. Pew, L. M. Hough, & J. R. Pomerantz (Eds.), *Psychology and the real world: Essays illustrating fundamental contributions to society* (pp. 140–146). New York: Worth.

Elias, M. J., Parker, S., & Rosenblatt, J. L. (2005). Building educational opportunity. In S. Goldstein & R. B. Brooks (Eds.), *Handbook of resilience in children* (pp. 315–336). New York: Kluwer Academic.

Elicker, J., Englund, M., & Sroufe, L. A. (1992). Predicting peer competence and peer relationships in childhood from early parent–child relationships. In R. D. Parke & G. W. Ladd (Eds.), *Family–peer relationships: Modes of linkage* (pp. 77–106). Hillsdale, NJ: Erlbaum.

Elliott, J. G. (1999). School refusal: Issues of conceptualization, assessment, and treatment. *Journal of Child Psychology and Psychiatry and Allied Disciplines, 40,* 1001–1012.

Ellis, A. E., & Oakes, L. M. (2006). Infants flexibly use different dimensions to categorize objects. *Developmental Psychology, 42,* 1000–1011.

Ellis, W. E., & Zarbatany, L. (2007). Explaining friendship formation and friendship stability: The role of children's and friends' aggression and victimization. *Merrill-Palmer Quarterly, 53,* 79–104.

Else-Quest, N. M. (2012). Gender differences in temperament. In M. Zentner & R. L. Shiner (Eds.), *Handbook of temperament* (pp. 479–496). New York: Guilford.

Else-Quest, N. M., Hyde, J. S., Goldsmith, H. H., & Van Hulle, C. A. (2006). Gender differences in temperament: A meta-analysis. *Psychological Bulletin, 132,* 33–72.

El-Sheikh, M., Bub, K. L.,Kelly, R. J., & Buckhalt, J. A. (2013). Children's sleep and adjustment: A residualized change analysis. *Developmental Psychology, 49,* 1591–1601.

El-Sheikh, M., Cummings, E. M., & Reiter, S. (1996). Preschoolers' responses to ongoing interadult conflict: The role of prior exposure to resolved versus unresolved arguments. *Journal of Abnormal Child Psychology, 24,* 665–679.

El-Sheikh, M., Kelly, R. J., Buckhalt, J. A., & Hinnant, B. (2010). Children's sleep and adjustment over time: The role of socioeconomic context. *Child Development, 81,* 870–883.

Eltzschig, H. K., Lieberman, E. S., & Camann, W. R. (2003). Regional anesthesia and analgesia for labor and delivery. *New England Journal of Medicine, 384,* 319–332.

Eluvathingal, T. J., Chugani, H. T., Behen, M. E., Juhasz, C., Muzik, O., Maqbook, M., et al. (2006). Abnormal brain connectivity in children after early severe socioemotional deprivation: A diffusion tensor imaging study. *Pediatrics, 117,* 2093–2100.

Emery, R. E., Sbarra, D., & Grover, T. (2005). Divorce mediation: Research and reflections. *Family Court Review, 43,* 22–37.

Ennemoser, M., & Schneider, W. (2007). Relations of television viewing and reading: Findings from a 4-year longitudinal study. *Journal of Educational Psychology, 99,* 349–368.

Entringer, S., Kumsta, R., Hellhammer, D. H., Wadhwa, P. D., & Wüst, S. (2009). Prenatal exposure to maternal psychosocial stress and HPA axis regulation in young adults. *Hormones and Behavior, 55,* 292–298.

Epstein, L. H., Roemmich, J. N., & Raynor, H. A. (2001). Behavioral therapy in the treatment of pediatric obesity. *Pediatric Clinics of North America, 48,* 981–983.

Epstein, L. H., Saelens, B. E., Myers, M. D., & Vito, D. (1997). Effects of decreasing sedentary behaviors on activity choice in obese children. *Health Psychology, 16,* 107–113.

Erath, S. A., Bierman, K. L., & the Conduct Problems Prevention Research Group. (2006). Aggressive marital conflict, maternal harsh punishment, and child aggressive-disruptive behavior: Evidence for direct and mediate relations. *Journal of Family Psychology, 20,* 217–226.

Erickson, J. D., Patterson, J. M., Wall, M., & Neumark-Sztainer, D. (2005). Risk behaviors and emotional well-being in youth with chronic health conditions. *Children's Health Care, 34,* 181–192.

Erikson, E. H. (1950). *Childhood and society.* New York: Norton.

Ernst, M., Moolchan, E. T., & Robinson, M. L. (2001). Behavioral and neural consequences of prenatal exposure to nicotine. *Journal of the American Academy of Child and Adolescent Psychiatry, 40,* 630–641.

Espy, K. A., Fang, H., Johnson, C., Stopp, C., & Wiebe, S. A. (2011). Prenatal tobacco exposure: Developmental outcomes in the neonatal period. *Developmental Psychology, 47,* 153–156.

Espy, K. A., Molfese, V. J., & DiLalla, L. F. (2001). Effects of environmental measures on intelligence in young children: Growth curve modeling of longitudinal data. *Merrill-Palmer Quarterly, 47,* 42–73.

Estourgie-van Burk, G. F., Bartels, M., van Beijsterveldt, T. C., Delemarre-van de Waal, H. A., & Boomsma, D. I. (2006). Body size in five-year-old twins: Heritability and comparison to singleton standards. *Twin Research and Human Genetics, 9,* 646–655.

Evanoo, G. (2007). Infant crying: A clinical conundrum. *Journal of Pediatric Health Care, 21,* 333–338.

Evans, G. W. (2003). A multimethodological analysis of cumulative risk and allostatic load among rural children. *Developmental Psychology, 39,* 924–933.

Evans, G. W. (2006). Child development and the physical environment. *Annual Review of Psychology, 57,* 424–451.

Evans, G. W., Fuller-Rowell, T. E., & Doan, S. N. (2012). Childhood cumulative risk and obesity: The mediating role of self-regulatory ability. *Pediatrics, 129,* e68–e73.

Evans, G. W., Gonnella, C., Marcynyszn, L. A. Gentile, L., & Slapekar, N. (2005). The role of chaos in poverty and children's socioemotional adjustment. *Psychological Science, 16,* 560–565.

Evans, G. W., & Schamberg, M. A. (2009). Childhood poverty, chronic stress, and adult working memory. *Proceedings of the National Academy of Sciences, 106,* 6545–6549.

Evans, N., & Levinson, S. C. (2009). The myth of language universals: Language diversity and its importance for cognitive science. *Behavioral and Brain Sciences, 32,* 429–492.

Eyler, L. T., Pierce, K., & Courchesne, E. (2012). A failure of left temporal cortex to specialize for language is an early emerging and fundamental property of autism. *Brain, 135,* 949–960.

F

Fabes, R. A., Eisenberg, N., Hanish, L. D., & Spinrad, T. L. (2001). Preschoolers' spontaneous emotion vocabulary: Relations to likability. *Early Education and Development, 12,* 11–27.

Fabes, R. A., Eisenberg, N., McCormick, S. E., & Wilson, M. S. (1988). Preschoolers' attributions of the situational determinants of others' naturally occurring emotions. *Developmental Psychology, 24,* 376–385.

Fabes, R. A., Martin, C. L., & Hanish, L. D. (2003). Young children's play qualities in same-, other-, and mixed-sex peer groups. *Child Development, 74,* 921–932.

Fagan, J. F., III., & Holland, C. R. (2007). Racial equality in intelligence: Predictions from a theory of intelligence as processing. *Intelligence, 35,* 319–334.

Fagan, J. F., III., Holland, C. R., & Wheeler, K. (2007). The prediction, from infancy, of adult IQ and achievement. *Intelligence, 35,* 225–231.

Fagan, J. F., III. (1973). Infants' delayed recognition memory and forgetting. *Journal of Experimental Child Psychology, 16,* 424–450.

Fagard, J., & Pezé, A. (1997). Age changes in interlimb coupling and the development of bimanual coordination. *Journal of Motor Behavior, 29,* 199–208.

Fagard, J., Spelke, E., & von Hofsten, C. (2009). Reaching and grasping a moving object in 6-, 8-, and 10-month-old infants: Laterality and performance. *Infant Behavior and Development, 32,* 137–146.

Fagot, B. I. (1985). Changes in thinking about early sex role development. *Developmental Review, 5,* 83–98.

Fagot, B. I., & Hagan, R. I. (1991). Observations of parent reactions to sex-stereotyped behaviors: Age and sex effects. *Child Development, 62,* 617–628.

Fahrmeier, E. D. (1978). The development of concrete operations among the Hausa. *Journal of Cross-Cultural Psychology, 9,* 23–44.

Falagas, M. E., & Zarkadoulia, E. (2008). Factors associated with suboptimal compliance to vaccinations in children in developed countries: A systematic review. *Current Medical Research and Opinion, 24,* 1719–1741.

Falbo, T. (2012). Only children: An updated review. *Journal of Individual Psychology, 68,* 38–49.

Falbo, T., Poston, D. L., Jr., Triscari, R. S., & Zhang, X. (1997). Self-enhancing illusions among Chinese schoolchildren. *Journal of Cross-Cultural Psychology, 28,* 172–191.

Falk, D. (2005). Brain lateralization in primates and its evolution in hominids. *American Journal of Physical Anthropology, 30,* 107–125.

Fantz, R. L. (1961, May). The origin of form perception. *Scientific American, 204*(5), 66–72.

Faraone, S. V., Biederman, J., & Mick, E. (2006). The age-dependent decline of attention deficit hyperactivity disorder: A meta-analysis of follow-up studies. *Psychological Medicine, 36,* 159–165.

Farmer, T. W., Irvin, M. J., Leung, M.-C., Hall, C. M., Hutchins, B. C., & McDonough, E. (2010). Social preference, social prominence, and group membership in late elementary school: Homophilic concentration and peer affiliation configurations. *Social Psychology of Education, 13,* 271–293.

Farr, R. H., Forssell, S. L., & Patterson, C. J. (2010). Parenting and child development in adoptive families: Does parental sexual orientation matter? *Applied Developmental Science, 14,* 164–178.

Farrant, K., & Reese, E. (2000). Maternal style and children's participation in reminiscing: Stepping stones in children's autobiographical memory development. *Journal of Cognition and Development, 1,* 193–225.

Farroni, T., Csibra, G., Simion, F., & Johnson, M. H. (2002). Eye contact detection in humans from birth. *Proceedings of the National Academy of Sciences, 99,* 9602–9605.

Farroni, T., Massaccesi, S., Menon, E., & Johnson, M. H. (2007). Direct gaze modulates face recognition in young infants. *Cognition, 102,* 396–404.

Farver, J. M., & Branstetter, W. H. (1994). Preschoolers' prosocial responses to their peers' distress. *Developmental Psychology, 30,* 334–341.

Fearon, R. P., Bakermans-Kranenburg, M. J., Lapsley, A., & Roisman, G. I. (2010). The significance of insecure attachment and disorganization in the development of children's externalizing behavior: A meta-analystic study. *Child Development, 81,* 435–456.

Federal Interagency Forum on Child and Family Statistics. (2013). *America's children: Key national indicators of well-being.* Retrieved from www.childstats.gov/pdf/ac2013/ac_13.pdf

Feeney, J. A., Hohaus, L., Noller, P., & Alexander, R. P. (2001). *Becoming parents: Exploring the bonds between mothers, fathers, and their infants.* New York: Cambridge University Press.

Feldman, R. (2003). Infant–mother and infant–father synchrony: The coregulation of positive arousal. *Infant Mental Health Journal, 24,* 1–23.

Feldman, R. (2006). From biological rhythms to social rhythms: Physiological precursors of mother–infant synchrony. *Developmental Psychology, 42,* 175–188.

Feldman, R. (2007a). Maternal–infant contact and child development: Insights from the kangaroo intervention. In L. L'Abate (Ed.), *Low-cost approaches to promote physical and mental health: Theory, research, and practice* (pp. 323–351). New York: Springer.

Feldman, R. (2007b). Maternal versus child risk and the development of parent–child and family relationships in five high-risk populations. *Development and Psychopathology, 19,* 293–312.

Feldman, R. (2007c). Parent–infant synchrony and the construction of shared timing: Physiological precursors, developmental outcomes, and risk conditions. *Journal of Child Psychology and Psychiatry, 48,* 329–354.

Feldman, R., Eidelman, A. I., & Rotenberg, N. (2004). Parenting stress, infant emotion regulation, maternal sensitivity, and the cognitive development of triplets: A model for parent and child influences in a unique ecology. *Child Development, 75,* 1774–1791.

Feldman, R., Gordon, I., Schneiderman, I., Weisman, O., & Zagoory-Sharon, O. (2010). Natural variations in maternal and paternal care are associated with systematic changes in oxytocin following parent–infant contact. *Psychoneuroendocrinology, 35,* 1133–1141.

Feldman, R., Granat, A., Pariente, C., Kanety, H., Kuint, J., & Gilboa-Schechtman, E. (2009). Maternal depression and anxiety across the postpartum year and infant social engagement, fear regulation, and stress reactivity. *Journal of the American Academy of Child and Adolescent Psychiatry, 48,* 919–927.

Feldman, R., & Klein, P. S. (2003). Toddlers' self-regulated compliance to mothers, caregivers, and fathers: Implications for theories of socialization. *Developmental Psychology, 39,* 680–692.

Feldman, R., Sussman, A. L., & Zigler, E. (2004). Parental leave and work adaptation at the transition to parenthood: Individual, marital, and social correlates. *Journal of Applied Developmental Psychology, 25,* 459–479.

Fenson, L., Dale, P. S., Reznick, J. S., Bates, E., Thal, D. J., & Pethick, S. J. (1994). Variability in early communicative development. *Monographs of the Society for Research in Child Development, 59*(5, Serial No. 242).

Ferguson, C. J. (2013). Spanking, corporal punishment and negative long-term outcomes: A meta-analytic review of longitudinal studies. *Clinical Psychology Review, 33,* 196–288.

Ferguson, T. J., Stegge, H., & Damhuis, I. (1991). Children's understanding of guilt and shame. *Child Development, 62,* 827–839.

Fernald, A., & Marchman, V. A. (2012). Individual differences in lexical processing at 18 months predict vocabulary growth in typically developing and late-talking toddlers. *Child Development, 82,* 203–222.

Fernald, A., Marchman, V. A., & Weisleder, A. (2013). SES differences in language processing skill and vocabulary are evident at 18 months. *Developmental Science, 16,* 234–248.

Fernald, A., & Morikawa, H. (1993). Common themes and cultural variations in Japanese and American mothers' speech to infants. *Child Development, 64,* 637–656.

Fernald, A., Perfors, A., & Marchman, V. A. (2006). Picking up speed in understanding: Speech processing efficiency and vocabulary growth across the 2nd year. *Developmental Psychology, 42,* 98–116.

Fernald, A., Taeschner, T., Dunn, J., Papousek, M, Boysson-Bardies, B., & Fukui, I. (1989). A cross-language study of prosodic modifications in mothers' and fathers' speech to preverbal infants. *Journal of Child Language, 16,* 477–502.

Fernald, L. C., & Grantham-McGregor, S. M. (1998). Stress response in school-age children who have been growth-retarded since early childhood. *American Journal of Clinical Nutrition, 68,* 691–698.

Fernyhough, C., & Fradley, E. (2005). Private speech on an executive task: Relations with task difficulty and task performance. *Cognitive Development, 20,* 103–120.

Ferrando, M., Prieto, M. D., Almeida, L. S., Ferándiz, C., Bermejo, R., López-Pina, J. A., et al. (2011). Trait emotional intelligence and academic performance: Controlling for the effects of IQ, personality, and self-concept. *Journal of Psychoeducational Assessment, 29,* 150–159.

Ferrari, P. F., & Coudé, G. (2011). Mirror neurons and imitation from a developmental and evolutionary perspective. In A. Vilain, C. Abry, J.-L. Schwartz, & J. Vauclair (Eds.), *Primate communication and human language* (pp. 121–138). Amsterdam, Netherlands: John Benjamins.

Ferrari, P. F., Tramacere, A., Simpson, E. A., & Iriki, A. (2013). Mirror neurons through the lens of epigenetics. *Trends in Cognitive Sciences, 17,* 450–457.

Ferrari, P. F., Visalberghi E., Paukner A., Fogassi L., Ruggiero A., Suomi, S. (2006). Neonatal imitation in rhesus macaques. *PLOS Biology, 4,* e302.

Ferry, A. L., Hespos, S. J., & Waxman, S. R. (2010). Categorization in 3- and 4-month-old infants: An advantage of words over tones. *Child Development, 81,* 472–479.

Ficca, G., Fagioli, I., Giganti, F., & Salzarulo, P. (1999). Spontaneous awakenings from sleep in the first year of life. *Early Human Development, 55,* 219–228.

Field, T. (2001). Massage therapy facilitates weight gain in preterm infants. *Current Directions in Psychological Science, 10,* 51–54.

Field, T. (2011). Prenatal depression effects on early development: A review. *Infant Behavior and Development, 34,* 1–14.

Field, T., Hernandez-Reif, M., & Freedman, J. (2004) Stimulation programs for preterm infants. *Social Policy Report of the Society for Research in Child Development, 18*(1).

Field, T. M. (1998). Massage therapy effects. *American Psychologist, 53,* 1270–1281.

Fiese, B. H., Foley, K. P., & Spagnola, M. (2006). Routine and ritual elements in family mealtimes: Contexts for child wellbeing and family identity. *New Directions for Child and Adolescent Development, 111,* 67–90.

Fiese, B. H., & Schwartz, M. (2008). Reclaiming the family table: Mealtimes and child health and well-being. *Social Policy Report of the Society for Research in Child Development, 22* (4), 3–18.

Fiese, B. H., & Winter, M. A. (2010). The dynamics of family chaos and its relation to children's socioemotional well-being. In G. W. Evans & T. D. Wachs (Eds.), *Chaos and its influence on children's development: An ecological perspective* (pp. 49–66). Washington, DC: American Psychological Association.

Fifer, W. P., Byrd, D. L., Kaku, M., Eigsti, I. M., Isler, J. R., Grose-Fifer, J., et al. (2010). Newborn infants learn during sleep. *Proceedings of the National Academy of Sciences, 107,* 10320–10323.

Findlay, L. C., & Coplan, R. J. (2008). Come out and play: Shyness in childhood and the benefits of organized sports participation. *Canadian Journal of Behavioural Science, 40,* 153–161.

Finger, B., Hans, S. L., Bernstein, V. J., & Cox, S. M. (2009). Parent relationship quality and infant–mother attachment. *Attachment and Human Development, 11,* 285–306.

Finkelhor, D. (2009). The prevention of childhood sexual abuse. *Future of Children, 19,* 169–194.

Finn, J. D., Gerber, S. B., & Boyd-Zaharias, J. (2005). Small classes in the early grades, academic achievement, and graduating from high school. *Journal of Educational Psychology, 97,* 214–233.

Finnilä, K., Mahlberga, N., Santtilia, P., & Niemib, P. (2003). Validity of a test of children's suggestibility for predicting responses to two interview situations differing in degree of suggestiveness. *Journal of Experimental Child Psychology, 85,* 32–49.

Fischer, K. W., & Bidell, T. (1991). Constraining nativisit inferences about cognitive capacities. In S. Carey & R. Gelman (Eds.), *The epigenesis of mind: Essays on biology and cognition* (pp. 199–235). Hillsdale, NJ: Erlbaum.

Fischer, K. W., & Bidell, T. R. (2006). Dynamic development of action and thought. In R. M. Lerner (Ed.), *Handbook of child psychology: Vol. 1. Theoretical models of human development* (6th ed., pp. 313–399). Hoboken, NJ: Wiley.

Fischman, M. G., Moore, J. B., & Steele, K. H. (1992). Children's one-hand catching as a function of age, gender, and ball location. *Research Quarterly for Exercise and Sport, 63,* 349–355.

Fish, M. (2004). Attachment in infancy and preschool in low socioeconomic status rural Appalachian children: Stability and change and relations to preschool and kindergarten competence. *Development and Psychopathology, 16,* 293–312.

Fisher, C. B. (1993, Winter). Integrating science and ethics in research with high-risk children and youth. *Social Policy Report of the Society for Research in Child Development, 4*(4).

Fisher, C. B., Hoagwood, K., Boyce, C., Duster, T., Frank, D. A., & Grisso, T. (2002). Research ethics for mental health science involving ethnic minority children and youths. *American Psychologist, 57,* 1024–1040.

Fisher, J. O., Mitchell, D. S., Smiciklas-Wright, H., & Birch, L. L. (2001). Maternal milk consumption predicts the tradeoff between milk and soft drinks in young girls' diets. *Journal of Nutrition, 131,* 246–250.

Fisher, J. O., Rolls, B. J., & Birch, L. L. (2003). Children's bite size and intake of an entrée are greater with large portions than with age-appropriate or self-selected portions. *American Journal of Clinical Nutrition, 77,* 1164–1170.

Fite, P. J., Stauffacher, K., Ostrov, J. M., & Colder, C. R. (2008). Replication and extension of Little et al.'s (2003) forms and functions of aggression measure. *International Journal of Behavioral Development, 32,* 238–242.

Fivush, R. (2001). Owning experience: Developing subjective perspective in autobiographical narratives. In C. Moore & K. Lemmon (Eds.), *The self in time: Developmental perspectives* (pp. 35–52). Mahwah, NJ: Erlbaum.

Fivush, R. (2009). Sociocultural perspectives on autobiographical memory. In M. L. Courage & N. Cowan (Eds.), *The development of memory in infancy and childhood* (pp. 283–301). Hove, UK: Psychology Press.

Fivush, R. (2011). The development of autobiographical memory. *Annual Review of Psychology, 62,* 559–582.

Fivush, R., & Haden, C. A. (2005). Parent–child reminiscing and the construction of a subjective self. In B. D. Homer & C. S. Tamis-LeMonda (Eds.), *The development of social cognition and communication* (pp. 315–336). Mahwah, NJ: Erlbaum.

Fivush, R., & Wang, Q. (2005). Emotion talk in mother–child conversations of the shared past: The effects of culture, gender, and event valence. *Journal of Cognition and Development, 6,* 489–506.

Flak, A. L., Su, S., Bertrand, J., Denny, C. H., Kesmodel, U. S., & Cogswell, M. E. (2014). The association of mild, moderate, and binge prenatal alcohol exposure and child neuropsychological outcomes: A meta-analysis. *Alcoholism: Clinical and Experimental Research, 38,* 214–226.

Flavell, J. H., Flavell, E. R., & Green, F. L. (2001). Development of children's understanding of connections between thinking and feeling. *Psychological Science, 12,* 430–432.

Flavell, J. H., Green, F. L., & Flavell, E. R. (1987). Development of knowledge about the appearance–reality distinction. *Monographs of the Society for Research in Child Development, 51*(1, Serial No. 212).

Flavell, J. H., Green, F. L., & Flavell, E. R. (1995). Young children's knowledge about thinking. *Monographs of the Society for Research in Child Development, 60*(1, Serial No. 243).

Flavell, J. H., Green, F. L., Flavell, E. R., & Grossman, J. B. (1997). The development of children's knowledge about inner speech. *Child Development, 68,* 39–47.

Fletcher, A. C., Nickerson, P., & Wright, K. L. (2003). Structured leisure activities in middle childhood: Links to well-being. *Journal of Community Psychology, 31,* 641–659.

Fletcher, E. N., Whitaker, R. C., Marino, A. J., & Anderson, S. E. (2014). Screen time at home and school among low-income children attending Head Start. *Child Indicators Research, 7,* 421–436.

Floccia, C., Christophe, A., & Bertoncini, J. (1997). High-amplitude sucking and newborns: The quest for underlying mechanisms. *Journal of Experimental Child Psychology, 64,* 175–198.

Flom, R. (2013). Intersensory perception of faces and voices in infants. In P. Belin, S. Campanella, & T. Ethofer (Eds.), *Integrating face and voice in person perception* (pp. 71–93). New York: Springer.

Flom, R., & Bahrick, L. E. (2007). The development of infant discrimination of affect in multimodal and unimodal stimulation: The role of intersensory redundancy. *Developmental Psychology, 43,* 238–252.

Flom, R., & Bahrick, L. E. (2010). The effects of intersensory redundancy on attention and memory: Infants' long-term memory for orientation in audiovisual events. *Developmental Psychology, 46,* 428–436.

Flom, R., & Pick, A. D. (2003). Verbal encouragement and joint attention in 18-month-old infants. *Infant Behavior and Development, 26,* 121–134.

Flynn, E., & Siegler, R. (2007). Measuring change: Current trends and future directions in microgenetic research. *Infant and Child Development, 16,* 135–149.

Flynn, J. R. (1999). Searching for justice: The discovery of IQ gains over time. *American Psychologist, 54,* 5–20.

Flynn, J. R. (2007). *What is intelligence? Beyond the Flynn effect.* New York: Cambridge University Press.

Flynn, J. R., & Rossi-Casé, L. (2011). Modern women match men on Raven's Progressive Matrices. *Personality and Individual Differences, 50,* 799–803.

Fogel, A., & Garvey, A. (2007). Alive communication. *Infant Behavior and Development, 30,* 251–257.

Fomon, S. J., & Nelson, S. E. (2002). Body composition of the male and female reference infants. *Annual Review of Nutrition, 22,* 1–17.

Fonnesbeck, C. J., McPheeters, M. L., Krishnaswami, S., Lindegren, M. L., & Reimschisel, T. (2013). Estimating the probability of IQ impairment from blood phenylalanine for phenylketonuria patients: A hierarchical meta-analysis. *Journal of Inherited Metabolic Disease, 36,* 757–766.

Forcada-Guex, M., Pierrehumbert, B., Borghini, A., Moessinger, A., & Muller-Nix, C. (2006). Early dyadic patterns of mother–infant interactions and outcomes of prematurity at 18 months. *Pediatrics, 118e,* 107–114.

Ford, D. Y. (2012). Gifted and talented education: History, issues, and recommendations. In K. R. Harris, S. Graham, T. Urdan, S. Graham, J. M. Royer, & M. Zeidner (Eds.), *APA educational psychology handbook: Vol. 2. Individual differences and cultural contextual factors* (pp. 83–110). Washington, DC: American Psychological Association.

Ford, L., Kozey, M. L., & Negreiros, J. (2012). Cognitive assessment in early childhood: Theoretical and practical perspectives. In D. P. Flanagan & P. L. Harrison (Eds.), *Contemporary intellectual assessment: Theories, tests, and issues* (pp. 585–622). New York: Guilford.

Fordham, K., & Stevenson-Hinde, J. (1999). Shyness, friendship quality, and adjustment during middle childhood. *Journal of Child Psychology and Psychiatry, 40,* 757–768.

Forman, D. R., Aksan, N., & Kochanska, G. (2004). Toddlers' responsive imitation predicts preschool-age conscience. *Psychological Science, 15,* 699–704.

Forman, D. R., O'Hara, M. W., Stuart, S., Gorman, L. L., Larsen, K. E., & Coy, K. C. (2007). Effective treatment for postpartum depression is not sufficient to improve the developing mother–child relationship. *Development and Psychopathology, 19,* 585–602.

Foster, W. A., & Miller, M. (2007). Development of the literacy achievement gap: A longitudinal study of kindergarten through third grade. *Language, Speech, and Hearing Services in Schools, 38,* 173–181.

Fox, C. L., & Boulton, M. J. (2006). Friendship as a moderator of the relationship between social skills problems and peer victimization. *Aggressive Behavior, 32,* 110–121.

Fox, N. A., & Davidson, R. J. (1986). Taste-elicited changes in facial signs of emotion and the asymmetry of brain electrical activity in newborn infants. *Neuropsychologia, 24,* 417–422.

Fox, N. A., Henderson, H. A., Pérez-Edgar, K., & White, L. K. (2008). The biology of temperament: An integrative approach. In C. A. Nelson & M. Luciana (Eds.), *Handbook of developmental cognitive neuroscience* (2nd ed., pp. 839–853). Cambridge, MA: MIT Press.

Fox, N. A., Nelson, C. A., III, & Zeanah, C. H. (2013). The effects of early severe psychosocial deprivation on children's cognitive and social development: Lessons from the Bucharest Early Intervention Project. In N. S. Landale, S. M. McHale, & A. Booth (Eds.), *Families and child health* (pp. 33–41). New York: Springer Science + Business Media.

Foy, J. G., & Mann, V. (2003). Home literacy environment and phonological awareness in preschool children: Differential effects for rhyme and phoneme awareness. *Applied Psycholinguistics, 24,* 59–88.

Fraiberg, S. (1971). *Insights from the blind.* New York: Basic Books.

Franchak, J. M., & Adolph, K. E. (2012). What infants know and what they do: Perceiving possibilities for walking through openings. *Developmental Psychology, 48,* 1254–1261.

Franco, P., Danias, A. P., Akamine, E. H., Kawamoto, E. M., Fortes, Z. B., Scavone, C., & Tostes, R. C. (2002). Enhanced oxidative stress as a potential mechanism underlying the programming of hypertension in utero. *Journal of Cardiovascular Pharmacology, 40,* 501–509.

Frank, J. B., Jarit, G. J., Bravman, J. T., & Rosen, J. E. (2007). Lower extremity injuries in the skeletally immature athlete. *Journal of the American Academy of Orthopaedic Surgeons, 15,* 356–366.

Franklin, V. P. (2012). "The teachers' unions strike back?" No need to wait for "Superman": Magnet schools have brought success to urban public school students for over 30 years. In D. T. Slaughter-Defoe, H. C. Stevenson, E. G. Arrington, & D. J. Johnson (Eds.), *Black educational choice: Assessing the private and public alternative to traditional K-12 public schools* (pp. 217–220). Santa Barbara, CA: Praeger.

Franks, P. W., Hanson, R. L., Knowler, W. C., Sievers, M. L., Bennett, P. H., & Looker, H. C. (2010). Childhood obesity, other cardiovascular risk factors, and premature death. *New England Journal of Medicine, 362,* 485–493.

Frazier, B. N., Gelman, S. A., & Wellman, H. M. (2009). Preschoolers' search for explanatory information within adult–child conversation. *Child Development, 80,* 1592–1611.

Fredricks, J. A., & Eccles, J. S. (2002). Children's competence and value beliefs from childhood through adolescence: Growth trajectories in two male-sex-typed domains. *Developmental Psychology, 38,* 519–533.

Freeman, H., & Newland, L. A. (2010). New directions in father attachment. *Early Child Development and Care, 180,* 1–8.

Freitag, C. M., Rohde, L. A., Lempp, T., & Romanos, M. (2010). Phenotypic and measurement influences on heritability estimates in childhood ADHD. *European Child and Adolescent Psychiatry, 19,* 311–323.

Frejka, T., Sobotka, T., Hoem, J. M., & Toulemon, L. (2008). Childbearing trends and policies in Europe. *Demographic Research, 19,* 5–14.

French, D. C., Chen, X., Chung, J., Li, M., Chen, H., & Li, D. (2011). Four children and one toy: Chinese and Canadian children faced with potential conflict over a limited resource. *Child Development, 82,* 830–841.

Freud, S. (1973). *An outline of psychoanalysis.* London: Hogarth. (Original work published 1938)

Friedlmeier, W., Corapci, F., & Cole, P. M. (2011). Socialization of emotions in cross-cultural perspective. *Social and Personality Psychology Compass, 5,* 410–427.

Fries, A. B. W., & Pollak, S. D. (2004). Emotion understanding in postinstitutionalized Eastern European children. *Development and Psychopathology, 16,* 355–369.

Fries, A. B. W., Ziegler, T. E., Kurian, J. R., Jacoris, S., & Pollak, S. D. (2005). Early experience in humans is associated with changes in neuropeptides critical for regulating social behavior. *Proceedings of the National Academy of Sciences, 102,* 17237–17240.

Frontline. (2012). *Poor kids.* Retrieved from www.pbs.org/wgbh/pages/frontline/poor-kids

Fry, D. P. (2014). Environment of evolutionary adaptedness, rough-and-tumble play, and the selection of restraint in human aggression. In D. Narvaez, K. Valentino, A. Fuentes, J. J. McKenna, & P. Gray (Eds.), *Ancestral landscapes in human evolution: Culture, childrearing and social wellbeing* (pp. 169–188). New York: Oxford University Press.

Fryer, S. L., Crocker, N. A., & Mattson, S. N. (2008). Exposure to teratogenic agents as a risk factor for psychopathology. In T. P. Beauchaine & S. P. Hinshaw (Eds.), *Child and adolescent psychopathology* (pp. 180–207). Hoboken, NJ: Wiley.

Fu, G., Xu, F., Cameron, C. A., Heyman, G., & Lee, K. (2007). Cross-cultural differences in children's choices, categorizations, and evaluations of truths and lies. *Developmental Psychology, 43,* 278–293.

Fulcher, M., Sutfin, E. L., & Patterson, C. J. (2008). Individual differences in gender development: Associations with parental sexual orientation, attitudes, and division of labor. *Sex Roles, 58,* 330–341.

Fuligni, A. J. (1998). Authority, autonomy, and parent–adolescent conflict and cohesion: A study of adolescents from Mexican, Chinese, Filipino, and European backgrounds. *Developmental Psychology, 34,* 782–792.

Fuligni, A. J. (2004). The adaptation and acculturation of children from immigrant families. In U. P. Gielen & J. Roopnarine (Eds.), *Childhood and adolescence: Cross-cultural perspectives* (pp. 297–318). Westport, CT: Praeger.

Fuligni, A. S., Han, W.-J., & Brooks-Gunn, J. (2004). The Infant–Toddler HOME in the 2nd and 3rd years of life. *Parenting: Science and Practice, 4,* 139–159.

Fuller, C., Keller, L., Olson, J., Plymale, A., & Gottesman, M. (2005). Helping preschoolers become healthy eaters. *Journal of Pediatric Health Care, 19,* 178–182.

Fuller-Thomson, E., & Minkler, M. (2005). Native American grandparents raising grandchildren: Findings from the Census 2000 Supplementary Survey and implications for social work practice. *Social Work, 50,* 131–139.

Fuller-Thomson, E., & Minkler, M. (2007). Mexican American grandparents raising grandchildren: Findings from the Census 2000 American Community Survey. *Families in Society, 88,* 567–574.

Fullerton, J. T., Navarro, A. M., & Young, S. H. (2007). Outcomes of planned home birth: An integrative review. *Journal of Midwifery and Women's Health, 52,* 323–333.

Furman, W., & Buhrmester, D. (1992). Age and sex differences in perceptions of networks of personal relationships. *Child Development, 63,* 103–115.

Furusawa, T., Naka, I., Yamauchi, T., Natsuhara, K., Kimura, R., Nakazawa, M., et al. (2010). The Q223r polymorphism in LEPR is associated with obesity in Pacific Islanders. *Human Genetics, 127,* 287–294.

Fushiki, S. (2013). Radiation hazards in children—lessons from Chernobyl, Three Mile Island and Fukushima. *Brain & Development, 35,* 220–227.

Fuson, K. C. (2009). Avoiding misinterpretations of Piaget and Vygotsky: Mathematical teaching without learning, learning without teaching, or helpful learning-path teaching? *Cognitive Development, 24,* 343–361.

Fuson, K. C., & Burghard, B. H. (2003). Multidigit addition and subtraction methods invented in small groups and teacher support of problem solving and reflection. In A. J. Baroody & A. Dowker (Eds.), *The development of arithmetic concepts and skills* (pp. 267–304). Mahwah, NJ: Erlbaum.

G

Gakidou, E., Cowling, K., Lozano, R., & Murray, C. J. L. (2010). Increased educational attainment and its effect on child mortality in 175 countries between 1970 and 2009: A systematic analysis. *Lancet, 376,* 959–974.

Galambos, S. J., & Maggs, J. L. (1991). Children in self-care: Figures, facts and fiction. In J. V. Lerner & N. L. Galambos (Eds.), *Employed mothers and their children* (pp. 131–157). New York: Garland.

Galbally, M., Lewis, J., van IJzendoorn, M., & Permezel, M. (2011). The role of oxytocin in mother–infant relations: A systematic review of human studies. *Harvard Review of Psychiatry, 19,* 1–14.

Galinsky, E., Aumann, K., & Bond, J. T. (2009). *Times are changing: Gender and generation at work and at home.* New York: Families and Work Institute.

Galland, B. C., Taylor, B. J., Elder, D. E., & Herbison, P. (2012). Normal sleep patterns in infants and children: A systematic review. *Sleep Medicine Reviews, 16,* 213–222.

Galler, J. R., Bryce, C. P., Waber, D. P., Hock, R. S., Harrison, R., Eaglesfield, G. D., et al. (2012). Infant malnutrition predicts conduct problems in adolescents. *Nutritional Neuroscience, 15,* 186–192.

Galler, J. R., Ramsey, C. F., Morley, D. S., Archer, E., & Salt, P. (1990). The long-term effects of early kwashiorkor compared with marasmus. IV. Performance on the National High School Entrance Examination. *Pediatric Research, 28,* 235–239.

Galloway, J. C., & Thelen, E. (2004). Feet first. Object exploration in young infants. *Infant Behavior and Development, 27,* 107–112.

Gallup. (2013). *Desire for children still norm in U.S.* Retrieved from www.gallup.com/poll/164618/desire-children-norm.aspx

Galvao, T. F., Thees, M. F., Pontes, R. F., Silva, M. T., & Pereira, M. G. (2013). Zinc supplementation for treating diarrhea in children: A systematic review and meta-analysis. *Pan American Journal of Public Health, 33,* 370–377.

Gambling, L., Kennedy, C., & McArdle, H. J. (2011). Iron and copper in fetal development. *Seminar in Cell Development Biology, 22,* 637–644.

Ganea, P. A., Allen, M. L., Butler, L., Carey, S., & DeLoache, J. S. (2009). Toddlers' referential understanding of pictures. *Journal of Experimental Child Psychology, 104,* 283–295.

Ganea, P. A., & Harris, P. A. (2010). Not doing what you are told: Early perseverative errors in updating mental representations via language. *Child Development, 81,* 457–463.

Ganea, P. A., Ma, L., & DeLoache, J. S. (2011). Young children's learning and transfer of biological information from picture books to real animals. *Child Development, 82,* 1421–1433.

Ganea, P. A., Shutts, K., Spelke, E., & DeLoache, J. S. (2007). Thinking of things unseen: Infants' use of language to update object representations. *Psychological Science, 8,* 734–739.

Ganger, J., & Brent, M. R. (2004). Reexamining the vocabulary spurt. *Developmental Psychology, 40,* 621–632.

Garcia, A. J., Koschnitzky, J. E., & Ramirez, J. M. (2013). The physiological determinants of sudden infant death syndrome. *Respiratory Physiology and Neurobiology, 189,* 288–300.

Garcia, M. M., Shaw, D. S., Winslow, E. B., & Yaggi, K. E. (2000). Destructive sibling conflict and the development of conduct problems in young boys. *Developmental Psychology, 36,* 44–53.

Garcia-Bournissen, F., Tsur, L., Goldstein, L. H., Staroselsky, A., Avner, M., & Asrar, F. (2008). Fetal exposure to isotretinoin—an international problem. *Reproductive Toxicology, 25,* 124–128.

García Coll, C., & Marks, A. K. (2009). *Immigrant stories: Ethnicity and academics in middle childhood.* New York: Basic Books.

Garde, J. B., Suryavanshi, R. K., Jawale, B. A., Deshmukh, V., Dadhe, D. P., & Suryavanshi, M. K. (2014). An epidemiological study to know the prevalence of deleterious oral habits among 6 to 12 year old children. *Journal of International Oral Health, 6,* 39–43.

Gardner, H. (1983). *Frames of mind: The theory of multiple intelligences.* New York: Basic Books.

Gardner, H. (1993). *Multiple intelligences: The theory in practice.* New York: Basic Books.

Gardner, H. (2000). *Intelligence reframed: Multiple intelligences for the twenty-first century.* New York: Basic Books.

Gardner, H. (2011). The theory of multiple intelligences. In M. A. Gernsbacher, R. W. Pew, L. M. Hough, & J. R. Pomerantz (Eds.), *Psychology and the real world: Essays illustrating fundamental contributions to society* (pp. 122–130). New York: Worth.

Gardner, M., & Sandberg, D. E. (2011). Growth hormone treatment for short stature: A review of psychosocial assumptions and empirical evidence. *Pediatric Endocrinology Reviews, 9,* 579–588.

Garner, P. W. (1996). The relations of emotional role taking, affective/moral attributions, and emotional display rule knowledge to low-income school-age children's social competence. *Journal of Applied Developmental Psychology, 17,* 19–36.

Garner, P. W. (2003). Child and family correlates of toddlers' emotional and behavioral responses to a mishap. *Infant Mental Health Journal, 24,* 580–596.

Garner, P. W., & Estep, K. (2001). Emotional competence, emotion socialization, and young children's peer-related social competence. *Early Education and Development, 12,* 29–48.

Gartrell, N. K., Bos, H. M. W., & Goldberg, N. G. (2011). Adolescents of the U.S. National Longitudinal Lesbian Family Study: Sexual orientation, sexual behavior, and sexual risk exposure. *Archives of Sexual Behavior, 40,* 1199–1209.

Gartstein, M. A., & Rothbart, M. K. (2003). Studying infant temperament via the revised infant behavior questionnaire. *Infant Behavior and Development, 26,* 64–86.

Gartstein, M. A., Slobodskaya, H. R., & Kinsht, I. A. (2003). Cross-cultural differences in temperament in the first year of life: United States of America (U.S.) and Russia. *International Journal of Behavioral Development, 27,* 316–328.

Gartstein, M. A., Slobodskaya, H. R., Zylicz, P. O., Gosztyla, D., & Nakagawa, A. (2010). A cross-cultural evaluation of temperament: Japan, USA, Poland and Russia. *International Journal of Psychology and Psychological Therapy, 10,* 55–75.

Gaskins, S. (1999). Children's daily lives in a Mayan village: A case study of culturally constructed roles and activities. In R. Göncü (Ed.), *Children's engagement in the world: Sociocultural perspectives* (pp. 25–61). Cambridge, UK: Cambridge University Press.

Gaskins, S. (2013). Pretend play as culturally constructed activity. In M. Taylor (Ed.), *Oxford handbook on the development of the imagination* (pp. 224–251). Oxford, UK: Oxford University Press.

Gaskins, S. (2014). Children's play as cultural activity. In L. Brooker, M. Blaise, & S. Edwards (Eds.), *Sage handbook of play and learning in early childhood* (pp. 31–42). London: Sage.

Gaskins, S., Haight, W., & Lancy, D. F. (2007). The cultural construction of play. In A. Göncü & S. Gaskins (Eds.), *Play and development: Evolutionary, sociocultural, and functional perspectives* (pp. 179–202). Mahwah, NJ: Erlbaum.

Gates, G. J. (2013). *LGBT parenting in the United States.* Los Angeles, CA: Williams Institute of the UCLA School of Law. Retrieved from http://williamsinstitute.law.ucla.edu/wp-content/uploads/LGBT-Parenting.pdf

Gathercole, S. E., Lamont, E., & Alloway, T. P. (2006). Working memory in the classroom. In S. Pickering (Ed.), *Working memory and education* (pp. 219–240). San Diego: Elsevier.

Gathercole, V., Sebastián, E., & Soto, P. (1999). The early acquisition of Spanish verbal morphology: Across-the-board or piecemeal knowledge? *International Journal of Bilingualism, 3,* 133–182.

Gauvain, M. (2004). Bringing culture into relief: Cultural contributions to the development of children's planning skills. In R. V. Kail (Ed.), *Advances in child development and behavior* (pp. 39–71). San Diego, CA: Elsevier.

Gauvain, M., de la Ossa, J. L., & Hurtado-Ortiz, M. T. (2001). Parental guidance as children learn to use cultural tools: The case of pictorial plans. *Cognitive Development, 16,* 551–575.

Gauvain, M., & Munroe, R. L. (2009). Contributions of societal modernity to cognitive development: A comparison of four cultures. *Child Development, 80,* 1628–1642.

Gauvain, M., Munroe, R. L., & Beebe, H. (2012). Children's questions in cross-cultural perspective: A four-culture study. *Journal of Cross-Cultural Psychology, 44,* 1148–1165.

Gauvain, M., & Rogoff, B. (1989a). Collaborative problem solving and children's planning skills. *Developmental Psychology, 25,* 139–151.

Gauvain, M., & Rogoff, B. (1989b). Ways of speaking about space: The development of children's skill in communicating spatial knowledge. *Cognitive Development, 4,* 295–307.

Gaylor, E. E., Burnham, M. M., Goodlin-Jones, B. L., & Anders, T. (2005). A longitudinal follow-up study of young children's sleep patterns using a developmental classification system. *Behavioral Sleep Medicine, 3,* 44–61.

Geangu, E., Benga, O., Stahl, D., & Striano, T. (2010). Contagious crying beyond the first days of life. *Infant Behavior and Development, 33,* 279–288.

Geary, D. C. (2006). Development of mathematical understanding. In D. Kuhn & R. Siegler (Eds.), *Handbook of child psychology: Vol. 2. Cognition, perception, and language* (6th ed., pp. 777–810). Hoboken, NJ: Wiley.

Geerts, C. C., Bots, M. L., van der Ent, C. K., Grobbee, D. E., & Uiterwaal, C. S. (2012). Parental smoking and vascular damage in their 5-year-old children. *Pediatrics, 129,* 45–54.

Gelman, R. (1972). Logical capacity of very young children: Number invariance rules. *Child Development, 43,* 75–90.

Gelman, R., & Shatz, M. (1978). Appropriate speech adjustments: The operation of conversational constraints on talk to two-year-olds. In M. Lewis & L. A. Rosenblum (Eds.), *Interaction, conversation, and the development of language* (pp. 27–61). New York: Wiley.

Gelman, S. A. (2003). *The essential child.* New York: Oxford University Press.

Gelman, S. A. (2006). Early conceptual development. In K. McCartney & D. Phillips (Eds.), *Blackwell handbook of early childhood development* (pp. 149–166). Malden, MA: Blackwell.

Gelman, S. A., & Kalish, C. W. (2006). Conceptual development. In D. Kuhn & R. Siegler (Eds.), *Handbook of child psychology: Vol. 2. Cognition, perception, and language* (6th ed., 687–733). New York: Wiley.

Gelman, S. A., Taylor, M. G., & Nguyen, S. P. (2004). Mother-child conversations about gender. *Monographs of the Society for Research in Child Development, 69*(1, Serial No. 275), pp. 1–127.

Gendler, M. N., Witherington, D. C., & Edwards, A. (2008). The development of affect specificity in infants' use of emotion cues. *Infancy, 13,* 456–468.

Genessee, F., & Jared, D. (2008). Literacy development in early French immersion programs. *Canadian Psychology, 49,* 140–147.

Gennetian, L. A., & Morris, P. A. (2003). The effects of time limits and make-work-pay strategies on the well-being of children: Experimental evidence from two welfare reform programs. *Children and Youth Services Review, 25,* 17–54.

Gentile, B., Grabe, S., Dolan-Pascoe, B., Twenge, J. M., Wells, B. E., & Maitino, A. (2009). Gender differences in domain-specific self-esteem: A meta-analysis. *Review of General Psychology, 13,* 34–45.

Gentile, D. A. (2011). The multiple dimensions of video game effects. *Child Development Perspectives, 5,* 75–81.

Geraci, A., & Surian, L. (2011). The developmental roots of fairness: Infants' reactions to equal and unequal distributions of resources. *Developmental Science, 14,* 1012–1020.

Gergely, G., & Watson, J. (1999). Early socio-emotional development: Contingency perception and the social-biofeedback model. In P. Rochat (Ed.), *Early social cognition: Understanding others in the first months of life* (pp. 101–136). Mahwah, NJ: Erlbaum.

Gershoff, E. T. (2002). Corporal punishment, physical abuse, and the burden of proof: Reply to Baumrind, Larzelere, and Cowan (2002), Holden (2002), and Parke (2002). *Psychological Bulletin, 128,* 602–611.

Gershoff, E. T., & Aber, J. L. (2006). Neighborhoods and schools: Contexts and consequences for the mental health and risk behaviors of children and youth. In L. Balter & C. S. Tamis-LeMonda (Eds.), *Child psychology: A handbook of contemporary issues* (2nd ed., pp. 611–645). New York: Psychology Press.

Gershoff, E. T., Grogan-Kaylor, A., Lansford, J. E., Chang, L., Zelli, A., Deater-Deckard, K., et al. (2010). Parent discipline practices in an international sample: Associations with child behaviors and moderation by perceived normativeness. *Child Development, 81,* 487–502.

Gershoff, E. T., Lansford, J. E., Sexton, H. R., Davis-Kean, P., & Sameroff, A. J. (2012). Longitudinal links between spanking and children's externalizing behaviors in a national sample of white, black, Hispanic, and Asian American families. *Child Development, 83,* 838–843.

Gershoff-Stowe, L., & Hahn, E. R. (2007). Fast mapping skills in the developing lexicon. *Journal of Speech, Language, and Hearing Research, 50,* 682–697.

Gershon, E. S., & Alliey-Rodriguez, N. (2013). New ethical issues for genetic counseling in common mental disorders. *American Journal of Psychiatry, 170,* 968–976.

Gerson, S., & Woodward, A. L. (2010). Building intentional action knowledge with one's hands. In S. P. Johnson (Ed.), *Neoconstructivism: The new science of cognitive development* (pp. 295–313). New York: Oxford University Press.

Gervai, J. (2009). Environmental and genetic influences on early attachment. *Child and Adolescent Psychiatry and Mental Health, 3,* 25. Retrieved from www.capmh.com/content/3/1/25

Gesell, A. (1933). Maturation and patterning of behavior. In C. Murchison (Ed.), *A handbook of child psychology.* Worcester, MA: Clark University Press.

Geuze, R. H., Schaafsma, S. M., Lust, J. M., Bouma, A., Schiefenhovel, W., Groothuis, T. G. G., et al. (2012). Plasticity of lateralization: Schooling predicts hand preference but not hand skill asymmetry in a non-industrial society. *Neuropsychologia, 50,* 612–620.

Gewirtz, A., Forgatch, M., & Wieling, E. (2008). Parenting practices as potential mechanisms for child adjustment following mass trauma. *Journal of Marital and Family Therapy, 34,* 177–192.

Ghim, H. R. (1990). Evidence for perceptual organization in infants: Perception of subjective contours by young infants. *Infant Behavior and Development, 13,* 221–248.

Gibbs, J. C. (2010). Beyond the conventionally moral. *Journal of Applied Developmental Psychology, 31,* 106–108.

Gibson, E. J. (1970). The development of perception as an adaptive process. *American Scientist, 58,* 98–107.

Gibson, E. J. (2000). Perceptual learning in development: Some basic concepts. *Ecological Psychology, 12,* 295–302.

Gibson, E. J. (2003). The world is so full of a number of things: On specification and perceptual learning. *Ecological Psychology, 15,* 283–287.

Gibson, E. J., & Walk, R. D. (1960). The "visual cliff." *Scientific American, 202,* 64–71.

Gibson, J. J. (1979). *The ecological approach to visual perception.* Boston: Houghton Mifflin.

Gibson-Davis, C., & Rackin, H. (2014). Marriage or carriage? Trends in union context and birth type by education. *Journal of Marriage and Family, 76,* 506–519.

Giedd, J. N., Lalonde, F. M., Celano, M. J., White, S. L., Wallace, G. L., Lee, N. R., et al. (2009). Anatomical brain magnetic resonance imaging of typically developing children and adolescents. *Journal of the American Academy of Child and Adolescent Psychiatry, 48,* 465–470.

Giles, A., & Rovee-Collier, C. (2011). Infant long-term memory for associations formed during mere exposure. *Infant Behavior and Development, 34,* 327–338.

Giles, J. W., & Heyman, G. D. (2005). Young children's beliefs about the relationship between gender and aggressive behavior. *Child Development, 76,* 107–121.

Giles-Sims, J., Straus, M. A., & Sugarman, D. B. (1995). Child, maternal, and family characteristics associated with spanking. *Family Relations, 44,* 170–176.

Gill, M., Daly, G., Heron, S., Hawi, Z., & Fitzgerald, M. (1997). Confirmation of association between attention deficit hyperactivity disorder and a dopamine transporter polymorphism. *Molecular Psychiatry, 2,* 311–313.

Gill, S. V., Adolph, K. E., & Vereijken, B. (2009). Change in action: How infants learn to walk down slopes. *Developmental Science, 12,* 888–902.

Gillies, R. M. (2003). Structuring co-operative learning experiences in primary school. In R. M. Gillies & A. F. Ashman (Eds.), *Co-operative learning: The social and intellectual outcomes of learning in groups* (pp. 36–53). New York: Routledge.

Gilliom, M., Shaw, D. S., Beck, J. E., Schonberg, M. A., & Lukon, J. L. (2002). Anger regulation in disadvantaged preschool boys: Strategies, antecedents, and the development of self-control. *Developmental Psychology, 38,* 222–235.

Gilmore, J. H., Shi, F., Woolson, S. L., Knickmeyer, R. C., Short, S. J., Lin, W., et al. (2012). Longitudinal development of cortical and subcortical gray matter from birth to 2 years. *Cerebral Cortex, 22,* 2478–2485.

Ginsburg, H. P., Lee, J. S., & Boyd, J. S. (2008). Mathematics education for young children: What it is and how to promote it. *Social Policy Report of the Society for Research in Child Development, 12*(1).

Giofré, D., Mammarella, I. C., & Cornoldi, C. (2013). The structure of working memory and how it relates to intelligence in children. *Intelligence, 41,* 396–406.

Giscombé, C. L., & Lobel, M. (2005). Explaining disproportionately high rates of adverse birth outcomes among African Americans: The impact of stress, racism and related factors in pregnancy. *Psychological Bulletin, 131,* 662–683.

Glade, A. C., Bean, R. A., & Vira, R. (2005). A prime time for marital/relational intervention: A review of the transition to parenthood literature with treatment recommendations. *American Journal of Family Therapy, 33,* 319–336.

Glazener, C. M., Evans, J. H., & Petro, R. E. (2005). Alarm interventions for nocturnal enuresis in children. *Cochrane Database of Systematic Reviews,* Issue 2. Art. No.: CD002911.

Gleason, J. B. (2013). The development of language: An overview and a preview. In J. B. Gleason & N. B. Ratner (Eds.), *The development of language* (8th ed., pp. 1–29). Upper Saddle River, NJ: Pearson.

Gleason, T. R. (2013). Imaginary relationships. In M. Taylor (Ed.), *Oxford handbook of the development of imagination* (pp. 251–271). New York: Oxford University Press.

Gleason, T. R., & Hohmann, L. M. (2006). Concepts of real and imaginary friendships in early childhood. *Social Development, 15,* 128–144.

Gleason, T. R., Sebanc, A. M., & Hartup, W. W. (2000). Imaginary companions of preschool children. *Developmental Psychology, 36,* 419–428.

Gleitman, L. R., Cassidy, K., Nappa, R., Papfragou, A., & Trueswell, J. C. (2005). Hard words. *Language Learning and Development, 1,* 23–64.

Glenright, M., & Pexman, P. M. (2010). Development of children's ability to distinguish sarcasm and verbal irony. *Journal of Child Language, 37,* 429–451.

Gluckman, P. D., Sizonenko, S. V., & Bassett, N. S. (1999). The transition from fetus to neonate—an endocrine perspective. *Acta Paediatrica Supplement, 88*(428), 7–11.

Gnepp, J. (1983). Children's social sensitivity: Inferring emotions from conflicting cues. *Developmental Psychology, 19,* 805–814.

Gnoth, C., Maxrath, B., Skonieczny, T., Friol, K., Godehardt, E., & Tigges, J. (2011). Final ART success rates: A 10 years survey. *Human Reproduction, 26,* 2239–2246.

Goble, P. Martin, C. L., Hanish, L. D., & Fabes, R. A. (2012). Children's gender-typed activity choices across preschool social contexts. *Sex Roles, 67,* 435–451.

Godfrey, K. M., & Barker, D. J. (2000). Fetal nutrition and adult disease. *American Journal of Clinical Nutrition, 71,* 1344S–1352S.

Goeke-Morey, M. C., Papp, L. M., & Cummings, E. M. (2013). Changes in marital conflict and youths' responses across childhood and adolescence: A test of sensitization. *Development and Psychopathology, 25,* 241–251.

Goering, J. (Ed.). (2003). Choosing a better life? *How public housing tenants selected a HUD experiment to improve their lives and those of their children: The Moving to Opportunity Demonstration Program.* Washington, DC: Urban Institute Press.

Gogate, L. J., & Bahrick, L. E. (1998). Intersensory redundancy facilitates learning of arbitrary relations between vowel sounds and objects in seven-month-old infants. *Journal of Experimental Child Psychology, 69,* 133–149.

Gogate, L. J., & Bahrick, L. E. (2001). Intersensory redundancy and 7-month-old infants' memory for arbitrary syllable–object relations. *Infancy, 2,* 219–231.

Goh, Y. I., & Koren, G. (2008). Folic acid in pregnancy and fetal outcomes. *Journal of Obstetrics and Gynaecology, 28,* 3–13.

Goldberg, A. E. (2010). *Lesbian and gay parents and their children: Research on the family life cycle.* Washington, DC: American Psychological Association.

Goldberg, A. E., Kashy, D. A., & Smith, J. Z. (2012). Gender-typed play behavior in early childhood: Adopted children with lesbian, gay, and heterosexual parents. *Sex Roles, 67,* 503–513.

Goldberg, A. E., & Perry-Jenkins, M. (2003). Division of labor and working-class women's well-being across the transition to parenthood. *Journal of Family Psychology, 18,* 225–236.

Goldenberg, C., Gallimore, R., Reese, L., & Garnier, H. (2001). Cause or effect? Immigrant Latino parents' aspirations and expectations, and their children's school performance. *American Educational Research Journal, 38,* 547–582.

Goldfield, B. A. (1987). Contributions of child and caregiver to referential and expressive language. *Applied Psycholinguistics, 8,* 267–280.

Goldhaber, D. (2012). *The nature–nurture debates: Bridging the gaps.* New York: Cambridge University Press.

Goldin-Meadow, S. (2003). *The resilience of language.* New York: Psychology Press.

Goldin-Meadow, S. (2009). Using the hands to study how children learn language. In J. Colombo, P. McCardle, & L. Freund (Eds.), *Infant pathways to language: Methods, models, and research directions* (pp. 195–210). New York: Psychology Press.

Goldin-Meadow, S., Gelman, S. A., & Mylander, C. (2005). Expressing generic concepts with and without a language model. *Cognition, 96,* 109–126.

Goldschmidt, L., Richardson, G. A., Cornelius, M. D., & Day, N. L. (2004). Prenatal marijuana and alcohol exposure and academic achievement at age 10. *Neurotoxicology and Teratology, 26,* 521–532.

Goldstein, M. H., & Schwade, J. A. (2008). Social feedback to infants' babbling facilitates rapid phonological learning. *Psychological Science, 19,* 515–523.

Goldstein, S. (2011a). Attention-deficit/hyperactivity disorder. In S. Goldstein & C. R. Reynolds (Eds.), *Handbook of neurodevelopmental and genetic disorders in children* (2nd ed., pp. 131–150). New York: Guilford.

Goldstein, S. (2011b). Learning disabilities in childhood. In S. Goldstein, J. A. Naglieri, & M. DeVries (Eds.), *Learning and attention disorders in adolescence and adulthood: Assessment and treatment* (2nd ed., pp. 31–58). Hoboken, NJ: Wiley.

Goldstein, S. E., & Tisak, M. S. (2004). Adolescents' outcome expectancies about relational aggression within acquaintanceships, friendships, and dating relationships. *Journal of Adolescence, 27,* 283–302.

Golinkoff, R. M., & Hirsh-Pasek, K. (2006). Baby wordsmith: From associationist to social sophisticate. *Current Directions in Psychological Science, 15,* 30–33.

Golinkoff, R. M., & Hirsh-Pasek, K. (2008). How toddlers begin to learn verbs. *Trends in Cognitive Sciences, 12,* 397–403.

Golomb, C. (2004). *The child's creation of a pictorial world* (2nd ed.). Mahwah, NJ: Erlbaum.

Golombok, S., Readings, J., Blake, L., Casey, P., Mellish, L., Marks, A., & Jadva, V. (2011). Children conceived by gamete donation: Psychological adjustment and mother-child relationships at age 7. *Journal of Family Psychology, 25,* 230–239.

Golombok, S., Rust, J., Zervoulis, K., Croudace, T., Golding, J., & Hines, M. (2008). Developmental trajectories of sex-typed behavior in boys and girls: A longitudinal general population study of children aged 2.5–8 years. *Child Development, 79,* 1583–1593.

Golombok, S., Rust, J., Zervoulis, K., Golding, J., & Hines, M. (2012). Continuity in sex-typed behavior from preschool to adolescence: A longitudinal population study of boys and girls aged 3–13 years. *Archives of Sexual Behavior, 41,* 591–597.

Gomez-Perez, E., & Ostrosky-Solis, F. (2006). Attention and memory evaluation across the life span: Heterogeneous effects of age and education. *Journal of Clinical and Experimental Neuropsychology, 28,* 477–494.

Gonzales, N. A., Cauce, A. M., Friedman, R. J., & Mason, C. A. (1996). Family, peer, and neighborhood influences on academic achievement among African-American adolescents: One-year prospective effects. *American Journal of Community Psychology, 24,* 365–387.

Gonzalez, A.-L., & Wolters, C. A. (2006). The relation between perceived parenting practices and achievement motivation in mathematics. *Journal of Research in Childhood Education, 21,* 203–217.

González-Rivera, M., & Bauermeister, J. A. (2007). Children's attitudes toward people with AIDS in Puerto Rico: Exploring stigma through drawings and stories. *Qualitative Health Research, 17,* 250–263.

Good, T. L., & Brophy, J. (2003). *Looking in classrooms* (9th ed.). Boston: Allyn and Bacon.

Goodman, A., Schorge, J., & Greene, M. F. (2011). The long-term effects of in utero exposures—the DES story. *New England Journal of Medicine, 364,* 2083–2084.

Goodman, C., & Silverstein, M. (2006). Grandmothers raising grandchildren: Ethnic and racial differences in well-being among custodial and coparenting families. *Journal of Family Issues, 27,* 1605–1626.

Goodman, J., Dale, P., & Li, P. (2008). Does frequency count? Parental input and the acquisition of vocabulary. *Journal of Child Language, 35,* 515–531.

Goodman, K. S. (2005). *What's whole in whole language.* Berkeley, CA: RDR Books.

Goodman, S. H., Gravitt, G. W., Jr., & Kaslow, N. J. (1995). Social problem solving: A moderator of the relation between negative life stress and depression symptoms in children. *Journal of Abnormal Child Psychology, 23,* 473–485.

Goodnight, J. A., Bates, J. E., Staples, A. D., Pettit, G. S., & Dodge, K. A. (2007). Temperamental resistance to control increases the association between sleep problems and externalizing behavior development. *Journal of Family Psychology, 21,* 39–48.

Goodnow, J. J. (2010). Culture. In M. H. Bornstein (Ed.), *Handbook of cultural developmental science* (pp. 3–20). New York: Psychology Press.

Goodvin, R., Meyer, S., Thompson, R. A., & Hayes, R. (2008). Self-understanding in early childhood: Associations with child attachment security and maternal negative affect. *Attachment and Human Development, 10,* 433–450.

Goodvin, R., & Romdall, L. (2013). Associations of mother–child reminiscing about negative past events, coping, and self-concept in early childhood. *Infant and Child Development, 22,* 383–400.

Gooren, E. M. J. C., Pol, A. C., Stegge, H., Terwogt, M. M., & Koot, H. M. (2011). The development of conduct problems and depressive symptoms in early elementary school children: The role of peer rejection. *Journal of Clinical Child and Adolescent Psychology, 40,* 245–253.

Gopnik, A., & Choi, S. (1990). Do linguistic differences lead to cognitive differences? A cross-linguistic study of semantic and cognitive development. *First Language, 11,* 199–215.

Gopnik, A., & Nazzi, T. (2003). Words, kinds, and causal powers: A theory theory perspective on early naming and categorization. In D. H. Rakison & L. M. Oakes (Eds.), *Early category and concept development* (pp. 303–329). New York: Oxford University Press.

Gopnik, A., & Tenenbaum, J. B. (2007). Bayesian networks, Bayesian learning and cognitive development. *Developmental Science, 10,* 281–287.

Gordon, I., Zagoory-Sharon, O., Leckman, J. F., & Feldman, R. (2010). Oxytocin and the development of parenting in humans. *Biological Psychiatry, 68,* 377–382.

Gordon, R. A., Chase-Lansdale, P. L., & Brooks-Gunn, J. (2004). Extended households and the life course of young mothers: Understanding the associations using a sample of mothers with premature, low-birth-weight babies. *Child Development, 75,* 1013–1038.

Gormally, S., Barr, R. G., Wertheim, L., Alkawaf, R., Calinoiu, N., & Young, S. N. (2001). Contact and nutrient caregiving effects on newborn infant pain responses. *Developmental Medicine and Child Neurology, 43,* 28–38.

Gorman, B. K., Fiestas, C. E., Peña, E. D., & Clark, M. R. (2011). Creative and stylistic devices employed by children during a storybook narrative task: A cross-cultural study. *Language, Speech, and Hearing Services in Schools, 42,* 167–181.

Gormley, W. T., Jr., & Phillips, D. (2009). *The effects of pre-K on child development: Lessons from Oklahoma.*

Washington, DC: National Summit on Early Childhood Education, Georgetown University.

Goswami, U. (1996). Analogical reasoning and cognitive development. In H. Reese (Ed.), *Advances in child development and behavior* (Vol. 26, pp. 91–138). New York: Academic Press.

Gottfried, A. E., Gottfried, A. W., & Bathurst, K. (2002). Maternal and dual-earner employment status and parenting. In M. H. Bornstein (Ed.), *Handbook of parenting: Vol. 3. Being and becoming a parent* (2nd ed., pp. 207–230). Mahwah, NJ: Erlbaum.

Gottlieb, G. (1998). Normally occurring environmental and behavioral influences on gene activity: From central dogma to probabilistic epigenesis. *Psychological Review, 105,* 792–802.

Gottlieb, G. (2003). On making behavioral genetics truly developmental. *Human Development, 46,* 337–355.

Gottlieb, G. (2007). Probabilistic epigenesis. *Developmental Science, 10,* 1–11.

Gottlieb, G., Wahlsten, D., & Lickliter, R. (2006). The significance of biology for human development: A developmental psychobiological systems of view. In R. M. Lerner (Ed.), *Handbook of child psychology: Vol. 1. Theoretical models of human development* (6th ed., pp. 210–257). Hoboken, NJ: Wiley.

Gottman, J. M., Gottman, J. S., & Shapiro, A. (2010). A new couples approach to interventions for the transition to parenthood. In M. S. Schulz, M. K. Pruett, P. K. Kerig, & R. D. Parke (Eds.), *Strengthening couple relationships for optimal child development* (pp. 165–179). Washington, DC: American Psychological Association.

Gould, F., Clarke, J., Heim, C., Harvey, P. D., Majer, M., & Nemeroff, C. B. (2010). The effects of child abuse and neglect on cognitive functioning in adulthood. *Journal of Psychiatric Research, 46,* 500–506.

Gould, J. L., & Keeton, W. T. (1996). *Biological science* (6th ed.). New York: Norton.

Graber, J. A., Nichols, T., Lynne, S. D., Brooks-Gunn, J., & Botwin, G. J. (2006). A longitudinal examination of family, friend, and media influences on competent versus problem behaviors among urban minority youth. *Applied Developmental Science, 10,* 75–85.

Graham-Bermann, S. A., & Howell, K. H. (2011). Child maltreatment in the context of intimate partner violence. In J. E. B. Myers (Ed.), *Child maltreatment* (3rd ed., pp. 167–180). Thousand Oaks, CA: Sage.

Gralinski, J. H., & Kopp, C. B. (1993). Everyday rules for behavior: Mothers' requests to young children. *Developmental Psychology, 29,* 573–584.

Granic, I., Hollenstein, T., Dishion, T. J., & Patterson, G. R. (2003). Longitudinal analysis of flexibility and reorganization in early adolescence: A dynamic systems study of family interactions. *Developmental Psychology, 39,* 606–617.

Granier-Deferre, C., Bassereau, S., Ribeiro, A., Jacquet, A. Y., & Lecanuet, J.-P. (2003). *Cardiac "orienting" response in fetuses and babies following in utero melody-learning.* Paper presented at the 11th European Conference on Developmental Psychology, Milan, Italy.

Grant, K. B., & Ray, J. A. (2010). *Home, school, and community collaboration: Culturally responsive family involvement.* Thousand Oaks, CA: Sage Publications.

Grantham-McGregor, S., & Ani, C. (2001). A review of studies on the effect of iron deficiency on cognitive development in children. *Journal of Nutrition, 131,* 649S–668S.

Grantham-McGregor, S., Powell, C., Walker, S., Chang, S., & Fletcher, P. (1994). The long-term follow-up of severely malnourished children who participated in an intervention program. *Child Development, 65,* 428–439.

Grantham-McGregor, S., Schofield, W., & Powell, C. (1987). Development of severely malnourished children who received psychosocial stimulation: Six-year follow-up. *Pediatrics, 79,* 247–254.

Grantham-McGregor, S., Walker, S. P., & Chang, S. (2000). Nutritional deficiencies and later behavioral development. *Proceedings of the Nutrition Society, 59,* 47–54.

Gratier, M., & Devouche, E. (2011). Imitation and repetition of prosodic contour in vocal interaction at 3 months. *Developmental Psychology, 47,* 67–76.

Grattan, M. P., De Vos, E., Levy, J., & McClintock, M. K. (1992). Asymmetric action in the human newborn: Sex differences in patterns of organization. *Child Development, 63,* 273–289.

Gray, K. A., Day, N. L., Leech, S., & Richardson, G. A. (2005). Prenatal marijuana exposure: Effect on child depressive symptoms at ten years of age. *Neurotoxicology and Teratology, 27,* 439–448.

Gray, M. R., & Steinberg, L. (1999). Unpacking authoritative parenting: Reassessing a multidimensional construct. *Journal of Marriage and the Family, 61,* 574–587.

Gray-Little, B., & Carels, R. (1997). The effects of racial and socioeconomic consonance on self-esteem and achievement in elementary, junior high, and high school students. *Journal of Research on Adolescence, 7,* 109–131.

Gray-Little, B., & Hafdahl, A. R. (2000). Factors influencing racial comparisons of self-esteem: A quantitative review. *Psychological Bulletin, 126,* 26–54.

Green, G. E., Irwin, J. R., & Gustafson, G. E. (2000). Acoustic cry analysis, neonatal status and long-term developmental outcomes. In R. G. Barr, B. Hopkins, & J. A. Green (Eds.), *Crying as a sign, a symptom, and a signal* (pp. 137–156). Cambridge, UK: Cambridge University Press.

Greenberg, J. P. (2013). Determinants of after-school programming for school-age immigrant children. *Children and Schools, 35,* 101–111.

Greenberger, E., O'Neil, R., & Nagel, S. K. (1994). Linking workplace and homeplace: Relations between the nature of adults' work and their parenting behaviors. *Developmental Psychology, 30,* 990–1002.

Greendorfer, S. L., Lewko, J. H., & Rosengren, K. S. (1996). Family and gender-based socialization of children and adolescents. In F. L. Smoll & R. E. Smith (Eds.), *Children and youth in sport: A biopsychological perspective* (pp. 89–111). Dubuque, IA: Brown & Benchmark.

Greene, S. M., Anderson, E. R., Forgatch, M. S., DeGarmo, D. S., & Hetherington, E. M. (2012). Risk and resilience after divorce. In F. Walsh (Ed.), *Normal family processes: Growing diversity and complexity* (4th ed., pp. 102–127). New York: Guilford.

Greenfield, P. M. (1992, June). *Notes and references for developmental psychology.* Conference on Making Basic Texts in Psychology More Culture-Inclusive and Culture-Sensitive, Western Washington University, Bellingham, WA.

Greenfield, P. M. (2004). *Weaving generations together: Evolving creativity in the Maya of Chiapas.* Santa Fe, NM: School of American Research.

Greenfield, P. M., Suzuki, L. K., & Rothstein-Fish, C. (2006). Cultural pathways through human development. In K. A. Renninger & I. E. Sigel (Eds.), *Handbook of child psychology: Vol. 4. Child psychology in practice* (6th ed., pp. 655–699). Hoboken, NJ: Wiley.

Greenhill, L. L., Halperin, J. M., & Abikoff, H. (1999). Stimulant medications. *Journal of the American Academy of Child and Adolescent Psychiatry, 38,* 503–512.

Greenough, W. T., & Black, J. E. (1992). Induction of brain structure by experience: Substrates for cognitive development. In M. Gunnar & C. A. Nelson (Eds.), *Minnesota symposia on child psychology* (pp. 155–200). Hillsdale, NJ: Erlbaum.

Greer, B. D., Neidert, P. L., Dozier, C. L., Payne, S. W., Zonneveld, K. L. M., & Harper, A. M. (2013). Functional analysis and treatment of problem behavior in early education classrooms. *Journal of Applied Behavior Analysis, 46,* 289–295.

Greer, T., & Lockman, J. J. (1998). Using writing instruments: Invariances in young children and adults. *Child Development, 69,* 888–902.

Groh, A. M., Fearon, R. M. P., Bakermans-Kranenburg, M. J., Van IJzendoorn, M. H., Steele, R. D., & Roisman, G. I. (2014). The significance of attachment security for children's social competence with peers: A meta-analytic study. *Attachment and Human Development, 16,* 103–136.

Groome, L. J., Swiber, M. J., Holland, S. B., Bentz, L. S., Atterbury, J. L., & Trimm, R. F., III. (1999). Spontaneous motor activity in the perinatal infant before and after birth: Stability in individual differences. *Developmental Psychobiology, 35,* 15–24.

Gropman, A. L., & Adams, D. R. (2007). Atypical patterns of inheritance. *Seminars in Pediatric Neurology, 14,* 34–45.

Grossmann, K., Grossmann, K. E., Fremmer-Bombik, E., Kindler, H., Scheuerer-Englisch, H., & Zimmermann, P. (2002). The uniqueness of the child–father attachment relationship: Fathers' sensitive and challenging play as a pivotal variable in a 16-year longitudinal study. *Social Development, 11,* 307–331.

Grossmann, K., Grossmann, K. E., Kindler, H., & Zimmermann, P. (2008). A wider view of attachment and exploration: The influence of mothers and fathers on the development of psychological security from infancy to young adulthood. In J. Cassidy & P. R. Shaver (Eds.), *Handbook of attachment: Theory, research, and clinical applications* (2nd ed., pp. 880–905). New York: Guilford.

Grossmann, K., Grossmann, K. E., Spangler, G., Suess, G., & Unzner, L. (1985). Maternal sensitivity and newborns' orientation responses as related to quality of attachment in Northern Germany. In I. Bretherton & E. Waters (Eds.), Growing points of attachment theory and research. *Monographs of the Society for Research in Child Development, 50*(1–2, Serial No. 209).

Grossmann, T., Striano, T., & Friederici, A. D. (2007). Developmental changes in infants' processing of happy and angry facial expressions: A neurobehavioral study. *Brain and Cognition, 64,* 30–41.

Grow-Maienza, J., Hahn, D.-D., & Joo, C.-A. (2001). Mathematics instruction in Korean primary schools: Structures, processes, and a linguistic analysis of questioning. *Journal of Educational Psychology, 93,* 363–376.

Gruendel, J., & Aber, J. L. (2007). Bridging the gap between research and child policy change: The role of strategic communications in policy advocacy. In J. L. Aber, S. J. Bishop-Josef, S. M. Jones, K. T. McLearn, & D. A. Phillips (Eds.), *Child development and social policy: Knowledge for action* (pp. 43–58). Washington, DC: American Psychological Association.

Grusec, J. E. (1988). *Social development: History, theory, and research.* New York: Springer-Verlag.

Grusec, J. E. (2006). The development of moral behavior and conscience from a socialization perspective. In M. Killen & J. Smetana (Eds.), *Handbook of moral development* (pp. 243–265). Philadelphia: Erlbaum.

Guedes, M., Pereira, M., Pires, R., Carvalho, P., & Canavarro, M. C. (2013). Childbearing motivations scale: Construction of a new measure and its preliminary psychometric properties. *Journal of Family Studies.* Retrieved from link.springer.com/article/10.1007%2Fs10826-013-9824-0

Guerra, N. G., Graham, S. & Tolan, P. H. (2011). Raising healthy children: Translating child development research into practice. *Child Development, 82,* 7–16.

Guerra, N. G., Williams, K. R., & Sadek, S. (2011). Understanding bullying and victimization during childhood and adolescence: A mixed methods study. *Child Development, 82,* 295–310.

Guest, A. M. (2013). Cultures of play during middle childhood: Interpretive perspectives from two distinct marginalized communities. *Sport, Education and Society, 18,* 167–183.

Guglielmi, R. S. (2008). Native language proficiency, English literacy, academic achievement, and occupational attainment in limited-English-proficient students: A latent growth modeling perspective. *Journal of Educational Psychology, 100,* 322–342.

Guignard, J.-H., & Lubart, T. I. (2007). A comparative study of convergent and divergent thinking in intellectually gifted children. *Gifted and Talented International, 22*(1), 9–15.

Guilford, J. P. (1985). The structure-of-intellect model. In B. B. Wolman (Ed.), *Handbook of intelligence* (pp. 225–266). New York: Wiley.

Guilleminault, C., Palombini, L., Pelayo, R., & Chervin, R. D. (2003). Sleepwalking and sleep terrors in prepubertal children: What triggers them? *Pediatrics, 111,* e17–e25.

Guimond, F. A., Brendgen, M., Forget-Dubois, N., Dionne, G., Vitaro, F., Tremblay, R. E., & Boivin, M. (2012). Associations of mother's and father's parenting practices with children's observed social reticence in a competitive situation: A monozygotic twin difference study. *Journal of Abnormal Child Psychology, 40,* 391–402.

Gullone, E. (2000). The development of normal fear: A century of research. *Clinical Psychology Review, 20,* 429–451.

Gulotta, T. P. (2008). How theory influences treatment and prevention practice within the family. In T. P. Gulotta (Ed.), *Family influences on child behavior and development: Evidence-based prevention and treatment approaches* (pp. 1–20). New York: Routledge.

Gunderson, E. A., Ramirez, G., Levine, S. C., & Beilock, S. L. (2012). The role of parents and teachers in the development of gender-related math attitudes. *Sex Roles, 66,* 153–166.

Gunnar, M. R., & Cheatham, C. L. (2003). Brain and behavior interfaces: Stress and the developing brain. *Infant Mental Health Journal, 24,* 195–211.

Gunnar, M. R., & de Haan, M. (2009). Methods in social neuroscience: Issues in studying development. In M. de Haan & M. R. Gunnar (Eds.), *Handbook of developmental social neuroscience* (pp. 13–37). New York: Guilford.

Gunnar, M. R., Morison, S. J., Chisholm, K., & Schuder, M. (2001). Salivary cortisol levels in children adopted from Romanian orphanages. *Development and Psychopathology, 13,* 611–628.

Gunnar, M. R., & Quevedo, K. (2007). The neurobiology of stress and development. *Annual Review of Psychology, 58,* 145–173.

Gunnarsdottir, I., Schack-Nielsen, L., Michaelson, K. F., Sørensen, T. I., & Thorsdottir, I. (2010). Infant weight gain, duration of exclusive breast-feeding, and childhood BMI—two similar follow-up cohorts. *Public Health Nutrition, 13,* 201–207.

Gupta, J. K., Hofmeyr, G. J., & Shehmar, M. (2012). Position in the second stage of labour for women without epidural anaesthesia. *Cochrane Database of Systematic Reviews, Issue 5*(Art. No. CD002006).

Guo, G., & VanWey, L. K. (1999). Sibship size and intellectual development: Is the relationship causal? *American Sociological Review, 64,* 169–187.

Guralnick, M. J. (2012). Preventive interventions for preterm children: Effectiveness and developmental mechanisms. *Journal of Developmental and Behavioral Pediatrics, 33,* 352–364.

Gustafson, G. E., Green, J. A., & Cleland, J. W. (1994). Robustness of individual identity in the cries of human infants. *Developmental Psychobiology, 27,* 1–9.

Gustafson, G. E., Wood, R. M., & Green, J. A. (2000). Can we hear the causes of infants' crying? In R. G. Barr & B. Hopkins (Eds.), *Crying as a sign, a symptom, and a signal: Clinical, emotional, and developmental aspects of infant and toddler crying* (pp. 8–22). New York: Cambridge University Press.

Guterman, N. B., Lee, S. J., Taylor, C. A., & Rathouz, P. J. (2009). Parental perceptions of neighborhood processes, stress, personal control, and risk for physical child abuse and neglect. *Child Abuse and Neglect, 33,* 897–906.

Guttentag, R., & Ferrell, J. (2004). Reality compared with its alternatives: Age differences in judgments of regret and relief. *Developmental Psychology, 40,* 764–775.

Guttmacher Institute. (2013, December). *Unintended pregnancy in the United States.* Retrieved from www.guttmacher.org/pubs/FB-Unintended-Pregnancy-US.html

Gweon, H., Dodell-Feder, D., Bedney, M., & Saxe, R. (2012). Theory of mind performance in children correlates with functional specialization of a brain region for thinking about thoughts. *Child Development, 83,* 1853–1868.

Gwiazda, J., & Birch, E. E. (2001). Perceptual development: Vision. In E. B. Goldstein (Ed.), *Blackwell handbook of perception* (pp. 636–668). Oxford, UK: Blackwell.

H

Hack, M., & Klein, N. (2006). Young adult attainments of preterm infants. *Journal of the American Medical Association, 295,* 695–696.

Hagerman, R. J., Berry-Kravis, E., Kaufmann, W. E., Ono, M. Y., Tartaglia, N., & Lachiewicz, A. (2009). Advances in the treatment of fragile X syndrome. *Pediatrics, 123,* 378–390.

Hahn, S., & Chitty, L. S. (2008). Noninvasive prenatal diagnosis: Current practice and future perspectives. *Current Opinion in Obstetrics and Gynecology, 20,* 146–151.

Haight, W. L., & Miller, P. J. (1993). *Pretending at home: Early development in a sociocultural context.* Albany: State University of New York Press.

Hainline, L. (1998). The development of basic visual abilities. In A. Slater (Ed.), *Perceptual development: Visual, auditory, and speech perception in infancy* (pp. 37–44). Hove, UK: Psychology Press.

Hakuta, K., Bialystok, E., & Wiley, E. (2003). Critical evidence: A test of the critical period hypothesis for second-language acquisition. *Psychological Science, 14,* 31–38.

Hale, C. M., & Tager-Flusberg, H. (2003). The influence of language on theory of mind: A training study. *Developmental Science, 6*, 346–359.

Hales, V. N., & Ozanne, S. E. (2003). The dangerous road of catch-up growth. *Journal of Physiology, 547*, 5–10.

Halfon, N., & McLearn, K. T. (2002). Families with children under 3: What we know and implications for results and policy. In N. Halfon & K. T. McLearn (Eds.), *Child rearing in America: Challenges facing parents with young children* (pp. 367–412). New York: Cambridge University Press.

Halford, G. S., & Andrews, G. (2006). Reasoning and problem solving. In D. Kuhn & R. Siegler (Eds.), *Handbook of child psychology: Vol. 2. Cognition, perception, and language* (6th ed., pp. 557–608). Hoboken, NJ: Wiley.

Halford, G. S., & Andrews, G. (2010). Information-processing models of cognitive development. In J. G. Bremner & T. D. Wachs (Eds.), *Wiley-Blackwell handbook of infant development: Vol. 1. Basic research* (2nd ed., pp. 698–722). Oxford, UK: Wiley.

Halford, G. S., & Andrews, G. (2011). Information-processing models of cognitive development. In U. Goswami (Ed.), *Wiley-Blackwell handbook of childhood cognitive development* (2nd ed., pp. 697–722). Hoboken, NJ: Wiley-Blackwell.

Halgunseth, L. C., Ispa, J. M., & Rudy, D. (2006). Parental control in Latino families: An integrated review of the literature. *Child Development, 77*, 1282–1297.

Halim, M. L., & Ruble, D. (2010). Gender identity and stereotyping in early and middle childhood. In J. C. Chrisler & D. R. McCreary (Eds.), *Handbook of gender research in psychology* (pp. 495–525). New York: Springer.

Halim, M. L., Ruble, D. N., & Tamis-LeMonda, C. S. (2013). Four-year-olds' beliefs about how others regard males and females. *British Journal of Developmental Psychology, 2013,* 128–135.

Hall, D. G., Burns, T., & Pawluski, J. (2003). Input and word learning: Caregivers' sensitivity to lexical category distinctions. *Journal of Child Language, 30*, 711–729.

Hall, G. S. (1904). *Adolescence.* New York: Appleton-Century-Crofts.

Halle, T. G. (2003). Emotional development and well-being. In M. H. Bornstein, L. Davidson, C. L. M. Keyes, K. A. Moore, & the Center for Child Well-Being (Eds.), *Well-being: Positive development across the life course* (pp. 125–138). Mahwah, NJ: Erlbaum.

Haller, J. (2005). Vitamins and brain function. In H. R. Lieberman, R. B. Kanarek, & C. Prasad (2005). *Nutritional neuroscience* (pp. 207–233). Philadelphia: Taylor & Francis.

Hamilton, B. E., Martin, J. A., Osterman, M. J. K., & Curtin, S. C. (2014). Births: Preliminary data for 2013. *National Vital Statistics Reports, 63*(2). Hyattsville, MD: National Center for Health Statistics. Retrieved from www.cdc.gov/nchs/data/nvsr/nvsr63/nvsr63_02.pdf

Hamlin, J. K., Hallinan, E. V., & Woodward, A. L. (2008). Do as I do: 7-month-old infants selectively reproduce others' goals. *Developmental Science, 11*, 487–494.

Hamlin, J. K., & Wynn, K. (2011). Young infants prefer prosocial to antisocial others. *Cognitive Development, 26*, 30–39.

Hammond, S. I., Müller, U., Carpendale, J. I. M., Bibok, M. B., & Lieberman-Finestone, D. (2012). The effects of parental scaffolding on preschoolers' executive function. *Developmental Psychology, 48*, 271–281.

Hammons, A. J., & Fiese, B. H. (2011). Is frequency of shared family meals related to the nutritional health of children and adolescents? *Pediatrics, 127*, e1565–e1574.

Hampton, T. (2014). Studies probe links between childhood asthma and obesity. *Journal of the American Medical Association, 311*, 1718–1719.

Hanawalt, B. A. (1993). *Growing up in medieval London: The experience of childhood in history.* New York: Oxford University Press.

Hanawalt, B. A. (2003). The child in the Middle Ages and the Renaissance. In W. Koops & M. Zuckerman (Eds.), *Beyond the century of childhood: Cultural history and developmental psychology.* Philadelphia: University of Pennsylvania Press.

Hanington, L., Heron, J., Stein, A., & Ramchandani, P. (2012). Parental depression and child outcomes—is marital conflict the missing link? *Child: Care, Health and Development, 38*, 520–529.

Hanioka, T., Ojima, M., Tanaka, K., & Yamamoto, M. (2011). Does secondhand smoke affect the development of dental caries in children? A systematic review. *International Journal of Environmental Research and Public Health, 8,* 1503–1509.

Hanish, L. D., Sallquist, J., DiDonato, M., Fabes, R. A., & Martin, C. L. (2012). Aggression by whom—aggression toward whom: Behavioral predictors of same- and other-gender aggression in early childhood. *Developmental Psychology, 48,* 1450–1462.

Hannon, E. E., & Johnson, S. P. (2004). Infants use meter to categorize rhythms and melodies: Implications for musical structure learning. *Cognitive Psychology, 50*, 354–377.

Hannon, E. E., & Trehub, S. E. (2005a). Metrical categories in infancy and adulthood. *Psychological Science, 16*, 48–55.

Hannon, E. E., & Trehub, S. E. (2005b). Tuning in to musical rhythms: Infants learn more readily than adults. *Proceedings of the National Academy of Sciences, 102*, 12639–12643.

Hans, S. L., & Jeremy, R. J. (2001). Postneonatal mental and motor development of infants exposed in utero to opiate drugs. *Infant Mental Health Journal, 22*, 300–315.

Hansell, N. K., Wright, M. J., Geffen, G. M., Geffen, L. B., Smith, G. A., & Martin, N. G. (2001). Genetic influence on ERP slow wave measures of working memory. *Behavioral Genetics, 31*, 603–614.

Hansen, M. B., & Markman, E. M. (2009). Children's use of mutual exclusivity to learn labels for parts of objects. *Developmental Psychology, 45*, 592–596.

Hao, L., & Woo, H. S. (2012). Distinct trajectories in the transition to adulthood: Are children of immigrants advantaged? *Child Development, 83*, 1623–1639.

Happé, F., & Frith, U. (2006). The weak coherence account: Detail-focused cognitive style in autism spectrum disorders. *Journal of Autism and Developmental Disorders, 1*, 1–21.

Harley, K., & Reese, E. (1999). Origins of autobiographical memory. *Developmental Psychology, 35*, 1338–1348.

Harlow, H. F., & Zimmerman, R. (1959). Affectional responses in the infant monkey. *Science, 130*, 421–432.

Harris, Y. R., & Graham, J. A. (2007). *The African American child: Development and challenges.* New York: Springer.

Harrison, A. O., Wilson, M. N., Pine, C. J., Chan, S. Q., & Buriel, R. (1994). Family ecologies of ethnic minority children. In G. Handel & G. G. Whitchurch (Eds.), *The psychosocial interior of the family* (pp. 187–210). New York: Aldine De Gruyter.

Hart, B. (2004). What toddlers talk about. *First Language, 24,* 91–106.

Hart, B., & Risley, T. R. (1995). *Meaningful differences in the everyday experience of young American children.* Baltimore: Paul H. Brookes.

Hart, C. H., Burts, D. C., Durland, M. A., Charlesworth, R., DeWolf, M., & Fleege, P. O. (1998). Stress behaviors and activity type participation of preschoolers in more and less developmentally appropriate classrooms: SES and sex differences. *Journal of Research in Childhood Education, 13.*

Hart, C. H., Newell, L. D., & Olsen, S. F. (2003). Parenting skills and social–communicative competence in childhood. In J. O. Greene & B. R. Burleson (Eds.), *Handbook of communication and social interaction skills* (pp. 753–797). Mahwah, NJ: Erlbaum.

Hart, C. H., Yang, C., Charlesworth, R., & Burts, D. C. (2003, April). *Kindergarten teaching practices: Associations with later child academic and social/emotional adjustment to school.* Paper presented at the biennial meeting of the Society for Research in Child Development, Tampa, FL.

Hart, C. H., Yang, C., Nelson, L. J., Robinson, C. C., Olsen, J. A., Nelson, D. A., et al. (2000). Peer acceptance in early childhood and subtypes of socially withdrawn behavior in China, Russia and the United States. *International Journal of Behavioral Development, 24*, 73–81.

Hart, D., Atkins, R., & Matsuba, M. K. (2008). The association of neighborhood poverty with personality change in childhood. *Journal of Personality and Social Psychology, 94*, 1048–1061.

Hart, H., & Rubia, K. (2012). Neuroimaging of child abuse: A review. *Frontiers in Human Neuroscience, 6*, 52.

Harter, S. (1999). *The construction of self: A developmental perspective.* New York: Guilford.

Harter, S. (2012). *The construction of the self: Developmental and sociocultural foundations* (2nd ed.). New York: Guilford.

Hartshorn, K. (2003). Reinstatement maintains a memory in human infants for 1½ years. *Developmental Psychobiology, 42*, 269–282.

Hartshorn, K., Rovee-Collier, C., Gerhardstein, P., Bhatt, R. S., Klein, P. J., Aaron, F., Wondoloski, T. L., & Wurtzel, N. (1998a). Developmental changes in the specificity of memory over the first year of life. *Developmental Psychobiology, 33*, 61–78.

Hartshorn, K., Rovee-Collier, C., Gerhardstein, P., Bhatt, R. S., Wondoloski, T. L., Klein, P., Gilch, J., Wurtzel, N., & Campos-deCarvalho, M. (1998b). The ontogeny of long-term memory over the first year-and-a-half of life. *Developmental Psychobiology, 32*, 69–89.

Hartup, W. W. (2006). Relationships in early and middle childhood. In A. L. Vangelisti & D. Perlman (Eds.), *Cambridge handbook of personal relationships* (pp. 177–190). New York: Cambridge University Press.

Hartup, W. W., & Abecassis, M. (2004). Friends and enemies. In P. K. Smith & C. H. Hart (Eds.), *Blackwell handbook of childhood social development* (pp. 285–306). Malden, MA: Blackwell.

Hasebe, Y., Nucci, L., & Nucci, M. S. (2004). Parental control of the personal domain and adolescent symptoms of psychopathology: A cross-national study in the United States and Japan. *Child Development, 75*, 815–828.

Hau, K.-T., & Ho, I. T. (2010). Chinese students' motivation and achievement. In M. H. Bond (Ed.), *Oxford handbook of Chinese psychology* (pp. 187–204). New York: Oxford University Press.

Hauf, P., Aschersleben, G., & Prinz, W. (2007). Baby do–baby see! How action production influences action perception in infants. *Cognitive Development, 22*, 16–32.

Hauser-Cram, P., Warfield, M. E., Stadler, J., & Sirin, S. R. (2006). School environments and the diverging pathways of students living in poverty. In A. C. Huston & M. N. Ripke (Eds.), *Developmental contexts in middle childhood* (pp. 198–216). New York: Cambridge University Press.

Hauspie, R., & Roelants, M. (2012). Adolescent growth. In N. Cameron & R. Bogin (Eds.), *Human growth and development* (2nd ed., pp. 57–79). London: Elsevier.

Havstad, S. L., Johnson, D. D., Zoratti, E. M., Ezell, J. M., Woodcroft, K., Ownby, D. R., et al. (2012). Tobacco smoke exposure and allergic sensitization in children: A propensity score analysis. *Respirology, 17*, 1068–1072.

Haws, R. A., Yakoob, M. Y., Soomro, T., Menezes, E. V., Darmstadt, G. L., & Bhutta, Z. A. (2009). Reducing stillbirths: Screening and monitoring during pregnancy and labour. *BMC Pregnancy and Childbirth, 9*(Suppl. S1).

Hay, D. F., Pawlby, S., Waters, C. S., Perra, O., & Sharp, D. (2010). Mothers' antenatal depression and their children's antisocial outcomes. *Child Development, 81,* 149–165.

Hayne, H. (2002). Thoughts from the crib: Meltzoff and Moore (1994) alter our views of mental representation during infancy. *Infant Behavior and Development, 25,* 62–64.

Hayne, H. (2004). Infant memory development: Implications for childhood amnesia. *Developmental Review, 24*, 33–73.

Hayne, H., Herbert, J., & Simcock, G. (2003). Imitation from television by 24- and 30-month-olds. *Developmental Science, 6*, 254–261.

Hayne, H., Rovee-Collier, C., & Perris, E. E. (1987). Categorization and memory retrieval by three-month-olds. *Child Development, 58*, 750–767.

Hayslip, B., Jr., & Kaminski, P. L. (2005). Grandparents raising their grandchildren. *Marriage and Family Review, 37*, 147–169.

Haywood, H. C., & Lidz, C. (2007). *Dynamic assessment in practice.* New York: Cambridge University Press.

Haywood, K., & Getchell, N. (2014). *Life span motor development* (6th ed.). Champaign, IL: Human Kinetics.

Hazen, N. L., McFarland, L., Jacobvitz, D., & Boyd-Soisson, E. (2010). Fathers' frightening behaviours and sensitivity with infants: Relations with fathers' attachment representations, father–infant attachment, and children's later outcomes. *Early Child Development and Care, 180,* 51–69.

Healthy Families America. (2011). *Healthy Families America FAQ.* Retrieved from www.healthyfamiliesamerica.org/about_us/faq.shtml

Heckman, J. J., Seong, H. M., Pinto, R., Savelyev, P., & Yavitz, A. (2010). A new cost-benefit and rate of return for the Perry Preschool Program: A summary. In

A. J. Reynolds, A. J. Rolnick, M. M. Englund, & J. Temple (Eds.), *Childhood programs and practices in the first decade of life: A human capital integration* (pp. 199–213). New York: Cambridge University Press.

Heinrich-Weltzien, R., Zorn, C., Monse, B., & Kromeyer-Hauschild, K. (2013). Relationship between malnutrition and the number of permanent teeth in Filipino 10- to 13-year-olds. *BioMed Research International, 2013,* Article ID 205950.

Hellemans, K. G., Sliwowska, J. H., Verma, P., & Weinberg, J. (2010). Prenatal alcohol exposure: Fetal programming and later life vulnerability to stress, expression and anxiety disorders. *Neuroscience and Biobehavioral Reviews, 34,* 791–807.

Helwig, C. C. (2006). Rights, civil liberties, and democracy across cultures. In M. Killen & J. G. Smetana (Eds.), *Handbook of moral development* (pp. 185–210). Philadelphia: Erlbaum.

Helwig, C. C., & Jasiobedzka, U. (2001). The relation between law and morality: Children's reasoning about socially beneficial and unjust laws. *Child Development, 72,* 1382–1393.

Helwig, C. C., & Prencipe, A. (1999). Children's judgments of flags and flag-burning. *Child Development, 70,* 132–143.

Helwig, C. C., & Turiel, E. (2004). Children's social and moral reasoning. In P. K. Smith & C. H. Hart (Eds.), *Blackwell handbook of childhood social development* (pp. 476–490). Malden, MA: Blackwell.

Helwig, C. C., & Turiel, E. (2011). Children's social and moral reasoning. In P. K. Smith & C. H. Hart (Eds.), *The Wiley-Blackwell handbook of childhood social development* (2nd ed., pp. 567–583). Chichester, UK: John Wiley & Sons.

Helwig, C. C., Zelazo, P. D., & Wilson, M. (2001). Children's judgments of psychological harm in normal and canonical situations. *Child Development, 72,* 66–81.

Henricsson, L., & Rydell, A.-M. (2004). Elementary school children with behavior problems: Teacher–child relations and self-perception. A prospective study. *Merrill-Palmer Quarterly, 50,* 111–138.

Hensley, E., & Briars, L. (2010). Closer look at autism and the measles-mumps-rubella vaccine. *Journal of the American Pharmacists Association, 50,* 736–741.

Hepper, P. G., Dornan, J., & Lynch, C. (2012). Sex differences in fetal habituation. *Developmental Science, 15,* 373–383.

Hepper, P. G., McCartney, G. R., & Shannon, E. A. (1998). Lateralised behaviour in first trimester human foetuses. *Neuropsychologia, 43,* 313–315.

Heraghty, J. L., Hilliard, T. N., Henderson, A. J., & Fleming, P. J. (2008). The physiology of sleep in infants. *Archives of Disease in Childhood, 93,* 982–985.

Herbert, J., Gross, J., & Hayne, H. (2007). Crawling is associated with more flexible memory retrieval by 9-month-old infants. *Developmental Science, 10,* 183–189.

Hernandez, D. J., Denton, N. A., & Blanchard, V. L. (2011). Children in the United States of America: A statistical portrait by race-ethnicity, immigrant origins, and language. *Annals of the American Academy of Political and Social Science, 633,* 102–127.

Hernandez, D. J., Denton, N. A., Macartney, S., & Blanchard, V. L. (2012). Children in immigrant families: Demography, policy, and evidence for the immigrant paradox. In C. García Coll & A. K. Marks (Eds.), *The Immigrant Paradox in Children and adolescents: Is becoming American a developmental risk?* (pp. 17–36). Washington, DC: American Psychological Association.

Hernando-Herraez, I., Prado-Martinez, J., Garg, P., Fernandez-Callejo, M., Heyn, H., Hvilsom, C., et al. (2013). Dynamics of DNA methyltion in recent human and great ape evolution. *PLOS Genetics, 9*(9), e1003763.

Heron, T. E., Hewar, W. L., & Cooper, J. O. (2013). *Applied behavior analysis.* Upper Saddle River, NJ: Pearson.

Heron-Delaney, M., Anzures, G., Herbert, J. S., Quinn, P. C., Slater, A. M., Tanaka, J. W., et al. (2011). Perceptual training prevents the emergence of the other race effect during infancy. *PLOS ONE, 6,* 231–255.

Herrnstein, R. J., & Murray, C. (1994). *The bell curve.* New York: Free Press.

Hespos, S. J., Ferry, A. L., Cannistraci, C. J., Gore, J., & Park, S. (2010). Using optical imaging to investigate functional cortical activity in human infants. In A. W. Roe (Ed.), *Imaging the brain with optical methods* (pp. 159–176). New York: Springer Science + Business Media.

Hesse, E., & Main, M. (2000). Disorganized infant, child, and adult attachment: Collapse in behavioral and attentional strategies. *Journal of the American Psychoanalytic Association, 48,* 1097–1127.

Hetherington, E. M. (2003). Social support and the adjustment of children in divorced and remarried families. *Childhood, 10,* 237–254.

Hetherington, E. M., & Kelly, J. (2002). *For better or for worse: Divorce reconsidered.* New York: Norton.

Hetherington, E. M., & Stanley-Hagan, M. (2000). Diversity among stepfamilies. In D. H. Demo, K. R. Allen, & M. A. Fine (Eds.), *Handbook of family diversity* (pp. 173–196). New York: Oxford University Press.

Hewlett, B. S. (1992). Husband–wife reciprocity and the father–infant relationship among Aka pygmies. In B. S. Hewlett (Ed.), *Father–child relations: Cultural and biosocial contexts* (pp. 153–176). New York: Aldine De Gruyter.

Hewlett, B. S. (2004). Fathers in forager, farmer, and pastoral cultures. In M. E. Lamb (Ed.), *The role of the father in child development* (4th ed., pp. 182–195). Hoboken, NJ: Wiley.

Heyes, C. (2005). Imitation by association. In S. Hurley & N. Chater (Eds.), *Perspectives on imitation: From neuroscience to social science: Vol. 1. Mechanisms of imitation and imitation in animals* (pp. 157–177). Cambridge, MA: MIT Press.

Heyes, C. M. (2010). Where do mirror neurons come from? *Neuroscience and Biobehavioral Reviews, 34,* 575–583.

Heyman, G. D., Dweck, C. S., & Cain, K. M. (1992). Young children's vulnerability to self-blame and helplessness: Relationship to beliefs about goodness. *Child Development, 63,* 401–415.

Heyman, G. D., & Gelman, S. A. (1999). The use of trait labels in making psychological inferences. *Child Development, 70,* 604–619.

Heyman, G. D., & Gelman, S. A. (2000). Preschool children's use of trait labels to make inductive inferences. *Journal of Experimental Child Psychology, 77,* 1–19.

Heyman, G. D., & Legare, C. H. (2004). Children's beliefs about gender differences in the academic and social domains. *Sex Roles, 50,* 227–239.

Heywood, C. (2013). *A history of childhood: Children and childhood in the West from medieval to modern times.* Oxford, UK: Polity.

Hickling, A. K., & Wellman, H. M. (2001). The emergence of children's causal explanations and theories: Evidence from everyday conversation. *Developmental Psychology, 37,* 668–683.

Hicks, J. H., & Goedereis, E. A. (2009). The importance of context and the gain-loss dynamic for understanding grandparent caregivers. In K. Shifren (Ed.), *How caregiving affects development: Psychological implications for child, adolescent, and adult caregivers* (pp. 169–190). Washington, DC: American Psychological Association.

High, P. C., LaGasse, L., Becker, S., Ahlgren, I., & Gardner, A. (2000). Literacy promotion in primary care pediatrics: Can we make a difference? *Pediatrics, 105,* 927–934.

Hilbert, D. D., & Eis, S. D. (2014). Early intervention for emergent literacy development in a collaborative community pre-kindergarten. *Early Childhood Education Journal, 42,* 105–113.

Hildreth, K., & Rovee-Collier, C. (2002). Forgetting functions of reactivated memories over the first year of life. *Developmental Psychobiology, 41,* 277–288.

Hildreth, K., Sweeney, B., & Rovee-Collier, C. (2003). Differential memory-preserving effects of reminders at 6 months. *Journal of Experimental Child Psychology, 84,* 41–62.

Hill, A. L., Degnan, K. A., Calkins, S. D., & Keane, S. P. (2006). Profiles of externalizing behavior problems for boys and girls across preschool: The roles of emotion regulation and inattention. *Developmental Psychology, 42,* 913–928.

Hill, D. B., Menvielle, E., Sica, K. M., & Johnson, A. (2010). An affirmative intervention for families with gender variant children: Parental ratings of child mental health and gender. *Journal of Sex and Marital Therapy, 36,* 6–23.

Hill, E. J., Mead, N. T., Dean, L. R., Hafen, D. M., Gadd, R., Palmer, A. A., & Ferris, M. S. (2006). Researching the 60-hour dual-earner workweek: An alternative to the "opt-out revolution." *American Behavioral Scientist, 49,* 1184–1203.

Hill, J. L., Brooks-Gunn, J., & Waldfogel, J. (2003). Sustained effects of high participation in an early intervention for

low-birth-weight premature infants. *Developmental Psychology, 39,* 730–744.

Hilt, L. M. (2004). Attribution retaining for therapeutic change: Theory, practice, and future directions. *Imagination, Cognition, and Personality, 23,* 289–307.

Hinojosa, T., Sheu, C.-F., & Michael, G. F. (2003). Infant hand-use preference for grasping objects contributes to the development of a hand-use preference for manipulating objects. *Developmental Psychobiology, 43,* 328–334.

Hipfner-Boucher, K., Milburn, T., Weitzman, E., Greenberg, J., Pelletier, J., & Girolametto, L. (2014). Relationships between preschoolers' oral language and phonological awareness. *First Language, 34,* 178–197.

Hirasawa, R., & Feil, R. (2010). Genomic imprinting and human disease. *Essays in Biochemistry, 48,* 187–200.

Hirsh-Pasek, K., & Burchinal, M. (2006). Mother and caregiver sensitivity over time: Predicting language and academic outcomes with variable- and person-centered approaches. *Merill-Palmer Quarterly, 52,* 449–485.

Hirsh-Pasek, K., & Golinkoff, R. M. (2003). *Einstein never used flash cards.* New York: Rodale.

Hobson, J. A., Hobson, R. P., Malik, S., Bargiota, K., & Calo, S. (2013). The relation between social engagement and pretend play in autism. *British Journal of Developmental Psychology, 31,* 114–127.

Hodges, J., & Tizard, B. (1989). Social and family relationships of ex-institutional adolescents. *Journal of Child Psychology and Psychiatry, 30,* 77–97.

Hodnett, E. D., Gates, S., Hofmeyr, G. J., & Sakala, C. (2012). Continuous support for women during childbirth. *Cochrane Database of Systematic Reviews, Issue 7* (Art. No. CD003766).

Hoehn, T., Hansmann, G., Bührer, C., Simbruner, G., Gunn, A. J., Yager, J., et al. (2008). Therapeutic hypothermia in neonates: Review of current clinical data, ILCOR recommendations and suggestions for implementation in neonatal intensive care units. *Resuscitation, 78,* 7–12.

Hoerr, T. (2004). How MI informs teaching at New City School. *Teachers College Record, 106,* 40–48.

Hoff, E. (2003). The specificity of environmental influence: Socioeconomic status affects early vocabulary development via maternal speech. *Child Development, 74,* 1368–1378.

Hoff, E. (2006). How social contexts support and shape language development. *Developmental Review, 26,* 55–88.

Hoff, E. (2013). Interpreting the early language trajectories of children from low-SES and language minority homes: Implications for closing achievement gaps. *Developmental Psychology, 49,* 4–14.

Hoff, E., Core, C., Place, S., Rumiche, R., Senor, M., & Parra, M. (2012). Dual language exposure and early bilingual development. *Journal of Child Language, 39,* 1–27.

Hoff, E., Laursen, B., & Tardif, T. (2002). Socioeconomic status and parenting. In M. H. Bornstein (Ed.), *Handbook of parenting: Vol. 2. Biology and ecology of parenting* (pp. 231–252). Mahwah, NJ: Erlbaum.

Hoff, E. V. (2005). A friend living inside me: The forms and functions of imaginary companions. *Imagination, Cognition and Personality, 24,* 151–189.

Hofferth, S. L. (2010). Home media and children's achievement and behavior. *Child Development, 81,* 1598–1610.

Hofferth, S. L., & Anderson, K. G. (2003). Are all dads equal? Biology versus marriage as a basis for paternal investment. *Journal of Marriage and the Family, 65,* 213–232.

Hofferth, S. L., Forry, N. D., & Peters, H. E. (2010). Child support, father–child contact, and preteens' involvement with nonresidential fathers: Racial/ethnic differences. *Journal of Family Economic Issues, 31,* 14–32.

Hoffman, L. W. (2000). Maternal employment: Effects of social context. In R. D. Taylor & M. C. Wang (Eds.), *Resilience across contexts: Family, work, culture, and community* (pp. 147–176). Mahwah, NJ: Erlbaum.

Hoffman, M. K., Vahratian, A., Sciscione, A. C., Troendle, J. F., & Zhang, J. (2006). Comparison of labor progression between induced and noninduced multiparous women. *Obstetrics and Gynecology, 107,* 1029–1034.

Hoffner, C., & Badzinski, D. M. (1989). Children's integration of facial and situational cues to emotion. *Child Development, 60,* 411–422.

Hokoda, A., & Fincham, F. D. (1995). Origins of children's helpless and mastery achievement patterns in the family. *Journal of Educational Psychology, 87,* 375–385.

Holditch-Davis, D., Belyea, M., & Edwards, L. J. (2005). Prediction of 3-year developmental outcomes from sleep development over the preterm period. *Infant Behavior and Development, 79,* 49–58.

Holland, A. L. (2004). Plasticity and development. *Brain and Language, 88,* 254–255.

Hollich, G. J., Hirsh-Pasek, K., & Golinkoff, R. M. (2000). Breaking the language barrier: An emergentist coalition model for the origins of word learning. *Monographs of the Society for Research in Child Development, 65*(3, Serial No. 262).

Holmes, J., Gathercole, S. E., & Dunning, D. L. (2010). Poor working memory: Impact and interventions. In P. Bauer (Ed.), *Advances in child development and behavior* (Vol. 39, pp. 1–43). London: Academic Press.

Hood, M., Conlon, E., & Andrews, G. (2008). Preschool home literacy practices and children's literacy development: A longitudinal analysis. *Journal of Educational Psychology, 100,* 252–271.

Hopf, L., Quraan, M. A., Cheung, M. J., Taylor, M. J., Ryan, J. D., & Moses, S. N. (2013). Hippocampal lateralization and memory in children. *Journal of the International Neuropsychological Society, 19,* 1042–1052.

Hopkins, B., & Westra, T. (1988). Maternal handling and motor development: An intracultural study. *Genetic, Social and General Psychology Monographs, 14,* 377–420.

Hopkins-Golightly, T., Raz, S., & Sander, C. J. (2003). Influence of slight to moderate risk for birth hypoxia on acquisition of cognitive and language function in the preterm infant: A cross-sectional comparison with preterm-birth controls. *Neuropsychology, 17,* 3–13.

Horner, S. L., & Gaither, S. M. (2004). Attribution retraining instruction with a second-grade class. *Early Childhood Education Journal, 31,* 165–170.

Horner, T. M. (1980). Two methods of studying stranger reactivity in infants: A review. *Journal of Child Psychology and Psychiatry, 21,* 203–219.

Houlihan, J., Kropp. T. Wiles, R., Gray, S., & Campbell, C. (2005). *Body burden: The pollution in newborns.* Washington, DC: Environmental Working Group.

Houts, R. M., Barnett-Walker, K. C., Paley, B., & Cox, M. J. (2008). Patterns of couple interaction during the transition to parenthood. *Personal Relationships, 15,* 103–122.

Hovdenak, N., & Haram, K. (2012). Influence of mineral and vitamin supplements on pregnancy outcome. *European Journal of Obstetrics & Gynecology and Reproductive Biology, 164,* 127–132.

Hoven, C. W., Duarte, C. S., Lucas, C. P., Wu, P., Mandell, D. J., Goodwin, R. D., et al. (2005). Psychopathology among New York City public school children 6 months after September 11. *Archives of General Psychiatry, 62,* 545–552.

Howard, K. S., & Brooks-Gunn, J. (2009). The role of home-visiting programs in preventing child abuse and neglect. *Future of Children, 19,* 119–146.

Howe, M. L., Courage, M. L., & Rooksby, M. (2009). The genesis and development of autobiographical memory. In M. L. Courage & N. Cowan (Eds.), *The development of memory in infancy and childhood* (pp. 177–196). Hove, UK: Psychology Press.

Howe, N., Aquan-Assee, J., & Bukowski, W. M. (2001). Predicting sibling relations over time: Synchrony between maternal management styles and sibling relationship quality. *Merrill-Palmer Quarterly, 47,* 121–141.

Howell, K. K., Coles, C. D., & Kable, J. A. (2008). The medical and developmental consequences of prenatal drug exposure. In J. Brick (Ed.), *Handbook of the medical consequences of alcohol and drug abuse* (2nd ed., pp. 219–249). New York: Haworth Press.

Howell, S. R., & Becker, S. (2013). Grammar from the lexicon: Evidence from neural network simulations of language acquisition. In D. Bittner & N. Ruhlig (Eds.), *Lexical bootstrapping: The role of lexis and semantics in child language* (pp. 245–264). Berlin: Walter de Gruyter.

Howes, C., & Matheson, C. C. (1992). Sequences in the development of competent play with peers: Social and social pretend play. *Developmental Psychology, 28,* 961–974.

Hsu, A. S., Chater, N., & Vitányi, P. (2013). Language learning from positive evidence, reconsidered: A simplicity-based approach. *Topics in Cognitive Science, 5,* 35–55.

Huang, C.-C. (2006). Child support enforcement and father involvement for children in never-married mother families. *Fathering, 4,* 97–111.

Hubbs-Tait, L., Nation, J. R., Krebs, N. F., & Bellinger, D. C. (2005). Neurotoxicants, micronutrients, and social environments: Individual and combined effects on children's development. *Psychological Science in the Public Interest, 6,* 57–121.

Hudson, J. A., Fivush, R., & Kuebli, J. (1992). Scripts and episodes: The development of event memory. *Applied Cognitive Psychology, 6,* 483–505.

Hudson, J. A., & Mayhew, E. M. Y. (2009). The development of memory for recurring events. In M. L. Courage & N. Cowan (Eds.), *The development of memory in infancy and childhood* (pp. 69–91). Hove, UK: Psychology Press.

Hudziak, J. J., & Rettew, D. C. (2009). Genetics of ADHD. In T. E. Brown (Ed.), *ADHD comorbidties: Handbook for ADHD complications in children and adults* (pp. 23–36). Arlington, VA: American Psychiatric Publishing.

Huebner, C. E., & Payne, K. (2010). Home support for emergent literacy: Follow-up of a community-based implementation of dialogic reading. *Journal of Applied Developmental Psychology, 31,* 195–201.

Huesmann, L. R., Moise-Titus, J., Podolski, C., & Eron, L. D. (2003). Longitudinal relations between children's exposure to TV violence and their aggressive and violent behavior in young adulthood: 1977–1992. *Developmental Psychology, 39,* 201–221.

Hughes, C., & Dunn, J. (1998). Understanding mind and emotion: Longitudinal associations with mental-state talk between young friends. *Developmental Psychology, 34,* 1026–1037.

Hughes, C., & Ensor, R. (2007). Executive function and theory of mind: Predictive relations from ages 2 to 4. *Developmental Psychology, 43,* 1447–1459.

Hughes, C., & Ensor, R. (2010). Do early social cognition and executive function predict individual differences in preschoolers' prosocial and antisocial behavior? In B. W. Sokol, U. Müller, J. I. M. Carpendale, A. R. Young, & G. Iarocci (Eds.), *Social interaction and the development of social understanding and executive functions* (pp. 418–441). New York: Oxford University Press.

Hughes, C., Ensor, R., & Marks, A. (2010). Individual differences in false belief understanding are stable from 3 to 6 years of age and predict children's mental state talk with school friends. *Journal of Experimental Child Psychology, 108,* 96–112.

Hughes, C., Marks, A., Ensor, R., & Lecce, S. (2010). A longitudinal study of conflict and inner state talk in children's conversations with mothers and younger siblings. *Social Development, 19,* 822–837.

Hughes, J. N. (2011). Longitudinal effects of teacher and student perceptions of teacher–student relationship qualities on academic adjustment. *Elementary School Journal, 112,* 38–60.

Hughes, J. N., Cavell, T. A., & Grossman, P. B. (1997). A positive view of self: Risk or protection for aggressive children? *Development and Psychopathology, 9,* 75–94.

Hughes, J. N., & Kwok, O. (2006). Classroom engagement mediates the effect of teacher–student support on elementary students' peer acceptance. *Journal of School Psychology, 43,* 465–480.

Hughes, J. N., & Kwok, O. (2007). Influence of student–teacher and parent–teacher relationships on lower achieving readers' engagement and achievement in the primary grades. *Journal of Educational Psychology, 99,* 39–51.

Hughes, J. N., Wu, J–Y., Kwok, O., Villarreal, V., & Johnson, A. Y. (2012). Indirect effects of child reports of teacher–student relationship on achievement. *Journal of Educational Psychology, 104,* 350–365.

Hughes, J. N., Zhang, D., & Hill, C. R. (2006). Peer assessments of normative and individual teacher–student support predict social acceptance and engagement among low-achieving children. *Journal of School Psychology, 43,* 447–463.

Humphrey, T. (1978). Function of the nervous system during prenatal life. In U. Stave (Ed.), *Perinatal physiology* (pp. 651–683). New York: Plenum.

Hunnius, S., & Geuze, R. H. (2004a). Developmental changes in visual scanning of dynamic faces and abstract stimuli in infants: A longitudinal study. *Infancy, 6,* 231–255.

Hunnius, S., & Geuze, R. H. (2004b). Gaze shifting in infancy: A longitudinal study using dynamic faces and abstract stimuli. *Infant Behavior and Development, 27,* 397–416.

Hunt, C. E., & Hauck, F. R. (2006). Sudden infant death syndrome. *Canadian Medical Association Journal, 174,* 1861–1869.

Hunt, E. (2011). *Human intelligence.* New York: Cambridge University Press.

Hunter, L. A. (2014). Vaginal breech birth: Can we move beyond the term breech trial? *Journal of Midwifery and Women's Health, 59,* 320–327.

Huntsinger, C., Jose, P. E., Krieg, D. B., & Luo, Z. (2011). Cultural differences in Chinese American and European American children's drawing skills over time. *Early Childhood Research Quarterly, 26,* 134–145.

Hurewitz, F., Brown-Schmidt, S., Thorpe, K., Gleitman, L. R., & Trueswell, J. C. (2000). One frog, two frog, red frog, blue frog: Factors affecting children's syntactic choices in production and comprehension. *Journal of Psycholinguistic Research, 29,* 597–626.

Hursti, U.-K. (1999). Factors influencing children's food choice. *Annals of Medicine, 31,* 26–32.

Hurt, H., Betancourt, L. M., Malmud, E. K., Shera, D. M., Giannetta, J. M., Brodsky, N. L., et al. (2009). Children with and without gestational cocaine exposure: A neurocognitive systems analysis. *Neurotoxicology and Teratology, 31,* 334–341.

Huston, A. C., Wright, J. C., Marquis, J., & Green, S. B. (1999). How young children spend their time: Television and other activities. *Developmental Psychology, 35,* 912–925.

Hutchinson, E. A., De Luca, C. R., Doyle, L. W., Roberts, G., & Anderson, P. J. (2013). School-age outcomes of extremely preterm or extremely low birth weight children. *Pediatrics, 131,* e1053–e1061.

Huttenlocher, J., Waterfall, H., Veasilyeva, M., Vevea J., & Hedges, L. (2010). Sources of variability in children's language growth. *Cognitive Psychology, 61,* 343–365.

Huttenlocher, P. R. (2002). *Neural plasticity: The effects of environment on the development of the cerebral cortex.* Cambridge, MA: Harvard University Press.

Huyck, M. H. (1996). Continuities and discontinuities in gender identity in midlife. In V. L. Bengtson (Ed.), *Adulthood and aging* (pp. 98–121). New York: Springer-Verlag.

Hyde, D. C., & Spelke, E. S. (2011). Neural signatures of number processing in human infants: Evidence for two core systems underlying numerical cognition. *Developmental Science, 14,* 360–371.

Hyde, J. S., Essex, M. J., Clark, R., & Klein, M. H. (2001). Maternity leave, women's employment, and marital incompatibility. *Journal of Family Psychology, 15,* 476–491.

Hymel, S., Schonert-Reichl, K. A., Bonanno, R. A., Vaillancourt, T., & Henderson, N. R. (2010). Bullying and morality: Understanding how good kids can behave badly. In S. Jimerson, S. M. Swearer, & D. L. Espelage (Eds.), *Handbook of bullying in schools: An international perspective* (pp. 101–118). New York: Routledge.

I

Iacoboni, M. (2009). Imitation, empathy, and mirror neurons. *Annual Review of Psychology, 60,* 653–670.

Imai, M., & Haryu, E. (2004). The nature of word-learning biases and their roles for lexical development: From a cross-linguistic perspective. In D. G. Hall & S. R. Waxman (Eds.), *Weaving a lexicon* (pp. 411–444). Cambridge, MA: MIT Press.

Imai, M., Li, L., Haryu, E., Okada, H., Hirsh-Pasek, K., Golinkoff, R. M., & Shigematsu, J. (2008). Novel noun and verb learning in Chinese-, English-, and Japanese-speaking children. *Child Development, 79,* 979–1000.

Ingoldsby, E. M., Shelleby, E., Lane, T., & Shaw, D. S. (2012). Extrafamilial contexts and children's conduct problems. In V. Maholmes & R. B. King (Eds.), *Oxford handbook of poverty and child development* (pp. 404–422). New York: Oxford University Press.

Insana, S. P., & Montgomery-Downs, H. E. (2012). Sleep and sleepiness among first-time postpartum parents: A field- and laboratory-based multimethod assessment. *Developmental Psychobiology, 55,* 361–372.

Ip, S., Chung, M., Raman, G. Trikalinos, T. A., & Lau, J. (2009). A summary of the Agency for Healthcare Research and Quality's evidence report on breastfeeding in developed countries. *Breastfeeding Medicine, 4*(Suppl. 1), S17–S30.

Isabella, R. (1993). Origins of attachment: Maternal interactive behavior across the first year. *Child Development, 64,* 605–621.

Isabella, R., & Belsky, J. (1991). Interactional synchrony and the origins of infant–mother attachment: A replication study. *Child Development, 62,* 373–384.

Ishihara, K., Warita, K., Tanida, T., Sugawara, T., Kitagawa, H., & Hoshi, N. (2007). Does paternal exposure to 2,3,7, 8-tetrachlorodibenzo-p-dioxin (TCDD) affect the sex ratio of offspring? *Journal of Veterinary Medical Science, 69,* 347–352.

Isles, A. R., & Wilkinson, L. S. (2011). Genomic imprinting effects on brain and behavior: Future directions. In A. Petronis & J. Mill (Eds.), *Brain, behavior and epigenetics* (pp. 169–184). New York: Springer.

Israel, M. Johnson, C., & Brooks, P. J. (2000). From states to events: The acquisition of English passive participles. *Cognitive Linguistics, 11,* 103–129.

Ivorra, J. L., Sanjuan, J., Jover, M., Carot, J. M., de Frutos, R., & Molto, M. D. (2010). Gene-environment interaction of child temperament. *Journal of Developmental and Behavioral Pediatrics, 31,* 545–554.

Izard, C. E., King, P. A., Trentacosta, C. J., Laurenceau, J. P., Morgan, J. K, Krauthamer-Ewing, E. S., & Finlon, K. J. (2008). Accelerating the development of emotion competence in Head Start children. *Development and Psychopathology, 20,* 369–397.

Izard, V., Dehaene-Lambertz, G., & Dehaene, S. (2008). Distinct cerebral pathways for object identity and number in human infants. *PLOS Biology, 6*(2), e11.

Izard, V., Sann, C., Spelke, E. S., & Streri, A. (2009). Newborn infants perceive abstract numbers. *Proceedings of the National Academy of Sciences, 106,* 10382–10385.

J

Jack, F., Simcock, G., & Hayne, G. (2012). Magic memories: Young children's verbal recall after a 6-year delay. *Child Development, 83,* 159–172.

Jackson, A. P., Bentler, P. M., & Franke, T. M. (2006). Employment and parenting among current and former welfare recipients. *Journal of Social Service Research, 33,* 13–25.

Jackson, L. A., von Eye, A., Witt, E. A., Zhao, Y., & Fitzgerald, H. E. (2011). A longitudinal study of the effects of Internet use and videogame playing on academic performance and the roles of gender, race and income in these relationships. *Computers in Human Behavior, 27,* 228–239.

Jacobs, J. E., Lanza, S., Osgood, D. W., Eccles, J. S., & Wigfield, A. (2002). Changes in children's self-competence and values: Gender and domain differences across grades one through twelve. *Child Development, 73,* 509–527.

Jacobs, J. N., & Kelley, M. L. (2006). Predictors of paternal involvement in childcare in dual-earner families with young children. *Fathering, 4,* 23–47.

Jacobson, J. L., & Jacobson, S. W. (2003). Prenatal exposure to polychlorinated biphenyls and attention at school age. *Journal of Pediatrics, 143,* 780–788.

Jacquet, P. (2004). Sensitivity of germ cells and embryos to ionizing radiation. *Journal of Biological Regulators and Homeostatic Agents, 18,* 106–114.

Jadallah, M., Anderson, R. C., Nguyen-Jahiel, K., Miller, B. W., Kim, I-H., Kuo, L-J., et al. (2011). Influence of a teacher's scaffolding moves during child-led small-group discussions. *American Educational Research Journal, 48,* 194–230.

Jadva, V., Casey, P., & Golombok, S. (2012). Surrogacy families 10 years on: Relationship with the surrogate, decisions over disclosure and children's understanding of their surrogacy origins. *Human Reproduction, 27,* 3008–3014.

Jaffari-Bimmel, N., Juffer, F., van IJzendoorn, M. H., Bakermans-Kranenburg, M. J., & Mooijaart, A. (2006). Social development from infancy to adolescence: Longitudinal and concurrent factors in an adoption sample. *Developmental Psychology, 42,* 1143–1153.

Jaffee, S. R., Bowes, L., Ouellet-Morin, I., Fisher, H. L., Moffitt, T. E., Merrick, M. T., & Arseneault, L. (2013). Safe, stable, nurturing relationships break the intergenerational cycle of abuse: A prospective nationally representative cohort of children in the United Kingdom. *Journal of Adolescent Health, 53,* S4–S10.

Jaffee, S. R., Caspi, A., Moffitt, T. E., Belsky, J., & Silva, P. (2001). Why are children born to teen mothers at risk for adverse outcomes in young adulthood? *Development and Psychopathology, 13,* 377–397.

Jaffee, S. R., & Christian, C. W. (2014). The biological embedding of child abuse and neglect: Implications for policy and practice. *Society for Research in Child Development Social Policy Report, 28*(1).

Jaffee, S. R., Moffitt, T. E., Caspi, A., & Taylor, A. (2003). Life with (or without) father: The benefits of living with two biological parents depend on the father's antisocial behavior. *Child Development, 74,* 109–126.

Jambon, M., & Smetana, J. G. (2014). Moral complexity in middle childhood: Children's evaluations of necessary harm. *Developmental Psychology, 50,* 22–33.

Jansen, A., Theunissen, N., Slechten, K., Nederkoorn, C., Boon, B., Mulkens, S., & Roefs, A. (2003). Overweight children overeat after exposure to food cues. *Eating Behaviors, 4,* 197–209.

Jansen, J., de Weerth, C., & Riksen-Walraven, J. M. (2008). Breastfeeding and the mother–infant relationship. *Developmental Review, 28,* 503–521.

Jansen, P. W., Roza, S. J., Jaddoe, V. W. V., Mackenbach, J. D., Raat, H., Hofman, A., et al. (2012). Children's eating behavior, feeding practices of parents and weight problems in early childhood: Results from the population-based Generation R Study. *International Journal of Behavioral Nutrition and Physical Activity, 9,* 130–138.

Janssens, J. M. A. M., & Deković, M. (1997). Child rearing, prosocial moral reasoning, and prosocial behavior. *International Journal of Behavioral Development, 20,* 509–527.

Jaudes, P. K., & Mackey-Bilaver, L. (2008). Do chronic conditions increase young children's risk of being maltreated? *Child Abuse and Neglect, 32,* 671–681.

Jedrychowski, W., Perera, F. P., Jankowski, J., Mrozek-Budzyn, D., Mroz, E., Flak, E., et al. (2009). Very low prenatal exposure to lead and mental development of children in infancy and early childhood. *Neuroepidemiology, 32,* 270–278.

Jeffrey, J. (2004, November). Parents often blind to their kids' weight. *British Medical Journal Online.* Retrieved from content.health.msn.com/content/article/97/104292.htm

Jenkins, J. M., Rasbash, J., & O'Connor, T. G. (2003). The role of the shared family context in differential parenting. *Developmental Psychology, 39,* 99–113.

Jenni, O. G., & Carskadon, M. A. (2012). Sleep behavior and sleep regulation from infancy through adolescence: Normative aspects. *Sleep Medicine Clinics, 7,* 529–538.

Jennifer, D., & Cowie, H. (2009). Engaging children and young people actively in research. In K. Bryan (Ed.), *Communication in healthcare* (pp. 135–163). New York: Peter Lang.

Jensen, A. R. (1969). How much can we boost IQ and scholastic achievement? *Harvard Educational Review, 39,* 1–123.

Jensen, A. R. (1998). *The g factor: The science of mental ability.* New York: Praeger.

Jensen, A. R. (2001). Spearman's hypothesis. In J. M. Collis & S. Messick (Eds.), *Intelligence and personality: Bridging the gap in theory and measurement* (pp. 3–24). Mahwah, NJ: Erlbaum.

Jensen, A. R. (2002). Galton's legacy to research on intelligence. *Journal of Biosocial Science, 34,* 145–172.

Jerome, E. M., Hamre, B. K., & Pianta, R. C. (2009). Teacher–child relationships from kindergarten to sixth grade: Early childhood predictors of teacher-perceived conflict and closeness. *Social Development, 18,* 915–945.

Jeynes, W. (2012). A meta-analysis of the efficacy of different types of parental involvement programs for urban students. *Urban Education, 47,* 706–742.

Ji, C. Y., & Chen, T. J. (2008). Secular changes in stature and body mass index for Chinese youth in sixteen major cities, 1950s–2005. *American Journal of Human Biology, 20,* 530–537.

Jiao, S., Ji, G., & Jing, Q. (1996). Cognitive development of Chinese urban only children and children with siblings. *Child Development, 67,* 387–395.

Jipson, J. L., & Gelman, S. A. (2007). Robots and rodents: Children's inferences about living and nonliving kinds. *Child Development, 78,* 1675–1688.

Joh, A. S., & Adolph, K. E. (2006). Learning from falling. *Child Development, 77,* 89–102.

Johnson, A. D., Ryan, R. M., & Brooks-Gunn, J. (2012). Child-care subsidies: Do they impact the quality of care children experience? *Child Development, 83,* 1444–1461.

Johnson, C., & Mindell, J. A. (2011). Family-based interventions for sleep problems of infants. In M. El-Sheikh (Ed.), *Sleep and development: Familial and socio-cultural considerations* (pp. 375–402). New York: Oxford University Press.

Johnson, E. K., & Seidl, A. (2008). Clause segmentation by 6-month-old infants: A crosslinguistic perspective. *Infancy, 13,* 440–455.

Johnson, E. K., & Tyler, M. D. (2010). Testing the limits of statistical learning for word segmentation. *Developmental Science, 13,* 339–345.

Johnson, J. G., Cohen, P., Smailes, E. M., Kasen, S., & Brook, J. S. (2002). Television viewing and aggressive behavior during adolescence and adulthood. *Science, 295,* 2468–2471.

Johnson, M. H. (1999). Ontogenetic constraints on neural and behavioral plasticity: Evidence from imprinting and face processing. *Canadian Journal of Experimental Psychology, 55,* 77–90.

Johnson, M. H. (2001). The development and neural basis of face recognition: Comment and speculation. *Infant and Child Development, 10,* 31–33.

Johnson, M. H. (2011). Developmental neuroscience, psychophysiology, and genetics. In M. H. Bornstein & M. E. Lamb (Eds.), *Developmental science: An advanced textbook* (6th ed., pp. 187–222). Mahwah, NJ: Erlbaum.

Johnson, M. H., & Mareschal, D. (2001). Cognitive and perceptual development during infancy. *Current Opinion in Neurobiology, 11,* 213–218.

Johnson, R. C., & Schoeni, R. F. (2011). Early-life origins of adult disease: National longitudinal population-based study of the United States. *American Journal of Public Health, 101,* 2317–2324.

Johnson, S., Li, J., Kendall, G., Strazdins, L., & Jacoby, P. (2013). Mothers' and fathers' work hours, child gender, and behavior in middle childhood. *Journal of Marriage and Family, 75,* 56–74.

Johnson, S. C., Dweck, C. S., & Chen, F. S. (2007). Evidence for infants' internal working models of attachment. *Psychological Science, 18,* 501–502.

Johnson, S. C., Dweck, C., Chen, F. S., Stern, H. L., Ok, S.-J., & Barth, M. (2010). At the intersection of social and cognitive development: Internal working models of attachment in infancy. *Cognitive Science, 34,* 807–825.

Johnson, S. L. (2000). Improving preschoolers' self-regulation of energy intake. *Pediatrics, 106,* 1429–1435.

Johnson, S. P. (1997). Young infants' perception of object unity: Implications for development of attentional and cognitive skills. *Current Directions in Psychological Science, 6,* 5–11.

Johnson, S. P. (2009). Developmental origins of object perception. In A. Woodward & A. Needham (Eds.), *Learning and the infant mind* (pp. 47–65). New York: Oxford University Press.

Johnson, S. P. (2010). How infants learn about the visual world. *Cognitive Science, 34,* 1158–1184.

Johnson, S. P. (2011). A constructivist view of object perception in infancy. In L. M. Oakes, C. H. Cashon, M. Casasola, & D. Rakison (Eds.), *Infant perception and cognition* (pp. 51–68). New York: Oxford University Press.

Johnson, S. P., Bremner, J. G., Slater, A., Mason, U., Foster, K., & Cheshire, A. (2003). Infants' perception of object trajectories. *Child Development, 74,* 94–108.

Johnson, S. P., Fernandes, K. J., Frank, M. C., Kirkham, N. Z., Marcus, G. F., et al. (2009). Abstract rule learning for visual sequences in 8- and 11-month-olds. *Infancy, 14,* 2–18.

Johnson, S. P., Slemmer, J. A., & Amso, D. (2004). Where infants look determines how they see: Eye movements and object perception performance in 3-month-olds. *Infancy, 6,* 185–201.

Johnson, S. P., & Shuwairi, S. M. (2009). Learning and memory facilitate predictive tracking in 4-month-olds. *Journal of Experimental Child Psychology, 102,* 122–130.

Johnston, M. V., Nishimura, A., Harum, K., Pekar, J., & Blue, M. E. (2001). Sculpting the developing brain. *Advances in Pediatrics, 48,* 1–38.

Jokhi, R. P., & Whitby, E. H. (2011). Magnetic resonance imaging of the fetus. *Developmental Medicine and Child Neurology, 53,* 18–28.

Jones, A., Charles, P., & Benson, K. (2013). A model for supporting at-risk couples during the transition to parenthood. *Families in Society, 94,* 166–173.

Jones, D. J., & Lindahl, K. M. (2011). Coparenting in extended kinship systems: African American, Hispanic, Asian heritage, and Native American families. In J. P. McHale & K. M. Lindahl (Eds.), *Coparenting* (pp. 61–79). Washington, DC: American Psychological Association.

Jones, H. E. (2006). Drug addiction during pregnancy: Advances in maternal treatment and understanding child outcomes. *Current Directions in Psychological Science, 15,* 126–130.

Jones, J., Lopez, A., & Wilson, M. (2003). Congenital toxoplasmosis. *American Family Physician, 67,* 2131–2137.

Jones, S. (2009). The development of imitation in infancy. *Philosophical Transactions of the Royal Society B, 364,* 2325–2335.

Jordan, B. (1993). *Birth in four cultures.* Prospect Heights, IL: Waveland.

Jorgenson, L. A., Sun, M., O'Connor, M., & Georgieff, M. K. (2005). Fetal iron deficiency disrupts and maturation of synaptic function and efficacy in area CA1 of the developing rat hippocampus. *Hippocampus, 15,* 1094–1102.

Jose, A., O'Leary, D., & Moyer, A. (2010). Does premarital cohabitation predict subsequent marital stability and marital quality? A meta-analysis. *Journal of Marriage and Family, 72,* 105–116.

Joseph, R. M., & Tager-Flusberg, H. (2004). The relationship of theory of mind and executive functions to symptom type and severity in children with autism. *Development and Psychopathology, 16,* 137–155.

Josselyn, S. A., & Frankland, P. W. (2012). Infantile amnesia: A neurogenic hypothesis. *Learning and Memory, 19,* 423–433.

Juby, H., Billette, J.-M., Laplante, B., & Le Bourdais, C. (2007). Nonresident fathers and children: Parents' new unions and frequency of contact. *Journal of Family Issues, 28,* 1220–1245.

Judge, S., Puckett, K., & Bell, S. M. (2006). Closing the digital divide: Update from the Early Childhood Longitudinal Study. *Journal of Educational Research, 100,* 52–60.

Juffer, F., & van IJzendoorn, M. H. (2012). Review of meta-analytical studies on the physical, emotional, and cognitive outcomes of intercountry adoptees. In J. L. Gibbons & K. S. Rotabi (Eds.), *Intercountry adoption: Policies, practices, and outcomes* (pp. 175–186). Burlington, VT: Ashgate Publishing.

Junge, C., Kooijman, V., Hagoort, P., & Cutler, A. (2012). Rapid recognition at 10 months as a predictor of language development. *Developmental Science, 15,* 463–473.

Jürgensen, M., Hiort, O., Holterhus, P.-M., & Thyen, U. (2007). Gender role behavior in children with XY karyotype and disorders of sex development. *Hormones and Behavior, 51,* 443–453.

Jusczyk, P. W. (2002). Some critical developments in acquiring native language sound organization. *Annals of Otology, Rhinology and Laryngology, 189,* 11–15.

Jusczyk, P. W., Johnson, S. P., Spelke, E. S., & Kennedy, L. J. (1999). Synchronous change and perception of object unity: Evidence from adults and infants. *Cognition, 71,* 257–288.

Jusczyk, P. W., & Luce, P. A. (2002). Speech perception. In H. Pashler & S. Yantis (Eds.), *Steven's handbook of experimental psychology: Vol. 1. Sensation and perception* (3rd ed., pp. 493–536). New York: Wiley.

Justice, E. M. (1986). Developmental changes in judgments of relative strategy effectiveness. *British Journal of Developmental Psychology, 4,* 75–81.

Jutras-Aswad, D., DiNieri, J. A., Harkany, T., & Hurd, Y. L. (2009). Neurobiological consequences of maternal cannabis on human fetal development and its neuropsychiatric outcome. *European Archives of Psychiatry and Clinical Neuroscience, 259,* 395–412.

K

Kaffashi, F., Scher, M. S., Ludington-Hoe, S. M., & Loparo, K. A. (2013). An analysis of the kangaroo care intervention using neonatal EEG complexity: A preliminary study. *Clinical Neurophysiology, 124,* 238–246.

Kagan, J. (2003). Behavioral inhibition as a temperamental category. In R. J. Davidson, K. R. Scherer, & H. H. Goldsmith (Eds.), *Handbook of affective sciences* (pp. 320–331). New York: Oxford University Press.

Kagan, J. (2008). Behavioral inhibition as a risk factor for psychopathology. In T. P. Beauchaine & S. P. Hinshaw

(Eds.), *Child and adolescent psychopathology* (pp. 157–179). Hoboken, NJ: Wiley.

Kagan, J. (2010). Emotions and temperament. In M. H. Bornstein (Ed.), *Handbook of cultural developmental science* (pp, 175–194). New York: Psychology Press.

Kagan, J. (2013a). Contextualizing experience. *Developmental Review, 33,* 273–278.

Kagan, J. (2013b). Equal time for psychological and biological contributions to human variation. *Review of General Psychology, 17,* 351–357.

Kagan, J. (2013c). *The human spark: The science of human development.* New York: Basic Books.

Kagan, J. (2013d). Temperamental contributions to inhibited and uninhibited profiles. In P. D. Zelazo (Ed.), *The Oxford handbook of developmental psychology* (142–164). New York: Oxford University Press.

Kagan, J., Snidman, N., Kahn, V., & Towsley, S. (2007). The preservation of two infant temperaments into adolescence. *Monographs of the Society for Research in Child Development, 72*(2, Serial No. 287).

Kagan, J., Snidman, N., Zentner, M., & Peterson, E. (1999). Infant temperament and anxious symptoms in school-age children. *Development and Psychopathology, 11,* 209–224.

Kahana-Kalman, R., & Walker-Andrews, A. S. (2001). The role of person familiarity in young infants' perception of emotional expressions. *Child Development, 72,* 352–362.

Kahn, R. S., Khoury, J., Nichols, W. C., & Lanphear, B. M. (2003). Role of dopamine transporter genotype and maternal prenatal smoking in childhood hyperactive–impulsive, inattentive, and oppositional behaviors. *Journal of Pediatrics, 143,* 104–110.

Kail, R. V. (2003). Information processing and memory. In M. H. Bornstein, L. Davidson, C. L. M. Keyes, K. A. Moore, and the Center for Child Well-Being (Eds.), *Well-being: Positive development across the life course* (pp. 269–280). Mahwah, NJ: Erlbaum.

Kail, R. V., & Ferrer, E. F. (2007). Processing speed in childhood and adolescence: Longitudinal models for examining developmental change. *Child Development, 78,* 1760–1770.

Kail, R. V., McBride-Chang, C., Ferrer, E., Cho, J.-R., & Shu, H. (2013). Cultural differences in the development of processing speed. *Developmental Science, 16,* 476–483.

Kaiser Family Foundation. (2014). *How will the uninsured fare under the Affordable Care Act?* Retrieved from kff.org/health-reform/fact-sheet/how-will-the-uninsured-fare-under-the-affordable-care-act

Kakihara, F., Tilton-Weaver, L., Kerr, M., & Stattin, H. (2010). The relationship of parental control to youth adjustment: Do youths' feelings about their parents play a role? *Journal of Youth and Adolescence, 39,* 1442–1456.

Kalra, L., & Ratan, R. (2007). Recent advances in stroke rehabilitation. *Stroke, 38,* 235–237.

Kaminsky, Z., Petronis, A., Wang, S–C., Levine, B., Ghaffar, O., Floden, D., et al. (2007). Epigenetics of personality traits: An illustrative study of identical twins discordant for risk-taking behavior. *Twin Research and Human Genetics, 11,* 1–11.

Kanazawa, S. (2012). Intelligence, birth order, and family size. *Personality and Social Psychology Bulletin, 38,* 1157–1164.

Kane, P., & Garber, J. (2004). The relations among depression in fathers, children's psychopathology, and father–child conflict: A meta-analysis. *Clinical Psychology Review, 24,* 339–360.

Kang, N. H., & Hong, M. (2008). Achieving excellence in teacher workforce and equity in learning opportunities in South Korea. *Educational Researcher, 37,* 200–207.

Kantaoka, S., & Vandell, D. L. (2013). Quality of afterschool activities and relative change in adolescent functioning over two years. *Applied Developmental Science, 17*(3), 123–134.

Kanters, M. A., Bocarro, J. N., Edwards, M., Casper, J., & Floyd, M. F. (2013). School sport participation under two school sport policies: Comparisons by race/ethnicity, gender, and socioeconomic status. *Annals of Behavioral Medicine 45*(Suppl. 1), S113–S121.

Kaplow, J. B., & Widom, C. S. (2007). Age of onset of child maltreatment predicts long-term mental health outcomes. *Journal of Abnormal Psychology, 116,* 176–187.

Karafantis, D. M., & Levy, S. R. (2004). The role of children's lay theories about the malleability of human attributes in beliefs about and volunteering for disadvantaged groups. *Child Development, 75,* 236–250.

Karasik, L. B., Adolph, K., Tamis-LeMonda, C. S., & Zuckerman (2012). Carry on: Spontaneous object carrying in 13-month-old crawling and walking infants. *Developmental Psychology, 48,* 389–397.

Karasik, L. B., Tamis-LeMonda, C. S., & Adolph, K. E. (2011). Transition from crawling to walking and infants' actions with objects and people. *Child Development, 82,* 1199–1209.

Karemaker, A., Pitchford, N., & O'Malley, C. (2010). Enhanced recognition of written words and enjoyment of reading in struggling beginner readers through whole-word multimedia software. *Computers and Education, 54,* 199–208.

Karevold, E., Ystrom, E., Coplan, R. J., Sanson, A. V., & Mathiesen, K. S. (2012). A prospective longitudinal study of shyness from infancy to adolescence: Stability, age-related changes, and prediction of socio-emotional functioning. *Journal of Abnormal Child Psychology, 40,* 1167–1177.

Karkhaneh, M., Rowe, B. H., Saunders, L. D., Voaklander, D. C., & Hagel, B. E. (2013). Trends in head injuries associated with mandatory bicycle helmet legislation targeting children and adolescents. *Accident Analysis and Prevention, 59,* 206–212.

Karrass, J., & Braungart-Rieker, J. M. (2005). Effects of shared parent–infant book reading on early language acquisition. *Applied Developmental Psychology, 26,* 133–148.

Kärtner, J., Keller, H., Chaudhary, N., & Yovsi, R. D. (2012). The development of mirror self-recognition in different sociocultural contexts. *Monographs of the Society for Research in Child Development, 77*(4, Serial No. 305).

Kastens, K. A., & Liben, L. S. (2007). Eliciting self-explanations improves children's performance on a field-based map skills task. *Cognition and Instruction, 25,* 45–74.

Kataoka, S., & Vandell, D. L. (2013). Quality of afterschool activities and relative change in adolescent functioning over two years. *Applied Developmental Science, 17,* 123–134.

Katz, J., Lee, A. C. C., Lawn, J. E., Cousens, S., Blencowe, H., Ezzati, M., et al. (2013). Mortality risk in preterm and small-for-gestational-age infants in low-income and middle-income countries: A pooled country analysis. *Lancet, 382,* 417–425.

Katzmarzyk, P. T., & Leonard, W. R. (1998). Climatic influences on human body size and proportions: Ecological adaptations and secular trends. *American Journal of Physical Anthropology, 106,* 483–503.

Katz-Wise, S. L., Priess, H. A., & Hyde, J. S. (2010). Gender-role attitudes and behavior across the transition to parenthood. *Developmental Psychology, 46,* 18–28.

Kaufmann, K. B., Büning, H., Galy, A., Schambach, A., & Grez, M. (2013). Gene therapy on the move. *EMBO Molecular Medicine, 5,* 1642–1661.

Kavanaugh, R. D. (2006a). Pretend play. In B. Spodek & O. N. Saracho (Eds.), *Handbook of research on the education of young children* (2nd ed., pp. 269–278). Mahwah, NJ: Erlbaum.

Kavanaugh, R. D. (2006b). Pretend play and theory of mind. In L. Balter & C. S. Tamis-LeMonda (Eds.), *Child psychology: A handbook of contemporary issues* (2nd ed., pp. 153–166). New York: Psychology Press.

Kavšek, M. (2004). Predicting later IQ from infant visual habituation and dishabituation: A meta-analysis. *Journal of Applied Developmental Psychology, 25,* 369–393.

Kavšek, M., & Bornstein, M. H. (2010). Visual habituation and dishabituation in preterm infants: A review and meta-analysis. *Research in Developmental Disabilities, 31,* 951–975.

Kavšek, M., Yonas, A., & Granrud, C. E. (2012). Infants' sensitivity to pictorial depth cues: A review and meta-analysis. *Infant Behavior and Development, 35,* 109–128.

Kearney, C. A., Spear, M., & Mihalas, S. (2014). School refusal behavior. In L. Grossman & S. Walfish (Eds.), *Translating psychological research into practice* (pp. 83–88). New York: Springer.

Keating-Lefler, R., Hudson, D. B., Campbell-Grossman, C., Fleck, M. O., & Westfall, J. (2004). Needs, concerns, and social support of single, low-income mothers. *Issues in Mental Health Nursing, 25,* 381–401.

Keefe, M. R., Barbosa, G. A., Froese-Fretz, A., Kotzer, A. M., & Lobo, M. (2005). An intervention program for families with irritable infants. *American Journal of Maternal/Child Nursing, 30,* 230–236.

Keen, R. (2011). The development of problem solving in young children: A critical cognitive skill. *Annual Review of Psychology, 62,* 1–24.

Keil, F. C. (1986). Conceptual domains and the acquisition of metaphor. *Cognitive Development, 1,* 72–96.

Keil, F. C., & Lockhart, K. L. (1999). Explanatory understanding in conceptual development. In E. K. Scholnick, K. Nelson, S. A. Gelman, & P. H. Miller (Eds.), *Conceptual development: Piaget's legacy* (pp. 103–130). Mahwah, NJ: Erlbaum.

Keller, H., Borke, Y. J., Kärtner, J., Jensen, H., & Papaligoura, Z. (2004). Developmental consequences of early parenting experiences: Self-recognition and self-regulation in three cultural communities. *Child Development, 75,* 1745–1760.

Keller, H., & Otto, H. (2009). The cultural socialization of emotion regulation during infancy. *Journal of Cross-Cultural Psychology, 40,* 996–1011.

Keller, S. S., Crow, T., Foundas, A., Amunts, K., & Roberts, N. (2009). Broca's area: Nomenclature, anatomy, typology and symmetry. *Brain and Language, 109,* 29–48.

Kelley, S. A., Brownell, C. A., & Campbell, S. B. (2000). Mastery motivation and self-evaluative affect in toddlers: Longitudinal relations with maternal behavior. *Child Development, 71,* 1061–1071.

Kellman, P. J., & Arterberry, M. E. (2006). Infant visual perception. In D. Kuhn & R. Siegler (Eds.), *Handbook of child psychology: Vol. 2. Cognition, perception, and language* (6th ed., pp. 109–160). Hoboken, NJ: Wiley.

Kelly, D. J., Liu, S., Ge, L., Quinn, P. C., Slater, A. M., Lee, K., et al. (2007). Cross-race preferences for same-race faces extend beyond the African versus Caucasian contrast in 3-month-old infants. *Infancy, 11,* 87–95.

Kelly, D. J., Quinn, P. C., Slater, A. M., Lee, K., Ge, L., & Pascalis, O. (2009). The other-race effect develops during infancy: Evidence of perceptual narrowing. *Psychological Science, 18,* 1084–1089.

Kelly, R., & Hammond, S. (2011). The relationship between symbolic play and executive function in young children. *Australasian Journal of Early Childhood, 36*(2), 21–27.

Kemeny, M. E. (2003). The psychobiology of stress. *Current Directions in Psychological Science, 12,* 124–129.

Kempe, C. H., Silverman, B. F., Steele, P. W., Droegemueller, P. W., & Silver, H. K. (1962). The battered-child syndrome. *Journal of the American Medical Association, 181,* 17–24.

Kendrick, D., Barlow, J., Hampshire, A., Stewart-Brown, S., & Polnay, L. (2008). Parenting interventions and the prevention of unintentional injuries in childhood: Systematic review and meta-analysis. *Child: Care, Health and Development, 34,* 682–695.

Kennedy, A. M., & Gust, D. A. (2008). Measles outbreak associated with a church congregation: A study of immunization attitudes of congregation members. *Public Health Reports, 123,* 126–134.

Kennedy, B. S., Doniger, A. S., Painting, S., Houston, L., Slaunwhite, M, Mirabella, F., et al. (2014). Declines in elevated blood lead levels among children, 1997–2011. *American Journal of Preventive Medicine, 46,* 259–264.

Kennell, J. H., Klaus, M., McGrath, S., Robertson, S., & Hinkley, C. (1991). Continuous emotional support during labor in a U.S. hospital. *Journal of the American Medical Association, 265,* 2197–2201.

Keren, M., Feldman, R., Namdari-Weinbaum, I., Spitzer, S., & Tyano, S. (2005). Relations between parents' interactive style in dyadic and triadic play and toddlers' symbolic capacity. *American Journal of Orthopsychiatry, 75,* 599–607.

Kernis, M. H. (2002). Self-esteem as a multifaceted construct. In T. M. Brinthaupt & R. P. Lipka (Eds.), *Understanding early adolescent self and identity* (pp. 57–88). Albany: State University of New York Press.

Kerns, K. A., Brumariu, L. E., & Seibert, A. (2011). Multi-method assessment of mother–child attachment: Links to parenting and child depressive symptoms in middle childhood. *Attachment and Human Development, 13,* 315–333.

Kessen, W. (1967). Sucking and looking: Two organized congenital patterns of behavior in the human newborn. In H. W. Stevenson, E. H. Hess, & H. L. Rheingold (Eds.), *Early behavior: Comparative and developmental approaches* (pp. 147–179). New York: Wiley.

Kessler, R. C., Adler, L. A., Barkley, R., Biederman, J., Conners, C. K., & Demler, O. (2006). The prevalence and correlates of adult ADHD in the United States: Results from the National Comorbidity Survey Replication. *American Journal of Psychiatry, 163,* 716–723.

Kessler, R. C., Adler, L. A., Barkley, R., Biederman, J., Conners, C. K., & Faraone, S. V. (2005). Patterns and predictors of attention-deficit/hyperactivity disorder persistence into adulthood: Results from the National Comorbidity Survey Replication. *Biological Psychiatry, 57,* 1442–1451.

Kew, K., Ivory, G., Muniz, M. M., & Quiz, F. Z. (2012). No Child Left Behind as school reform: Intended and unintended consequences. In M. A. Acker-Hocevar, J. Ballenger, W. A. Place, & G. Ivory (Eds.), *Snapshots of school leadership in the 21st century: Perils and promises of leading for social justice, school improvement, and democratic community* (pp. 13–30). Charlotte, NC: IAP Information Age Publishing.

Khaleefa, O., Sulman, A., & Lynn, R. (2009). An increase of intelligence in Sudan, 1987–2007. *Journal of Biosocial Science, 41,* 279–283.

Khaleque, A., & Rohner, R. P. (2012). Pancultural associations between perceived parental acceptance and psychological adjustment of children and adults: A meta-analytic review of worldwide research. *Journal of Cross-Cultural Psychology, 43,* 784–800.

Kieras, J. E., Tobin, R. M., Graziano, W. G., & Rothbart, M. K. (2005). You can't always get what you want: Effortful control and children's responses to undesirable gifts. *Psychological Science, 16,* 391–396.

Killen, M., Crystal, D., & Watanabe, H. (2002). The individual and the group: Japanese and American children's evaluations of peer exclusion, tolerance of difference, and prescriptions for conformity. *Child Development, 73,* 1788–1802.

Killen, M., Kelly, M. C., Richardson, C., Crystal, D., & Ruck, M. (2010). European American children's and adolescents' evaluations of interracial exclusion. *Group Processes and Intergroup Relations, 13,* 283–300.

Killen, M., Lee-Kim, J., McGlothlin, H., & Stangor, C. (2002). How children and adolescents evaluate gender and racial exclusion. *Monographs of the Society for Research in Child Development, 67*(4, Serial No. 271).

Killen, M., Margie, N. G., & Sinno, S. (2006). Morality in the context of intergroup relationships. In M. Killen & J. G. Smetana (Eds.), *Handbook of moral development* (pp. 155–183). Mahwah, NJ: Erlbaum.

Killen, M., Mulvey, K. L., Richardson, C., Jampol, N., & Woodward, A. (2011). The accidental transgressor: Morally relevant theory of mind. *Cognition, 119,* 197–215.

Killen, M., Rutland, A., & Ruck, M. (2011). Promoting equity, tolerance, and justice in childhood. *Society for Research in Child Development Social Policy Report, 25*(4).

Killen, M., & Stangor, M. (2001). Children's social reasoning about inclusion and exclusion in gender and race peer group contexts. *Child Development, 72,* 174–186.

Kilmer, R. P., Cook, J. R., Crusto, C., Strater, K. P., & Haber, M. G. (2012). Understanding the ecology and development of children and families experiencing homelessness: Implications for practice, supportive services, and policy. *American Journal of Orthopsychiatry, 82,* 389–401.

Kim, G., Walden, T. A., & Knieps, L. J. (2010). Impact and characteristics of positive and fearful emotional messages during infant social referencing. *Infant Behavior and Development, 33,* 189–195.

Kim, J.-Y., McHale, S. M., Osgood, D. W., & Crouter, A. C. (2006). Longitudinal course and family correlates of sibling relationships from childhood through adolescence. *Child Development, 77,* 1746–1761.

Kim, J. M. (1998). Korean children's concepts of adult and peer authority and moral reasoning. *Developmental Psychology, 34,* 947–955.

Kim, J.-Y., McHale, S. M., Crouter, A. C., & Osgood, D. W. (2007). Longitudinal linkages between sibling relationships and adjustment from middle childhood through adolescence. *Developmental Psychology, 43,* 960–973.

Kim, S., & Kochanska, G. (2012). Child temperament moderates effects of parent–child mutuality on self-regulation: A relationship-based path for emotionally negative infants. *Child Development, 83,* 1275–1289.

Kim, S., Kochanska, G., Boldt, L. J., Nordling, J. K., & O'Bleness, J. J. (2014). Developmental trajectory from early responses to transgressions to future antisocial behavior: Evidence for the role of the parent–child relationship from two longitudinal studies. *Development and Psychopathology, 26,* 93–103.

King, A. C., & Bjorklund, D. F. (2010). Evolutionary developmental psychology. *Psicothema, 22,* 22–27.

King, V. (2007). When children have two mothers: Relationships with nonresident mothers, stepmothers, and fathers. *Journal of Marriage and Family, 69,* 1178–1193.

King, V. (2009). Stepfamily formation: Implications for adolescent ties to mothers, nonresident fathers, and stepfathers. *Journal of Marriage and Family, 71,* 954–968.

Kinney, H. C. (2009). Brainstem mechanisms underlying the sudden infant death syndrome: Evidence from human pathologic studies. *Developmental Psychobiology, 51,* 223–233.

Kinnunen, M.-L., Pietilainen, K., & Rissanen, A. (2006). Body size and overweight from birth to adulthood. In L. Pulkkinen & J. Kaprio (Eds.), *Socioemotional development and health from adolescence to adulthood* (pp. 95–107). New York: Cambridge University Press.

Kinsella, M. T., & Monk, C. (2009). Impact of maternal stress, depression and anxiety on fetal neurobehavioral development. *Clinical Obstetrics and Gynecology, 52,* 425–440.

Kiriakidis, S. P., & Kavoura, A. (2010). Cyberbullying: A review of the literature on harassment through the Internet and other electronic means. *Family and Community Health, 33,* 82–93.

Kirkham, N. Z., Cruess, L., & Diamond, A. (2003). Helping children apply their knowledge to their behavior on a dimension-switching task. *Developmental Science, 6,* 449–476.

Kirkorian, H. L., Pempek, T. A., Murphy, L. A., Schmidt, M. E., & Anderson, D. R. (2009). The impact of background television on parent–child interaction. *Child Development, 80,* 1350–1359.

Kisilevsky, B. S., & Hains, S. M. J. (2011). Onset and maturation of fetal heart rate response to the mother's voice over late gestation. *Developmental Science, 14,* 214–223.

Kisilevsky, B. S., Hains, S. M. J., Brown, C. A., Lee, C. T., Cowperthwaite, B., & Stutzman, S. S. (2009). Fetal sensitivity to properties of maternal speech and language. *Infant Behavior and Development, 32,* 59–71.

Kisilevsky, B. S., Hains, S. M. J., Lee, K., Muir, D. W., Xu, F., Fu, G., Zhao, Z. Y., & Yang, R. L. (1998). The still-face effect in Chinese and Canadian 3- to 6-month-old infants. *Developmental Psychology, 34,* 629–639.

Kisilevsky, B. S., & Low, J. A. (1998). Human fetal behavior: 100 years of study. *Developmental Review, 18,* 1–29.

Kit, B. K., Ogden, C. L., & Flegal, K. M. (2014). Epidemiology of obesity. In W. Ahrens & I. Pigeot (Eds.), *Handbook of Epidemiology* (2nd ed., pp. 2229–2262). New York: Springer Science + Business Media.

Kitsantas, P., Gaffney, K. F., & Cheema, J. (2012). Life stressors and barriers to timely prenatal care for women with high-risk pregnancies residing in rural and nonrural areas. *Women's Health Issues, 22,* e455–e460.

Kitzman, H. J., Olds, D. L., Cole, R. E., Hanks, C. A., Anson, E. A., Arcoleo, K. J., et al. (2010). Enduring effects of prenatal and infancy home visiting by nurses on children: Follow-up of a randomized trial among children at age 12 years. *Archives of Pediatric and Adolescent Medicine, 164,* 412–418.

Kitzmann, K. M., Cohen, R., & Lockwood, R. L. (2002). Are only children missing out? Comparison of the peer-related social competence of only children and siblings. *Journal of Social and Personal Relationships, 19,* 299–316.

Kjønniksen, L., Anderssen, N., & Wold, B. (2009). Organized youth sport as a predictor of physical activity in adulthood. *Scandinavian Journal of Medicine and Science in Sports, 19,* 646–654.

Kjønniksen, L., Torsheim, T., & Wold, B. (2008). Tracking of leisure-time physical activity during adolescence and young adulthood: A 10-year longitudinal study. *International Journal of Behavioral Nutrition and Physical Activity, 5,* 69.

Klahr, D., Matlen, B., & Jirout, J. (2013). Children as scientific thinkers. In G. J. Feist & M. E. Gorman (Eds.), *Handbook of the psychology of science* (pp. 223–247). New York: Springer.

Klaus, M. H., & Kennell, J. H. (1982). *Parent–infant bonding.* St. Louis: Mosby.

Klebanov, P. K., Brooks-Gunn, J., McCarton, C., & McCormick, M. C. (1998). The contribution of neighborhood and family income to developmental test scores over the first three years of life. *Child Development, 69,* 1420–1436.

Kleinsorge, C., & Covitz, L. M. (2012). Impact of divorce on children: Developmental considerations. *Pediatrics in Review, 33,* 147–155.

Klemfuss, J. Z., & Ceci, S. J. (2012). Legal and psychological perspectives on children's competence to testify in court. *Developmental Review, 32,* 81–204.

Klemmensen, A.K., Tabor, A., Østerdal, M. L., Knudsen, V.K., Halldorsson, T. I., Mikkelsen, T. B., et al. (2009). Intake of vitamin C and E in pregnancy and risk of pre-eclampsia: Prospective study among 57,346 women. *BJOG, 116,* 964–974.

Kliegman, R. M., Behrman, R. E., Jenson, H. B., & Stanton, B. F. (Eds.). (2008). *Nelson textbook of pediatrics e-dition* (18th ed. text with continually updated online references.) Philadelphia: Saunders.

Kliewer, W., Fearnow, M. D., & Miller, P. A. (1996). Coping socialization in middle childhood: Tests of maternal and paternal influences. *Child Development, 67,* 2339–2357.

Klimes-Dougan, B., & Kistner, J. (1990). Physically abused preschoolers' responses to peers' distress. *Developmental Psychology, 26,* 599–602.

Klingman, A. (2006). Children and war trauma. In K. A. Renninger & I. E. Sigel (Eds.), *Handbook of child psychology: Vol. 4. Child psychology in practice* (6th ed., pp. 619–652). Hoboken, NJ: Wiley.

Kloess, J. A., Beech, A. R., & Harkins, L. (2014). Online child sexual exploitation: Prevalence, process, and offender characteristics. *Trauma, Violence, & Abuse, 15,* 126–139.

Kluwer, E. S., & Johnson, M. D. (2007). Conflict frequency and relationship quality across the transition to parenthood. *Journal of Marriage and Family, 69,* 1089–1106.

Knafo, A., & Plomin, R. (2006). Parental discipline and affection and children's prosocial behavior: Genetic and environmental links. *Journal of Personality and Social Psychology, 90,* 147–164.

Knafo, A., Zahn-Waxler, C., Davidov, M., Hulle, C. V., Robinson, J. L., & Rhee, S. H. (2009). Empathy in early childhood: Genetic, environmental, and affective contributions. In O. Vilarroya, S. Altran, A. Navarro, K. Ochsner, & A. Tobena (Eds.), *Values, empathy, and fairness across social barriers* (pp. 103–114). New York: New York Academy of Sciences.

Knickmeyer, R. C., Gouttard, S., Kang, C., Evans, D., Wilber, K., Smith, J. K., et al. (2008). A structural MRI study of human brain development from birth to 2 years. *Journal of Neuroscience, 28,* 12176–12182.

Knobloch, H., & Pasamanick, B. (Eds.). (1974). *Gesell and Amatruda's Developmental Diagnosis.* Hagerstown, MD: Harper & Row.

Knopf, M., Kraus, U., & Kressley-Mba, R. A. (2006). Relational information processing of novel unrelated actions by infants. *Infant Behavior and Development, 29,* 44–53.

Knudsen, E. I. (2004). Sensitive periods in the development of the brain and behavior. *Journal of Cognitive Neuroscience, 16,* 1412–1425.

Kobayashi, T., Hiraki, K., & Hasegawa, T. (2005). Auditory-visual intermodal matching of small numerosities in 6-month-old infants. *Developmental Science, 8,* 409–419.

Kobayashi, T., Kazuo, H., Ryoko, M., & Hasegawa, T. (2004). Baby arithmetic: One object plus one tone. *Cognition, 91,* B23–B34.

Kochanska, G. (1991). Socialization and temperament in the development of guilt and conscience. *Child Development, 62,* 1379–1392.

Kochanska, G., & Aksan, N. (2006). Children's conscience and self-regulation. *Journal of Personality, 74,* 1587–1617.

Kochanska, G., Aksan, N., & Carlson, J. J. (2005). Temperament, relationships, and young children's receptive cooperation with their parents. *Developmental Psychology, 41,* 648–660.

Kochanska, G., Aksan, N., & Nichols, K. E. (2003). Maternal power assertion in discipline and moral discourse contexts: Commonalities, differences, and implications for children's moral conduct and cognition. *Developmental Psychology, 39,* 949–963.

Kochanska, G., Aksan, N., Prisco, T. R., & Adams, E. E. (2008). Mother–child and father–child mutually responsive orientation in the first 2 years and children's outcomes at preschool age: Mechanisms of influence. *Child Development, 79,* 30–44.

Kochanska, G., Forman, D. R., Aksan, N., & Dunbar, S. B. (2005). Pathways to conscience: Early mother–child mutually responsive orientation and children's moral emotion, conduct, and cognition. *Journal of Child Psychology and Psychiatry, 46,* 19–34.

Kochanska, G., Gross, J. N., Lin, M.-H., & Nichols, K. E. (2002). Guilt in young children: Development, determinants, and relations with broader system standards. *Child Development, 73,* 461–482.

Kochanska, G., & Kim, S. (2012). Difficult temperament moderates links between maternal responsiveness and children's compliance and behavior problems in low-income families. *Journal of Child Psychology and Psychiatry, 54,* 323–332.

Kochanska, G., & Kim, S. (2014). A complex interplay among the parent–child relationship, effortful control, and internalized rule-compatible conduct in young children: Evidence from two studies. *Developmental Psychology, 50,* 8–21.

Kochanska, G., Kim, S., Barry, R. A., & Philibert, R. A. (2011). Children's genotypes interact with maternal responsive care in predicting children's competence: Diathesis-stress or differential susceptibility? *Development and Psychopathology, 23,* 605–616.

Kochanska, G., & Knaack, A. (2003). Effortful control as a personality characteristic of young children: Antecedents, correlates, and consequences. *Journal of Personality, 71,* 1087–1112.

Kochanska, G., Murray, K. T., & Harlan, E. T. (2000). Effortful control in early childhood: Continuity and change, antecedents, and implications for social development. *Developmental Psychology, 36,* 220–232.

Kochanska, G., Philibert, R. A., & Barry, R. A. (2009). Interplay of genes and early mother–child relationship in the development of self-regulation from toddler to preschool age. *Journal of Child Psychology and Psychiatry, 50,* 1331–1338.

Kochel, K. P., Ladd, G. W., & Rudolph, K. D. (2012). Longitudinal associations among youth depressive symptoms, peer victimization, and low peer acceptance: An interpersonal process perspective. *Child Development, 83,* 637–650.

Kohen, D. E., Leventhal, T., Dahinten, V. S., & McIntosh, C. N. (2008). Neighborhood disadvantage: Pathways of effects for young children. *Child Development, 79,* 156–169.

Kohlberg, L. (1966). A cognitive-developmental analysis of children's sex-role concepts and attitudes. In E. E. Maccoby (Ed.), *The development of sex differences* (pp. 82–173). Stanford, CA: Stanford University Press.

Kolak, A. M., & Volling, B. L. (2011). Sibling jealousy in early childhood: Longitudinal links to sibling relationship quality. *Infant and Child Development, 20,* 213–226.

Koletzko,B., Beyer, J., Brands, B., Demmelmair, H., Grote, V., Haile, G., et al. (2013). Early influences of nutrition on postnatal growth. *Nestlé Nutrition Institute Workshop Series, 71,* 11–27.

Kollmann, M., Haeusler, M., Haas, J., Csapo, B., Lang, U., & Klaritsch, P. (2013). Procedure-related complications after genetic amniocentesis and chorionic villus sampling. *Ultraschall in der Medizen, 34,* 345–348.

Konner, M. (2010). *The evolution of childhood: Relationships, emotion, mind.* Cambridge, MA: Harvard University Press.

Konner, M. J. (1977). Infancy among the Kalahari Desert San. In P. H. Leiderman, S. R. Tulkin, & A. Rosenfield (Eds.), *Culture and infancy: Variations in the human experience* (pp. 287–328). New York: Academic Press.

Kontos, A. P., Elbin, R. J., Fazio-Sumrock, V. C., Burkhart, S., Swindell, H., Maroon, J., et al. (2013). Incidence of sports-related concussion among youth football players aged 8–12 years. *Journal of Pediatrics, 163,* 717–720.

Kooijman, V., Hagoort, P., & Cutler, A. (2009). Prosodic structure in early word segmentation: ERP evidence from Dutch ten-month-olds. *Infancy, 14,* 591–612.

Kopp, C. B., & Neufeld, S. J. (2003). Emotional development during infancy. In R. Davidson, K. R. Scherer, & H. H. Goldsmith (Eds.), *Handbook of affective sciences* (pp. 347–374). Oxford, UK: Oxford University Press.

Kowalski, R. M., & Limber, S. P. (2013). Psychological, physical, and academic correlates of cyberbullying and traditional bullying. *Journal of Adolescent Health, 53,* S13–S20.

Kowalski, R. M., Limber, S. P., & Agatston, P. W. (2008). *Cyber bullying: Bullying in the digital age.* Malden, MA: Blackwell.

Kozer, E., Costei, A. M., Boskovic, R., Nulman, I., Nikfar, S., & Koren, G. (2003). Effects of aspirin consumption during pregnancy on pregnancy outcomes: Meta-analysis. *Birth Defects Research: Part B, Developmental and Reproductive Toxicology, 68,* 70–84.

Kozulin, A. (Ed.). (2003). *Vygotsky's educational theory in cultural context.* Cambridge, UK: Cambridge University Press.

Kraebel, K. S. (2012). Redundant amodal properties facilitate operant learning in 3-month-old infants. *Infant Behavior and Development, 35,* 12–21.

Krafft, K., & Berk, L. E. (1998). Private speech in two preschools: Significance of open-ended activities and make-believe play for verbal self-regulation. *Early Childhood Research Quarterly, 13,* 637–658.

Krähenbühl, S., Blades, M., & Eiser, C. (2009). The effect of repeated questioning on children's accuracy and consistency in eyewitness testimony. *Legal and Criminological Psychology, 14,* 263–278.

Kral, T. V. E., & Faith, M. S. (2009). Influences on child eating and weight development from a behavioral genetics perspective. *Journal of Pediatric Psychology, 34,* 596–605.

Krcmar, M., Grela, B., & Lin, K. (2007). Can toddlers learn vocabulary from television? An experimental approach. *Media Psychology, 10,* 41–63.

Kreppner, J., Kumsta, R., Rutter, M., Beckett, C., Castle, J., Stevens, S., et al. (2010). Developmental course of deprivation-specific psychological patterns: Early manifestations, persistence to age 15, and clinical features. *Monographs of the Society for Research in Child Development, 75*(1, Serial No. 295), 79–101.

Kreppner, J., Rutter, M., Beckett, C., Castle, J., Colvert, E., Groothues, C., et al. (2007). Normality and impairment following profound early institutional deprivation: A longitudinal follow-up into early adolescence. *Developmental Psychology, 43,* 931–946.

Kretch, K. S., & Adolph, K. E. (2013a). Cliff or step? Posture-specific learning at the edge of a drop-off. *Child Development, 84,* 226–240.

Kretch, K. S., & Adolph, K. E. (2013b). No bridge too high: Infants decide whether to cross based on the probability of falling not the severity of the potential fall. *Developmental Science, 16,* 336–351.

Krueger, R. F., & Johnson, W. (2008). Behavior genetics and personality. In L. Q. Pervin, O. P. John, & R. W. Robins (Eds.), *Handbook of personality: Theory and research* (3rd ed., pp. 287–310). New York: Guilford.

Krumhansl, C. L., & Jusczyk, P. W. (1990). Infants' perception of phrase structure in music. *Psychological Science, 1,* 70–73.

Kuczynski, L. (1984). Socialization goals and mother–child interaction: Strategies for long-term and short-term compliance. *Developmental Psychology, 20,* 1061–1073.

Kuczynski, L., & Lollis, S. (2002). Four foundations for a dynamic model of parenting. In J. R. M. Gerris (Ed.), *Dynamics of parenting.* Hillsdale, NJ: Erlbaum.

Kuhl, P. K., Ramirez, R. R., Bosseler, A., Lin, J. L., & Imada, T. (2014). Infants' brain responses to speech suggest analysis by synthesis. *Proceedings of the National Academy of Sciences, 111,* 11238–11245.

Kuhl, P. K., Tsao, F.-M., & Liu, H.-M. (2003). Foreign-language experience in infancy: Effects of short-term exposure and social interaction on phonetic learning. *Proceedings of the National Academy of Sciences, 100,* 9096–9101.

Kuhn, D. (1995). Microgenetic study of change: What has it told us? *Psychological Science, 6,* 133–139.

Kulkarni, A. D., Jamieson, D. J., Jones, H. W., Jr., Kissin, D. M., Gallo, M. F., Macaluso, M., et al. (2013). Fertility treatments and multiple births in the United States. *New England Journal of Medicine, 369,* 2218–2225.

Kumar, M., Chandra, S., Ijaz, Z., & Senthilselvan, A. (2014). Epidural analgesia in labour and neonatal respiratory distress: A case-control study. *Archives of Disease in Childhood—Fetal and Neonatal Edition, 99,* F116–F119.

Kunnen, S. (Ed.). (2012). *A dynamic systems approach to adolescent development.* London: Routledge.

Kuppens, S., Laurent, L., Heyvaert, M., & Onghena, P. (2013). Associations between parental control and relational aggression in children and adolescents: A multilevel and sequential meta-analysis. *Developmental Psychology, 49,* 1697–1712.

Kurdziel, L., Duclos, K., & Spencer, R. M. C. (2013). Sleep spindles in midday naps enhance learning in preschool children. *Proceedings of the National Academy of Sciences, 110,* 17267–17271.

Kurganskaya, M. E. (2011). Manual asymmetry in children is related to parameters of early development and familial sinistrality. *Human Physiology, 37,* 654–657.

Kurian, M. A., Gissen, P., Smith, M., Heales, S. J. R., & Clayton, P. T. (2011). The monoamine neurotransmitter disorders: An expanding range of neurological syndromes. *Lancet Neurology, 10,* 721–733.

Kurtz-Costes, B., Rowley, S. J., Harris-Britt, A., & Woods, T. A. (2008). Gender stereotypes about mathematics and science and self-perceptions of ability in late childhood and early adolescence. *Merrill-Palmer Quarterly, 54,* 386–409.

Kushnir, J., Kushnir, B., & Sadeh, A. (2013). Children treated for nocturnal enuresis: Characteristics and trends over a 15-year period. *Child and Youth Care Forum, 42,* 119–129.

Kwak, K. W., Lee, Y. S., Park, K. H., & Baek, M. (2010). Efficacy of desmopressin and enuresis alarm as first and second line treatment for primary monosymptomatic nocturnal enuresis: Prospective randomized crossover study. *Journal of Urology, 184,* 2521–2526.

L

Ladd, G. W. (2005). *Children's peer relationships and social competence: A century of progress.* New Haven, CT: Yale University Press.

Ladd, G. W., Birch, S. H., & Buhs, E. S. (1999). Children's social and scholastic lives in kindergarten: Related spheres of influence? *Child Development, 70,* 1373–1400.

Ladd, G. W., Buhs, E. S., & Seid, M. (2000). Children's initial sentiments about kindergarten: Is school liking an antecedent of early classroom participation and achievement? *Merrill-Palmer Quarterly, 46,* 255–279.

Ladd, G. W., & Burgess, K. B. (1999). Charting the relationship trajectories of aggressive, withdrawn, and aggressive/withdrawn children during early grade school. *Child Development, 70,* 910–929.

Ladd, G. W., Kochenderfer-Ladd, B., Eggum, N. D., Kochel, K. P., & McConnell, E. M. (2011). Characterizing and comparing the friendships of anxious-solitary and unsociable preadolescents. *Child Development, 82,* 1434–1453.

Ladd, G. W., LeSieur, K., & Profilet, S. M. (1993). Direct parental influences on young children's peer relations. In S. Duck (Ed.), *Learning about relationships* (Vol. 2, pp. 152–183). London: Sage.

Lagattuta, K. H., Sayfan, L., & Blattman, A. J. (2010). Forgetting common ground: Six- to seven-year-olds have an overinterpretive theory of mind. *Developmental Psychology, 46,* 1417–1432.

Lagattuta, K. H., & Thompson, R. A. (2007). The development of self-conscious emotions: Cognitive processes and social influences. In J. L. Tracy, R. W. Robins, & J. P. Tangney (Eds.). *The self-conscious emotions: Theory and research* (pp. 91–113). New York: Guilford Press.

Lagattuta, K. H., Wellman, H. M., & Flavell, J. H. (1997). Preschoolers' understanding of the link between thinking and feeling: Cognitive cuing and emotional change. *Child Development, 68,* 1081–1104.

Lagnado, L. (2001, November 2). Kids confront Trade Center trauma. *Wall Street Journal,* pp. B1, B6.

Laible, D. (2007). Attachment with parents and peers in late adolescence: Links with emotional competence and social behavior. *Personality and Individual Differences, 43,* 1185–1197.

Laible, D. (2011). Does it matter if preschool children and mothers discuss positive vs. negative events during reminiscing? Links with mother-reported attachment, family emotional climate, and socioemotional development. *Social Development, 20,* 394–411.

Laible, D., & Song, J. (2006). Constructing emotional and relational understanding: The role of affect and mother–child discourse. *Merrill-Palmer Quarterly, 52,* 44–69.

Laible, D., & Thompson, R. A. (2002). Mother–child conflict in the toddler years: Lessons in emotion, morality, and relationships. *Child Development, 73,* 1187–1203.

Lakshman, R., Elks, C. E., & Ong, K. K. (2012). Childhood obesity. *Circulation, 126,* 1770–1779.

Lalonde, C. E., & Chandler, M. J. (1995). False-belief understanding goes to school: On the social-emotional consequences of coming early or late to a first theory of mind. *Cognition and Emotion, 9,* 167–185.

Lalonde, C. E., & Chandler, M. J. (2002). Children's understanding of interpretation. *New Ideas in Psychology, 20,* 163–198.

Lam, C. B., McHale, S. M., & Crouter, A. C. (2012). Parent–child shared time from middle childhood to late adolescence: Developmental course and adjustment correlates. *Child Development, 83,* 2089–2103.

Lamarche, V., Brendgen, M., Boivin, M., Vitaro, F., Perusse, D., & Dionne, G. (2006). Do friendships and sibling relationships provide protection against peer victimization in a similar way? *Social Development, 15,* 373–393.

Lamaze, F. (1958). *Painless childbirth.* London: Burke.

Lamb, M. E. (2012). Mothers, fathers, families, and circumstances: Factors affecting children's adjustment. *Applied Developmental Science, 16,* 98–111.

Lamb, M. E., & Ahnert, L. (2006). Nonparental child care: Context, concepts, correlates, and consequences. In K. A. Renninger & I. E. Sigel (Eds.), *Handbook of child psychology: Vol. 4. Child psychology in practice* (6th ed., pp. 700–778). Hoboken, NJ: Wiley.

Lamb, M. E., & Lewis, C. (2004). The development and significance of father–child relationships in two-parent families. In M. E. Lamb (Ed.), *The role of the father in child development* (4th ed., pp. 272–306). Hoboken, NJ: Wiley.

Lamb, M. E., & Lewis, C. (2013). Father–child relationships. In N. J. Cabrera & C. S. Tamis-LeMonda (Eds.), *Handbook of father involvement* (2nd ed., pp. 119–134). New York: Routledge.

Lamb, M. E., Thompson, R. A., Gardner, W., Charnov, E. L., & Connell, J. P. (1985). Infant–mother attachment: The origins and developmental significance of individual differences in the Strange Situation: Its study and biological interpretation. *Behavioral and Brain Sciences, 7,* 127–147.

Lambert, S. M., Masson, P., & Fisch, H. (2006). The male biological clock. *World Journal of Urology, 24,* 611–617.

Lampl, M. (1993). Evidence of saltatory growth in infancy. *American Journal of Human Biology, 5,* 641–652.

Lampl, M., & Johnson, M. L. (2011). Infant growth in length follows prolonged sleep and increased naps. *Sleep, 34,* 641–650.

Langer, J., Gillette, P., & Arriaga, R. I. (2003). Toddlers' cognition of adding and subtracting objects in action and in perception. *Cognitive Development, 18,* 233–246.

Langosch, D. (2012). Grandparents parenting again: Challenges, strengths, and implications for practice. *Psychoanalytic Inquiry, 32,* 163–170.

Lanphear, B., Hornung, R., Khoury, J., Yolton, K., Baghurst, P., Bellinger, D., et al. (2005). Low-level environmental lead exposure and children's intellectual function: An international pooled analysis. *Environmental Health Perspectives, 113,* 894–899.

Lansford, J. E. (2009). Parental divorce and children's adjustment. *Perspectives on Psychological Science, 4,* 140–152.

Lansford, J. E., Criss, M. M., Dodge, K. A., Shaw, D. S., Pettit, G. S., & Bates, J. E. (2009). Trajectories of physical discipline: Early childhood antecedents and developmental outcomes. *Child Development, 80,* 1385–1402.

Lansford, J. E., Criss, M. M., Laird, R. D., Shaw, D. S., Pettit, G. S., Bates, J. E., & Dodge, K. A. (2011). Reciprocal relations between parents' physical discipline and children's externalizing behavior during middle childhood and adolescence. *Development and Psychopathology, 23,* 225–238.

Lansford, J. E., Malone, P. S., Castellino, D. R., Dodge, K. A., Pettit, G., & Bates, J. E. (2006). Trajectories of internalizing, externalizing, and grades for children who have and have not experienced their parents' divorce or separation. *Journal of Family Psychology, 20,* 292–301.

Lansford, J. E., Malone, P. S., Dodge, K. A., Pettit, G. S., & Bates, J. E. (2010). Developmental cascades of peer rejection, social information processing biases, and aggression during middle childhood. *Development and Psychopathology, 22,* 593–602.

Lansford, J. E., Wagner, L. B., Bates, J. E., Dodge, K. A., & Pettit, G. S. (2012). Parental reasoning, denying privileges, yelling, and spanking: Ethnic differences and associations with child externalizing behavior. *Parenting: Science and Practice, 12,* 42–56.

Lapierre, M. A., Piotrowski, J., & Klinebarger, D. L. (2012). Background television in the homes of U.S. children. *Pediatrics, 130,* 839–846.

Laranjo, J., Bernier, A., Meins, E., & Carlson, S. M. (2010). Early manifestations of children's theory of mind: The roles of maternal mind-mindedness and infant security of attachment. *Infancy, 15,* 300–323.

Larroque, B., Ancel, P.-Y., Marret, S., Marchand, L., André, M., Arnaud, C., et al. (2008). Neurodevelopmental disabilities and special care of 5-year-old children born before 33 weeks of gestation (the EPIPAGE study): A longitudinal cohort study. *Lancet, 371,* 813–820.

Larsen, J. A., & Nippold, M. A. (2007). Morphological analysis in school-age children: Dynamic assessment of a word learning strategy. *Language, Speech, and Hearing Services in Schools, 38,* 201–212.

Larzelere, R. E., Cox, R. B., Jr., & Mandara, J. (2013). Responding to misbehavior in young children: How authoritative parents enhance reasoning with firm control. In R. E. Larzelere, A. S. Morris, & A. W. Harrist (Eds.), *Authoritative parenting: Synthesizing nurturance and discipline for optimal child development* (pp. 89–111). Washington, DC: American Psychological Association.

Larzelere, R. E., Schneider, W. N., Larson, D. B., & Pike, P. L. (1996). The effects of discipline responses in delaying toddler misbehavior recurrences. *Child and Family Behavior Therapy, 18,* 35–7.

Lashley, F. R. (2007). *Essentials of clinical genetics in nursing practice.* New York: Springer.

Latendresse, G., & Ruiz, R. J. (2011). Maternal corticotropin-releasing hormone and the use of selective serotonin reuptake inhibitors independently predict the occurrence of preterm birth. *Journal of Midwifery and Women's Health, 56,* 118–126.

Latz, S., Wolf, A. W., & Lozoff, B. (1999). Sleep practices and problems in young children in Japan and the United States. *Archives of Pediatric and Adolescent Medicine, 153,* 339–346.

Lau, Y. L., Cameron, C. A., Chieh, K. M., O'Leary, J., Fu, G., & Lee, K. (2012). Cultural differences in moral justifications enhance understanding of Chinese and Canadian children's moral decisions. *Journal of Cross-Cultural Psychology, 44,* 461–477.

Lauer, P. A., Akiba, M., Wilkerson, S. B., Apthorp, H. S., Snow, D., & Martin-Glenn, M. (2006). Out-of-school time programs: A meta-analysis of effects for at-risk students. *Review of Educational Research, 76,* 275–313.

Laughlin, L. (2013). *Who's minding the kids? Child care arrangements: Spring 2011.* Current Population Reports, P70-135. Washington, DC: U.S. Census Bureau.

Laurent, H., Kim, H., & Capaldi, D. (2008). Prospective effects of interparental conflict on child attachment security and the moderating role of parents' romantic attachment. *Journal of Family Psychology, 22,* 377–388.

Lauricella, A. R., Gola, A. A H., & Calvert, S. L. (2011). Toddlers' learning from socially meaningful video characters. *Media Psychology, 14,* 216–232.

Laursen, B., Bukowski, W. M., Aunola, K., & Nurmi, J.-E. (2007). Friendship moderates prospective associations between social isolation and adjustment problems in young children. *Child Development, 78,* 1395–1404.

Lavelli, M., & Fogel, A. (2005). Developmental changes in the relationship between the infant's attention and emotion during early face-to-face communication: The 2-month transition. *Developmental Psychology, 41,* 265–280.

Law, E. C., Sideridis, G. D., Prock, L. A., & Sheridan, M. A. (2014). Attention-deficit/hyperactivity disorder in young children: Predictors of diagnostic stability. *Pediatrics, 133,* 659–667.

Law, K. L., Stroud, L. R., Niaura, R., LaGasse, L. L., Liu, J., & Lester, B. M. (2003). Smoking during pregnancy and newborn neurobehavior. *Pediatrics, 111,* 1318–1323.

Lawn, J. E., Mwansa-Kambafwile, J., Horta, B. L., Barros, F. C., & Cousens, S. (2010). "Kangaroo mother care" to prevent neonatal deaths due to preterm birth complications. *International Journal of Epidemiology, 39,* i144–i154.

Lawrence, E., Rothman, A., Cobb, R. J., & Bradbury, T. N. (2010). Marital satisfaction across the transition to parenthood. In M. S. Schulz, M. K. Pruett, P. K. Kerig, & R. D. Parke (Eds.), *Strengthening couple relationships for optimal child development* (pp. 97–114). Washington, DC: American Psychological Association.

Lawson, K. R., & Ruff, H. A. (2004). Early attention and negative emotionality predict later cognitive and behavioral function. *International Journal of Behavioral Development, 28,* 157–165.

Lazar, I., & Darlington, R. (1982). Lasting effects of early education: A report from the Consortium for Longitudinal Studies. *Monographs of the Society for Research in Child Development, 47*(2–3, Serial No. 195).

Lazarus, R. S., & Lazarus, B. N. (1994). *Passion and reason.* New York: Oxford University Press.

Lazinski, M. J., Shea, A. K., & Steiner, M. (2008). Effects of maternal prenatal stress on offspring development: A commentary. *Archives of Women's Mental Health, 11,* 363–375.

Leaper, C. (1994). Exploring the correlates and consequences of gender segregation: Social relationships in childhood, adolescence, and adulthood. In C. Leaper (Ed.), *New directions for child development* (No. 65, pp. 67–86). San Francisco: Jossey-Bass.

Leaper, C. (2000). Gender, affiliation, assertion, and the interactive context of parent—child play. *Developmental Psychology, 36,* 381–393.

Leaper, C. (2013). Gender development during childhood. In P. D. Zelazo (Ed.), *Oxford handbook of developmental psychology, Vol. 2: Self and other* (pp. 326–377). New York: Oxford University Press.

Leaper, C., Anderson, K. J., & Sanders, P. (1998). Moderators of gender effects on parents' talk to their children: A meta-analysis. *Developmental Psychology, 34,* 3–27.

Leaper, C., & Friedman, C. K. (2007). The socialization of gender. In J. E. Grusec & P. D. Hastings (Eds.), *Handbook of socialization: Theory and research* (pp. 561–587). New York: Guilford.

Learmonth, A. E., Lamberth, R., & Rovee-Collier, C. (2004). Generalization of deferred imitation during the first year of life. *Journal of Experimental Child Psychology, 88,* 297–318.

Leavell, A. S., Tamis-LeMonda, C. S., Ruble, D. N., Zosuls, K. M, & Cabrera, N. J. (2011). African American, White, and Latino fathers' activities with their sons and daughters in early childhood. *Sex Roles, 66,* 53-65.

Lebel, C., & Beaulieu, C. (2011). Longitudinal development of human brain wiring continues from childhood into adulthood. *Journal of Neuroscience, 31,* 10937–10947.

Lecanuet, J.-P., Granier-Deferre, C., & DeCasper, A. (2005). Are we expecting too much from prenatal sensory experiences? In B. Hopkins & S. P. Johnson (Eds.), *Prenatal development of postnatal functions* (pp. 31–49). Westport, CT: Praeger.

Lecanuet, J.-P., Granier-Deferre, C., Jacquet, A.-Y., Capponi, I., & Ledru, L. (1993). Prenatal discrimination of a male and female voice uttering the same sentence. *Early Development and Parenting, 2,* 217–228.

LeCuyer, E., & Houck, G. M. (2006). Maternal limitsetting in toddlerhood: Socialization strategies for the development of self-regulation. *Infant Mental Health Journal, 27,* 344–370.

LeCuyer, E. A., Christensen, J. J., Kearney, M. H., & Kitzman, H. J. (2011). African American mothers' self-described discipline strategies with young children. *Issues in Comprehensive Pediatric Nursing, 34,* 144–162.

Lee, C.-Y. S., & Doherty, W. J. (2007). Marital satisfaction and father involvement during the transition to parenthood. *Fathering, 5,* 75–96.

Lee, E. A., Torrance, N., & Olson, D. R. (2001). Young children and the say/mean distinction: Verbatim and paraphrase recognition in narrative and nursery rhyme contexts. *Journal of Child Language, 28,* 531–543.

Lee, E. H., Zhou, Q., Eisenberg, N., & Wang, Y. (2012). Bidirectional relations between temperament and parenting styles in Chinese children. *International Journal of Behavioral Development, 37,* 57–67.

Lee, G. Y., & Kisilevsky, B. S. (2013). Fetuses respond to father's voice but prefer mother's voice after birth. *Developmental Psychobiology, 56,* 1–11.

Lee, K., Xu, F., Fu, G., Cameron, C. A., & Chen, S. (2001). Taiwan and Mainland Chinese and Canadian children's categorization and evaluation of lie- and truth-telling: A modesty effect. *British Journal of Developmental Psychology, 19,* 525–542.

Lee, S. J., Ralston, H. J., Partridge, J. C., & Rosen, M. A. (2005). Fetal pain: A systematic multidisciplinary review

of the evidence. *Journal of the American Medical Association, 294,* 947–954.

Lee, S. J., Taylor, C. A., Altschul, I., & Rice, J. C. (2013). Parental spanking and subsequent risk for child aggression in father-involved families of young children. *Children and Youth Services Review, 35,* 1476–1485.

Lee, V. E., & Burkam, D. T. (2002). *Inequality at the starting gate.* Washington, DC: Economic Policy Institute.

Leerkes, E. M. (2010). Predictors of maternal sensitivity to infant distress. *Parenting: Science and Practice, 10,* 219–239.

Leet, T., & Flick, L. (2003). Effect of exercise on birth weight. *Clinical Obstetrics and Gynecology, 46,* 423–431.

Legare, C. H., & Gelman, S. A. (2008). Bewitchment, biology, or both: The co-existence of natural and supernatural explanatory frameworks across development. *Cognitive Science, 32,* 607–642.

Legare, C. H., Zhu, L., & Wellman, H. (2013). Examining biological explanations in Chinese preschool children: A cross-cultural comparison. *Journal of Cognition and Culture, 13,* 67–93.

Legerstee, M., & Markova, G. (2007). Intentions make a difference: Infant responses to still-face and modified still-face conditions. *Infant Behavior and Development, 30,* 232–250.

Lehman, M., & Hasselhorn, M. (2007). Variable memory strategy use in children's adaptive intratask learning behavior: Developmental changes and working memory influences in free recall. *Child Development, 78,* 1068–1082.

Lehman, M., & Hasselhorn, M. (2012). Rehearsal dynamics in elementary school children. *Journal of Experimental Child Psychology, 111,* 552–560.

Lehnung, M., Leplow, B., Ekroll, V., Herzog, A., Mehdorn, M., & Ferstl, R. (2003). The role of locomotion in the acquisition and transfer of spatial knowledge in children. *Scandinavian Journal of Psychology, 44,* 79–86.

Lehr, V. T., Zeskind, P. S., Ofenstein, J. P., Cepeda, E., Warrier, I., & Aranda, J. V. (2007). Neonatal facial coding system scores and spectral characteristics of infant crying during newborn circumcision. *Clinical Journal of Pain, 23,* 417–424.

Lejeune, F., Marcus, L., Berne-Audeoud, F., Streri, A., Debillon, T., & Gentaz, E. (2012). Intermanual transfer of shapes in preterm human infants from 33 to 34 + 6 weeks postconceptional age. *Child Development, 83,* 794–800.

Lemche, E., Lennertz, I., Orthmann, C., Ari, A., Grote, K., Hafker, J., & Klann-Delius, G. (2003). Emotion-regulatory process in evoked play narratives: Their relation with mental representations and family interactions. *Praxis der Kinderpsychologie und Kinderpsychiatrie, 52,* 156–171.

Lempert, H. (1989). Animacy constraints on preschoolers' acquisition of syntax. *Child Development, 60,* 237–245.

Lenhart, A., Purcell, K, Smith, A., & Zickuhr, K. (2010). *Social media & mobile Internet use among teens and young adults.* Washington, DC: Pew Research Center.

Lerman, R. I. (2010). Capabilities and contributions of unwed fathers. *Future of Children, 20,* 63–85.

Lerner, R. M., Leonard, K., Fay, K., & Issac, S. S. (2011). Continuity and discontinuity in development across the life span: A developmental systems perspective. In K. L. Fingerman, C. A. Berg, J. Smith, & T. C. Antonucci (Eds.), *Handbook of life-span development* (pp. 141–160). New York: Springer.

Lerner, R. M., & Overton, W. F. (2008). Exemplifying the integrations of the relational developmental system. *Journal of Adolescent Research, 23,* 245–255.

Lernout, T., Theeten, H., Hens, N., Braeckman, T., Roelants, M., Hoppenbrouwers, K., & Van Damme, P. (2013). Timeliness of infant vaccination and factors related with delay in Flanders, Belgium. *Vaccine, 32,* 284–289.

Leslie, A. M. (2004). Who's for learning? *Developmental Science, 7,* 417–419.

Lester, B. M., & Lagasse, L. L. (2010). Children of addicted women. *Journal of Addictive Diseases, 29,* 259–276.

Lett, D. (1997). *L'enfant des miracles: Enfance et société au Moyen Age (XIIe–XIIIe siecle).* Paris: Aubier.

Leuner, B., Glasper, E. R., & Gould, E. (2010). Parenting and plasticity. *Trends in Neurosciences, 33,* 465–473.

Levendosky, A. A., Bogat, G. A., Huth-Bocks, A. C., Rosenblum, K., & von Eye, A. (2011). The effect of domestic violence on the stability of attachment from infancy to preschool. *Journal of Clinical Child and Adolescent Psychology, 40,* 398–410.

Leventhal, T., & Brooks-Gunn, J. (2003). Children and youth in neighborhood contexts. *Current Directions in Psychological Science, 12,* 27–31.

Leventhal, T., & Dupéré, V. (2011). Moving to opportunity: Does long-term exposure to "low-poverty" neighborhoods make a difference for adolescents? *Social Science and Medicine, 73,* 737–743.

Levin, I., & Bus, A. G. (2003). How is emergent writing based on drawing? Analyses of children's products and their sorting by children and mothers. *Developmental Psychology, 39,* 891–905.

LeVine, R. A., Dixon, S., LeVine, S., Richman, A., Leiderman, P. H., Keefer, C. H., & Brazelton, T. B. (1994). *Child care and culture: Lessons from Africa.* New York: Cambridge University Press.

LeVine, R. A., LeVine, S. E., Rowe, M. L., & Schnell-Anzola, B. (2004). Maternal literacy and health behavior: A Nepalese case study. *Social Science and Medicine, 58,* 863–877.

LeVine, R. A., LeVine, S., Schnell-Anzola, B., Rowe, M. L., & Dexter, E. (2012). *Literacy and mothering: How women's schooling changes the lives of the world's children.* New York: Oxford University Press.

Levy, G. D., Taylor, M. G., & Gelman, S. A. (1995). Traditional and evaluative aspects of flexibility in gender roles, social conventions, moral rules, and physical laws. *Child Development, 66,* 515–531.

Levy, S. R., & Dweck, C. S. (1999). The impact of children's static vs. dynamic conceptions of people on stereotype information. *Child Development, 70,* 1163–1180.

Lewis, M. (1992). *Shame: The exposed self.* New York: Free Press.

Lewis, M. (1995). Embarrassment: The emotion of self-exposure and evaluation. In J. P. Tangney & K. W. Fischer (Eds.), *Self-conscious emotions* (pp. 198–218). New York: Guilford.

Lewis, M. (1998). Emotional competence and development. In D. Pushkar, W. M. Bukowski, A. E. Schwartzman, E. M. Stack, & D. R. White (Eds.), *Improving competence across the lifespan* (pp. 27–36). New York: Plenum.

Lewis, M. (2014). *The rise of consciousness and the development of emotional life.* New York: Guilford.

Lewis, M., & Brooks-Gunn, J. (1979). *Social cognition and the acquisition of self.* New York: Plenum.

Lewis, M., & Ramsay, D. (2002). Cortisol response to embarrassment and shame. *Child Development, 73,* 1034–1045.

Lewis, M., & Ramsay, D. (2004). Development of self-recognition, personal pronoun use, and pretend play during the 2nd year. *Child Development, 75,* 1821–1831.

Lewis, M., Ramsay, D. S., & Kawakami, K. (1993). Differences between Japanese infants and Caucasian American infants in behavioral and cortisol response to inoculation. *Child Development, 64,* 1722–1731.

Lewis, M. D. (2008). Emotional habits in brain and behavior: A window on personality development. In A. Fogel, B. J. King, & S. G. Shanker (Eds.), *Human development in the twenty-first century* (pp. 72–80). New York: Cambridge University Press.

Lewis, T. L., & Maurer, D. (2005). Multiple sensitive periods in human visual development: Evidence from visually deprived children. *Developmental Psychobiology, 46,* 163–183.

Lew-Williams, C., Pelucchi, B., & Saffran, J. R. (2011). Isolated words enhance statistical language learning in infancy. *Developmental Science, 14,* 1323–1329.

Li, D.-K., Willinger, M., Petitti, D. B., Odouli, R., Liu, L., & Hoffman, H. J. (2006). Use of a dummy (pacifier) during sleep and risk of sudden infant death syndrome (SIDS): Population based case-control study. *British Medical Journal, 332,* 18–21.

Li, J., Johnson, S. E., Han, W., Andrews, S., Kendall, G., Strazdins, L. & Dockery, A. (2014). Parents' nonstandard work schedules and child well-being: A critical review of the literature. *Journal of Primary Prevention, 35,* 53–73.

Li, K., Zhu, D., Guo, L., Li, Z., Lynch, M. E., Coles, C., et al. (2013). Connectomics signatures of prenatal cocaine exposure affected adolescent brains. *Human Brain Mapping, 34,* 2494–2510.

Li, S.-C., Lindenberger, U., Hommel, B., Aschersleben, G., Prinz, W., & Baltes, P. B. (2004). Transformation in the couplings among intellectual abilities and constituent cognitive processes across the life span. *Psychological Science, 15,* 155–163.

Li, W., Farkas, G., Duncan, G. J., Burchinal, M. R., & Vandell, D. L. (2013). Timing of high-quality child care and cognitive, language, and preacademic development. *Developmental Psychology, 49,* 1440–1451.

Li, X., Atkins, M. S., & Stanton, B. (2006). Effects of home and school computer use on school readiness and cognitive development among Head Start children: A randomized control trial. *Merrill-Palmer Quarterly, 52,* 239–263.

Li, X. Q., Zhu, P., Myatt, L., & Sun, K. (2014). Roles of glucocorticoids in human parturition: A controversial fact? *Placenta, 35,* 291–296.

Liben, L. S. (2006). Education for spatial thinking. In K. A. Renninger & I. E. Sigel (Eds.), *Handbook of child psychology: Vol. 4. Child psychology in practice* (6th ed., pp. 197–247). Hoboken, NJ: Wiley.

Liben, L. S. (2009). The road to understanding maps. *Current Directions in Psychological Science, 18,* 310–315.

Liben, L. S., & Bigler, R. S. (2002). The developmental course of gender differentiation: Conceptualizing, measuring, and evaluating constructs and pathways. *Monographs of the Society for Research in Child Development, 67*(2, Serial No. 269).

Liben, L. S., Bigler, R. S., & Krogh, H. R. (2001). Pink and blue collar jobs: Children's judgments of job status and job aspirations in relation to sex of worker. *Journal of Experimental Child Psychology, 79,* 346–363.

Liben, L. S., & Downs, R. M. (1993). Understanding person–space–map relations: Cartographic and developmental perspectives. *Developmental Psychology, 29,* 739–752.

Liben, L. S., Kastens, K. A., & Stevenson, L. M. (2002). Real-world knowledge through real-world maps: A developmental guide for navigating the educational terrain. *Developmental Review, 22,* 267–322.

Liben, L. S., Myers, L. J., Christensen, A. E., & Bower, C. A. (2013). Environmental-scale map use in middle childhood: Links to spatial skills, strategies, and gender. *Child Development, 84,* 2047–2063.

Lickliter, R., & Honeycutt, H. (2013). A developmental evolutionary framework for psychology. *Review of General Psychology, 17,* 184–189.

Lidstone, J. S. M., Meins, E., & Fernyhough, C. (2010). The roles of private speech and inner speech in planning during middle childhood: Evidence from a dual task paradigm. *Journal of Experimental Child Psychology, 107,* 438–451.

Lidz, C. S. (2001). Multicultural issues and dynamic assessment. In L. A. Suzuki & J. G. Ponterotto (Eds.), *Handbook of multicultural assessment: Clinical, psychological, and educational applications* (2nd ed., pp. 523–539). San Francisco: Jossey-Bass.

Lidz, J. (2007). The abstract nature of syntactic representations. In E. Hoff & M. Shatz (Eds.), *Blackwell handbook of language development* (pp. 277–303). Malden, MA: Blackwell.

Lidz, J., Gleitman, H., & Gleitman, L. (2004). Kidz in the 'hood: Syntactic bootstrapping and the mental lexicon. In D. G. Hall & S. R. Waxman (Eds.), *Weaving a lexicon* (pp. 603–636). Cambridge, MA: MIT Press.

Liew, J., Eisenberg, N., Spinrad, T. L., Eggum, N. D., Haugen, R. G., Kupfer, A., et al. (2010). Physiological regulation and fearfulness as predictors of young children's empathy-related reactions. *Social Development, 20,* 111–134.

Li-Grining, C. P. (2007). Effortful control among low-income preschoolers in three cities: Stability, change, and individual differences. *Developmental Psychology, 43,* 208–221.

Lillard, A. (2007). *Montessori: The science behind the genius.* New York: Oxford University Press.

Lillard, A., & Else-Quest, N. (2006). Evaluating Montessori education. *Science, 313,* 1893–1894.

Lillard, A. S., Nishida, T., Massaro, D., Vaish, A., Ma, L., & McRoberts, G. (2007). Signs of pretense across age and scenario. *Infancy, 11,* 130.

Lillard, A. S., & Peterson, J. (2011). The immediate impact of different types of television on young children's executive function. *Pediatrics, 128,* 644–649.

Lillard, A. S., & Witherington, D. (2004). Mothers' behavior modifications during pretense snacks and their possible signal value for toddlers. *Developmental Psychology, 40,* 95–113.

Lin, T-J., Anderson, R. C., Hummel, J. E., Jadallah, M., Miller, B. W., Nguyen-Jahiel, K., et al. (2012). Children's use of analogy during collaborative reasoning. *Child Development, 83,* 1429–1443.

Lincove, J. A., & Painter, G. (2006). Does the age that children start kindergarten matter? Evidence of long-term educational and social outcomes. *Educational Evaluation and Policy Analysis, 28,* 153–179.

Lind, J. N., Li, R., Perrine, C. G., & Shieve, L. A. (2014). Breastfeeding and later psychosocial development of children at 6 years of age. *Pediatrics, 134,* S36–S41.

Lindblad, F., & Hjern, A. (2010). ADHD after fetal exposure to maternal smoking. *Nicotine and Tobacco Research, 12,* 408–415.

Lindsay-Hartz, J., de Rivera, J., & Mascolo, M. F. (1995). Differentiating guilt and shame and their effects on motivation. In J. P. Tangney & K. W. Fischer (Eds.), *Self-conscious emotions* (pp. 274–300). New York: Guilford.

Lindsey, E. W., & Colwell, M. J. (2013). Pretend and physical play: Links to preschoolers' affective social competence. *Merrill-Palmer Quarterly, 59,* 330–360.

Lindsey, E. W., Colwell, M. J., Frabutt, J. M., Chambers, J. C., & MacKinnon-Lewis, C. (2008). Mother–child dyadic synchrony in European-American and African-American families during early adolescence: Relations with self-esteem and prosocial behavior. *Merrill-Palmer Quarterly, 54,* 289–315.

Lindsey, E. W., & Mize, J. (2000). Parent–child physical and pretense play: Links to children's social competence. *Merrill-Palmer Quarterly, 46,* 565–591.

Linebarger, D. L., & Piotrowski, J. T. (2010). Structure and strategies in children's educational television: The roles of program type and learning strategies in children's learning. *Child Development, 81,* 1582–1597.

Linscheid, T. R., Budd, K. S., & Rasnake, L. K. (2005). Pediatric feeding problems. In M. C. Roberts (Ed.), *Handbook of pediatric psychology and psychiatry* (3rd ed., pp. 481–488). New York: Guilford.

Linver, M. R., Martin, A., & Brooks-Gunn, J. (2004). Measuring infants' home environment: The IT-HOME for infants between birth and 12 months in four national data sets. *Parenting: Science and Practice, 4,* 115–137.

Lipsitt, L. P. (2003). Crib death: A biobehavioral phenomenon? *Psychological Science, 12,* 164–170.

Lipton, J. S., & Spelke, E. S. (2003). Origins of number sense: Large-number discrimination in human infants. *Psychological Science, 14,* 396–401.

Liszkowski, U., Carpenter, M., & Tomasello, M. (2007). Pointing out new news, old news, and absent referents at 12 months of age. *Developmental Science, 10,* F1–F7.

Liszkowski, U., Carpenter, M., & Tomasello, M. (2008). Twelve-month-olds communicate helpfully and appropriately for knowledgeable and ignorant partners. *Cognition, 108,* 732–739.

Litovsky, R. Y., & Ashmead, D. H. (1997). Development of binaural and spatial hearing in infants and children. In R. H. Gilkey & T. R. Anderson (Eds.), *Binaural and spatial hearing in real and virtual environments* (pp. 571–592). Mahwah, NJ: Erlbaum.

Little, C., & Carter, A. S. (2005). Negative emotional reactivity and regulation in 12-month-olds following emotional challenge: Contributions of maternal—infant emotional availability in a low-income sample, *Infant Mental Health Journal, 26,* 354–368.

Liu, D., Sabbagh, M. A., Gehring, W. J., & Wellman, H. M. (2009). Neural correlates of children's theory of mind development. *Child Development, 80,* 318–326.

Liu, J., Raine, A., Venables, P. H., Dalais, C., & Mednick, S. A. (2003). Malnutrition at age 3 years and lower cognitive ability at age 11 years. *Archives of Paediatric and Adolescent Medicine, 157,* 593–600.

Liu, J., Raine, A., Venables, P. H., & Mednick, S. A. (2004). Malnutrition at age 3 years and externalizing behavior problems at ages 8, 11, and 17 years. *American Journal of Psychiatry, 161,* 2005–2013.

Lleras, C., & Rangel, C. (2009). Ability grouping practices in elementary school and African American/Hispanic achievement. *American Journal of Education, 115,* 279–304.

Lloyd, M. E., Doydum, A. O., & Newcombe, N. S. (2009). Memory binding in early childhood: Evidence for a retrieval deficit. *Child Development, 80,* 1321–1328.

Lobo, M. A., & Galloway, J. C. (2013). The onset of reaching significantly impacts how infants explore both objects and their bodies. *Infant Behavior and Development, 36,* 14–24.

Lochman, J. E., & Dodge, K. A. (1998). Distorted perceptions in dyadic interactions of aggressive and nonaggressive boys: Effects of prior expectations, context, and boys' age. *Development and Psychopathology, 10,* 495–512.

Locke, J. (1892). Some thoughts concerning education. In R. H. Quick (Ed.), *Locke on education* (pp. 1–236). Cambridge, UK: Cambridge University Press. (Original work published 1690).

Lockhart, K. L., Chang, B., & Story, T. (2002). Young children's beliefs about the stability of traits: Protective optimism? *Child Development, 73,* 1408–1430.

Lockhart, K. L., Nakashima, N., Inagaki, K., & Keil, F. C. (2008). From ugly duckling to swan? Japanese and American beliefs about the stability and origins of traits. *Cognitive Development, 23,* 155–179.

Loehlin, J. C., Horn, J. M., & Willerman, L. (1997). Heredity, environment, and IQ in the Texas Adoption Project. In R. J. Sternberg & E. L. Grigorenko (Eds.), *Intelligence, heredity, and environment* (pp. 105–125). New York: Cambridge University Press.

Loganovskaja, T. K., & Loganovsky, K. N. (1999). EEG, cognitive and psychopathological abnormalities in children irradiated in utero. *International Journal of Psychophysiology, 34,* 213–224.

Loganovsky, K. N., Loganovskaja, T. K., Nechayev, S. Y., Antipchuk, Y. Y., & Bomko, M. A. (2008). Disrupted development of the dominant hemisphere following prenatal irradiation. *The Journal of Neuropsychiatry and Clinical Neurosciences, 20,* 274–291.

Lohman, D. F. (2000). Measures of intelligence: Cognitive theories. In A. E. Kazdin (Ed.), *Encyclopedia of psychology: Vol. 5* (pp. 147–150). Washington, DC: American Psychological Association.

Lohrmann, S., & Bambara, L. M. (2006). Elementary education teachers' beliefs about essential supports needed to successfully include students with developmental disabilities who engage in challenging behaviors. *Research and Practice for Persons with Severe Disabilities, 31,* 157–173.

Loman, M. M., & Gunnar, M. R. (2010). Early experience and the development of stress reactivity and regulation in children. *Neuroscience and Biobehavioral Reviews, 34,* 867–876.

Longstaffe, S., Moffatt, M. E., & Whalen, J. C. (2000). Behavioral and self-concept changes after six months of enuresis treatment: A randomized, controlled trial. *Pediatrics, 105,* 935–940.

Lonigan, C. J., Purpura, D. J., Wilson, S. B., Walker, J., & Clancy-Menchetti, J. (2013). Evaluating the components of an emergent literacy intervention for preschool children at risk for reading difficulties. *Journal of Experimental Child Psychology, 114,* 111–130.

Looker, D., & Thiessen, V. (2003). *The digital divide in Canadian schools: Factors affecting student access to and use of information technology.* Ottawa: Statistics Canada, Catalogue no. 81-597-X. Retrieved from www.statcan.ca/bsolc/english/bsolc?catno=81-597-X

Loomans, E. M., Van der Stelt, O., van Eijsden, M., Gemke, R. J., Vrijkotte, T., & den Bergh, B. R. (2011). Antenatal maternal anxiety is associated with problem behaviour at age five. *Early Human Development, 87,* 565–570.

Lorenz, K. Z. (1952). *King Solomon's ring.* New York: Crowell.

Louie, V. (2001). Parents' aspirations and investment: The role of social class in the educational experiences of 1.5- and second-generation Chinese Americans. *Harvard Educational Review, 71,* 438–474.

Louis, J., Cannard, C., Bastuji, H., & Challamel, M.-J. (1997). Sleep ontogenesis revisited: A longitudinal 24-hour home polygraphic study on 15 normal infants during the first two years of life. *Sleep, 20,* 323–333.

Lourenço, O. (2003). Making sense of Turiel's dispute with Kohlberg: The case of the child's moral competence. *New Ideas in Psychology, 21,* 43–68.

Lourenço, O. (2012). Piaget and Vygotsky: Many resemblances, and a crucial difference. *New Ideas in Psychology, 30,* 281–295.

Love, J. M., Chazan-Cohen, R., & Raikes, H. (2007). Forty years of research knowledge and use: From Head Start to Early Head Start and beyond. In J. L. Aber, S. J. Bishop-Josef, S. M. Jones, K. T. McLearn, & D. Phillips (Eds.), *Child development and social policy: Knowledge for action* (pp. 79–95). Washington, DC: American Psychological Association.

Love, J. M., Harrison, L., Sagi-Schwartz, A., van IJzendoorn, M. H., Ross, C., & Ungerer, J. A. (2003). Child care quality matters: How conclusions may vary with context. *Child Development, 74,* 1021–1033.

Love, J. M., Kisker, E. E., Ross, C., Raikes, H., Constantine, J., Boller, K., & Brooks-Gunn, J. (2005). The effectiveness of early Head Start for 3-year-old children and their parents: Lessons for policy and programs. *Developmental Psychology, 41,* 885–901.

Low, M., Farrell, A., Biggs, B., & Pasricha, S. (2013). Effects of daily iron supplementation in primary-school-aged children: Systematic review and meta-analysis of randomized controlled trials. *Canadian Medical Association Journal, 185,* E791–E802.

Low, S. M., & Stocker, C. (2012). Family functioning and children's adjustment: Associations among parents' depressed mood, marital hostility, parent–child hostility, and children's adjustment. *Journal of Family Psychology, 19,* 394–403.

Lubart, T. I. (2003). In search of creative intelligence. In R. J. Sternberg, J. Lautrey, & T. I. Lubart (Eds.), *Models of intelligence: International perspectives* (pp. 279–292). Washington, DC: American Psychological Association.

Lubart, T. I., Georgsdottir, A., & Besançon, M. (2009). The nature of creative giftedness and talent. In T. Balchin, B. Hymer, & D. J. Matthews (Eds.), *The Routledge international companion to gifted education* (pp. 42–49). New York: Routledge.

Luby, J., Belden, A., Sullivan, J., Hayen, R., McCadney, A., & Spitznagel, E. (2009). Shame and guilt in preschool depression: Evidence for elevations in self-conscious emotions in depression as early as age 3. *Journal of Child Psychology and Psychiatry, 50,* 1156–1166.

Lucas-Thompson, R., & Clarke-Stewart, K. A. (2007). Forecasting friendship: How marital quality, maternal mood, and attachment security are linked to children's peer relationships. *Journal of Applied Developmental Psychology, 28,* 499–514.

Lucassen, N., Tharner, A., Van IJzendoorn, M. H., Bakermans-Kranenburg, M. J., Volling, B. L., Verhulst, F. C., et al. (2011). The association between paternal sensitivity and infant–father attachment security: A meta-analysis of three decades of research. *Journal of Family Psychology, 25,* 986–992.

Luecken, L. J., Lin, B., Coburn, S. S., MacKinnon, D. P., Gonzales, N. A., & Crnic, K. A. (2013). Prenatal stress, partner support, and infant cortisol reactivity in low-income Mexican American families. *Psychoneuroendocrinology, 38,* 3092–3101.

Lukowski, A. F., Koss, M., Burden, M. J., Jonides, J., Nelson, C. A., Kaciroti, N., et al. (2010). Iron deficiency in infancy and neurocognitive functioning at 19 years: Evidence of long-term deficits in executive function and recognition memory. *Nutritional Neuroscience, 13,* 54–70.

Luna, B., Thulborn, K. R., Monoz, D. P., Merriam, E. P., Garver, K. E., Minshew, N. J., et al. (2001). Maturation of widely distributed brain function subserves cognitive development. *Neuroimage, 13,* 786–793.

Lund, N., Pedersen, L. H., & Henriksen, T. B. (2009). Selective serotonin reuptake inhibitor exposure in utero and pregnancy outcomes. *Archives of Pediatrics and Adolescent Medicine, 163,* 949–954.

Lundy, B. L. (2002). Paternal socio-psychological factors and infant attachment: The mediating role of synchrony in father–infant interactions. *Infant Behavior and Development, 25,* 221–236.

Luo, L. Z., Li, H., & Lee, K. (2011). Are children's faces really more appealing than those of adults? Testing the baby schema hypothesis beyond infancy. *Journal of Experimental Child Psychology, 110,* 115–124.

Lussier, P., Corrado, R., & Tzoumakis, S. (2012). Gender differences in physical aggression and associated developmental correlates in a sample of Canadian preschoolers. *Behavioral Sciences and the Law, 30,* 643–671.

Luthar, S. S., & Barkin, S. H. (2012). Are affluent youth truly "at risk"? Vulnerability and resilience across diverse samples. *Development and Psychopathology, 24,* 429–449.

Luthar, S. S., & Goldstein, A. S. (2008). Substance use and related behaviors among suburban late adolescents: The importance of perceived parent containment. *Development and Psychopathology, 20,* 591–614.

Luthar, S. S., & Latendresse, S. J. (2005a). Children of the affluent: Challenges to well-being. *Current Directions in Psychological Science, 14,* 49–53.

Luthar, S. S., & Latendresse, S. J. (2005b). Comparable "risks" at the socioeconomic status extremes: Preadolescents' perceptions of parenting. *Development and Psychopathology, 17,* 207–230.

Luthar, S. S., & Sexton, C. (2004). The high price of affluence. In R. V. Kail (Ed.), *Advances in child development* (Vol. 32, pp. 126–162). San Diego, CA: Academic Press.

Lynch, S. K., Turkheimer, E., D'Onofrio, B. M., Mendle, J., Emery, R. E., Slutske, W. S., & Martin, N. G. (2006). A genetically informed study of the association between harsh punishment and offspring behavioral problems. *Journal of Family Psychology, 20,* 190–198.

Lyon, T. D., & Flavell, J. H. (1994). Young children's understanding of "remember" and "forget." *Child Development, 65,* 1357–1371.

Lyons-Ruth, K., Bronfman, E., & Parsons, E. (1999). Maternal frightened, frightening, or aytpical behavior and disorganized infant attachment patterns. *Monographs of the Society for Research in Child Development, 64*(3, Serial No. 258), 67–96.

Lyster, R., & Genesee, F. (2012). Immersion education. In Carol A. Chapelle (Ed.), *Encyclopedia of Applied Linguistics* (pp. 2608–2614). Hoboken, NJ: Wiley.

Lytton, H., & Gallagher, L. (2002). Parenting twins and the genetics of parenting. In M. H. Bornstein (Ed.), *Handbook of parenting: Vol. 1. Children and parenting* (pp. 227–253). Mahwah, NJ: Erlbaum.

M

Ma, F., Xu, F., Heyman, G. D., & Lee, K. (2011). Chinese children's evaluations of white lies: Weighing the consequences for recipients. *Journal of Experimental Child Psychology, 108,* 308–321.

Ma, L., & Lillard, A. S. (2006). Where is the real cheese? Young children's ability to discriminate between real and pretend acts. *Child Development, 77,* 1762–1777.

Ma, W., Golinkoff, R. M., Hirsh-Pasek, K., McDonough, C., & Tardif, T. (2009). Imagine that! Imageability predicts the age of acquisition of verbs in Chinese children. *Journal of Child Language, 36,* 405–423.

Ma, W., Golinkoff, R. M., Houston, D., & Hirsh-Pasek, K. (2011). Word learning in infant- and adult-directed speech. *Language Learning and Development, 7,* 209–225.

Maas, F. K. (2008). Children's understanding of promising, lying, and false belief. *Journal of General Psychology, 13,* 301–321.

Maccoby, E. E. (1984). Middle childhood in the context of the family. In W. A. Collins (Ed.), *Development during middle childhood* (pp. 184–239). Washington, DC: National Academy Press.

Maccoby, E. E. (1998). *The two sexes: Growing up apart, coming together.* Cambridge, MA: Belknap/Harvard University Press.

Maccoby, E. E. (2002). Gender and group process: A developmental perspective. *Current Directions in Psychological Science, 11,* 54–58.

MacKenzie, M. J., Nicklas, E., Waldfogel, J., & Brooks-Gunn, J. (2013). Spanking and child development across the first decade of life. *Pediatrics, 132,* e1118–e1125. Retrieved from http://pediatrics.aappublications.org/content/132/5/e1118.full.html

Mackey, K., Arnold, M. L., & Pratt, M. W. (2001). Adolescents' stories of decision making in more and less authoritative families: Representing the voices of parents in narrative. *Journal of Adolescent Research, 16,* 243–268.

Mackie, S., Show, P., Lenroot, R., Pierson, R., Greenstein, D. K., & Nugent, T. F., III. (2007). Cerebellar development and clinical outcome in attention deficit hyperactivity disorder. *American Journal of Psychiatry, 164,* 647–655.

MacLeod, J. (2009). *Ain't no makin' it: Aspirations and attainment in a low-income neighborhood.* Boulder, CO: Westview Press.

MacWhinney, B. (2005). Language development. In M. H. Bornstein & M. E. Lamb (Eds.), *Developmental science: An advanced textbook* (5th ed., pp. 359–387). Mahwah, NJ: Erlbaum.

Madigan, S., Bakermans-Kranenburg, M. J., van IJzendoorn, M. H., Moran, G., Pederson, D. R., & Benoit, D. (2006). Unresolved states of mind, anomalous parental behavior, and disorganized attachment: A review and meta-analysis of a transmission gap. *Attachment and Human Development, 8,* 89–111.

Madole, K. L., Oakes, L. M., & Rakison, D. H. (2011). Information-processing approaches to infants' developing representation of dynamic features. In L. M. Oakes, C. H. Cashon, M. Casasola, & D. Rakison (Eds.), *Infant perception and cognition* (153–178). New York: Oxford University Press.

Madon, S., Willard, J., Guyll, M., & Scherr, K. C. (2011). Self-fulfilling prophecies: Mechanisms, power, and links to social problems. *Social and Personality Psychology Compass, 5/8,* 578–590.

Madsen, S. A., & Juhl, T. (2007). Paternal depression in the postnatal period assessed with traditional and male depression scales. *Journal of Men's Health and Gender, 4,* 26–31.

Magnuson, K., & Shager, H. (2010). Early education: Progress and promise for children from low-income families. *Children and Youth Services Review, 32,* 1186–1198.

Main, M., & Goldwyn, R. (1998). *Adult attachment classification system.* London: University College.

Main, M., & Solomon, J. (1990). Procedures for identifying infants as disorganized/disoriented during the Ainsworth Strange Situation. In M. Greenberg, D. Cicchetti, & M. Cummings (Eds.), *Attachment in the preschool years: Theory, research, and intervention* (pp. 121–160). Chicago: University of Chicago Press.

Majdandžić, M., & van den Boom, D. C. (2007). Multimethod longitudinal assessment of temperament in early childhood. *Journal of Personality, 75,* 121–167.

Malatesta, C. Z., Grigoryev, P., Lamb, C., Albin, M., & Culver, C. (1986). Emotion socialization and expressive development in preterm and full-term infants. *Child Development, 57,* 316–330.

Malina, R. M., & Bouchard, C. (1991). *Growth, maturation, and physical activity.* Champaign, IL: Human Kinetics.

Mandara, J., Varner, F., Greene, N., & Richman, S. (2009). Intergenerational family predictors of the black–white achievement gap. *Journal of Educational Psychology, 101,* 867–878.

Mandel, D. R., Jusczyk, P. W., & Pisoni, D. B. (1995). Infants' recognition of the sound patterns of their own names. *Psychological Science, 6,* 314–317.

Mandler, J. M. (2004). Thought before language. *Trends in Cognitive Sciences, 8,* 508–513.

Mandler, J. M., & McDonough, L. (1998). On developing a knowledge base in infancy. *Developmental Psychology, 34,* 1274–1288.

Mangelsdorf, S. C., Schoppe, S. J., & Buur, H. (2000). The meaning of parental reports: A contextual approach to the study of temperament and behavior problems. In V. J. Molfese & D. L. Molfese (Eds.), *Temperament and personality across the life span* (pp. 121–140). Mahwah, NJ: Erlbaum.

Mao, A., Burnham, M. M., Goodlin-Jones, B. L., Gaylor, E. E., & Anders, T. F. (2004). A comparison of the sleep–wake patterns of cosleeping and solitary-sleeping infants. *Child Psychiatry and Human Development, 35,* 95–105.

Maratsos, M. (2000). More overregularizations after all: New data and discussion on Marcus, Pinker, Ullman, Hollander, Rosen, & Xu. *Journal of Child Language, 27,* 183–212.

Marcon, R. A. (1999). Positive relationships between parent–school involvement and public school innercity preschoolers' development and academic performance. *School Psychology Review, 28,* 395–412.

Marcus, G. F. (1995). Children's overregularization of English plurals: A quantitative analysis. *Journal of Child Language, 22,* 447–459.

Marcus, G. F., Vijayan, S., Rao, S. B., & Vishton, P. M. (1999). Rule learning by seven-month-old infants. *Science, 283,* 77–80.

Mares, M.-L., & Acosta, E. E. (2010). Teaching inclusiveness via TV narratives in the US: Young viewers need help with the message. *Journal of Children and Media, 4,* 231–247.

Mares, M.-L., & Pan, Z. (2013). Effects of Sesame Street: A meta-analysis of children's learning in 15 countries. *Journal of Applied Developmental Psychology, 34,* 140–151.

Marian, V., Neisser, U., & Rochat, P. (1996). *Can 2-month-old infants distinguish live from videotaped interactions with their mothers* (Emory Cognition Project, Report #33). Atlanta, GA: Emory University.

Marin, T. J., Chen, E., Munch, T., & Miller, G. (2009). Double exposure to acute stress and chronic family stress is associated with immune changes in children with asthma. *Psychosomatic Medicine, 71*, 378–384.

Markant, J. C., & Thomas, K. M. (2013). Postnatal brain development. In P. D. Zelazo (Ed.), *Oxford handbook of developmental psychology: Vol. 1. Body and mind* (pp. 129–163). New York: Oxford University Press.

Markman, E. M. (1992). Constraints on word learning: Speculations about their nature, origins, and domain specificity. In M. R. Gunnar & M. P. Maratsos (Eds.), *Minnesota Symposia on Child Psychology* (Vol. 25, pp. 59–101). Hillsdale, NJ: Erlbaum.

Markova, G., & Legerstee, M. (2006). Contingency, imitation, and affect sharing: Foundations of infants' social awareness. *Developmental Psychology, 42*, 132–141.

Marlier, L., & Schaal, B. (2005). Human newborns prefer human milk: Conspecific milk odor is attractive without postnatal exposure. *Child Development, 76*, 155–168.

Marsee, M. A., & Frick, P. J. (2010). Callous-unemotional traits and aggression in youth. In W. F. Arsenio & E. A. Lemerise (Eds.), *Emotions, aggression, and morality in children: Bridging development and psychopathology* (pp. 137–156). Washington, DC: American Psychological Association.

Marsh, H. W. (1990). The structure of academic self-concept: The Marsh/Shavelson model. *Journal of Educational Psychology, 82*, 623–636.

Marsh, H. W., & Ayotte, V. (2003). Do multiple dimensions of self-concept become more differentiated with age? The differential distinctiveness hypothesis. *Journal of Educational Psychology, 95*, 687–706.

Marsh, H. W., Craven, R., & Debus, R. (1998). Structure, stability, and development of young children's self-concepts: A multicohort–multioccasion study. *Child Development, 69*, 1030–1053.

Marsh, H. W., Ellis, L. A., & Craven, R. G. (2002). How do preschool children feel about themselves? Unraveling measurement and multidimensional self-concept structure. *Developmental Psychology, 38*, 376–393.

Marsh, H. W., Gerlach, E., Trautwein, U., Lüdtke, O., & Brettschneider, W.-D. (2007). Longitudinal study of predadolescent sport self-concept and performance: Reciprocal effects and causal ordering. *Child Development, 78*, 1640–1656.

Marsh, H. W., Trautwein, U., Lüdtke, O., Koller, O., & Baumert, J. (2005). Academic self-concept, interest, grades, and standardized test scores: Reciprocal effects models of causal ordering. *Child Development, 76*, 397–416.

Marshall, P. J., & Meltzoff, A. N. (2011). Neural mirroring systems: Exploring the EEG mu rhythm in human infancy. *Developmental Cognitive Neuroscience, 1*, 110–123.

Marshall-Baker, A., Lickliter, R., & Cooper, R. P. (1998). Prolonged exposure to a visual pattern may promote behavioral organization in preterm infants. *Journal of Perinatal and Neonatal Nursing, 12*, 50–62.

Martin, C. L., Eisenbud, L., & Rose, H. (1995). Children's gender-based reasoning about toys. *Child Development, 66*, 1453–1471.

Martin, C. L., & Fabes, R. A. (2001). The stability and consequences of young children's same-sex peer interactions. *Developmental Psychology, 37*, 431–446.

Martin, C. L., Fabes, R. A., Evans, S. M., & Wyman, H. (1999). Social cognition on the playground: Children's beliefs about playing with girls versus boys and their relations to sex segregated play. *Journal of Social and Personal Relationships, 16*, 751–771.

Martin, C. L., Fabes, R. A., Hanish, L., Leonard, S., & Dinella, L. M. (2011). Experienced and expected similarity to same-gender peers: Moving toward a comprehensive model of gender segregation. *Sex Roles, 65*, 421–434.

Martin, C. L., & Halverson, C. F. (1987). The role of cognition in sex role acquisition. In D. B. Carter (Ed.), *Current conceptions of sex roles and sex typing: Theory and research* (pp. 123–137). New York: Praeger.

Martin, C. L., Kornienko, O., Schaefer, D. R., Hanish, L. D., Fabes, R. A., & Goble, P. (2013). The role of sex of peers and gender-typed activities in young children's peer affiliative networks: A longitudinal analysis of selection and influence. *Child Development, 84*, 921–937.

Martin, C. L., & Ruble, D. (2004). Children's search for gender cues: Cognitive perspectives on gender development. *Current Directions in Psychological Science, 13*, 67–70.

Martin, C. L., Ruble, D. N., & Szkrybalo, J. (2002). Cognitive theories of early gender development. *Psychological Bulletin, 128*, 903–933.

Martin, E. K., & Silverstone, P. H. (2013). How much child sexual abuse is "below the surface," and how can we help adults identify it early? *Frontiers in Psychiatry, 4*, 1–10.

Martin, J. A., Hamilton, B. E., Osterman, J. K., Curtin, S. C., & Matthews, T. J. (2013). Births: Final data for 2012. *National Vital Statistics Reports, 62*(9). Hyattsville, MD: National Center for Health Statistics. Retrieved from www.cdc.gov/nchs/data/nvsr/nvsr62/nvsr62_09.pdf

Martinez-Frias, M. L., Bermejo, E., Rodríguez-Pinilla, E., & Frías, J. L. (2004). Risk for congenital anomalies associated with different sporadic and daily doses of alcohol consumption during pregnancy: A case-control study. *Birth Defects Research, Part A, Clinical and Molecular Teratology, 70*, 194–200.

Martinot, D., Bagès, C., & Désert, M. (2012). French children's awareness of gender stereotypes about mathematics and reading: When girls improve their reputation in math. *Sex Roles, 66*, 210–219.

Martinot, D., & Désert, M. (2007). Awareness of a gender stereotype, personal beliefs, and self-perceptions regarding math ability: When boys do not surpass girls. *Social Psychology of Education, 10*, 455–471.

Martins, N., & Harrison, K. (2012). Racial and gender differences in the relationship between children's television use and self-esteem: A longitudinal panel study. *Communication Research, 39*, 338–357.

Martinson, M. L., McLanahan, S., & Brooks-Gunn, J. (2012). Race/ethnic and nativity disparities in child overweight in the United States and England. *Annals of the American Association for the Psychological Study of Social Issues, 643*, 219–238.

Martlew, M., & Connolly, K. J. (1996). Human figure drawings by schooled and unschooled children in Papua New Guinea. *Child Development, 67*, 2743–2762.

Marzolf, D. P., & DeLoache, J. S. (1994). Transfer in young children's understanding of spatial representations. *Child Development, 65*, 1–15.

Masataka, N. (1996). Perception of motherese in a signed language by 6-month-old deaf infants. *Developmental Psychology, 32*, 874–879.

Mascolo, M. F., & Fischer, K. W. (1995). Developmental transformations in appraisals for pride, shame, and guilt. In J. P. Tangney & K. W. Fischer (Eds.), *Self-conscious emotions* (pp. 114–139). New York: Guilford.

Mascolo, M. F., & Fischer, K. W. (2007). The codevelopment of self and sociomoral emotions during the toddler years. In C. A. Brownell & C. B. Kopp (Eds.), *Socioemotional development in the toddler years: Transitions and transformations* (pp. 66–99). New York: Guilford.

Mash, C., & Bornstein, M., H. (2012). 5-month-olds' categorization of novel objects: Task and measure dependence. *Infancy, 17*, 179–197.

Mashburn, A. J., Pianta, R. C., Hamre, B. K., Downer, J. T., Barbarin, O. A., Bryant, D., et al. (2008). Measures of classroom quality in prekindergarten and children's development of academic, language, and social skills. *Child Development, 79*, 732–749.

Mason, C. A., Walker-Barnes, C. J., Tu, S., Simons, J., & Martisez-Arrue, R. (2004). Ethnic differences in the affective meaning of parental control behaviors. *Journal of Primary Prevention, 25*, 601–631.

Massey, Z., Rising, S. S., & Ickovics, J. (2006). CenteringPregnancy group prenatal care: Promoting relationship-centered care. *JOGNN, 35*, 286–294.

Masten, A. S. (2007). Resilience in developing systems: Progress and promise as the fourth wave rises. *Development and Psychopathology, 19*, 921–930.

Masten, A. S. (2011). Resilience in children threatened by extreme adversity: Frameworks for research, practice, and translational synergy. *Development and Psychopathology, 23*, 493–506.

Masten, A. S. (2014). Global perspectives on resilience in children and youth. *Child Development, 85*, 6–20.

Masten, A. S., & Cicchetti, D. (2010). Developmental cascades. *Development and Psychopathology, 22*, 491–495.

Masten, A. S., & Reed, M. J. (2002). Resilience in development. In C. R. Snyder & S. J. Lopez (Eds.), *Handbook of positive psychology* (pp. 74–88). New York: Oxford University Press.

Masten, A. S., & Shaffer, A. (2006). How families matter in child development: Reflections from research on risk and resilience. In A. S. Masten & A. Shaffer (Eds.), *Families count: Effects on child and adolescent development* (pp. 5–25). New York: Cambridge University Press.

Mastropieri, D., & Turkewitz, G. (1999). Prenatal experience and neonatal responsiveness to vocal expressions of emotion. *Developmental Psychobiology, 35*, 204–214.

Mastropieri, M. A., Scruggs, T. E., Guckert, M., Thompson, C. C., & Weiss, M. P. (2013). Inclusion and learning disabilities: Will the past be prologue? In J. P. Bakken, F. E. Oblakor, & A. Rotatori (Eds.), *Advances in special education* (Vol. 25, pp. 1–17). Bingley, UK: Emerald Group Publishing.

Masur, E. F., & Rodemaker, J. E. (1999). Mothers' and infants' spontaneous vocal, verbal, and action imitation during the second year. *Merrill-Palmer Quarterly, 45*, 392–412.

Mather, M. (2010, May). *U.S. children in single-mother families* (PRB Data Brief). Washington, DC: Population Reference Bureau.

Matthews, H. (2014, January 14). A billion dollar boost for child care and early learning. CLASP: Policy solutions that work for low-income people. Retrieved from www.clasp.org/issues/child-care-and-early-education/in-focus/a-billion-dollar-boost-for-child-care-and-early-learning

Mattson, S. N., Calarco, K. E., & Lang, A. R. (2006). Focused and shifting attention in children with heavy prenatal alcohol exposure. *Neuropsychology, 20*, 361–369.

Mattson, S. N., Crocker, N., & Nguyen, T. T. (2012). Fetal alcohol spectrum disorders: Neuropsychological and behavioral features. *Neuropsychological Review, 21*, 81–101.

Maurer, D., & Lewis, T. (2013). Human visual plasticity: Lessons from children treated for congenital cataracts. In J. K. E. Steeves & L. R. Harris (Eds.), *Plasticity in sensory systems* (pp. 75–93). New York: Cambridge University Press.

Maurer, D., Mondloch, C. J., & Lewis, T. L. (2007). Sleeper effects. *Developmental Science, 10*, 40–47.

May, L. E., Glaros, A., Yeh, H., Clapp, J. E., & Gustafson, K. M. (2010). Aerobic exercise during pregnancy influences fetal cardiac autonomic control of heart rate and heart rate variability. *Early Human Development, 86*, 213–217.

Mayberry, R. I. (2010). Early language acquisition and adult language ability: What sign language reveals about the critical period for language. In M. Marshark & P. E. Spencer (Eds.), *Oxford handbook of deaf studies, language, and education* (Vol. 2, pp. 281–291). New York: Oxford University Press.

Mayes, L. C., & Zigler, E. (1992). An observational study of the affective concomitants of mastery in infants. *Journal of Child Psychology and Psychiatry, 33*, 659–667.

Mayeux, L., & Cillessen, A. H. N. (2003). Development of social problem solving in early childhood: Stability, change, and associations with social competence. *Journal of Genetic Psychology, 164*, 153–173.

Mayeux, L., Houser, J. J., & Dyches, K. D. (2011). Social acceptance and popularity: Two distinct forms of peer status. In A. H. N. Cillessen, D. Schwartz, & L. Mayeux (Eds.), *Popularity in the peer system* (pp. 79–102). New York: Guilford.

Maynard, A. E. (2002). Cultural teaching: The development of teaching skills in Maya sibling interactions. *Child Development, 73*, 969–982.

Maynard, A. E., & Greenfield, P. M. (2003). Implicit cognitive development in cultural tools and children: Lessons from Maya Mexico. *Cognitive Development, 18*, 489–510.

Mazumdar, M., Bellinger, D. C., Gregas, M., Abanilla, K., Bacic, J., & Needleman, H. L. (2011). Low-level environmental lead exposure in childhood and adult intellectual function: A follow-up study. *Environmental Health, 10*, 24.

McAdoo, H. P., & Younge, S. N. (2009). Black families. In H. A. Neville, B. M. Tynes, & S. O. Utsey (Eds.), *Handbook of African American psychology* (pp. 103–115). Thousand Oaks, CA: Sage.

McAlister, A., & Peterson, C. C. (2006). Mental playmates: Siblings, executive functioning and theory of mind. *British Journal of Developmental Psychology, 24*, 733–751.

McAlister, A., & Peterson, C. C. (2007). A longitudinal study of child siblings and theory of mind development. *Cognitive Development, 22*, 258–270.

McBride-Chang, C., Wagner, R. K., Muse, A., Chow, B. W.-Y., & Shu, H. (2005). The role of morphological awareness in children's English reading and vocabulary acquisition. *Applied Psycholinguistics, 26,* 415–435.

McCabe, A. (1997). Developmental and cross-cultural aspects of children's narration. In M. Bamberg (Ed.), *Narrative development: Six approaches* (pp. 137–174). Mahwah, NJ: Erlbaum.

McCabe, A., Tamis-LeMonda, C. S., Bornstein, M. H., Cates, C. B., Golinkoff, R., Guerra, A. W., et al. (2013). Multilingual children: Beyond myths and toward best practices. *Society for Research in Child Development Social Policy Report, 27*(4).

McCarter-Spaulding, D., Lucas, J., & Gore, R. (2011). Employment and breastfeeding outcomes in a sample of black women in the United States. *Journal of National Black Nurses' Association, 22,* 38–45.

McCartney, K., Dearing, E., Taylor, B., & Bub, K. (2007). Quality child care supports the achievement of low-income children: Direct and indirect pathways through caregiving and the home environment. *Journal of Applied Developmental Psychology, 28,* 411–426.

McCartney, K., Owen, M., Booth, C., Clarke-Stewart, A., & Vandell, D. (2004). Testing a maternal attachment model of behavior problems in early childhood. *Journal of Child Psychology and Psychiatry, 45,* 765–778.

McCarton, C. (1998). Behavioral outcomes in low birth weight infants. *Pediatrics, 102,* 1293–1297.

McCarty, M. E., & Ashmead, D. H. (1999). Visual control of reaching and grasping in infants. *Developmental Psychology, 35,* 620–631.

McCarty, M. E., & Keen, R. (2005). Facilitating problem-solving performance among 9- and 12-month-old infants. *Journal of Cognition and Development, 6,* 209–228.

McClelland, M. M., Cameron, C. E., Wanless, S. B., & Murray, A. (2007). Executive function, behavioral self-regulation, and social-emotional competence: Links to school readiness. In O. Saracho & B. Spodek (Eds.), *Contemporary perspectives on social learning in early childhood education* (pp. 83–107). Charlotte, NC: Information Age Publishing.

McColgan, K. L., & McCormack, T. (2008). Searching and planning: Young children's reasoning about past and future event sequences. *Child Development, 79,* 1477–1479.

McCormack, T., & Atance, C. M. (2011). Planning in young children: A review and synthesis. *Developmental Review, 31,* 1–31.

McCormack, V. A., dos Santos Silva, I., Koupil, I., Leon, D. A., & Lithell, H. O. (2005). Birth characteristics and adult cancer incidence: Swedish cohort of over 11,000 men and women. *International Journal of Cancer, 115,* 611–617.

McCormick, M. C., Brooks-Gunn, J., Buka, S. L., Goldman, J., Yu, J., Salganik, M., Scott, D. T., et al. (2006). Early intervention in low birth weight premature infants: Results at 18 years of age for the Infant Health and Development Program. *Pediatrics, 117,* 771–780.

McCrink, K., & Wynn, K. (2004). Large-number addition and subtraction by 9-month-old infants. *Psychological Science, 15,* 776–781.

McCune, L. (1993). The development of play as the development of consciousness. In M. H. Bornstein & A. O'Reilly (Eds.), *New directions for child development* (No. 59, pp. 67–79). San Francisco: Jossey-Bass.

McDonough, C., Song, L., Hirsh-Pasek, K., & Golinkoff, R. M. (2011). An image is worth a thousand words: Why nouns tend to dominate verbs in early word learning. *Developmental Science, 14,* 181–189.

McDonough, L. (1999). Early declarative memory for location. *British Journal of Developmental Psychology, 17,* 381–402.

McDowell, D. J., & Parke, R. D. (2000). Differential knowledge of display rules for positive and negative emotions: Influences from parents, influences on peers. *Social Development, 9,* 415–432.

McElwain, N. L., & Booth-LaForce, C. (2006). Maternal sensitivity to infant distress and nondistress as predictors of infant–mother attachment security. *Journal of Family Psychology, 20,* 247–255.

McFarland-Piazza, L., Hazen, N., Jacobvitz, D., & Boyd-Soisson, E. (2012). The development of father–child attachment: Associations between adult attachment representations, recollections of childhood experiences and caregiving. *Early Child Development and Care, 182,* 701–721.

McGee, L. M., & Richgels, D. J. (2004). *Literacy's beginnings: Supporting young readers and writers* (4th ed.). Boston: Allyn and Bacon.

McGee, L. M., & Richgels, D. J. (2012). *Literacy's beginnings: Supporting young readers and writers* (6th ed.). Boston: Allyn and Bacon.

McGonigle-Chalmers, M., Slater, H., & Smith, A. (2014). Rethinking private speech in preschoolers: The effects of social presence. *Developmental Psychology, 50,* 829–836.

McGrath, S. K., & Kennell, J. H. (2008). A randomized controlled trial of continuous labor support for middle-class couples: Effect on cesarean delivery rates. *Birth: Issues in Perinatal Care, 35,* 9–97.

McHale, J. P., Kazali, C., Rotman, T., Talbot, J., Carleton, M., & Lieberson, R. (2004). The transition to coparenthood: Parents' prebirth expectations and early coparental adjustment at 3 months postpartum. *Development and Psychopathology, 16,* 711–733.

McHale, J. P., & Rotman, T. (2007). Is seeing believing? Expectant parents' outlooks on coparenting and later coparenting solidarity. *Infant Behavior and Development, 30,* 63–81.

McHale, S. M., Updegraff, K. A., Helms-Erikson, H., & Crouter, A. C. (2001). Sibling influences on gender development in middle childhood and early adolescence: A longitudinal study. *Developmental Psychology, 37,* 115–125.

McHale, S. M., Updegraff, K. A., & Whiteman, S. D. (2012). Sibling relationships and influences in childhood and adolescence. *Journal of Marriage and Family, 74,* 913–930.

McIntyre, S., Blair, E., Badawi, N., Keogh, J., & Nelson, K. B. (2013). Antecedents of cerebral palsy and perinatal death in term and late preterm singletons. *Obstetrics and Gynecology, 122,* 869–877.

McKenna, J. J. (2001). Why we never ask "Is it safe for infants to sleep alone?" *Academy of Breast Feeding Medicine News and Views, 7*(4), 32, 38.

McKenna, J. J. (2002, September/October). Breastfeeding and bedsharing: Still useful (and important) after all these years. *Mothering, 114,* 28–37.

McKenna, J. J., & McDade, T. (2005). Why babies should never sleep alone: A review of the co-sleeping controversy in relation to SIDS, bedsharing, and breastfeeding. *Paediatric Respiratory Reviews, 6,* 134–152.

McKenna, J. J., & Volpe, L. E. (2007). Sleeping with baby: An Internet-based sampling of parental experiences, choices, perceptions, and interpretations in a Western industrialized context. *Infant and Child Development, 16,* 359–385.

McKinney, C., Donnelly, R., & Renk, K. (2008). Perceived parenting, positive and negative perceptions of parents, and late adolescent emotional adjustment. *Child and Adolescent Mental health, 13,* 66–73.

McKown, C. (2013). Social equity theory and racial-ethnic achievement gaps. *Child Development, 84,* 1120–1136.

McKown, C., Gregory, A., & Weinstein, R. S. (2010). Expectations, stereotypes, and self-fulfilling prophecies in classroom and school life. In J. L. Meece & J. S. Eccles (Eds.), *Handbook of research on schools, schooling and human development* (pp. 256–274). New York: Routledge.

McKown, C., & Strambler, M. J. (2009). Developmental antecedents and social and academic consequences of stereotype-consciousness in middle childhood. *Child Development, 80,* 1643–1659.

McKown, C., & Weinstein, R. S. (2003). The development and consequences of stereotype consciousness in middle childhood. *Child Development, 74,* 498–515.

McKown, C., & Weinstein, R. S. (2008). Teacher expectations, classroom context, and the achievement gap. *Journal of School Psychology, 46,* 235–261.

McLanahan, S. (1999). Father absence and the welfare of children. In E. M. Hetherington (Ed.), *Coping with divorce, single parenting, and remarriage: A risk and resiliency perspective* (pp. 117–145). Mahwah, NJ: Erlbaum.

McLaughlin, K. A., Fox, N. A., Zeanah, C. H., & Nelson, C. A. (2011). Adverse rearing environments and neural development in children: The development of frontal electroencephalogram asymmetry. *Biological Psychiatry, 70,* 1008–1015.

McLeskey, J., & Waldron, N. L. (2011). Educational programs for elementary students with learning disabilities: Can they be both effective and inclusive? *Learning Disabilities: Research and Practice, 26,* 48–57.

McLoyd, V. C., Aikens, N. L., & Burton, L. M. (2006). Childhood poverty, policy, and practice. In K. A. Renninger & I. E. Sigel (Eds.), *Handbook of child psychology: Vol. 4. Child psychology in practice* (6th ed., pp. 700–778). Hoboken, NJ: Wiley.

McLoyd, V. C., Kaplan, R., Hardaway, C. R., & Wood, D. (2007). Does endorsement of physical discipline matter? Assessing moderating influences on the maternal and child psychological correlates of physical discipline in African-American families. *Journal of Family Psychology, 21,* 165–175.

McLoyd, V. C., & Smith, J. (2002). Physical discipline and behavior problems in African-American, European-American, and Hispanic children: Emotional support as a moderator. *Journal of Marriage and the Family, 64,* 40–53.

McMahon, C. A., Barnett, B., Kowalenko, N. M., & Tennant, C. C. (2006). Maternal attachment state of mind moderates the impact of postnatal depression on infant attachment. *Journal of Child Psychology and Psychiatry and Allied Disciplines, 47,* 660–669.

McNeil, D. G., Jr. (2014, March 5). Early treatment is found to clear H.I.V. in a 2nd baby. *New York Times,* p. A1.

Mead, G. H. (1934). *Mind, self, and society.* Chicago: University of Chicago Press.

Meazza, C., Pagani, S., & Bozzola, M. (2011). The Pygmy short stature enigma. *Pediatric Endocrinology Reviews, 8,* 394–399.

Meece, D. & Mize, J. (2011). Preschoolers' cognitive representations of peer relationships: Family origins and behavioural correlates. *Early Childhood Development and Care, 181,* 63–72.

Meins, E., Fernyhough, C., Fradley, E., & Tuckey, M. (2001). Rethinking maternal sensitivity: Mothers' comments on infants' mental processes predict security of attachment at 12 months. *Journal of Child Psychology and Psychiatry and Allied Disciplines, 42,* 637–648.

Meins, E., Fernyhough, C., Wainwright, R., Clark-Carter, D., Gupta, M. D., Fradley, E., & Tucker, M. (2003). Pathways to understanding mind: Construct validity and predictive validity of maternal mind-mindedness. *Child Development, 74,* 1194–1211.

Melby, J. N., Conger, R. D., Fang, S., Wichrama, K. A. S., & Conger, K. J. (2008). Adolescent family experiences and educational attainment during early adulthood. *Developmental Psychology, 44,* 1519–1536.

Melby-Lervag, M., & Hulme, C. (2010). Serial and free recall in children can be improved by training: Evidence for the importance of phonological and semantic representations in immediate memory tasks. *Psychological Science, 21,* 1694–1700.

Melinder, A., Endestad, T., & Magnussen, S. (2006). Relations between episodic memory, suggestibility, theory of mind, and cognitive inhibition in the preschool child. *Scandinavian Journal of Psychology, 47,* 485–495.

Meltzoff, A. N. (2007). "Like me": A foundation for social cognition. *Developmental Science, 10,* 126–134.

Meltzoff, A. N. (2013). Origins of social cognition: Bidirectional self-other mapping and the "like-me" hypothesis. In M. Banaji & S. A. Gelman (Eds.), *Navigating the social world: What infants, children, and other species can teach us* (pp. 139–144). New York: Oxford University Press.

Meltzoff, A. N., & Kuhl, P. K. (1994). Faces and speech: Intermodal processing of biologically relevant signals in infants and adults. In D. J. Lewkowicz & R. Lickliter (Eds.), *The development of intersensory perception: Comparative perspectives* (pp. 335–369). Hillsdale, NJ: Erlbaum.

Meltzoff, A. N., & Moore, M. K. (1977). Imitation of facial and manual gestures by human neonates. *Science, 198,* 75–78.

Meltzoff, A. N., & Moore, M. K. (1994). Imitation, memory, and the representation of persons. *Infant Behavior and Development, 17,* 83–99.

Meltzoff, A. N., & Moore, M. K. (1999). Persons and representation: Why infant imitation is important for theories of human development. In J. Nadel & G. Butterworth (Eds.), *Imitation in infancy* (pp. 9–35). Cambridge, UK: Cambridge University Press.

Meltzoff, A. N., & Williamson, R. A. (2010). The importance of imitation for theories of social-cognitive development. In J. G. Bremner & T. D. Wachs (Eds.), *Wiley-Blackwell handbook of infant development* (2nd ed., pp. 345–364). Oxford, UK: Wiley.

Melzi, G., & Schick, A. R. (2013). Language and literacy in the school years. In J. B. Gleason & N. B. Ratner (Eds.), *Development of language* (8th ed., pp. 329–365). Upper Saddle River, NJ: Pearson.

Memo, L., Gnoato, E., Caminiti, S., Pichini, S., & Tarani, L. (2013). Fetal alcohol spectrum disorders and fetal alcohol syndrome: The state of the art and new diagnostic tools. *Early Human Development, 89S1,* S40–S43.

Menesini, E., Calussi, P., & Nocentini, A. (2012). Cyberbullying and traditional bullying: Unique, additive, and synergistic effects on psychological health symptoms. In Q. Li, D. Cross, & P. K. Smith (Eds.), *Cyberbullying in the global playground* (pp. 245–265). Malden, MA: Wiley-Blackwell.

Menesini, E., Nicocenti, A., & Calussi, P. (2011). The measurement of cyberbullying: Dimensional structure and relative item severity and discrimination. *Cyberspsychology and Behavior, 14,* 267–274.

Menesini, E., & Spiel, C. (2012). Introduction: Cyberbullying: Development, consequences, risk and protective factors. *European Journal of Developmental Psychology, 9,* 163–167.

Mennella, J. A., & Beauchamp, G. K. (1998). Early flavor experiences: Research update. *Nutrition Reviews, 56,* 205–211.

Mennella, J. A., Jagnow, C. P., & Beauchamp, G. K. (2001). Prenatal and postnatal flavor learning by human infants. *Pediatrics, 107,* e88.

Ment, L. R., Vohr, B., Allan, W., Katz, K. H., Schneider, K. C., Westerveld, M., Cuncan, C. C., & Makuch, R. W. (2003). Change in cognitive function over time in very low-birth-weight infants. *Journal of the American Medical Association, 289,* 705–711.

Menyuk, P., Liebergott, J. W., & Schultz, M. C. (1995). *Early language development in full-term and premature infants.* Hillsdale, NJ: Erlbaum.

Meredith, N. V. (1978). *Human body growth in the first ten years of life.* Columbia, SC: State Printing.

Messinger, D. S., & Fogel, A. (2007). The interactive development of social smiling. In R. Kail (Ed.), *Advances in child development and behavior* (Vol. 35, pp. 327–366). Oxford, UK: Elsevier.

Meyer, R. (2009). Infant feeding in the first year. 1: Feeding practices in the first six months of life. *Journal of Family Health Care, 19,* 13–16.

Meyer, S., Raikes, H. A., Virmani, E. A., Waters, S., & Thompson, R. A. (2014). Parent emotion representations and the socialization of emotion regulation in the family. *International Journal of Behavioral Development, 38,* 164–173.

Meyers, A. B., & Berk, L. E. (2014). Make-believe play and self-regulation. In L. Brooker, M. Blaise, & S. Edwards (Eds.), *Sage handbook of play and learning in early childhood* (pp. 43–55). London: Sage.

Mezulis, A. H., Hyde, J. S., & Clark, R. (2004). Father involvement moderates the effect of maternal depression during a child's infancy on child behavior problems in kindergarten. *Journal of Family Psychology, 18,* 575–588.

Michalik, N. M., Eisenberg, N., Spinrad, T. L., Ladd, B., Thompson, M., & Valiente, C. (2007). Longitudinal relations among parental emotional expressivity and sympathy and prosocial behavior in adolescence. *Social Development, 16,* 286–309.

Michiels, D., Grietens, H., Onghena, P., & Kuppens, S. (2010). Perceptions of maternal and paternal attachment security in middle childhood: Links with positive parental affection and psychological adjustment. *Early Child Development and Care, 180,* 211–225.

Migliano, A. B., Vinicius, L., & Lahr, M. M. (2007). Life history trade-offs explain the evolution of human pygmies. *Proceedings of the National Academy of Sciences, 104,* 20216–20219.

Mikami, A. Y., Griggs, M. S., Lerner, M. D., Emeh, C. C., Reuland, M. M., Jack, A., & Anthony, M. R. (2013). A randomized trial of a classroom intervention to increase peers' social inclusion of children with attention-deficit/hyperactivity disorder. *Journal of Consulting and Clinical Psychology, 81,* 100–112.

Mikami, A. Y., Lerner, M. D., & Lun, J. (2010). Social context influences on children's rejection by their peers. *Child Development Perspectives, 4,* 123–130.

Milan, S., Snow, S., & Belay, S. (2007). The context of preschool children's sleep: Racial/ethnic differences in sleep locations, routines, and concerns. *Journal of Family Psychology, 21,* 20–28.

Milevsky, A., Schlechter, M., Netter, S., & Keehn, D. (2007). Maternal and paternal parenting styles in adolescents: Associations with self-esteem, depression, and life satisfaction. *Journal of Child and Family Studies, 16,* 39–47.

Miller, C. F., Lurye, L. E., Zosuls, K. M., & Ruble, D. N. (2009). Accessibility of gender stereotype domains: Developmental and gender differences in children. *Sex Roles, 60,* 870–881.

Miller, G. E., Chen, E., Fok, A. K., Walker, H., Lim, A., Hiholls, E. F., et al. (2009). Low early-life social class leaves a biological residue manifested by decreased glucocorticoid and increased proinflammatory signaling. *Proceedings of the National Academy of Sciences, 106,* 14716–14721.

Miller, L. E., Grabell, A., Thomas, A., Bermann, E., & Graham-Bermann, S. A. (2012). The associations between community violence, television violence, parent–child aggression, and aggression in sibling relationships of a sample of preschoolers. *Psychology of Violence, 2,* 165–178.

Miller, P. H. (2009). *Theories of developmental psychology* (5th ed.) New York: Worth.

Miller, P. H. (2011). Piaget's theory: Past, present, and future. In U. Goswami (Ed.), *Wiley-Blackwell handbook of childhood cognitive development* (2nd ed., pp. 649–672). Chicester, UK: Wiley-Blackwell.

Miller, P. J., Fung, H., & Koven, M. (2007). Narrative reverberations: How participation in narrative practices co-creates persons and cultures. In S. Kitayama & D. Cohen (Eds.), *Handbook of cultural psychology* (pp. 595–614). New York: Guilford.

Miller, P. J., Fung, H., Lin, S., Chen, E. C., & Boldt, B. R. (2012). How socialization happens on the ground: Narrative practices as alternate socializing pathways in Taiwanese and European-American families. *Monographs of the Society for Research in Child Development, 77*(1, Serial No. 302).

Miller, P. J., Fung, H., & Mintz, J. (1996). Self-construction through narrative practices: A Chinese and American comparison of early socialization. *Ethos, 24,* 1–44.

Miller, P. J., Hengst, J. A., & Wang, S. (2003). Ethnographic methods: Applications from developmental cultural psychology. In P. M. Camic & J. E. Rhodes (Eds.), *Qualitative research in psychology* (pp. 219–242). Washington, DC: American Psychological Association.

Miller, P. J., Wang, S., Sandel, T., & Cho, G. E. (2002). Self-esteem as folk theory: A comparison of European American and Taiwanese mothers' beliefs. *Parenting: Science and Practice, 2,* 209–239.

Miller, P. J., Wiley, A. R., Fung, H., & Liang, C.-H. (1997). Personal storytelling as a medium of socialization in Chinese and American families. *Child Development, 68,* 557–568.

Miller, S. A., Hardin, C. A., & Montgomery, D. E. (2003). Young children's understanding of the conditions for knowledge acquisition. *Journal of Cognition and Development, 4,* 325–356.

Miller, W. B. (2009). The reasons people give for having children. In W. B. Miller (Ed.), *Why we have children: Building a unified theory of the reproductive mind* (pp. 1–19). Aptos, CA: Transnational Family Research Institute.

Milligan, K., Astington, J. W., & Dack, L. A. (2007). Language and theory of mind: Meta-analysis of the relation between language ability and false-belief understanding. *Child Development, 78,* 622–646.

Mills, C. M. (2013). Knowing when to doubt: Developing a critical stance when learning from others. *Developmental Psychology, 49,* 404–418.

Mills, D., & Conboy, B. T. (2005). Do changes in brain organization reflect shifts in symbolic functioning? In L. Namy (Ed.), *Symbol use and symbolic representation* (pp. 123–153). Mahwah, NJ: Erlbaum.

Mills, D., Plunkett, K., Prat, C., & Schafer, G. (2005). Watching the infant brain learn words: Effects of language and experience. *Cognitive Development, 20,* 19–31.

Mills, M., Rindfuss, R. R., McDonald, P., & te Velde, E. (2011). Why do people postpone parenthood? Reasons and social policy incentives. *Human Reproduction Update, 17,* 848–860.

Mills, R. S. L. (2005). Taking stock of the developmental literature on shame. *Developmental Review, 25,* 26–63.

Mills, R. S. L., & Grusec, J. E. (1989). Cognitive, affective, and behavioral consequences of praising altruism. *Merrill-Palmer Quarterly, 35,* 299–326.

Mills, T. L., Gomez-Smith, Z., & De Leon, J. M. (2005). Skipped generation families: Sources of psychological distress among grandmothers of grandchildren who live in homes where neither parent is present. *Marriage and Family Review, 37,* 191–212.

Mindell, J. A., Sadeh, A., Kwon, R., & Goh, D. Y T. (2013). Cross-cultural differences in the sleep of preschool children. *Sleep Medicine, 14,* 1283–1289.

Minkler, M., & Fuller-Thomson, E. (2005). African American grandparents raising grandchildren: A national study using the Census 2000 American Community Survey. *Journal of Gerontology, 60B,* S82–S92.

Miranda, A., Presentacion, M. J., Siegenthaler, R., & Jara, P. (2013). Effects of a psychosocial intervention on the executive functioning in children with ADHD. *Journal of Learning Disabilities, 46,* 363–376.

Misailidi, P. (2006). Young children's display rule knowledge: Understanding the distinction between apparent and real emotions and the motives underlying the use of display rules. *Social Behavior and Personality, 34,* 1285–1296.

Mischel, W., & Liebert, R. M. (1966). Effects of discrepancies between observed and imposed reward criteria on their acquisition and transmission. *Journal of Personality and Social Psychology, 3,* 45–53.

Mistry, R. S., Biesanz, J. C., Chien, N., Howes, C., & Benner, A. D. (2008). Socioeconomic status, parental investments, and the cognitive and behavioral outcomes of low-income children from immigrant and native households. *Early Childhood Research Quarterly, 23,* 193–212.

Miura, I. T., & Okamoto, Y. (2003). Language supports for mathematics understanding and performance. In A. J. Baroody & A. Dowker (Eds.), *The development of arithmetic concepts and skills* (pp. 229–242). Mahwah, NJ: Erlbaum.

Mize, J., & Pettit, G. S. (2010). The mother–child playgroup as socialisation context: A short-term longitudinal study of mother–child–peer relationship dynamics. *Early Child Development and Care, 180,* 1271–1284.

Mok, M. M. C., Kennedy, K. J., & Moore, P. J. (2011). Academic attribution of secondary students: Gender, year level and achievement level. *Educational Psychology, 31,* 87–104.

Moll, H., & Meltzoff, A. N. (2011). How does it look? Level 2 perspective-taking at 36 months of age. *Child Development, 82,* 661–673.

Moll, H., & Tomasello, M. (2006). Level I perspective-taking at 24 months of age. *British Journal of Developmental Psychology, 24,* 603–613.

Moll, K., Ramus, F., Bartling, J., Bruder, J., Kunze, S., Neuhoff, N., et al. (2014). Cognitive mechanisms underlying reading and spelling development in five European orthographies. *Learning and Instruction, 29,* 65–77.

Moller, K., Hwang, C. P., & Wickberg, B. (2008). Couple relationship and transition to parenthood: Does workload at home matter? *Journal of Reproductive and Infant Psychology, 26,* 57–68.

Molloy, C. S., Wilson-Ching, M., Anderson, V. A., Roberts, G., Anderson, P. J., Doyle, L. W., et al. (2013). Visual processing in adolescents born extremely low birth weight and/or extremely preterm. *Pediatrics, 132,* e704–e712.

Molnar, D. S., Levitt, A., Eiden, R. D., & Schuetze, P. (2014). Prenatal cocaine exposure and trajectories of externalizing behavior problems in early childhood: Examining the role of maternal negative affect. *Development and Psychopathology, 26,* 515–528.

Mondloch, C. J., Lewis, T., Budreau, D. R., Maurer, D., Dannemillier, J. L., Stephens, B. R., & Kleiner-Gathercoal, K. A. (1999). Face perception during early infancy. *Psychological Science, 10,* 419–422.

Monk, C., Georgieff, M. K., & Osterholm, E. A. (2013). Research review: Maternal prenatal distress and poor nutrition—mutually influencing risk factors affecting infant neurocognitive development. *Journal of Child Psychology and Psychiatry, 54,* 115–130.

Monk, C. S., Weng, S.-J., Wiggins, J. L., Kurapati, N., Louro, H. M. C., Carrasco, M., et al. (2010). Neural circuitry of emotional face processing in autism spectrum disorders. *Journal of Psychiatry and Neuroscience, 35,* 105–114.

Montague, D. P. F., & Walker-Andrews, A. S. (2001). Peekaboo: A new look at infants' perception of emotion expressions. *Developmental Psychology, 37,* 826–838.

Montemayor, R., & Eisen, M. (1977). The development of self-conceptions from childhood to adolescence. *Developmental Psychology, 13,* 314–319.

Moon, C., Cooper, R. P., & Fifer, W. P. (1993). Two-day-old infants prefer their native language. *Infant Behavior and Development, 16,* 495–500.

Moon, R. Y., Horne, R. S. C., & Hauck, F. R.(2007). Sudden infant death syndrome. *The Lancet, 370,* 1578–1587.

Moore, C., Mealiea, J., Garon, N., & Povinelli, D. (2007). The development of body self-awareness. *Infancy, 11,* 157–174.

Moore, E. G. J. (1986). Family socialization and the IQ test performance of traditionally and transracially adopted black children. *Developmental Psychology, 22,* 317–326.

Moore, G. A., Cohn, J. E., & Campbell, S. B. (2001). Infant affective responses to mother's still face at 6 months differentially predict externalizing and internalizing behaviors at 18 months. *Developmental Psychology, 37,* 706–714.

Moore, K. L., & Persaud, T. V. N. (2008). *Before we are born* (7th ed.). Philadelphia: Saunders.

Moore, K. L., Persaud, T. V. N., & Torchia, M. G. (2013). *Before we are born: Essentials of embryology and birth defects* (8th ed.). Philadelphia, PA: Saunders.

Moore, M., & Mindell, J. A. (2012). Sleep-related problems in childhood. In C. M. Morin & C. A. Espie (Eds.), *Oxford handbook of sleep and sleep disorders* (pp. 729–745). New York: Oxford University Press.

Moore, M. K., & Meltzoff, A. N. (1999). New findings on object permanence: A developmental difference between two types of occlusion. *British Journal of Developmental Psychology, 17,* 563–584.

Moore, M. K., & Meltzoff, A. N. (2004). Object permanence after a 24-hr delay and leaving the locale of disappearance: The role of memory, space, and identity. *Developmental Psychology, 40,* 606–620.

Moore, M. K., & Meltzoff, A. N. (2008). Factors affecting infants' manual search for occluded objects and the genesis of object permanence. *Infant Behavior and Development, 31,* 168–180.

Moore, M. R., & Stambolis-Ruhstorfer, M. (2013). LGBT sexuality and families at the start of the twenty-first century. *Annual Review of Sociology, 39,* 491–507.

Moran, G., Forbes, L., Evans, E., Tarabulsy, G. M., & Madigan, S. (2008). Both maternal sensitivity and atypical maternal behavior independently predict attachment security and disorganization in adolescent mother–infant relationships. *Infant Behavior and Development, 31,* 321–325.

Moran, G. F., & Vinovskis, M. A. (1986). The great care of godly parents: Early childhood in Puritan New England. *Monographs of the Society for Research in Child Development, 50*(4–5, Serial No. 211).

Moran, S., & Gardner, H. (2006). Extraordinary achievements: A developmental and systems analysis. In D. Kuhn & R. S. Siegler (Eds.), *Handbook of child psychology: Vol. 2. Cognition, perception, and language* (6th ed., pp. 905–949). Hoboken, NJ: Wiley.

Morawska, A., & Sanders, M. (2011). Parental use of time out revisited: A useful or harmful parenting strategy? *Journal of Child and Family Studies, 20,* 1–8.

Morelli, G. A., Rogoff, B., & Angelillo, C. (2003). Cultural variation in young children's access to work or involvement in specialized child-focused activities. *International Journal of Behavioral Development, 27,* 264–274.

Morelli, G. A., Rogoff, B., Oppenheim, D., & Goldsmith, D. (1992). Cultural variation in infants' sleeping arrangements: Questions of independence. *Developmental Psychology, 28,* 604–613.

Moreno, A. J., Klute, M. M., & Robinson, J. L. (2008). Relational and individual resources as predictors of empathy in early childhood. *Social Development, 17,* 613–637.

Morgan, I. G., Ohno-Matsui, K., & Saw, S.-M. (2012). Myopia. *Lancet, 379,* 1739–1748.

Morgan, P. L., Farkas, G., Hillemeier, M. M., & Maczuga, S. (2009). Risk factors for learning-related behavior problems at 24 months of age: Population-based estimates. *Journal of Abnormal Child Psychology, 37,* 401–413.

Morra, S., Gobbo, C., Marini, Z., & Sheese, R. (Eds.). (2008). *Cognitive development: Neo-Piagetian perspectives.* New York: Erlbaum.

Morrill, M. I., Hines, D. A., Mahmood, S., & Córdova, J. V. (2010). Pathways between marriage and parenting for wives and husbands: The role of coparenting. *Family Process, 49,* 59–73.

Morris, A. S., Silk, J. S., Morris, M. D. S., & Steinberg, L. (2011). The influence of mother–child emotion regulation strategies on children's expression of anger and sadness. *Developmental Psychology, 47,* 213–225.

Morris, A. S., Silk, J. S., Steinberg, L., Myers, S. S., & Robinson, L. R. (2007). The role of the family context in the development of emotion regulation. *Social Development, 16,* 362–388.

Morris, G., & Baker-Ward, L. (2007). Fragile but real: Children's capacity to use newly acquired words to convey preverbal memories. *Child Development, 78,* 448–458.

Morrissey, T., Dunifon, R. E., & Kalil, A. (2011). Maternal employment, work schedules, and children's body mass index. *Child Development, 82,* 66–81.

Morrissey, T. W. (2013). Multiple child care arrangements and common communicable illnesses in children aged 3 to 54 months. *Maternal and Child Health Journal, 17,* 1175–1184.

Morrongiello, B. A., Fenwick, K. D., & Chance, G. (1998). Crossmodal learning in newborn infants: Inferences about properties of auditory-visual events. *Infant Behavior and Development, 21,* 543–554.

Morrongiello, B. A., Kane, A., & Zdzieborski, D. (2011). "I think he is in his room playing a video game": Parental supervision of young elementary-school children at home. *Journal of Pediatric Psychology, 36,* 708–717.

Morrongiello, B. A., & Kiriakou, S. (2004). Mothers' home-safety practices for preventing six types of childhood injuries: What do they do, and why? *Journal of Pediatric Psychology, 29,* 285–297.

Morrongiello, B. A., Midgett, C., & Shields, R. (2001). Don't run with scissors: Young children's knowledge of home safety rules. *Journal of Pediatric Psychology, 26,* 105–115.

Morrongiello, B. A., Ondejko, L., & Littlejohn, A. (2004). Understanding toddlers' in-home injuries: I. Context, correlates, and determinants. *Journal of Pediatric Psychology, 29,* 415–431.

Morrongiello, B. A., & Rennie, H. (1998). Why do boys engage in more risk taking than girls? The role of attributions, beliefs, and risk appraisals. *Journal of Pediatric Psychology, 23,* 33–43.

Morrongiello, B. A., Widdifield, R., Munroe, K., & Zdzieborski, D. (2014). Parents teaching young children home safety rules: Implications for childhood injury risk. *Journal of Applied Developmental Psychology, 35,* 254–261.

Morse, S. B., Zheng, H., Tang, Y., & Roth, J., (2009). Early school-age outcomes of late preterm infants. *Pediatrics, 123,* e622–e629.

Mosby, L., Rawls, A. W., Meehan, A. J., Mays, E., & Pettinari, C. J. (1999). Troubles in interracial talk about discipline: An examination of African American child rearing narratives. *Journal of Comparative Family Studies, 30,* 489–521.

Mosely-Howard, G. S., & Evans, C. B. (2000). Relationships and contemporary experiences of the African-American family: An ethnographic case study. *Journal of Black Studies, 30,* 428–451.

Moses, L. J., Baldwin, D. A., Rosicky, J. G., & Tidball, G. (2001). Evidence for referential understanding in the emotions domain at twelve and eighteen months. *Child Development, 72,* 718–735.

Moss, E., Cyr, C., Bureau, J.-F., Tarabulsy, G. M., & Dubois-Comtois, K. (2005). Stability of attachment during the preschool period. *Developmental Psychology, 41,* 773–783.

Moss, E., Cyr, C., & Dubois-Comtois, K. (2004). Attachment at early school age and developmental risk: Examining family contexts and behavior problems of controlling-caregiving, controlling-punitive, and behaviorally disorganized children. *Developmental Psychology, 40,* 519–532.

Moss, E., Smolla, N., Guerra, I., Mazzarello, T., Chayer, D., & Berthiaume, C. (2006). Attachment and self-reported internalizing and externalizing behavior problems in a school period. *Canadian Journal of Behavioural Science, 38,* 142–157.

Mossey, P. A., Little, J., Munger, R. G., Dixon, M. J., & Shaw, W. C. (2009). Cleft lip and palate. *Lancet, 374,* 1773–1785.

Mosteller, F. (1995). The Tennessee Study of Class Size in the Early School Grades. *Future of Children, 5*(2), 113–127.

Mota, J., Silva, P., Santos, M. P., Ribeiro, J. C., Oliveira, J., & Duarte, J. A. (2005). Physical activity and school recess time: Differences between the sexes and the relationship between children's playground physical activity and habitual physical activity. *Journal of Sports Sciences, 23,* 269–275.

Mottus, R., Indus, K., & Allik, J. (2008). Accuracy of only children stereotype. *Journal of Research in Personality, 42,* 1047–1052.

Mottweiler, C. M., & Taylor, M. (2014). Elaborated role play and creativity in preschool age children. *Psychology of Aesthetics, Creativity, and the Arts, 8,* 277–286.

Mounts, N. S., Valentiner, D. P., Anderson, K. L., & Boswell, M. K. (2006). Shyness, sociability, and parental support for the college transition: Relation to adolescents' adjustment. *Journal of Youth and Adolescence, 35,* 71–80.

Mrug, S., Hoza, B., & Gerdes, A. C. (2001). Children with attention-deficit/hyperactivity disorder: Peer relationships and peer-oriented interventions. In D. W. Nangle & C. A. Erdley (Eds.), *The role of friendship in psychological adjustment* (pp. 51–77). San Francisco: Jossey-Bass.

Mu, Q., & Fehring, R. J. (2014). Efficacy of achieving pregnancy with fertility-focused intercourse. *American Journal of Maternal Child Nursing, 39,* 35–40.

Muenssinger, J., Matuz, T., Schleger, F., Kiefer-Schmidt, I., Goelz, R. Wacker-Gussmann, A., et al. (2013). Auditory habituation in the fetus and neonate: An fMEG study. *Developmental Science, 16,* 287–295.

Müller, O., & Krawinkel, M. (2005). Malnutrition and health in developing countries. *Canadian Medical Association Journal, 173,* 279–286.

Mullett-Hume, E., Anshel, D., Guevara, V., & Cloitre, M. (2008). Cumulative trauma and posttraumatic stress disorder among children exposed to the 9/11 World Trade Center attack. *American Journal of Orthopsychiatry, 78,* 103–108.

Mulvaney, M. K., McCartney, K., Bub, K. L., & Marshall, N. L. (2006). Determinants of dyadic scaffolding and cognitive outcomes in first graders. *Parenting: Science and Practice, 6,* 297–310.

Mulvaney, M. K., & Mebert, C. J. (2007). Parental corporal punishment predicts behavior problems in early childhood. *Journal of Family Psychology, 21,* 389–397.

Mumme, D. L., Bushnell, E. W., DiCorcia, J. A., & Lariviere, L. A. (2007). Infants' use of gaze cues to interpret others' actions and emotional reactions. In R. Flom, K. Lee, & D. Muir (Eds.), *Gaze-following: Its development and significance* (pp. 143–170). Mahwah, NJ: Erlbaum.

Munakata, Y. (2001). Task-dependency in infant behavior: Toward an understanding of the processes underlying cognitive development. In F. Lacerda, C. von Hofsten, & M. Heimann (Eds.), *Emerging cognitive abilities in early infancy* (pp. 29–52). Mahwah, NJ: Erlbaum.

Munakata, Y. (2006). Information processing approaches to development. In D. Kuhn & R. S. Siegler (Eds.), *Handbook of child psychology: Vol. 2. Cognition, perception, and language* (6th ed., pp. 426–463). Hoboken, NJ: Wiley.

Muños-Hoyos, A., Molina-Carballo, A., Augustin-Morales, M., Contreras-Chova, F., Naranjo-Gómez, A., Justicia-Martínez, F., et al. (2011). Psychosocial dwarfism: Psychopathological aspects and putative neuroendocrine markers. *Psychiatry Research, 188,* 96–101.

Munroe, R. L., & Romney, A. K. (2006). Gender and age differences in same-sex aggregation and social behavior. *Journal of Cross-Cultural Psychology, 37,* 3–19.

Muret-Wagstaff, S., & Moore, S. G. (1989). The Hmong in America: Infant behavior and rearing practices. In J. K. Nugent, B. M. Lester, & T. B. Brazelton (Eds.), *Biology, culture, and development* (Vol. 1, pp. 319–339). Norwood, NJ: Ablex.

Muris, P., & Field, A. P. (2011). The "normal" development of fear. In W. K. Silverman, & A. P. Field (Eds.), *Anxiety disorders in children and adolescents* (2nd ed., pp. 76–89). Cambridge, UK: Cambridge University Press.

Muris, P., & Meesters, C. (2014). Small or big in the eyes of the other: On the developmental psychopathology of self-conscious emotions as shame, guilt, and pride. *Clinical Child and Family Psychology Review, 17,* 19–40.

Muris, P., Merckelbach, H., Ollendick, T. H., King, N. J., & Bogie, N. (2001). Children's nighttime fears: Parent–child ratings of frequency, content, origins, coping behaviors and severity. *Behaviour Research and Therapy, 39,* 13–28.

Murphy, J. B. (2013). Access to in vitro fertilization deserves increased regulation in the United States. *Journal of Sex and Marital Therapy, 39,* 85–92.

Murphy, R. F., Penuel, W. R., Means, B., Korbak, C., Whaley, A., & Allen, J. E. (2002). *A review of recent evidence on the effectiveness of discrete educational software.* Washington, DC: U.S. Department of Education.

Murphy, T. H., & Corbett, D. (2009). Plasticity during recovery: From synapse to behaviour. *Nature Reviews Neuroscience, 10,* 861–872.

Murphy, T. P., & Laible, D. J. (2013). The influence of attachment security on preschool children's empathic concern. *International Journal of Behavioral Development, 37,* 436–440.

Murray, A. D. (1985). Aversiveness is in the mind of the beholder. In B. M. Lester & C. F. Z. Boukydis (Eds.), *Infant crying* (pp. 217–239). New York: Plenum.

Murray, L. K., Nguyen, A., & Cohen, J. A. (2014). Child sexual abuse. *Pediatric Clinics of North America, 23,* 321–337.

Mussen, P. H., & Eisenberg-Berg, N. (1977). *Roots of caring, sharing, and helping.* San Francisco: Freeman.

Mutchler, J. E., Baker, L. A., & Lee, S. (2007). Grandparents responsible for grandchildren in Native-American families. *Social Science Quarterly, 88,* 990–1009.

Myant, K. A., & Williams, J. M. (2005). Children's concepts of health and illness: Understanding of contagious illnesses, noncontagious illnesses and injuries. *Journal of Health Psychology, 10,* 805–819.

Myers, L. J., & Liben, L. S. (2008). The role of intentionality and iconicity in children's developing comprehension and production of cartographic symbols. *Child Development, 79,* 668–684.

Myowa-Yamakoshi, M., Tomonaga, M., Tanaka, M., & Matsuzawa, T. (2004). Imitation in neonatal chimpanzees *(Pan troglodytes). Developmental Science, 7,* 437–442.

N

Nadel, J., Prepin, K., & Okanda, M. (2005). Experiencing contingency and agency: First step toward self-understanding in making a mind? *Interaction Studies, 6,* 447–462.

Nader, P. R., O'Brien, M., Houts, R., Bradley, R., Belsky, J., Crosnoe, R., et al. (2006). Identifying risk for obesity in early childhood. *Pediatrics, 118,* e594–e601.

Nærde, A., Ogden, T., Janson, H., & Zachrisson, H. D. (2014). Normative development of physical aggression from 8 to 26 months. *Developmental Psychology, 6,* 1710–1720.

Nagy, E., Compagne, H., Orvos, H., Pal, A., Molnar, P., & Janszky, I. (2005). Index finger movement imitation by human neonates: Motivation, learning, and lefthand preference. *Pediatric Research, 58,* 749–753.

Naigles, L. R., & Swenson, L. D. (2007). Syntactic supports for word learning. In E. Hoff & M. Shatz (Eds.), *Blackwell handbook of language development* (pp. 212–231). Malden, MA: Blackwell.

Naito, M., & Seki, Y. (2009). The relationship between second-order false belief and display rules reasoning: Integration of cognitive and affective social understanding. *Developmental Science, 12,* 150–164.

Nánez, J., Sr., & Yonas, A. (1994). Effects of luminance and texture motion on infant defensive reactions to optical collision. *Infant Behavior and Development, 17,* 165–174.

Narr, K. L., Woods, R. P., Lin, J., Kim, J., Phillips, O. R., Del'Homme, M., et al. (2009). Widespread cortical thinning is a robust anatomical marker for attention-deficit/hyperactivity disorder. *Journal of the American Academy of Child and Adolescent Psychiatry, 48,* 1014–1022.

National Association for Sport and Physical Education. (2009). *Active start: A statement of physical activity guidelines for children from birth to age 5* (2nd ed.). Reston, VA: Author.

National Association for Sport and Physical Education. (2012). *Shape of the nation report: Status of physical education in the USA.* Retrieved from www.shapeamerica .org/advocacy/son/2012/upload/2012-Shape-of-Nation-full-report-web.pdf

National Center for Biotechnology Information. (2014). *Online Mendelian inheritance in man.* Retrieved from www.omim.org

National Center for Injury Prevention and Control. (2013). *WISQARS fatal injury reports, national and regional, 1999–2012.* Retrieved from webappa.cdc.gov/sasweb/ncipc/mortrate10_us.html

National Coalition for the Homeless. (2009). How many people experience homelessness? Retrieved from www .nationalhomeless.org/factsheets/How_Many.html

National Council of Youth Sports. (2008). Report on trends and participation in organized youth sports. Stuart, FL: Author.

National Early Literacy Panel. (2008). *Developing early literacy: A scientific synthesis of early literacy development and implications for intervention.* Jessup, MD: National Institute for Literacy.

National Institutes of Health. (2011). *Dental caries (tooth decay) in children (age 2 to 11).* Retrieved from www.nidcr .nih.gov/DataStatistics/FindDataByTopic/DentalCaries/DentalCariesChildren2to11.htm

National Institutes of Health. (2014). *Genes and disease.* Retrieved from www.ncbi.nlm.nih.gov/books/NBK22183

National Survey of Children's Health. (2012). *Data Research Center for Child & Adolescent Health.* Retrieved from www.childhealthdata.org/learn/NSCH

Nauta, J., van Mechelen, W., Otten, R. H. J., & Verhagen, E. A. L. M. (2014). A systematic review on the effectiveness of school and community-based injury prevention programmes on risk behaviour and injury risk in 8–12 year old children. *Journal of Science and Medicine in Sport, 17,* 165–172.

Needham, A. (2001). Object recognition in 4.5-month-old infants. *Journal of Experimental Child Psychology, 78,* 3–24.

Needleman, H. L., MacFarland, C., Ness, R. B., Reinberg, S., & Tobin, M. J. (2002). Bone lead levels in adjudicated delinquents: A case control study. *Neurotoxicology and Teratology, 24,* 711–717.

Neff, K. D., & Helwig, C. C. (2002). A constructivist approach to understanding the development of reasoning about rights and authority within cultural contexts. *Cognitive Development, 17,* 1429–1450.

Neitzel, C., & Stright, A. D. (2003). Mothers' scaffolding of children's problem solving: Establishing a foundation of academic self-regulatory competence. *Journal of Family Psychology, 17,* 147–159.

Nelson, C. A. (2002). Neural development and lifelong plasticity. In R. M. Lerner, F. Jacobs, & D. Wertlieb (Eds.), *Handbook of applied developmental science* (Vol. 1, pp. 31–60). Thousand Oaks, CA: Sage.

Nelson, C. A. (2007a). A developmental cognitive neuroscience approach to the study of atypical development: A model system involving infants of diabetic mothers. In D. Coch, G. Dawson, & K. W. Fischer (Eds.), *Human behavior, learning, and the developing brain: Atypical development* (2nd ed., pp. 37–59). New York: Guilford.

Nelson, C. A. (2007b). A neurobiological perspective on early human deprivation. *Child Development Perspectives, 1,* 13–18.

Nelson, C. A., & Bosquet, M. (2000). Neurobiology of fetal and infant development: Implications for infant mental health. In C. H. Zeanah, Jr. (Ed.), *Handbook of infant mental health* (2nd ed., pp. 37–59). New York: Guilford.

Nelson, C. A., Fox, N. A., & Zeanah, C. H. (2014). *Romania's abandoned children: Deprivation, brain development, and the struggle for recovery.* Cambridge, MA: Harvard University Press.

Nelson, C. A., Thomas, K. M., & de Haan, M. (2006). Neural bases of cognitive development. In D. Kuhn & R. Siegler (Eds.), *Handbook of child psychology: Vol. 2. Cognition, perception, and language* (6th ed., pp. 3–57). Hoboken, NJ: Wiley.

Nelson, C. A., Wewerka, S., Borscheid, A. J., deRegnier, R., & Georgieff, M. K. (2003). Electrophysiologic evidence of impaired cross-modal recognition memory in 8-month-old infants of diabetic mothers. *Journal of Pediatrics, 142,* 575–582.

Nelson, C. A., Wewerka, S., Thomas, K. M., Tribby-Walbridge, S., deRegnier, R., & Georgieff, M. K. (2000). Neurocognitive sequelae of infants of diabetic mothers. *Behavioral Neuroscience, 114,* 950–956.

Nelson, C. A., III. (2011). Neural development and lifelong plasticity. In D. P. Keating (Ed.), *Nature and nurture in early child development* (pp. 45–69). New York: Cambridge University Press.

Nelson, D. A., & Coyne, S. M. (2009). Children's intent attributions and feelings of distress: Associations with maternal and paternal parenting practices. *Journal of Abnormal Child Psychology, 37,* 223–237.

Nelson, D. A., Nelson, L. J., Hart, C. H., Yang, C., & Jin, S. (2006). Parenting and peer-group behavior in cultural context. In X. Chen, D. French, & B. Schneider (Eds.), *Peer relations in cultural context* (pp. 213–246). New York: Cambridge University Press.

Nelson, D. A., Robinson, C. C., & Hart, C. H. (2005). Relational and physical aggression of preschool-age children: Peer status linkages across informants. *Early Education and Development, 16,* 115–139.

Nelson, D. A., Yang, C., Coyne, S. M., Olsen, J. A., & Hart, C. H. (2013). Parental psychological control dimensions: Connections with Russian preschoolers' physical and relational aggression. *Journal of Applied Developmental Psychology, 34,* 1–8.

Nelson, E. L., Campbell, J. M., & Michel, G. F. (2013). Unimanual to bimanual: Tracking the development of handedness from 6 to 24 months. *Infant Behavior and Development, 36,* 181–188.

Nelson, K. (1973). Structure and strategy in learning to talk. *Monographs of the Society for Research in Child Development, 38*(1–2, Serial No. 149).

Nelson, K. (2003). Narrative and the emergence of a consciousness of self. In G. D. Fireman & T. E. McVay, Jr. (Eds.), *Narrative and consciousness: Literature, psychology, and the brain* (pp. 17–36). London: Oxford University Press.

Nemet, D., Barkan, S., Epstein, Y., Friedland, O., Kowen, G., & Eliakim, A. (2005). Short- and long-term beneficial effects of a combined dietary–behavioural–physical activity intervention for the treatment of childhood obesity. *Pediatrics, 115,* e443–e449.

Nepomnyaschy, L., & Waldfogel, J. (2007). Paternity leave and fathers' involvement with their young children. *Community, Work and Family, 10,* 427–453.

Nesdale, D., Durkin, K., Maas, A., & Griffiths, J. (2004). Group status, outgroup ethnicity, and children's ethnic attitudes. *Applied Developmental Psychology, 25,* 237–251.

Nesdale, D., Durkin, K., Maas, A., & Griffiths, J. (2005). Threat, group identification, and children's ethnic prejudice. *Social Development, 14,* 189–205.

Neuman, S. B. (2003). From rhetoric to reality: The case for high-quality compensatory prekindergarten programs. *Phi Delta Kappan, 85*(4), 286–291.

Neuman, S. B. (2006). The knowledge gap: Implications for early education. In D. K. Dickinson & S. B. Neuman (Eds.), *Handbook of early literacy research* (Vol. 2, pp. 29–40). New York: Guilford.

Neuman, S. B., & Celano, D. (2001). Access to print in middle- and low-income communities: An ecological study of four neighborhoods. *Reading Research Quarterly, 36,* 8–26.

Neville, H. J., & Bavelier, D. (2002). Human brain plasticity: Evidence from sensory deprivation and altered language experience. In M. A. Hofman, G. J. Boer, A. J. G. D. Holtmaat, E. J. W. van Someren, J. Berhaagen, & D. F. Swaab (Eds.), *Plasticity in the adult brain: From genes to neurotherapy* (pp. 177–188). Amsterdam: Elsevier Science.

Neville, H. J., & Bruer, J. T. (2001). Language processing: How experience affects brain organization. In D. B. Bailey, Jr., J. T. Bruer, F. J. Symons, & J. W. Lichtman (Eds.), *Critical thinking about critical periods* (pp. 151–172). Baltimore: Paul H. Brookes.

Nevin, R. (2006). Understanding international crime trends: The legacy of preschool lead exposure. *Environmental Research, 104,* 315–316.

Newcombe, N. S., Sluzenski, J., & Huttenlocher, J. (2005). Preexisting knowledge versus on-line learning: What do young infants really know about spatial location? *Psychological Science, 16,* 222–227.

Newheiser, A., Dunham, Y., Merrill, A., Hoosain, L., & Olson, K. R. (2014). Preference for high status predicts implicit outgroup bias among children from low-status groups. *Developmental Psychology, 50,* 1081–1090.

Newland, L. A., Coyl, D. D., & Freeman, H. (2008). Predicting preschoolers' attachment security from fathers' involvement, internal working models, and use of social support. *Early Child Development and Care, 178,* 785–801.

Newnham, C. A., Milgrom, J., & Skouteris, H. (2009). Effectiveness of a modified mother—infant transaction program on outcomes for preterm infants from 3 to

24 months of age. *Infant Behavior and Development, 32,* 17–26.

Newson, J., & Newson, E. (1975). Intersubjectivity and the transmission of culture: On the social origins of symbolic functioning. *Bulletin of the British Psychological Society, 28,* 437–446.

Ng, F. F., Pomerantz, E. M., & Deng, C. (2014). Why are Chinese mothers more controlling than American mothers?: "My child is my report card." *Child Development, 85,* 355–369.

Ng, F. F., Pomerantz, E. M., & Lam, S. (2007). European-American and Chinese parents' responses to children's success and failure: Implications for children's responses. *Developmental Psychology, 43,* 1239–1255.

Ni, Y. (1998). Cognitive structure, content knowledge, and classificatory reasoning. *Journal of Genetic Psychology, 159,* 280–296.

NICHD (National Institute for Child Health and Human Development) Early Child Care Research Network. (1997). The effects of infant child care on infant–mother attachment security: Results of the NICHD Study of Early Child Care. *Child Development, 68,* 860–879.

NICHD (National Institute of Child Health and Human Development) Early Child Care Research Network. (1998). Relations between family predictors and child outcomes: Are they weaker for children in child care? *Developmental Psychology, 34,* 1119–1128.

NICHD (National Institute for Child Health and Human Development) Early Child Care Research Network. (1999). Child care and mother–child interaction in the first 3 years of life. *Developmental Psychology, 35,* 1399–1413.

NICHD (National Institute of Child Health and Human Development) Early Child Care Research Network. (2000a). Characteristics and quality of child care for toddlers and preschoolers. *Applied Developmental Science, 4,* 116–135.

NICHD (National Institute of Child Health and Human Development) Early Child Care Research Network. (2000b). The relation of child care to cognitive and language development. *Child Development, 71,* 960–980.

NICHD (National Institute of Child Health and Human Development) Early Child Care Research Network. (2001). Before Head Start: Income and ethnicity, family characteristics, child care experiences, and child development. *Early Education and Development, 12,* 545–575.

NICHD (National Institute of Child Health and Human Development) Early Child Care Research Network. (2002a). Child-care structure → process → outcome: Direct and indirect effects of child-care quality on young children's development. *Psychological Science, 13,* 199–206.

NICHD (National Institute of Child Health and Human Development) Early Child Care Research Network. (2002b). The interaction of child care and family risk in relation to child development at 24 and 36 months. *Applied Developmental Science, 6,* 144–156.

NICHD (National Institute of Child Health and Human Development) Early Child Care Research Network. (2003a). Does amount of time spent in child care predict socioemotional adjustment during the transition to kindergarten? *Child Development, 74,* 976–1005.

NICHD (National Institute of Child Health and Human Development) Early Child Care Research Network. (2003b). Does quality of child care affect child outcomes at age *Developmental Psychology, 39,* 451–469.

NICHD (National Institute of Child Health and Human Development) Early Child Care Research Network. (2004). Type of child care and children's development at 54 months. *Early Childhood Research Quarterly, 19,* 203–230.

NICHD (National Institute of Child Health and Development) Early Child Care Research Network. (2005). *Child care and development: Results from the NICHD Study of Early Child Care and Youth Development.* New York: Guilford.

NICHD (National Institute of Child Health and Human Development) Early Child Care Research Network. (2006). Child-care effect sizes for the NICHD Study of Early Child Care and Youth Development. *American Psychologist, 61,* 99–116.

Nicholls, A. L., & Kennedy, J. M. (1992). Drawing development: From similarity of features to direction. *Child Development, 63,* 227–241.

Nicholls, D. E., & Viner, R. M. (2009). Childhood risk factors for lifetime anorexia nervosa by age 30 in a national birth cohort. *Journal of the American Academy of Child and Adolescent Psychiatry, 48,* 791–799.

Nichols, K. E., Fox, N., & Mundy, P. (2005). Joint attention, self-recognition, and neurocognitive function in toddlers. *Infancy, 7,* 35–51.

Nickman, S. L., Rosenfeld, A. A., Fine, P., MacIntyre, J. C., Pilowsky, D. J., & Howe, R.-A. (2005). Children in adoptive families: Overview and update. *Journal of the American Academy of Child and Adolescent Psychiatry, 44,* 987–995.

Nicolopoulou, A., & Ilgaz, H. (2013). What do we know about pretend play and narrative development? A response to Lillard, Lerner, Hopkins, Dore, Smith, and Palmquist on "The impact of pretend play on children's development: A review of the evidence." *American Journal of Play, 6,* 55–81.

Niehaus, M. D., Moore, S. R., Patrick, P. D., Derr, L. L., Lorntz, B., Lima, A. A., & Gurerrant, R. L. (2002). Early childhood diarrhea is associated with diminished cognitive function 4 to 7 years later in children in a northeast Brazilian shantytown. *American Journal of Tropical Medicine and Hygiene, 66,* 590–593.

Nielsen, G. L., Andersen, E., & Lundbye-Christensen, S. (2010). Maternal blood glucose in diabetic pregnancies and cognitive performance in offspring in young adulthood: A Danish cohort study. *Diabetic Medicine, 27,* 786–790.

Nielsen, L. S., Danielsen, K. V., & Sørensen, T. I. (2011). Short sleep duration as a possible cause of obesity: Critical analysis of the epidemiological evidence. *Obesity Reviews, 12,* 78–92.

Nielsen, M. (2012). Imitation, pretend play, and childhood: Essential elements in the evolution of human culture? *Journal of Comparative Psychology, 126,* 170–181.

Nielsen, M., & Christie, T. (2008). Adult modeling facilitates young children's generation of novel pretend acts. *Infant and Child Development, 17,* 151–162.

Nielsen, N. M., Hansen, A. V., Simonsen, J., & Hviid, A. (2011). Prenatal stress and risk of infectious diseases in offspring. *American Journal of Epidemiology, 173,* 990–997.

Nievar, M. A., & Becker, B. J. (2008). Sensitivity as a privileged predictor of attachment: A second perspective on De Wolff & van IJzendoorn's meta-analysis. *Social Development, 17,* 102–114.

Nikulina, V., & Widom, C. S. (2013). Child maltreatment and executive functioning in middle adulthood: A prospective examination. *Neuropsychology, 27,* 417–427.

Nippold, M. A., Taylor, C. L., & Baker, J. M. (1996). Idiom understanding in Australian youth: A cross-cultural comparison. *Journal of Speech and Hearing Research, 39,* 442–447.

Nisbett, R. E. (2009). *Intelligence and how to get it.* New York: Norton.

Nisbett, R. E., Aronson, J., Blair, C., Dickens, W., Flynn, J., Halpern, D. F., et al. (2012). Intelligence: New findings and theoretical developments. *American Psychologist, 67,* 130–159.

Nishitani, S., Miyamura, T., Tagawa, M., Sumi, M., Takase, R., Doi, H., Moriuchi, H., & Shinohara, K. (2009). The calming effect of a maternal breast milk odor on the human newborn infant. *Neuroscience Research, 63,* 66–71.

Noble, K. G., Fifer, W. P., Rauh, V. A., Nomura, Y., & Andrews, H. F. (2012). Academic achievement varies with gestational age among children born at term. *Pediatrics, 130,* e257–e264.

Noonan, C. W., Kathman, S. J., Sarasua, S. M., & White, M. C. (2003). Influence of environmental zinc on the association between environmental and biological measures of lead in children. *Journal of Exposure Analysis and Environmental Epidemiology, 13,* 318–323.

Noroozian, M., Shadloo, B., Shakiba, A., & Panahi, P. (2012). Educational achievement and other controversial issues in left-handedness: A neuropsychological and psychiatric view. In T. Dutta & M. K. Mandal (Eds.), *Bias in human behavior* (pp. 41–82). Hauppauge, NY: Nova Science.

Northstone, K., Joinson, C., Emmett, P., Ness, A., & Paus, T. (2012). Are dietary patterns in childhood associated with IQ at 8 years of age? A population-based cohort study. *Journal of Epidemiological Community Health, 66,* 624–628.

Norwitz, E. R. (2009). A blood test to predict preterm birth: Don't mess with maternal—fetal stress. *Journal of Clinical Endocrinology and Metabolism, 94,* 1886–1889.

Nosarti, C., Walsh, M., Rushe, T. M., Rifkin, L., Wyatt, J., Murray, R. M., et al. (2011). Neonatal ultrasound results following very preterm birth predict adolescent behavioral and cognitive outcome. *Developmental Neuropsychology, 36,* 118–135.

Noterdaeme, M., Mildenberger, K., Minow, F., & Amorosa, H. (2002). Evaluation of neuromotor deficits in children with autism and children with a specific speech and language disorder. *European Child and Adolescent Psychiatry, 11,* 219–225.

Nowicki, E. A., Brown, J., & Stepien, M. (2014). Children's thoughts on the social exclusion of peers with intellectual or learning disabilities. *Journal of Intellectual Disability Research, 58,* 346–357.

Nucci, L. (2005). Culture, context, and the psychological sources of human rights concepts. In W. Edelstein & G. Nunner-Winkler (Eds.), *Morality in context* (pp. 365–394). Amsterdam: Elsevier.

Nucci, L. (2008). *Nice is not enough: Facilitating moral development.* Upper Saddle River, NJ: Prentice Hall.

Nucci, L. P., & Gingo, M. (2011). The development of moral reasoning. In U. Goswami (Ed.), *The Wiley-Blackwell handbook of childhood cognitive development* (2nd ed., pp. 420–444). Hoboken, NJ: Wiley.

Nye, B., Hedges, L. V., & Konstantopoulos, S. (2001). Are effects of small classes cumulative? Evidence from a Tennessee experiment. *Journal of Educational Research, 94,* 336–345.

O

Oakes, L. M., Coppage, D. J., & Dingel, A. (1997). By land or by sea: The role of perceptual similarity in infants' categorization of animals. *Developmental Psychology, 33,* 396–407.

Obeidallah, D., Brennan, R. T., Brooks-Gunn, J., & Earls, F. (2004). Links between pubertal timing and neighborhood contexts: Implications for girls' violent behavior. *Journal of the American Academy of Child and Adolescent Psychiatry, 43,* 1460–1468.

Oberecker, R., & Friederici, A. D. (2006). Syntactic event-related potential components in 24-month-olds' sentence comprehension. *NeuroReport, 17,* 1017–1021.

Obradović, J., Long, J. D., Cutuli, J. J., Chan, C.-K., Hinz, E., Heistad, D., & Masten, A. S. (2009). Academic achievement of homeless and highly mobile children in an urban school district: Longitudinal evidence on risk, growth, and resilience. *Development and Psychopathology, 21,* 493–518.

O'Brien, M., Weaver, J. M., Nelson, J. A., Calkins, S. D., Leerkes, E. M., & Marcovitch, S. (2011). Longitudinal associations between children's understanding of emotions and theory of mind. *Cognition and Emotion, 25,* 1074–1086.

O'Connor, E., & McCartney, K. (2007). Examining teacher–child relationships and achievement as part of an ecological model of development. *American Educational Research Journal, 44,* 340–369.

O'Connor, T. G., & Croft, C. M. (2001). A twin study of attachment in preschool children. *Child Development, 72,* 1501–1511.

O'Connor, T. G., Marvin, R. S., Rutter, M., Olrich, J. T., Britner, P. A., & the English and Romanian Adoptees Study Team. (2003). Child–parent attachment following early institutional deprivation. *Development and Psychopathology, 15,* 19–38.

O'Connor, T. G., Rutter, M., Beckett, C., Keaveney, L., Dreppner, J. M., & the English and Romanian Adoptees Study Team. (2000). The effects of global severe privation on cognitive competence: Extension and longitudinal follow-up. *Child Development, 71,* 376–390.

O'Dea, J. A. (2003). Why do kids eat healthful food? Perceived benefits of and barriers to healthful eating and physical activity among children and adolescents. *Journal of the American Dietetic Association, 103,* 497–501.

O'Dea, J. A. (2012). Body image and self-esteem. In T. F. Cash (Ed.), *Encyclopedia of body image and human appearance* (pp. 141–147). London: Elsevier.

OECD (Organisation for Economic Cooperation and Development). (2013a). *Health at a glance 2013: OECD indicators.* Retrieved from www.oecd.org/els/health-systems/Health-at-a-Glance-2013.pdf

OECD (Organisation for Economic Cooperation and Development). (2013b). *OECD health statistics 2013–Frequently requested data.* Retrieved from www.oecd.org/social/soc/oecdfamilydatabase.htm

OECD (Organisation for Economic Cooperation and Development). (2014). *OECD family data base.* Retrieved from www.oecd.org/social/soc/oecdfamilydatabase.htm

Office of Head Start. (2014). *Head Start program facts: Fiscal year 2013.* Retrieved from eclkc.ohs.acf.hhs.gov/hslc/data/factsheets/2013-hs-program-factsheet.html

Ogan, A., & Berk, L. E. (2009, April). *Effects of two approaches to make-believe play training on self-regulation in Head Start children.* Paper presented at the biennial meeting of the Society for Research in Child Development, Denver, CO.

Ogden, C. L., Carroll, M. D., Kit, B. K., & Flegal, K. M. (2014). Prevalence of childhood and adult obesity. *Journal of the American Medical Association, 311,* 806–814.

Ohgi, S., Arisawa, K., Takahashi, T., Kusumoto, T., Goto, Y., Akiyama, T., & Saito, H. (2003a). Neonatal behavioral assessment scale as a predictor of later developmental disabilities of low-birth-weight and/or premature infants. *Brain and Development, 25,* 313–321.

Ohgi, S., Takahashi, T., Nugent, J. K., Arisawa, K., & Akiyama, T. (2003b). Neonatal behavioral characteristics and later behavioral problems. *Clinical Pediatrics, 42,* 679–686.

Ojha, S., Robinson, L., Symonds, M. E., & Budge, H. (2013). Suboptimal maternal nutrition affects offspring health in adult life. *Early Human Development, 89,* 909–913.

Okagaki, L., & Sternberg, R. J. (1993). Parental beliefs and children's school performance. *Child Development, 64,* 36–56.

Okami, P., Weisner, T., & Olmstead, R. (2002). Outcome correlates of parent–child bedsharing: An eighteen-year longitudinal study. *Developmental and Behavioral Pediatrics, 23,* 244–253.

Olafson, E. (2011). Child sexual abuse: Demography, impact, and interventions. *Journal of Child and Adolescent Trauma, 4,* 8–21.

Olds, D. L., Eckenrode, J., Henderson, C., Kitzman, H., Cole, R., Luckey, D., et al. (2009). Preventing child abuse and neglect with home visiting by nurses. In K. A. Dodge & D. L. Coleman (Eds.), *Preventing child maltreatment* (pp. 29–54). New York: Guilford.

Olds, D. L., Kitzman, H., Cole, R., Robinson, J., Sidora, K., Luckey, D. W., et al. (2004). Effects of nurse home-visiting on maternal life course and child development: Age 6 follow-up results of a randomized trial. *Pediatrics, 114,* 1550–1559.

Olds, D. L., Kitzman, H., Hanks, C., Cole, R., Anson, E., Sidora-Arcoleo, K., et al. (2007). Effects of nurse home visiting on maternal and child functioning: Age-9 follow-up of a randomized trial. *Pediatrics, 120,* e832–e845.

Olds, D. L., Robinson, J., O'Brien, R., Luckey, D. W., Pettitt, L. M., Henderson, C. R., Jr., et al. (2002). Home visiting by paraprofessionals and by nurses: A randomized, controlled trial. *Pediatrics, 110,* 486–496.

Olineck, K. M., & Poulin-Dubois, D. (2009). Infants' understanding of intention from 10 to 14 months: Interrelations among violation of expectancy and imitation tasks. *Infant Behavior and Development, 32,* 404–415.

Ollendick, T. H., King, N. J., & Muris, P. (2002). Fears and phobias in children: Phenomenology, epidemiology, and aetiology. *Child and Adolescent Mental Health, 7,* 98–106.

Oller, D. K. (2000). *The emergence of the speech capacity.* Mahwah, NJ: Erlbaum.

Olson, D., Sikka, R. S., Hayman, J., Novak, M., & Stavig, C. (2009). Exercise in pregnancy. *Current Sports Medicine Reports, 8,* 147–153.

Olson, S. L., Lopez-Duran, N., Lunkenheimer, E. S., Chang, H., & Sameroff, A. J. (2011). Individual differences in the development of early peer aggression: Integrating contributions of self-regulation, theory of mind, and parenting. *Development and Psychopathology, 23,* 253–266.

Omar, H., McElderry, D., & Zakharia, R. (2003). Educating adolescents about puberty: What are we missing? *International Journal of Adolescent Medicine and Health, 15,* 79–83.

Ondrusek, N., Abramovitch, R., Pencharz, P., & Koren, G. (1998). Empirical examination of the ability of children to consent to clinical research. *Journal of Medical Ethics, 24,* 158–165.

O'Neil, R., Welsh, M., Parke, R. D., Wang, S., & Strand, C. (1997). A longitudinal assessment of the academic correlates of early peer acceptance and rejection. *Journal of Clinical Child Psychology, 26,* 290–303.

O'Neill, M., Bard, K. A., Kinnell, M., & Fluck, M. (2005). Maternal gestures with 20-month-old infants in two contexts. *Developmental Science, 8,* 352–359.

Ong, K. K., Ahmed, M. L., & Dunger, D. B. (2006). Lessons from large population studies on timing and tempo of puberty (secular trends and relation to body size): The European trend. *Molecular and Cellular Endocrinology, 254–255,* 8–12.

Ontai, L. L., & Thompson, R. A. (2008). Attachment, parent–child discourse and theory-of-mind development. *Social Development, 17,* 47–60.

Oosterwegel, A., & Openheimer, L. (1993). *The self-system: Developmental changes between and within self-concepts.* Hillsdale, NJ: Erlbaum.

Opinion Research Corporation. (2009). *American teens say they want quality time with parents.* Retrieved from www.napsnet.com/pdf_archive/47/68753.pdf

Ordonana, J. R., Caspi, A., & Moffitt, T. E. (2008). Unintentional injuries in a twin study of preschool children: Environmental, not genetic risk factors. *Journal of Pediatric Psychology, 33,* 185–194.

O'Reilly, A. W. (1995). Using representations: Comprehension and production of actions with imagined objects. *Child Development, 66,* 999–1010.

Ornstein, P. A., Haden, C. A., & Elischberger, H. B. (2006). Children's memory development: Remembering the past and preparing for the future. In E. Bialystok & F. I. M. Craik (Eds.), *Lifespan cognition: Mechanisms of change* (pp. 143–161). New York: Oxford University Press.

Orobio de Castro, B., Veerman, J. W., Koops, W., Bosch, J. D., & Monshouwer, H. J. (2002). Hostile attribution of intent and aggressive behavior: A meta-analysis. *Child Development, 73,* 916–934.

Oshima-Takane, Y., & Robbins, M. (2003). Linguistic environment of secondborn children. *First Language, 23,* 21–40.

Osterholm, E. A., Hostinar, C. E., & Gunnar, M. R. (2012). Alterations in stress responses of the hypothalamic-pituitary-adrenal axis in small for gestational age infants. *Psychoneuroendocrinology, 37,* 1719–1725.

Osterman M. J., & Martin J. A. (2011). Epidural and spinal anesthesia use during labor. *National Vital Statistics Report, 59*(5), 1–13.

Ostrov, J. M., Crick, N. R., & Stauffacher, K. (2006). Relational aggression in sibling and peer relationships during early childhood. *Applied Developmental Psychology, 27,* 241–253.

Ostrov, J. M., Gentile, D. A., & Mullins, A. D. (2013). Evaluating the effect of educational media exposure on aggression in early childhood. *Journal of Applied Developmental Psychology, 34,* 38–44.

Ostrov, J. M., Murray-Close, D., Godleski, S. A., & Hart, E. J. (2013). Prospective associations between forms and functions of aggression and social and affective processes during early childhood. *Journal of Experimental Child Psychology, 116,* 19–36.

Otter, M., Schrander-Stempel, C. T. R. M., Didden, R., & Curfs, L. M. G. (2013). The psychiatric phenotype in triple X syndrome: New hypotheses illustrated in two cases. *Developmental Neurorehabilitation, 15,* 233–238.

Oude, L. H., Baur, L., Jansen, H., Shrewsbury, V. A., O'Malley, C., Stolk, R. P., & Summerbell, C. D. (2009). Interventions for treating obesity in children. *Cochrane Database of Systematic Reviews,* Issue 1, CD001872.

Ouko, L. A., Shantikumar, K., Knezovich, J., Haycock, P., Schnugh, D. J., & Ramsay, M. (2009). Effect of alcohol consumption on CpG methylation in the differentially methylated regions of H19 and IG-DMR in male gametes: Implications for fetal alcohol spectrum disorders. *Alcoholism, Clinical and Experimental Research, 33,* 1615–1627.

Overton, W. F. (2010). Life-span development: Concepts and issues. In W. F. Overton (Ed.), *Handbook of lifespan development: Cognition, biology, and methods* (pp. 1–29). Hoboken, NJ: Wiley.

Owen, C. G., Whincup, P. H., Kaye, S. J., Martin, R. M., Smith, G. D., Cook, D. G., et al. (2008). Does initial breastfeeding lead to lower blood cholesterol in adult life? A quantitative review of the evidence. *American Journal of Clinical Nutrition, 88,* 305–314.

Oyserman, D., Bybee, D., Mowbray, C., & Hart-Johnson, T. (2005). When mothers have serious mental health problems: Parenting as a proximal mediator. *Journal of Adolescence, 28,* 443–463.

Özçaliskan, S. (2005). On learning to draw the distinction between physical and metaphorical motion: Is metaphor an early emerging cognitive and linguistic capacity? *Journal of Child Language, 32,* 291–318.

P

Pacella, R., McLellan, M., Grice, K., Del Bono, E. A., Wiggs, J. L., & Gwiazda, J. E. (1999). Role of genetic factors in the etiology of juvenile-onset myopia based on a longitudinal study of refractive error. *Optometry and Vision Science, 76,* 381–386.

Padilla-Walker, L. M. (2008). "My mom makes me so angry!": Adolescent perceptions of mother–child interactions as correlates of adolescent emotions. *Social Development, 17,* 306–325.

Palacios, J., & Brodzinsky, D. M. (2010). Adoption research: Trends, topics, outcomes. *International Journal of Behavioral Development, 34,* 270–284.

Palincsar, A. S., & Herrenkohl, L. R. (1999). Designing collaborative contexts: Lessons from three research programs. In A. M. O'Donnell & A. King (Eds.), *Cognitive perspectives on peer learning. The Rutgers Invitational Symposium on Education Series* (pp. 151–177). Mahwah, NJ: Erlbaum.

Palosaari, E., Punamäki, R., Diab, M., & Qouta, A. (2013). Posttraumatic cognitions and posttraumatic stress symptoms among war-affected children: A cross-lagged analysis. *Journal of Abnormal Psychology, 122,* 656–661.

Pan, B. A., & Snow, C. E. (1999). The development of conversation and discourse skills. In M. Barrett (Ed.), *The development of language* (pp. 229–249). Hove, UK: Psychology Press.

Pan, C. W., Ramamurthy, D., & Saw, S. M. (2012). Worldwide prevalence and risk factors for myopia. *Ophthalmic and Physiological Optics, 32,* 3–16.

Pan, H. W. (1994). Children's play in Taiwan. In J. L. Roopnarine, J. E. Johnson, & F. H. Hooper (Eds.), *Children's play in diverse cultures* (pp. 31–50). Albany: SUNY Press.

Papousek, M. (2007). Communication in early infancy: An arena of intersubjective learning. *Infant Behavior and Development, 30,* 258–266.

Paradis, J. (2007). Second language acquisition in childhood. In E. Hoff & M. Shatz (Eds.), *Blackwell handbook of language development* (pp. 387–405). Malden, MA: Blackwell.

Paradis, J., Genesee, F., & Crago, M. B. (2011). *Dual language development and disorders: A handbook on bilingualism and learning* (2nd ed.). Baltimore, MD: Brookes.

Paradise, R., & Rogoff, B. (2009). Side by side: Learning by observing and pitching in. *Ethos, 27,* 102–138.

Parameswaran, G. (2003). Experimenter instructions as a mediator in the effects of culture on mapping one's neighborhood. *Journal of Environmental Psychology, 23,* 409–417.

Parent, A., Teilmann, G., Juul, A., Skakkebaek, N. E., Toppari, J., & Bourguignon, J. (2003). The timing of normal puberty and the age limits of sexual precocity: Variations around the world, secular trends, and changes after migration. *Endocrine Reviews, 24,* 668–693.

Paris, S. G., & Paris, A. G. (2006). Assessments of early reading. In K. A. Renninger & I. E. Sigel (Eds.), *Handbook of child psychology: Vol. 4. Child psychology in practice* (6th ed., pp. 48–74). Hoboken, NJ: Wiley.

Parish-Morris, J., Golinkoff, R. M., & Hirsh-Pasek, K. (2013). From coo to code: A brief story of language development. In P. D. Zelazo (Ed.), *Oxford handbook of developmental psychology: Vol. 1. Body and mind* (pp. 867–908). New York: Oxford University Press.

Parish-Morris, J., Pruden, S., Ma, W., Hirsh-Pasek, K., & Golinkoff, R. M. (2010). A world of relations: Relational words. In B. Malt & P. Wolf (Eds.), *Words and the mind: How words capture human experience* (pp. 219–242). New York: Oxford University Press.

Parke, R. D. (2002). Fathers and families. In M. H. Bornstein (Ed.), *Handbook of parenting: Vol. 3* (2nd ed., pp. 27–73). Mahwah, NJ: Erlbaum.

Parke, R. D., & Buriel, R. (2006). Socialization in the family: Ethnic and ecological perspectives. In N. Eisenberg (Ed.), *Handbook of child psychology: Vol. 3. Social, emotional, and personality development* (6th ed., pp. 429–504). Hoboken, NJ: Wiley.

Parke, R. D., Coltrane, S., Fabricius, W., Powers, J., & Adams, M. (2004a). Assessing father involvement in Mexican-American families. In R. Day & M. E. Lamb (Eds.), *Conceptualizing and measuring paternal involvement* (pp. 17–38). Mahwah, NJ: Erlbaum.

Parke, R. D., Simpkins, S. D., McDowell, D. J., Kim, M., Killian, C., Dennis, J., Flyr, M. L., Wild, M., & Rah, Y. (2004b). Relative contributions of families and peers to children's social development. In P. K. Smith & C. H. Hart (Eds.), *Blackwell handbook of childhood social development* (pp. 156–177). Malden, MA: Blackwell.

Parker, P. D., Schoon, I., Tsai, Y.-M., Nagy, G., Trautwein, U., & Eccles, J. (2012). Achievement, agency, gender, and socioeconomic background as predictors of postschool choices: A multicontext study. *Developmental Psychology, 48*, 1629–1642.

Parker, S. W., Nelson, C. A., & the Bucharest Early Intervention Project Core Group. (2005). The impact of early institutional rearing on the ability to discriminate facial expressions of emotion: An event-related potential study. *Child Development, 76*, 54–72.

Parten, M. (1932). Social participation among preschool children. *Journal of Abnormal and Social Psychology, 27*, 243–269.

Pascalis, O., de Haan, M., & Nelson, C. A. (1998). Long-term recognition memory for faces assessed by visual paired comparison in 3- and 6-month-old infants. *Journal of Experimental Psychology: Learning, Memory, and Cognition, 24*, 249–260.

Pascalis, O., de Haan, M., & Nelson, C. A. (2002). Is face processing species-specific during the first year of life? *Science, 296*, 1321–1323.

Pasley, K., & Garneau, C. (2012). Remarriage and stepfamily life. In F. Walsh (Ed.), *Normal family processes: Growing diversity and complexity* (4th ed., pp. 149–171). New York: Guilford.

Patel, S., Gaylord, S., & Fagen, J. (2013). Generalization of deferred imitation in 6-, 9-, and 12-month-old infants using visual and auditory contexts. *Infant Behavior and Development, 36*, 25–31.

Pathman, T., Larkina, M., Burch, M. M., & Bauer, P. J. (2013). Young children's memory for the times of personal past events. *Journal of Cognition and Development, 14*, 120–140.

Pattenden, S., Antova, T., Neuberger, M., Nikiforov, B., De Sario, M., Grize, L., & Heinrich, J. (2006). Parental smoking and children's respiratory health: Independent effects of prenatal and postnatal exposure. *Tobacco Control, 15*, 294–301.

Patterson, C. J. (2013). Children of lesbian and gay parents: Psychology, law, and policy. *Psychology of Sexual Orientation and Gender Diversity, 1*(S), 27–34.

Patterson, G. R., & Fisher, P. A. (2002). Recent developments in our understanding of parenting: Bidirectional effects, causal models, and the search for parsimony. In M. H. Bornstein (Ed.), *Handbook of parenting* (Vol. 5, pp. 59–88). Mahwah, NJ: Erlbaum.

Patton, G. C., Coffey, C., Carlin, J. B., Sawyer, S. M., Williams, J., Olsson, C. A., et al. (2011). Overweight and obesity between adolescence and young adulthood: A 10-year prospective cohort study. *Journal of Adolescent Health, 48*, 275–280.

Paukner A., Ferrari P. F., & Suomi, S. J. (2011). Delayed imitation of lipsmacking gestures by infant rhesus macaques (*Macaca mulatta*). *PLOS ONE 6*(12): e28848.

Paul, J. J., & Cillessen, A. H. N. (2003). Dynamics of peer victimization in early adolescence: Results from a four-year longitudinal study. *Journal of Applied School Psychology, 19*, 25–43.

Paulussen-Hoogeboom, M. C., Stams, G. J. J. M., Hermanns, J. M. A., & Peetsma, T. T. D. (2007). Child negative emotionality and parenting from infancy to preschool: A meta-analytic review. *Developmental Psychology, 43*, 438–453.

Pearlman, D. N., Zierler, S., Meersman, S., Kim, H. K., Viner-Brown, & Caron, C. (2006). Race disparities in childhood asthma: Does where you live matter? *Journal of the National Medical Association, 98*, 239–247.

Pedersen, S., Vitaro, F., Barker, E. D., & Anne, I. H. (2007). The timing of middle-childhood peer rejection and friendship: Linking early behavior to early adolescent adjustment. *Child Development, 78*, 1037–1051.

Pederson, D. R., & Moran, G. (1996). Expressions of the attachment relationship outside of the Strange Situation. *Child Development, 67*, 915–927.

Peirano, P., Algarin, C., & Uauy, R. (2003). Sleep-wake states and their regulatory mechanisms throughout early human development. *Journal of Pediatrics, 143*, S70–S79.

Pellegrini, A. D. (2003). Perceptions and functions of play and real fighting in early adolescence. *Child Development, 74*, 1522–1533.

Pellegrini, A. D. (2004). Rough-and-tumble play from childhood through adolescence: Development and possible functions. In P. K. Smith & C. H. Hart (Eds.), *Blackwell handbook of childhood social development* (pp. 438–453). Malden, MA: Blackwell.

Pellegrini, A. D., Huberty, P. D., & Jones, I. (1995). The effects of recess timing on children's playground and classroom behaviors. *American Educational Research Journal, 32*, 845–864.

Pellegrini, A. D., Kato, K., Blatchford, P., & Baines, E. (2002). A short-term longitudinal study of children's playground games across the first year of school: Implications for social competence and adjustment to school. *American Educational Research Journal, 39*, 991–1015.

Pellicano, E., Maybery, M., Durkin, K., & Maley, A. (2006). Multiple cognitive capabilities/deficits in children with an autism spectrum disorder: "Weak" central coherence and its relationship to theory of mind and executive control. *Development and Psychopathology, 18*, 77–98.

Pennisi, E. (2012). ENCODE Project writes eulogy for junk DNA. *Science, 337*, 1160–1161.

Penny, H., & Haddock, G. (2007). Anti-fat prejudice among children: The "mere proximity" effect in 5–10 year olds. *Journal of Experimental Social Psychology, 43*, 678–683.

Peralta de Mendoza, O. A., & Salsa, A. M. (2003). Instruction in early comprehension and use of a symbol–referent relation. *Cognitive Development, 18*, 269–284.

Perlmutter, M. (1984). Continuities and discontinuities in early human memory: Paradigms, processes, and performances. In R. V. Kail, Jr., & N. R. Spear (Eds.), *Comparative perspectives on the development of memory* (pp. 253–287). Hillsdale, NJ: Erlbaum.

Perren, S., von Wyl, A., Burgin, D., Simoni, H., & von Klitzing, K. (2005). Depressive symptoms and psychosocial stress across the transition to parenthood: Associations with parental psychopathology and child difficulty. *Journal of Psychosomatic Obstetrics and Gynaecology, 26*, 173–183.

Perry, G. H., & Dominy, N. J. (2009). Evolution of the human pygmy phenotype. *Trends in Ecology and Evolution, 24*, 218–225.

Pesonen, A.-K., Räikkönen, K., Heinonen, K., & Komsi, N. (2008). A transactional model of temperamental development: Evidence of a relationship between child temperament and maternal stress over five years. *Social Development, 17*, 326–340.

Petch, J., & Halford, W. K. (2008). Psycho-education to enhance couples' transition to parenthood. *Clinical Psychology Review, 28*, 1125–1137.

Peters, R. D. (2005). A community-based approach to promoting resilience in young children, their families, and their neighborhoods. In R. D. Peters, B. Leadbeater, & R. J. McMahon (Eds.), *Resilience in children, families, and communities: Linking context to practice and policy* (pp. 157–176). New York: Kluwer Academic.

Peters, R. D., Bradshaw, A. J., Petrunka, K., Nelson, G., Herry, Y., Craig, W. M., et al. (2010). The Better Beginnings, Better Futures Project: Findings from grade 3 to grade 9. *Monographs of the Society for Research in Child Development, 75* (3, Serial No. 297).

Peters, R. D., Petrunka, K., & Arnold, R. (2003). The Better Beginnings, Better Futures Project: A universal, comprehensive, community-based prevention approach for primary school children and their families. *Journal of Clinical Child and Adolescent Psychology, 32*, 215–227.

Peterson, C. (2012). Children's autobiographical memories across the years: Forensic implications of childhood amnesia and eyewitness memory for stressful events. *Developmental Review, 32*, 287–306.

Peterson, C., Parsons, T., & Dean, M. (2004). Providing misleading and reinstatement information a year after it happened: Effects on long-term memory. *Memory, 12*, 1–13.

Peterson, C., & Rideout, R. (1998). Memory for medical emergencies experienced by 1- and 2-year-olds. *Developmental Psychology, 34*, 1059–1072.

Peterson, C., Warren, K. L., & Short, M. M. (2011). Infantile amnesia across the years: A 2-year follow-up of children's earliest memories. *Child Development, 82*, 1092–1105.

Petitto, L. A., Holowka, S., Sergio, L. E., Levy, B., & Ostry, D. J. (2004). Baby hands that move to the rhythm of language: Hearing babies acquiring sign languages babble silently on the hands. *Cognition, 93*, 43–73.

Petitto, L. A., Holowka, S., Sergio, L. E., & Ostry, D. (2001). Language rhythms in babies' hand movements. *Nature, 413*, 35–36.

Petitto, L. A., & Marentette, P. F. (1991). Babbling in the manual mode: Evidence for the ontogeny of language. *Science, 251*, 1493–1496.

Petrill, S. A., & Deater-Deckard, K. (2004). The heritability of general cognitive ability: A within-family adoption design. *Intelligence, 32*, 403–409.

Pettigrew, T. F., & Tropp, L. R. (2006). A meta-analytic test of intergroup contact theory. *Journal of Personality and Social Psychology, 90*, 751–783.

Pettit, G. S., Brown, E. G., Mize, J., & Lindsey, E. (1998). Mothers' and fathers' socializing behaviors in three contexts: Links with children's peer competence. *Merrill-Palmer Quarterly, 44*, 173–193.

Pew Research Center. (2013). *Among 38 nations, U.S. is the outlier when it comes to paid parental leave.* Retrieved from www.pewresearch.org/fact-tank/2013/12/12/among-38-nations-u-s-is-the-holdout-when-it-comes-to-offering-paid-parental-leave

Pfeffer, C. R., Altemus, M., Heo, M., & Jiang, H. (2007). Salivary cortisol and psychopathology in children bereaved by the September 11, 2001 terror attacks. *Biological Psychiatry, 61*, 957–965.

Pfeifer, J. H., Ruble, D. N., Bachman, M. A., Alvarez, J. M., Cameron, J. A., & Fuligni, A. J. (2007). Social identities and intergroup bias in immigrant and nonimmigrant children. *Developmental Psychology, 43*, 496–507.

Pfeiffer, S. I., & Yermish, A. (2014). Gifted children. In L. Grossman & S. Walfish (Eds.), *Translating psychological research into practice* (pp. 57–64). New York: Springer.

Phillips, D. A., & Lowenstein, A. E. (2011). Early care, education, and child development. *Annual Review of Psychology, 62*, 483–500.

Piaget, J. (1926). *The language and thought of the child.* New York: Harcourt, Brace & World. (Original work published 1923)

Piaget, J. (1930). *The child's conception of the world.* New York: Harcourt, Brace, & World. (Original work published 1926)

Piaget, J. (1951). *Play, dreams, and imitation in childhood.* New York: Norton. (Original work published 1945)

Piaget, J. (1952). *The origins of intelligence in children.* New York: International Universities Press. (Original work published 1936)

Piaget, J. (1971). *Biology and knowledge.* Chicago: University of Chicago Press.

Pickens, J., Field, T., & Nawrocki, T. (2001). Frontal EEG asymmetry in response to emotional vignettes in preschool age children. *International Journal of Behavioral Development, 25*, 105–112.

Pierroutsakos, S. L., & Troseth, G. L. (2003). Video verite: Infants' manual investigation of objects on video. *Infant Behavior and Development, 26*, 183–199.

Pierson, L. (1996). Hazards of noise exposure on fetal hearing. *Seminars in Perinatology, 20*, 21–29.

Piirto, J. (2007). *Talented children and adults* (3rd ed.). Waco, TX: Prufrock Press.

Pine, J. M. (1995). Variation in vocabulary development as a function of birth order. *Child Development, 66*, 272–281.

Ping, R. M., & Goldin-Meadow, S. (2008). Hands in the air: Using ungrounded iconic gestures to teach children conservation of quantity. *Developmental Psychology, 44*, 1277–1287.

Pinker, S. (1999). *Words and rules: The ingredients of language.* New York: Basic Books.

Pinker, S., Lebeaux, D. S., & Frost, L. A. (1987). Productivity and constraints in the acquisition of the passive. *Cognition, 26*, 195–267.

Pipp, S., Easterbrooks, M. A., & Brown, S. R. (1993). Attachment status and complexity of infants' self- and other-knowledge when tested with mother and father. *Social Development, 2,* 1–14.

Pipp, S., Easterbrooks, M. A., & Harmon, R. J. (1992). The relation between attachment and knowledge of self and mother in one-year-old infants to three-year-old infants. *Child Development, 63,* 738–750.

Pleck, J. H., & Masciadrelli, B. P. (2004). Paternal involvement by U.S. residential fathers: Levels, sources, and consequences. In M. E. Lamb (Ed.), *The role of the father in child development* (4th ed., pp. 222–271). Hoboken, NJ: Wiley

Plante, I., Théoret, M., & Favreau, O. E. (2009). Student gender stereotypes: Contrasting the perceived maleness and femaleness of mathematics and language. *Educational Psychology, 29,* 385–405.

Platt, M. P. W. (2014). Neonatology and obstetric anaesthesia. *Archives of Disease in Childhood—Fetal and Neonatal Edition, 99,* F98.

Plomin, R. (1994). *Genetics and experience: The interplay between nature and nurture.* Thousand Oaks, CA: Sage.

Plomin, R. (2009). The nature of nurture. In K. McCartney & R. A. Weinberg (Eds.), *Experience and development: A festschrift in honor of Sandra Wood Scarr* (pp. 61–80). New York: Psychology Press.

Plomin, R. (2013). Commentary: Missing heritability, polygenic scores, and gene–environment interactions. *Journal of Child Psychology and Psychiatry and Allied Disciplines, 54,* 1147–1149.

Plomin, R., DeFries, J. C., & Knopik, V. S. (2013). *Behavioral genetics* (6th ed.). New York: Worth.

Plomin, R., & Spinath, F. M. (2004). Intelligence: Genetics, genes, and genomics. *Journal of Personality and Social Psychology, 86,* 112–129.

Plucker, J. A., & Makel, M. C. (2010). Assessment of creativity. In J. C. Kaufman & R. J. Sternberg (Eds.), *Cambridge handbook of creativity* (pp. 48–73). New York: Cambridge University Press.

Pluess, M., & Belsky, J. (2011). Prenatal programming of postnatal plasticity? *Development and Psychopathology, 23,* 29–38.

Poehlmann, J. (2003). An attachment perspective on grandparents raising their very young grandchildren: Implications for intervention and research. *Infant Mental Health Journal, 24,* 149–173.

Poehlmann, J., Schwichtenberg, A. J. M., Shlafer, R. J., Hahn, E., Bianchi, J.-P., & Warner, R. (2011). Emerging self-regulation in toddlers born preterm or low birth weight: Differential susceptibility to parenting. *Developmental and Psychopathology, 23,* 177–193.

Polakowski L. L., Akinbami, L. J., & Mendola, P. (2009). Prenatal smoking cessation and the risk of delivering preterm and small-for-gestational-age newborns. *Obstetrics and Gynecology, 114,* 318–325.

Polderman, T. J. C., de Geus, J. C., Hoekstra, R. A., Bartels, M., van Leeuwen, M., Verhulst, F. C., et al. (2009). Attention problems, inhibitory control, and intelligence index overlapping genetic factors: A study in 9-, 12-, and 18-year-old twins. *Neuropsychology, 23,* 381–391.

Polka, L., & Rvachew, S. (2005). The impact of otitis media with effusion on infant phonetic perception. *Infancy, 8,* 101–117.

Pomerantz, E. M., & Dong, W. (2006). Effects of mothers' perceptions of children's competence: The moderating role of mothers' theories of competence. *Developmental Psychology, 42,* 950–961.

Pomerantz, E. M., & Eaton, M. M. (2000). Developmental differences in children's conceptions of parental control: "They love me, but they make me feel incompetent." *Merrill-Palmer Quarterly, 46,* 140–167.

Pomerantz, E. M., Grolnick, W. S., & Price, C. E. (2013). The role of parents in how children approach achievement: A dynamic process perspective. In A. J. Elliott & C. J. Dweck (Eds.), *Handbook of confidence and motivation* (pp. 259–278). New York: Guilford.

Pomerantz, E. M., & Kempner, S. G. (2013). Mothers' daily person and process praise: Implications for children's theory of intelligence and motivation. *Developmental Psychology, 13,* 2040–2046.

Pomerantz, E. M., Ng, F. F., & Wang, Q. (2008). Culture, parenting, and motivation: The case of East Asia and the United States. In M. L. Maehr, S. A., Karabenick, & T. C. Urdan (Eds.), *Advances in motivation and achievement: Social psychological perspectives* (Vol. 15, pp. 209–240). Bingley, UK: Emerald Group.

Pomerantz, E. M., & Ruble, D. N. (1998). The multidimensional nature of control: Implications for the development of sex differences in self-evaluation. In J. Heckhausen & C. S. Dweck (Eds.), *Motivation and self-regulation across the life span* (pp. 159–184). New York: Cambridge University Press.

Pomerantz, E. M., & Saxon, J. L. (2001). Conceptions of ability as stable and self-evaluative processes: A longitudinal examination. *Child Development, 72,* 152–173.

Pomerantz, E. M., & Wang, Q. (2009). The role of parental control in children's development in Western and East Asian countries. *Current Directions in Psychological Science, 18,* 285–289.

Pong, S., Johnston, J., & Chen, V. (2010). Authoritarian parenting and Asian adolescent school performance. *International Journal of Behavioral Development, 34,* 62–72.

Pong, S., & Landale, N. S. (2012). Academic achievement of legal immigrants' children: The roles of parents' pre- and postmigration characteristics in origin-group differences. *Child Development, 83,* 1543–1559.

Pons, F., Lawson, J., Harris, P. L., & de Rosnay, M. (2003). Individual differences in children's emotion understanding: Effects of age and language. *Scandinavian Journal of Psychology, 44,* 347–353.

Poole, D. A., & Bruck, M. (2012). Divining testimony? The impact of interviewing props on children's reports of touching. *Developmental Review, 32,* 165–180.

Poplinger, M., Talwar, V., & Crossman, A. (2011). Predictors of children's prosocial lie-telling: Motivation, socialization variables, and moral understanding. *Journal of Experimental Child Psychology, 110,* 373–392.

Portes, A., & Rumbaut, R. G. (2005). Introduction: The second generation and the Children of Immigrants Longitudinal Study. *Ethnic and Racial Studies, 28,* 983–999.

Posner, M. I., & Rothbart, M. K. (2007a). *Educating the human brain.* Washington, DC: American Psychological Association.

Posner, M. I., & Rothbart, M. K. (2007b). Temperament and learning. In M. I. Posner & M. K. Rothbart (Eds.), *Educating the human brain* (pp. 121–146). Washington, DC: American Psychological Association.

Potter, D. (2012). Same-sex parent families and children's academic achievement. *Journal of Marriage and Family, 74,* 556–571.

Poudevigne, M., & O'Connor, P. J. (2006). A review of physical activity patterns in pregnant women and their relationship to psychological health. *Sports Medicine, 36,* 19–38.

Poulin-Dubois, D., Serbin, L. A., Eichstedt, J. A., Sen, M. G., & Beissel, C. F. (2002). Men don't put on make-up: Toddlers' knowledge of the gender stereotyping of household activities. *Social Development, 11,* 166–181.

Povinelli, D. J. (2001). The self—Elevated in consciousness and extended in time. In C. Moore & K. Lemmon (Eds.), *The self in time: Developmental perspectives* (pp. 75–95). Mahwah, NJ: Erlbaum.

Powell, M. P., & Schulte, T. (2011). Turner syndrome. In S. Goldstein & C. R. Reynolds (Eds.), *Handbook of neurodevelopmental and genetic disorders in children* (2nd ed.) (pp. 261–275). New York: Guilford Press.

Prechtl, H. F. R., & Beintema, D. (1965). *The neurological examination of the full-term newborn infant.* London: Heinemann Medical.

Pressley, M., & Hilden, D. (2006). Cognitive strategies. In D. Kuhn & R. Siegler (Eds.), *Handbook of child psychology: Vol. 2. Cognition, perception, and language* (6th ed., pp. 511–556). Hoboken, NJ: Wiley.

Pressley, M., Wharton-McDonald, R., Raphael, L. M., Bogner, K., & Roehrig, A. (2002). Exemplary first-grade teaching. In B. M. Taylor & P. D. Pearson (Eds.), *Teaching reading: Effective schools, accomplished teachers* (pp. 73–88). Mahwah, NJ: Erlbaum.

Preuss, T. M. (2012). Human brain evolution: From gene discovery to phenotype discovery. *Proceedings of the National Academy of Sciences, 109*(Suppl. 1), 10709–10716.

Previc, F. H. (1991). A general theory concerning the prenatal origins of cerebral lateralization. *Psychological Review, 98,* 299–334.

Principi, N., Baggi, E., & Esposito, S. (2012). Prevention of acute otitis media using currently available vaccines. *Future of Microbiology, 7,* 457–465.

Proctor, M. H., Moore, L. L. Gao, D., Cupples, L. A., Bradlee, M. L., Hood, M. Y., & Ellison, R. C. (2003). Television viewing and change in body fat from preschool to early adolescence: The Framingham Children's Study. *International Journal of Obesity, 27,* 827–833.

Proffitt, D. R., & Bertenthal, B. I. (1990). Converging operations revisited: Assessing what infants perceive using discrimination measures. *Perception and Psychophysics, 47,* 1–11.

Programme for International Student Assessment. (2012). *PISA 2012 Results.* Retrieved from nces.ed.gov/surveys/pisa/pisa2012/index.asp

Proietti, E., Röösli, M., Frey, U., & Latzin, P. (2013). Air pollution during pregnancy and neonatal outcome: A review. *Journal of Aerosol Medicine and Pulmonary Drug Delivery, 26,* 9–23.

Proulx, M., & Poulin, F. (2013). Stability and change in kindergartners' friendships: Examination of links with social functioning. *Social Development, 22,* 111–125.

Pruden, S. M., Hirsh-Pasek, K., Golinkoff, R. M., & Hennon, E. A. (2006). The birth of words: Ten-month-olds learn words through perceptual salience. *Child Development, 77,* 266–280.

Pruett, M. K., & Donsky, T. (2011). Coparenting after divorce: Paving pathways for parental cooperation, conflict resolution, and redefined family roles. In J. P. McHale & K. M. Lindahl (Eds.), *Coparenting: A conceptual and clinical examination of family systems* (pp. 231–250). Washington, DC: American Psychological Association.

Pryor, J. (2014). *Stepfamilies: A global perspective on research, policy, and practice.* New York: Routledge.

Psychiatric Genomics Consortium. (2013). Identification of risk loci with shared effects of five major psychiatric disorders. *Lancet, 381,* 1371–1379.

Puhl, R. M., Heuer, C. A., & Brownell, D. K. (2010). Stigma and social consequences of obesity. In P. G. Kopelman, I. D. Caterson, & W. H. Dietz (Eds.), *Clinical obesity in adults and children* (3rd ed., pp. 25–40). Hoboken, NJ: Wiley.

Puhl, R. M., & Latner, J. D. (2007). Stigma, obesity, and the health of the nation's children. *Psychological Bulletin, 133,* 557–580.

Pujol, J., Soriano-Mas, C., Ortiz, H., Sebastián-Gallés, N., Losilla, J. M., & Deus, J. (2006). Myelination of language-related areas in the developing brain. *Neurology, 66,* 339–343.

Puma, M., Bell, S., Cook, R., Heid, C., Broene, P., Jenkins, F., et al. (2012). *Third grade follow-up to the Head Start Impact Study final report.* OPRE Report #2012-45b. Washington, DC: U.S. Department of Health and Human Services.

Punamaki, R. L. (2006). Ante- and perinatal factors and child characteristics predicting parenting experience among formerly infertile couples during the child's first year: A controlled study. *Journal of Family Psychology, 20,* 670–679.

Purcell-Gates, V. (1996). Stories, coupons, and the TV guide: Relationships between home literacy experiences and emergent literacy knowledge. *Reading Research Quarterly, 31,* 406–428.

Putallaz, M., Grimes, C. L., Foster, K. J., Kupersmidt, J. B., Coie, J. D., & Dearing, K. (2007). Overt and relational aggression and victimization: Multiple perspectives within the school setting. *Journal of School Psychology, 45,* 523–547.

Putnam, S. P., Samson, A. V., & Rothbart, M. K. (2000). Child temperament and parenting. In V. J. Molfese & D. L. Molfese (Eds.), *Temperament and personality across the life span* (pp. 255–277). Mahwah, NJ: Erlbaum.

Q

Qin, L., and Pomerantz, E. M. (2013). Reciprocal pathways between American and Chinese early adolescents' sense of responsibility and disclosure to parents. *Child Development, 84,* 1887–1895.

Quas, J. A., Malloy, L. C., Melinder, A., Goodman, G. S., & D'Mello, M. (2007). Developmental differences in the effects of repeated interviews and interviewer bias on young children's event memory and false reports. *Developmental Psychology, 43,* 823–837.

Quinn, P. C. (2008). In defense of core competencies, quantitative change, and continuity. *Child Development, 79,* 1633–1638.

Quinn, P. C., & Intraub, H. (2007). Perceiving "outside the box" occurs early in development: Evidence for boundary extension in three- to seven-month-old infants. *Child Development, 78,* 324–334.

Quinn, P. C., Kelly, D. J., Lee, K., Pascalis, O., & Slater, A. (2008). Preference for attractive faces extends beyond conspecifics. *Developmental Science, 11,* 76–83.

Quinn, P. C., Yahr, J., Kuhn, A., Slater, A. M., & Pascalis, O. (2002). Representation of the gender of human faces by infants: A preference for female. *Perception, 31,* 1109–1121.

R

Raabe, T., & Beelman, A. (2011). Development of ethnic, racial, and national prejudice in childhood and adolescence: A multinational meta-analysis of age differences. *Child Development, 82,* 1715–1737.

Racanello, A., & McCabe, P. C. (2010). Role of otitis media in hearing loss and language deficits. In P. C. McCabe & S. R. Shaw (Eds.), *Pediatric disorders* (pp. 22–31). Washington, DC: Corwin Press

Racz, S. J., McMahon, R. J., & Luthar, S. S. (2011). Risky behavior in affluent youth: Examining the co-occurrence and consequences of multiple problem behaviors. *Journal of Child and Family Studies, 20,* 120–128.

Radesky, J. S., Kistin, C. J., Zuckerman, B., Nitzberg, K., Gross, J., Kaplan-Sanoff, M., et al. (2014). Patterns of mobile device use by caregivers and children during meals in fast food restaurants. *Pediatrics, 133,* e843–e849.

Rahi, J. S., Cumberland, P. M., & Peckham, C. S. (2011). Myopia over the life course: Prevalence and early life influences in the 1958 British birth cohort. *Ophthalmology, 118,* 797–804.

Raikes, H. A., Robinson, J. L., Bradley, R. H., Raikes, H. H., & Ayoub, C. C. (2007). Developmental trends in self-regulation among low-income toddlers. *Social Development, 16,* 128–149.

Raikes, H. H., Chazan-Cohen, R., Love, J. M., & Brooks-Gunn, J. (2010). Early Head Start impacts at age 3 and a description of the age 5 follow-up study. In A. J. Reynolds, A. J. Rolnick, M. M. Englund, & J. Temple (Eds.), *Childhood programs and practices in the first decade of life: A human capital integration* (pp. 99–118). New York: Cambridge University Press.

Rakison, D. H. (2005). Developing knowledge of objects' motion properties in infancy. *Cognition, 96,* 183–214.

Rakison, D. H. (2010). Perceptual categorization and concepts. In J. G. Bremner & T. D. Wachs (Eds.), *Wiley-Blackwell handbook of infant development* (2nd ed., pp. 243–270). Oxford, UK: Wiley.

Rakison, D. H., & Lawson, C. A. (2013). Categorization. In P. D. Zelazo (Ed.), *Oxford handbook of developmental psychology: Vol. 1. Body and mind* (pp. 591–627). New York: Oxford University Press.

Rakoczy, H., Tomasello, M., & Striano, T. (2004). Young children know that trying is not pretending: A test of the "behaving-as-if" construal of children's early concept of pretense. *Developmental Psychology, 40,* 388–399.

Rakoczy, H., Tomasello, M., & Striano, T. (2005). How children turn objects into symbols: A cultural learning account. In L. Namy (Ed.), *Symbol use and symbol representation* (pp. 67–97). New York: Erlbaum.

Ramachandrappa, A., & Jain, L. (2008). Elective cesarean section: Its impact on neonatal respiratory outcome. *Clinics in Perinatology, 35,* 373–393.

Raman, L., & Gelman, S. A. (2004). A cross-cultural developmental analysis of children's and adults' understanding of illness in South Asia (India) and the United States. *Journal of Cognition and Culture, 4,* 293–317.

Ramchandani, P. G., Stein, A., O'Connor, T. G., Heron, J., Murray, L., & Evans, J. (2008). Depression in men in the postnatal period and later child psychopathology: A population cohort study. *Journal of the American Academy of Child and Adolescent Psychiatry, 47,* 390–398.

Ramey, C. T., Ramey, S. L., & Lanzi, R. G. (2006). Children's health and education. In K. A. Renninger & I. E. Sigel (Eds.), *Handbook of child psychology: Vol. 4. Child psychology in practice* (6th ed., pp. 864–892). Hoboken, NJ: Wiley.

Ramirez, M. M. (2011). Labor induction: A review of current methods. *Obstetrics and Gynecology Clinics of North America, 38,* 215–225.

Ramos, M. C., Guerin, D. W., Gottfried, A. W., Bathurst, K., & Oliver, P. H. (2005). Family conflict and children's behavior problems: The moderating role of child temperament. *Structural Equation Modeling, 12,* 278–298.

Ramsey-Rennels, J. L., & Langlois, J. H. (2006). Differential processing of female and male faces. *Current Directions in Psychological Science, 15,* 59–62.

Ramus, F. (2002). Language discrimination by newborns: Teasing apart phonotactic, rhythmic, and intonational cues. *Annual Review of Language Acquisition, 2,* 85–115.

Rasmussen, C., Ho, E., & Bisanz, J. (2003). Use of the mathematical principle of inversion in young children. *Journal of Experimental Child Psychology, 85,* 89–102.

Rasmussen, C., Neuman, R. J., Heath, A. C., Levy, F., Hay, D. A., & Todd, R. D. (2004). Familial clustering of latent class and DSM-IV defined attention-deficit hyperactivity disorder (ADHD) subtypes. *Journal of Child Psychology and Psychiatry, 45,* 589–598.

Rathunde, K., & Csikszentmihalyi, M. (2005). The social context of middle school: Teachers, friends, and activities in Montessori and traditional school environments. *Elementary School Journal, 106,* 59–79.

Rauber, M. (2006, May 18). Parents aren't sitting still as recess disappears. *Parents in Action.* Retrieved from www.parentsaction.org/news/parents-in-action/index.cfm?i=410

Rautava, L., Lempinen, A., Ojala, S., Parkkola, R., Rikalainen, H., Lapinleimu, H., et al. (2007). Acoustic quality of cry in very-low-birth weight infants at the age of 1½ years. *Early Human Development, 83,* 5–12.

Raver, C. C. (2003). Does work pay psychologically as well as economically? The role of employment in predicting depressive symptoms and parenting among low-income families. *Child Development, 74,* 1720–1736.

Ravid, D., & Tolchinsky, L. (2002). Developing linguistic literacy: A comprehensive model. *Journal of Child Language, 29,* 417–447.

Ravitch, D. (2010). *The death and life of the great American school system: How testing and choice are undermining education.* New York: Basic Books.

Ray, E., & Heyes, C. (2011). Imitation in infancy: The wealth of the stimulus. *Developmental Science, 14,* 92–105.

Ray, R., Gornick, J. C., & Schmitt, J. (2008). *Parental leave policies in 21 countries: Assessing generosity and gender equality.* Washington, DC: Center for Economic and Policy Research.

Ray, S., Reddy, P. J., Jain, R., Gollapalli, K., Moiyadi, A., & Srivastava, S. (2011). Proteomic technologies for the identification of disease biomarkers in serum: Advances and challenges ahead. *Proteomics, 11,* 2139–2161.

Rayner, K., Pollatsek, A., & Starr, M. S. (2003). Reading. In A. F. Healy & R. W. Proctor (Eds.), *Handbook of psychology: Experimental psychology* (Vol. 4, pp. 549–574). New York: Wiley.

Reed, C. E., & Fenton, S. E. (2013). Exposure to diethylstilbestrol during sensitive life stages: A legacy of heritable health effects. *Birth Defects Research. Part C, Embryo Today: Reviews, 99,* 134–146.

Reed, R. K. (2005). *Birthing fathers.* New Brunswick, NJ: Rutgers University Press.

Reese, E., & Newcombe, R. (2007). Training mothers in elaborative reminiscing enhances children's autobiographical memory and narrative. *Child Development, 78,* 1153–1170.

Reese, E., Newcombe, R., & Bird, G. M. (2006). The emergence of autobiographical memory: Cognitive, social, and emotional factors. In C. M. Flinn-Fletcher & G. M. Haberman (Eds.), *Cognition and language: Perspectives from New Zealand* (pp. 177–189). Bowen Hills, Australia: Australian Academic Press.

Reis, S. M. (2004). We can't change what we don't recognize: Understanding the special needs of gifted females. In S. Baum (Ed.), *Twice-exceptional and special populations of gifted students* (pp. 67–80). Thousand Oaks, CA: Corwin Press.

Reiss, D. (2003). Child effects on family systems: Behavioral genetic strategies. In A. C. Crouter & A. Booth (Eds.), *Children's influence on family dynamics* (pp. 3–36). Mahwah, NJ: Erlbaum.

Rentner, T. L., Dixon, L. D., & Lengel, L. (2012). Critiquing fetal alcohol syndrome health communication campaigns targeted to American Indians. *Journal of Health Communication, 17,* 6–21.

Repacholi, B. M., & Gopnik, A. (1997). Early reasoning about desires: Evidence from 14- and 18-month-olds. *Developmental Psychology, 33,* 12–21.

Repetti, R., & Wang, S. (2010). Parent employment and chaos in the family. In G. W. Evans & T. D. Wachs (Eds.), *Chaos and its influence on children's development: An ecological perspective* (pp. 191–208). Washington, DC: American Psychological Association.

Reschly, A. L., & Christenson, S. L. (2009). Parents as essential partners for fostering students' learning outcomes. In R. Gilman & E. Scott Huebner (Eds.), *Handbook of positive psychology in schools* (pp. 257–272). New York: Routledge.

Resnick, G. (2010). Project Head Start: Quality and links to child outcomes. In A. J. Reynolds, A. J. Rolnick, M. M. Englund, & J. Temple (Eds.), *Childhood programs and practices in the first decade of life: A human capital integration* (pp. 121–156). New York: Cambridge University Press.

Resnick, M., & Silverman, B. (2005). *Some reflections on designing construction kits for kids.* Proceedings of the Conference on Interaction Design and Children, Boulder, CO.

Resta, R., Biesecker, B. B., Bennett, R. L., Blum, S., Hahn, S. E., Strecker, M. N., & Williams, J. L. (2006). A new definition of genetic counseling: National Society of Genetic Counselors' Task Force Report. *Journal of Genetic Counseling, 15,* 77–83.

Reynolds, A. J., & Temple, J. A. (1998). Extended early childhood intervention and school achievement: Age thirteen findings from the Chicago Longitudinal Study. *Child Development, 69,* 231–246.

Rhoades, B. L., Greenberg, M. T., & Domitrovich, C. E. (2009). The contribution of inhibitory control to preschoolers' social-emotional competence. *Journal of Applied Developmental Psychology, 30,* 310–320.

Rhodes, M., Leslie, S.-J., & Tworek, C. M. (2012). Cultural transmission of social essentialism. *Proceedings of the National Academy of Sciences, 109,* 13526–13531.

Richardson, H. L., Walker, A. M., & Horne, R. S. C. (2008) Sleep position alters arousal processes maximally at the high-risk age for sudden infant death syndrome. *Journal of Sleep Research, 17,* 450–457.

Richler, J., Luyster, R., Risi, S., Hsu, W.-L., Dawson, G., & Bernier, R. (2006). Is there a 'regressive phenotype' of autism spectrum disorder associated with the measles-mumps-rubella vaccine? A CPEA study. *Journal of Autism and Developmental Disorders, 36,* 299–316.

Richmond, J., Colombo, M., & Hayne, H. (2007). Interpreting visual preferences in the visual paired-comparison task. *Journal of Experimental Psychology: Learning, Memory, and Cognition, 33,* 823–831.

Rideout, V., & Hamel, E. (2006). *The media family: Electronic media in the lives of infants, toddlers, preschoolers and their parents.* Menlo Park, CA: Henry J. Kaiser Family Foundation.

Rideout, V. J., Foehr, U. G., & Roberts, D. F. (2010). *Generation M²: Media in the lives of 8- to 18-year-olds.* Menlo Park, CA: Henry J. Kaiser Family Foundation.

Rieffe, C., Terwogt, M. M., & Cowan, R. (2005). Children's understanding of mental states as causes of emotions. *Infant and Child Development, 14,* 259–272.

Riggins, T., Cheatham, C., Stark, E., & Bauer, P. J. (2013). Elicited imitation performance at 20 months predicts memory abilities in school age children. *Journal of Cognition and Development, 14,* 593–606.

Riggins, T., Miller, N. C., Bauer, P., Georgieff, M. K., & Nelson, C. A. (2009). Consequences of low neonatal iron status due to maternal diabetes mellitus on explicit memory performance in childhood. *Developmental Neuropsychology, 34,* 762–779.

Riggs, K. J., Jolley, R. P., & Simpson, A. (2013). The role of inhibitory control in the development of human figure drawing in young children. *Journal of Experimental Child Psychology, 114,* 537–542.

Rijlaarsdam, J., Stevens, G. W. J. M., van der Ende, J., Arends, L. R., Hofman, A., Jaddoe, V. W. V., et al. (2012). A brief observational instrument for the assessment of infant home environment: Development and psychometric testing. *International Journal of Methods in Psychiatric Research, 21,* 195–204.

Rijsdijk, F. V., & Boomsma, D. I. (1997). Genetic mediation of the correlation between peripheral nerve conduction velocity and IQ. *Behavior Genetics, 27,* 87–98.

Rindermann, H., & Ceci, S. J. (2008). *Education policy and country outcomes in international cognitive competence studies*. Graz, Austria: Institute of Psychology, Karl-Franzens-University Graz.

Ripley, A. (2013). *The smartest kids in the world: And how they got that way*. New York: Simon and Schuster.

Ripple, C. H., & Zigler, E. (2003). Research, policy, and the federal role in prevention initiatives for children. *American Psychologist, 58*, 482–490.

Ris, M. D., Dietrich, K. N., Succop, P. A., Berger, O. G., & Bornschein, R. L. (2004). Early exposure to lead and neuropsychological outcome in adolescence. *Journal of the International Neuropsychological Society, 10*, 261–270.

Ritz, B., Oiu, J., Lee, P. C., Lurmann, F., Penfold, B., Erin Weiss, R., et al. (2014). Prenatal air pollution exposure and ultrasound measures of fetal growth in Los Angeles, California. *Environmental Research, 130*, 7–13.

Riva, D., & Giorgi, C. (2000). The cerebellum contributes to higher functions during development: Evidence from a series of children surgically treated for posterior fossa tumors. *Brain, 123*, 1051–1061.

Rivkees, S. A. (2003). Developing circadian rhythmicity in infants. *Pediatrics, 112*, 373–381.

Rizzolatti, G., & Craighero, L. (2004). The mirror-neuron system. *Annual Review of Neuroscience, 27*, 169–192.

Roben, C. K. P., Bass, A. J., Moore, G. A., Murray-Kolb, L., Tan, P. Z., Gilmore, R. O., et al. (2012). Let me go: The influences of crawling experience and temperament on the development of anger expression. *Infancy, 17*, 558–577.

Roberts, B. W., & DelVecchio, W. F. (2000). The rankorder consistency of personality traits from childhood to old age: A quantitative review of longitudinal studies. *Psychological Bulletin, 126*, 3–25.

Roberts, D. F., Foehr, U. G., & Rideout, V. (2005). *Generation M: Media in the lives of 8–18 year olds*. Menlo Park, CA: Henry J. Kaiser Family Foundation.

Roberts, J. E., Burchinal, M. R., & Durham, M. (1999). Parents' report of vocabulary and grammatical development of American preschoolers: Child and environment associations. *Child Development, 70*, 92–106.

Robertson, J. (2008). Stepfathers in families. In J. Pryor (Ed.), *International handbook of stepfamilies: Policy and practice in legal, research, and clinical environments* (pp. 125–150). Hoboken, NJ: Wiley.

Robila, M. (2012). Family policies in Eastern Europe: A focus on parental leave. *Journal of Child and Family Studies, 21*, 32–41.

Robin, D. J., Berthier, N. E., & Clifton, R. K. (1996). Infants' predictive reaching for moving objects in the dark. *Developmental Psychology, 32*, 824–835.

Robins, R. W., Tracy, J. L., Trzesniewski, K., Potter, J., & Gosling, S. D. (2001). Personality correlates of self-esteem. *Journal of Research in Personality, 35*, 463–482.

Robinson, C. C., Anderson, G. T., Porter, C. L., Hart, C. H., & Wouden-Miller, M. (2003). Sequential transition patterns of preschoolers' social interactions during child-initiated play: Is parallel-aware play a bidirectional bridge to other play states? *Early Childhood Research Quarterly, 18*, 3–21.

Robinson, S., Goddard, L., Dritschel, B., Wisley, M., & Howlin, P. (2009). Executive functions in children with autism spectrum disorders. *Brain and Cognition, 71*, 362–368.

Robinson-Zañartu, C., & Carlson, J. (2013). Dynamic assessment. In K. F. Geisinger (Ed.), *APA handbook of testing and assessment in psychology: Vol. 3. Testing and assessment in school psychology and education* (pp. 149–168). Washington, DC: American Psychological Association.

Roca, A., Carcia-Esteve, L., Imaz, M. L., Torres, A., Hernández, S., & Botet, F. (2011). Obstetrical and neonatal outcomes after prenatal exposure to selective serotonin reuptake inhibitors: The relevance of dose. *Journal of Affective Disorders, 135*, 208–215.

Rochat, P. (1989). Object manipulation and exploration in 2- to 5-month-old infants. *Developmental Psychology, 25*, 871–884.

Rochat, P. (1998). Self-perception and action in infancy. *Experimental Brain Research, 123*, 102–109.

Rochat, P. (2001). *The infant's world*. Cambridge, MA: Harvard University Press.

Rochat, P. (2013). Self-conceptualizing in development. In P. Zelazo (Ed.), *Oxford handbook of developmental psychology* (Vol. 2, pp. 378–397). New York: Oxford University Press.

Rochat, P., & Goubet, N. (1995). Development of sitting and reaching in 5- to 6-month-old infants. *Infant Behavior and Development, 18*, 53–68.

Rochat, P., & Hespos, S. J. (1997). Differential rooting responses by neonates: Evidence for an early sense of self. *Early Development and Parenting, 6*, 105–112.

Rochat, P., & Striano, T. (2002). Who's in the mirror? Self–other discrimination in specular images by four- and nine-month-old infants. *Child Development, 73*, 35–46.

Rodgers, J. L., Cleveland, H. H., van den Oord, E., & Rowe, D. C. (2000). Resolving the debate over birth order, family size, and intelligence. *American Psychologist, 55*, 599–612.

Rodgers, J. L., & Wänström, L. (2007). Identification of a Flynn effect in the NLSY: Moving from the center to the boundaries. *Intelligence, 35*, 187–196.

Rodkin, P. C., Farmer, T. W., Pearl, R., & Van Acker, R. (2006). They're cool: Social status and peer group supports for aggressive boys and girls. *Social Development, 15*, 175–204.

Rodriguez, E. M., Dunn, M. J., & Compas, B. E. (2012). Cancer-related sources of stress for children with cancer and their parents. *Journal of Pediatric Psychology, 37*, 185–197.

Roelfsema, N. M., Hop, W. C., Boito, S. M., & Wladimiroff, J. W. (2004). Three-dimensional sonographic measurement of normal fetal brain volume during the second half of pregnancy. *American Journal of Obstetrics and Gynecology, 190*, 275–280.

Rogan, W. J., Dietrich, K. N., Ware, J. H., Dockery, D. W., Salganik, M., & Radcliffe, J. (2001). The effect of chelation therapy with succimer on neuropsychological development in children exposed to lead. *New England Journal of Medicine, 344*, 1421–1426.

Rogers, J. M. (2009). Tobacco and pregnancy. *Reproductive Toxicology, 28*, 152–160.

Rogoff, B. (1996). Developmental transitions in children's participation in sociocultural activities. In A. J. Sameroff & M. M. Haith (Eds.), *The five to seven year shift: The age of reason and responsibility* (pp. 273–294). Chicago: University of Chicago Press.

Rogoff, B. (1998). Cognition as a collaborative process. In D. Kuhn & R. S. Siegler (Eds.), *Handbook of child psychology: Vol. 2. Cognition, perception, and language* (5th ed., pp. 679–744). New York: Wiley.

Rogoff, B. (2003). *The cultural nature of human development*. New York: Oxford University Press.

Rogoff, B., Correa-Chavez, M., & Silva, K.G. (2011). Cultural variation in children's attention and learning. In M. A. Gernsbacher, R. W. Pew, L. M. Hough, & J. R. Pomerantz (Eds.), *Psychology and the real world: Essays illustrating fundamental contributions to society* (pp. 154–163). New York: Worth.

Rogoff, B., Malkin, C., & Gilbride, K. (1984). Interaction with babies as guidance in development. In B. Rogoff & J. V. Wertsch (Eds.), *Children's learning in the "zone of proximal development"* (New directions for child development, No. 23, pp. 31–44). San Francisco: Jossey-Bass.

Rogoff, B., & Waddell, K. J. (1982). Memory for information organized in a scene by children from two cultures. *Child Development, 53*, 1224–1228.

Rohner, R. P., & Veneziano, R. A. (2001). The importance of father love: History and contemporary evidence. *Review of General Psychology, 5*, 382–405.

Roid, G. (2003). *The Stanford-Binet Intelligence Scales, Fifth Edition, interpretive manual*. Itasca, IL: Riverside Publishing.

Roid, G. H., & Pomplun, M. (2012). The Stanford-Binet Intelligence Scales, Fifth Edition. In D. P. Flanagan & P. L. Harrison (Eds.), *Contemporary intellectual assessment: Theories, tests and issues* (pp. 249–268). New York: Guilford.

Roisman, G. I., & Fraley, R. C. (2006). The limits of genetic influence: A behavior-genetic analysis of infant–caregiver relationship quality and temperament. *Child Development, 77*, 1656–1667.

Roisman, G. I., & Fraley, R. C. (2008). Behavior-genetic study of parenting quality, infant-attachment security, and their covariation in a nationally representative sample. *Developmental Psychology, 44*, 831–839.

Romano, A. M., & Lothian, J. A. (2008). Promoting, protecting, and supporting normal birth: A look at the evidence. *Journal of Obstetric, Gynecologic, and Neonatal Nursing, 37*, 94–104.

Roman-Rodriguez, C. F., Toussaint, T., Sherlock, D. J., Fogel, J., & Hsu, C-D. (2014). Preemptive penile ring block with sucrose analgesia reduces pain response to neonatal circumcision. *Urology, 83*, 893–898.

Rome-Flanders, T., & Cronk, C. (1995). A longitudinal study of infant vocalizations during mother–infant games. *Journal of Child Language, 22*, 259–274.

Ronald, A., & Hoekstra, R. (2014). Progress in understanding the causes of autism spectrum disorders and autistic traits: Twin studies from 1977 to the present day. In S. H. Rhee & A. Ronald (Eds.), *Advances in Behavior Genetics* (Vol. 2, pp. 33–65). New York: Springer.

Rönnqvist, L., & Domellöf, E. (2006). Quantitative assessment of right and left reaching movements in infants: A longitudinal study from 6 to 36 months. *Developmental Psychobiology, 48*, 444–459.

Rönnqvist, L., & Hopkins, B. (1998). Head position preference in the human newborn: A new look. *Child Development, 69*, 13–23.

Roopnarine, J. L., & Evans, M. E. (2007). Family structural organization, mother–child and father–child relationships and psychological outcomes in English-speaking African Caribbean and Indo Caribbean families. In M. Sutherland (Ed.), *Psychology of development in the Caribbean*. Kingston, Jamaica: Ian Randle.

Roopnarine, J. L., Hossain, Z., Gill, P., & Brophy, H. (1994). Play in the East Indian context. In J. L. Roopnarine, J. E. Johnson, & F. H. Hooper (Eds.), *Children's play in diverse cultures* (pp. 9–30). Albany: SUNY Press.

Roopnarine, J. L., Krishnakumar, A., Metindogan, A., & Evans, M. (2006). Links between parenting styles, parent–child academic interaction, parent–school interaction, and early academic skills and social behaviors in young children of English-speaking Caribbean immigrants. *Early Childhood Research Quarterly, 21*, 238–252.

Roopnarine, J. L., Talukder, E., Jain, D., Joshi, P., & Srivastav, P. (1990). Characteristics of holding, patterns of play, and social behaviors between parents and infants in New Delhi, India. *Developmental Psychology, 26*, 667–673.

Rosander, K., & von Hofsten, C. (2004). Infants' emerging ability to represent occluded object motion. *Cognition, 91*, 1–22.

Rosander, K., & von Hofsten, C. (2011). Predictive gaze shifts elicited during observed and performed action in 10-month-old infants and adults. *Neuropsychologia, 49*, 2911–2917.

Rose, A. J., Swenson, L. P., & Waller, E. M. (2004). Overt and relational aggression and perceived popularity: Developmental differences in concurrent and prospective relations. *Developmental Psychology, 40*, 378–387.

Rose, L. (2000). Fathers of full-term infants. In N. Tracey (Ed.), *Parents of premature infants: Their emotional world* (pp. 105–116). London: Whurr.

Rose, S. A., Feldman, J. F., & Jankowski, J. J. (2001a). Attention and recognition memory in the 1st year of life: A longitudinal study of preterm and full-term infants. *Developmental Psychology, 37*, 135–151.

Rose, S. A., Feldman, J. F., & Jankowski, J. J. (2001b). Visual short-term memory in the first year of life: Capacity and recency effects. *Developmental Psychology, 37*, 539–549.

Rose, S. A., Feldman, J. F., Jankowski, J. J., & Van Rossem, R. (2011). The structure of memory in infants and toddlers: An SEM study with full-terms and preterms. *Developmental Science, 14*, 83–91.

Rose, S. A., Jankowski, J. J., & Senior, G. J. (1997). Infants' recognition of contour-deleted figures. *Journal of Experimental Psychology: Human Perception and Performance, 23*, 1206–1216.

Roseberry, S., Hirsh-Pasek, K., & Golinkoff, R. M. (2014). Skype me! Socially contingent interactions help toddlers learn language. *Child Development, 85*, 956–970.

Roseberry, S., Hirsh-Pasek, K., Parish-Morris, J., & Golinkoff, R. M. (2009). Live action: Can young children learn verbs from video? *Child Development, 80*, 1360–1375.

Rosen, A. B., & Rozin, P. (1993). Now you see it, now you don't: The preschool child's conception of invisible particles in the context of dissolving. *Developmental Psychology, 29*, 300–311.

Rosen, C. S., & Cohen, M. (2010). Subgroups of New York City children at high risk of PTSD after the September 11 attacks: A signal detection analysis. *Psychiatric Services, 61*, 64–69.

Rosenbloom, A. L. (2009). Idiopathic short stature: Conundrums of definition and treatment. *International Journal of Pediatric Endocrinology*, Article ID 470378.

Roseth, C. J., Pellegrini, A. D., Bohn, C. M., van Ryzin, M., & Vance, N. (2007). Preschoolers' aggression, affiliation, and social dominance relationships: An observational, longitudinal study. *Journal of School Psychology, 45,* 479–497.

Roskos, K. A., & Christie, J. F. (2013). Gaining ground in understanding the play–literacy relationship. *American Journal of Play, 6,* 82–97.

Ross, H. S., Conant, C., Cheyne, J. A., & Alevizos, E. (1992). Relationships and alliances in the social interactions of kibbutz toddlers. *Social Development, 1,* 1–17.

Ross, J. L., Roeltgen, D. P., Kushner, H., Zinn, A. R., Reiss, A., Bardsley, M. Z., et al. (2012). Behavioral and social phenotypes in boys with 47, XYY syndrome or 47, XXY Klinefelter syndrome. *Pediatrics, 129,* 769–778.

Ross, N., Medin, D. L., Coley, J. D., & Atran, S. (2003). Cultural and experiential differences in the development of folkbiological induction. *Cognitive Development, 18,* 25–47.

Rossi, B. V. (2014). Donor insemination. In J. M. Goldfarb (Ed.), *Third-party reproduction* (pp. 133–142). New York: Springer.

Ross-Sheehy, S., Oakes, L. M., & Luck, S. J. (2003). The development of visual short-term memory capacity in infants. *Child Development, 74,* 1807–1822.

Rothbart, M. K., (2011). *Becoming who we are: Temperament and personality in development.* New York: Guilford.

Rothbart, M. K. (2003). Temperament and the pursuit of an integrated developmental psychology. *Merrill-Palmer Quarterly, 50,* 492–505.

Rothbart, M. K., Ahadi, S. A., & Evans, D. E. (2000). Temperament and personality: Origins and outcome. *Journal of Personality and Social Psychology, 78,* 122–135.

Rothbart, M. K., & Bates, J. E. (2006). Temperament. In N. Eisenberg (Ed.), *Handbook of child psychology: Vol. 3. Social, emotional, and personality development* (6th ed., pp. 99–166). Hoboken, NJ: Wiley.

Rothbart, M. K., Posner, M. I., & Kieras, J. (2006). Temperament, attention, and the development of self-regulation. In K. McCartney & D. Phillips (Eds.), *Blackwell handbook of early childhood development* (pp. 338–357). Malden, MA: Blackwell.

Rothbaum, F., Kakinuma, M., Nagaoka, R., & Azuma, H. (2007). Attachment and *amae:* Parent–child closeness in the United States and Japan. *Journal of Cross-Cultural Psychology, 38,* 465–486.

Rothbaum, F., Weisz, J., Pott, M., Miyake, K., & Morelli, G. (2000). Attachment and culture: Security in the United States and Japan. *American Psychologist, 55,* 1093–1104.

Rouselle, L., Palmers, E., & Noël, M.-P. (2004). Magnitude comparison in preschoolers: What counts? Influence of perceptual variables. *Journal of Experimental Child Psychology, 87,* 57–84.

Rovee-Collier, C. (1999). The development of infant memory. *Current Directions in Psychological Science, 8,* 80–85.

Rovee-Collier, C., & Barr, R. (2001). Infant learning and memory. In G. Bremner & A. Fogel (Eds.), *Blackwell handbook of infant development* (pp. 139–168). Oxford, UK: Blackwell.

Rovee-Collier, C., & Bhatt, R. S. (1993). Evidence of long-term memory in infancy. *Annals of Child Development, 9,* 1–45.

Rovee-Collier, C., & Cuevas, K. (2009). Multiple memory systems are unnecessary to account for infant memory development: An ecological model. *Developmental Psychology, 45,* 160–174.

Rovers, M. M., Numans, M. E., Langenbach, E., Grobbee, D. E., et al. (2008). Is pacifier use a risk factor for acute otitis media? A dynamic cohort study. *Family Practice, 25,* 233–236.

Rowe, M. L. (2008). Child-directed speech: Relation to socioeconomic status, knowledge of child development and child vocabulary skill. *Journal of Child Language, 35,* 185–205.

Rowe, M. L., & Goldin-Meadow, S. (2009a). Differences in early gesture explain SES disparities in child vocabulary size at school entry. *Science, 323,* 951–953.

Rowe, M. L., & Goldin-Meadow, S. (2009b). Early gesture selectively predicts later language learning. *Developmental Science, 12,* 182–187.

Rowe, M. L., Raudenbush, S. W., & Goldin-Meadow, S. (2012). The pace of vocabulary growth helps predict later vocabulary skill. *Child Development, 83,* 508–525.

Rowe, R., Maughan, B., & Goodman, R. (2004). Childhood psychiatric disorder and unintentional injury: Findings from a national cohort study. *Journal of Pediatric Psychology, 29,* 119–130.

Rowland, C. F. (2007). Explaining errors in children's questions. *Cognition, 104,* 106–134.

Rowland, C. F., & Pine, J. M. (2000). Subject-auxiliary inversion errors and wh-question acquisition: "What children do know?" *Journal of Child Language, 27,* 157–181.

Rowley, S. J., Kurtz-Costes, B., Mistry, R., & Feagans, L. (2007). Social status as a predictor of race and gender stereotypes in late childhood and early adolescence. *Social Development, 16,* 150–168.

Rubin, D. M., O'Reilly, A. L., Luan, X., Dai, D., Localio, A. R., et al. (2011). Variation in pregnancy outcomes following statewide implementation of a prenatal home visitation program. *Archives of Pediatrics and Adolescent Medicine, 165,* 198–204.

Rubin, K. H., Begle, A. S., & McDonald, K. L. (2012). Peer relations and social competence in childhood. In V. Anderson & M. H. Beauchamp (Eds.), *Developmental social neuroscience and childhood brain insult: Theory and practice* (pp. 23–44). New York: Guilford.

Rubin, K. H., Bowker, J. C., McDonald, K. L., & Menzer, M. (2013). Peer relationships in childhood. In P. D. Zelazo (Ed.), *Oxford handbook of developmental psychology, Vol. 2: Self and other* (pp. 242–275). New York: Oxford University Press.

Rubin, K. H., Bukowski, W. M., & Parker, J. G. (2006). Peer interactions, relationships, and groups. In N. Eisenberg (Ed.), *Handbook of child psychology: Vol. 3. Social, emotional, and personality development* (6th ed., pp. 571–645). Hoboken, NJ: Wiley.

Rubin, K. H., & Burgess, K. (2002). Parents of aggressive and withdrawn children. In M. Bornstein (Ed.), *Handbook of parenting* (2nd ed., pp. 383–418). Hillsdale, NJ: Erlbaum.

Rubin, K. H., Burgess, K. B., & Hastings, P. D. (2002). Stability and social-behavioral consequences of toddlers' inhibited temperament and parenting behaviors. *Child Development, 73,* 483–495.

Rubin, K. H., Coplan, R., Chen, X., Bowker, J., & McDonald, K. L. (2011). Peer relationships in childhood. In M. E. Lamb & M. H. Bornstein (Eds.), *Social and personality development: An advanced textbook* (pp. 309–360). New York: Psychology Press.

Rubin, K. H., Fein, G. G., & Vandenberg, B. (1983). Play. In E. M. Hetherington (Ed.), *Handbook of child psychology: Vol. 4. Socialization, personality, and social development* (4th ed., pp. 693–744). New York: Wiley.

Rubin, K. H., Stewart, S. L., & Coplan, R. J. (1995). Social withdrawal in childhood: Conceptual and empirical perspectives. In T. H. Ollendick & R. J. Prinz (Eds.), *Advances in clinical child psychology* (Vol. 17, pp. 157–196). New York: Plenum.

Rubin, K. H., Watson, K. S., & Jambor, T. W. (1978). Free-play behaviors in preschool and kindergarten children. *Child Development, 49,* 539–536.

Ruble, D. N., Alvarez, J., Bachman, M., Cameron, J., Fuligni, A., Garcia Coll, C. T., & Rhee, E. (2004). The development of a sense of "we": The emergence and implications of children's collective identity. In M. Bennett & F. Sani (Eds.), *The development of the social self* (pp. 29–76). Hove, UK: Psychology Press.

Ruble, D. N., Martin, C. L., & Berenbaum, S. A. (2006). Gender development. In N. Eisenberg (Ed.), *Handbook of child psychology: Vol. 3. Social, emotional, and personality development* (6th ed., pp. 858–932). Hoboken, NJ: Wiley.

Ruble, D. N., Taylor, L. J., Cyphers, L., Greulich, F. K., Lurye, L. E., & Shrout, P. E. (2007). The role of gender constancy in early gender development. *Child Development, 78,* 1121–1136.

Ruff, C. (2002). Variation in human body size and shape. *Annual Review of Anthropology, 31,* 211–232.

Ruff, H. A., & Capozzoli, M. C. (2003). Development of attention and distractibility in the first 4 years of life. *Developmental Psychology, 39,* 877–890.

Ruffman, T., & Langman, L. (2002). Infants' reaching in a multi-well A not B task. *Infant Behavior and Development, 25,* 237–246.

Ruffman, T., Slade, L., Devitt, K., & Crowe, E. (2006). What mothers say and what they do: The relation between parenting, theory of mind, language, and conflict/cooperation. *British Journal of Developmental Psychology, 24,* 105–124.

Runco, M. A. (1992). Children's divergent thinking and creative ideation. *Developmental Review, 12,* 233–264.

Rushton, J. P. (2012). No narrowing in mean black–white IQ differences—Predicted by heritable g. *American Psychologist, 67,* 500–501.

Rushton, J. P., & Jensen, A. R. (2006). The totality of available evidence shows the race IQ gap still remains. *Psychological Science, 17,* 921–922.

Rushton, J. P., & Jensen, A. R. (2010). The rise and fall of the Flynn effect as a reason to expect a narrowing of the black–white IQ gap. *Intelligence, 38,* 213–219.

Russell, A., Mize, J., & Bissaker, K. (2004). Parent–child relationships. In P. K. Smith & C. H. Hart (Eds.), *Blackwell handbook of childhood social development* (pp. 204–222). Malden, MA: Blackwell.

Russell, J., Alexis, D., & Clayton, N. S. (2010). Episodic future thinking in 3- to 5-year-old children: The ability to think of what will be needed from a different point of view. *Cognition, 114,* 56–71.

Russell, S. T., & Muraco, J. A. (2013). Representative data sets to study LGBT-parent families. In A. E. Goldberg & K. R. Allen (Eds.), *LGBT-parent families: Innovations in research and implications for practice* (pp. 343–356). New York: Springer.

Russo, A., Semeraro, F., Romano, M. R., Mastropasqua, R., Dell'Omo, R., & Costagliola, C. (2014). Myopia onset and progression: Can it be prevented? *International Ophthalmology, 34,* 693–705.

Rust, J., Golombok, S., Hines, M., Johnston, K., Golding, J., & the ALSPAC Study Team. (2000). The role of brothers and sisters in the gender development of preschool children. *Journal of Experimental Child Psychology, 77,* 292–303.

Ruthsatz, J., & Urbach, J. B. (2012). Child prodigy: A novel cognitive profile places elevated general intelligence, exceptional working memory and attention to detail at the root of prodigiousness. *Intelligence, 40,* 419–426.

Rutland, A., Killen, M., & Abrams, D. (2010). A new social-cognitive developmental perspective on prejudice: The interplay between morality and group identity. *Perspectives on Psychological Science, 5,* 279–291.

Rutter, M. (2007). Gene–environment interdependence. *Developmental Science, 10,* 12–18.

Rutter, M. (2011). Biological and experiential influences on psychological development. In D. P. Keating (Ed.), *Nature and nurture in early child development* (pp. 7–44). New York: Cambridge University Press.

Rutter, M., Colvert, E., Kreppner, J., Beckett, C., Castle, J., & Groothues, C. (2007). Early adolescent outcomes for institutionally deprived and non-deprived adoptees. I: Disinhibited attachment. *Journal of Child Psychology and Psychiatry, 48,* 17–30.

Rutter, M., & the English and Romanian Adoptees Study Team. (1998). Developmental catch-up, and deficit, following adoption after severe global early privation. *Journal of Child Psychology and Psychiatry, 39,* 465–476.

Rutter, M., O'Connor, T. G., & the English and Romanian Adoptees Study Team. (2004). Are there biological programming effects for psychological development? Findings from a study of Romanian adoptees. *Developmental Psychology, 40,* 81–94.

Rutter, M., Pickles, A., Murray, R., & Eaves, L. (2001). Testing hypotheses on specific environmental causal effects on behavior. *Psychological Bulletin, 127,* 291–324.

Rutter, M., Sonuga-Barke, E. J., Beckett, C., Castle, J., Kreppner, J., Kumsta, R., et al. (2010). Deprivation-specific psychological patterns: Effects of institutional deprivation. *Monographs of the Society for Research in Child Development, 75*(1, Serial No. 295).

Ryan, R. M., Fauth, R. C., & Brooks-Gunn, J. (2006). Childhood poverty: Implications for school readiness and early childhood education In B. Spodek & O. N. Saracho (Eds.), *Handbook of research on the education of young children* (2nd ed., pp. 323–346). Mahwah, NJ: Erlbaum.

Ryding, M., Konradsson, K., Kalm, O., & Prellner, K. (2002). Auditory consequences of recurrent acute purulent otitis media. *Annals of Otology, Rhinology, and Laryngology, 111* (3, Pt. 1), 261–266.

S

Saarni, C. (2000). Emotional competence: A developmental perspective. In R. Bar-On & J. D. A. Parker (Eds.), *Handbook of emotional intelligence* (pp. 68–91). San Francisco: Jossey-Bass.

Saarni, C., Campos, J. J., Camras, L. A., & Witherington, D. (2006). Emotional development: Action, communication, and understanding. In N. Eisenberg (Ed.), *Handbook of child psychology: Vol. 3. Social, emotional, and personality development* (6th ed., pp. 226–299). Hoboken, NJ: Wiley.

Sabo, D. and Veliz, P. (2011). *Progress without equity: The provision of high school athletic opportunity in the United States, by gender 1993–94 through 2005–06*. East Meadow, NY: Women's Sports Foundation.

Sadeh, A. (1997). Sleep and melatonin in infants: A preliminary study. *Sleep, 20,* 185–191.

Sadeh, A., Flint-Ofir, E., Tirosh, T., & Tikotzky, L. (2007). Infant sleep and parental sleep-related cognitions. *Journal of Family Psychology, 21,* 74–87.

Sadler, T. W. (2010). *Langman's medical embryology* (11th ed.). Baltimore, MD: Lippincott Williams & Wilkins.

Saenger, P. (2003). Dose effects of growth hormone during puberty. *Hormone Research, 60*(Suppl. 1), 52–57.

Safe Kids Worldwide. (2008). *Report to the nation: Trends in unintentional childhood injury mortality and parental views on child safety.* Retrieved from www.safekids.org/research-report/report-nation-trends-unintentional-childhood-injury-mortality-and-parental-views

Safe Kids Worldwide (2011). *A look inside American family vehicles: National study of 79,000 car seats, 2009–2010.* Retrieved from www.safekids.org/research-report/look-inside-american-family-vehicles-national-study-79000-car-seats-2009-2010

Safe Kids Worldwide. (2013). *Overview of childhood injury morbidity and mortality in the U.S. Fact Sheet.* Retrieved from www.safekids.org/fact-sheet/overview-childhood-injury-morbidity-and-mortality-us-fact-sheet-pdf

Saffran, J. R. (2009). What can statistical learning tell us about infant learning? In A. Woodward & A. Needham (Eds.), *Learning and the infant mind* (pp. 29–48). New York: Oxford University Press.

Saffran, J. R., Aslin, R. N., & Newport, E. L. (1996). Statistical learning by 8-month-old infants. *Science, 27,* 1926–1928.

Saffran, J. R., & Thiessen, E. D. (2003). Pattern induction by infant language learners. *Developmental Psychology, 39,* 484–494.

Saffran, J. R., Werker, J. F., & Werner, L. A. (2006). The infant's auditory world: Hearing, speech, and the beginnings of language. In D. Kuhn & R. Siegler (Eds.), *Handbook of child psychology: Vol. 2. Cognition, perception, and language* (6th ed., pp. 58–108). Hoboken, NJ: Wiley.

Saigal, S., Stoskopf, B., Streiner, D., Boyle, M., Pinelli, J., & Paneth, N. (2006). Transition of extremely low-birthweight infants from adolescence to young adulthood. *Journal of the American Medical Association, 295,* 667–675.

Saitta, S. C., & Zackai, E. H. (2005). Specific chromosome disorders in newborns. In H. W. Taeusch, R. A. Ballard, & C. A. Gleason (Eds.), *Avery's diseases of the newborn* (8th ed., pp. 204–215). Philadelphia: Saunders.

Sale, A., Berardi, N., & Maffei, L. (2009). Enrich the environment to empower the brain. *Trends in Neurosciences, 32,* 233–239.

Salihu, H. M., Shumpert, M. N., Slay, M., Kirby, R. S., & Alexander, G. R. (2003). Childbearing beyond maternal age 50 and fetal outcomes in the United States. *Obstetrics and Gynecology, 102,* 1006–1014.

Salisbury, A. L., Ponder, K. L., Padbury, J. F., & Lester, B. M. (2009). Fetal effects of psychoactive drugs. *Clinics in Perinatology, 36,* 595–619.

Salley, B. J., & Dixon, W. E., Jr. (2007). Temperamental and joint attentional predictors of language development. *Merrill-Palmer Quarterly, 53,* 131–154.

Salmivalli, C., & Voeten, M. (2004). Connections between attitudes, group norms, and behaviour in bullying situations. *International Journal of Behavioral Development, 28,* 246–258.

Salomo, D., & Liszkowski, U. (2013). Sociocultural settings influence the emergence of prelinguistic deictic gestures. *Child Development, 84,* 1296–1307.

Salter, D., McMillan, D., Richards, M., Talbot, T., Hodges, J., Bentovim, A., & Hastings, R. (2003). Development of sexually abusive behavior in sexually victimized males: A longitudinal study. *Lancet, 361,* 471–476.

Sameroff, A. (2006). Identifying risk and protective factors for healthy child development. In A. Clarke-Stewart & J. Dunn (Eds.), *Families count: Effects on child and adolescent development* (pp. 53–76). New York: Cambridge University Press.

Sanders, O. (2006). Evaluating the Keeping Ourselves Safe Programme. Wellington, NZ: Youth Education Service, New Zealand Police. Retrieved from www.nzfvc.org.nz/accan/papers-presentations/abstract11v.shtml

Sann, C., & Streri, A. (2007). Perception of object shape and texture in human newborns: Evidence from cross-modal transfer tasks. *Developmental Science, 10,* 399–410.

Sann, C., & Streri, A. (2008). The limits of newborn's grasping to detect texture in a cross-modal transfer task. *Infant Behavior and Development, 31,* 523–531.

Sansavini, A., Bertoncini, J., & Giovanelli, G. (1997). Newborns discriminate the rhythm of multisyllabic stressed words. *Developmental Psychology, 33,* 3–11.

Sarnecka, B. W., & Gelman, S. A. (2004). Six does not just mean a lot: Preschoolers see number words as specific. *Cognition, 92,* 329–352.

Sarnecka, B. W., & Wright, C. E. (2013). The idea of an exact number: Children's understanding of cardinality and equinumerosity. *Cognitive Science, 37,* 1493–1506.

Sato, T., Matsumoto, T., Kawano, H., Watanabe, T., Uematsu, Y., & Semine, K. (2004). Brain masculinization requires androgen receptor function. *Proceedings of the National Academy of Sciences, 101,* 1673–1678.

Saucier, J. F., Sylvestre, R., Doucet, H., Lambert, J., Frappier, J. Y., Charbonneau, L., & Malus, M. (2002). Cultural identity and adaptation to adolescence in Montreal. In F. J. C. Azima & N. Grizenko (Eds.), *Immigrant and refugee children and their families: Clinical, research, and training issues* (pp. 133–154). Madison, WI: International Universities Press.

Saudino, K. J. (2003). Parent ratings of infant temperament: Lessons from twin studies. *Infant Behavior and Development, 26,* 100–107.

Saudino, K. J., & Plomin, R. (1997). Cognitive and temperamental mediators of genetic contributions to the home environment during infancy. *Merrill-Palmer Quarterly, 43,* 1–23.

Saxe, G. B. (1988, August–September). Candy selling and math learning. *Educational Researcher, 17*(6), 14–21.

Saxton, M., Backley, P., & Gallaway, C. (2005). Negative input for grammatical errors: Effects after a lag of 12 weeks. *Journal of Child Language, 32,* 643–672.

Sayfan, L., & Lagatutta, K. H. (2009). Scaring the monster away: What children know about managing fears of real and imaginary creatures. *Child Development, 80,* 1756–1774.

Saygin, A. P., Leech, R., & Dick, F. (2010). Nonverbal auditory agnosia with lesion to Wernicke's area. *Neuropsychologia, 48,* 107–113.

Saygin, A. P., Wilson, S. M., Dronkers, N. F., & Bates, E. (2004). Action comprehension in aphasia: Linguistic and non-linguistic deficits and their lesion correlates. *Neuropsychologia, 42,* 1788–1804.

Saylor, M. M. (2004). Twelve- and 16-month-old infants recognize properties of mentioned absent things. *Developmental Science, 7,* 599–611.

Saylor, M. M., Sabbagh, M. A., & Baldwin, D. A. (2002). Children use whole–part juxtaposition as a pragmatic cue to word meaning. *Developmental Psychology, 38,* 993–1003.

Saylor, M. M., & Troseth, G. L. (2006). Preschoolers use information about speakers' desires to learn new words. *Cognitive Development, 21,* 214–231.

Scarr, S., & McCartney, K. (1983). How people make their own environments: A theory of genotype–environment effects. *Child Development, 54,* 424–435.

Scarr, S., & Weinberg, R. A. (1983). The Minnesota adoption studies: Genetic differences and malleability. *Child Development, 54,* 260–267.

Schaal, B., Marlier, L., & Soussignan, R. (2000). Human fetuses learn odours from their pregnant mother's diet. *Chemical Senses, 25,* 729–737.

Schauwers, K., Gillis, S., Daemers, K., De Beukelaer, C., De Ceulaer, G., Yperman, M., & Govaerts, P. J. (2004). Normal hearing and language development in a deaf-born child. *Otology and Neurotology, 25,* 924–929.

Scher, A., Epstein, R., & Tirosh, E. (2004). Stability and changes in sleep regulation: A longitudinal study from 3 months to 3 years. *International Journal of Behavioral Development, 28,* 268–274.

Scher, A., Tirosh, E., Jaffe, M., Rubin, L., Sadeh, A., & Lavie, P. (1995). Sleep patterns of infants and young children in Israel. *International Journal of Behavioral Development, 18,* 701–711.

Scherrer, J. L. (2012). The United Nations Convention on the Rights of the Child as policy and strategy for social work action in child welfare in the United States. *Social Work, 57,* 11–22.

Schlaggar, B. L., & Barnes, K. A. (2011). Developmental cognitive neuroscience: Infancy to young adulthood. In K. L. Fingerman, C. A. Berg, J. Smith, & T. C. Antonucci (Eds.), *Handbook of life-span development* (pp. 363–385). New York: Springer.

Schlagmüller, M., & Schneider, W. (2002). The development of organizational strategies in children: Evidence from a microgenetic longitudinal study. *Journal of Experimental Child Psychology, 81,* 298–319.

Schmid, R. G., Tirsch, W. S., & Scherb, H. (2002). Correlation between spectral EEG parameters and intelligence test variables in school-age children. *Clinical Neurophysiology, 113,* 1647–1656.

Schmidt, A. T., Waldow, K. J., Grove, W. M., Salinas, J. A., & Georgieff, M. K. (2007). Dissociating the long-term effects of fetal/neonatal iron deficiency on three types of learning in the rat. *Behavioral Neuroscience, 121,* 475–482.

Schmidt, L. A., Fox, N. A., Rubin, K. H., Sternberg, E. M., Gold, P. W., & Smith, C. C. (1997). Behavioral and neuroendocrine responses in shy children. *Developmental Psychobiology, 35,* 119–135.

Schmidt, L. A., Fox, N. A., Schulkin, J., & Gold, P. W. (1999). Behavioral and psychophysiological correlates of self-presentation in temperamentally shy children. *Developmental Psychobiology, 30,* 127–140.

Schmidt, M. E., Crawley-Davis, A. M., & Anderson, D. R. (2007). Two-year-olds' object retrieval based on television: Testing a perceptual account. *Media Psychology, 9,* 389–409.

Schmidt, S. (2013). *Early Head Start participants, programs, families and staff in 2012.* Washington, DC: CLASP. Retrieved from www.clasp.org/resources-and-publications/files/EHS-PIR-2012-Fact-Sheet.pdf

Schmitz, S., Fulker, D. W., Plomin, R., Zahn-Waxler, C., Emde, R. N., & DeFries, J. C. (1999). Temperament and problem behaviour during early childhood. *International Journal of Behavioral Development, 23,* 333–355.

Schneider, B. H., Atkinson, L., & Tardif, C. (2001). Child–parent attachment and children's peer relations: A quantitative review. *Developmental Psychology, 37,* 86–100.

Schneider, D. (2006). Smart as we can get? *American Scientist, 94,* 311–312.

Schneider, W. (1986). The role of conceptual knowledge and metamemory in the development of organizational processes in memory. *Journal of Experimental Child Psychology, 42,* 218–236.

Schneider, W. (2002). Memory development in childhood. In U. Goswami (Ed.), *Blackwell handbook of childhood cognitive development* (pp. 236–256). Malden, MA: Blackwell.

Schneider, W., & Bjorklund, D. F. (1992). Expertise, aptitude, and strategic remembering. *Child Development, 63,* 461–473.

Schneider, W., & Bjorklund, D. F. (1998). Memory. In D. Kuhn & R. S. Siegler (Eds.), *Handbook of child psychology: Vol. 2. Cognition, perception, and language* (5th ed., pp. 467–521). New York: Wiley.

Schneider, W., & Pressley, M. (1997). *Memory development between two and twenty* (2nd ed.). Mahwah, NJ: Erlbaum.

Schonberg, R. L., & Tifft, C. J. (2007). Birth defects and prenatal diagnosis. In M. L. Batshaw, L. Pellegrino, & N. J. Roizen (Eds.), *Children with disabilities* (6th ed., pp. 83–96). Baltimore: Paul H. Brookes.

Schöner, G., & Thelen, E. (2006). Using dynamic field theory to rethink infant habituation. *Psychological Review, 113,* 273–299.

Schoon, I., Jones, E., Cheng, H., Maughan, B. (2012). Family hardship, family instability, and cognitive development. *Journal of Epidemiology and Community Health, 66,* 716–722.

Schoppe-Sullivan, S. J., Brown, G. L., Cannon, E. A., Mangelsdorf, S. C., & Sokolowski, M. S. (2008). Maternal gatekeeping, coparenting quality, and fathering behavior in families with infants. *Journal of Family Psychology, 22,* 389–398.

Schoppe-Sullivan, S. J., Mangelsdorf, S. C., Brown, G. L., & Sokolowski, M. S. (2007). Goodness-of-fit in family context: Infant temperament, marital quality, and early coparenting behavior. *Infant Behavior and Development, 30,* 82–96.

Schott, J. M., & Rossor, M. N. (2003). The grasp and other primitive reflexes. *Journal of Neurological and Neurosurgical Psychiatry, 74,* 558–560.

Schroeder, R. D., Bulanda, R. E., Giordano, P. C., & Cernkovich, S. A. (2010). Parenting and adult criminality: An examination of direct and indirect effects by race. *Journal of Adolescent Research, 25,* 64–98.

Schuetze, P., & Eiden, R. D. (2006). The association between maternal cocaine use during pregnancy and physiological regulation in 4- to 8-week-old infants: An examination of possible mediators and moderators. *Journal of Pediatric Psychology, 31,* 15–26.

Schull, W. J. (2003). The children of atomic bomb survivors: A synopsis. *Journal of Radiological Protection, 23,* 369–394.

Schulte-Ruther, M., Markowitsch, H. J., Fink, G. R., & Piefke, M. (2007). Mirror neuron and theory of mind mechanisms involved in face-to-face interactions: A functional magnetic resonance imaging approach to empathy. *Journal of Cognitive Neuroscience, 19,* 1354–1372.

Schultz, T. R. (2011). Computational modeling of infant concept learning: The developmental shift from features to correlations. In L. M. Oakes, C. H. Cashon, M. Casasola, & D. Rakison (Eds.), *Infant perception and cognition* (125–152). New York: Oxford University Press.

Schulz, M. S., Cowan, C. P., & Cowan, P. A. (2006). Promoting healthy beginnings: A randomized controlled trial of a preventive intervention to preserve marital quality during the transition to parenthood. *Journal of Consulting and Clinical Psychology, 74,* 20–31.

Schulze, C., Grassmann, S., & Tomasello, M. (2013). 3-year-old children make relevant inferences in indirect verbal communication. *Child Development, 84,* 2079–2093.

Schunemann, N., Sporer, N., & Brunstein, J. C. (2013). Integrating self-regulation in whole-class reciprocal teaching: A moderator–mediator analysis of incremental effects on fifth graders' reading comprehension. *Contemporary Educational Psychology, 38,* 289–305.

Schunk, D. H., & Pajares, F. (2005). Competence perceptions and academic functioning. In A. J. Andrew & C. S. Dweck (Eds.), *Handbook of competence and motivation* (pp. 85–104). New York: Guilford.

Schunk, D. H., & Zimmerman, B. J. (2013). Self-regulation and learning. In W. M. Reynolds, G. E. Miller, & I. B. Weiner (Eds.), *Handbook of psychology: Vol. 7. Educational psychology* (pp. 45–68). Hoboken, NJ: Wiley.

Schwanenflugel, P. J., Henderson, R. L., & Fabricius, W. V. (1998). Developing organization of mental verbs and theory of mind in middle childhood: Evidence from extensions. *Developmental Psychology, 34,* 512–524.

Schwartz, C. E., Kunwar, P. S., Greve, D. N., Kagan, J., Snidman, N. C., & Bloch, R. B. (2012). A phenotype of early infancy predicts reactivity of the amygdala in male adults. *Molecular Psychiatry, 17,* 1042–1050.

Schwarz, N. (1999). Self-reports: How the questions shape the answers. *American Psychologist, 54,* 93–105.

Schwebel, D. C., & Bounds, M. L. (2003). The role of parents and temperament on children's estimation of physical ability: Links to unintentional injury prevention. *Journal of Pediatric Psychology, 28,* 505–516.

Schwebel, D. C., & Brezausek, C. M. (2007). Father transitions in the household and young children's injury risk. *Psychology of Men and Masculinity, 8,* 173–184.

Schwebel, D. C., Brezausek, C. M., Ramey, S. L., & Ramey, C. T. (2004). Interactions between child behavior patterns and parenting: Implications for children's unintentional injury risk. *Journal of Pediatric Psychology, 29,* 93–104.

Schwebel, D. C., & Gaines, J. (2007). Pediatric unintentional injury: Behavioral risk factors and implications for prevention. *Journal of Developmental and Behavioral Pediatrics, 28,* 245–254.

Schwebel, D. C., Roth, D. L., Elliott, M. N., Chien, A. T., Mrug, S., Shipp, E., et al. (2012). Marital conflict and fifth-graders' risk for injury. *Accident Analysis and Prevention, 47,* 30–35.

Schwebel, D. C., Roth, D. L., Elliott, M. N., Windle, M., Grunbaum, J. A., Low, B., et al. (2011). The association of activity level, parent mental distress, and parental involvement and monitoring with unintentional injury risk in fifth graders. *Accident Analysis and Prevention, 43,* 848–852.

Schweinhart, L. J. (2010). The challenge of the High/Scope Perry Preschool study. In A. J. Reynolds, A. J. Rolnick,

M. M. Englund, & J. Temple (Eds.), *Childhood programs and practices in the first decade of life: A human capital integration* (pp. 199–213). New York: Cambridge University Press.

Schweinhart, L. J., Montie, J., Xiang, Z., Barnett, W. S., Belfield, C. R., & Nores, M. (2005). *Lifetime effects: The High/Scope Perry Preschool Study through age 40.* Ypsilanti, MI: High/Scope Press.

Schweizer, K., Moosbrugger, H., & Goldhammer, F. (2006). The structure of the relationship between attention and intelligence. *Intelligence, 33,* 589–611.

Schwenck, C., Bjorklund, D. F., & Schneider, W. (2007). Factors influencing the incidence of utilization deficiencies and other patterns of recall/strategy-use relations in a strategic memory task. *Child Development, 22,* 197–212.

Schwier, C., van Maanen, C., Carpenter, M., & Tomasello, M. (2006). Rational imitation in 12-month-old infants. *Infancy, 10,* 303–311.

Scott, L. S. (2009). *Two is enough.* Berkeley, CA: Seal Press.

Scott, L. S., & Monesson, A. (2009). The origin of biases in face perception. *Psychological Science, 20,* 676–680.

Scott, R. M., & Fisher, C. (2012). 2.5-year-olds use cross-situational consistency to learn verbs under referential uncertainty. *Cognition, 122,* 163–180.

Scrutton, D. (2005). Influence of supine sleeping positioning on early motor milestone acquisition. *Developmental Medicine and Child Neurology, 47,* 364.

Seethaler, P. M., Fuchs, L. S., Fuchs, D., & Compton, D. L. (2012). Predicting first graders' development of calculation versus word-problem performance: The role of dynamic assessment. *Journal of Educational Psychology, 104,* 224–234.

Seibert, A. C., & Kerns, K. A. (2009). Attachment figures in middle childhood. *International Journal of Behavioral Development, 33,* 347–355.

Seidl, A., Hollich, G., & Jusczyk, P. (2003). Early understanding of subject and object wh-questions. *Infancy, 4,* 423–436.

Sekido, R., & Lovell-Badge, R. (2009). Sex determination and SRY: Down to a wink and a nudge? *Trends in Genetics, 25,* 19–29.

Senechal, M., & LeFevre, J. (2002). Parental involvement in the development of children's reading skill: A five-year longitudinal study. *Child Development, 73,* 445–460.

Senghas, R. J., Senghas, A., & Pyers, J. E. (2005). The emergence of Nicaraguan Sign Language: Questions of development, acquisition, and evolution. In J. Langer, S. T. parker, & C. Milbrath (Eds.), *Biology and knowledge revisited: From neurogenesis to psychogenesis* (pp. 287–306). Mahwah, NJ: Erlbaum.

Sengpiel, V., Elind, E., Bacelis, J., Nilsson, S., Grove, J., Myhre, R., et al. (2013). Maternal caffeine intake during pregnancy is associated with birth weight but not with gestational length: Results from a large prospective observational cohort study. *BMC Medicine, 11,* 42.

Senju, A., Csibra, G., & Johnson, M. H. (2008). Understanding the referential nature of looking: Infants' preference for object-directed gaze. *Cognition, 108,* 303–319.

Senn, T. E., Espy, K. A., & Kaufmann, P. M. (2004). Using path analysis to understand executive function organization in preschool children. *Developmental Neuropsychology, 26,* 445–464.

Serbin, L. A., Powlishta, K. K., & Gulko, J. (1993). The development of sex typing in middle childhood. *Monographs of the Society for Research in Child Development, 58*(2, Serial No. 232).

Sermon, K., Van Steirteghem, A., & Liebaers, I. (2004). Preimplantation genetic diagnosis. *Lancet, 363,* 1633–1641.

Serratrice, L. (2013). The bilingual child. In T. K. Bhatia & W. C. Ritchie (Eds.), *Handbook of bilingualism and multilingualism* (pp. 87–108). Chichester, UK: Wiley-Blackwell.

Sesame Workshop. (2014). *Where we work: All locations.* Retrieved from www.sesameworkshop.org/where-we-work/all-locations

Sevigny, P. R., & Loutzenhiser, L. (2010). Predictors of parenting self-efficacy in mothers and fathers of toddlers. *Child Care, Health and Development, 36,* 179–189.

Sewell, A., St George, A., & Cullen, J. (2013). The distinctive features of joint participation in a community of learners. *Teaching and Teacher Education, 31,* 46–55.

Seymour, S. C. (1999). *Women, family, and child care in India.* Cambridge, UK: Cambridge University Press.

SFIA (Sports & Fitness Industry Association). (2013). 2013 U.S. trends in team sports report. Retrieved from www.sfia.org/reports/305

Shah, T., Sullivan, K., & Carter, J. (2006). Sudden infant death syndrome and reported maternal smoking during pregnancy. *American Journal of Public Health, 96,* 1757–1759.

Shahaeian, A., Peterson, C. C., Slaughter, V., & Wellman, H. M. (2011). Culture and the sequence of steps in theory of mind development. *Developmental Psychology, 47,* 1239–1247.

Shapka, J. D., & Keating, D. P. (2005). Structure and change in self-concept during adolescence. *Canadian Journal of Behavioural Science, 37,* 83–96.

Shaw, D. S., Lacourse, E., & Nagin, D. S. (2005). Developmental trajectories of conduct problems and hyperactivity from ages 2 to 10. *Journal of Child Psychology and Psychiatry, 46,* 931–942.

Shaw, D. S., Winslow, E. B., & Flanagan, C. (1999). A prospective study of the effects of marital status and family relations on young children's adjustment among African-American and European-American families. *Child Development, 70,* 742–755.

Shaw, P., Brierley, B., & David, A. S. (2005). A critical period for the impact of amygdala damage on the emotional enhancement of memory? *Neurology, 65,* 326–328.

Shaw, P., Eckstrand, K., Sharp, W., Blumenthal, J., Lerch, J. P., & Greenstein, D. (2007, November 16). Attention-deficit/hyperactivity disorder is characterized by a delay in cortical maturation. *Proceedings of the National Academy of Sciences Online.* Retrieved from www.pnas.org/cgi/content/abstract/0707741104v1

Sheehan, G., Darlington, Y., Noller, P., & Feeney, J. (2004). Children's perceptions of their sibling relationships during parental separation and divorce. *Journal of Divorce and Remarriage, 41,* 69–94.

Sherman, S. L., Freeman, S. B., Allen, E. G., & Lamb, N. E. (2005). Risk factors for nondisjunction of trisomy 21. *Cytogenetic Genome Research, 111,* 273–280.

Sherry, B., McDivitt, J., Brich, L. L., Cook, F. H., Sanders, S., Prish, J. L., Francis, L. A., & Scanlon, K. S. (2004). Attitudes, practices, and concerns about child feeding and child weight status among socioeconomically diverse white, Hispanic, and African-American mothers. *Journal of the American Dietetic Association, 104,* 215–221.

Shimada, S., & Hiraki, K. (2006). Infant's brain responses to live and televised action. *NeuroImage, 32,* 930–939.

Shipman, K. L., Zeman, J., Nesin, A. E., & Fitzgerald, M. (2003). Children's strategies for displaying anger and sadness: What works with whom? *Merrill-Palmer Quarterly, 49,* 100–122.

Shonkoff, J. P., & Bales, S. N. (2011). Science does not speak for itself: Translating child development research for the public and its policymakers. *Child Development, 82,* 17–32.

Shriver, L. H., Harrist, A. W., Page, M., Hubbs-Tait, L., Moulton, M., & Topham, G. (2013). Differences in body esteem by weight status, gender, and physical activity among young elementary school-aged children. *Body Image, 10,* 78–84.

Shuwairi, S. M., Albert, M. K., & Johnson, S. P. (2007). Discrimination of possible and impossible objects in infancy. *Psychological Science, 18,* 303–307.

Shwalb, D. W., Nakawaza, J., Yamamoto, T., & Hyun, J.-H. (2004). Fathering in Japanese, Chinese, and Korean cultures: A review of the research literature. In M. E. Lamb (Ed.), *The role of the father in child development* (4th ed., pp. 146–181). Hoboken, NJ: Wiley.

Shweder, R. A., Goodnow, J. J., Hatano, G., LeVine, R. A., Markus, H. R., & Miller, P. J. (2006). The cultural psychology of development: One mind, many mentalities. In R. M. Lerner (Ed.), *Handbook of child psychology: Vol. 1. Theoretical models of human development* (6th ed., pp. 716–792). Hoboken, NJ: Wiley.

Sidappa, A., Georgieff, M. K., Wewerka, S., Worwa, C., Nelson, C. A., & deRegnier, R. (2004). Iron deficiency alters auditory recognition memory in newborn infants of diabetic mothers. *Pediatric Research, 55,* 1034–1041.

Sidebotham, P., Heron, J., & the ALSPAC Study Team. (2003). Child maltreatment in the "children of the nineties": The role of the child. *Child Abuse and Neglect, 27,* 337–352.

Siebert, A. C., & Kerns, K. A. (2009). Attachment figures in middle childhood. *International Journal of Behavioral Development, 33,* 347–355.

Siegal, M., Iozzi, L., & Surian, L. (2009). Bilingualism and conversational understanding in young children. *Cognition, 110,* 115–122.

Siega-Riz, A. M., Deming, D. M., Reidy, K. C., Fox, M. K., Condon, E., & Briefel, R. R. (2010). Food consumption patterns of infants and toddlers: Where are we now? *Journal of the American Dietetic Association, 110,* S38–S51.

Siegler, R. S. (1996). *Emerging minds: The process of change in children's thinking.* New York: Oxford University Press.

Siegler, R. S. (2002). Microgenetic studies of self-explanation. In N. Granott & J. Parziale (Eds.), *Microdevelopment: Transition processes in development and learning* (pp. 31–58). New York: Cambridge University Press.

Siegler, R. S. (2006). Microgenetic analyses of learning. In D. Kuhn & R. Siegler (Eds.), *Handbook of child psychology: Vol. 2. Cognition, perception, and language* (6th ed., pp. 464–510). Hoboken, NJ: Wiley.

Siegler, R. S. (2009). Improving preschoolers' number sense using information-processing theory. In O. A. Barbarin & B. H. Wasik (Eds.), *Handbook of child development and early education: Research to practice* (pp. 429–454). New York: Guilford.

Siegler, R. S., & Crowley, K. (1991). The microgenetic method: A direct means for studying cognitive development. *American Psychologist, 46,* 606–620.

Siegler, R. S., & Mu, Y. (2008). Chinese children excel on novel mathematics problems even before elementary school. *Psychological Science, 19,* 759–763.

Siegler, R. S., & Svetina, M. (2006). What leads children to adopt new strategies? A microgenetic/cross-sectional study of class inclusion. *Child Development, 77,* 997–1015.

Silk, J. S., Sessa, F. M., Morris, A. S., Steinberg, L., & Avenevoli, S. (2004). Neighborhood cohesion as a buffer against hostile maternal parenting. *Journal of Family Psychology, 18,* 135–146.

Silk, T. J., & Wood, A. G. (2011). Lessons about neurodevelopment from anatomical magnetic resonance imaging. *Journal of Developmental and Behavioral Pediatrics, 32,* 158–168.

Silvén, M. (2001). Attention in very young infants predicts learning of first words. *Infant Behavior and Development, 24,* 229–237.

Simcock, G., & DeLoache, J. (2006). Get the picture? The effects of iconicity on toddlers' reenactment from picture books. *Developmental Psychology, 42,* 1352–1357.

Simcock, G., Garrity, K., & Barr, R. (2011). The effect of narrative cues on infants' imitation from television and picture books. *Child Development, 82,* 1607–1619.

Simcock, G., & Hayne, H. (2003). Age-related changes in verbal and nonverbal memory during early childhood. *Developmental Psychology, 39,* 805–814.

Simion, F., Cassia, V. M., Turati, C., & Valenza, E. (2001). The origins of face perception: Specific versus nonspecific mechanisms. *Infant and Child Development, 10,* 59–65.

Simons, L. G., Chen, Y. F., Simons, R. L., Brody, G., & Cutrona, C. (2006). Parenting practices and child adjustment in different types of households: A study of African-American families. *Journal of Family Issues, 27,* 803–825.

Simons, L. G., Simons, R. L., & Su, X. (2013). Consequences of corporal punishment among African Americans: The importance of context and outcome. *Journal of Youth and Adolescence, 42,* 1273–1285.

Simonton, D. K. (2009). Giftedness: The gift that keeps on giving. In T. Balchin, B. Hymer, & D. J. Matthews (Eds.), *The Routledge international companion to gifted education* (pp. 26–31). New York: Routledge.

Simpson, E. A., Varga, K., Frick, J. E., & Fragaszy, D. (2011). Infants experience perceptual narrowing for nonprimate faces. *Infancy, 16,* 318–328.

Simpson, J. A., Rholes, W. S., Campbell, L., Tran, S., & Wilson, C. L. (2003). Adult attachment, the transition to parenthood, and depressive symptoms. *Journal of Personality and Social Psychology, 84,* 1172–1187.

Simpson, K. R. (2011). Clinician's guide to the use of oxytocin for labor induction and augmentation. *Journal of Midwifery and Women's Health, 56,* 214–221.

Singer, D. G., & Singer, J. L. (2005). *Imagination and play in the electronic age.* Cambridge, MA: Harvard University Press.

Singleton, J. L., & Newport, E. L. (2004). When learners surpass their models: The acquisition of American Sign Language from inconsistent input. *Cognitive Psychology, 49,* 370–407.

Sirois, S., & Jackson, I. (2007). Social cognition in infancy: A critical review of research on higherorder abilities. *European Journal of Developmental Psychology, 4,* 46–64.

Sirois, S., & Jackson, I. R. (2012). Pupil dilation and object permanence in infants. *Infancy, 17,* 61–78.

Skinner, E. A., Zimmer-Gembeck, M. J., & Connell, J. P. (1998). Individual differences and the development of perceived control. *Monographs of the Society for Research in Child Development, 63*(2–3, Serial No. 254).

Skipper, Y., & Douglas, K. (2012). Is no praise good praise? Effects of positive feedback on children's and university students' responses to subsequent failures. *British Journal of Educational Psychology, 82,* 327–339.

Slack, K. S., & Yoo, J. (2005). Food hardship and child behavior problems among low-income children. *Social Service Review, 79,* 511–536.

Slater, A., & Johnson, S. P. (1999). Visual sensory and perceptual abilities of the newborn: Beyond the blooming, buzzing confusion. In A. Slater & S. P. Johnson (Eds.), *The development of sensory, motor and cognitive capacities in early infancy* (pp. 121–141). Hove, UK: Sussex Press.

Slater, A., Quinn, P. C., Kelly, D. J., Lee, K., Longmore, C. A., McDonald, P. R., & Pascalis, O. (2011). The shaping of the face space in early infancy: Becoming a native face processor. *Child Development Perspectives, 4,* 205–211.

Slater, A., Riddell, P., Quinn, P. C., Pascalis, O., Lee, K., & Kelly, D. J. (2010). Visual perception. In J. G. Bremner & T. D. Wachs (Eds.), *Wiley-Blackwell handbook of infant development: Vol. 1. Basic research* (2nd ed., pp. 40–80). Chichester, UK: Wiley-Blackwell.

Slonims, V., & McConachie, H. (2006). Analysis of mother–infant interaction in infants with Down syndrome and typically developing infants. *American Journal of Mental Retardation, 111,* 273–289.

Small, M. (1998). *Our babies, ourselves.* New York: Anchor.

Smart, J., & Hiscock, H. (2007). Early infant crying and sleeping problems: A pilot study of impact on parental well-being and parent-endorsed strategies for management. *Journal of Paediatrics and Child Health, 43,* 284–290.

Smetana, J. G. (2006). Social-cognitive domain theory: Consistencies and variations in children's moral and social judgments. In M. Killen & J. G. Smetana (Eds.), *Handbook of moral development* (pp. 119–154). Mahwah, NJ: Erlbaum.

Smetana, J. G., Rote, W. M., Jambon, M., Tasopoulos-Chan, M., Villalobos, M., & Comer, J. (2012). Developmental changes and individual differences in young children's moral judgments. *Child Development, 83,* 683–696.

Smit, D. J. A., Boersma, M., Schnack, H. G., Micheloyannis, S., Doomsma, D. I., Pol, H. E. H., et al. (2012). The brain matures with stronger functional connectivity and decreased randomness of its network. *PLOS ONE, 7*(5), e36896.

Smith, B. H., Barkley, R. A., & Shapiro, C. J. (2006). Attention-deficit/hyperactivity disorder. In E. J. Mash & R. A. Barkley (Eds.), *Treatment of childhood disorders* (3rd ed., pp. 65–136). New York: Guilford.

Smith, C. L., Calkins, S. D., Keane, S. P., Anastopoulos, A. D., & Shelton, T. L. (2004). Predicting stability and change in toddler behavior problems: Contributions of maternal behavior and child gender. *Developmental Psychology, 40,* 29–42.

Smith, J., & Ross, H. (2007). Training parents to mediate sibling disputes affects children's negotiation and conflict understanding. *Child Development, 78,* 790–805.

Smith, J. P., & Forrester, R. (2013). Who pays for the health benefits of exclusive breastfeeding? An analysis of maternal time costs. *Journal of Human Lactation, 29,* 547–555.

Smith, J. R., Brooks-Gunn, J., Kohen, D., & McCarton, C. (2001). Transitions on and off AFDC: Implications for parenting and children's cognitive development. *Child Development, 72,* 1512–1533.

Smith, L. B., Jones, S. S., Landau, B., Gershkoff-Stowe, L., & Samuelson, L. (2002). Object name learning provides on-the-job training for attention. *Psychological Science, 13,* 13–19.

Smith, P. K., Mahdavi, J., Carvalho, M., Fisher, S., Russell, S., & Tippett, N. (2008). Cyberbullying: Its nature and impact in secondary school pupils. *Journal of Child Psychology and Psychiatry, 49,* 376–385.

Smith, R., Smith, J. I., Shen, X., Engel, P. J., Bowman, M. E., McGrath, S. A., et al. (2009). Patterns of plasma corticotrophin-releasing hormone, progesterone, estradiol and estriol change and the onset of human labor. *Journal of Clinical Endocrinology and Metabolism, 94,* 2066–2074.

Smits, J., & Monden, C. (2011). Twinning across the developing world. *PLOS ONE, 6*(9), e25239.

Smyke, A. T., Zeanah, C. H., Fox, N. A., Nelson, C. A., & Guthrie, D. (2010). Placement in foster care enhances quality of attachment among young institutionalized children. *Child Development, 81,* 212–223.

Snell, E. K., Adam, E. K., & Duncan, G. J. (2007). Sleep and the body mass index and overweight status of children and adolescents. *Child Development, 78,* 309–323.

Snidman, N., Kagan, J., Riordan, L., & Shannon, D. C. (1995). Cardiac function and behavioral reactivity. *Psychophysiology, 32,* 199–207.

Snow, C. E., & Beals, D. E. (2006). Mealtime talk that supports literacy development. In R. W. Larson, A. R. Wiley, & K. R. Branscomb (Eds.), *Family mealtime as a context of development and socialization* (pp. 51–66). San Francisco: Jossey-Bass.

Snow, C. E., Pan, B. A., Imbens-Bailey, A., & Herman, J. (1996). Learning how to say what one means: A longitudinal study of children's speech act use. *Social Development, 5,* 56–84.

Snyder, J., Brooker, M., Patrick, M. R., Snyder, A., Schrepferman, L., & Stoolmiller, M. (2003). Observed peer victimization during early elementary school: Continuity, growth, and relation to risk for child antisocial and depressive behavior. *Child Development, 74,* 1881–1898.

Sobel, D. M. (2006). How fantasy benefits young children's understanding of pretense. *Developmental Science, 9,* 63–75.

Society for Research in Child Development. (2007). *SRCD ethical standards for research with children.* Retrieved from www.srcd.org/index.php?option=com_content&task= view&id=68&Itemid=110

Soderstrom, M. (2008). Early perception–late comprehension of grammar? The case of verbal –s: A response to de Villiers & Johnson (2007). *Journal of Child Language, 35,* 671–676.

Soderstrom, M., Seidl, A., Nelson, D. G. K., & Jusczyk, P. W. (2003). The prosodic bootstrapping of phrases: Evidence from prelinguistic infants. *Journal of Memory and Language, 49,* 249–267.

Solomon, G. B., & Bredemeier, B. J. L. (1999). Children's moral conceptions of gender stratification in sport. *International Journal of Sport Psychology, 30,* 350–368.

Solomon, J., & George, C. (2011). The disorganized attachment-caregiving system. In J. Solomon & C. George (Eds.), *Disorganized attachment and caregiving* (pp. 3–24). New York: Guilford.

Sonuga-Barke, E. J., Schlotz, W., & Kreppner, J. (2010). Differentiating developmental trajectories for conduct, emotion, and peer problems following early deprivation. *Monographs of the Society for Research in Child Development, 75*(1, Serial No. 295), 102–124.

Sorkhabi, N., & Mandara, J. (2013). Are the effects of Baumrind's parenting styles culturally specific or culturally equivalent? In R. E. Larzelere, A. S. Morris, & A. W. Harrist (Eds.), *Authoritative parenting: Synthesizing nurturance and discipline for optimal child development* (pp. 113–135). Washington, DC: American Psychological Association.

Sosa, R., Kennell, J., Klaus, M., Robertson, S., & Urrutia, J. (1980). The effect of a supportive companion on perinatal problems, length of labor, and mother–infant interaction. *New England Journal of Medicine, 303,* 597–600.

Soska, K. C., Adolph, K. E., & Johnson, S. P. (2010). Systems in development: Motor skill acquisition facilitates three-dimensional object completion. *Developmental Psychology, 46,* 129–138.

South African Department of Health. (2009). *2008 National Antenatal Sentinel HIV and Syphilis Prevalence Survey.* Retrieved from www.doh.gov.za/docs/nassps-f.html

Sowell, E. R., Trauner, D. A., Camst, A., & Jernigan, T. (2002). Development of cortical and subcortical brain structures in childhood and adolescence: A structural MRI study. *Developmental Medicine and Child Neurology, 44,* 4–16.

Sowislo, J. F., & Orth, U. (2013). Does low self-esteem predict depression and anxiety? A meta-analysis of longitudinal studies. *Psychological Bulletin, 139,* 213–240.

Spangler, G., Fremmer-Bomik, E., & Grossmann, K. (1996). Social and individual determinants of attachment security and disorganization during the first year. *Infant Mental Health Journal, 17,* 127–139.

Spangler, G., Johann, M., Ronai, Z., & Zimmermann, P. (2009). Genetic and environmental influence on attachment disorganization. *Journal of Child Psychology and Psychiatry, 50,* 952–961.

Sparling, J., Wilder, D., Kondash, J., Boyle, M. & Compton, M. (2011). Effects of interviewer behavior on accuracy of children's responses. *Journal of Applied Behavior Analysis, 44,* 587–592.

Speece, D. L., Ritchey, K. D., Cooper, D. H., Roth, F. P., & Schatschneider, C. (2004). Growth in early reading skills from kindergarten to third grade. *Contemporary Educational Psychology, 29,* 312–332.

Spelke, E. S., & Hermer, L. (1996). Early cognitive development: Objects and space. In R. Gelman & T. K. Au (Eds.), *Perceptual and cognitive development* (pp. 71–114). San Diego: Academic Press.

Spelke, E. S., & Kinzler, K. D. (2007). Core knowledge. *Developmental Science, 10,* 89–96.

Spelke, E. S., Phillips, A., & Woodward, A. L. (1995). Infants' knowledge of object motion and human action. In D. Sperber, D. Premack, & A. J. Premack (Eds.), *Causal cognition: A multidisciplinary debate* (pp. 44–78). New York: Oxford University Press.

Spence, M. J., & DeCasper, A. J. (1987). Prenatal experience with low-frequency maternal voice sounds influences neonatal perception of maternal voice samples. *Infant Behavior and Development, 10,* 133–142.

Spencer, J. P., Perone, S., & Buss, A. T. (2011). Twenty years and going strong: A dynamic systems revolution in motor and cognitive development. *Child Development Perspectives, 5,* 260–266.

Spere, K. A., Schmidt, L. A., Theall-Honey, L. A., & Martin-Chang, S. (2004). Expressive and receptive language skills of temperamentally shy preschoolers. *Infant and Child Development, 13,* 123–133.

Spilt, J., Hughes, J. N., Wu, J-Y., & Kwok, O-M. (2012). Dynamics of teacher–student relationships: Stability and change across elementary school and the influence on children's academic success. *Child Development, 83,* 1180–1195.

Spinrad, T. L., & Eisenberg, N. (2009). Empathy, prosocial behavior, and positive development in schools. In R. Gilman, E. S. Huebner, & M. J. Furlong (Eds.), *Handbook of positive psychology in schools* (pp. 119–129). New York: Routledge.

Spock, B., & Needlman, R. (2012). *Dr. Spock's baby and child care* (9th ed.). New York: Gallery Books.

Spoelstra, M. N., Mari, A., Mendel, M., Senga, E., van Rheenen, P., van Dijk, T. H., et al. (2012). Kwashiorkor and marasmus are both associated with impaired glucose clearance related to pancreatic β-cell dysfunction. *Metabolism: Clinical and Experimental, 61,* 1224–1230.

Sporer, N., Brunstein, J. C., & Kieschke, U. (2009). Improving students' reading comprehension skills: Effects of strategy instruction and reciprocal teaching. *Learning and Instruction, 19,* 272–286.

Sroufe, L. A. (2002). From infant attachment to promotion of adolescent autonomy: Prospective, longitudinal data on the role of parents in development. In J. G. Borkowski & S. L. Ramey (Eds.), *Parenting and the child's world* (pp. 187–202). Mahwah, NJ: Erlbaum.

Sroufe, L. A., Coffino, B., & Carlson, E. A. (2010). Conceptualizing the role of early experience: Lessons from the Minnesota Longitudinal Study. *Developmental Review, 30,* 36–51.

Sroufe, L. A., Egeland, B., Carlson, E., & Collins, W. (2005). *Minnesota Study of Risk and Adaptation from birth to maturity: The development of the person.* New York: Guilford.

Sroufe, L. A., & Waters, E. (1976). The ontogenesis of smiling and laughter: A perspective on the organization of development in infancy. *Psychological Review, 83,* 173–189.

Sroufe, L. A., & Wunsch, J. P. (1972). The development of laughter in the first year of life. *Child Development, 43,* 1324–1344.

St James-Roberts, I. (2007). Infant crying and sleeping: Helping parents to prevent and manage problems. *Sleep Medicine Clinics, 2,* 363–375.

St James-Roberts, I. (2012). *The origins, prevention and treatment of infant crying and sleep problems.* London: Routledge.

Stams, G. J. M., Juffer, F., & van IJzendoorn, M. H. (2002). Maternal sensitivity, infant attachment, and temperament in early childhood predict adjustment in middle childhood: The case of adopted children and their biologically unrelated parents. *Developmental Psychology, 38,* 806–821.

Staniford, L. J., Breckon, J. D., & Copeland, R. J. (2012). Treatment of childhood obesity: A systematic review. *Journal of Child and Family Studies, 21,* 545–564.

Stanovich, K. E. (2013). *How to think straight about psychology* (10th ed.). Upper Saddle River, NJ: Pearson.

Staub, F. C., & Stern, E. (2002). The nature of teachers' pedagogical content beliefs matters for students' achievement gains: Quasi-experimental evidence from elementary mathematics. *Journal of Educational Psychology, 94,* 344–355.

Steckel, R. H. (2012). Social and economic effects on growth. In N. Cameron & R. Bogin (Eds.), *Human growth and development* (2nd ed., pp. 225–244). London: Elsevier.

Steele, H., Steele, M., & Fonagy, P. (1996). Associations among attachment classifications of mothers, fathers, and their infants. *Child Development, 67,* 541–555.

Steele, L. C. (2012). The forensic interview: A challenging intervention. In P. Goodyear-Brown (Ed.), *Handbook of child sexual abuse: Identification, assessment, and treatment* (pp. 99–119). Hoboken, NJ: Wiley.

Steele, S., Joseph, R. M., & Tager-Flusberg, H. (2003). Developmental change in theory of mind abilities in children with autism. *Journal of Austism and Developmental Disorders, 33,* 461–467.

Stehr-Green, P., Tull, P., Stellfeld, M., Mortenson, P. B., & Simpson, D. (2003). Autism and thimerosal-containing vaccines: Lack of consistent evidence for an association. *American Journal of Preventive Medicine, 25,* 101–106.

Stein, Z., Susser, M., Saenger, G., & Marolla, F. (1975). *Famine and human development: The Dutch hunger winter of 1944–1945.* New York: Oxford.

Steinberg, L., Blatt-Eisengart, I., & Cauffman, E. (2006). Patterns of competence and adjustment among adolescents from authoritative, authoritarian, indulgent, and neglectful homes: A replication in a sample of serious juvenile offenders. *Journal of Research on Adolescence, 16,* 47–58.

Steinberg, L., Darling, N. E., & Fletcher, A. C. (1995). Authoritative parenting and adolescent development: An ecological journey. In P. Moen, G. H. Elder, Jr., & K. Luscher (Eds.), *Examining lives in context* (pp. 423–466). Washington, DC: American Psychological Association.

Steinberg, L., & Silk, J. S. (2002). Parenting adolescents. In M. H. Bornstein (Ed.), *Handbook of parenting: Vol. 1. Children and parenting* (pp. 103–134). Mahwah, NJ: Erlbaum.

Steiner, J. E. (1979). Human facial expression in response to taste and smell stimulation. In H. W. Reese & L. P. Lipsitt (Eds.), *Advances in child development and behavior* (Vol. 13, pp. 257–295). New York: Academic Press.

Steiner, J. E., Glaser, D., Hawilo, M. E., & Berridge, D. C. (2001). Comparative expression of hedonic impact: Affective reactions to taste by human infants and other primates. *Neuroscience and Biobehavioral Reviews, 25,* 53–74.

Stenberg, C. R., & Campos, J. J. (1990). The development of anger expressions in infancy. In N. Stein, B. Leventhal, & T. Trabasso (Eds.), *Psychological and biological approaches to emotion* (pp. 247–282). Hillsdale, NJ: Erlbaum.

Stenberg, G. (2003). Effects of maternal inattentiveness on infant social referencing. *Infant and Child Development, 12,* 399–419.

Stephens, B. E., & Vohr, B. R. (2009). Neurodevelopmental outcome of the premature infant. *Pediatric Clinics of North America, 56,* 631–646.

Stern, D. (1985). *The interpersonal world of the infant.* New York: Basic Books.

Sternberg, R. J. (2005). The triarchic theory of successful intelligence. In D. P. Flanagan & P. L. Harrison (Eds.), *Contemporary intellectual assessment: Theories, tests, and issues* (pp. 103–119). New York: Guilford.

Sternberg, R. J. (2008). The triarchic theory of successful intelligence. In N. Salkind (Ed.), *Encyclopedia of educational*

psychology (Vol. 2, pp. 988–994). Thousand Oaks, CA: Sage.

Sternberg, R. J. (2011). The theory of successful intelligence. In R. J. Sternberg & S. B. Kaufman (2011). *Cambridge handbook of intelligence* (pp. 504–527). New York: Cambridge University Press.

Sternberg, R. J. (2013). Contemporary theories of intelligence. In W. M. Reynolds & G. E. Miller (Eds.), *Handbook of psychology: Vol. 7. Educational psychology* (2nd ed., pp. 23–44). Hoboken, NJ: Wiley.

Sternberg, R. J., & Grigorenko, E. L. (2002). *Dynamic testing.* New York: Cambridge University Press.

Sternberg, R. J., & Jarvin, L. (2003). Alfred Binet's contributions as a paradigm for impact in psychology. In R. J. Sternberg (Ed.), *The anatomy of impact: What makes the great works of psychology great* (pp. 89–107). Washington, DC: American Psychological Association.

Stevenson, H. W., Lee, S., & Mu, X. (2000). Successful achievement in mathematics: China and the United States. In C. F. M. van Lieshout & P. G. Heymans (Eds.), *Developing talent across the lifespan* (pp. 167–183). Philadelphia: Psychology Press.

Stevenson, R., & Pollitt, C. (1987). The acquisition of temporal terms. *Journal of Child Language, 14,* 533–545.

Stewart, P. W., Lonky, E., Reihman, J., Pagano, J., Gump, B. B., & Darvill, T. (2008). The relationship between prenatal PCB exposure and intelligence (IQ). *Environmental Health Perspectives, 116,* 1416–1422.

Stewart, R. B., Jr. (1990). *The second child: Family transition and adjustment.* Newbury Park, CA: Sage.

Stifter, C. A., & Braungart, J. M. (1995). The regulation of negative reactivity in infancy: Function and development. *Developmental Psychology, 31,* 448–455.

Stiles, J. (2008). *Fundamentals of brain development.* Cambridge, MA: Harvard University Press.

Stiles, J. (2012). The effects of injury to dynamic neural networks in the mature and developing brain. *Developmental Psychobiology, 54,* 343–349.

Stiles, J., Moses, P., Roe, K., Akshoomoff, N. A., Trauner, D., & Hesselink, J. (2003). Alternative brain organization after prenatal cerebral injury: Convergent fMRI and cognitive data. *Journal of the International Neuropsychological Society, 9,* 604–622.

Stiles, J., Nass, R. D., Levine, S. C., Moses, P., & Reilly, J. S. (2009). Perinatal stroke: Effects and outcomes. In K. O. Yeates, M. D. Ris, H. G. Taylor, & B. Pennington (Eds.), *Pediatric neuropsychology: Research, theory and practice* (2nd ed., pp. 181–210). New York: Guilford.

Stiles, J., Reilly, J. S., & Levine, S. C. (2012). *Neural plasticity and cognitive development.* New York: Oxford University Press.

Stiles, J., Reilly, J., Paul, B., & Moses, P. (2005). Cognitive development following early brain injury: Evidence for neural adaptation. *Trends in Cognitive Sciences, 9,* 136–143.

Stiles, J., Stern, C., Appelbaum, M., & Nass, R. (2008). Effects of early focal brain injury on memory for visuospatial patterns: Selective deficits of global–local processing. *Neuropsychology, 22,* 61–73.

Stipek, D. (2004). Teaching practices in kindergarten and first grade: Different strokes for different folks. *Early Childhood Research Quarterly, 19,* 548–568.

Stipek, D. (2011). Classroom practices and children's motivation to learn. In E. Zigler, W. S. Gilliam, & W. S. Barnett (Eds.), *The pre-K debates: Current controversies and issues* (pp. 98–103). Baltimore, MD: Paul H. Brookes.

Stipek, D. J., & Byler, P. (2001). Academic achievement and social behaviors associated with age of entry into kindergarten. *Journal of Applied Developmental Psychology, 22,* 175–189.

Stipek, D. J., Feiler, R., Daniels, D., & Milburn, S. (1995). Effects of different instructional approaches on young children's achievement and motivation. *Child Development, 66,* 209–223.

Stipek, D. J., Gralinski, J. H., & Kopp, C. B. (1990). Self-concept development in the toddler years. *Developmental Psychology, 26,* 972–977.

Stochholm, K., Bojesen, A., Jensen, A. S., Juul, S., & Grayholt, C. H. (2012). Criminality in men with Klinefelter's syndrome and XYY syndrome: A cohort study. *British Medical Journal, 2,* e000650.

Stoltenborgh, M., van IJzendoorn, M. H., Euser, E. M., & Bakermans-Kranenburg, M. J. (2011). A global perspective on child sexual abuse: Meta-analysis of prevalence around the world. *Child Maltreatment, 16,* 79–101.

Stone, R. (2005). *Best classroom management practices for reaching all learners: What award-winning classroom teachers do.* Thousand Oaks, CA: Corwin Press.

Stoner, R., Chow, M. L., Boyle, M. P., Sunkin, S. M., Mouton, P. R., Roy, S., et al. (2014). Patches of disorganization in the neocortex of children with autism. *New England Journal of Medicine, 370,* 1209–1219.

Storch, S. A., & Whitehurst, G. J. (2001). The role of family and home in the literacy development of children from low-income backgrounds. In P. R. Britto & J. Brooks-Gunn (Eds.), *The role of family literacy environments in promoting young children's emerging literacy skills (New directions for child and adolescent development,* No. 92, pp. 53–71). San Francisco: Jossey-Bass.

Stormshak, E. A., Bierman, K. L., McMahon, R. J., Lengua, L. J., & the Conduct Problems Prevention Research Group. (2000). Parenting practices and child disruptive behavior problems in early elementary school. *Journal of Clinical Child Psychology, 29,* 17–29.

Strapp, C. M., & Federico, A. (2000). Imitations and repetitions: What do children say following recasts? *First Language, 20,* 273–290.

Straus, M. A., & Stewart, J. H. (1999). Corporal punishment by American parents: National data on prevalence, chronicity, severity, and duration, in relation to child and family characteristics. *Clinical Child and Family Psychology Review, 2,* 55–70.

Strayer, L., & Roberts, W. (2004). Children's anger, emotional expressiveness, and empathy: Relations with parents' empathy, emotional expressiveness, and parenting practices. *Social Development, 13,* 229–254.

Strazdins, L., Clements, M. S., Korda, R. J., Broom, D. H., & D'Souza, R. M. (2006). Unsociable work? Nonstandard work schedules, family relationships, and children's well-being. *Journal of Marriage and the Family, 68,* 394–410.

Strazdins, L., O'Brien, L. V., Lucas, N., & Roders, B. (2013). Combining work and family: Rewards or risks for children's mental health? *Social Science and Medicine, 87,* 99–107.

Streissguth, A. P., Treder, R., Barr, H. M., Shepard, T., Bleyer, W. A., Sampson, P. D., & Martin, D. (1987). Aspirin and acetaminophen use by pregnant women and subsequent child IQ and attention decrements. *Teratology, 35,* 211–219.

Streri, A. (2005). Touching for knowing in infancy: The development of manual abilities in very young infants. *European Journal of Developmental Psychology, 2,* 325–343.

Stretesky, P., & Lynch, M. (2004). The relationship between lead and crime. *Journal of Health and Social Behavior, 45,* 214–229.

Striano, T., & Rochat, P. (2000). Emergence of selective social referencing in infancy. *Infancy, 1,* 253–264.

Striano, T., Tomasello, M., & Rochat, P. (2001). Social and object support for early symbolic play. *Developmental Science, 4,* 442–455.

Stright, A. D., Herr, M. Y., & Neitzel, C. (2009). Maternal scaffolding of children's problem solving and children's adjustment in kindergarten: Hmong families in the United States. *Journal of Educational Psychology, 101,* 207–218.

Stright, A. D., Neitzel, C., Sears, K. G., & Hoke-Sinex, L. (2002). Instruction begins in the home: Relations between parental instruction and children's self-regulation in the classroom. *Journal of Educational Psychology, 93,* 456–466.

Strohschein, L. (2005). Parental divorce and child mental health trajectories. *Journal of Marriage and Family, 67,* 1286–1300.

Strohschein, L., Gauthier, A. H., Campbell, R., & Kleparchuk, C. (2008). Parenting as a dynamic process: A test of the resource dilution hypothesis. *Journal of Marriage and Family, 70,* 670–683.

Stromquist, N. P. (2007). Gender equity education globally. In S. S. Klein, B. Richardson, D. A. Grayson, L. H. Fox, & C. Kramarae (Eds.), *Handbook for achieving gender equity through education* (2nd ed., pp. 33–42). Mahwah, NJ: Erlbaum.

Stronach, E. P., Toth, S. L., Rogosch, F., Oshri, A., Manle, J. T., & Cicchetti, D. (2011). Child maltreatment, attachment security and internal representations of mother and mother–child relationships. *Child Maltreatment, 16,* 137–154.

Stroub, K. J., & Richards, M. P. (2013). From resegregation to reintegration: Trends in the racial/ethnic segregation of metropolitan public schools, 1993–2009. *American Educational Research Journal, 50,* 497–531

Stryer, B. K., Tofler, I. R., & Lapchick, R. (1998). A developmental overview of child and youth sports in society. *Child and Adolescent Psychiatric Clinics of North America, 7,* 697–719.

Sturge-Apple, M. L., Davies, P. T., Winter, M. A., Cummings, E. M., & Schermerhorn, A. (2008). Interparental conflict and children's school adjustment: The explanatory role of children's internal representations of interparental and parent–child relationships. *Developmental Psychology, 44,* 1678–1690.

Su, T. F., & Costigan, C. L. (2008). The development of children's ethnic identity in immigrant Chinese families in Canada: The role of parenting practices and children's perceptions of parental family obligation expectations. *Journal of Early Adolescence, 29,* 638–663.

Suárez-Orozco, C., Pimental, A., & Martin, M. (2009). The significance of relationships: Academic engagement and achievement among newcomer immigrant youth. *Teachers College Record, 111,* 712–749.

Subrahmanyam, K., Gelman, R., & Lafosse, A. (2002). Animate and other separably moveable things. In G. Humphreys (Ed.), *Category-specificity in brain and mind* (pp. 341–371). London: Psychology Press.

Subramanian, S. V., Perkins, J. M., Emre, O., & Smith, G. D. (2011). Weight of nations: A socioeconomic analysis of women in low- to middle-income countries. *American Journal of Clinical Nutrition, 93,* 232–233.

Substance Abuse and Mental Health Services Administration. (2013). *Results from the 2012 National Survey on Drug Use and Health: Summary of national findings.* Rockville, MD: Author.

Suddendorf, T., Simcock, G., & Nielsen, M. (2007). Visual self-recognition in mirrors and live videos: Evidence for a developmental asynchrony. *Cognitive Development, 22,* 185–196.

Sullivan, J., Beech, A. R., Craig, L. A., & Gannon, T. A. (2011). Comparing intra-familial and extra-familial child sexual abusers with professionals who have sexually abused children with whom they work. *International Journal of Offender Therapy and Comparative Criminology, 55,* 56–74.

Sullivan, M. C., McGrath, M. M. Hawes, K., & Lester, B. M. (2008). Growth trajectories of preterm infants: Birth to 12 years. *Journal of Pediatric Health Care, 22,* 83–93.

Sullivan, M. W., & Lewis, M. (2003). Contextual determinants of anger and other negative expressions in young infants. *Developmental Psychology, 39,* 693–705.

Sullivan, P. F., Daly, M. J., & O'Donovan, M. (2012). Genetic architectures of psychiatric disorders: The emerging picture and its implications. *Nature Reviews Genetics, 13,* 537–551.

Sullivan, S., & Glanz, J. (2006). *Building effective learning communities: Strategies for leadership, learning, and collaboration.* Thousand Oaks, CA: Corwin Press.

Sullivan, S. A., & Birch, L. L. (1990). Pass the sugar, pass the salt: Experience dictates preference. *Developmental Psychology, 26,* 546–551.

Sun, H., Ma, Y., Han, D., Pan, C. W., & Xu, Y. (2014). Prevalence and trends in obesity among China's children and adolescents, 1985–2010. *PLOS ONE, 9*(8), r105469j.

Sunderam, S., Kissin, D. M., Crawford, S., Anderson, J. E., Folger, S. G., Jamieson, D. J., et al. (2013, December 6). Assisted reproductive technology surveillance—United States. *Morbidity and Mortality Weekly Report, 62*(9), 1–24.

Sundet, J. M., Barlaug, D. G., & Torjussen, T. M. (2004). The end of the Flynn effect? A study of secular trends in mean intelligence test scores of Norwegian conscripts during half a century. *Intelligence, 32,* 349–362.

Super, C. M. (1981). Behavioral development in infancy. In R. H. Monroe, R. L. Monroe, & B. B. Whiting (Eds.), *Handbook of cross-cultural human development* (pp. 181–270). New York: Garland.

Super, C. M., & Harkness, S. (2002). Culture structures the environment for development. *Human Development 45,* 270–274.

Super, C. M., & Harkness, S. (2009). The developmental niche of the newborn in rural Kenya. In J. K. Nugent, B. J. Petrauskas, & T. B. Brazelton (Eds.), *The newborn as a person: Enabling healthy development worldwide* (pp. 85–97). Hoboken, NJ: Wiley.

Super, C. M., & Harkness, S. (2010). Culture and infancy. In J. G. Bremner & T. D. Wachs (Eds.), *Wiley-Blackwell handbook of infant development: Vol. 1. Basic research* (2nd ed., pp. 623–649). Chichester, UK: Wiley-Blackwell.

Super, C. M., Harkness, S., van Tijen, N., van der Vlugt, E., Fintelman, M., & Dijkstra, J. (1996). The three R's of Dutch childrearing and the socialization of infant arousal. In S. Harkness & C. M. Super (Eds.), *Parents' cultural belief systems* (pp. 447–466). New York:

Supple, A. J., & Small, S. A. (2006). The influence of parental support, knowledge, and authoritative parenting on Hmong and European American adolescent development. *Journal of Family Issues, 27,* 1214–1232.

Survey USA. (2005). *Disciplining a child.* Retrieved from www.surveyusa.com/50StateDisciplineChild0805Sortedby Teacher.htm

Svirsky, M. A., Teoh, S. W., & Neuburger, H. (2004). Development of language and speech perception in congenitally profoundly deaf children as a function of age at cochlear implantation. *Audiology and Neuro-Otology, 9,* 224–233.

Swain, M. E. (2014). Surrogacy and gestational carrier arrangements: Legal aspects. In J. M. Goldfarb (Ed.), *Third-party reproduction* (pp. 133–142). New York: Springer.

Swan, S. H., Liu, F., Kruse, R. L., Wang, C., Redmon, J. B., Sparks, A., & Weiss, B. (2010). Prenatal phthalate exposure and reduced masculine play in boys. *International Journal of Andrology, 33,* 259–269.

Swanson, H. L. (2011). Intellectual growth in children as a function of domain specific and domain general working memory subgroups. *Intelligence, 39,* 209–219.

Sweet, M. A., & Appelbaum, M. L. (2004). Is home visiting an effective strategy? A meta-analytic review of home visiting programs for families with young children. *Child Development, 75,* 1435–1456.

Swingley, D. (2005). Statistical clustering and the contents of the infant vocabulary. *Cognitive Psychology, 50,* 86–132.

Swinson, J., & Harrop, A. (2009). Teacher talk directed to boys and girls and its relationship to their behaviour. *Educational Studies, 35,* 515–524.

Szaflarski, J. P., Rajogopal, A., Altaye, M., Byars, A. W., Jacola, L., Schmithorst, V. J., et al. (2012). Left-handedness and language lateralization in children. *Brain Research, 1433,* 85–97.

Szepkouski, G. M., Gauvain, M., & Carberry, M. (1994). The development of planning skills in children with and without mental retardation. *Journal of Applied Developmental Psychology, 15,* 187–206.

T

Tabibi, Z., & Pfeffer, K. (2007). Finding a safe place to cross the road: The effect of distractors and the role of attention in children's identification of safe and dangerous road-crossing sites. *Infant and Child Development, 16,* 193–206.

Tacon, A., & Caldera, Y. (2001). Attachment and parental correlates in late adolescent Mexican American women. *Hispanic Journal of Behavioral Sciences, 23,* 71–88.

Takahashi, K. (1990). Are the key assumptions of the "Strange Situation" procedure universal? A view from Japanese research. *Human Development, 33,* 23–30.

Talaulikar, V. S., & Arulkumaran, S. (2011). Folic acid in obstetric review. *Obstetrics and Gynecological Survey, 66,* 240–247.

Tamis-LeMonda, C. S., & Bornstein, M. H. (1989). Habituation and maternal encouragement of attention in infancy as predictors of toddler language, play, and representational competence. *Child Development, 60,* 738–751.

Tamis-LeMonda, C. S., Shannon, J. D., Cabrera, N. J., & Lamb, M. E. (2004). Fathers and mothers at play with their 2- and 3-year-olds: Contributions to language and cognitive development. *Child Development, 75,* 1806–1820.

Tamm, L., Nakonezny, P. A., & Hughes, C. W. (2014). An open trial of metacognitive executive function training for young children with ADHD. *Journal of Attention Disorders, 18,* 551–559.

Tandon, S. D., Colon, L. Vega, P., Murphy, J., & Alonso, A. (2012). Birth outcomes associated with receipt of group prenatal care among low-income Hispanic women. *Journal of Midwifery & Women's Health, 57,* 476–481.

Tangney, J. P., Stuewig, J., & Mashek, D. J. (2007). Moral emotions and moral behavior. *Annual Review of Psychology, 58,* 345–372.

Tanimura, M., Takahashi, K., Kataoka, N., Tomita, K., Tanabe, I., Yasuda, M., et al. (2004). Proposal: Heavy television and video viewing poses a risk for infants and young children. *Nippon Shonika Gakkai Zasshi, 108,* 709–712 (in Japanese).

Tanner, J. M., Healy, M., & Cameron, N. (2001). *Assessment of skeletal maturity and prediction of adult height* (3rd ed.). Philadelphia: Saunders.

Tanskanen, P., Valkama, M., Haapea, M., Barnes, A., Ridler, K., Miettunen, J., et al. (2011). Is prematurity associated with adult cognitive outcome and brain structure? *Pediatric Neurology, 44,* 12–20.

Taras, V., Sarala, R., Muchinsky, P., Kemmelmeier, M., Singelis, T. M., Avsec, A., et al. (2014). Opposite ends of the same stick? Multi-method test of the dimensionality of individualism and collectivism. *Journal of Cross-Cultural Psychology, 45,* 213–245.

Tardif, T. (2006). But are they really verbs? Chinese words for action. In K. Hirsh-Pasek & R. M. Golinkoff (Eds.), *Action meets word: How children learn verbs* (pp. 477–498). New York: Oxford University Press.

Tardif, T., Fletcher, P., Liang, W., Zhang, Z., Kaciroti, N., & Marchman, V. A. (2008). Baby's first 10 words. *Developmental Psychology, 44,* 929–938.

Tarren-Sweeney, M. (2006). Patterns of aberrant eating among preadolescent children in foster care. *Journal of Abnormal Child Psychology, 34,* 623–634.

Tarullo, A. R., Balsam, P. D., & Fifer, W. P. (2011). Sleep and infant learning. *Infant and Child Development, 20,* 35–46.

Tarullo, A. R., & Gunnar, M. R. (2006). Child maltreatment and the developing HPA axis. *Hormones and Behavior, 50,* 632–639.

Taumoepeau, M., & Ruffman, T. (2006). Mother and infant talk about mental states relates to desire language and emotion understanding. *Child Development, 77f* 465–481.

Taylor, C. A., Manganello, J. A., Lee, S. J., & Rice, J. C. (2010). Mothers' spanking of 3-year-old children and subsequent risk of children's aggressive behavior. *Pediatrics, 125,* e1057–e1065.

Taylor, M., & Carlson, S. M. (1997). The relation between individual differences in fantasy and theory of mind. *Child Development, 68,* 436–455.

Taylor, M., & Carlson, S. M. (2000). The influence of religious beliefs on parental attitudes about children's fantasy behavior. In K. S. Rosengren, C. N. Johnson, & P. L. Harris (Eds.), *Imagining the impossible* (pp. 247–268). New York: Cambridge University Press.

Taylor, M., Carlson, S. M., Maring, B. L., Gerow, L., & Charley, C. M. (2004). The characteristics and correlates of fantasy in school-age children: Imaginary companions, impersonation, and social understanding. *Developmental Psychology, 40,* 1173–1187.

Taylor, M., Esbensen, B. M., & Bennett, R. T. (1994). Children's understanding of knowledge acquisition: The tendency for children to report that they have always known what they have just learned. *Child Development, 65,* 1581–1604.

Taylor, M. C., & Hall, J. A. (1982). Psychological androgyny: Theories, methods, and conclusions. *Psychological Bulletin, 92,* 347–366.

Taylor, M. G., Rhodes, M., & Gelman, S. A. (2009). Boys will be boys; cows will be cows: Children's essentialist reasoning about gender categories and animal species. *Child Development, 80,* 461–481.

Taylor, R. D. (2010). Risk and resilience in low-income African American families: Moderating effects of kinship social support. *Cultural Diversity and Ethnic Minority Psychology, 16,* 344–351.

Taylor, R. L. (2000). Diversity within African-American families. In D. H. Demo & K. R. Allen (Eds.), *Handbook of family diversity* (pp. 232–251). New York: Oxford University Press.

Taylor, Z. E., Eisenberg, N., Spinrad, T. L., Eggum, N. D., & Sulik, M. J. (2013). The relations of ego-resiliency and emotion socialization to the development of empathy and prosocial behavior across early childhood. *Emotion, 15,* 822–831.

Team Up for Youth. (2014). *The perils of poverty: The health crisis facing our low-income girls . . . and the power of sports to help.* Retrieved from www.ussoccerfoundation.org/uploads/Health_of_Low_Income_Girls_Coaching_Corps.pdf

Tecwyn, E. C., Thorpe, S. K. S., & Chappell, J. (2014). Development of planning in 4- to 10-year-old children: Reducing inhibitory demands does not improve performance. *Journal of Experimental Child Psychology, 125,* 85–101.

Temple, C. M., & Shephard, E. E. (2012). Exceptional lexical skills but executive language deficits in school starters and young adults with Turner syndrome: Implications for X chromosome effects on brain function. *Brain and Language, 120,* 345–359.

Temple, J. L., Giacomelli, A. M., Roemmich, J. N., & Epstein, L. H. (2007). Overweight children habituate slower than nonoverweight children to food. *Physiology and Behavior, 9,* 250–254.

Tenenbaum, H. R., Hill, D., Joseph, N., & Roche, E. (2010). "It's a boy because he's painting a picture": Age differences in children's conventional and unconventional gender schemas. *British Journal of Psychology, 101,* 137–154.

Tenenbaum, H. R., & Leaper, C. (2002). Are parents' gender schemas related to their children's gender-related cognitions? A meta-analysis. *Developmental Psychology, 38,* 615–630.

Tenenbaum, H. R., & Leaper, C. (2003). Parent–child conversations about science: The socialization of gender inequities? *Developmental Psychology, 39,* 34–57.

Tenenbaum, H. R., Snow, C. E., Roach, K. A., & Kurland, B. (2005). Talking and reading science: Longitudinal data on sex differences in mother–child conversations in low-income families. *Journal of Applied Developmental Psychology, 26,* 1–19.

ten Tusscher, G. W., & Koppe, J. G. (2004). Perinatal dioxin exposure and later effects—A review. *Chemosphere, 54,* 1329–1336.

Teti, D. M., Saken, J. W., Kucera, E., & Corns, K. M. (1996). And baby makes four: Predictors of attachment security among preschool-age firstborns during the transition to siblinghood. *Child Development, 67,* 579–596.

Teyber, E. (2001). *Helping children cope with divorce* (rev. ed.). San Francisco: Jossey-Bass.

Thakur, G. A., Sengupta, S. M., Grizenko, N., Schmitz, N., Pagé, V., & Joober, R. (2013). Maternal smoking during pregnancy and ADHD: A comprehensive clinical and neurocognitive characterization. *Nicotine & Tobacco Research, 15,* 149–157.

Thatcher, R. W., Walker, R. A., & Giudice, S. (1987). Human cerebral hemispheres develop at different rates and ages. *Science, 236,* 1110–1113.

Theil, S. (2006, September 4). Beyond babies. *Newsweek: International Edition.* Retrieved from www.msnbc.msn.com/id/14535863/site/newsweek

Thelen, E., & Adolph, K. E. (1992). Arnold Gesell: The paradox of nature and nurture. *Developmental Psychology, 28,* 368–380.

Thelen, E., & Corbetta, D. (2002). Microdevelopment and dynamic systems: Applications to infant motor development. In N. Granott & J. Parziale (Eds.), *Microdevelopment: Transition processes in development and learning* (pp. 59–79). New York: Cambridge University Press.

Thelen, E., Fisher, D. M., & Ridley-Johnson, R. (1984). The relationship between physical growth and a newborn reflex. *Infant Behavior and Development, 7,* 479–493.

Thelen, E., Schöner, G., Scheier, C., & Smith, L. B. (2001). The dynamics of embodiment: A field theory of infant perseverative reaching. *Behavioral and Brain Sciences, 24,* 1–34.

Thelen, E., & Smith, L. B. (1998). Dynamic systems theories. In R. M. Lerner (Ed.), *Handbook of child psychology: Vol. 1. Theoretical models of human development* (5th ed., pp. 563–634). New York: Wiley.

Thelen, E., & Smith, L. B. (2006). Dynamic systems theories. In R. M. Lerner (Ed.), *Handbook of child psychology: Vol. 1. Theoretical models of human development* (6th ed., pp. 258–312). Hoboken, NJ: Wiley.

Thiessen, E. D., Kronstein, A. T., & Hufnagle, D. G. (2012). The extraction and integration framework: A two-process account of statistical learning. *Psychological Bulletin, 139,* 792–814.

Thiessen, E. D., & Saffran, J. R. (2007). Learning to learn: Infants' acquisition of stress-based strategies for word segmentation. *Language Learning and Development, 3,* 75–102.

Thoermer, C., Woodward, A., Sodian, B., & Perst, H. (2013). To get the grasp: Seven-month-olds encode and selectively reproduce goal-directed grasping. *Journal of Experimental Child Psychology, 116,* 499–509.

Thomaes, S., Brummelman, E., Reijntjes, A., & Bushman, B. J. (2013). When Narcissus was a boy: Origins, nature, and consequences of childhood narcissism. *Child Development Perspectives, 7,* 22–26.

Thomaes, S., Stegge, H., Bushman, B. J., & Olthof, T. (2008). Trumping shame by blasts of noise: Narcissism, self-esteem, shame, and aggression in young adolescents. *Child Development, 79,* 1792–1801.

Thoman, E., & Ingersoll, E. W. (1993). Learning in premature infants. *Developmental Psychology, 29,* 692–700.

Thomas, A., & Chess, S. (1977). *Temperament and development.* New York: Brunner/Mazel.

Thomas, K. A., & Tessler, R. C. (2007). Bicultural socialization among adoptive families: Where there is a will, there is a way. *Journal of Family Issues, 28,* 1189–1219.

Thombs, B. D., Roseman, M., & Arthurs, E. (2010). Prenatal and postpartum depression in fathers and mothers. *Journal of the American Medical Association, 304,* 961.

Thompson, A., Hollis, C., & Richards, D. (2003). Authoritarian parenting attitudes as a risk for conduct problems: Results of a British national cohort study. *European Child and Adolescent Psychiatry, 12,* 84–91.

Thompson, A. L., & Bentley, M. E. (2013). The critical period of infant feeding for the development of early disparities in obesity. *Social Science and Medicine, 97,* 288–296.

Thompson, P. M., Giedd, J. N., Woods, R. P., MacDonald, D., Evans, A. C., & Toga, A. W. (2000). Growth patterns in the developing brain detected by using continuum mechanical tensor maps. *Nature, 404,* 190–192.

Thompson, R. A. (1990). Vulnerability in research: A developmental perspective on research risk. *Child Development, 61,* 1–16.

Thompson, R. A. (2006). The development of the person: Social understanding, relationships, conscience, self. In N. Eisenberg (Ed.), *Handbook of child psychology: Vol. 3. Social, emotional, and personality development* (6th ed., pp. 24–98). Hoboken, NJ: Wiley.

Thompson, R. A. (2008). Early attachment and later development: Familiar questions, new answers. In J. Cassidy & P. R. Shaver (Eds.), *Handbook of attachment* (2nd ed., pp. 348–365). New York: Guilford.

Thompson, R. A. (2009). Early foundations: Conscience and the development of moral character. In D. Narvaez & D. K. Lapsley (Eds.), *Personality, identity, and character: Explorations in moral psychology* (pp. 159–184). New York: Cambridge University Press.

Thompson, R. A. (2011). The emotionate child. In D. Cicchetti & G. I. Roisman (Eds.), *Minnesota symposium on child psychology: The origins and organization of adaptation and maladaptation* (pp. 13–53). Hoboken, NJ: Wiley.

Thompson, R. A. (2013). Attachment theory and research: Précis and prospect. In P. D. Zelazo (Ed.), *Oxford handbook of developmental psychology: Vol. 2. Self and other* (pp. 191–216). New York: Oxford University Press.

Thompson, R. A., & Goodman, M. (2010). Development of emotion regulation: More than meets the eye. In A. M. Kring & D. M. Sloan (Eds.), *Emotion regulation and psychopathology: A transdiagnostic approach to etiology and treatment* (pp. 38–58). New York: Guilford.

Thompson, R. A., & Goodvin, R. (2007). Taming the tempest in the teapot. In C. A. Brownell & C. B. Kopp (Eds.), *Socioemotional development in the toddler years: Transitions and transformations* (pp. 320–341). New York: Guilford.

Thompson, R. A., & Meyer, S. (2007). Socialization of emotion regulation in the family. In J. J. Gross (Ed.), *Handbook of emotion regulation* (pp. 249–268). New York: Guilford.

Thompson, R. A., Meyer, S., & McGinley, M. (2006). Understanding values in relationships: The development of conscience. In M. Killen & J. G. Smetana (Eds.), *Handbook of moral development* (pp. 267–298). Mahwah, NJ: Erlbaum.

Thompson, R. A., & Nelson, C. A. (2001). Developmental science and the media. *American Psychologist, 56,* 5–15.

Thompson, R. A., Winer, A. C., & Goodvin, R. (2011). The individual child: Temperament, emotion, self, and personality. In M. H. Bornstein & M. E. Lamb (Eds.),

Developmental science: An advanced textbook (6th ed., pp. 427–468). Hoboken, NJ: Taylor & Francis.

Thompson, W. W., Price, C., Goodson, B., Shay, D. K., Benson, P., Hinrichsen, V. L., et al. (2007). Early thimerosal exposure and neuropsychological outcomes at 7 to 10 years. *New England Journal of Medicine, 357*, 1281–1292.

Thorne, B. (1993). *Gender play: Girls and boys in school.* New Brunswick, NJ: Rutgers University Press.

Thornton, S. (1999). Creating conditions for cognitive change: The interaction between task structures and specific strategies. *Child Development, 70*, 588–603.

Thorpe, K. (2006). Twin children's language development. *Early Human Development, 82*, 387–395.

Tien, A. (2013). Bootstrapping and the acquisition of Mandarin Chinese: A natural semantic metalanguage perspective. In D. Bittner & N. Ruhlig (Eds.), *Lexical bootstrapping: The role of lexis and semantics in child language* (pp. 39–72). Berlin: Walter de Gruyter.

Tienari, P., Wahlberg, K. E., & Wynne, L. C. (2006). Finnish adoption study of schizophrenia: Implications for family interventions. *Families, Systems, and Health, 24*, 442–451.

Tienari, P., Wynne, L. C., Laksy, K., Moring, J., Nieminen, P., Sorri, A., et al. (2003). Genetic boundaries of the schizophrenia spectrum: Evidence from the Finnish adoptive family study of schizophrenia. *The American Journal of Psychiatry, 160*, 1587–1594.

Tiet, Q. Q., Huizinga, D., & Byrnes, H. F. (2010). Predictors of resilience among inner city youths. *Journal of Child and Family Studies, 19*, 360–378.

Tiggemann, M., & Anesbury, T. (2000). Negative stereotyping of obesity in children: The role of controllability beliefs. *Journal of Applied Social Psychology, 30*, 1977–1993.

Tincoff, R., & Jusczyk, P. W. (1999). Some beginnings of word comprehension in 6-month-olds. *Psychological Science, 10*, 172–175.

Tinsley, B. J. (2003). *How children learn to be healthy.* Cambridge, UK: Cambridge University Press.

Tishkoff, S. A., & Kidd, K. K. (2004). Implications of biogeography of human populations for "race" and medicine. *Nature Genetics, 36* (11s): S21–7.

Tizard, B., & Rees, J. (1975). The effect of early institutional rearing on the behaviour problems and affectional relationships of four-year-old children. *Journal of Child Psychology and Psychiatry, 16*, 61–73.

Tomasello, M. (2000). Do young children have adult syntactic competence? *Cognition, 74*, 209–253.

Tomasello, M. (2003). *Constructing a language: A usage-based theory of language acquisition.* Cambridge, MA: Harvard University Press.

Tomasello, M. (2006). Acquiring linguistic constructions. In D. Kuhn & R. Siegler (Eds.), *Handbook of child psychology: Vol. 2: Cognition, perception, and language* (6th ed., pp. 255–298). Hoboken, NJ: Wiley.

Tomasello, M. (2011). Language development. In U. Goswami (Ed.), *Wiley-Blackwell handbook of childhood cognitive development* (2nd ed., pp. 239–257). Malden, MA: Wiley-Blackwell.

Tomasello, M., & Akhtar, N. (1995). Two-year-olds use pragmatic cues to differentiate reference to objects and actions. *Cognitive Development, 10*, 201–224.

Tomasello, M., Akhtar, N., Dodson, K., & Rekau, L. (1997). Differential productivity in young children's use of nouns and verbs. *Journal of Child Language, 24*, 373–387.

Tomasello, M., & Brandt, S. (2009). Flexibility in the semantics and syntax of children's early verb use. *Monographs of the Society for Research in Child Development, 74*(2, Serial No. 293), 113–126.

Tomasello, M., Call, J., & Hare, B. (2003). Chimpanzees understand psychological states—the question is which ones and to what extent. *Trends in Cognitive Sciences, 7*, 153–156.

Tomasello, M., Carpenter, M., & Liszkowski, U. (2007). A new look at infant pointing. *Child Development, 78*, 705–722.

Tomasetto, C., Alparone, F. R., & Cadinu, M. (2011). Girls' math performance under stereotype threat: The moderating role of mothers' gender stereotypes. *Developmental Psychology, 47*, 943–949.

Tomyr, L., Ouimet, C., & Ugnat, A. (2012). A review of findings from the Canadian Incidence Study of reported child abuse and neglect (CIS). *Canadian Journal of Public Health, 103*, 103–112.

Tong, S., Baghurst, P., Vimpani, G., & McMichael, A. (2007). Socioeconomic position, maternal IQ, home environment, and cognitive development. *Journal of Pediatrics, 151*, 284–288.

Tong, S., McMichael, A. J., & Baghurst, P. A. (2000). Interactions between environmental lead exposure and sociodemographic factors on cognitive development. *Archives of Environmental Health, 55*, 330–335.

Toomela, A. (1999). Drawing development: Stages in the representation of a cube and a cylinder. *Child Development, 70*, 1141–1150.

Toomela, A. (2002). Drawing as a verbally mediated activity: A study of relationships between verbal, motor, visuospatial skills and drawing in children. *International Journal of Behavioral Development, 26*, 234–247.

Torquati, J. C., Raikes, H. H., Huddleston-Casas, C. A., Bovaird, J. A., & Harris, B. A. (2011). Family income, parent education, and perceived constraints as predictors of observed program quality and parent rated program quality. *Early Childhood Research Quality, 26*, 453–464.

Torrance, E. P. (1988). The nature of creativity as manifest in its testing. In R. J. Sternberg (Ed.), *The nature of creativity: Contemporary psychological perspectives* (pp. 43–75). New York: Cambridge University Press.

Tottenham, N., Hare, T. A., & Casey, B. J. (2009). A developmental perspective on human amygdala function. In P. J. Whalen & E. A. Phelps (Eds.), *The human amygdala* (pp. 107–117). New York: Guilford.

Tottenham, N., Hare, T. A., Millner, A., Gilhooly, T., Zevin, J. D., & Casey, B. J. (2011). Elevated amygdala response to faces following early deprivation. *Developmental Science, 14*, 190–204.

Tough, S. C., Vekved, M., & Newburn-Cook, C. (2012). Do factors that influence pregnancy planning differ by maternal age? A population-based survey. *Journal of Obstetrics and Gynaecology Canada, 34*, 39–46.

Townsend, D. A., & Rovee-Collier, C. (2007). The transitivity of 6-month-olds' preconditioned memories in deferred imitation. Paper presented at the annual meeting of the Eastern Psychological Association, Philadelphia.

Tracy, J. L., Robins, R. W., & Lagattuta, K. H. (2005). Can children recognize pride? *Emotion, 5*, 251–257.

Tran, P., & Subrahmanyam, K. (2013). Evidence-based guidelines for informal use of computers by children to promote the development of academic, cognitive, and social skills. *Ergonomics, 56*, 1349–1362.

Träuble, B., & Pauen, S. (2011). Cause or effect: What matters? How 12-month-old infants learn to categorize artifacts. *British Journal of Developmental Psychology, 29*, 357–374.

Traurig, M., Mack, J., Hanson, R. L., Ghoussaini, M., Meyre, D., Knowler, W., et al. (2009). Common variation in SIM1 is reproducibly associated with BMI in Pima Indians. *Diabetes, 58*, 1682–1689.

Trautner, H. M., Gervai, J., & Nemeth, R. (2003). Appearance-reality distinction and development of gender constancy understanding in children. *International Journal of Behavioral Development, 27*, 275–283.

Trautner, H. M., Ruble, D. N., Cyphers, L., Kirsten, B., Behrendt, R., & Hartman, P. (2005). Rigidity and flexibility of gender stereotypes in childhood: Developmental or differential? *Infant and Child Development, 14*, 365–381.

Trehub, S. E. (2001). Musical predispositions in infancy. *Annals of the New York Academy of Sciences, 930*, 1–16.

Tremblay, R. E. (2000). The development of aggressive behavior during childhood: What have we learned in the past century? *International Journal of Behavioral Development, 24*, 129–141.

Trentacosta, C. J., & Shaw, D. S. (2009). Emotional self-regulation, peer rejection, and antisocial behavior: Developmental associations from early childhood to early adolescence. *Journal of Applied Developmental Psychology, 30*, 356–365.

Trevarthen, C. (2003). Infant psychology is an evolving culture. *Human Development, 46*, 233–246.

Triandis, H. C. (2005). Issues in individualism and collectivism research. In R. M. Sorrentino, D. Cohen, J. M. Olson, & M. P. Zanna (Eds.), *Culture and social behavior: The Ontario Symposium* (Vol. 10, pp. 207–225). Mahwah, NJ: Erlbaum.

Triandis, H. C. (2007). Culture and psychology: A history of their relationship. In S. Kitahama (Ed.), *Handbook of cultural psychology* (pp. 59–76). New York: Guilford.

Triandis, H. C., & Gelfand, M. J. (2012). A theory of individualism and collectivism. In P. A. M. Van Lange,

A. W. Kruglanski, & E. T. Higgins (Eds.), *Handbook of theories of social psychology* (Vol. 2, pp. 498–520). Thousand Oaks, CA: Sage.

Trickett, P. K., Noll, J. G., & Putnam, F. W. (2011). The impact of sexual abuse on female development: Lessons from a multigenerational, longitudinal research study. *Development and Psychopathology, 23*, 453–476.

Trionfi, G., & Reese, E. (2009). A good story: Children with imaginary companions create richer narratives. *Child Development, 80*, 1301–1313.

Trocmé, N., & Wolfe, D. (2002). *Child maltreatment in Canada: The Canadian Incidence Study of Reported Child Abuse and Neglect.* Retrieved from www.hcsc.gc.ca/pphb-dgspsp/cm-vee

Troilo, J., & Coleman, M. (2012). Full-time, part-time full-time, and part-time fathers: Father identities following divorce. *Family Relations, 61*, 601–614.

Tronick, E., & Lester, B. M. (2013). Grandchild of the NBAS: The NICU Network Neurobehavioral Scale (NNNS): A review of the research using the NNNS. *Journal of Child and Adolescent Psychiatric Nursing, 26*, 193–203.

Tronick, E. Z., Morelli, G., & Ivey, P. (1992). The Efe forager infant and toddler's pattern of social relationships: Multiple and simultaneous. *Developmental Psychology, 28*, 568–577.

Tronick, E. Z., Thomas, R. B., & Daltabuit, M. (1994). The Quechua manta pouch: A caretaking practice for buffering the Peruvian infant against the multiple stressors of high altitude. *Child Development, 65*, 1005–1013.

Trønnes, H., Wilcox, A. J., Lie, R. T., Markestad, T., & Moster, D. (2014). Risk of cerebral palsy in relation to pregnancy disorders and preterm birth: A national cohort study. *Developmental Medicine and Child Neurology, 56*, 779–785.

Troop-Gordon, W., & Asher, S. R. (2005). Modifications in children's goals when encountering obstacles to conflict resolution. *Child Development, 76*, 568–582.

Troseth, G. L. (2003). Getting a clear picture: Young children's understanding of a televised image. *Developmental Science, 6*, 247–253.

Troseth, G. L., & DeLoache, J. S. (1998). The medium can obscure the message: Young children's understanding of video. *Child Development, 69*, 950–965.

Troseth, G. L., Saylor, M. M., & Archer, A. H. (2006). Young children's use of video as a source of socially relevant information. *Child Development, 77*, 786–799.

Troutman, D. R., & Fletcher, A. C. (2010). Context and companionship in children's short-term versus long-term friendships. *Journal of Social and Personal Relationships, 27*, 1060–1074.

True, M. M., Pisani, L., & Oumar, F. (2001). Infant–mother attachment among the Dogon of Mali. *Child Development, 72*, 1451–1466.

Trzesniewski, K. H., Donnellan, M. B., & Robins, R. W. (2003). Stability of self-esteem across the life span. *Journal of Personality and Social Psychology, 84*, 205–220.

Tsang, C. D., & Conrad, N. J. (2010). Does the message matter? The effect of song type on infants' pitch preferences for lullabies and playsongs. *Infant Behavior and Development, 33*, 96–100.

Tuchfarber, B. S., Zins, J. E., & Jason, L. A. (1997). Prevention and control of injuries. In R. Weissberg, T. P. Gullotta, R. L. Hampton, B. A. Ryan, & G. R. Adams (Eds.), *Enhancing children's wellness* (pp. 250–277). Thousand Oaks, CA: Sage.

Tucker, C. J., McHale, S. M., & Crouter, A. C. (2001). Conditions of sibling support in adolescence. *Journal of Family Psychology, 15*, 254–271.

Tudge, J. R. H., Hogan, D. M., Snezhkova, I. A., Kulakova, N. N., & Etz, K. E. (2000). Parents' child-rearing values and beliefs in the United States and Russia: The impact of culture and social class. *Infant and Child Development, 9*, 105–121.

Turati, C., Cassia, V. M., Simion, F., & Leo, I. (2006). Newborns' face recognition: Role of inner and outer facial features. *Child Development, 77*, 297–311.

Turiel, E., & Killen, M. (2010). Taking emotions seriously: The role of emotions in moral development. In W. F. Arsenio & E. A. Lemerise (Eds.), *Emotions, aggression, and morality in children: Bridging development and psychopathology* (pp. 33–52). Washington, DC: American Psychological Association.

Turnbull, K. P., Anthony, A. B., Justice, L., & Bowles, R. (2009). Preschoolers' exposure to language stimulation in classrooms serving at-risk children: The contribution of group size and activity context. *Early Education and Development, 20,* 53–79.

Turner, P. J., & Gervai, J. (1995). A multidimensional study of gender typing in preschool children and their parents: Personality, attitudes, preferences, behavior, and cultural differences. *Developmental Psychology, 31,* 759–772.

Turner, R. N., Hewstone, M., & Voci, A. (2007). Reducing explicit and implicit outgroup prejudice via direct and extended contact: The mediating role of self-disclosure and intergroup anxiety. *Journal of Personality and Social Psychology, 93,* 369–388.

Twenge, J. M., & Campbell, W. K. (2001). Age and birth cohort differences in self-esteem: A cross-temporal meta-analysis. *Personality and Social Psychology Review, 5,* 321–344.

Twenge, J. M., & Crocker, J. (2002). Race and self-esteem: Meta-analyses comparing whites, blacks, Hispanics, Asians, and American Indians and comment on Gray-Little and Hafdahl (2000). *Psychological Bulletin, 128,* 371–408.

Tyano, S., Keren, M., Herrman, H., & Cox, J. (2010). *Parenthood and mental health.* Oxford, UK: Wiley-Blackwell.

U

Uccelli, P., & Pan, B. A. (2013). Semantic development. In J. B. Gleason & N. B. Ratner (Eds.), *Development of language* (8th ed., pp., 89–119). Upper Saddle River, NJ: Pearson.

Udechuku, A., Nguyen, T., Hill, R., & Szego, K. (2010). Antidepressants in pregnancy: A systematic review. *Australian and New Zealand Journal of Psychiatry, 44,* 978–996.

Ukrainetz, T. A., Justice, L. M., Kaderavek, J. N., Eisenberg, S. L., Gillam, R., & Harm, H. M. (2005). The development of expressive elaboration in fictional narratives. *Journal of Speech, Language, and Hearing Research, 48,* 1363–1377.

Ullrich-French, S., & Smith, A. L. (2006). Perceptions of relationships with parents and peers in youth sport: Independent and combined prediction of motivational outcomes. *Psychology of Sport and Exercise, 7,* 193–214.

Underwood, M. K. (2003). *Social aggression in girls.* New York: Guilford.

UNAIDS. (2012). *Global report: UNAIDS report on the global AIDS epidemic.* Retrieved from www.unaids.org/en/resources/publications/2012/name,76121,en.asp

Unger, C. C., Salam, S. S., Sarker, M. S. A., Black, R., Cravioto, A., & Arifeen, S. E. (2014). Treating diarrhoeal disease in children under five: The global picture. *Archives of Diseases of Childhood, 99,* 273–278.

UNICEF (United Nations Children's Fund). (2011). *Children in conflict and emergencies.* Retrieved from www.unicef.org/protection/armedconflict.html

UNICEF (United Nations Children's Fund). (2012). *Measuring child poverty: New league tables of child poverty in the world's richest countries* (Innocenti Report Card 10). Florence, Italy: UNICEF Innocenti Research Centre.

UNICEF (United Nations Children's Fund). (2013a). *Child info: Monitoring the situation of infants and children.* Retrieved from www.childinfo.org/statistical_tables.html

UNICEF (United Nations Children's Fund). (2013b). *Making education a priority in the post-2015 development agenda: Report of the Global Thematic Consultation on Education in the Post-2015 Development Agenda.* Retrieved from www.unicef.org/education/files/Education_Thematic_Report_FINAL_v7_EN.pdf

United Nations. (2012). *World population prospects: The 2012 revision. Population database.* Retrieved from esa.un.org/wpp/unpp/panel_population.htm

U.S. Census Bureau. (2011). *Marital events of Americans: 2009.* Retrieved from www.census.gov/prod/2011pubs/acs-13.pdf

U.S. Census Bureau. (2014a). International database. Retrieved from www.census.gov/population/international/data/idb/informationGateway.php

U.S. Census Bureau. (2014b). *Statistical abstract of the United States* (133rd ed.). Washington, DC: U.S. Government Printing Office.

U.S. Department of Agriculture. (2012). *WIC: The Special Supplemental Nutrition Program for Women, Infants, and Children.* Nutrition program facts. Retrieved from www.fns.usda.gov/sites/default/files/WIC-Fact-Sheet.pdf

U.S. Department of Agriculture. (2013a). *Expenditures on children by families, 2012.* Retrieved from www.cnpp.usda.gov/Publications/CRC/crc2012.pdf

U.S. Department of Agriculture. (2013b). *Household food security in the United States in 2013.* Retrieved from www.ers.usda.gov/publications/err-economic-research-report/err173.aspx#.VCGVHUg28dU

U.S. Department of Agriculture. (2014). *Fact sheet: WIC—The Special Supplemental Program for Women, Infants, and Children.* Retrieved from www.fns.usda.gov/wic/about-wic-wic-glance

U.S. Department of Education. (2006). *Calories in, calories out: Food and exercise in public elementary schools, 2005.* Retrieved from nces.ed.gov/Pubs2006/ nutrition

U.S. Department of Education. (2014). *Digest of education statistics: 2012.* Washington, DC: U.S. Government Printing Office.

U.S. Department of Health and Human Services. (2006). *Research to practice: Preliminary findings from the Early Head Start Prekindergarten Follow-Up, Early Head Start Research and Evaluation Project.* Washington, DC: Author.

U.S. Department of Health and Human Services. (2010a). *Breastfeeding.* Retrieved from www.womenshealth.gov/breastfeeding/index.cfm

U.S. Department of Health and Human Services. (2010b). *Head Start Impact Study: Final report.* Washington, DC: U.S Government Printing Office.

U.S. Department of Health and Human Services. (2012). *Who is at risk for sickle cell anemia?* Retrieved from www.nhlbi.nih.gov/health/health-topics/topics/sca/atrisk.html

U.S. Department of Health and Human Services. (2013). *Child Maltreatment 2012.* Retrieved from www.acf.hhs.gov/programs/cb/resource/child-maltreatment-2012

U.S. Department of Health and Human Services. (2014). *What causes Down syndrome?* Retrieved from www.nichd.nih.gov/health/topics/down/conditioninfo/Pages/causes.aspx

Usta, I. M., & Nassar, A. H. (2008). Advanced maternal age. Part I: Obstetric complications. *American Journal of Perinatology, 25,* 521–534.

Uttal, D. H., Meadow, N. G., Tipton, E., Hand, L. L., Alden, A. R., Warren, C., & Newcombe, N. S. (2013). The malleability of spatial skills: A meta-analysis of training studies. *Psychological Bulletin, 139,* 352–402.

Uziel, Y., Chapnick, G., Oren-Ziv, A., Jaber, L., Nemet, D., & Hashkes, P. J. (2012). Bone strength in children with growing pains: Long-term follow-up. *Clinical and Experimental Rheumatology, 30,* 137–140.

V

Vaillancourt, T., Brittain, H., Bennett, L., Arnocky, S., McDougall, P., Hymel, S., et al. (2010a). Places to avoid: Population-based study of student reports of unsafe and high bullying areas at school. *Canadian Journal of School Psychology, 25,* 40–54.

Vaillancourt, T., Brittain, H. L., McDougall, P., & Duku, E. (2013). Longitudinal links between childhood peer victimization, internalizing and externalizing problems, and academic functioning: Developmental cascades. *Journal of Abnormal Child Psychology, 41,* 1203–1215.

Vaillancourt, T., & Hymel, S. (2006). Aggression and social status: The moderating roles of sex and peer-valued characteristics. *Aggressive Behavior, 32,* 396–408.

Vaillancourt, T., Hymel, S., & McDougall, P. (2013). The biological underpinnings of peer victimization: Understanding why and how the effects of bullying can last a lifetime. *Theory into Practice, 52,* 241–248.

Vaillancourt, T., McDougall, P., Hymel, S., & Sunderani, S. (2010b). Respect or fear? The relationship between power and bullying behavior. In S. R. Jimerson, S. M. Swearer, & D. L. Espelage (Eds.), *Handbook of bullying in schools: An international perspective* (pp. 211–222). New York: Routledge.

Vaillant-Molina, M., Bahrick, L. E., & Flom, R. (2013). Young infants match facial and vocal emotional expressions of other infants. *Infancy, 18,* E97–E111.

Vaish, A., Missana, M., & Tomasello, M. (2011). Three-year-old children intervene in third-party moral transgressions. *British Journal of Developmental Psychology, 29,* 124–130.

Vaish, A., & Striano, T. (2004). Is visual reference necessary? Contributions of facial versus vocal cues in 12-month-olds' social referencing behavior. *Developmental Science, 7,* 261–269.

Vakil, E., Blachstein, H., Sheinman, M., & Greenstein, Y. (2009). Developmental changes in attention tests norms: Implications for the structure of attention. *Child Neuropsychology, 15,* 21–39.

Valdés, G. (1998). The world outside and inside schools: Language and immigrant children. *Educational Researcher, 27*(6), 4–18.

Valentine, J. C., DuBois, D. L., & Cooper, H. (2004). The relation between self-beliefs and academic achievement: A meta-analytic review. *Educational Psychologist, 39,* 111–133.

Valian, V. (1999). Input and language acquisition. In W. C. Ritchie & T. K. Bhatia (Eds.), *Handbook of child language acquisition* (pp. 497–530). San Diego: Academic Press.

Valiente, C., Eisenberg, N., Fabes, R. A., Shepard, S. A., Cumberland, A., & Losoya, S. H. (2004). Prediction of children's empathy-related responding from their effortful control and parents' expressivity. *Developmental Psychology, 40,* 911–926.

Valiente, C., Lemery-Chalfant, K., & Swanson, J. (2010). Prediction of kindergartners' academic achievement from their effortful control and emotionality: Evidence for direct and moderated relations. *Journal of Educational Psychology, 102,* 550–560.

Valkenburg, P. M., & Calvert, S. L. (2012). Media and the child's developing imagination. In D. G. Singer & J. L. Singer (Eds.), *Handbook of children and the media* (pp.157–170). Thousand Oaks, CA: Sage.

Valli, L., Croninger, R. G., & Buese, D. (2012). Studying high-quality teaching in a highly charged policy environment. *Teachers College Record, 114*(4), 1–33.

van Aken, C., Junger, M., Verhoeven, M., van Aken, M. A. G., & Deković, M. (2007). The interactive effects of temperament and maternal parenting on toddlers' externalizing behaviours. *Infant and Child Development, 16,* 553–572.

Vandell, D. L., Belsky, J., Burchinal, M., Steinberg, L., Vandergrift, N., & the NICHD Early Child Care Research Network. (2010). Do effects of early child care extend to age 15 years? Results from the NICHD Study of Early Child Care and Youth Development. *Child Development, 81,* 737–756.

Vandell, D. L., & Mueller, E. C. (1995). Peer play and friendships during the first two years. In H. C. Foot, A. J. Chapman, & J. R. Smith (Eds.), *Friendship and social relations in children* (pp. 181–208). New Brunswick, NJ: Transaction.

Vandell, D. L., & Posner, J. K. (1999). Conceptualization and measurement of children's after-school environments. In S. L. Friedman & T. D. Wachs (Eds.), *Measuring environment across the life span* (pp. 167–196). Washington, DC: American Psychological Association.

Vandell, D. L., Reisner, E. R., & Pierce, K. M. (2007). *Outcomes linked to high-quality after-school programs: Longitudinal findings from the Study of Promising After-School Programs.* Retrieved from www.gse.uci.edu/childcare/pdf/afterschool/PP%20Longitudinal%20Findings%20Final%20Report.pdf

Vandell, D. L., Reisner, E. R., Pierce, K. M., Brown, B. B., Lee, D., Bolt, D., & Pechman, E. M. (2006). *The study of promising after-school programs: Examination of longer term outcomes after two years of program experiences.* Madison, WI: University of Wisconsin. Retrieved from www.wcer.wisc.edu/childcare/statements.html

Vandell, D. L., & Shumow, L. (1999). After-school child care programs. *Future of Children, 9*(2), 64–80.

van den Akker, A. L. Deković, M., Prinzie, P., & Asscher, J. J. (2010). Toddlers' temperament profiles: Stability and relations to negative and positive parenting. *Journal of Abnormal Child Psychology, 38,* 485–495.

Van den Bergh, B. R. H., & De Rycke, L. (2003). Measuring the multidimensional self-concept and global self-worth of 6- to 8-year-olds. *Journal of Genetic Psychology, 164,* 201–225.

Van den Bergh, B. R. H., Van Calster, B., Smits, T., Van Huffel, S., & Lagae, L. (2008). Antenatal maternal anxiety is related to HPA-axis dysregulation and self-reported depressive symptoms in adolescence: A prospective study on the fetal origins of depressed mood. *Neuropsychopharmacology, 33,* 536–545.

van den Dries, L., Juffer, F., van IJzendoorn, M. H., & Bakermans-Kranenburg, M. J. (2009). Fostering security?

A meta-analysis of attachment in adopted children. *Children and Youth Services Review, 31,* 410–421.

van den Eijnden, R., Vermulst, A., van Rooij, A. J., Scholte, R., & van de Mheen, D. (2014). The bidirectional relationships between online victimization and psychosocial problems in adolescents: A comparison with real-life victimization. *Journal of Youth and Adolescence, 43,* 790–802.

Vanderbilt, K. E., Liu, D., & Heyman, G. D. (2011). The development of distrust. *Child Development, 82,* 1372–1380.

Vanderbilt-Adriance, E., & Shaw, D. S. (2008). Protective factors and the development of resilience in the context of neighborhood disadvantage. *Journal of Abnormal Child Psychology, 36,* 887–901.

van der Meer, A. L. (1997). Keeping the arm in the limelight: Advanced visual control of arm movements in neonates. *European Journal of Paediatric Neurology, 4,* 103–108.

van de Vijver, F. J. R. (2011). Bias and real difference in cross-cultural differences: Neither friends nor foes. In F. J. R. van de Vijver, A. Chasiotis, & H. F. Byrnes (Eds.), *Fundamental questions in cross-cultural psychology* (pp. 235–258). Cambridge, UK: Cambridge University Press.

Vandewater, E. A., Bickham, D. S., Lee, J. H., Cummings, H. M., Wartella, E. A., & Rideout, V. J. (2005). When the television is always on: Heavy television exposure and young children's development. *American Behavioral Scientist, 48,* 562–577.

van Geel, M., & Vedder, P. (2011). The role of family obligations and school adjustment in explaining the immigrant paradox. *Journal of Youth and Adolescence, 40,* 187–196.

van Gelderen, L., Bos, H. M. W., Gartrell, N., Hermanns, J., & Perrin, E. C. (2012). Quality of life of adolescents raised from birth by lesbian mothers: The U.S. National Longitudinal Family Study. *Journal of Developmental and Behavioral Pediatrics, 33,* 17–23.

van Grieken, A., Renders, C. M., Wijtzes, A. I., Hirasing, R. A., & Raat, H. (2013). Overweight, obesity and underweight is associated with adverse psychosocial and physical health outcomes among 7-year-old children: The "Be Active, Eat Right" Study. *PLOS ONE, 8*(6), e67383.

Van Hulle, C. A., Goldsmith, H. H., & Lemery, K. S. (2004). Genetic, environmental, and gender effects on individual differences in toddler expressive language. *Journal of Speech, Language, and Hearing Research, 47,* 904–912.

van IJzendoorn, M. H., & Bakermans-Kranenburg, M. J. (2006). DRD4 7-repeat polymorphism moderates the association between maternal unresolved loss or trauma and infant disorganization. *Attachment and Human Development, 8,* 291–307.

van IJzendoorn, M. H., Bakermans-Kranenburg, M. J., & Ebstein, R. P. (2011). Methylation matters in child development: Toward developmental behavioral epigenetics. *Child Development Perspectives, 5,* 305–310.

van IJzendoorn, M. H., Belsky, J., & Bakermans-Kranenburg, M. J. (2012). Serotonin transporter genotype 5-HTTLPR as a marker of differential susceptibility: A meta-analysis of child and adolescent gene-by-environment studies. *Translational Psychiatry, 2,* e147.

van IJzendoorn, M. H., Juffer, F., & Poelhuis, C. W. K. (2005). Adoption and cognitive development: A meta-analytic comparison of adopted and nonadopted children's IQ and school performance. *Psychological Bulletin, 131,* 301–316.

van IJzendoorn, M. H., & Kroonenberg, P. M. (1988). Cross-cultural patterns of attachment: A meta-analysis of the Strange Situation. *Child Development, 59,* 147–156.

van IJzendoorn, M. H., & Sagi, A. (1999). Cross-cultural patterns of attachment. In J. Cassidy & P. R. Shaver (Eds.), *Handbook of attachment: Theory, research, and clinical applications* (pp. 713–734). New York: Guilford.

van IJzendoorn, M. H., & Sagi-Schwartz, A. (2008). Cross-cultural patterns of attachment: Universal and contextual dimensions. In J. Cassidy & P. R. Shaver (Eds.), *Handbook of attachment* (2nd ed., pp. 880–905). New York: Guilford.

van IJzendoorn, M. H., Vereijken, C. M. J. L., Bakermans-Kranenburg, M. J., & Riksen-Walraven, J. M. (2004). Assessing attachment security with the Attachment Q Sort: Meta-analytic evidence for the validity of the Observer AQS. *Child Development, 75,* 1188–1213.

Varela-Silva, M. I., Frisancho, A. R., Bogin, B., Chatkoff, D., Smith, P. K., Dickinson, F., & Winham, D. (2007). Behavioral, environmental, metabolic, and intergenerational components of early life undernutrition leading to later obesity in developing nations and in minority groups in the U.S.A. *Collegium Antropologicum, 31,* 39–46.

Varnhagen, C. (2007). Children and the Internet. In J. Gackenbach (Ed.), *Psychology and the Internet* (2nd ed., pp. 37–54). Amsterdam: Elsevier.

Vaughn, B. E., Bost, K. K., & van IJzendoorn, M. H. (2008). Attachment and temperament. In J. Cassidy & P. R. Shaver (Eds.), *Handbook of attachment: Theory, research, and clinical applications* (2nd ed., pp. 192–216). New York: Guilford.

Vaughn, B. E., Colvin, T. N., Azria, M. R., Caya, L., & Krzysik, L. (2001). Dyadic analyses of friendship in a sample of preschool-age children attending Head Start: Correspondence between measures and implications for social competence. *Child Development, 72,* 862–878.

Vaughn, B. E., Kopp, C. B., & Krakow, J. B. (1984). The emergence and consolidation of self-control from eighteen to thirty months of age: Normative trends and individual differences. *Child Development, 55,* 990–1004.

Vaughn, B. E., Vollenweider, M., Bost, K. K., Azria-Evans, M. R., & Snider, J. B. (2003). Negative interactions and social competence for preschool children in two samples: Reconsidering the interpretation of aggressive behavior for young children. *Merrill-Palmer Quarterly, 49,* 245–278.

Veenstra, R., Lindenberg, S., Munniksma, A., & Dijkstra, J. K. (2010). The complex relation between bullying, victimization, acceptance, and rejection: Giving special attention to status, affection, and sex differences. *Child Development, 81,* 480–486.

Velderman, M. K., Bakermans-Kranenburg, M. J., Juffer, F., & van IJzendoorn, M. H. (2006). Effects of attachment-based interventions on maternal sensitivity and infant attachment: Differential susceptibility of highly reactive infants. *Journal of Family Psychology, 20,* 266–274.

Velez, C. E., Wolchik, S. A., Tien, J., & Sandler, I. (2011). Protecting children from the consequences of divorce: A longitudinal study of the effects of parenting on children's coping processes. *Child Development, 82,* 244–257.

Venezia, M., Messinger, D. S., Thorp, D., & Mundy, P. (2004). The development of anticipatory smiling. *Infancy, 6,* 397–406.

Veneziano, R. A. (2003). The importance of paternal warmth. *Cross-Cultural Research, 37,* 265–281.

Verhulst, F. C. (2008). International adoption and mental health: Long-term behavioral outcome. In M. E. Garralda & J.-P. Raynaud (Eds.), *Culture and conflict in adolescent mental health* (pp. 83–105). Lanham, MD: Jason Aronson.

Verissimo, M., & Salvaterra, F. (2006). Maternal secure-base scripts and children's attachment security in an adopted sample. *Attachment and Human Development, 8,* 261–273.

Vernon-Feagans, L., & Cox, M. (2013). The Family Life Project: An epidemiological and developmental study of young children living in poor rural families. *Monographs of the Society for Research in Child Development, 78*(5, Serial No. 310).

Vernon-Feagans, L., Hurley, M. M., Yont, K. M., Wamboldt, P. M., & Kolak, A. (2007). Quality of childcare and otitis media: Relationship to children's language during naturalistic interactions at 18, 24, and 36 months. *Journal of Applied Developmental Psychology, 28,* 115–133.

Vernon-Feagans, L., Pancsofar, N., Willoughby, M., Odom, E., Quade, A., & Cox, M. (2008). Predictors of maternal language to infants during a picture book task in the home: Family SES, child characteristics and the parenting environment. *Journal of Applied Developmental Psychology, 29,* 213–226.

Vest, A. R., & Cho, L. S. (2012). Hypertension in pregnancy. *Cardiology Clinics, 30,* 407–423.

Vinden, P. G. (1996). Jun'n Quechua children's understanding of mind. *Child Development, 67,* 1707–1716.

Vinden, P. G. (2002). Understanding minds and evidence for belief: A study of Mofu children in Cameroon. *International Journal of Behavioral Development, 26,* 445–452.

Vinik, J., Almas, A., & Grusec, J. (2011). Mothers' knowledge of what distresses and what comforts their children predicts children's coping, empathy, and prosocial behavior. *Parenting: Science and Practice, 11,* 56–71.

Visher, E. B., Visher, J. S., & Pasley, K. (2003). Remarriage families and stepparenting. In F. Walsh (Ed.), *Normal family processes: Growing diversity and complexity* (pp. 153–175). New York: Guilford.

Vistad, I., Cvancarova, M., Hustad, B. L., & Henriksen, T. (2013). Vaginal breech delivery: Results of a prospective registration study. *BMC Pregnancy and Children, 13,* 153.

Vitaro, F., Boivin, M., Brendgen, M., Girard, A., & Dionner, G. (2012). Social experiences in kindergarten and academic achievement in grade 1: A monozygotic twin difference study. *Journal of Educational Psychology, 2,* 366–380.

Vitaro, F., & Brendgen, M. (2012). Subtypes of aggressive behaviors: Etiologies, development, and consequences. In T. Bliesner, A. Beelmann, & M. Stemmler (Eds.), *Antisocial behavior and crime: Contributions of developmental and evaluation research to prevention and intervention* (pp. 17–38). Cambridge, MA: Hogrefe.

Vitrup, B., & Holden, G. W. (2010). Children's assessments of corporal punishment and other disciplinary practices: The role of age, race, SES, and exposure to spanking. *Journal of Applied Developmental Psychology, 31,* 211–220.

Vivanti, G., Nadig, A., Ozonoff, S., & Rogers, S. J. (2008). What do children with autism attend to during imitation tasks? *Journal of Experimental Psychology, 101,* 186–205.

Vizard, E. (2013). Practitioner review: The victims and juvenile perpetrators of child sexual abuse—assessment and intervention. *The Journal of Child Psychology and Psychiatry, 54,* 503–515.

Voegtline, K. M., Costigan, K. A., Pater, H. A., & DiPietro, J. A. (2013). Near-term fetal response to maternal spoken voice. *Infant Behavior and Development, 36,* 526–533.

Vogel, C. A., Xue, Y., Maiduddin, E. M., Carlson, B. L., & Kisker, E. E. (2010). *Early Head Start children in grade 5: Long-term follow-up of the Early Head Start Research and Evaluation Study sample* (OPRE Report No. 2011-8). Washington, DC: U.S. Department of Health and Human Services.

Vohr, B. R., Stephens, B. E., McDonald, S. A., Ehrenkranz, R. A., Laptook, A. R., Pappas, A., et al. (2013). Cerebral palsy and growth failure at 6 to 7 years. *Pediatrics, 132,* e905–e914.

Volling, B. L. (2001). Early attachment relationships as predictors of preschool children's emotion regulation with a distressed sibling. *Early Education and Development, 12,* 185–207.

Volling, B. L. (2012). Family transitions following the birth of a sibling: An empirical review of changes in the firstborn's adjustment. *Psychological Bulletin, 138,* 497–528.

Volling, B. L., & Belsky, J. (1992). Contribution of mother–child and father–child relationships to the quality of sibling interaction: A longitudinal study. *Child Development, 63,* 1209–1222.

Volling, B. L., Mahoney, A., & Rauer, A. J. (2009). Sanctification of parenting, moral socialization, and young children's conscience development. *Psychology of Religion and Spirituality, 1,* 53–68.

Volling, B. L., McElwain, N. L., & Miller, A. L. (2002). Emotion regulation in context: The jealousy complex between young siblings and its relations with child and family characteristics. *Child Development, 73,* 581–600.

Vondra, J. I., Shaw, D. S., Searingen, L., Cohen, M., & Owens, E. B. (2001). Attachment stability and emotional and behavioral regulation from infancy to preschool age. *Development and Psychopathology, 13,* 13–33.

von Gontard, A., Heron, J., & Joinson, C. (2011). Family history of nocturnal enuresis and urinary incontinence: Results from a large epidemiological study. *Journal of Urology, 185,* 2303–2306.

von Hofsten, C. (1993). Prospective control: A basic aspect of action development. *Human Development, 36,* 253–270.

von Hofsten, C. (2004). An action perspective on motor development. *Trends in Cognitive Sciences, 8,* 266–272.

von Hofsten, C., & Rosander, K. (1998). The establishment of gaze control in early infancy. In S. Simion & G. Butterworth (Eds.), *The development of sensory, motor and cognitive capacities in early infancy* (pp. 49–66). Hove, UK: Psychology Press.

Vouloumanos, A. (2010). Three-month-olds prefer speech to other naturally occurring signals. *Language Learning and Development, 6,* 241–257.

Vuoksimaa, E., Koskenvuo, M., Rose, R. J., & Kaprio, J. (2009). Origins of handedness: A nationwide study of 30,1671 adults. *Neuropsychologia, 47,* 1294–1301.

Vygotsky, L. S. (1978). *Mind in society: The development of higher psychological processes.* Cambridge, MA: Harvard

University Press. (Original works published 1930, 1933, and 1935)
Vygotsky, L. S. (1987). Thinking and speech. In R. W. Rieber, A. S. Carton (Eds.), & N. Minick (Trans.), *The collected works of L. S. Vygotsky: Vol. 1. Problems of general psychology* (pp. 37–285). New York: Plenum. (Original work published 1934)

W

Waber, D. P. (2010). *Rethinking learning disabilities.* New York: Guilford.
Waber, D. P., Bryce, C. P., Girard, J. M., Zichlin, M., Fitzmaurice, G. M., & Galler, J. R. (2014). Impaired IQ and academic skills in adults who experienced moderate to severe infantile malnutrition: A 40-year study. *Nutritional Neuroscience, 17,* 58–64.
Wadell, P. M., Hagerman, R. J., & Hessl, D. R. (2013). Fragile X syndrome: Psychiatric manifestations, assessment and emerging therapies. *Current Psychiatry Reviews, 9,* 53–58.
Wadsworth, M. E., Rindlaub, L., Hurwich-Reiss, E., Rienks, S., Bianco, H., & Markman, H. J. (2013). A longitudinal examination of the adaptation to poverty-related stress model: Predicting child and adolescent adjustment over time. *Journal of Clinical Child and Adolescent Psychology, 42,* 713–725.
Wagenaar, K., van Wessenbruch, M. M., van Leeuwen, F. E., Cohen-Kettenis, P. T., Delemarre-van de Waal, H. A., Schats, R., et al. (2011). Self-reported behavioral and socioemotional functioning of 11- to 18-year-old adolescents conceived by in vitro fertilization. *Fertility and Sterility, 95,* 611–616.
Wainryb, C., & Ford, S. (1998). Young children's evaluations of acts based on beliefs different from their own. *Merrill-Palmer Quarterly, 44,* 484–503.
Walberg, H. J. (1986). Synthesis of research on teaching. In M. C. Wittrock (Ed.), *Handbook of research on teaching* (3rd ed., pp. 214–229). New York: Macmillan.
Waldfogel, J., Craigie, T.-A., & Brooks-Gunn, J. (2010). Fragile families and child wellbeing. *Future of Children, 20,* 87–112.
Waldfogel, J., & Zhai, F. (2008). Effects of public preschool expenditures on the test scores of fourth graders: Evidence from TIMMS. *Educational Research and Evaluation, 14,* 9–28.
Waldman, I. D., Rowe, D. C., Abramowitz, A., Kozel, S. T., Mohr, J. H., & Sherman, S. L. (1998). Association and linkage of the dopamine transporter gene and attention-deficit hƒyperactivity disorder in children: Heterogeneity owing to diagnostic subtype and severity. *American Journal of Human Genetics, 63,* 1767–1776.
Waldorf, K. M. A., & McAdams, R. M. (2013). Influence of infection during pregnancy on fetal development. *Reproduction, 146,* R151–R162.
Walenski, M., Tager-Flusberg, H., & Ullman, M. T. (2006). Language in autism. In S. O. Moldin & J. L. R. Rubenstein (Eds.), *Understanding autism: From basic neuroscience to treatment* (pp. 175–203). Boca Raton, FL: CRC Press.
Walker, C. M., Walker, L. B., & Ganea, P. A. (2012). The role of symbol-based experience in early learning and transfer from pictures: Evidence from Tanzania. *Developmental Psychology, 49,* 1315–1324.
Walker, L. J., & Taylor, J. H. (1991). Family interactions and the development of moral reasoning. *Child Development, 62,* 264–283
Walker, O. L., Degnan, K. A., Fox, N. A., & Henderson, H. A. (2013). Social problem solving in early childhood: Developmental change and the influence of shyness. *Journal of Applied Developmental Psychology, 34,* 185–193.
Walker, O. L., & Henderson, H. A. (2012). Temperament and social problem solving competence in preschool: Influences on academic skills in early elementary school. *Social Development, 21,* 761–779.
Walker, S. M. (2013). Biological and neurodevelopmental implications of neonatal pain. *Clinics in Perinatology, 40,* 471–491.
Wall, M., & Côté, J. (2007). Developmental activities that lead to dropout and investment in sport. *Physical Education and Sport Pedagogy, 12,* 77–87.
Walton, G. E., Armstrong, E. S., & Bower, T. G. R. (1998). Newborns learn to identify a face in eight-tenths of a second? *Developmental Science, 1,* 79–84.
Wang, Q. (2004). The emergence of cultural self-constructs: Autobiographical memory and self-description in European American and Chinese children. *Developmental Psychology, 40,* 3–15.
Wang, Q. (2006a). Earliest recollections of self and others in European American and Taiwanese young adults. *Psychological Science, 17,* 708–714.
Wang, Q. (2006b). Relations of maternal style and child self-concept to autobiographical memories in Chinese, Chinese immigrant, and European American 3-year-olds. *Child Development, 77,* 1794–1809.
Wang, Q. (2008). Emotion knowledge and autobiographical memory across the preschool years: A cross-cultural longitudinal investigation. *Cognition, 108,* 117–135.
Wang, Q., Doan, S. N., & Song, Q. (2010). Talking about internal states in mother–child reminiscing influences children's self-representations: A cross-cultural study. *Cognitive Development, 25,* 380–393.
Wang, Q., Shao, Y., & Li, Y. J. (2010). "My way or mom's way?" The bilingual and bicultural self in Hong Kong Chinese children and adolescents. *Child Development, 81,* 555–567.
Wang, S., Baillargeon, R., & Paterson, S. (2005). Detecting continuity violations in infancy: A new account and new evidence from covering and tube effects. *Cognition, 95,* 129–173.
Wang, Z., & Deater-Deckard, K. (2013). Resilience in gene–environment transactions. In S. Goldstein & R. B. Brooks (Eds.), *Handbook of resilience in children* (2nd ed., pp. 57–72). New York: Springer Science + Business Media.
Warnock, F., & Sandrin, D. (2004). Comprehensive description of newborn distress behavior in response to acute pain (newborn male circumcision). *Pain, 107,* 242–255.
Warren, A. R., & Tate, C. S. (1992). Egocentrism in children's telephone conversations. In R. M. Diaz & L. E. Berk (Eds.), *Private speech: From social interaction to self-regulation* (pp. 245–264). Hillsdale, NJ: Erlbaum.
Warren, S. L., & Simmens, S. J. (2005). Predicting toddler anxiety/depressive symptoms: Effects of caregiver sensitivity on temperamentally vulnerable children. *Infant Mental Health Journal, 26,* 40–55.
Wasik, B. A., & Bond, M. A. (2001). Beyond the pages of a book: Interactive book reading and language development in preschool classrooms. *Journal of Educational Psychology, 93,* 243–250.
Washington, J. A., & Thomas-Tate, S. (2009). How research informs cultural-linguistic differences in the classroom: The bi-dialectal African American child. In S. Rosenfield & V. Berninger (Eds.), *Implementing evidence-based academic interventions in school settings* (pp. 147–164). New York: Oxford University Press.
Washington, T., Gleeson, J. P., & Rulison, K. L. (2013). Competence and African American children in informal kinship care: The role of family. *Children and Youth Services Review, 35,* 1305–1312.
Wasserman, E. A., & Rovee-Collier, C. (2001). Pick the flowers and mind your As and 2s! Categorization by pigeons and infants. In M. E. Carroll & J. B. Overmier (Eds.), *Animal research and human health: Advancing human welfare through behavioral science* (pp. 263–279). Washington, DC: American Psychological Association.
Watamura, S. E., Donzella, B., Alwin, J., & Gunnar, M. R. (2003). Morning-to-afternoon increases in cortisol concentrations for infants and toddlers at child care: Age differences and behavioral correlates. *Child Development, 74,* 1006–1020.
Watamura, S. E., Phillips, D., Morrissey, T. W., McCartney, K., & Bub, K. (2011). Double jeopardy: Poorer social–emotional outcomes for children in the NICHD SECCYD experiencing home and child-care environments that confer risk. *Child Development, 82,* 48–65.
Waters, E., de Silva-Sanigorski, A., Brown, T., Campbell, K. J., Goa, Y., Armstrong, R., et al. (2011). Interventions for preventing obesity in children. *Cochrane Database of Systematic Reviews,* Issue 12. Art. No.: CD0011871.
Waters, E., Merrick, S., Treboux, D., Crowell, J., & Albersheim, L. (2000). Attachment security in infancy and early adulthood: A twenty-year longitudinal study. *Child Development, 71,* 684–689.
Waters, E., Vaughn, B. E., Posada, G., & Kondo-Ikemura, K. (Eds.). (1995). Caregiving, cultural, and cognitive perspectives on secure-base behavior and working models: New growing points of attachment theory and research. *Monographs of the Society for Research in Child Development, 60*(2–3, Serial No. 244).
Waters, S. F., & Thompson, R. A. (2014). Children's perceptions of the effectiveness of strategies for regulating anger and sadness. *International Journal of Behavioral Development, 38,* 174–181.
Watrin, J. P., & Darwich, R. (2012). On behaviorism in the cognitive revolution: Myth and reactions. *Review of General Psychology, 16,* 269–282.
Watson, J. B., & Raynor, R. (1920). Conditioned emotional reactions. *Journal of Experimental Psychology, 3,* 1–14.
Watson, M. (1990). Aspects of self development as reflected in children's role playing. In D. Cicchetti & M. Beeghly (Eds.), *The self in transition: Infancy to childhood* (pp. 281–307). Chicago: University of Chicago Press.
Wax, J. R., Pinette, M. G., & Cartin, A. (2010). Home versus hospital birth—process and outcome. *Obstetric and Gynecological Survey, 65,* 132–140.
Waxman, S. R., & Lidz, J. L. (2006). Early word learning. In D. Kuhn & R. Siegler (Eds.), *Handbook of child psychology: Vol. 2. Cognition, perception, and language* (6th ed., pp. 464–510). Hoboken, NJ: Wiley.
Waxman, S. R., & Senghas, A. (1992). Relations among word meanings in early lexical development. *Developmental Psychology, 28,* 862–873.
Webb, N. M., Franke, M. L., Ing, M., Chan, A., De, T., Freund, D., & Battey, D. (2008). The role of teacher instructional practices in student collaboration. *Contemporary Educational Psychology, 33,* 360–381.
Webb, N. M., Nemer, K. M., & Chizhik, A. W. (1998). Equity issues in collaborative group assessment: Group composition and performance. *American Educational Research Journal, 35,* 607–651.
Webb, S. J., Monk, C. S, & Nelson, C. A. (2001). Mechanisms of postnatal neurobiological development: Implications for human development. *Developmental Neuropsychology, 19,* 147–171.
Weber, C., Hahne, A., Friedrich, M., & Friederici, A. (2004). Discrimination of word stress in early infant perception: Electrophysiological evidence. *Cognitive Brain Research, 18,* 149–161.
Webster-Stratton, C., & Reid, M. J. (2010). The Incredible Years Parents, Teachers, and Children Training Series: A multifaceted treatment approach for young children with conduct disorders. In J. R. Weisz & A. E. Kazdin (Eds.), *Evidence-based psychotherapies for children and adolescents* (2nd ed., pp. 194–210). New York: Guilford.
Webster-Stratton, C., Rinaldi, J., & Reid, J. M. (2011). Long-term outcomes of Incredible Years parenting program: Predictors of adolescent adjustment. *Child and Adolescent Mental Health, 16,* 38–46.
Wechsler, D. (2002). *WPPSI-III: Wechsler Preschool and Primary Scale of Intelligence* (3rd ed.). San Antonio, TX: Psychological Corporation.
Wechsler, D. (2003). *WISC-IV: Wechsler Intelligence Scale for Children* (4th ed.). San Antonio, TX: Psychological Corporation.
Weems, C. F., & Costa, N. M. (2005). Developmental differences in the expression of childhood anxiety symptoms and fears. *Journal of the American Academy of Child and Adolescent Psychiatry, 44,* 656–663.
Wehren, A., DeLisi, R., & Arnold, M. (1981). The development of noun definition. *Journal of Child Language, 8,* 165–175.
Weikart, D. P. (1998). Changing early childhood development through educational intervention. *Preventive Medicine, 27,* 233–237.
Weikum, W. M., Vouloumanos, A., Navarra, J., Soto-Faraco, S., Sebastián-Gallés, N., & Werker, J. F. (2007). Visual language discrimination in infancy. *Science, 316,* 1159.
Weiland, C., & Yoshikawa, H. (2013). Impacts of a prekindergarten program on children's mathematics, language, literacy, executive function, and emotional skills. *Child Development, 84,* 2112–2130.
Weinberg, M. K., & Tronick, E. Z. (1994). Beyond the face: An empirical study of infant affective configurations of facial, vocal, gestural, and regulatory behaviors. *Child Development, 65,* 1503–1515.
Weinfield, N. S., Sroufe, L. A., & Egeland, B. (2000). Attachment from infancy to early adulthood in a high-risk sample: Continuity, discontinuity, and their correlates. *Child Development, 71,* 695–702.
Weinfield, N. S., Whaley, G. J. L., & Egeland, B. (2004). Continuity, discontinuity, and coherence in attachment from infancy to late adolescence: Sequelae of organization

and disorganization. *Attachment and Human Development, 6,* 73–97.
Weinstein, R. S. (2002). *Reaching higher: The power of expectations in schooling.* Cambridge, MA: Harvard University Press.
Weinstock, M. (2008). The long-term behavioural consequences of prenatal stress. *Neuroscience and Biobehavioral Reviews, 32,* 1073–1086.
Weisberg, D. S., Zosh, J. M., Hirsh-Pasek, K., & Golinkoff, R. M. (2013). Talking it up: Play, language development, and the role of adult support. *American Journal of Play, 6,* 39–54.
Weisgram, E. S., Bigler, R. S., & Liben, L. S. (2010). Gender, values, and occupational interests among children, adolescents, and adults. *Child Development, 81,* 778–796.
Weisman, O., Magori-Cohen, R., Louzoun, Y., Eidelman, A. I., & Feldman, R. (2011). Sleep–wake transitions in premature neonates predict early development. *Pediatrics, 128,* 706–714.
Weiss, K. M. (2005). Cryptic causation of human disease: Reading between the germ lines. *Trends in Genetics, 21,* 82–88.
Weizman, Z. O., & Snow, C. E. (2001). Lexical output as related to children's vocabulary acquisition: Effects of sophisticated exposure and support for meaning. *Developmental Psychology, 37,* 265–279.
Wekerle, C., & Wolfe, D. A. (2003). Child maltreatment. In E. J. Mash & R. A. Barkley (Eds.), *Child psychopathology* (2nd ed., pp. 632–684). New York: Guilford.
Weller, E. B., Kloos, A. L., & Weller, R. A. (2006). Mood disorders. M. K. Dulcan & J. M. Wiener (Eds.), *Essentials of child and adolescent psychiatry* (pp. 267–320). Washington, DC: American Psychiatric Association.
Wellman, H. M. (2002). Understanding the psychological world: Developing a theory of mind. In U. Goswami (Ed.), *Blackwell handbook of child cognitive development* (pp. 167–187). Malden, MA: Blackwell.
Wellman, H. M. (2011). Developing a theory of mind. In U. Goswami (Ed.), *Wiley-Blackwell handbook of childhood cognitive development* (2nd ed., pp. 258–284). Malden, MA: Wiley-Blackwell.
Wellman, H. M. (2012). Theory of mind: Better methods, clearer findings, more development. European *Journal of Developmental Psychology, 9,* 313–330.
Wellman, H. M., Fang, F., Liu, D., Zhu, L., & Liu, G. (2006). Scaling of theory-of-mind understandings in Chinese children. *Psychological Science, 17,* 1075–1081.
Wellman, H. M., & Hickling, A. K. (1994). The mind's "I": Children's conception of the mind as an active agent. *Child Development, 65,* 1564–1580.
Wellman, H. M., Lopez-Duran, S., LaBounty, J., & Hamilton, B. (2008). Infant attention to intentional action predicts preschool theory of mind. *Developmental Psychology, 44,* 618–623.
Weng, S. F., Redsell, S. A., Swift, J. A., Yang, M., & Glazebrook, C. P. (2012). Systematic review and meta-analyses of risk factors for childhood overweight identifiable during infancy. *Archives of Disease in Childhood, 97,* 1019–1026.
Wentworth, N., Benson, J. B., & Haith, M. M. (2000). The development of infants' reaches for stationary and moving targets. *Child Development, 71,* 576–601.
Wentzel, K. R., & Brophy, J. E. (2014). *Motivating students to learn.* Hoboken, NJ: Taylor & Francis.
Werner, E. E. (1989, April). Children of the garden island. *Scientific American, 260(4),* 106–111.
Werner, E. E. (2001). *Journeys from childhood to midlife: Risk, resilience, and recovery.* Ithaca, NY: Cornell University Press.
Werner, E. E. (2013). What can we learn about resilience from large-scale longitudinal studies? In S. Goldstein & R. Brooks (Eds.), *Handbook of resilience in children* (2nd ed., pp. 87–102). New York: Springer Science + Business Media.
Werner, E. E., & Smith, R. S. (1982). *Vulnerable but invincible: A study of resilient children.* New York: McGraw-Hill.
Werner, E. E., & Smith, R. S. (1992). *Overcoming the odds: High risk children from birth to adulthood.* Ithaca, NY: Cornell University Press.
Werner, N. E., & Crick, N. R. (2004). Maladaptive peer relationships and the development of relational and physical aggression during middle childhood. *Social Development, 13,* 495–514.
Westermann, G., Sirois, S., Shultz, T. R., & Mareschal, D. (2006). Modeling developmental cognitive neuroscience. *Trends in Cognitive Sciences, 10,* 227–232.
Whaley, S. E., Koleilat, M., & Jiang, L. (2012). WIC infant food package issuance data are a valid measure of infant feeding practices. *Journal of Human Lactation, 28,* 134–138.
Whaley, S. E., Koleilat, M., Whaley, M., Gomez, J., Meehan, K., & Saluja, K. (2012). Impact of policy changes on infant feeding decisions among low-income women participating in the Special Supplemental Nutrition Program for Women, Infants, and Children. *American Journal of Public Health, 102,* 2269–2273.
Whipple, E. E. (2006). Child abuse and neglect: Consequences of physical, sexual, and emotional abuse of children. In H. E. Fitzgerald, B. M. Lester, & B. Zuckerman (Eds.), *The crisis in youth mental health: Vol 1. Childhood disorders* (pp. 205–229). Westport, CT: Praeger.
Whipple, N., Bernier, A., & Mageau, G. A. (2011). Broadening the study of infant security of attachment: Maternal autonomy-support in the context of infant exploration. *Social Development, 20,* 17–32.
White, B., & Held, R. (1966). Plasticity of sensorimotor development in the human infant. In J. F. Rosenblith & W. Allinsmith (Eds.), *The causes of behavior* (pp. 60–70). Boston: Allyn and Bacon.
White, M. A., Wilson, M. E., Elander, G., & Persson, B. (1999). The Swedish family: Transition to parenthood. *Scandinavian Journal of Caring Sciences, 13,* 171–176.
White, Y. A., Woods, D. C., Takai, Y., Ishihara, O., Seki, H., & Tilly, J. L. (2012). Oocyte formation by mitotically active germ cells purified from ovaries of reproductive-age women. *Nature Medicine, 18,* 413–421.
Whitehurst, G. J., & Lonigan, C. J. (1998). Child development and emergent literacy. *Child Development, 69,* 848–872.
Whiteman, S. D., & Loken, E. (2006). Comparing analytic techniques to classify dyadic relationships: An example using siblings. *Journal of Marriage and Family, 68,* 1370–1382.
Whitesell, N. R., Mitchell, C. M., Spicer, P., and the Voices of Indian Teens Project Team. (2009). A longitudinal study of self-esteem, cultural identity, and academic success among American Indian adolescents. *Cultural Diversity and Ethnic Minority Psychology, 15,* 38–50.
Whiteside-Mansell, L., Bradley, R. H., Owen, M. T., Randolph, S. M., & Cauce, A. M. (2003). Parenting and children's behavior at 36 months: Equivalence between African-American and European-American mother–child dyads. *Parenting: Science and Practice, 3,* 197–234.
Whiting, B., & Edwards, C. P. (1988). *Children in different worlds.* Cambridge, MA: Harvard University Press.
Whitney, C. G., Zhou, F., Singleton, J., & Schuchat, A. (2014). Benefits from immunization during the Vaccines for Children Program Era—United States, 1994–2013. *Morbidity and Mortality Weekly Report, 63,* 352–355.
Wichman, A. L., Rodgers, J. L., & MacCallum, R. C. (2007). Birth order has no effect on intelligence: A reply and extension of previous findings. *Personality and Social Psychology Bulletin, 33,* 1195–1200.
Wichmann, C., Coplan, R. J., & Daniels, T. (2004). The social cognitions of socially withdrawn children. *Social Development, 13,* 377–392.
Wichstrøm, L. (2006). Sexual orientation as a risk factor for bulimic symptoms. *International Journal of Eating Disorders, 39,* 448–453.
Widen, S. C., & Russell, J. A. (2011). In building a script for an emotion do preschoolers add its cause before its behavior consequence? *Social Development, 20,* 471–485.
Wigfield, A., Battle, A., Keller, L. B., & Eccles, J. S. (2002). Sex differences in motivation, self-concept, career aspiration, and career choice: Implications for cognitive development. In A. McGillicudy-De Lisi & R. De Lisi (Eds.), *Biology, society, and behavior: The development of sex differences in cognition* (pp. 93–124). Westport, CT: Ablex.
Wigfield, A., Eccles, J. S., Schiefele, U., Roeser, R. W., & Davis-Kean, P. (2006). Development of achievement motivation. In N. Eisenberg (Ed.), *Handbook of child psychology: Vol. 3. Social, emotional, and personality development* (6th ed., pp. 933–1002). Hoboken, NJ: Wiley.
Wigfield, A., Eccles, J. S., Yoon, K. S., Harold, R. D., Arbreton, A. J., Freedman-Doan, C., & Blumenfeld, P. C. (1997). Changes in children's competence beliefs and subjective task values across the elementary school years: A three-year study. *Journal of Educational Psychology,* 89, 451–469.
Wilcox, T., & Woods, R. (2009). Experience primes infants to individuate objects. In A. Woodward & A. Needham (Eds.), *Learning and the infant mind* (pp. 117–143). New York: Oxford University Press.
Willatts, P. (1999). Development of means—end behavior in young infants: Pulling a support to retrieve a distant object. *Developmental Psychology, 35,* 651–667.
Williams, G. R. (2008). Neurodevelopmental and neurophysiological actions of thyroid hormone. *Journal of Neuroendocrinology, 20,* 784–794.
Williams, K., & Dunne-Bryant, A. (2006). Divorce and adult psychological well-being: Clarifying the role of gender and age. *Journal of Marriage and Family, 68,* 1178–1196.
Williams, K., Haywood, K. I., & Painter, M. (1996). Environmental versus biological influences on gender differences in the overarm throw for force: Dominant and nondominant arm throws. *Women in Sport and Physical Activity Journal, 5,* 29–48.
Williams, P. E., Weiss, L. G., & Rolfhus, E. (2003). *WISC-IV: Theoretical model and test blueprint.* San Antonio, TX: Psychological Corporation.
Williams, S. C., Lochman, J. E., Phillips, N. C., & Barry, T. D. (2003). Aggressive and nonaggressive boys' physiological and cognitive processes in response to peer provocations. *Journal of Clinical Child and Adolescent Psychology, 32,* 568–576.
Williams, S. T., Mastergeorge, A. M., & Ontai, L. L. (2010). Caregiver involvement in infant peer interactions: Scaffolding in a social context. *Early Childhood Research Quarterly, 25,* 251–266.
Williamson, J., Softas-Nall, B., & Miller, J. (2003). Grandmothers raising grandchildren: An exploration of their experiences and emotions. *Counseling and Therapy for Couples with Families, 11,* 23–32.
Wilson-Ching, M., Molloy, C. S., Anderson, V. A., Burnett, A., Roberts, G., Cheong, J. L., et al. (2013). Attention difficulties in a contemporary geographic cohort of adolescents born extremely preterm/extremely low birth weight. *Journal of the International Neuropsychological Society, 19,* 1097–1108.
Wimmer, M. B. (2013). *Evidence-based practices for school refusal and truancy.* Bethesda, MD: NASP.
Winkler, I., Háden, G. P., Ladinig, O., Sziller, I., & Honing, H. (2009). Newborn infants detect the beat in music. *Proceedings of the National Academy of Sciences, 106,* 2468–2471.
Winner, E. (1986, August). Where pelicans kiss seals. *Psychology Today, 20*(8), 25–35.
Winner, E. (1988). *The point of words: Children's understanding of metaphor and irony.* Cambridge, MA: Harvard University Press.
Winner, E. (2000). The origins and ends of giftedness. *American Psychologist, 55,* 159–169.
Winsler, A. (2009). Still talking to ourselves after all these years: A review of current research on private speech. In A. Winsler, C. Fernyhough, & I. Montero (Eds.), *Private speech, executive functioning, and the development of self-regulation.* New York: Cambridge University Press.
Winsler, A., Abar, B., Feder, M. A., Rubio, D. A., & Schunn, C. D. (2007). Private speech and executive functioning among high functioning children with autism spectrum disorders. *Journal of Autism and Developmental Disorders, Online First*™.
Winsler, A., Fernyhough, C., & Montero, I. (2009). *Private speech, executive functioning, and the development of verbal self-regulation.* New York: Cambridge University Press.
Witherington, D. C. (2005). The development of prospective grasping control between 5 and 7 months: A longitudinal study. *Infancy, 7,* 143–161.
Witherington, D. C., Campos, J. J., Harriger, J. A., Bryan, C., & Margett, T. E. (2010). Emotion and its development in infancy. In G. Bremner & T. D. Wachs (Eds.), *Wiley-Blackwell handbook of infant development: Vol. 1. Basic research* (2nd ed., pp. 568–591). Hoboken, NJ: Wiley-Blackwell.
Wolchik, S. A., Sandler, I. N., Millsap, R. E., Plummer, B. A., Greene, S. M., Anderson, E. R., et al. (2002). Six-year follow-up of preventive interventions for children of divorce: A randomized controlled trial. *Journal of the American Medical Association, 288,* 1874–1881.

Wolf, A. W., Jimenez, E., & Lozoff, B. (2003). Effects of iron therapy on infant blood lead levels. *Journal of Pediatrics, 143,* 789–795.

Wolfberg, A. J. (2012). The future of fetal monitoring. *Reviews in Obstetrics and Gynecology, 5,* e132–e136.

Wolfe, D. A. (2005). *Child abuse* (2nd ed.) Thousand Oaks, CA: Sage.

Wolfe, V. V. (2006). Child sexual abuse. In E. J. Mash & R. A. Barkley (Eds.), *Treatment of childhood disorders* (3rd ed., pp. 647–727). New York: Guilford.

Wolff, P. H. (1966). The causes, controls and organization of behavior in the neonate. *Psychological Issues, 5*(1, Serial No. 17).

Wolff, P. H., & Fesseha, G. (1999). The orphans of Eritrea: A five-year follow-up study. *Journal of Child Psychology and Psychiatry and Allied Disciplines, 40,* 1231–1237.

Wood, E., Desmarais, S., & Gugula, S. (2002). The impact of parenting experience on gender stereotyped toy play of children. *Sex Roles, 47,* 39–49.

Wood, J. J., Emmerson, N. A., & Cowan, P. A. (2004). Is early attachment security carried forward into relationships with preschool peers? *British Journal of Developmental Psychology, 22,* 245–253.

Wood, J. N., Kouider, S., & Carey, S. (2009). Acquisition of singular-plural morphology. *Developmental Psychology, 45,* 202–206.

Wood, R. M. (2009). Changes in cry acoustics and distress ratings while the infant is crying. *Infant and Child Development, 18,* 163–177.

Woodward, A. (2009). Infants' grasp of others' intentions. *Current Directions in Psychological Science, 18,* 53–57.

Woodward, J., & Ono, Y. (2004). Mathematics and academic diversity in Japan. *Journal of Learning Disabilities, 37,* 74–82.

Woolley, J. D. (1997). Thinking about fantasy: Are children fundamentally different thinkers and believers from adults? *Child Development, 68,* 991–1011.

Woolley, J. D. (2000). The development of beliefs about direct mental–physical causality in imagination, magic, and religion. In K. S. Rosengren, C. N. Johnson, & P. L. Harris (Eds.), *Imagining the impossible* (pp. 99–129). New York: Cambridge University Press.

Woolley, J. D., Browne, C. A., & Boerger, E. A. (2006). Constraints on children's judgments of magical causality. *Journal of Cognition and Development, 7,* 253–277.

Woolley, J. D., & Cornelius, C. A. (2013). Beliefs in magical beings and cultural myths. In M. Taylor (Ed.), *Oxford handbook of the development of imagination* (pp. 61–74). New York: Oxford University Press.

Woolley, J. D., Cornelius, C. A., & Lacy, W. (2011). Developmental changes in the use of supernatural explanations for unusual events. *Journal of Cognition and Culture, 11,* 311–337.

Woolley, J. D., & Cox, V. (2007). Development of beliefs about storybook reality. *Developmental Science, 10,* 681–693.

World Health Organization. (2008). *World report on child injury prevention.* Geneva, Switzerland: Author.

World Health Organization. (2012a). *Countdown to 2015: Building a future for women and children.* Geneva, Switzerland: Author.

World Health Organization. (2012b). *The World Health Organization's infant feeding recommendation.* Retrieved from www.who.int/nutrition/topics/infantfeeding_recommendation/en/index.html

World Health Organization (2013a). *Levels and trends in child mortality: Report 2013.* Geneva, Switzerland: Author.

World Health Organization. (2013b). *World health statistics 2013.* Retrieved from apps.who.int/iris/bitstream/10665/81965/1/9789241564588_eng.pdf?ua=1

World Health Organization. (2014a). *Immunization, vaccines, and biologicals: Data, statistics and graphics.* Retrieved from www.who.int/immunization/monitoring_surveillance/data/en/

World Health Organization. (2014b). Rubella. Fact Sheet No. 367. Retrieved from www.who.int/mediacentre/factsheets/fs367/en

World Health Organization. (2014c). *WHO global infobase.* Retrieved from apps.who.int/infobase/Comparisons.aspx

World Health Organization. (2014d). *World health statistics 2014.* Retrieved from www.who.int/gho/publications/world_health_statistics/2014/en

Wörmann, V., Holodynski, M., Kärtner, J., & Keller, H. (2012). A cross-cultural comparison of the development of the social smile: A longitudinal study of maternal and infant imitation in 6 and 12-week-old infants. *Infant Behavior and Development, 35,* 335–347.

Worthman, C. M. (2011). Developmental cultural ecology of sleep. In M. El-Sheikh (Ed.), *Sleep and development: Familial and socio-cultural considerations* (pp. 167–194). New York: Oxford University Press.

Worthy, J., Hungerford-Kresser, H., & Hampton, A. (2009). Tracking and ability grouping. In L. Christenbury, R. Bomer, & P. Smargorinsky (Eds.), *Handbook of adolescent literacy research* (pp. 220–235). New York: Guilford.

Wright, B. C. (2006). On the emergence of the discriminative mode for transitive inference. *European Journal of Cognitive Psychology, 18,* 776–800.

Wright, B. C., Robertson, S., & Hadfield, L. (2011). Transitivity for height versus speed: To what extent do the under-7s really have a transitive capacity? *Thinking and Reasoning, 17,* 57–81.

Wright, J. C., Huston, A. C., Murphy, K. C., St. Peters, M., Pinon, M., Scantlin, R., & Kotler, J. (2001). The relations of early television viewing to school readiness and vocabulary of children from low-income families: The Early Window Project. *Child Development, 72,* 1347–1366.

Wright, J. P., Dietrich, K., Ris, M., Hornung, R., Wessel, S., Lanphear, B., et al. (2008). Association of prenatal and childhood blood lead concentrations with criminal arrests in early adulthood. *PLOS Medicine, 5,* e101.

Wright, M. O., & Masten, A. S. (2005). Resilience processes in development. In S. Goldstein & R. B. Brooks (Eds.), *Handbook of resilience in children* (pp. 17–37). New York: Springer.

Wright, R. O., Tsaih, S. W., Schwartz, J., Wright, R. J., & Hu, H. (2003). Associations between iron deficiency and blood lead level in a longitudinal analysis of children followed in an urban primary care clinic. *Journal of Pediatrics, 142,* 9–14.

Wright, W. E. (2013). Bilingual education. In T. K. Bhatia & W. C. Ritchie (Eds.), *Handbook of bilingualism and multilingualism* (pp. 598–623). Chichester, UK: Wiley-Blackwell.

Wrotniak, B. H., Epstein, L. H., Raluch, R. A., & Roemmich, J. N. (2004). Parent weight change as a predictor of child weight change in family-based behavioral obesity treatment. *Archives of Pediatric and Adolescent Medicine, 158,* 342–347.

Wu, G., Bazer, F. W., Cudd, T. A., Meininger, C. J., & Spencer, T. E. (2004). Maternal nutrition and fetal development. *Journal of Nutrition, 134,* 2169–2172.

Wu, L. L., Bumpass, L. L., & Musick, K. (2001). Historical and life course trajectories of nonmarital childbearing. In L. L. Wu & B. Wolfe (Eds.), *Out of wedlock: Causes and consequences of nonmarital fertility* (pp. 3–48). New York: Russell Sage Foundation.

Wulczyn, F. (2009). Epidemiological perspectives on maltreatment prevention. *Future of Children, 19,* 39–66.

Wyman, E., Rakoczy, H., & Tomasello, M. (2009). Normativity and context in young children's pretend play. *Cognitive Development, 24,* 146–155.

Wynn, K. (1992). Addition and subtraction by human infants. *Nature, 358,* 749–750.

Wynn, K., Bloom, P., & Chiang, W.-C. (2002). Enumeration of collective entities by 5-month-old infants. *Cognition, 83,* B55–B62.

Wynne-Edwards, K. E. (2001). Hormonal changes in mammalian fathers. *Hormones and Behavior, 40,* 139–145.

X

Xu, F., Han, Y., Sabbagh, M. A., Wang, T., Ren, X., & Li, C. (2013). Developmental differences in the structure of executive function in middle childhood and adolescence. *PLOS ONE, 8,* e77770.

Xu, F., Spelke, E., & Goddard, S. (2005). Number sense in human infants. *Developmental Science, 8,* 88–101.

Y

Yamada, T., Yamada, T., Morikawa, M., & Minakami, H. (2012). Clinical features of abruptio placentae as a prominent cause of cerebral palsy. *Early Human Development, 88,* 861–864.

Yang, B., Ollendick, T. H., Dong, Q., Xia, Y., & Lin, L. (1995). Only children and children with siblings in the People's Republic of China: Levels of fear, anxiety, and depression. *Child Development, 66,* 1301–1311.

Yang, C.-K., & Hahn, H.-M. (2002). Cosleeping in young Korean children. Developmental and Behavioral Pediatrics, 23, 151–157.

Yarrow, M. R., Scott, P. M., & Waxler, C. Z. (1973). Learning concern for others. *Developmental Psychology, 8,* 240–260.

Yeates, K. O., Schultz, L. H., & Selman, R. L. (1991). The development of interpersonal negotiation strategies in thought and action: A social-cognitive link to behavioral adjustment and social status. *Merrill-Palmer Quarterly, 37,* 369–405.

Yeh, C. J., Kim, A. B., Pituc, S. T., & Atkins, M. (2008). Poverty, loss, and resilience: The story of Chinese immigrant youth. *Journal of Counseling Psychology, 55,* 34–48.

Yirmiya, N., Erel, O., Shaked, M., & Solomonica-Levi, D. (1998). Meta-analyses comparing theory of mind abilities of individuals with autism, individuals with mental retardation, and normally developing individuals. *Psychological Bulletin, 124,* 283–307.

Yook, J.-H., Han, J.-Y., Choi, J.-S., Ahn, H.-K., Lee, S.-W., Kim, M.-Y., et al. (2012). Pregnancy outcomes and factors associated with voluntary pregnancy termination in women who had been treated for acne with isotretinoin. *Clinical Toxicology, 50,* 896–901.

Yoshida, H., & Smith, L. B. (2003). Known and novel noun extensions: Attention at two levels of abstraction. *Child Development, 74,* 564–577.

Yoshikawa, H., Aber, J. L., & Beardslee, W. R. (2012). The effects of poverty on the mental, emotional, and behavioral health of children and youth: Implications for prevention. *American Psychologist, 67,* 272–284.

Yoshikawa, H., Weiland, C., Brooks-Gunn, J., Burchinal, M. R., Espinosa, L. M., Gormley, W. T., et al. (2013). *Investing in our future: The evidence base on preschool education.* Ann Arbor, MI: Society for Research in Child Development. Retrieved from fcd-us.org/resources/evidence-base-preschool

Youn, M. J., Leon, J., & Lee, K. J. (2012). The influence of maternal employment on children's learning growth and the role of parental involvement. *Early Child Development and Care, 182,* 1227–1246.

Young, S. E., Friedman, N. P., Miyake, A., Willcutt, E. G., Corley, R. P., Haberstick, B. C., et al. (2009). Behavioral disinhibition: Liability for externalizing spectrum disorders and its genetic and environmental relation to response inhibition across adolescence. *Journal of Abnormal Psychology, 118,* 117–130.

Young-Hyman, D., Tanofsky-Kraff, M., Yanovski, S. Z., Keil, M., Cohen, M. L., & Peyrot, M. (2006). Psychological status and weight-related distress in overweight or at-risk-for-overweight children. *Obesity, 14,* 2249–2258.

Yousafzai, A. K., Yakoob, M. Y., & Bhutta, Z. A. (2013). Nutrition-based approaches to early childhood development. In P. R. Britto, P. L. Engle, & C. M. Super (Eds.), *Handbook of early childhood development research and its impact on global policy* (pp. 202–226). New York: Oxford University Press.

Yu, R. (2002). On the reform of elementary school education in China. *Educational Exploration, 129,* 56–57.

Yuill, N., & Pearson, A. (1998). The developmental bases for trait attribution: Children's understanding of traits as causal mechanisms based on desire. *Developmental Psychology, 34,* 574–586.

Yule, W., Dyregov, A., Raundalen, M., & Smith, P. (2013). Children and war: The work of the Children and War Foundation. *European Journal of Psychotraumatology, 4,* 1–8.

Yumoto, C., Jacobson, S. W., & Jacobson, J. L. (2008). Fetal substance exposure and cumulative environmental risk in an African-American cohort. *Child Development, 79,* 1761–1776.

Yunger, J. L., Carver, P. R., & Perry, D. G. (2004). Does gender identity influence children's psychological well-being? *Developmental Psychology, 40,* 572–582.

Z

Zachrisson, H. D., Dearing, E., Lekhal, R., & Toppelberg, C. O. (2013). Little evidence that time in child care causes externalizing problems during early childhood in Norway. *Child Development, 84,* 1152–1170.

Zadjel, R. T., Bloom, J. M., Fireman, G., & Larsen, J. T. (2013). Children's understanding and experience of mixed emotions: The roles of age, gender, and empathy. *The Journal of Genetic Psychology, 174,* 582–603.

Zafeiriou, D. I. (2000). Plantar grasp reflex in high-risk infants during the first year of life. *Pediatric Neurology, 22,* 75–76.

Zahn-Waxler, C., Kochanska, G., Krupnick, J., & McKnew, D. (1990). Patterns of guilt in children of depressed and well mothers. *Developmental Psychology, 26,* 51–59.

Zajac, R., O'Neill, S., & Hayne, H. (2012). Disorder in the courtroom? Child witnesses under cross-examination. *Developmental Review, 32,* 181–204.

Zalewski, M., Lengua, L. J., Wilson, A. C., Trancik, A., & Bazinet, A. (2011). Emotion regulation profiles, temperament, and adjustment problems in preadolescents. *Child Development, 82,* 951–966.

Zaslow, M. J., Weinfield, N. S., Gallagher, M., Hair, E. C., Ogawa, J. R., Egeland, B., Tabors, P. O., & De Temple, J. M. (2006). Longitudinal prediction of child outcomes from differing measures of parenting in a low-income sample. *Developmental Psychology, 42,* 27–37.

Zeanah, C. H. (2000). Disturbances of attachment in young children adopted from institutions. *Journal of Developmental and Behavioral Pediatrics, 21,* 230–236.

Zeifman, D. M. (2003). Predicting adult responses to infant distress: Adult characteristics associated with perceptions, emotional reactions, and timing of intervention. *Infant Mental Health Journal, 24,* 597–612.

Zelazo, N. A., Zelazo, P. R., Cohen, K. M., & Zelazo, P. D. (1993). Specificity of practice effects on elementary neuromotor patterns. *Developmental Psychology, 29,* 686–691.

Zelazo, P., & Paus, T. (2010). Developmental social neuroscience: An introduction. In M. K. Underwood & L. H. Rosen (Eds.), *Social development: Relationships in infancy, childhood, and adolescence* (pp. 29–43). New York: Guilford.

Zelazo, P. D., & Carlson, S. M. (2012). Hot and cool executive function in childhood and adolescence: Development and plasticity. *Child Development Perspectives, 6,* 354–360.

Zelazo, P. D., Carlson, S. M., & Kesek, A. (2008). The development of executive function in childhood. In C. A. Nelson & M. Luciana (Eds.), *Handbook of cognitive developmental neuroscience* (2nd ed., pp. 553–574). Cambridge, MA: MIT Press.

Zelazo, P. D., Muller, U., Frye, D., & Marcovitch, S. (2003). The development of executive function: Cognitive complexity and control—revised. *Monographs of the Society for Research in Child Development, 68*(3), 93–119.

Zeller, M. H., & Modi, A. C. (2006). Predictors of health-related quality of life in obese youth. *Obesity Research, 14,* 122–130.

Zellner, D. A., Loaiza, S., Gonzales, Z., Pita, J., Morales, J., et al. (2006). Food selection changes under stress. *Physiology & Behavior, 87,* 789–793.

Zeskind, P. S., & Barr, R. G. (1997). Acoustic characteristics of naturally occurring cries of infants with "colic." *Child Development, 68,* 394–403.

Zhang, T.-Y., & Meaney, M. J. (2010). Epigenetics and the environmental regulation of the genome and its function. *Annual Review of Psychology, 61,* 439–466.

Zhou, Q., Lengua, L. J., & Wang, Y. (2009). The relations of temperament reactivity and effortful control to children's adjustment problems in China and the United States. *Developmental Psychology, 45,* 724–739.

Zhou, X., Huang, J., Wang, Z., Wang, B., Zhao, Z., Yang, L., & Zheng-zheng, Y. (2006). Parent–child interaction and children's number learning. *Early Child Development and Care, 176,* 763–775.

Ziemer, C. J., Plumert, J. M., & Pick, A. D. (2012). To grasp or not to grasp: Infants' actions toward objects and pictures. *Infancy, 17,* 479–497.

Zimmer-Gembeck, M. J., & Skinner, E. A. (2011). The development of coping across childhood and adolescence: An integrative review and critique of research. *International Journal of Behavioral Development, 35,* 1–17.

Zimmerman, B. J., & Labuhn, A. S. (2012). Self-regulation of learning: Process approaches to personal development. In K. R. Harris, S. Graham, T. Urdan, C. B. McCormick, G. M. Sinatra, & J. Sweller (Eds.), *APA educational psychology handbook: Vol. 1. Theories, constructs, and critical issues* (pp. 399–425). Washington, DC: American Psychological Association.

Zimmerman, F. J., & Christakis, D. A. (2005). Children's television viewing and cognitive outcomes. *Archives of Pediatrics and Adolescent Medicine, 159,* 619–625.

Zimmerman, F. J., Christakis, D. A., & Meltzoff, A. N. (2007). Television and DVD/video viewing in children younger than 2 years. *Archives of Pediatrics and Adolescent Medicine, 161,* 473–479.

Zimmermann, L. K., & Stansbury, K. (2004). The influence of emotion regulation, level of shyness, and habituation on the neuroendocrine response of three-year-old children. *Psychoneuroendocrinology, 29,* 973–982.

Zitzmann, M. (2013). Effects of age on male fertility. *Best Practice & Research Clinical Endocrinology and Metabolism, 27,* 617–628.

Ziv, Y. (2013). Social information processing patterns, social skills, and school readiness in preschool children. *Journal of Experimental Child Psychology, 114,* 306–320.

Zoëga, H., Rothman, K. J., Huybrechts, K. F., Olafsson, O., Baldursson, G., Almarsdottir, A. B., et al. (2012). A population-based study of stimulant drug treatment of ADHD and academic progress in children. *Pediatrics, 130,* e53–e62.

Zolotor, A. J., & Puzia, M. E. (2010). Bans against corporal punishment: A systematic review of the laws, changes in attitudes and behaviours. *Child Abuse Review, 19,* 229–247.

Zolotor, A. J., Theodore, A. D., Runyan, D. K., Chang, J. J., & Laskey, A. L. (2011). Corporal punishment and physical abuse: Population-based trends for three-to-11-year-old children in the United States. *Child Abuse Review, 20,* 57–66.

Zosuls, K. M., Ruble, D. N., Tamis-LeMonda, C. S., Shrout, P. E., Bornstein, M. H., & Greulich, F. K. (2009). The acquisition of gender labels in infancy: Implications for gender-typed play. *Developmental Psychology, 45,* 688–701.

Zucker, K. J. (2006). "I'm half-boy, half-girl": Play psychotherapy and parent counseling for gender identity disorder. In R. L. Spitzer, M. B. First, J. B. W. Williams, & M. Gibbon (Eds.), *DSM-IVTR Casebook: Vol. 2. Experts tell how they treated their own patients* (pp. 322–334). Washington, DC: American Psychiatric Publishing.

Zukow-Goldring, P. (2002). Sibling caregiving. In M. H. Bornstein (Ed.), *Handbook of parenting: Vol. 3* (2nd ed., pp. 253–286). Hillsdale, NJ: Erlbaum.

Zukowski, A. (2013). Putting words together. In J. B. Gleason & N. B. Ratner (Eds.), *The development of language* (pp. 120–162). Upper Saddle River, NJ: Pearson.

Zur, O., & Gelman, R. (2004). Young children can add and subtract by predicting and checking. *Early Childhood Research Quarterly, 19,* 121–137.

Zwart, M. (2007). The Dutch system of perinatal care. *Midwifery Today with International Midwife, 81*(Spring), 46.

Name Index

Italic *n* following page numbers indicates source note accompanying an illustration, figure, or table.

Figures and tables are indicated by f and t following page numbers.